FAMILY ADVOCACY PROGRAM
3rd Medical Group
24800 Hospital Dr
Elmendorf AFB AK 99506

CLINICAL HANDBOOK OF COUPLE THERAPY

CLINICAL HANDBOOK
OF
COUPLE THERAPY

Edited by
Neil S. Jacobson
Alan S. Gurman

THE GUILFORD PRESS
New York   London

©1995 The Guilford Press
A Division of Guilford Publications, Inc.
72 Spring Street, New York, NY 10012

Printed in the United States of America

This book is printed on acid-free paper.

Last digit is print number: 9 8 7 6 5 4 3 2 1

Library of Congress Cataloging-in-Publication Data

Clinical handbook of couple therapy / edited by Neil S. Jacobson, Alan S.
  Gurman.
      p. cm.
   Includes bibliographical references and index.
   ISBN 0-89862-855-5
   1. Marital psychotherapy, I. Jacobson, Neil S., 1949–   , II.
Gurman, Alan S.
   RC488.5.C584 1995
   616.89′156—dc20   95-17655
                                                               CIP

Contributors

Carol M. Anderson, Ph.D., Professor, Department of Psychiatry, University of Pittsburgh, Pittsburgh, Pennsylvania

Kimberly Anglin, Ph.D., Postdoctoral Fellow, Western Psychiatric Institute and Clinic, University of Pittsburgh, Pittsburgh, Pennsylvania

Julia C. Babcock, M.S., Research Assistant, Department of Psychology, University of Washington Center for Clinical Research, Seattle, Washington

Donald H. Baucom, Ph.D., Professor, Department of Psychology, University of North Carolina at Chapel Hill, Chapel Hill, North Carolina

Steven R. H. Beach, Ph.D., Associate Professor, Department of Psychology, University of Georgia, Athens, Georgia

Stacia Beak Beatty, Ph.D., Clinical Psychologist, McGregor and Associates Psychological Services, Winchester, Kentucky

Susan L. Blumberg, Ph.D., Private Practice, Denver, Colorado

Laura S. Brown, Ph.D., Clinical Professor, Department of Psychology, University of Washington, and Independent Practice, Seattle, Washington

Andrew Christensen, Ph.D., Professor, Department of Psychology, University of California, Los Angeles, Los Angeles, California

Judith Coché, Ph.D., Director, The Coché Center, Philadelphia, Pennsylvania

Michelle G. Craske, Ph.D., Professor, Department of Psychology, University of California, Los Angeles, Los Angeles, California

Sona A. Dimidjian, M.S.W., Family Therapist, Family Therapy Center, Western Psychiatric Institute and Clinic, Pittsburgh, Pennsylvania

Beatrice Ellis, Ph.D., Clinical Instructor, Department of Psychiatry and Behavioral Sciences, University of Washington School of Medicine, Seattle, Washington

Pamela Hill Epps, Ph.D., Assistant Professor, Florida Mental Health Institute, University of South Florida, Tampa, Florida

Elizabeth E. Epstein, Ph.D., Research Assistant Professor, Center of Alcohol Studies, Rutgers, The State University of New Jersey, Piscataway, New Jersey

Norman Epstein, Ph.D., Professor, Department of Family and Community Development, University of Maryland, College Park, Maryland

Celia Jaes Falicov, Ph.D., Associate Clinical Professor, Department of Psychology, University of California, San Diego, San Diego, California

Frank J. Floyd, Ph.D., Associate Professor, Department of Psychology, University of North Carolina at Chapel Hill, Chapel Hill, North Carolina

Ian H. Gotlib, Ph.D., Professor and Director of Clinical Training, Department of Psychology, Northwestern University, Evanston, Illinois

Leslie S. Greenberg, Ph.D., Professor, Department of Psychology, York University, North York, Ontario, Canada

Alan S. Gurman, Ph.D., Professor, Department of Psychiatry, University of Wisconsin Medical School, Madison, Wisconsin

Julia R. Heiman, Ph.D., Professor, Department of Psychiatry and Behavioral Sciences, University of Washington School of Medicine, Seattle, Washington

Amy Holtzworth-Munroe, Ph.D., Associate Professor, Department of Psychology, Indiana University, Bloomington, Indiana

Lynn Jacob, L.C.S.W., President, Academy of Family Mediators, and Faculty, Chicago Center for Family Health, Chicago, Illinois

Neil S. Jacobson, Ph.D., Professor, Department of Psychology, University of Washington Center for Clinical Research, Seattle, Washington

Susan M. Johnson, Ed.D., Professor of Psychology and Psychiatry, Department of Psychology, University of Ottawa, Ottawa, Ontario, Canada

Shalonda Kelly, M.A., Graduate Student, Department of Psychology, Michigan State University, East Lansing, Michigan

Howard J. Markman, Ph.D., Professor, Department of Psychology, University of Denver, Denver, Colorado

Barbara S. McCrady, Ph.D., Professor, Graduate School of Applied and Professional Psychology, and Clinical Director, Center of Alcohol Studies, Rutgers, The State University of New Jersey, Piscataway, New Jersey

Apryl Miller, L.S.W., Director, Family Therapy Center, Western Psychiatric Institute and Clinic, Pittsburgh, Pennsylvania

Daniel V. Papero, Ph.D., M.S.S.W., Georgetown Family Center, Washington, D.C.

JoEllen Patterson, Ph.D., Marriage and Family Therapy Program, School of Education, University of San Diego, San Diego, California

Frank S. Pittman III, M.D., Private Practice, Atlanta, Georgia

Cheryl Rampage, Ph.D., Director of Graduate Education, The Family Institute, Northwestern University, Evanston, Illinois

Lynn A. Rankin, M.A., Graduate Student, Department of Psychology, University of North Carolina at Chapel Hill, Chapel Hill, North Carolina

Michael Rohrbaugh, Ph.D., Professor, Department of Psychology, University of Arizona, Tucson, Arizona

Maria P. P. Root, Ph.D., Clinical Associate Professor, Department of Psychology, University of Washington, and Clinical Psychologist, Private Practice, Seattle, Washington

Jill Savege Scharff, M.D., Co-Director, International Institute of Object Relations Therapy, and Clinical Professor, Department of Psychiatry, Georgetown University, Washington, D.C.

Varda Shoham, Ph.D., Associate Professor and Clinical Director, Department of Psychology, University of Arizona, Tucson, Arizona

Virginia Simons, L.C.S.W., Co-Director, Evanston Family Therapy Center, Chicago Center for Family Health, Chicago, Illinois

Samuel Slipp, M.D., Clinical Professor of Psychiatry, New York University School of Medicine, New York, New York

Scott M. Stanley, Ph.D., Co-Director, Center for Marital and Family Studies, and Department of Psychology, University of Denver, Denver, Colorado

Tina Pittman Wagers, M.S.W., Psy.D., Kaiser Permanente Medical Group, Denver, Colorado

Froma Walsh, Ph.D., Co-Director, Chicago Center for Family Health and Professor, University of Chicago, Chicago, Illinois

Daniel B. Wile, Ph.D., Private Practice, Oakland, California

Lori A. Zoellner, M.A., Graduate Student, Department of Psychology, University of California, Los Angeles, Los Angeles, California

Contents

1. Therapy with Couples: A Coming of Age   1
   Alan S. Gurman and Neil S. Jacobson

Part I
MODELS OF INTERVENTION WITH COUPLES

Section A
MAJOR THEORIES OF COUPLE THERAPY

2. Bowen Family Systems and Marriage   11
   Daniel V. Papero

3. Integrative Behavioral Couple Therapy   31
   Andrew Christensen, Neil S. Jacobson, and Julia C. Babcock

4. Cognitive Aspects of Cognitive-Behavioral Marital Therapy   65
   Donald H. Baucom, Norman Epstein, and Lynn A. Rankin

5. The Ego-Analytic Approach to Couple Therapy   91
   Daniel B. Wile

6. The Emotionally Focused Approach to Problems in Adult Attachment   121
   Susan M. Johnson and Leslie S. Greenberg

7. Problem- and Solution-Focused Couple Therapies: 142
   The MRI and Milwaukee Models
   Varda Shoham, Michael Rohrbaugh, and JoEllen Patterson

8. Psychoanalytic Marital Therapy   164
   Jill Savege Scharff

Section B
GROUP METHODS

 9. Group Therapy with Couples   197
     Judith Coché

10. Preventive Intervention and Relationship Enhancement   212
     Frank J. Floyd, Howard J. Markman, Shalonda Kelly,
     Susan L. Blumberg, and Scott M. Stanley

Part II
COUPLE THERAPY AND RELATIONALLY
DEFINED PROBLEMS AND ISSUES

Section A
ISSUES OF CULTURE, GENDER, AND SEXUAL ORIENTATION

11. Cross-Cultural Marriages   231
     Celia Jaes Falicov

12. Redefining the Past, Present, and Future: Therapy with Long-Term 247
     Marriages at Midlife
     Carol M. Anderson, Sona A. Dimidjian, and Apryl Miller

13. Gendered Aspects of Marital Therapy   261
     Cheryl Rampage

14. Therapy with Same-Sex Couples: An Introduction   274
     Laura S. Brown

Section B
RUPTURES OF THE RELATIONAL BOND

15. Crises of Infidelity   295
     Frank S. Pittman III and Tina Pittman Wagers

16. The Assessment and Treatment of Marital Violence: 317
     An Introduction for the Marital Therapist
     Amy Holtzworth-Munroe, Stacia Beak Beatty, and Kimberly Anglin

17. Facilitating Healthy Divorce Processes: 340
     Therapy and Mediation Approaches
     Froma Walsh, Lynn Jacob, and Virginia Simons

**Part III
COUPLE THERAPY AND COMMON
PSYCHIATRIC DISORDERS**

18. Marital Therapy in the Treatment of Alcohol Problems 369
     Barbara S. McCrady and Elizabeth E. Epstein

19. Anxiety Disorders: The Role of Marital Therapy 394
     Michelle G. Craske and Lori A. Zoellner

20. A Marital/Family Discord Model of Depression: 411
     Implications of Therapeutic Intervention
     Ian H. Gotlib and Steven R. H. Beach

21. Conceptualization and Treatment of Eating Disorders in Couples 437
     Maria P. P. Root

22. Object Relations Marital Therapy of Personality Disorders 458
     Samuel Slipp

23. Treating Sexual Desire Disorders in Couples 471
     Julia R. Heiman, Pamela Hill Epps, and Beatrice Ellis

INDEX 497

CLINICAL HANDBOOK OF COUPLE THERAPY

1

Therapy with Couples: A Coming of Age

ALAN S. GURMAN
NEIL S. JACOBSON

I<small>T IS HARD</small> to believe that we first began our collaboration on the *Clinical Handbook of Marital Therapy*, the parent publication of the present volume, well over a decade ago. While we wish we could deny the graying of our heads, we acknowledge with pleasure the evolving unfolding life cycle of the first *Handbook*. Typically such books reach their old age within a handful of years, and all but disappear from professional visibility. To our great gratification, the *Handbook* has remained healthy since its conception. It has become a primary reference source in the field, and it has been widely adopted for use in courses in both university and independent institute training centers. It has aged well in our aim to compile the first comprehensive guide to the clinical practice of therapy with couples.

But just as relationships change over time, so, too, do professional practices and beliefs, as well as the broader social contexts within which these practices and beliefs exist. The most obvious change in this second edition of the *Handbook* is, ironically, its new title. Undoubtedly, most intimate, long-term adult relationships continue to be constituted by what we know as "marriage," a term that refers simultaneously to both the relational and legal nature of a committed adult union. In this era of the increasing viability and visibility of alternative relationship styles and family structures, however, it seems more appropriate to think in terms of "couples" than

"marriages." The word "couple" is more universally descriptive of the link and bond between two people, without at the same time conveying the judgmental tone of social value implied by the word "marriage." Not all contributors to this volume (or professional writings in general) adopt this more neutral word, even when not referring to traditional "marriage" per se. Yet we believe that the ideas set forth here about clinical practice are salient even outside the traditional relational construction of marriage. Arguing that the psychology of alternative forms of committed, intimate adult relationships is fundamentally different from that of traditional "marriage" would logically require a vastly different array of clinical methodologies than currently exists. While different forces come to bear on different types of relationships, established principles of human behavior are established principles of human behavior. To understand and intervene clinically with couple relationships, there are no principles that transcend these.

Clinical work with couples today also exists in a different professional atmosphere than it did a decade ago when we began to edit the first edition of this *Handbook*. At least three major trends inside the field and three outside the field can be noted. First, outside the consultation room, the credibility of the profession of marriage [sic] and family therapy has increased, as conveyed by the large number of states that now license practioners of such therapies. In part, this reflects the increased political influence of major professional organizations. It also reflects an increased awareness in the public-at-large of the centrality of long-term adult relationships to a wide variety of difficulties in adult living.

A second, related trend is that therapy with couples has become a much more widely accepted clinical practice within the politically and economically dominant mental health discipline of psychiatry. This shift is due, in no small measure, to the significant advances of the past decade in the use of couple therapy in the treatment of a number of very commonly occurring psychiatric disorders (see below).

A third trend of practical relevance from outside the domain of couple and family therapy per se, has been the extraordinary growth of managed health care delivery systems. These treatment systems place a premium on the efficiency, as well as the efficacy, of clinical practice, and naturally foster the use of interventions that are focused and brief. While some influential approaches to couple therapy are designed as long-term projects, certainly the overwhelming majority of couple therapists practice in ways that are consistent with the projected economic constraints of the psychotherapeutic marketplace circa the year 2000.

Three recent trends within the broader field of couple and family therapy that make revision of this *Handbook* timely can also be cited. First, in the last decade, the number of graduate school training programs in marital and family therapy that have received professional approval and accreditation has increased substantially. The expansion of this list is attributable not only to the enhanced respect of couple and family treatment alluded to before, but also to the tightening of academic standards within many of these programs and the achievement of higher quality education and training.

Second, one might say that the standards of discourse in the field-at-large have been enhanced in recent years. Manus argued persuasively in 1966 that couple therapy was a "technique in search of a theory," with little conceptual clarity in evidence. The present volume documents that psychotherapy with couples, rather than being the hodgepodge it used to be, now includes some of the most significant conceptual, clinical, and empirical advances of the last twenty years in any branch of the world of psychotherapy.

Finally, and hardly independent of some of the above-noted trends and changes in the field,

there seems recently to have been a virtual cessation of arguments about the relationship between couple therapy and family therapy. This seems quite remarkable in light of the fact that, in the opening chapter of the first edition of this *Handbook,* we identified (accurately we believe) this matter as the most controversial issue in constructing a history of couple therapy. Whether couple therapy is (read: is seen as) a subtype or variant of family therapy, or a distinct clinical entity, simply does not seem to be the discord-inducing concern it was a few short years ago. Perhaps therapists, clinical educators, and even clinical theorists have too much to worry about these days to allow time for such concerns. Or, perhaps as the field of behavior therapy has illustrated for many years, once you demonstrate your clinical robustness beyond a reasonable empirical doubt, the nay-sayers look for someone else to pick on. To offer a "Forrest Gumpism" of our own, "Effective is as effective does."

Given these very significant changes in the landscape of the field of couple therapy, a revised *Handbook* seemed fully warranted, despite the continuing vigor of the first edition. In this edition, as in the first, we have attempted to present a balanced admixture of the clinical theories and methods of working with couples that have endured and sustained their vitality and prominence over a substantial period of time, and truly significant recent advances in the treatment of couples. These advances range from the refinement of existing theories or the development of new major theories of couple therapy, to thoughtful and coherent considerations of the implications of cultural and political awareness for couple therapy, to increasing specificity in the planning and prescribing of therapeutic regimens for the treatment of various relational and individually diagnosed problems.

To these ends, we have made significant changes from the first edition of the *Handbook* in both the roster of our contributors and the game plan for the volume. Thus, for example, two major theory chapters on behavioral couple therapy appear here because, taken together, they represent the most up-to-date thinking in this realm, within which there are two complementary, yet divergent patterns of recent conceptual and clinical development. Likewise, "Emotionally Focused Therapy," which appeared in the section on "Emerging Models of Intervention" in the first edition now appears as a major theory because it has become just that. A piece on the problem- and solution-focused therapies complements, but takes the place of, the

"Structural-Strategic" chapter in the original *Handbook,* and a less eclectically leaning chapter on psychoanalytic couple therapy than appeared in the first *Handbook* is now included in order to highlight the unique contributions of that method. The ego-analytic approach to couple therapy included here likewise has some of its roots in psychoanalytic thinking.

In some areas, we have, in effect, combined the topics of chapters in the first *Handbook,* for example, a single chapter now addresses separation and divorce, divorce mediation, and remarriage, and preventive and enrichment methods are considered together. And, as noted, our couple therapy roster has changed a good deal; thus, about two thirds of the authors (or senior authors) in this revised edition were not among our esteemed contributors to the first edition. So, while this is a revised edition of the original *Handbook* in terms of much of its topical coverage, it is also a new volume, insofar as no two authors can present identical perspectives on the same body of knowledge.

The format for chapters in this edition has not changed substantially. Authors of chapters in Part I, Section A, "Major Theories of Couple Therapy," Section B, "Group Methods," and Part III, "Couple Therapy and Common Psychiatric Disorders," were given detailed guidelines for constructing their contributions (see below). In presenting these author guidelines, we hoped to fall in a midrange between totally controlling the authors' format, and thereby limiting the creativity of our colleagues, and giving complete freedom to authors' expository preferences, and thereby losing comparability across chapters.

MODELS OF INTERVENTION WITH COUPLES

Part I of this *Handbook* includes presentations of the major current theories of couple therapy (listed in alphabetical order) and two innovative group methods. The rationale for including the new topics in Section A, "Major Theories of Couple Therapy," has already been noted. Authors in that Section were given the following guidelines to address in preparing their chapters.

1. The theoretical model of couple distress/dysfunction
2. The theory of therapeutic change
   a. Rationale for how the treatment approach follows from the model of distress/dysfunction
   b. Overall strategy for bringing about relationship change (e.g., diagnostic/assessment procedures, typical goals, typical structure of therapy sessions, hypothesized active ingredients of the approach)
3. The role of the therapist (e.g., how a working alliance is fostered; whether the therapist–patient relationship is used explicitly to foster change; the stance of the therapist [self-disclosing vs. more distant, leading vs. following, confronting vs. supporting, etc.]; changes in the therapist's role over the course of therapy; typical technical errors)
4. Specific techniques and the therapy process (description/illustration of major techniques/strategies; common obstacles to successful treatment; limitations of and contraindications to the approach; use of other interventions, e.g., medication, individual sessions)
5. Common significant clinical issues (e.g., working with "difficult" couples; managing resistance/noncompliance; handling acute relationship distress; dealing with termination)

A close reading of the "Major Theories" section reveals some intriguing, emerging conceptual and technical trends in the field of couple therapy. Significant shifts seem to have been occurring conceptually in the last decade or so regarding the therapist–patient relationship, and the relevance of inner versus outer experience. While psychoanalytically oriented therapists have emphasized the centrality of the therapist–patient relationship, other couple therapy theorists have not always put those relationships as close to center stage as they now do. Psychoanalytic therapists view the therapist–patient relationship as having curative potential in and of itself. Most other couple therapists do not attribute such change-inducing power to the relationshsip, yet they do repeatedly identify the quality of the working alliance as essential for creating a context in which change within the couple relationship may take place. For many years, the field of couple (and family) therapy seemed so taken with its own cleverness that it lost sight of the self-evident observation that effective therapy is not merely a series of inventive "moves," but is, more than anything else, a person-to-person connection. Compared to the past, there seems to be much less emphasis on the therapist's outwitting patients to behave in new ways, and an accompanying greater emphasis on acceptance. Forging a therapeutic bond involves both establishing a condition of safety within which relationship experiements and risks may be attempted, and modeling styles of relating for the couples themselves. Not many years ago, it was rare to read, or hear at a professional conference, couple and family therapists underlining the importance of listening, reflecting, and acknowledging. The notion of empathy, an old standby for therapists trained in other traditions, almost never crossed the lips or flowed from the pens of systems therapists. The Duhls (1981) noted this trend in pointing out that "It is hard to kiss a system."

Relatedly, couple therapists have recently been attending more to emotions. While it may seem odd to therapists outside the couple/family field not to devote special attention to emotions, such was the case for many years. Focused so much on observable interpersonal transactions, couple therapists often seemed to treat emotions as mere noise and epiphenomena of the more important overt behaviors which, if modified, would lead everyone toward relational tranquility and inner harmony. This renewed interest in emotions as irreducible experience in intimate adult attachments can also be seen as part of a wider trend in the field in the last decade, one in which there is less talk of the supremacy of outer/overt/interpersonal variables versus inner/covert/intrapersonal variables. Indeed, as couple and family therapists have rediscovered the self, the artificial split between what occurs within and without the skin has faded, and the field has become genuinely more "systemic." Indeed, we believe it is not an exaggeration to say that, in the last decade, the field of couple therapy has been rehumanized.

On the technical front, flexibility and specificity are increasingly evident. We see no change from the time of the first edition of the *Handbook* in terms of most of the major models of couple therapy being sufficiently conceptually coherent as to be able to incorporate specific intervention techniques typically associated with alternative models. Thus, for example, we find Bowen therapists incorporating behavioral techniques such as biofeedback and relaxation training; behavior therapists promoting the "empathic joining" of couples in the face of problems; and psychoanalytic therapists including directive sex therapy strategies in their work. In none of these, or other similar cases, are such seemingly foreign methods called upon willy-nilly. Rather, they are integrated into a central theory with a clear justification and rationale. At the same time, the majority of major models of couple therapy have striven, successfully we believe, to become more explicit and specific in describing what they believe to be the active interventions in their approaches that make a therapeutic difference. And such increased specificity has not been limited to the practitioners of behavior therapy and problem- and solution-focused therapies, as one might expect. Perhaps the *Zeitgeist* in the psychotherapy field-at-large—of treatment manuals, expectations of controlled clinical trials, accountability for outcomes, etc.—has seeped into the couple therapy domain. Couple therapy seems to have become more modest in its claims, yet more credible in its appearance.

COUPLE THERAPY AND RELATIONALLY DEFINED PROBLEMS AND ISSUES

Couple therapy may be used in two major psychotherpeutic domains. First, there is the application of various treatment methods to problems which are reliably seen as interactive and interpersonal. Second, couple therapy is also increasingly being called upon as a first-line treatment of choice for problems that are traditionally viewed in most mental health fields as disorders of individuals.

Part II addresses these relational problems in Sections devoted to "Issues of Culture, Gender, and Sexual Orientation," and to "Ruptures of the Relational Bond." While values play important roles in all psychotherapies, some problems brought to therapists have particular value salience in two ways. First, many couples request help in resolving conflict which straightforwardly involves deeply felt personal values in areas such as gender, religion, race, and ethnicity. Second, some clinical problems, such as those involving issues of sex-role identity and culture identification, have particular potential for eliciting antitherapeutic reactions from therapists.

In recent years, therapists have become far more aware of the impact on couples' relationships of both social change and of assumptions about mental health embedded in the dominant social fabric. Likewise, therapists have become more sensitized to the implications of such changes and assumptions for couple therapy. What becomes more evident year after year is that couple therapists need to recognize three major facets of how these types of value considerations should play out in the clinical encounter.

First, couple therapists must seek education and information about the kinds of value issues that affect the therapeutic discourse. The assumption of good intentions is not sufficient to the task, but must be complemented by substantive knowledge in such areas as ethnicity, gender, sexual orientation, and midlife adult development. Second, couple therapists need to recognize that the primary therapeutic aim is not to proselytize any particular set of new values to couples, but rather, to help couples increase the variety of narratives, or constructions, available within which these most human issues can be considered. In brief, the danger to couples' relational health is value rigidity, or what George Kelly (1955) referred to many years ago as "hardening of the categories." Finally, couple therapists would be wise to recognize that the mere existence of value differences within a couple does not automatically elevate such matters to the status of "primary problem." How a given couple constructs (perceives and evaluates) these differences is what matters; value differences are more or less important at different times with different types of problems. Obviously, effective couple therapists will often identify problems (or, more likely, problem themes) that underlie couples' stated concerns, and it is their responsibility to make clear to couples the connection between these two levels. At the same time, it is the task of therapists to solve problems, not to create them.

These "hardened categories" often become evident in clinical work that involves "Ruptures of the Relational Bond" (Section B). Creating new narratives, dispelling old myths, and generally increasing couples' cognitive and action options are major operative themes in this realm. They may be expressed in such varied ways as demystifying and demythologizing commonly held beliefs about infidelity; refraining from reflexively assuming that couple therapy is so powerful that it can usually stand alone in the treatment of couple violence; or challenging widely held assumptions about what constitutes the normal intact family, or widely disseminated, yet incorrect, information about the presumed inevitable destructiveness of divorce for children.

COUPLE THERAPY AND COMMON PSYCHIATRIC DISORDERS

The kinds of clinical problems addressed in Part III have traditionally been viewed as residing within individuals, in terms of both their origins and their maintenance. Despite the enormous numbers of mental health consumers beset by problems of depression, anxiety, etc., couple and family therapists have largely ignored these areas of clinical concern until very recently. In a parallel way, couple/family therapists have too often paid insufficient attention to eating disorders among their adult clientele.

We view problems such as anxiety, depression, alcoholism, eating disorders, inadequate sexual desire, and personality disorders as genuine clinical syndromes which exist apart from, as well as in significant connection with, relationship dynamics. We requested that the authors of chapters in this section, in addition to considering the issues put to the authors of "Major Models" chapters, also consider the following questions:

1. What is the usual (diagnostic) definition of this problem?
2. How do relationship issues contribute to this (individual) problems?
3. How does the (individual) problem contribute to relationship discord?
4. What nondyadic factors, if any, play an important role in either the etiology or maintenance of this disorder?
5. Are there limitations of a purely "relational therapy" approach to treating this problem?
6. Are other interventions (e.g., medications) used in treating this problem within a relatively focused therapy?

Given that couple/family therapists generally have had little to say about the treatment of many common diagnosable adult disorders, it is ironic that these disorders have recently come to comprise one of the most scientifically based areas of clinical practice in the entire couple/family therapy field. Recognizing the existence of real psychiatric disorders has not, as some in the couple/family field feared, led to a negation of the relevance of couple therapy. Indeed, by drawing upon the canons of traditional scientific methodology, clinical researchers have actually enhanced the credibility of couple therapy interventions for these problems. Research on the couple treatment of such disorders in the last decade has shown strikingly that individual problems and relational problems influence each other reciprocally. These data have important implications for what is still perhaps the most controversial issue in the realm of systems-oriented treatment of psychiatric disorders, that is, whether individual problems are functional for relationships. We suggested in the first edition of the *Handbook* that the more appropriate form of the question might be "*When* do symptoms serve such functions?" A thoughtful reading of several of the chapters in this section of the present volume seems to confirm, as we suggested earlier, that (1) some individual symptoms seem often to serve interpersonal functions; (2) some individual symptoms seem rarely to serve interpersonal functions; and (3) some individual symptoms are quite variably interpersonally functional. As Maria Root in this section of the *Handbook* (p. 456) states the matter, "At times it is hard to distinguish an etiological factor from a reaction." Recent research has confirmed what some of us in the field (e.g., Gurman, Kniskern, & Pinsof, 1986) have long asserted, against the prevailing clinical wisdom, that functions are dangerously confused with consequences.

CONCLUSION

In sum, we see seven very telling trends in the theory and practice of couple therapy since the first edition of this *Handbook:* greater awareness of the significance of personal and cultural values; a more balanced appreciation of the interdependence of interpersonal and intrapsychic factors in couple relationships; increased attention to the importance of the therapist–patient relationship; a continuous strengthening of support for technical flexibility in practice; an increasing emphasis on specifying and operationalizing interventions; a less self-congratulatory and more honest assessment of the efficacy of couple therapies; and the forging of more solid linkages with psychology, psychiatry, and other relevant professions and disciplines. In all these ways, we believe that couple therapy has come of age.

REFERENCES

Duhl, B. S., & Duhl, F. J. (1981). Integrative family therapy. In A. S. Gurman & D. P. Kniskern (Eds.), *Handbook of family therapy.* New York: Brunner/Mazel.

Gurman, A. S., Kniskern, D. P., & Pinsof, W. M. (1986). Research on the process and outcome of family therapy. In S. Garfield & A. E. Bergin (Eds.), *Handbook of psychotherapy and behavior change* (3rd ed.). New York: Wiley.

Kelly, G. A. (1955). *The psychology of personal constructs.* New York: Norton.

Manus, G. I. (1966). Marriage counseling: A technique in search of a theory. *Journal of Marriage and the Family, 28,* 449–453.

I

MODELS OF INTERVENTION WITH COUPLES

A

Major Theories
of Couple Therapy

2

Bowen Family Systems and Marriage

DANIEL V. PAPERO

Fᴿᴼᴹ ɴᴀᴛᴜʀᴇ'ѕ ɪɴꜰɪɴɪᴛᴇ ᴡᴇʙ of breeding pairs, some of which link together for life and most of which do not, humankind elevates and endows its own variant with the status of marriage. To define or explain *marriage*, however, is about as difficult as defining or explaining the term "love." When does a marriage begin? When does it end? What determines what occurs in between? Is each marriage unique or do common areas exist? What part does each person play, and what functions do other people serve? Individuals and generations have ever-fresh opinions about such questions, views shaped by their families, by the challenges of their own world to adjust, by their own biology, and by the partner they have picked, hope to find, or have renounced as their own particular opportunity to learn about marriage.

Bowen family systems theory (BFST) is not primarily a theory about marriage. Rather, it addresses human capability and functioning, the uniqueness of each person, and the connections between people. It looks at what people do repeatedly, not at what they say about what they do. It views the person in the context of an emotional field of relationships to important others and the impact of that shifting emotional field on each individual's ability to be at his/her best. Marriage is but one of the relationships in the emotional field of any person. Whether people are at their best or something less with their marriage partners is determined in part by who each person is, by the nature of the relationship between them, and by the status of the emotional field in which the marriage is embedded.

EMOTIONAL SYSTEM

Eight concepts form the body of BFST. Each describes a variable that influences the behavior of individuals and families. In addition to these concepts, which will be discussed more fully in the following pages, BFST is essentially incomprehensible without an understanding of the term "emotional system" (Papero, 1990; Kerr & Bowen, 1988; Bowen, 1978). As used in BFST, the *emotional system* refers to processes shaped by evolution that form an innate or instinctive guidance system for an organism. Learned responses are also a part of the emotional system to the degree that they are automatic. Such processes unfold in response to both simple and complex stimuli. The human emotional system is a version of that system present in all living things. Many of the biochemical and mechanical processes are similar and even identical in all living creatures.

The emotional system provides the drumbeat to which the organism marches. Feeding, mating, resting, and nesting, among many other types of behavior, all are determined for most species by the emotional system. The term can also be applied to an organism-like unit of individuals acting as a whole. Animals behave in their characteristic ways because they must. They have no alternative to what nature has programmed into their cells and whatever capacity they possess for learning. The emotional system is the only guidance system available to them. BFST posits that much of human behavior is governed by the emotional system as well, far more so, perhaps, than many of us have ever imagined. But in addition to the emotional system, the human being possesses a *feeling system* and a *intellectual system.*

The feeling system appears to be a link between the emotional system, which is generally not felt, and the intellectual system. It resembles the tip of an iceberg, the part that projects into the realm of awareness, while most of the remainder lies below the surface and beyond awareness. The feeling system is believed to be a product of fairly recent brain evolution and is not possessed by many living things. The intellectual system refers to the ability to know and to understand, to reason abstractly, and to communicate complicated ideas (Kerr & Bowen, 1988). It serves as a second guidance system for the individual, although the capacity to employ this system is more fully developed in some people than in others.

Kerr and Bowen (1988) list three purposes served by the concept of the emotional system. First, it presents as a cornerstone of BFST the assumption that the same or very similar life processes regulate all living things. Second, it provides a way of thinking that supercedes or bridges the compartmentalization of knowledge about biological forms and processes. And third, the emotional system extends beyond the lone individual to the surrounding relationship system. The swarming of soldier ants in a colony to repel invaders is not based on an individual ant's assessment of thoughts or feelings. The ant acts as it must, in response to the presence of threat and the stimulus of its co-workers' behavior. The emotional system governs the behavior of the individual ant and that of the colony as a unit. In a sense, then, emotionally based behavior is the common denominator of all living things. From the point of view of BFST, the relationship phenomena referred to as "marital symptoms" reflect the operation of the emotional system of each individual and of the broader unit in which the particular twosome is embedded. From a theoretical perspective, the symptoms reflect the automatic response of the individual, the twosome, and the broader unit to shifts in the condition of the unit and of the

broader environment in which the unit is situated.

A second important element forming a background to discussing the eight concepts of BFST is captured in the term "anxiety." In a general manner, "anxiety" can be defined as the organism's response to real or imagined threat. More specifically, anxiety refers to physiological and psychological changes that occur as the emotional system of the organism responds to the perception of danger. Anxiety can be further delineated with the terms "acute" and "chronic." *Acute anxiety* describes the organism's response to a real and current threat. It lasts generally only as long as the perception of threat persists. *Chronic anxiety*, however, is manifested in the fear of what might happen and can be longlasting. Chronic anxiety may involve changes in physiology and psychology that persist in spite of the conditions surrounding the individual. Among its manifestations are sustained wariness and suspicion, physical tension, fears about what might be, fatigue, irritability, and a host of physical symptoms. Chronic anxiety wears down human resiliency, and its debilitating effects tend to reduce people's ability to manage episodes of acute anxiety. Anxiety is an intense manifestation of the emotional system. It impedes the person's ability to use the intellectual system to guide the self through the world. Chronic anxiety, therefore, can represent a permanent impediment to the inherent flexibility in the human being. Anxiety, and particularly chronic anxiety, has a major influence on human functioning.

BOWEN FAMILY SYSTEMS THEORY

BFST consists of eight formal concepts, each of which plays a role in the observable behavior of the individual and the family unit. Each of the concepts are presented briefly.

Differentiation of Self

The concept of differentiation of self forms the foundation of BFST. What Bowen observed was variation among individuals, based on functioning. Some people appear to behave automatically, using only instinct and feeling as a guide. Decisions seem based on avoiding discomfort of any sort and on what feels good or right. Others also have the ability to employ their thinking capacity under some conditions (generally low anxiety) but quickly revert to automatic behavior when anxious. Still other people display the capacity to maintain their thinking under a variety of conditions. They seem to have choice between which guidance system they employ, switching back and forth from the automatic to the thoughtful essentially at will. Both guidance systems, the emotional and the intellectual, are useful, depending on the conditions facing the person.

Under many circumstances, the automatic behavior of the emotional system works remarkably well to navigate the person through a shifting environment. This is only to be expected, given the evolutionary development of the emotional system and its countless refinements wrought through the process of natural selection. But occasionally, the person can be confronted by a set of conditions to which the emotional response is inadequate for optimal adjustment. The emotional response could, in fact, compound the challenge of adjustment. The ability to shift to the intellectual system to govern behavior is an important asset.

Bowen described a continuum based on the ability of the person to keep separate the emotional and intellectual systems and to maintain choice between them, which he called the "scale of differentiation of self." People with no ability whatsoever to separate them, no matter what the conditions, were assigned the rank of zero on the continuum. They had no ability to differentiate between the emotional and intellectual systems and operated continuously under the guidance of the emotional system. From the zero point, individuals could be assigned a position on the continuum based on an assessment of their ability to separate emotional and intellectual systems and to maintain choice between them. Bowen assigned the number 100 to the opposite end of the continuum, to designate the individual displaying full ability to separate and choose between the emotional and intellectual systems to guide behavior.

No one has described the scale of differentiation better than Bowen himself:

This scale is an effort to classify all levels of human functioning, from the lowest possible levels to the highest potential level, on a single dimension. In broad terms it would be similar to an emotional maturity scale, but it deals with factors that are different from "maturity" concepts. The scale eliminates the need for the concept "normal." It has nothing to do with emotional health or illness or pathology. There are people low on the scale who keep their lives in emotional equilibrium without psychological symptoms, and there are some higher on the scale who develop symptoms under severe stress. (1972, p. 117)

Bowen went on to add that people lower on the scale were more vulnerable to stress and had greater difficulty recovering from symptoms than those higher on the scale. The scale, furthermore, had no direct correlation with socioeconomic level or intelligence.

In addition to a basic level of differentiation of self resulting from the developmental processes, Bowen added the idea of a functional level of differentiation of self. The general idea is that with some practice and effort people can function better than they automatically might. A person with a basic level of 35 could, with hard work, perseverance and good fortune, be able to function like a person with a basic level of 50. The latter would function at that level without so much effort and travail. Functional level of differentiation is important in a clinical process. What people essentially work on is the enhancing of functional differentiation.

Functional level of differentiation of self can be influenced by the relationship network, and from a theoretical point of view, a person could function below his/her basic level. For example, a young husband made the following observation of what happened to him in relationship to his wife: He noted that they both appeared to have about the same capability in the world and the same ability to think about things. He reported, however, that shortly after marriage he lost sight of what he thought and believed. He began to guide himself by what he thought his wife wanted from him. The harder he would try to interpret her wishes and meet her needs, the more critical of him she became. As time passed, he did less and less for himself, exhibiting the classic indicators of depression. He lost his zest for life, and the harder he tried, the less responsive to his wife he became. When, finally, the wife indicated that she was considering divorce, he began to think again. He reported that he felt as if a great weight had been lifted from him. He no longer was responsible to meet this woman's needs. His thinking was free to turn to his own goals and to consider more carefully his relationship to his wife. As he governed his behavior more from his own thinking, his wife's criticism decreased, and each found the relationship more interesting. His functioning had risen to his basic level.

At the heart of the concept of differentiation of self is the basic relationship to one's parents. Physical separation occurs in a regular developmental sequence from conception forward. Emotional separation, the ability to employ and follow either the intellectual or the emotional system in the relationship with the parents, is less obvious. To the degree that emotional separation is incomplete, the parents and the child remain attached emotionally. The attachment can be complete, a symbiosis in which neither can survive without the other. There are infinite degrees of separation from that point. Bowen referred to the remaining attachment as *unresolved emotional attachment* (Bowen, 1978).

Unresolved emotional attachment is equivalent to the degree of undifferentiation in a person and in a family. The higher the level of differentiation, the less undifferentiation or unresolved attachment must be handled by the involved individuals and the less intense the mechanisms to deal with the undifferentiation. The amount of such attachment to the parents is determined by several factors. The first is the degree of unresolved attachment of the parents themselves, a legacy of their own families. The second is the manner in which the parents have managed the attachment in their marriage. The third factor is the degree of anxiety to which the parents and the family have been exposed and have generated at important periods in life, and how this anxiety has been handled. Bowen's view, incorporated in BFST, was that the unresolved emotional attachment to parents is established relatively early in life, essentially a product of the relationship to the parents. If the parents manage their attachment and their relationship well and/or if they enjoy good fortune, the amount of unresolved attachment may decrease in a given generation. With poor management and less favorable circumstances, it can also increase.

Differentiation of self can be thought of along many axes. How life energy is expended can be one. Below a level of 50 on the differentiation continuum, people give much of their life energy to relationships and to other people. Giving and seeking approval, trying to please another, supporting another or seeking support oneself, and gaining love or reacting to the failure of not gaining love are a few examples of how life energy can be expended on the lower end of the continuum. In his classic 1966 paper, Bowen wrote about this aspect of differentiation in the following manner:

From 50 down it is increasingly a *feeling* world except for those at the extreme lower end who can be too miserable to feel. A typical *feeling* person is one who is responsive to emotional harmony or disharmony about him. . . . So much life energy goes into "loving" and seeking "love" and approval that there is little energy left for self-determined, goal-directed activity. (p. 358)

Differentiation can also be thought of in terms of the degree to which people depend on another. Perhaps the most extreme version of dependency occurs in the symbiosis in which none of the individuals involved can live without the others. In a relationship network in which people are heavily dependent upon one another, a change in one can produce a great discomfort and hardship for others. BFST suggests that the dependence between people can be much more than psychological. The actual functioning of the physical organism can come to be linked to the functioning of others, and well-being depends on the others not changing too drastically. Below the midpoint on the differentiation continuum, dependency or the need for another plays an increasing role in how people function. Bowen used the term "fusion" to refer to the degree of dependence that can occur at the lower levels of differentiation of self. People present themselves as if they were a common self, as if they shared a common ego boundary, within which there could be no meaningful distinction among individuals. The thoughts, fantasies, feelings, and even the physical pain of one became a part of the other(s).

Differentiation can also be thought of in terms of chronic anxiety. The opposite of differentiation, which Bowen often referred to as "undifferentiation," has come to be seen as virtually synonymous with chronic anxiety. Essentially, the degree of undifferentiation is the same as the level of chronic anxiety with which the individual and the group must come to terms. Chronic anxiety is manifested in the lability of relationship networks, the intense need for another, and heightened vulnerability to symptoms of all sorts.

Triangles

Bowen's discovery of the triangle as the basic building block of the human relationship system ranks in importance alongside the discovery of differentiation of self. What Bowen realized was that no two-person system stands in isolation. Bowen's own words described his observation:

In calm periods, two members of the triangle have a comfortable emotional alliance, and the third, in the unfavored "outsider" position, moves either toward winning the favor of one of the others or toward rejection, which may be planned as winning favor. In tense situations, the "outsider" is in the favored position and both of the emotionally overinvolved ones will predictably make efforts to involve the third in the conflict. (1966, pp. 160–161)

Triangles emerge most clearly in the presence of a moderate amount of anxiety. Then, various movements of the triangling process can be observed, yet the process is mild enough to be contained within a single triangle. It does not spill over to involve the interlocking triangles characteristic of higher intensities of anxiety. When interlocking triangles are activated, the interactions can be so complicated and chaotic that the observation of triangling is very difficult.

The triangle consists of three two-person relationships. It is a configuration of shifting alliances and reactive processes. The communication from one to another about yet a third affects the sensitivity, perception/interpretation, and behavior of each. People become more sensitized to one another, interpret the behavior of others in a personalized manner, and behave reactively on the basis of that heightened sensitivity and personalized interpretation. Triangles are dynamic and constantly shifting, although the particular configuration can become fixed and occur repeatedly when the proper conditions are present (generally a particular intensity of anxiety and a particular cast of characters). More than simple movements of closeness and distance, the triangling process involves shifts in perception and behavior due to the interaction.

For example, a man, while talking to his pastor, mentions that his wife has a drinking problem, and he thinks she is an alcoholic. Following this communication, he feels better briefly. The wife is not aware that the husband has told this to the pastor. The clergywoman, meanwhile, begins to worry some about the wife. Her view of the woman changes to one of pity and concern. When she next sees the wife, the pastor is in a predicament. Should she or should she not tell the woman that she knows? Should she reveal her source? Should she express her concern or remain silent? Should she intervene? In short, her view of her parishioner has changed along with her response to her. The discussion with the husband has led to an increase in the pastor's anxiety. Unless she is extremely good at managing herself, the shift in her perception and in her feeling system will be communicated to the other woman, and there is a good chance that the nature of the relationship between them

will change. The change is evident in how each sees the other and in the automatic response of each to the other. And this shifting is based on the comments of the husband, not on any clear fact. The woman, meanwhile, knows that the relationship has changed, but she may well not know why. She may be less open with the pastor or become angry. In this manner, the interpersonal environment with which each person in the triangle has to contend has changed, and the wife does not know what has occurred.

If the anxiety driving the triangle is sufficiently intense, the triangling process may reach out to involve other triangles in an interlocking fashion. The same husband may make a similar communication to the church deacon, who in turn mentions the communication to the pastor and to his own wife. The deacon may feel sorry for the husband and more angry at the wife. The next time he sees her, he may avoid looking at her or talking to her. The wife, who has always enjoyed the deacon's sense of humor, is perplexed and does not know what has happened. The deacon's wife, meanwhile, may comment to her closest friend that she is worried about the wife and is thinking about how to lend a hand. In this manner, the "news" spreads through the congregation. Each person has a different reaction to the news, which is played out in the relationship network. The outcome can be a shift in the relative positions of the original wife and husband within the congregation, he the recipient of compassion and she more isolated. And, in this example, the process began simply with a comment, not a fact. A process of interlocking triangles surely propelled the Salem witch trials.

The triangling process appears to be built into the human emotional system, presumably a legacy of evolution. Under certain circumstances, the activation of triangles appears useful and anxiety moderating. Under other circumstances, triangles result in the isolation and even injury to one or more people. Primatologist Frans de Waal commented on the process among primates, which he refers to as "triadic awareness":

The term "triadic awareness" means the capacity to perceive social relationships between other individuals and to form varied triangular relationships: that is the ability of individual A in his relationship with B and C not only to be aware of and allow for his own relationship with both B and C individually (A-B and A-C), but also to be aware of and allow for the relationship B-C. Elementary forms of threedimensional group life are found in many bird and mammal species, but the primates are undoubtedly supreme in this respect. (1982, p. 182)

From the perspective of BFST, a marriage is but one side of a triangle, an intense relationship that can run hot or cold in response to shifts of the emotional field in which it exists and in response to the various processes of the triangle.

The triangling process is sensitive to anxiety and is influenced by differentiation of self. The more intense the anxiety in a field at a particular time, the more triangling will occur as the anxiety spreads through the field. The higher a person's level of differentiation of self, however, the better he/she will manage anxiety without following the triangling process. If anxiety is intense enough, however, any person or group will display triangling. The process is characteristic of the emotional system when conditions are suitable.

Nuclear Family Emotional Process, Family Projection Process, Sibling Position, Multigenerational Transmission Process, Emotional Cutoff, and Emotional Process in Society

The breeding pairs of most mammalian species do not unite for a lifetime. For many species, mating is a very casual encounter indeed, whereas for others the duration of the breeding twosome as a unit is linked to the conditions to which the animals must adjust at any point in time. The conditions comprise the hereditary and learned characteristics of each animal, the nature of the group to which the breeding pair belongs, and the changing environmental conditions that challenge the ability of all living things to adapt—availability of resources, competition, climate change, population pressures, and so on. The human being appears to fall within this latter group, and the viability of the union is determined by the particular qualities of each person, the resources available to the unit, and the conditions to which it must adjust at a particular moment in time.

All living things are wonderfully flexible creatures. Species differ in terms of the capabilities each possesses and the ability to apply those capabilities to the situation at hand. Such variation essentially forms the basis for the process of natural selection. Some species are better suited to specific conditions than others, and if the conditions are persistent enough, the better suited species predominate, and those less well suited decrease in number or even become extinct. Variation, in terms of natural selection, is defined as genetic. Various random genetic mutations provide the basis for the differences essential to the process of natural selection.

Individuals within a species also differ from one another in much the same way that species differ. This difference can be attributed in part to genetics, but experience also plays a role. "Experience" can be defined as those processes and behaviors developed or influenced by the individual's interaction with a particular environment and retained by the organism. Such effects can be so fundamental as to appear gene-like or so ephemeral that they are easily eroded by another interactional sequence. The combination of genes plus experience expresses itself in the behavior of the individual. This combination also determines the behavioral potential of the individual, the ability to develop new behaviors or modify existing ones to adjust to changing conditions. In short, an individual's past, both long-term and more recent, determines capability in the here and now.

From the BFST point of view, the hereditary and experientially based behaviors and capabilities that each person brings to a marriage are incorporated under differentiation of self. The ability of each to maintain separation of the emotional and feeling systems from the intellectual system is determined by the multigenerational past and by the life experiences in one's own family. Two concepts of BFST address the mechanisms by which the past impacts upon the present. The first, the *family projection process*, addresses how the parental level of differentiation of self is passed on to the children in an uneven fashion. Within a group of siblings, some may emerge with a somewhat higher level of differentiation than the parents, some with a lower level, and some with an identical level. Those children who emerge with a lower level of differentiation of self are more exposed to parental immaturity than their more fortunate siblings. They have greater difficulty separating smoothly from their parents, and in extreme cases may not separate at all. They emerge with less ability to separate the emotional and feeling systems from the intellectual system, and their lives are governed more by feeling than are the lives of their siblings. Those children who are freest from unresolved emotional attachment to their parents emerge with somewhat higher levels of differentiation than their parents. More of their life energy can be invested in their life goals, and they are freer to experience the world for themselves. The *multigenerational transmission process* addresses how this process, repeated generation after generation, results in different branches of a family moving toward higher and lower levels of differentiation and lesser or greater vulnerability to dysfunction.

Theory also postulates that the level of differentiation of each partner is very similar, if not identical.[1] The level of undifferentiation (immaturity, chronic anxiety, and emotional reactivity) is also similar or identical. The degree of undifferentiation determines the degree of dependency between the pair. The greater the degree of undifferentiation, the less each possesses a self apart from the relationship and the more each requires the presence of the other, behaving in certain acceptable ways to maintain his/her own functioning. The greater the dependency, the less tolerance each has for difference in the other and the more anxiety can be generated when differences inevitably appear.

When calm, a two-person relationship can appear mature and stable. As anxiety mounts, however, the characteristic symptoms of the anxious twosome appear. These processes are rarely static. They shift from person to person and appear or disappear in response to shifting levels of anxiety and the emergence of other symptoms in the broader system. The level of differentiation of the partners and the intensity of anxiety determine the threshold beyond which symptoms appear. The various symptom presentations of the two-person relationship comprise the *nuclear family emotional process.* An early and frequent symptom of relationship anxiety is *emotional distance.* Among its numerous manifestations are silence, physical avoidance of one another, distractibility or apparent disinterest in what the other is saying, preoccupation, and even the clinical symptoms of depression. Each person can become distant from the other, or one can draw back from a puzzled other. In this case, if the distance is uncomfortable enough, the less distant one will make efforts to reinvolve the more distant person. This may sometimes be successful, but if it is not, the distancing one tends to become more distant, and the other steps up the efforts to reinvolve him/her. The result is a repetitive pattern of one withdrawing and the other trying to engage, often called pursuit and distance.

Conflict is a second symptom that can appear in a twosome. It can occur in an alternating cycle with emotional distance, or it can stand alone. Conflict can range in severity from simple bickering to severe violence. Each person focuses intently on what he/she believes the other to be doing wrong, and neither is shy about pointing out the other's problem. The basic dependency between people is most clearly seen in conflict. Each tells the other clearly and forcefully how he/she has violated the dependence and what needs to be done to correct the situation.

A third symptom can be called a functioning shift in both partners, manifested primarily as a *dysfunction of one partner or spouse.* The programming of each partner fits like a tongue and groove with that of the other. One partner tends to take charge of situations and take care of the other, who yields to the partner decisions and responsibility for self. If this process is prolonged, the yielding one can appear weak and helpless. He/she turns increasingly to the other to spell out what needs to be done and how to do it. The other gains the appearance of functioning increasingly well. He/she comes to make and carry out the decisions for the other. Each pays a price in this reciprocal process. The yielding one becomes vulnerable to physical and emotional dysfunction. The basic posture toward life becomes one of helpless surrender. The caretaking partner bears a sense of enormous responsibility that can serve as a ball and chain, limiting that person's freedom to pursue goals important to self. Bowen once referred to a consequence of this posture as "being pinned down in the one-up position" (personal communication). Sometimes the reciprocal balance can appear peaceful and the partners devoted to one another. But violence can also flare with this symptom, generally when anxiety is very high and the overresponsible one feels at the breaking point. It can also flare when the high functioner feels unappreciated or betrayed by the behavior of the other, or when the underfunctioner perceives self to be oppressed or abused. Then, either one can strike suddenly and violently.

The fourth symptom presentation of the two-person system expands the configuration to a three-person system. In this case, parental anxiety becomes focused upon a particular child. The special child may have certain problems from birth, but the process can occur without obvious difficulty in the child. The general process begins usually with the mother, who identifies strongly with the child and responds to her own anxiety with a worry about the child. The other parent, generally the father, can either support this worry or hand the anxious mother and child off to a series of professionals, thus keeping himself relatively buffered from the crescendos of anxiety in the pair. Bowen referred to this as the *projection of the problem to a child.* Often the relationship between the parents is cooperative and relatively calm, and the child does frequently develop a symptom that seems to justify the parents' concern.

These symptoms are mechanisms that automatically appear when conditions are right. These various symptoms function as mechanisms for absorbing, binding, or handling a certain amount of anxiety and relieving the rest of the system of that anxiety. A small segment of the system is impaired, but the impairment is limited to the smallest segment of the system that can contain the anxiety. The symptom, therefore, appears to serve a maintenance function for the unit as a whole. If the anxiety is intense enough, more than one symptom can crop up in the same or in a different part of the unit. If the anxiety becomes chronic, so may the symptom, becoming part of the regular processes of the system. On the other hand, when the anxiety is acute, the symptom can disappear with the lessening of anxiety. Such symptoms are not pathological. They are a natural part of all human systems and appear whenever anxiety surpasses the particular tolerance of the people involved. All families have one or more of these symptoms at times. Some families have only mild, temporary versions of them, whereas others have severe and prolonged episodes of symptomatology.

The remaining three concepts of BFST further spell out how emotional process impacts the resources available to each person and each nuclear family, and how emotional process in society influences the environment with which each individual and each family must contend.

In the course of developing his theory, Bowen realized that *sibling position* played an important role in the process of the family and in the characteristic postures people assumed under the pressure of anxiety. He had not systematically organized his thinking about this important component when he fortuitously discovered the work of Walter Toman (1961) on sibling position. By systemically collecting data from thousands of families in the United States and Europe, Toman was able to develop profiles of the thinking and behavioral characteristics common to the 10 possible sibling positions into which everyone must fall. No one person has all these characteristics, and no sibling position is more fortunate than another. Each has advantages and disadvantages, primarily in terms of the fit with other people in relationship. Aided by these profiles, Toman was able to make predictions about how a person may behave in the presence of another with a different sibling position, particularly when both are anxious.

Bowen developed the concept of "emotional cutoff" to refer to extreme emotional distancing. The distance can be actual, with miles and no contact between people, or it can be internal, with each person employing various intrapsychic and even physiological mechanisms to avoid contact with the other, even though both persons may live in the same house. The cutoff develops as a way of managing the unresolved emotional attachment to the parents (see the previous discussion of differentiation of self). Bowen describes the relevance of cutoff in the following manner:

> The person who runs away from home is as emotionally attached as the one who stays at home and uses internal mechanisms to control the attachment. The one who runs away does have a different life course. He needs emotional closeness but is allergic to it. He runs away kidding himself that he is achieving "independence." The more intense the cut-off with his parents, the more he is vulnerable to repeating the same pattern in future relationships. (1978, p. 535)

Emotional cutoffs can have particularly important consequences for marriage. Each partner must manage his/her own unresolved emotional attachment to parents, and the cutoff is a frequently observed phenomenon. The more distant each partner is from his/her own family, the more intense the emotional process within the marriage tends to be. Furthermore, a person who has employed cutoff to manage the attachment to the parents is also likely to employ distance, even cutoff, to manage the intense attachment to the spouse. When a person can become aware of his/her proclivity to cut off from important others, and when major cutoffs can be reversed, the marital unit can function with decreased emotional intensity.

The final concept of BFST, *emotional process in society*, addresses the environment in which everyone must live and with which all marriages must contend. Basically, Bowen observed that the same processes operate in society that operate in the family. Anxiety, which Bowen believed to be fueled by increasing population and dwindling resources, moves through society in waves. Groups of people respond to increases in anxiety with greater difficulty in thinking and with more automatic responses. Fads and panics come to determine social behavior during periods of heightened anxiety, and the more thoughtful segment are hard-pressed to maintain their own beliefs and principles in the face of such pressure.

ON CHANGE

Few ideas in any field seem as elusive as the concept of change when applied to human behavior. In fact, behavior is rarely static and fixed. What people do changes from moment to moment and from season to season. People behave differently with different people, but not always. Even when a symptom is present in a family, the symptom is not active all the time. Marital conflict is rarely continuous, and the stimuli that lead to fighting one day may be completely ignored the next. Some behaviors and interactional sequences reoccur in a predictable fashion, like the carefully choreographed movements of an intricate ballet in coordination with the music and the set. Some of these repetitions are desired and pursued, whereas others are considered aversive and to be avoided at all costs. At times, the human organism is perversely recalcitrant, and the more one tries to change, the more one seems to stay the same.

Any symptom in a family is the product of the interplay of the level of differentiation of its members plus the intensity of anxiety at a given moment. The symptom is not considered an indicator of a defect or pathology in the person or the family, but is reflective of the state of the family, determined by the family history, by the processes at work within it, and the challenges to which it must adjust. Furthermore, the symptom is a regulatory mechanism, a protective device that is deployed to counteract the erosive and often toxic effects of chronic and acute anxiety. A symptom represents a quantity of bound anxiety, a focal point around which others can assume various postures and roles.

Much, therefore, of what is called *change* merely represents simple shifts in the state of the system or unit, reflecting the ebb and flow of anxiety. The symptom can emerge, disappear, and reemerge, reflecting the intensity of anxiety in the characters and in the system. If change is to be measured by feeling better or feeling worse, the ground is even more uncertain. Through the process of triangling and the infectious quality of anxiety, one person's efforts and success at feeling better may produce distress and even impairment in another.

Similarly, a symptom in a person or interpersonal segment of a unit may serve a prophylactic function. As long as the symptom regulates or absorbs the excess anxiety in the unit, the remainder of the unit may be relatively symptom free and functional. When a symptom becomes severe, however, it can generate further increases in the intensity of anxiety. An additional symptom can then appear, one that is more effective at blunting the effect of anxiety. As anxiety increases in a family or unit, greater symptom severity and the involvement of previously unaffected individuals are predictable. Any decrease in anxiety, consequently, can also lead to a shift in the functioning of the unit. The symptom can disappear, people can feel better, and their functioning can improve according to their own standards of performance. This sort of shift in the unit, colored with positive feeling, is often considered change.

Shifts in anxiety and functioning levels can occur slowly or very rapidly in a particular unit. In spite of these fluctuations, however, the essential vulnerability of the individual and the unit has not significantly been altered. Vanished symptoms may never reappear if the unit is fortunate, and if nothing stirs up anxiety once again to a critical threshold. But nothing has actually changed. The basic vulnerability of the unit is unaffected. Vulnerability is reduced when the basic and functional levels of differentiation are increased. Therefore, the most basic goal of family psychotherapy is enhanced differentiation of self for motivation individuals and for the unit.

The Role of the Clinician

The BFST definition of the clinician's role is so basically different from that of other theoretical systems that Bowen was reluctant to use the traditional word "therapist" to refer to the clinician. He selected, instead the word "coach" and referred to the clinical process as *coaching*. He drew the term from athletics, where the coach functions to create a climate in which each player can come close to his/her best level of performance, and in which the interaction of the team assists each player to develop further than he/she could alone. The family unit is the patient, not a particular person or relationship within it. The clinician attempts to manage self in a manner that lends a hand to the natural restorative processes inherent in the family.

The clinician attempts to be in contact with the family emotionally. This means, in part, being aware of the emotional processes at work in the family across time. Where have the symptoms appeared historically? Which of the processes defined by theory appear to apply to this particular family? What environmental pressures and what events within the family appear to be contributing to the family's anxiety? How have triangles played themselves out across time? How are they active currently? How is emotional reactivity manifested in various family members, and what is the part each person plays in contributing to another's emotional reaction? Such information emerges continually during the clinical process, sometimes as the result of the clinician's questions and often contributed by the family during the discussion of the situation.

A number of emotionally charged issues lurk in the emotional field of any family. An emotionally charged issue is one that, when presented to members of the family, triggers feeling-laden emotional reactivity. The ability of people to consider facts, to maintain a broad perspective of time, events, and some objectivity varies with the intensity of the emotional response—the more intense the response, the less the ability to think. Emotionally charged issues produce intense feelings in vulnerable people and activate the triangling process, resulting in judgmental decisions, side taking, avoidance, and blaming. People subjectively color such issues negatively or positively, generally based on their own experience. One person's positive can be another person's negative within the same emotional unit.

To be in contact with a family emotionally also means that the clinician can manage his/her own emotional vulnerabilities when these issues increase reactivity in the unit. When the clinician can touch upon any of these emotionally charged issues in a manner that allows people to talk about the intense feelings and tone down the reactivity associated with them, the emotional chain reaction in the unit can be slowed down. This requires that the clinician have a thorough understanding of his/her own emotional reactivity, recognize it when it is occurring, and have enough mastery of self to prevent his/her own emotional response from becoming part of the family problem.

Bowen used several terms to refer to the important effort of the therapist to retain his/her own level of differentiation of self during the clinical process. "Emotional neutrality," "staying outside the emotional system of the family," and "detriangling" all refer to the effort of the clinician to maintain differentiation of self while in emotional contact with the family. In an early paper Bowen described the process in the following manner:

If the therapist is to develop the capacity to stay outside the family emotional system in his clinical work, it is essential that he devote a continuing effort to differentiate his own self from the emotional system of his own family and also from the emotional system in which he works. Said in another way, it is necessary that he learn about triangles, and that he use his knowledge successfully in the emotional systems most important to him. However, there are some rules and principles that are important in the clinical situation. It is essential that he always stay focused on process, and that he defocus the content of what is being said. (1978, p. 250)

There are no particular styles of interaction prescribed by BFST. The clinician is not advised to be self-disclosing or distant, leading or following, confronting or supporting. For the clinician working on emotional neutrality, the ideal position is to be able to see the many sides of what another is saying and to be able to comment about any side either seriously or with humor.

The efforts of the clinician to attain and retain emotional neutrality remain the same throughout the course of the clinical process. The major difficulties for the clinician occur in the recognition and management of his/her own anxiety. An anxious clinician can drive a family away. His/her anxiety can play itself out in an overly responsible posture, benevolently or harshly, and infantalize a family. The clinician can take sides in an emotionally charged issue, becoming part of the emotional process of the family. The anxious clinician can assume responsibility for fixing the problem in the family, pouring life energy into the clinical family. The common outcome is frequently called "burnout," a rise (from a BFST point of view) in chronic anxiety related to the erosion of self (life energy and direction) in the process of lending self to another. The anxious clinician can also drain precious life energy from the family, stirring family anxiety through his/her need to be needed.

The Clinical Process

The clinical endeavor includes from the onset a survey of the family emotional fields (Bowen, 1978). The information gathered is recorded on a family diagram, which becomes a tool both for the clinician and for the family in learning about family process, differentiation of self, and the effect of anxiety upon the emotional unit. In a general sense, the clinician collects factual information about the entire family, person to person, and about events that have occurred in the recent and more distant past.

The survey often begins with the basic history of each spouse. Date and place of birth, education and employment history, current employment, health history, and date and cause of death (where indicated) form the core information gathered. The same information is collected for their children and for the members of their extended families. Information about the relationship between the spouses is also gathered. How and when did they meet? When did they decide to marry? What factors influenced that decision? How does each recollect the period of courtship? What were the significant events of that period, and how did people react to them? The facts of the marriage itself are recorded: when people were married, who attended, where the newlyweds lived, and so forth. Information about pregnancies, miscarriages, and births is gathered. Moves from one location to another are also important, and the clinician gathers facts about the timing and the impact of the move on the family. In a similar fashion, information is gathered about the families of each spouse. The clinician aims to formulate a picture of a family emotional system functioning both in the nuclear family and in the extended family across at least two generations.

The survey of the family emotional fields highlights the anxiety-sensitive symptoms of the family system, reveals the mechanisms used across time to manage the sensitivity and reactivity in the unit, and aids in seeing the unfolding reactivity that leads to the current symptom. Of particular interest are emotional cutoffs and the phenomenon referred to as the "emotional shock wave," the emergence of symptoms across the family unit following an event of particular emotional significance, often the death of an important family member.

Bowen (1971) listed the four main functions of the clinician in the clinical process with spouses. Each will now be briefly considered.

1. *Defining and clarifying the emotional process between spouses.* The emotional process between spouses (or for that matter, between any two connected individuals) can best be thought of as a chain reaction. The pair are preferentially sensitive: that is, they are more sensitive to each other than either is to some less connected person with less emotional significance. A behavior in one, set off in response to some sort of stimulus, is perceived, interpreted, and reacted to by the other. The reaction is based in the emotional system and is guided more by feeling than by thinking. Each reaction leads to a counterreaction, resulting in one of the four characteristic processes of relationship—distance, conflict, the loss of functioning in one and the gain of functioning in another, or the involvement of a child

in the process. Not all variations of emotional process are perceived by people as problematic. Falling in love, for example, is as much an automatic chain reaction as conflict, but is rarely considered a negative. One person's anxious effort to promote love and create togetherness, however, is often seen as an irritation by the other.

The chain reaction defined as problematical can also be thought of as a series of anxiety transfers from one person to the other and back. Fear is among the most infectious feelings known to human beings, and it can pass virtually instantaneously between people. People have always know this when they are calm. One does not cry "Fire!" in a crowded theater, precisely because anxiety is transmitted so rapidly, and such feeling-based behavior can be dangerous. The anxiety can increase in intensity with each transfer. Each increase in anxiety leads to greater reactivity, and the process can continue, at times forcing outside intervention to bring it to a halt. The intensity of the process varies with the level of differentiation of self and the intensity of anxiety of the participants.

The clinician works to keep his/her eye on the emotional process between people, not on whatever issue serves momentarily as the vehicle for emotional expression. The clinician approaches each person directly with questions about reactivity, feelings, and mentational processes. What is it that each person reacts to so strongly? What is the reaction like for each of them? What is it about the other person that serves as a stimulus to such a response? What makes the other so special that one reacts differently than with another person? The questions about process are infinite, and it can be explored in greater and greater detail. The goal is for people to talk and think about the process between them, not to enact it.

Learning about the chain reaction, becoming aware of one's own part in it, and thinking about how to change self are essential if people are to be able to let one another know about themselves, their thoughts, hopes, fears, and the principles that guide their lives. Few researchers have described the dilemma more clearly than did Bowen:

> Most spouses are caught in feeling worlds in which they react and respond to the feeling complex in the other, without ever really knowing the other. Most spouses probably have the most open relationships in their adult lives during the courtship. After marriage, each quickly begins to learn the subjects

that make the other anxious. To avoid the discomfort in self when the other is anxious, each avoids anxious issues, and an increasing number of subjects become taboo for discussion in the marriage. This breakdown in communication is present to some degree in most marriages. (1978, p. 227)

The clinician's stance is an active one. An important ingredient is often referred to as a "research attitude" or the clinician's interest in learning more about the process rather than trying to fix it. Many questions come from such a focus on inquiry. Such questions are honest: that is, they are designed to acquire new information, not to communicate an opinion or an ideal in an indirect fashion. The clinician works to keep each person in contact with him/herself, thinking about the problem rather than reacting to it. When the chain reaction ignites issues between people, the clinician works to bring the focus back once again to the process between them. For example, when one partner raises his/her voice angrily, or when tears start, the clinician can ask the other if he/she noticed the change in voice or the tears, and what happened in them in response. Is this response typical or unusual? How effective is the response in resolving the dilemma, in communicating to the other, in managing one's own feelings, and so forth? A reasonable goal for the clinician is to touch upon any emotionally charged issue presented by the family, to assist the people in thinking about the role of the issue and the emotional process behind it, and to help both the family and the clinician emerge from the discussion with less anxiety.

People work on managing their own reactivity in many ways. Many people find that some of the techniques of various popular therapies take on new significance when placed within the context of the emotional system. Biofeedback training can be a useful tool for persons interested in studying their own reactivity and response to important others. Although learning relaxation procedures may be a by-product of biofeedback training, most people find it extremely useful in two ways. In the first place, people learn to recognized the physical and mental markers of their own reactivity. Second, the connection between reactivity and relationship becomes more tangible. People can actually see their reaction as they talk about, think about, and actually interact with an important other. Advances in computerized biofeedback equipment allow the clinician to be monitored in the session as well, so that the family members can know both his/her

reactivity and sensitivity and their own. Such techniques can be useful for the interested person, but many people discover their own ways to recognize and work on reactivity without ever employing another therapeutic technique.

2. *Keeping self detriangled from the emotional process.* When the clinician sees both spouses together, he/she becomes the third element in the triangle involving the pair. How the clinician conducts self is governed by the knowledge of triangles. Bowen explains the process most clearly:

> This is part of central concept about triangles: Conflict between two people will resolve automatically if both remain in emotional contact with a third person who can relate actively to both without taking sides with either. This reaction is so predictable that it can be used in other areas of the family system and in social systems. (1978, p. 224)

The effort of the clinician to be in emotional contact with people and to maintain emotional neutrality has been discussed extensively earlier. The side taking among people is ubiquitous and often subtle. The clinician possesses a reservoir of knowledge of his/her own emotional reactivity, acquired through the continual work on differentiation of self in his/her own family and in all arenas. Personal training in biofeedback can also aid the clinician to know self better. This knowledge is essential to the management of self in the clinical arena. In addition, the clinician acquires with experience an ability to distinguish the emotional interplay between people from the issues that they present as the problem. With such knowledge, the clinician is presumably equipped to recognize the triangling process as it inevitably presents itself and to manage self within it without taking sides emotionally.

An important element of keeping self detriangled is the clinician's ability, mentioned previously, to defocus the issues presented by people and direct attention and observation to the emotional chain reaction between them. For people engaged in conflict, the emotional process resembles a fierce tennis match. One person serves an issue with just enough feeling-laden spin that the other cannot ignore it. He/she volleys back with another spinning shot, and the match is on! Subtle adjustments can end the immediate volley, but another is ready and waiting, needing only the initial serve to set it off. The issues are similar to the can of tennis balls that players bring to the court. When one volley is finished, the server grabs a new ball and initiates another volley. When the emotional process moves toward an over- and underfunctioning reciprocity, the chain reaction is not so readily apparent, but the erosion of the self of the underfuntioning one can sometimes be seen directly.

An example may help to illustrate the point. A young couple sought clinical assistance after the husband told his wife that he wanted a divorce. For the preceding few years, each had become increasingly distant from the other. Efforts to talk with one another would end in feeling-laden exchanges and heightened frustration. The husband became extremely involved with his job, spending long hours at work and time at home thinking about and preparing for his assignments. The wife became increasingly moody and unhappy. Her drinking increased to problem levels. During the clinical sessions, the wife would be quite expressive of feelings. She would cry, at times be angry, and generally act like a fountain of effervescent feeling. At these times, the husband would remain quiet, appearing somewhat withdrawn, and respond very little to her. After a period of this behavior, however, she would become more thoughtful and clearer about the dilemma she faced. She would tone down the feeling, and her inherent strength would begin to emerge. At this point, an interesting transformation occurred in the husband. His eyes would glisten with pregnant tears, his voice would crack, and he gave every appearance of struggling with intense feeling. He would talk of love, of his sense of guilt, and comment that the dissolution of the marriage was all his fault. During these moments, the wife would appear to wilt in her chair. Her head would fall, her erect posture would collapse in a slump, her voice would assume a little-girl quality, and she would give the appearance of complete helplessness. She reported that she felt intensely suicidal at these moments, and that it took her a long time to recover. She observed that at such moments she lost all ability to think for herself and was overcome by intense feelings.

Such situations present frequent opportunities for the clinician to respond emotionally to the family, to respond with simplistic remedies, and to feel sorry for one or the other and blame the opposite. Any such response tends to related to the immature side of the participants, to reinforce their own uncertainty about their lives and their abilities to be responsible for themselves. When the clinician can see the emotional process, manage his/her automatic emotional response, and stay in viable contact with each person, the strength of each can emerge,

and a way through the dilemma becomes possible.

3. Teaching the functions of emotional systems. Any clinical situation is sometimes didactic. BFST is best seen as a tool that motivated people can learn to apply to the dilemmas besetting them. The single most important variable governing the teaching process in clinical activity is anxiety, both in the clinician and in the family. When the clinician and the family are both relatively calm, a teaching exchange is possible. An anxious clinician will often resort to lectures on theory, explanation of the meaning of some particular interaction, and so forth, in an effort to cover his/her own uncertainty and to feel more comfortable. Attempting to teach theory and the functions of emotional systems at such times is a futile effort. The clinician is often seen as lecturing or scolding the family, and at the very least, the process is boring. When the family is anxious, the clinician's effort to convey an idea is often heard as a criticism or concrete suggestion to employ some particular technique or take a particular action. Anxious people hear things that are not said and say things that are not heard.

Teaching can often occur with the use of simple diagrams drawn on a chalkboard in the clinician's office. The clinician tries to convey the ideas and concepts of BFST. Virtually any sort of teaching device is possible. Bowen would often tell a story to illustrate a point. Much of the teaching occurs, however, by example. Emotional neutrality is best conveyed by demonstration, and the clinician is presented many opportunities to demonstrate this quality. Serving as an example is also central to the fourth function of the clinician.

4. Demonstrating differentiation of self during the clinical process. The culmination of the clinician's efforts to manage self occurs when he/she must define self in the face of pressures to join in the emotional process of the family. The pressure can be subtle or overt and intense. An early situation involves the use of names. Does the clinician slip into the use of first names with people, or is a respectful boundary better maintained with the more formal use of surnames? There is no correct answer to such a question, but if a clinician has not thought through some of these details, he/she is likely to become, perhaps inadvertently, a participant in the family emotional process. In Bowen's words,

When one member of a family can calmly state his own convictions and belief, and take action on his convictions without criticism of the beliefs of others and without becoming involved in emotional debate, then other family members will start the same process of becoming more sure of self and more accepting of others. The "I position" is very useful early in therapy as an operating position in relation to the family. It is advantageous to use it whenever possible through therapy. The more the therapist can clearly define himself in relation to the families, the easier it is for family members to define themselves to each other. (1978, p. 252)

Being sure of one's own viewpoint and principles, and how one will act in response to a situation is the essence of differentiation of self. Statements for self are not presented as a criticism of others or as a demand that someone else be different. Nor are they offered as a subject for debate. The family is free to stop their effort at any time, and the clinician is free to spell out his/her part in the process at any point along the way.

With experience, a clinician can learn how to handle the routine situations (like the use of names) which require some definition of self. An I position can be very simple, for example, "I think I understand what you're saying, and my thoughts go a different direction." The definition of self can also be more involved, requiring much though on the clinician's part and a great deal of self-management in order to present his/her position calmly and clearly. Much of the teaching function of the clinical process can also be made from the I position. As Bowen described the effort, "the therapist presents his views, beliefs, and operating principles in such a way that they can be accepted or rejected by the family" (1978, pp. 231–232). An active and lively family can present the clinician with a situation for which he/she has no precedent, and principles must be relied upon to guide the definition of self. Often, such situations occur when the family is pressuring the clinician to take some sort of action that will make the family feel better but leads the clinician to some sort of irresponsible action. Common areas in which such pressures occur include the prescription and use of medication, and the hospitalization of a symptomatic person.

The clinical process can proceed with both spouses or with only one. A major consideration is the degree of reactivity between the partners. Can they stop the debate long enough to let one of them talk to the clinician without interruption? Can they listen to what the other is saying

to the clinician, without automatically creating in their heads the counterresponse? Can the emotional chain reaction be contained at least for the clinical session? If so, and if both are willing to participate, the sessions can include both spouses.

When seeing spouses together, a simple principle governs the overall effort: "It is a clinical fact that the original two-person tension system will resolve itself automatically when contained within a three-person system, one of whom remains emotionally detached" (Bowen, 1978, p. 224). Bowen (1978) also stated this principle in the following manner: "Conflict between two people will resolve automatically if both remain in emotional contact with a third person who can relate actively to both without taking sides with either. This reaction is so predictable that it can be used in other areas of the family system and in social systems" (p. 175). The significant factor in each statement is the ability of the third person to remain in emotional contact with each partner while remaining emotional neutral.

Although the four functions of the clinician always apply in a general way, the main technique when seeing spouses together involves shifting the focus from the content of issues and clarifying the emotional process between the partners. The clinical process aims to externalized the emotional process behind the issues and assist people to separate their fantasy, feeling, and thinking systems from one another internally and interpersonally.

The general format is for the clinician to talk with one person while the other listens. The clinician has a series of low-key questions aimed at clarifying the emotional reactivity of the person and the chain reaction between partners. The questions vary with the information presented by the person and reflect the clinician's own general interest as well. The questions aim to elicit the thinking of the other, not to persuade him/her of a particular viewpoint or to lead to a particular observation. How objective can the person be about a process in which he/she participates? How clear is one's own role in such an interaction? What is one person so sensitive to in the other? What occurs in self when the other presents the sensitive stimulus (a tone of voice, a look, a gesture, a topic, etc.)? The question can assist the other person to clarify the details of his/her reactivity and thinking.

Sometimes the response of the person is intense with feeling. The clinician's questions assist the individual to tone down the feeling response from a volcanic eruption to a bubbling fountain that is less overwhelming and more accessible to both the person and his/her partner, less likely to set off a counterfeeling in the other. When the chain reaction erupts in the session, the clinician can step up the tempo of the questions while maintaining a low-key approach. Did the husband note the change in the tone of his wife's voice when she made her last comment? What was his reaction to the tone? How did the reaction affect what he was thinking and feeling? In this manner, the clinician moves from person to person, asking about their thoughts and reaction in response to what their partner has been saying.

During the clinical course, one or the other person may drop out for awhile. Occasionally, the clinician may suggest that only one partner come in for awhile, generally the one who is making the most progress, leaving it to the spouses to determine who that one is. Such a suggestion often occurs when the partners have been unable to manage the reactive process in the clinical sessions, which then become extensions of the intense debate that goes on at home. Sometimes, only one partner is motivated to seek assistance from the very beginning. At such times, the methodology shifts from family psychotherapy with two spouses to family psychotherapy with one partner.

Another principle guides the effort with one person. A deadlocked family can loosen up when some differentiation can rise up out of the family quagmire (Bowen, 1978). The goal of the clinical process is to assist the person to greater objectivity and an initial effort toward differentiation of self (Bowen, 1978). The basic procedures of the effort toward differentiation of self are communicated to the person. In general, these include shifting one's critical focus on another by reducing the other-directed thinking, verbal action, and energy designed to change the other. The reduction of energy designed to change the other is accompanied by a redirection of energy to the task of changing self:

Changing self involves finding a way to listen to the attacks of the other without responding, of finding a way to live with what is without trying to change it, of defining one's own beliefs and convictions without attacking those of the other, and in observing the part that self plays in the situation. (Bowen, 1978, p. 178)

The task of becoming a better observer of one's own life and one's own part in the relationship difficulties is important. Much of the subsequent clinical sessions are taken up with the person's reports about what he/she has observed, what is being worked on, where difficulties have been encountered, what has been done to meet the difficulties, and what success or lack of success has resulted.

Finally, the clinician advises the other partner of what may be expected if he/she is successful in moving a little toward differentiation. The initial response from the emotionally important other(s) will reflect intense criticism along the following lines: "You are selfish, mean, uncaring, and vicious. If you loved me and understood me, you would not be the way you are. You are deliberately trying to hurt me." If the differentiating one continues on course, this phase of criticism is followed by a withdrawal, characterized by the attitude, "To heck with you, I don't need you." This reaction may be the most difficult of all for the person working on differentiation. One's dependency on the other is painfully exposed, and the person has only his/her own conviction and motivation to rely upon. If the differentiating one can continue on, following the general procedures outlined previously, the other will ultimately shift his/her functioning to reflect the increased autonomy.

The emotional process between spouses can be so intense at times that it becomes extremely difficult for either of them to make much progress toward management of the emotional chain reaction by changing self. Such stalemates can slow down an effort considerably. In the period 1967–1968, Bowen observed that several residents were practicing better family psychotherapy than any previous group. Upon investigation, he learned that these residents had been making serious efforts to work on differentiation of self in the families they came from. Further inquiry revealed that these residents were also handling the predictable emotional difficulties with their own spouses and children differently from other previous groups. They seemed to be applying what they learned from the efforts with their extended families automatically with their spouses and children. In essence, they had bypassed some of the marital stalemate (Bowen, 1978). From this observation, Bowen developed another clinical suggestion: the effort to work on differentiation of self in one's original family as an aid to enhancing functioning in the current family.

With this addition, it became possible for the motivated person to bypass the inevitable stalemates that arise in a given relationship by turning to the extended family for relationships of similar intensity. Often, the knowledge and skill gained with the extended family allowed the person to find resolutions to stalemates that had seemed irresolvable. When the effort bogged down in the extended family, the person could turn again to the dilemma with the spouse, moving from one intense relationship to another, always with the goal of learning to manage self more responsibly while remaining in emotional contact with important others.

The effort with one's extended family assumes a motivation to learn about the family with an eye toward greater objectivity. A person sets out essentially to conduct a research study on his/her own family. As Bowen explained the effort,

> The study requires that the researcher begins to gain control over his emotional reactivity to his family, that he visit his parental family as often as indicated, and that he develop the ability to become a more objective observer in his own family. As the system becomes more "open" and he can begin to see the triangles and the part he plays in the family reaction patterns, he can begin the more complex process toward differentiating himself from the myths, images, distortions, and triangles he had not previously seen. (1978, pp. 539–540)

The learning in this process comes mostly from the person's own work toward the management of self in the family. He/she is aware that progress depends upon personal effort and responsibility. The effort with the extended family falls into three general categories, all of which are equally important:

1. Establishing person-to-person relationships in the extended family
2. Becoming a better observer of oneself and others
3. Detriangling oneself from emotional situations

The motivated individual is encouraged to work toward establishing person-to-person relationships with as many people as possible in the family:

> In broad terms, a person to person relationship is one in which two people can relate personally to each other about each other, without talking about others (triangling), and without talking about impersonal "things." Few people can talk personally to anyone for more than a few minutes without increasing anxiety, which results in silences, talking about others, or talking about impersonal things. (Bowen, 1978, p. 540)

In the course of the effort, the person comes face to face with the effect of his/her immatur-

ity on others, and with his/her sensitivity to the thoughts and feelings of the other person. An added benefit is the improvement of the relationship system that develops over time in the family.

Bowen also described the task as developing an individual relationship to each parent. All kinds of obstacles can develop when one sets out on such an effort. Time-honored and congenial family roles, preserving a calm congeniality, can block the effort of each to know the other. Feeling-endowed images of the parent and emotionally programmed responses in the offspring can deflect efforts to know the other. The clinician who has experience in his/her own family can help avoid emotionally based roadblocks that can absorb vast amounts of time.

The motivated person also takes on the task of becoming a better observer of self and the family. A related task is to control one's own emotional reactiveness. Whenever a person can be a bit outside the emotional process of the family, simply watching it unfold rather than playing a direct part in it, he/she gets a different view of people and the interactional process. It is easier not to be angry at people and not to blame others for emotional dilemmas. When one person can be freer in the family, not being so quick to take sides and to blame, the entire family gains. Bowen warns that it is impossible to tell the family what one is trying to do and still make it work. Telling other leads to automatic reactions and debates that hinder the effort to observe and manage one's own automatic response differently. The ability to observe and manage one's own reactiveness, even a little bit, is a skill with great application in all areas of living. One can follow one's own automatic responses much of the time with little or no problem, and also have the skill to step out of the reactive position into that of the observer to slow reactivity down, and to exert greater control of self and the situation when necessary.

Finally, the effort with the extended family involves detriangling oneself from emotional situations. The effort toward personal relationships and observing and controlling one's own reactiveness opens up the relationship system and restores the emotional process to what it was before one cut off from it. One is exposed to the emotional issues of the family and the various triangles that surface and submerge when such issues dominate. When one can see the triangles, it is possible to be different in relation to them.

Detriangling self from emotional situations, as a process, has been discussed previously. Bowen (1978) describes the efforts succinctly: "The overall goal is to be constantly in contact with an emotional issue involving two other people and self, without taking sides, without counterattacking or defending self, and to always have a neutral response" (p. 542).

Bowen cautions that confrontation is the single biggest error made by people in the effort with their extended families. Confrontation is fundamentally an effort to change another, radically different from the focus of differentiation of self in which the effort is to change self.

Bowen was interested in the future and in the functioning of generations still to come. He thought knowledge and science were extremely important to the future. He captured what he meant in one of the last pieces he wrote:

> My life work has been based on an opposing viewpoint [to the view that there can never be a science of human behavior]. It says merely that the physical structure of the human is scientific, that the human brain *functions* to create feelings and subjective states, and that the brain is capable of separating structure from function. My premise merely states that the human is a passenger on planet earth and that sometime in the future the human can clarify the difference between *what the human is* from *what the human feels, imagines and says.* (Kerr & Bowen, 1988, pp. 354–355)

The list of areas to be explored through the lens of BFST is infinite. Each investigation produces many more new questions than it answers. Theory development and application guide one another. All serious work with BFST aims to increase and transmit knowledge effectively to the future.

A different theoretical lens permits old questions to be reformulated and reexamined. What is natural in human nature, and how does it work? Do the principles of evolutionary theory apply to the human being and the human family? How is *Homo sapiens* similar and different from other species? Are the similarities analogies or homologies? Are the differences real or simply variations on a theme? Can knowledge of human nature and the human family challenge current scientific thinking?

Old problems are also open to new approaches guide by theory. Can the theoretical concepts of the emotional system and differentiation of self contribute to the resolution of contemporary and future personal, family, societal, and planetary dilemmas as they play out into the 21st century? Current projects investigate human health symptoms (AIDS, cancer, asthma, etc.), societal dilemmas (homelessness, violence, the health

industry, etc.), the functioning of large and small organizations and institutions (leadership, productivity, etc.), among many others, utilizing the lens of BFST.

As for marriage—women and men will continue to form breeding pairs into the foreseeable future. Many will also, if current and past society is any guide, debate the necessity, viability, and purpose of marriage. They will experiment with contrived variations of all sorts. But babies will be born, and how their parents manage themselves with one another and in the world will continue to be important to those children, who, in their turn, become partners and parents themselves. BFST provides one way of thinking about the management of self as a partner, as a parent, and as an autonomous individual.

POSTSCRIPT

Following their initial review of the completed chapter, the editors requested that three commonly asked questions be addressed in these concluding paragraphs:

1. How is resistance handled?
2. How is termination handled?
3. What are the contraindications to BFST?

The following discussion pertains to the clinical application of BFST in general and is not limited to the context of marriage. The first two questions reflect a different theoretical perspective from BFST about the role of the clinician and the clinical process itself. The concepts of resistance and termination come from a theoretical perspective stressing the relative importance of the therapist and the primacy of the therapeutic relationship in the clinical process.

In the original psychoanalytic context, the general term "resistance" referred to anything that impeded the emergence of unconscious in the conscious. Resistance could be triggered by interactional pressures between analyst and analysand, but also occurred mostly as a natural and expected part of the analytic process. Where resistance represented an interactional impasse, the analyst and the patient each played a part. Otherwise, it could be described as the patient's process of self-deception or inability to accept the truth of his/her own mental reality. The patient's transference to the analyst of feelings and reactions developed in an early relationship to a parent lay most often at the core of resistance.

In the contemporary world of therapy, resistance can mean many things, from the psychoanalytic usage in all its nuances and refinements to the judgmental labeling of a person or family that does not cooperate with a clinician. Historically, the concept of resistance comes from a theory of the individual, not of the family. Within BFST, it falls within the general parameters of reactivity and emotional system functioning. In one's efforts to manage self in relationship to important others, one automatically comes to recognize and address the forces in self working against nonreactive communication with another and against differentiation. When the term refers more coarsely to the reluctance of a person or family to accept the notions of the clinician and cooperate with his/her concept of what is best, then the coach works to understand his/her own part of the interactional process and to manage self differently. The coach does not attempt to change another, but to define and manage self in the context of the clinical process.

Both the concepts of resistance and termination come from a theoretical framework stressing the importance of the therapeutic relationship and of the transference by the patient toward the therapist of feelings and reactions developed in the early relationship to a parent. BFST directs the person back to the original relationships or to their closest current approximation, downplaying the relationship to the coach. When the important relationships are activated, whether to a spouse, parent, or other significant emotional figure, the transference becomes less important.

The dilemma of transference could arise when seeing one person individually. To meet this possibility, Bowen (1978) refined the clinical skill which he called "staying outside the transference," which he defined as the clinician's ability to keep him/herself emotionally disengaged. The clinician works to manage his/her sensitivity, interpretive mindset, and emotional reactivity to the other person.

Staying out of the transference begins with initial contact with the family and the clinician's task of establishing the orientation of the theoretical–therapeutic system. Bowen describes his thinking in the following manner:

> Most families are referred with a diagnosis for the dysfunction. They think in terms of the medical model and expect that the therapist is going to change the diagnosed family member, or the parents may expect the therapist to show or tell them how to change the child without understanding and

modifying their part in the family system. . . . I persistently oppose the tendency of the family to view me as a "therapist." . . . When the therapist allows himself to become a "healer" or "repairman," the family goes into dysfunction to wait for the therapist to accomplish his work. (1978, pp. 157–158)

Many of the techniques associated with family systems therapy serve the accomplishment of this task—the avoidance of the diagnosis of any family member, the effort to establish the clinician as a consultant for the initial sessions and as supervisor of the effort if the process continues, and the focus on observation rather than therapy. The family makes a research project of itself.

The clinician's definition of him/herself to the family becomes important. Bowen explains what he means:

> One of the most important processes in this method of psychotherapy is the therapist's continuing attention to defining his "self" to the families. This beings from the first contact which defines this theoretical and therapeutic system and its differences from others. It proceeds in almost every session around all kinds of life issues. Of importance are the "action" stands which have to do with "what I will do and will not do." I believe a therapist is in a poor position to ask a family to do something he does not do. (1978, p. 177)

The positions defined by the clinician are always presented in terms of what he/she will or will not do, never in terms of what is best for the family.

Bowen sums up his basic notion of "staying out of the transference" in the following paragraph:

> The life style of this low level of differentiation is the investment of psychic energy in the "self" of another. When this happens in therapy, it is transference. A goal of this therapy is to help the other person make a research project out of life. It is important to keep "self" contained with the therapist as the other spouse. If the person understands the life-goal nature of the effort and that progress will slow down or stop with energy invested in the "self" of the therapist, he is in a better position to help keep the energy focused on the goal. (1978, p. 179)

To the degree that the clinician has been successful in functioning as coach rather than therapist and staying out of the transference, many of the dilemmas associated with the therapeutic relationship can be avoided. Each clinician develops his/her way of presenting self and the theoretical-therapeutic orientation to the family. Some elements are relatively common, including the respectful attitude of the clinician toward the family; the relative infrequency of appointments, often determined by the family; and the focus on learning more about the family, rather than fixing the family problem.

Common dilemmas between clinician and family generally indicate that the clinician has not defined him/herself clearly enough to the family. The family's behavior may reflect the clinician's slipping from the role of coach to that of change agent, pressuring the family in the process to accept his/her interpretation of reality and to conduct themselves in the manner he/she deems appropriate. The clinician may have inadequately addressed the anxiety of an agency, a court system or even the broader society, functioning as a part of an intense triangle. The family may respond with its own intensity and anxiety, an apparent reluctance to cooperate or to participate fully in the clinician's treatment plan. The beginning of a person's effort toward differentiation within the family may not match the clinician's notion of what ought to occur, creating anxious discomfort in the therapist. The clinician may define the patient as resistant. In whatever situation that may develop, the coach works always to see and modify his/her part of an emotional process.

The main thrust of the effort to learn and apply BFST occurs outside the clinical hour in the important relationships of the family, the work system, and the community. The learning occurs in each family member's efforts to become familiar with the emotional system of family, work, and community and to manage self differently within it. The effort to improve functional differentiation of self is continuous. A person's or family's efforts may occur in spurts and may or may not involve a clinician. Many families keep contact with a clinician across many years but may only speak with him/her infrequently. Some families end contact with a particular clinician but maintain contact with BFST through reading, conferences, and through their own private efforts toward greater differentiation.

From the first contact, therefore, the clinician works to establish the theoretical orientation of the clinical process. The family is responsible for its own decisions, and the coach for his/hers. Each can end participation in the clinical process at any time, for any reason. This is not a matter of technique but is built into the contact between coach and family from the beginning. The ending of clinical contact can occur in innumerable ways. Typically, the family decides when to begin and end the contact. There is no concept of right timing, at least from the clinician. The

family determines its priorities in much the same way that it determines how often to see a personal physician, a banker, or any other sort of consultant. And the clinician determines how and to what degree he/she is willing to be involved. In short, the concept of termination applies to a different way of thinking about the process between clinician and family and a different focus and approach.

BFST is a theory of the human family with clinical applications derived from it. A theory is a way of thinking about a set of facts and is always subject to refinement and alteration if the facts so warrant. As theory is refined, clinical applications can change. There are no family symptoms that cannot be addressed by BFST, and consequently, no contraindications. There are various situations in which the coach may well disqualify him/herself from entering or continuing clinical activity. Such situations are marked by the clash of theories and clinical applications so discrepant that no assistance to the family seems likely.

A common situation concerns the active participation of several therapists in a family dilemma. A spouse may have an individual therapist, a child may have a child therapist, and the marital pair may be referred for marital therapy. The likelihood is high that each of these therapists has a different way of thinking about the nature of the problem and how best to approach it. Transferences usually exist between family members and the various therapists, intensifying feelings and complicating each person's ability to be responsible for and to represent self. From the viewpoint of BFST, all the symptoms are a product of the family emotional unit. To divide them into separate problems to be addressed by different practitioners confuses the situation and adds additional relationship variables and triangles that can be extremely complex. Such a situation cannot really be called a contraindication, for a coach may occasionally tackle this complicated situation. Some have even been able to navigate these tricky waters, defining self in a variety of triangles around a large number of emotionally charged subjects.

BFST addresses the family unit as the patient, not the particular symptomatic individual or relationship. This viewpoint allows any family member to work on his/her part of a symptom. BFST is not well suited to the eclectic therapist, because its application requires a thorough grounding in theory and an understanding of emotional system functioning. The mixing of techniques from different theoretical origins at best produces a haphazard approach, based more in the therapist's subjectivity than on fact and knowledge. If the term "contraindication" is to be applied at all, it should be restricted to the clinician, not to the family. Whatever rules are derived from BFST, they exist for the clinician, not for application to the family.

NOTES

1. In his writings, Bowen described the level of differentiation of self of each partner as identical. In his personal comments, he would sometimes describe the levels as similar rather than identical.

REFERENCES

Bowen, M. (1966). The use of family theory in clinical practice. *Comprehensive Psychiatry, 7*(5), 345–374.

Bowen, M. (1972). On the differentiation of self. In J. Framo (Ed.), *Family interaction: A dialogue between family researchers and family therapists* (pp. 111–173). New York: Springer.

Bowen, M. (1978). *Family therapy in clinical practice.* New York: Aronson.

deWaal, F. (1982). *Chimpanzee politics: Power and sex among apes.* New York: Harper & Row.

Kerr, M. E., & Bowen, M. (1988). *Family evaluation: An approach based on Bowen theory.* New York/London: Norton.

Papero, D. V. (1990). *Bowen family systems theory.* Boston/London: Allyn & Bacon.

Toman, W. (1961). *Family constellation.* New York: Springer.

3

Integrative Behavioral Couple Therapy

ANDREW CHRISTENSEN
NEIL S. JACOBSON
JULIA C. BABCOCK

Integrative behavioral couple therapy (IBCT) represents both a continuation and a marked departure from previous attempts to apply behavioral theory to intervention with married couples. Similar to approaches developed by Jacobson and his colleagues (Jacobson & Holtzworth-Monroe, 1986; Jacobson & Margolin, 1979; Holtzworth-Monroe & Jacobson, 1991), Stuart (1980), and Patterson and Weiss (e.g., Weiss, Hops, & Patterson, 1973), IBCT makes use of reinforcement principles to conceptualize and intervene with couples. Also, most of the assessment instruments and treatment strategies of these earlier approaches also appear in IBCT. Readers familiar with behavioral approaches will recognize instruments such as the Spouse Observation Checklist (Weiss et al., 1973) and the Areas of Change Questionnaire (Margolin, Talovic, & Weinstein, 1983) and procedures such as behavioral exchange and communication/problem-solving training (Jacobson & Holtzworth-Monroe, 1986).

IBCT represents a marked departure from these earlier behavioral approaches in two important ways. First, IBCT eschews the term "marriage" or "marital" in its title in an attempt to apply the approach to a larger group of dyads than just married couples. It is our belief that this approach can be used successfully with adult couples in close, romantic relationships, whether they be living together couples, gay and lesbian couples, or married couples. Furthermore, we wish to avoid the "heterosexism" and "marriageism" that comes from an exclusive focus on married couples. Nevertheless, we realize that the most common application of this approach is to married couples, and most of our examples concern this group.

Second, IBCT incorporates the notion of "acceptance" into its behavioral theory and into its strategies for assisting couples. While the idea of promoting acceptance in psychotherapeutic work is hardly new, behavioral approaches to marriage have emphasized behavioral change rather than acceptance of the partner's behavior as is. IBCT attempts to balance this traditional emphasis on change with an equivalent emphasis on acceptance. Furthermore, IBCT delineates a series of procedures designed to foster acceptance in couples.

IBCT was developed by Andrew Christensen and Neil S. Jacobson. This chapter represents the first, complete, published account of IBCT although the treatment was briefly mentioned by Jacobson (1991), briefly described by Jacobson (1992), and described more fully in an unpublished treatment manual (Christensen & Jacobson, 1991). A monograph detailing the approach

(Jacobson & Christensen, in press) and a guide for couples (Christensen & Jacobson, in press) are being developed.

The impetus for the development of IBCT came from our clinical experience, as well as from our research on traditional behavioral couple therapy (TBCT). In our clinical work, we were independently experimenting with methods for increasing acceptance in couples as we were experiencing the limitations of traditional change strategies. Furthermore, the data on TBCT, although impressive in both quantity and outcome, showed that many couples were not achieving lasting benefit from therapy. About one third of the couples treated by TBCT do not show any benefit from therapy. Of those who do benefit, about one third relapse within 1 to 2 years. Thus, only about one half of couples treated with TBCT improve and maintain their improvement over the long term (Jacobson et al., 1984; Jacobson, Schmaling, & Holtzworth-Munroe, 1987). Clearly, more is needed for at least half the couples who present for marital therapy. It is our belief that the addition of procedures for promoting acceptance can reach many of these couples who could not achieve lasting benefit from TBCT, while increasing the power of treatment for those couples who could benefit from TBCT.

In this chapter we first describe our theoretical model of relationship distress, emphasizing the development of that distress. Couples start out happy and in love. Any viable theory of marital distress must explain how they go from this harmonious state to the discordant state that couples find themselves in when they come to therapy or divorce court. Next, we focus on our theory of therapeutic change. How can behavioral theory inform a specific therapy for complex marital problems? We focus on assessment, emphasizing a functional analysis of behavior, as well as intervention. After presenting this theoretical material, we focus on the "how-to-do-it" practice of IBCT. We first describe several stages in this therapy, then focus on particular strategies for bringing about change and promoting acceptance.

THEORETICAL MODEL OF RELATIONSHIP DISTRESS

There are a great many misconceptions about behaviorism, and what it means to apply a behavioral approach to couples. These misconceptions are reflected in much of the commentary about behavioral approaches within the family therapy field (e.g., Johnson & Greenberg, 1991; Gurman, 1991; Snyder & Wills, 1991), and even in much of the traditional writings by behavior therapists (cf. Jacobson, 1991). These misconceptions, which arise from the notoriety of early behavioral models such as John Watson's, include, but are not limited to, the following: Behaviorists are less concerned than others with unobservable phenomena such as thinking and feeling; behaviorists believe that all behaviors are learned, and that genetic factors are relatively unimportant; and behaviorists do not believe that early childhood experiences are important in determining adult behavior. On the contrary, contemporary behaviorists are concerned about and attempt to explain the same subject matter as do all other theoretical frameworks. Moreover, there is nothing in the contemporary behavioral framework that even implies that genetic factors are not important; in fact, behaviorism attempts to account for how simple and complex behaviors are acquired after genetic constraints have been taken into account. Finally, behaviorism is a learning model, and the influence of early childhood is not only acknowledged but it is also considered important.

So how does this contemporary behaviorism apply to couples? The behavioral model provides a method, called "functional analysis," for identifying how individuals in a relationship are influenced by each other, and how aspects of the relationship itself are influenced by factors external to it. In theory, once these events have been identified, they can be influenced, and we end up with a prescription for couple therapy. Thus, when we are trying to explain an individual's marital distress, we look to the partner's behavior and hypothesize how that person influences the other's marital satisfaction. When we are trying to explain dysfunctional marital interaction, we look for its antecedents and consequences. These antecedents and consequences lead to our prescriptions for intervention. When these antecedents and consequences are integrated with notions of the couples' and individual partners' histories, we have a complete behavioral account of the evolution of a relationship. The history is paramount, because it determines, along with genetic makeup, our susceptibility to current environmental events. But the history is not static: It keeps changing with every new experience, and in the end, the couple therapist is really trying to contribute to a revisionist relationship history, so that by the time therapy is over, the relationship environment is maintaining those aspects of the relationship that maximize couple satisfaction.

Despite an emphasis upon the external environment as the cause of human behavior, behaviorists acknowledge that human beings bring something causal to the behavior–environment transaction. Human beings are not simply pushed around by the environment. As a result of their genetic endowment and previous exposure to the environment, they push back. In the couple area, theorists have conceptualized that couples bring communication skills and conflict resolution skills to their interactions, which then influence and are influenced by these interactions (Christensen, 1983; Jacobson & Margolin, 1979). If couples are proficient in these skills, or are trained in them through proper therapy, they can deal with conflict that arises between them in a constructive manner that does not deteriorate into negative interaction. If, however, couples do not have these skills, they may engage in destructive interaction that adversely affects their satisfaction and further deteriorates their skills.

In the last couple of decades, behavioral approaches have experienced a shift away from external determinants to "cognitive determinants" of behavior, such as schemas, irrational thoughts, and attributions. This so-called "cognitive revolution" meant a shift toward dualism, the positing of hypothetical constructs beneath the skin as causes in addition to external stimuli as causes. Similarly, behavioral approaches to marriage have experienced a move away from external determinants toward internal cognitive–affective states. For example, Baucom, Epstein, Sayers, and Sher (1989) delineated five types of cognitive processes that they deemed important in marriage: (1) selective perception, (2) attributions, (3) assumptions, (4) standards, and (5) expectations.

IBCT represents a return to behaviorists' traditional emphasis on the functional analysis and external determinants of behavior. Whereas IBCT attempts to integrate approaches from a variety of different sources, it does so within a traditional behavioral approach. It retains certain mediational concepts, such as skills that reflect learning history, but it reiterates behaviorists' traditional distrust of hypothetical constructs as explanatory concepts.

Development of Relationship Distress

How then does IBCT describe the development of relationship distress? IBCT assumes that mate selection is an outcome produced by an inter-action between the genetic predispositions of both partners, their learning histories prior to meeting, and the mutual reinforcement provided during courtship. Partners enter into a relationship based on the actual and anticipated reinforcers that they receive in the relationship. Their tenure in the relationship and their commitments to the relationship, such as marriage, result from the complex interplay of these features. Reinforcers can refer to benefits external to the relationship itself, such as the wealth, status, and prestige that being with a particular partner provides, as well as to benefits internal to the relationship, such as the emotional support, companionship, or sexual pleasure that partners get from their interaction. Actual and potential punishments also play a role, such as when partners stay in a relationship to avoid the aversive consequence of religious sanctions, the loss of financial resources, or the loss of the partner's emotional support.

Why do partners not select a mate with whom they can maintain high levels of mutual gratification and then live their lives together in mutual satisfaction? Several developmental processes may play havoc with this utopian view of relationships. First, the reinforcement value of a partner can decrease over time because of "reinforcement erosion"—the tendency for behaviors that were once reinforcing to diminish in reinforcement with repeated experience (Jacobson & Margolin, 1979). As partners habituate to each other and become satiated with the reinforcers that the other provides, experiences that were once novel and exciting may become routine and ordinary. If couples have a limited range of reinforcers and are unable to expand their repertoire of reinforcers, then they may experience a loss of satisfaction.

A second developmental process is the exposure of incompatibilities through greater contact. Any two people who start a close relationship will be different in important ways. No matter how careful their mate-selection process, at some point they will find themselves confronted with situations in which they do not want the same things at the same time in the same way. Furthermore, these differences will at times be important. Partners will not be able to shrug them off as trivial; they will be invested in having it done their way. During courtship, partners may be shielded from these incompatibilities. Their contact may be limited to recreational times, so that their differing habits and schedules do not conflict. In addition, they may be on their best behavior with each other, so that any incompatibilities are minimized. However, as the relationship progresses, particularly to the point at which they live together, partners' incompatibilities are likely to be exposed.

A third developmental process is the generation of incompatibilities through shared life experiences. Some incompatibilities may not be apparent until the couple shares some life event. Perhaps the best example is having children. A couple might plan on having children, and agree in advance on their number, timing, and manner of rearing. However, their presence may affect husband and wife in incompatible and largely unpredictable ways. Even though they agreed in advance that childrearing would be shared equally, he may believe child care can be entrusted to others, while she believes the two of them must themselves do most child care. He may think a crying baby should always be responded to, while she thinks babies can cry themselves to sleep.

A fourth developmental process is the creation of incompatibilities as both partners experience their own individual life events. For example, a couple may be compatible in their desire for closeness with each other until the wife's career "takes off" and she desires less closeness in the relationship and more devotion to her career. Similarly, a couple may be compatible in their manner of dealing with in-laws until the wife's mother has a stroke and the wife wants her mother to live with them. The husband cannot fathom having his disabled mother-in-law living with them.

Whatever their source, incompatibilities can have enormous impact on the reinforcement exchange within the couple. One or both partners will be deprived of reinforcement or exposed to punishment. For the couple in which the wife's career "takes off," either the wife is deprived of career opportunities, or the husband of his desired level of closeness, or both. The couple who disagrees about the use of baby-sitters will either deprive the husband of contact alone with his wife, or expose the wife to painful anxiety and guilt.

Coercion theory (Patterson, 1982) and other postulates regarding aversive control play a central role in the behavioral model of couple distress. They suggest that in situations of incompatibility, one or both partners often engage in coercive techniques. Partners will apply aversive stimulation until the other gives in and does it their way. "Aversive stimulation" in relationships can refer to such things as crying, guilt induction, withdrawal, withholding, even physical violence. Partners can be quite creative in the way they apply aversive stimulation until the other complies. When one partner does "give in," either partially or completely, positive and negative reinforcement occur. The partner who was coercive gets positively reinforced for his/her coercive efforts (by getting what he/she wanted). The partner who is the recipient of the coercion gets negatively reinforced, in that the aversive stimuli stop once he/she has complied. Therefore, both members are reinforced for their responses in this coercive situation and can be expected to engage in their respective behaviors again.

Although both partners get reinforced, it is at some cost, at least to the partner being coerced. This partner had to give up his/her position in order to reduce the negative stimulation. Therefore, the coerced one may not comply immediately. He/she may progressively habituate to coercive responses and may unintentionally shape the partner to apply increasingly stronger levels of coercion before he/she complies. Also, the partner may not comply on every occasion. The coerced one may hold out on some occasions, thus providing the partner with a more powerful intermittent reinforcement for being coercive.

Although it seems to be a temporary solution to the incompatibility between partners, coercion may actually increase that incompatibility. The husband who coerces his career-minded wife to skip a meeting so she can go out to dinner with him may have achieved a Pyrrhic victory. Angry at him for the coercion and concerned about her work, she may be less than a desirable dinner partner. With his repeated coercive efforts she may withdraw from him in anger, stiffen her resistance to his coercion, and resolve not to abandon her work responsibilities ever again. Thus, the coercive solution may make an incompatibility between a pair even greater.

We have described coercion as an interaction between the coercer and the coerced. It is unlikely, however, that one partner solely maintains the coercive role while the other maintains the coerced role. More likely, both partners engage in coercive acts but possibly use different kinds of coercive behavior. This reciprocal use of coercion in combination with intermittent reinforcement for coercion, the shaping of higher levels of coercion, and the greater incompatibility that often results from the coercion, makes the relationship a source of mutual pain. If we add to these processes the phenomenon of reinforcement erosion, we have a picture of distressed couples entering therapy—experiencing much pain and little pleasure from their relationship. Thus, with these simple notions of positive and negative reinforcement, combined with the notion of inevitable incompatibilites between partners, the behavioral perspective can explain how a loving couple can become an angry, pain-inducing, distressed couple.

THEORY OF THERAPEUTIC CHANGE

IBCT represents a return to traditional behavioral roots, but its approach is a marked departure from both traditional and contemporary behavioral couple therapy. IBCT contends that much previous behavioral work did not capture the true, important controlling variables in marital interaction. Instead, they often captured variables that were derivative of the controlling ones and thus were trivial by contrast. An example clarifies this distinction. Let us assume that for a particular couple, a major set of controlling variables for the marital satisfaction of the wife, Margo, are actions from her husband, Dave, that communicate to her that she is deeply loved and valued. Her childhood history made her question whether she was loved and lovable, so finding a man who was devoted to her was essential for marital satisfaction. For Dave, a major class of reinforcers are those things Margo does that provide him with the experience that she admires and believes in him. Because of his childhood history, Dave is driven to succeed as a writer. He is both embarrassed and dismayed that he must work as a high school English teacher while he struggles with writing on his off-hours. The fact that Margo saw talent in him, believed that he could be a writer, and actively encouraged him in that dream was a major facet of his attachment to her.

During the first few years of their marriage, Dave and Margo began to take each other for granted, got focused on their own needs, and found the needs of the other annoying and interfering. As a result, Margo missed out on the reassurance that she needed from Dave and Dave missed out on the support he depended on from Margo. Feeling deprived by the other, both began to withhold from the other, not just in the crucial areas of love and support, but in other areas as well. They spent less time in companionate activities together. Their sexual frequency and satisfaction deteriorated. They began to bicker a lot.

IBCT describes the decreases in companionship and sexual frequency and the increase in bickering as derivative problems. These problems came about only because of the decreases in the more central problems of love and support. Although these derivative problems may have their own dynamics and ultimately achieve a life of their own, they are originally fueled by other factors. For example, an argument over a blouse that Margo chooses to wear may be based on a genuine difference in how Dave and Margo view that blouse; the argument may produce hurt feeling in one or both of them; and the argument could escalate so that one or both of them take dramatic action, such as tearing up the blouse. However, had Dave not been so angry at Margo over other, more important matters, he would have brought up the matter in a kinder way or ignored it altogether. Likewise, had Margo not been so mad at Dave over other, more important matters, she could have heard his comments with more objectivity.

We believe that TBCT often targets derivative problems rather than the crucial, controlling problems. TBCT often focuses on specific, discrete, current observable behavior, such as can be obtained with the Spouse Observation Checklist (Weiss et al., 1973), and focuses on specific, discrete behavioral changes that are desired, such as can be obtained with the Areas of Change Questionnaire (Margolin, Talovic, & Weinstein, 1983). This strategy of assessment, as well as these particular assessment instruments, would likely reveal the lack of companionship, the infrequent sex, and the frequent arguments that characterize Dave and Margo, but they would be unlikely to reveal the lack of love and value that Margo experiences and the lack of encouragement and support that Dave experiences. Thus, TBCT would likely focus on derivative rather than major, controlling variables.

Functional Analysis of Behavior

What is the alternative to an assessment focus on specific, discrete, observable behavior or desired changes in that behavior? The hallmark of behavioral asessment, a functional analysis of behavior, focuses not on the size of the unit, its specificity, or even its observability. Rather, a functional analysis examines the variables that control a given behavior by manipulating conditions that are antecedent to that behavior and consequent to that behavior. By observing how the behavior fluctuates in response to these changes, one determines the conditions that control the behavior.

Our ability to conduct a functional analysis of

couple interaction is greatly limited in three respects. First, we are not present during most of a couple's behavior, so we cannot observe the conditions that precede and follow any instance of marital distress. We are forced to rely on the couple's report of their behavior and the conditions that surround it. Certainly we are able to observe their interaction during the session, and this may provide important information. However, in-session behavior represents only a small and not necessarily representative, sample of the couple's interaction. A second limitation that impairs our ability to conduct a functional analysis is the idiosyncratic nature of learning histories that often result in diverse stimulus conditions serving similar functions, or even apparently opposite stimulus conditions. Margo may often get distressed when a day goes by without Dave telling her that he loves her. If we were able to gather that information, we might have a good candidate for a possible controlling variable for Margo's distress. If we learn, however, that Margo also gets distressed when Dave tells her that he *does* love her, we might get confused, not to mention Dave's confusion and frustration. However, if Dave's attempts to assure her of his love are done out of obligation, rather than out of any strong experience of love for her at the time he voices the feeling, her similar response to both the absence and apparent presence of a particular condition makes perfect sense. A third and even more important limitation in conducting a functional analysis with couples is that we have very limited power to directly influence any conditions in their lives. We certainly do not have the luxury of manipulating a series of conditions until we find the true controlling variables that affect a couple's life. Altering any condition in a couple's life may be difficult. If we choose any unimportant one, by the time we have changed it, the couple may be too frustrated or feel too much failure to allow us to try another. For example, if we decided that a lack of companionship was the key to Dave and Margo's unhappiness, we would try to increase their contact with each other. Since it is not the right variable and since they are so angry with each other, they might well be resistant to the idea. Even without resistance, they might find it genuinely difficult to make more time for movies, dinners, and the like. Furthermore, the events may produce at best only limited and temporary satisfaction for them. By the time we give up on increased companionship as the key for them, they might have given up on us.

These limitations notwithstanding, couples can provide us with useful information that can aid us in our functional analysis of the controlling variables for their distress. First, couples can often articulate something about controlling variables. They are aware of their unhappiness and can voice, not just the unhappiness, but the reasons for it as well. These reasons that couples offer may, unfortunately, be as confusing as they are enlightening. Because they are so angry and dissatisfied, their descriptions may sound more like accusations than explanations. Margo may accuse Dave of being selfish rather than describe what she is missing in the relationship. Also, these accusations may be broad, exaggerated, and overgeneralized. Rather than specify the lack of support he feels in his efforts to become a writer, Dave may simply say that "she doesn't support anything I do." Finally, couples may describe not only the controlling variables in their marital distress but also what we have called the derivative variables. Margo and Dave may be so upset over their recent argument about whether to go to Dave's bosses' party that they focus on that conflict and the derogatory things each said during the conflict rather than on the more important controlling variables in their relationship. Thus, couples can often tell us something about their controlling variables, but it requires a skilled clinician to sort out the important from the unimportant and the description from the accusation.

Sometimes couples cannot articulate what is bothering them. They may not have been able to put together exactly what is bothering them or they may feel too embarrassed or feel too vulnerable to articulate the exact reasons. Nevertheless, despite this inability to articulate the source of their distress, they may be able to recognize and acknowledge it if the therapist states it, particularly if the therapist can state it in a way that does not cause them to feel accused, attacked, or on the defensive.

Value of Affect

In searching for the controlling variables for relationship distress, the affective expressions of each member of the couple are an important clue. Their absence suggests a variable of little importance to the couple. If the therapist notes how little time the couple spends in companionate activities, but the couple expresses little affect about that apparent loss, the therapist would be wise to search in other areas. Often, anger is a clue to an important controlling variable. Couples often have some idea of what is important to their partner and in the throes of distress will attack their partner where it most hurts. These attacks and the anger they generate can offer useful insight to the therapist. For example, if Margo charges that Dave will never be anything but a high school English teacher, Dave's bristling anger and hurt can be a clue to the importance of his writing career for him and the lack of support he feels from Margo. Although often useful, anger can be a misleading clue, as well as a helpful one. Couples can sometimes get so frustrated with each other that a variety of unimportant actions or inactions spark an angry response. Couples can get angry over what we have called the derivative variables, as well as over the controlling ones.

Perhaps the more important affective clues are softer, sadder feelings. These feelings may express the loss that a partner has experienced in the relationship. If the therapist suggests to Margo that she no longer feels valued or important to Dave and Margo nods quietly with tears coming to her eyes, the therapist has some assurance that he/she has touched an important chord and targeted an important variable in their relationship.

Definition, Specification, and Themes

A hallmark of behavioral approaches to assessment has been definition and specification. When potential controlling variables are identified, they are carefully defined in observational terms and are behaviorally pinpointed. A well-defined, concrete behavior is more likely to be understood and sets a clearer target for change than some abstract, ill-defined concept. However, too great a focus on specification and definition can lead to narrow problem descriptions. Assessment may generate a long list of specific changes that could affect a couple's distress.

While endorsing the value of definition and specification, IBCT is alert to linkages among the problems the clients bring in to therapy. Similar to systemic, psychodynamic, and experiential approaches, the IBCT therapist looks for themes in the diverse array of complaints that clients present. Jan may want more time together with Bart and more attention from him; she may complain about his lack of self-disclosure, or get her feelings hurt by his unenthusiastic responses and vacant stares, and she may see his questions of her and conversations with her as perfunctory. The IBCT therapist would see the theme of greater closeness in all of her marital complaints and would want to highlight that theme rather

than merely getting behaviorally specific definitions of each complaint.

This focus on themes is useful for several reasons. First, these themes often represent "response classes," which are behaviors serving similar functions. Because the specific behaviors that comprise the theme share similar functions, changes in different aspects or specific behaviors relevant to a theme may reduce the need for change in other behaviors in the response class. If Jan gets a more affectionate and energetic response from her husband, she may have less need for more total time together with him. Second, identification of a theme allows the therapist possibly to detect areas of concern that were not even mentioned by the client, and relate areas that were mentioned. For example, seeing Jan's problems as resulting from a lack of closeness may enable the IBCT therapist to conjecture about her unwillingness to accommodate to Bart's needs for contact with his family of origin. If she does not feel close to him, she may not want to be in a situation in which she will feel even more left out (while he interacts with his family), and she may want to punish him by disallowing what she sees as one of the few things he wants from her. Third, a focus on theme allows the IBCT therapist to see the universality and the common threads in diverse complaints. Like family systems theorists, the IBCT theorist believes there are certain fundamental issues that must be resolved in close relationships, such as the calibration of closeness and distance between the pair, and the allocation of power and responsibility. Fourth, an interpersonal relationship theme can never be adequately specified behaviorally. Consider the following extended example concerning Ray, a stockbroker, and his wife Lucy, a registered nurse. Assume that their conflictual interpersonal theme concerns equal respect, attention, and regard for each one's professional accomplishments. Assume that one could carefully define two behavioral aspects of that theme: namely, Ray's jokes about the relative size of Lucy's salary, and the unequal conversational time devoted to his career versus her career. These two classes of acts could be defined and specified but they would be unlikely to exhaust the ways in which this theme is manifested in their current relationship. Furthermore, it is unlikely that these two behavioral classes exhaust the potential ways in which this theme could manifest itself in the future. If Ray rigidly devoted equal talk time to Lucy's career as well as his own, and if he religiously abstained from jokes about the size of her salary, there would still be millions of ways in which this differential respect and attention could occur. Closing of a big deal in his job deserves a major dinner out to celebrate, but there are no comparable celebrations for the achievements of her job. The Christmas letter they send to friends each year provides greater depths of coverage to his career achievements than to hers. The attention and interest each provides the other regarding the details of their work lives differs despite their rigid adherence to an equal allocation of time. Thus, IBCT would rather focus on a theme itself than on specific examples of the theme. Certainly, IBCT finds it useful for clients to articulate specific instances of the theme, but IBCT never assumes that those specific instances completely capture the theme.

Intervention

Once an assessment has revealed the probable controlling variables for a couple's relationship distress, the therapist must intervene to alter those variables. Historically, behavioral approaches to couple therapy have emphasized change. Excesses or deficits in one member's behavior were thought to account for the other's marital distress. The solution to marital distress was then to get each partner to do more of the behavior in which they were deficient and to do less of the behavior in which they were deemed excessive. These changes would then increase the satisfaction of both.

Change

Historically, there have been two major strategies for generating change in couples: behavior exchange strategies (BE) and communication/problem-solving training (CPT). BE are direct efforts to identify and change the frequency with which behaviors are reinforced and punished. Specifically, couples pinpoint behaviors that are more likely to be reinforced (and reinforcing) and less likely to be punished (or punishing), and then, through a series of directives, apply these prinicples to improving the quality of their marital interaction. It is important to note here the difference between functional and topographical definitions of reinforcers and punishers. "Topographical definitions" refer to features of the event or behavior itself (e.g., that it looks or feels good or bad), whereas "functional definitions" refer to the relationship or contingency between behavior and its consequences. When we discuss behaviors that get reinforced, we are

referring to the functions of those behaviors, and thus are not simply pulling for behaviors that "feel good," but rather behaviors that are effective, that is, behaviors that generate reinforcing consequences or terminate aversive ones. Hence, the IBCT therapist is advised to go to great lengths to consider the context in which apparently desired changes occur, with the assumption that the same behaviors might have very different effects depending on the nature of the therapist's directives, the timing of the change, and other factors that surround them. For example, Susan's compliments to Harry may indeed be reinforcers for him, except when they are given in response to a therapist's directive that she be more complimentary to Harry.

Usually, BE is placed strategically at the beginning of a treatment program in order to increase the positivity of the relationship which, the therapist hopes, will enable partners to approach negotiation over their more difficult conflicts in a better position. Consistent with this strategy, a common historical characteristic of BE procedures is to focus primarily on *nonconflictual* behaviors.

In CPT, the second avenue for creating change, the couple is taught to talk about conflict in noncoercive ways, to negotiate resolutions of their conflict in noncoercive ways, and thus to positively create change in their relationship. Initially, these skills are taught with reference to the couple's current conflicts. However, the goal is to teach the couple these skills so that they may use them when future conflicts arise. For example, the therapist may help couples to negotiate changes in who does household chores now, but in so doing hopes to teach them conflict resolution skills, so that they can make changes when future conflicts, such as ones around money, arise.

The behavioral (Skinner, 1966) distinction between contingency-shaped and rule-governed behavior is important in considering IBCT strategies for changing behavior. In rule-governed behavior, people are reinforced for following a rule and punished for violating it. The consequences are determined by the extent to which the behavior matches the rule, not by any natural consequences related to the rule. For example, most people who learn to play a song on the piano do so by following the rules specified in the sheet music for that song (i.e., the notes on the music that tell one what keys to press). In contrast, contingency-shaped behavior is determined by the natural consequences that accrue from that behavior, not from the match of that behavior to a particular rule. For example, those who learn to play a song on the piano "by ear" do not follow the rule of music notes but are shaped by the sounds from the keys they press.

BE and CPT create changes in couples primarily through rule governed behavior. In BE, couples identify potential reinforcing behaviors and are explicitly or implicitly given the rule to increase the frequency of those behaviors. The therapist reinforces the couple for compliance with that rule but also hopes that natural contingencies will maintain those behaviors. For example, the husband increases the frequency with which he compliments his wife based on the BE "rule" developed in therapy. However, the behavior continues because of the natural reinforcement provided by his wife to those compliments (e.g., smiles, laughter, etc.). Similarly, in CPT, a couple defines a conflictual problem, negotiates a solution to that problem, and implements a contract or agreement for change (i.e., a rule). The therapist reinforces compliance with that rule but hopes that naturalistic reinforcers will maintain the rule. For example, a couple negotiates a schedule for housework (i.e., a rule) that is maintained because its use helps them to avoid negative interaction.

Many of the changes that couples desire in therapy do not lend themselves to rule control. As Skinner (1966) noted, rule-governed behavior and contingency-shaped behavior may look alike, but there are some subtle differences between them. From the inside, contingency-shaped behavior may feel more "right" or more "genuine" than rule-governed behavior. From the outside, contingency shaped behavior may look more "authentic" than rule-governed behavior. For example, even though a lover and a prostitute may engage in similar sexual behaviors, the lover probably feels more passion when making love than does the prostitute while turning a trick. Furthermore, unless the prostitute is skilled in deception, the sexual act may seem routine, like doing a job, rather than expressing desire.

Many of the changes that couples want in therapy have to do with the subtleties of contingency shaped behavior rather than the bald compliance of rule governed behavior. Increased trust, greater interest in sex, or greater respect for the partner's achievements are not easily attained through rule-governed behavior. One cannot prescribe them in BE or negotiate for them in CPT. Consider Joe's sexual dissatisfaction with Mary. While Joe would like more frequent sex with greater variety from Mary, what really disturbs him is her lack of passion. Even if she obligingly complied with his request for frequency and variety, he would still not be satisfied because her level of enjoyment or passion, her hunger, does not match what he would like. Even if she willingly tried to comply with his request, and put more enthusiasm in her sexual responsiveness, there still would be a high likelihood of failure. Her acting might feel unauthentic to her and be perceived as false to him. It is unlikely that the couple could maintain their sexual charade for long, or that it would be really fulfilling to them.

Therefore, although rule-governed processes of making change, such as BE and CPT, have a major role in the intervention strategies of IBCT, other strategies are needed for changes that cannot be brought about through these processes. Also, additional strategies are needed for cases in which couples are simply unwilling or unable to make the changes that the other desires.

Emotional Acceptance

Emotional acceptance (EA) in IBCT refers to a situation in which behavior change does not occur, or does not occur as much as the spouse requesting it would like. However, rather than the partner doing more of the behavior in which he/she was deemed deficient, or less of the behavior in which he/she was deemed excessive, the requesting spouse experiences the problematic behavior, or lack of behavior, in a new way. Whereas before, the behavior was experienced as offensive, unacceptable, and blameworthy, now it is experienced at one extreme as understandable and tolerable, if not necessarily desirable, or at the other extreme, as something valuable, to be appreciated.

It might be tempting to think in terms of a dichotomy in which, at one extreme, change occurs, and at the other extreme, acceptance occurs instead of change, thereby obviating the necessity for behavior change. Whereas earlier approaches to behavioral couple therapy emphasized change rather than acceptance, IBCT attempts to establish balance by adding an acceptance focus. As tempting as this dialectical view might be, it is oversimplified for at least two reasons. First, the type of change emphasized in traditional approaches is very specific, and fails to cover the gamut of changes that are possible in a couple relationship. In particular, "change" was traditionally defined as accommodating to another partner's request, compromising on some issue, or collaborating to find a solution for a couple problem. Although acceptance may be the antithesis of this type of change, acceptance is actually, in itself, a form of change. Presumably, when EA occurs, there has been a shift in the context in which the behavior that was formerly of concern occurred, such that change on the part of the perpetrator is no longer necessary. In short, although as a matter of convenience we will contrast the two intervention strategies by using terms such as "change versus acceptance," we are really talking about different levels of change. Second, the two types of change are viewed as mutually facilitative rather than opposing. For example, at times, couple problems can be maintained and even exacerbated by the way partners talk about the problem. Indeed, at times, the way couples talk about the problem, or at least their efforts to "solve" it, can become the primary problem. By promoting acceptance of the behavior, the problem, or the person, the dysfunctional reaction to the problem is eliminated and the problem can sometimes be solved when efforts to solve it cease.

The primary goal of EA is not, however, to subtly or paradoxically induce change in behavior. If that happens, so much the better. But the primary goal is straightforward—to alter the reaction of spouses to their partner's behavior. This behavior once felt unacceptable, intolerable, and painful. If they react differently to this behavior, experiencing it perhaps as an unpleasant and unfortunate but integral part of the package of qualities that is their spouse, or in the best of all possible cases, as a desirable though not always pleasant quality of their spouse, the problem that brought them to therapy is nonetheless resolved.

STAGES OF THERAPY

Assessment Phase

IBCT begins with a three- to four-session evaluation phase. During this period, IBCT therapists try to answer the following six questions:

1. How distressed is this couple?
2. How committed is this couple to this relationship?
3. What are the issues that divide them?
4. Why are these issues such a problem for them?
5. What are the strengths holding them together?
6. What can treatment do to help them?

Each of these questions has important implications for IBCT therapy.

The first question, the severity of the marital distress, may determine how therapy initially proceeds. If couples are mildly to moderately distressed, the assessment phase can proceed without interruption. However, if the couple is in crisis or cannot tolerate a more leisurely assessment procedure, an immediate intervention may be necessary. Examples include homicide or suicide risks, spouse or child physical abuse, or psychosis.

Level of distress can be ascertained through the conjoint couple interview. Couples may discuss desires to separate or inform the therapist that they have recently separated. In addition to these content indicators, the process by which the couples discuss their problems can reveal their level of distress. Some spouses are so angry at each other that they have a hard time being quiet and listening to their partner without interrupting and attempting to "correct" their partner. Questionnaire measures can be used to gain a more precise indication of distress. Marital satisfaction inventories such as the Dyadic Adjustment Scale (Spanier, 1976) and the Marital Status Inventory (Snyder, 1979) provide quantitative indicants and normative data for assessing a couple's level of distress. Whatever the actual level of distress a couple has, assessments of violence should also be undertaken. This can be done through interview. However, it is often best to supplement interview indications with questionnaire instruments such as the Conflict Tactics Scale (Strauss, 1979).

The second question to be addressed during assessment is the level of commitment of the couple. Although commitment is usually inversely related to level of distress (a couple in extreme distress is likely to have their commitment eroded), discrepancies between the two constructs are frequent enough to merit a separate assessment of commitment. A couple may have high distress and still have high commitment. Likewise, a couple may have low distress but still have low commitment. The level of distress of a couple tells the therapist roughly how much must be done to help the couple. The level of commitment gives the therapist a rough indication of the couple's willingness to put effort into this task.

Commitment can be assessed through self-report questionnaires. For example, the Dyadic Adjustment Scale has a question at the end that assesses the couple's desire for the relationship to succeed and their willingness to put effort into making it succeed. The Marital Status Inventory (Weiss & Cerreto, 1980) asks couples to check off items that reflect steps toward divorce (e.g., discussing the matter with a trusted friend, setting up an independent bank account, consulting an attorney). The more steps one has taken toward separation and divorce, the lower the commitment to the marriage.

Individual interviews with each spouse may provide the clearest assessment of commitment. These interviews may indicate that one or both spouses are ready to give up the marriage and see this therapy as a last-ditch effort. Some partners may have already decided to leave the marriage, but are entering therapy only to provide a safe haven for their partner or to show the world that they tried everything to save the marriage. An individual interview may reveal that one or both spouses are engaged in an ongoing affair that severely limits their commitment to the marriage. Couple therapy is not possible if one partner's or both partners' commitment is too low. To the extent that commitment is low, but couple therapy is still possible, couples will be less amenable to treatment interventions requiring accomodations, compromise, and collaborating. Thus, EA will more likely be emphasized.

Assessment should answer a third question concerning the issues that divide the couple. We are interested here not just in the controversial topics about which they argue but also in their positions on these topics. We may discover, for example, that a couple, Michael and Donna, disagree about money, but we also want to know each spouse's position on this controversial topic. Perhaps Michael wants to spend money as it comes in, whereas Donna is more interested in saving. We also would like to know some environmental factors that may affect this controversy. For example, maybe Donna brings in more money than Michael and provides that fact as justification for having a greater say than he in how money is spent.

Consider another common issue that divides couples: the problem of different desires for closeness between them. Perhaps Donna desires more time together, more expressions of affection and love, and greater personal disclosure, whereas Michael desires more time apart for work and friends, feels uncomfortable with expressions of affection and love, and likes personal privacy. Environmental factors that exacerbate this difference are their separate work worlds, which provide Donna with little social stimulation, but provide Michael with a lot. Consequently, he comes home from work seeking privacy, whereas she comes home from work seeking social contact with him.

The therapist can assess controversial issues quite easily in the conjoint interview. Spouses are usually aware of their disagreements and can be articulate about them. However, there are questionnaires that can be useful in this regard. The Areas of Change Questionnaire presents spouses with a list of common changes that married couples may desire in their marriage. Each spouse indicates the amount and direction of change he/she seeks in the partner, as well as his/her perception of the change the spouse seeks in them. The Areas of Change Questionnaire can be helpful in targeting areas that spouses may not think of during the therapy session, or may be reluctant to mention (e.g., changes in sexual behavior).

The answer to the fourth question—why these issues are such a problem for them—can be found in their attempts to solve the problem through their interaction. Do they avoid discussing it all together? Do they complain bitterly to each other and bicker ceaselessly? Does one try to pressure the other for change, while the other withdraws in anger? Consider the issue of money discussed previously. Perhaps Michael makes large purchases without consulting Donna. She gets furious at these acts of his and punishes him through criticism and complaint. When he does discuss the possibility of a purchase, she often dismisses it as unnecessary and too expensive. Because he sees no likelihood of a positive outcome through negotiation with Donna, and because he is not open to much compromise, Michael unilaterally decides on purchases and suffers the consequences from his wife of criticism and complaint. Because of her anger at these unilateral purchases, Donna is not open to discussion with him and tries to stem what she sees as his extensive spending by dismissing most of his suggestions for purchases.

The search for why closeness is such a problem for Michael and Donna can also be found in their attempts to deal with the problem through their interaction. Donna may initiate conversation with Michael and pour affection upon him as her way of opening him up and generating a reciprocal response from him. He does not want to disappoint her or hurt her feelings, so he often goes along with her, but unenthusiastically. She often finds him distracted, only going through the motions, only there physically but not emotionally. Eventually, she blows up at him for being such a "cold fish," for having "no feelings," for being such a bore. He is furious at her accusations;

after all, he has been trying to please her by going along with her even when he has not felt like it. This is what he gets for his efforts. He withdraws, angry and pouting. Later she feels guilty for what she said and tries to reconcile with him, setting the stage again for a repeat of their struggle over closeness.

The therapist should be sensitive to the vicious cycles that often occur in a couple's interaction around a controversial issue. As in the examples above, each partner's well-intentioned efforts to solve the problem often elicit problematic behavior in the other, which in turn elicits problematic behavior in him/herself. Donna's efforts at initiating contact with her husband overwhelm him and make him want to pull back. His desire not to hurt her feelings make him go along with her, but make him dishonest emotionally by being with her only in body. She sees through his efforts and gets hurt and angry at him. It is important during the feedback session to give the couple a new perspective on the problem as a vicious cycle involving a circular causal chain between the two of them.

A fifth question for assessment concerns the current strengths that keep the couple together. What are the characteristics that attracted the two to each other in the first place? Which of these characteristics are now making them value each other and the relationship? The therapist discovers these positive features of the pair by asking them to look at their relationship historically as well as currently. As the couple describe what attracted them to each other and provide a brief history of their early relationship, the therapist is attentive to once-attractive features of the two that are now related to their problems. For example, among other things, Donna mentions Michael's spontaneity and unpredictability that attracted her to him, while Michael mentions the comfortable, secure "nest" that was Donna's apartment, which he found so attractive. Clearly, Michael's spontaneity can be seen in his present purchasing habits, while Donna's orientation toward comfort and security can be seen in her desire to save.

Differences that attract can also repel. If therapy can teach the couple to experience both the positive and negative side of differences, then therapy may also facilitate the couple's acceptance of their differences. In the case of Donna and Michael, IBCT may want to place their current differences about spending money in the context of their attractive features of spontaneity and security. Therefore, the therapist keeps a careful eye open for material about attrac-

tion that can be used to reformulate current problems.

The therapist also asks what strengths are working now to keep the couple together in the face of the serious difficulties that brought them to therapy. The couple's answers may reveal something about their level of distress (An extremely angry couple may have difficulty acknowledging any positive features of each other.), or their level of commitment (A strongly committed couple may discuss the importance of their relationship even in the face of great distress.). However, questions about strengths also provide the therapist with material for later therapy discussions. Knowing that a couple still has an active and fulfilling sex life or that they can have productive, even intimate conversations, when they talk about their children, gives the therapist perspective about their problems and provides information that may inform later interventions. For example, the therapist might ask a couple to consider how their discussions about their children, which are so productive even when the focus is on a problem, are different from their discussions about marital issues, which are so unproductive.

The keys to change can often be found in couples' past successes and strengths. To the extent that IBCT therapists can delineate what happens when couples are getting along, and distinguish it from the interaction sequences that are associated with arguments and negative experiences, they have a clue as to how the partners need to change. Often, the BE tasks that work most effectively are those derived from partners' existing repertoires of reinforcers. Similarly, the clues to effective conflict resolution often involve scrutinizing what happens when conflict is dealt with effectively. Thus, it is important to put at least as much emphasis on how things work when they work, as on how things break down when they break down. For the vast majority of distressed couples, they get along at least on occasion, and they resolve conflict successfully now and then.

The delineation of these success strategies is often considerably more important than the rules listed in communication training manuals. The careful scrutiny of individual cases emphasizes the functional analytic perspective and provides another prototype for the emphasis in IBCT on contingency shaped as opposed to rule-governed behavior. In the end, IBCT places greater importance on what works for couples, not on what the rules say.

The final question—what treatment can do to

help—is perhaps the most important. However brilliant a therapist's understanding of a marital problem, if he/she has no goals or strategies for treatment, then this treatment will proceed without direction and with little chance for success. The goals of IBCT therapists are almost always some combination of change and acceptance: acceptance of differences between the pair, and change in the way they handle those differences. Change typically involves more open, nonblaming, and nondefensive communication about the problem, as well as some accommodation to each other's specific needs. The therapist should consider in assessment what possible accommodation the pair could make toward each other, as well as what kind of acceptance may be necessary.

Consider Donna and Michael's money problems. They may need to accept that they have a fundamental difference about the value of "living for today" versus "saving for tomorrow." However, they may only be able to accept this difference and make some accommodation to each other if they are able to discuss these differences openly, without attack and defense. If Michael could share with Donna his interests in making a major purchase before he actually does so, and if Donna could listen to him without dismissing his ideas, they might be able to have a constructive discussion about the problem. Such a series of discussions over a variety of incidents might enable them to accommodate to each other's needs. If Michael did not feel so controlled by Donna, his genuine desires to please her, his rational knowledge about the desirability of saving, and his own interests in the long-term purchases for which she is saving might enable him to forego certain purchases and increase his contribution to savings. Similarly, if Donna did not feel so manipulated by Michael's covert purchases and if she saw the significance of some of them to him, her own genuine desire to please him, as well as her own rational knowledge that one cannot put off all pleasure until tomorrow, might enable her to support some of his purchases and be more generous to herself in the present. As they become less entrenched in their positions, they may be able to negotiate and problem solve about (1) an amount to contribute to savings each month, (2) an amour t for each to use at their personal discretion, and (3) purchase amounts that require prior discussion and approval by the other.

An important component of the assessment of "how treatment can help" involves evaluating each partner's capacity for change *and* accept-

ance. At one extreme are couples who are able to work together on problems, who recognize that they need to change themselves if the relationship is going to improve, and who seem predisposed toward compromise and accommodation. At the other extreme are couples who seem to have irreconcilable differences, who believe that they have already done everything they can do to improve the situation, and who are unable to work well together on problems. Since most couples fall somewhere in between these two extremes, it is a difficult task to determine how much to emphasize change versus acceptance strategies early in therapy. In our experience, more accurate assessments of capacity to change can be derived from individual interviews with partners. We also know from our research that capacity for change is negatively associated with severity of distress, proximity to divorce, the total or near-total cessation of a sexual relationship, and traditional sex-role constellations.

Perhaps the most important factor in determining the relative emphasis on change and acceptance is the extent to which partners manifest a "collaborative set." This set refers to a shared perspective on the part of each that they are mutually responsible for the problems in the relationship, and that they both need to change themselves if the relationship is going to improve. To the extent that couples bring this set into therapy, change strategies are more likely to be successful. In contrast, to the extent that partners present themselves as innocent victims of the other's oppression, and enter therapy hoping that the therapist will convince the other to change, acceptance strategies need to be emphasized. Because only a minority of couples manifest a collaborative set at the beginning of therapy, acceptance work tends to predominate, especially at the beginning. This particular approach to the collaborative set exemplifies the differences between TBCT and IBCT. In TBCT, we would attempt to induce a collaborative set where none existed (Jacobson & Margolin, 1979). Although we were often successful in the induction of such a set, the end result amounted to the force feeding of change, with rapid relapse following termination occurring all too frequently. Now we react to however couples present themselves. If they do not present with a collaborative set, we do not try to induce it, but rather "accept" its absence.

As we shall see in more detail later, strategies for promoting acceptance always include discussions of the problem with the therapist as mediator. Typically, these discussions occur at four levels: (1) a general discussion of the problem (2) discussion of an upcoming incident that may trigger the problem, (3) discussion of a recent negative incident illustrating the problem, and (4) discussion of a recent positive incident in which either or both partners tried to "do it better," even if the ultimate outcome was not positive. For certain problems, discussions about upcoming incidents may not be possible, because anticipating those incidents may be impossible. However, general discussions and discussions of recent positive and negative incidents are applicable to virtually all couple problems.

During assessment, the therapist needs to learn enough about each of the couple's major problems to know (1) where to focus a general discussion and (2) what incidents to look for in treatment. To focus the general discussion, the therapist needs to determine the general destructive pattern that occurs during the problem, how each partner contributes to the pattern, and how understandable human reactions motivate these unfortunate contributions. In the case of Donna and Michael's money problems, the destructive pattern is a lack of open communication, followed by unilateral action and punishment. Michael's contribution is his failure to discuss his ideas and his resorting to unilateral action, but these actions of his result in part from Donna's resistance to any of his purchases and her dismissal of his views. Donna's contribution is her immediate dismissal of Michael's ideas about purchases and her punishment of any of his actions, but her behavior results in part from his unwillingness to consult her and consider her an equal partner.

The therapist must also learn in assessment what incidents to look for during treatment that reflect this problematic pattern and could be a focus of therapeutic discussion. In the case of Donna and Michael's money problems, of great use would be discussion of an upcoming event for which Michael might desire (or even now plan) to purchase something controversial (e.g., Michael's desire to purchase something at an upcoming computer fair). In such a situation, the therapist gets an opportunity to do *in vivo* training of the couple in the very presence of a concrete problem. Neither general discussions or *in vivo* training will completely prevent a recurrence of the problematic sequence between the couple. Furthermore, future episodes of the problem often cannot be predicted. Therefore, discussions of recent incidents, both good and bad, that illustrate the problem will be useful. With regard to Michael and Donna's money problems, a recent purchase by Michael without consulting Donna, or a recent attempt by Michael to discuss a potential purchase that Donna dismissed, would illustrate negative instances. Any recent incident in which Michael tried a more open sharing of his desires to make a purchase, or in which Donna tried to be more open to his desires, would be useful for discussion as positive instances, even if those initial efforts did not lead ultimately to a constructive episode.

In summary, through answering the final question—what treatment can do to help—the therapist makes an initial determination of what acceptance and accommodation may be possible for the couple, as well as sufficient to solve the problem. Also, the therapist learns enough about the problem to provide a framework for the therapy discussions to follow.

Feedback Session

After the assessment phase, the IBCT therapist provides clients with feedback about assessment findings and a treatment plan. With this information in hand, the couple can make a rational decision about whether to proceed with treatment.

The six questions IBCT therapists ask during assessment provide the outline for the feedback session. Therapists describe these questions and their answers to the couple. The answers have a descriptive purpose, in that they provide to the couple information that the therapist discovered. However, more important, the answers often have a clinical purpose for moving the couple in a positive direction. Both purposes are discussed later.

It should also be noted that the feedback session is a dialogue between therapist and clients, rather than a lecture from the therapist. Notions are presented tentatively, and feedback is sought throughout the presentation. The partners themselves are viewed as the experts on what ails them, and they contribute actively to the formulation of problems. Perhaps the sessions should be thought of as an exchange of ideas, with initial hypotheses tentatively put forth by the therapist, and the purpose being to arrive at a mutually acceptable treatment plan.

For the first question, IBCT therapists indicate to the couple their current level of relative distress. Therapists may tell the couple their actual scores on relevant instruments (e.g., the Dyadic Adjustment Scale and Marital Satisfaction Inventory) and provide some normative

3. Integrative Behavioral Couple Therapy

benchmarks to aid the couple's interpretations of their scores (e.g., mean scores of "happy" couples, cutoff scores for distress, mean scores for divorcing couples). At a clinical level, IBCT therapists may want to use this information to reassure some anxious couples (e.g., most couples entering therapy score worse), or to underscore the seriousness of the difficulties for other couples.

For the commitment question, IBCT therapists indicate to the couple their general level of commitment to the relationship. At the high end of commitment, therapists may say something like "I see you two as very committed to the relationship, despite the problems you have mentioned." At the middle level of commitment, therapists may acknowledge both commitment and doubt, as in "I think both of you still want this relationship to work, but the problems have been so severe that both of you have seriously faced the possibility of separation and divorce." At low levels of commitment, therapists focus primarily on the doubt. "I think this therapy represents a last-ditch effort for you two. You are willing to try one more time, but neither of you has much hope." For all levels, therapists use information from the questionnaires and the interviews to support their observations. The last item of the Dyadic Adjustment Scale and all the items on the Marital Status Inventory are relevant commitment items. The clinical purpose of this feedback, like that on distress, is reassurance for some couples and an underscoring of seriousness for others. Another clinical purpose for couples who present themselves as low in commitment is to challenge them and place major responsibility for success upon them. Do they really want this relationship to work? Are they willing to put forth effort? The success of this therapy depends primarily on the couple; therapists' skills are only beneficial with a couple who wants improvement in the relationship and will put forth effort for that improvement.

Feedback about the third question focuses on the two or three major controversial areas that trouble the couple. For each of these areas, IBCT therapists describe each partner's position in ways that validate that position as reasonable but point out the differences between the positions and the conflict of interest that results. When possible, therapists add information to show the couple that this difference is part of a larger difference between them that has been a source of attraction. The clinical purpose of this feedback is to move the partners away from a blaming stance with regard to their differences and toward

a more accepting stance. For example, in giving Donna and Michael feedback about their money problems, the therapist might say:

"The two of you clearly have a problem about spending money. I see this problem as reflecting a difference between you about the relative value of focusing on today or tomorrow. Michael, you are clearly a 'live for today' type of person, while you Donna are clearly a 'prepare for tomorrow' type of person. Both positions are reasonable. Only in the extreme are they invalid. But neither of you would argue that you should never prepare for tomorrow or never live for today. It's just a different emphasis. It is interesting to me that this difference that bothers you now is part of a larger difference that was a source of attraction for you. You said, Donna, that you were attracted to Michael because he was a spontaneous person, which in my view is a 'live for today' kind of person. You said, Michael, that you really appreciated the comfortable, secure 'nest' that Donna could provide for you. Only 'prepare for tomorrow' people can ever build a nest."

In answering the fourth assessment question for the couple, IBCT therapists point to the couple's interaction, not to the difference between them itself, as the source of their problems. Therapists describe each partner's understandable and often well-intentioned actions to deal with the difference between them, but point out how these actions often generate distress rather than resolution. The clinical purpose of this feedback is to show each partner how they are contributing to the problem and thus how they could change to better the situation. However, IBCT therapists emphasize the understandable feelings that motivate each partner's contributions, so that each partner can hear this feedback about their role in the struggle nondefensively. For example, consider what an IBCT therapist might say to Michael and Donna:

"This difference between the two of you about the value of saving for tomorrow versus spending for today—which is a common difference between couples—comes up for the two of you when you, Michael, want to purchase something. I think you have tried to talk to Donna about potential purchases at times in the past, but find her so resistant to your ideas, and she seems to you so controlling about money, that you think the only way to have any financial choice in the relationship is just to take unilateral action and buy the item. Yes, Donna will find out and get angry at you, but that price, however unpleasant, seems worth it to you to have some power and autonomy in financial decisions. On your side, Donna, you see Michael's unilateral actions as completely shutting you out of any role in these financial decisions. Far from feeling in control, you feel unimportant, unconsulted, and neglected. So it is not surprising that you get upset when he does make a unilateral purchase, or that you are not particularly open to his ideas if he does pass them by you. You assume he may go buy whatever he wants no matter what you say, and the only way to rein him in is to discourage any purchase in advance."

In discussing these problematic methods for dealing with differences, we introduce three concepts that play important roles in later acceptance work: the "mutual trap," the "minefield," and the "credibility gap." The mutual trap is a situation in which both partners are trying to "get out of" or resolve the conflict, but everything they try seems to exacerbate the problem. They are trapped because they know of no other strategy to reduce the conflict or resolve the argument, and, on the face of it, what they are doing seems to be the best possible strategy. Yet, its effect is the opposite of that intended. Mutual traps characterize most recursive, dysfunctional interaction patterns.

For example, consider Frank and Lorna. Frank is extremely sensitive to conflict, and would go to great lengths to minimize, eliminate, or resolve conflict. His "conflict phobia" makes good sense in light of his upbringing, having been raised in a family where overt expressions of conflict were severely punished. Lorna comes from a family in which conflict was freely expressed, and she reports that conflict is helpful to her. When Lorna becomes irritated with Frank, he cannot stand it, so he tries to talk her out of it, denies what he did that made her angry, or tries to compensate for the anger by making a conciliatory gesture. Yet, she cannot turn off her limbic system and thus she remains angry, at least for a short period of time. When his efforts to get rid of her anger are unsuccessful, he becomes angry at her, accusing her of being stubborn, contentious, and unwilling to let go of her anger. From his perspective, she is stubbornly holding on to the anger, and will not let him get out of it, thus prolonging the conflict unnecessarily. From her perspective, he is asking her to turn

off experiences that are beyond her voluntary control. His pressure actually increases her anger. They are both trapped and cannot extricate themselves. The trap for him is that he finds conflict extremely aversive, and it is quite natural for him to do everything in his power to try to dissipate it. Yet the harder he works to get rid of the conflict, the angrier she gets, because he appears to be invalidating her feelings. The trap for her is that the only way to please him is to stop being angry, but she cannot do that easily and the effort may make her more angry. They are stuck. All short-term solutions for one partner come at great cost to the other, and thus there is no apparent solution that would work for both of them.

The "minefield" or "land mine" refers to those buttons that partners push, which, once pushed, seem to lead inexorably to severe conflict. With Frank and Lorna, one land mine involves money. Any time he brings up money, she gets furious. A functional analysis reveals a long history of money being used as a method of control in this relationship, and when Frank brings up Lorna's spending habits, she bristles, because she has never felt control over what she can and cannot spend. To her, money signifies his lack of trust (insisting on a prenuptial agreement), his lack of commitment (he must be planning to leave her someday), and his dominance in the relationship. Thus, no matter how innocent the discussion seems, money has great functional significance in this relationship and is a minefield for the couple.

A credibility gap refers to a point in an argument where an impasse develops because one person's position is simply not credible to the partner. Problem solving is impossible in such situations. Many impasses are characterized by credibility gaps. With Frank and Lorna, there was a credibility gap when Frank tried to backtrack from a statement that had angered Lorna. When he would try to apologize, clarify, or minimize a remark that she had experienced as critical, she simply would not believe him. Her expression of disbelief always resulted in escalation of his level of anger, because she was dismissing his genuine efforts to provide her with more perspective on his remark. Mutual traps, land mines, and credibility gaps are often at the core of how people get stuck when enacting their dysfunctional dance or theme.

Feedback about the sixth assessment question—what treatment can do to help—often follows the previously discussed feedback about the analysis of the problem. IBCT therapists describe for couples the goals for treatment, as well as the procedures to achieve those goals. The goals will almost always emphasize acceptance, as well as change. The goal of change will usually include more open communication about the problem, as well as specific changes relevant to that particular problem. Therapeutic procedures to achieve these goals include (1) discussions in session about the general issue, as well as discussion of particular instances where the problem arose; and (2) outside homework to further session work. These procedures are described in detail in the next section of this chapter. The clinical purpose of the feedback about treatment is to give the couple some notion of what to expect and to orient them toward the goals of accommodation and acceptance through more open communication. For example, consider how feedback about a treatment plan for their money issue is described to Donna and Michael:

"How can treatment help this money problem between the two of you? First of all, let me describe what I think the goals of that treatment should be. One goal would be better communication between the two of you about major purchases. That goal may sound desirable and even simple in the abstract, but it would mean, Donna, that you would be more open to hearing Michael's ideas. Being more open would not mean that you agree to go along with all of his ideas, just that you give him a hearing. Being more open for you, Michael, means that you discuss your intentions before taking action, but it doesn't mean that you agree to take no action. So neither of you have to give up any of your options by engaging in discussion. However, discussion offers you some hope of accommodation to each other.

Accommodation to each other and acceptance of each other would be the remaining two goals of treatment for this problem. I'm not sure what mix of the two will work for you as a couple, but I'm sure some of both will be required for successful treatment. The two of you are different in your positions about money, as we have discussed, but both of your positions are reasonable. Therapy can help you accept this difference and not blame each other for being the way you are. Therapy may also help you negotiate some accommodation to each other—for example, guidelines for amounts to save each month, amounts for discretionary use, and purchase amounts that require consultation with the other.

How will we achieve these goals? Mainly by talking in here, with me as moderator. We will discuss the issue in general, but more important, we will discuss specific instances that come up. I will be interested in discussing positive instances where the two of you try to discuss a purchase more openly, as well as negative instances where you are unable to discuss a purchase and get angry at each other—for example, because, Michael, you think that Donna dismissed your idea or because, Donna, you think that Michael made a unilateral purchase without consulting you. I may also ask you to try doing some things outside of this session, such as implementing an agreement that we have reached in here."

In addition to delineating the problem areas and explaining the treatment plan, the feedback session can be an opportunity to begin the *intervention stage*. In particular, two types of clinical interventions fit nicely into the feedback format. The first pertains to the delineation of strengths. By spending a substantial portion of time during the session delineating strengths, couples often see the beginnings of the solutions to their problems. This feedback itself can change their perspective on their problems, and thus begin the process of change. One has to be careful when presenting these strengths not to invalidate spouses' pain. At the same time, an exclusive emphasis on the pain can have iatrogenic effects, and can actually create a perspective in which the problems are experienced as worse than they were prior to therapy.

The second type of intervention that can be usefully employed during the feedback session is the *collaborative probe*. It is often useful to probe couples as to their capacity for collaboration. Their responses to this probe and their replies to their partners' responses can be useful guides to the sequencing of "change" and "acceptance" interventions. Sample questions that are useful in such a probe include, "How do you contribute to the problems in this relationship?" or "What are some of the changes that you need to make if this relationship is going to improve?" To the extent that partners have trouble pinpointing their own shortcomings and/or changes that may be required of them, the prognosis for a collaborative set decreases. One has to be careful to get specifics when this probe is undertaken. It is one thing to respond in a socially desirable way (e.g., "It takes two to tango," "I know that I am not perfect, and that I need to change too . . ."); it is quite another to have specific ideas as to how one contributes to the other partner's unhappiness. If a person's only ideas for self-change involve less reactivity to his/her partner's obnoxious behavior, then the therapist is not going to make progress by assuming a collaborative set.

Considerations for Implementing Treatment Phases

Order of Discussion

Most couples, like Donna and Michael, have more than one major issue for which they seek help. What should determine the order in which the therapist deals with these issues? Sometimes the clinical exigencies of the case determine the order of treatment. Issues of violence or separation obviously demand immediate attention, often before assessment is completed. Occasionally, an issue will be so volatile for the couple that it may be "too hot to handle" right away, and the therapist chooses to work first on a less volatile, although still major problem, hoping that success will pave the way for more fruitful discussions of the volatile area. However, barring these clinical exigencies, the IBCT therapist lets the couple determine which issue to focus on each week, based on its current salience to them. Usually, the couple focuses on a relevant incident during the previous week. The rationale for letting couples determine the focus each week is based on four ideas:

1. Couples will be more interested and motivated to discuss something that is salient for them.
2. Couples will be able to recall more of the details of a relevant instance when it has happened during the last week.
3. Couples can learn the most when issues are hot. While Donna and Michael may be able to discuss their money problems quite well when they have not had an incident for months, what IBCT therapists want them to achieve is a better discussion in the face of, or soon after, a relevant problematic instance.
4. Most intense marital conflicts will involve one of the couple's main themes, despite differences in content.

IBCT therapists, however, put some constraints on the selection of problems for discussion. First, therapists encourage some continuity from one week to the next. If Donna and Michael discuss their money problem during treatment session 5 and their closeness problem during treatment session 6, the IBCT therapist will take some time during session 6 to follow up on what was discussed about money in session 5. Did the couple have further thoughts and feelings about the discussion? If an agreement was reached in session 5, did the couple implement it during the week? Second, the therapist keeps the couple "on task" in terms of discussion about major problems. Sometimes couples will drift into incidents that are not relevant to their reasons for being in therapy. For example, perhaps Donna's and Michael have a quarrel on the way to therapy about Donna being late in getting ready. If they focus on that in the session, because it is so recent for them, the therapist would want to be sure it was related to one of the delineated major problems or represented a new, major problem before focusing a lot of time on it. If it just represents an isolated minor quarrel, it should not take up a large portion of the session.

Integration of Change and Acceptance Strategies

IBCT focuses on both change and acceptance, but the order and emphasis vary from couple to couple. It is not necessary that partners agree on everything before change strategies are introduced. Indeed, such couples probably do not exist, and if they do, they certainly do not seek couple therapy. But change strategies are often greatly facilitated when partners experience each other's positions as understandable and reasonable, given who they are and their particular context and learning history. For example, Michael will probably be unwilling to change if Donna's efforts to control money are experienced as malevolent. However, he may be willing to compromise and be more accommodating if he experiences her behavior around money within the context of knowing that her previous husband abandoned her and left her with nothing.

Change strategies are also more likely to succeed when partners accept the inevitability of problems, and the fact that no matter how much change occurs, some conflict is inevitable. Finally, change strategies are more successful if people know how to take care of themselves, so that they can survive without getting what they want from their partner whenever they want it. For all of these reasons, it often makes sense to begin with acceptance work, and proceed to change strategies only after achieving at least a modicum of acceptance.

For some couples, particularly those who are highly collaborative and exhibit mild to moderate degrees of marital distress, change-oriented strategies could be pursued first, although the therapist would shift to EA as needed. Even when change oriented strategies are used initially and proceed smoothly, however, EA interventions are integrated into communication and problem-solving training. Even if change is easy for a couple, EA principles are often utilized for prevention of future problems. Moreover, even though some couples' marital problems can be solved by change-oriented strategies alone, maintenance may be more likely and the level of change more profound if EA is included as part of the solution.

For other couples, change and EA strategies are introduced concurrently. For example, BE may begin from the first treatment session, but discussion of themes within an EA context would receive "equal time." This balancing act is more common than the sequence in which exclusively change-oriented interventions are used initially, with EA as the default option. When the collaborative set seems firm but incompatibility is high, this equal attention to acceptance and change is the preferred strategy. Or, when couples seem only mildly distressed but noncollaborative, this strategy is preferred.

But for a plurality of couples, IBCT promotes certain kinds of acceptance before initiating change strategies. Many partners need to accept each other's different positions on a problem or become more compassionate and "soften" toward the other's negative behavior before change is introduced. Otherwise, they may be resistant to change, or the changes that do occur are likely to be short-lived. For example, Michael will not be open to change if he interprets Donna as trying to control how money is spent because of her neurotic needs for security. Change on his part would only promote her need to control and relinquish his reasonable position. Likewise, Donna will not be open to change if she hears Michael expressing that view of her. Change on her part would signal that she thinks his view of her is correct!

Another kind of acceptance is necessary before change is introduced: the experience that one's own actions, while understandable and often well-intentioned, create pain for the partner. This kind of acceptance of one's own role in the problem may often promote change on its own. If one can see the partner's position as reasonable and pinpoint the functional relationship between one's own action and the other's pain, change may begin on behalf of the partner, or at least one avenue will be open to that kind of change. For example, if Donna experiences Michael's intimidation when discussing a potential purchase with her, and his hurt when she dismisses his ideas, she might spontaneously give him a better hearing.

Spontaneous change, based on growing acceptance of the partner, is ideal in IBCT. Although negotiation and problem solving carry the connotation of two *self-interested* people *working* at something and having to *give up* something that they desire in order to reach an agreement for change that represents a *compromise*, the spontaneous change we are discussing carries little of this negative tone of self-interest, work, giving up, and compromise. Rather, this kind of change seems to come naturally from the partners' caring for each other.

From a behavioral perspective, the spontaneous change that results from EA is contingency shaped, whereas that resulting from change-oriented strategies is rule governed. As many behavior analysts have noted, changes that are naturally shaped by contingencies are often preferred to changes that are under the control of rules. For one thing, changes responding to natural fluctuations in contingencies are more likely to be durable; furthermore, rule-governed changes are more ritualized, less reinforcing, and therefore less likely to promote increased marital satisfaction.

When IBCT therapists see this spontaneous, contingency-shaped change, they provide positive feedback to the couple. They make sure that partners acknowledge the changes that the other has made. But they also provide a note of caution. The partner may not always be able to behave differently. Each may slip back into old habits. Therefore, while rejoicing in the improvement, partners should prepare themselves for a relapse in which they will be faced again with each other's aversive actions. Here, the IBCT therapist moves toward acceptance strategies that emphasize tolerance and self-care in the face of the other's painful actions (details of these strategies to follow). This strategy of relapse preparation is not intended as a paradoxical intervention to prevent relapse. If it works in that way, so much the better. However, it is designed because of the low probability that partners can make sudden, permanent changes in their behavior. Some relapse or return to an old pattern is virtually inevitable.

Despite a preference for spontaneous change, IBCT recognizes that such change may not be forthcoming. Even if a couple has accepted each other's positions as valid and sees how their actions cause each other pain, they may be unable or unwilling to make spontaneous changes that reduce each other's pain. IBCT therapists may need to move the couple explicitly toward behavior exchange or problem solving, much as it is practiced in TBCT. However, while conducting problem solving with couples, IBCT therapists continue to work for further acceptance by the partners. In a manner similar to the preceding strategy, they communicate to the couple that no matter how successful the attempts at problem solving, the couple will at times slip back into old habits. Therefore, it is necessary to build each other's tolerance and ability to take care of self in the face of the partner's actions. Thus, problem solving often goes hand in hand with tolerance-building and self-care efforts.

SPECIFIC THERAPEUTIC TECHNIQUES AND STRATEGIES

Strategies for Promoting Change in Couples

Behavior Exchange

When couples enter therapy, they are usually providing and receiving little gratification from each other. Compared with earlier periods in their relationship, their potential to reinforce each other may have been eroded. Furthermore, because of the struggles between them, they may not be utilizing whatever potential still exists. Their efforts to reinforce each other may have been extinguished, or they may, out of hurt and anger, be actively withholding benefits from the other. Whatever the reasons, couples entering therapy are often caught in a downward spiral of doing less and less for each other.

One goal of BE strategies is to provide some immediate relief for couples in this predicament by increasing their mutual reinforcement without great cost to either partner. If successful, BE also puts couples in a better position for dealing with the incompatible differences they may have to face in each other during later stages of therapy.

These goals are achieved through two deceptively simple steps: (1) identifying desired behaviors that may be reinforcing for each other, and (2) increasing the frequency of those behaviors. In order for the couple to achieve the immediate increase in benefit, the desired be-haviors should provide maximum gratification to the receiver, at little cost to the giver. Usually spouses can list many desired behaviors that could benefit them. The trick is in selecting behaviors that can be delivered with minimal cost to the giver. Minimal-cost behaviors usually have several characteristics. First, these behaviors are not a source of controversy between the pair. If a couple is engaged in a struggle over contact with the wife's mother, the husband's going with his wife to see her mother would not be an appropriate BE target, even though it might be reinforcing to the wife. Second, a low-cost behavior would not require new skills by either partner. If a wife is inhibited about sexual expression, adventuresome sexual acts would not be an appropriate target for BE, even if it might be reinforcing for her husband. Finally, less cost is usually involved to increase a positive behavior than to decrease a negative behavior (Weiss, 1978; Weiss, Birchler, & Vincent, 1974). Increasing praise is usually easier than reducing criticism. Furthermore, because doing an act is more noticeable than suppressing an act, the giver of praise is more likely to be reinforced for that act than for the suppression of criticism.

Weiss and Birchler (1978) have suggested that therapists conduct a cost-benefit analysis of possible BE targets by having spouses rate a series of behaviors for their potential benefit to the receiver and cost to the giver. In this way, the therapist could empirically determine those behaviors that would best serve the purposes of BE. Of course, spouses cannot anticipate exactly what costs and benefits might accrue from specific behaviors. Furthermore, those costs and benefits depend on the context in which those behaviors occur.

Whether established through a cost-benefit analysis or more informally through an interview, the targets for BE were traditionally selected by the potential receiver identify desired behaviors and having the potential giver select which behaviors he/she is willing to do (i.e., the least costly). In one interesting variation described in Jacobson and Margolin (1979), the giver attempts to determine empirically which of his/her behaviors have impact on the partner's marital satisfaction. Spouses are asked to track the daily occurrence of a number of marital behaviors and their daily satisfaction levels through the Spouse Observation Checklist (Weiss et al., 1973). They are then asked to form hypotheses about which of their behaviors are most beneficial to their partners and to test those hypotheses by increasing the frequency of the hypothesized behaviors and observing the effects on the partner's daily rating of marital satisfaction. In this way, a giver can determine what behaviors under his/her control have maximal impact on the partner's daily marital satisfaction.

Currently, we begin the selection of targets for BE by having the "giver" try to figure out what would improve the relationship for the potential recipient. For example, each partner might be asked to independently and concurrently develop his/her version of the other's wish list, without any input from the recipient at all. Then, in the following therapy session, the therapist helps both partners operationalize and add to the lists, but still avoids input from the recipient. This task helps the giver focus on his/her own role in improving the relationship and virtually forces partners to take responsibility for changing themselves. Later, we allow and encourage input from the potential recipient (to be discussed), but not when the assignment is first introduced.

The second step in BE—to increase the frequency of specified behaviors—is done directly. Traditionally, the therapist asks the potential giver to do more of the identified behaviors within a particular time frame. For example, in the "love days" procedure developed by Weiss and his associates (Weiss & Birchler, 1978; Weiss et al., 1973), the therapist has couples schedule specific days when one spouse will attempt to double his/her output of "pleasing" behaviors. In the "caring days" procedure of Stuart (1980), the therapist asks couples to set aside specific days in which one spouse will demonstrate his/her caring for the other in as many ways as possible.

Rather than asking the giver to do more, the therapist may ask the receiver to make specific requests of the giver. Couples are often unaccustomed to asking for direct changes from the other, yet this skill of direct communication may be an important one for them to learn. However, in this procedure, it is important that the therapist make clear that it is up to the giver to determine which requests he/she will grant. A forced gift is unlikely to be reinforcing for either the giver or the receiver. In general, BE works better when the giver has a range of behaviors from which to choose. In that way, the giver can exercise effective control over which behaviors requested by the recipient the giver does, and the recipient can interpret the behaviors as done willingly by the giver.

Our most recent version of BE allows the giver greater latitude in what is given and when. Now, we typically begin by asking givers to attempt an increase in their partners' daily marital satisfaction at times they (the givers) choose, using items of their "choice" from *their* lists of potentially reinforcing behaviors. When the giver chooses which behaviors to increase and when, the recipient is more likely to experience the increase as positive. Moreover, the more general the directive, the more options the giver has as to which behaviors to increase and when, the more likely that compliance will occur. We have found that this focus on the giver is much more effective than the traditional BE interventions described previously.

Besides these two basic procedures of BE—identifying and increasing the frequency of desired behaviors—a third step is often added. Partners are trained to recognize and acknowledge the behaviors that the other has done for them. BE can sometimes go awry if one spouse puts energy into doing something positive for the other, but the other shows no appreciation for those actions, or worse, is angry that the partner did not do them before. The only way that new, positive actions can be maintained is if those actions get some reinforcement from the partner. Direct intervention may be necessary to ensure such reinforcement.

Although the traditional emphasis in BE has been on increasing nonconflictual behaviors, there are times when partners make major changes in core areas. For some couples, when behaviors are specifically targeted for change, and partners discover that they have the ability to do things that significantly improve the relationship climate, the effects of BE snowball. This is not the norm, nor should couples expect it. But it can and does happen. As long as the therapist warns couples to attempt only those changes that will not be costly to them, they are free to choose any item or items from their lists, be they major or minor problems. At times, the effort they make is more important than whether they choose the right behaviors to increase.

Communication/Problem-Solving Training

The goal of CPT is the systematic training of communication skills in couples while solving some of their specific problems. Although the solution of the specific problems provides immediate gratification for them, the more important goal is the teaching of skills with which they can solve future problems that inevitably arise between them.

Other approaches to marital therapy have emphasized communication training (e.g., Ables &

Brandsma, 1977), but they have usually focused on communication for expression rather than communication for change. That is to say, they have emphasized the expression and reception of feelings, whereas CPT teaches couples skills for resolving conflicts. Although the skills for resolving conflict certainly involve the expression of feelings, additional skills are needed. Furthermore, CPT differs from other approaches to communication training in its systematic method of training, as well as its particular repertoire of skills.

CPT differs from BE in three respects. First, CPT is process oriented, whereas BE is content oriented. BE is concerned with making changes in specific behaviors, whereas CPT focuses on creating change in particular behaviors only as a way of teaching couples how to solve problems. Second, BE instigates new behaviors by direct instruction, whereas CPT generates new behaviors through the process of discussion, negotiation, and skill development. Finally, CPT normally requires more time and effort than BE. Because the focus of CPT is on issues that are more complicated and controversial than the behaviors that are the focus of BE, CPT normally accounts for more therapeutic attention than BE.

Description of Communication/Problem-Solving Training. IBCT teach couples an important distinction between arguments and CPT. Arguments are a competitive struggle between the two partners, characterized by attack and defense. Although arguments are inevitable in marriage and may serve some useful functions for the couple, they are different from CPT, which is a collaborative effort to solve problems. IBCT therapists help couples distinguish, inside and outside therapy, which occasions are arguments and which are CPT. To make the distinction more concrete, therapists may designate particular areas of the therapy session for "fighting" and for "problem solving," and encourage the couple to designate areas of their home similarly.

Within CPT itself, IBCT therapists teach an important distinction between problem definition and problem solution. During problem definition, which occurs first, the couple formulates a specific statement of what the problem is. During problem solution, the couple generates possible solutions, negotiates those solutions, and reaches an agreement about a particular solution. Keeping these two processes separate facilitates effective CPT by preventing premature solutions during problem definition and by maintaining focus during problem solution.

There are general guidelines for conducting CPT, as well as specific guidelines for the definition and solution phases. Review of these guidelines provides an overview of CPT.

The first general guidelines is that only one problem is discussed at a time. Although relationship problems are often related, an attempt to deal with too much may make the task so complex and overwhelming that no solution is possible. Second, partners are to discuss their own views, rather than speculate about their partner. In particular, partners are to avoid inferences about the other person's motivation, attitudes, or feelings. Such mind reading is usually perceived by the partner as an attack (often a correct perception) and leads to defensiveness and counterattack, which then derails problem solving. In fact, any kind of attack or verbal abuse is inappropriate for CPT. Third, each partner is encouraged to begin his/her statement with a paraphrase or summary of what the other just said. Although such a procedure might appear somewhat unusual or mechanical for couples, it ensures that partners listen to each other. By so doing, interruptions are limited, miscommunication may be averted, and partners may be more likely to adopt the other's perspective.

There are several guidelines for the definition stage. First, IBCT therapists encourage partners to look for and mention some positive aspect of the stated problem. For example, rather than saying "You never help with the kids," a wife might comment that "You are really good at playing with the kids. They really look forward to that and enjoy it. But I need more help from you with their homework." If partners can genuinely endorse something positive about the other in the problem area, it can facilitate collaboration between them.

Second, IBCT therapists train couples to state their problems in specific, descriptive, behavioral terms. Rather than using personality descriptions (e.g., "lazy," "neurotic") and overgeneralizations (e.g., "you always . . ." or "you never . . ."), partners pinpoint the problematic behaviors or sequences that occur between them.

This emphasis on specific, behavioral prescriptions is not meant to preclude feeling expression. In fact, the third guideline is that partners are encouraged to express their feelings about the pinpointed problem. The experiential impact of a problem is part of the problem and must be included in its definition. Partners may have difficulty both in defining their problems and in articulating their feelings about these problems. They may have only limited awareness of what specific behaviors cause them distress and what feelings those behaviors generate. Therefore, both defining behaviors and expressing feelings may require time and exploration by the couple.

Fourth, partners are encouraged to acknowledge their own role in perpetuating the problem. IBCT therapists promote the view that most relationship problems are jointly caused and maintained. Therefore, partners need not be defensive about admitting that they have something to do with the problem. Such admissions are often helpful for partners to hear, because in previous arguments both partners may have charged that the other was solely to blame for the problem. Acknowledgment of each other's role also lays the groundwork for the solution phase, in which both partners often end up agreeing to make changes. However, it is important during the problem definition phase to avoid any implication that admission of a role in the problem obligates either partner to a particular change. Partners can be freer to aknowledge their roles if there are no necessary obligations attached.

Finally, couples should devise a brief, succinct summary of their problem that will function as their problem definition. As an example of a good summary problem definition, let us consider the issue of husband helping more with homework, which was mentioned previously. The therapist tries to focus the discussion until material like the following appears. Then the therapist summarizes the problem or encourages the couple to summarize the problem as follows:

"The problem is that Judy has most of the responsibility for monitoring and assisting with the kids' homework, which makes her feel unequally burdened and angry at George for his lack of participation. George, on the other hand, feels that he does not have authority over the homework when he does do it. He acknowledges that Judy is better than he is at doing homework with the kids, but he is angry that she interrupts his work with the children to correct him, and that she checks the homework to make sure he checked over it correctly! As a result, both partners end up angry and withdraw from the other."

When a problem definition like this has been established, the couple is ready to move on to the problem solution phase. There are three guidelines for this phase. First, the discussion should be focused on finding solutions rather than on further elaborations of the problem. The IBCT therapist makes this happen by clearly demarcating the two phases and by promoting brainstorming in the solution phase. During brainstorming, couples generate as many solutions to the problem as possible, without regard to their quality. Even funny or absurd solutions are encouraged in order to deemphasize quality, promote creativity in generating imaginative solutions, and add humor to the situation. The therapist may suggest some odd solutions as a way of creating a brainstorming atmosphere. Second, the couple evaluates the brainstormed solutions, based on their benefits and costs. Absurd ideas are eliminated and possible solutions are considered for their advantages and disadvantages. Third, the discussion of possible solutions should emphasize mutual negotiation and compromise. Partners are encouraged to discuss possible trade-offs with each other. ("I would do this if you would do that"). Although therapists encourage this kind of discussion, they try to ensure that there is no coercion in the negotiation and that couples do not offer concessions that they may not be able to follow through on. Finally, any agreement that is reached should be specific and in writing. Spouses need to be clear on what they have agreed to do. Such clarity makes misunderstanding less likely and compliance with the agreement more likely.

An agreement on the homework issue discussed previously might be reached as follows: George agrees to help out more with the kids' homework and Judy agrees to not interfere with George. Specifically, George agrees to do homework with the kids two or three nights a week, depending on his and Judy's work schedules. Each night at dinner, Judy and George will agree on who is responsible for helping the kids with homework. If George is responsible, Judy will not interrupt his efforts with the kids or check over his work. However, Judy can talk with George about effective ways of dealing with homework.

Training Methods. Systematic methods involving instructions, feedback, behavioral rehearsal, and fading are used to train couples in CPT skills. The content of the program is imparted through verbal instructions and role playing. For example, the therapist might explain the skill of paraphrasing to a couple and then illustrate by modeling paraphrasing in a conversation with the wife. To insure that couples learn the principles behind each skill, the therapist should explain reasons for each skill, as well as the skill itself. For example, in addition to explaining and illustrating paraphrasing, the therapist should explain how paraphrasing ensures that partners listen to each other and makes them more likely to see the other person's position.

Once instruction has taken place, couples must practice the skills themselves, first in therapy and later at home. This behavioral rehearsal is essential for skills learning. Initially the therapist may prompt and reinforce these skills, but eventually the couple must learn to engage in them without these therapeutic supports.

As couples practice their new skills, IBCT therapists provide generous feedback about both the desirable and undesirable aspects of their performance, emphasizing the desireable aspects. Feedback tends to be descriptive rather than interpretive and focuses on the functional value rather than the content of the behavior. For example, a therapist might note: "You didn't first paraphrase what she said, so she is not certain you heard what she said." Feedback is normally provided verbally, but video- or audiotape feedback can also be used. Taped feedback is very powerful, and therapists must be careful to insure that the feedback is not overwhelming for couples who are not used to seeing or hearing themselves on tape.

As training proceeds, the therapist becomes less and less active in the CPT discussions. The goal is for couples to learn skills, not just to respond to therapist cues. Therefore, the therapist must reduce those cues to ensure that the skills are learned. Typically, therapy will not be terminated abruptly; rather, sessions will be spaced at longer and longer intervals to ensure that skills are being practiced and maintained. This fading of the therapist's contact and influence underscores the major goal of CPT—to teach skills that are applicable to a variety of problems rather than simply to solve a specific, current problem.

Strategies to Promote Emotional Acceptance between Partners

IBCT employs four strategies to promote emotional acceptance: (1) acceptance through empathic joining around the problem, (2) acceptance through detachment from the problem, (3) acceptance through greater tolerance of the partner's aversive actions, and (4) acceptance through increased ability to take care of oneself when confronted with the partner's aversive actions. In the first two strategies, the therapist enhances acceptance by helping couples experience the problem in a different way, either as an understandable dilemma that causes both partners

pain, or as a common, external enemy that they share. In the last two strategies, acceptance is enhanced by reducing the aversiveness of the partner's actions, either by increasing one's tolerance or self-care in the face of those actions.

Emotional Acceptance through Empathic Joining around the Problem

When couples come into therapy, they typically are distressed at each other's actions or inactions, because these behaviors are experienced within a particular context. Partners may often experience their spouses as "bad"—mean, selfish, inconsiderate, deceitful, or the like—or they may label their partners as mentally or emotionally disturbed—hysterical, compulsive, overly emotional, pathologically underemotional, dependent, hostile, or the like. If they do not experience their partners as bad or label them as emotionally disordered, they might call them inadequate—unable to communicate, unable to love, unable to be intimate, or the like. Experiencing the partner in this context makes emotional acceptance difficult. How can one accept a mate that is bad, emotionally disturbed, or inadequate? Even if emotional acceptance occurs in this situation, it is less than desirable because it creates an implicit or explicit hierarchy between the pair. "He is selfish, but I am not." "She is emotionally disturbed, but I am not." "He is inadequate, but I am not." "I am okay, but she is not."

To create emotional acceptance, the therapist reformulates the problem and the partner's behavior in terms of common differences between people, and understandable emotional reactions to those differences. Of special importance in this reformulation is to underscore the pain that each partner experiences and the efforts, however misdirected, that each makes to accommodate the other. We have found two metaphors helpful here, one with students and one with couples. To our statistically minded students we often describe the negative reaction by a partner as a dependent variable (e.g., a complaint), the behavior producing the reaction as an independent variable, and the accusation that is implicit in the independent variable as a covariate. Once the blaming or accusatory stance is covaried out, a pure, unbridled expression of pain is left, and its association with the dependent variable is decreased. With couples, we sometimes present them with the equation

$$\text{PAIN} + \text{ACCUSATION} = \text{MARITAL DISCORD}$$

whereas

PAIN – ACCUSATION = ACCEPTANCE.

Initially, the therapist simply provides this reformulation of the couple's problem during the feedback session. For example, in providing feedback to Michael and Donna about their closeness problem, the therapist might say:

"A major problem that I see the two of you as having comes from a difference between you in your desired level of intimacy or closeness. You, Donna, want more closeness, more expression of love, and more togetherness between the two of you, while you, Michael, want more independence and autonomy in your relationship. This is a common difference between people, but it gets the two of you in trouble because of an unpleasant sequence of communication between the two of you as you try to deal with this difference. It is hard to say how it starts, but after some period of distance between the two of you, at some point, Donna, you feel deprived of Michael's company or are anxious about the distance between you, and you approach Michael, seeking more contact. However, when you make this request, you are often tense because you are annoyed or angry that he does not initiate contact, you are worried about his response to you, and you can anticipate the negative cycle that often happens. When you, Michael, hear her request, you sense the tension, and you feel pressured, controlled, and put upon. However, even when she approaches you without tension, you are now so sensitive to this issue and so expectant of these requests, that you may respond with tension of your own. When either of you senses or anticipates tension from the other, you are liable to go to your emotional corners—you feel rejected, hurt, and angry, Donna, while you feel pressured, controlled, and put upon, Michael. In this state it is hardly surprising that you, Donna, express your anger by blaming Michael and demanding things from him, while you, Michael, retreat in sullen silence. And neither of you gets what you wanted."

A couple will often agree with this reformulation when it is given in the feedback session, but this does not mean that they have achieved emotional acceptance of the other. Perhaps the therapist's reformulation is the first step toward that acceptance, but they will need many experiences in which the problem is experienced in a different context or in which they talk to each other about the problem in a different way before they move substantially toward greater acceptance of the other.

The Language of Acceptance. To promote acceptance, IBCT therapists both guide couples in a different way of talking about problems and provide this different perspective in their formulations. At the expressive level, this language of acceptance emphasizes talking about one's own experience versus talking about the other. Therapists encourage spouses to talk about their own feeling and thinking rather than to describe what the other did or what they think the other is thinking and feeling. IBCT therapists may prompt partners with statements such as "Michael, you are describing now what you think Donna is feeling during these scenarios. Would you talk about what is going on with you?" This emphasis on talk about self is consistent with the common therapeutic admonition to use "I statements" versus "you statements." However, IBCT therapists are concerned more with content than with syntax, because syntax can be a mask for content. Many a focus on the other has been camouflaged with an "I statement," as in "I feel you are trying to control me." Therefore, IBCT therapists may not emphasize this distinction between "I statements" and "you statements" in their efforts to get partners to talk about self.

When clients talk about themselves, IBCT therapists encourage disclosures about "soft" feelings and thoughts versus "hard" ones. Hard disclosures reveal the self in a stronger, more dominant position vis-à-vis the partner. They are emotions such as anger and resentment, and cognitions around assertion, power, and control (e.g., "I won't let myself be taken advantage of; I will get what I want; I won't be controlled"). Soft disclosures reveal the self as vulnerable to the partner. They reflect feelings of hurt, fear, and disappointment and thoughts of doubt, uncertainty, and danger (e.g., "I wasn't sure he cared about me; I didn't know if I could do it alone; I thought she might get upset; I wanted to please him"). Hard disclosures are easier to make because they do not reveal the self as vulnerable, but harder for the partner to hear because they imply blame and dominance over the partner. Soft disclosures are harder to make because they reveal the self as vulnerable but are easier for the partner to empathize with and hear. Because of their capacity to generate empathy, soft disclosures are more likely to promote closeness between the couple.

IBCT therapists assume that there is a soft feeling and thinking associated with almost all hard feelings and thinking. Hurt usually accompanies anger; disappointment often comes with resentment; fear and insecurity often breed assertiveness and aggression. When IBCT therapists encourage self-disclosure by couples, hard disclosures are most likely to occur first. For example, a withdrawn spouse is likely to voice anger or resentment before soft feelings. These disclosures are important because they are true statements about what is going on with the client. However, they may not, by themselves, lead to acceptance unless they are accompanied by and framed in terms of soft disclosures. Michael will not be able to accept Donna if he sees her as just angry at him for not giving her enough attention. However, he may be able to accept her if he sees her doubt about his love, her anguish in his withdrawal, and her loneliness when he is absent. Donna will not be able to accept Michael if she sees him as just angry and resistant to her requests, but she may be able to accept him if she sees his anger and resistance coming from a fear of being overwhelmed by her.

Ideally, IBCT therapists create a safe atmosphere in therapy where couples can reveal this softness. However, these disclosures often do not come spontaneously. Therapists may need to suggest them to couples. When Michael discloses his anger and resolute determination not to be controlled by Donna's efforts for greater closeness, the therapist might say, "I wonder, Michael, if this anger at Donna and this determination to hold your own with her comes from a sense of almost being overwhelmed by her." Similarly, the therapist might reflect one of Michael's statements by saying, "It sounds like you want to take a strong stand with Donna. You must fear that if you don't, you won't have any say at all."

The emphasis in IBCT on soft disclosures is similar to the emphasis on unexpressed feelings in emotionally focused couple therapy (Greenberg & Johnson, 1986). The soft feelings and thoughts that are disclosed in IBCT are likely to be unexpressed feelings. However, as emotionally focused couple therapy points out, often anger and resentment are unexpressed feelings. Both therapies might encourage the expression of unexpressed anger and resentment, but IBCT would be less willing to end the matter at that point. It would want to explore what pain, hurt, and disappointment (soft feelings) are associated with the anger and resentment without in any way minimizing or denying the validity of the anger and resentment.

Up to now, we have been discussing the language of acceptance at the expressive level. What do listeners do? If speakers focus on their own experience, then listeners may be freed from the demanding tasks of coming up with defenses, explanations, contrary examples, and counterattacks. They may be able to listen and understand. Furthermore, as they experience the therapist guiding them away from defenses and explanations, they may be further motivated to listen and understand when the partner is speaking rather than develop rebuttals. IBCT therapists may encourage "active listening" by training spouses to paraphrase and reflect what their partners have said. However, IBCT therapists are hesitant about promoting a formula for communication and are concerned about integrating therapeutic procedures with the client's style. Therefore, they emphasize active listening at points where the communication breaks down, or where the speaker's message is not heard, rather than insisting that each speaker's message be met with a listener's paraphrase.

Whenever IBCT therapists focus on promoting acceptance through these types of reformulations, they always have a choice between trying to teach the couple to talk to each other differently, and simply using their own reformulations to produce acceptance. Thus far, we have been emphasizing the language of clients, but in many ways the language of therapists is more important. For many couples, it is very difficult to talk about the problem in the ways described previously, no matter how often they practice. The difficulty is that when strong affect is aroused, the content takes precedence over the process, and these distinctions between blaming and nonblaming disappear. Luckily, we have found that it is not necessary for couples to actually use this language regularly. As long as therapists use it and consistently reformulate the problem in the ways described, acceptance can occur. Couples now have something that they did not have before, namely, the therapist's perspective, which becomes a part of their learning history and influences the impact that the problem has on them. They become more accepting in a number of ways: They may recover from their arguments more quickly; they may debrief the problem in a nonblaming manner, even though the arguments continue; and perhaps most important, they may accept the inevitability of these conflicts.

The Focus of Therapeutic Conversations. What are the topics of discussion through which therapists promote acceptance? IBCT therapists guide couples through four types of conversations:

1. A general discussion of the basic differences between them and the resultant interaction pattern
2. Discussion of an upcoming event that may trigger the problem
3. Discussion of a recent negative event during which the problem occurred
4. Discussion of a recent positive event in which they handled the problem better

A general discussion about the problem can come on the heels of a discussion of a relevant incident or may occur in the absence of any immediate incident. The clinical purposes of a general discussion are (1) to promote a view of the problem as arising from differences between the partners and (2) to promote a more sympathetic context for the partners' behavior in the face of those differences. Such a discussion may focus on the understandable reasons why partners are different. Personal history, current environmental pressures, and gender-related differences may help explain to the couple why they are different. For example, Michael's siblings were so much older than he that he was raised almost as an only child, whereas Donna was raised with two close-in-age siblings. These differences in family history might explain their different comfort levels with intimacy. Donna's current job requires considerable solitary activity, whereas Michael's job requires extensive social contact—a difference that might explain their different inclinations for contact at the end of the day. Also, their differences reflect common gender stereotypes that may result from socialization and/or biological differences. IBCT therapists do not attempt any extensive analysis of personal history, environmental pressures, or gender stereotypes with couples. Rather, they use whatever information is easily available to them to underscore the differences between partners and to frame those differences as coming about through understandable human experience.

During these general discussions, IBCT therapists also try to elucidate the sequence of negative interaction that occurs around these differences. These sequences are often referred to as "themes" or "dances." Even though they may be painful for both partners, IBCT therapists try to reframe them as resulting from understandable reactions and counterreactions of the spouses

to their differences. Donna pressures Michael for contact, in part because she desires more closeness than he, and in part because she reacts to his withdrawal. Similarly, Michael withdraws from Donna, in part because he desires more independence than Donna, and in part because he reacts to her pressure.

However beneficial these general discussions of the problem are, a focus on individual incidents is usually necessary to promote acceptance between partners. The most fruitful incident to discuss is an upcoming one. Here, therapist and spouses can discuss anticipated reactions, develop an understanding and acceptance of those reactions, and possibly problem solve to alter the situation. For example, Michael may want to spend an upcoming weekend away with a group of his male friends, but is afraid to broach the topic with Donna because of what her reaction may be. Even before he has mentioned the idea to her, he may be developing resentment about her anticipated response, so that his tension will be evident in his first utterance on the matter. Or Donna may want a special celebration of their upcoming anniversary but be concerned that Michael will not give it much attention. Already she may be angry about his anticipated response, so that her first comment on the matter may be negative. Discussion in therapy of these anticipated events can do much to promote acceptance, as well as allow for some resilience and debriefing after the event to promote closeness.

Because couples can anticipate only a fraction of the incidents concerning a problem, IBCT therapists usually deal with recent incidents rather than upcoming ones. Therapists should seize upon any problem-related incident that went well. If Michael and Donna were able to work out a way to spend quality time either together or apart, IBCT therapists would want to discuss this incident in therapy to understand how it went well and to reinforce the partners for their respective actions. For example, perhaps Donna was especially accommodating to Michael's desire for time alone on a recent weekend. An analysis in therapy reveals that her ease in accommodation came about in part because she felt they were able to relate so intimately two nights earlier. This reaction in her—that intimacy with Michael enables her to accept his time apart—would be underscored in therapy for its obvious importance, but also because it counteracts a secret fear of Michael's—that the more she gets the more she wants.

The discussions of positive events serve an additional function: They help prepare couples for the inevitability of slipups. There is no better time to deal with slipups than when things are going well. After the couple has been thoroughly debriefed regarding a positive event, IBCT therapists commonly ask, "What will happen if it does not go as well next time?" This often leads to "tolerance" interventions (described later), or to further discussion of the problem. The question in and of itself communicates that slipups are inevitable, and helps partners become more accepting of their inevitability. Without such caveats, they are likely to become demoralized when the inevitable slipup occurs, or when they have their next bad week.

IBCT therapists often do not have the luxury of dealing with positive incidents around problems. They must be prepared to deal with many incidents that went badly and for which strong emotions still exist. In order to promote acceptance, rather than merely replay a bad scene with its plethora of negative emotions, IBCT therapists focus on the initial stages of the incident, even on preincident material, rather than the middle and closing stages of the incident. Once a negative incident gets underway, partners typically go through a sequence of aversive exchanges that can provide much blameworthy material for each ("Donna just yelled at me hysterically"; "Michael wouldn't even look at me"). However, in the beginning stages, each partner's actions may be more understandable and acceptable, at least when elucidated in therapy. Consider an incident in which Michael comes home late from work and Donna greets him with an accusatory "You don't care anything about me, do you?" Michael gets furious at this attack, especially since his delay was only due to an accident that tied up the freeway. They yell at each other briefly, then retreat into cold distance the rest of the evening. During the discussion of this incident, an IBCT therapist would want to understand what was going on with Donna before Michael came home. Perhaps she had become increasingly distressed at the distance between them and this incident of lateness only served as a trigger for the release of her distress. What she was really saying was "I am unhappy about the distance between us. I fear it means that you don't care much about me. Your being late gives me an opportunity to say this." From Michael's side, he, too, is aware of the distance between them, but he has no chance to miss it because he is too worried about her reaction to it. To avoid any angry outburst, he tries to be home at agreed upon times. This day, despite leaving at the usual time, he is late. He is distressed by this, but tells himself that it is not his fault and any complaint by her would be unjustified. What he might have been saying was "Yes, we have not been close, but I have been trying to do what I can. I can't stand it when I try and you still criticize me." By focusing the couple on this *early* material, IBCT therapists not only promote acceptance but make it easier for the couple to "return to normal" after the incident, if they have not done so already.

Emotional Acceptance through Detachment from the Problem

Whereas our first strategy counteracts blame and promotes acceptance by engendering empathy and compassion in each member for the other, our second strategy works for these same goals by promoting a detached, descriptive, externalized view of the problem. Rather than eliciting soft emotional expression, this approach engages partners in an intellectual analysis of the problem. The therapist engages the couple in a conversation about the sequence of conflict between them, about what "triggers" their reactions, and about the interconnection of specific incidents to each other and to their overriding theme. In these discussions, the therapist carefully avoids any evaluative analysis that might place blame or responsibility for change on one person. The emphasis is on a detached description of the problematic sequence. The problem is not a "you" or "me" but an "it."

The use of humor and metaphor can be useful in promoting a detached analysis of problems as long as it does not demean, embarrass, or show disrespect for either member. Consider, for example, Georgia and Dan, who have a problem coordinating housework and child care between them. When Georgia is under pressure and feels that Dan has not been doing his share, she angrily takes control and orders Dan to do a series of chores. In response, Dan finds any excuse to get out of the situation, which, of course, further angers Georgia. If a discussion of this problem could lead to a humorous characterization of the sequence as the "General Georgia and Deserter Dan syndrome," the couple could use this label to see the problem and their own roles in it, while maintaining some humorous distance from it. They might even use the label as a means of recovering from a conflict, such as by saying that "We've just had another episode from Deserter Dan and General Georgia."

Like acceptance through emphatic joining, acceptance through detachment from the problem can be conducted at each of the four levels described previously:

1. A general discussion of basic differences and the resultant conflictual interaction sequences
2. Discussion of an upcoming event that may trigger the problem
3. Discussion of a recent positive event relevant to the problem
4. Discussion of a recent negative event relevant to the problem

In fact, although we separate our discussion of the two strategies for promoting acceptance because they have a different conceptual focus, practically speaking, a therapist will often mix the two. For example, in debriefing the couple regarding a recent negative event, the therapist might have the couple describe their own behavior that served as a trigger for their partner's reaction, but then focus on their emotional reactions in an attempt to expose the softer, more vulnerable side of each partner.

The two concepts that unify detachment interventions are the notions of "continuity" and "description." If work on detachment is going well, couples should be increasingly able to experience their themes and prototypical, destructive interactional sequences descriptively, with detachment and insight into the interconnectedness of various incidents. Therapists need to remind clients of what happened last week, and draw connections between incidents being discussed in the current session and those discussed in previous sessions. Every incident should be related to the one or two overriding themes that characterize the destructive interaction patterns. Couples should learn to critique their own enactments of recurring destructive patterns without blame and accusation.

This increased ability to "debrief" arguments and recognize patterns can be called "developing a platform for viewing the relationship," to use Wile's (1981) terminology. What is important is that one of two things happen to increasing degrees during the course of therapy: Either the couple develops increased capacity to discuss their problems as an "it" that they share, a cross they have to bear, rather than as adversaries, or, if they do not learn to talk this way, they at least change the way they talk about their problems when they refer to them *after* an argument. Over time, it becomes increasingly apparent that they use descriptive and detached, rather than accusatory, language. Or, at the very least, they learn

to talk to each other in a nonaccusatory way about the fact that they are using accusatory language.

We have a number of exercises that we use from time to time in helping couples put the problem outside of themselves. At times, the therapist simply brings in a fourth chair, and says, "Let's put the problem in the chair and talk about it. But whenever you refer to it, talk about it as an 'it' sitting in this chair." Another effective task is to have the couple imagine that the therapist is present during their arguments at home. Perhaps a chair can be set for the therapist. Often, couples are better able to discuss the problem as an "it" in the therapist's office than when they are at home. Part of the reason is that they are talking, in part, to the therapist. For example, Michael may turn to the therapist and say, "I felt like there was no way I could win." We sometimes enourage couples to turn to the imaginary therapist in the chair at home to explain what is going on, because this is often easier than saying it directly to the partner. This task often gets couples to talk about their desire to blame and accuse each other, rather than actually doing the blaming or accusing. The more people talk about their desire to make accusations rather than actually make them, the more acceptance is fostered.

One of many ironies in EA work is that by giving up on change strategies, change is often facilitated. Often, as couples stop trying to solve the problem using their self-defeating strategies, the solution becomes straightforward. For example, when Alex and Jill stopped fighting over how Alex could change his priorities so that family would come first, and instead discussed the difficulties Alex had in changing his priorities (due to a drive to be more successful than his dad, a desire to please everyone, etc.) they became closer, and his priorities became less important.

Emotional Acceptance through Tolerance Building

Human beings find it hard to accept pain. They are wired genetically to do all possible to prevent, avoid, or escape from pain. What makes emotional acceptance of a partner so difficult for couples is the pain induced by some of the partner's behaviors. One way to facilitate acceptance is to increase a spouse's tolerance for the partner's behavior, which will reduce the pain caused by that behavior. But tolerance can occur only if spouses stop their frantic efforts to prevent, avoid, and escape from a partner's behavior by trying to change the partner or escape from him/her. If they can experience the partner's behavior without so much struggle, they may find themselves less sensitive to it. The key to tolerance building is actually to give up the struggle to change the partner, and to experience the behavior in a context in which acceptance is promoted. The strategies that follow are designed to achieve this.

Positive Features of Negative Behavior. IBCT therapists point out to a spouse the positive features of the partner's negative behavior. If couples see the benefits of negative behavior, they may be more able to tolerate it. This strategy is quite similar to that of "positive connotation" in family systems therapy. However, as used in IBCT, pointing out positive features differs from "positive connotation" in two ways. First, IBCT continues to acknowledge the negative features while pointing out positive features. It does not attempt a wholesale reframing of problem behavior into positive behavior. IBCT therapists are skeptical as to whether such a complete reframing is possible for couples. Furthermore, such a reframing ignores the reality of the current pain. Second, IBCT seeks positive features that are really there for the couple. It is less strategic than "positive connotation," because IBCT is not after any interpretation that might alter perception, but only those that reflect some reality for the couple. For example, if IBCT therapists understood Donna's criticisms as coming from her anger at Michael and her desire to hurt his feelings, they would *not* interpret her criticisms as her positive efforts to help Michael. Rather, they would interpret her criticisms as coming from her own deep hurt and her view, however incorrect, that the only way she can get through to him is through her criticisms. They might note to Michael that these criticisms are not a sign of his own failings, but rather a clear indication of how badly Donna is feeling.

This IBCT strategy of pointing out the positive in the negative is easiest when therapists can frame that negative behavior as part of a characteristic that originally attracted or now attracts the other. For example, assume that Donna's discussion of her attraction to Michael included information comparing him to other men. Whereas other men pressured her for greater sexual intimacy and expressed their love for her as a means, she suspected, of getting greater sexual intimacy, Michael was different. He never pushed her for greater sexual or emotional intimacy. In fact, she was the initiator, sexually and emotionally,

and thus could regulate their level of intimacy. When discussing the current problem of Michael's lack of sexual or emotional initiation, IBCT therapists would want to discuss this difference between Michael and other men. For example, a therapist might say to Donna:

"Early on you appreciated Michael's respect for you and your boundaries, and his willingness to let you determine the pace of intimacy. I know that now you wish he would take more initiative and you feel bad when he doesn't, but I think he may still be letting you set the pace, as long as it doesn't push him to where he is uncomfortable. I think this does give you some freedom to express intimacy as you wish and you need put no energy in setting up boundaries, but I think now you are mainly feeling the negative side of this, that you are more the giver than the receiver."

Even if spouses do not provide information that allows IBCT therapists to interpret negative behavior as partly positive, therapists can point to a common function of individual differences: that they create balance in the relationship so it can function more smoothly. For example, an IBCT therapist might say to Michael and Donna:

"I'm not surprised that you two got together, because, in terms of intimacy, both of you need what the other has. If you, Michael, had gotten together with someone like yourself, both of you would been so distant that a relationship might not have been possible. On the other hand, Donna, if you had gotten together with someone like yourself, both of you would have been so entangled that much of your individuality might not have been possible. So in this relationship, Donna, you see to it that intimacy is taken care of, while, Michael, you see to it that independence is taken care of."

Framing a couple's differences in terms of a positive balance may facilitate both acceptance and change. The balance suggests that what each gives is necessary for the relationship, but also that each needs to move in the direction of the other. For example, in a couple in which the wife is very critical and the husband is very noncritical, an IBCT therapist might praise the wife for being so discriminating in her judgment and the husband for being so accepting of others. The IBCT therapist would also indicate that each characteristic is important in a relationship, but their problem is that these positive traits are too one-sided. Therefore, each partner needs to learn from the other's positive trait.

Role Playing or Behavior Rehearsal of Negative Behavior. Role playing or behavior rehearsal is a common strategy for change in behavioral marital therapy. Couples practice new behaviors in the session so that they can use them later, outside the session. However, these new behaviors that couples practice are often more constructive ways of communicating about each partner's needs and desires. Change is not directed toward the needs and desires themselves. For example, Michael and Donna practice constructive ways of signaling each other that they want time together or time apart. However, change efforts are not directed at Donna needing less time together (which is what Michael may hope for) or at Michael needing less time apart (which is what Donna may hope for). Thus, even in these traditional, change-oriented procedures, the therapist promotes acceptance of the couple's divergent needs and desires, while trying to change the way they communicate about them.

IBCT goes one step further. It promotes acceptance not only of partners' divergent needs, but also of their old, ineffective ways of communicating these needs. IBCT therapists give couples the message that no matter how effective they are in making changes, at times they will "slip up" and lapse into old patterns. Therefore, it is essential that IBCT therapists prepare the couple for those slipups, so that the couple does not misinterpret a lapse as a relapse and conclude that all their good efforts have failed. With this rationale in place, IBCT therapists ask couples to rehearse a slipup in the session. For example, IBCT therapists might ask Michael to role play a situation in which he tells Donna he is going out with friends that evening, without having discussed this with her in advance. Or they might ask Donna to role play a situation in which she attacks Michael for not caring about her.

During these role-playing situations, IBCT therapists are active in helping the couple discuss the feelings and thinking that arise in them or might arise if this episode occurred in real life. As in the strategies described earlier for debriefing of recent events, the therapist's goal is to elucidate the reactions of each, however strong, but put them in a sympathetic context by showing how understandable they are. The therapist may highlight the dilemma that these reactions create. For example, after role playing a scene in which Donna attacks Michael for not caring, the therapist might say to Donna and Michael:

"So it seems to me, Donna, that when there hasn't been much closeness between the two of you, you sense it but are likely to experience it as neglect by Michael. After all, he doesn't initiate much contact or seem available for it. So in this situation, it is hard for you not to attack Michael with a charge of not caring. It doesn't seem like he does care. However, on your side, Michael, the attack feels so 'out of the blue' and so unjustified. You have just been attending to your own business. Had she asked for time together, chances are, you would have responded positively. But now with this attack, your feelings are hurt, too. You get defensive, and you don't want to be close to her."

The primary goal of this exercise is to expose couples to likely scenarios without the destructive forces of attack, defense, and counterattack. With the therapist's assistance, couples express their feelings in these scenario rather than acting them out. Ideally, this exposure serves to desensitize couples to these scenarios and enables couples to face them with greater acceptance in the future. If couples are not so sensitive and reactive to each other's negative behavior, then they can accept the occasional occurrence of that behavior.

IBCT therapists also explore the possibility of "self-care" efforts during these potentially destructive scenarios. What can each partner do to take care of and protect self during these slipups? These strategies are discussed later.

Faked Incidents of Negative Behavior. To further promote acceptance of negative behavior by desensitizing partners to that behavior, IBCT therapists ask couples to fake incidents of negative behavior when they are really not inclined to do that behavior. For example, Donna may be asked to attack Michael as not caring about her, when she really does not feel that way.

IBCT therapists ask couples to fake negative behavior rather than wait until it occurs naturally, because a faked behavior can be done without the faker experiencing negative emotion. The faker may feign negative emotion as part of the negative behavior, but he/she can do so with calmness. This calmness allows the faker to more clearly observe the partner's pain and can prevent the incident from escalating. In fact, the faker is told to reveal the fake soon after it is initiated, so that escalation will be prevented and the couple can discuss their reactions to the incident. The instructions to fake are given in front of the partner, so that the partner knows that some negative behavior in the future may be faked. This knowledge could interrupt the partner's stereotypical reactions to negative behavior. For example, if Donna attacks Michael as not caring, when she really does not feel that way, she can see his upset and defensiveness more clearly, because she is not angry. She may be able to empathize with him. Furthermore, the instructions cast over her attacks a shadow of doubt that may interrupt Michael's defensiveness.

The powerful aspect of this task is that it can work in so many different ways. By instructing one partner to behave negatively in the presence of the other, the potential recipient of the negative behavior is now going to wonder, every time the behavior occurs, whether this instance is the assignment or a "spontaneous" example of the problem. This aspect of the directive tends to ritualize the transaction and change its function. Because the function of the negative behavior has changed, it no longer has the same impact as it once did. Thus, by ritualizing the problem, and thereby changing its function, the problem may go away.

This assignment is similar to the technique of "prescribing the symptom" in systems therapies. However, the goal in IBCT is not to reduce the likelihood of the symptom through a paradoxical directive. If that does occur, so much the better. However, IBCT therapists' rationale for this assignment is greater desensitization and thus acceptance of inevitable negative behavior. Unlike systems approaches, the IBCT rationale can be shared with the couple.

Emotional Acceptance through Greater Self-Care

If spouses are especially needy or vulnerable, they may have difficulty accepting the partner when the partner is unable to fulfill their needs or accommodate their vulnerabilities. One avenue toward greater acceptance is to increase each spouse's self-reliance, so they can manage better when their partner is unavailable to them. For example, if Donna were not so needy for closeness from Michael, she could accept his independence and his distancing from her more easily. Likewise, if Michael were not so vulnerable to approval from Donna, he could accept her criticism and displeasure more easily. IBCT promotes self-care activities as a means of increasing acceptance.

Alternative Means of Need Satisfaction. IBCT therapists explore with clients alternative means, other than their partner, for need satisfaction. This exploration must be done sensitively, because alternative means are likely to be second-best means for need satisfaction. Yes, Donna could get greater closeness through her friends, but what she wants is greater closeness with Michael, not with her friends. Also, the exploration must be done conditionally—for those times when partner is unable to satisfy needs— not as a way of releasing the partner from responsibility for need satisfaction. For example, if Donna sees this exploration as a way of getting Michael "off the hook" so that he does not have to be close to her, she will understandably resist such an exploration. However, if the thrust of therapy is to promote greater closeness but help her take care of herself better when Michael is unable to be close to her, then she may be more amenable to this exploration.

Because IBCT therapists are seeking greater acceptance between partners, this intervention can be successful, even if it does not lead to specific efforts by one or both spouses to seek alternative means of need satisfaction. The discussion itself introduces the notion of personal responsibility for need satisfaction. Thus, the discussion can lead to greater acceptance of the partner's inability to always fulfill needs. For example, even if Donna does not attempt greater closeness with her friends, this discussion could move her toward acceptance of Michael as being distant at times when she desires closeness.

Self-Care in the Face of Negative Behavior. Spouses' vulnerability to each other is often most apparent in the immediate presence of provocative, negative behavior. When Donna accuses Michael of not caring about her, he recoils at what he feels is such an unjust assault on him. His anger and frustration are painfully apparent in his rush to defend himself and prove that his actions are beyond reproach. Of course, his efforts only intensify her accusations and escalate the process. What spouses need in the presence of provocative behavior such as this by the other is often some means of protecting and caring for themselves. If IBCT therapists promote the idea that change efforts, however successful, will rarely be exhaustive (i.e., eliminate all future occurrences of the problem), then IBCT therapists must help arm spouses to face those incidents in ways that protect themselves while minimizing escalation.

Common means of protecting and caring for

oneself in the face of stress include leaving the situation, seeking solace from others, assertively altering the situation, and defining the situation differently. For example, in the face of Donna's accusations, Michael could leave the scene of the interaction, call one of his friends for comfort, tell Donna assertively that he will not sit and listen to attacks on his character, or define the situation differently in his head (e.g., as a temporary slipup that, however painful, will be over soon).

These different means of self-protection should not be considered in isolation from the partner's response, since some of them may further escalate the situation. For example, Donna may react even more strongly if Michael leaves the situation or calls certain friends or family. IBCT therapists help clients explore strategies that protect self without further alienating the partner or worsening the situation. Therefore, greater emphasis is put upon assertive expression and redefinition than on "time-outs" or contact with friends.

As with the earlier strategy of seeking alternative means of need fulfillment, exploration of self-care possibilities may promote acceptance of the partner, even if spouses do not identify clear actions that they can use when the partner is being provocatively negative. The exploration itself promotes several notions that can further acceptance. Occasionally provocative behavior will happen; spouses have a personal responsibility to take care of self in these situations; the provocative behavior does not imply that the relationship has fallen apart.

Summary

We have described four strategies to enhance emotional acceptance. In *emotional acceptance through empathic joining around the problem*, IBCT therapists reformulate problems in terms of the pain each partner experiences, rather than in terms of the blame each partner deserves. In *emotional acceptance through detachment from the problem*, the therapist promotes discussion of problems through detached description, rather than through emotional accusation. In *emotional acceptance through tolerance building*, IBCT therapists engage couples in actions that may desensitize them to each other's negative behavior. With lessened pain, partners may be more tolerant and accepting of each other's shortcomings. Finally, in *emotional acceptance through greater self-care*, IBCT therapists promote greater independence and self-reliance in members of couples, particularly in the face of a partner's

negative behaviors. With greater self-care, partners may experience less pain, greater tolerance, and greater acceptance. These four strategies lead not only to greater acceptance by partners but also by removing the pressure to change, they remove one of the greatest barriers to change. Thus, these strategies can often achieve on their own the twin goals of IBCT: acceptance and change.

REFERENCES

Ables, B. S., & Brandsma, J. M. (1977). *Therapy for couples.* San Francisco: Jossey-Bass.

Baucom, D. H., Epstein, N., Sayers, S. L., & Sher, T. G. (1989). The role of cognitions in marital relationships: Definitional, methodological, and conceptual issues. *Journal of Consulting and Clinical Psychology, 57,* 31–38.

Christensen, A. (1983). Intervention. In H. H. Kelley, E. Berscheid, A. Christensen, J. H. Harvey, T. L. Huston, G. Levinger, E. McClintock, L. A. Peplau, & D. R. Peterson, *Close relationships* (pp. 397–448). New York: Freeman.

Christensen, A., & Jacobson, N. S. (1991). *Integrative behavioral couple therapy.* Unpublished treatment manual.

Christensen, A., & Jacobson, N. S. (in press). *When lovers make war: Building intimacy from conflict through acceptance and change.*

Greenberg, L. S., & Johnson, S. M. (1986). Emotionally focused couples therapy. In N. S. Jacobson & A. S. Gurman (Eds.), *Clinical handbook of marital therapy* (pp. 253–276). New York: Guilford Press.

Gurman, A. S. (1991). Back to the future, ahead to the past: Is marital therapy going in circles? *Journal of Family Psychology, 4,* 402–406.

Holzworth-Munroe, A., & Jacobson, N. S. (1991). Behavioral marital therapy. In A. S. Gurman & D. P. Kniskern (Eds.), *Handbook of family therapy* (2nd ed., pp. 96–133). New York: Brunner/Mazel.

Jacobson, N. S. (1991). To be or not to be behavioral when working with couples: What does it mean? *Journal of Family Psychology, 4,* 436–445.

Jacobson, N. S. (1992). Behavioral couple therapy: A new beginning. *Behavior Therapy, 23,* 493–506.

Jacobson, N. S., & Christensen, A. (in press). *Integrative behavioral couple therapy.* New York: Norton.

Jacobson, N. S., Follette, W. C., Revenstorf, D., Baucom, D. H., Hahlweg, K., & Margolin, G. (1984). Variability in outcome and clinical significance of behavioral marital therapy: A reanalysis of outcome data. *Journal of Consulting and Clinical Psychology, 52,* 497–564.

Jacobson, N. S., & Holtzworth-Munroe, A. (1986). Marital therapy: A social learning/ cognitive perspective. In N. S. Jacobson & A. S. Gurman (Eds.), *Clinical handbook of marital therapy* (pp. 29–70). New York: Guilford Press.

Jacobson, N. S., & Margolin, G. (1979). *Marital therapy: Strategies based on social learning and behavior exchange principles.* New York: Brunner/Mazel.

Jacobson, N. S., Schmaling, K. B., & Holtzworth-Munroe, A. (1987). Component analysis of behavioral marital therapy: Two-year follow-up and prediction of relapse. *Journal of Marital and Family Therapy, 13,* 187–195.

Johnson, S. M., & Greengerg, L. S. (1991). There are more things in heaven and earth than are dreamed of in BMT: A response to Jacobson. *Journal of Family Psychology, 4,* 407–415.

Margolin, G., Talovic, S., & Weinstein, C. D. (1983). Areas of Change Questionnaire: A practical approach to marital assessment. *Journal of Consulting and Clinical Psychology, 51,* 920–931.

Patterson, G. R. (1982). *Coercive family process.* Eugene, OR: Castalia.

Skinner, B. F. (1966). An operant analysis of problem solving. In B. Kleinmuntz (Ed.), *Problem solving: Research method teaching* (pp. 225–257). New York: Wiley.

Snyder, D. K. (1979). Multidimensional assessment of marital satisfaction. *Journal of Marriage and the Family, 41,* 813–823.

Snyder, D. K., & Wills, R. M. (1991). Facilitating change in marital therapy and research. *Journal of Family Psychology, 4,* 426–435.

Spanier, G. B. (1976). Measuring dyadic adjustment: New scales for assessing the quality of marriage and similar dyads. *Journal of Marriage and the Family, 38,* 15–28.

Strauss, M. A. (1979). Measuring intrafamily conflict and violence: The Conflict Tactics (CT) scales. *Journal of Marriage and the Family, 41,* 75–88.

Stuart, R. B. (1980). *Helping couples change: A social learning approach to marital therapy.* New York: Guilford Press.

Weiss, R. L. (1978). The conceptualization of marriage from a behavioral perspective. In T. J. Paolino & B. S. McCrady (Eds.), *Marriage and marital therapy: Psychoanalytic, behavioral, and systems perspectives* (pp. 165–239). New York: Brunner/Mazel.

Weiss, R. L., & Birchler, G. R. (1978). Adults with marital dysfunction. In M. Hersen & A. S. Bellack (Eds.), *Behavior therapy in the psychiatric setting* (pp. 331–364). Baltimore: Williams & Wilkins.

Weiss, R. L., Birchler, G. R., & Vincent, J. P. (1974). Contractual models for negotiation training in marital dyads. *Journal of Marriage and the Family, 36,* 321–331.

Weiss, R. L., & Cerreto, M. C. (1980). The Marital Status Inventory: Development of a measure of dissolution potential. *American Journal of Family Therapy, 8,* 80–85.

Weiss, R. L., Hops, H., & Patterson, G. R. (1973). A framework for conceptualizing marital conflict, technology for altering it, some data for evaluating it. In L. A. Hamerlynck, L. C. Handy, & E. J. Mash (Eds.), *Behavior change: Methodology, concepts, and practice* (pp. 309–342). Champaign, IL: Research Press.

Wile, D. B. (1981). *Couples therapy: A nontraditional approach.* New York: Wiley.

4

Cognitive Aspects of Cognitive-Behavioral Marital Therapy

DONALD H. BAUCOM
NORMAN EPSTEIN
LYNN A. RANKIN

RECENT YEARS have witnessed a mushrooming of interest in cognitive factors of marriage and marital distress among researchers, theoreticians, and clinicians who have traditionally approached marriage from a behavioral perspective. In part, this incorporation of cognitive factors into behavioral formulations of marriage is consistent with the general trend within behavioral therapy to include cognitive factors. In addition, the success of attribution theory within social psychology as one theoretical framework for understanding interpersonal interactions (Heider, 1958) has served as a natural bridge for considering cognitive factors in marriage. Furthermore, within recent years, the overlap between marital distress and depression has become increasingly apparent (Beach, Whisman, & O'Leary, 1994). The attributional reformulation of the learned helplessness theory as a model of depression again brought attention to the important role of cognitive factors in clinical phenomena (Seligman, Abramson, & Teasdale, 1978). It was but a small step for marital researchers to investigate whether attributional factors that appeared prevalent in depression also existed in maritally distressed couples, thus helping to explain the co-occurrence of these two disorders.

As a result of these various influences, behavioral marital therapy (BMT) has increasingly incorporated cognitive factors, such that it has been renamed cognitive-behavioral marital therapy (CBMT) by many authors. As suggested by this term, behavioral factors have not been eliminated from the treatment; instead, the treatment strategies merely have been broadened to include a focus on cognitive factors. Nor is the role of emotional factors minimized in this treatment approach. In fact, in their recent volume on CBMT, Baucom and Epstein (1990) devoted approximately equal space to a consideration of cognitive, behavioral, and emotional factors in marital distress and marital therapy.

Any consideration of these three broad domains of marital functioning must also recognize that separation of these factors is somewhat artificial because cognitions, behaviors, and emotions are inextricably interwoven. However, for heuristic purposes, it is helpful to differentiate among these variables in order to highlight the various factors that need to be considered in understanding marital discord and to recognize the potentially widespread impact that any specific intervention might have on marital functioning. Thus, an intervention that focuses on altering spouses' behaviors might additionally impact the way that the couple thinks about and feels toward each other. The current chapter highlights the role of cognitive factors in marital functioning and marital therapy. Behavioral factors in marital therapy are addressed elsewhere in this volume. The reader should recognize that the disproportionate focus given to cognitive factors herein should not be interpreted as the totality of treatment in working with distressed couples. Without elaborating on other forms of intervention, brief mention is given to demonstrate how cognitive interventions interact with behavioral and emotionally focused interventions. A more complete discussion of integrating and sequencing cognitive, behavioral, and emotional interventions in CBMT is provided elsewhere (Baucom & Epstein, 1990, Chap. 11).

CATEGORIES OF COGNITIVE FACTORS IN MARRIAGE

The term "cognitions" is a rather broad term and implies little more than thought. Consequently, proclaiming that the ways that couples think about marriage is relevant in understanding marital discord is a rather obvious and unenlightening statement. In order to be of assistance to clinicians attempting to assist maritally distressed couples, a delineation of various types of cognitive factors in marriage is necessary. Baucom, Epstein, Sayers, and Sher (1989) have proposed that there are at least five different types of cognition that appear to impact marital functioning. They include (1) selective attention, (2) attributions, (3) expectancies, (4) assumptions, and (5) standards.

Selective attention refers to the fact that spouses are not attentive to all relationship-relevant events that occur, and what they attend to likely influences how they feel about the relationship. Onces spouses do attend to certain marital events, they might try to explain why at least some events have occurred, and in the case of negative events, whether someone is responsible and deserves to be blamed for the event; these cognitive processes are referred to as *attributions*. Whereas attributions focus on explaining and evaluating past events, spouses often attempt to predict what will occur in the future in their relationships; that is, they develop *expectancies* about the future. Spouses also have a number of basic beliefs about relationships, themselves, and their partners. These beliefs about the ways the relationships actually work, what males and females

are like, how a partner operates—in essence, one's beliefs about the ways that things are—are referred to as one's *assumptions* about marriage. Whereas marital assumptions involve a spouse's beliefs about the way that relationship-oriented aspects of the marriage actually operate and how things are, relationship *standards* address a spouse's beliefs about what a relationship and the marital partners should be like. Standards involve one's values for what form a relationship should take and how each partner should conduct oneself within that context.

A full discussion of the research validating the importance of these five cognitive variables in marital functioning is beyond the scope of this chapter; however, brief mention of selected findings, along with clinical implications, can provide a context for understanding the rationale for many of the interventions discussed later in the chapter. The most important implication of selective attention is that the events that spouses notice become those that are available for further cognitive processing, for influencing future behavior, and serving as the basis for emotional responses to the partner and the marriage. A number of studies confirm that husbands and wives have different perceptions of what behaviors have occurred during a brief time period (e.g., 24 hours) and that distressed couples show lower rates of agreement than do nondistressed couples (cf. Christensen & Nies, 1980; Christensen, Sullaway, & King, 1983; Jacobson & Moore, 1981). Compared to the observation of trained raters in couples' homes, distressed spouses appear to underestimate the number of pleasurable events that occur between spouses by 50% (Robinson & Price, 1980). Attempting to assist distressed couples becomes increasingly difficult when they have different memories about what events have actually occurred. In particular, if spouses underattend to the positive events that occur and do not note when the partner engages in positive behavior, then behavioral changes brought about by therapy might not be noticed and likely will have minimal impact on improving the quality of the relationship. Thus, assisting the couple in attending to relationship events in a manner that more reasonably reflects their interaction can be of utmost importance if other treatment interventions are to be of success.

One of the most important aspects of marital behavior is that it occurs within the context of an intimate, ongoing relationship in which behaviors can carry great meaning. Thus, canceling a luncheon appointment with one's partner can be interpreted by the partner in various ways that can have different impacts on the partner's behavior and emotional responses. A great deal of research has been conducted demonstrating that spouses' attributions for relationship events are related to level of marital adjustment (for a review see Bradbury & Fincham, 1990). Overall, the findings from these studies suggest that distressed couples tend to make attributions that might be labeled as "distress-maintaining," whereas nondistressed couples interpret events in ways that are "relationship-enhancing" (Holtzworth-Munroe & Jacobson, 1985). More specifically, when explaining marital events, distressed spouses tend to focus on negative aspects of the partner and/or the relationship. On the other hand, nondistressed spouses explain events that accent the positive aspects of the partner and the relationship, while minimizing negative features of the marriage. These distress-maintaining attributions from unhappy couples can lead to a wide range of negative feelings toward the partner and the relationship, as well as inhibiting the types of behavioral changes needed to improve the marriage.

Whereas numerous investigations have demonstrated the negativistic attributions of distressed couples, these investigations have not attempted to differentiate between negative and distorted attributions. This differentiation between negative and distorted cognitions is important when considering clinical interventions. That is, if one spouse is providing explanations for a partner's behavior in a manner that appears to be distorted, then interventions are likely to focus on assisting the spouse in thinking of different ways to understand the partner's behavior. However, if the attributions are negative but realistic, then attempting to alter the attributions would lead to a distortion of reality. For example, if a wife interprets her husband's late hours at work as resulting from his aversion to being around her and the children at night, and he confirms her interpretation, then the clinician would be unlikely to attempt to alter her attribution for her husband's behavior. Instead, interventions might more productively focus on clarifying what factors contribute to the husband's dislike for being with his family at night; altering the family's behaviors during the evening hours might become the treatment of choice in this instance.

Whereas attributions focus on explanations for events that have occurred, expectancies involve couples' predictions regarding future relationship behavior and functioning. Less research has been

conducted focusing on this type of relationship cognition, but the findings thus far indicate that relationship expectancies are important factors in marital functioning. Both Pretzer, Epstein, and Fleming (1985) and Vanzetti and Notarius (1991) have found that positive expectancies about the relationship are related to higher levels of marital adjustment. In addition, Vanzetti and Notarius have demonstrated that positive relationship expectancies also predict marital adjustment longitudinally. Positive expectancies also are correlated with actual behavior in laboratory interactions. Vanzetti, Notarius, and Nee-Smith (1992) have found that couples with general negative expectancies about the relationship make specific predictions when interacting with their partners, such that they anticipate few positive behaviors and many negative behaviors. Vanzetti and Notarius (1991) also found that couples with negative expectancies actually preceive more negative behaviors when interacting.

Not only are expectancies related to behavior, they appear to be correlated with other cognitive variables. Both Pretzer et al. (1985) and Vanzetti et al. (1992) concluded that couples' expectancies are related to their attributions for partner behavior. Spouses with negative expectancies appear to provide distress-maintaining attributions for their major relationship problems and for specific behaviors that their partners demonstrate in laboratory interactions. Finally, Pretzer et al. found that expectancies that the the relationship would improve were correlated with affective functioning; spouses with such expectancies demonstrated lower levels of depression. Consequently, the results to date indicate that relationship expectancies are correlated with marital behaviors, cognitions, and emotions.

Couples' assumptions about the nature of marriage, the two genders, and the individual to whom one is married also are important factors in designing treatment strategies. At present there has been only limited research investigating the role of assumptions in marital functioning, but the findings thus far demonstrate the importance of this cognitive factor. Epstein and Eidelson have developed the Relationship Belief Inventory (Eidelson & Epstein, 1982; Epstein & Eidelson, 1981) to assess selected marital assumptions. Their results indicate that the more an individual believes spouses cannot change relationships and the more they believe that disagreement is destructive, then the lower their estimates that their marital problems would improve with treatment. Thus, there appears to be a set of beliefs about the way that things are that contributes to a sense of hopelessness for improving the relationship. Such beliefs are likely to impact the extent to which spouses are willing to become involved in the therapeutic process and persist in their therapeutic efforts in the face of difficulty.

Finally, couples' standards for how the relationship *should be* can serve as a template against which they evaluate their partners' and their own behavior to determine the acceptability of each person's behavior and the relationship. That is, a spouse at times seems to be distressed because the partner is not "living up" to what the spouse views as acceptable marital behavior. Thus, a husband's behavior might not be explicitly destructive, but his wife might be distressed because it does not mirror how she believes a husband should behave toward his wife. Baucom, Epstein, Rankin, and Burnett (1990) have developed the Inventory of Specific Relationship Standards in an attempt to assess important relationship standards. Their findings indicate that for both husbands and wives, those individuals who hold strong relationship-focused standards (i.e., standards that ask a great deal from both partners in contributing to a close, caring relationship that considers the needs and wishes of both partners) are more satisfied with their marriages. The findings further point out that when the partners are not satisfied that their standards are being met in the relationship, they are more unhappy with the marriage (Baucom et al., 1990). Thus, therapist are likely to work more effectively with couples if they understand what the couples' standards for a marriage are, rather than attempting to have all couples conform to a preconceived notion of marriage. In developing a treatment plan, therapists will want to evaluate whether a couple's behavior is in need of change or whether one partner holds unreasonable or unrealistic standards that need to be targeted for intervention. Consequently, on a number or occasions, the focus of treatment is likely to become cognitive change rather than behavioral change.

ASSESSMENT OF COGNITIONS

In order to obtain a broad understanding of the couple, an assessment of the cognitive variables described previously can be of assistance to the clinician. To assess cognitive variables, the clinician must learn what the spouses are thinking, and there are a variety of strategies available for this purpose (e.g., self-report inventories, observation of interaction, verbal self-report, etc.). In this section, we examine some general strategies for assessing a couple's cognitions and discuss the intergration of information gathered by those strategies.

Whereas discrete cognitions and behaviors are often and appropriately the focus of attention during assessment of a couple, it is worthwhile to consider the ways that these specific cognitions and/or behaviors may contribute to an integrated psychological pattern of relationship functioning. For many couples, one or two major relationship themes underlie and provide the context for understanding the dysfunctional cognitions and behaviors in their relationship. For example, a couple may struggle with each other for control in the relationship, and this struggle may be expressed in a number of domains of the relationship. They may argue over who controls the finances, whose friends to spend more time with, and how clean to keep the house. These areas may initially seem separate but might actually all be driven by an underlying power struggle. A recognition of this theme is quite helpful for the clinician as he/she makes intervention choices for this particular couple.

It is important to recognize that a consideration of the major themes characterizing a relationship expands the CBMT model beyond one that primarily focuses on skills deficits. Skills training continues to be an important part of CBMT, but if a clinician focuses only on potential skill deficits, he/she may miss the major psychological issues that are giving the couple difficulty. That is, a couple may have become quite skilled at problem solving and emotional expressiveness and use both skills appropriately, yet still have not addressed a major overriding theme in their relationship.

One of us recently worked with a couple that exemplifies the importance of seeking major relationship themes. Both members of the couple were quite bright and invested in making the relationship work. They quickly became competent at emotional expressiveness and problem solving, bringing up one issue after another as a problem to solve. Each spouse stated his/her belief that the problems being addressed were minor, yet they painfully addressed each problem, and continued to produce issue after issue. It became clear to the clinician that this couple was in the middle of a struggle for control that was being expressed in countless problem-solving sessions. As an example, the couple spent three sessions developing an elaborate schedule for cleaning up the dog's messes, each fearing that he/she would be taken advantage of without such a contract. When the theme of a power struggle was introduced to the couple, they quickly agreed that a constant theme running through their problem solving and emotional expressiveness was individual concerns of being taken advantage of and consequent jockeying for control in the relationship. The couple continued to explore the power struggle with the clinician in various ways, including expression of their feelings about why they worried so about being taken advantage of, and how the fears had developed. Eventually they began to trust each other and the relationship, and looked back on their previous elaborate schedules and schemes as quite humorous. Therefore, for some couples, problems in the relationship may not be addressed completely with skills training, and the introduction of major relationship themes is helpful to both the clinician and the couple.

While looking for major relationship themes and specific area of dysfunction, a clinician can make use of a number of specific strategies for assessing cognitions within a marriage. The initial assessment phase typically comprises several components, utilizing different strategies. The first information available about the couple is often a set of questionnaires that the spouses have completed prior to their first session with the clinician. During the interview phase, a marital history is obtained, current concerns are examined, and the clinician spends some time observing the couple's conununication with each other. These various components are considered in some detail and in the order in which they are typically used. Selecting which strategies to use, and the way that themes can be extrapolated from the information given are also important parts of the assessment process, and are explored as well.

Self- and Spouse Reports

While the interview can yield a great deal of information about the cognitive variables being examined, paper-and-pencil inventories can significantly add to and help direct the interview. It may be especially helpful to have couples complete and return the inventories prior to the first interview. If this occurs, the clinician will have the opportunity to examine the inventories and direct the interview based on specific areas of concern. In addition, the clinician may be able to begin formulating possible themes for the couple from the completed inventories. For assessing cognitive variables in marital discord, a

number of useful self-report and spouse-report inventories exist. Although a wide selection of cognitive inventories are examined, it is impossible to make use of all of them, necessitating the need for a selection strategy. A typical scenario is to send several inventories to the couple for completion prior to beginning the assessment phase (an example of a set of such inventories are given in the following paragraphs), and then, as the assessment phase continues, to use additional inventories as needed in order to explore the cognitions of a particular couple. Thus, the inventories described below are each useful for exploring a particular area of difficulty for couples.

The Spouse Observation Checklist (Weiss, Hops, & Patterson, 1973) is useful for examining whether spouses have similar perceptions about the events that take place in their relationship. Spouses mark the behaviors that occurred in the past 24 hours on a checklist containing 408 behaviors. The items focus primarily on the spouse, with additional items focused on the relationship. By comparing a husband and wife's responses, the clinician can establish the extent of agreement between the couple's perceptions about the events that occurred.

An additional method of comparing spouses' perceptions is also a behaviorally oriented measure, the Areas of Change Questionnaire (Weiss et al., 1973). In the first part of this inventory, each spouse answers questions about the behavior changes that he/she would like from the partner (e. g. "I would like very much for my partner to show more affection"). In the second part, each spouse answers questions about their perceptions of the behavior changes their spouse would like from them (e.g., "My partner would very like for me to show more affection"). By comparing spouses' inventories, the clinician can develop an understanding of the accuracy of spouses' perceptions. Therefore, if a clinician began to suspect during the initial interview that the couple might have different perceptions of their relationship, he/she might administer the Spouse Observation Checklist or Areas of Change Questionnaire to test this hypothesis.

A number of measures for assessing the attributions that couples make in their relationship have been developed and include the Dyadic Attributional Inventory (Baucom, Sayers, & Duhe, 1987), the Relationship Attribution Questionnaire (Baucom, Epstein, Daiuto, & Carels, 1991), and the Attribution Questionnaire (Fincham & O'Leary, 1983). The measures differ on whether they focus on hypothetical events or events that might have occurred in the couple's relationship. A respondent may be asked to imagine a hypothetical event that might have occurred in his/her relationship and then to provide an explanation for why that event might have occurred. Conversely, the respondent might be asked to check off on a list those events that had actually occurred in his/her relationship, and provide attributions for those events. Both methods for assessing attributions offer assets and drawbacks. Whereas the use of an actual event is likely to be more relevant to the couple, it may not be representative of the spouse's style of attributions. That is, when asked to pick a recent event to describe, the spouse may pick an event that is atypical (e.g., a husband may attribute the prior evening's argument to losing his job that day, an event that never happened before, and is unlikely to happen often in the future), and therefore may provide atypical attributions. On the other hand, a concern with using hypothetical events is the generalizability from the attributions made for that event to attributions for actual events. However, using hypothetical situations can help to determine if an attributional style exists. Because the respondent is not responding to particular events, he/she may provide the typical response for why events occur in the relationship. For example, if a wife is asked to explain why her husband came home late, she may answer based on what she thinks is the husband's most likely reason for this behavior. As mentioned earlier, prior to beginning the assessment phase, an attributional inventory may be used which provides the clinician with a preliminary understanding of the attributions that the spouses make about their relationship, and therefore may pinpoint areas of concern before the interviews begin. If an attributional inventory is not used prior to beginning the interviews, it may become obvious during the interviews or treatment phase that one or both spouses are making attributions that are problematic for the relationship. At this point, it may be of use to administer an attributional inventory to further clarify attributional tendencies.

A cognitive measure of expectancies is found on a subscale of the Marital Agendas Protocol (Notarius & Vanzetti, 1983). On this inventory, spouses give predictions about specific and generalized expectancies for their marital interaction (e.g., how much improvement they expect they will make in their relationship; the extent to which the respondent believes that the couple has the ability to make changes). This informa-tion is useful to the clinician, not just as an example of the types of experiences spouses may have, but also as an indirect way of assessing investment in the therapeutic process. Similar to measures already discussed, the Marital Agendas Protocol would be appropriately used when the clinician had reason to question the problematic nature of these specific cognitions. For example, if the spouses made comments about expecting that therapy would be of no use, predicted that their relationship would not improve, and/or that the spouse would not change, it would be of use to pursue the expectancies of the couple in more detail.

No comprehensive inventory has been developed to assess a couple's assumptions about their relationship. However, several inventories include subscales that measure various specific assumptions. For example, the Relationship Belief Inventory (Eidelson & Epstein, 1982), includes subscales that focus on spouses' beliefs about how much partners change, how much spouses think that the two sexes understand each other, and finally, on whether spouses believe that disagreement is destructive. Couples are often unaware of the assumptions that they hold, and when the clinician judges that their assumptions might be causing problems in the relationship, it is useful to measure this more fully. The use of an inventory such as the Relationship Belief Inventory provides a method for pinpointing problematic areas for further discussion with the couple. In many cases, the spouses have given little thought to their own or each other's assumptions, making such a discussion quite useful.

To assess the standards that spouses hold for their relationship, two new measures, the Inventory of General Relationship Standards and the Inventory of Specific Relationship Standards (Baucom et al., 1990) may prove to be useful. The inventories assess the standards that couples hold for several relationship dimensions, including boundaries, power/control, and investment. The boundary dimension measures the extent to which the respondent believes the partners should share and attempt to "be one" in various aspects of their relationship; the power/control dimension measures the extent to which spouses believe that they should convince each other of their own perspectives, as well as the extent to which they believe that decision making should be shared equally by the spouses; the investment dimension measures the extent to which the spouses believe that one partner should give to the relationship by doing tasks for the marriage, and through demonstrating acts of caring and love to the other person.

Standards can be examined at two levels, a general or global level, and a more specific, content-related level. The Inventory of General Relationship Standards assesses global standards that couples hold in the thrree dimensions, whereas the Inventory of Specific Relationship Standards assesses more specific standards in the three dimensions. For example, a respondent may generally see the need for closeness in the relationship (i.e., endorsing general standards on the Inventory of General Relationship Standards for closeness, or few boundaries), yet in some specific areas (e.g., finances on the Inventory of Specific Relationship Standards) may endorse standards for being more separate. Following each item on the standards inventories, a respondent answers two additional questions that help to clarify the impact of holding that standard. The first question asks about the degree to which this standard is met in the relationship, since it may be that a spouse holds a standard that the partner meets, resulting in few problems in this area. Conversely, the spouse may not be able to meet that standard; thus, an additional question addresses the extent to which it is upsetting when a standard is not met. Similar to assumptions, the standards that spouses hold may not be immediately apparent to the clinician. Therefore, as the assessment and treatment phases continue, it may become clear that a particular couple holds some problematic standards. In this case, the clinician could make use of the Inventory of General Relationship Standards or the Inventory of Specific Relationship Standards to help clarify the nature of the problematic standards. For some couples, each spouse may hold reasonable standards, but those standards are incompatible with each other. On the other hand, one or both spouses may hold extreme standards that are impossible for anyone to meet. In this event, cognitive restructuring would be indicated.

In addition to assessing the standards that couples hold for their relationship, the Inventory of General Relationship Standards and Inventory of Specific Relationship Standards, as well as other inventories, provide information that allows the clinician to formulate hypotheses about the major themes that may characterize the couple's relationship. For example. a couple may consistently endorse incompatible standards in the boundary dimension across a number of content areas. The husband may endorse standards for more boundaries (or separation) in leisure activities, friends shared, finances shared, and

amount of time one should spend with in-laws, while the wife endorses standards for few boundaries (or more closeness) between them on the same issues. In other words, she believes they should have similar ideas and share most of their activities, while he believes they should have more aspects of their lives separate from each other. Because these incompatible standards cut across a number of content areas, but all are related to the amount of boundaries the spouses believe should be between them, the clinician could begin to formulate a theory that boundary issues are a problematic theme for this couple.

Each inventory described previously has the potential to be useful, yet it would be unreasonable to try to use them all with each couple. Therefore, a clinician must decide which inventory will be most useful for a particular couple, The clinician may decide to send the couple several inventories prior to their first session, and an example of such a set might include a measure of marital adjustment (e.g., the Dyadic Adjustment Scale; Spanier, 1976) and a behaviorally oriented measure of areas of desired change (e.g., Areas of Change Questionnaire; Weiss et al., 1973). The additional cognitive inventories described could then be used at the discretion of the clinician as specific cognitive issues arise during the interview and treatment sessions.

Interview

Initial interviews with the couple include a marital history and a discussion of current concerns and relationship strengths, including a general attempt at understanding the cognitions of the couple. Each of these areas are examined for their role in exploring the cognition of the couple.

In covering the history of a couple's marriage, several points are worth attention, and are often covered in chronological order. For example, the clinician may begin by asking about the couple's initial encounter (e.g., how they met, what was attractive about each other, etc.), and then about the development of the relationship, the decision to marry, development after marriage, and finally the current concerns (e.g., when they each perceived difficulties in the relationship, etc.). Each of these areas has the potential to yield information about the cognitions of the couple that may direct the clinician to further question the spouses in that area. For example, in examining the major events that have occurred as the relationship progressed, the clinician solicits each partner's cognition about those events (e.g., why the event happened, spouses' relative roles in the event, consequences of the event, standards for handling relationship problems, etc.).

Therefore, during the course of the marital history interview(s), a number of cognitive variables can be appraised. For example, it is not possible for spouses to attend to all of the events that occur between partners. Therefore, selective attention to negative behaviors on the part of one's spouse may be a contributing factor to the couple's presenting problems. During the assessment interview, it may become clear that the spouses have different memories for various relationship events. For example, one spouse may remember a number of major problematic events in their relationship history, with significant negative affect attached to those events, while the partner may remember the development of the relationship as having been uneventful. In addition, spouses may offer different memories of more current problems, and may see the roles that each partner plays in the problem in a very different light. It is worthwhile for the clinician to address these different perspectives if they are expressed, questioning each spouse about his/her memory and understanding of the events.

Another cognitive variable that is potentially assessed in the interview is the attributions that spouses make for relationship events. For example, as the couple descibes the development of their relationship, covering difficult transitions, major events, and the development of their current problems, negative attributions are likely to be offered. Likewise, when discussing current concerns, spouses may spontaneously offer the reason they believe a problem exists (e.g., "He gets home late every night because he just does not care about me"). If the couple does not offer a reason for major events or development of current problems, the clinician should actively question the couple more fully about these areas to gain a sense of each spouse's attributions. In addition, the interview is an appropriate time for the clinician to question the spouses about their answers on any inventories that they might have completed. To explore more fully the attributions that spouses make, the clinician could point out areas of concern on the inventory and ask each spouse why he/she thinks they have a problem in that area. For example, the clinician might ask each spouse to explain why he/she thinks that they disagree so often about their demonstrations of affection (a question found on the Dyadic Adjustment Scale; Spanier, 1976).

Expectancies are another cognition that can be assessed from the interview. For example, it may become clear during the marital history that the wife has an expectancy that the relationship will not work out because she never had one work out before. Therefore, her behavior (e.g., constantly seeking the attention of others) and thoughts (e.g., Why should I do anything nice for him?) might be seen as a way of protecting herself when the relationship fails. Understanding this wife's expectancies might help to put her actions in a new context for both herself and her husband (e.g., he may have thought she did not care about him, when, in fact, she was afraid of losing him). During the interview process, the clinician should be aware of the potentially destructive role that irrational or dysfunctional expectancies can play and he/she should question spouses further when it becomes apparent that one or both have problematic expectancies.

Occasionally linked to expectancies are the assumptions that spouses may make (i.e., how the person assumes that things are in the world, their relationship, etc.); it is possible to gain an understanding of these during the interview. In the example of the wife who does not expect her relationship to work out, it may be that she developed this expectancy from her assumption that "relationships never work out." As the interview progresses, the clinician should listen for hints that a spouse may hold irrational assumptions or assumptions that may be detrimental to the relationship, and pursue these further should they arise.

A final cognitive variable that can be assessed in the interview is the standards that a couple holds for their relationship. As the interview progresses through the marital history and discussion of current concerns, the standards that couples hold for their relationship might become clear. In addition, when spouses are asked to discuss issues focal to their relationship, standards may become more obvious. The clinician should be particularly vigilant for incompatible standards between the spouses, as well as extreme standards held by one or both spouses. In the case of incompatible standards, it might be worthwhile to help the spouses clarify their individual standards and then discuss how they might handle the situation of holding incompatible standards. For example, in some areas spouses might hold different standards, but both might judge that area as not very important. In other cases, only one spouse might feel the area is important and the other may be willing to go along with the partner in that area (e.g., one spouse might feel very strongly that their finances should be kept separate, while the partner feels that they should be combined, but does not feel as strongly about it). When one spouse holds extreme standards (i.e., standards that no one could achieve), this is likely to cause problems in the relationship. The spouse holding the standard might feel disappointed, whereas the partner feels bad or resentful at being unable to meet the standard.

Current Concerns

Once an understanding of the development of the relationship is obtained, it is important to address the current concerns of the couple that contributed to their decision to undergo marital therapy. Whereas a number of these concerns may already have been mentioned during the marital history phase, it is important for the clinician to establish that all of the presenting concerns have been addressed and understood. The clinician may structure this phase by using the inventories completed by the couple prior to beginning the assessment. He/she can discuss with the couple the major points revealed by the inventories and question them further about these areas. The clinician should then ask the couple if there are additional issues that were not covered on the inventories, hopefully arriving at a full picture of the couple's concerns. These issues are likely to focus on problematic behavioral excesses and deficits that concerns either partner. However, as these behavioral concerns are discussed, the clinician can obtain information about the couple's cognitions (e.g., exploring the individual's attributions for why the problem exists along with that person's standards for how he/she believes the relationship should function in that area).

Observation of Communication

In addition to exploring a couple's marital history and current concerns, spouses are often asked to interact with each other in a variety of conversations so that the clinician can assess their communication directly, both the ability to problem solve and share feelings and thoughts with each other effectively. In addition to the rest of the interview and inventories that the spouses may have completed, observation of communication can yield valuable information about the spouses' cognitions.

Spouses' selective attention may become obvious during the couple's communication, because the clinician can see directly whether

spouses actually listen to each other, or whether, as is often the case with distressed couples, one or both spouses are selectively hearing negative comments. In planning the intervention for the couple, it is useful for the clinician to ascertain whether one or both spouses fail to understand or distort what the other has said.

Similarly, the attributions that spouses make for various relationship events are likely to surface during the observed communication. During their discussion of problems, many distressed couples focus on assigning blame for a problem rather than on seeking a solution for the issue. Therefore, in addition to clarifying their level of ability to problem solve, the couple may also be giving the clinician useful information about their attributions.

The clinician might also find examples of the expectancies that spouses hold during the observation of conununication. While problem solving, couples often spontaneously give a prediction about the likelihood of a solution working. Often this prediction is a negative one and exhibits the hopelessness that brought the spouses to therapy (e.g., "That will never work; I don't think we'll ever be able to agree on anything"). Similarly, while addressing areas of concern, some spouses include, either explicitly or more indirectly, their standards for how partners should relate in the problem area being discussed. Thus, a couple's communication can not only elucidate communication strengths and weakness but also contribute to the clinician's growing understanding of the couple's cognitions surrounding the marriage.

Selecting Assessment Strategies

A number of assessment strategies have been discussed, and it is impossible to employ all of them, making it necessary for the clinician to choose carefully among them. Most clinicians rely primarily upon the initial interviews (including the marital history, discussion of current concerns, and observation of communication), and as detailed previously, a great deal of information about a couple's cognitions can be discovered during this phase of the assessment. Often, the initial interviews flag potential problematic cognitions that the clinician can address in future sessions.

Although it might prove helpful to have couples complete cognitive inventories prior to the first session, time constraints make it unlikely that a comprehensive set of cognitive measures can be employed with each couple. Instead, once the assessment interviews have begun, the clinician may choose to include additional inventories based on the problems of a particular couple. For example, if the clinician senses that the spouses seem to selectively attend to negatives in each other, the Spouse Observation Checklist could help the clinician gather more information about the couple in this area. In this particular scenario, using an attributional questionnaire might provide additional information. For example, positive behaviors that the spouses do perceive may be minimized through providing negative attributions for the partner's behaviors (e.g.. "He just did that because he knew we would talk about it in therapy").

Whereas the initial assessment is designed to be comprehensive, it is unlikely to uncover all problematic cognitions. Some cognitions (e.g., assumptions, standards) may be particularly difficult to elicit early in the therapy process, merely because these cognitions are not always immediately available to the spouses themselves. Therefore, it is vital that the clinician continue to assess cognitions throughout the therapeutic process.

Integrating the Information

Perhaps the most important aspect of the assessment process is integrating all of the information supplied by the couple. For a number of couples, this integration can take the form of major relationship themes. That is, most of the information about the couple can be seen to fit within one or two major themes for that couple. Disparate content areas of problems (e.g., sexual relations, finances) as well as distorted cognitions (e.g., selective attention, extreme standards) may actually be rooted in the same theme. For example, a couple with incompatible standards for the amount of boundaries that they think should be between them (as assessed by the Inventory of Specific Relationship Standards) could easily present for marital therapy with all of the above difficulties. Whereas each problematic area could be addressed separately, it is quite useful for the clinician as well as the couple to understand the larger context within which those individual difficulties fit.

Using major relationship themes is a convenient way to structure the feedback session that most clinicians provide at the end of the assessment phase. During this session, the clinician describes for the couple his/her understanding of their relationship and current difficulties. Placing these difficulties within one or two major themes is quite useful in helping the couple understand what may be a large amount of information. The clinician could begin with a description of the major theme (e.g., "You two seem to be locked in a struggle for control"), providing evidence gathered in the assessment of the couple (e.g., "When I asked you to solve a problem, neither of you would let the other suggest a problem"; You report that when the two of you argue, neither will be the first to apologize"; "On the Inventory of Specific Relationship Standards you both endorsed some problematic control standards"). The clinician can then question the couple about whether they agree with the assessment, and whether there are any other issues that were not addressed.

An important part of integrating the assessment information gathered is selecting the intervention strategies that will be most helpful for a particular couple, as well as the order in which those strategies would best be implemented. Once a clinician has developed an understanding of the couple's current difficulties and personal styles, he/she can make choices about the intervention strategies that would be most useful for that particular couple. As an example, for a couple who experienced a number of significant negative events in their relationship that were never discussed between the spouses, the clinician might decide to begin with teaching the couple to share their thoughts and feelings with each other. With this particular couple, the clinician may have discovered that neither spouse seemed to understand why the partner behaved in the way that he/she did, and therefore early in therapy might want to discuss attributions for various events in the relationship (e.g., "he spent 4 years ignoring me in graduate school because he felt that we were no longer intellectual equals").

Whereas it is valuable to recognize problematic cognitions, it is often not necessary to plan a phase of treatment focused solely on cognitions. Rather, the clinicians can maintain an awareness of the cognitions that the assessment phase pinpointed as potentially problematic, and address those cognitions within the context of skills training. For example, it may become evident during emotional expressiveness that a spouse makes very skewed attributions about the partner. The clinician can stop the emotional expressiveness for a few minutes and switch to some cognitive restructuring, returning to emotional expressiveness after addressing the problematic attribution. The role of cognitive restructuring within the broader context of marital therapy is discussed in this chapter and elsewhere (Baucom & Epstein, 1990, Chap. 11).

Understanding a couple's difficulties within the context of a theme is useful when planning skills training. For example, if a couple appears to be engaged in a power struggle, teaching problem solving to them may take a particular direction. The couple would likely need additional instruction on the use of compromise solutions, or on willingness to consider each other's proposed solutions. Likewise, the same couple might have a more difficult time learning emotional expressiveness (e.g., needing additional instruction to carefully listen instead of preparing a defense). Therefore, although the same skills may be taught to a variety of couples, the exact manner of instruction for particular couples may change, depending on the issues that characterize their relationship.

In addition to selecting the interventions to be used and their order, it is important for the clinician to recognize the appropriate situations for using cognitive restructuring: that is, not all negative cognitions are distorted and therefore should not be restructured. At times, spouses may make negative comments about the relationship that are based in reality (e.g., the husband states that he is not sure he wants to remain in the marriage). In this case, the clinician might attempt to address the basis for the husband's attitude toward the marriage, including behavioral changes that are needed, rather than attempting to directly alter the husband's negative statement that he is not committed to the relationship. On the other hand, if the husband's cognition was distorted (e.g., he thought his wife was going to leave when she had no intention of doing so), cognitive restructuring would be appropriate. Therefore, the clinician must evaluate whether cognitions are distorted before intervening to change them.

Assessment of the cognitions of the couple, although a primary focus of the formal assessment phase, should not be considered as completed during this phase: that is, the clinician will continue to gather information about each spouse's cognitions in the ongoing interactions between the couple. For example, if during emotional expressiveness training a wife makes evident for the first time that she has problematic assumptions about men (e.g., "men are never faithful"), it might be appropriate for the clinician to address that assumption at that time, and more fully assess other cognitions she may have in this area.

It can be seen that the assessment phase of marital therapy is a rich source of information

about a couple's cognitions. Information about the ways that spouses think is available from a number of sources: verbal report, pencil-and-paper inventories, observation of interaction, and more. It is important for a clinician to make use of all of these, but also to recognize that he/she cannot rely on the spouses to spontaneously offer examples of problematic cognitions. The clinician must also seek information about such cognitions, not only by following clues provided by the spouses, but also by being aware of potentially problematic areas and directing questions about these areas (e.g., during the marital history, he/she asks about each spouse's understanding of why they decided to get married, what the perception of the other person's decision was based on, etc.). In addition, it is important to note that whereas this chapter has covered cognitions in detail, the assessment phase of marital therapy consists of assessing behavior and emotions with equal emphasis. The three domains are interrelated, and this chapter, although emphasizing cognitions, does not intend to suggest that behavior and emotions are any less important to understand.

THE STRUCTURE OF THERAPY SESSIONS

To a great extent, BMT has been described and implemented in research contexts in a modular format: that is, within the context of a skills training approach to marital therapy, behavioral marital therapists often have decided to teach couples a set of skills that involve a specified series of steps. These steps are presented systematically in a didactic format to the couple; the couple is asked to practice the skills during the session, with the therapist acting as a coach–educator. Finally, the couple is assigned homework to build on this set of skills. Thus, the therapy might devote a number of consecutive sessions to teaching the problem-solving process to a couple. A major issue when expanding the behavioral model to include a focus on cognitions is whether to proceed in a similar manner, attempting to address cognitive issues from a skills-oriented perspective, and whether to organize the therapy in a modular manner with cognitive interventions serving as a module or series of modules.

As will be discussed later in the chapter, treatment outcome research involving cognitive intervention is still in the early stages of evaluation, and most of these questions are yet to be addressed empirically. Consequently, we must rely upon the limited research that exists, as well as clinical observations to date when considering these issues. Our experience has been that in attempting to intervene on couples' cognitions, therapists have some similar goals to what they attempt in intervening on couples' behaviors. Most important, in both instances the therapist wants to assist the couple in dealing with current concerns as well as to equip the couple in dealing with other issues in the future. In this sense, the therapist hopes to teach the couple skills (either behavioral or cognitive) so that they can assist themselves in the future.

However, this common focus on teaching skills to the couple does not necessarily imply that cognitive changes are most effectively obtained through a modular strategy in which the couple devotes a number of weeks to cognitive restructuring, either preceded or followed by behavioral intervention. In fact, one of us (DHB) conducted two marital therapy outcome studies in which cognitive restructuring and behavioral interventions were presented in a modular fashion as a set of skills to be learned over several weeks (Baucom & Lester, 1986; Baucom, Sayers, & Sher, 1990). The results of those investigations demonstrated that the interventions were successful in producing cognitive changes along with increases in marital adjustment; however, comments from some couples and therapists suggested that this modular approach was less than optimal. For example, once a couple had a better understanding of an issue cognitively, the spouses often were ready to make behavioral changes in that area. Asking them to wait several weeks to address the issue from a behavioral perspective appeared to disrupt the continuity for the couple. As a result, our recommendation is that CBMT be viewed more from an integrative perspective in which cognitive, behavioral, and emotional intervention are interwoven as needed to address the couples concerns when the issues arise.

Although some distressed couples enter therapy complaining that their partners think about the relationship and each other in distorted ways, typically couples' major concerns are that they do not like the way that the other is behaving, along with related emotional consequences (e.g., anger, depression, emotional disengagement). Consequently, in an attempt to be responsive to the couples' concerns and address the issues most pertinent to them, in the majority of cases intervention begins with an emphasis on behavior change, with the anticipation that emotional changes will follow from the behavioral changes.

At other times the intervention begins by focusing directly on attempting to alter dysfunctional emotions (see Baucom & Epstein, 1990, for a discussion of the latter instance). A shift to cognitive intervention occurs when the therapist perceives that there are important cognitive factors that are contributing to the emotional upset or interfering with optimal behavior change.

How to make these shifts to a cognitive focus becomes a matter of importance for the therapist. For example, a frequent problem of distressed couples is that they often become distracted when interacting with each other, demonstrating difficulty in maintaining focus on the given issue under consideration. Consequently, frequent shifts between a focus on cognitive, behavior, and emotional issues during a single session can prove disruptive, confusing, and maintains the couple's style of lack of focus. Therefore, unless necessary, the therapist should attempt to shift to cognitive interventions at times that will minimize disrupting other interventions that are the focus of the session. This can be done in a number of ways. For example, at the beginning of the session, the therapist often is discussing the couple's homework assignment with them. If the assignment had a cognitive focus, then a discussion of cognitive factors follows naturally. On other occasions, the homework might have had a focus on altering behavior. In these instances, the couple might report that the behavior changes did not occur, or they did occur but did not have the anticipated positive impact. In attempting to understand these experiences, the therapist might explore and determine that cognitive factors played a major role in the unsuccessful behavioral homework. For example, in one instance the homework involved a husband agreeing to talk more with his wife after dinner. The wife reported that even though he did so, the conversations were not gratifying. In discussing the reasons for her reaction, the therapist uncovered the fact that she concluded that her husband did not really want to talk with her; he only did so because he did not want to look bad in front of the therapist. This initiated a discussion of her attributions for her husband's recent behavior changes that were more relationship focused. Thus, discussions of homework or experiences during the couple's week, reviewed at the beginning of the session, provide an opportunity to address cognitive factors that do not require a shift from other interventions in the midst of the session.

In a somewhat different vein, the therapist might initiate the discussion of a cognitive theme at the beginning of the session that will be important for the current session's success. For example, the therapist's plans might call for the couple to engage in problem solving for the current session. The therapist has uncovered a theme for the couple that both spouses believe that they should not disagree with each other or say anything that would make the partner feel bad. Consequently, the couple's problem-solving sessions take the form of one person offering a possible solution to a problem and the partner quickly agreeing to the solution, without any real discussion of each person's thoughts and feelings about the solution. Thus, the therapist might have them discuss at the beginning of the session whether it is acceptable to disagree on an issue in an attempt to set the stage for more effective problem solving.

There are other opportunities for the therapist to intervene on cognitive issues without creating significant shifts in the flow of the session. The CBMT therapist typically leaves time near the end of the session to discuss with couples their experience of the session. Not infrequently, one or both of the spouses react to the session in a manner that the therapist would not have predicted. A discussion of the spouse's reaction often illuminates important cognitive factors that have contributed to the experience of the session. This awareness might usher in a discussion of the cognitive issue to the extent that time permits at the end of the session, or the therapist might decide to begin the next session with a discussion of the cognitive issue.

The previous discussion provides examples of ways that the therapist can focus on cognitive factors at the beginning and end of sessions without disrupting other interventions. However, there clearly are occasions in the midst of a session when a shift to a cognitive focus is appropriate. Both behavioral and emotional cues can suggest that important cognitive factors need to be addressed. For example, a major behavioral indicator that cognitive factors might be interfering with behavior change is when the therapist becomes convinced that the couple has the skills needed and the environment has been altered in ways to facilitate behavior change, yet the behavior change is not occurring. This phenomenon can be seen both during and outside of the session. For example, a couple might have been learning conununication and problem-solving skills for several weeks and demonstrate a high level of skill attainment, yet during a given session, the therapist comments to the wife several times that she continues to reject

her husband's suggestions but refuses to clarify what she would like. The therapist believes that the wife understands his/her statements and is capable of offering her own suggestions, but for some reason is not doing so. On such an occasion, the therapist might suspend the problem solving to clarify the basis for the wife's behavior. Such a discussion might point out that the wife believes that her husband should know what she wants and that if she has to verbalize her wishes, then her husband's agreement to behave that way has no meaning (i.e., mind reading is expected). Such a belief must be addressed before effective problem solving can proceed.

The preceding examples demonstrate that attention to cognitive factors can become critical in increasing the likelihood of success of other treatment interventions. However, cognitive interventions should not be relegated to the role of auxiliary interventions to be employed solely when other interventions are not successful. On many occasions, the primary issues that a couple needs to address are cognitive issues. For example, one distressed couple was struggling with their standards for what a marital relationship should be and what was realistic to expect from each other. They got along well with each other and experienced few aversive interactions. In addition, they engaged in a number of pleasurable joint activities with each other that they both enjoyed. However the wife had a sense of a personal mission or focus in life, and for her a marital relationship should involve a clear sense of a couple's joint mission beyond getting along well and meeting external criteria of success. Along with this perspective, she believed that partners should be soul mates, persons who are on the same "wavelength" and who view the world in similar ways. Her husband, who was very committed to the relationship and cared a great deal about his wife, found these "philosophical" views of life hard to understand. They were somewhat unrelated to his belief that what was critical was for two people to love each other, be respectful to each other, provide a loving home environment for their family, and enjoy doing things together. Whereas there were some behavioral concerns that flowed from these different standards for relationships, a primary focus on helping the couple come to grips with their different relationship standards was the critical element in assisting this couple. Thus, at times cognitive interventions are a primary focus of marital therapy with certain couples, and on other occasions cognitive interventions help to buttress behavioral and affective interventions.

THE ROLE OF THE THERAPIST

A wide variety of cognitive interventions are available to the CBMT therapist, and some of the specific interventions are discussed here. In order to employ these interventions most effectively, a clearer understanding of the therapist's role, or how the therapist operates during the session, is in order. In part, the therapist's role is dictated by the structure of the sessions as described previously. The therapist's role can be viewed as active and directive, helping to provide structure to the session. These descriptors are consistent with a behavioral approach to marital therapy that employs a major skills-training focus. However, there is at least one difference that exists when the therapist is focusing on cognitive restructuring versus teaching the couple behavioral skills.

This difference involves the therapist's role in attending to the process versus the content of the couple's relationship and interaction patterns. Whereas most marital therapists are likely to attend to both process and content to some extent, different therapies differentially focus on one versus the other. For example, when couples are learning the behavioral skill of problem solving, the therapist's primary focus is on process, or the way that couples communicate and interact with each other. Do they make eye contact; do they stay solution oriented; do they avoid blaming each other for past occurrences of the problem; do they accept responsibility for their roles in the problem; do they offer specific solutions that take both spouses' needs into account? Thus, problem solving is a series of steps involving a process, and the therapist's primary role is to assist couples in learning this process. Often, the behavioral marital therapist refrains from focusing on the content of the problem and does not offer solutions to the problem under consideration; addressing the content of what solution will work best for the couple is seen as the couple's task. This focus on process is exemplified in behavioral research on marriage, with its major emphases on communication patterns and sequences, with little attention to what the couple is actually discussing in terms of content. However, this emphasis on process during behavioral skills is merely a relative emphasis. During the assessment process and throughout treatment, the therapist remains attentive to certain relationship themes that are central to understanding and assisting the couple. For example, the therapist might conclude that a significant factor in the couple's distress is the husband's belief that he must ignore his own needs and devote almost all of his energy to pleasing his wife. The therapist will likely point out this theme to the couple and note when it is impacting behavioral skills training, such as solutions derived during problem solving or other behavioral activities (e.g., engaging in joint pleasurable activities for the couple).

When considering cognitive factors in marriage, the therapist's role often involves a relative shift to a greater focus on content. This shift results from the nature of the phenomenon under consideration: that is, negativistic, extreme, and distorted cognitions are evaluated by their content and the extent to which they are incongruent with other information. Thus, when a wife presents the standard that her husband should be able to read her mind, the therapist likely will need to focus on this specific content. Because the wife is the individual who holds this standard, the therapist is likely to focus on the wife when addressing this issue. Consequently, in the midst of the couple's session, a discussion between the therapist and one spouse is likely to ensue. Even though the therapist might be addressing one partner's cognitions to a great extent, the relationship focus is maintained in various ways. First, the content of the cognition ("My partner should be able to read my mind") deals with the relationship. Second, the therapist likely will inquire as to how this belief impacts the relationship, both in positive and negative ways. Both partners are likely to participate in this discussion. Third, the therapist is likely to address the other partner's beliefs in this domain and how the combination of these two beliefs influences their relationship. Fourth, the therapist might ask the couple to participate in a homework assignment in which the partners agree to interact with each other in a new way, based on a modified version of the standard agreed on during the therapy session. Consequently, the therapist's role is to help isolate dysfunctional cognitions held by one or both spouses and then to relate these cognitions to relationship functioning, thus moving flexibly between a focus on the individual and the couple.

This focus on the content of the standard does not mean that the therapist ignores process aspects of cognitive restructuring. Process issues related to the previous example might be addressed in two different ways. First, the therapist challenges the couple to become aware of times when the wife appears to be employing the standard for mind reading in everyday life and to attempt to change her cognitions and resulting behaviors. Thus, the couple is asked to become sensitive to specific ways in which the cognition operates in their lives and how this is related to behavior and emotions; that is, the process by which this particular cognition impacts relationship functioning is evaluated. Second, the couple is given a broader framework for understanding marital discord that includes the role of cognitive factors in relationship functioning. Although the model need not be taught in a complex manner, the couple is introduced to the notion of standards along with other cognitions. The therapist in this case would explain how people have standards or beliefs for what relationships should be like and how each partner's behavior is assessed relative to those standards. The couple is taught how emotional and behavioral responses can follow from this cognitive processing. Within this context, the specific standard (mind reading is expected) is introduced. In addition and at a much broader level, the therapist is beginning an educational process in which couples are being taught to become more aware of their cognitions, how to evaluate them, and when needed, how to challenge these thoughts. The specific intervention strategies directed toward these ends are discussed next.

Although the therapist makes an ongoing attempt to educate couples to the cognitive process and to have them take over the role of uncovering dysfunctional cognitions as therapy progresses, this continues to be a difficult process for many couples. Whereas most couples can learn the specific and concrete behavioral steps of problem-solving and communications training (e.g., do not interrupt; offer specific behavioral solutions to problem issues, etc.), uncovering and challenging dysfunctional cognitions without the aid of the therapist requires a fair amount of psychological mindedness on the part of couples. In actuality, even the identification of dysfunctional cognitions involves several different steps, and different spouses attain various levels of proficiency at each step. First, spouses have to recognize that they might be having thoughts that are contributing to their discord in a given instance. Thus, when a husband becomes angry at his wife for coming home late from work, he may or may not recognize that he is likely making an attribution for her behavior that is contributing to his upset feelings (i.e., that his emotional response is mediated by what he is thinking).

Second, the cognition that is focal to the specific circumstance or a set of circumstances must be isolated. In this same example, the husband's belief that his wife is purposely late as an attempt to demonstrate her power in the relationship must be clarified. Some couples are not able to isolate the important cognitive themes in their relationship on their own, but once the therapist helps shed light on these issues, the couple is capable of identifying when this same issue arises in other instances. In the previous example, the therapist might have to help the husband become aware that he seems to view his wife as attempting to demonstrate her power. However, once this theme has been clarified, the husband might become competent in recognizing when this same theme is operating in other instances. Assuming that there seems to be little evidence to support this belief about his wife, he is then in a position to challenge his own thinking. Whereas the husband's ability to become aware of this theme can be of great assistance to the couple in the present, it in no way assures that when other themes arise in the future, once therapy is terminated, that the couple will be prepared to uncover the themes on their own.

This third level of identifying cognitions, isolating new cognitive themes without significant assistance from the therapist, is the most difficult for couples because it asks them to become their own cognitive therapists. This is the ultimate in cognitive skills training and increases the likelihood that when new cognitive issues arise in the future, the couple will be able to identify and evaluate the cognition without a therapist. Consequently, will the husband in the previous example be able to isolate other attributional themes unrelated to control/power after therapy is completed? In working with cognitive interventions, the therapist's goal is help the couple become as skilled in the cognitive process as is possible for them as individuals. Whereas some couples can become competent at uncovering new cognitive distortions that are not isolated by the therapist, other couples remain more limited in the process.

Overall, the therapist's role can be viewed as an active, somewhat directive role in which the therapist is attempting to isolate and help the couple produce needed change in cognitive, behavioral, and emotional realms. At times, the therapist will be focusing on process aspects of the relationship (e.g., noting ways that the couple interacts and the patterns of conununication that ensue). On other occasions, particularly early in the process of cognitive restructuring, the therapist attends a great deal to the content of the couple's thoughts in order to help them come to recognize certain dysfunctional cognitions. Over time, the couple hopefully becomes more attuned to the role of cognitive functioning in relationships, allowing the therapist to become more process-focused in the cognitive realm. Consequently, the role of the therapist is a rather complex one, with alternating focus on (1) cognitive, behavioral, or emotional aspects of the spouses and the relationship; (2) the individual as the primary focus versus the relationship as the focus of an intervention; and (3) relative emphasis on content versus process aspects of the relationship.

COGNITIVE RESTRUCTURING INTERVENTIONS

As noted already,the overall goals of cognitive interventions are to develop spouses' abilities to identify their cognitions that are associated with marital discord, to test the validity or appropriateness of those cognitions, and to modify dysfunctional cognitions. It is not assumed that negative cognitions are distorted, but couples are helped to see when relationship events are distressing due to the particular views that they have of those events. In the discussion that follows, we describe a variety of cognitive interventions used to increase couples' skills for identifying and modifying their own cognitions. For the purpose of clarity, this material is divided into two major sections dealing with (1) techniques for identification/monitoring of cognitions and (2) techniques for modifying potentially problematic cognitions. Within each of these two sections, useful techniques for addressing the five types of cognitions described earlier (selective attention, attributions, expectancies, assumptions, and standards) are described. As noted previously, it is assumed that in clinical practice all of these cognitive restructuring techniques are integrated with interventions focused on behavioral and affective aspects of marital interaction. More extended descriptions of cognitive interventions and their integration with behavioral and affective interventions can be found in the Baucom and Epstein (1990) text.

Developing Self-Monitoring of Cognition

As is typical in cognitive therapy (cf. Beck & Emery, 1985; Beck, Rush, Shaw, & Emery, 1979), in CBMT the therapist emphasizes the idea that an individual's affect and behavior can be influenced by "automatic thoughts" that occur without planning and commonly seem plausible to the individual. It is stressed that in order to understand one's responses to events in an intimate relationship, it is important to monitor the content and process of the associated automatic thoughts, The therapist also explains how some of these thoughts are fully within the individual's awareness, whereas others may occur so rapidly that they are not noticed, and still others (e.g., basic assumptions and standards about marriage) may be "dormant" until a specific relevant event triggers them (as described more fully in the next section). Consequently, spouses are coached in monitoring and recording cognitions associated with pleasing and distressing relationship events.

Increasing Spouses' Awareness of Selective Attention

As has been noted by family therapists, members of intimate relationships tend to "punctuate" their perceptions of their interactions (i.e., to view the ongoing sequence of events) in linear causal terms, such that their own negative behaviors are caused by the other's actions. Although there clearly are instances in which one partner has had a major impact on an event, the tendency to focus on linear causality impedes the spouses' ability to identify more complex circular processes in their interactions, and fosters destructive mutual blaming. Consequently, one of the initial goals in developing couples' self-monitoring of cognition is to broaden their selective attention to encompass circular patterns in ongoing couple interaction. Commonly, this is accomplished initially by the therapist drawing the couples' attention to such sequences, either in their reports of interactions that have occurred in daily life or in their immediate interactions in the therapist's office. On the one hand, information about naturalistic interactions is potentially invaluable because it may be more representative of the life events influencing couples' marital satisfaction. On the other hand, such data rely on retrospective accounts that may be inaccurate and even biased. As described earlier, there is considerable evidence that spouses have low rates of agreement about the occurrence of marital events. Consequently, the marital therapist should be conservative in relying on retrospective reports of marital interaction, at least until couples have had experience monitoring sequences and circular processes in therapy sessions. Nevertheless, when a therapist notices a common circular pattern in couples', reports of several distressing interactions over time, he/she may summarize that observation for couples and suggest that they attempt to notice further instances of that pattern in the future. This intervention not only shifts the spouses' perceptions of events outside the therapist's office, but it also has the potential to make couples more self-conscious about negative patterns, and possibly disrupt what have become relatively automatic responses. For example, in one couple, the wife repeatedly complained that her husband made her uncomfortable by asking for reassurance of her love and by physically clinging to her. In turn, the husband reported distress that his wife commonly acted aloof and physically withdrew from him. Each partner had perceived that his/her own behavior was caused by the other's behavior, and each felt helpless to get the partner to change the aversive behavior. The therapist noted the circular process in this pattern, gave the couple the homework of monitoring the pattern at home, and stressed that the partners were influencing each other mutually. This led into a discussion of how, instead of focusing on inducing the other person to change his/her part of the circular process, each spouse could interrupt the pattern by taking responsibility for changing his/her own behaviors. The therapist conveyed a sense of optimism that the couple had it within their power to change a mutually distressing cycle. During the next session, the couple reported that they had in fact noticed themselves getting caught up in the old pattern and that they had experienced some success at interrupting it by altering their own typical behaviors. Over time, with additional coaching from the therapist, the couple became more skilled at noticing a variety of sequences and circular patterns in their interactions.

During treatment sessions, the therapist can interrupt an ongoing interaction and coach the spouses in identifying the sequence of events, including not only behaviors, but also associated cognitions and emotional responses. In addition, when a therapist has audiotape or videotape equipment available, sessions can be taped and played back to a couple, so that they can observe their interaction pattern. For example, a therapist might interrupt a couple's fruitless and frustrating debate about who was to blame for escalating an argument during a session by suggesting that they stop and replay the tape to examine the process. Then, the therapist and couple can identify the behaviors on each spouse's part that contributed to the escalation of conflict. Again, the goals of such interventions during therapy sessions are to broaden the spouses' awareness of complex contingencies that link their responses, and to increase their sense of personal responsibility and potential efficacy in changing negative patterns. The advantages to conducting this type of analysis in an ongoing session are that it avoids the pitfalls of retrospective reporting and that the therapist can monitor the sequence of couple interactions and ask the spouses questions to elicit more information about their responses as they occur.

A second approach to increasing spouses' identification of their selective attention to marital events focuses on the process by which distressed spouses tend to engage in "negative tracking" (Jacobson & Margolin, 1979), noticing negative behaviors in partners and overlooking positive ones. As behavioral marital therapists have noted, such a focus on negative behavior is likely to elicit distress, and positive behavior that is not noticed will not be reinforced. Consequently, in CBMT, it is not only important to increase spouses' exchanges of positive behaviors and decrease exchanges of negative behaviors, but it also is crucial to reduce the selective attention involved in negative tracking.

One technique for broadening spouses' perceptions of each other's behaviors in daily life is to ask them to keep daily logs of relationship behaviors. For example, spouses may be asked to complete the Spouse Observation Checklist (Weiss et al., 1973), logging, and rating as pleasing or displeasing, the occurrence of 408 behaviors (mostly by the partner, but some couple behaviors as well) during 24-hour periods. Although the Spouse Observation Checklist typically is used more for assessment than for intervention, therapists can instruct couples who engage in negative tracking to be on the lookout for pleasing as well as displeasing events.

Another technique for increasing clients' attention to positive relationship events is asking them to complete logs of interactions with their partners that elicit pleasant or unpleasant moods. For example, spouses may complete the Daily Record of Dysfunctional Thoughts (Beck et al., 1979), recording concrete descriptions of situations associated with particular emotional states, as well as detailed wording of their automatic thoughts while in the situations. Although the Daily Record of Dysfunctional Thoughts is used more commonly for testing the validity of negative cognitions (the description of this procedure follows), it can be used in this manner to focus spouses' attention on pleasant events, as well as the cognitions associated with experiencing pleasure in those situations. As spouses complete the Daily Record of Dysfunctional Thoughts across a variety of situations, they often become more introspective, differentiating variations in their emotions and cognitions. They also tend to notice instances in which their cognitions tend to mediate their affective and behavioral responses to their partners' behaviors, again broadening their perceptions of the complexities of their marital interactions. One note of caution concerning use of the original Daily Record of Dysfunctional Thoughts form developed for use with depressed individuals is that some distressed spouses may be put off by the term "dysfunctional thoughts" in the title. This defensiveness about the suggestion that marital problems might be caused by their having dysfunctional thinking (especially when they tend to blame their partners for the problems) can be reduced by making the title of the form more benign, for example, "Daily Record of Automatic Thoughts."

Increasing Spouses' Awareness of Attributions and Expectancies

The marital therapist can sensitize a couple to the existence of inferences such as attributions and expectancies by presenting case examples unrelated to the couple's own functioning. Furthermore, spouses' awareness of the types of inferences that they make about their own relationship can be increased by having them complete self-report inventories assessing attributions and expectancies (e.g., Baucom, Sayers, & Duhe, 1987; Bradbury & Fincham, in press; Pretzer, Epstein, & Fleming, 1991). However, it is our experience that much more consistent and systematic monitoring of inferences concerning ongoing marital events is required to develop spouses' abilities for noticing their own attributions and expectancies.

During treatment sessions, the therapist can look for shifts in each spouse's affect and behavior and can interrupt the couple's interaction to inquire about the cognitions and emotions the individuals are experiencing at such moments. It is important that the therapist not ask leading questions, based on his/her hypotheses about the clients' possible attributions or expectancies. Instead, the therapist inquires about the emotions that the individuals were feeling at the time, as well as any thoughts that had occurred. Relatively open-ended questions of the form, "And what

did that mean to you when she said that?" can be used to elicit the spouses' inferences. As is the case in efforts to increase couples' awareness of selective perception, this procedure of assessing ongoing attributions and expectancies also is used to "socialize" clients into the cognitive therapy approach to self-monitoring of automatic thoughts. The goal is for the spouses to become adept at using shifts in their own affect and behavior as cues for exploration of their attributions and expectancies, such that they need less prompting and coaching from the therapist over time.

Written logs such as the Daily Record of Dysfunctional Thoughts also can be used on a routine basis for clients' monitoring of attributions and expectancies associated with distress and conflict (as well as positive events) during daily life. The therapist can instruct the spouses to record all thoughts that they experience in these situations, and can suggest that they be aware of any inferences they make about causes of partner behavior and predictions of future events. Caution should be exercised in not creating "demand characteristics" when instructing clients about their self-monitoring (i.e., putting thoughts into clients' heads). However, there is sufficient evidence that spouses generate attributions and other inferences spontaneously (cf. Bradbury & Fincham, 1990), and that alerting couples to their existence seems to be an important aspect of teaching them about cognitive restructuring skills.

Increasing Spouses' Awareness of Assumptions and Standards

Because assumptions and standards about intimate relationships tend to be more long-standing cognitive schemata that comprise part of an individual's worldview, the degree to which they are conscious and accessible to introspection can vary considerably. As described earlier, self-report questionnaires such as the Relationship Belief Inventory and the Inventory of Specific Relationship Beliefs can be used to elicit assumptions and standards of which the individual is aware and open to disclosing. Similarly, one of us (NE) commonly asks spouses to fill out a sentence completion form with instructions to describe the way they would prefer a close romantic relationship to be. The 21 items include sentence stems such as "The amount of time spent per week sharing our feelings and thoughts would be . . . ," "The roles of careers would be . . . ," "We'd show our appreciation for each other by . . . ," and "We'd demonstrate commitment to each other by . . . ,"

Although the sharing of responses to these instruments during conjoint marital therapy sessions can increase spouses' awareness of both their own and their partners' assumptions and standards, there is no guarantee that this awareness will generalize to self-monitoring of schemata that elicit distress during their daily interactions. Consequently, once again it is important to give couples homework that involves identification of schemata triggered by specific relationship events that occur between sessions. For example, when spouses complete the Daily Record of Dysfunctional Thoughts to log affect and cognitions in specific situations, they can be instructed in the use of self-questioning designed to identify any underlying assumptions and standards associated with their responses to the events. Clients' skills at such self-questioning can be developed through modeling and coaching by the therapist during treatment sessions, using the Daily Record of Dysfunctional Thoughts or other logging forms to analyze an upsetting event during a session.

The client begins by identifying and writing down any automatic thoughts associated with the experienced affective state. At times, the initial automatic thought explicitly includes the content of an assumption or standard that was triggered by the relationship event. For example, a man who was angered by his wife's apparent indifference to household chores reported the thought, "Anyone who cared about her marriage would do things to make her home environment more pleasant." This assumption about the types of behavior that naturally follow from caring was highly accessible, and thus readily discussed by the couple and therapist.

In contrast, some underlying assumptions and standards are only identified through processes of (1) following a line of Socratic questioning of the form, "And if that is so, then what would be upsetting about it?" or (2) looking for common themes in the various situations that upset a spouse. An example of the second procedure was a woman who became angry in situations in which her husband invited friends to watch football on weekend days, stayed late at work to complete a project, failed to tell her what his parents discussed with him during a recent phone call, and bought a new compact disc player without consulting her. When the therapist coached the woman in searching for a common theme in these events, she concluded that they all meant to her that she was not a high priority in her husband's life. When the therapist subsequently asked her what types of behavior by her husband

would reflect greater valuing of her, she was able to specify a pattern in which he would share information, decision making, and more time with her. Thus, this inferential process helped to uncover one of this woman's standards about an intimate relationship that was violated repeatedly by her husband's behavior. Her homework between sessions then included monitoring other situations in which this standard affected her responses to her husband's behavior.

All of the previous procedures are intended to make spouses better observers of their own behaviors, cognitions, and emotional states. In a CBMT approach, a central goal is to help couples develop the cognitive-monitoring and restructuring skills that allow them to deal with their own cognitions, independent of a therapist. The following section describes techniques for evaluating and modifying cognitions that couples identify during their self-monitoring.

Developing Cognitive Restructuring Skills

As noted earlier, in CBMT it is not assumed that spouses' cognitions concerning distressing marital events are distorted, and a central task of therapy is to develop clients' skills at examining the validity or appropriateness of their cognitions in a systematic manner. When a negative cognition appears to be valid, for example, when evidence supports the attribution that one's partner's actions were based on malicious intent, cognitive restructuring is not likely the next step. However, in many instances spouses may discover that their cognitions are distorted or unrealistic in some manner, and the realization of this bias may set the stage for interventions to modify the cognitions, The following are common approaches to the evaluation and modification of selective attention, attributions, expectancies, assumptions, and standards.

Evaluation and Modification of Selective Attention

The goal of interventions in this area is to identify whether each spouse's perceptions are accurate representations or biased views of marital events. It is important for the therapist to understand and to convey to couples that identifying the ultimate "truth" about what has occurred during marital interactions usually is impossible. The amount of information available during even a brief interaction is immense, and consequently, everyone's attention (including the therapist's) necessarily tends to be selective. Therefore, the goal of examining perceptions is not to prove who is right or wrong, but rather to develop the best estimate of what events have occurred, and what factors appear to have influenced their occurrence. In essence, the therapist coaches the couple in conducting a functional analysis of distressing and pleasing events in their relationship, focusing on circular processes, as described earlier.

In order to conduct an analysis of their perceptions, spouses are instructed to ask themselves a number of questions. First, whenever they find themselves thinking or saying that their partner "always" or "never" does a particular thing, they should use it as a cue to examine whether there are identifiable exceptions to the rule. Furthermore, they should ask themselves under what conditions the behavior tends to occur, versus the conditions under which the exceptions occur. The goal of cognitive restructuring in this instance is to shift the narrow view of the partner's behavior (i.e., counteract the tendency to attribute the behavior to a global, stable trait) and increase awareness of situational factors that can be used to modify desirable behaviors. Data from logs such as the Spouse Observation Checklist and Daily Record of Dysfunctional Thoughts can be invaluable in challenging biased perceptions of relationship events.

The use of functional analysis in examining one's perceptions also is relevant when a spouse blames a partner for a negative event. The therapist can ask the spouse to try to identify all the factors (including the spouse's own behavior) that existed when the unpleasant event occurred. These data then can be used to compare alternative causes of the event. Further description of how this procedure is used to test the validity of negative attributions is provided next.

Evaluation and Modification of Attributions and Expectancies

As noted earlier, research on couples' attributions has indicated systematic tendencies for distressed spouses to attribute each other's negative behaviors to stable, global traits and to negative intent and other blameworthy characteristics. Similar to other types of cognition that we have discussed, these attributions occur in an unplanned manner and typically seem plausible to the individual as explanations for a partner's behavior. The major goal of cognitive restructuring is to coach the individual in identifying alternative attributions for the target behavior and to evaluate the relative validities of the original and alternative attributions. Although this

process sometimes results in the conclusion that an initial negative attribution is accurate, in other instances the spouse concludes that another explanation is more reasonable. When the alternative attribution is more benign than the original one, the spouse's affect and behavior toward his/her partner may become more positive. However, even though the link between attributions and marital behavioral interactions has been demonstrated in recent research (e.g., Bradbury & Fincham, 1992), there is little direct evidence as yet that changes in attributions necessarily result in behavioral changes. It has been our clinical experience that cognitive shifts often facilitate modification of negative behavior exchanges between spouses, but that often they must be integrated with behavioral interventions. It appears that at times the behavioral sequences between spouses have become so over learned and automatic that changes in attributions and other cognitions may have limited impact on their own.

For example, when the husband who had attributed his wife's minimal interest in household chores to a lack of caring about him and their marriage found a plausible alternative attribution that her behavior reflected a learned, lifelong devaluing of chores, his anger decreased. He nevertheless continued to become angry with her on weekend days, when she spent her time reading rather than working on chores, because she either failed to respond to his hints about "doing something constructive before the day slips away" or acted in a defensive way, saying that she deserved some leisure time. However, when the therapist engaged the couple in systematic problem-solving communication, focused on generating possible solutions to this conflict about use of weekend time, both spouses' behaviors became more cooperative, and the husband's belief in the more benign attribution about his wife's behavior concerning chores increased.

Logical analysis is a procedure commonly used in cognitive therapy (cf. Beck et al., 1979) that can be applied in the modification of spouses' problematic attributions about each other. In logical analysis, the individuals essentially ask themselves the question, "Does this inference I have made make sense logically?" They are taught about particular types of cognitive distortions that can influence inferences (see Baucom & Epstein, 1990, and Beck et al., 1979, for descriptions of cognitive distortions such as arbitrary inference, overgeneralization, and personalization), and are asked to search for instances of such distortions in their own thinking.

For example, one husband became angry when he overheard his wife making plans on the telephone to go shopping with a woman friend and subsequently failed to mention her plans to him. His attribution about her behavior was, "She didn't want to include me. She feels closer to her friend than to me." When the therapist asked the husband to identify any possible cognitive distortions in his attribution, he noted that he may have been engaging in personalization, wherein the individual concludes that the cause of an event is related to himself/herself. His wife reinforced this view by stating that, in fact, she preferred to spend their limited leisure time together, but that she remembered hearing him say that he wanted to watch a sports event on television that day and that she also knew from past experiences that he did not enjoy shopping. The husband became less upset when he acknowledged the looseness in his logic and found his wife's alternative explanation for her behavior plausible. Thus, the cognitive restructuring in this situation involved a combination of the husband's identifying a possible logical error in his inference and in his consideration of alternative attributions for his wife's behavior.

Logical analysis and the examination of alternative inferences also can be used to test the validity of spouses' expectancies about the probabilities that particular events will occur in their relationships in the future. For example, chronic emotional distance in one couple was influenced at least in part by the husband's tendency to withhold sharing his personal thoughts and emotions with his wife. During an exploration of his cognitions associated with his low level of self-disclosure, the husband explained that he was aware of fearing that if his wife really got to know him well, she would become bored with him and eventually leave him. He related this fear to the fact that a woman whom he had loved very much had left him for another man approximately a year before he met his wife. Through logical analysis, he was able to see that his prediction that one woman would leave him because another woman had done so involved overgeneralization and, in fact, he was able to describe a number of significant differences between the two women and the relationships he had with them. He also was able to recount past experiences in a variety of romantic relationships and friendships in which people seemed to like him more as they learned more about him. This analysis reduced his reported fear of disclosure, especially when his wife noted that she believed she would feel closer to him if he shared more

of himself with her. In fact, the couple discussed the irony of how the husband's lack of disclosure had contributed in the marriage to some of the emotional distance that he had feared.

Nevertheless, the therapist did not want to rely on logical analysis alone to alter an expectancy associated with considerable anxiety on this husband's part. Consequently, the spouses were coached in designing and implementing a "behavioral experiment" (cf. Baucom & Epstein, 1990) in which the husband's expectancy was tested directly. The experiment involved the husband's disclosure of increasingly personal thoughts and emotions to the wife, and the wife, in turn, providing the husband feedback about what is was like for her to hear his disclosures. The husband was to select the level of his disclosure such that his anxiety level was maintained at a manageable level. He reported considerable relief as he observed that his disclosures were met with warmth and appreciation from his wife. Over time, his belief in original negative expectancy was weakened significantly.

Evaluation and Modification of Assumptions and Standards

Theoretical and clinical literature on schemata such as assumptions and standards suggests that these long-standing cognitive structures develop on the basis of life experiences, often beginning in childhood, and function as templates by which daily events are categorized and understood. Epstein and Baucom (1993) noted that individuals also are likely to develop assumptions and standards based on, and specific to, their current intimate relationship. It has been assumed that new experiences have the potential to alter schemata, but basic social cognition research also has indicated that individuals' perceptions and memories of present events are shaped by preexisting schemata (see reviews relevant to marital functioning by Epstein & Baucom, 1993). Thus, as part of individuals' basic cognitive structures for organizing life experiences, assumptions and standards may be difficult to change. Nevertheless, a number of clinical techniques are used in CBMT to address potentially problematic assumptions and standards.

Research with the Relationship Belief Inventory (e.g., Bradbury & Fincham, in press; Eidelson & Epstein, 1982; Epstein, Pretzer, & Fleming, 1987) has indicated that spouses' beliefs in extreme or unrealistic assumptions and standards (e.g., that partners should be able to mind read each other's thoughts and emotions) tend to be associated with marital distress and negative behavioral interactions. Consequently, when the clinician's cognitive assessment has revealed that one or both members of a couple hold such assumptions and standards, some time is usually spent on interventions intended to modify the schemata, making them more realistic or appropriate for the "real-life" context of the couple's relationship.

In CBMT, the therapist conunonly provides a rationale to couples for examining how realistic or appropriate their assumptions and standards are. Although rational-emotive therapists (e.g., Ellis, Sichel, Yeager, DiMattia, & DiGiuseppe, 1989) tend to emphasize to clients that their extreme standards are irrational and the source of their relationship problems, we prefer a more Socratic approach in which the clients are coached in evaluating the consequences of living according to their current assumptions and standards. Consequently, the therapist discusses with a couple how all people develop a variety of assumptions about how relationships work, as well as standards for an acceptable relationship. The therapist explains that assumptions are crucial for making sense of experiences, and standards guide people in making important life decisions, such as selecting mates whose interests, values, and personal ethics are compatible with their own. However, depending on the kinds of personal experiences that have shaped an individual's assumptions and standards, these beliefs sometimes may be extreme or inappropriate to his/her present intimate relationships. The therapist may present an example of how a person who was exposed as a child to frequent violent conflict between his/her parents may develop a standard that partners should never express anger openly. Then, the therapist discusses the advantages (e.g., upsetting emotional expression is avoided) and disadvantages (e.g., sources of anger and dissatisfaction are not resolved and may lead to alienation of the partners) that occur when the individual applies such a standard to a current relationship. This rationale typically concludes with the therapist noting that it is important to examine one's assumptions and standards to see how well they contribute to the quality of a couple's relationship, as well as to identify any unrealistic ones that may be producing conflict or distress.

Following the presentation of a rationale for evaluating the consequences of adhering to particular assumptions and standards, the therapist can open exploration of a couple's schemata by reviewing their responses to a self-report questionnaire such as the Relationship Belief Inventory, Inventory of Specific Relationship Beliefs, or the sentence-completion form described earlier. The goal of this review is to assist spouses in identifying advantages and disadvantages of their schemata. In conjoint sessions, it is often a person's partner who points out negative consequences of his/her particular assumption or standard. In such cases, it is important for the therapist to minimize the couple's tendency to engage in debates about who is right or wrong about the merits or drawbacks of a spouse's schema. The therapist stresses the goal of uncovering any assumptions and standards that appear to cause friction and distress between the partners, and then engaging in problem solving (see the description of problem-solving procedures by Shoham, Rorhbaugh, & Patterson in Chapter 7, this volume) to determine a way that the couple can deal with the existence of the schemata that are contributing to conflict. It is noted that some of the possible solutions are as follows:

1. The spouse who holds the assumption or standard can modify it so that it no longer is inconsistent with the realities of the couple's ongoing interactions.
2. The partner can alter his/her assumptions, standards, and associated behavior to comply with the conditions of the spouse's schema.
3. The spouses can find a mutually palatable view that represents a compromise between their schemata.
4. The spouses can agree to tolerate the differences in their schemata and associated behaviors.

A therapist can help spouses evaluate the consequences of living according to particular standards or assumptions by coaching them in writing down lists of a particular schema's advantages and disadvantages. When a spouse can see that there are significant drawbacks to a particular standard, the therapist can assist him or her in "rewriting" it in less extreme terms. For example, an individual who held a standard that "Spouses should not express anger toward each other openly, " and who recognized its drawbacks in leaving conflicts unresolved, might revise the standard to read, "When we feel anger toward each other, we will use it as a sign that some issue is important to us and needs to be addressed. We then will use constructive communication skills to convey our upset feelings to our partner in a manner that respects him/her but specifies the issue and what we would like done about it." Logical analysis can be used to examine the degree to which the more extreme version of the standard is a realistic view of what members of a marriage are capable of achieving. A key to inducing spouses to modify extreme standards and assumptions is communicating respect for their basic values and belief systems, while demonstrating to them how these can be modified in a manner that improves their relationships.

Whereas the techniques for identifying and altering cognitions within couples are described in a straightforward manner, changing spouses' beliefs about relationships, their partners, and themselves is anything but a simple task. Consequently, addressing any cognitive theme is likely to require repeated interventions. For example, frequently a spouse will respond, "I know on an intellectual level that what I am thinking does not make sense, but on an emotional level it seems real." Thus, in the above example of a partner who has revised a standard for expressing anger in appropriate ways, the person might suggest that, of course, it makes sense to express negative feelings to each other in a constructive manner; however, on an emotional level, it still feels very dangerous. Likely it will require much behavioral practice in expressing emotions adaptively before the partner comes to believe cognitively and experience emotionally that sharing negative feelings with a spouse is adaptive for the couple and safe for the individuals. Consequently, repeated discussions of the cognition under consideration and review of behavioral experiments designed to test and alter the cognition are needed to promote effective cognitive change.

TREATMENT OUTCOME RESEARCH ON THE ROLE OF COGNITIVE RESTRUCTURING IN MARITAL THERAPY

Although there are some exceptions (e.g., Johnson & Greenberg, 1985; Snyder, Wills, & Grady-Fletcher, 1991), overall the results indicate that when different theoretical approaches to marital therapy have been compared empirically, the various treatment strategies have been found to be equally effective in assisting distressed couples (Baucom & Epstein, 1990). As will be demonstrated, these same findings hold when cognitive restructuring is compared to BMT that has excluded an explicit focus on cognitive restructuring. This could lead one to conclude (1) that focusing solely on behaviors is sufficient in

assisting couples, and (2) that helping couples think differently about their relationship is all that is needed, without the requirement that they behave differently toward each other. Thus, a cursory glance at the findings could lead one to believe that within these treatment parameters, any of the interventions seem to be equally effective; however, such a conclusion appears to be premature for several reasons. There are a number of drawbacks to the studies conducted involving cognitive restructuring that limits what we can conclude about the utility of cognitive restructuring in appropriate contexts. First, no studies have matched interventions to the specific needs of each individual couple. That is, in order to satisfy empirical standards, couples have been randomly assigned to treatment groups. This practice allows for comparison between treatments, but does not take the specific characteristics of the couples into account. In essence, what this means is that cognitive restructuring and behavioral interventions are equally effective when the needs of the couple are not taken into account. Not all couples need a significant amount of cognitive restructuring; nor do all couples require large amounts of behavior change. There is a great need for matching studies that indicate whether the overall effectiveness of marital therapy can be improved when the specific needs of the couple are matched with the treatment provided to them.

Second, protocols for studies have employed a set period of time for each treatment component (e.g., 6 weeks of communication training, 3 weeks of cognitive restructuring, etc.). This presents a somewhat unnatural scenario in therapy, because in most clinical contexts, therapy normally would move as needed between the components. For example, it might become obvious during problem-solving training that one spouse holds unrealistic standards for the marriage (e.g., "We should alwsys agree"). The clinican would likely find it more useful to use cognitive restructuring at this point, rather than waiting until the end of a 6-week communication skills component. At present, no integrative study has been conducted in which the clinician moves between cognitive restructuring and BMT as necessary, based on the needs of the couple.

In addition, the cognitive restructuring phase of some treatment outcome studies has been relatively short. Changing the beliefs that someone has held for along time likely requires more clinical intervention than has been allotted in the studies conducted to date. In fact, Baucom,

Sayers, and Sher (1990) found connsistent cognitive changes only after six cognitive sessions; after three sessions the changes were inconsistent. Furthermore, Baucom and Epstein (1990) concluded that even six sessions are probably too few.

Although researchers are aware of the limitations of CBMT investigations, there is still utility in examining the current set of outcome studies. The outcome studies investigating the effectiveness of cognitive restructuring fall into two categories. Four studies have examined the usefulness of cognitive restructuring as an addition to traditional BMT (Baucom & Lester, 1986; Baucom et al., 1990; Behrens, Sanders, & Halford, 1990; Halford, Sanders, & Behrens, 1993); three additional studies have examined the effectiveness of cognitive restructuring alone, relative to BMT (Emmelkamp et al., 1988; Epstein, Pretzer, & Fleming, 1982; Huber & Milstein, 1985).

Overall, the studies indicate that cognitive restructuring produces meaningful cognitive changes for couples in marital therapy, and the treatments (either cognitive restructuring alone, or in combination with BMT) were found to be effective in increasing marital adjustment. Furthermore, all of the studies suggest that when compared to BMT alone, cognitive restructuring and BMT are equally effective in improving marital adjustment.

It is worthwhile to consider some of the specific changes that cognitive restructuring has been shown to produce in these investigations. In all of the treatment outcome studies, the cognitive interventions designed to alter cognitions did, in fact, have the desired effects. However, the studies varied in the cognitions targeted for restructuring. Huber and Milstein (1985) found that brief cognitive therapy produced significant changes in couples' expectancies for the outcome of therapy. That is, couples receiving the cognitive therapy were more likely to exhibit increased desire to improve their relationship, as well as to predict that they would benefit from therapy. Epstein et al. (1982) found that cognitive restructuring was more effective than a communications training intervention in altering standards. Baucom and Lester (1986) and Baucom et al. (1990) demonstrated that their cognitive restructuring altered relationship standards and assumptions. Behrens et al. (1990) focused on cognitions specific to interactions (e.g., negative and positive partner referent thoughts), finding the cognitive changes occurring in this area. Therefore, it can be seen that the use of CBMT encompasses a wide range of cognitions and interventions, adding to the difficulty of comparing CBMT to traditional BMT. It is unlikely that each of these cognitive changes would be necessary for every couple, which provides support for the need for a study personalizing treatment approaches to each couple.

In summary, there is evidence to suggest that cognitive restructuring produces meaningful changes in the way that couples think about their relationship, as well as increasing marital adjustment. As discussed, a number of factors have limited the conclusions that can be drawn from the available investigations. A study that assigns couples to treatment groups based on individual needs would aid in further clarifying the effectiveness of cognitive restructuring. Likewise, a study designed to alternate among cognitive, behavioral, and emotional interventions based on the situational demands of a particular treatment session would provide additional clarification of the utility of cognitive restructuring within the broader context of marital therapy.

REFERENCES

Abramson, L. Y., Seligman, M. E. P., & Teasdale, J. (1978). Learned helplessness in humans: Critique and reformulation. *Journal of Abnormal Psychology, 87,* 49–94.

Baucom, D. H., & Epstein, N. (1990) *Cognitive behavioral marital therapy.* New York: Brunner/Mazel.

Baucom, D. H., Epstein, N., Daiuto, A., & Carels, R. A. (1991, November). *The Relationship Attribution Questionnaire: A new instrument for assessing relationship attributions and their impact.* Paper presented at the 25th Annual Convention of the Association for Advancement of Behavior Therapy, New York.

Baucom, D. H., Epstein, N., Rankin, L. A., & Burnett, C. K. (1990, November). *New measures for assessing couples' standards.* Paper presented at the 24th Annual Convention of the Association for Advancement of Behavior Therapy, San Francisco.

Baucom, D. H., Epstein, N., Sayers, S., & Sher, T. G. (1989). The role of cognitions in marital relationships: Definitional, methodological, and conceptual issues. *Journal of Consulting and Clinical Psychology, 57,* 31–38.

Baucom, D. H., & Lester, G. W. (1986). The usefulness of cognitive restructuring as an adjunct to behavioral marital therapy. *Behavior Therapy, 17,* 385–403.

Baucom, D. H., Sayers, S. L., & Duhe, A. D. (1987,

November). *Attributional style and attributional pattern among married couples.* Paper presented at the 21st Annual Convention of the Association for Advancement of Behavior Therapy, Boston.

Baucom, D. H., Sayers, S. L., & Sher, T. G. (1990). Supplementing behavioral marital therapy with cognitive restructuring and emotional expressiveness training: An outcome investigation. *Journal of Consulting and Clinical Psychology, 58,* 636–645.

Beach, S. R. H., Whisman, M. A., & O'Leary, K. D. (1994). Marital therapy for depression: Theoretical foundation, current status and future directions. *Behavior Therapy, 25,* 345–371.

Beck, A. T., & Emery, G. (1985). *Anxiety disorders and phobias: A cognitive perspective.* New York: Basic Books.

Beck, A. T., & Rush, A. J., Shaw, B. F., & Emery, G. (1979). *Cognitive therapy of depression.* New York: Guilford Press.

Behrens, B. C., Sanders, M. R., & Halford, W. K. (1990). Behavioral marital therapy: An evaluation of treatment effects across high and low risk settings. *Behavior therapy, 21*(4), 423–434.

Bradbury, T. N., & Fincham, F. D. (1990). Attribution in marriage: Review and critique. *Psychological Bulletin, 107,* 3–33.

Bradbury, T. N., & Fincham, F. D. (1993). Attributions and behavior in marital interaction. *Journal of Personality and Social Psychology, 63,* 613–628.

Bradbury, T. N., & Fincham, F. D. (in press). Assessing dysfunctional cognition in marriage: A reconsideration of the Relationship Belief Inventory. *Psychological Assessment.*

Christensen, A., & Nies, D. C. (1980). The Spouse Observation Checklist: Empirical analysis and critique. *American Journal of Family Therapy, 8,* 69–79.

Christensen, A., Sullaway, M., & King, C. (1983). Systematic error in behavioral reports of dyadic interaction: Egocentric bias and content effects. *Behavioral Assessment, 5,* 131–142.

Eidelson, R. J., & Epstein, N. (1982). Cognition and relationship maladjustment: Development of a measure of dysfunctional relationship beliefs. *Journal of Consulting and Clinical Psychology, 50,* 715–720.

Ellis, A., Sichel, J. L., Yeager, R. J., DiMattia, D. J., & DiGiuseppe, R. (1989). *Rational-emotive couples therapy.* New York: Pergamon.

Emmelkamp, P.N.G., van den Heuvell, C., Ruphan, M., Sanderman, R., Scholing, A., & Stroink, F. (1988). Cognitive and behavioral interventions: A comparative evaluation with clinically distressed couples. *Journal of Family Psychology, 1,* 365–367.

Epstein, N., & Baucom, D. H. (1993). Cognitive factors in marital disturbance. In K. S. Dobson & P. C. Kendall (Eds.), *Psychopathology and cognition* (pp. 351–385). San Diego: Academic Press.

Epstein, N., & Eidelson, R. J. (1981). Unrealistic beliefs of clinical couples: Their relationship to expectations, goals and satisfaction. *American Journal of Family Therapy, 9*(4), 13–22.

Epstein, N., Pretzer, J. L., & Fleming, B. (1982, November). *Cognitive therapy and communication training: Comparisons of effects with distressed couples.* Paper presented at the 16th Annual Convention of the Association for Advancement of Behavior Therapy, Los Angeles.

Epstein, N., Pretzer, J. L., & Fleming, B. (1987). The role of cognitive appraisal in self-reports of marital communication. *Behavior Therapy, 18,* 51–69.

Fincham, F. D, & O'Leary, K. D. (1983). Causal inferences for spouse behavior in maritally distressed and nondistressed couples. *Journal of Social and Clinical Psychology, 1,* 42–57.

Halford, W. K., Sanders, M. R., & Behrens, B. C. (1993). A comparison of the generalization of behavioral marital therapy and enhanced behavioral marital therapy. *Journal of Consulting and Clinical Psychology, 61,* 51–60.

Heider, F. (1958). *The psychology of interpersonal relations.* New York: Wiley.

Holtzworth-Munroe, A., & Jacobson, N. S. (1985). Causal attributions of married couples: When do they search for causes? What do they conclude when they do? *Journal of Personality and Social Psychology, 48,* 1398–1412.

Huber, C. H., & Milstein, B. (1985). Cognitive restructuring and a collaborative set in couples' work. *American Journal of Family Therapy, 13*(2), 17–27.

Jacobson, N. S., & Margolin, G. (1979). *Marital therapy: Strategies based on social learning and behavior exchange principles.* New York: Brunner/Mazel.

Jacobson, N. S., & Moore, D. (1981). Spouses as observers of the events in their relationship. *Journal of Consulting and Clinical Psychology, 49,* 269–277.

Johnson, S. M., & Greenberg, L. S. (1985). Differential effects of experiential and problem-solving interventions in resolving marital conflicts. *Journal of Consulting and Clinical Psychology, 53,* 175–184.

Notarius, C., & Vanzetti, N. (1983). The Marital Agendas Protocol. In L. Filsinger (Ed.), *A sourcebook of marital and family assessment.* Beverly Hills: Sage.

Pretzer, J., Epstein, N., & Fleming, B. (1991). The Marital Attitudes Survey: A measure of dysfunctional attributions and expectancies. *Journal of Cogntive Psychotherapy, 5,* 131–148.

Robinson, E. A., & Price, M. G. (1980). Pleasurable behavior in marital interaction: An observational study. *Journal of Consulting and Clinical Psychology, 48,* 117–118.

Synder, D. K., Wills, R. M., & Grady-Fletcher, A. (1991). Long-term effectiveness of behavioral versus insight-oriented marital therapy. *Journal of Consulting and Clinical Psychology, 59,* 138–141.

Spanier, G. G. (1976). Measuring dyadic adjustment: New scales for assessing the quality of marriage and similar dyads. *Journal of Marriage and the Family, 38,* 15–28.

Vanzetti, N. A., & Notarius, C. I. (1991, November). *Relational efficacy: A summary of findings.* Paper presented at the 25th Annual Convention of the Association for Advancement of Behavior Therapy, New York.

Vanzetti, N. A., Notarius, C. I., & NeeSmith, D. (1992). Specific and generalized expectancies in marital interaction. *Journal of Family Psychology, 6,* 171–183.

Weiss, R. L., Hops, H., & Paterson, G. R. (1973). A framework for conceptualizing marital conflict, a technology for altering it, some data for evaluating it. In L. A. Hamerlynck, L. C. Handy, & E. J. Mash (Eds.), *Behavior change: Methodology, concepts and practice* (pp. 309–342). Champaign, IL: Research Press.

Weiss, R. L., & Perry, B. A. (1983). The Spouse Observation Checklist: Development and clinical applications. In E. E. Filsinger (Ed.), *Marriage and family assessment: A sourcebook for family therapy.* (pp. 65–84). Beverly Hills: Sage.

5

The Ego-Analytic Approach to Couple Therapy

DANIEL B. WILE

Mᴀʏ PURPOSE in this chapter is to show how the world looks from an ego-analytic perspective. Ego analysis is a psychodynamic approach that focuses on self-reproach (negative self-talk) and nonpejorative interventions and thus has much in common with cognitive therapy and narrative approaches.

Here is ego-analytic thinking in a nutshell: In addition to the obvious problem that comes to be defined in the therapy, there is typically a hidden problem, which is the client's intolerance of the obvious problem—the client's anxious, discouraged, despairing, counterphobic, self-reproaching, unable-to-tolerate-having-the-problem, anxiously-trying-to-solve-it-or-to-brush-it-away, flinching reaction to the obvious problem. Taken together, such responses constitute an inability to "have" the problem or, to say the same thing in another way, to feel entitled to it.

Ego analysis is about this inability to "have" a problem—and, more generally, to "have" whatever feeling, thought, or experience is there.

> We feel sad and we think we shouldn't feel sad. (We feel unentitled to our sadness.) We tell ourselves: "Being sad doesn't help; I shouldn't let things get to me the way I do; I should be able to look on the positive side, and, anyway, I should be over it by now."
>
> We feel angry and we think we shouldn't feel angry. We feel unentitled to our anger. So

we suppress it. But then, sometime later, we blurt it out in a more eruptive and provocative form than if we had expressed it directly in the first place. Feeling unentitled to a feeling (in this case, anger) has produced a problem. But we also feel unentitled to the problem—that is, we see ourselves as weak, inhibited, immature, or lacking self-control for having this problem of suppressing our anger and then blurting it out. We fail to recognize that suppressing, which leads to blurting, is unavoidable. Everyone repeatedly does it. It is unavoidable because "feeling unentitled to feelings," which *leads* to suppressing, is unavoidable.

As these examples suggest, life is to an important extent the relationship we have with ourselves about our feelings, experiences, and problems—following, in large part, from our ability or inability to have, inhabit, or feel entitled to them. As these examples also suggest, the major contributor to this sense of *unentitlement* is self-reproach (i.e., shame, guilt, superego injunctions, negative self-talk, self-blame, self-criticism, and self-hate). Self-reproach shuts down productive thinking; it impairs a person's problem-solving ability much as an immune deficiency impairs the ability to fight disease. A therapist with an ego-analytic approach is alert to the danger of his/her interventions feeding into the client's self-reproach.

Certain interventions that therapists commonly make and find helpful are seen from an ego-analytic perspective to have such a reproaching element, which can reinforce clients' self-reproaches and impair their ability to think. For example, no matter how tactfully therapists suggest to clients that they just made a "you statement," these clients are likely at some level to feel reproached—as they also will feel no matter how tactfully therapists suggest that they are "afraid of intimacy," are "codependent" or that they "expect the therapist to magically solve" their problems. It is hard for clients to hear such statements—even buffered versions of them—without feeling rebuked. They feel they are being told that they should *not* have made a "you statement," be codependent, and so on. And the problem, as I have said, is that such rebukes can reinforce a client's self-rebuke and impair his/her ability to think.

In making these statements, therapists do not see themselves as rebuking—particularly if they make them in buffered forms. They see themselves as pointing out reality, as giving clients needed information, or as confronting them with their maladaptive behavior. In fact, given the theoretical framework within which these therapists work, they feel they would not be doing their job if they failed to make these statements.

Given the theoretical framework within which I work—the ego-analytic framework—I feel that I would not be doing my job if I *were* to make these interventions, since I see them as rebukes. But don't these interventions express crucial truths that clients need to know? From an ego-analytic view, they represent misleading partial truths. The more complete "truth"—the information that from an ego-analytic viewpoint the client needs to know—requires a fuller statement. Instead of just saying, "You're being codependent," which the person is likely to hear as, "You *shouldn't* be codependent," I would add:

> "And, *of course*, you're being 'codependent.' It's hard for a person to sit there and do nothing when someone he or she really cares about—and depends on—is destroying himself or herself right in front of your eyes, even if everyone tells you, and you tell yourself, that what you're doing is only making things worse."

How does my extended statement differ from the traditional one? To explain, I shall use the familiar metaphor of the mind as a courtroom with a prosecuting attorney and a defense attorney. The traditional therapeutic statement,

"You're being codependent," provides material for the person's inner prosecuting attorney. My elaboration on the traditional therapeutic intervention provides material for the person's inner defense attorney. My hope is to free the client from the charges of the inner prosecuting attorney so that the client can think about the matter. That is the goal of ego-analytic interpretations: to free people from self-condemnation so that they can think.

Here are other examples of ego-analytic interpretations that, by providing a defense attorney to reveal and balance the person's inner prosecuting attorney, create the possibility for neutrality and objectivity so that the person can think.

Instead of just saying, "You're afraid of intimacy," which the client is likely to hear as "You *shouldn't* be afraid of intimacy" (since there is nothing to be afraid of), I would immediately want to present the defense attorney's case and say:

> "And, *of course*, you're afraid of intimacy. Anyone would be who views relationships as you do—which is the way that practically everyone does—as requiring the sacrifice of your wishes to the wishes of someone else. You're afraid of intimacy because intimacy is dangerous."

Here is another example. Instead of just saying, "You made a 'you statement,'" which the client is likely to hear as "You shouldn't have made that 'you statement,'" I would want to present the defense attorney's case and say:

> "And, *of course*, you made a 'you statement.' You're feeling completely misunderstood—and you're *being* misunderstood. And when a person is being misunderstood, he doesn't feel like making an 'I statement.' He feels like making a 'you statement.' Sometimes, nothing but a good 'you statement' will do."

Instead of just saying, "You expect me to magically solve your problems," which the person is likely to hear as "You *shouldn't* expect me to magically solve your problems," I would immediately want to present the defense attorney's case and say:

> "And, *of course*, you expect me to magically solve your problems. You've been struggling with them yourself for so long, and without success, that by this time you probably feel that

no one can solve them—not you, not me, not anyone. But, since you feel you really need to solve them, you're hoping that maybe I might be able to come up with something anyway. In fact, you might be *counting* on it. It's a way you've found to maintain hope."

Ego analysis is based on recognizing that the root of the problem is the pejorative attitude that clients have toward themselves and on how common therapeutic interventions feed into and reinforce these attitudes, that is, how these interventions stimulate the client's inner prosecuting attorney and silence the client's inner defense attorney. Ego-analytic thinking, recognizing as it does the morally tinged cultural slogans with which people reproach themselves, is alert to how certain traditional psychotherapeutic interventions contribute to the problem.

In an effort to prevent partners in therapy from interrupting one another, many couple therapists tell the interrupting partner something to the effect of: "Don't interrupt; give your partner a chance to finish; you had your turn, now give her a chance to have hers." The problem with such an instruction is that the person interrupting can feel that he is being told that he is doing something wrong; that is, that he should *not* have interrupted. Here is the ego-analytic alternative:

"It's hard to just sit there and say nothing when you feel you're being so misunderstood and misrepresented—even if what you're trying to do is to give your partner her chance."

In this ego-analytic alternative, the therapist acknowledges the interrupting partner's experience: that is, the therapist makes a case for the urgency of the client's need to interrupt. In any given exchange, the ego-analytic therapist tries to make a case for both partners or, in Apfelbaum's (1982b, p. 16) words, function as a "lawyer hired by both sides."

Another common therapist-to-partner instruction is, "Say it to him, not to me," which the partner is likely to hear as, "You should have said it to him in the first place." Since I do not mind if partners say it to me rather than to one another, I have no need to instruct them not to do so. If a partner were to reproach *herself* for saying it to me rather than to him, however, I would immediately want to present the defense attorney's case and say:

"It makes sense that you might say it to me rather than to him. When you say it to him,

he doesn't listen. And he doesn't listen because he's trying to convince you of the opposite—he feels that *you* don't listen. So you're saying it to me because you're hoping *someone* will listen—and that, if you convince me, maybe I'll convince *him*."

Here is a list of other common therapeutic interventions that, even if stated in buffered forms, are seen from an ego-analytic perspective to have an accusatory element:

"You're mind reading."
"You have unrealistic expectations."
"That's not a feeling—I asked you what you were *feeling*."
"You're engaging in negative self-talk."
"Don't both talk at the same time."
"You must be angry at someone; depression is anger turned inward."
"You haven't dealt with your anger at your mother for dying."
"You're triangling your son into your relationship."
"You're trying to control the hour."
"You're resisting."
"That's defensive."
"You bring up issues at the end of the hour so there won't be time to talk about them."
"You blame others rather than accept responsibility for your problems."
"You're angry at me just as you were angry at your father long ago."
"That is the angry 2-year-old in you talking."

The problem with these classic interventions, and with those I described earlier, is that they are accusatory and run the risk of feeding into the client's self-accusation. On the other hand, these interventions also contain useful information. Clients are sometimes able to overlook the accusatory element, and instead:

Profit from the information. Clients might feel grateful, for example, to hear that they just made a "you statement" (since that helps them understand why, in response, their partner got so defensive) even though the way the therapist informed them might have been accusatory: that is, the therapist's intervention might itself have been a "you statement" ("You just made a you statement").

Feel relieved. Clients might feel relieved rather than accused when told, for example, "Your anger at your partner is really anger at your father," since this might enable them to not have to hate their partner so much.

Feel inspired. Clients might feel heartened rather than accused when told, for example, "That's the two-year-old in you talking," since they might be inspired by the idea that they can change.

Of course, the accusatory element in the intervention might catch up with them later. The man who felt inspired at the prospect of eliminating the "angry-two-year-old" from his reactions might feel demoralized and self-reproachful if he finds this difficult to do. The woman who felt relief at the idea that her anger at her husband was really anger at her father might become upset at the thought: "My husband and the therapist blame it all on me; they see it as *my* problem rather than as *our* problem."

As an ego-analytic therapist, I look for ways to inform, relieve, and inspire clients that are not accusatory and thus do not run the risk of contributing to their self-reproach.

Some people might wonder whether my effort to avoid reinforcing clients' self-reproach might prevent me from confronting clients with important but painful truths about themselves. As I see it, clients are *already* confronting themselves with painful "truths." For example, they are criticizing themselves for being "codependent," afraid of intimacy," or "narcissistic." And *that* is the problem: this self-reproach and their effort to defend themselves against it.

But let us examine this self-reproach. Self-reproach appears early in our lives. Children instinctively blame themselves. They think it is their fault, for example, when a parent dies or when their parents get a divorce ("It's because I've been bad"). Self-reproach has an insistent, oppressive, all-encompassing quality, which is why people have difficulty avoiding it and why therapists have difficulty refuting it. As soon as someone suggests to us that we are codependent or afraid of intimacy, we immediately feel the weight of public opinion against us. We feel the weight of our own opinion against us. And being accused is being convicted. Once you are labeled defensive, codependent, and so on, you find it hard to defend yourself. Everyone just immediately thinks it is true about you.

As this presentation of the ego-analytic version of standard therapeutic interventions reveals, ego-analytic therapy is based on

Providing a defense attorney to reveal and balance the client's inner prosecuting attorney so that the client can think.

Finding the hidden validity in clients' responses, that is, showing how these responses are not as inappropriate and irrational as they might seem, but in important ways make sense in the present situation.

In doing these things, ego-analytic therapists adopt what I call the "hidden-validity principle," the first of four major principles that together constitute ego-analytic therapy. Ego-analytic therapists show how the clients' responses make sense in the present situation because from their point of view the root problem is the tendency of clients to invalidate their responses, that is, to focus on how they do *not* make sense.

Ego-analytic thinking thus differs from certain traditional forms of psychodynamic explanation that focus on the inappropriateness or maladaptiveness of clients' responses and thus have the effect of invalidating these responses, that is, of showing how they do not make sense in the present situation. The reactions of clients are attributed, for example, to developmental deficits, holdovers from childhood, secondary gain, skills deficits, irrational ideas, unrealistic expectations, and commitment to the pathological couple system.

I do not suggest that we eliminate these traditional forms of psychodynamic reasoning. People *do*, after all, have character defects; their problems *do* go back to childhood; they *do* obtain secondary gain from their symptoms; they *do* have skills deficits, bad habits, and unrealistic expectations; and they *are* caught in pathological couple systems.

What I do suggest is that we look both at how a client's responses are valid and at how they are *invalid*.[1] The problem with these traditional psychodynamic explanations is that they so convincingly demonstrate what is invalid in clients' response that:

I can easily lose interest in looking for what is valid in them.

I can lose sight of what for me is the crucial issue: what is keeping the client from feeling entitled to those responses and how the heart of the problem is clients' *own* beliefs that certain of their responses are invalid.

To prevent my own use of these traditional ideas from distracting me from looking for what is valid in my clients' responses, I adopt five guidelines. Whenever I find myself focusing on how a client's responses are irrational, pathological, childish, the result of developmental deficits, inappropriate holdovers from the past, and so on—that is, whenever I find myself focusing on how these responses are invalid—I look for

Guideline 1. Ordinary adult feelings that the person is expressing in distorted forms because he/she feels unentitled to them.

Guideline 2. A hidden appropriateness in the person's seemingly inappropriate behavior.

Guideline 3. How the person's childhood-based special sensitivity improves his/her ability to notice a provocation that is occurring at the moment.

Guideline 4. Important information about the relationship for which the pathological-appearing behavior is a rough first approximation, that is, a clue.

Guideline 5. Universal or common human issues that the person is experiencing in clear and intense forms.

These are all ways of shifting the focus in a client's reactions from what is invalid to what is valid in them.

How does adopting the hidden-validity principle affect a therapist's work? In a couple therapy session with me, Carol turns to her lover, Sue, and says, "Why are you angry at me?"

If I were to adopt a communication skills training approach, and point out Carol's communication error, I might say:

"That's *mind reading*. How do you know she's angry? You can't know what Sue is feeling. Only Sue knows what she's feeling. Let her speak for herself."

But, adopting the hidden-validity principle, I do some mind reading myself and say to Carol:

"My guess is that what you are feeling here and what you might want to tell Sue is, "I'm *worried* that you're angry at me; you've been quiet lately and when you're quiet, I can easily worry that you're angry at me.""

In making this intervention, I would be showing Carol's symptomatic response (her accusatory "Why are you angry at me?") to be, to have, to reveal, or to be traceable to

Guideline 1. An ordinary feeling: her *worry* that Sue might be angry at her.

Guideline 2. A hidden appropriateness. Carol is reacting to a provocation on Sue's part: Sue's withdrawal.

Guideline 3. A provocation that Carol's childhood-based special sensitivity improves her ability to notice. Her early experience with withdrawn and unavailable parents makes her reactive to Sue's withdrawals. But she is reacting to something that *is* happening: Sue *is* withdrawing.

Guideline 4. A potentially useful clue. Both Carol and Sue would prefer that Carol not be so reactive to Sue's silences. But her reactivity has one benefit: At least they will never wake up one day to find themselves in a mutually withdrawn relationship without knowing how they got there. Carol is their protection against that.

Guideline 5. A common couple issue: Carol has a clear and intense version of a common couple concern. People often wonder when their partners become quiet whether they might be upset with them about something.

Carol's inability to get across the feeling "I'm worried that you might be angry at me" led to her symptomatic response: *accusing* Sue of being angry at her. This brings up the second of the four major ego-analytic principles—need-to-get-something-across. According to this principle, people react in offensive, provocative, compulsive, or impulsive ways—that is, they become symptomatic—when they have important thoughts or feelings that they are unable to get across.

How did I come up with the intervention? "My guess, Carol, is that what you might want to tell Sue is, 'I'm *worried* that you're angry at me; you've been quiet lately and when you're quiet, I can easily worry that you're angry at me' "? I asked myself, "What is the ordinary feeling that, since Carol was unable to get it across, led her to blurt out to Sue, 'Why are you angry at me'?"

How does adopting the need-to-get-something-across principle affect a therapist's work? You become a different therapist if you focus on how clients' symptomatic responses are the result of an inability to get across ordinary adult feelings than if you focus on how these responses represent immature reactions, pathological motives, primitive drives, infantile impulses, faulty thinking, or childish wishes.

Sue responds to Carol's "Why are you angry at me?" with an outraged, "I'm tired of your always thinking I'm angry at you when I'm not."

And they get into a fight:

CAROL: Yes, but look at you—you *are* angry.
SUE: No I'm not.

CAROL: You aren't? Listen to your tone of voice.

SUE: Well, I didn't *have* a tone of voice until you accused me of being angry.

CAROL: You've been furious with me for *days*—it's just finally coming out now.

SUE: Well congratulations! You've just turned a person who was feeling perfectly okay about you into someone who's ready to tear out your hair—and her own. Are you satisfied? Do you always do that with all your lovers?

CAROL: Only the ones who act like you.

The problem, from an ego-analytic view, is not the argument itself. There are always going to be arguments, if not at this moment about this issue, then later about another. There are always going to be disappointments, disagreements, and conflicts. If partners do not get into out-and-out fights, then they will, at the least, exchange sour looks, make under-the-breath comments, or retreat into angry silence.

Since there is no way to avoid fights entirely, I put my emphasis on helping partners recover from them by having "recovery conversations." In a recovery conversation, the partners try to figure out how they got into the fight, what the fight was about, and what it reveals about the relationship. They try to make sense of the fight and, by so doing, arrive at a sense of resolution about it.

But how are partners going to talk about a fight without simply rekindling it? They need a neutral, objective, nonblaming, nondefensive, shared perspective or vantage point. And this brings up the third major principle of ego-analytic couple therapy: the joint platform. Ego-analytic couple therapy is dedicated to creating such a platform.

You become a different therapist if, instead of focusing on *solving* the problem, you focus on creating a joint platform from which the partners can integrate the problem into the relationship.

Some therapists might see Carol's accusatory, "Why are you angry at me?" as an effort to start a fight to protect against too much intimacy. Sue's silence, which provoked Carol's anger, might be seen as her own attempt to protect against too much intimacy. The interaction as a whole might be seen as serving the purpose of maintaining homeostasis—keeping intimacy within tolerable limits. According to such serves-a-purpose therapeutic thinking, whatever happens is seen as what the people involved *want*

to happen, at least unconsciously. This is the "self-responsibility ethic," according to which

There are no accidents.
There are no victims.
People are architects of their own destinies; they are creators of their own problems, and
Only *they* can solve their problems.
If a problem persists, it is because the person is getting something out of it—"secondary gain" (although, since it is the major force maintaining the problem, it might more accurately be called "primary gain").

Ego-analytic therapists are concerned about how the self-responsibility ethic converges with clients' tendencies to blame themselves for their problem and, in general, for whatever happens to them ("It's my own fault; I'm doing it to myself"; "I'm sitting here feeling sorry for myself and blaming others rather than making an effort to change"; "I could change if I wanted to, and the fact that I don't means I must be getting something out of it").

From an ego-analytic point of view, whatever secondary gain clients get from their symptoms is secondary indeed. The disadvantages far outweigh the advantages. The pain and distress that people suffer in panic attacks, for example, or in depression, far outweigh the secondary gain of getting others to take care of them, of controlling others, or of fulfilling dependency needs.

To guard against the self-responsibility ethic, ego-analytic therapists adopt the victims principle: the last of the four major ego-analytic principles. You become a different therapist if you focus on how people are victims—how they are stuck, trapped, and deprived of what they need—than if you adopt the self-responsibility ethic and focus on how they are getting too much from their symptoms to be willing to give them up.

It is unfashionable to think of ourselves as victims since it sounds too much like having a "victim mentality." So why did I choose the graphic and culturally shocking term "victim" to define this principle, rather than the less provocative, less controversial, less burdened-with-unwanted-connotations "stuck" "trapped," or "deprived"? Because I wanted to make clear that I am challenging the self-responsibility ethic, and adopting the term "victims principle" allows me to do just that. To a person who adopts this ethic, there is no such thing as a victim.

In this chapter, I demonstrate how these four ego-analytic principles generate a distinctive therapeutic approach, concentrating on two of these principles: need to get something across and joint platform. The other two principles—hidden validity and joint victims—are implicit.

In addition, I show how all four principles are derivatives of a supraordinate principle: entitlement to feelings.

Ego analysis has its roots in Freud (1926/1959), emerged in the work of Fenichel (1941), and was further developed by Gray (1982) and Apfelbaum (Apfelbaum, 1977, 1982a, 1988; B. Apfelbaum & C. Apfelbaum, 1985; Apfelbaum & Gill, 1989). My own work (Wile, 1981, 1984, 1985a, 1985b, 1987, 1988, 1993, 1994) follows the line of thinking developed by Apfelbaum.

Ego analysis is not to be confused with Hartmann and Rapaport's ego psychology. As Apfelbaum (1966, 1983) demonstrated, ego psychology is an extension of id-analytic thinking, whereas ego analysis is an alternative to it.

THE EGO-ANALYTIC THEORY OF RELATIONSHIP DYSFUNCTION

As just described, partners become symptomatic (i.e., they get into fights, become mutually withdrawn, or engage in pursuer–distancer interactions) when they are unable to get across certain important thoughts, feelings, and wishes.

Mark walks into the bedroom and sees his wife, Peg, cooing over their 3-month-old son, Joey. Mark has the following sequence of thoughts and feelings.

As you read through the sequence, you might be surprised by the number of thoughts and feelings, especially since they all occur in the course of just a few seconds. But this is how our minds work—like computers ratcheting through possibilities. When I tried to write down the thoughts and feelings that partners had in the course of a single evening, it took the better part of a book (Wile, 1993).

Seeing Peg cooing with the baby, Mark feels left out. That is his first feeling.
He thinks he *shouldn't* feel left out, that it means he is self-centered. That is the next feeling: self-reproach for feeling left out. "If I were a loving father," he tells himself, "I'd be *touched* by Peg paying a lot of attention to Joey. I'd feel proud. I'd run for a camera. The fact that I feel left out means that I must be like another child needing Peg's attention."

"And the *reason* I'm another child needing Peg's attention is that I'm still competing with my brother for my *father's* attention—Peg and the baby are just stand-ins." And immediately he feels angry at his father for favoring his brother and fostering this competition. "If my father hadn't been like *that*, I wouldn't be like *this*."
"But I should be *over* it by now—I should have forgiven my father long ago." This is Mark's next feeling: self-reproach for not being over his anger at his father and for taking it out on Peg and Joey.
"But wait a minute! Peg didn't even notice that I came into the room. She didn't even look up. So it's not just that I *feel* left out—it's that I'm *being* left out." This is Mark's next feeling: anger at Peg for leaving him out.
"But a new mother is supposed to be totally involved in her baby," Mark quickly tells himself. "So the problem isn't Peg's involvement with Joey; it's my minding it." Here, Mark is experiencing a resurgence of self-reproach.
"Of course, maybe all fathers feel this way. Maybe it's normal." Here, Mark is defending himself against this self-reproach. He is trying to give himself the benefit of the doubt.
"I shouldn't be obsessing like this. If something is bothering me, I should do something about it or at least learn to live with. In any event, I should stop thinking about it. It doesn't help to go back and forth like this." Here, Mark is suffering yet another resurgence of self-reproach.

Here are alternative ways that therapists might understand Mark's stream of thoughts and feelings:

Hypothesis 1. Mark *is* still competing with his brother for his father's attention, just as he says.
Hypothesis 2. Mark *is* like another child that his wife has to take care of, also just as he says.
Hypothesis 3. Mark was damaged in childhood—he is a victim of unempathic parenting—which is a variant of Mark's view that he is still suffering from his father's having preferred his brother.
Hypothesis 4. Mark has a narcissistic sensitivity to not being the center of attention, which is a variant of Mark's view that his feeling left out means that he is self-centered.

Hypothesis 5. The source of the problem is Peg's symbiotic involvement with Joey, which is a variant of Mark's own view that Peg is over involved with Joey.

Hypothesis 6. Mark's problem is a readiness to blame others (his externalizing) and his failure to take responsibility for his feelings, which approximates Mark's own view that he should be over his anger at his father by now and, in any event, that he should not take out his feelings on Peg and Joey.

Hypothesis 7. Mark is obsessing about the problem rather than dealing with his feelings, which is what he says, too.

Hypothesis 8. Mark should realize that he is dealing with the common experience that new fathers have of feeling left out—just as he says.

Many of these hypotheses might turn out to be true. In fact, all of them might be true. From an ego-analytic perspective, however, each hypothesis misses the crucial issue: Mark's sense of unentitlement to his experience. He feels he should not be having the feelings he is having, which means, to start with, he feels he should not be feeling left out.

As a result of feeling unentitled to feeling left out, Mark starts anxiously obsessing, which is an experience to which he *also* feels unentitled. But what does it mean to say that Mark feels *unentitled to the experience of anxious obsessing? It means that he is unable to sympathize with himself for anxiously obsessing; instead, he condemns himself for it.

Here is how it might sound *were* Mark to sympathize with himself:

"Hmm, I feel left out seeing Peg cooing over Joey. And that's a problem because, if I know me, that means that I'm going to get crazy—I'm going to spend the rest of the day accusing myself, trying to justify myself, trying to get the blame off me by blaming others, thinking I'm the only one on the earth who has this problem and that there's something wrong with me, and trying to reassure myself by telling myself, 'No, *lots* of fathers feel this way.' And it's too bad that I have to do all that—I'd much rather wash the car and have a beer."

What is important to notice in this statement that I just imagined for Mark is that all his original thoughts and feelings are there; he simply has a different attitude toward them:

As Mark originally experienced these thoughts and feelings, he anxiously ping-ponged among them. Each thought reminded of another, which, in turn, reminded him of still another. And he kept doubling back on them, shuttling between accusing himself and justifying himself.

In my imagined statement for Mark, he *sympathized* with himself for anxiously ping-ponging among them and, in that sense, felt entitled to his experience of anxiously obsessing.

And now we can see what "feeling entitled to one's experience" means. It means feeling entitled to whatever feeling, thought, or problem you have at the moment, or to put it another way, being able to *have* the feeling, thought, or problem you have. By "being able to *have* a thought, feeling, or problem," I mean

Having a neutral, nonanxious, self-accepting, not-blaming-yourself, not-blaming-others, self-sympathizing, self-forgiving attitude about the thought, feeling, or problem and about yourself for having it.

Being able to sit with the thought, feeling, or problem, that is, not anxiously having to solve, resolve, or come to a conclusion about it right away, but not giving up on it either.

Being sufficiently unpanicked and non-self-blaming about the thought, feeling, or problem that you are able to think about it and can even afford to be curious about it.

Being able to engage with it without being drawn into its undertow.

Staying connected with it without getting tangled in it.

And here is where the idea "sense of entitlement to experience" becomes complex, because it *also* means, as shown in the example, feeling entitled to the problem of feeling unentitled to a problem (or to a thought or feeling). It means having a neutral attitude about being nonneutral. It means, in addition:

Having a . . .	Attitude about being . . .
nonanxious	anxious
self-accepting	non-self-accepting
non-self-blaming	self-blaming
non-other-blaming	other-blaming
self-sympathizing	non-self-sympathizing
self-forgiving	non-self-forgiving
able to think about it	unable to think about it

able to be curious about it	unable to be curious about it
able to sit with it without giving up on it	unable to sit with it without giving up on it
able to engage with it without being drawn into its undertow	unable to engage with it without being drawn into its undertow
able to stay connected without getting tangled	unable to stay connected without getting tangled.

From certain non-ego-analytic perspectives, the crucial point is that Mark has a developmental deficit, an unresolved childhood conflict, a traumatic history, a narcissistic vulnerability—or, for that matter, skills deficits, irrational ideas, a three-generational problem, a need for punishment, and so on.

From an ego-analytic perspective, the crucial point is that Mark is accusing himself of having a developmental deficit, an unresolved childhood conflict, a traumatic history, and so on, and that is the problem: his self-reproach (and, in general, his sense of unentitlement to whatever experience he is having), leading to a loss of much of his ability to think, talk, and problem solve.

It is too bad that Mark feels unentitled to his experience (of feeling left out and of anxious ping-ponging as a result of feeling left out) since, if he were to feel entitled to it, he might be able to confide in Peg about it. He might be able to say:

"I know I'm supposed to be the proud father, but instead I just feel left out. And I'm worried that it means that I'm selfish and immature. I'm angry at my father for making me this way, but then I think I shouldn't still be blaming him. I think that you're too involved with Joey, but then I think you're just being a good mother. I think that maybe all fathers feel this way, but then I think that I'm the only one and there's something wrong with me. So I'm really spinning around here. And I feel I shouldn't be. I feel I shouldn't be feeling left out in the first place. And wait. If all that weren't enough, I'm worried about everything I've just told you, because I'm afraid that you too will think that something is wrong with me—that I'm immature and selfish."

It is hard to imagine anyone being sufficiently self-aware and articulate to be able to say all this. But if Mark were able to do so, he might feel better. Of course, he would not feel better if Peg were to reply:

"I'm only doing what a mother is supposed to do. Can't you take care of yourself? Do you have to be like another child I have to take care of?"

If Peg were to say this, it could mean either that she has her own strong feelings about the issue or that Mark's comment stimulated her worry that she is not being the attentive wife she thinks she should be. She would be defending herself by attacking Mark.

So here is Mark's situation. He feels unentitled to his experience of feeling left out and of anxious ping-ponging as a result of feeling left out. As a consequence, he is unable to formulate this experience in his own mind or tell Peg about it. And if he were to tell her about it, she might just criticize him. Mark is thus in the difficult situation of having important feelings that he is unable to get across to Peg or even formulate clearly in his own mind (i.e., get them across to himself). He does what people generally do when they have important feelings that they are unable to get across. He has what I call "symptoms":

He feels a little down.

He asks fewer questions than he usually does about what his mother—who took care of Joey that day—said about how things went with Joey.

He loses the wish to tell Peg about a success he had at work, even though he had been looking forward all day to doing so.

He temporarily forgets about the success.

He takes a tenth of a second longer than usual to respond when Peg asks him what happened at work that day—and then he says, "Nothing special. The same old thing."

He makes a slightly less elaborate dinner than usual.

He has little to say during dinner.

He loses a decibel in his usually hearty laugh.

He eats more than he usually does at dinner (even though he has been trying to lose weight).

He feel sluggish and weary.

He worries that he is coming down with something.

He thinks that marriage is overrated as a source of satisfaction and that his major pleasure in life will have to come from work.

He has a sudden wish to be in the desert on a Harley.

I know that when we use the word "symptoms" we typically think of maladaptive or pathological reactions such as insomnia, loss of appetite, and excessive drinking. But I am using the word in a broader way to include reactions such as worrying about coming down with something, having little to say during dinner, or suddenly wishing to be totally alone. In so doing, I am following in Freud's footsteps when he talked about "symptomatic acts." Freud saw symptomatic acts—for example, forgetting names or making Freudian slips—as normal everyday events: the psychopathology of everyday life. I am saying that the major psychopathology of everyday life is the subtle, everyday ways that we continually becomes alienated—from ourselves and from one another.

The symptoms that Mark is having at the moment are subtle, so subtle that no one observing him would notice any of them—except Peg, of course, and she notices many of them. She is sensitive to subtle indications of Mark's feeling, as most people are to subtle shifts in their partner's feelings. She worries that Mark's withdrawal means that he is angry at her.

So as soon as they put Joey to bed, she begins the following exchange:

PEG: You've been quiet tonight. Is something wrong?
MARK: No, I'm just tired.

Peg can tell from Mark's response that he doesn't want to talk about it. She doesn't know, however, that the reason he doesn't is that he experiences her question as a reproach—as "You *shouldn't* have been quiet"—which is difficult to take because it feeds into his *self*-reproach. *He* feels he shouldn't have been so quiet (i.e., detached and withdrawn).

PEG (*persisting*): Are you angry with me about something?

Mark also takes this as a reproach. He hears it as "You *are* angry and you *shouldn't* be angry." So he defends himself.

MARK: I'm not angry. I'm just frustrated.
PEG: About what?

Mark does not know "about what"—or even that he is frustrated at all. He just said it to convince Peg that he was not angry. But now he is in a spot in which he feels he has to come up with something that is frustrating him.

MARK: There just isn't enough time in the day. Life is a buzz and a whir—it's too busy—what with work, the baby, the house, and everything else.

Mark is saying that *life* is too busy. More to the point, however, he feels that *Peg* is too busy—with the baby—and, as a result, he feels left out.

Mark is telling Peg that life is a buzz and a whir. More to the point is the buzz and whir in his own mind, that is, his anxious ping-ponging that results from his reproaching himself for feeling left out.

Peg is glad that Mark is finally talking to her.

PEG: I know; it's been crazy.

As just described, Mark has been having important feelings throughout the evening that he has been unable to tell Peg (or even clearly formulate in his own mind) because he feels unentitled to them. At the same time, Peg has been having her own important feelings or experiences that she has been unable to tell *him*. Here is the feeling she has at the moment, or rather, here is how it would sound were she able to tell Mark about it:

"You know, I've been having a hard time tonight—I've been sitting here getting more and more distressed. I always have a hard time when you're quiet. I worry that I've done something to make you mad—that's why I blurted out a moment ago, 'Are you angry at me about something?' "

Peg is unable to say this to Mark, however, or even to formulate it clearly in her own mind. That is because she feels unentitled to her sensitivity to Mark's silences; she thinks she should not mind them. She thinks that it is *her* problem and that she should not burden Mark with it. The reason she is sensitive to Mark's silences, she believes, is that her mother used to punish her by giving her the silent treatment.

Peg is thus in agreement with those therapists who believe that partners should take personal responsibility for their feelings: that is, they should not burden their relationships with leftover issues from childhood. As an ego-analytic therapist, however, I take the position that:

Much of the problem is the partner's, Peg's effort *not* to burden her relationship with leftover issues from childhood, which leaves her unable to elicit Mark's help in dealing with them. She would be eliciting his help were she to confide in him in the way I just suggested ("You know, I've been having a hard time tonight. I always have a hard time when you're quiet. I worry that I've done something to make you mad—that's why I blurted out a moment ago, 'Are you angry at me about something?' ")

The ultimate purpose of a relationship is to be curative, that is, to help both partners with their childhood-based problems. The goal of therapy is to help fulfill this potential, that is, to transform the relationship into more of a curative agent.

Peg's problem is not her childhood-based special sensitivity. Everyone has childhood-based special sensitivities and usually of several sorts (although, of course, those of some clients are more extreme, as well as more intrinsically debilitating, than those of others). Peg's problem is that she does not have a way to talk with Mark about her childhood-based special sensitivity, or even to think clearly about it. (If it were a friend of hers who had such a sensitivity, Peg would have gone over and put her arms around her. Peg is unable to be such a friend to herself; she is unable to put her arms around herself.)

And *that* is the crucial childhood-based problem: Peg's sensitivity about her sensitivity, that is, her discomfort, self-consciousness, shame, self-hate, negative self-talk, anxiety, or sense of unentitlement to her sensitivity and her resulting inability to confide in Mark about it and to recruit him as a resource in dealing with it. She cannot say to Mark, "When you're quiet, I worry that you're silently angry at me the way my mother used to be."

Peg does what people do (and what Mark himself did throughout the evening) when they are unable to give adequate expression to their thoughts and feelings. She generates symptoms. She jumps to the conclusion that Mark is angry, and she condemns him for it.

PEG: Well, it would help if you didn't always have to get so angry at me.

MARK: I'm not angry. I already told you: I'm just frustrated.

PEG: Well, you *look* angry.

MARK: You always think I'm angry when I'm not.

PEG: You were angry when you came home.

MARK: No I wasn't.

PEG: Yes, you were.

Here is what happened. When Mark came home, he seemed a little quiet. Peg asked what was wrong. They got into a squabble—the kind that partners get into all the time. In fact, the whole interaction seems ordinary and unremarkable. Nothing much really happened. But, demonstrated here are three important ego-analytic ideas:

Idea 1. Leading-edge feelings. Everyone experiences a continuous series of leading-edge, uppermost, top-of-the-mind, major-and-immediate feelings. In this example, Mark felt left out (that was his first leading-edge feeling), which led to self-reproach for feeling left out (that was his second leading-edge feeling), and so on. Peg worried that Mark's silence meant that he was angry at her. That was one of her leading-edge feelings.

Idea 2. Generating symptoms. When people are unable to get across their leading-edge feelings, they generate symptoms. Mark's symptoms included withdrawal, cooking a less ambitious dinner than usual, and experiencing a sudden wish to be in the desert on a Harley. Peg's symptoms included jumping to the conclusion that Mark was angry at her and scolding him for it.

Idea 3. Sense of entitlement. The ultimate source of psychological problems, that is, the major reason that people are unable to get across their leading-edge feelings, is feeling unentitled to these feelings. Mark felt unentitled first to feeling left out, then to his self-reproach for feeling left out, and so on. He felt he should not be having these feelings. Peg felt unentitled to her fear that Mark's quietness meant that he was angry at her; she felt she was overreacting.

THE RESULTING CLINICAL APPROACH

These ideas lead to a couple therapy approach based on recognizing how feeling unentitled to feelings interferes with the partners' ability to get across these feelings, produces symptoms, and disrupts their ability to think, talk, and problem solve. The therapist's task, accordingly, is

1. To discover at any moment each partner's leading-edge feeling, that is, what each partner needs to get across to avoid generating symptoms.
2. To create a joint platform (a neutral, non-

accusing, nondefensive, vantage point) from which the partners can look at the situation that they are in and, in particular, how they feel unentitled to their feelings, are unable to get them across, and generate symptoms. These symptoms (e.g., feeling withdrawn or angry) then become the new feelings that they now need to get across.

Creating such a joint platform would mean, in the example of Peg and Mark, giving them the advantage of jointly being able to appreciate that:

- As a consequence of Mark's inability to get across his leading-edge feeling (e.g., "I feel left out and I feel I shouldn't feel left out"), he became symptomatic and, among other things, fell silent.
- As a consequence of Peg's inability to get across her leading-edge feeling ("When you're quiet the way you are right now, I worry that you're silently angry at me"), she became symptomatic: that is, she jumped to the conclusion that Mark was angry and criticized him for it.

Here, in paradigmatic form, is the ego-analytic approach to couple therapy. I now show what a couples therapy session looks like when conducted from such a perspective, that is, when attention is focused on (1) discovering the thoughts, feelings, and wishes that the partners are suffering from being unable to get across, and (2) creating a joint platform.

The day after the evening I just described, Peg and Mark come to see me for their weekly couple therapy session. It is their third session.

PEG: We had a horrible night last night.

MARK (*to Peg*): Well, it wouldn't have been so horrible if you hadn't gotten on my back.

THERAPIST (*to himself*): Peg is not going to like that "on my back" remark. If, as I suspect, she is unable to put into words (give adequate expression to) her hurt or anger about it (i.e., her leading-edge feeling), she is going to generate symptoms. She is going to call Mark names, withdraw, become confused, or something. Mark already is generating symptoms—that is what his "get off my back" remark is: a symptom. So he, too, needs help in getting across his leading-edge feeling. I could direct attention to what I think each partner needs to get across. I

could say, "That 'get off my back' remark is strong stuff, Mark; it's clear that you're distressed about what happened last night. And, Peg, since it *is* strong stuff, you're likely to be bridling under it." That might be all that is needed to slow the action and direct their attention to the respective leading-edge feelings they are suffering from being unable to get across. But the session is barely five seconds old. Instead of immediately jumping in, I'll wait to see what happens.

PEG: Well, that's all you gave me—your back. You turned your back to me—emotionally. You hardly said two words the whole evening.

THERAPIST (*to himself*): That was clever of Peg. She turned Mark's "get off my back" remark against him, which means that Mark probably now has a new and even more urgent leading-edge feeling to get across, something to the effect of: "I hate it when you take something I say, twist it, and use it against me; I feel totally foolish and feel like doing the same thing to you." If Mark is unable to say this—or to give adequate representation to his feelings in some way—he is going to generate symptoms: shrug disgustedly, withdraw, drop a verbal bomb.

MARK (*to Peg*): You know, you're getting to be more like your mother every day.

THERAPIST (*to himself*): Right! There's the bomb. Just last session Peg said that she hates it when Mark compares her to her mother. That Mark did it anyway means he clearly felt assaulted by what Peg just said. Let's see if I can say something about that. (*to Mark*): That was the bomb, Mark. As Peg said last week, she hates it when you compare her to her mother—it's like dropping the bomb on her. Of course, you might have needed to drop it. You might have felt really squelched by what Peg just said—seeing it as unfair and uncalled for.

In saying this, I am trying to accomplish both ego-analytic tasks:

Task 1. Pointing to what each partner needs to get across. I am trying to direct attention to—that is, get the partners interested in looking for—the leading-edge feeling that, because Mark was unable to get it across, led to his symptomatic reaction: his dropping the bomb. At the same time, I am trying to direct attention to the leading-edge feeling that Peg is likely to have as a consequence of Mark's dropping the bomb, which, if she is *unable* to get it across, will lead her to generate symptoms of her own.

Task 2. Creating a joint platform. I am trying to create a nonfighting vantage point from which Peg and Mark can look at their fighting. This joint platform would consist of a nonblaming view of how Peg understandably dislikes having the bomb dropped on her and how Mark understandably had the urge to drop it.

Here is how they respond:

MARK (*to Peg*): I didn't turn my back to you last night. (*to the therapist*): I hate it when she uses what I say against me.

PEG (*to Mark*): Well, I hate it when you accuse me of getting on your back.

MARK: Well, you *did* get on my back.

In response to my comment, Mark came closer to getting across what he needed to say. He shifted from his nonspecific, blunderbuss, dropping-the-bomb comment ("You're getting to be more like your mother every day") to discussing more directly what he was upset about: Peg's using his "get off my back" remark against him. And Peg came closer to what she needed to say ("I hate it when you accuse me of getting on your back"). My comment thus led Peg and Mark to approximate more closely the leading-edge feeling each needed to get across.

But Mark and Peg are clearly not on the joint platform. They have a shared vantage point: They are talking about the situation they were just in (i.e., Mark's accusing Peg of getting on his back and Peg's turning his accusation against him), but it is an *adversarial* rather than a nonadversarial shared vantage point and is thus not a joint platform.

They continue:

PEG (*to Mark*): I hate it when you say I'm getting to be like my mother.

MARK: Well, you *are*.

PEG: Well, if I'm getting to be like my mother, you're getting to be like your father—you're completely out to lunch, just like he always was. You haven't a clue about how to how to have a relationship with anyone.

I try to create a joint platform from which Peg and Mark can look at what is happening:

THERAPIST (*to both*): How much are you enjoying this chance to tell the other off, get a few things off your chest, and set the other person straight—and how much are you feeling frustrated and misunderstood and just wish you weren't in this dispute?

MARK: We're getting nowhere.

PEG (*to Mark*): It doesn't help, you know, that the first thing out of your mouth is how I was on your back last night.

MARK: Well, last night was pretty horrible.

PEG: That's what *I* just said.

THERAPIST (*to himself*): Last night appears to be the major locus of their symptom-generating for the week. (*to both*): Maybe we should talk about last night.

MARK: I think so.

PEG: It's a shame. Things had been going so well *until* last night.

THERAPIST (*to himself*): Right, Peg. Before we get into last night, let's establish how things had been going so we can put last night in context. (*to Mark*): Do you agree with Peg that things had been going well until last night?

MARK: For the most part.

PEG (*to Mark*): Only "for the most part"? I thought things were going *really* well.

MARK: They were going *pretty* well.

THERAPIST (*to himself*): Peg and Mark seem to have been having somewhat different weeks together. (*to Peg*): Peg, what made it a week that went "really well"? (*to Mark*): And, Mark, what made it a week that went "just pretty well"?

PEG: I don't know. I felt close—you know, Mark, me, and the baby—we're a family.

MARK: That's what I was thinking, too: We're a family, except I was thinking about the money problems *because* we're a family—and the *responsibilities*, and the *complications*.

THERAPIST (*to himself*): What does Mark mean by "complications"? Does Peg know what he means by it?

PEG: Yes, well, there are those things, too. I guess I see the glass as half-full and you see it as half-empty.

THERAPIST (*to himself*): Mark is not going to like being told he sees the glass as half-empty—meaning that he looks only on the negative side of things. He's probably going to have to sit there and take it, though, since "You see the glass as half-empty" is practically unanswerable. As soon as someone says that, everyone immediately thinks it's true about the person—being accused is being convicted. And since Mark isn't going to have an answer, he's going to generate symptoms. So,

I'd better prepare for symptoms. He's probably going to shrug, look glum, shift a couple of inches further away from Peg, become a couple of degrees more discouraged, and perhaps think again about reducing these sessions to every other week.

MARK: I don't know. Maybe I'm just seeing the glass as too big for the water that's in it.

THERAPIST (*to himself*): Wow! What a surprise! Mark thought of an answer—and such a clever one. It's the first time I've heard anyone come up with any kind of answer at all to the charge, "You see the glass as half-empty."

How did Mark come up with that answer? Well, it took several steps:

Mark reacted to Peg's "You see the glass as half-empty" with a tenth-of-a-second crestfallen state in which he felt unappreciated and misjudged.

Which led to the "Who-needs-this?" tenth-of-a-second mental divorce state in which, for that moment, he was ready to give up the whole relationship and ride off into the desert on that Harley. "I could tell her that, as far as I'm concerned, the glass is broken."

Which gave him enough pleasure and relief to inspire him to try to come up with something that he would still enjoy saying but that would be less provocative. "What I really want to tell her is that I'm being realistic and she's being a Pollyanna."

That is the chain of thoughts that led to Mark's statement, "Maybe I'm just seeing the glass as too big for the water that's in it."

Although Mark's response is clever, it is still a symptom—a *successful* one. It is a symptom because Mark is not getting across his leading-edge feeling, which is that Peg's comment about seeing the glass as half-empty bothers him—he feels reproached. Instead, he is acting as if it does not bother him. It is a *successful* symptom in that it

Enables Mark to make an active response—to be masterful.

Provides him with an alternative to having to sit there and take it.

Enables him to avoid less desirable symptoms, such as feeling glum, becoming a couple of degrees more discouraged, and threatening divorce.

Provides him with a sense of relief and enjoyment.

Shifts Peg and him into a collaborative state.

Peg enjoys this expression of Mark's wit. She laughs. Mark enjoys Peg's enjoyment. *He* laughs.

THERAPIST (*joining Peg and Mark in admiring Mark's wit*): That's clever.

PEG: He's always doing that.

THERAPIST: He's always . . . ?

PEG: You know, making witty comments.

THERAPIST: Do you like his doing it?

PEG: Not always. Sometimes he'll make a joke in the middle of a conversation—and it disrupts the whole train of thought. I don't like that. But when he does it right in the middle of a fight, sometimes I just have to laugh—which, of course, immediately ends the fight. And I do *like* it then. What he said just now was one of his best.

MARK: It *was* pretty good, wasn't it?

THERAPIST (*to Mark*): How much was it just a joke and how much do you feel that the glass *is* too big for the water you've got?

MARK: It was really just a joke—but, if I think about it, it *is* sort of true: The family *is* too big for the money we've got. *Any* family is too big for the money we've got.

THERAPIST (*to himself*): Here's a good place to ask Mark what he meant earlier about the "complications" of a family. (*to Mark*): Yes, you talked earlier about the "money problems" in having a family—and also about the "responsibilities" and "complications." What *are* the "complications"?

MARK: Well, since Joey came along, Peg and I hardly have a moment for one another.

PEG: All we can do these days is wave in passing.

Mark has just taken the first step toward realizing and saying that he feels Peg does not have enough time for *him*, that is, that she seems to him totally wrapped up in the baby and, as a result, he feels left out. Mark is circling in on this crucial leading-edge feeling from last night.

I do not know this, however.

THERAPIST (*to himself*): I don't see where this is going. Sure, Peg and Mark are busy, but almost every couple tells me they're busy. So now might be a good time to get us back to what happened last night.

I did not realize that, in an important way, Mark had already gotten us back to that—or, at least, to an important issue underlying what happened last night.

THERAPIST (*to both*): Okay, so there you are. You're having these different weeks together.

Peg, you're feeling close—feeling that the three of you are a family; you're seeing the glass as half-full. Mark, you're worried about the complications—particularly, those of having no time for one another; you're seeing the glass as half-empty or, as you just said, "as too big for the water that's in it." And then, last night, something happened. What was it?

PEG (*to the therapist*): Mark started yelling at me.

MARK (*to Peg*): I didn't yell.

PEG: Okay, you raised your voice.

MARK: I was just being emphatic. Anyway, the argument started way before that.

PEG: I don't remember how it started.

MARK: I don't either, but I know it was before I began yelling—I mean, before I got emphatic.

PEG: I don't even remember what the fight was about.

MARK: Me either.

PEG: It was really upsetting at the time, but now I can't remember anything about it.

MARK: It's a blur.

Here I am faced with the situation—familiar to couple therapists—in which partners tell you that something important happened but they cannot remember much about it.

THERAPIST: Is there some part about it you can remember?

PEG: Wait a minute! I know. It all started when Mark came home from work angry.

MARK: I didn't come home angry.

PEG: Yes, you did.

This is the situation—also familiar to couple therapists—in which the partners disagree on the facts of the matter.

THERAPIST: Well, let's get each of your versions. In fact, let's go back to earlier in the day and see if we can figure out what might have led up to the fight. How were you feeling about one another that *morning?*

PEG: I didn't even *see* Mark that morning. I got up really early to take the baby to Mark's mother's—she's our sitter.

MARK: We didn't have any contact until that evening. In fact, I got home even later than usual because I stopped to pick up dinner.

THERAPIST: Okay, Mark, there you were, coming up the walk, dinner in hand. What were you feel—?

MARK (*interrupting*): We don't have a walk. We live in an apartment. I was coming up the stairs.

THERAPIST: Okay, so you were coming up the stairs. How were you feeling about Peg?

MARK: I don't remember.

THERAPIST: How did you think things would go that evening between you and Peg?

MARK: I wasn't thinking about it one way or another.

Earlier in my career, I might have concluded that Mark was being "resistant." And I might have been right, although, as I now see it, putting it this way fails to emphasize what is most crucial. If Mark feels uncertain or suspicious about where my questions are leading, if he feels bombarded by them, or if he feels I might be taking Peg's side, and if he does not have a way to talk with me about these feelings, he could easily and *understandably* become symptomatic and resist.

As this reasoning suggests, my theory of resistance and defensiveness is influenced by my people-become-symptomatic-if-they-are-unable-to-get-across-their-leading-edge-feeling principle. As I see it, "resistance" and "defensiveness"—by which therapists typically mean subtle, unconscious, or indirect forms of resistance and defensiveness—are consequences of the client's inability to discuss his/her apprehensions, reservations, and objections in straightforward ways. They are the result of the client's sense of unentitlement to his/her resistance and defensiveness. If Mark cannot say, for example, "I feel that you're siding with Peg and trying to prove that I came home grumpy," he might have no choice but to act upon his suspicion and resist.

Also, these days I make sure that any conclusion I might arrive at that a client is being defensive or resistant is not a consequence of becoming symptomatic myself, that is, of my own inability to get across leading-edge feelings. For example, if I do not have a way to think through—to get across to myself—how I feel blocked by Mark's responses, I am likely to make the logical error of inferring intention from effect and jump to the conclusion that he is being purposefully obstructionistic.

As this reasoning suggests, my view of countertransference is influenced by my people-become-symptomatic-if-they-are-unable-to-get-across-their-leading-edge-feeling principle. My therapeutic judgment can become impaired if I am unable to think through (i.e., get across to myself) my leading-edge feelings.

THERAPIST (*to himself*): Although Mark might be being obstructionistic, I'll look first to see if there is a simpler explanation. (*to Mark*): Okay, Mark, so you're coming up the stairs, but you don't remember exactly what you were feeling. Peg, where were you at the time? What were you doing?

PEG: I was straightening things up in the living room.

MARK: You were in the baby's room.

PEG: Oh yes, that's right.

Of course, Mark would remember Peg's being in the baby's room when he first came home, since from his point of view, that is when and where the crucial event of the evening took place: Mark's seeing Peg attending to the baby and his feeling left out. If I had an inkling of this, I would have directed my next question to him rather than to Peg.

THERAPIST (*to Peg*): Do you remember what you were feeling about Mark?

PEG: I wasn't feeling anything about him at all. I was worried about Joey—his forehead was hot.

THERAPIST (*to Peg*): Okay, so you—

PEG (*to Mark*): I know we need the money, but maybe it was a mistake for me to go back to work so soon. If Joey gets sick, I ought to be home with him.

THERAPIST (*to Peg*): Okay, so you—

PEG: And then Mark came home grouchy.

MARK: I wasn't grouchy. I was feeling good. My boss had just complimented me for doing the best job of framing he'd seen in years.

PEG: You didn't tell me that.

MARK: I was *going* to tell you.

THERAPIST (*to himself*): Now, that's interesting. If Mark *was* going to tell Peg about his success but didn't, something must have happened to change his mind, and whatever it was might have something to do with how they got into the fight. (*to Mark*): What happened that changed your mind about telling her?

MARK: Well, she seemed so caught up in the baby, I didn't think she'd be interested.

PEG (*breaking in*): I already told you. Joey's forehead was hot. I was worried that he had a fever.

THERAPIST (*to himself*): Peg is defending herself, which means that she feels reproached. Mark's comment didn't seem reproachful to me, but Peg might be on to something. Clients are often better than I am at picking up how their partner is reacting.

MARK: You're *always* fussing over Joey about something.

THERAPIST (*to himself*): Even if Mark wasn't accusing Peg before, he is now.

In saying "Peg seemed so involved in Joey, I didn't think she'd be interested in hearing about my success," Mark is saying, in essence, that he just figured out why he did not tell her about his success. But Mark is also making a complaint. He is saying that it is her fault that he did not tell her about his success; she was too caught up in Joey.

All Peg hears, of course, is the complaint. So she defends herself. She says, "I already told you: Joey's forehead was hot; I was worried that he had a fever." Feeling frustrated by Peg's response —she is justifying what she had done rather than listening to what he is trying to say—Mark attacks. He says, "You're *always* fussing over Joey about something," to which Peg now snaps back:

PEG: He's your son, too. He had a fever. *You* should have been worried.

THERAPIST (*to himself*): Let's see if I can help Peg state her leading-edge feeling. (*to Peg*): That's strong stuff, Peg—telling Mark that he's not concerned about Joey. How much are you saying that to deal with his criticizing you for being *over*concerned and how much do you really mean it—and that it's something you might want us to talk about?"

PEG (*more calmly*): Well, I don't like his criticizing me.

THERAPIST (*to himself*): I take that to mean that Peg didn't mean it.

MARK (*to Peg*): I don't like *your* criticizing *me*, either.

THERAPIST (*to himself*): Let's see if I can help them pick out their leading-edge feelings. (*to both*): Let's look at this criticizing. It began when you, Mark, said that Peg seemed so caught up in Joey that you didn't think she'd be interested in hearing about your success that day. When Mark said that, Peg, what did you feel? Angry? Hurt? What?

PEG: If Mark was going to tell me about what his boss said, I ought to have been paying more attention. I felt really bad that I wasn't.

THERAPIST (*to himself*): So *that's* what lay behind Peg's criticizing Mark: *self*-criticism. (*to Peg*): Oh, so you blamed *yourself*.

PEG: I *always* blame myself. Right now I'm blaming myself for leaving Mark out. Last night I blamed myself for getting upset when Mark left *me* out. It's ridiculous!

MARK: Yes, well, I blamed myself, too. I felt I shouldn't be jealous of my own kid.

Feeling ashamed of how upset she was about Mark's quietness last night (since she saw her upset as a sign of weakness), Peg had been trying not to think about it. The nonaccusing way in which I said "Oh, so you blamed *yourself*" enabled her to feel that it wasn't such a terrible thing to be self-blaming. That is all she needed to enable her to say "I *always* blame myself."

Feeling humiliated by his jealousy, Mark had been trying to conceal it. But now, suddenly, he is talking about it easily as if it were no big deal. Peg's "I always blame myself" has for the moment changed *Mark's* whole way of thinking. For this moment, it feels safe—even meritorious—to admit self-blame. Peg's "I always blame myself," followed by Mark's "Yes, well, I blamed myself, too" is, in fact, a 3-second competitive exchange over who is the more clearly self-blaming.

Earlier, I distinguished between the obvious and the hidden problem and described how ego analysis focuses on the hidden problem. The obvious problem here is Peg's fear of abandonment and Mark's jealousy of his son. Most people would immediately view such feelings as the heart of matter. It is easy to miss, despite being right in front of our eyes, the *real* heart of the matter: Peg's *self-blame* for her fear of abandonment and Mark's *self-blame* for his jealousy of his son. This is the hidden problem that, according to ego-analytic thinking, is the heart of the matter: self-blame—the person's feeling that he/she shouldn't be having the obvious problem. Peg's belief that she shouldn't mind Mark's being quiet, and Mark's belief that he shouldn't be jealous of his son, led them to try to fight off these feelings rather than confide in one another about them.

Without such confiding, Peg and Mark's evening became one of guardedness and brittleness—the kind of low-grade alienation and quarreling that is so much a part of everyday couple life that it generally escapes our notice. It is hidden because it is so taken for granted. My point in detailing Peg and Mark's evening was to reveal this low-grade alienation and quarreling. I did this by demonstrating what it would be like—how dramatically the evening would change—were Peg and Mark to confide in one another. What immediately became clear is that, at any given moment, Peg and Mark—and by extension all of us—are in need of (i.e., are lacking) a conversation.

The therapeutic task is to give partners a taste of this conversation. For a brief moment, now that I have helped Peg and Mark discover the conversation they needed to have, their alienated and adversarial tone is replaced by one of collaboration and intimacy.

THERAPIST (*to himself*): Okay, that sounds like the key to understanding last night. Peg and Mark were having these soft-underbelly feelings that they were unable to express. They're talking about them now—I can feel a collaborative spirit beginning—but I don't think it's going to last. In a moment, they're probably going to go back to arguing. So I'll tag what has just happened. (*to both*): Did both of you hear what I just heard? While each of you was blaming the other, privately each of you was blaming yourself.

The session had taken a positive turn. We had discovered the *obvious problem* of Peg's fear of abandonment and Mark's jealousy of his son, as well as the *hidden problem* of their self-blame for having these reactions. Peg and Mark's confiding in each other about these things had produced the beginnings of a collaborative spirit. But immediately they said:

PEG: Yes, but what do we do about it?
MARK: How do we change?

These questions told me that Peg and Mark were *not* on the joint platform. They were *not* looking self-sympathetically and non-self-blamingly at their reactions: Peg at her fear of abandonment, Mark at his jealousy toward his son, and both at their self-blame. Instead, they were caught up in the self-blame (as revealed in the need to find an immediate solution). They were acting on it rather than looking at it. The self-blame had again become hidden.

THERAPIST (*to himself*): We've only barely begun to talk about the problem and Peg and Mark are already impatiently looking for a solution and are discouraged about ever finding one. And *of course* they are. That's the intolerance they feel about having the problem.

The urgency of Peg's "Yes, but what do we do about it?" and Mark's "How do we change?" indicate their self-blame for having the reactions they are having and being the way they are. Their questions demonstrate their inability to inhabit or "have" the problem and, instead, their need to eliminate it right away.

THERAPIST: And what you want to change is . . . ?

PEG: There's something wrong with a person who gets rattled when her husband becomes a little quiet.

MARK: And with a husband who gets jealous of someone who barely knows how to crawl.

THERAPIST: So, the main thing at the moment is that each of you feels *self-critical.*

PEG: Of course! How can I be a good mother when I can't stop acting like a child myself?

MARK (*to the therapist*): You can't be saying that it's *normal* for a father to be jealous of his son?

THERAPIST: Okay, so the two of you are telling me that it's *not* that you're self-critical, but rather that you *deserve* criticism. You have these faults. You feel you *should* be self-critical.

MARK (*to the therapist*): What other way is there to see it?

PEG: I've got to stop acting like a 2-year old.

THERAPIST (*to himself*): Mark means, of course, that "There *isn't* any other way to see it." His question is rhetorical; he doesn't really expect an answer. So he and Peg are going to be surprised that I can come up with one. (*to both*): You could see it as. . . . Well, let's say that it wasn't you but instead those friends of yours—Marie and Carlos—who had the night you just described. And they tell you about it. Carlos says, "Things were awful last night. I felt so ashamed of being jealous of my son that I couldn't tell Marie anything about it; I just got quiet." Marie says, "And I can't stand how upset I got when he *became* quiet. What kind of mother can I be if I act like a kid myself?" If Marie and Carlos were to say this to you, how would you feel? What would you say?

PEG: I wouldn't say anything. I'd go over and give them each a big hug.

MARK: You wouldn't be able to—there wouldn't be room—because I'd be there already with my arms around them.

THERAPIST: And, as you were hugging them, you'd be thinking . . . what? That there's something wrong with them? That they're not normal? That they're acting like 2-year olds?

PEG: I'd just be feeling bad for them.

MARK: Somehow it's different when it's someone else.

THERAPIST: So the problem, then, is that there's no one around to throw their arms around *you* and to feel bad for *you.*

My goal in picturing *friends* of Peg and Mark having the difficult evening is to reveal the hidden problem of self-blame and to create a joint platform—a nonaccusing vantage point—from which Peg and Mark can sympathize with each other about this self-blame.

PEG (*to the therapist*): I see what you're saying. You're telling us that we should nicer to *ourselves.*

MARK: Well, we *should* be nicer to ourselves—a whole lot nicer. But I don't see how we're going to do it. We certainly didn't do it last night.

PEG: I don't see how we ever could.

The self-blame has taken a new form. Peg and Mark are blaming themselves for not being nicer to themselves.

THERAPIST: Okay, so you see me as telling you that you should be nicer to yourselves.

PEG: Aren't you?

THERAPIST: Well, what I'd *like* to tell you is how *hard* it is to be nice to yourself about something that you feel as bad about as you, Mark, feel about being jealous of your son and as you, Peg, feel about your sensitivity to Mark's silences.

I am trying to create a non-self-blaming, not-anxiously-having-to-change-it-right-away vantage point—a joint platform—from which Peg and Mark can look at their self-blame.

An effect of Peg and Mark's self-blame is to impair the problem-solving capacity of the relationship. Peg's problem is *not* fear of abandonment, but how she abandons herself when she has such a fear. Her self-blame for feeling abandoned (i.e., her sense of unentitlement to her sensitivity to abandonment) prevents her from thinking constructively about the problem and from appealing to Mark as a resource in dealing with it. There wouldn't even be a problem were Peg able to tell Mark: "I'm getting the panicky feeling I always get when you're quiet, and I hate myself for overreacting and behaving like such a child."

Similarly, Mark's problem is his sense of unentitlement to his experience of feeling jealous of his son and his resulting inability to confide in Peg about it. There wouldn't even be a problem were Mark able to tell Peg: "I'm so ashamed about feeling jealous of Joey that I can hardly bring myself to tell you about it."

Ego-analytic couple therapy is devoted to look-

ing at how, at any given moment, partners abandon themselves in dealing with their problems.
They lose track of (they reject) their leading-edge
feelings, making it impossible to think through
or confide in one another about them.

As a result of this session, we have made a first
step toward uncovering the hidden problem of
self-blame. And we now have a slogan for picturing the non-self-blaming, non-self-abandoning
alternative. At any moment that Peg and Mark
become self-blaming, I can tell them: "This
sounds like one of those times when there isn't
anybody to throw their arms around you and feel
bad for you." I now have this probe light for revealing the hidden problem of self-blame. My
goal is to create a joint platform—a non-self-
blaming vantage point—from which, among
other things, Peg and Mark can observe their
self-blame.

Insight in therapy, that is, the use of interpretation, has been criticized in some quarters as ineffectual. Many interpretations are ineffectual
because they focus on the obvious problem and
neglect the hidden one. A typical interpretation
would be to trace Peg's sensitivity to abandonment to traumatic losses in childhood, or Mark's
jealousy of his son to sibling rivalry in *his* childhood. The danger is that such insight might simply confirm in Peg and Mark's minds that
something is wrong with them, that is, that their
reactions—Peg's fear of abandonment and Mark's
jealousy of his son—are inappropriate, pathological, and childish. Such interpretations would
stamp in the self-blame rather than reveal it.

My purpose in describing these sessions with
Peg and Mark is to demonstrate the following
points about ego-analytic couple therapy:

1. These two ego-analytic principles—leading-
edge feelings and the joint platform—are embedded in practically everything I do. At any given
moment, I am trying to discover what feelings
partners suffer from being unable to get across
and give them a joint platform from which to
look at their situation. My view of symptom formation, resistance, countertransference, childhood etiology, the purpose of relationships, the
purpose of therapy, and a great many other
things, is based on these two principles.

2. Behavior is interrelated. The behavior of
one partner, if unable to get across what he/she
needs to, typically elicits symptomatic behavior
from the other.

3. The goal of ego-analytic therapy is to increase the partners' *own* abilities to track leading-
edge feelings and to create a joint platform.

4. Effectively tracking leading-edge feelings
means not letting the obvious problem completely block out the hidden problem, which is the
person's intolerance of the obvious problem. It
means appreciating how quickly a leading-edge
feeling, such as jealousy or fear of abandonment
(the obvious problem), leads to self-reproach for
having this feeling (the hidden problem). It
means appreciating how life is, in large part, the
relationship that we have with ourselves *about*
our feelings.

5. The methods I use to track partners'
leading-edge feelings and create a joint platform
include interviewing the partners, setting the
scene, and creating a nonhostile environment
that makes it possible for them to discover what
they feel. Other methods, demonstrated elsewhere (Wile, 1981, 1988, 1993), include suggesting to partners what these feelings might be;
restating what they have just said in a neutral,
nonaccusing, nondefensive way; and making up
the conversations they might have were they already on the joint platform.

A question I am often asked by people is "After you help partners discover their leading-edge
feelings, and after you help them create joint
platforms, what do you do then?" What these
people mean is, "All this sounds nice—you are
clearly taking an important first step—but when
and how is the real therapy going to take place?
How is the real change to occur?"

When people ask this, I know that I have not
made clear how powerful are getting across
leading-edge feelings and operating from a joint
platform. Your entire outlook changes. Your partner looks different to you. Your relationship looks
different to you. *You* look different to you.

In many cases, creating a joint platform and
getting across leading-edge feelings are the solution to the problem. They are *not* the solution
to the problem, of course, if, for example, the
problem is that one partner really wants to have
a baby and the other really does not. They *are*
the solution to the extent that the problem is
how the partners talk (or are unable to talk) about
their conflict over whether to have a baby.

The vignette I just described is an example of
an early couple therapy session. As I said, it was
Peg and Mark's third session. What do I do,
however, in a later session—a 10th, 20th, or final session? The same thing I did in this one.
I use whatever the partners report from the
week—and whatever happens in the session—to
reveal leading-edge feelings and to create a joint
platform. Each session is the next lesson in ap-

plying these two ego-analytic principles. The goal is to make these principles increasingly a part of the couple's everyday thinking.

Where do these two principles come from? They emerge from a more general principle—the sense of entitlement to feelings—which is the core idea of ego-analytic thinking.

> At the root of Mark's problem last night was his feeling unentitled to feeling left out, feeling unentitled to his self-reproach for feeling left out, and so on.
>
> At the root of Peg's problem was feeling unentitled to her fear that Mark's silence meant that he was angry at her. If Peg were to feel entitled to this fear, she would be able to think about it, take it into account, plan for it, sympathize with herself for having it, confide in Mark about it, and appeal to him as a resource in dealing with it, rather than simply feel flooded by it.

Here is *how* the two ego-analytic principles that I have emphasized in this chapter—the need-to-get-something-across and the joint platform—emerge from this more general principle (the sense of entitlement to feelings):

> *The need-to-get-something-across principle.* People are unable to get across their leading-edge feelings and, as a result, generate symptoms primarily *because they feel unentitled to these feelings.*
>
> *The joint-platform principle.* Since we are inevitably going to feel unentitled to certain feelings, be unable to get them across, and generate symptoms, we need a way to deal with the problem. And the way to deal with such a we're-inevitably-going-to-fall-prey-to-it problem is to create a platform—and with our partner a joint platform—from which to monitor it.

In other words, our inability to get across our leading-edge feelings is the main problem produced by feeling unentitled to our feelings; creating a platform or a joint platform is our main way to deal with this problem. Creating a joint platform is the solution because the lack of a joint platform, that is, the lack of an ability to recruit our partners as resources in dealing with our problems with them, *is* the problem.

Implicit in the idea of the joint platform are the two other ego-analytic principles that I described at the beginning of this chapter: the hidden-validity and the joint-victims prin-

ciples. Both of these principles also emerge from the idea of a sense of entitlement to feelings.

In the hidden-validity principle, the therapist focuses on what is valid rather than on what is invalid in clients' reactions:

> When Mark reported feeling jealous of Joey, I focused on how he was reacting to a common or universal couple problem (fathers of newborns typically do feel left out) and how it was not just a matter of his distorting the present in terms of the past (displacing his jealousy toward his brother on Joey) or of his being characterologically prone to jealousy.
>
> When Peg became upset at Mark's silence, I focused on the ways her reaction was valid rather than on the ways in which it was invalid: that is, I focused on how, by his silence, Mark, in a subtle way, was abandoning her rather than on how her reaction might simply (or not at all) be a displacement of her experience long ago with her punishing mother.

I focus on what is valid rather than on what is invalid in their responses, first, to even the balance, because Peg and Mark *themselves* focus on what is invalid in their responses. My goal is not simply to reassure Peg and Mark and to make them feel better; it is much more to enable them to think and talk about the issue:

> If Mark is going to be able to think and talk about his jealousy of Joey, that is, if he is going to be able to establish a joint platform with Peg from which to talk about it, he needs to feel that his reaction is not as totally invalid, irrational, and unacceptable as he presently thinks it is.
>
> If Peg is going to be able to think and talk about her sensitivity to Mark's silence, that is, if she is going to be able to establish a joint platform with Mark from which to talk about it, she needs to feel that her sensitivity is not as totally invalid, irrational, and unacceptable as she presently thinks.

So one reason I focus on what is valid rather than invalid in clients' responses is to dig them out of their self-accusing, reflexively-accusing-their-partners, anxious, withdrawn, or defensive positions that make it impossible for them to think. Another reason is to help them *recognize* that they are invalidating their responses, and that this is the heart of the problem. By demonstrating how it would improve the situation (and might even solve the problem) if Mark were to confide in Peg that he felt left out, and if she were to confide in him that she is sensitive to his silences, I show them that the problem is their inability to confide in one another in this way. Or, to be more exact, the problem is that their sense of unentitlement to their feelings (i.e., their invalidating of their responses) prevents such confiding.

In adopting the fourth ego-analytic principle—the joint-victims principle—I take the position that partners are joint victims of the relationship. In so doing, I take issue with the modern pop-psychology view (based on Freud's principle of unconscious determinism) that

We design our destinies.

Whatever happens is what unconsciously we want to happen.

There are no accidents.

There are no victims (e.g., "Why would you rent a ground-floor apartment if you didn't want it to be broken into and yourself raped?")

According to this pop-psychology view, people are too quick to deny responsibility for what happens to them, to feel powerless over their lives, and to see themselves as victims. According to ego-analytic thinking, people are too quick to do the opposite—to accept responsibility for everything that happens to them and, in particular, to blame themselves for their problems. (Weighed down by all of this, they then may put the blame on others.) People criticize themselves, among other things, for being self-indulgent, behaving like spoiled children, wallowing in self-pity, being unwilling to grow up and accept the responsibilities of an adult, and getting too much gratification from their symptomatic behavior to be willing to give it up.

A major purpose of the victims principle is to remind the therapist that people in a troubled relationship are deprived rather than gratified. I describe elsewhere (Wile, 1981) how ego analysis rejects the traditional image of partners as gratifying regressive impulses and seeking exploitive control and views them as deprived of the minimal satisfaction and control necessary to make a relationship livable.

Viewed from a traditional perspective, Mark might be seen as seeking the regressive narcissistic gratification of claiming Peg's full attention, that is, being another child she has to take care of. My objection to this formulation is that it causes the therapist to miss that the crucial factor is Mark's *self-reproach* for these very thing—for

seeking what *he* feels to be the regressive narcissistic gratification of claiming Peg's full attention, that is, acting like another child she has to take care of.

Because of his self-reproach, Mark is unable to tell Peg about his feelings. He is unable to get the relief, satisfaction, and sense of resolution that might come from being able to confide in Peg about his feelings (and about his self-reproach about having these feelings). And now we see the manner in which, and the mechanism by which, Mark is being deprived: His inability to formulate his leading-edge feelings keeps him getting his wishes stated, or met—or even knowing what they are. As a result, he lacks the control in the relationship that anyone would need to make it livable.

Many therapists hesitate to think of clients as victims. For example, clients who as children were sexually abused by a parent are thought of as "incest survivors" rather than as "incest victims." Therapists are concerned about their clients' developing a "victim mentality," by which they mean a sense of hopelessness, helplessness, passivity, resignation, "It's ultimately my own fault," "I deserve what I get."

I am concerned about this danger, also. But I do not believe that avoiding the word "victim" protects against it. On the contrary, taking a stand *against* clients' seeing themselves as victims and *against* their victim mentality may feed into their self-reproach. There is a one-two punch here. The first punch is clients having to suffer the effects of being a victim. The second punch is reproaching themselves for having a victim mentality, that is, for any tendency they have to feel helpless, hopeless, passive, resigned, and so on. Such self-reproach is a major barrier to clients being able to sympathize with themselves for being victims.

The purpose of the victims principle is thus threefold. It is to help the therapist realize (or remember) that clients suffer:

1. The self-responsibility ethic, that is, their tendency to blame themselves for their problems ("It's my own fault; I'm doing it to myself").

2. Failure to appreciate that they are victims, that is, that they are deprived, stuck, trapped, and lack adequate control in the situation.

3. Self-blame for having a victim mentality, that is, for reacting in what they themselves feel to be too passive, helpless, and self-reproachful a way.

I said that I chose the unfashionable and jarring term "*victim* principle" to distinguish it from "everything-serves-a-purpose, you-must-have-wanted-it-that-way" thinking and the self-responsibility ethic, both of which reject the idea that people are victims. A *further* reason is to emphasize that part of the problem is clients' own inability to sympathize with themselves for being victims and their tendency to reproach themselves for having a victim mentality.

When I say that partners are joint victims, do I mean to say that the physically abusing husband is a victim? Yes! As is well known, many physically abusing partners were themselves physically abused as children. As is also well known, the typical abusing or battering husband is an extreme example of a person who is aggressive because he cannot be assertive: that is, he is a person who has difficulty holding up his end in an argument. He strikes out physically when he feel helpless in the face of his wife's verbal attack, real or imagined.

But although I see the battering husband himself as a victim (of his attack against himself and of this whole pattern), I must state two important qualifications.

The first is that until the abuse has stopped, there is no way to *care* whether the husband himself is a victim. Our first priority has to be to the wife's safety and to her feelings—how she feels terrorized, how she blames herself, how the abuse undermines her self-confidence. Unless the therapist attends to these feelings, this woman might be unable to extricate herself from the abusive situation; attending to her feelings might enable her to free herself.

The second qualification arises from the confusion between understanding and excusing. Or, to put it another way, at issue here are two meanings of the word, "understanding." The wife's and therapist's *understanding* that the physically abusing husband is himself a victim (i.e., is caught up in a cycle of feeling helpless and lashing out) does not mean that she and the therapist have to be *understanding* in the sense of excusing, forgiving, accepting, or tolerating the abuse.

Unfortunately, a battered wife often does confuse understanding with excusing. She confuses the two when she says to herself, "Poor guy, he can't help himself, so I don't have the right to leave him." She thinks she has to excuse him, feel forgiving, or tolerate his behavior. She would *not* confuse understanding with excusing were she to say to herself, "Poor guy, he can't help himself, but I don't care: I hate him" or "Poor guy,

he can't help himself, but I can help *myself*; I'm leaving."

To summarize all four ego-analytic principles, as a result of feeling unentitled to their feelings, clients

1. Discount, disqualify, dismiss, discredit, impugn, or invalidate their feelings, which I deal with therapeutically by validating their reactions (the hidden-validity principle). My purpose is to reveal that the problem is their *invalidation* of their reactions and, beyond that, their sense of unentitlement to their feelings.
2. Are unable to get their feelings across, which I deal with therapeutically by trying to figure out at any given moment in a therapy session what the client needs to get across to avoid generating symptoms (the need-to-get-something-across principle).
3. Conclude that their problems are their own fault ("I'm doing it to myself"), which I deal with therapeutically by recognizing how clients are stuck, trapped, and deprived, that is, how they are victims (the victims principle).
4. Are unable to establish a platform (a neutral, objective, non-blame-oriented, nondefensive, nonanxious vantage point) from which to monitor their feelings and problems, which I deal with therapeutically by trying to create such a platform (the platform principle).

A platform is needed because the root problem—feeling unentitled to feelings—is unsolvable, and creating a platform is the premier way to deal with unsolvable problems.

The ultimate goal of ego-analytic therapy is to create this nonanxious, able-to-"have"-the-problem, not-having-to-solve-the-problem-right-away vantage point, from which clients can look at this root problem of feeling unentitled to their feelings.

Having an ego-analytic orientation means approaching clients with these four ego-analytic principles in mind (along with the supraordinate principle: sense of entitlement to feelings).

PERSONAL QUALITIES OF THE THERAPIST

Some therapists develop their own informal version of ego-analytic therapy: that is, they adopt elements of or tendencies toward ego-analytic thinking, despite the fact that (1) they have not heard of ego analysis and (2) the theory to which they officially subscribe is not compatible with ego-analytic thinking. They develop their own informal version of ego-analytic therapy much as mothers in the 1930s developed their own informal version of demand feeding while officially subscribing to the infant-feeding philosophy of the day: schedule feeding.[2]

Just as these mothers instinctively felt that a rigid schedule feeding did not make sense and was not good for their babies, so these therapists instinctively feel that many of the interventions prescribed by their official theory do not make sense and are not good for their clients—interventions such as confronting clients with their dependency, need to control the hour, unconscious wish to keep symptoms, fear of intimacy, defensiveness, or narcissistic demandingness. These therapists intuitively feel that such interpretations are pejorative and countertherapeutic. Or, they believe that such formulations, although valid about people in general, somehow never seem to apply to the particular client that they have in front of them at the moment.

Conversely, there are therapists who know about ego-analytic therapy, subscribe to it, and believe they are doing it, but who, in part because of their character tendencies or personal philosophy, instinctively adopt a *non*-ego-analytic stance and, for example, view clients as dependent, as exploitatively seeking to control the hour, as unconsciously wishing to keep their symptoms, and so on.

The ego-analytic perspective is difficult to maintain even for therapists whose character tendencies and personal philosophy *are* consistent with it. The difficulty is, in part, the pressure under which all therapists operate. For example, we feel responsible to help the client but, with some clients, we feel powerless to do so. As a result, we become symptomatic: that is, we become symptomatic if we are unable to recruit ourselves as resources in dealing with these feelings of responsibility and powerlessness.

For an ego-analytic therapist, "becoming symptomatic" means, among other things, losing the ego-analytic perspective. It means

Forgetting that the source of the problem is the client's sense of unentitlement to his/her feelings, inability to get across leading-edge feelings, lack of a platform, and tendency to invalidate his/her own reactions—and, instead, focusing on how the client is immature, irrational, or pathological.

Forgetting that the client is a victim—that he/she is stuck, trapped, and deprived—and, instead, seeing the client as getting too much from his/her symptoms to be willing to give them up.

MORE ABOUT THE JOINT PLATFORM

Partners frequently say about couple therapy: "It's a safe place to talk about our problems"; "It's only here that we can really talk"; "We can talk here without things immediately escalating." Couple therapy is an experiment to see whether, in the presence and with the help of a third party (the therapist), the partners will be able to talk in a better way than they can at home. Partners remain interested in coming to couple therapy only to the extent that it provides such a safe place in which to talk.

Ego analysis makes this familiar theme of safety the core of an entire therapeutic approach. As I just described

The goal in *any given session* is to provide partners with a joint platform or safe setting in which to talk.

The goal for the *therapy* is to enable partners to create *for themselves* a joint platform or safe setting.

My goal for Peg and Mark is to enable them to create for themselves a safe setting in which to talk, among other things, about how Mark falls quiet when he gets self-critical about feeling left out and how Peg responds by accusing him of being angry at her.

To the extent that Peg and Mark are able to create such a safe setting or joint platform, they will have established a *new* relationship—a relationship about their relationship—based on the following:

Being able to recruit each other as resources and confidants in dealing with this problem that they have with each other.

Becoming a two-person consciousness-raising group in dealing with this problem.

Talking intimately about their alienation from each other and, in so doing, reestablishing a sense of intimacy.

As I said, the creation of a joint platform is in itself a solution. The problem is not eliminated. Mark might continue to deal with self-blame by withdrawing. Peg might continue to deal with

Mark's withdrawal by accusing him of being angry. Mark might continue to deal with Peg's accusation by counterattacking. At a crucial moment, however, one of them will go to the other and say:

MARK: Hey, we did it again!
PEG: Hmm. I guess we did. And we did it the way we *always* do it. You got a little quiet and I immediately accused you of being angry.
MARK: Right. And, like always, the reason I *got* quiet was that I was beating myself up about something. Except this time I think I figured out more about it, which is that . . .

Peg and Mark would be creating a supraordinate perspective—a joint platform; a relationship about the relationship; an ongoing, developing conversation about the problem; a getting together about how they had begun to become alienated—which itself is the solution to their alienation.

Partners can become increasing adept in adopting such a supraordinate perspective. As time goes on, Peg and Mark might be able to catch themselves earlier in the chain of events. In the middle of the fight, one of them might say (feeling proud at being able to spot it):

Hey, we're *doing* it again.

As even more time goes by, they might be able to catch themselves earlier still. One of them might say:

Hey, I think we're *about* to do it again.

As an ego-analytic couple therapist, my primary attention is not on solving problems in the sense of eliminating them. Rather, it is on creating a joint platform from which partners can look at these problems—and *that*, the joint platform, is the solution. But why not *try* to eliminate problems? Well, I do that, too.

In an effort to deal with Mark's self-reproach for feeling left out (i.e., to help him to feel less self-reproach), I told him that most fathers of newborns feel left out and, in addition, that most fathers of newborns feel self-reproachful about feeling left out.
I asked Peg and Mark if they thought Mark's taking responsibility for the baby's supplementary bottle-feeding might make him feel less left out.
I tried to give Peg the advantage of knowing that behind her "Why do you always have

to get so angry at me?" is "I'm *worried* that your silence means that you're angry at me." To the extent she remembers that behind this accusation is a worry, she might in the future be able to express the worry rather than the accusation.

At the same time that I make these direct attempts to help partners solve (in the sense of *eliminate*) the problem, I try to enable partners to "have" the problem, that is, to not *have* to solve it, but instead to create a joint platform from which to look at it. I do this because many of the most important problems cannot be eliminated. All couples have recurrent periods of disagreement and friction, of not seeing eye to eye. All couples have their own set of ongoing difficult-to-resolve or impossible-to-resolve conflicts, and there are always new problems waiting in the wings.

Partners need a way to deal with these disagreements and conflicts. This is where the joint platform comes in. To the extent that Peg and Mark are able to create a joint platform, they

Can mutually observe these inevitable problems.
And, in the process of observing, can commiserate with each other.
And, in the process of commiserating, can establish a collaborative spirit, an experience of being in it together, a sense of intimacy.

Thus, the first point about a joint platform is that it is a solution in itself—a solution that does not require eliminating the problem. But the second point is that the joint platform frees partners to do their best thinking, collaborating, and problem solving and, in the process, increases partners' abilities to arrive at whatever concrete solutions (i.e., ways of eliminating the problem) might be possible.

The fact that the joint platform is so crucial to ego-analytic couple therapy immediately raises the following obvious questions:

1. What if I am unable to create a joint platform with a particular couple?
2. What if I am able to create such a platform, but the partners do not go to the next step, which is to start creating it for themselves outside the sessions?
3. What if my creation of a joint platform—a nonblaming, nondefensive forum in which the partners can talk about their relationship—just makes clear the fact that

they have relationship-threatening un-reconcilable wishes (e.g., one partner really wants children and the other really does not; one partners wants a traditional marriage and the other does not; one partner wants to return to live in the inner city to help others of his/her class or race, and the other does not)?

What do I do? I try to create a platform from which to talk with them about the following:

My inability to create a joint platform for them right there in the sessions. I might discuss with them, for example, how whatever conciliatory, reaching-out, potentially-platform-generating comment I help one partner make just immediately and painfully strikes the other as too little, too late.

The failure of the therapy to positively affect their lives outside the therapy. I might create a platform from which the three of us can talk about the failure of the therapy to result in the two of them's creating a platform for themselves outside the therapy. If a platform is a good way to deal with problems in the relationship, then a platform is a good way to deal with problems in the therapy—in this case, our failure so far to accomplish the purposes for which the partners came.

The existence of these relationship-threatening un-reconcilable wishes. I try to create a joint platform from which partners can commiserate with each other about having such wishes and about the possibility of the relationship's ending. This contrasts with what they have been doing, which is to argue about the problem or try to avoid talking or even thinking about it. I try to help them recruit each other as resources in dealing with this problem—to enable them to be together (to commiserate with each other) about how they might end up apart.

There is no natural point at which I stop trying to create a platform. No matter what the problem is—even if it is the inability to create a platform—there is always the possibility of creating a vantage point from which to look at it.

I said that my therapeutic goal is to enable partners to be able to create joint platforms for themselves. I do not expect, however, that they will be able to create the full-blown platforms that I create for them in the sessions. As I describe elsewhere (Wile, 1981, 1988, 1993), partners by themselves are typically able to cre-ate only bits and fragments of a joint platform. Fortunately, that can be enough. Any move in the direction of creating a joint platform can often make a big difference. Just knowing that there *is* such a thing as a joint platform can often make a big difference.

For example, in the week following the session I just described, Peg and Mark got caught up again in the pattern of Mark's feeling left out and withdrawing and Peg's accusing him of being angry at her. But this time they were able to remember that, at least for a moment in the previous session (and as a result of the joint platform I created for them), they had a new way to look at this pattern. In the old way, each saw the other as maliciously trying to thwart him/her. In the new way, each partner saw the other, instead, as caught up in struggles of his/her own. Although they were unable to re-create that joint platform for themselves right there in the moment, their memory that, at least for a few minutes in the session they'd had this alternative view, gave them a less-grimly-hating-the-other-person-and-privately-hating-themselves perspective.

THE EGO-ANALYTIC APPROACH TO COMMON COUPLE-THERAPY METHODS

As an ego-analytic couple therapist, do I ever use the familiar couple therapy methods of communication skills training, cognitive restructuring, paradoxical intervention, and tracing problems to childhood? I have my own ego-analytic versions of them.

Communication Skills Training

I want Peg to have the benefit of knowing that when she says to Mark, "Why are you so angry at me?" she is "mind reading": that is, she is violating one of the rules of good communication. As I show elsewhere (Wile, 1988, 1993), each of these rules is based on an important piece of information—in the case of the "Do not mind read" rule: Others generally do not like it if you tell them what they feel.

But, applying the ego-analytic hidden-validity principle, I would immediately want to justify Peg's disobeying the "No mind reading" rule: that is, I would want to point out the ways in which her disobeying it makes sense. I would want to tell her:

"Nearly everyone jumps to conclusions at times about things that really worry them—that they have a particular disease, for example, or that they might have just failed the important test they just took or, when their kids are late, that something awful happened to them. When Mark is quiet, Peg, you jump to the feared conclusion that he is angry at you. You 'mind read.' But, instead of saying 'You shouldn't mind read,' I want to say that you're *going* to mind read, and so am I, and so is everyone else. As I said, at times everyone jumps to feared conclusions. What you *can* do, though, is become increasingly good at noticing that your 'mind reading'—in this case, your telling Mark that he is angry at you—*is* jumping to a feared conclusion."

I want to create a joint platform from which Peg and Mark can appreciate the inevitability of Peg's mind reading—and of Mark's mind reading—and of their disobeying the other rules of good communication. I have recently reconceptualized the rules of good communication as the *impossible-to-obey* rules of good communication (Wile, 1993).

I want to tell Peg, in addition, that she might be correct: Mark might indeed be angry at her in ways that he does not realize—and that I do not realize. It is hard to be certain about the truth in such matters.

Cognitive Restructuring

In telling Mark that fathers of newborns often feel left out, I engaged in cognitive restructuring: that is, I tried to refute Mark's negative self-talk (his belief that something was wrong with him for feeling left out). In the ego-analytic version of refuting negative self-talk, however;

I do it, not so much as an end in itself (i.e., to straighten out Mark's thinking and to make him feel better), but as a means to an end: to clear away the self-blame that interferes with his ability to think.

I do it, not just to eliminate Mark's negative self-talk, but even more so to *reveal* this negative self-talk. It is often difficult to eliminate negative self-talk. So instead of putting my total effort (and the full power of my therapeutic authority) behind refuting negative self-talk, I try to create a platform from which Mark can monitor his negative self-talk, take it into account, appreciate its inevitability, and deal with its negative effects.

I am concerned about stimulating negative self-talk about negative self-talk. If Mark tries and fails to eliminate his negative self-talk, he could easily become self-reproachful, that is, engage in negative self-talk about his inability to eliminate his negative self-talk. Instead of telling him that his negative self-talk is irrational and that he should stop it, I tell him that negative self-talk is often difficult to stop, despite its being irrational.

I tell Mark that negative self-talk is a set of Furies with which nearly everyone contends; it does not always yield to reason. There are certain states of mind that we all experience that have negative self-talk built into them. I try to create a platform from which he can commiserate with himself for having to deal with his negative self-talk.

Paradoxical Interventions

In the paradoxical intervention of "positive reframing" or "positive connotation," strategic therapists redefine negative intentions or destructive behavior in positive terms (e.g., a destructive fight is redefined as an effort to reinvigorate the relationship). Strategic therapists do so to shake up the family system, to put the partners off guard, or to produce change in some other way. These therapists do not make these interventions because they think they are true. They do not care what is true; they do not think that it possible to know what is true. They are interested only in producing change.

Strategic therapists are on to something important here, but I think there is a more precise way to say what it is. As I see it, partners profit from positive reframing or positive connotation because they suffer from their own negative framing or negative connotation. In ego-analytic terms, they suffer from feeling unentitled to their feelings, which leads them to invalidate their own and their partner's reactions.

In the ego-analytic version of positive reframing, the therapist positively reframes to reveal and balance the client's negative framing, so that the client can really think about the matter.

A second type of paradoxical intervention is "prescribing the symptom." A strategic therapist might give Peg and Mark the following instructions: "Three times in the coming week, Peg, I want you deliberately to leave Mark out, at which time, Mark, I want you to withdraw, following which, Peg, I want you to accuse Mark of being angry at you."

Here again, strategic therapists are on to something important but, again, I think there is a more precise way to describe it. Peg and Mark's problem, from an ego-analytic viewpoint, is their discomfort with, sense of unentitlement to, and phobic reaction to their experience. Mark is unable to tell Peg that he feels left out; instead, he just withdraws. Peg is unable to tell Mark that she is worried that his withdrawal means he is angry at her; instead, she *accuses* him of being angry.

The problem, in other words, is the lack of a joint platform—a non-self-reproachful, nonphobic vantage point—from which they can confide in one another about these experiences, and about their self-reproachful and phobic reactions to these experiences.

Prescribing the symptom—telling Peg and Mark to engage in their pattern deliberately—might enable them to stand back, discuss, and even laugh together about the pattern. To the extent that they are able to do this, they would be taking a step toward inhabiting this part of their relationship and creating a joint platform from which to view it.

A third type of paradoxical intervention is "predicting a relapse." Let us say that several weeks pass without Peg and Mark engaging in their familiar pattern of Mark's feeling left out and withdrawing and Peg's accusing him of being angry at her. A strategic therapist might predict a relapse. I might, also. But, whereas the strategic therapist would predict a relapse to prevent it from happening, I would predict it to prepare the partners for it. Anticipating the recurrence of a problem is part of creating a joint platform from which to look at it.

Tracing Problems to Childhood

Tracing problems to childhood can contribute to the creation of a joint platform from which partners can look at their conflicts:

In listening to Mark describe the details of how he felt left out in childhood, Peg felt sympathetic—in contrast to her usual experience, which was to feel impatient with him for feeling left out. And, in listening to *himself*, Mark felt sympathetic toward himself—in contrast to his usual experience, which was self-reproach for still being so affected by events in his childhood.

In listening to Peg describe how she felt tyrannized by her mother's silences, Mark felt sympathetic—in contrast to his usual ex-

perience, which was to feel impatient with how she felt tyrannized by *his* silences. And, listening to *herself*, Peg felt sympathetic toward herself—in contrast to her usual experience, which was self-reproach for not being over her mother by now.

Our tracing their reactions to childhood thus helped Peg and Mark create a sympathizing-rather-than-blaming vantage point—a joint platform—from which they could look at their situation.

At a certain point, however, our tracing their problems to childhood began to *interfere* with the establishment of a joint platform:

Mark began to feel that our tracing his feeling left out with Peg to his feeling left out in childhood was blaming him for the problem. He needed us to appreciate that Peg, in fact, *was* leaving him out when she was preoccupied with the baby.

Peg began to feel that our tracing her sensitivity to Mark's silence to her childhood experience with her mother was blaming her for the problem. She needed us to appreciate that Mark had, after all, stopped talking to her, that is, that there *was* an immediate and present provocation.

So I shifted from the tracing-problems-to-childhood mode to the showing-how-each-was-responding-to-something-that-was-going-on-at-the-moment mode. I *validated* their responses. I showed how their responses made sense in the immediate situation and were not simply displacements from the past. And I *universalized* their responses. I suggested that

In reacting to Peg's involvement with the baby, Mark was in touch with a common reality in couple relationships: Fathers of newborns often do get left out.

In reacting to Mark's quietness, Peg was in touch with a common reality in couple relationships: Partners often do become subtly withdrawn, which over time can have an insidious effect on the relationship.

An ego-analytic approach requires paying attention to the ways that tracing problems to childhood decreases or increases self-reproach and contributes to or interferes with the creation of a joint platform. More important than that, an ego-analytic approach requires recognizing how the relationship itself is a potential solution to childhood-based problems. I told Peg and Mark that

> The problem is *not* so much Mark's sensitivity to feeling left out or Peg's sensitivity to Mark's quietness. Everyone is sensitive to something.
>
> The problem is *not* so much Peg's leaving Mark out or Mark's becoming quiet. Every partner at times leaves the other out, becomes quiet, or in one way or another becomes withdrawn or preoccupied.
>
> The problem (which all couples experience to one extent or another) *is* not having a way to get together to sort out what happened, that is, to create an intimate, nonadversarial vantage point from which to talk about the alienating experience and, by so doing, to reestablish a sense of connection and intimacy.

In the ego-analytic version of tracing problems to childhood, I place emphasis, not on partners' childhood-based sensitivities or developmental deficits in themselves, but on how partners relate to themselves and to one another about these sensitivities or deficits and, in particular, how they are able or unable to confide in each other about them, appeal to each other as resources in dealing with them, and create a joint platform from which to look at them.

Here, Peg and Mark are appealing to each other as resources in dealing with their childhood-based special sensitivities:

> Instead of just feeling self-critical for feeling left out and becoming quiet, Mark could *confide* in Peg that he felt self-critical for feeling left out and, as a result, became quiet.
>
> Instead of reacting to Mark's quietness by accusing him of being angry at her, Peg could *confide* in him that she was worried that his quietness meant that he was angry at her.

By confiding in each other in these ways, Peg and Mark would be invoking the curative power of the relationship. They would be recruiting each other in dealing with their problems with each other.

And now we see what the *master* childhood-based problem is. It's the childhood-based special sensitivities and developmental deficits that prevent partners from

> Confiding in each other.
>
> Recruiting each other as resources in dealing with their problems with each another.
>
> Invoking the curative potential of the relationship.
>
> Creating a joint platform from which to look at their childhood-based special sensitivities and developmental deficits.

Ego-analytic thinking starts with the assumption that the ultimate purpose of a relationship is to be curative, that is, to provide partners with a built-in confidant to help deal with problems, including the problems they bring to the relationship from their childhoods—their childhood-based special sensitivities and developmental deficits. At the same time, these sensitivities and deficits make it difficult for them to appeal to each other as resources. In fact, a major debilitating effect of the partners' childhood-based special sensitivities and developmental deficits is to *disable* the curative function of the relationship.

So this is what the world looks like from an ego-analytic perspective:

> Certain familiar interventions of other approaches (e.g., "You're codependent"; "You're afraid of intimacy") are seen as having a pejorative element: that is, they provide material for the partners' inner prosecuting attorneys' charges.
>
> An important ego-analytic task is to provide a defense attorney to reveal and balance the client's inner prosecuting attorney so that the client can think.
>
> Everyone's root problem is this inner prosecuting attorney: that is, self-reproach, self-blame, self-hate, negative self-talk, shame, guilt, or more broadly, the sense of unentitlement to feelings.
>
> Ego analysis focuses on what it calls the *hidden* problem—the relationship we have with ourselves about our thoughts, feelings, wishes, problems, and experiences—rather than the *obvious* problem, that is, the thoughts, feelings, wishes, problems, and experiences themselves.
>
> A major effect of feeling unentitled to feelings is difficulty in formulating these feelings and getting them across to others.
>
> An important ego-analytic task is to discover at any given moment the leading-edge feeling that each partner is unable to get across, that is, that he/she needs to get across to avoid generating symptoms.

A couple relationship *is* the relationship the partners have with one another about the continuous series of leading-edge feelings simultaneously being generated within each partner.

The ultimate purpose of a relationship is to be curative, that is, to provide partners with a built-in confidant to deal with their problems (particularly those they have with one another) and with the leading-edge feelings to which they feel unentitled.

The goal of couple therapy is to establish more fully the relationship as a curative agent, that is, to enable partners to create a joint platform from which they can monitor their relationship and recruit each other as resources in dealing with their problems with each other.

A joint platform is the solution—it is the goal of couple therapy—because the problem, feeling unentitled to feelings, is unsolvable, and creating a platform is the premier way to deal with unsolvable problems.

Tracing couple's problems to childhood is helpful to the extent that it contributes to rather than interferes with the development of a joint platform. An important ego-analytic task is to increase partners' abilities to recruit each other as resources in dealing with their childhood-based special sensitivities and developmental deficits.

In their concept of negative self-talk, cognitive-behavior therapists deal essentially with the inner prosecuting attorney's attack, which I see as lying at the heart of everyone's problems. The ego-analytic task is to create a platform from which the person can appreciate that negative self-talk is often difficult to silence (and a lifelong problem) and that there is the danger of generating negative self-talk about negative self-talk.

The rules of good communication contain crucial bits of information. I recommend making use of this information and at the same time recognizing that these rules are impossible to obey and can lead to a sense of failure if a person expects to be able to obey them.

Ego analysis has its own view of why paradoxical interventions are useful. "Positive framing" is useful because the client is suffering from his/her own negative framing (i.e., self-reproach, a sense of unentitlement to feelings). "Prescribing the symptom" is useful because the client is suffering from his/her own *non*prescribing of the symptom, that is, from

the avoidance of and phobic reaction to the symptom. "Predicting a relapse" is useful because the client is suffering from his/her *not* predicting a relapse, that is, from counting on the symptom not to recur and thus being unprepared when it does.

Ego-analytic therapy redefines certain classic couple therapy interventions (e.g., "You're afraid of intimacy"; "Say it to her, not to me") in its own terms. It takes familiar couple therapy methods (e.g., communication skills training, cognitive restructuring, paradoxical interventions, childhood-oriented interpretations) and recasts them. Therapists who adopt the five ego-analytic principles—the hidden-validity, need-to-get-something-across, joint-platform, joint-victims principles, and the supraordinate sense-of-entitlement-to-feelings principle—will automatically see themselves, their partners, and their clients in a new way.

NOTES

1. Hoffman (1983) describes the controversy between therapists who emphasize how a client's transference reactions are *in*valid (a distortion from the past) and those who emphasize how they are invalid *and* valid (an understandable reaction to the therapist's behavior.)

2. The metaphor of 1930s mothers is borrowed from Kohut (1984, pp. 171, 191), who used it to describe the attitude of certain classical analysts who— "whatever their consciously held and openly professed theoretical beliefs—have always, subtly or not so subtly, discarded their straitlaced reserve, [and provided] the emotional responsiveness" that Kohut felt some patients need.

REFERENCES

Apfelbaum, B. (1966). On ego psychology: A critique of the structural approach to psychoanalysis. *International Journal of Psycho-Analysis, 47*, 451–475.

Apfelbaum, B. (1977). A contribution to the development of the behavioral-analytic sex therapy model. *Journal of Sex and Marital Therapy, 3*, 128–138.

Apfelbaum, B. (1982a). The clinical necessity for Kohut's self theory. *Voices, 18*, 43–49.

Apfelbaum, B. (1982b, Spring). Letter to the editor. *California State Psychologist*, p. 16.

Apfelbaum, B. (1983, August). *Introduction to the symposium "Ego Analysis and Ego Psychology."*

Paper presented at the Annual Convention of the American Psychological Association, Anaheim, CA.

Apfelbaum, B. (1988). An ego-analytic perspective on desire disorders. In S. R. Leiblum & R. C. Rosen (Eds.), *Sexual desire disorders* (pp. 75–104). New York: Guilford Press.

Apfelbaum, B., & Apfelbaum, C. (1985). The ego-analytic approach to sexual apathy. In D. C. Goldberg (Ed.), *Contemporary marriage: Special issues in couples therapy* (pp. 439–481). Homewood, IL: Dorsey.

Apfelbaum, B., & Gill, M. M. (1989). Ego analysis and the relativity of defense: Technical implications of the structural theory. *Journal of the American Psychoanalytic Association, 37,* 1071–1096.

Fenichel, O. (1941). *Problems of psychoanalytic technique.* New York: Psychoanalytic Quarterly.

Freud, S. (1959). Inhibitions, symptoms and anxiety. In J. Strachey (Ed. and Trans.) *Standard edition of the complete psychological works of Sigmund Freud* (Vol. 20, pp. 77–174). London: Hogarth Press. (Original work published 1926)

Gray, P. (1982). "Developmental lag" in the evolution of technique for psychoanalysis of neurotic conflict. *Journal of the American Psychoanalytic Association, 30,* 621–655.

Hoffman, I. Z. (1983). The patient as interpreter of the analyst's experience. *Contemporary Psychoanalysis, 19*(3), 389–422.

Kohut, H. (1984). *How does analysis cure?* Chicago: University of Chicago Press.

Wile, D. B. (1981). *Couples therapy: A nontraditional approach.* New York: Wiley.

Wile, D. B. (1984). Kohut, Kernberg, and accusatory interpretations. *Psychotherapy: Theory, Research, Practice, and Training, 21*(3), 353–364.

Wile, D. B. (1985a). Psychotherapy by precedent: Unexamined legacies from pre-1920 psychoanalysis. *Psychotherapy: Theory, Research, Practice, and Training, 22*(4): 793–802.

Wile, D. B. (1985b). Phases of relationship development. In D. C. Goldberg (Ed.), *Contemporary marriage: Special issues in couples therapy* (pp. 35–61). Homewood, IL: Dorsey.

Wile, D. B. (1987). An even more offensive theory. In W. Dryden (Ed.), *Key cases in psychotherapy* (pp. 78–102). London: Croom Helm.

Wile, D. B. (1988). *After the honeymoon: How conflict can improve your relationship.* New York: Wiley.

Wile, D. B. (1993). *After the fight: A night in the life of a couple.* New York: Guilford Press.

Wile, D. B. (1994). The ego-analytic approach to emotion in couples therapy. In S. M. Johnson & L. S. Greenberg (Eds.), *The heart of the matter: Perspective on emotion in marital therapy* (pp. 27–45). New York: Brunner/Mazel.

6

The Emotionally Focused Approach to Problems in Adult Attachment

SUSAN M. JOHNSON
LESLIE S. GREENBERG

Emotionally focused couple therapy (EFT) is an empirically validated approach to couple therapy (Johnson & Greenberg, 1987; Alexander, Holtzworth-Munroe, & Jameson, 1994) that focuses on compelling intrapsychic emotional responses and the patterns implicit in the process of interaction. The inner experience of the partners and the relationship events are assumed to be mutually determining and are reprocessed and restructured in therapy to create a more secure bond between partners. Distressed relationships are viewed as insecure bonds in which essentially healthy attachment needs are unable to be met due to rigid interaction patterns that block emotional engagement. Without such engagement and need fulfillment, insecurity and methods of coping with this insecurity control the relationship, resulting in problems in the attachment process. EFT is the only couple therapy explicitly based on attachment theory, which at the moment appears to be one of the most promising theoretical perspectives on adult love relationships (Hazan & Shaver, 1987; Paterson & Moran, 1989). EFT gives a primary place to the role of emotion in defining and redefining close relationships. It is one of the few psychodynamic approaches to marital therapy that has been empirically validated and subject-ed to process research aimed at relating specific in-session changes to positive outcomes (Johnson & Greenberg, 1988).

THEORETICAL MODEL OF MARITAL DISTRESS

EFT views marital distress from an integrative interpersonal–intrapsychic perspective, synthesizing experiential and systemic concepts into a theory of marital dysfunction. Interactional positions in distressed couples tend to be rigidly defined and interact to create powerful, repetitive negative interaction cycles. From an EFT perspective, these positions are maintained both by the compelling emotional experiences of the partners and by prototypical interactional patterns that take on a life of their own and become self-reinforcing. These patterns then restrict accessibility and responsiveness, which are the basis of a secure sense of attachment and emotional connectedness (Sroufe, 1979; Stern, 1977, 1985).

This perspective fits well with recent research suggesting that the essential elements of marital distress are negative affect, negative content patterns such as criticism and blaming, and negative repetitive, highly structured interaction patterns (Gottman, 1979). In such relationships, the typical interaction is one of reciprocal aversiveness resulting in hostility and/or withdrawal from the encounter. Gottman (1991) has recently reported that in marital interaction tasks in which areas of disagreement were discussed, physiological arousal, especially of the husbands, as well as negative interactional patterns in which wives were critical and husbands withdrew or stonewalled, predicted marital dissatisfaction three years later. These husbands typically exhibited immobility in the face and neck and little or no eye contact, and the couples' facial expression of emotion predicted marital separation four years later. In couples more likely to separate, the wife facially expressed disgust and the husband expressed fear, while both displayed "miserable smiles." Accompanying these expressions were the interactional patterns referred to previously in which one partner, generally the wife, complained, criticized, or expressed contempt and the other partner, generally the husband, was defensive, disagreed, and withdrew. Thus, according to Gottman, couples likely to separate tend to fend off contact, become emotionally distant, and seem more critical and fearful than couples who stay together.

This pattern, without suggesting linear causality, appears to be one in which the husband becomes intensely physiologically aroused and possibly because of males' slower recovery rates to physiological arousal, learns to withdraw from conflict, because arousal that endures is aversive. The wife, in attempting to reengage, also becomes physiologically aroused and then blames and complains. It is important to note that this sequence describes the process as beginning at the point of the husband's withdrawal; however, presumably this withdrawal is in part due to the wife's pursuit, just as her pursuit is a function of his disengagement; ultimately both withdraw and marital dissolution is in process. This innovative research program by Gottman and his colleagues lends strong support to the importance given by EFT to affective experience and communication in marital distress. EFT targets the experience and expression of emotion and uses these to shift interactions toward accessibility and responsiveness. The inability to respond to the other, inaccessibility, and the resulting lack of engagement or contact, are seen as the central problems in distressed relationships. The patterns that are the most prominent in distressed couples seem then to be attack–withdraw or pursue–distance (Napier, 1978; Greenberg & Johnson, 1988), which eventually evolve into at-

tack–attack or withdraw–withdraw patterns. Sustaining emotional engagement and resolving any difficulty that arises here, perhaps as a result of partner and/or gender differences in affect regulation, are of crucial importance in resolving marital difficulties (Gottman & Krokoff, 1979; Gottman & Levenson, 1986).

In the EFT model, inner experience refers particularly to emotional experience and how it is processed. In close adult relationships, powerful emotional responses such as fear–mistrust, and associated prototypical models of self and other learned in past attachment contexts (e.g., "I am defective and unlovable, so others will leave me") are evoked, particularly when conflict arises. This inner experience orients one partner to the other and helps to organize interactional responses. These responses then become the basis of the habitual positions that the partners take with each other, particularly around issues of affiliation–closeness and control–dependence. These positions, especially when they become rigid and laden with intense affect, then act to curtail the probable responses of the other partner; hostility, for example, evokes reciprocal aggression or self-protective distancing. The positions the couple take with each other then create relationship-defining events that in a mutually determining fashion also feed back into the inner experience of each partner. These events may create, maintain, or modify each partner's experience of the relationship. In a distressed relationship, inner and outer realities, context and experience, mesh into a tight negative system that becomes an absorbing state and precludes the evolution of new patterns or responses. To paint this in terms of a clinical picture, one partner becomes so angry and resentful that all she sees are the negative aspects of her spouse, and that anger organizes all her responses to him; she becomes more and more demanding and less and less easy to please. Her spouse becomes so intimidated and fearful that all he can see is his partner's anger, and his fear ensures that he will either be vigilant or distant. Neither partner can exit from this system, and neither can attain the security and intimacy that most couples hope for in marriage. This is a stalemate, a dead end.

The marital therapist has then to modify *the inner experience* of both partners, the *positions* they take in the relationship dance, and the *relationship events* that define the quality of attachment and also influence the definition of self for both the partners. A summary of this process may be found in Figure 6.1.

The power of the self-reinforcing interaction-

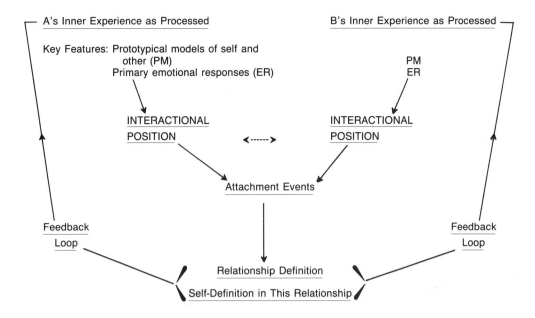

FIGURE 6.1. EFT model of relationship process.

al patterns in distressed relationships is a phenomenon that challenges all marital therapists. Systems theory partially explains such patterns (Steinglass, 1987), suggesting that interactions concerning control and affiliation naturally become organized over time and through homeostasis tend to repeat and maintain themselves. While systems theory states that each partner's behavior is constrained and dictated by the other, it does not address the issue of motivation and dynamics internal to the individual. The theoretical perspective of attachment theory suggests that it is the innate need for security, as well as the concomitant vulnerability to rejection by, or loss of, the attachment figure, that underlies the habitual responses each partner has to the other. The compelling responses each partner has to the other are most understandable, it seems to us, if they are seen not only in the context of systems theory but also as a reflection of each partner's need for security and protection, and as the arena where the schema defining self and other are appraised and formulated. The relevance of the attachment process theory to the ongoing organization and definition of self has been addressed by theorists such as Guidano and Liotti (1983) and Sroufe (1989).

From a theoretical perspective, the most crucial elements in EFT are the nature of attachment and the role of emotion in defining or redefining intimate relationships. The following discussion focuses on these elements.

Attachment and Marriage

Attachment theory is often placed under the general umbrella of object relations theory, from which it was derived, but from which it also differs greatly (Bowlby, 1969). Both theories give a prime place in human functioning to relatedness to intimate others rather than to drive theories of motivation. Both also concern themselves with internal representations of such "objects" or intimate others, and how such representations guide personality development and the creation of future relationships. However, in attachment theory the focus is *not* on the structure of the psyche and specific contents, such as ego states and fantasy objects, or on mechanisms such as projective identification, but on human beings as information-processing organisms with innate goals of security and protection. Maintaining closeness to others is considered to be an innate evolutionary survival mechanism. Attachment theory has also given rise to a body of specific empirical research documenting attachment styles in children and adults and relating such styles to variables such as exploratory behavior in children and marital happiness in adults (Senchak & Leonard, 1992). Attachment is more parsimonious in its theoretical explanations and focuses upon emotion much more emphatically (Hazan & Shaver, 1994; Thompson, 1990). It has logically given rise then to interventions such as EFT, rather than interventions that focus on past conflicts and the creation of insight.

Adult love relationships are more and more being viewed in terms of attachment theory (Shaver, Hazan, & Bradshaw, 1988; Bartholomew & Horowitz, 1991), which focuses on such relationships as emotional bonds, addressing innate adaptive needs for protection, security, and connectedness with significant others. A bond is conceptualized as an emotional tie and a set of attachment behaviors, activated by emotional experience, that regulate closeness and distance. A full discussion of attachment theory may be found elsewhere (Bowlby, 1969, 1988) and is beyond the scope of this chapter. Only the chief tenets of bonding theory with clear relevance for the marital therapist are addressed here. The accessibility and responsiveness of attachment figures are essential to a sense of personal security, so that issues of trust, safety, and dependence are foremost in marital therapy. Since attachment needs are an essential and adaptive part of being human, so the emotions associated with these needs are an essential and primary element in close relationships.

In terms of bonding theory, marital distress may generally be considered to represent the failure of an attachment relationship to provide a secure base for one or both partners. The basic attachment needs for security, protection, and closeness have not been met. The resulting anxiety and the efforts to cope with this anxiety and create a response in the caregiver, evoke similar behaviors in both infant–caregiver relationships and adult romantic relationships (Johnson, 1986). There is an intensification of attachment behaviors such as protest and clinging by one partner, or an avoidance of the distressing interaction by withdrawal. In distressed relationships, this situation evolves until neither partner is able to be responsive or accessible to the other. The context the partners create continues to generate more and more insecurity until emotional engagement cannot be sustained. The problem here is in the interaction and the lack of emotional attunement in the partners' response to each other. The subtlety of this process has been captured more adequately by developmental theorists (Stern, 1977) than by theorists considering problems in adult relationships. Attunement here implies a sensitive moment-to-moment *being with* a partner as he/she experiences and expresses an emotion, as well as exhibiting behaviors that convey that one can empathically enter into and share the other's affective state, as when a baby lets out an exuberant yell and the mother's face lights up and she laughs, or when a partner recoils in fear and the spouse's face softens in compassion. (Stern, 1985).

On a more intrapsychic level, attachment theory suggests that rigid, insecure attachment styles (Ainsworth, 1982; Hazan & Shaver, 1987) contribute to the creation of dysfunctional relationships in adults. Bowlby (1969) suggests that working models of self and other, and their accompanying affective responses and affect-regulation strategies, guide behavior in close relationships. These models are always being modified and changed by experience. If a child did not trust his/her parents he/she may, as an adult, learn to trust his/her partner. However, as insecure attachment styles become extreme and impermeable, they may render partners almost incapable of the open responsiveness that is the foundation of secure bonds with others. In such cases, the other partner is usually perceived as the cause of the problem (e.g., "I cannot trust him. I know he will desert me if I become vulnerable"). Such positions tend to evoke interpersonal responses in others that confirm the insecure partner's attachment style. Attachment theory suggests then that insecure, that is, anxious ambivalent and avoidant attachment styles, may create problems in intimacy with partners, but may also be modified by new interactional experiences that facilitate safety and the growth of trust. Avoidance of engagement and extreme insecurity, however, make such modification more difficult. In very distressed relationships, style, or how one processes events, and present recurring interactions, reinforce each other in a negative spiral of hostility and distance. At any point in time, security is then a function of both present relationships and individual attachment style. Research into attachment in infants (Fox, Kimmerly, & Schafer, 1991) also suggests that attachment style is not a trait, but a function of individual predispositions to have confidence in the availability of others and to regulate distressing affect in attachment contexts in a particular manner, in response to the patterns of interaction in present relationships. Attachment style is assumed to reflect relationship history and as such to influence current relationship functioning.

The relational needs of the partners for contact and security are not considered problematic here, but rather are aspects of healthy functioning. This view, central to attachment theory, parallels the humanistic–experiential perspective of functioning (Rice & Greenberg, 1992; Rogers, 1961), which emphasizes the potentially adaptive nature of most needs and desires, and views problems as arising from the distortion or disowning of such needs (Perls, 1973). Attachment needs are conceptualized as adaptive and life enhancing, and dependency is seen as an essential part of the human experience (Bowlby, 1988). The task for adult relationships is to develop a secure interdependence that nurtures both partners. This theoretical perspective allows the marital therapist to validate the needs of each partner and gives him/her a map that focuses upon issues such as safety, dependence, trust, and vulnerability.

Emotion in Marriage

The formation, maintenance, disruption, and renewal of affectional bonds is a primary source of intense human emotion (Bowlby, 1973), and attachment theory emphasizes that emotional experience and expression are of primary importance in close relationships and organize proximity-seeking behaviors. This focus upon emotion as an adaptive, orienting, and organizing factor in human experience parallels the approach to emotion taken by other theorists of human functioning (Izard, 1979). Emotion, which has previously been somewhat eclipsed by a focus upon behavior and cognition, is now being recognized as playing a primary and unique role in self-regulation and in social interaction (Frijda, 1986; Tronick, 1989; Greenberg & Johnson, 1990). Emotion is a relational action tendency that acts to establish, maintain, or disrupt a relationship with the environment in the form of a readiness to act. Emotions, particularly anger, sadness, and fear, are felt predominantly in response to other people's actions. The emotional system is also a primary signaling system that allows for the prediction of individual behavior and regulates social interaction, (e.g., the expression of fear signals the need for help and in many situations evokes affiliative behaviors). Emotion and emotional communication are, therefore, key regulators of marital interaction (Johnson & Greenberg, 1994).

Emotion is viewed by attachment theorists and by us in constructivist information processing terms. Emotional experience is seen as being constantly constructed from a variety of levels or sources of information. Leventhal (1979, 1984) suggests three levels: (1) the expressive motor, system, which is an innate response system; (2) the conceptual level, which stores rules and beliefs about emotional experiences; and (3) a schematic or emotional memory level, which builds complex internal representations linking one's emotional experience, the situational contexts in which this experience occurred, and conceptually processed thoughts and beliefs about the experience. These emotional schemata, which represent complex integrative structures coding and reproducing emotional experience, are of fundamental importance in emotional life. These levels of processing are all aspects of a person's current information processing, many of which may be out of awareness and all of which are integrated to form conscious emotional experience. Emotion thus involves highly complex information processing and provides us with feedback about our reaction to situations. It is a rapid appraisal system that appraises a situation in relation to a need or a goal (Frijda, 1986) and leads to adaptive action. In intimate relationships, appraisals of one's partner's actions in relation to one's attachment needs are most salient. *Emotion in marital therapy provides us with information about, and access to, partners' needs, to their appraisals and beliefs, and to their response tendencies.*

The experience and expression of underlying emotions are central in the restructuring of attachment bonds, occurring as they do at the interface between the organism and the environment, the self and the system. They simultaneously involve self-regulatory and other regulatory behavior, and render self-definition and relationship definition essentially two sides of the same coin. In intimate relationships, patterns of relating to the other, engaging and disengaging, regulate each partner's inner affective state, just as these inner responses are communicated to the other, and tend to create interaction patterns (Tronick, 1989). Emotion is of crucial importance in working with a marital system and with systems in general, because *emotion links the intrapsychic and the social.* Emotions are simultaneously biological and social, and thereby give us access to the interpersonal and intrapsychic determinants of action. Emotion is the synthesis that occurs at the interface of the dichotomies, inner–outer, organism–environment, mind–body, integrating appraisal of relational events with relational action tendencies and expressive and sensory responses. They offer us a means of understanding the essential interconnectedness of people's experience and interaction and how these give rise to each other. Emotions are both felt subjectively and expressed socially. Consideration of emotions is thus essential in marital therapy, because emotions speak to the core of subjective experience within people, as well as to the core of the connectedness between people. *A major task of therapy is then to explore, unravel, and resynthesize the complex elements and levels constituting emotion, constructed by individuals throughout their lives.* The processing of emotional experience specifically accesses core cognitions, or working models of self and other, which often interfere with the creation of intimacy, and allows for the reprocessing of painful affect in the relationship, thus reducing the need for self-protective strategies that limit contact and involvement. *The second major task of therapy is the expression of underlying emotions to change interactions.* Here, the other (as opposed to self) regulatory aspect of emotion comes into play, because it provides a context that influences the other's behavior.

Greenberg and Safran (1987) suggest that different types of emotional expression should be assessed in therapy in order to facilitate differential intervention. Recognizing that emotions are both biologically based and culturally determined, and are caused both by rapid autonomic appraisals and by time-consuming conscious deliberation, they have suggested that distinctions be made between primary, secondary, and instrumental emotions. In this categorization, primary emotions are viewed as essentially biologically adaptive, orienting the organism to the personal significance of outside events in relation to needs and goals. Thus, in marriage, primary emotions, such as anger at being violated or diminished, sadness at the loss of a partner's attention or company, and fear in response to threatened rejection by a partner, provide adaptive action tendencies to help organize appropriate behavior. Anger mobilizes a partner to defend against attack, fear mobilizes for withdrawal from threat, and sadness mobilizes for recovery of that which is lost. Often these emotions are not initially in awareness and need to be accessed and intensified in therapy and used as aids to marital problem solving.

Secondary, reactive emotional responses are often problematic and are not the organism's direct, immediate, goal-relevant response to the environment. Rather, they are secondary to more primary generating process, or are reactions to primary responses being thwarted. Defensive or reactive responses such as expressing anger or blaming when afraid, or crying in frustration or withdrawing when angry, are secondary emotional responses to underlying emotional processes.

Secondary emotions also occur as responses to primary emotions, for example, as in fear of one's anger, or shame at one's sadness or vulnerability. In addition, secondary emotions, such as hopelessness in response to negative expectations, occur in reaction to underlying cognitive processes. Secondary reactive responses of this type are not to be focused on or intensified in therapy, rather they are to be explored in order to access underlying processes. Secondary emotions are generally readily available to awareness and often are part of the presenting problem. Instrumental emotional responses, on the other hand, are functional emotional behavioral patterns that people have learned to use in influencing others. These are emotions that are expressed in order to achieve some intended effect, such as crying in order to evoke sympathy or expressing anger in order to dominate. Instrumental expressions of this type are not information about responses to situations, but are attempts to influence others or manage one's image. In therapy, these expressions are best bypassed, confronted, or interpreted, not explored or differentiated to access adaptive information.

In addition to adaptive primary emotions, maladaptive primary emotions need to be recognized, such as fear in response to benevolence or anger in response to caring. Although the emotional response system generally plays an adaptive role in human functioning, maladaptive responses can be learned as a function of trauma or strongly negative environmental contingencies in childhood. These emotions then need to be accessed in therapy, but for the purpose of modification rather than for orientation.

Assessing the type of emotion being expressed in therapy thus provides the clinician with a map for intervention (Greenberg & Johnson, 1986). *Primary adaptive emotion is accessed for its orienting information, whereas maladaptive emotion is accessed to make it more amenable to modification and restructuring. Secondary or instrumental expression is expanded or bypassed in order to access an underlying experience.*

THEORY OF CHANGE

The perspective taken on relationships and relationship problems defines the goals of any particular marital therapy and the key interventions used. In accordance with the theory discussed earlier, the goals of EFT are, then, to access and reprocess the emotional responses underlying couple's interactional positions and, when necessary, to restructure emotional schemes and internal models, so that new positions, conducive to increased accessibility and responsiveness, can be experienced in therapy. New interactional cycles then facilitate the growth of safety and trust, and allow for the formation of a secure attachment bond between partners, which facilitates the development of the new emotional schemes and internal working models of attachment. This process evolves in the following manner. First, the underlying emotion is accessed in the session. This indicates that an emotion scheme has been activated and is "up and running." When this emotion, say fear, is accessed and communicated, rather than the secondary or instrumental emotion, such as angry blaming, both partners reprocess their experience through this framework. Partners who recognize their fear begin to reconstrue their experience and the relationship, whereas the partners who observe their partner's fear begin to see the other in new ways (Greenberg, James, & Conry, 1988). The experience is thus reprocessed. This leads to a change in both partners' response and in the interaction.

On other occasions, either the primary emotion is already available, or when it becomes available, is recognized as being a maladaptive response. Thus, a fear of abandonment, fear of engulfment, or of being attacked may be recognized as having been learned from prior experience, for example, as in adults who have been sexually abused as children and learned to associate physical closeness with fear. In this case, more individually focused restructuring of the person's emotion schemes and internal working models may be needed. One of the best ways of achieving this individual change is through a new experience with the partner. Thus, restructuring the interaction so that the partner does not withdraw or attack, helps to provide the abandoned or fearful partner with a new relational experience, an opportunity to develop trust and to create new ways of relating. This leads to the restructuring of old schemes and/or the creation of new ones. The result is a new experience of being in the world and a new way of interacting. No longer does this partner react with fear, anticipate what is dreaded, and act in terms of this anticipation; rather, the person develops a sense of security, a secure base, with his/her partner.

The process of therapy focuses on emotional experience and expression because affect is seen as so crucial in attachment contexts and in the process of therapeutic change in general. There is also a constant focus on the structure and process of interaction, with each partner's responses being framed in terms of the pull of the interpersonal field, that is, in relation to the other's behavior, and the reaction that a particular response is likely to evoke. The content of therapy focuses on themes of closeness–separateness, deprivation and longing associated with attachment needs, and boundaries and control. The therapist heightens attachment-related affects such as fear, vulnerability, and sadness, and experiences such as isolation and abandonment that are evoked in interactions with the partner, validating the need for safety, comfort, closeness, and protection. The therapist also focuses on autonomy-related affects such as anger and experiences of submission and dependence, validating the need for self-assertion and boundary definition.

The active ingredients of change in this model are considered to be (1) an accessing and engagement in emotional experience in the session; (2) a reprocessing and, when necessary, a restructuring of this internal experience; and (3) a shift in interactional positions toward affiliation and engagement. Specific change events that incorporate these elements have been found to be associated with positive outcomes (Johnson & Greenberg, 1988). An event labeled a "softening," in which both spouses are emotionally engaged and discover new elements of their experience in the relationship, is associated with successful outcomes in EFT. In this event, a blaming, hostile partner is able to reach for his/her previously withdrawn but now available spouse and ask that his/her needs be met. A transcript of this change event is included later in this chapter. It is the lived experience of new aspects of self and other engaging in new interaction patterns that creates new relationship definitions: that is, it is new experience, rather than insight or new skills, that is crucial. Both elements, a reprocessing of the emotion underlying interactional patterns and an enactment of new interaction patterns, are seen as necessary for change. The EFT therapist has to be comfortable focusing on intrapsychic experience and evoking powerful affects, and be able to track and restructure interpersonal events, using one to expand on and redefine the other. *The two main tasks of therapy are then (1) to access and reprocess the emotional experience of partners and (2) to restructure interaction patterns.*

By the end of therapy, couples generally see their partners differently, and the picture is less threatening and includes both partners' vulnerabilities and insecurities. The interaction patterns have changed from negative cycles of hostility and/or distance to sustained emotional engagement and intimacy (Greenberg, Ford, Alden, & Johnson, 1993; Dandeneau & Johnson, 1994).

No matter what the content of the marital problem, the assumption is that reprocessing problematic emotional responses, facilitating emotional attunement, and structuring the interaction to facilitate accessibility and responsiveness creates a secure base from which couples can problem solve effectively and make new agreements to change other behaviors (e.g., parenting or coping with finances). If couples are relatively undistressed and flexible in their interactional positions, this process can be very brief. Even with such couples, the EFT therapist would focus on vulnerabilities, patterns of closeness, distance, and control, and facilitating emotional engagement, rather than prescribing behavior change or creating insight. Instances where the process of EFT is contraindicated or inappropriate are addressed in the Clinical Issues section of this Chapter.

Change Strategies

The EFT treatment process involves nine steps that are generally implemented in 12 to 20 therapy sessions, in the following sequence:

1. The delineating of conflict issues in the core struggle.
2. Identifying the negative interaction cycle.
3. Accessing the unacknowledged feelings underlying interactional positions.
4. Reframing the problem in terms of underlying feelings, attachment needs, and negative cycles.
5. Promoting identification with disowned needs and aspects of self, and integrating these into relationship interactions.
6. Promoting acceptance of the partner's experience and new interaction patterns.
7. Facilitating the expression of needs and wants, and creating emotional engagement.
8. Facilitating the emergence of new solutions.
9. Consolidating new positions.

It is not possible in this chapter to elaborate on each step of therapy. The steps and details of the associated interventions are elaborated elsewhere (Greenberg & Johnson, 1988). In terms of assessment, the most important goal in the first session is to build a hypothesized map of the interaction and the way it is experienced by each partner. Essentially, this involves identifying positions/cycles and vulnerabilities/protective strategies. The rigidity and reactivity of responses are particularly noted. The therapist explores the problems and strengths of the relationship from each partner's viewpoint, probes for the emotional response underlying interactional positions, asks about attachment histories and the history of the relationship, delineates prototypical problematic situations, observes present interaction patterns, experiments with each partner's responsiveness, builds an alliance, and sets a clear agenda for therapy. We have often found it helpful to have two individual sessions that allow the therapist to cement the alliance, to pursue information that may be withheld in the presence of the spouse, and to probe for underlying vulnerabilities and therapy agendas. By the end of the fourth session the therapist should have a clear understanding of the interaction and a plan of intervention, and has usually already delineated the cycle and begun to hone in on underlying feelings. A diagnostic picture of the relationship, the problem, and the task of therapy are then presented to the couple and discussed. An expectation is set up that treatment will last from 12 to 20 sessions. If, at this point, the partners' agendas for therapy are incompatible or if other contraindications for EFT are apparent, such as violence in the relationship, the couple is referred elsewhere. An interaction pattern that includes violence precludes the expressing and processing of vulnerability and the authentic building of trust. When a partner's anger is closely linked to physical aggressiveness toward the other, it is also difficult to validate it without validating the action tendency inherent in the emotion. This topic has also been addressed elsewhere (Greenberg & Johnson, 1988). If there are significant blocks to the effectiveness of marital therapy, such as an inability to trust due to unresolved childhood sexual abuse, individual as well as marital therapy may be recommended (Johnson, 1989). A more complete elaboration of the assessment procedure, including the transcript of a first session, has been presented elsewhere (Johnson & Greenberg, 1992).

Rather than describe each step in the process of therapy, a synopsis of a typical change process follows. A couple enters therapy with the male partner complaining of being criticized and seeing his wife as aggressive and unreasonable. The female partner feels depressed and lonely. She angrily describes her spouse as a frozen workaholic who is indifferent to her and her distress. The therapist builds an alliance with both partners and assesses the strengths and weaknesses of the relationship, noting the level of reactivity, the rigidity of interaction patterns, and the quality of affective responses. The therapist then delineates the pattern in the interaction as pursue and blame / withdraw and placate. The therapist validates each partner's experience of the relationship and describes how both are trapped in this pattern and unwittingly creating it. The key moments in therapy are then as follows: The male withdrawn partner accesses and expresses his sense of failure and inadequacy, and his fear of losing his wife. He acknowledges that he distances himself from his own feelings and his wife's distress by working excessively. He accesses, processes, and shares congruently his insecurity in his own sense of self and in his relationship with his wife. This constitutes a change in his level of accessibility; he moves in the session from distant detachment to present engagement. His partner denies the validity of his new behaviors, refuses to believe him, and remains angry. The therapist validates her reluctance to trust him, works at enabling her to touch the sense of desertion and fear of being abandoned that fuels her anger, and frames her aggression as desperateness. The male partner now begins to focus on how afraid he is of her anger and how obsessed he has become with avoiding it. The couple replay and reprocess key incidents in their relationship and he begins to draw boundaries, refuses to accept blame, and requests that she begin to risk trusting him. This now moves him to a stance of equality and contact with his wife and he demands to be let in. The wife now expresses her consuming fear of trusting him and her certainty that if he came close, he would see her neediness and reject her. She experiences in the session her overwhelming fear of being judged by others as unlovable, and he stays involved and responsive to her. She is then able to ask for reassurance and comfort. She moves now from a blaming hostile position to a more accessible, vulnerable, and affiliative stance. The partners consolidate their new positions, strengthen their sense of intimacy and trust, and resolve long-standing conflicts in their relationship. Many things occur in this process and it can be considered from many perspectives and on many levels. To the therapist, it is clear that the partners experience and share new aspects of themselves that evoke new perceptions and responses in the other. Problematic cycles are enacted and expanded to create a different kind of dialogue that allows new kinds of interactions to occur. In the sessions, each partner experiences and reprocesses his/her fears and vulnerabilities. The vulnerabilities of each partner then become integrated into the relationship, forming the basis for closer contact, rather than motivating attack or withdrawal. The therapist structures new interactions (e.g., "Can you tell him how afraid you are of his criticism?") that challenge each partner's original position and allow for the creation of more emotional engagement. The way the partners experience the relationship changes; the way they express their sense of themselves changes, and the way they respond to each other changes. *The stages in this process may be summarized as conflict deescalation, reengagement of the withdrawer, softening the blaming spouse, integration, and termination.* It is important to stress that this process does not occur in separate linear steps: rather, these steps are repeated circular microsequences of one partner reengaging, the other ceasing complaint, and so on, until they achieve a marked level of softening and new engagement.

In terms of the process of change in any particular session, it will vary with the stage of treatment and the nature of the couple's problems; however, it is possible to sketch a typical EFT session in general terms. A typical session starts with the therapist inquiring about the present status of the relationship and how the couple experienced the last week. This might include discussing the impact of the last session or homework assignments, which are usually awareness exercises. These may involve noting and bringing to the next session an incident in in which the subject withdrew from the interaction and how that was accomplished and experienced by himself/herself, and its effect on the partner. If the couple is currently engaged in some form of interactional cycle, or the partners are feeling some distress or dissatisfaction, this is explored. Attempts are made to make explicit the implicit processes and to begin framing them in terms of the couple's cycle. If an event perceived by the couple as significant for the relationship has occurred since the last session, the therapist inquires about it, and it is often reevoked and enacted in the session. The therapist then uses this to pursue the therapy goals judged most pertinent at that time. If the couple does not bring in this kind of event, the therapist discusses the last session and may repeat/replay significant pieces of dialogue from the last session. The therapist has to track the experiencing of each partner and validate this experience whenever possible, as well as tracking interactional events. He/she then makes judgements as to where to focus and help a partner reprocess a particular emotion, or replay, heighten, and expand interactions with their spouse. The therapist has to be able to switch from being immersed in the client's phenomenological world with the client, to stepping back, directing an interaction, and tracking the process of that interaction. Each session ends with a summary of each partner's emotional processes and the interactional events that were particularly salient. In general, after the building of the alliance and the assessment phase, the therapist focuses to a greater extent on the less hostile and more withdrawn partner. This partner is usually two steps ahead of the other in the therapy process. In EFT, it is clear when the therapy process is complete, because the couple is able to exit from negative cycles in the session, to sustain emotional engagement, and to be accessible and responsive to each other.

THE ROLE OF THE THERAPIST

A positive working alliance is a prerequisite for the implementation of EFT and has been found to be associated with positive outcome (Johnson & Talitman, 1995). This is fostered in the beginning by the therapist's ability to provide structure, safety, and a sense of direction that makes sense to the clients, and by the therapist's sensitive tracking and reflection of each partner's experience. EFT is a synthesis of experiential and systemic approaches to change; in both these schools, the ability to form a strong alliance is seen as crucial to the therapy process. Systems theory refers to the therapist's joining with each partner and the system *as it is* before beginning to create change (Minuchin, 1974). In experiential therapies, a therapist's empathy and respect for the client's experience are essential and curative elements (Rogers, 1961), creating the safety that enables people to risk encountering threatening aspects of their experience in the interest of change. The concept of expanding experiencing is important here; clients are not told to try to be different, but to allow themselves to be more completely who they are, that is, not to be less angry but to be directly angry and have that anger legitimized by the therapist so that more primary aspects of experience, such as the hurt or fear or sadness, also arise. This only occurs if the therapist creates a safe place. The therapist's ability to listen, to reflect, accept, and acknowledge each partner's experience is facili-

tated by the philosophy advocated by experientialists and by bonding theorists, that each partner's needs and emotions are essentially healthy and adaptive. Both partners are viewed as doing their best to protect themselves and hold on to the relationship, defining it in a way that creates for them some sense of safety.

The alliance can be viewed in terms of three elements: task, bond, and goal (Bordin, 1979). A positive alliance in EFT implies that the tasks structured by the therapist are perceived as relevant, the goals of therapy are congruent with the couple's needs, and the therapist is perceived as accepting and supportive, that is, as providing a context of safety to facilitate engagement in the tasks. The bond aspect of the alliance in EFT is fostered by the therapist's attuning to the couple's emotional experience and engaging each partner on an emotional level. The therapist sees and responds to the clients' pain. This is a potent event in terms of building bonds. The therapist also accepts and validates aspects of the clients' experience that they may never have accepted, and that their partner may be unable to accept in the present context. The tasks of EFT set by the therapist, based as they are on compelling emotions, tend to be perceived by the participants as powerful and directly relevant to the clients' concerns. The process, if it is possible to speak analogically, goes to the "heart of the matter" and addresses people's innate (according to attachment theory) longings and fears. In terms of goals, the focus on patterns and attachment needs provides a nonpathologizing, nonblaming way of conceptualizing the system and appears easy for couples to relate to and understand. The formulation of the problem in terms of patterns and cycles includes both partners in the maintenance of the problem, without blaming either person for the present distress in the relationship. Changing a distressing pattern is also a goal that both partners can agree on.

It may be that different aspects of the alliance are particularly crucial at different times in therapy; however, in general, all three elements form a prerequisite base for effective engagement in EFT. If any one aspect is missing, the client will not allow the therapist to evoke emotional experience, set up new interactions that appear dangerous and difficult, and suggest or interpret feelings and thoughts when necessary. At any moment in therapy, the tasks of the therapist are dependent on a positive alliance with both spouses. The therapist has to be able to block the usual pattern of interactions and focus the clients on their underlying feelings. This will not occur unless the clients are comfortable with including the therapist as a partner in the processing of their experience. Partners also have to be able to rely on the fact that unfamiliar, newly evoked aspects of self will be prized by the therapist, especially in the face of possible rejection by their spouses. The therapist provides a safe area for exploring new aspects of self, and this usually results in a strong bond between the therapist and each partner, especially by the end of therapy. The alliance in EFT is, however, considered a necessary condition for effective intervention, rather than an explicit active ingredient in change, as in classical Rogerian approaches (Rogers, 1961). Intrapsychic reprocessing of experience with the therapist also is not sufficient for relational change. What is crucial is the use of this reprocessing to create new relationship events, which then redefine the relationship between the couple.

The marital therapist must monitor the alliance with both spouses and explicitly address and repair it wherever necessary. This has been discussed in detail elsewhere (Johnson & Greenberg, 1989). The main requirement of the therapist in EFT is flexibility. He/she has to be able to move close to the couple and track their moment-to-moment experience and also choreograph new interactions with authority. The therapist then has to be able both to follow and to lead, to confront and to support, to practice self-disclosure and maintain professional distance, as the process of therapy demands. The therapist may be more or less active at various times in therapy; for example, at the end of therapy the therapist can be less active, handing over the initiative to the couple and affirming their achievements.

What are the kinds of errors that novice therapists typically make while learning EFT? First, there are mistakes in the area of the alliance. The alliance may not be balanced: for example, the therapist may identify, or through insensitive interventions, appear to identify with one client and blame the other. The novice therapist sometimes finds it difficult to validate one partner's experience and perceptions in such a way as to avoid implying judgment or negative intent on the part of the other. This situation improves when the therapist becomes more aware of the interpersonal implications of any intrapsychically oriented intervention. The therapist has to be engaged with an individual partner and also be conscious of the implications of this process for the other partner and the relationship. In general, to create and maintain an alliance, the therapist has to adapt to the client's style; this is part of the attunement to the client's experience mentioned earlier. If the client has particular difficulty accessing emotion, for example, the therapist may have to interpret more in the beginning of therapy than he/she would with more expressive clients. Experienced therapists adapt their pace, language, and level of intervention to the client.

The ability to maintain a clear focus on the processing of emotional responses and the restructuring of interactions is also essential. An inexperienced therapist will allow the focus to become diffuse or derailed in the session, or will not complete the process. For example, a withdrawn husband risks coming forward and reaches for his spouse, but his wife attacks him. The therapist may become confused or begin to lecture the attacking spouse, rather than focusing on the experience of the attacker and using evocative responding to explore her response, before then returning to the interaction in which the withdrawer attempts to contact his wife. The novice therapist may also access emotion and neglect to use this emotion to create new interactions. A client who has softened in a previous session may return after this session and exhibit high levels of hostility: The experienced therapist frames this in terms of the client's increased vulnerability in the last session and is able to continue the process of integrating the new experiences and responses into the relationship.

As the therapist gains experience in EFT, he/she becomes more and more discriminating as to the quality of emotional response required for change to occur. As discussed elsewhere (Greenberg & Johnson, 1988) *the superficial discussion of emotion is ineffective, as is the indiscriminate ventilation of reactive emotions.* The therapist learns to evoke vivid and intense emotional experience by "being skillfully" with the client (Kempler, 1981), rather than simply being skillful. He/she is then able to stay close to the client's experience and also help the client crystallize elements of that experience in a new way.

The EFT therapist does not usually engage in direct confrontation, but rather allows the process or the responses of one partner to confront the other with the nature or consequences of the other's actions. For example, the therapist may replay an interactional sequence in which a previously withdrawn wife made an assertive response that was dismissed by her partner, after which she again withdrew. The therapist tracks this process and either encourages the wife to express how she experienced this interaction, or replays the interaction so that the husband can see how he evokes the behavior he finds so distressing in his spouse.

Compliance also is not an issue in EFT; if the client cannot respond to a suggestion made by the therapist, then this is explored, and becomes part of the process of therapy. The classic example occurs when a husband has openly experienced new and powerful emotions with the therapist while his wife is present, but refuses to express these same emotions to his wife directly. The exploration of this refusal usually provides powerful material about how this individual experiences the relationship. It is often just as useful to tune into the unwillingness or difficulty that the client has in completing the tasks set by the therapist as it is to have the client acquiesce and complete the task.

GENERAL TECHNIQUES

The techniques used in EFT vary according to the steps of therapy. In all steps, however, the therapist is engaged in two main tasks: (1) working with emotional experiences, accessing, validating, reprocessing, and restructuring emotional responses, and (2) creating new relationship-defining events by reframing, restructuring, and consolidating interactions. The first task requires the use of techniques taken predominantly from Gestalt and client-centred approaches to change. The moment-to-moment experience of the clients is the key reference point in therapy. The therapist tracks how the partners construct their emotional experience and how this, in turn, creates their positions relative to each other. This is a process of discovery and creation; it is not simply more intimate self-disclosure.

The second task involves the reframing and restructuring of interactions toward accessibility and responsiveness. The reprocessed emotional experience of the partners is used to expand the previously negative patterns and to create new relationship events. Interactions are tracked and refocused, replayed and restructured. As the nature of the dialogue between partners changes, previously unresolvable problems become less relevant and problematic because they are able to be addressed on a completely different level in the context of the newly defined relationship (Johnson & Greenberg, 1991).

In order to demonstrate the EFT process, there follows a transcript of a change event. The specific interventions in EFT have been described in detail elsewhere (Greenberg & Johnson, 1988), and will not be listed here, but their application will be demonstrated. In this change event, the husband has already moved from a detached, submissive position and has taken a more accessible and assertive stance with his wife, who has at last seen him "without his business suit, his uniform on" in the therapy sessions. She had been generally angry and critical up to this point in therapy, threatening to leave the relationship and requiring that her spouse prove himself worthy of her trust. This was a typical couple in that this pursue–blame and withdraw–placate pattern is exceedingly common, with the female partner in the pursuing role and showing depressive symptoms at various times, as was the case here. Both partners were referred to a hospital clinic for severe marital distress and were seen by one of us (SMJ). This couple's score on the Dyadic Adjustment Scale (Spanier, 1976) was 63 (a score of 70 is typical of divorcing couples). The process of this therapy was also typical in that the therapist focused more intensely on the withdrawn spouse in the first sessions, although the therapist actively works with both partners throughout therapy, because without modifying the withdrawer's position, engagement is impossible, and the other partner will resist changing from his/her self-protective stance.

Transcript 1: A Softening Change Event (Session 14)

A *softening* is defined as a previously hostile/critical spouse asking, from a position of vulnerability, a newly accessible partner for what he/she needs.

THERAPIST: What happened in the fight?

PRUE: I was disappointed he was not home but when he came in, he'd been drinking, and I got mad.

MARK: You were mad and you left . . . I can deal with you mad, but you accused me of accepting this job to get more involved at work and spend less time with you, of withdrawing—and that hurt—it's not true—then you walked out after you threw that at me.

PRUE: I talked about feelings and you got very defensive.

THERAPIST1 (*to Mark*): You feel accused, whatever actually happened. You experienced it that way?

MARK: Yes.

THERAPIST: How do you feel about that accusation?

MARK: I get hurt—I try so hard to be there. You never asked me about the job, so I try to go insensitive—shut it down—(*to the therapist*) then she cries and leaves. [This accurate description of the interaction pattern and the awareness of feelings and of how he copes reflects the work already done.]

PRUE: Well, the job he's been offered will take all his time. He'll be off—off on the computer—in his office downstairs.

THERAPIST (*to Prue*): How do you feel when you talk about this?

PRUE: Sad and very angry.

THERAPIST: Angry? What I pick up is sad and *afraid*. Maybe I'm off the wall here, but it feels familiar to me (*slows pace, drops voice*). What I'm hearing, if I'm hearing it right, is the piece of music that says, "I can't trust you, I daren't trust you, you're not going to be there for me, you're not going to be there—you'll go off and do your own thing—I'll never be first with you (*pause*). You're not going to be there. I can't trust you. I'll fight, I won't let you hurt me—you're not going to be there." That's what I'm hearing (*long pause*). [The therapist heightens and empathically interprets, frames Prue's response in terms of fear and abandonment. The goal is to access the more primary emotions underlying Prue's anger.]

PRUE (*slowly, quietly*): I can't even be clear. I can't say how he's not going to be there for me.

THERAPIST: Does that fit, Prue?

PRUE: Yes, yes (*tears*). I get angry instead—I guess I've just never recognized it as being afraid—as fear.

THERAPIST: So, it's like there's an alarm inside of you honed to Mark deserting you, leaving you alone, and you felt this when you moved the first time and after the baby was born (*Prue nods*) and so when he comes home and says, "I've been offered a new job," the alarm goes off? [The therapist uses simple images to crystallize the couple's experience.]

PRUE: Yeah, right (*cries*), the alarm goes off. . . . (*to Mark*) I was proud you got offered the job, but then I thought—for me it's going to be so lonely—you're not going to be around and it's a job—it has to be done, (*to the Therapist*) I don't feel like I can tell him to be with me.

THERAPIST: You don't have the right to say, "I need you. Come and be with me." [The therapist heightens the attachment need and the sense of unentitlement.]

PRUE: No, it's work—he has to do it.

THERAPIST (*very softly*): What would it be like, Prue, to go to Mark and say, "Mark, I need you. Come and be with me"?

PRUE: I don't do that—I don't, I don't know (*agitated*).

THERAPIST (*softly, slowly*): You don't feel that your needs, that who you are is special and important enough that you can ask—have the right to say, "I need you; be with me." [The therapist interprets, explicating and heightening the sense of unentitlement.]

PRUE (*sobbing*): I'm not working—pulling my weight (*sobs*).

THERAPIST: You're not special enough. You have no right to be first—no right—no. (*Prue nods, sobs.*) How does that feel? [The therapist shows empathic reflection, with a focus on emotional experience.]

PRUE: Awful.

THERAPIST (*softly*): Yeah, to have all that need and all that fear and feel like you can't go and get some reassurance (*pause*)—no wonder you get mad. What else can you do?

PRUE: Yes.

THERAPIST: Have you ever been with anyone where you felt really entitled to go and say, "I need—come—just because I need you"? [The therapist evokes longing and deprivation.]

PRUE: Maybe my mom, when I was little—not to a man. No, no (*shakes her head*) . . . (*calmer*). I feel guilty about not working. I've never felt totally okay about it. (*Repeats this, becoming cooler and more detached.*)

THERAPIST [refocusing]: So what happens inside you is you feel, "I've disappointed Mark. I haven't met his expectations—I should be different, I should be working—so I can't ask." Your loneliness isn't that important. You don't allow yourself to do that.

PRUE: Well, once in a blue moon, maybe. Well, no—no, I don't let it come out of my mouth.

THERAPIST: In fact, I think that's when you say, like you did the other night, "I'm going out"—it's like "You won't take care of me, so I'll take care of me"—and he hears that you don't need him at all. And the two of you never get close—you don't risk it. When you need him most, you get angry and up and leave. Am I going too far here? [The therapist relates her response to Mark's experience and to the relationship cycle. Her working model of attachment is that she is unworthy and unentitled and the other will abandon her.]

PRUE: That's right, I can't. I don't feel comfortable talking about these needs with Mark

THERAPIST: Right (*pause*). Can you tell him, "I'm too scared to tell you how much I need you"? [The therapist uses reprocessed feeling to create new relationship event.]

PRUE (*long pause, crying*): I can't. (*her eyes widen, shakes her head.*)

THERAPIST: Ah-ha. (*softly*) Even that's scary, right (*pause*). Can you look at him right now? (*She does.*) You're too scared to show him that fear? [The therapist reflects her fear.]

PRUE (*crying*): I never get it out the right way. I don't communicate it. (*Mark is engaged, present, leaning forward.*)

THERAPIST: Alarm bells. You can't let him see how afraid you are. What will happen if he sees, Prue, if he sees how scared you are, scared that you will reach for him and he won't be there? If he sees that . . . [The therapist focuses on the catastrophic fear of exposure and abandonment.]

PRUE: He would be there. I do think he would—but . . .

THERAPIST: But?

PRUE: He hasn't supported me to stay at home—well, maybe it's the way I ask— well

THERAPIST [refocusing]: In your head you say, "Yeah, he'd be there—he would. Yeah, most of the time, he would, he likes to be needed" Right? (*Prue nods.*) I think he would too, but there's another level—here we're talking about fear. This is like the fear a little child feels—a little Prue that starts screaming her head off. Dangerous, dangerous—I can't, I can't. He won't be there—I'll die, it will be so awful—I'll ask and he won't be there. [The therapist heightens the fear event.]

PRUE (*crying*): Yes, yes, yes. (*sobs*)

THERAPIST (*long pause, leaning toward Prue*): What's happening right now?

PRUE: I don't know if he could understand . . .

THERAPIST: You don't know if you could reach him?

PRUE: Yes.

THERAPIST: What do you feel listening to Prue, Mark?

MARK: I'm not sure—I feel sorry for us as a couple—I'm trying to think how we communicated after the move. We never talk on that level.

THERAPIST: Can you tell her how you feel right now—right now? [The therapist directs the interaction.]

MARK: I feel sad.

THERAPIST: Can you tell her?

MARK: I feel sad you can't come and say you need me. If you did, I'd be there in a flash—I would.

THERAPIST: Are you asking her to give you a chance? You'd like to be there? [The therapist heightens his accessibility to facilitate restructuring the interaction.]

MARK: Absolutely. I want to be needed (*leaning toward her*). I'm not going to turn you away.

THERAPIST (*to Prue*): Do you hear him talking to that tiny afraid person inside you and he's saying, "Try me out. Risk it—reach for me—let me be there for you. Let go. I'll catch you—come and be close." He's inviting you. [The therapist replays and heightens interaction event.]

PRUE: Yes (*sobs*).

MARK: It's the issue. If I could just find a way round—solve the . . . why this happens (*looks off into the distance*).

THERAPIST [focusing, blocking, Mark's distancing]: Mark, I'd like you to just see that she's afraid and just stay with her—never mind the solution. Can you see she's afraid? I want you to meet your wife. Will you please come out of your head, come and meet your wife—like you took your business suit off to meet her—and now here she is. (*Prue bursts into tears.*) [The therapist directs interaction toward engagement].

THERAPIST (*to Prue*): What's happening, Prue?

PRUE: He probably doesn't want to meet me. I don't want him to meet me—I don't want anyone to ever meet this person. [The therapist moves closer, hands Prue a tissue as she sobs, puts her hand on Prue's arm, long pause.]

THERAPIST: You don't want anyone to see that needy scared part of you—no one could like her, right? [Empathic reflection; core model of self is enacted here.]

PRUE: I don't like her. I won't show anymore—

THERAPIST: Hmm—you don't see that part of you as lovable. Mark certainly wouldn't want to put his arms around her and hold her—he couldn't possibly feel that. [The therapist evokes her longing/fear of rejection.]

PRUE: He'd feel disappointed.

THERAPIST: Disappointed?

PRUE: She's weak, she's needy . . .

THERAPIST: Ah, ha! What do you want, Prue, right now? Need, right now?

PRUE: I want Mark to hold me.

THERAPIST: Ask him. [Directs interaction.]

PRUE: Please hold me. I'm scared. (*Mark holds her; the therapist looks out window. Prue cries.*)

After a session of this kind, it is wise for the therapist to caution clients not to expect that all will be resolved between them and not to be disappointed if they find they are unable to be nurtured by, or close to, their partners during the week. After all, these painful feelings have kept them protecting themselves for years and will not suddenly disappear, nor will the partner be able to be sufficiently comforting to soothe them away in one week.

After this particular session, Prue distanced Mark until the next session, when she began the session with a loaded, angry issue. The therapist refocused the session and continued the process from the previous week. Prue then shared all the "failings" that she was sure Mark would see and disapprove of if she let down her guard. She agreed that when she began to let him in, she then "got scared, so I'd run or smack him." He was protective, warm and reassuring, stating, "I fell in love with that soft part of you. I want it back, I want to hold and protect you." In the present, she struggled with her fear, feeling "physical panic" and avoiding Mark's eyes, in which she knew that she would see "disapproval." The therapist directed her to tell Mark how much she needed his approval and acceptance. She struggled and then complied. He responded lovingly and commented, "The soft childish scared part of you that you don't like, that's the easiest part to connect with." The remaining sessions consisted of consolidating the changes, which were now apparent, in each partner's position.

As previously mentioned, this kind of change event has been linked to successful outcome in EFT (Johnson & Greenberg, 1988), as have general indices of the processes involved in these events, such as depth of experiencing, affective self-disclosure, and affiliative interaction (Greenberg et al., 1993). The specification of the client performances that lead to change, and the therapist interventions that facilitate them, enables clinicians to train therapists efficiently because it is then possible to say what works and when.

CLINICAL ISSUES

Who are the couples for whom EFT is particularly suited? Couples who do well in EFT tend to show at least a minimal level of basic trust and goodwill, can learn to take some responsibility for their part in the creation of relationship cycles, and have an emotional investment in maintaining the relationship. Couples who show little progress in EFT usually contain one partner who is rigidly unable or unwilling to shift his/her position or reprocess key emotional responses. No matter what the other partner does in the session, this partner is unable to tolerate the experience of vulnerability in relation to the spouse. This may be a matter of motivation. Perhaps one partner has already become detached and is unwilling to reengage, or has a personal style that prohibits the trusting openness, and responsiveness that foster a close bond. Frequently, partners for whom trusting another is extremely problematic have never experienced any kind of secure attachment in their past. There is evidence that the experience of even one secure, safe relationship in childhood may mitigate the results of parental abuse and allow an abused person to create positive relationships (Egeland, Jacobvitz, & Sroufe, 1988). People who have never experienced such safety have extremely negative expectations of relationships and view intimacy as a strange and unknown phenomenon. If trust, or a willingness to put one's fate in the hands of another (Holmes & Rempel, 1989), is viewed as containing three elements—predictability, dependability, and faith—it seems likely that for those who have never experienced a safe attachment, trust would be hard to come by. Such partners may have low threat thresholds, and anxiety levels that evoke coercion or avoidance in relation to their spouse, and are easier to prime and harder to dispel than in those who have known safe closeness. The vigilance and risk-aversive strategies that such partners employ tend to nullify expectancy-disconfirming events and create the negative relationships they fear. It is generally true that negative behavior is treated as more diagnostically relevant in intimate relationships, even by trusting partners, perhaps because our emotional system is keyed to issuing warnings (Berscheid, 1983); however, this may be unassailable in such partners. Clinically, the best prognostic indicators appear to be, not distress level per se, but whether the partners, and female partners in particular, still have some trust for the other (Johnson & Talitman, 1995), as well as whether they are able, in the sessions, to respond at all to the other's vulnerability when it is expressed. Trust difficulties may also be the result of attachment history in the past or in the present relationship. Violence, for example, or any particularly meaningful incident in which one partner felt betrayed, abandoned, or rejected by the other may block the willingness to trust.

The crucial importance of trust is also underlined by the fact that the line between self-regulation and other-regulation, self-representation and other-representation, is very thin in intimate relationships (Tronick, 1989). The partner has incredible power to influence the ongoing construal of self and the regulation of positive and negative emotions arising from without and within the relationship. Either the attachment figure can give feedback that facilitates a positive sense of self and aids in the regulation of any negative emotions that occur, or he/she can define the partner in distressing, demeaning, or disorienting ways and contribute negatively to the partner's ability to manage negative affect.

The effectiveness of EFT does not seem to vary with the emotional expressiveness of the partners; in fact, EFT can be a powerful intervention with an emotionally stilted partner perhaps because, once engaged upon, the process of discovering one's emotional life is often empowering and enriching (Johnson & Talitman, 1995). The therapist begins by validating the partner's inhibition and/or lack of awareness of his/her emotions, and is then able to help such a partner to experience new aspects of himself/herself. For example, a husband who recognizes that he is always "numb" emotionally, is able to own the fact that he numbs himself and then access the sadness that he feels when relating to others. This experience of sadness tends to be very powerful, both for this partner personally and for redefining his relationship, precisely because these emotions are newly experienced and expressed. EFT is not suited for couples who are clearly separating, for whom the goal of a secure and intimate bond is not appropriate. It is also not suited for abusive relationships, which may or may not include physical violence, where vulnerability will be taken advantage of and used to harm.

What are some of the difficulties that arise in the practice of EFT? First, it is necessary for the therapist to see how responses are created by the relationship pattern, that is, how they are evoked by the responses of the other, and as a product of intrapsychic emotional processing and attempts at self-regulation. Novice therapists find this double perspective difficult at first. It involves a therapist's seeing, for example, a husband's withdrawal and frustrating passivity as a reflection of his fear of contact with his spouse, his perception of his spouse as judgmental and

rejecting, and his sense of inadequacy, as well as seeing the impact of his wife's aggressive response when he does try to make contact, and the cycle they both create in the relationship. Similarly, it involves a therapist's seeing a wife's aggressive, complaining attack as a reflection of her frustrated needs for contact with her unavailable spouse, who avoids her, her perception of him as rejecting her, and her sense of unlovableness in the relationship. Then, the therapist learns to alternate between reprocessing intrapsychic realities and recreating interpersonal realities. The therapist's level of experience and interaction is also crucial here. It is not the partner's discussion or ventilation of already formulated emotional responses or the enactment of "nicer" responses to each other that create change, but the engagement in new, emotionally charged experience and the translation of that engagement into new attachment events. For example, it is a partner's new experience of anger that is owned and stated to the spouse as, "I'll shut you out, I won't let you control and destroy me," that creates a new contact between spouses.

As we have stated elsewhere (Johnson & Greenberg, 1987), part of the process of learning to implement EFT is to learn how to track inner experience and the relationship dance, and to use process diagnosis to judge when interventions are appropriate, to know what emotion is waiting to be accessed and what the effect of the expression of this emotion is likely to be at a certain point in therapy. The experiential techniques of tuning into and accepting each partner's experience are crucial here. The nonjudgmental stance of the therapist is learned and maintained by a self-monitoring process. The therapist empathizes with each person's position, and attempts to tune in to the most poignant aspects of this experience. The stance of "difficult" partners then becomes grist for the mill of therapy rather than a hurdle the therapist has to circumvent. For example, the very aggressive blamer who begins to soften and engage his/her spouse only to then react with even more virulent hostility, is helped by the therapist to connect with his/her deep fear of depending on anyone and his/her refusal to be vulnerable. The partners then have to deal with this reality.

The main techniques, apart from those already mentioned, for dealing with difficult impasses, whether in the intrapsychic processing of an individual partner or in the interactional process, are to conduct individual sessions and/or to provide a diagnostic picture to the client. Individual sessions, if used, are always balanced between partners. These sessions would typically involve the use of experiential or Gestalt techniques to resynthesize strong emotional responses that block contact between spouses. It is also possible to make present and reprocess specific incidents in the attachment history of couples that impact the present relationship. This process would focus on specific problematic responses and how past emotional experiences influence the partners' present perceptions and responses, rather than on general family of origin issues. For example, in one couple, the husband would attempt to leave during a fight and the wife would block the doorway. This experience was so negative for the husband that he would become verbally abusive and threatening, undermining the trust his wife was learning to have for him. In an individual session, this experience was explored as a prototypical situation in which this individual felt completely overwhelmed and experienced catastrophic panic. As he reprocessed this situation, the object of his responses shifted from his wife to his mother. He began to deal with the painful abuse that he had experienced as a child and never as yet recognized, owned, or communicated to anyone. In the following marital sessions, his presentation of self changed dramatically and he was able to communicate his pain to his wife. The main work continued to be focused in the here and now between the couple; this facet, however, brought a vital missing piece into the context of the interaction. To be specific, the therapist did not work on this client's relationship with his mother per se; rather, she helped the client recognize how a past interaction directed his response toward his wife, and used the sharing of this to create new interactions between the couple. Insight into his attachment history was not the goal here, but a deeper experiencing of the fears that arose when he related to his wife in a conflict situation.

A diagnostic picture involves the presentation of process patterns and the therapist's conclusions drawn from those patterns about the nature of the present relationship and the possibilities for the future. The process tends to be confrontational but the therapist, as relationship consultant, does not take a confrontational stance. The therapist might say,

"It seems like we get stuck here doesn't it? We have been here before. Jim, you reach for Anne but it seems that it's hard for you, Anne, to take the risk and respond. It's almost like there is nothing he can do to persuade you to take the risk. The sad thing is that this leaves you, Jim, feeling helpless and depressed, and you, Anne, feeling alone and angry. I don't know how to help the two of you get closer."

The therapist describes the problematic interaction and the consequences of the interaction in the here and now and in terms of the possibilities for relationship satisfaction in the future. The partners are then in a context where a choice has to be made: to risk change, to live with the present impasse, or to separate. The therapist focuses on and heightens the choice that the couple faces. The "diagnostic picture intervention" is also used in the termination process of EFT. The therapist describes the original relationship cycles and partner's positions and then delineates the present interactions, highlighting the changes and their consequences for the couple's sense of security and intimacy.

Two problematic types of couple interaction that typically arise in the process of EFT are (1) interactions involving an inaccessible and/or self-deprecating withdrawer and (2) those involving a rigidly hostile, mistrustful blamer. The latter interaction is the most difficult and is the point at which EFT is most likely to fail with chronically distressed couples. Let us look at these two situations and consider the interventions typically used in each one. The first prerequisite to facilitating the emergence of an inaccessible withdrawer is a positive therapeutic relationship. The therapist has to join with the withdrawn partner and create a sense of safety that acts as an antidote to the anxiety and self-protectiveness of such partners. The position this partner takes and his/her experience in the relationship is accepted and framed as legitimate. Empathic reflection encourages such partners to touch emotions they habitually avoid and to begin accessing and expressing feared or despised (by the self and/or by the spouse) aspects of self. The therapist reflects as respectfully as possible the pain inherent in the withdrawer's experience in the relationship, using evocative responding and replays to connect the partner with his/her own experience.

THERAPIST: How do you feel when your wife uses that word, "wimp", and she is talking about you?
JIM: Maybe I am, maybe I am a wimp.
THERAPIST: How are you feeling right now, Jim? What happened when you put your hand over your eyes?

JIM: Maybe she's right. I don't know how I feel. She says it lots.

THERAPIST: So, it happens often? Yes, and you are used to it, is that it? (*Jim nods.*) So, you know how to duck?

JIM: (*laughs*) I just don't listen, I guess.

THERAPIST: You tune her out, or switch off, or go somewhere else? [The therapist uses simple images and metaphors.]

JIM: Yeah, I switch off (*he makes a switch gesture*).

THERAPIST: Right, then she can't reach you. You're not there. How does it feel when you do this, right now, when you turn the switch?

JIM: Bad (*tears in his eyes*).

The therapist then works on accessing the feelings, often of inadequacy, loneliness, and hopelessness, that underlie this partner's avoidance of engagement. If the client is really lost and cannot access any feeling the therapist will interpret.

THERAPIST: Perhaps I'm wrong, but right now, although you say you don't feel anything, I'm picking up incredible sadness just sitting here. [The therapist will then get the withdrawer to explicitly enact his position.] Can you tell your spouse, "I switch off, I go away, I can't stay and listen to you telling me I'm nothing, I won't stay"? [The therapist makes his position active and explicit but frames it in terms of the message the client gets from his wife.]

As the withdrawer's need for self-protection lessens and the vulnerable aspects of self he is protecting emerge in the sessions and are legitimized, he/she begins to move to a less submissive and/or passive position in relationship to the spouse and to access other emotions, such as anger. The therapist supports these moves and directs the partner to take risks that are, in themselves, a reversal of his/her previous stance.

THERAPIST: Can you tell her now, "I won't let you do this to me. Don't tell me who I am"? (*Jim does his version of this.*) How did that feel, Jim? (*Jim beams and replies positively.*) Good, can you say it again, please?

The therapist has to help contain the other partner's anxiety, because the blaming spouse often reacts with alarm and may become more hostile. The therapist has to frame the husband's responses as the first step to being present with and for his wife and to use empathy and validation to support her and help her tolerate this interactional shift. By the end of therapy, with-

drawers usually reach for and reassure the spouse and frame themselves more positively as individuals and partners. It is also empowering for them to see that they have helped to create the partner's responses by their avoidance of contact. They also see the partner's vulnerability, and so feel less threatened by his/her hostility.

The hostile, mistrustful blamer is the potential nemesis of most marital therapists, including the EFT therapist. The worst-case scenario is that he/she refuses to take any responsibility for the creation of the negative cycles in the relationship and the impact of his/her behavior on the partner. This is usually coupled with an implicit refusal to be vulnerable in and outside the session. The therapist structures interactions to render this position explicit, "Can you tell him, I won't put my weapon down, I won't be vulnerable to you, no matter what you do," and follows this with interventions, such as presenting a diagnostic picture. However, most blamers, demanders, and aggressive partners, do soften. What interventions does the therapist typically use here? The therapist's first task is to help this partner access the emotions underlying his/her position. These are typically, from a bonding perspective, feelings of abandonment, rejection, and a fear of trusting and depending on the other. In attachment terms, if you cannot get your attachment figure to respond to your distress by coming closer, then panic and helplessness naturally follow. Empathic reflection and evocative responding help the therapist tune into and elaborate particular responses that occur in the session.

THERAPIST: What happens to you when your spouse says, "I do my best, Maria." What is happening right now?

MARIA: I don't want to hear it, I feel so angry.

THERAPIST: It's hard to hear this, that he is trying, when you feel so (*pause*).

MARIA: Lonely. What am I supposed to do then? Say, "Fine, okay"?

THERAPIST: You feel helpless? (*Maria nods.*) Like, he says he's trying and you still feel empty and alone, yes? (*Maria nods.*) Can you tell him about that helplessness?

Here, the therapist moves to restructure the interaction around this partner's helplessness rather than her anger. The therapist will then help the husband to respond to this emotional expression and in the process, the blamer's fears of trusting and disorientation at her partner's recent availability emerge.

The therapist engages in intense sequences of

helping the blamer process his/her emotions, catastrophic fears, and attachment longings that particularly arise here, validating and supporting the processor, preventing any loss of focus with redirections and replays, and setting tasks that involve the blamer allowing him/herself to become vulnerable and ask for what he/she needs from the spouse. One version of this process is contained in the previous transcript. It is important to note that this situation is experienced as a potent crisis by the blaming spouse; it constitutes a letting go of defenses that have evolved as the only security available for this partner and confronting the danger and exquisite hope of reaching for the partner in a new way. It is also a crisis for the relationship, in that at this moment the withdrawer is available (or the therapist would not be initiating these interventions) and responsive, and the blaming partner struggles toward a new kind of contact. He/she struggles in the face of past disappointments to believe that the other is, in fact, available, and that it is safe to experience and express his/her attachment needs. In our experience, this softening event is a watershed for the relationship and a powerful attachment event that initiates a new sense of safety, trust, and contact in the relationship. The remaining sessions consist of consolidating the emotional engagement between spouses and dealing with termination.

A potential problem arises in EFT at Step 6 of the process. when the blaming partner is particularly hostile. If the therapist, having accessed one partner's experience, is working with the hostile spouse to promote acceptance of the other's expressed experience (e.g., "I am intimidated by you, so I hide"), and this spouse is unable to accept the other's experience or begins to attack, a potential crisis exists, in that this could confirm the first partner's belief that it is unsafe to express underlying feelings and needs, and solidify the dysfunctional interactional cycle. This may be handled in a number of ways. First, the therapist is continually assessing how open the system is to change and does not try to access underlying vulnerabilities in one partner until it appears that the other has some openness to hearing the disclosure and that the system is developing some flexibility. In the situation in which the partner does become vulnerable, the therapist is alert to the first signs of nonacceptance in the spouse and can intervene immediately to block this response and reframe it. It can be reframed and explored as an internal block in the listener that makes it difficult for him/her to hear the other. This block may then also be

explored in terms of how it operates to prevent contact between the spouses, and contributes to the negative cycle of pursue–distance. The therapist also needs to support and validate the disclosing partner and may suggest that it is very difficult for the other spouse to be able to hear and respond immediately to this behavior; in fact, there is usually a period of confusion, disorientation, and testing before the other can respond.

FUTURE DIRECTIONS

If a particular therapy has been found to be generally effective, and attempts have been made to specify the change processes involved in that treatment, then a next logical step is to ascertain if this set of interventions benefits particular couples more than others. Research into client variables that might predict success in EFT has begun, and we will also continue to look at the process of change, because understanding these phenomena is so crucial in this field (Johnson & Greenberg, 1991). The examination of the effectiveness of EFT interventions targeted at particular miniprocesses, such as the creation of intimacy, has been conducted (Dandeneau & Johnson, 1994) and will continue. It is also important to keep the link between intervention and the theoretical view of adult intimacy espoused by any particular school of marital therapy clear. As attachment theory continues to be applied to adult relationships and our understanding of this phenomenon deepens, its application to the field of marital therapy should become more and more fruitful (Johnson, in press). For example, it may be that particular kinds of couples with particular attachment styles are more suited for one kind of marital therapy than another, or respond better to certain interventions than other couples. Partners with avoidant–dismissing attachment styles, for example, may need particular kinds of intervention in order to maximize their response to marital therapy.

The use of EFT with special populations is also a promising area. Some preliminary work has been conducted using EFT with couples in which the female partner is clinically depressed and maritally distressed, and the results, albeit with a small sample, are promising (Dessaulles, 1991). More research is needed here, but certainly from the EFT perspective, it is possible to hypothesize several ways in which EFT might be expected to impact this particular individual symptomatology. First, interactional patterns that make secure attachment and intimacy difficult are likely to help create and/or maintain depression: in fact, one of the signs of separation distress in attachment theory is depression (Bowlby, 1969). In the face of an innate need for connection and engagement, depression is a natural response to isolation and deprivation. Symptoms tend to be maintained by the rules of the relationship, and the relationship as experienced, also tends to solidify those rules. The model of self, often negative in depressed partners, may be viewed as being constantly defined in relation to one's intimate other, and the creation of a more secure bond, in which each individual is defined so as to enhance self-esteem and self-efficacy, is a powerful antidote to the sense of loss and inadequacy that often seems to underlie depressive symptoms. EFT has also been applied to populations in which marital relationships are excessively stressed: for example, it has been used for the parents of chronically ill children (Walker, Johnson, Manion, Cloutier, 1995). Attachment theory states that a secure bond buffers individuals against stress and increases their ability to cope effectively with problematic situations in this population. EFT improved not only the marital satisfaction of these couples but also their ability to cope with the parenting stress inherent in this situation.

Marital therapy is still a relatively new field and has many challenges to face (Johnson, 1991). If we can respond to these challenges and refine our strategies and techniques, as well as begin to understand how and when they work, perhaps marital intervention can take its place as a powerful means of creating change, not just in specific relationships, but also in both family systems and individual functioning.

REFERENCES

Ainsworth, M. D. (1982). Attachment: Retrospect and prospect. In C. M. Parkos & J. J. Stevenson-Hinde (Eds.), *The place of attachment in human behavior* (pp. 3–30). New York: Basic Books.

Alexander, J. F., Holtzworth-Munroe, A., & Jameson, P. (1994). The process and outcome of marital and family therapy: Research review and evaluation. In A. E. Bergin & S. L. Garfield (Eds.), *Handbook of psychotherapy and behavior change* (4th ed., pp. 595–612). New York: Wiley.

Bartholomew, K., & Horowitz, L. (1991). Attachment styles among young adults. *Journal of Personality and Social Psychology, 61,* 226–244.

Berscheid, E. (1983). Emotion. In H. H. Kelley, E. Ber-

scheid, A. Christensen, J. H. Harvey, T. L. Huston, G. Levinger, E. McClintock, L. A. Peplau, & D. R. Peterson, *Close relationships* (pp. 110–168). New York: Freeman.

Bordin, E. S. (1979). The generalizability of the psychoanalytic concept of the working alliance. *Psychotherapy, 16,* 252–260.

Bowlby, J. (1969). *Attachment and loss: Vol. 1. Attachment.* New York: Basic Books.

Bowlby, J. (1973). *Attachment and loss: Vol. 2. Separation.* New York: Basic Books.

Bowlby, J. (1988). *A secure base.* New York: Basic Books.

Dandeneau, M., & Johnson, S. M. (1994). Facilitating intimacy: A comparative outcome study of emotionally focused and cognitive interventions. *Journal of Marital and Family Therapy, 20,* 17–33.

Dessaulles, A. (1991). *The treatment of clinical depression in the context of marital distress.* Unpublished doctoral dissertation, University of Ottawa, Canada.

Egeland, B., Jacobvitz, D., & Sroufe, A. L. (1988). *Child Development, 59,* 1080–1088.

Fox, N., Kimmerly, N. L., & Schafer, W. D. (1991). Attachment to mother/attachment to father: A meta-analysis. *Child Development, 62,* 210–225.

Frijda, N. H. (1986). *The emotions.* Cambridge, England: Cambridge University Press.

Gottman, J. M. (1979). *Marital interaction: Experimental investigations.* New York: Academic Press.

Gottman, J. M. (1991). Predicting the longitudinal course of marriages. *Journal of Marital and Family Therapy, 17,* 3–7.

Gottman, J. M., & Krokoff, L. F. (1989). Marital interaction and satisfaction: A longitudinal view. *Journal of Consulting and Clinical Psychology, 57,* 47–52.

Gottman, J. M., & Levenson, R. W. (1986). Assessing the role of emotion in marriage. *Behavioral Assessment, 8,* 31–48.

Greenberg, L. S., Ford, C., Alden, L., & Johnson, S. M. (1993). Change processes in emotionally focused therapy. *Journal of Consulting and Clinical Psychology, 61,* 78–84.

Greenberg, L. S., James, P., & Conry, R. (1988). Perceived change processes in emotionally focused couples therapy. *Family Psychology, 2,* 4–23.

Greenberg, L. S., & Johnson, S. M. (1986). Affect in marital therapy. *Journal of Marital and Family Therapy, 12,* 1–10.

Greenberg, L. S., & Johnson, S. M. (1988). *Emotionally focused therapy for couples.* New York: Guilford Press.

Greenberg, L. S., & Johnson, S. M. (1990). Emotional change processes in couples therapy. In E. A. Blechman (Ed.), *Emotions and the family* (pp. 137–154), Hillsdale, NJ: Erlbaum.

Greenberg, L. S., & Safran, J. D. (1987). *Emotion in psychotherapy*. New York: Guilford Press.

Guidano, V. F., & Liotti, G. (1983). *Cognitive processes and emotional disorders: A structural approach to psychotherapy*. New York: Guilford Press.

Hazan, C., & Shaver, P. (1987). Conceptualizing romantic love as an attachment process. *Journal of Personality and Social Psychology, 52*, 511–524.

Hazan, C., & Shaver, P. R. (1994). Attachment as an organizational framework for research on close relationships. *Psychological Inquiry, 5*, 1–22.

Holmes, J. G., & Rempel, J. K. (1989). Trust in close relationships. *Review of Personality and Social Psychology, 19*, 187–220.

Izard, C. E. (1979). *Emotion in personality and psychopathology*. New York: Plenum.

Johnson, S. M. (1986). Bonds and bargains: Relationship paradigms and their significance for marital therapy. *Journal of Marital and Family Therapy, 12*, 259–267.

Johnson, S. M. (1989). Integrating marital and individual therapy for incest survivors. *Psychotherapy: Theory, Research, and Practice, 26*, 96–103.

Johnson, S. M. (1991). Marital therapy: Issues and challenges. *Journal of Psychiatry and Neuroscience, 16*, 176–181.

Johnson, S. M., & Greenberg, L. S. (Eds.). (1994). *The heart of the matter: Emotion in marital therapy*. New York: Brunner/Mazel.

Johnson, S. M. (in press). Marital therapy: Research status and directions. In G. P. Sholevar (Ed.), *Textbook of family and marital therapy*. Washington, DC: APPI Press.

Johnson, S. M., & Greenberg, L. S. (1987). Emotionally focused marital therapy: An overview. *Psychotherapy, 24*, 552–560.

Johnson, S. M., & Greenberg, L. S. (1988). Relating process to outcome in marital therapy. *Journal of Marital and Family Therapy, 14*, 175–183.

Johnson, S. M., & Greenberg, L. S. (1989). The therapeutic alliance in marital therapy. *Journal of Cognitive Psychotherapy, 3*, 97–110.

Johnson, S. M., & Greenberg, L. S. (1991). There are more things in heaven and earth than are dreamed of in BMT: A reply to Jacobson. *American Journal of Family Psychology, 4*, 407–415.

Johnson, S. M., & Greenberg, L. S. (1992). Emotionally focused therapy: Restructuring attachment. In S. H. Budman, M. F. Hoyt, & S. Friedman (Eds.), *The first session in brief therapy* (pp. 204–224). New York: Guilford Press.

Kempler, W. (1981). *Experiential psychotherapy within families*. New York: Brunner/Mazel.

Leventhal, H. (1979). A perceptual motor processing model of emotion. In P. Pliner, K. R. Blankstein, & I. M. Spigel (Eds.), *Advances in the study of communication and affect: Vol. 5. Perceptions of emotions in self and others* (pp. 1–46). New York: Plenum.

Leventhal, H. (1984). A perceptual motor theory of emotion. In L. Berkowitz (Ed.), *Advances in experimental social psychology* (Vol. 17, pp. 117–182). New York: Academic Press.

Minuchin, S. (1974). *Families and family change*. Cambridge, MA: Harvard University Press.

Napier, A. Y. (1978). The rejection–intrusion pattern: A central dynamic. *Journal of Marriage and Family Counseling, 14*, 5–12.

Paterson, R. J., & Moran, G. (1989). Attachment theory: Personality development and psychotherapy. *Clinical Psychology Review, 8*, 611–636.

Perls, F. S. (1973). *The Gestalt approach and eye witness to therapy*. Palo Alto, CA: Science & Behavior Books.

Rice, L. N., & Greenberg, L. S. (1992). Humanistic approaches to psychotherapy. In H. Freedheim & J. Norcross (Eds.), *History of psychotherapy*. VA: APA Publications.

Rogers, C. R. (1961). *On becoming a person*. Boston: Houghton-Mifflin.

Senchak, M., & Leonard, K. (1992). Attachment styles and marital adjustment among newlywed couples. *Journal of Social and Personal Relationships, 9*, 51–64.

Shaver, P., Hazan, C., Bradshaw, D. (1988). Love as attachment. In R. J. Sternberg & M. L. Barnes (Eds.), *The psychology of love* (pp. 68–99). New Haven: Yale University Press.

Spanier, G. (1976). Measuring dyadic adjustment. *Journal of Marriage and the Family, 38*, 15–28.

Stoufe, A. L. (1979). Socioemotional development. In J. D. Osofsky (Ed.), *Handbook of infant development* (pp. 462–516).

Sroufe, A. L. (1989). Relationships and individual adaptation. In A. J. Sameroff & R. N. Emde (Eds.), *Relationship disturbances in early childhood* (pp. 70–94). New York: Basic Books.

Steinglass, P. (1987). A systems view of family interaction and psychopathology. In T. Jacob (Ed.), *Family interaction and psychopathology* (pp. 25–63). New York: Plenum.

Stern, D. N. (1977). *The first relationship: Infant and mother*. Cambridge, MA: Harvard University Press.

Stern, D. N. (1985). *The interpersonal world of the infant: A view from psychoanalysis and developmental psychology*. New York: Basic Books.

Thompson, R. A. (1900). Emotion and self-regulation. In R. Dienstbier (Ed.), *Socioemotional development* (pp. 365–467). Lincoln, NE: University of Nebraska Press.

Tronick, E. Z. (1989). Emotions and emotional communication in infants. *American Psychologist, 44*, 112–119.

7

Problem- and Solution-Focused Couple Therapies: The MRI and Milwaukee Models

VARDA SHOHAM[1]
MICHAEL ROHRBAUGH
JOELLEN PATTERSON

DESPITE THEIR MARGINAL status as diagnosable (and reimbursable) mental disorders, marital and couple problems are difficult—and important—for therapists to treat. With two in three marriages ending in divorce (Bray & Hetherington, 1993), the consequences for children and families of *not* resolving couple complaints can be enormous (Amato & Keith, 1991; Bray, 1990). Yet in dealing with couple complaints, a therapist often meets partners who are unequally committed to change or who have drastically different reasons for coming to therapy—for example, to enlist the therapist's help in changing the other, to comply with an ultimatum, or even to leave the relationship. The therapist's job is no easier when spouses with longstanding resentments blame each other for their problems rather than taking responsibility themselves, or when the couple's difficulties affect or are affected by the behavior of other people (e.g., children, parents). In addition, some clients "solve" a marital problem by leaving the marriage, an option not available with individual complaints such as anxiety or depression or with family complaints that focus on a child. Indeed, the task of therapeutic engagement is likely to be more complex—and the grace period for ef-

fective intervention shorter—when a therapist deals with two clients rather than one. And this is not to mention the reluctance of insurance companies to reimburse treatment of marital and couple problems per se. Thus, there are good reasons why brief, efficient treatment for couple problems has special appeal. Of the many approaches to treating these problems, few are as parsimonious as the two we discuss here.

This chapter outlines two closely related but distinct models of brief therapy, each applicable to many problems, including couple problems. *Brief problem-focused therapy*, developed in the late 1960s and '70s by Richard Fisch, John Weakland, Paul Watzlawick, and their colleagues at the Mental Research Institute (MRI) in Palo Alto (Weakland, Watzlawick, Fisch, & Bodin, 1974; Watzlawick, Weakland, & Fisch, 1974; Fisch, Weakland, & Segal, 1982; Weakland & Fisch, 1992), grew from ideas originating in Gregory Bateson's seminal research project on communication, which many regard as the intellectual foundation of the family therapy movement (Watzlawick, Beavin, & Jackson, 1967; Sluzki & Ransom, 1976). The second model, *brief solution-focused therapy*, was developed in the late 1970s and '80s by Steve de Shazer and his associates at the Brief Family Therapy Center in Milwaukee (de Shazer et al., 1986; de Shazer, 1982, 1985, 1988, 1991; Berg & Miller, 1992). Inspired by the work at MRI, the Milwaukee group took "focused problem resolution" (Weakland et al., 1974) as a starting point and evolved a complementary form of brief therapy called "focused solution development" (de Shazer et al., 1986). Although both brief therapy approaches continue to be taught and practiced at the two centers, the basic principles and tactics of MRI's problem-focused model have remained fairly constant, whereas the Milwaukee solution-focused model has undergone progressive revision. The Milwaukee model now appears to have a substantially different emphasis than the parent (MRI) model—and a higher profile in the mental health marketplace.

The hallmark of these models is conceptual and technical parsimony. The aim of therapy is simply to resolve the presenting complaint as quickly and efficiently as possible so that clients can get on with life: Goals such as promoting personal growth, working through underlying emotional issues, or teaching couples better problem-solving and communication skills are not emphasized. Both therapies offer minimal theory, focusing narrowly on the presenting complaint and relevant solutions, and both are nonnormative in that neither attempts to specify what constitutes a normal or dysfunctional marriage. Both pay close attention not only to what clients *do* but also to how they *view* the problem, themselves, and each other; in fact, both therapies assume that the "reality" of problems and change is constructed more than discovered. Both therapies also attach considerable importance to clients' "customership" for change and to the possibility that therapy itself may play a role in maintaining (rather than resolving) problems. Finally, in contrast to most other treatments for couples, therapists following the MRI and Milwaukee models often see the partners individually, even when the focus of intervention is a complaint about the marriage itself.

The most fundamental difference between problem- and solution-focused therapy concerns the emphasis each gives to the concept of "solution": While the MRI approach aims to interdict existing solutions that maintain the problem and to promote "less of the same," the Milwaukee model seeks to identify exceptions to the problem and develop new solutions that work. (Indeed, the semantics of "solutions" can be confusing.) Following from this are differences in the

therapist's usual tactics and stance. For example, MRI therapists tend to focus interventions on behavioral change at home, whereas Milwaukee therapists are more likely to promote cognitive change in the session. A striking tactical difference is that MRI therapists usually adopt a cautious, restraining stance, especially when clients begin to change, whereas solution-focused therapists are quick with compliments and praise. Another difference, at least partly semantic, is that the MRI group identifies its therapy as "strategic," a self-characterization that the Milwaukee group now avoids. Fisch, Weakland, Watzlawick, and their colleagues portray their therapy as a process of deliberate influence in which the therapist assumes responsibility for outcome, while de Shazer, Berg, and associates describe their solution-focused therapy as coconstructivist, collaborative, and (by implication) not so manipulative (de Shazer, 1991).

Whatever the "strategic" status of these two therapies, our chapter deals primarily with them and not with the strategic approach to treating couples developed by Jay Haley (who coined the term "strategic") and his associate Cloe Madanes (Haley, 1980, 1987; Madanes, 1981, 1991). Although interventions based on the Haley–Madanes model are sometimes similar to those practiced by the MRI group (which should not be surprising because Haley was an early member of the MRI Brief Therapy Center), their strategic therapy makes assumptions about relational structure and the adaptive (protective) function of symptoms that the MRI and Milwaukee groups reject. A useful description of strategic marital therapy drawing on the Haley–Madanes model can be found in Todd's (1986) chapter in the first edition of this *Handbook*.

Our chapter deals primarily with applications of problem- and solution-focused brief therapy to *couple* complaints, but this is a somewhat arbitrary delimitation. As general models of problem resolution, the MRI and Milwaukee therapies approach couple problems in essentially the same way they do other complaints. Because both are concerned with systems of interaction, however, they also focus on marital interaction when working with many "individual" problems—for example, depression (Watzlawick & Coyne, 1980; Coyne, 1986a) and problem drinking (Fisch, 1986; Berg & Miller, 1992)—and for tactical reasons they may avoid calling this "couple therapy" in dealings with the clients. This, along with the fact that brief and solution-focused therapists often treat couple problems nonconjointly (by seeing individuals), leaves fuzzy any distinction between what is and is not "couple therapy."

The first two sections of the chapter describe, in turn, the problem-focused (MRI) and solution-focused (Milwaukee) brief therapy models. Here, we review the background of each approach, outline the main principles of practice, and consider applications in therapy with couples.[2] The third section presents critical commentary concerning prospects for reconciliation, the question of strategy, some possible perils of parsimony, and whether these therapies really work. Of particular interest is whether the MRI and Milwaukee models are as effective and efficient as their proponents claim, and what we know (or can learn) about them from systematic empirical research.

FOCUSED PROBLEM RESOLUTION: THE MRI MODEL

MRI's brief therapy is a pragmatic embodiment of the "interactional view" (Watzlawick & Weakland, 1978), which explains behavior—especially problem behavior—in terms of what happens between people rather than within them. The interactional view grew from attempts by members of Bateson's research group (which included Weakland, Haley, and MRI founder Don D. Jackson) to apply ideas from cybernetics and systems theory to the study of communication. After the Bateson project ended, Watzlawick, Beavin, and Jackson (1967) brought many of these ideas together in *Pragmatics of Human Communication*. Around the same time, Fisch, Weakland, Watzlawick, and others (including Haley) formed the Brief Therapy Center at MRI to study ways of doing therapy briefly. Their work was also influenced by the uncommon therapeutic techniques of Arizona psychiatrist Milton Erickson, whom Haley and Weakland visited many times during the Bateson project (Haley, 1967).

Since 1966, the Brief Therapy Center (BTC) has followed a consistent format in treating over 400 cases. Staff members meet weekly as a team to treat unselected cases for a maximum of 10 sessions. One member of the team serves as a primary therapist while the others consult from behind a one-way mirror. After treatment (at roughly 3 and 12 months following termination), another team member conducts a telephone follow-up interview with the client(s) to evalu-

ate change in the original presenting problem and to determine if clients developed additional problems or sought further treatment elsewhere. The Center's pattern of practice—like the participation of its core members, Fisch, Weakland, and Watzlawick—has been remarkably consistent for over a quarter century, an unusual achievement in the history of psychotherapy research. Although research at MRI has been mostly qualitative, the BTC archives offer rich possibilities for investigating brief strategic intervention.

From the work of the BTC emerged a model of therapy that focuses on observable interaction in the present, makes no assumptions about normality or pathology, and remains "as close as possible to practice." The first formal statement of this model appeared in a 1974 *Family Process* paper by Weakland et al., entitled "Brief Therapy: Focused Problem Resolution." Around the same time Watzlawick et al. (1974) also published *Change: Principles of Problem Formation and Problem Resolution*, a widely recognized theoretical treatise that distinguished first- and second-order change and exemplified the MRI view of problem resolution. Eight years later, Fisch et al. (1982) offered *The Tactics of Change: Doing Therapy Briefly*, essentially a how-to do-it manual that remains the most comprehensive and explicit statement to date of the BTC's clinical method. A more recent and concise statement of the MRI model (Weakland & Fisch, 1992) appears as a book chapter unlikely to receive the attention it deserves. Although these sources do not deal with marital therapy per se, couple complaints figure prominently in the clinical principles and examples. In addition, a recent analysis of the BTC's archival data suggests that at least 40% of the cases treated there have involved some form of marital or couple complaint (Rohrbaugh, Shoham, & Schlanger, 1992).

In the literature on MRI-style brief therapy, the work of James Coyne (1985, 1986a, 1986b, 1988) deals with couples complaints most systematically and directly. Coyne, who affiliated with the BTC in the late 1970s and early '80s, is perhaps best known for his research on marital interaction and depression. Coyne's clinical papers highlight the significance of the interview in strategic marital therapy, particularly how the therapist works to (re)frame the couple's definition of the problem in a way that sets the stage for later interventions. These papers give many examples of problem-focused intervention with couples, especially when one of the partners is depressed.

Principles of Practice

The MRI brief therapy model is based on two interlocking assumptions about problems and change:

> Regardless of their origins and etiology—if, indeed, these can ever be reliably determined—the problems people bring to psychotherapists persist only if they are maintained by ongoing current behavior of the client and others with whom he interacts. Correspondingly, if such problem-maintaining behavior is appropriately changed or eliminated, the problem will be resolved or vanish, regardless of its nature, or origin, or duration. (Weakland et al., 1974, p. 144)

How problems persist is thus more important than how they originate, and their persistence depends mainly on social interaction, with the behavior of one person both stimulated and shaped by the response of others (Weakland & Fisch, 1992). Moreover—and this is the central observation of the MRI group—what people do in order to control, prevent, or eliminate a problem usually plays a crucial role in perpetuating it. In this sense, "the problem is the solution" (Watzlawick et al., 1974).

In *Pragmatics*, Watzlawick et al. (1967) highlight the familiar demand–withdraw cycle associated with many marital complaints:

> Suppose a couple have a marital problem to which he contributes passive withdrawal while her 50% is nagging and criticism. In explaining their frustrations, the husband will state that withdrawal is his only *defense against* her nagging, while she will label this explanation gross and willful distortion of what "really" happens in their marriage: namely, that she is critical of him *because* of his passivity. Stripped of all ephemeral and fortuitous elements, their fights consist in a monotonous exchange of the messages, "I will withdraw because you nag" and "I nag because you withdraw." (p. 56, italics in the original)

Watzlawick et al. (1974) elaborate a similar pattern in *Change*:

> In marriage therapy, one can frequently see both spouses engaging in behaviors which they individually consider the most appropriate reaction to something wrong that the other is doing. That is, in the eyes of each of them the particular corrective behavior of the other is seen as that behavior which needs correction. For instance, a wife may have the impression that her husband is not open enough for her to know where she stands with him, what is going on in his head,what he is doing when he is away from home, etc. Quite naturally, she will there-fore attempt to get the needed information by asking him questions, watching his behavior, and checking on him in a variety of other ways. If he considers her behavior as too intrusive, he is likely to withhold from her information which in and by itself would be quite harmless and irrelevant to disclose—"just to teach her that she need not know everything." Far from making her back down, this attempted solution not only does not bring about the desired change in her behavior but provides further fuel for her worries and her distrust—"if he does not even talk to me about these little things, there *must* be something the matter." The less information he gives her, the more persistently she will seek it, and the more she seeks it, the less he will give her. By the time they see a psychiatrist, it will be tempting to diagnose her behavior as pathological jealousy—provided that no attention is paid to their pattern of interaction and their attempted solutions, which *are* the problem. (pp. 35–36, italics in the original)

The "solutions" of demand and withdrawal in these examples make perfectly good sense to the participants, yet their interactional consequences serve only to confirm each partner's unsatisfactory "reality." How such a cycle began is likely to remain obscure, and what causes what is a matter of more or less arbitrary punctuation: From an interactional view, the system is its own explanation.

A problem, then, consists of a vicious cycle involving a positive feedback loop between some behavior someone considers undesirable (the complaint) and some other behavior(s) intended to modify or eliminate it (the attempted solution). Given that problems persist because of people's current attempts to solve them, therapy need consist only of identifying and deliberately interdicting these well-intentioned "solutions," thereby breaking the vicious cycles (positive feedback loops) that maintain the impasse. If this can be done—even in a small way—virtuous cycles may develop in which "less of the solution leads to less of the problem, leading to less of the solution, and so on" (Fisch et al., 1982). In pursuing this goal, the MRI therapist is careful to speak the clients' language and to avoid argumentation. And for a limited subset of problems, resolution can also occur by virtue of clients reevaluating the original complaint as "no problem" (Weakland & Fisch, 1992).

The MRI formula for doing therapy briefly is simple in concept, if not in execution. The first step is to get a very specific, behavioral picture of the complaint, who sees it as a problem, and why it is a problem now. Since the problem is not assumed to be the tip of a psychological or interactional iceberg, the aim is simply to be clear about who is doing what. A useful guideline is for the therapist to have enough details to answer the question, "If we had a video of this, what would I see?" Later the therapist also tries to get a clear behavioral picture of what the clients will accept as a minimum change goal. For example, "What would he (or she, or both) be doing differently that will let you know this is taking a turn for the better?"

The next step of brief therapy requires an equally specific inquiry into the behaviors most closely related to the problem, namely, what the clients (and any other people concerned about it) are doing to handle, prevent, or resolve the complaint, and what happens after these attempted solutions. From this emerges a formulation of a problem–solution loop, and particularly of the specific solution behaviors that will be the focus of intervention. The therapist (or team) can then develop a picture of what "less of the same" will look like—that is, of what behavior, by whom, in what situation, will suffice to reverse the problem-maintaining solution. Ideally this strategic objective constitutes a 180° reversal of what the clients have been doing. While interventions typically involve prescribing some alternative behavior, the key element is stopping the performance of the attempted solution (Weakland & Fisch, 1992). Understanding problem-maintaining solution patterns also helps the therapist be clear about what positions and suggestions to avoid—what the MRI group calls the "minefield."

The most relevant problem-maintaining solutions are current ones, but the therapist investigates solutions tried and discarded in the past as well, because these give hints about what has worked before (and may again). In one of our alcohol-treatment cases (Rohrbaugh, Shoham, Spungen, & Steinglass, 1995), a wife who in the past had taken a hard line with her husband about not drinking at the dinner table later reversed this stance because she did not want to be controlling. As his drinking problem worsened, she dealt with it less and less directly, by busying herself in other activities or retreating to her study to meditate. Careful inquiry revealed that the former hard-line approach, though distasteful, had actually worked—when the wife had set limits, the husband had controlled his drinking. By relabeling her former stance as caring and reassuring to the husband, the therapist was later able to help the wife reverse her stance in a way that broke the problem cycle. The MRI approach thus makes some use of problem-*resolving* solu-

tions, but these receive much less emphasis than they do in the solution-focused Milwaukee model describe later.

The most direct way to interrupt a problem–solution loop is to suggest some specific action in some specific situation that will require someone to do less of the same (Fisch et al., 1982). It is crucial that the suggestion be framed in terms compatible with the clients' own language, position, or worldview—especially with how they prefer to see themselves. Some spouses, for example, will be attracted to the idea of making a loving sacrifice, but others may want to teach the partner a lesson. A less direct way to break the pattern is to redefine what one partner is doing in a way that stops short of prescribing change, yet makes it difficult for them to continue (e.g., "I've noticed that your reminding him and telling him what you think seems to give him an excuse to keep doing what he's doing without feeling guilty—he can justify it to himself simply by blaming you").

Grasping and using clients' views—what Fisch et al. (1982) call "patient position"—is almost as fundamental to brief therapy as the behavioral prescriptions that interdict problem-maintaining solutions. In discussing frame development, Coyne (1986b, 1988) emphasizes that strategic therapists not only elicit clients' beliefs, but also shape and structure those beliefs to set the stage for later interventions. For example, a therapist might accept a wife's view that her husband is uncommunicative and unemotional, then extend this view to suggest that the husband's defensiveness indicates vulnerability. The extension paves the way for suggesting a different way of dealing with a husband who is vulnerable, rather than simply withholding (Coyne, 1988).

Two important tactical principles in brief therapy are *work with the customer* and *preserve maneuverability*. The customership principle means simply that the therapist works with the person or persons most concerned about the problem (the "sweater" or "sweaters"). Thus, a therapist treating a marital complaint would not require or even encourage the participation of a reluctant spouse, especially if this is what the principal complainant has been doing. To preserve maneuverability is to maximize possibilities for therapeutic influence—the therapist's main responsibility. In *Tactics*, Fisch et al. (1982) make plain the importance of control: "The therapist, to put it bluntly, needs to maintain his own options while limiting those of the patients" (p. 23), and they outline tactics for gaining (and regaining) control, even in initial phone contacts, since " . . . treatment is likely to go awry if the therapist is not in control of it" (p. xii). Preserving maneuverability also means that the therapist avoids taking a firm position or making a premature commitment to what clients should do, and that he/she constructs task assignments in a way that clients are likely to do more than they agreed to do (Coyne, 1988).

Customership and maneuverability are both relevant to why brief therapists often treat marital complaints by seeing one or both partners separately. The brief therapist would rather address a marital complaint by seeing a motivated spouse alone than by struggling to engage a spouse who is not a customer. In theory, this should not decrease the possibility of successful outcome, because the interactional view assumes that problem resolution can follow from a change by any participant in the relevant interactional system (Weakland & Fisch, 1992). Coyne (1988), in fact, notes that a systems perspective *encourages* consideration of "how a motivated spouse can influence the less motivated spouse and the quality of their relationship" (p. 95, cf. Hoebel, 1976; Watzlawick & Coyne, 1980). Another reason to see spouses separately, even when both are customers, is to preserve maneuverability. If the spouses have sharply different views of their situation, for example, separate sessions give the therapist more flexibility in accepting each viewpoint and framing suggestions one way for her and another way for him (appealing to their better instincts). The split format also helps the therapist avoid being drawn into the position of referee or possible ally. The goal, however, remains to promote change in what happens between the partners.

A final reason for interviewing spouses separately is to facilitate assessment. Some couples relentlessly enact their arguments and conflicts in the therapy room and others lapse into silence and withdrawal. As Coyne (1988) points out, seeing such patterns at least once is useful, but their repetition can easily handicap the therapist's efforts to track important problem–solution loops that occur outside the therapy session. Strategic therapists like Coyne also make a point of seeing the partners alone at least once to inquire about their commitment to the relationship; if either is pessimistic, Coyne requests a moratorium on separation long enough to give treatment a chance to make a difference. In no case, however, does the therapist express more commitment to saving the marriage or to the likely success of therapy than the client being interviewed (Coyne, 1988).

In addition to interventions that target specific problem–solution loops, the MRI group uses several *general interventions* applicable to a broad range of problems and to promoting change in all stages of therapy. General interventions include telling clients to go slow, cautioning them about dangers of improvement, making a U-turn, and giving instructions about how to make the problem worse (Fisch et al., 1982). Most of these tactics are variations of therapeutic restraint, a stance that is highly characteristic of this approach. The most common tactic is the injunction to "go slow," given with a credible rationale such as "change occurring slowly and step by step makes for a more solid change than change which occurs too suddenly" (1982, p. 159). This tactic is used to prepare clients for change, to convey acceptance of reluctance to change, and to solidify change once it begins to occur. Fisch et al. suggest two reasons why "go slow" messages work: (1) they make clients more likely to cooperate with therapeutic suggestions, and (2) they relax the sense of urgency that often fuels clients' problem-maintaining-solution efforts.

Coyne (1988) describes several other general interventions that he uses in the first or second session with couples. One involves asking the couple to collaborate in performing the problem pattern (e.g., an argument) deliberately, for the ostensible purpose of helping the therapist better understand how they get involved in such a no-win encounter, and specifically, how each partner is able to get the other to be less reasonable than he/she would be normally. This task is more than diagnostic, however, because it undercuts negative spontaneity, creates an incentive for each partner to resist provocation, and sometimes introduces a shift in the usual problem–solution pattern.

Published case reports notwithstanding, the outcome of brief therapy rarely turns on a single intervention. Much depends on how the therapist nurtures incipient change and manages termination. When a small change occurs, the therapist acknowledges and emphasizes the clients' part in making it happen, but avoids encouraging further change directly. The most common stance in responding to change is gentle restraint (e.g., "go slow") and continuation of the interdiction strategy that produced it. Special tactics may be used with clients who are overly optimistic or overly anxious (e.g., predicting or prescribing a relapse) or who minimize change or relapse (e.g., exploring "dangers of improvement"). Termination occurs without celebration or fanfare. If change is solid, the therapist acknowledges progress, inquires about what the clients are doing differently, suggests that they anticipate other problems, and implies they will be able to cope with whatever problems do arise. Otherwise, various restraining tactics may be used. If clients ask to work on other problems, the therapist suggests taking time out to adapt to change and offers to reassess the other problems later (Fisch et al., 1982; Rosenthal & Bergman, 1986).

Approaches to Couple Problems

In terms of Bateson's (1958) distinction between complementary and symmetrical interaction[3] (cf. Watzlawick et al., 1967), the most common foci of solution interdiction in MRI-style couple therapy seem to involve complementary patterns such as the familiar demand–withdraw sequence described earlier. For example, one partner may press for change in some way, while the other withdraws or refuses to respond; one partner may attempt to initiate discussion of some problem, while the other avoids discussion; one partner may criticize what the other does, while the other defends his/her actions; or one may accuse the other of thinking or doing something that the other denies (Christensen & Heavy, 1993). Each of these variations—demand–refuse, discuss–avoid, criticize–defend, accuse–deny—fits the problem–solution-loop formula, because more demand leads to more withdrawal, which leads to more demand, and so on. Although the MRI group avoids (normative) a priori assumptions about adaptive or maladaptive family relations, the clinical relevance of demand–withdraw interaction appears well established by research indicating that this pattern is substantially more prevalent in divorcing couples and clinic couples than in couples who are not distressed (Christensen & Schenk, 1991). Interestingly, many authors have described the demand–withdraw pattern and speculated about its underlying dynamics (e.g., Fogarty, 1976; Napier, 1978; Wile, 1981), but few have been as concerned as the MRI group with practical ways to change it.

To the extent that the partner on the demand side of the sequence is the main customer for change, intervention will focus on encouraging that person to do less of the same. In the demand–refuse cycle, one spouse may press for change by exhorting, reasoning, arguing, lecturing, and so on—a solution pattern that Fisch and associates call "seeking accord through opposition." If the wife is the main complainant,[4]

achieving less of the same usually depends on helping her suspend overt attempts to influence the husband, for example, by declaring helplessness or in some other specific way taking a one-down position, or by performing an observational–diagnostic task to find out "what he'll do on his own" or "what we're really up against." How the therapist frames specific suggestions depends on what rationale the customer will buy: An extremely religious client, for example, might be amenable to the suggestion that she silently pray for her husband instead of exhorting him. Successful solution interdiction in several MRI cases (Watzlawick & Coyne, 1980; Fisch et al., 1982) followed from developing the frame that behavior one partner sees as stubbornness is actually motivated by the other's pride. Since proud people need to discover and do things on their own, without feeling pressed or that they are giving in, it makes sense to encourage the spouse by discouraging (restraining) him. If the demand-side partner follows suggestions for doing this, she will effectively reverse her former solution to the stubborn behavior.

For some couples the demand–withdraw cycle involves one partner attempting to initiate discussion (e.g., to get the other to open up, be more expressive, etc.) while the other avoids it. One of us (VS) had the experience of being the primary therapist for one such couple during her training at MRI. The wife, herself a therapist and the main complainant, would repeatedly encourage her inexpressive husband to get his feelings out, especially when he came home from work "looking miserable." When the husband responded to this with distraught silence, the wife would encourage him to talk about his feeling toward her and the marriage (thinking that this would bring out positive associations). In a typical sequence the husband would then begin to get angry and tell the wife to back off, but she, encouraged by his expressiveness, would continue to push for meaningful discussion, in response to which—on more than one occasion—the husband stormed out of the house and disappeared overnight. The intervention that eventually broke the cycle in this case came from Fisch, who entered the therapy room with a suggestion: In the next week, at least once, the husband was to come home, sit at the kitchen table, and pretend to look miserable. The wife's task, when she saw this look, was to go to the kitchen, prepare chicken soup, and serve it to him *silently* with a worried look on her face. The couple came to the next session looking anything but miserable; they reported that their attempt to carry out the assignment had failed because she—and then he—could not keep a straight face, yet they were delighted that the humor so characteristic of the early days of their relationship had "resurfaced." While the intervention served to interdict the wife's attempted solution of pursuing discussion, it also interrupted the heaviness and deadly seriousness in the couple's relationship.[5]

When the demand–withdraw pattern involves criticism and defense, both partners are more likely to be customers for change, so change can be introduced though either partner or both. One strategy, noted previously, is to develop a rationale for the criticizing partner to observe the behavior he/she is criticizing without commenting on it. Another is to get the defending, partner to do something other than defending—for example, to simply agree with the criticism, or to help the criticizer "lighten up" by not taking the criticism seriously ("I guess you're probably right—therapy is helping me see I'm not much fun and probably too old to change"; or "You're right—I don't know if I inherited this problem from my parents or our kids"). In *Change*, Watzlawick et al. (1974) also describe a more indirect interdiction of a wife's attempts to avoid marital fights by defending herself. As homework, the therapist asked the combative husband to pick a fight deliberately with someone outside the marriage. In the next session, the husband recounted in detail how his attempts to do this had failed because he had not been able to get the other person to lose his temper. In the authors' view, hearing this "made the wife more aware of her contribution to the problem than any insight-oriented explanation or intervention could have done" (p. 120).

Another approach to interdicting accusation–denial cycles is an intervention the MRI group calls "jamming" (Fisch et al., 1982). When one partner accuses the other of something both agree is wrong (e.g., dishonesty, infidelity, insensitivity), and the other partner's denial seems only to confirm the accuser's suspicions, leading to more accusations and more denials, the jamming intervention aims to promote less of the same by both parties. After disavowing any ability to determine who is right or wrong in the situation, the therapist proposes to help the couple improve their communication, which obviously has broken down, and particularly, to improve the accuser's perceptiveness about the problem. Achieving this, the therapist continues (in a conjoint session), will require that the defender (e.g., the wife) deliberately randomize the behavior of

which she is accused (e.g., sometimes acting "as if" she is attracted to other men and sometimes not), while the accuser (e.g., the husband) tests his perceptiveness about what she is "really" doing. Each should keep a record of what they did or observed, they are told in a conjoint session, but they must not discuss the experiment or compare notes until the next session. The effect of such a prescription is to free the defender from (consistently) defending and the accuser from accusing; the circuit is thus "jammed" because verbal exchanges (accusations and denial) now have less information value.

Sometimes a problem cycle is characterized by indirect demands related to the paradoxical form of communication Fisch et al. (1982) call "seeking compliance through voluntarism." For instance, a wife may complain that her husband not only ignores her needs, but that he also should know what to do without her having to tell him, since otherwise he would be doing it only because she asked him and not because he really wanted to. Or a husband may be reluctant to ask his wife to do something because he thinks she may not really want to do it. The brief therapy strategy recommended in these situations is to get the person who is asking for something to do so directly, even if arbitrarily. If clients want to appear benevolent, the therapist can use this position by defining their indirection as unwittingly destructive: for example, "a husband's reticence to ask favors of his wife can be redefined as an 'unwitting deprivation of the one thing she needs most from you, a sense of your willingness to take leadership'" (Fisch et al., 1982, p. 155). Intervening through the nonrequesting partner might also be possible if that person can be persuaded to take the edge off the paradoxical "be spontaneous" demand by saying something like, "I'm willing to do it and I will, but let's face it, I don't enjoy cleaning up."

In other complaint-maintaining complementary exchanges, one partner may be domineering or explosive and the other placating or submissive. Here, less of the same usually requires getting the submissive, placating partner to take some assertive action. This was the approach taken in a controversial case reported by Bobele (1987), who describes the interactional analysis and successful interdiction of a cycle of violence involving a woman and her boyfriend. (Woody & Woody, 1988, criticized Bobele's approach on legal and ethical grounds, but see rejoinders by Weakland, 1988.)

Symmetrical patterns of problem-maintaining behavior, although less common, often offer more possibilities for intervention because customership, too, is balanced. For combative couples embroiled in symmetrically escalating arguments, the strategy could be to get at least one of them to take a one-down position, or to prescribe the argument under conditions likely to undermine it (Coyne, 1988). Another symmetrical solution pattern stems from miscarriage of the (usually sensible) belief that problems are best solved by talking them through. Yet some couples—including some who are very psychologically minded—manage to perpetuate relationship difficulties simply by trying to talk about them. In a case treated at MRI, for example, a couple's problem-solving "talks" about issues in their relationship usually escalated into full-blown arguments. Therapy led them to a different, more workable solution: When either partner felt the need to talk about their relationship, they would first go bowling (R. Fisch, personal communication, 1992).

Interestingly, despite their emphasis on interaction, the MRI group acknowledges a "self-referential" aspect of complaints such as anxiety states, insomnia, obsessional thinking, sexual dysfunction, and other "be spontaneous" problems. These complaints "can arise and be maintained without help from anyone else. This does not mean that others do not aid in maintaining such problems; often they do. We simply mean that these kinds of problems do not need such 'help' in order to occur and persist" (Fisch et al., 1982, pp. 136–137). Treatment of such problems in a couple context may involve simultaneous interdiction of both interactional and self-referential problem–solution loops. For example, with a woman who experienced difficulty reaching orgasm, the MRI team targeted two problem–solution loops, one self-referential (the harder she tried, the more she failed) and one interactional (the more the husband inquired how aroused she was and whether she had an orgasm, the harder she tried to perform). One strand of the intervention was a prescription that, for the wife to become more aware of her feelings during intercourse, she should "notice her bodily sensations, *regardless of how much or how little* pleasure she may experience" (1982, p. 158, italics in the original). The second (interactional) strand was a version of jamming: In the wife's presence, the therapist asked the husband not to interfere with this process by checking her arousal, but if he did, the wife was simply to say "I didn't feel a thing." Other strategies aimed at combined interdiction of interactional and self-referential solution patterns have been applied in the treatment of "individual" complaints such as depression (Coyne, 1986a, 1988) and anxiety (Rohrbaugh & Shean, 1988).

Interventions for marital complaints usually focus on one or both members of the couple, yet there are circumstances in which other people—relatives, friends, or even another helper—figure prominently in MRI-style couple therapy, especially when the third party is a key customer for change. For example, a mother who is understandably concerned about her daughter's marital difficulties may counsel or console the daughter in a way that unwittingly amplifies the problem or makes the young couple less likely to deal with their differences directly. In this case, brief therapy might focus first on helping the mother—an important complainant—reverse her own solution efforts, and take up later (if at all) the interaction between the young couple, which is likely to change when the mother becomes less involved. Brief therapists have also found ways to involve third parties who may *not* be customers for change, particularly for problems related to marital infidelity (Teisman, 1979; Green & Bobele, 1988).

Finally, for a small subset of marital complaints, the goal of brief therapy is to help couples reevaluate their problem as "no problem," or as a problem they can live with, and strategies for achieving this typically involve some sort of reframing. Indeed, marriage is fertile ground for what Watzlawick et al. (1974) call the "utopia syndrome":

> Quite obviously, few—if any—marriages live up to the ideals contained in some of the classic marriage manuals or popular mythology. Those who accept these ideas about what a marital relationship should "really" be are likely to see their marriage as problematic and to start working toward its solution until divorce do them part. Their concrete problem is not their marriage, but their attempts at finding the solution to a problem which in the first place is not a problem, and which, even if it were one, could not be solved on the level on which they attempt to change it. (p. 57)

FOCUSED SOLUTION DEVELOPMENT: THE MILWAUKEE MODEL

Solution-focused therapy grew from the work of de Shazer, Berg, and their colleagues at the Brief Family Therapy Center (BFTC) in Milwaukee. Founded in 1978, the BFTC adopted many of the principles of brief therapy articulated earlier at MRI, especially the Ericksonian principle of "utilizing what clients bring" (Haley, 1967). As their work evolved, however, it came to focus more on *exceptions* to problems—on helping clients do more of what has already worked—than on the problems themselves. De Shazer et al. (1986) describe "focused solution development" in a *Family Process* paper with obvious parallels to the Weakland et al. (1974) paper on "focused problem resolution." The fullest descriptions of the Milwaukee model, however, are de Shazer's books, which have appeared at 3-year intervals since 1982. These include: *Patterns of Brief Family Therapy* (1982), *Keys to Solution in Brief Therapy* (1985), *Investigating Solutions in Brief Therapy* (1988), and *Putting Difference to Work* (1991). Solution-focused therapy has been the subject of many other publications as well. The most notable, in our view, are books by Lipchik (1988), O'Hanlon and Weiner-Davis (1989) and Berg and Miller (1992).

The Milwaukee BFTC prefers to conduct therapy in a consultation–team format similar to that used at MRI, although de Shazer (1985) emphasizes that the team is "stimulating but not necessary" for this type of therapy. The Milwaukee team format is somewhat more structured than MRI's, with a planned intrasession break for consultation occurring about 30–40 minutes into the interview. The average number of sessions for BFTC cases is less than 5 (slightly fewer than at MRI). Although follow-up is apparently not done on all cases, de Shazer (1991) reports outcome data for 164 cases based on an unpublished follow-up study by Kiser (1988). The Milwaukee group has also undertaken several informal research projects on the *process* of their therapy, investigating factors that influence client "change talk" (Gingerich, de Shazer, & Weiner-Davis, 1988) and responses to specific therapeutic tasks (de Shazer & Molnar, 1984; Weiner-Davis, de Shazer, & Gingerich, 1987). According to de Shazer (1985, 1988), this research had an important influence on practice patterns at the BFTC.

Unlike the MRI model, the theory and practice of solution-focused therapy have undergone progressive revision.[6] The first and most fundamental shift was from describing interaction patterns around complaints (à la MRI) to focusing on what clients do that works. Then, in the mid-1980s, the group declared the "death of resistance" (de Shazer et al., 1986) to underscore their assumption that clients do want to change, and that the therapist's job is to identify and use each client's unique way of cooperating. Another shift was from using the interview mainly as a staging ground for an end-of-session intervention

to emphasizing the interventive value of interviewing itself (Lipchik & de Shazer, 1986; Lipchik, 1992), namely, asking questions that amplify exceptions to the problem and help clients construct a more hopeful future. The team made "exception questions" and the related "miracle question" increasingly central to the approach, using these interventions as soon as possible in therapy. Interest also developed in "formula tasks," likened by de Shazer (1985) to skeleton keys that seemed to stimulate expectations of change regardless of the nature of the problem (or lock). This fueled the conviction that solution-focused interventions "can initiate change without the therapist's knowing much, if anything, about the problem" (O'Hanlon & Weiner-Davis, 1989, p. 24). The revisions of the Milwaukee model also imply that de Shazer and associates have come to view cognitive processes—particularly the coconstruction of meaning by therapist and client—as more fundamental than behavioral processes to therapeutic change.

In his 1991 book, de Shazer aligns solution-focused therapy with the intellectual tradition of "poststructuralism" and with the new postmodern therapeutic tradition represented by authors such as Anderson and Goolishian (1990) and Hoffman (1990). The coin of the poststructural realm is language and meaning, and in de Shazer's view therapy is a "negotiated, consensual, cooperative endeavor in which the solution-focused therapist and client jointly produce various language games focused on a) exceptions, b) goals, and c) solutions" (1991, p. 74). Like the MRI constructivists, post-structualists view knowledge and "reality" as constructed rather than discovered, but go further in denouncing any conceptual split between subject and object or knower and known. There is little place for objective description of problem–solution loops in this perspective, let alone for concepts like "client resistance" or "deliberate therapeutic influence." And since the entire "objectivist" bias of social science is suspect (Harland, 1987; Hoffman, 1990), poststructuralist therapists would naturally question how (or whether) one should evaluate clinical outcome. Interestingly, parts of de Shazer's work through 1988 showed a countervailing emphasis on disciplined observation, informal (but objectivist) research, and "expert systems" designed to reduce solution-focused therapy to flowcharts that "make the knowledge of the team at BFTC more communicable and explicit" (de Shazer, 1988, p. 15).[7]

Any description of solution-focused therapy by outsiders will be, at best, a partial snapshot of a moving target. Not only have de Shazer, Berg, and the core BFTC group revised their ideas over the years, but some of the original members have left the group and now pursue related but somewhat different interests (e.g., Lipchik, 1992; Weiner-Davis, 1992). Moreover, some of the most explicit and, in our view, useful formulations of the model—the "expert system" flowcharts noted previously—have not been favored in the group's recent writings. In any case, we attempt to summarize here the main (current or recent) principles of solution-focused practice, including applications to couples.

Principles of Practice

The Milwaukee model is complaint based, yet solution oriented. Like MRI problem-focused therapists, solution-focused therapists treat only what clients complain about: Therapy starts with a complaint and ends when the complaint is alleviated. Unlike MRI therapists, however, the solution-focused therapist requires only a broad statement of the complaint before shifting to "solution talk" and asking about what happens (or will happen) when the problem is not present. The search for solutions—the "behavioral and/or perceptual changes that the therapist and client construct to alter the difficulty" (de Shazer et al., 1986, p. 210)—proceeds through making "fluke exceptions" to the problem into "a difference that make a difference" (de Shazer, 1988, p. xvii). It is assumed that clients have effective solutions in their repertoires, and once these are identified, the therapist need only guide clients to do more of them. Most radical, perhaps, is that solution-focused therapy entails no theory of problems and whenever possible "bypasses even looking for a problem" (de Shazer, 1990).

Although the Milwaukee model is concerned with behavioral as well as cognitive change, de Shazer assumes that behavior change follows naturally after clients see things differently:

> Problems are seen to maintain themselves simply because they maintain themselves and because clients depict the problem as *always happening.* Therefore, times when the complaint is absent are dismissed as trivial by the client or even remain completely unseen, hidden from the client's view. Nothing is actually hidden, but although these exceptions are open to view, they are not seen by the clients as differences that make a difference. For the client, the problem is seen as primary (and the exceptions, if seen at all, are seen as secondary), while for therapists the exceptions are seen as primary; interventions are meant to help clients make a similar

inversion, which will lead to the development of a solution. (1991, p. 58, italics in the original)

In addition to *deconstructing* the complaint through inducing doubt in the clients' construal of it, solution-focused therapy pursues another kind of cognitive change through *reconstructing* the clients' sense of their ability to resolve, control, or contain the problem. Thus, solution-focused interventions aim not only to help clients *see* that problems have exceptions, but also to *own* these exceptions as solutions they themselves have already applied successfully. For example, to preempt the view that an exception "just happened," the therapist typically asks, "How did you do that?" An increased sense of mastery over one's problems is one of the model's most important principles of change (Weiner-Davis, 1992). If the problem is not always happening, and if clients have already mastered ways to make it not happen, the possibility of a problem-free future becomes much more feasible (de Shazer, 1990).

The first session of solution-focused therapy typically begins with the question, "What brings you in?" But after listening respectfully to the clients' story (without encouraging elaboration), the therapist shifts the conversation to goals and outcomes. One way to do this is by asking a "miracle question:" "Suppose that one night, while you were asleep, there was a miracle and this problem was solved. How would you know? What would be different? How will your husband know without your saying a word to him about it?" (de Shazer, 1988, p. 5). To make the prospect of a problem-free future more vivid, the therapist presses for details (e.g., "What will that look like? What else will be different? Who will notice?"). This also sets the stage for inquiring about ways in which pieces of the miracle are already happening, what it will take to keep them happening, and so on. For clients reluctant to accept the miracle idea, other goal-oriented questions of the form, "How will you know treatment has been successful?" serve the same purpose. In any case, negotiating goals in this way is a crucial building block for solution-focused therapy, and according to Berg and Miller (1992) "well-formed" treatment goals have certain characteristics: They are small, specific, behavioral, positive, realistic (indicating the presence rather than the absence of something), and preliminary (indicating a beginning rather than an end).

Establishing and maintaining a cooperative client–therapist relationship, a task interwoven with negotiating goals, also begins early in therapy and continues throughout. Here the distinction between customer, complainant, and visitor-type relationships offers guidelines for therapeutic cooperation or "fit" (de Shazer, 1988; Berg & Miller, 1992). If the relationship involves a visitor with whom the therapist cannot define a clear complaint or goal, cooperation requires nothing more than sympathy, politeness, and compliments for whatever the clients are successfully doing (with no tasks or requests for change). In a complainant relationship, where clients present a complaint but appear unwilling to take action or want someone else to change, the therapist cooperates by accepting their views, giving compliments, and sometimes prescribing observational tasks (e.g., to notice exceptions to the complaint pattern). Finally, with customers who want to do something about a complaint, the principle of fit allows the therapist to be more direct in guiding them toward solutions. It is important to note also that solution-focused therapists (unlike MRI therapists) use compliments and praise "with all cases . . . regardless of the type of client–therapist relationship, and throughout the treatment process" (Berg & Miller, 1992, p. 101).

Both de Shazer (1988) and Berg and Miller (1992) emphasize that the customer–complainant–visitor categories represent dynamic, changing attributes of the therapist–client relationship, not static characteristics of the clients themselves. Visitors and complainants can become customers and vice versa. In fact, one of the main reasons to cooperate with clients in this way is to increase possibilities for customership. On the other hand, solution-focused therapists like Lipchik (1992) no longer use the categories since to do so may risk "confining by defining."

At the heart of the method are purposeful interviewing techniques designed to "influence the clients' view of the problem in a manner that leads to solution" (Berg & Miller, 1992, p. 70). Future-oriented questions (like the miracle question) are probably the most important of these, but therapists use past- and present-oriented questions to seed and accentuate possibilities for change as well. Since complaints typically show some variability, the therapist can search for exceptions in the present by asking about times when the complaint is absent or less pressing ("What is different about the days when you two are getting along? What are you doing differently then? What do you notice that is different about each other?"). Questions can also be historical ("Tell me about a problem the two of you as a couple handled well in the past? How did

you do that?"). How clients answer such questions is less important than how they are asked, since the purpose is less to gather information than to seed ideas about possible change. One guideline, for example, is to phrase future-oriented questions in a manner that presupposes change ("What *will* you be doing differently together *when* Bill stops drinking?" rather than "What *would* you be doing differently *if* he stops?"). And, of course, it is not individual questions that make a difference, but the way questions are woven together to develop a solution-focused theme.

In addition to the miracle question, purposeful interviewing may also include scaling questions, coping questions, and questions about presession change. *Scaling questions* serve to help clients be more specific about a variety of issues such as treatment goals, readiness to change, commitment to their relationship, and progress already made. ("On a scale ranging from 0 to 10 where 0 represents things at their worst, and 10 represents how things will be when these problems are resolved, where would you place yourself today?" [Cade & O'Hanlon, 1993, pp. 105–106]; "What would it take for you to say you are at 6?") The message conveyed by the scale metaphor is that change is a continuous, dynamic, expected, and fairly controllable process (Kowalski & Kral, 1989). *Coping questions* ("How do you manage to keep going? What do you do to keep things from getting worse?") gently challenge the belief that a situation is hopeless by implying that small change may already be happening. Finally, *questions about presession change* highlight what clients may have already done on their own ("Many times people notice in between the time they make the appointment for therapy and the first session that things already seem different. What have you noticed about your situation?" [Weiner-Davis et al., 1987, p. 360]). Weiner-Davis and associates found that 20 of 30 clients who asked this question reported some positive change at the first session, and many solution-focused therapists now routinely ask clients to watch for such changes when they schedule their first session (cf. Talmon, 1990).

Solution-focused therapists also prescribe tasks, although this now appears less central to the model than it used to be. Customers may simply be asked to *do* more of what works. Clients who are less committed to change may be asked only to *observe* what they do related to exceptions or their goals ("Keep track of what you do this week that makes you feel more in control of things," or "Keep track of what your husband does that indicates he is more responsive"). Other clients, describing only "spontaneous" exceptions may be asked to *predict* when such exceptions will occur (de Shazer, 1988).

In addition to individualized tasks, the Milwaukee group has made good use of "formula" tasks applicable to a broad range of clients and complaints. The best known of these is the formula first-session task, typically given at the end of the first session: "Between now and the next time we meet, we would like you to observe, so you can describe it to us next time, what happens in your life that you would like to continue to have happen" (de Shazer et al., 1986, p. 217). de Shazer and associates report that the great majority of their clients (50 of 56 in one survey) respond favorably to this request, usually noticing "new and different" things they want to continue. Adams, Piercy, and Jurich (1991) studied the formula first-session task experimentally, with positive but less dramatic results, and Talmon (1990) reported using it to good effect in the initial phone call *before* clients come to his single-session therapy. In our experience (Rohrbaugh et al., 1995), this intervention is especially well suited for couples ("Pay attention to what it is about your *relationship* that you would like to continue").

The later stages of solution-focused therapy build upon and amplify what has happened before. The therapist continues to inquire about positive changes ("What's been better? What else?"); amplifies the details of what has gone right ("What happened exactly? How did you do that?"); and reinforces with praise, compliments, and heightened interest any changes the clients have made ("You did what? That's great!"). Setbacks are also handled in a way that accentuates the positive ("What have you learned from this? How have you managed to get back on track?"). As for termination, solution-focused brief therapists approach each session as potentially the last (de Shazer, 1991)—and as treatment goals are met, the therapist is alert to ask clients if it makes sense to stop (O'Hanlon & Weiner-Davis, 1989).

Application to Couples

Solution-focused therapy for marital and couple complaints follows the same principles as therapy for other complaints. Because the Milwaukee group does not define or distinguish complaint patterns, we cannot review their contributions in this area in the way we did MRI's. Still, it is apparent from published clinical examples that much of the BFTC's work involves couples. Wylie (1990) provides the following description of a BFTC training tape:

> Steve de Shazer elicits in about 10 minutes an abbreviated account of marital difficulty (the husband gets angry when his wife isn't available to him, but won't admit he's angry and retreats to sulk; she pursues him, tries to "communicate," ends up furiously yelling). During the next two sessions, first de Shazer, then codirector Insoo Kim Berg, reiterate variations of the same few questions about "exceptions" to the problem, which are the hallmarks of their work. "When was the last time things were okay or better than okay between you?" "What were you doing differently during those times?" "How can you make that happen again?" "What do you need to do to keep things going this way?" There is an almost hypnotic quality to the droning repetition of the same questions ("What else did you do to make things different?" "What else did you do?" "What else?") that would seem to induce coma, except that the one-note refrain evokes a gradual flowering and transformation in the couple. Two people, folded in their cocoons of tension and anger, begin to emerge, growing by turns interested, hopeful, eager, enthusiastic, confident, giggly, and affectionate. It is hard to doubt that they will think about each other differently and be nicer to one another then before they came into therapy. (p. 30)

This is in striking contrast to the MRI group's approach(es) to demand–withdraw patterns described earlier, since the apparently successful solution-focused intervention required very little attention to the problematic interaction sequence per se. Indeed, bypassing the problem in this way is as characteristic of treating couple complaints as any other complaint. In another case, where the problem was that a couple "always bickered," de Shazer's questioning led the couple to discover by the end of the first session that they actually bickered only 60% of the time, and by the third session they reported *not* bickering 80% of the time: "At no point during any of the three sessions did we discuss bickering, the pattern(s) involved, its possible causes, or its possible meaning. We only talked about what they did when they did not bicker" (1990, p. 95).

Not surprisingly, customership is crucial to determining who to see in couples therapy, as well as what to do. Like the MRI group, de Shazer and associates do not hesitate to treat marital complaints by seeing only one spouse if the other spouse is disinterested in therapy or only a visitor. In a case study reminiscent of the MRI approach, de Shazer and Berg (1984) describe the successful one-person treatment of a marital complaint presented by a woman distraught about her detective/husband going out without her. The "solution" suggested by the team and adopted by the wife, a clear customer, was to bring more mystery to the marriage (a rather different tact than she had been pursuing). Elsewhere, de Shazer (1988) makes clear that the customer/complainant/visitor guidelines apply to the therapist's relationship with the members of a couple: "If a couple has a joint complaint, give them a joint, cooperative task. If only one member of a couple presents the complaint like a customer, give the 'customer' a task that involves doing something and the other person an observation task" (p. 99).

Solution-focused techniques also figure prominently in two recent books about couples: *Rewriting Love Stories*, by Hudson and O'Hanlon (1991), and *Divorce-Busting*, a successful self-help book by Weiner-Davis (1992). Neither is a "pure" application of the Milwaukee model, however, because both incorporate ideas and techniques from other sources, including the MRI model. Although both are complaint-focused and highly pragmatic, they also include some "normative" ideas about why couples have problems and what, in general, they should do to change.

Interestingly, the solution-focused parts of Hudson and O'Hanlon's (1991) approach draw on the couple's past at least as much as their future. (In fact, *Rewriting Love Stories* makes no mention of the miracle question.)

> Whatever people's experiences are at the moment, they are likely to feel that they have felt the same way for a long time, even if that has not been the case. . . . We try to coax people out of the global negative thinking about the marriage by asking about when things were better. This not only tends to move them from thinking that everything is negative to adopting a more positive view, but also helps us identify what has worked in the past. (p. 47)
>
> . . . To locate strengths and resources that the couple has but has neglected, we ask about what was happening when things were better, we hold positive strength-oriented assumptions, and we ask for exceptions to the rule of the problem. Implicit in our questions and comments is an assumption that the couple has resources for change. (p. 50)

Weiner-Davis's (1992) book incorporates much more of the Milwaukee model and translates solution-oriented principles into prescriptions that are accessible to the general reader. For example, she offers suggestions such as "Notice what is different about the times the two of you are getting along," "Pay attention to how your conflicts end," and "If there are no exceptions, identify the best of the worst." In another chapter she poses future-focused questions such as "When you feel happier, what will you be able (or want) to do that you haven't been doing lately?" "If your mate were to die suddenly or leave abruptly, how would you rearrange your life?" and, of course, "If you went to sleep tonight and a miracle happened . . . ?" Also, by including some problem-focused recommendations such as "Identify your 'more of the same' behaviors" and "Do a 180°," Weiner-Davis brings Milwaukee and MRI together in the service of self-help.

CRITICAL COMMENTARY

Reconciliation

Having reviewed the main principles and applications to couples of the problem- and solution-focused brief therapies, we next consider possibilities for reconciling these models with each other, both theoretically and tactically, and comment briefly on the prospect of using them in tandem with other approaches to treating couple problems.

Against the backdrop of diverse therapies represented in this volume, the similarities between the MRI and Milwaukee models appear to far outweigh the differences. As noted in our introduction, both are complaint based, minimalist models that make no explicit assumptions about the nature of healthy or dysfunctional relationships. Both do assume, however, that small changes, even in one partner's behavior, can lead to further changes that the couple can essentially amplify on their own. And when change begins, the brief therapist's main concern is getting out of the way.

At a conceptual level, the differences between these two models seem mainly a matter of emphasis—one aims to help clients do less of what does not work while the other identifies and promotes more of what does. Weakland and Fisch (1992) sum up the relationship this way:

> We agree that both our approach and that of de Shazer . . . can be considered "minimalistic," not only in seeking a small initial change that will lead on to more but also in seeking theoretical simplicity—though it should be emphasized that applying either of these orientations in practice may be far from simple. Beyond that we do not see these two approaches as opposed or contradictory. De Shazer was in contact with and influenced by the work of MRI at least from 1972, when he took one

of our early brief therapy workshops, and our approaches have much in common. However, we focus primarily on attempted solutions that do not work and maintain the problem; de Shazer and his followers, in our view, have the inverse emphasis. *The two are complementary.* (p. 317, italics added)

Another major difference between the models —that problem-focused therapy emphasizes clients *doing* something differently whereas solution-focused therapy emphasizes *viewing* things differently—can also be reconciled theoretically if one considers that behavioral and cognitive change processes are not mutually exclusive but reciprocal and complementary, with one often leading to the other (cf. Bandura, 1977; Shoham-Salomon, Avner, & Neeman, 1989). Thus, clients' increased sense of agency following solution-focused questioning may instigate a change in a behavior sequence, just as beneficent consequences of less-of-the-same solution behavior may stimulate hope and a sense of mastery over the problem. In other words, interventions based on the two models may enter the same chain of change events, but at different points.

A more important question is how readily the two models can be reconciled in practice—and about this we are less sanguine. The principal authors who have applied the solution-focused variations to couples (Hudson & O'Hanlon, 1991; Weiner-Davis, 1992) are unabashedly eclectic, presenting a potpourri of techniques drawn from both models with relatively few guidelines for differential treatment selection. This is a common and probably reasonable way to approach therapy, yet the MRI and Milwaukee models themselves, as presented by Fisch, Weakland, and associates and by de Shazer, Berg, and associates, are much more systematic—so much so, in fact, that what-to-do-when in each model has been represented in the form of flowcharts (de Shazer, 1988; Rosenthal & Bergman, 1986). We have seen no similarly systematic attempts to integrate these models by specifying when, or under what circumstances, a therapist would use principles or tactics from one approach rather than another. This is no easy task, because despite similarities, there are also many ways in which specific tactics and the general therapeutic stance prescribed by the two models can be quite incompatible (e.g., investigating complaints vs. exceptions to complaints, offering optimism and encouragement vs. pessimism and restraint). O'Hanlon & Weiner-Davis (1989) approximate a sequential principle of integration in recommending that a therapist fall back to MRI tactics (e.g., therapeutic restraint) when solution-focused techniques do not work or appear to become more of the same: "When pursuing exceptions, solution, and problem-free futures feels like swimming upstream, change directions and either become problem-focused . . . or become pessimistic and observe what follows" (p. 113). But beyond such general guidelines, it is not clear how problem- and solution-focused therapy might fit together coherently in practice.[8]

Apart from the problem of reconciling the MRI and Milwaukee models with each other, there is a question of how well they mix or fit with other approaches based on different assumptions about problems and change. While many therapists can (and do) use problem- and solution-focused techniques in conjunction with other approaches, what they lose in doing so is the parsimony of the brief therapy models—arguably their most essential and useful ingredient.

Strategy or Conversation?

An interesting divergence between the two models is that solution-focused therapists increasingly identify their work as collaborative and conversational rather than strategic. Like Haley, who coined the term "strategic therapy," the MRI group continues to emphasize the therapist's responsibility to intervene deliberately, on the basis of a specific strategy or plan, to resolve the presenting complaint as quickly and efficiently as possible. Problem resolution is most efficient, they claim, when the therapist frames interventions in a manner calculated to fit the clients' way of construing the world, and achieving this does not require (and may be handicapped by) the therapist's telling clients the "true" rationale for a given intervention. As we noted earlier, de Shazer and his followers began to distance themselves from the strategic theme in the late 1980s, a shift reflecting changes in their own practice patterns (e.g., from between-session tasks to within-session purposeful interviewing) as well as the emerging influence of postmodern and narrative ideas in the therapy field generally (McNamee & Gergen, 1992).

More recently, de Shazer (1991) located his work in a post structural framework that would seem to preclude "strategic" intervention. The structural (modern) view informing most therapies fails to recognize the impossibility of separating subject from object—the therapist/observer from the observed individual/couple/family system. The problem with this, according to poststructuralists, is that drawing such a boundary sets up imaginary oppositions and implies an adversarial relationship between therapists and clients. De Shazer asserts that the MRI model, although embracing constructivist conceptions of reality (Watzlawick) and rejecting normative views of problems, nonetheless retains the subject–object split between therapist and problem-maintaining behavior pattern and for this reason "can be seen as transitional, as fitting into a position between structuralism and post-structuralism" (1991, p. 56). Not surprisingly, the idea of deliberate (strategic) influence is anathema to poststructuralism. As de Shazer puts it, "the use of 'strategy' (Haley, 1963) and 'tactics' (Fisch et al., 1983 [sic]), meant to suggest careful planning on the part of the therapist, implies *at the very least* that the therapist and the client are involved in a contest" (1991, p. 33, italics in the original).

Given this (de)construction of strategic therapy, it seems fair to ask if the therapeutic conversation that characterizes the solution-focused approach is as collaborative and nonstrategic as de Shazer and associates would like to believe. At least one set of critics (Efran & Schenker, 1993) finds the invariant praise and positive feedback of the Milwaukee approach manipulative and an affront to therapeutic candor. Indeed, one might wonder how a therapy that involves "purposeful questioning," can be summarized in an if-this-do-that flowchart, and relies from time to time on calculated messages from a team behind the mirror could be considered anything *but* planful and strategic. Turning the table full circle, Weakland (1992) criticizes use of the term "therapeutic conversation" as not only vague but misleading, because it implies that therapy is nonhierarchical and that the therapist has no intention of influencing the clients' thoughts and behavior. And in the foreword to de Shazer's (1991) book, Weakland says, "I do not think that use of the term 'strategy' necessarily implies a contest between therapist and client; indeed, I would propose that de Shazer carries on his therapeutic conversations strategically" (p. viii).

Whether or not these approaches are strategic, applications of covert therapeutic agendas in which therapists do not make their rationale for particular interventions explicit to clients have been criticized as manipulative and potentially harmful to the client–therapist relationship (Wendorf & Wendorf, 1985; Ryder, 1987). Defenders of strategic therapy, on the other hand, argue that responsible therapy is inherently manipulative (Fisch, 1990), that therapeutic truthtelling can be not only naive but discour-

teous (Haley, 1987), and that good strategic therapists are profoundly respectful of clients' "subjective truths" (Coyne, 1985; Cade & O'Hanlon, 1993). It may be possible to determine empirically whether strategic interdiction of a problem–solution loop is any more efficient than a straightforward coaching approach, but the controversy about covert strategy is unlikely to be resolved by research. Even if what Haley (1987) calls benevolent lies do produce better therapeutic results, critics such as Wendorf and Wendorf (1985) worry about the ecological consequences of this, not only for the specific therapist–client relationships in which benevolent deceptions occur, but also for how therapists view themselves as helping persons and for the credibility of therapy in society generally.

Ethical issues may be especially salient in work with couples because the therapist must deal with the (often conflicting) agendas of two adults rather than one. A further complication arises when a therapist intervenes through one member of a couple with the implicit or explicit goal of changing not only the behavior of the motivated client, but also the behavior of the nonparticipating spouse (e.g., Watzlawick & Coyne, 1980; Hoebel, 1976): What responsibility, if any, does the therapist have to obtain informed consent from other people likely to be affected by an intervention? Such questions have no easy answer.

The Perils of Parsimony

The most common criticism of the MRI and Milwaukee models is that they oversimplify, either by making unrealistic assumptions about how people change, or by ignoring aspects of the clinical situation that may be crucial to appropriate intervention. Some critics find implausible the rolling-snowball idea that a few well-targeted interventions that produce small changes in clients' cognitions or behavior can kick off a process that will lead to significant shifts in the problem pattern; others grant that brief interventions sometimes produce dramatic changes, but doubt that those changes last (Wylie, 1990). Not surprisingly, therapists of competing theoretical persuasions object to the fact that these brief therapies pointedly ignore personality and relationship dynamics that, from other perspectives, may be fundamental to the problems couples bring to therapists. For example, Gurman (quoted by Wylie, 1990) suggests that "doing no more than interrupting the sequence of behaviors in marital conflict may solve the problem, but not if one spouse begins fights in order to maintain distance because of a lifelong fear of intimacy" (p. 31). Defenders of the brief therapy faith reply that such "iceberg" assumptions about what lies beneath a couple's complaint serve only to complicate the therapist's task and make meaningful change more difficult to achieve. Unfortunately, it is unlikely that research evidence will soon resolve these arguments one way or the other.

A related criticism is that the brief therapies typically ignore feelings and do not make affect a primary focus of intervention, even in work with couples. Coyne (1986c) replies that working with emotion-laden exchanges is very much a part of strategic marital therapy, but warns that attempts by therapists to evoke or increase emotional expression risk recapitulating "be spontaneous" paradoxical demands that perpetuate the problem. Furthermore, "when there has been a polarization around differences about the desired level of intimacy or emotional expressiveness, too central a focus on the evocation of feelings may inhibit change" (p. 12). In another commentary on this issue, Kleckner, Frank, Bland, Amendt, and Bryant (1992) refute the "myth of the unfeeling strategic therapist," pointing out, like Coyne, that strategic therapists do deal with feelings—they just don't talk or write much about them (cf. Cade & O'Hanlon, 1993).

A final and potentially more serious criticism is that, because brief therapies are complaint focused, they may ignore problems such as spouse abuse and substance abuse if clients do not present them as overt complaints in the first session (Wylie, 1990). This may be a particular risk in the solution-focused approach, where therapists not only give limited attention to eliciting complaints but purposefully attempt to shift therapist–client conversation away from them, to exceptions, as soon as possible. Yet even in MRI's focused problem resolution, where therapists explore complaint patterns in great detail and often meet with partners separately, the focus of intervention remains almost exclusively on what clients say they want to change. The nonnormative, constructivist premise of brief therapy, which rejects the idea of objective standards for what is normal or abnormal or good or bad behavior, also excuses the therapist from attempting to "discover" conditions such as alcoholism or spouse abuse. According to Fisch (as cited by Wylie, 1990), an MRI therapist would inquire about suspected wife beating only if it were in some way alluded to in the interview. Thus, although brief therapists no doubt respect

statutory obligations to report certain kinds of suspected abuse and warn potential victims of violence, they clearly distinguish therapy from social control and reserve the former for customers with explicit complaints.

The recent proliferation of books and workshops on solution-focused therapy has given this approach a higher profile than the MRI model in the mental health marketplace, but has also attracted more focused criticism. For example, Efran and Schenker (1993), in reviewing five new books, find solution-focused therapy "excruciatingly formulaic" and warn that "overprogramming the therapist can be a problem with the method" (p. 72). With the fundamental agenda fixed in advance and little room for spontaneity or authenticity, this "conversational" therapy impressed Efran and Schenker as ironically *uncon*versational. These reviewers also worry that such a relentless pursuit of positivity may invalidate the client's perceptions and compromise the therapist's credibility. Another line of criticism (Fraser, 1993) faults solution-focused therapy for ignoring complaint patterns, especially the kinds of problem–solution sequences investigated so thoroughly by the MRI group. While amplifying exceptions without defining problem patterns may suffice to resolve some complaints, there are also situations where deemphasizing or deflecting attention from a problem (related, say, to grief, depression, or recovery from a trauma) constitutes more of what the clients have been doing themselves, or more of what other people are trying to get them to do. A therapist who does not recognize these patterns risks repeating them, in which case solution-focused therapy may itself become a problem-maintaining solution.

DO THE BRIEF THERAPIES REALLY WORK?

The last critical issue we raise about the MRI and Milwaukee therapies is in our view the most important. These are therapies that justify themselves as pragmatic, efficient, effective approaches to resolving problems. Yet, the evidence that they *do* really work is sparse, largely anecdotal, and not nearly so persuasive as their proponents sometimes claim. To our knowledge, neither approach in its pure form has yet been subjected to a controlled clinical trial.[9] And although both brief therapy centers have conducted follow-up studies of their cases, they have not measured outcome in ways that are persuasive to the behavioral science mainstream.

Since their therapies are complaint based, the MRI and Milwaukee centers have both evaluated outcome by asking clients whether the complaint has been resolved (Weakland et al., 1974; de Shazer, 1991). The MRI procedure, from the outset, has been for a team member other than the primary therapist to conduct a telephone follow-up interview with clients approximately 3 and 12 months following termination. The questions concern (1) attainment of the treatment goal; (2) the status of the presenting problem, including whether any further treatment has been sought; (3) improvements in areas not specifically aggressed in treatment; and (4) the emergence of any new problems. Based on the answers to these questions, the team then meets to classify each case as attaining success (substantial or complete relief of the presenting complaint with no new problems), significant improvement (clear but not complete relief of the complaint), or failure (little or no change, negative change, or further treatment for the presenting complaint). The Milwaukee group apparently follows a similar follow-up procedure (Kiser, 1988; de Shazer, 1991), although we are less familiar with how they determine "success."

At first blush, the success rates presented by both centers are impressive. For the first 97 cases followed up at MRI, Weakland et al. (1974) reported success, significant improvement, and failure rates of 40%, 32% and 28%, respectively. In a more recent review of 285 cases treated there through 1991, for which we could find interpretable follow-up data, the success, partial success, and failure rates were 44%, 24%, and 32%, respectively (Rohrbaugh et al., 1992). Thus, at least two thirds of the MRI cases reportedly improved, and the average length of therapy was six sessions. A follow-up study at the Milwaukee center found even higher success rates: Kiser (1988) tabulated outcomes for 164 BFTC clients according to the MRI categories, with follow-up intervals ranging to 18 months. Here there was "an 80.4% success rate (65.6% of the clients met their goal while 14.7% made significant improvement) within an average of 4.6 sessions . . . [and] . . . at 18 months, the success rate had increased to 86%" (de Shazer, 1991, p. 161).

There are several reasons, of course, why outcome figures like these must be interpreted cautiously. One limitation is that the researchers have not described their follow-up procedures in enough detail to permit critical evaluation of the reliability and validity of the results obtained.[10] For example, we do not know how precisely the resolution of target complaints was defined in the interview, how goal attainment was scaled, whether collateral interviews were conducted in couple and family cases, or how demand characteristics might have colored the clients' responses. The last problem is of special concern in solution-focused therapy, in which the relentless shaping of solution-talk makes clients' later reports of outcome suspect (Efran & Schenker, 1993). Another issue is that the classification of outcome (at least at MRI) was based on the judgment of the clinical team, which leaves open the possibility of a positive bias. Still, the two-thirds improvement figure for brief therapy at MRI is roughly in line with success rates reported in the literature for other, usually longer forms of therapy (Smith, Glass, & Miller, 1980). On the other hand, the 80–90% success rate claimed by the Milwaukee group is well above the norm for psychotherapy research and strikes some observers as unbelievable (Wylie, 1990).

Despite the limitations of in-house success rates, the MRI and Milwaukee follow-up studies provide some tentative data on how brief these therapies can be, and on what client variables might predict outcome, at least at MRI. Although therapy at both centers is brief (less than 10 sessions), outcomes may depend on the number of sessions clients have. The MRI group undertook an experiment in the mid-1970s to test the feasibility of shortening treatment to 5 sessions: Cases randomly assigned to a 5 session limit ($n = 13$) fared substantially worse than control cases ($n = 14$) allowed the usual 10 sessions, leading to rejection of the 5-session limit on empirical grounds (Rohrbaugh et al., 1992). A similar pattern may hold at the Milwaukee center, where de Shazer (1991) reports a higher success rate for cases seen 4 or more times than for those seen 3 times or less.

In studying the MRI archives, we also attempted to compare samples of unambiguous success and failure cases, and the main positive finding will bring us back to the topic of treating couples. To identify these samples, we began with the team's outcome classifications, read the follow-up reports, and applied some additional, rather stringent inclusion criteria that limited the final comparison groups to 39 clear success cases with sustained positive outcomes and 33 clear treatment failures. When we compared these groups on a number of client pretreatment variables (e.g., demographics, problem history, nature of the presenting complaint) and on variables having to do with the format of treatment, there were surprisingly few differences. In fact, only one variable—the number of different people seen—differentiated the groups clearly, and this difference appeared specific to cases involving a marital or couple complaint. Thus, couple therapy cases were well represented in both groups (< 40%), but were more likely to be successful when at least two people (the two partners) participated in treatment. This finding would not seem to fit well with the MRI view that marital complaints can be treated effectively by intervening through one spouse. On the other hand, we have not evaluated the potentially confounding role of customership in these cases, or the possibility that the absent partners were as uncommitted to the relationship as they apparently were to therapy. In any case, these MRI results do little to undermine Gurman, Kniskern, and Pinsof's (1986) empirical generalization that "when both spouses are involved in therapy conjointly for marital problems, there is a greater chance of positive outcome than when only one spouse is treated" (p. 572).

The peculiar combination of promises and problems associated with evaluating the MRI and Milwaukee models would seem reason enough to subject these methods to controlled clinical trials. In theory, this should not be difficult to do, since both therapies are quite specific and would not be difficult to manualize. In the only controlled study we have seen, Adams, Piercy, and Jurich (1991) found no difference in overall improvement between cases who received 10 sessions of solution-focused therapy versus a like amount of problem-focused (structural/strategic/systemic) therapy. Another study by Goldman and Greenberg (1992) incorporated some aspects of the MRI model (e.g., identifying and interrupting interaction cycles) in a comparison of strategic and emotion-focused couple therapy, although this cannot be considered a pure test of the MRI approach. Interestingly, however, follow-up results favored the strategic treatment and the investigators suggested that this approach may be well suited for couples with rigidly entrenched, complementary interaction patterns.

To some extent, the paucity of rigorous research on problem- and solution-focused brief therapy reflects skepticism among social-constructivist and poststructural thinkers about knowledge gained through the "objectivist" methods of social science. It nevertheless seems ironic that therapies claiming to resolve problems so efficiently should treat the measurement of outcome so superficially. Much will be gained, we think, when proponents of the MRI and Milwaukee approaches pay as much attention to

documenting results as they do to describing treatment procedures—and when mainstream researchers view these therapies as worthy of rigorous study.

Beyond the question of outcome, traditional research methods will help to clarify how and why the brief therapies work. Again, possibilities for investigating the *process* of therapy multiply when one considers that many of the interventions in these models are very well specified. The formula tasks and purposeful interview techniques so fundamental to the solution-focused approach are a case in point. Adams et al. (1991), in the study cited previously, found that clients who received de Shazer's formula first-session task ("Observe what you want to continue to have happen . . . ") reported more compliance, clearer goals, and more improvement in the presenting problem at the next session than those who received a problem-focused task. On the other hand, Adams and associates had also hypothesized, following de Shazer (1985), that the formula task would increase clients' optimism and sense of mastery, yet client reports and observer ratings gave no indication that this was the case. Further research along these lines should help to clarify the presumed importance of such processes in mediating change following solution-focused interviews and interventions. Process studies might also be used to address some of the questions about solution-focused therapy raised by Efran and Schenker (1993), mentioned previously. For example, do clients (or outside observers) perceive therapists who focus exclusively on solution-talk to be less credible than therapists who allow or encourage problem-talk? Is credibility related to the discrepancy between therapist positivity and the clients' self perceptions? Does solution-talk in the session correlate with solution-talk (and behavior change) at home?

On balance, the treatment of marital complaints will benefit from cross-fertilization between the disparate clinical cultures represented by the MRI and Milwaukee models on the one hand, and by mainstream behavioral research and therapy on the other. Intriguing parallels—between MRI's problem–solution sequences and cognitive-behaviorist's reciprocal-influence processes (Bandura, 1977), between solution-focused techniques and "motivational" interviewing (DiClemente, 1991; Miller & Rollnick, 1991), and between MRI's reframing and what Jacobson (1992) calls "acceptance" interventions—are among the many points of intersection that remain largely unacknowledged and unexplored.[11] An obstacle to rapprochement is the postmodern, constructivist epistemology that discourages some proponents of the MRI and Milwaukee therapies from taking "objectivist" research seriously. Although this may not dissolve, we hope that researchers interested in identifying effective interventions for marital distress will take these therapies seriously.

NOTES

1. The order of the first two authors is arbitrary.

2. Two of us (VS and MR) have had considerably more direct experience with the MRI model than with the Milwaukee model. Nevertheless, we value both approaches and now use both in our practice and research (e.g., Rohrbaugh, Shoham, Spungen, & Steinglass, 1994).

3. Bateson (1958) distinguished *complementary* interaction patterns, in which participants exchange opposite behavior (e.g., nagging and withdrawal, dominance and submission), from *symmetrical* patterns, in which they exchange similar behavior (e.g., mutual blame or avoidance).

4. Christensen's research suggests that women are on the demand side of demand–withdraw interaction more often than men (Christensen & Heavy, 1993).

5. This may owe partly to the fact that Fisch, Shoham, and the wife shared a cultural familiarity with chicken soup as a credible—and potentially nonverbal—remedy for familial distress.

6. To the title of an essay entitled "What is it about brief therapy that works?" de Shazer attached the footnote, "as of August, 1988" (1990, p. 90).

7. How this squares with de Shazer's more recent poststructural emphasis is not entirely clear to us.

8. We recently explored the possibility of integrating problem- and solution-focused interventions in a systemic treatment manual for problem drinking (Rohrbaugh et al., 1994). Both methods proved useful in the project, but apart from specifying how and when certain questions should be asked (e.g., the miracle question and formula first session task), we could not construct a coherent rationale for when to use one approach rather than the other. Since attempting to use both simultaneously seemed to produce confused, unfocused interventions, the only firm selection guideline was that therapists be clear about which approach they were pursuing at any given time.

9. Without control groups it is difficult to evaluate a therapy's effectiveness and impossible to calculate the effect sizes necessary to include studies of brief therapy in quantitative reviews of therapy outcome research (Shadish et al., 1993).

10. The report of Kiser's study exists only as an unpublished master's thesis. According to Kiser (personal communication, 1994), manuscripts based on the study have been rejected by three journals, primarily on methodological grounds.

11. Even the miracle question has found a place in both cultures, though its application in therapy goes back at least to Alfred Adler's "magic wand."

REFERENCES

Adams, J. F., Piercy, F. P., & Jurich, J. A. (1991). Effects of solution focused therapy's "formula first session task" on compliance and outcome in family therapy. *Journal of Marital and Family Therapy, 17,* 277–290.

Amato, P. R., & Keith, B. (1991). Parental divorce and the well-being of children: A meta-analysis. *Psychological Bulletin, 110,* 26–46.

Anderson, H., & Goolishian, H. A. (1990). Beyond cybernetics: Comments on Atkinson and Heath's "Further thoughts on second-order family therapy." *Family Process, 29,* 157–163.

Bandura, A. (1977). Self-efficacy: Toward a unifying theory of behavioral change. *Psychological Review, 84,* 191–215.

Bateson, G. (1958). *Naven* (2nd ed.). Stanford, CA: Stanford University Press.

Berg, I. K., & Miller, S. D. (1992). *Working with the problem drinker: A solution-focused approach.* New York: Norton.

Bobele, M. (1987). Therapeutic interventions in life-threatening situations. *Journal of Marital and Family Therapy, 13,* 225–240.

Bray, J. H. (1990). Impact of divorce on the family. In R. E. Rekel (Ed.), *Textbook of family practice* (4th ed., pp. 111–122). Philadelphia: Saunders.

Bray, J. H., & Hetherington, E. M. (1993). Families in transition: Introduction and overview. *Journal of Family Psychology, 7,* 3–8.

Cade, B., & O'Hanlon, W. H. (1993). *A brief guide to brief therapy.* New York: Norton.

Christensen, A., & Heavy, C. L. (1993). Gender differences in marital conflict: The demand/withdraw interaction pattern. In S. Oskamp & M. Costanzo (Eds.), *Gender issues in contemporary society* (pp. 113–141). Newbury Park, CA: Sage.

Christensen, A., & Shenk, J. L. (1991). Communication, conflict, and psychological distance in nondistressed, clinic, and divorcing couples. *Journal of Consulting and Clinical Psychology, 59,* 458–463.

Coyne, J. C. (1985). Toward a theory of frames and reframing: The social nature of frames. *Journal of Marital and Family Therapy, 11,* 337–344.

Coyne, J. C. (1986a). Strategic marital therapy for

depression. In N. S. Jacobson & A. S. Gurman (Eds.), *Clinical handbook of marital therapy* (pp. 495–511). New York: Guilford Press.

Coyne, J. C. (1986b). The significance of the interview in strategic therapy. *Journal of Strategic and Systemic Therapies, 5,* 63–70.

Coyne, J. C. (1986c). Evoked emotion in marital therapy: Necessary or even useful? *Journal of Marital and Family Therapy, 12,* 11–14.

Coyne, J. C. (1988). Strategic therapy. In J. F. Clarkin, G. L. Haas, & I. O. Glick (Eds.), *Affective disorders and the family: Assessment and treatment* (pp. 89–113). New York: Guilford Press.

de Shazer, S. (1982). *Patterns of brief family therapy.* New York: Guilford Press.

de Shazer, S. (1985). *Keys to solution in brief therapy.* New York: Norton.

de Shazer, S. (1988). *Clues: Investigating solutions in brief therapy.* New York: Norton.

de Shazer, S. (1990). What is it about brief therapy that works? In J. K. Zeig (Ed.), *Brief therapy: Myths, methods, and metaphors* (pp. 90–99). New York: Brunner/Mazel.

de Shazer, S. (1991). *Putting differences to work.* New York: Norton.

de Shazer, S., & Berg, I. (1984). A part is not apart: Working with only one of the partners present. In A. S. Gurman (Ed.), *Casebook of marital therapy* (pp. 97–110). New York: Guilford Press.

de Shazer, S., Berg, I., Lipchik, E., Nunnally, E., Molnar, A., Gingerich, W., & Weiner-Davis, M. (1986). Brief therapy: Focused solution development. *Family Process, 25,* 207–222.

DiClemente, C. C. (1991). Motivational interviewing and the stages of change. In W. R. Miller & S. Rollnick, *Motivational interviewing: Preparing people to change addictive behavior* (pp. 191–202). New York: Guilford Press.

Efran, J. S., & Schenker, M. D. (1993). A potpourri of solutions: How new and different is solution-focused therapy? *Family Therapy Networker, 17,* 71–74.

Fisch, R. (1986). The brief treatment of alcoholism. *Journal of Strategic and Systemic Therapies, 5,* 40–49.

Fisch, R. (1990). "To thine own self be true . . . " Ethical issues in strategic therapy. In J. K. Zeig (Ed.), *Brief therapy: Myths, methods, and metaphors* (pp. 429–436). New York: Brunner/Mazel.

Fisch, R., Weakland, J. H., & Segal, L. (1982). *The tactics of change.* San Francisco: Jossey-Bass.

Fogarty, F. (1976). Marital crisis. In P. J. Guerin (Ed.), *Family therapy: Theory and practice* (pp. 325–334). New York: Gardner.

Fraser, J. S. (1993, March). *Solution-focused therapy—as a problem.* Paper presented at conference honoring J. H. Weakland, New Orleans, LA.

Gingerich, W. J., de Shazer, S., & Weiner-Davis, M. (1987). Constructing change: A research view of interviewing. In E. Lipchik (Ed.), *Interviewing.* Rockville, MD: Aspen.

Goldman, A., & Greenberg, L. (1992). Comparison of integrated systemic and emotionally focused approaches to couples therapy. *Journal of Consulting and Clinical Psychology, 60,* 962–969.

Green, S., & Bobele, M. (1988). An interactional approach to marital infidelity. *Journal of Strategic and Systemic Therapies, 7,* 35–47.

Gurman, A. S., Kniskern, D. P., & Pinsof, W. (1986). Research on the process and outcome of marital and family therapy. In S. L. Garfield & A. E. Bergin (Eds.), *Handbook of psychotherapy and behavior change* (pp. 565–624). New York: Wiley.

Haley, J. (Ed.). (1967). *Advanced techniques of hypnosis and therapy: Selected papers of Milton H. Erickson, M.D.* New York: Grune & Stratton.

Haley, J. (1980). *Leaving home.* New York: McGraw-Hill.

Haley, J. (1987). *Problem-solving therapy: New strategies for effective family therapy* (2nd ed.). San Francisco: Jossey-Bass.

Harland, R. (1987). *Superstructuralism: The philosophy of structuralism and post-structuralism.* London: Methuen.

Hoebel, F. C. (1976). Brief family-interactional therapy in the management of cardiac-related high-risk behaviors. *Journal of Family Practice, 3,* 613–618.

Hoffman, L. (1990). Constructing realities: An art of lenses. *Family Process, 29,* 1–12.

Hudson, P. O., & O'Hanlon, W. H. (1991). *Rewriting love stories: Brief marital therapy.* New York: Norton.

Jacobson, N. S. (1992). Behavioral couple therapy: A new beginning. *Behavior Therapy, 23,* 493–506.

Kiser, D. (1988). *A follow-up study conducted at the Brief Family Therapy Center of Milwaukee.* Unpublished master's thesis, University of Wisconsin, Milwaukee.

Kleckner, T., Frank, L., Bland, C., Amendt, J. H., & Bryant, R. (1992). *Journal of Marital and Family Therapy, 18,* 41-51.

Kowalski, K., & Kral, R. (1989). The geometry of solution: Using the scaling technique. *Family Therapy Case Studies, 4,* 59–66.

Lipchik, E. (Ed.). (1987). *Interviewing.* Rockville, MD: Aspen.

Lipchik, E. (1992). A "reflecting interview." *Journal of Strategic and Systemic Therapies, 11,* 59–74

Lipchik, E., & de Shazer, S. (1986). The purposeful interview. *Journal of Strategic and Systemic Therapies, 5,* 88–99.

Madanes, C. (1981). *Strategic family therapy*. San Francisco: Jossey-Bass.

Madanes, C. (1991). Strategic family therapy. In A. S. Gurman & D. P. Kniskern (Eds.), *Handbook of family therapy* (Vol. 2, pp. 396–416). New York: Brunner/Mazel.

McNamee, S., & Gergen, K. J. (Eds.). (1992). *Therapy as social construction*. Newbury Park, CA: Sage.

Miller, W. R., & Rollnick, S. (1991). *Motivational interviewing: Preparing people to change addictive behavior*. New York: Guilford Press.

Napier, A. Y. (1978). The rejection–intrusion pattern: A central family dynamic. *Journal of Marriage and Family Counseling, 4*, 5–12.

O'Hanlon, W., & Weiner-Davis, M. (1989). *In search of solutions: A new direction in psychotherapy*. New York: Norton.

Rohrbaugh, M., & Shean, G. (1988). Anxiety disorders: An interactional view of agoraphobia. In F. Walsh & C. Anderson (Eds.), *Chronic illness and the family* (pp. 66–85). New York: Brunner/Mazel.

Rohrbaugh, M., Shoham, V., & Schlanger, K. (1992). In the brief therapy archives: A progress report. Unpublished manuscript.

Rohrbaugh, M., Shoham, V., Spungen, C., & Steinglass, P. (1995). A systemic couples therapy for problem drinking. In B. Bongar & L. Beutler (Eds.), *Foundations of psychotherapy: Theory, research and practice* (pp. 228–253). London: Oxford University Press.

Rosenthal, M. K., & Bergman, Z. (1986). A flow-chart presenting the decision-making process of the MRI Brief Therapy Center. *Journal of Strategic and Systemic Therapies, 5*, 1–6.

Ryder, R. G. (1987). *The realistic therapist: Modesty and relativism in therapy and research*. Newbury Park, CA: Sage.

Shoham-Salomon, V., Avner, R., & Neeman, R. (1989). You are changed if you do and changed if you don't: Mechanisms underlying paradoxical interventions. *Journal of Consulting and Clinical Psychology, 57*, 590–598.

Sluzki, C. E., & Ransom, D. C. (1976). *Double bind: The foundation of the communicational approach to the family*. New York: Grune & Stratton.

Smith, M. L., Glass, G. U., & Miller, T. I. (1980). *The benefits of psychotherapy*. Baltimore, MD: Johns Hopkins University Press.

Talmon, M. (1990). *Single-session therapy*. San Francisco: Jossey-Bass.

Teisman, M. (1979). Jealousy: Systematic, problem-solving therapy with couples. *Family Process, 18*, 151–160.

Todd, T. C. (1986). Structural–strategic marital therapy. In N. S. Jacobson & A. S. Gurman (Eds.), *Clinical handbook of marital therapy* (pp. 71–105). New York: Guilford Press.

Watzlawick, P., Beavin, J., & Jackson, D. D. (1967). *Pragmatics of human communication*. New York: Norton.

Watzlawick, P., & Coyne, J. C. (1980). Depression following stroke: Brief, problem-focused treatment. *Family Process, 19*, 13–18.

Watzlawick, P., & Weakland, J. H. (Eds.). (1978). *The interactional view*. New York: Norton.

Watzlawick, P., Weakland, J. H., & Fisch, R. (1974). *Change: Principles of problem formation and problem resolution*. New York: Norton.

Weakland, J. H. (1988). Weakland on the Woodys–Bobele exchange. *Journal of Marital and Family Therapy, 14*, 205.

Weakland, J. H. (1992). Conversation—but what kind? In S. Gilligan & M. Price (Eds.), *Therapeutic conversations* (pp. 136–145). New York: Norton.

Weakland, J. H., & Fisch, R. (1992). Brief therapy—MRI style. In S. H. Budman, M. F. Hoyt, & S. Friedman (Eds.), *The first session in brief therapy* (pp. 306–323). New York: Guilford Press.

Weakland, J. H., Watzlawick, P., Fisch, R., & Bodin, A. (1974). Brief therapy: Focused problem resolution. *Family Process, 13*, 141–168.

Weiner-Davis, M. (1992). *Divorce-busting*. New York: Summit Books.

Weiner-Davis, M., de Shazer, S., & Gingerich, W. J. (1987). Using pretreatment change to construct a therapeutic solution: An exploratory study. *Journal of Marital and Family Therapy, 13*, 359–356.

Wendorf, D. J., & Wendorf, R. J. (1985). A systemic view of family therapy ethics. *Family Process, 24*, 443–460.

Wile, D. B. (1981). *Couples therapy: A non-traditional approach*. New York: Wiley.

Woody, J. D., & Woody, R. H. (1988). Public policy in life-threatening situations: A response to Bobele. *Journal of Marital and Family Therapy, 14*, 133–138.

Wylie, M. S. (1990). Brief therapy on the couch. *Family Therapy Networker, 14*, 26–35, 66.

8

Psychoanalytic Marital Therapy

JILL SAVEGE SCHARFF

PSYCHOANALYTIC MARITAL therapy can be distinguished from the other major models of marital therapy by the history of its development, its theoretical underpinnings, and their application in clinical practice. It derives from the psychoanalytic theory and therapy invented by Freud (1910a) and uses many of his ways of thinking and working, but it bears little resemblance to classical analysis and yet can be quite compatible with it because of the shared ideology. In practice, psychoanalytic marital therapy has some features in common with the two other major models, behavioral and systems approaches (Gurman, 1978) that are arrived at from quite different theoretical viewpoints. This technical flexibility has been welcomed by Gurman and Jacobson (1986) as a sign of willingness to learn from other models so as to identify the common ground of therapeutic efficacy. While psychoanalysis, a time-consuming and costly undertaking, remains an important treatment option for individual patients (many of whom are themselves therapists), who are deeply committed to learning about themselves, who need to undertake a major revision of their personality structure, and who are in life circumstances that support the analysis, its main value lies in its continuing contribution to the theory of personal development in relation to significant others through the life cycle, and its application to more affordable therapies such as marital therapy.

Psychoanalytic marital therapy derives from a psychoanalytic model. Paolino and McCrady (1978) argued that the term "psychoanalytic" should not be used interchangeably with the term "psychodynamic" but should be reserved only for those forms of marital therapy that operate on Freudian principles. According to this idea, marital therapy using Sullivanian, Fairbairnian, or Kleinian principles would not qualify for inclusion in this chapter. In my experience the term "psychoanalytic" has been avoided because the associated cartoon image of an individual patient lying on the couch of a blank screen analyst is patently at odds with the practice of the marital therapist. The term "psychodynamic," like "psychoanalytic," describes a theory of therapy that focuses on mental conflict between the conscious part of the mind and the unconscious part, where powerful, unacceptable thoughts and feelings are pushed away; between various substructures of the mind; and between thoughts and feelings. In practice, psychoanalytic marital therapy is a nondirective, relatively unstructured method that follows the couple's associations, that values past and present experience equally in order to understand *why* rather than *how* destructive patterns occur, and that relies on interpretation of resistance, defense, and transference of unconscious thoughts and feelings to the person of the therapist (Finkelstein, 1987). But even though the term "psychodynamic therapy" captures the dynamic relation between parts of the self and the other, it obscures its psychoanalytic origin. This disavowal was felt necessary at a time when psychoanalysis, even though applicable to family studies (Flugel, 1921; Grotjahn, 1960), was not as relevant to the emerging field of family and marital therapy as more modern communications and systems theories (von Bertalannfy, 1950; Katz & Kahn, 1966).

Nevertheless, psychoanalysis continued to influence the development of structural and strategic approaches to family therapy—and by extension, marital therapy—through the contributions of analysts such as Ackerman, Bowen, Cooklin, Lidz, Minuchin, Selvini Palazzoli, Stierlin, Shapiro, Watzlawick, Wynne, Zilbach, and Zinner; others who had analytic training, such as Andolfi, Byng-Hall, and Jackson; Framo and Paul, who were influenced by analytic theory; and group analyst Skynner. According to Bodin (1981), Jackson acknowledged his indebtedness to Sullivan's (1953) interpersonal theory of etiology and psychotherapy, whereas the Chicago Institute of Psychoanalysis influenced Satir's training at the Chicago School of Social Work and led to her interest in corrective emotional experience and the importance of self-concept and self-esteem for the individual. Working in the 1960s and 1970s with Haley, Bateson, and Weakland, the communications and systems family theorists at the Mental Research Institute, Satir and the Institute's directors Jackson and Riskin, both of whom had analytic training, along with Watzlawick, formerly a Jungian training analyst, integrated psychoanalytic understanding with systems models, and preserved a concern for the individual as well as for the family life group.

Now that psychoanalysis has some newer models of the mind that are more applicable to the interpersonal situation and the family, and the marital therapy field has come of age, we seem to be ready to give psychoanalytic marital therapy its rightful name and place among the major models of family therapy.

Granted that all the major models deal with thoughts, feelings, and behavior and the interactions between the mind, the body, the significant other, and the environment, what distinguishes the psychoanalytic approach? It is based on a psychoanalytic model of the marriage, derived from a psychoanalytic model of the mind of the individual and from group analytic theory applied to the small group of two, and it employs a technique that is generally psychoanalytic in orientation, although not in format.

THE PSYCHOANALYTIC MODEL OF MARITAL DYSFUNCTION

The Psychoanalytic Model of the Mind of the Individual

The Duality of Instincts

Freud held that the human infant is motivated by two opposing instincts. At first, Freud (1905, 1915a) saw these as "the sexual instinct" (also called "libido") for getting on with life and enjoying sexual pleasure and the "self-preservative instinct" for repressing the sexual instinct in order to face reality. Later, he saw opposition to the sexual instinct more in terms of "the death instinct," the manifestations of which were harder for him to see, but which he thought were diverted into the external world in the form of destructiveness and aggressiveness (Freud, 1930). These instincts, or "drives" as they are now more commonly called, have the "aim" of gratification by the "object" that they fall upon. Their "source" is the pool of instincts, impulses or drives seething untamed in the unconscious mind (1915b) and located in what Freud called the "id" (1923). These instincts have to be tamed in order not to lose the love object. The infant takes inside successive versions of the love object that have to be given up at each stage of development and out of these introjections are formed the child's "ego," the conscious, executive part of the self, and "superego," the critical, forbidding, guiding part of the self based on selective internalization of parental attributes (1923). Although well aware of the mother's holding and handling of her infant, Freud underemphasized the quality of the relationship. Instead, he focused on the structure and function of the child's mind only, and developed for this task a model of the mind based on science. The organism seeks (1) discharge of instinctual tension; (2) repetition of tension-reducing behavior so as to return to a state of "homeostasis"; or (3) "narcissistic" retreat into the self where needs either do not disturb or their satisfaction can be imagined as vividly as if it were occurring (1914b).

Preoedipal Development

The instincts go through a series of "psychosexual stages of development" that unfold in a predetermined, universal sequence. At first, predominantly "oral" in nature, they propel the infant to suck, both for survival through being fed and for pleasure. When the "oral" gives way to the "anal" as the dominant "erogenous zone," the child gains pleasure from the feces and from the control the anus can exert over them. In the "phallic" stage of development, the child is now aware of and seeks genital sensations, often confused with the urethral sensations of urination. As always, the drives seek objects to gratify their expressions. Naturally, the mother is training her child to gain control over these impulses, and so she becomes forbidding as well as gratifying of her child's wishes. Aware of differences in the genitalia between the sexes, the female child imagines that the more obvious penis affords the boy greater pleasure than she enjoys. This is a source of unhappiness and sometimes shame and poor self-esteem. The sequence now moves on to the "oedipal phase."

Oedipal Development

The little girl develops the fantasy of getting a penis for herself: the best and biggest is the one that she seeks, namely her father's. The child does not want to admit that this is her mother's territory and imagines that she may have to get rid of Mommy so as to have Daddy, and any babies that he might give her, all to herself. The girl is then afraid of an angry mother who will kill her or her unborn babies. The boy notices that his mother is interested in his father and assumes that her interest has to do with her wish for his penis. Size comparisons notwithstanding, the boy hopes that his mother will find his penis more attractive than her husband's. If not, the boy imagines, he may have to kill his rival, the father who, if he should find this out, might angrily retaliate by killing the boy or at least cutting off his penis to punish him for wanting his mother. Freud called the boy's fear of retaliation "castration anxiety." Images of the forbidding parents are internalized as a part of the mind called the "superego" that operates as a conscience and matures in its capacity for maintaining altruistic as well as moral values (Freud, 1923). Capable now of more complex thinking, the child realizes that there is no way of having everything and gives up the forbidden sexual and murderous wishes in favor of being the child of two parents who are together. The oedipus complex is more or less resolved and the child moves on into the "latency stage" in which ego and superego defenses against regression are strengthened and issues of autonomy and skills building come to the fore. If unable to master the challenges of a particular developmental stage, a child may be-

come "fixated" there or even "regress" to an earlier developmental stage inappropriate to chronological age.

The nature of the "resolution of the oedipus complex" (Freud, 1924) determines the child's character structure by 7 years of age, with one qualifier: The oedipus constellation comes up for reworking during the sexually energized phase of adolescence. Its state of resolution by that time determines the ego's degree of disengagement from the old incestuous objects, which, in turn, determines how free the young person is to develop age-appropriate, sexually experimental, love relationships with peers. The mate who is eventually selected will offer attraction and passionate attachment powerful enough to defeat the tie to the old objects, and yet similar enough to inherit the transference to them.

The Psychoanalytic Model Applied to the Two-Person System

Skynner (1976) applied Freud's (1905) concept of fixation and regression to family functioning. Shapiro (1979) and Zinner and Shapiro (1972) showed how families that are more in tune with the attitudes of an earlier developmental stage are unable to proceed to the developmental tasks of adolescence. Although all of these writers address the subject of marriage, they tend not to emphasize developmental regression and fixation in marital dynamics. Bowen (1978) noted that spouses tend to operate at a similar level of differentiation, by which he meant that each spouse was the same distance along the developmental path toward personal integrity, with a capacity for tolerating anxiety, appreciating self and otherness, and taking responsibility for one's own being and destiny (Friedman, 1991). Zilbach (1988), taking off from Erickson (1950), applied a developmental perspective to the family life cycle and described how changes in family needs appropriate to changing developmental stages alter the parents' functioning as a couple, but marriage was not her primary focus. Marriage as a developmental process has received little consideration (Winer, 1990).

Although equally rare, the developmental perspective on marriage can be quite revealing: By applying Freudian theory to the couple relationship, a psychoanalytic marital therapist can be quite specific about the developmental level at which the couple in treatment tends to operate, as shown in the following extract in which Willi (1982) notes the latent conjunctions that underlie couples' quarrels and arguments:

In the narcissistic couple conflict, behind all the bitter fighting, there is a common yearning for an absolute ideal of peaceful symbiosis whose unreality demands continual accentuation by the addition of frustrations.

Despite all the arguments in oral marital conflict, partners agree that love should function as a mother–child care-oriented relationship.

In the anal–sadistic conflict, the partners draw up an unspoken agreement knowing that their relationship would disintegrate were it not safeguarded by bondage, control and authority.

In the phallic conflict, both parties assume that the husband should always be superior to the wife. (p. 147)

Continuing his study of the mind, Freud (1921) explored group psychology in a paper that seems to presage a more interactional model. Instead of moving in that direction, however, he returned to the individual again and developed his "structural theory of personality" that emphasized internal conflict between the agencies of the self: ego, superego, and id. Alger (1967), Sander (1989), Giovacchini (1965), and Graller (1981) applied Freudian structural theory concepts to couple dynamics. Sager and colleagues (Sager, 1976; Sager et al., 1971), who noted that intrapsychic factors determine transactional aspects of a marital relationship, found that conflict dynamics specific to the marriage contract must be interpreted in terms of the spouses' unconscious wishes and aims. Bergmann (1987) and Person (1988, 1990) amplified Fruedian psychoanalytic theory with studies of culture and literature in their treatises on romantic love. Freud's structural personality theory appealed to many North American analysts and led most of them to an intensely intrapsychic focus that was not generally used to illuminate the study of relationships.

This is where analysis and family and marital therapy largely parted company, except in the following instances: Sullivan's (1953) interpersonal psychiatry offered a relational view that was kept out of the mainstream of psychoanalysis, but succeeded in influencing Ryckoff (Ryckoff, Day, & Wynne 1959) and Wynne (1965) who, however, were mainly interested in families, not couples. In his historical review, Martin (1976) tells us that analyst Oberndorf (1938) practiced analysis of two spouses married to each other and claimed to have treated their marriage by analyzing their complementary neuroses separately and consecutively. (Pity the one who had to wait!) Giovacchini (1965) and Drellich (1968) described the psychoanalysis of marital partners by separate

analysts; Thomas (1956) treated each spouse himself in simultaneous analytic psychotherapy; Mittlemann (1944), who described the complementary neuroses of spouses, advocated concurrent psychotherapy with a separate therapist for each spouse (Mittlemann, 1948), to which Martin and Bird (1953) added collaborative meetings between the therapists, an approach also used by Dicks (1967) in Britain. By the late 1950s, the partners were seen together by the same therapist, an approach that Mittlemann had used but for which the term "conjoint marital therapy" was coined by Jackson (Jackson & Weakland, 1961). Greene (1970) and collaborating cotherapists used individual, concurrent, and conjoint psychoanalytic therapy sessions in a combination that, although flexible, had to adhere to a predictable sequence (Hollender, 1971; Zinner, 1989).

Against the mainstream, some psychoanalysts persevered to understand the effects of complementary neuroses of the marriage partners on mate selection and in married life. Kohut's (1971, 1977, 1982) self-psychology theory of narcissistic character pathology, and Kernberg's (1975) theory of ego splits and alternating ego states in borderline pathology, have been applied to the couple relationship by Lansky (1986), Kernberg (1991) and Solomon (1989). Meissner (1978) developed a coherent psychoanalytic perspective on marriage as part of family life, yet he maintained that since psychoanalysis lent understanding to family dynamics and therapy, psychoanalysis itself was "inherently, if implicitly, a form of family therapy" (p. 83). Many psychoanalytic marital therapists could not support that claim, but they do agree that psychoanalysis of a spouse affects the balance of the unconscious forces at work in the marriage. Kohl (1962) expressed concern for the untreated spouse of the analytic patient, and Kubie (1956) suggested that perhaps psychoanalysis should not be undertaken when the marriage is in crisis. Dare (1986) responsibly delays analysis of a prospective patient until a conjoint meeting with the spouse assures him that the spouse will not be adversely affected by the decision and that marital therapy is not needed more urgently than analysis. He also checks to see whether a child is part of the problematic marital system; if so, he prefers a family therapy approach, as does Zilbach (1986).

Although psychoanalysis was a dominant, early influence on marital therapy, psychoanalytic marital therapy has not always been recognized as a major model for two main reasons: (1) individually trained psychoanalytic therapists could not readily apply their models of the mind to conjoint situations, and (2) marital therapists looking for information applicable to marital dynamics found more of it in the family systems literature. Psychoanalysis needed a revised model of the mind if it were to be of greater use to the marital therapist.

A Revised Psychoanalytic Model of the Mind: Object Relations Theory

The psychoanalytic theory that has emerged as the one most applicable to a model of marital interaction is that of object relations theory, which also illuminates family dynamics (D. Scharff & J. Scharff, 1987, 1991; J. Scharff, 1989). An individual psychology drawn from study of the relationship between patient and therapist, object relations theory holds that the motivating factor in growth and development of the human infant is the need to be in a relationship with a mothering person, not the discharge of energy from some instinct. Impulses and driven activity are now seen not as primary elemental forces, but as desperate attempts to relate, or as breakdown products of failed relationships. According to Sutherland (1980), object relations theory is an amalgam of the work of British Independent group analysts Balint (1968), Fairbairn (1952), Guntrip (1961, 1969), and Winnicott (1951, 1958, 1965, 1971), and of Klein (1948, 1957) and her followers. Of them all, Fairbairn (1963) gave the most systematic challenge to Freudian theory. His schema of the endopsychic situation was picked up by Dicks (1967), who applied it to his work with spouses. In Britain, Bannister and Pincus (1965), Clulow (1985), Dare (1986), Main (1966), Pincus (1960), and Skynner (1976); in Germany, Willi (1984); and in the United States, Boszormenyi-Nagy and Spark (1973), Frank (1989), Framo (1970), Martin (1976), Meissner (1978), Nadelson (1978), D. Scharff and J. Scharff (1987, 1991), and Zinner (1976, 1988) all acknowledge the influence of Dicks's work on the psychoanalytic model of marital interaction. In his study of unconsummated marriages, Friedman (1962) integrated Dicks's concepts with those of Balint. Bergmann (1990) applied Dicks's formulation to his study of love. McCormack (1989), who applied Winnicott's concept of the holding environment to the borderline–schizoid marriage, Finkelstein (1987), Siegel (1992), Slipp (1984), and Stewart, T. Peters, Marsh, and M. Peters (1975) all advocated an object relations approach to the theory of marital therapy.

Before I describe Dicks's model of marital dynamics, I need to summarize Fairbairn's (1944, 1952, 1954) theory of the individual.

The Individual Psychology of Fairbairn

The infant is not the inchoate conglomerate of drives that Freud described. The infant is born with a whole self through which it executes behaviors that secure the necessary relatedness. Infant research (Stern, 1985) has now corroborated this view of the infant as competent. The infant is looking for attachment, not discharge. As the infant relates to the mother (or mothering person), attachment develops. Out of the vicissitudes of this experience, psychic structure is built. The experience—even with a reasonably good mother who responds well to her infant's regulatory cycles (Brazelton 1982; Brazelton & Als, 1979)—is always somewhat disappointing, in that unlike the situation in the womb, needs cannot be met before they cause discomfort. When the frustration is intolerable, the infant perceives the mother as rejecting. To cope with the pain, the infant takes in ("introjects") the experience of the mother as a rejecting object and rejects that image inside the self by "splitting" it off from the image of the ideal mother and pushing it out of consciousness ("repressing" it). This is called the "rejected object." It is further split into its need-exciting and need-rejecting aspects, associated with feelings of longing and rage, respectively. The part of the self that related to this aspect of the mother is also split off from the original whole self and is repressed along with the relevant, unbearable feelings. Now the personality consists of (1) a "central self" attached with feelings of satisfaction and security to an "ideal internal object"; (2) a "craving self" longingly, but unsatisfyingly, attached to an "exciting internal object"; and (3) a "rejecting self" angrily attached to a "rejecting internal object."

Fairbairn's terminology for the unconscious parts of self and object were "libidinal ego" and "exciting object," "antilibidinal ego" and "rejecting object," but these terms have been discarded in favor of the "exciting" and "rejecting" parts of the self and objects, respectively. The exciting part of the self is sometimes called the "craving self" as suggested by Ogden (1982). Along with the relevant affects, these parts comprise two repressed, unconsciously operating systems of self in relation to object, called "internal object relationships." Fairbairn's genius was to recognize that the rejecting object relationship system further suppressed the exciting object relationship system. Now, we have a view of the personality in which subsystems of the object relationship are in dynamic interaction with each other. Dicks's genius was to see how two personalities in a marriage united not just at the level of conscious choice, compatibility, and sexual attraction, but also at the unconscious level, where they experienced an extraordinary fit, of which they were unaware. Glimmers of lost parts of the self are seen in the spouse and this excites the hope that, through marriage, unacceptable parts of the self can be expressed vicariously.

Dicks (1967) noted that the fit between spouses, their "unconscious complementarity," leads to the formation of a "joint personality." In the healthy marriage, this allows for *derepression* of the repressed parts of one's object relations, and so one can *refind* lost parts of the self in relation to the spouse. In the unhealthy marriage, the fit cements previous repression because undoing of the defenses would also undo the spouse's similar defensive armament that the marriage is supposed to consolidate rather than threaten. Now, we have a model of two minds united in marriage, their boundaries changing and their internal economies in flux, for better or worse.

Spouses' Unconscious Communication: Projective Identification

To account for unconscious communication between spouses, Dicks turned to Klein's (1946) concept of "projective identification" as the crucial bridging concept between the intrapsychic and the interpersonal. Klein's ideas were further elaborated by Segal (1964) and Heimann (1973) who drew attention to introjective identification as well. Projective identification is a mental process that is used to defend against anxiety during the earliest months of life. Like Freud, Klein remained true to instinct theory. Klein thought that the infant had to defend against harm from the aggression of the death instinct by splitting it off from the self and deflecting it by projecting aggressively tinged parts of the self into the maternal object, especially her breast. Boundaries between self and object being unformed, the infant sees those parts of the self as if they were parts of the object. Now the infant fears attack from the breast as an aggressive object. Klein called this stage of personality development, the "paranoid–schizoid position." Under the influence of the life instinct, the infant also projects loving parts of itself into the breast and experiences it as a loving object. Aspects of the breast, sorted in primitive fashion into all good or all bad, are identified with and taken into the infant through "introjective identification" (Klein, 1946, Heimann, 1973). According to Klein, psychic structure forms through repeated cycles of projective and introjective identification. Maturation over the course of the first half-year of life enables the infant to leave behind primitive splitting between good and bad, and to develop an appreciation of a whole object that is felt to be both good and bad. The infant becomes capable of tolerating ambivalence, recognizing the destructive effect of its aggression, feeling concern for the object, and making reparation for damage done to it. When this is accomplished, the infant has achieved the "depressive position."

At this early age, according to Klein, the infant already has a concept of the parents as a couple involved in mutually gratifying intercourse, perceived by the infant at first as a feeding experience and later as a genital relationship from which the child is excluded. This image forms the basis for another aspect of the child's psychic structure, namely the "internal couple" (D. Scharff & J. Scharff, 1991; J. Scharff, 1992). Understanding the functioning of the internal couple as part of the therapist's personality is particularly important in marital therapy, where it is stirred by interaction with the patient couple. Marital therapy may founder or be avoided by the therapist who cannot face the pain of exclusion by, or frightening fusion with, the couple.

The paranoid–schizoid and depressive positions remain active throughout the life cycle as potential locations along a continuum from pathology to health. Projective identification is retained as a mental process of unconscious communication that functions along a continuum from defense to mature empathy. It is difficult to describe exactly how the process of projective and introjective identification actually takes place. We can become aware of it from its effect upon us as therapists (and in our domestic life as spouses or family members). It is usually experienced as a feeling that is alien or unexplainable, perhaps a feeling of excitement or numbness. It could be a sudden idea, a fantasy, a sense of in-touchness, or a fear, such as a fear of going mad. Fantasies can be communicated by tone of voice, gesture, changes in blood flow to the skin, or in other overt macro- or microbehaviors. But at other times the experience is not detectable with present methods. To some, this may sound a bit mystical, but others are willing to accept the occurrence of projective and introjective identification on the basis of their own experience of complexity, ambiguity, and awe in relationships.

Marriage, like infancy, offers a relationship of devotion, commitment, intimacy, and physicality. It fosters regression and offers the partners a durable setting in which to explore the self and the other. Repressed parts of the self seek expression directly in relation to an accepting spouse or indirectly through uninhibited aspects of the spouse. There is a mutual attempt to heal and make reparation to the object refound in the spouse through projective identification, and then to find through introjective identification a new, more integrated self. The dynamic relation between parts of the self described by Fairbairn can now be conceptualized as occurring between the conscious and unconscious subsystems of two personalities united in marriage. Figure 8.1 illustrates this process diagrammatically.

The Steps of Projective and Introjective Identification in Marriage

Figure 8.1 summarizes the mutuality of the processes. They have been described as a series of interlocking steps (D. Scharff & J. Scharff, 1991; J. Scharff, 1992). To describe them more fully, I have to begin at some point along the chain of reciprocity. I will start arbitrarily from the wife's original projection.

Projection. The wife expels a part of herself that is denied (or overvalued) and sees her spouse as if he were imbued with these qualities,- whether he is or not. He will probably be imbued with some of them, accounting for the attraction that his wife felt for him. In other words the projection may or may not fit. If it does, the spouse has a "valency" (Bion, 1961) for responding to the projection.

Projective identification. The husband may or may not identify with the projection. If he does, he may do so passively under the influence of his wife's capacity to induce in him a state of mind corresponding to her own, even if it feels foreign to him, or actively by the force of his valency compelling him to be identified that way. He tends to identify either with the projected part of the wife's *self* ("concordant identification") or with the *object* ("complementary identification") that applies to that part of herself (Racker, 1968). Although the husband inevitably has been chosen because of his psychological valencies and physical (including sexual) characteristics that resonate with parts of the wife's self and object, he also has his own personality and body that are different from those of his wife and her external objects on whom her internal objects are based. In this gap between the original and the new object lies the healing potential of these bilateral processes. The husband as a new object transforms his wife's view of herself and her objects through accepting each projection, temporarily identifying with it, modifying it, and returning it in a detoxified form through a mental process of "containment," analogous to the mother's way of bearing the pain of her infant's distress and misperceptions of her (Bion, 1962). Now, through "introjective identification" the wife takes in this modified version

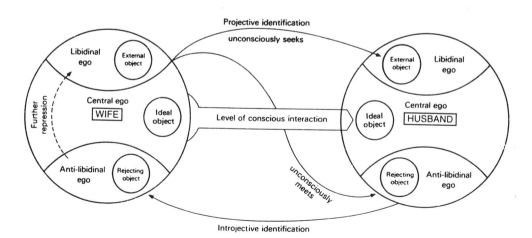

FIGURE 8.1. Projective and introjective identification. Adapted from D. Scharff (1982). Copyright by David E. Scharff. Adapted by permission of Routledge & Kegan Paul.

of herself and assimilates her view of herself to it. She grows in her capacity to distinguish self and other. If her husband is not willing or able to offer her the containment that she needs and instead returns her projections to her either unaltered or exaggerated, growth is blocked.

Mutual projective and introjective identificatory processes. The wife is simultaneously receiving projections from her husband and returning them to him. Together, they are containing and modifying each other's internal versions of self and object. Mutual projective and introjective processes govern mate selection, falling in love, the quality of the sexual relationship, the level of intimacy, and the nature of the marriage in general and its effect on the partners' development as adults (D. Scharff, 1982, D. & J. Scharff, 1991). In a mutual process, husband and wife connect according to unconscious complementarity of object relations. Similarly, couple and therapist relate through the reciprocal actions of transference and countertransference.

How is unconscious complementarity of object relations different from the familiar term "collusion" (Willi, 1982)? I think that "collusion" is another way of describing the same process, at least in those writings in which collusion refers to an unconscious dynamic between a couple. I tend to avoid the term "collusion" because to me it seems to judge and blame the husband and wife, as if they were intentionally colluding to thwart each other, their families, and their therapists. Nevertheless, I agree that mutual projective and introjective identificatory processes cement the couple in an unconscious collusive attempt to avoid anxiety.

The psychoanalytic model of marriage allows for a balance between satisfaction and distress. Marital dysfunction occurs when more distress than can be tolerated upsets the balance. This happens when some of the following conditions apply:

1. Projective and introjective identificatory processes are not mutually gratifying.
2. Containment of the spouse's projections is not possible.
3. Cementing of the object relations set happens instead of its modification.
4. Projective identification of the genital zone as an unarousing or rejecting object cannot be modified by sexual experience.
5. Aspects of the love object have to be split off and experienced in a less threatening situation, leading to triangulation involving a child, hobby, work, friend, parent, or lover.

The following snapshot, taken from a vignette that is described later in the chapter, illustrates the way the balance in a couple may shift and lead to breakup.

Michelle and Lenny were drawn to each other by mutual projective and introjective identificatory processes. She saw in him a solid, loving, thoughtful, and successful man who treated her well and whom her hatefulness could not destroy, whereas he was proud to be her stable base, and in return, he enjoyed her vivacity and outrageous disregard of his sensibilities, loving her in spite of herself and treating her like a queen. Lenny treated Michelle as special, the way his mother had treated him, and as Michelle's mother had treated her and her brother even more so. Michelle treated Lenny as she had felt treated: he was special to her, as she was to her mother, but not as wonderful as the other person, namely her brother, corresponding to herself in relation to Lenny as her brother. The problem arose when Lenny could not contain Michelle's projective identification of him as her brother, because he was not as exciting, not as aggressive, and not as enviable as her brother. Michelle could not contain his projective identification of her as his adored self, because she was so hateful and destroyed by envy. Michelle longed for Lenny to be more aggressive, but the more she pestered him to be so, the less space she gave to his initiative, and the more she became like a repressed, nagging image of his mother, whom he preferred to think of as adoring. Lenny had helped Michelle with her fear of sex, and so, to some extent, she had managed to modify her projective identification of the genital zone as an unarousing and rejecting object spoiled by her envy of her brother's genitalia and preferred status, but not sufficiently to reinvest her vagina as a gratifying organ of pleasure and bonding for the couple. No actual triangulation had occurred, but in fantasy Michelle kept herself attached to the hope of a better man who would fulfill all her expectations of virility. She wished to break up, but could not. Against Lenny's wishes, but facing the reality of the destructiveness of their attachment, Lenny decided to break up, because the balance of the re-creation of projective and introjective identificatory processes had shifted from the gratifying into the intolerable range and his hope of their modification was lost.

THE THEORY
OF THERAPEUTIC CHANGE

Psychoanalytic marital therapy creates a therapeutic environment in which the couple's pattern of defenses can be displayed, recognized, and analyzed until the underlying anxieties can be named, experienced, and worked through together. In the language of object relations couple therapy, we conceptualize the process as one of improving the couple's capacity for containment of projections. Spouses learn to modify each other's projections, to distinguish them from aspects of the self, and then take back their projections. The wife is then free to perceive her husband accurately as a separate person whom she chooses to love for himself, rather than for the gratification he had afforded to repressed parts of herself. Through this process, reinforced by the joy of more mature loving, the wife *re*finds herself and becomes both more loving and more lovable. Doing the same work for himself, her husband grows in the same direction. Sometimes, however, their improved capacities for autonomy and mature love will take them in opposite directions than marriage to each other. Saving the marriage is not the primary goal. Ideally, freeing the marriage from the grip of its obligatory projective and introjective identificatory processes is the goal of treatment. In practice, something short of the ideal may be all that the couple needs to be on their way again. More realistically, the goal of treatment is to enable the projective identificatory cycle to function at the depressive rather than the paranoid–schizoid end of the continuum more often than before therapy (Ravenscroft, 1991).

This is accomplished through a number of techniques. These are not the familiar techniques of communications-trained or behavioral marital therapists. The techniques of object relations couple therapy comprise a series of attitudes toward the couple and the therapeutic process. Later in the chapter, I will look more closely at technique in marital therapy. For now, I will show how psychoanalytically trained marital therapists use these techniques during the assessment process.

The Diagnostic Assessment Process

Setting the Frame

We set a frame (Langs, 1976; Zinner, 1989) within which to establish a reliable space for work. The frame may be established at the beginning or may emerge according to need as the consultation proceeds. The frame includes the number and length of sessions, the setting of the fee, the therapist's management of the beginning and end of sessions, and the establishment of the way of working. Usually about five sessions are needed before we are ready with a formulation and recommendation. This allows for one or two couple sessions, one or more individual sessions for each spouse as indicated, and a couple session in which formulations and recommendations about treatment are given. The couple's reactions to the frame and any attempts to bend it are explored in terms of the couple's transference to the therapist's attempts to provide a safe therapeutic space. This exploration is undertaken both to secure the frame against unconscious forces tending to distort it and to discover the nature of the flaws in the couple's holding capacity.

Creating Psychological Space for Understanding

The object relations therapist creates psychological space for understanding (Box, 1981) by containing the couple's anxieties as therapy is begun. We do this through our way of dealing with the couple relationship, rather than with the individuals who comprise it, and by the way we listen, allow feelings to be expressed, experience those feelings in relation to ourselves, and interpret our experience. The couple identifies with our containing function and so develops the capacity to create space for understanding.

Listening to the Unconscious

We listen in a relaxed way that is both attentive and yet not closely focused. We try to be free of the need to get information and to make sense of things. We listen, not to the individuals alone, but to the communication from the couple as a system in relation to us. We listen not only to the conscious communication, but also to the unconscious communication. We do this by following the themes emerging from the verbal associations, by noting the meaning of silences, by integrating our observation of nonverbal language with words and silence, and by working with fantasy and dream material. We also attend to the unconscious communication expressed in the physical aspects of sexual functioning. As we listen, we let our senses be impinged on, we hold the experience inside, and then we allow meaning to emerge from within.

Following the Affect

We are interested in moments of emotion, because these provide access to the unconscious areas from which the feeling has emerged. These moments bring us a living history of the relationships in the families of origin that is more immediate and useful than a formally obtained social history or genogram. Some psychoanalytic marital therapists, however, such as Dare (1986), recommend the use of the genogram.

Transference and Countertransference

Creating the space, listening, and following the affect come together in the "countertransference" (Freud, 1910b)—namely, our feelings about the couple and the individual spouses—in response to the couple's "transference" (Freud, 1917)—namely, their feelings about us as new editions of figures from their family histories. At times, our countertransference remains unconscious in a way that supports our being in tune with the couple and doing our work. At other times, it obtrudes as a feeling of discomfort, a fantasy or a dream, and then we can take hold of it and get to work on what it means. How does our feeling correspond to the internal object relations set of the couple?

Interpretation of Defense

We point out the couple's recurring pattern of interactions that serve a defensive purpose. Then, speaking from our own emotional experience of joining in unconscious communication with the couple, we interpret the couple's pattern of defenses. Only when we can point out the pattern and the way in which we have been involved in it can we work out what they and we have been defending ourselves against.

Confronting Basic Anxiety

Last, we work with the couple's basic anxieties that have seemed too intolerable to bear in consciousness. When they are named, faced, and adapted to, the couple can proceed to the next developmental phase of the couple's life cycle. During assessment, we are content to identify some aspect of the basic anxiety revealed in the defensive patterns that we have pointed out, without any attempt at thorough exploration.

In general, the diagnostic process is designed as a fair trial of therapy. We are not concerned with getting answers to our questions. We simply create an environment in which issues may be raised, especially the immediate the issue of whether to invest in therapy. The therapist gets an in-depth sample of the couple relationship, while the couple has an opportunity to be in unconscious communication with the therapist and to subject that experience to process and review. Although our intention is to arrive at understanding, our main goal is to facilitate entry into treatment, if that is what we recommend. In other words, we do not worry about finding out everything or making magical interpretations or complete formulations. We just want to secure the therapeutic space and give the couple a sample on which to base their decision about commitment to marital therapy.

Some couples come to us already seeking couple therapy. Others have to be shown that this is the approach most likely to help them, rather than the individual therapy that one of the partners had requested. In this case, an individual problem has to be redefined as a symptom of the relationship. I do not suppose, however, that couple therapy is always best, or that every couple is ready for it. I find it best to start wherever the spouses are, and to recommend the form of treatment that they will accept and follow through on, including referral for adjunctive medication or behavioral treatment where indicated, or for individual psychoanalysis when that is an appropriate, definitive choice, not a defense against couple therapy.

Typical Treatment Goals

Goals are not closely specified, because we find this to be restricting. We do not tailor our approach to the removal of a symptom, because we value the symptom as a beacon that leads us through the layers of defense and anxiety from which it stems. In any case, goals tend to change over time as the couple is freed to experience the potential of their relationship. So we prefer a somewhat open-ended formulation of a couple's aims for treatment. We are content with a general statement of the wish to change behavior, to become more accommodating, to improve communication and understanding, and to function better as a couple. In technical terms, our therapeutic goals are listed in Table 8.1.

Typical Structure of Therapy Sessions

The marital therapy session may be of any predetermined length, from 45 minutes to 1½ hours, and may occur weekly or twice weekly for

TABLE 8.1. The Goals of Object Relations Couple Therapy

• To recognize and rework the couple's mutual projective and introjective identifications.
• To improve the couple's contextual holding capacity so that the partners can provide for each other's needs for attachment, autonomy, and developmental progression.
• To recover the centered holding relationship that allows for unconscious communication between the spouses, shown in their capacity for empathy, intimacy, and sexuality.
• To promote individuation of the spouses and differentiation of needs, including the need for individual therapy or psychoanalysis.
• To return the couple with confidence to the tasks of the current developmental stage in the couple's life cycle.

as long as necessary, 2 years being the average duration of treatment. Although psychoanalytic marital therapy is a long-term method for in-depth work, the same approach can be applied by those at work in managed care situations. In such a limited time frame, we offer as much understanding as we can of the couple's defensive system, without feeling under pressure to produce quick changes. We admit the limits of what we can offer rather than delude ourselves, the families, and their health-care planners into thinking that the minimum is all that is necessary, just because it is all that we are authorized to provide.

Family therapists of various orientations share a common goal in seeking to improve technique, so that more families can be helped more economically. Fewer sessions can be quite effective in crises and in families with short-term goals. When families see that their presenting symptom is part of a broader dysfunction, some of them make it a financial priority to work for more fundamental change in the family system and in their internal object relations. These are the families for whom short-term, focused methods provide a window of opportunity through which to move on to in-depth family therapy, with plenty of time to do the work.

Both in brief therapy and in long-term therapy formats, beginnings and endings of the sessions are important. Anxiety is often most accessible at these times of separation and reunion. The psychoanalytic marital therapist is attentive to boundary phenomena because they illuminate the interior of the couple relationship.

Other than having a beginning, a middle, and an end, the psychoanalytic marital therapy session has no structure imposed upon it, because the therapist does not direct how the couple will use the session. Instead, we follow the couple's lead and comment on how their use of the session reflects their way of dealing with other times, tasks, authorities, and intimate situations.

The main ingredient of the approach is the working space provided by the therapeutic relationship. Training, supervision, peer discussion, and personal therapy ensure that the therapist maximizes the availability of the therapeutic self and calibrates it for use as an effective therapeutic instrument.

The Role of the Therapist

The working alliance is fostered mainly by the therapist's capacity for tolerating anxiety. The therapist is neither aloof nor gratifying, but is willing to be accommodating, to share knowledge when that will be helpful, and to negotiate a way of working that meets the couple's needs without compromising the therapist's integrity. Some couples may need more support or advice than others (including behavioral sex therapy for some), yet the principle of remaining fundamentally nondirective at the unconscious level still applies. That is to say, when the couple responds to some parenting advice or resists an assignment in sex therapy, for example, the therapist waits for associations to the spouses' reactions, including any dreams and fantasies, through which to trace the unconscious thread and its relation to the transference.

The general attitude is one of not doing too much so as to let themes emerge in their own form and time. Once the shape of the couple's experience declares itself, then the therapist takes hold of it, interacts, shares the experience, and puts words on it. Reaching in to the couple's unconscious life in this way gives the couple the feeling of being understood and "held" psychologically in the treatment situation. This fosters the working alliance and sustains the couple and the therapist through times when the relationship to the therapist inevitably bears the brunt of the couple's distress.

As therapists we aim to become an object that the couple can use—and abuse—if necessary, becoming a transitional object that their relationship encompasses and uses, as a child uses a toy or a pet to deflect yet express feelings about self, sibling, or parent. In the quality of their relationship to us, we can discover and reveal to the couple the defenses and anxieties that confound their relationship. We are not traditional blank screen analysts, impassively awaiting the onslaught from the id. As psychoanalytic marital therapists we are personable yet not seductive, and remain neutral as to how the couple chooses to use therapy, following rather than leading. We are both supportive and confrontational when communicating to the couple our experience of the use they have made of us, using our own presence and feelings and yet remaining somewhat distant and not allowing our personality or mood to dominate the session. We do not share information from our personal lives, but may share a fantasy or a feeling that occurs to us in association to the couple's material. The therapeutic stance changes little over the course of the therapy, but the way that the therapist interacts with the couple will change as couple and therapist become progressively more able to give up defensive patterns, to tolerate shared anxiety, and to engage in a collaborative relationship. In the following section on technique, I will return to a more detailed examination of the use of the therapist's self.

The most usual error is that of doing too much. We may get anxious about being worthwhile and so take action to dispel the uneasy, helpless feeling. We may end a session early, start late, forget an appointment, make a slip, lose a couple's check, or call them by the wrong name. We may speak too much, cut off the flow of communication, or retreat into a witholding silence. We may substitute asking questions for realizing how little we know or how frustrated we have been by a witholding couple. All of these happenings are to be expected as part of the work of allowing ourselves to be affected. Instead of calling them errors, we can call them deviations from which we can recover as soon as we subject them to process and review.

Another common error is to deviate from the neutral position: Now, we are siding with the husband; now, we take the wife's point of view. Psychoanalytic marital therapists agree that a neutral position is important and that partiality to either spouse is an error. But we disagree about the need to avoid it. Dare (1986) advises scrupulous fairness to spouses and absolute symmetry in the seating arrangements. We share his ideal of fairness as an intention, but we leave room for error. Rather than rigidly guarding against them, we prefer to work with deviations and jealousies that arise, and to understand their source in difficulties with triangles in the family of origin.

Technique of Marital Therapy

Object relations couple therapists observe the couple relationship primarily through noticing the way the couple deals with us, but we are also interested in how the spouses interact with each other. We are concerned not just with the conscious aspects of their bond, but also with the internal object relations operating through mutual projective identificatory processes in the couple's unconscious.

In keeping with this focus, our psychoanalytic technique employs nondirective listening for the emergence of unconscious themes, following the affect, analyzing dream, fantasy material, and associations offered by both members of the couple, and exploring the family history of each spouse as it relates to the current couple relationship. We point out patterns of interaction that tend to recur and look for unconscious forces that drive the repetition. Gradually we become familiar with the defensive aspects of these repeating cycles. We do this over and over, covering the same ground and making inroads into defended territory, which we find particularly accessible at times when the couple's transference has stirred a countertransference response through which we can appreciate the couple's vulnerability. As their trust builds, we can help the couple figure out and face the nameless anxiety behind the defense. Our help comes in the form of interpretations of resistance, defense, and conflict, conceptualized as operating through unconscious object relation systems that support and subvert the marriage. These interpretations are imparted after metabolization in the countertransference. Interpretation may lead to insight that produces change in the unconscious object relations of the couple, or it may lead to increased resistance to the unconscious conflict. Progression and regression succeed each other in cycles as we work through the defensive structures of the marriage to the point where these are no longer interfering with the couple's capacity for working together as life partners, now loving each other, integrating good and bad, and building a relationship of intimacy and sexuality that is free to develop through the developmental life cycle of the marriage.

What does all this mean in practice? Our technique can be explored through its components, as summarized in Table 8.2.

Setting the Frame

Our first priority is to set a frame (Langs, 1976) for therapy. This offers "a secure and consistent

TABLE 8.2. The Tasks of Object Relations Couple Therapy

1. Setting the frame
2. Maintaining a neutral position of involved impartiality
3. Creating a psychological space
4. Use of the therapist's self: negative capability
5. Transference and countertransference
6. Interpretation of defense, anxiety, fantasy, and inner object relations: the "because clause"
7. Working through
8. Termination

environment in which highly sensitive, private feelings and fantasies can be expressed and explored without the threat of actualizing the feared consequences" (Zinner, 1989, p. 321). The couple tries to bend the frame so that unconscious wishes can be gratified, but their efforts are frustrated by the therapist who holds firm. The ensuing conflict brings into the treatment the issues that have been dividing the marriage.

How is the frame set in the first place? By being clear about the arrangements and by staying with the agreed treatment format. For instance, when clearly indicated, the couple is given a firm recommendation for marital therapy. Couples who are not ready for couple therapy and who have not responded to interpretations of their resistance to it will be given a choice of psychoanalytically oriented, separate or concurrent family and individual therapies, with or without necessary or preferred adjunctive treatment or referral for behavioral or communications-based therapy as either an alternative or preliminary treatment. Given a free choice, they can then sometimes move in the direction of the therapist's original emphasis on the marital relationship, but, if not, their right to begin therapy as they see fit must be respected and accommodated. If they choose to work with us, then by mutual agreement, couple and therapist settle upon the treatment plan. Then the policy of sticking to the plan is explained and discussed: Unless future experience dictates a shift, no change in the arrangements will be undertaken except after thorough discussion and mutual agreement. So the frame is secure, but flexible.

Then we outline other policies, such as fees, vacations, and billing practice. Our billing practice is to bill at the end of the month and to have the couple's check by the 10th of the month. We do this because it helps us to keep in mind the moment when the bill was rendered and to focus on how the couple is dealing with the financial aspects of the commitment. We sell our time not by item of service but by long-term commitment, so we expect the couple to attend as planned. If they have to be absent, we are willing to reschedule within the week, but if that is not possible, then we hold them responsible for the time. Unlike our work with families in which we will see the family with a member absent, in couple therapy we do not work unless both members of the couple are present. Suddenly doing individual therapy with one spouse poses a threat to the therapist's neutrality and capacity to help the couple. Of course, in keeping with the flexible frame, individual sessions can be scheduled by plan and by mutual agreement, but not as filler for absences from therapy.

At the moment of moving from assessment to treatment, the couple is given the choice of accepting the frame or accepting referral to another therapist whose conditions seem preferable. Here is an example from such a session.

Mr. and Mrs. Melville both had previous individual therapies and now wanted to work with me in marital therapy. He was a successful organizational consultant who loved his work, enjoyed food, sports, and sex and felt great about himself, except in his marriage, where he felt unloved. She was a good homemaker, mother of three little ones, and ran a small business selling jewelry from her home. She felt exhausted, unaccomplished, and uninterested in sex. Both tended to overspend and so short-term cash flow problems created financial stress in addition to their marital tension.

I told them my fee and my billing policy. They had no problem agreeing to the amount of my fee and my payment schedule. But charging for missed sessions was another matter.

"Do you mean to say this would apply to my traveling on business?" asked Mr. Melville.

"I'm willing to reschedule within that week if I can," I replied. "But when I can't, then I have to hold you responsible for the time, if we have agreed to meet weekly as I recommend."

"But I'm very punctual and never miss an appointment," he protested. "My previous therapist will tell you that. And he never charged me, because he knew I wasn't acting out. This business travel is out of my control."

Mrs. Melville's concern was different. "Do I have to take vacation when you do? And when do you go away?" she wanted to know. I thought she resented being tied to my plans, but without saying so, I answered her question.

"I tend to take three weeks in August, sometimes

one at Christmas, and another in late March," I replied.

"Oh, good!" she exclaimed. "That's what I do. So it's not a problem. It's more a problem for him, traveling."

I said, "I see that you react differently to my policy. You, Mr. Melville, feel that since you are a good, responsible person, you do not deserve to be charged, which to you feels like a punishment and a rejection of your worth. You, Mrs. Melville, feel afraid of being trapped in the relationship with me. I assume these feelings also come up between you as you deal with the consequences of the marriage commitment."

"Oh, yes," Mrs. Melville rushed to concur. "I feel so trapped in marriage. I need my own space, and especially my own money, but he feels punished by that."

"I sure do," said Mr. Melville. "I feel punished for the way your first husband left you feeling destitute. I'm not like that. I insist on sharing my inheritance with you, even though you insist yours goes directly to the children."

"It's true," she agreed. "And you were very fair with your first wife. But you just don't understand how it freaks me out to think of merging our accounts. I feel I'd be losing myself. I never, ever want to feel financially and emotionally destitute, as I did when my first marriage broke up."

"I've been through divorce and if it happened again and I lost everything to her, I'd still know I could start over," he said.

She said, "But I'm terrified I couldn't."

He said, "But I'm not your first husband."

Quietly now, Mrs. Melville said, "You just don't know how afraid I am of losing myself."

In early transference reactions to the frame, the Melvilles revealed their fundamental problems. His self-worth was tied to his earning capacity rather than to being loved, because the former was more dependable than the latter. His willingness to provide for his wife could not assuage her sense of insecurity, because it emphasized his independence from her and defended against love. How could anyone so apparently confident ever understand her terror of dependency and her fears of annihilation? How could someone so generous be married to someone to whom it meant so little? The answer must lie in their mutual projection into him of the good, abundant, nourishing, energetic breast (the feeding, gratifying part of the mother experienced by the infant, which in this case resided in their fathers, as I later learned), and into her shriveled, nonreplenishing breast, depleted by

their neediness (an image that derived from their shared views of their mothers). As the therapist expecting to be paid, I was a replenishing breast to which they had to contribute in partnership, an expectation that threatened them in ways unique to each individual in reflection of the object relations set.

Listening to the Unconscious

At the conscious level we listen to what the couple is saying, which of the partners is saying what, in what order, and with what affect. We try to listen just as carefully to the silence and to the nonverbal communications in the form of gestures. Yet this careful listening is not as consciously attentive as our description sounds so far. Instead, we experience a drifting state of mind, at one level interacting, maybe even asking a question and hearing the answer, at another level not listening for anything in particular. Freud (1912) described this as "evenly-suspended attention," the therapist turning "his own unconscious like a receptive organ toward the transmitting unconscious of the patient" (pp. 112–115). Through experience, supervision, peer consultation, ongoing process, and review of our work in sessions, therapy, and self-analysis, we develop an understanding of our own unconscious so that we can separate our own from the patients' material. We tune in our calibrated, unconscious receiving apparatus at the deepest level of communication to the unconscious signals from the couple, coming through to us as a theme that emerges from the flow of associations and silences, amplified by dream and fantasy, and resonating in us as countertransference experience from which we can share in and reconstruct the couple's unconscious object relations. When we give the couple our reconstruction in the form of an interpretation, we can check out its validity by evaluating the ensuing associative flow.

Maintaining a Neutral Position

We maintain a position of neutrality with no preference for one spouse or the other, for one type of object relationship versus another, for lifestyle choices, or treatment outcome. Our attention hovers evenly between the intrapsychic dimensions of each spouse, their interpersonal process, and their interaction with us. While we obviously value marriage as an institution, we do not have a bias about continuation of a couple's marriage or divorce. We are invested in our work with the couple and in the possibility of growth and development, but we do not want to invest in the couple's achievement. We want to hold a position described as one of "involved impartiality" (Stierlin, 1977). Any deviations from that occur in directions that are quite unique to each couple. From reviewing the specific pull exerted upon us, we learn about the couple's unconscious object relationships.

Creating the Psychological Space

This willingness to work with one's experience demonstrates an attitude of valuing process and review. It offers the couple a model for self-examination and personal sharing and creates the psychological space into which the couple can move and there develop its potential for growth.

We offer a therapeutic environment in which the couple can experience its relationship in relation to the therapist. Our therapeutic stance derives from our integration of the concepts of "container–contained" (Bion, 1962) and the "holding environment" (Winnicott, 1960). The relationship to the therapist creates a transitional space in which the couple can portray and reflect upon its current way of functioning, learn about and modify its projective identificatory system, and invent new ways of being. Through clinical experience, training and supervision, and intensive personal psychotherapy or psychoanalysis, the therapist develops a "holding capacity," the capacity to bear the anxiety of the emergence of unconscious material and affect through containment and to modify it through internal processing of projective identifications. The therapist contributes this capacity to the transitional space that is thereby transformed into an expanded psychological space for understanding. The couple then takes in this space and finds within the marital relationship the capacity to deal with current and future anxiety. Once this happens, the actual therapeutic relationship can be terminated because the therapeutic function has been internalized.

The Use of the Therapist's Self

Clearly, the use of the therapist's self is central to our technique. Some of this can be learned from reading (Jacobs, 1991; J. Scharff, 1992), but mainly we must develop an openness to learning from experience, nurtured in training and supervision. For fullest use of the self in the clinical setting, we need to have had the personal experience of understanding our own family his-

tory and object relations in psychoanalysis or intensive psychotherapy, including couple and family therapy, even in the rare instance when this has not been necessary for a satisfactory personal life. This gives the therapist the necessary base of self-knowledge to calibrate the self as a diagnostic and therapeutic instrument. Its continued refinement is a lifelong task, accomplished mainly through process and review in the clinical situation, discussion with colleagues, and through teaching and writing.

Negative Capability. Once the therapist's self is cleared for use as a receiving apparatus and as a space that can be filled with the experience of the couple, the therapist is able to know, without seeking to know actively, about the couple's unconscious. Striving to find out distorts the field of observation. Instead we recommend a nondirective, unfocused, receptive attitude best described as "negative capability," a term invented by the poet Keats to describe Shakespeare's capacity as a poet for "being in uncertainties, mysteries, doubts, without any irritable reaching after fact and reason" (Murray, 1955, p. 261). Bion (1970), expanding on Keats's term, urged the therapist to be without memory or desire, that is, to abandon the need to know and impose meaning. Negative capability, however, is an ideal state and we do not advocate irritably reaching for it. Instead, it is a state to sink into, best achieved by not doing too much and allowing understanding to come from inside our experience. In their anxiety to be understood and cared about, some couples will react with frustration to the therapist's apparent lack of directiveness, activity, and omniscience. As long as their reactions are recognized and intepreted, these couples usually come to value the deeper level of understanding that is promoted by the therapist's inhibition of surface engagement activity. Some couples will not be able to tolerate the initial frustration or the ensuing depth of intimacy offered by the analytic therapist, and will do better with a therapist who relates in a more obviously supportive way and does not intend to offer an in-depth, growth experience.

Transference and Countertransference. Negative capability fosters our capacity to respond to the couple's transference, namely, their shared feelings about the therapist. The transference gives rise to ideas, feelings, or behavior in the therapist, namely our countertransference. As Heimann (1950) pointed out, "the analyst's countertransference is an instrument of research into the patient's unconscious" (p. 81). The analyst must value and study his countertranference because "the emotions roused in him are often nearer to the heart of the matter than his reasoning" (Heimann, 1950, p. 82). This elaboration of countertransference stresses an understanding of the normal countertransference and its deviations (Money-Kyrle, 1956), rather than emphasizing the pathology of the therapist's responses.

In studying our reactions to unconscious material in psychoanalysis, psychotherapy, and couple and family therapy, we have found that our countertransference experiences tend to cluster in relation to two kinds of transferences. These are the "contextual" and the "focused" transferences (D. Scharff & J. Scharff, 1987). "Contextual countertransference" refers to the therapist's reaction to the patient's contextual transference, namely, the patient's response to the therapeutic environment, shown in attitudes about the frame of treatment, unconscious resistance in general, specific conscious feelings, and behavior toward the therapist as an object for providing a holding situation. "Focused countertransference" occurs in response to the focused transference, namely feelings the patient transfers to the therapist as an object for intimate relating. Usually the contextual transference–countertransference predominates in the opening and closing phases of individual treatment and throughout family therapy. In couple therapy, there is often rapid oscillation between the contextual and focused countertransference, as the following vignette shows:

Mrs. Rhonda Clark, a tall, angular woman with a short, burgundy-colored, spiked hairdo stormed ahead of her husband, Dr. Clark, a short, round-faced, gentle-looking man. She wore high-style black leather pants and a studded jacket, which she threw on the couch. He meekly laid down his own sheepskin coat and looked expectantly at her through his traditional, rimmed glasses, which were, however, unexpectedly bright purple. She was emitting hostility but no words.

I asked if they were waiting for me to start. He said that she almost didn't come today.

I said, "How come? You, Mrs. Clark, were the one who called me and made the arrangements."

"I'm just mad, today, at him, the big shot, Mr. Doctor God," she said. Facing him, she shouted angrily, "You are *not* God!" Turning back to me, she continued, "I just thought, 'What's the use?' He's always berating me and belittling me. His nurses have no respect for me, he says, and that's just bull-

shit. They *seem* to have no respect for me because *he* has no respect for me."

"Well, after you've called the office three times in a half-hour they get wary," he replied. To me, he said, "And I do blame her for having such a short trigger and causing turmoil in our life and at my office. All I ask is to be in a happy situation with a decent sex life and no ruckus. My friends think I should bail out, but I want to stay for the children."

"He's just selfish," she responded. "Why be there for him sexually when he's putting me down? I'm a good person. I've got friends. He's just fucked up and dumps all his shit on me and makes me sound like a lunatic."

I felt some revulsion toward Mrs. Clark. I felt ashamed to be thinking that she didn't look or act like a doctor's wife. My sympathies were with the doctor, calm and reasonable and not asking much. But I knew from experience that this was not an opinion, it was just a temporary reaction, not just to her, but to them as a couple. For some reason, as this couple crossed the boundary into the therapy space, Mrs. Clark became dominating, interruptive, and crude.

I said, "I can see, Mrs. Clark, you are so angry as to feel therapy will be no use, but I think maybe you, Dr. Clark, also feel anxious about what will come of it."

"Yes," said Dr. Clark, "*She* always acts this anxious way."

I said, "Is Mrs. Clark the only one who is anxious or do you have questions, too?"

"No, I'm not anxious, but, yes, I do have questions. I want to interview you about where you went to school."

This is one question that must always be answered. Without commenting on the denigrating, aggressive tone in his question, I told him my professional background. He was glad to learn that I had graduated from medical school in 1967. He had thought that I was a psychologist (which he would not like) and that I seemed too young. So he felt relieved that I had been practicing as a board certified psychiatrist for 15 years. I was temporarily protected from his denigration by the fact of my sharing his medical background, which he and his wife overvalued.

I said that I was glad to hear of his concerns, because until now, it had appeared as though Mrs. Clark was the one who had all the feelings about therapy being no use. I told them that I had the impression that she expressed her anxiety by getting angry, but that he expressed his anxiety through her. Now, usefully, he was admitting to it. Both of them, for their own reasons and in their individual ways, were anxious about therapy and about their marriage.

In my countertransference, I experienced a deviation from "involved impartiality" (Stierlin, 1977) and realized that the wife was expressing a focused transference toward me as the doctor (the same profession as her husband) and that this was a cover for the couple's shared contextual transference of distrust in the context of treatment. My task was to address the contextual transference with them so that the couple could modify their reluctance to begin treatment.

In an assessment interview, we do not focus on the details of the individual, focused transferences. Indeed, they may remain subordinate to the shared transference throughout a marital treatment, but more commonly, we find ourselves dealing with a rapid oscillation between the two poles of focused and contextual transferences. This example serves, however, to illustrate another idea that is helpful in work with our reactions to focused transferences, namely Racker's (1968) concept of "concordant" and "complementary" transference.

Racker described countertransference as a fundamental condition of receiving the patient's projections and tolerating them inside him as projective identifications. His reception of the projections was unconscious, out of his awareness until he subjected his experience to process and review. In Racker's view, countertransference is a fundamental means of understanding the patient's internal world, a view that object relations couple therapists share.

Racker further pointed out that the therapist might identify with parts either of the patient's self or objects. Identification with the patient's self he called "concordant identification." Identification with the object was called "complementary identification." As marital therapists, we can now think of our therapeutic task as the reception and clarification of the couple's projections, followed by analysis of the interpersonal conditions under which these occur.

In the session with the Clarks described above, the wife experienced me as a contemptuous and rejecting object like the object that she projected into her husband, and she evoked in me an unwelcome state of mind in which I felt contempt for her. My countertransference was one of complementary identification to her object. The husband experienced me as a denigrated object like the one he projected into his wife and then switched to seeing me as a part of himself, the wise physician. To him, my countertrans-

ference was one of concordant identification with part of his self. I did not experience an identification with his object, perhaps because my identity as a physician protected me from it, but more likely because I was tuning in to an internal process in which he used his ideal object to repress his rejected object, which he split and projected more readily into Mrs. Clark than into me at this stage of the assessment.

Interpretation of Defense and Anxiety about Intimacy Early in the Midphase

Aaron and Phyllis had had a fulfilling marriage for 10 years—until Aaron's 16-year-old daughter, Susie, came to live with them. Phyllis had raised their shared family without much criticism from Aaron, and without challenge from their very young son and daughter. She felt supported by Aaron in her role as an efficient mother who ran a smooth household. She felt loved by him and by her dependent children. Her self-esteem was good because she was a much better mother than her mother had been.

But when her step-daughter Susie came to stay, trouble began. Phyllis had firm ideas on what was appropriate for Susie and, in contrast, Aaron was extremely permissive. So Phyllis became the target for Susie's animosity. Aaron saw no need for limits and, indeed, saw no problem between Phyllis and Susie. Phyllis became increasingly angry at Aaron. He bore the situation stoically, only occasionally confronting the problem. Then, he would tell Phyllis that she was being small-minded and awful because she was acting out her jealousy and "making his kid miserable." She was angry at that attack on her self-esteem and never did recover from it.

They saw a family counselor who verified the 16-year-old's need for limits, supported Phyllis's views, and worked to get Aaron's cooperation. Aaron turned around and in a short time his daughter was behaving well and Phyllis could enjoy her. To this day, 10 years later, Phyllis enjoys visits from her.

This seemed to have been a spectacular therapeutic success. I asked Aaron how he conceptualized the amazing turnabout. He said that once the therapist had made the situation clear to him, he simply told his daughter, "You do what Phyllis says or you're out." But Phyllis's anger at Aaron's ignoring her pleas until then was still there. Although she continued to enjoy sex with Aaron, Phyllis walked out emotionally for several years, in an equal retribution for the years in which she felt Aaron had walked out on her. The family counselor had treated the family symptom and its effect on the couple with a useful prescription that removed the symptom. But she did it so rapidly that the underlying problem in the marriage was not recognized. The use of the focus upon a problem child as a defense against problems of intimacy had not been addressed, and so the issue came up again in their second treatment opportunity.

The force of Aaron's ultimatum, "Do what Phyllis says or you're out" suggested to me that he had lived by the same rule himself for the preceding 10 years. Then, however, he began to challenge Phyllis's rule, by expressing his alternative way of coping with children—with predictable results. Now, the same old problem they had had with Susie was surfacing with their shared older daughter, who was now 15. Because no work had been done on their differences, they had not developed a shared method of childrearing. Now that Aaron was challenging Phyllis, they fought about the right way to do everything, but nowhere so painfully as over the care of their children.

Phyllis went on to give an example, however, that concerned not the problem daughter, but their 11-year-old son. He had asked at dinner, "If I wanted to go out with a girl on a date, would that be all right?" Phyllis had promptly told him that this was inappropriate because he was too young. Aaron had immediately interjected, "If you want to take a girl to the movies, that's fine. I'll drive you." Phyllis told me that she had felt undermined. Aaron said that he had spoken up because he felt that she was being unhelpful to their son's social development. I said that I could see that either position could be defended, but that the problem was that they had not discussed things so as to arrive at a shared position that met their anxiety about their 11-year-old's burgeoning social independence.

Phyllis was furious at me for a whole day. She thought that I had been unaccommodating and controlling. But to my surprise, and to her credit, she said that she had had to laugh when it struck her that it was not what *I* was doing but what *she* was bringing to the session. "I was angry at what you said, but the words could have fallen out of my own mouth," she exclaimed.

I realized that Phyllis was seeing me in the transference as Aaron saw her, and I was speculating on the origin of this projective identification and admiring her insight.

Phyllis returned to her argument: "I don't feel every decision requires a conference, as you seem to suggest, Dr. Scharff. I wouldn't think dating by an 11-year-old was a subject for discussion. It's the same as if a child had asked 'Can I cut off my hand?' and I had said 'I'll ask your father.' "

I had three responses. I felt put down, as though I had not a clue about an 11-year-old's social development. I felt I was being small-minded getting into the fight with them about a child, when I knew they had come for help not with childrearing but with their marriage. My third response was the thought that dating, meaning independence and intimacy, was equated with severe damage and loss.

Perhaps Phyllis felt that she needed her son close to her and could not yet face being cut off from him. Perhaps Aaron, while wishing to facilitate their son's date, was offering to drive in order to stay close to him, too, or possibly to stay close to the issue of intimacy vicariously. I also wondered if dating signaled sexuality as causing loss, but that was probably not the case since sexuality was relatively free of conflict for them. So I concluded that the loss referred to sexuality being cut off from intimacy in the rest of the relationship.

I said, "I'm not really talking about whether or not an 11-year-old should date. I'm taking you up on the effect of sticking to alternative positions and not talking about them together."

Here I was confronting their defense of using a child to portray their conflict about intimacy.

Aaron said, "I feel cramped in every part of my life. I can't say what I feel at all because Phyllis is so vulnerable."

Phyllis said, "I don't want to live like this. We now argue about stuff we agree on. These patterns are vicious. They're killing us. We can't share a job because each of us is instructing the other on how to do it right. We even argue over how to load the grocery bags. I say, 'Put the chips on top.' he says 'Put the heavy stuff together.' I say, 'Okay do it your own way—and you'll have smashed chips!' "

I said to them, "Although you argue about what is the right way, you actually share an assumption that there is a right way and that, if you don't do it right, things will get smashed."

Phyllis said, "I see the marriage as something that got cracked and can't be repaired. It's irretrievable. When things get sore, I leave. I'm trying to give up that idea now. But I had to leave once, to get away from my family. My mother was a dreadful, intrusive person and I was very unhappy. I got out by being perfect, an overachiever. I'm proud of rising above that background. Having struggled so hard not to be evil like her, I was very threatened when Aaron said I was small-minded and evil. I felt so wronged. Never compare me to her!"

Now, I understood my countertransference response of feeling small, no-good, and ignorant as reflecting a complementary identification with Phyllis's internal maternal object, and at the same time a concordant identification with Phyllis's most repressed part of her self. Using the explanation that Phyllis had worked out, I was able to make an interpretation integrating her words and my countertransference.

I said to Phyllis, "Now, I can see that you retreated from Aaron because you wished to keep your relationship together as the harmonious marriage it used to be, and occasionally is, when you have enjoyable sex. You were trying to protect yourself and him from your becoming as horrible as the angry, intrusive mother spoiling the relationship, or else facing the calamity of having to leave the marriage in order to leave that part of you behind."

This interpretation illustrates the use of the "because clause" (Ezriel, 1952). Ezriel noted that transference contains three aspects: (1) a required relationship that defended against (2) an avoided relationship, both of which were preferable to (3) a calamity. We have found it useful in couple's therapy to follow his interpretive model, because it brings the avoided relationship into focus as both anxiety and defense.

Aaron had not yet told me enough about himself to let me complete the picture. It was clear that Phyllis was still using projection and overfunctioning within the marriage to keep herself above being horrible. And Aaron, feeling cramped like the children, was finding her control just as horrible. When he suppressed his angry or critical feelings, as he did most of the time except in irrational fights, he also suppressed his warm, affectionate feelings, except when he and Phyllis had sex.

In this example, the sexually exciting object relationship was the "required" relationship being used to repress the "avoided" rejecting object constellation. Aaron's conscious suppression felt withholding to Phyllis, who longed for feedback and emotional involvement. Aaron's eventual outbursts against her led her to relentless pursuit for his attention, approval, and affection. The emergence of the avoided relationship unleashed the energy of the exciting object constellation, because it was no longer needed for repression. When Phyllis failed to get what she hoped for from Aaron, she then suppressed her longings and withdrew. Now the rejecting object system was repressing the exciting one. But when this happened, she appeared to Aaron to be pouting, and he withdrew. The cycle continued—their needs for intimacy defended against and frustrated by their mutual projective identifications. I could see this pattern, but would have to wait for more object relations information from him to clarify his contribution. Incidentally, we cannot always achieve the same depth or specificity in interpretation, but the "because clause" is still useful as an intention in which we can ask the family to join as we move toward understanding.

Working with Fantasy and Inner Object Relations in the Midphase

Instead of taking a genogram in evaluation and telling couples about their relationship to their family of origin, we prefer to wait for a living history of inner objects to emerge through our attention to object relations' history at affectively charged moments in therapy.

Dr. and Mrs. Clark had been working with me for a year. We had worked on Arthur's passivity, his inability to earn Rhonda's admiration of him as a successful, ambitious, caring man, and his need to denigrate her by comparison to the nurses at the office. We worked on her tirades and her outrageous behavior that alienated him, his office staff, and his family, and that left her feeling contemptible. Their sex life had improved because he was less demanding and she less likely to balk and cause a fight. Their tenacious defensive system, in which she was assigned the blame and was the repository for the rage, greed, ambition, and badness in the couple, had not yet yielded to interpretation, although Rhonda was no longer on such a short fuse. I could see improvement in the diminution in the volume and frequency of her reactions and in the degree of his contempt, but the basic pattern stayed in place until Arthur felt safe enough to tell Rhonda and me the full extent of his sadistic and murderous fantasies in which he raped and axed various women who had abandoned him. Catharsis played a part in securing some relief for him, but the major therapeutic effect came from work done in the countertransference on the way he was treating the two actual women in the room with him, his wife and me, as he told his fantasies about other women.

As he concluded, Arthur said that he was terrified that people would think that he would act out his fantasies, which he had never done and would not do. Turning to me, he said, "You would understand that fear."

I felt extremely uncomfortable. If I acknowledged that I was familiar with such a fear, I felt that I would be siding with him in assuming that his wife was ignorant.

Excluded and put down, Rhonda retorted, "You said *she* would understand as if *I* wouldn't."

"She's a psychiatrist. She's heard all this before. She'll know I don't have any urges to do this in real sex," he replied.

Rhonda had a good point to make: "How does

she know you're not gonna act those out? How do I know? Do *you* know? Because you seem really scared."

I said, "There is no evidence that Arthur will act out the fantasies in their murderous form. But there is evidence that he's scared they'll get out of hand. We also have evidence right here that you do sadistic things to each other in this relationship, not physically, but emotionally. 'Put-downs,' you call them."

"Like what just happened here," exclaimed Rhonda. "Sure, she's trained, but I can understand it, too."

"Not that I'm gonna go out and do it," he reminded her.

"Right," she rejoined. "It's how you're gonna feel it. Arthur, I feel so relieved that it's not just been me. All these years I've been taking the shit for fucking up the marriage. Do you know, I feel so relieved. Finally, after all these years he's taking responsibility. Finally."

"But I told you about my sadistic fantasies," he said.

"You never did," Rhonda objected. "I'm not saying you never talked about fantasies before, but you never went into your real self, never in this detail. You've always said that I'm this, I'm that. It's always been me. Now I see in our marriage that your fantasies are totally in the way. Now rape I could maybe see as exciting, but why do you have to picture murders? That is scary."

I said, "To some extent the threatening part of the fantasy is arousing to both of you. But by the end of it, Arthur, you are terrified of losing control, and Rhonda, you are frightened for your life." They were nodding thoughtfully. I went on, "We're not talking put down, here. We're talking put *out*. These are compelling and forceful fantasies."

"This has been a big interference to you and to us," Rhonda replied. "This is like what you would call a breakthrough for us."

I felt inclined to agree with the wife's evaluation. The longer her husband kept the fantasy to himself, the more it seemed to be the real man terrified of being found out; it was hidden inside yet demanding to be heard. Furthermore, the way it got heard was through projection into his wife, who identified with it: In her rages and attacks on her husband she gave expression to the fantasy of attacking and chopping up the frustrating loved object. Meanwhile, he contained for her the greater calamity of the wish for death, a wish and fear that stemmed from early loss of an envied and hated older brother.

Working Through Late in the Midphase

Following the revelation, the Clarks had a session in which Rhonda talked of her continued sense of gratitude that her husband had shared his fantasies with her. Although she felt unusually tentative about responding to him sexually, she felt close to him and committed to working things out. For the first time, she felt an equal level of commitment from him. Summer was approaching and she was taking the children to visit her family in Maine for a month, as usual. Until now, Rhonda had viewed her annual summer trip as a chance to get away from Arthur's criticizing her and demanding sex of her. For the first time, she felt sad that they would have to spend the summer apart.

The sharing of the fantasy had been a healing experience. The couple could now move beyond a level of functioning characteristic of the paranoid–schizoid position toward the depressive position, in which there is concern for the object whose loss can be appreciated.

In a session following their vacation, Rhonda reported that she had got so much from the last session, it kept her thinking and working for 4 weeks. Even when Arthur expressed no affection during his phone call to her in Maine, when he did not even say he missed her, she felt hurt but not outraged as before. She realized that in some way he just was not there.

I suggested that Arthur had been unaware of feeling angry that Rhonda had left him alone for a few weeks and had dealt with it by killing her off.

"I was kind of pissed off at her being in Maine, getting to lie around on the family boat," Arthur admitted.

"He just cut me dead," Rhonda confirmed.

I said, "Well, there's the fantasy of killing operating again."

"Right," Rhonda replied. "But I didn't take it personally. It's just him. These last two weeks, I've been able to have grown-up feelings. Even though he belittles me, I don't live in a world of little feelings any more. That's a big change for me."

The husband's revelation of his murderous fantasies released his wife's capacity for growth, confirming that the silent operation of the unconscious projective identification expressed in the fantasy had been cutting her down and killing off her adult capacities.

As we peel away layers of repression, we experience more resistance. Sometimes, it feels as though the further we go the more we fall behind. The couple is suffering from a defensive system of object relationships that are mutually gratifying in an infantile way inside the marital system. Until more mature forms of gratification are found within the system, it is going to resist efforts at change. "Working through" is the term Freud (1914a) gave to the therapeutic effort to keep working away at this resistance and conflict. Sessions in this phase can feel plodding, laborious, repetitive, and uninspired. Resolution comes piecemeal, until one day the work is almost done.

Common Obstacles to Successful Treatment

Obstacles to treatment include secrets witheld from spouse or therapist: an ongoing affair that dilutes commitment to the marriage; severe intrapsychic illness in one spouse; financial strain from paying for treatment; severe acting out in the session in the form of violence or nonattendance; and the intrusion of the therapist's personal problems into the therapeutic space, unchecked by training or personal therapy. Unresolved countertransference can lead to premature termination (Dickes & Strauss, 1979).

If we can assume an adequate therapist, then the main obstacle to treatment is a lack of psychological mindedness in the couple. Despite a therapist's best effort, the spouses may not want to deal with frightening areas of unconscious experience. They might do better with a more focused, short-term, symptom-oriented approach. But it is better to discover this from experience than to assume it from a single diagnostic session. Every couple deserves a chance to work in depth. Some will take to the waters and others will not.

Indications, Contraindications, and Limitations

Psychoanalytic marital therapy is indicated for those couples who are interested in understanding and growth. It is not for the couple whose thinking style is concrete. The capacity to think psychologically does not correlate with low intelligence or social disadvantage. So, psychoanalytic marital therapy is not contraindicated in couples from lower social classes, some of whom will be capable of in-depth work. My co-author and I (D. Scharff & J. Scharff, 1991) have described its usefulness for developmental crises, grief, and mourning (Paul, 1967); communication problems; lack of intimacy, including sexuality (D. Scharff, 1982); unwelcome affairs and secrets (D. Scharff, 1978); remarriage (Waller-stein & Blakeslee, 1989); perversions and homosexuality; unwanted pregnancy and infertility; and apparently individual symptomatology that predates the marriage. It is not good for couples who require support and direction, financial assistance and budgetary planning. Alone, it is not sufficient for couples in which one partner has an addiction to alcohol or drugs that requires peer group abstinence support, addiction counseling or rehabilitation. It cannot produce major character change, although it produces enough change that spouses comes to view their characters as modifiable. Although in managed care situations the use of psychoanalytic marital therapy has been eschewed as a luxury, therapists who are constrained to work in a brief format with specific, limited goals will gain more understanding if they apply psychoanalytic marital therapy theory to their conceptualization of the problem, even though they cannot work as fully in that way as they might like.

Integration with Other Interventions and Concepts

Psychoanalytic marital therapy integrates well with other psychoanalytic interventions with which it may be combined sequentially or concurrently. It is fully compatible with individual psychoanalytic therapy, because the theory shares with psychoanalysis a common base. Particularly in the case of object relations couple therapy, the theory is compatible both with individual therapy and with couple, group or family therapy, because the theory refers to endopsychic systems that are expressed in the interpersonal dimension. The therapist can integrate a structural or strategic approach with in-depth object relations' understanding of defensive patterns (Slipp, 1988).

When a patient in psychoanalysis needs couple therapy, psychoanalytic marital therapy is the treatment of choice because of compatibility between the underlying theories. Then, the patient will not be told to quit analysis, as happened to a patient in analysis with me, in favor of a short-term intervention which, however helpful, will not effect major character change for which analysis has been recommended. Sometimes, individual problems cannot be managed with couple therapy alone, but this should not be concluded too early. Individual referral is not resorted to readily because it tends to load the marital problem in the individual arena, but when the couple can correctly recognize and meet individual needs, referral for one of the spouses may be helpful to the treatment process and to the marriage. Psychoanalytic marital therapy can then be combined with other treatment for the individual spouse, such as medication, addiction rehabilitation, phobia desensitization programs, individual psychotherapy, or psychoanalysis. When intensive individual therapy or psychoanalysis is required, the couple therapist may become anxious that the greater intensity of individual treatment will devalue the couple therapy. This is not at all inevitable. When it occurs, it does so because one therapist is being idealized while the other is being denigrated due to a splitting of the transference, which will need to be addressed. This risk to couple therapy is more likely to be a major problem if the couple therapist secretly admires individual psychoanalytic psychotherapy or psychoanalysis and puts down couple therapy. It is helpful for the concurrent treatments if both therapists are comfortable communicating with each other, but some analysts will not collaborate because they are dedicated to preserving the boundaries of the psychoanalysis for good reason and will not betray the patient's confidentiality. To my mind, the greater betrayal lies in not confronting the acting out of split transference.

Psychoanalytic marital therapy may be combined with a family session with children, who helpfully may say things about which the grownups are unaware. Sessions for one spouse with parents and/or siblings may be added and then the couple reviews that spouse's experience and its implications for their marriage (Framo, 1981). A couple may also be treated in a couples' group, either as an adjunct to their marital therapy or as a primary treatment method (Framo, 1973).

Psychoanalyic marital therapy can be combined serially or concurrently with behavioral sex therapy (Levay & Kagle, 1978; Lief, 1989; D. Scharff, 1982; D. Scharff & J. Scharff, 1991). The sex research of Masters and Johnson (1966, 1970) has vastly improved the marital therapist's understanding of sexuality. In addition, the psychoanalytic marital therapist finds Kaplan's work particularly helpful. Kaplan (1974) links psychoanalytic psychotherapy with sex therapy methodology. She shows how blockade in the progression through the behavioral steps requires psychoanalytic interpretation to get over underlying anxieties. She describes hypoactive sexual desire (1977, 1979) as a spectrum of disorders usually relating to psychodynamic issues that require psychoanalysis or psychoanalytic therapy, sometimes in conjunction with medication (1987). The psychoanalytic marital therapist can apply this knowledge within the usual frame of therapy or may switch to a specific sex therapy format if qualified to do so. I prefer to refer the couple to a colleague temporarily or concurrently, partly to free me from the strain of holding to the nondirective attitude at the unconscious level during directive behavioral formats, and partly because I do not feel as experienced and qualified in sex therapy or behavioral methods as some other therapists. Psychoanalytic marital therapists who work regularly in nonanalytic modes combine them without compromising the integrity of their analytic stance, by recognizing and working with the couple's transference to their directiveness in the nonanalytic role. Systems-oriented or structurally trained marital therapists can integrate the analytic stance into their current way of working by attending to the impact of their personality and directive behavior on the couple's attitude toward them. The object relations perspective gives more access to the use of therapists' psyches (Aponte & VanDeusen, 1981) and provides systems therapists with greater understanding of the system through its patterns that they will find re-created in relation to themselves (Van Trommel, 1984, 1985).

An illustration of the link between internal object relations, psychosexual stages of development, and sexual symptomatology is provided in the following vignette from an initial couple therapy evaluation that I did with David Scharff as my cotherapist.

Michelle and Lenny had a hateful attachment. Although diametrically opposite in character and family background, they had been together for 4 years, but Michelle, an outgoing social activist, had been unable to marry quiet, conservative Lenny because he seemed so passive. A nice, attractive man from an upper-class family, successful in business, loyal to her, he had many appealing qualities. He treated her well, he adored her, he was a rock, but she hated his steadfastness. He just could not meet her expectations. Her ideal man would be like her amazingly energetic, confident, and admirable brother. Unlike steady Lenny, Michelle was bubbling with energy, like a river running over the rock. So, why was she still with Lenny?

"Because I can't seem to dump the guy. He's a great boyfriend, classiest guy I've ever known," Michelle admitted. "But with him I'd be trapped in a boring marriage, always lighting a fire under his tush!"

Lenny was not put off by her contempt for him. "I love everything about her," he affirmed, "the way she speaks, the way she feels. I don't mind her being in the forefront: good protection! She's the world to me."

The therapists felt uncomfortable with this frustrating relationship and David Scharff, who is normally rather energetic, almost fell asleep to avoid the pain of being with Michelle and Lenny. His countertransference response led us to see the underlying sadness in their relationship and to experience the void they would have to face if their destructive bantering were to stop. Lenny's void came from the lack of a father when he was growing up. Michelle's came from her perception of herself as a girl whose brother had more than she did.

"Lenny is so average," Michelle went on. "Average is boring, whereas I'm special. So why do I hate myself? My mother did that to me. I used to dread being feminine. Now I wouldn't change it for the world. But I was such a tomboy. My brother has that specialness, but he has all the confidence to go with it. A complete winner! And I really envy him because of it. Because I'm missing that little part. There's a part of me that constantly finds holes in herself."

To an analyst, these words speak of penis envy from the phallic stage of development. Usually, we address this issue in the broader terms of envy of the man's world. But in this case, both aspects of Michelle's envy were close to consciousness.

"Whatever it is that he has—the confidence that makes him a complete *mensch*—I'm missing," she added.

"You feel this envy for Lenny, too, as his mother's great little kid," I suggested.

"Yes," said Lenny. "In my family, I'm the confident male. In her family, it's her brother. But he's self-confident, cocky. He knows he's good. I'd love to be him, myself."

"Lenny doesn't have that confidence," Michelle continued. "When he's called upon to be a *mensch*, he can be in certain cases, but not where it counts to me."

I was thinking of her feelings about the penis and all that it meant to her. Boldly, I asked, "What about where it counts in bed?"

For once, Michelle was nonplussed. "You talk about that, dear," she said, yielding the floor to Lenny.

Now, we learned that in bed Lenny was the confident sexual partner, who had shown great sensitivity to Michelle's vaginismus. He helped her to tolerate intercourse and find sexual release with him. He found her beautiful whether she was fat or thin. For Michelle, who hated her body, Lenny's adoration was both gratifying and contemptible.

"Sex is a pain to me but I'm as comfortable with Lenny as I can be," Michelle said with resignation. "You know, for a girl who had penis envy as a child, I hate them now. So, there's something obviously wrong with me."

"One thing about Lenny you appreciate is that he doesn't force himself on you in intercourse," I said.

Michelle said, "Right. He's very good to me."

I said, "But as a child, you admired the penis as a source of power."

"I don't remember anything about the penis itself," Michelle corrected me.

I had taken my cue from her use of the words "penis envy." But Michelle had generalized her envy.

"I mean the boy's world," I amended. "The things boys had that you didn't. What I'm saying is, now that you've taken possession of your adult femininity and enjoy a woman's world, it's sad for you that you can't take pleasure from the penis. You see it as a source of enviable and threatening power."

Michelle said, "I see it as an intrusion! I hate it. I've come a little distance, but I used to see it as a man sticking it to a woman."

I said, "Now you don't *see* it that way, but you still *feel* it like that."

Michelle said, "Not as much as I did. I used to see it as another way of a man's control, which I hate. But it's never, ever been like that with Lenny."

Applying Freudian theory, we can say that as a child, Michelle had thought that a boy like her brother did not feel the emptiness and longing that she felt in relation to her rejecting mother, because he had the penis that she was missing, while her vagina felt like an empty hole. In her adulthood, the penis continued to be threatening because it could enter that painful hole. She now felt that childhood hatred for the penis toward the man in her adult sexual relationship. The better Lenny did with her sexually, the more she enviously had to attack him. Lenny, although sexually competent, had some inhibition against being assertive, generally and sexually, and used Michelle as a phallic front for himself so that he could avoid castration anxiety. In this way, he avoided the fear of retaliation from an angry male, the forbidding father who resented the child's aggressive sexual longing to possess his mother.

In object relations terms, each partner was using Michelle as a manic defense against emptiness and sadness, and using Lenny as a depository for the schizoid defense against emptiness. Painful longing was projected into Michelle's vagina, for which she had a psychophysiological valency. In therapy they would need to take back these projective identifications of each other and develop a holding capacity for bearing their shared anxieties.

COMMON SIGNIFICANT CLINICAL ISSUES

Working with the Difficult Couple

There are many varieties of difficult couples. Difficulty depends partly on the degree of fixity of the couple's unconscious complementariness and the severity of their pathology, and partly on their fit with the object relations set of their therapist. Difficult couples may transfer from previous therapists in whom they were disappointed. A common trap for therapists is to suppose that we will be better than the previous therapist. Sometimes, treatment does go better, usually because of the couple's projection of negative objects into the former therapist. Unless we can address that issue, the couple will seem better but will not have developed the capacity to integrate good and bad objects. The turning point in treatment of the difficult couple often comes when the therapist is able to experience fully in the countertransference the hopelessness and despair that underlie their "difficult" defense (D. Scharff & J. Scharff, 1991). Sometimes the couple cannot use the assessment process to develop sufficient trust in the therapist to make a commitment to therapy. The disappointment that the therapist feels in failing to make an alliance activates guilt about not being able to repair the damage of the therapist's internal parental couple (J. Scharff, 1992).

Managing Resistance and Noncompliance

At worst, the couple may remain too resistant to engage in couple therapy. Nevertheless, one of the spouses may be willing to have individual therapy. It is important to start where the couple is. Change in one partner will effect change in the system, so that marital therapy may be possible later. Before arriving at that conclusion, however, psychoanalytic marital therapists try to understand the reasons for the resistance. We do not try to seduce the couple into making a commitment, or promise symptomatic relief. We do not remove the resistance by paradoxical prescription. We analyze the resistance with the aim of freeing the couple from the inhibition imposed by their defenses against intervention, and giving them control over their decision about treatment.

Sometimes, a couple can make the commitment but cannot keep it when anxieties surface. They may miss appointments, forget or refuse to pay the bill, or substitute a single partner for the couple. We discuss all these attempts to bend the frame in the hope that making conscious the unconscious reluctance will help the couple to confront the therapist about the treatment process and the therapist's style. But we do not agree to work without pay, because (1) we cannot allow our worth and earning potential to be attacked in that way, and (2) it produces unconscious guilt in the couple. Our policy is that we do not see a spouse alone to fill a session from which the other spouse is missing. On the other hand, each of us has at times done so when the situation seemed to call for it. Policies differ among psychoanalytic marital therapists as they do among therapists of other backgrounds, but the important thing is to establish a policy and a way of working and hold to it as a standard from which to negotiate, experiment, and learn.

Working with the Couple When There Is an Affair

Greene (1970) warned that premature discussion of the affair can disrupt the marriage, and Martin (1976) agreed that the mate should not always be told the secret. D. Scharff (1978) advocated revelation of the secret in every case, but has since modified the rigidity of his view (D. Scharff & J. Scharff, 1991). Revelation puts the couple and the therapist in a position to learn from the affair and to understand the meaning of the secret in developmental terms (Gross, 1951), the significance of the affair (Strean, 1976, 1979), and the attraction of the lover for the spouse. Only when the affair is known can the therapist work with the couple's expression of disappointment, envy, rage, love, and sadness. In the affair (as in a fantasy) lies important information about repressed object relations that cannot be expressed and contained within the marriage. It is worth remembering that the affair is an attempt to maintain the marriage, even while threatening its existence.

Working with a History of Trauma

The couple who is overwhelmed by recent trauma will experience it in terms of any previous trauma. One of the possible accommodations to trauma is to dissociate from it, and so the couple may split off their awareness of traumatic experience or sequester it inside the marriage in traumatic nuclei. An apparently satisfactory marital relationship may cover these traumatic nuclei or gaps which marital therapists may get access to by examining gaps in the treatment process or their own feelings of discomfort.

Tony and Theresa (described more fully in J. Scharff & D. Schraff, 1994) had been happy together in their marriage and now had three children, the eldest adopted from Theresa's first marriage. Tony and Theresa both worked to support the family and both shared household chores. Suddenly a fulminating infection in Tony's right arm could not be treated medically and he had to have his shoulder and arm amputated to save his life. An easy-going, cheerful man, Tony bounced right back at first, and then depression hit, as he realized the enormity of his loss. He refused rehabilitation work and prosthesis fittings. He sat around at home while his wife went out and worked his shift as well as her own. Then when she came home he complained about her being away. They were arguing an unusual amount, their daughter was avoiding the home, the middle child was doing badly in school, and the younger one seemed simply sad.

Telling the therapist about the trauma relieved their stress somewhat, and then it was possible to reveal the trauma base against which their marriage had been organized. Both of them had been physically abused by their parents, and both had taken the role of the child who will get hit to protect the others. When they got married, each promised to respect the other. There would never be any violence in their relationship. When tempers flared, they punched the wall instead. The bricks absorbed their anger and in so doing built a wall between them and their feelings. Now Tony had lost his punching arm, and without it, he did not know how to express his rage and grief.

The therapist noted the improvement in their capacity to acknowledge anger, but he was puzzled by a new pattern of skipping sessions. Their silences and his own discomfort led him to guess that they were creating a gap to cover over another traumatic nucleus. Perhaps another recent trauma lay beneath the loss of Tony's arm. Since they had already told him about their problems with anger, he wondered if they might be avoiding discussing their sexual life. Theresa replied that she had had a hysterectomy some years earlier, and since then had suffered from recurrent vaginal infections. Previously the couple had enjoyed a vigorous sexual life, and now sex had become less frequent. Theresa admitted that she avoided sex because it was painful for her, a secret that she had kept from Tony until that moment.

Prior to the loss of Tony's arm, the couple had lost the use of Theresa's vagina as an accepting, sexually responsive organ. They lost one body part that stood for the control of aggression and one that stood for their loving connectedness, both of them vital to the maintenance of their commitment to each other. Work with the couple would have to focus on mourning their losses and then finding gratifying ways to express love and anger.

In couples where current sexual interaction is traumatic, compulsively enacted or phobically avoided, we inquire about earlier sexual experience including unwanted sexual experience in the family of origin. We help the couple that tends to invoke abusive behavior in one spouse by showing that this is a way of repeating the abuse instead of remembering it. Other couples need to see that their efforts to avoid repetition of abuse can lead to a degree of control that is inhibiting not only to the marital relationship, but also to the next generation. We try to put words to experience. We help the couple to develop a narrative of the abuse history to share with their family as an alternative to the reenactment of trauma and the defenses against it.

Handling Acute Marital Distress

The prompt offer of a consultation appointment is usually enough to contain the distressful situation. In more extreme cases, a suicidal or psychotic spouse may require medication or hospitalization, while a violent one will need to be separated from the spouse temporarily. When distress is acute, and we have no time to deal with an emergency, it is better to refer the case to someone who has time than to make the couple wait for an appointment. During the delay, a couple's problem may be redefined as an individual illness, and the advantage of the healing potential of the crisis in the system is lost. If we do take the referral, a longer appointment time than usual is required to allow enough time for the couple to express their distress, and for the therapist to develop the necessary holding capacity to contain the partners' anxiety, to offer them a therapeutic relationship on which they can count, and to demonstrate the possibility of understanding their overwhelming emotion. Another appointment time within the week is scheduled before the couple leaves the session.

Termination

The couple has had some rehearsal for termination when ending each time-limited session and facing breaks in treatment due to illness, business commitments, or vacations. We work with the couple's habitual way of dealing with separations in preparation for the final parting. Our criteria for judging when that will be are summarized in Table 8.3.

TABLE 8.3. Criteria for Termination

1. The couple has internalized the therapeutic space and now has a reasonably secure holding capacity.
2. Unconscious projective identifications have been recognized, owned, and taken back by each spouse.
3. The capacity to work together as life partners is restored.
4. Relating intimately and sexually is mutually gratifying.
5. The couple can envision its future development and can provide a vital holding environment for its family.
6. The couple can differentiate among and meet the needs of each partner.
7. Alternatively, the couple recognizes the failure of the marital choice and understands the unconscious object relations' incompatibility; the partners separate with some grief work done and with a capacity to continue to mourn the loss of the marriage individually.

These goals that provide the criteria for termination are really only markers of progress. Couples decide for themselves what their goals are and whether they have been met. Sometimes they coincide with our idea of completion and sometimes not. We have to let ourselves become redundant and tolerate being discarded. As we mourn with the couple the loss of the therapy relationship (and in some cases, the loss of the marriage), we rework all the earlier losses. The couple now relives issues from earlier phases of the treatment with greater capacity for recovery from regression. Separating from the therapeutic relationship, therapist and couple demonstrate their respective capacities for acknowledging experience, dealing with loss, understanding defensive regressions, and mastering anxiety. As the couple terminates, now able to get on with life and love without us, we take our leave from them and at the same time, resolve another piece of our ambivalent attachment to our internal couple. Such a thorough experience of termination seasons therapists and prepares us to be of use to the next couple.

REFERENCES

Alger, I. (1967). Joint psychotherapy of marital problems. In J. Masserman (Ed.), Current psychiatric therapies (Vol. 7, pp. 112–117). New York: Grune & Stratton.

Aponte, H. J., & Van Deusen, J. M. (1981). Structural family therapy. In A. S. Gurman & D. P. Kniskern (Eds.), Handbook of family therapy (pp. 310–360). New York: Brunner/Mazel.

Balint M. (1968). The basic fault: Therapeutic aspects of regression. London: Tavistock.

Bannister, K., & Pincus, L. (1965). Shared phantasy in marital problems: Therapy in a four-person relationship. London: Tavistock.

Bergmann, M. S. (1987). The anatomy of loving. New York: Columbia University Press.

Bergmann, M. S. (1990, November). Love and hate in the life of a couple. Paper presented at the Washington School of Psychiatry Conference on Romantic Love, Washington, DC.

Bion, W. R. (1961). Experiences in groups. London: Tavistock; New York: Basic Books.

Bion, W. R. (1962). Learning from experience. London: Heinemann; New York: Basic Books.

Bion, W. R. (1970). Attention and interpretation. London: Tavistock.

Bodin, A. M. (1981). The interactional view: Family therapy approaches of the Mental Research Institute. In A. S. Gurman & D. P. Kniskern (Eds.), Handbook of family therapy (pp. 267–309). New York: Brunner/Mazel.

Boszormenyi-Nagy, I., & Sparks, G. (1973). Invisible royalties: In intergenerational family therapy. Hagerstown, MD: Harper & Row.

Bowen, M. (1978). Family therapy in clinical practice. New York: Aronson.

Box, S. (1981). Introduction: Space for thinking in families. In S. Box, B. Copley, J. Magagna, & E. Moustaki (Eds.), Psychotherapy with families (pp. 1–8). London: Routledge & Kegan Paul.

Brazelton, T.B. (1982). Joint regulation of neonate–parent behavior. In E. Tronick (Ed.), Social interchange in infancy (pp. 7–22). Baltimore: University Park Press.

Brazelton, T. B., & Als, H. (1979). Four early stages in the development of mother–infant interaction. Psychoanalytic Study of the Child, 34, 349–369.

Clulow, C. (1985). Marital therapy: An inside view. Aberdeen, Scotland: Aberdeen University Press.

Dare, C. (1986). Psychoanalytic marital therapy. In N. S. Jacobson & A. S. Gurman (Eds.), Clinical handbook of marital therapy (pp. 13–28). New York: Guilford Press.

Dickes, R., & Strauss, D. (1979). Countertransference as a factor in premature termination of apparently successful cases. *Journal of Sex and Marital Therapy, 5,* 22–27.

Dicks, H. V. (1967). *Marital tensions; Clinical studies towards a psycho-analytic theory of interaction.* London: Routledge & Kegan Paul.

Drellich, M. G. (1968). Psychoanalysis of marital partners by separate analysts. In S. Rosenbaum & I. Alger (Eds.), *The marriage relationship* (pp. 237–250). New York: Basic Books.

Erickson, E. H. (1950). *Childhood and society.* New York: Norton.

Ezriel, H. (1952). Notes on psychoanalytic group therapy II: Interpretation and research. *Psychiatry, 15,* 119–126.

Fairbairn, W. R. D. (1944). Endopsychic structure considered in terms of object relationships. In *Psychoanalytic studies of the personality* (pp. 82–135). London: Routledge & Kegan Paul, 1952.

Fairbairn, W. R. D. (1952). *Psychoanalytic studies of the personality.* London: Routledge & Kegan Paul.

Fairbairn, W. R. D. (1954). Observations on the nature of hysterical states. *British Journal of Medical Psychology, 27,* 105–125.

Fairbairn, W. R. D. (1963). Synopsis of an object-relations theory of the personality. *International Journal of Psycho-Analysis, 44,* 224–225.

Finkelstein, L. (1987). Toward an object relations approach in psychoanalytic marital therapy. *Journal of Marital and Family Therapy, 13,* 287–298.

Flugel, J. C. (1921). *The psychoanalytic study of the family.* (International Psycho-Analytical Library. No. 3). London: International Psycho-Analytical Press.

Framo, J. L. (1970). Symptoms from a family transactional viewpoint. In *Explorations in marital and family therapy: Selected papers of James L. Framo* (pp. 11–57). New York: Springer, 1982.

Framo, J. L. (1973). Marriage therapy in a couples' group. *Seminars in Psychiatry, 5,* 207–217.

Framo, J. L. (1981). The integration of marital therapy with sessions with family of origin. In A. S. Gurman & D. P. Kniskern (Eds.), *Handbook of family therapy* (pp. 133–158). New York: Brunner/Mazel.

Freud, S. (1905). Three essays on the theory of sexuality. *Standard Edition, 7,* 135–243.

Freud, S. (1910a). Five lectures on psychoanalysis. *Standard Edition, 11,* 1–55.

Freud, S. (1910b). The future prospects of psychoanalytic therapy. *Standard Edition, 11,* 141–151.

Freud, S. (1912). Recommendations to physicians practicing psychoanalysis. *Standard Edition, 12,* 111–120.

Freud, S. (1914a). Remembering, repeating, and working through. *Standard Edition, 12,* 147–156.

Freud, S. (1914b). On narcissism: An introduction. *Standard Edition, 14,* 67–107.

Freud, S. (1915a). Instincts and their vicissitudes. *Standard Edition, 14,* 109–140.

Freud, S. (1915b). The unconscious. *Standard Edition, 14,* 161–215.

Freud, S. (1917). Transference. *Standard Edition, 16,* 431–447.

Freud, S. (1921). Group psychology and the analysis of the ego. *Standard Edition, 18,* 69–134.

Freud, S. (1923). The ego and the id. *Standard Edition, 19,* 1–66.

Freud, S. (1924). The dissolution of the oedipus complex. *Standard Edition, 19,* 173–179.

Freud, S. (1930). Civilization and its discontents. *Standard Edition, 21,* 57–145.

Friedman, E. H. (1991). Bowen theory and therapy. In A. S. Gurman & D. P. Kniskern (Eds.), *Handbook of family therapy* (Vol. 2, pp. 134–170). New York: Brunner/Mazel.

Friedman, L. (1962). *Virgin wives: A study of unconsummated marriages.* London: Tavistock.

Giovacchini, P. L. (1965). Treatment of marital disharmonies: The classical approach. In B. L. Greene (Ed.), *The psychotherapies of marital disharmony* (pp. 39–82). New York: Free Press.

Graller, J. (1981). Adjunctive marital therapy. *The Annual of Psychoanalysis, 9,* 175–187.

Greene, B. L. (1970). *A clinical approach to marital problems.* Springfield, IL: Thomas.

Gross, A. (1951). The secret. *Bulletin of the Menninger Clinic, 15,* 37–44.

Grotjahn, M. (1960). *Psychoanalysis and family neurosis.* New York: Norton.

Guntrip, H. (1961). *Personality structure and human interaction: The developing synthesis of psychodynamic theory.* London: Hogarth Press and the Institute of Psycho-Analysis.

Guntrip H. (1969). *Schizoid phenomena, object relations and the self.* New York: International Universities Press.

Gurman, A. S. (1978). Contemporary marital therapies: A critique and analysis of psychoanalytic, behavioral and system approaches. In T. J. Paolino, Jr., & B. S. McCrady (Eds.), *Marriage and marital therapy* (pp. 455–566). New York: Brunner/Mazel.

Gurman, A. S., & Jacobson, N. S. (1986). Marital therapy: From technique to theory, back again, and beyond. In N. S. Jacobson & A. S. Gurman (Eds.), *Clinical handbook of marital therapy* (pp. 1–9). New York: Guilford Press.

Heimann, P. (1950). On counter-transference. *International Journal of Psycho-Analysis, 31,* 81–84.

Heimann, P. (1973). Certain functions of introjection and projection in early infancy. In M. Klein, P. Heimann, S. Isaacs, & J. Riviere (Eds.), *Developments in psycho-analysis* (pp. 122–168. London:

Hogarth Press and the Institute of Psycho-Analysis.

Hollender, M. H. (1971). Selection of therapy for marital problems. In J. H. Masserman (Ed.), *Current psychiatric therapies* (Vol. 11, pp. 119–128. New York: Grune & Stratton.

Jackson, D. D., & Weakland, J. H. (1961). Conjoint family therapy. *Psychiatry, 24,* 30–45.

Jacobs, T. J. (1991). *The use of the self.* Madison, CT: International Universities Press.

Kaplan, H. S. (1974). *The new sex therapy: Active treatment of sexual dysfunctions.* New York: Brunner/Mazel.

Kaplan, H. S. (1977). Hypoactive sexual desire. *Journal of Sex and Marital Therapy, 3,* 3–9.

Kaplan, H. S. (1979). *Disorders of sexual desire and other new concepts and techniques in sex therapy.* New York: Brunner/Mazel.

Kaplan, H. S. (1987) *Sexual aversion, sexual phobias, and panic disorder.* New York: Brunner/Mazel.

Katz, D., & Kahn, R. L. (1966). Common characteristics of open systems. In *The social psychology of organizations* (pp. 14–29). New York: Wiley.

Kernberg, O. F. (1975). *Borderline conditions and pathological narcissism.* New York: Jason Aronson.

Kernberg, O. F. (1991). Aggression and love in the relationship of the couple. *Journal of the American Psychoanalytic Association, 39,* 45–70.

Klein, M. (1946). Notes on some schizoid mechanisms. *International Journal of Psycho-Analysis, 27,* 99–100.

Klein, M. (1948). *Contributions to psycho-analysis 1921–1945.* London: Hogarth Press.

Klein, M. (1957). *Envy and gratitude.* London: Tavistock; New York: Basic Books.

Kohl, R. N. (1962). Pathological reactions of marriage partners to improvement of patients. *American Journal of Psychiatry, 118,* 1036–1041.

Kohut H. (1971). *The analysis of the self.* New York: International Universities Press.

Kohut, H. (1977). *The restoration of the self.* New York: International Universities Press.

Kohut, M. (1982). Introspection, empathy, and the semi-circle of mental health. *International Journal of Psycho-Analysis, 63,* 395–407.

Kubie, L. S. (1956). Psychoanalysis and marriage. In V. W. Eisenstein (Ed.), *Neurotic interaction in marriage* (pp. 10–43). New York: Basic Books.

Langs, R. (1976). *The therapeutic interaction: Vol. II. A critical overview and synthesis.* New York: Jason Aronson.

Lansky, M. (1986). Marital therapy for narcissistic disorders. In N. S. Jacobson & A. S. Gurman (Eds.), *Clinical handbook of marital therapy* (pp. 557–574). New York: Guilford Press.

Levay, A. N., & Kagle, A. (1978). Recent advances in sex therapy: Integration with the dynamic therapies. *Psychiatric Quarterly, 50,* 5–16.

Lief, H. F. (1989, October). *Integrating sex therapy with marital therapy.* Paper presented at the 47th Annual Conference of the American Association of Marriage and Family Therapists, San Francisco, CA.

Main, T. (1966). Mutual projection in a marriage. *Comprehensive Psychiatry, 7,* 432–449.

Martin, P.A. (1976). *A marital therapy manual.* New York: Brunner/Mazel.

Martin, P. A., & Bird, H. W. (1953). An approach to the psychotherapy of marriage partners—the stereoscopic technique. *Psychiatry, 16,* 123–127.

Masters, W. H., & Johnson, V. E. (1966). *Human sexual response.* Boston: Little Brown.

Masters, W. H., & Johnson, V. E. (1970). *Human sexual inadequacy.* Boston: Little Brown.

McCormack, C. (1989). The borderline–schizoid marriage. *Journal of Marital and Family Therapy, 15,* 299–309.

Meissner, W. W. (1978). The conceptualization of marriage and marital dynamics from a psychoanalytic perpective. In T. J. Paolino & B. S. McCrady (Eds.), *Marriage and marital therapy* (pp 25–28). New York: Brunner/Mazel.

Mittelmann, B. (1944). Complementary neurotic reactions in intimate relationships. *Psychoanalytic Quarterly, 13,* 479–491.

Mittelmann, B. (1948). The concurrent analysis of married couples. *Psychoanalytic Quarterly, 17,* 182–197.

Money-Kyrle, R. (1956). Normal countertransference and some of its deviations. *International Journal of Psycho-Analysis, 37,* 360–366.

Murray, J. M. (1955). *Keats.* New York: Noonday Press.

Nadelson, C. C. (1978). Marital therapy from a psychoanalytic perspective. In T. J. Paolino & B. S. McCrady (Eds.) *Marriage and marital therapy* (pp. 101–164). New York: Brunner/Mazel.

Oberndorf, P. (1938). Psychoanalysis of married couples. *Psychoanalytic Review, 25,* 453–475.

Ogden, T. H. (1982). *Projective identification and psychotherapeutic technique.* New York: Jason Aronson.

Paolino, T. J., Jr., & McCrady, B. S. (Eds.). (1978). *Marriage and marital therapy: Psychoanalytic, behavioral and systems theory perspectives.* New York: Brunner/Mazel.

Paul, N. (1967). The role of mourning and empathy in conjoint marital therapy. In G. Zuk & I. Boszormeny-Nagy (Eds.), *Family therapy and disturbed families* (pp. 186–205). Palo Alto, CA: Science & Behavior Books.

Person, E. S. (1988). *Dreams of love and fateful encounters.* New York: Norton.

Person, E. S. (1990, November). *Romantic love and the*

cultural unconscious. Paper presented at the Washington School of Psychiatry Conference on Romantic Love, Washington, DC.

Pincus, L. (Ed.). (1960). *Marriage: Studies in emotional conflict and growth.* London: Methuen.

Racker, H. (1968). *Transference and countertransference.* New York: International Universities Press.

Ravenscroft, K. (1991, March). *Changes in projective identification during treatment.* Paper presented at the Washington School of Psychiatry Object Relations Couple and Family Therapy Training Program Conference, Bethesda, MD.

Ryckoff, I., Day, J., & Wynne L. (1959). Maintenance of stereotyped roles in the families of schizophrenics. *AMA Archives of Psychiatry, 1,* 93–98.

Sager, C. J. (1976). *Marriage contracts and couple therapy: Hidden forces in intimate relationships.* New York: Brunner/Mazel.

Sager, C. J., Kaplan, H. S., Gundlach, R. H., Kremer, M., Lenz, R., & Royce, J. R. (1971). The marriage contract. *Family Process, 10,* 311–326.

Sander, F. (1989). Marital conflict and psychoanalytic therapy in the middle years. In J. Oldyam & R. Liebert (Eds.), *The middle years: New psychoanalytic perspectives* (pp. 160–176). New Haven, CT: Yale University Press.

Scharff, D. (1978). Truth and consequences in sex and marital therapy: The revelation of secrets in the therapeutic setting. *Journal of Sex and Marital Therapy, 4,* 35–49.

Scharff, D. E. (1982). *The sexual relationship: An object relations view of sex and the family.* Boston, London: Routledge & Kegan Paul.

Scharff, D., & Scharff, J. S. (1987). *Object relations family therapy.* Northvale, NJ: Jason Aronson.

Scharff, D., & Scharff, J. S. (1991). *Object relations couple therapy.* Northvale, NJ: Jason Aronson.

Scharff, J. S. (Ed.). (1989). *Foundations of object relations family therapy.* Northvale, NJ: Jason Aronson.

Scharff, J. S. (1992). *Projective and introjective identification and the use of the therapist's self.* Northvale NJ: Jason Aronson.

Scharff, J. S., & Scharff, D. E. (1994). *Object relations therapy of physical and sexual trauma.* Northvale, NJ: Jason Aronson.

Segal, H. (1964). *Introduction to the work of Melanie Klein.* London: Heinemann.

Siegel, J. (1992). *Repairing intimacy: An object relations approach to couples therapy.* Northvale, NJ: Jason Aronson.

Shapiro, R. L. (1979). Family dynamics and object relations theory: An analytic, group-interpretive approach to family therapy. In J. S. Scharff (Ed.), *Foundations of object relations family therapy* (pp. 225–245). Northvale, NJ: Jason Aronson.

Skynner, A. C. R. (1976). *Systems of family and marital psychotherapy.* New York: Brunner/Mazel.

Slipp, S. (1984). *Object relations: A dynamic bridge between individual and family treatment.* New York: Jason Aronson.

Slipp, S. (1988). *Theory and practice of object relations family therapy.* Northvale, NJ: Jason Aronson.

Solomon, M. (1989). *Narcissism and intimacy.* New York: Norton.

Stern, D. N. (1985) *The interpersonal world of the infant: A view from psychoanalysis and developmental psychology.* New York: Basic Books.

Stewart, R. H., Peters, T. C., Marsh, S., & Peters, M. J. (1975). An object relations approach to psychotherapy with married couples, families and children. *Family Process, 14,* 161–178.

Stierlin, H. (1977). *Psychoanalysis and family therapy.* New York: Jason Aronson.

Strean, H. S. (1976). The extra-marital affair: A psychoanalytic view. *Psychoanalytic Review, 63,* 101–113.

Strean, H. S. (1979). *The extramarital affair.* New York: Free Press

Sutherland, J. (1980). The British object relations theorists: Balint, Winnicott, Fairbairn, Guntrip. *Journal of the American Psychoanalytic Association, 28,* 829–860.

Sullivan, H. S. (1953). *The interpersonal theory of psychiatry.* New York: Norton.

Thomas, A. (1956). Simultaneous psychotherapy with marital partners. *American Journal of Psychotherapy, 10,* 716–727.

Van Trommel, M. J. (1984). A consultation method addressing the therapist–family system. *Family Process, 23,* 469–480.

Van Trommel, M. J. (1985, October). Presentation at the annual meeting of the American Association of Marriage and Family Therapy, New York, NY.

von Bertalanffy, L. (1950). The theory of open systems in physics and biology. *Science, 3,* 23–29.

Wallerstein, J. S., & Blakeslee, S. (1989). *Second chances.* New York: Ticknor & Fields.

Willi, J. (1982). *Couples in collusion.* Claremont, CA: Hunter House.

Willi, J. (1984). *Dynamics of couples therapy.* New York: Jason Aronson.

Winer, R. (1990, March). *Marriage's destiny.* Paper presented at the Washington School of Psychiatry Object Relations Family and Marital Therapy Conference, Bethesda, MD.

Winnicott, D. W. (1951). Transitional objects and transitional phenomena. In *Collected papers: Through paediatrics to psycho-analysis* (pp. 249–242).

London: Tavistock, 1958, and Hogarth Press, 1975.

Winnicott, D. W. (1958). *Collected papers: Through paediatrics to psycho-analysis.* London: Tavistock, 1958, and Hogarth Press, 1975.

Winnicott, D. W. (1960). The theory of the parent–infant relationship. *International Journal of Psycho-Analysis, 41,* 585–595.

Winnicott, D. W. (1965). *The maturational processes and the facilitating environment.* London: Hogarth Press.

Winnicott, D. W. (1971). *Playing and reality.* London: Tavistock.

Wynne, L. (1965). Some indications and contraindications for exploratory family therapy. In I. Boszormenyi-Nagy & J. Framo (Eds.), *Intensive family therapy* (pp. 289–322). New York: Harper & Row.

Zilbach, J. (1986). *Young children in family therapy.* New York: Brunner/Mazel.

Zilbach, J. (1988). The family life cycle: A framework for understanding children in family therapy. In L. Combrinck-Graham (Ed.), *Children in family contexts* (pp. 46–66). New York: Guilford Press.

Zinner, J. (1976). The implications of projective identification for marital interaction. In H. Grunebaum & J. Christ (Eds.), *Contemporary marriage: Structure, dynamics, and therapy* (pp. 293–308). Boston: Little, Brown.

Zinner, J. (1988, March). *Projective identification is a key to resolving marital conflict.* Paper presented at the Washington School of Psychiatry Psychoanalytic Family and Couple Therapy Conference, Bethesda, MD.

Zinner, J. (1989). The use of concurrent therapies: Therapeutic strategy or reenactment. In J. S. Scharff (Ed.), *Foundations of object relations family therapy* (pp. 321–333). Northvale, NJ: Jason Aronson.

Zinner, J., & Shapiro, R. (1972). Projective identification as a mode of perception and behavior in families of adolescents. *International Journal of Psycho-Analysis, 53,* 523–530.

B

Group Methods

9

Group Therapy with Couples

JUDITH COCHÉ

D URING THE MID- and late 1980s, I invited my husband to join me in beginning a group for couples in our private practice. We were pleased, if a bit surprised, at the power of the treatment modality that began to develop. In the course of the next 5 years, we altered and refined "the couples group" until it emerged as a distinct therapeutic model with a specific conceptual base and its own set of techniques. We fashioned the refinements through discussions with colleagues in the group and marital therapy fields, independent discussions with one another, feedback from our clients, experimentation with the techniques, and a modestly scaled clinical research study on the model.

We presented the model in depth in *Couples Group Psychotherapy* (J. Coché & E. Coché, 1990) and in a companion training videotape, *Techniques in Couples Group Therapy.* This chapter is not intended to give a condensed version of the book. Instead, I would like to address the theoretical, technical, and clinical issues involved in using the small group as a treatment modality for couples.

SYNOPSIS OF THE MODEL

A brief synopsis of the model acts as an orientation for the rest of the chapter. The couples group is a closed-ended group experience. Four couples begin and end the "group year" together. Members commit themselves to stay with the group for the entire 22-session treatment pack-

age. Groups meet twice monthly for 11 months. The pattern was initially born out of expedience: Couples found it easier to meet less frequently for longer sessions, rather than getting together weekly. Serendipitously, the model has turned out to be wise and efficient therapeutically: Longer sessions allow for greater intensity, and the time between sessions can be used for therapeutic homework assignments and trying out new behaviors.

Each session lasts 2½ hours. The first half of a session is a traditional group therapy session. Members work on their individual and couples' concerns within the flow of the group. In the second half of each session, the leaders conduct a structured exercise that is designed to deepen the learning from the first half of the session. The structured intervention can be a guided fantasy, a role play, a sociogram, a communication exercise (e.g., teaching listening skills) or a paper-and-pencil task. The structured interventions can also be designed to get the group moving again when it appears to be stuck.

The model I codeveloped is clearly not the only way to conduct couples group therapy. Yet, the literature we found in couples group therapy was sparse. A literature search turned up an occasional personal account by practitioners experimenting with the then novel combination of the two modalities of couples therapy and group therapy (e.g., P. Low & M. Low, 1975). When we began to develop the model, we received great encouragement and many technical innovations from colleagues in the disciplines of marital and group psychotherapy. Colleagues applauded the professional teaming between my husband, trained in research in group psychotherapy and existential philosophy, and myself with a background in supervising and teaching clinical work in group, family and marital, and individual psychotherapy.

THE THEORETICAL MODEL

The model presented here applies group psychotherapy techniques to marital therapy. As such, it forms an inclusive and unique model of couples group psychotherapy. Theoretical and conceptual foundations from the fields of individual personality development, family systems theory, and group psychotherapy theory form the basis of the model. In developing the model with my late husband, I adapted the conceptual framework to the actual clinical application of theoretical principles and clinical research in the fields of group and family therapy.

To use the model wisely, clinicians need prior knowledge and training in both group psychotherapy and psychotherapy with couples and families. It is essential that at least one—and preferably both—of the group leaders conceptualize client change via the psychotherapy process in contextual terms. I believe that human change occurs most powerfully within an interpersonal context and can, therefore, happen most efficiently when the psychotherapy process is conducted in a vibrant and interpersonal context and can, therefore, happen most efficiently when the psychotherapy process is conducted in a vibrant and interpersonal arena. I agree with Harry Stack Sullivan that it takes people to make people sick and people to make them well.

This model is a synthesis of two approaches that are brought together under the theoretical umbrella of general systems theory. Although some of the conceptual origins come from the worlds of biology (von Bertalanffy, 1968) and social psychology (Lewin, 1951), their application in mental health services comes from two often separate but not incompatible sectors: family therapy and group psychotherapy, because the fields are conceptually compatible. A group sometimes operates like a family, and a family has the properties of a small group. Both are greater than the sum of their parts, and the subsystems of each can be fully understood only through a knowledge of the working of the whole (Spitz, 1979).

An Existential Base

An existential foundation provides a philosophical stance for the proves of behavioral and interpersonal change. through clinical interventions that strengthen the use of self, I teach clients the basic attitudes toward a way of being in the world. Contributions from existential philosophy (Nietzsche, 1960; Sartre, 1948; Kaufman, 1975) and from philosophical–theologians (Buber, 1958; Tillich, 1952) provide conceptual underpinnings for clinical interventions. From the professional mental health literature, the thinking of Whitaker and Keith (1981), Bugental (1981, 1984), Watzlawick (1978, 1983, 1984) and Watzlawick, Weakland and Fisch (1974), have been adapted for this fast-paced, cognitive, systemic model. Although existential psychotherapy is a varied field with many individualistic thinkers, three unifying principles run throughout this model of couples group therapy:

1. *Clients seek to be more of a person in an intimate context than they have been able to achieve.* I agree with Whitaker and Keith (1981) that the goals of psychotherapy should be to establish a sense of belonging, to provide the freedom for persons to individuate, and to increase personal and systemic creativity. People enter psychotherapy to learn to be more of a person than they have been able to figure out from their life experience to date. The obstacles that clients construct to the intimacy they say they want maintain stability within the personality structure, blocking growth in the desired direction. Being more of a person means freeing up new levels of energy and creativity by overcoming some of the obstacles that have been constructed by oneself and by one's family. This, in turn, creates a sense of greater personal freedom for each member of the couple without necessitating the same repeated and unsuccessful behaviors. Personal and interpersonal meaning increases and the members of a couple need no longer return to the earlier and frustrating *modus operandi.*

2. *Adult intimacy involves taking responsibility for one's actions.* Intimacy is at its best for adults when each partner is able to take responsibility for his/her own thoughts, feelings, and behavior in relation to the other person. Therefore, adult intimacy is best achieved when partners are skillful and careful in their communication with one another. This translates into learning to respect personal boundaries in being close to someone else. This way of viewing intimacy also necessitates that each person learns how he/she feels,

learns to communicate feelings, learns to listen to the thoughts and feelings of another person, and learns to negotiate conflict in a respectful manner. These are skills that I teach couples. They are hard to master.

3. *Living life fully and responsibly entails making life choices.* No matter what happens in life, each person is faced with continual choices. For the most part, barring unforeseen natural disasters and illnesses, life choices belong to the person. People have to decide, for the most part, whether and when to divorce or separate, when and whether to have and raise children, and how to feed and care for their bodies and intellect.

I do not mean to imply that people are to blame for the choices they make, but simply that living life fully requires that people own their choices. This enables people to enjoy their pleasures fully and learn from their mistakes. Blame is superfluous to both enjoyment and learning. People make unconscious choices based on hidden conflicts that echo the legacy of an earlier family in pain in the world. During childhood and adolescence, the powerful force of the family of origin, with its beliefs, traditions, and adaptive styles, exerts its pull and shapes the person's beliefs about the ways in which decisions are made. In treating a couple, I often magnify the existential theme for them as they struggle with what seems to be an everyday problem.

Drawing attention to the larger existential issue often opens new ways to "unstick" the everyday dilemma.

Sue and George married despite concerns over family background. He was Israeli and she was German. Both had been warned not to marry outside their own worlds. Less than 3 months after the wedding, they became obsessed with which country to move to after Sue's completion of graduate training, although they were satisfied living in the United States. The conflict turned into a haunting argument, and George finally sought treatment. He needed help less with the decision regarding their living place, than because of disabling depression. As treatment progressed, we began to explore what it meant to them that each family of origin was against their marrying someone of different ethnic origins. The couple actually went to members of each side of the family as part of a homework assignment and invited the families to discuss their views on the other spouses' country. What the couple learned was very enlightening: Susan, raised a German, said that in the opinion of George's family, she had been responsible for the deaths of many of George's great aunts and uncles in the Second World War. She was not to be trusted. And some members of Susan's family still thought of George as a "dark-haired" foreigner, too different from them to be trusted. The couple began to realize that they were caught in a battle not of their own making. This realization marked the beginning of new approaches to their dilemma, as they began to negotiate dialogues with and about each other's family.

The Principle of Isomorphism

The principle of isomorphism, well known to systems theorists, states that similar structures and processes occur on several levels in related systems. Accordingly, a troublesome issue can manifest itself—with some variations—on an individual level (i.e., within a member of a couple), on a couple level (between members of a couple), on a subgroup level (e.g., for all men, or all victims of abuse), and on a group level (for each group member). Applying this principle to a couples group enables the therapist to think on several levels simultaneously, to respond with more flexibility to the challenges of the group, and too unravel otherwise bewildering shifts in levels.

THE THERAPEUTIC MODEL

Incorporating Listening and Communication Skills

Some of the couples work I do is very basic. For example, when couples have had no therapy experience as a unit, getting couples unstuck often means teaching adults how to know and discuss what they feel, how to listen actively to someone else, and how to communicate clearly. This is harder than it sounds. Part of the assessment procedure is an evaluation of these factors in a marriage. The therapeutic process is partially one of learning a new language, and a couple's starting point is with the skills of the least skilled partner. I have finally come to understand that some people are more naturally skilled than others. Within a couple, the woman frequently has more natural skills in the language of feelings, and the man often shows better problem-solving ability.

Following are four useful steps in increasing fluency in couples' communication:

1. Teach each partner to recognize what he/she feels.
2. Teach couples to listen actively to the partner.

3. Teach partners to communicate clearly and carefully.
4. Teach couples to negotiate differences respectfully.

The components of communication fluency are adapted from schools of humanistic psychotherapy (Wexler & Rice, 1974; Rogers, 1957; Truax & Carkhuff, 1967) and from Satir's work (1967, 1988) in couples' communication, and from my original work alone and with Erick Coché.

These four basic steps cut across the usual areas of trouble (sex, money, children, etc.) and provide process tools by which couples can build stronger relationships within the self of each member, between themselves, and between the couple and other group members. This kind of skill building increases the likelihood that, after therapy is completed, the marriage will be one in which change is maintained in the desired direction because the tools to maintain the change have been internalized.

The Intervention Hierarchy: Four Levels

When I apply the principle of isomorphism to a group, I deduce that the activity of a group can take place on any one of four levels at any time, as well as on a combination or more than one level simultaneously.

1. *Personal level.* At this level, group talk is intensively centered on one individual. At times, this looks like individual therapy in the presence of others. There are moments at which this is the intervention of choice in order to have the most powerful impact on a person.

2. *Couples level.* A group working in the couples mode spends time on the dynamics of one particular couple.

3. *Interpersonal level.* The activity of the group is directed to interpersonal relationships between two or more members of the group, or between nonrelated individuals or couples in the group. Members learn that others are struggling with similar issues and discover that they can be helpful to each other by sharing their similar struggles and attempted solutions with others. Often, the attention is given to subgroups that show some relevant characteristics (e.g., couple with children, the men). Many of Yalom's (1975) "curative factors," such as *universality* and *altruism*, come to full bloom in this mode of working. At times, the mere discovery of similarities

is healing; at other times, only a more extensive sharing of experiences can bring about therapeutic change.

4. *Group-as-a-whole level.* The group, with or without help from the leader, takes on a group issue. Directional shifts, group decisions, norm enforcement, or explorations of participants' roles in the group are all topics of discussion that fall into the group-as-a-whole category (Agazarian & Peters, 1981). In order to be a successful working group, the members have to work out problems in the group's own dynamics. Lewin (1951) provided seminal thinking on the "centrality of context." Some of these problems are part of the natural development of groups described elsewhere (Schein & Bennis, 1965; Thelen, 1954; MacKenzie & Livesley, 1983). Themes such as developing a mature relationship with the leader, with minimal dependence or counterdependence, fall into this category. Other problems are not common to all groups, but are unique and stem from the particular constellation of people in the room. For example, a monopolizer can drain group energies, and an acerbic relationship between two members can prevent the group from working independently. Group-as-a-whole work enables the group to progress developmentally from dependence through cohesiveness to interdependence. Without this intervention level, a group is in danger of remaining stuck in an early developmental stage. While it is possible to gain therapeutic benefits in such a group, the results are likely to be less substantial than those in a group that has gained some mastery over its group dynamics.

Mixing Interactive Levels

At times, it is difficult to detect the level of group interaction. Work on two levels can go on simultaneously. For example, one group member may focus intensively on family-of-origin conflicts, while a couple is working out something critical to their own marriage by helping the person who is working on the family-of-origin material. Thus, while the one member is working at an individual level, two other members are working on a couples level.

The Choice of Intervention Levels: Therapists' Guidelines

Knowledge of and sensitivity to the processes on all four interactive levels can be bewildering and may leave the therapist with the need for a rule of thumb to judge which level is likely to be the most advantageous at a given time. No easy guidelines exist as to which level of intervention works best, because the most effective level of intervention depends on the stages of the development of the group and on the different styles of the members themselves. In general, however, the most effective interventions in the early stage of the group are those that build cohesiveness, whereas more confronting interventions are most advantageous in the later phases. In the final phases of the group, interventions that provide some kind of closure, and enable members to say goodbye to one another, seem to be apt. The decision about intervention levels needs to be made over and over in response to the changing dynamics of the group. However, there is an optimistic note in choosing a level of intervention: Because there is no one level that is better than others, the clinician has a number of options available at all times. It is a bit like a trial balloon: If the balloon lands, everyone knows. If the balloon does not land, the clinician has done relatively little harm to the workings of the group.

SPLIT SESSIONS

Essential to the model is the format of unstructured and structured portions.

First Half: Unstructured Couples Group Psychotherapy

During the first half of an evening's session, the floor is open to anyone. The couples know this, plan ahead, and raise their own issues without delay. They bring up whatever pressing problems have arisen, or they give a follow-up report on something that they have worked on in previous sessions. Some couples "save" a hot topic for the safety of the group. A natural flow develops; one couple may open with a problem that is currently "hot" and others chime in with observations on the dynamics in this couple, or with experiences of their own on similar issues. There is a fluidity, an easy give-and-take. When a specific couple's problem has been dealt with, another couple may raise an issue in their marriage, or a particular couple's problem may expand into a more general group discussion of the underlying issue. Because the group members

genuinely enjoy and care about each other, a high level of interest in one another's problems develops. Although only one couple may be the focus of the group's attention, most group members become involved in the discussion and contribute their observations and personal experiences related to the problem at hand. The therapists simultaneously focus attention on the couple in the foreground and on the group as a whole, thereby generating a wide range of intervention options.

Second Half: Structured Exercises

A brief 5-minute break midway through the evening gives everyone the opportunity to stretch. The second half of the session is usually reserved for structured exercises designed to increase the group members' understanding of a relevant issue of concern to many group members at a given time (Wienecke, 1984). I actually choose or design the exercise *during* the 5-minute break, in response to a common theme or prevailing emotion in the group. The exercise may focus on anger, fear of intimacy, sadness, affection, death, addictions, or any of a wide variety of topics.

Twice Monthly, Longer Sessions

Psychotherapy is a consumer service. Our couples lead complex lives that are riddled with business trips, babysitters and fatigue at a day's end. Meeting less frequently than weekly but for longer sessions was originally decided merely for the sake of our consumers' convenience. We know that many couples who lead rich lives find it much more manageable to commit to two evenings per month for a year than to a weekly meeting. When we instituted the new pattern a few years ago, two unforeseen psychological advantages emerged: (1) the session seemed even greater in intensity than in the weekly groups, and (2) the time span between session gave couples more opportunity to work on matters on their own between sessions. They could and did try out new behaviors, performed therapeutic homework assignments, and discussed and tried to work out disagreements. Many sessions open with reports on what was accomplished between sessions, with couples reporting a genuine sense of accomplishment, as if to say, "Look at what we did without you!" As far as I am concerned, so much the better.

STRUCTURING AND SCREENING AS PREPARATORY ACCTIVITIES

Goals of Couples Group Preparation

Our preparatory meetings have a number of goals: altering the way a couple thinks of changing, sparking enthusiasm, explaining boundaries, and inducing effective group behaviors. One of the best forms of preparation involves a discussion of the policies by which the group operates.

Group Policies

Consistent and clearly spelled-out group policies are part of intelligent group psychotherapy preparation. The literature (Mayerson, 1984; Nichols, 1976) demonstrates that well-prepared group participants have a better concept of what they are supposed to do. They also have a higher expectation that their group will be successful. Well-prepared groups build cohesiveness more speedily and have lower rates of absences and dropout. One of the most significant aspects of group preparation is clarity about group rules.

Group policies function as a structure that provides an outer frame within which the group process can unfold and flourish. If all participants, leaders and members, have the same conceptual framework in respect to the boundaries within which everyone operates, an atmosphere of safety develops. Inside these boundaries, the group can pursue its task of improving marriages rather than using group time for interminable debates over group rules.

Group policies set the norm for appropriate member behavior. basic policies include the following:

We limit out-of-group contacts between members.

We encourage and set guidelines for how members can attend regularly, despite the inevitable complications of busy and successful lives.

We sign written confidentiality agreements within the first 30 minutes of meeting one another.

We openly discuss members who are delinquent in payment in the group meetings, so that finances become an integral part of the workings of the group.

We discuss openly in the group in an ongoing manner the evaluation process for the progress of each member and each couple, with regular time set aside for more formal evaluations

In this way, the structure of the therapy group becomes an integral part of the working process of the group. Every member understands that there are certain "rules of the road" that go along with being a group member. Research in group therapy has indicated that preparing members for group therapy is an advantage in that it helps them to benefit most from the experience. We prepare members in a clear and forthright manner.

Screening for the Group

In our groups, all members are expected to meet certain membership criteria:

1. An intimate relationship of at least 3 years' duration with the current partner.
2. Marital or couple problems for which solutions have been attempted with insufficient or unsatisfying results.
3. Ongoing or previous individual, couple, or family psychotherapy, either with one of the group leaders or elsewhere.
4. An interest in learning from and participating with other adults.
5. An intense desire to improve the intimacy and mutual satisfaction in the relationship.

Cognitively, members are average or above average in intellectual functioning and have a variety of "cognitive styles," (i.e., ways of organizing their experience to form their own definition of interpersonal reality). Some members are gifted in warm, nurturing ways of thinking about others, whereas others may be cool and distant, yet very insightful and incisive. Others are very concrete and matter-of-fact, whereas others are facile in thinking psychodynamically, systemically, or metaphorically. Some are remarkably articulate, whereas others have great difficulty in knowing and/or expressing how they feel. Most members appreciate humor and enjoy the laughter that is central to the fluidity of group functioning.

Heterogeneity/Homogeneity of Members in a Group

The couples groups are heterogeneous in relation to the members' ages, diagnoses, and severity of marital problems. Groups include people as old as 75 years and as young as 25. When there is a large age range, therapeutically useful transference phenomena occur in which the older people relate tot he other couples as they might relate to their own adult children, while younger couples get into various aging-parent issues with the older members.

I also prefer groups that vary in the severity of marital problems and/or individual diagnoses. My experience is that one borderline in a group is difficult, but two borderline work fairly well. The groups do not work well for members of average or lower average intelligence, nor do they work well for members who are psychotic or who have multiple personality diagnoses. The groups do work well for adults with learning disabilities, and other diagnostic categories.

Many couples are relatively high functioning, but need couples group therapy to refresh and revitalize marriages that seem to have gone stale. Some couples believe that their marriage is fundamentally solid but that "the spark has gone out of the relationship"; they choose to participate in the group in order to enhance and revitalize the marital foundation. Other members are going through a very serious crisis and actually see the group as their "last hope." Many couples have had marriage therapy before but found the experience disappointing. Having both types of couples in the group is encouraging. Those couples with the serious problem find much to learn from the others, whereas the latter are relieved to learn that they are "not as bad off" as their peers in the group or as they has thought. Common individual diagnoses of group members are personality disorders, neuroses, adult learning disabilities, and adjustment disorders. Many clients enter a group with mild to moderate forms of depression; there have been quite a few persons with serious depression and many with addictive disorders. I do not invite anyone with an overt psychosis, but have had one or two persons with borderline diagnoses.

Assessment

Assessment of a couples's problem begins long before they are considered for group participation; it begins with the first phone call and continues through the marital therapy sessions. I form hypotheses about the ways in which the partners function with each other and with their families of origin, how the balance of power works between them, and about the patterns they engage in that maintain, avoid or limit intimacy. I also inquire about attempts the partners have used to deal with their problems, and about the results they obtained with these strategies. Once a couple is invited to join a group, a more formal assessment procedure takes place. The

partners complete a variety of measures designed to provide the therapists with additional diagnostic information. These measures include the Couples Assessment Inventory, the Symptom Checklist, and at times, the Myers–Briggs Questionnaire.

Couples are asked to work on the assessment forms between the first and second session and to be ready for a discussion of their responses in the second session. In that session, the clients read excerpts from their forms and discuss their answers to the degree to which they choose to divulge the material. Most couples are willing to get moving toward their goal and are, therefore, prepared to share the assessment form responses with the group. In fact, many of them show a surprising frankness that helps to create an expectation that self-disclosure is the order of the day. This, in turn, contributes to the development of rapid cohesiveness.

Why Do Assessments?

Assessments serve four valuable functions:

1. *Assessment provides additional diagnostic input.* It is very important to carefully diagnose a couple before inviting them to join the group, in order to prevent later calamities (Spitz, 1979). Not infrequently, a couple appears quite different on paper than in the initial pregroup interview or even in the couple's therapy sessions before the group. Having the assessment data is analogous to receiving an outside consultation from a trusted clinician. I may discover unforeseen troublespots or hidden strengths. At the very least, I receive a confirmation of my prior impressions and can share these impressions with the clients themselves.

2. *Assessment provides a view of the defensive structure.* The assessment data, especially the Symptom Checklist, can provide glimpses not only of the depth of despair but also of the degree of denial.

3. *Assessment assists in goal setting.* The Couples Assessment Inventory, in particular, pushes the couple to think of the problem in very specific terms and in ways that conceptualize it as solvable and systemic. Members are encouraged to think about the reciprocity involved in those marital processes that cause them unhappiness, rather than blaming each other. They often derive hope and encouragement from getting away from the blame pattern. Thus, early in the development of the group the assessment form enhances the motivation to stop

denial and go to work on the most important issues.

4. *Assessment lays the foundation for treatment evaluation.* Later in the group, my cotherapist and I want to know how far a couple has come, and refer to the initial assessment forms. We ask the couple how they see issues routinely in the termination phase of the group. Members and leaders discuss the couple's progress, whether more therapy is indicated, and if so, what kind, and so on.

A CATALOG OF TECHNIQUES

Couples group psychotherapy includes a variety of therapeutic interventions. Many have been adapted from skills developed by other psychotherapists or researchers in related disciplines. Other interventions are the product of the creativity of our own clinical skill. A brief description of a few organizing techniques orients the reader to the range of interventions possible.

Making the Most of the Stages of Development

Groups have developmental stages. Very much like the stages of human development, a group had to go through certain processes that repeat themselves as a group progresses from its first meeting to a working stage of development (Bennis & Shephard, 1956; Bion, 1960; Thelen, 1954). The stages of group development are relatively predictable. Frequently, they have marker events, by which one can tell that a group has reached a stage or is moving from one stage to the next. The notion of stages implies that there is a certain developmental task that the group has to master. Often, the atmosphere in the group will convey to the leaders that the group is struggling with such a task. Understanding these tasks and working with them maximizes the effectiveness of the group. Thus, if a group is dealing with issues of joining and acceptance, the leader is ill-advised to focus on issues of mutuality and intimacy in the group; these are issues that belong in later stages. Instead, it is advantageous for the therapists to help the group clarify the current-stage task and guide the group in its search for stage-appropriate solutions to its issues. I believe that there are a number of repetitive patterns that can best be understood as developmental stages (Kirschenbaum & Glinder, 1972). Assuming a sequence of stages provides

help in understanding group phenomena that would otherwise be puzzling.

The five major stages in the development of a group are (1) Joining, (2) the Initial Working Phase, (3) Group Crisis and Expression of Dissatisfaction, (4) the Intensive Working Phase, and (5) Termination.

Joining is the first stage in a group. Characteristics of this stage include fear of acceptance by group members, anxiety over the wisdom of joining a group, and social politeness. A group is often dependent on its leaders, and members fear too much self-disclosure.

In the *Initial Working Phase* (and prelude to crisis), members begin to work on marital problems. Frequently, it is the impatience of those group members who are already fluent in the language of family systems work through previous therapy that moves the group to this stage. These members settle the self-disclosure issue simply by "taking the plunge" and modeling openness for the others, which catalyzes the group. One of the hallmarks of this stage is what might be called "moving from couple identity to personal identity." Members, who at first were seen by the others in the group merely as partners in a couple, begin to emerge as individuals with their own unique style and their own unique problems.

In the third stage, *Group Crisis and Expression of Dissatisfaction,* what often began in stage 2 as dissatisfaction turns into a real battle. The onset is usually sudden: One couple may come into a session and threaten the group with dropping out if the "bullshitting" does not stop. Or, a person suddenly loses his/her temper and noisily attacks the leaders or another member, and the battle is joined. The fight is usually a struggle for more depth and intimacy. The people who are ready to move on need deeper levels of self-disclosure in order to work on painful and embedded marital problems, rather than remain at the level of superficial fights. Yet, with each important group movement there will be a countermovement. There will be some members who resist by whatever means they can devise. The countermovement against greater disclosure and intimacy in a group is usually motivated by fear. Although some members in the group are ready and eager to expose themselves a great deal, others are frightened by, and resist, this prospect. They are afraid of what they might find if they take a closer look at their marriage or at themselves as individuals.

Once the crisis has been overcome, the group tacitly agrees on a comfortable level of self-disclosure that creates an atmosphere in which therapeutic work can be done. The group enters its second phase, the *Intensive Working Phase*. At this stage, the group is very cohesive, and members express genuine liking and affection for each other. They enjoy coming to the group and lateness and complaints about how hard it is to get to group meetings are heard less frequently. The group is then least resistant to serious work, and one painful situation after another becomes the work of the group, as members produce moving emotional experiences. A group working at this level is more skilled at systems therapy than most therapists trained in an individual treatment model. Leaders can literally enjoy the fruits of their own and the members' labors. Having successfully overcome earlier struggles, the group is now able to tackle the more significant problems of power, mutuality, and intimacy in their marriages and in the group. The group has become central in the lives of its members. It is a time of exciting, significant, and permanent personal and couples' changes.

About 2 months before the last meeting, one of the leaders reminds everyone that the group will end in 8 weeks. Group members usually react to this announcement of their entry into the *Termination* Stage with denial: "We (the group) don't have to deal with termination." Despite the denial, the knowledge is there that the group will end. Even though some members may reenlist for the next group, the group, as it is, will cease to exist. Inevitably, the denial is broken and the termination phase begins. Termination is marked by members' experiencing sadness and loss. During this phase, recontracting becomes a major issue. Couples decide if they want to end their membership or join again for another year. They ask for feedback from the rest of the group and report to the group on their progress during the group year. Much of that progress is clearly visible to the group. There is an atmosphere of sadness about ending the remarkable experience of the group, mixed with the pride and a sense of "team spirit" that comes from shared hard work.

Self-Disclosure

Research during the last two decades has indicated numerous positive therapeutic effects for members of psychotherapy groups. One of the benefits in psychotherapy within a group involves the willingness for members to self-disclose (Coché & Dies, 1981). Members experience a subjective sense of belonging and acceptance when they are invited to talk about issues that are anxiety provoking to them within a group

that is understanding and interested in the lives and issues of each member. Some depressed patients benefit from being helpful to others; thus, they can show improvement without a high degree of self-disclosure, but these clients are the exception. For most clients, the standard remains: Success in group therapy for any member depends on his/her degree of openness to the others in the group. It is valuable to explain to new group members that there are two kinds of self-disclosure in groups: One is telling the group about your life situation, about your background, your marriage, and so on; the other type of self-disclosure is of the here-and-now kind (i.e., letting the group know what you feel at this moment). Teaching members effective self-disclosure methods increases group cohesiveness.

DESIGNING EFFECTIVE STRUCTUREED INTERVENTIONS

Much of the second half of each session is spent executing a specially designed structured exercise. During the break after the unstructured part of the group, the leaders meet and design or choose an activity that is likely to deepen or refine the learning begun in the first portion of the session. If, for example, the group members have been discussing parts of themselves that embarrass, humiliate, or shame them, the leaders might design an exercise on the impact of poor self-esteem in a marriage and on careers. The exercises are *not* a grab bag of things to spring on a group, but are formulated by leaders' thinking of the entire group as a system and structuring a clinical intervention that is likely to "unstick" some members, or the group as a whole. There are five basic exercise modalities, each performing a specific function for the life and growth of the group and its members: writing exercises, guided imagery, direct verbal sharing, sociogram activities, and dramatic activities.

1. *Writing exercises.* Each group member takes paper and pencil and responds to a question. Each member or couple then writes down his/her/their responses to the question posed. After sufficient time, couples share their responses with each other. Writing tasks enable members to make a cognitive exploration of a particular issue, sharing thoughts and feelings with partner or with whole group. A broad range of topics is possible.

2. *Guided imagery.* Therapists can put group members into a relaxed state through some mild

hypnotic-induction or muscle-relaxation instructions (e.g., Lazarus, 1971), or may give the group members instructions to visualize a particular scene or encounter (Singer & Pope, 1978; Leuner, 1969). After allowing sufficient time for the members to become involved in their visual adventures, they are gently "brought back into the room." Individual members are then encouraged to share with the group some of the discoveries they made while in the slightly altered state of consciousness that helped them get somewhat closer to their unconscious processes. Guided imagery enable members to get in touch with preconscious feelings and beliefs about issues in relation to self, spouse, family of origin, children, other people.

3. *Direct verbal sharing.* In this simple group exercise a question is posed to the group—for example, "How do you feel about your first name?" or "How is your relationship with your spouse similar to or different from the one with your opposite parent?" Each person takes a turn at reflecting on his/her response to the question, and the group discusses the similarities between members and the meaning of the question for their marriage. Directed verbal sharing functions to help people to get to know each other, to build cohesiveness, and to foster universality or member identification with one another.

4. *Sociogram activities.* A "sociogram" gives a group a diagram of its own structure. Sociograms encompass a variety of forms (Moreno, 1951). Group members may be asked something on the order of "Whom in the group would you choose as your friend if you could? You are limited to three choices." Many other forms of the sociograms have evolved (e.g., the whole group may be standing up and members may express their choices through their body position to each other). Sociogram activities function to increase members awareness of the group structure and of each member's position in the group.

5. *Dramatic activities.* In this group of exercises, modifications of psychodrama (J. Moreno & Z. Moreno, 1959), role playing (D. Langley & G. Langley, 1983), and sculpting (Papp, 1976) are included. At times, it is worthwhile for a couple to sculpt a particular family problem (Papp, 1982). At other times, a couple may role play a particular scene that another couple has described.

Dealing with Resistance

The best way to deal with therapeutic resistance is to begin with the language used. If "resistance" implies doing something that is counter to someone's judgment, "hesitancy" implies moving carefully and slowly. If "denial" implies overlooking something that is obvious, "caution" implies taking care of what exists. Thus, it becomes obvious that any couple in their right (collective) mind would be hesitant about any commitment of 11 months that could harm as well as help their marriage. It also becomes obvious that a couple experiencing active distress would be cautious about further disturbing a rocky status quo. If the therapist puts himself/herself in the shoes of the client couple, it becomes much easier to identify with what the couple needs. Psychological resistance is always mutual, although it may seem implanted in one partner or the other. Frequently the male carries the resistance for the couple. As one husband put it, "It pains me to say that, but I also must confess that I really did not want to come to group therapy. I was kind of holding onto the doorframe out there as my wife dragged me in here for the first session." Respectful inquiry into the nature of the hesitancy, analysis of the function of the hesitancy for the couple, and patient guidance thorough strategically placed clinical interventions enable a couple to tip the balance of the stability–change scale toward the "change" vector.

Coleadership: Marriage between Equals

Male–female coleadership of the group contributes to its efficacy. Coleadership provides both a technical advantage and a therapeutic gain. Because there are two leaders, it is possible for the group to continue working even if one of the leaders has to be absent. On a therapeutic level, the leaders provide a valuable complement to each other: If one of them either overlooks or exaggerates the importance of a particular issues at hand, the other can provide balance, bring in an additional point of view and prevent potential iatrongenic problems. Rutan and Stone (1984) list a variety of advantages of coleadership, but also point out its drawbacks, citing a number of authors who note that the complexities of the relationship between the coleaders may detract from the power of the group. Nevertheless, cotherapy is quite common in couples groups, and I believe that its advantages usually outweigh its drawbacks.

It is a further advantage to the group if the leaders are of different genders (Kluge, 1974). Members of heterosexual couples have the opportunity to project their own feelings toward the opposite sex onto one of the leaders and work them out in the transference (Cividini & Klain, 1973; Cooper, 1976).

In working with one another, it is essential that the coleaders have a positive working relationship. They may have different therapeutic styles, but they must agree on their basic therapeutic theoretical framework. Considerable differences in the theory of what is helpful to people in a group could severely undermine the efficacy of the therapy (Hellwig & Memmott, 1974).

Out-of-Group Psychotherapy Work

Working with a therapist in individual, couples, or family sessions at least once every 3 weeks is a necessary part of the treatment package. Some group therapy practitioners disagree with this guideline and believe that such a procedure drains away energies from the group. Concurrent psychotherapy is necessary, because the group moves very quickly and it is impossible to contain all of the issues for each member, and for each couple, within one brief 5-hour clinical group meeting per month. It is not necessary, however, to have weekly meetings for members, because the group is powerful enough to catch the central concerns of each couple. The evolution of an adjunctive therapeutic meeting once or twice monthly has proven to be very successful: The treatment model is efficient in terms of energy and financial expenditure, but serves to personalize the psychotherapy for each member and couple in the group. In my experience, the other danger, that a couple's problem "falls through the cracks," is the larger concern.

There is some flexibility regarding who provides the out-of-group sessions. It is often one of the group therapists, but it can also be an outside therapist. If one of the group leaders also sees a couple outside of the group, this couple is likely to believe that it has a special relationship to this therapist and feel superior to the other couples. It is important for the group leader to be aware of such transference issues and deal with them as needed (Ormont, 1981).

WHAT MAKES COUPLES GROUP PSYCHOTHERAPY EFFECTIVE?

The treatment package presented here has a variety of ingredients that contribute to a constructive psychotherapy experience. Many of the ingredients could be varied to fit the needs of a different institutional setting. However, even

if varied, it is the complete package that helps couples work through their difficulties in an optimal manner.

The two most important ingredients are the couples' work and the group work. The presence of the partner allows the other people in the group to see the couple in action and to offer firsthand observations on the ways in which the partners "wind each other up" to have an argument, the ways in which they set "traps" for each other, and the ways in which they avoid or limit intimacy.

In addition, all the curative factors of a stronger group therapy come into play. Ever since Yalom's (1975) first efforts to map the ways that groups are therapeutic, more and more has been understood about what constitutes the healing forces in groups, and how they occur at different stages of the group's development. In the early stages of the therapy, group *universality* plays an important role in getting couples going, whereas in the middle phases *learning from each other* appears to be a crucial ingredient. Furthermore, due to its particular composition of members, each group also develops its own preferred style of working. Thus, whereas *insight* may be crucial in some groups, *experiential learning, altruism* and *receiving feedback* may be much more important in others.

Moreover, the group represents a microcosm of a marital community, in which couples show their interactive styles. The necessity for individuals in the couple to relate to a variety of people created opportunities to see the nuances of their interactional styles—for example, whether a husband in the group shows condescending behavior only toward his spouse, or with a variety of women only, or with both men and women.

As I reflect on 6 years of experience with over 75 couples in couples group psychotherapy, couples have expressed to me the benefits that they have received from the group. Advantages that have come from the group include a sense of universality, that is, a sense that a couple gets of other couples' experiencing some of the same difficulties they do, and that every couple is working on issues all of the time. A second benefit from the intensive working phase of the group is a sense of community that is developed from the high level of trust, which provides the foundation for the exceptional self-disclosure about each couple's marriage in particular, and about what marriage is about in general. A third benefit from the working climate in the group is that the group offers enough solid support that couples are able to counteract their own resistance to change in order to move forward in areas that are exceptionally painful. The rousing support offered when a couple makes changes provides the enthusiasm and the energy needed to help couples make decisions that would be too painful to make without this level of support.

OUTCOME RESEARCH ON PAST COUPLES GROUPS

Assessments made at the beginning of group participation form the basis for later evaluations of a couple's progress and eventual success or failure in therapy (Coché, 1983). Most of the evaluations are formal. I may bring a couple's initial assessment form into the final sessions of a group and have the whole group evaluate how far a couple has come in nearing the goals the partners had set. In addition to these informal evaluations, my husband and I designed a small study in which we sent questionnaires to couples who had completed couples groups over the preceding few years. As Marett (1988) points out, actual outcome research on couples groups is sparse and the few existing studies have serious methodological shortcomings. Still, we wanted answers to questions such as: How effective are the groups? Assuming that they are effective, what are the particular areas of improvement, as seen by the couples? Furthermore, in the eyes of the participants, what was it about the groups that made them effective for the couples?

A brief questionnaire was sent to members who had participated in a couples group within the past 3 years. Of the 13 couples who received a questionnaire, 9 couples returned it in time to be included in this analysis. We designed the questionnaire to approach the issue of therapeutic outcome from two angles: (1) What about the marriage is going better now and what is not? (2) What was there about the group that made it successful? We also added some questions regarding the goal with which the couple entered the group and ways to improve the couples' group experience.

In Their Own Words

We invited couples to tell us, in their own words, what they had gained that they believe to be worthy of mention. Here are four couples' responses:

Paul and Amy: "We learned about each other as individuals and have appreciated each other more."

Jack and Deidre: "After experiencing honest and personalized contact with other couples, the ratings of our problems diminished from 'this is a real big problem' to 'Aw, so what, no big deal.' "

Dale and Gerry: "We learned to accept our families of origin. Now, less energy is wasted on trying to 'fix' or change them and more energy is left for us as a couple."

Will and Denise: "We do communicate more effectively and some of that resulted from the group. . . . In some sense, we do know more about being a couple. We both had definite individual issues which we tended not to look at. They were clarified as part of the group."

Todd and Catherine represent the faction who resonated to structure and guided learning: "We believe more therapist control earlier on in each session would prevent a feeling of time restrictions at the end of each session. It's great to let the group talk things through but the therapists must control more frequently and earlier for the optimal benefits for the couples."

OUR CONCLUSIONS ON ASSESSMENT AND EVALUATION

Couples told us that they learned most in the areas of intimacy, communication, and the appreciation of one another's individuality. Having more fun ranked surprisingly low. This could mean that having more fun was not much of an issue before the couples joined, which was our belief, or that we did not sufficiently attend to the issue in the groups. It certainly deserves some thought.

Couples stated emphatically that they had achieved both their initial goals, and the later goals that they had set during the course of the group. The high rating that the course received on the goal attainment question was very rewarding to us, because it means that the group functioned to help people make changes in desired directions.

Couples found the positive, or cohesive, tone of the group to be very helpful to them. Perceived as less helpful were structures exercises, despite the number of couples who requested more structured leaders' interventions. Here again, I need further research. I suspect that different individuals in different couples, with different cognitive styles, experience various kinds of leadership differently, and this seemingly contradictory set of data may, in fact, represent different subgroups responding consistently within their own experience. For example, couples like Catherine and Todd need and respond well to structure, whereas couples like Ben and Karen grow more quickly through the capacity to be involved in direct leadership behaviors in the group. The interpersonal aspects of the group were the most important: honesty, trust, helping, and being in a group. The structure imposed by the therapists, important though it may be to the overall functioning of the group, was not paramount in the minds of the participants.

Asked how to improve the group, some couples, like Todd and Catherine, requested greater direction in leadership and a higher degree of structure. This presents an interesting therapeutic dilemma: Should I as coleader, at the risk of making the group more dependent (Bion, 1960), become more directive, or should I let the group search for answers, believing, as I do, that people change when there is nothing left to do? If so, I shall continue to invite the leadership behaviors to come from the group, even at the risk of being perceived as "wasting time" or "floundering" by members whose anxiety skyrockets at a lack of evident structure. Although I believe that each therapy team has to find its own answers to this issue, any extreme in leadership style, either too *laissez-faire* or too autocratic, is likely to be detrimental to the group (Lewin, 1951).

FUTURE DIRECTIONS

In 1985, Erich Coché and I began to construct a model for psychotherapeutic intervention that combined group psychotherapy principles with principles from family therapy. This model has proven to be an efficient and effective way for couples to receive the treatment that they desperately need and want. The model has proven effective over a range of ages, symptoms, and stages in marital development. The success of the model is due to a number of factors. The model is efficient, at a time and in an era when psychotherapy costs and profit margins are of great concern to clients and colleagues. The model is enjoyable for clinicians who are well trained: Fast-paced, challenging, and stimulating, the model provide intellectual nuturance both to members and therapists. The appreciation of the

couples who have changed as a result of the model provides further reason for its continuance.

Future directions for couples group psychotherapy are clear. First, it is necessary for the therapist to be willing to invest their own time and energy in dual training, both in group and family therapy skills: A therapist who is trained in only one modality is not trained to lead a couples psychotherapy group. A second direction includes research on issues that have been covered in this chapter, but that must remain at the level of impressions until more solid research is generated. A third direction moves beyond the psychotherapy model to the psychoeducational model. Many of the skills that are now taught in couples group psychotherapy would be better taught within a psychoeducational course in which couples learn how to communicate effectively in relation to intimacy and problem solving. Although reimbursement for psychoeducational work might be somewhat difficult, the benefits to the consumer would far outweigh the logistical concerns in repayment. A psychoeducational model could be constructed in a way that would be financially advantageous enough to make it worth the small financial outlay that it would cost members. A combination of such psychoeducational principles, followed by personalized treatment for each couple and the issues they bring to treatment, could be a next step in the direction for couples group psychotherapy. When Erich and I began to conceptualize couples group psychotherapy, we thought we were designing a highly esoteric treatment model that made sense theoretically but that would not have much appeal to couples or to therapists. Instead, in the 6 years I have been doing this work, both before and after Erich's death, I have been informed by its popularity. To date, I have trained over 800 therapists in workshops, and have worked with nearly 75 couples.

As I reflect on the success of the model, I attribute its reception to a few factors. First, it is efficient as a treatment model, at a time when psychotherapy costs and profit margins are of great concern to clients and colleagues. Second, it is great fun to do, once a therapist is skillful in the model. Fast-paced, challenging, and intensely stimulating, the model is nurturing to group members and therapists alike. Finally, the couples' appreciation in having the opportunity to learn about marriage is very richly rewarding for the therapist.

What next? The more I treat couples, the more convinced I become that two directions are necessary. First, I would like to know more about how the experience is therapeutic. Couples tell us that the therapy helps, but how and why? Couples groups provide a rich source of data about couples, about groups, and about bonding. We are sitting on a vast resource of valuable data.

And finally, I am certain that all couples everywhere could benefit from a couples school that teaches them the basic skills involved in coupling before the couple needs treatment. Much of what I do now in treatment could be best taught psychoeducationally as prevention skills. Couples group therapy teaches couples the skills they needed when they first met, in order to couple better. I look forward to a time when couples actively seek education in coupling. That day is approaching.

ACKNOWLEDGMENTS

Appreciation goes to Jason Satterfield, M.A., and Hazele Goodridge for manuscript assistance. Although I authored this chapter, I dedicate it to my late husband, Erich Coché. Erich died 1 year before the submission of this chapter. Before he died, he and I planned its substance. It was his final academic contribution after a 15-year career producing over 40 publications. His spirit remains in these pages.

REFERENCES

Agazarian, Y., & Peters, R. (1981). *The visible and invisible group: Two perspectives on group psychotherapy and group process.* London: Routledge & Kegan Paul.

Bennis, W., & Shephard, H. (1956). A theory of group development. *Human Relations, 9,* 415–437.

Bion, W. R. (1960). *Experiences in groups.* New York: Basic Books.

Buber, M. (1958). *I and thou* (2nd ed., R. G. Smith, Trans.) New York: Scribner's.

Bugental, J.F.T. (1981). *The search for authenticity: An existential–analytic approach to psychotherapy.* New York: Irvington.

Bugental, J.F.T. (1984). *The art of the psychotherapist: Evoking the healing/growth potential.* Santa Rosa, CA: Psychology Corp.

Cividini, E., & Klain, E. (1973). Psychotherapy in the cotherapeutic group. *Socijalna-Psihijatrija, 1,* 65–74.

Coché, E. (1983). Change measures and clinical practice in group psychotherapy. In R. R. Dies & K. R. MacKenzie (Eds.), *Advances in group psychotherapy* (pp. 79–99). New York: International Universities Press.

Coché, J., & Coché, E. (1990). *Couples group psychotherapy: A clinical practice model.* New York: Brunner/Mazel.

Coché, E., & Dies, R. R. (1981). Integrating research findings into the practice of group psychotherapy. *Psychotherapy: Theory, Research and Practice, 18,* 410–416.

Cooper, L. (1976). Co-therapy relationships in groups. *Small Group Behavior, 7,* 473–498.

Hellwig, K., & Memmott, R. J. (1974). Co-therapy: The balancing act. *Small Group Behavior, 5,* 175–181.

Kaufmann, W., (1975). *Existentialism from Dostoevsky to Sartre.* New York: Meridian.

Kirschenbaum, M. J., & Glinder, M. G. (1972). Growth processes in married-couples group therapy. *Family Therapy, 1,* 85–104.

Kluge, P. (1974). Group psychotherapy for married couples. *Psychotherapie und medizinische Psychologie, 24,* 132–137.

Langley, D. M., & Langley, G. E. (1983). *Dramatherapy and psychiatry.* London: Croon Helm.

Lazarus, A. A. (1971). *Behavior therapy and beyond.* New York: McGraw-Hill.

Leuner, H. (1969). Guided affective imagery: A method of intensive psychotherapy. *American Journal of Pschotherapy, 23,* 4–22.

Lewin, K. (1951). *Field theory in social science: Selected theoretical papers.* Chicago: University of Chicago Press.

Low, P., & Low, M. (1975). Treatment of married couples in a group run by a husband and wife. *International Journal of Group Psychotherapy, 25,* 54–66.

MacKenzie, K. R., & Livesley, W. J. (1983). A developmental model for brief group therapy. In R. R. Dies & K. R. Mackenzie (Eds.), *Advances in group psychotherapy* (pp. 101–116). New York: International Universities Press.

Marett, K. M. (1988). A substantive and methodological review of couples group therapy outcome research. *Group, 12,* 241–246.

Mayerson, N. H. (1984). Preparing clients for group therapy: A critical review and theoretical formulation. *Clinical Psychology Review, 4,* 191–213.

Moreno, J. L. (1951). *Sociometry, experimental method, and the science of society.* Beacon, NY: Beacon House.

Moreno, J. L., & Moreno, Z. T. (1959). *Psychodrama.* Beacon, NY: Beacon House.

Nichols, K. A. (1976). Preparation for membership in a group. *Bulletin of the British Psychological Society, 29,* 353–359.

Nietzsche, F. (1960). *Also sprach Zarathustra: Ein buch fur alle und keinen.* Munchen: Goldmann.

Ormont, L. R. (1981). Principles and practice of conjoint psychoanalytic treatment. *American Journal of Psychiatry, 138,* 69–73.

Papp, P. (1976). Family choreography. In P. J. Guerin (Ed.), *Family therapy: Theory and practice.* New York: Gardner Press.

Papp, P. (1982). Staging reciprocal metaphors in a couples group. *Family Process, 21,* 453–467.

Pittman, F. (1989). *Private lies: Infidelity and the betrayal of intimacy.* New York: Norton.

Rogers, C. R. (1957). The necessary and sufficient conditions of therapeutic personality change. *Journal of Consulting Psychology, 21,* 95–103.

Rutan, J. S., & Stone, W. N. (1984). *Psychodynamic group psychotherapy.* New York: Macmillan.

Sartre, J.-P. (1948). *Existentialism and humanism.* London: Methuen.

Satir, V. (1967). *Conjoint family therapy* (rev. ed.). Palo Alto, CA: Science & Behavior Books.

Satir, V. (1988). *The new peoplemaking.* Mountain View, CA: Science & Behavior Books.

Schein, E. H., & Bennis, W. G. (1965). *Personal and organizational change through group methods.* New York: Wiley.

Singer, J. L., & Pope, K. S. (1978). *The power of human imagination.* New York: Plenum.

Spitz, H. I. (1979). Group approaches in treating marital problems. *Psychiatric Annals, 9,* 318–330.

Thelen, H. (1954). *Dynamics of groups at work.* Chicago: University of Chicago Press.

Tillich, P. (1952). *The courage to be.* New Haven: Yale University Press.

Truax, C. B., & Carkhuff, R. R. (1967). *Towards effective counseling and psychotherapy: Training and practice.* Chicago: Aldine.

von Bertalanffy, L. (1968). *General system theory: Foundations, development, applications.* New York: Braziller.

Watzlawick, P. (1978). *The language of change: Elements of therapeutic communication.* New York: Basic Books.

Watzlawick, P. (1983). *The situation is hopeless, but not serious: The pursuit of unhappiness.* New York: Norton.

Wexler, D. A., & Rice, L. N. (Eds.). (1974). *Innovations in client-centered therapy.* New York: Wiley.

Wienecke, H. (1984). Thermenzentrtierte interaktion in einer ehepaargruppe [Report on a marital therapy group using theme-centered interaction]. *Partnerberatung, 21,* 114–126.

Yalom, I. D. (1975). *The theory and practice of group psychotherapy.* New York: Basic Books.

10

Preventive Intervention and Relationship Enhancement

FRANK J. FLOYD
HOWARD J. MARKMAN
SHALONDA KELLY
SUSAN L. BLUMBERG
SCOTT M. STANLEY

Preventive intervention and relationship enhancement share a common goal of helping couples to improve their relationships before problems develop, in order to prevent the occurrence of relationship deterioration that can lead to distress, contentiousness, and eventual dissolution. The rationale for preventive intervention seems self-evident. If we can help couples put into place mechanisms that strengthen the relationship, making it a more consistent source of rewards for the partners and more adaptable to developmental demands and external stressors, then we should be able to prevent the development of marital distress. Furthermore, because the marital relationship is the foundation for the family system, enhancing this subsystem should improve the functioning of parent–child and sibling relationships, and should improve the well-being of all family members.

Despite its appeal, this rationale may be deceptively oversimplified in some important ways. First, as Bradbury and Fincham (1990) note, finding a way to prevent relationship problems requires understanding the causal mechanisms that produce problems for couples, and then targeting those specific mechanisms in intervention. These authors emphasize the need for more re-

fined causal models and more sophisticated longitudinal research to identify the causal predictors of marital distress over time. However, a system as complex and fluid as a marital relationship never lends itself to exact prediction, and no one pathological agent or set of agents is likely to emerge that will account for a majority of the variance in marital quality over time. Thus, our efforts to enhance relationships and prevent distress must be directed at the types of activities and skills that improve opportunities for growth and reduce exposure to deleterious events, recognizing that solving any one problem or improving some aspect of the relationship can never be "the key" to marital success. Furthermore, it would be naive to forget that various couples have myriad ways of reaching the same point, so that interventions to help a couple achieve marital success must be flexible to fit with that couple's specific goals, characteristic style, relationship strengths, and so on.

A second complicating factor is that preventive interventions are not readily accessible, and tend to be used least often by those who seem to need them the most. At present, there is no empirical evidence to clarify which couples actually seek out preventive interventions. However, we can assume that couples who recognize that such an intervention may be helpful to them are the same couples who would be relatively diligent about monitoring and working to maintain marital harmony, even without a preventive intervention. Of course, this possibility does not reduce the value of making interventions readily accessible to couples who wish them, but it also suggests that we need to face the challenge of reaching a wider range of couples who are not seeking intervention. Perhaps more difficult is the problem of motivating couples who are relatively content with their current relationship and do not feel a need to use the new skills taught to them in the intervention. As Guerney, Brock, and Coufal (1986) argue, the preventionist is like a teacher who daily faces the formidable task of motivating students who see no immediate benefit in learning the day's lessons. Thus, our interventions must incorporate mechanisms for inducing couples to learn and practice new ways of relating, as well as marketing strategies for reaching potential consumers of prevention.

With these challenges facing us, 15 years ago we set out to develop an intervention strategy to enhance the relationship skills of young couples planning marriage, in order to prevent marital distress and dissolution. In this chapter we present an overview of the theoretical and research bases for the program, describe how our strategies relate to other interventions in the field, summarize the typical intervention format and procedures, and review the results of our own and other research on the effectiveness of preventive and relationship enhancement interventions with couples. In a final section, we discuss some of the innovations we have incorporated into the program over the years, and suggest some future directions for improving prevention and enhancement interventions.

THEORETICAL FRAMEWORK

The theoretical framework guiding the intervention addresses the goals of both preventing distress and enhancing adaptive functioning. Thus, the intervention draws upon both our knowledge about marital distress and its treatment, and theory and research on "normal" developmental transitions associated with the family life cycle.

Development of Marital Distress

The most vital work in understanding and treating marital distress over the past 20 years is the voluminous body of research and treatment manuals based on social learning theory (Gottman, 1979; Gottman, Notarius, Gonso, & Markman, 1976; Jacobson & Margolin, 1979; Stuart, 1980; Weiss, 1980). The premise of this approach is that marital satisfaction results from the exchange of rewarding behaviors between spouses, paired with the ability to resolve conflicts in a mutually satisfying way, without resorting either to escalation of negative affect and aggression, or withdrawal and avoidance. Recent extensions have also focused on the role of cognitive mediators such as irrational beliefs, unrealistic expectations, and attributional biases in promoting negative marital interaction and distress (Baucom & Epstein, 1990).

Much research documents the fact that these behavioral patterns and cognitive factors do indeed distinguish distressed from happy couples (e.g., Weiss & Heyman, 1990). The key question for prevention, however, is whether these conditions *predict* the development of distress in couples who are currently satisfied with their relationship. Although much less predictive research has been completed, some studies do show that unrewarding communication exchanges before marriage predict future distress (Markman, 1979, 1981), that both physiological arousal (Levenson & Gottman, 1985) and behavioral withdrawal (Gottman & Krokoff, 1989; Markman & Hahlweg, 1992) for men during marital discussions predict declines in marital satisfaction over time, and that marital violence and other aggressive precursors to violence can be detected early on in relationships (O'Leary et al., 1989).

Clearly, there are many other predictors of marital distress, including depression or alcoholism for one partner (Coyne et al., 1987; O'Farrell & Birchler, 1987); and situational factors, such as poverty, teenage marriage, and extreme differences in educational backgrounds for the partners. Although interventions directed at individual psychopathology have shown some success at improving couples' relationships, this occurs only when the marriage is a specific focus of intervention. Also, demographic and individual status factors do not address causal mechanisms in relationships, and they are not generally amenable to change by relationship interventionists. Thus, the behavioral framework is useful not only because of the research support, but also because it specifies factors that are potentially alterable and are proximally linked to the quality of the relationship.

Transition to Marriage and the Family Life Cycle

Prevention and relationship enhancement require a developmental perspective on couples' relationships. The family life cycle is a framework for viewing family development and family transitions across time. The framework derives from life-span development theory, which posits that development proceeds throughout the life span and is influenced by both normative and non-normative events (Baltes, 1987). As applied to family development, normative events are the typical transitions that occur in an expected sequence, such as coupling, engagement, marriage, birth of the first child, children entering school, and so on (Carter & McGoldrick, 1980). Non-normative events are generally uncommon and unexpected, or are occurrences for which the individual receives little preparation. Nonnormative events that can influence family development include stressful events such as unemployment (Broman, Hamilton, & Hoffman, 1990), or the birth of a child with a handicapping condition (Benson & Gross, 1989). Presumably, other fortuitous events that enhance family life also contribute to family development, but these events have not been adequately studied in psychological research. Also, some events such as divorce, job loss, and poverty are common for at least some segments of the population, but nevertheless, are not "normative" in the sense of expected transitions for families (Seltzer & Ryff, 1993).

In family development, transitions and nonnormative events serve as developmental turning points that can alter the trajectory for the next phase of development. These are the times when new demands come to bear, new roles are assumed, and new ways of relating are established. Family development theory proposes that the form of adaptation established at each transition influences the array of new opportunities or stressors encountered at later points in development. Thus, the earlier in development an intervention is implemented, the greater the possibility for far-reaching effects. For couples' relationships, the transition to marriage marks the most significant early change in roles and demands on the partners. If a growth-enhancing course is set early on, it should not only improve satisfaction in early phases of the relationship, but also should help the couple access more opportunities and avoid significant stressors in the future.

At each transition, couples confront developmental demands that must be mastered. Research on marriage suggests six development tasks that are particularly relevant to couples at the transition to marriage:

1. To develop constructive communication and conflict resolution skills.
2. To develop realistic, constructive, compatible attitudes and expectations regarding marriage in general, and their own relationship.
3. To develop behavioral-interaction patterns that satisfy the basic emotional and psychological needs of each partner.
4. To move toward each other as primary sources of gratification and anxiety reduction.
5. To develop constructive mechanisms for regulating closeness–distance and dependency–independence (cohesion) within the relationship.
6. To develop constructive mechanisms for regulating the pace and path of change (adaptability) within the relationship.

Given these challenges, preventive intervention with couples must be *future oriented*. Clearly, learning to resolve disagreements in a mutually rewarding way, having realistic expectations, and meeting emotional needs and providing rewards early in the relationship should help couples to maintain satisfaction in the short run. More important, these activities set the course for future development. For example, the ability to resolve conflicts in a timely manner and problem solve effectively should prevent the development of avoidant patterns that may lead to a buildup of unresolved conflicts for the couple and cause feelings of resentment and helplessness for the spouses. Furthermore, effective problem-solving skills help couples engage in the type of planning that can actually enhance future opportunities for them, thus allowing them greater control over their own future well-being.

A frequently ignored implication of family development theory is that the course of development is never firmly set. Mastery of early developmental transitions may increase resources for coping with later transitions, but the very nature of new transitions is that they make new demands that exceed existing resources and require a shift in existing patterns. For couples, communication skills, realistic relationship beliefs, and confidence about handling future disagreements are coping resources that they can bring to the task of managing the stress of new transitions and nonnormative events. This process is consistent with models of coping and adaptation to life stressors, in which the goal is to return the organism to a state of equilibrium similar to that in the period before the event (e.g., Lazarus & Folkman, 1984; McCubbin & Patterson, 1983). However, developmental transitions also move a relationship into a new developmental phase that requires new skills and roles. Merely attempting to return to preexisting ways of relating may be deleterious for development. Instead, new forms of relating must be established.

The family development model thus provides a framework for early preventive intervention with couples, and it also suggests that interventions should be implemented repeatedly throughout the course of family development as new transitions are encountered. Although giving couples skills early on may have a positive effect on coping with daily stressors in the short run and may set a course for more positive long-term adjustment, sustaining that positive course through various developmental transitions may be further aided by "booster" interventions at those times. However, to date, our prevention work has focused almost exclusively on working with couples only during the transition to marriage.

THE PREVENTION AND RELATIONSHIP ENHANCEMENT PROGRAM

The Prevention and Relationship Enhancement Program (PREP) has undergone several revisions since 1980, as research provides up-to-date information on the critical factors in relationship functioning. Here we present an overview of the newest version currently being offered at the Center for Marital and Family Studies at the University of Denver.

PREP is now provided in two formats. In the extended version, couples attend a series of six weekly sessions, each lasting 2 to 2½ hours. In each of the weekly sessions, groups of 4–10 couples hear a series of brief lectures presenting the skills or related relationship issues. Each couple is assigned a communication consultant who works with them as they practice the skills in a private room. The consultant acts as a coach, giving the couple active feedback to facilitate their acquisition of the skills. The couples also receive weekly homework assignments of skills practice and readings. This format is helpful for

couples who need time to integrate and understand the skills and to learn how the skills fit best into their relationship.

In the second format, 20 to 60 couples at a time hear the lectures in a large group setting over the course of a single weekend. The program is typically held at a hotel, and couples use their private rooms to practice the skills on their own. This format allows couples to focus intensively on their relationship over a short period of time.

In addition, the PREP material is now available on both videotape and audiotape for couples to use at home. Plans are under-way for a videotape series for trainers, and a new book by Markman, Stanley, and Blumberg (1994) presents this information.

It is important for couples to have the proper "set" for the program. One concept presented is that relationship problems can be prevented before they set in or become entrenched, if the couple is willing to work at change. Another concept is that the program is skills-based, and that relationship behaviors are modifiable with work. Along with this, we request that couples adopt a "try and see" attitude in exploring some new ways of relating. Couples are told that it will be up to them to work out how they want to best incorporate the ideas presented into their relationship. Essentially, we want the couples to believe that it is possible to really improve and strengthen their relationship, both for the present and for the future.

Overview of PREP

Each presentation or unit involves a brief lecture of 15- to 45-minutes duration and an accompanying exercise in which couples can learn to use the new skills presented or apply the related issues to their own relationship.

Session 1

In the first presentation, couples are introduced to the flow and structure of the program. Couples learn what to expect from the program and how the sessions will be run, and also learn something about those running the program. The first lecture also presents the research bases underlying the program. The couples are told that the material presented in PREP is based on sound, ongoing research. In addition, important research on gender roles in communication is discussed, in order to focus on important differences in how men and women communicate. We address the typical pattern of women pursuing in-timacy by bringing up issues and the typical male response of withdrawal in order to avoid conflict. Couples are encouraged to clearly define a time and a structure for constructive discussion of is-sues. We discuss the concepts of "safety" and "structure" in communication and how PREP provides a safe environment for good communi-cation. In fact, PREP provides safety by allow-ing both partners to bring up issues and concerns without risk of deteriorating into old, negative communication patterns.

This presentation also includes the basic model of communication, called the Intent–Impact Model (Gottman et al., 1976). In this model, the "speaker" is defined as the one who has a mes-sage to send, and the "listener" is the one who receives that message. Good communication oc-curs when the message the speaker intended to send matches the message the listener hears (ex-cept when the intended message is meant to harm the listener): that is, intent equals impact. "Filters" are cognitions, beliefs, expectations, emotions, or physical distractions that interrupt this process and cause intent not to equal im-pact, leading to miscommunication. Couples are encouraged to begin to identify filters that may be negatively impacting their communication.

The second presentation includes the descrip-tion of the skills for effective speaking and listen-ing. The communication skills and the rationale for them are presented, and an exercise to prac-tice the speaker–listener format is explained. Couples are instructed in the use of the "floor," a device to help them keep clear who is the as-signed speaker ("the speaker has the floor") and who is the listener. They are taught to paraphrase and validate what the speaker is saying, while the speaker learns to speak for him/herself and to speak about specific behaviors, feelings, and situations. The remainder of the session is spent in practice, with the consultant providing feed-back on the couples' progress.

Session 2

In the third presentation, destructive and con-structive styles of communicating are described in some detail. In this session, partners learn to give specific, direct feedback to one another, while talking about specific behaviors in specif-ic situations. This gives couples techniques (a structure) to accomplish the simultaneous goals of constructive expression of feelings and ap-propriate editing of destructive or negative con-tent and affect. Throughout the session, there is

a continued emphasis on good listening skills, such that as couples practice skills in this ses-sion, they are partly practicing how to listen to appropriately worded concerns of their partners. One of the key skills couples learn is to simply listen when in the listener role, rather than to prepare your next response or focus on their own feelings engendered by what the speaker is saying.

The role of expectations about communication and about relationships in general is illustrated in the fourth lecture. Couples are encouraged to look more deeply into their own beliefs about these issues, whether they are expressed openly or hidden, in order to identify expectations that may cause damage to the relationship. These ex-pectations act powerfully on a relationship be-cause they serve as filters that can distort communication, and because they lead to as-sumptions and behaviors that are directly hurt-ful to the partner.

Session 3

The fifth presentation discusses hidden issues or expectations and how they are directly linked to communication processes and problems. Hidden issues are any of a range of more powerful issues (e.g., caring, power, interest, fear of rejection, or desire for acceptance) that often underlie the dis-cussion of more "surface" topics. Couples are pre-sented with information on the types of hidden issues, their effects on communication, and how to identify them in their interactions. They are taught to look for issues that never seem to be resolved but just keep coming up, apparently triv-ial issues that blow up into big fights, or couples "gathering evidence," when one partner appears to be collecting instances of the misbehavior of the partner. Strategies to deal with such issues focus on the couple's use of the communication skills to uncover the deeper issues and face them together. An exercise in which the couple can begin this process is facilitated by the consultant, who can help the couple to identify the signs of hidden issues in their relationship.

The sixth presentation turns the focus to the role of fun in relationship maintenance and sta-bility. Many couples lose sight of how to have fun together over time, or believe that time and effort only need to be spent on problems. We suggest ways to put fun back into the relation-ship, and discuss fun as an important part of a healthy, growing relationship. Finally, we sug-gest some ways to help make fun happen and give homework consistent with this goal.

Session 4

The focus of the seventh presentation is on problem solving. The goal here is to present and practice a model for solving problems that leaves couples with a structure to help them more effectively negotiate their differences. We make a strong distinction between "problem discussion" and "problem solution" phases of handling problems. We stress that full and complete problem discussion is necessary for problem solution to be successful. In fact, problem solution should only be attempted when both members of the couple feel completely heard and understood by their partner. The biggest obstacle to follow-through on a problem solution is when there are unresolved feelings. The exercise allows couples to go through a complete problem discussion–problem solution process on a concrete issue, with the consultant providing feedback on the flow through the stages, as well as on the use of the skills.

Next, in the eighth presentation, couples are offered some suggestions on how good communication can revitalize and maintain the friendship and intimacy that is so important to good relationships. Once again, couples are taught that effort in this area of their relationship can pay off with increased feelings of closeness and intimacy. The idea of "friendship talks" is introduced, in which all relationship issues are banned and the couple must talk about something personally relevant to each member (e.g., work, family of origin, friends, personal goals, dreams, etc.).

Session 5

The issue of team building is introduced in the ninth presentation as a way for couples to focus on positive ways they can increase commitment and intimacy in their relationship. The lecture describes the different components of relationship commitment and their impact on relationships. A strong argument for the importance of this topic is highlighted with interesting research findings and discussion of ways to directly improve the level of commitment in a relationship. The exercise involves ranking one's own and the partner's level of commitment in different domains. This allows a starting point for further discussion of the impact that commitment issues have on the couple.

The tenth presentation serves to introduce the couples to four spiritual values that may impact their relationship. These values (honor, respect, intimacy, and forgiveness) are defined and illustrated through the traditional Judeo–Christian framework prevalent in this country. We are not describing a rigid set of beliefs. Rather, we are offering a flexible model of how communication and spiritual values are important in relationships. This presentation is designed to help couples recognize how spiritual values or beliefs impact their relationships. We divide the research in this area into two factors: (1) commitment and (2) the idea of the shared worldview. The role of communication in enhancing this component of their relationship is emphasized and an exercise around defining their own practice of spiritual and religious values and behaviors is presented.

Session 6

In the eleventh presentation, it is suggested that couples need to enhance, maintain, or improve their communication around their physical relationship. We present an overview of basic information on sensual communication and sexual dysfunction. Masters and Johnson's (1970) sensate focus task, with the massage of a nonthreatening part of the body (e.g., hands or feet), is described as a way for couples to focus on this issue. Our intention here is not to do sex therapy in any manner, but to help couples learn skills for better physical communication. As they practice the sensate focus task, concentrating on the communication aspect, they give each other feedback on how the massaging and touching feels.

The twelfth and final presentation brings home to couples the material taught in the program. In this final lecture, the importance of "engaging" the skills at times when they are most needed is emphasized, although those are the same times that it is most difficult to want to communicate in a constructive manner. Both partners must take responsibility to use the skills they have found helpful. We also encourage ongoing practice in the form of couples meetings.

We encapsulate the basic ground rules that set a framework for handling differences before disagreements arise. Although couples have been learning these ground rules throughout the program, here they are summarized and clearly defined as the core of the structure for communication. We encourage couples to develop their own set of ground rules that reflect their own communication needs and styles. We emphasize their taking personal responsibility for their own communication, as well as mutual commitment through agreements to have couples meetings at which they use the skills. The couples review a list of the five basic ground rules and agree to use them as is or modify them to fit their own needs. The consultant is present to answer questions and reinforce the couples' good use of the skills.

OUTCOME EVALUATION

Meta-analyses of prevention and relationship enhancement interventions show that, immediately following the intervention, couples improve more than 67–79% of controls who received either no intervention or a placebo condition (Giblin, 1986; Hahlweg & Markman, 1988). Short-term improvement is more pronounced on observational measures of communication behaviors than on self-report measures of relationship quality, probably because couples begin the intervention satisfied, and thus have little room for growth on self-report measures (Hahlweg & Markman, 1988). This ceiling effect might also account for why prevention and relationship enhancement programs show less pronounced effects than does marital therapy with distressed couples (Halhweg & Markman, 1988). However, among a variety of marital and family treatments, premarital couples in prevention programs show greater improvement than any other group (Giblin, Sprenkle, & Sheehan, 1985). Followup from 6–18 months later showed sustained effects, although longer term positive effects are less well documented (Hahlweg & Markman, 1988). In fact, the PREP intervention is the only prevention program that has been evaluated beyond an 18-month period.

Short-Term Effects of PREP

An initial evaluation of the immediate outcomes of PREP compared premarital couples randomly assigned to an intervention group with couples in a no treatment control condition (Markman, Floyd, Stanley, & Storaasli, 1988). Consistent with the meta-analyses results, immediately following PREP the intervention couples showed improved communication proficiency on observational measures, but they were not significantly different from controls on self-reports of satisfaction and relationship quality. Although the couples in the intervention group had learned the skills taught in the program and remained happy with their relationships, the couples in the

control group also remained happy with their relationships before marriage.

Other studies evaluated how couples receiving PREP fared compared to couples receiving an alternative intervention offered by their church. Blumberg (1991) compared PREP to engagement encounter, one of the most common premarital counseling programs offered by religious institutions in the United States. Following the intervention, PREP couples showed an overall increase in positive problem solving, and greater support–validation during interactions as compared to couples who received engagement encounter. Two months later, the PREP couples also tended to report higher levels of relationship satisfaction. In a similar study, Heavrin (1992) randomly assigned couples to receive PREP or a traditional pre-Canaan group intervention through the Catholic church. A waiting-list control group also received the traditional intervention later. At posttest, the PREP couples displayed more positive nonverbal communication skills than the other groups, and at follow up they were more stable and satisfied than the other couples.

An interesting gender difference that was found in the Blumberg (1991) study relates to the role of commitment for involving couples in preventive intervention groups. In both the PREP and engagement encounter conditions, the men rated themselves as being more personally dedicated to the relationship than did the women, although the women increased their dedication ratings over time. Furthermore, the men in 12 couples who declined to participate in either program were significantly less dedicated to their relationships than those who did participate. Perhaps a high dedication level for men, in particular, is necessary to engage couples in premarital intervention (Renick, Blumberg, & Markman, 1992).

Long-Term Effects of PREP

For over 10 years, the effectiveness of PREP has been evaluated as part of a large-scale investigation of the development of marital distress and its early identification. Out of an initial group of 135 couples, 83 couples from both the PREP and control groups have fully participated in the 8 follow-up sessions undertaken in this study. Attrition rates have primarily been due to couples who have broken up before marriage, 80% of whom were in the control rather than the PREP group. The multiple measures used included self-report inventories, videotaped interaction tasks, and communication measures (see Renick et al., 1992, for a review). Couples were assessed prior to participation in PREP, immediately following this participation, and at 1½-, 3-, 4-, 5-, 6-, 7-, 8-, and 9-year follow-ups. To date, data have been examined up to the 5-year follow-up.

One and one-half years after the intervention, the PREP couples had maintained high levels of relationship satisfaction, and continued to rate the impact of their communication behaviors positively, whereas control couples tended to show decreases in these areas over time. These differences were significant at the 3-year point. Also, the intervention couples reported fewer problems with their sexual relationship than control couples at this time (Markman et al., 1988). At both 3 and 4 years after the intervention, the PREP couples had experienced significantly fewer divorces or breakups and engaged in lower levels of negative communication (Markman, Renick, Floyd, Stanley, & Clements, 1993). Four years after PREP, these couples also showed a trend toward the display of more positive affect, a greater usage of communication skills, and fewer instances of dominance and conflict. At the 5-year follow-up, twice as many control couples as PREP couples had divorced or separated (16% and 8%, respectively). Furthermore, between 3 and 5 years after PREP, the intervention couples reported significantly fewer instances of marital violence than did the control couples. Interestingly, beginning at the 4-year follow-up, the PREP effects differed by gender, with only the husbands showing significant differences in satisfaction and interactions between the PREP and control groups.

CLINICAL ISSUES IN IMPLEMENTING PREVENTION AND RELATIONSHIP ENHANCEMENT

Therapist/Consultant Factors

Three broad features of the therapist's or consultant's approach are distinctive to preventive intervention and relationship enhancement. First, the consultant must adopt a competency orientation toward intervention. In PREP, this orientation is built into the content of the program, as reflected by the majority of the program's focus on teaching couples new, effective problem-solving skills. Competency also is promoted by persuading the partners to attend to and reward positive, relationship-enhancing behaviors from each other, and by encouraging them to monitor relationship quality and engage in relationship-maintenance activities. By keeping the focus on these activities, the consultant helps the couples to become aware of relationship strengths and draw upon these strengths when needed to handle the inevitable problems that arise in any relationship. A second feature of the consultant's approach is that it should focus on helping couples control the process of their interaction, rather than offering specific advice about issues at hand. Many couples seek an "expert on marriage" to tell them secrets to success or suggest solutions to current problems. However, in PREP, the consultant is an expert on communication, not on the particular circumstances confronting each couple. In a related vein, the third feature of the approach is that the consultant must adopt a teacher/consultant role in relation to the couples, so as to discourage the type of dependency that can develop with direct caregivers.

In addition to these three attributes, the consultant must exercise good basic relationship-building skills. Gurman and Kniskern (1978) concluded that the therapist's ability to establish a positive, supportive relationship with clients is the single therapist factor that is most consistently associated with positive therapy outcomes. This also holds true for behavioral interventions (Barton & Alexander, 1981). Similarly, the couples' receptiveness to preventive intervention is probably largely determined by their acceptance of the group leaders and consultants as understanding, caring, and genuine.

Intervention outcome studies are frequently criticized for using relatively inexperienced therapists to conduct sophisticated clinical interventions (e.g., Jacobson, 1991). Yet, PREP is specifically designed to use paraprofessionals as the primary contact persons with the couples. This practice originated from research documenting the effectiveness of many interventions with paraprofessional providers (Durlak, 1979). Furthermore, the outcome studies of PREP use paraprofessionals in order to simulate the practice in most community and church settings that implement prevention and relationship-enhancement programs. Nevertheless, all sessions are overseen by a senior-level clinician who supervises all interventions with the couples. We have no evidence that the program would be effective without this leadership.

Unfortunately, the quality of the client–clinician relationship in PREP has not yet received empirical attention. Also, we are only beginning to evaluate other characteristics of clinicians, such as adherence to the program as stipulated in the manuals. We hope that future research will help clarify and refine many of the clinical impressions presented here.

Instilling Hope and Confidence

Almost all couples enter prevention programs feeling good about their relationships, although some of them may be "at risk" for future distress. The goal of prevention programs is actually to alter the factors that put couples at risk. However, Gurman (1980) has argued that premarital intervention that "teaches couples how to express directly their doubts and dissatisfaction" (p. 93) is dangerous because it attacks the requisite idealization that helps couples manage the stress associated with the transition to marriage. Actually, there are no data to suggest that idealization is indeed predictive of a smoother transition to marriage, or that communication-based intervention alters idealized views of the partner or the relationship. In fact, PREP is specifically designed to increase couples' sense of relationship efficacy (Notarius & Vanzetti, 1983) by giving them the skills to confront and resolve problems as they emerge. The reports of individual couples suggest that instead of bursting bubbles of romanticism and idealism, PREP helps to instill hope, optimism, and confidence that inevitable disagreements and conflicts can be dealt with effectively. In fact, this sense of efficacy may be as important as the skills and information provided in the program. Nevertheless, we continue to be vigilant to the issues raised here, and feel that it is an important ethical responsibility to monitor continually the potential for raising problems that couples have not previously experienced.

A related issue involves therapists' sharing with couples impressions about the couples' relationships. This practice is specifically avoided in PREP, with the exception of pointing out specific, ineffective communication strategies as they emerge, and suggesting more effective communication skills. However, the availability of instruments such as PREPARE (Olson & Fowers, 1986), which is specifically designed to identify relationship problems predictive of marital failure, raises the possibility of widespread use of this procedure as an intervention strategy by practitioners who are unable to help couples improve in the problem areas identified. In the context of marital therapy with distressed couples, it may be appropriate for an experienced therapist to help a couple reach the decision that divorce

should be considered (Jacobson, 1983). However, in preventive intervention and relationship enhancement, the implicit (and sometimes explicit) contract with the couple is to help them enhance their relationship and improve their chances for marital success, and pointing out unresolvable problems or suggesting dissolution of the relationship would violate this contract.

OTHER APPROACHES

A variety of prevention and enrichment programs for couples are currently available to the consumer. This brief overview highlights some of the strengths and weaknesses of each program.

Relationship Enhancement

Guerney, Brock, & Coufal (1986) describe their approach as "integrated," incorporating elements of communication skills training, empathy training, client-centered, and behavioral techniques. Relationship enhancement (RE) is presented in a once-a-week format or in marathon format (4- and 8-hour sessions). Research conducted by Guerney and his colleagues suggests that RE benefits couples more than other programs; however, the research uses measures developed specifically for the purpose by Guerney and cannot be compared to research on the effectiveness of other programs.

RE focuses on teaching couples the skills they need in order to strengthen attitudes and feelings involved in caring, understanding, trusting, sharing, and loving. The skills are taught through didactic presentation and skills practice in each session. The therapist reinforces and facilitates practice of the skills. Guerney believes that the difference between RE and traditional marital therapy is the emphasis on the role of the therapist as a teacher of skills rather than a doctor who will cure or remove pain, even though RE is frequently used with couples who are having difficulties.

Practical Application of Intimate Relationship Skills

Practical Application of Intimate Relationship Skills (PAIRS) (Gordon, 1990) is a 12- to 16-week program that incorporates many components of both therapy and communication skills training. The couple participates in group and individual treatment, as well as a skills training component. Therefore, this approach is time-intensive and very expensive, limiting access to only affluent couples. Little research on the effectiveness of PAIRS has been published, so the relative effectiveness of this program cannot be readily assessed, even compared with traditional marital therapy.

Association for Couples in Marriage Enrichment

The Association for Couples in Marital Enrichment is a national organization dedicated to relationship enhancement, particularly through participation in Marriage Encounter, a weekend enrichment program for couples. Marriage Encounter focuses on raising couples' awareness of pertinent issues, including communication, problem solving, intimacy, spirituality, and sexuality. Group leaders are married couples who have been through the Marriage Encounter experience and have received some additional training. Group discussions are followed by private discussion for each couple on the topic of concern. An evaluation study by Milholland and Avery (1982) showed positive effects on trust and marital satisfaction. However, other research (Doherty, Lester, & Leish, 1986; Doherty & Walker, 1982) suggests that at least some couples may experience increased conflict that remains unresolved as a result of participating in Marriage Encounter.

Getting the Love You Want

A particularly popular book for couples lately is *Getting The Love You Want: A Guide for Couples,* by Harville Hendrix (1988). This well-written book provides separate sections on discussion of his theory of relationships and a program for couples to follow. Hendrix gives weekend seminars to couples across the country, introducing and promoting his program and book. This program is intended to be therapeutic in nature, inviting couples to attempt to address issues often raised in a therapy setting. This approach is based on general clinical principles and Hendrix's personal theory of relationships.

ENHANCING OUR ENHANCEMENT PROGRAMS

Identifying Effective Interventions

The prevention programs reviewed previously share a focus on improving couples' communi-

cations, but each also proposes unique goals or areas of intervention. For example, PREP focuses on problem solving, expectations, and sexuality, and emphasizes promoting future adjustment over increasing current satisfaction. Other approaches emphasize improving self-awareness (e.g., Marriage Encounter) and strengthening intimacy and love (e.g., RE). A review of these procedures for the programs, however, reveals more similarities than differences. Nevertheless, in marital relationships there probably are multiple trajectories to reaching satisfaction and stability. Thus, perhaps the best way to improve interventions is to conduct more basic research to discover more of the pathways to marital success used by different couples. Also, intervention studies are particularly valuable because they provide the only experimental manipulation of variables hypothesized to relate to marital success (Markman & Hahlweg, 1992).

Dissemination through Existing Institutions

Several studies are being conducted at this time regarding the effectiveness of PREP as disseminated in religious and other contexts. For example, in addition to the Heavrin (1992) study (discussed previously that evaluated PREP as compared to traditional pre-Canaan counseling in the Catholic church, another collaborative effort between the Archdiocese of Washington, DC, and Nordling and Brown at the University of Maryland is now underway to develop, implement, and evaluate PREP's effectiveness in a religious setting. In Germany, the Catholic Church and the federal government are sponsoring an evaluation of Ehevorbereitung Ein Partnerschaftliches Lernprogramm, an adaptation of PREP. Preliminary short-term results are consistent with the findings from U.S. samples in which EPL couples show no significant differences from controls on self-reports of marital quality, but do show more effective patterns of communication when discussing relationship problems (Markman & Hahlweg, 1992). Last, the Center for Marital and Family Studies, University of Denver, is working with U.S. Navy clergy and social workers to provide PREP to Navy couples globally.

Ethnic and Cultural Sensitivity

In order to improve the applicability of preventive intervention, and enhancement programs for a wider range of people, more research and program development are needed that focus on couples from different ethnic and cultural groups.

For example, a Dutch version of PREP is being offered to couples in which one partner comes from a divorced home or has a parent with a psychiatric disorder (Van Widenfelt & Schaap, 1991). This study is notable, not only because it uses a non-U.S. sample, but also because it applies PREP procedures to address the concerns of "at risk" couples. More work is needed also to make PREP more applicable to historically underserved populations, such as people of color and people from low socioeconomic backgrounds, who may face circumstances that are unusual for white, middle-class couples. For example, many African American and Latino couples have strong extended family relationships that persist after the couple's marriage, with some couples actually living in the same home with their families of origin (Mindel, 1980). Becoming closer as a dyadic unit and working together as a couple thus may be relatively complicated during the early stages of marriage. Also, for African American couples, the pressures caused by societal racism and the underavailability of men may make negotiating satisfactory levels of trust particularly difficult in marriage (Aborampah, 1989). As we revise and improve our interventions, a goal is to discover ways to make prevention better serve the needs of all people.

Booster Sessions

The notion of ongoing change throughout the family life course suggests that preventive intervention should move from a strictly "inoculation" model to more of a long-term maintenance model: that is, although research findings suggest that one can inoculate couples against short-term deterioration in their relationships by teaching effective communication and conflict-management skills, sustained effects may require ongoing interventions at key points in time in the family life cycle (e.g., the transition to parenthood). Booster interventions could help couples to maintain their use of the skills and to make modifications in their styles of interaction with the changes in their circumstances. Also, providing materials for home use, training paraprofessionals and natural caregivers in the community (e.g., ministers), providing weekend retreats, and presenting media-based interventions can be used to reinforce "healthy" marital practices. For PREP, we have recently developed a set of videotapes, based on the intervention program, that couples can use to review the basic skills and principles for good conflict management, and we

have begun to evaluate the effectiveness of booster sessions given at the transition to parenthood.

Evaluating Family Outcomes

Apart from helping couples, preventive marital intervention has implications for preventing or reducing the risks to children posed by exposure to destructive marital conflict. A clear association exists between marital conflict and children's problems (Grych & Fincham, 1989), and one potential causal pathway links ineffective marital conflict-management skills with negative parent–child interactions (Floyd & Zmich, 1991). Preliminary longitudinal results suggest that the ability to regulate affect and to manage conflict constructively at the premarital stage is related to positive children's outcomes and more positive parent–child communication (Lindahl & Markman, 1990). Thus, an important next step for evaluating preventive intervention and relationship enhancement is to explore the effects of intervention on future parent–child relationships and family adjustment.

CASE EXAMPLE

John, age 34, and Merm, age 33, came to PREP after 3 years of marriage. Both felt they had a strong marriage, but had noticed tensions building lately, and were concerned. Merm had dropped hints that they needed to work on their communication, and John enrolled them in the PREP program as a surprise for her. He wanted her to know that, like her, he was concerned and that he was serious about keeping their marriage strong.

Merm is a dental hygienist and John is a water resources engineer. They have no children yet. Like many couples, John and Merm had anxieties about marriage and divorce. Merm had two sisters and many friends who had divorced, and John's parents had divorced. They promised each other before marriage that if they ever had significant problems, they would seek help.

The following dialogues illustrate how their problem-solving communication evolved during the course of the intervention from an unstructured, unproductive conflict, to a more productive, structured conversation using the techniques learned in the program. The conflict involves her concerns about the time he spends on the computer.

MERM: I come home and I've got, you know, house work and stuff and then you're on the computer. What could you possibly have to do on the computer all the time?

JOHN: Well, I have my "to do" list to do and um, I use it for bills and stuff and for accounting and for things that you're not really involved in. I don't question you on how you spend your time.

MERM: But I just don't see how you have that much stuff that you're always doing every day . . .

JOHN: Yeah, but I don't judge you for how you spend time with your bunnies.

MERM: Well, yeah, but bunnies are pets. Pets are alive! But your computer's like this thing and . . .

JOHN: Yeah, but you're judging me.

MERM: And you're always on it and I—like if I need help around house or something—I can't ask you for help because . . .

JOHN: But I do help around the house. You just won't give me credit.

MERM: I think that you probably do more on the computer than you help around the house.

JOHN: I come home from work and we usually eat and then kind of do our own thing for a while, and I choose to spend my time how I want to spend it. And when I am doing it, I feel guilty 'cause I feel like you're going to be walking in any second, give me this look like, you know, "Why are you doing this?"

MERM: And like our vacation a couple years ago. We were going to have that place for a week, and you wanted to bring your computer . . .

JOHN: But you have to bring that up! Oh, okay, go on. And all I wanted to do was write letters and um, maybe do some journaling and that kind of thing. It's just like having a tablet of paper and yet you felt so threatened . . .

MERM: Well, I think when you go on vacation, I mean, I would think that vacation would just be me and you and not, you know, your huge computer. It's like if you have the computer there, I know you're going to be on the computer all day long and we're never going to spend any time together.

JOHN: But you bring a book with you, right, on vacation? Or paints, you do some painting or, . . . we took your bunny with on that vacation.

MERM: Well, she was sick and I had to. That's not . . . I had no choice on that. I mean . . .

JOHN: My computer could have had a virus!

MERM: Computer virus. I wish it would and then it would die! Then we don't have this problem.

Although this final joke demonstrates their ability to deescalate negative affect somewhat, the conversation is filled with examples of cross-complaining, blaming, denial of responsibility, and poor listening skills that are typical of unproductive conflicts. After learning about active listening skills, the couple was instructed to continue the discussion using the "Speaker–Listener Technique." One partner at a time holds "the floor" (a card with the rules for the technique on it), and as speaker, speaks only for him/herself, without mind reading the listener. The listener is instructed to paraphrase back to the speaker what he/she heard in order to demonstrate understanding and, ideally, concern for the speaker's viewpoint. We stress that agreement is not important, but respectful listening and validation of each other's viewpoints are essential.

MERM: The problem is, I feel like you don't pay any attention to me, or not enough attention to me, when you're on the computer all the time, and it kind of makes me feel like I'm not very important.

JOHN: Okay, so what you're saying is that, you don't feel like I'm paying enough attention to you and maybe I'm spending too much time on the computer.

MERM: Yeah, and you know, it hurts my feelings. I get really angry at that stupid computer and I get angry at you for wanting to spend so much time with it, or *I feel like* you are wanting to spend so much time with it. Um . . .

JOHN: So, okay, you feel neglected and therefore hurt. You feel like I maybe pay too much attention to the computer instead of you. (*Merm hands John the floor so that he can express his point of view.*) My point of view is that I've just chosen this like a hobby, and it's just how I choose to spend some time. And then, I feel like I can't even enjoy the time that I've chosen to work on the computer because I always feel like you're judging me or you're telling me I shouldn't be working on it.

MERM: Okay, I hear what you're saying. You're telling me now that this whole computer thing is mostly a hobby. And that you really enjoy the time that you spend on the computer and that this is something that's important to you, to be able to have that time to mess around on the computer and that . . .

JOHN: "Mess around" may not be the best choice.

MERM: Okay, um, effectively use it, okay? Um, and also that, if I got this correctly, you're feeling guilty or something if you're using it and I catch you using it, something like that?

JOHN: Yeah, kind of. Sometimes I feel like I can't use it without feeling that you're somewhere in the house thinking that I should be doing something more constructive, in your opinion.

MERM: Okay, so if I find you on the computer, then you're afraid that I'm going to say something about how you're not using your time constructively, or you should be helping me more around the house instead of enjoying yourself.

JOHN: Exactly.

At this point, the consultant asked them to explore potentially "hidden" issues that may be involved in the current problem. As a result, themes involving vulnerability emerge more and more clearly as their conversation continues. The discussion illustrates how hidden themes become clearer when couples learn to communicate with more structure. Here they are safe from attack, and thus less likely to respond defensively.

JOHN: So, is there something, I mean, is it just the computer that's bothering you or is there something deeper that the computer represents? And here, have the card. (*He hands her the floor card.*)

MERM: Um, I feel ah, I guess a lack of caring . . . I'm feeling at this time that you're so into this computer and you just have to get these things done. I feel neglected so I feel a lack of care or um, a lack of desire that you want to be with me.

JOHN: You feel like I'm choosing the computer over you and ah, that I don't care for you, is that what you said, or that . . .

MERM: Yeah, not quite that extreme. I mean I know you care for me but I . . . I guess I'm a little threatened that maybe you would want to spend time doing something else other than spending time with me, and it's something I don't want to get worse, and so then I end up feeling neglected or abandoned.

JOHN: So you're worrying about it escalating maybe, almost like addictive kind of be-

havior or maybe you even see it now as being kind of addictive.

As they continued their conversation, they were able to move through the problem-solving procedures that we teach couples. They came to an agreement for how to handle time with the computer that pleased them both and addressed the important concerns raised by each of them over the course of their conversation.

This example demonstrates how PREP focuses on teaching couples skills and structures to guide them through the difficult issues, so that they can deepen and enhance their relationship rather than build walls. Merm and John are like so many couples in our culture today. They are aware of the risks of divorce, and are aware of some patterns in their relationship that make them vulnerable. Because of their strong bond, they were motivated to do the work of prevention, before more serious patterns developed. This is the goal of PREP and the hope of preventive intervention.

REFERENCES

Aborampha, O. (1989). Black male–female relationships: Some observations. *Journal of Black Studies, 19,* 320–342.

Baltes, P. B. (1987). Theoretical propositions of life-span developmental psychology: On the dynamics between growth and decline. *Developmental Psychology, 23,* 611–626.

Barton, C., & Alexander, J. (1981). Functional family therapy. In A. S. Gurman & D. Kniskern (Eds.), *Handbook of family therapy* (pp. 403–443). New York: Brunner/Mazel.

Baucom, D. H., & Epstein, N. (1990). *Cognitive-behaviorial marital therapy.* New York: Brunner/Mazel.

Benson, B. A., & Gross, A. M. (1989). The effect of a congenitally handicapped child upon the marital dyad: A review of the literature. *Clinical Psychology Review, 9,* 747–758.

Blumberg, S. L. (1991). *Premarital intervention programs: A comparison study.* Unpublished doctoral dissertation, University of Denver, Denver, CO.

Bradbury, T. N., & Fincham, F. D. (1990). Preventing marital dysfunction: Review and analysis. In F. D. Fincham & T. N. Bradbury (Eds.), *The psychology of marriage: Basic issues and applications* (pp. 375–401). New York: Guilford Press.

Broman, C. L., Hamilton, V. L., & Hoffman, W. S. (1990). Unemployment and its effect on families:

Evidence from a plant closing study. *American Journal of Community Psychology, 18,* 643–659.

Carter, E. A., & McGoldrick, M. (1980). *The family life cycle: A framework for family therapy.* New York: Gardner.

Coyne, J. C., Kessler, R. C., Tal, M., Turnbull, J., Wortman, C. B., & Greden, J. F. (1987). Living with a depressed person. *Journal of Consulting and Clinical Psychology, 55,* 347–352.

Doherty, W. J., Lester, M. E., & Leigh, G. K. (1986). Marriage Encounter Weekends: Couples who win and couples who lose. *Journal of Marital and Family Therapy, 12,* 49–61.

Doherty, W. J., & Walker, B. J. (1982). Marriage Encounter casualties: A preliminary investigation. *American Journal of Family Therapy, 10.* 15–25.

Durlak, J. A. (1979). Comparative effectiveness of paraprofessional and professional helpers. *Psychological Bulletin, 86,* 80–92.

Floyd, F. J., & Zmich, D. E. (1991). Marriage and the parenting partnership: Perception and interactions of parents with mentally retarded and typically developing children. *Child Development, 62,* 1434–1448.

Giblin, P. (1986). Research and assessment in marriage and family enrichment: A meta-analysis study. *Journal of Psychotherapy and the Family, 2,* 79–86.

Giblin, P., Sprenkle, D. H., & Sheehan, R. (1985). Enrichment outcome research: A meta-analysis of premarital, marital, and family interventions. *Journal of Marital and Family Therapy, 11,* 257–271.

Gordon, L. (1990). *Love knots.* New York: Bantam.

Gottman, J. M. (1979). *Marital interaction: Empirical investigations.* New York: Academic Press.

Gottman, J. M., & Krokoff, L. J. (1989). Marital interaction and marital satisfaction: A longitudinal view. *Journal of Consulting and Clinical Psychology, 57,* 47–52.

Gottman, J. M., Notarius, C. I., Gonso, J., & Markman, H. J. (1976). *A couple's guide to communication.* Champaign, IL: Research Press.

Grych, J. H., & Fincham, F. D. (1990). Marital conflict and children's adjustment: A cognitive–contextual framework. *Psychological Bulletin, 108,* 267–290.

Guerney, B., Jr., Brock, G., & Coufal, J. (1986). Integrating marital therapy and enrichment: The relationship enhancement approach. In N. S. Jacobson & A. S. Gurman (Eds.), *Clinical handbook of marital therapy* (pp. 151–172). New York: Guilford Press.

Gurman, A. S. (1980). Behavioral marriage therapy in the 1980's: The challenge of integration. *American Journal of Family Therapy, 8,* 86–96.

Gurman, A. S., & Kniskern, D. P. (1978). Deterioration in marital and family therapy: Empirical, clin-ical, and conceptual issues. *Family Process, 17,* 3–20.

Hahlweg, K., & Markman, H. J. (1988). Effectiveness of behavioral marital therapy: Empirical status of behavioral techniques in preventing and alleviating marital distress. *Journal of Consulting and Clinical Psychology, 56,* 440–447.

Heavrin, J. (1992). *Marital preparation: A comparison of skill training and lecture of factors related to marital success.* Unpublished doctoral dissertation, Hofstra University, New York.

Hendrix, H. (1988). *Getting the love you want: A guide for couplse.* New York: Harper & Row.

Jacobson, N. S. (1983). Beyond empiricism: The politics of marital therapy. *American Journal of Family Therapy, 11,* 11–24.

Jacobson, N. S. (1991). Toward enhancing the efficacy of marital therapy and marital therapy research. *Journal of Family Psychology, 4,* 373–393.

Jacobson, N. S., & Margolin, G. (1979). *Marital therapy.* New York: Brunner/Mazel.

Lazarus, R. S., & Folkman, S. (1984). *Stress, appraisal, and coping.* New York: Springer.

Levenson, R. W., & Gottman, J. M. (1985). Physiological and affective predictors of change in relationship satisfaction. *Journal of Personality and Social Psychology, 49,* 85–94.

Lindahl, K., & Markman, H. J. (1990). Communication and negative affect regulation in the family. In E. Blechman (Ed.), *Emotions and families* (pp. 99–116). New York: Plenum.

Markman, H. J. (1979). The application of a behavioral model of marriage in predicting relationship satisfaction of couples planning marriage. *Journal of Consulting and Clinical Psychology, 45,* 743–749.

Markman, H. J. (1981). The prediction of marital distress: A five year follow-up. *Journal of Consulting and Clinical Psychology, 49,* 760–762.

Markman, H. J., Floyd, F. J., Stanley, S. M., & Storaasli, R. (1988). The prevention of marital distress: A longitudinal investigation. *Journal of Consulting and Clinical Psychology, 56,* 210–217.

Markman, H. J., & Hahlweg, K. (1993). Prediction and prevention of marital distress: A cross-cultural perspective. *Clinical Psychology Review, 13,* 29–43.

Markman, H. J., Renick, M. J., Floyd, F. J., Stanley, S. M., & Clements, M. (1993). Preventing marital distress through communication and conflict management training: A 4- and 5-year follow-up. *Journal of Consulting and Clinical Psychology, 61,* 70–77.

Markham, H. J., Stanley, S., & Blumberg, S. L. (1994). *Fighting for your marriage: Positive steps for preventing divorse and preserving a lasting love.* San Francisco: Jossey-Bass.

Masters, W., & Johnson, V. (1980). *Human sexual inadequacy.* Boston, Little, Brown.

McCubbin, H. I, & Patterson, J. M. (1983). Family stress and adaptation to crisis: A double ABCX model of family behavior. In D. H. Olson & B. C. Miller (Eds.), *Family studies review yearbook* (Vol. 1, pp. 87–106). Beverly Hills, CA: Sage.

Milholland, T. A., & Avery, A. W. (1982). Effect of Marriage Encounter on self-disclosure, trust and marital satisfaction. *Journal of Marital and Family Therapy, 8,* 87–89.

Mindel, C. H. (1980). Extended familism among urban Mexican Americans, Anglos and Blacks. *Hispanic Journal of Behavioral Sciences, 2,* 21–34.

Notarius, C. I., & Vanzetti, N. A. (1983). The Marital Agendas Protocol. In E. E. Filsinger (Ed.), *Marriage and family assessment* (pp. 209–227). Beverly Hills: Sage.

O'Farrell, T. J., & Birchler, G. R. (1987). Marital relationships of alcoholic, conflicted, and nonconflicted couples. *Journal of Marital and Family Therapy, 13,* 259–274.

O'Leary, K. D., Barling, J., Arias, I., Rosenbaum, A., Malone, J., & Tyree, A. (1989). Prevalence and stability of physical aggression between spouses: A longitudinal analysis. *Journal of Consulting and Clinical Psychology, 57,* 263–268.

Olson, D. H., & Fowers, B. J. (1986). Predicting marital success with PREPARE: A predictive validity study. *Journal of Marital and Family Therapy, 12,* 403–413.

Renick, M. J., Blumberg, S., & Markman, H. J. (1992). The prevention and relationship enhancement program (PREP): An empirically based preventive intervention program for couples. *Family Relations, 41,* 141–147.

Seltzer, M. M., & Ryff, C. D. (1993). Parenting across the lifespan: The normative and nonnormative cases. In D. L. Featherman, R. Lerner, & M. Perlmutter (Eds.), *Lifespan development and behavior* (Vol. 12). Hillsdale, NJ: Lawrence Erlbaum.

Stuart, R. B. (1980). *Helping couples change: A social learning approach to marital therapy.* New York: Guilford Press.

Van Widenfelt, B., & Schaap, C. (1991, November). *Preventing marital distress and divorce in a risk group in the Netherlands.* Presented at the convention of the Association for Advancement of Behavior Therapy, New York.

Weiss, R. L. (1980). Strategic Behavioral marital therapy: Toward a model for assessment and intervention. In J. P. Vincent (Ed.), *Advances in family intervention, assessment and theory* (Vol. 1, pp. 229–271). Greenwich, CT: JAI Press.

Weiss, R. L., & Heyman, R. E. (1990). Observation of marital interaction. In F. D. Fincham & T. N. Bradbury (Eds.), *The psychology of marriage: Basic issues and applications* (pp. 87–117). New York: Guilford Press.

II

COUPLE THERAPY
AND RELATIONALLY
DEFINED PROBLEMS
AND ISSUES

A

Issues of Culture, Gender, and Sexual Orientation

11

Cross-Cultural Marriages

CELIA JAES FALICOV

If you are not going to marry the boy next door—and if you do you may die of boredom—then you are going to have to work much harder.

—MARGARET MEAD

STRICTLY SPEAKING, we all intermarry, even if we marry the boy next door. Husband and wife generally belong to social units of one sort or another that differ in terms of family traditions, occupations, or political ideologies. Even the fact that the people marrying are of different genders can introduce considerable discrepancies in worldviews and experiences. Since it is rare to find entirely parallel background experiences, all marriages involve some degree of mutual accommodation.

But it is also probable that the inevitable accommodation may be longer and more complicated as the differences in background widen. With increasing frequency in the modern world, marriages occur between partners of diverse ethnicity, religion, social class, race, and nationality (Barron, 1972; Gordon, 1964; Ho, 1984). The terms "intermarriage," "intercultural marriage," and "cross-cultural marriages" will be used here to encompass those couples. Demographically, interethnic marriages are very common; interfaith marriages follow in frequency, with interracial marriages being the least frequent. Interclass marriages are comparatively rare (Leslie, 1982; Schulz, 1976).

Interethnic, interfaith, and interracial marriages offer unique possibilities for creative and enriching relationships. There are, however, potential conflicts if the worldviews of the spouses are very discrepant. Strains can also come from the disapproval of family, friends, and institutions. Families of origin may differ greatly in their values and rituals. Either or both families may object to the "cultural outsider." The new spouse may experience "culture shock" or feel ill-at-ease with the family of the other.

The factors that make for success or failure, happiness or unhappiness, in a marriage are extremely complex and cannot merely be reduced to degrees of cultural commonalities and differences. Because of the enormous complexity and variety of cross-cultural marriages, it is extremely difficult to make generalizations useful to the clinician without delving further into the attendant family processes.

In this chapter, the conditions under which cultural differences interact with family processes are explored. Problematic outcomes are described, and a number of clinical directions are offered. First, sociological theories about marital love and cultural consonance are briefly reviewed. Second, the idea is introduced that couples who intermarry enter a form of cultural transition, the task of which is to arrive at a balanced view of their similarities and differences. Variations in the way couples adapt to this task of dealing with their cultural differences, and the use they make of the cultural material, are diagnostic in and of themselves. Third, three commonly found clinical pictures in which cultural differences play a part are illustrated, along with suggestions for therapeutic interactions that require different positions of the therapist, vis-à-vis the cultural differences. The clinical examples emphasize the therapeutic use of culture as a valuable resource for change and highlight the dangers of dealing with cultural issues in a purely descriptive or explanatory manner.

MARITAL LOVE AND CULTURAL CONSONANCE

Social scientists offer two groups of theories linking marital love with cultural consonance or dissonance. The ideology of our society dictates that marriages should be based on a romantic foundation, that is, on the experience of mutual love. One group of theories maintains that such love has a better chance of flourishing when the partners share similarities in background. According to Reiss (1976), the experience of rapport that is so essential to the development of love is greatly facilitated by commonality of social and cultural experiences.

> One's social and cultural background is a key basis from which to predict the range of types of people for whom one could feel rapport. Broad factors such as religious upbringing and educational background would make one able to understand a person with similar religious and educational background, and thus make rapport more likely. (p. 93)

Theories that stress the importance of similarities for marital compatibility regard cross-cultural marriages rather pessimistically and cite the high incidence of divorce as proof of the difficulties involved in these marriages (Berman, 1968). In fact, most interfaith premarital counseling emphasizes finding areas of commonality between the prospective spouses (Crohn, 1986).

Another group of theories about love are predicated on just the opposite reasoning, emphasizing the importance of differences for individual need fulfillment in a relationship. A widespread belief is that "opposites attract" and complement each other (Winch, 1955). Most of the early computerized dating systems were based on this notion of complementary psychological needs (Schulz, 1976). Psychodynamic authors also view the cultural differences as mere masks behind which lie the partners' complementary needs.

> The bottom line is whether the union provides the necessary warmth, love, affection, excitement, caring, intimacy, and solidarity all human beings require. This is the prerequisite behind the masks of

two racially different people. "It takes two to tango," and, consciously or unconsciously, a person selects a marriage partner who complements a particular dance step and road in life. (Jester, 1982, p. 111)

Although the complementary differences referred to are personality differences, a similar argument might be used to find value in cultural differences between partners (Falicov, 1982). Such a view would stress the opportunities open to spouses in cross-cultural marriages. For example, a workaholic, task-oriented WASP man could benefit from marrying a person-oriented woman from a Latin culture. The integration of the two complementary backgrounds may produce a richer and more satisfying whole than if each had married a person within his/her own culture. A contemporary, positive view of intermarriage could propose that, like other types of "blended" families (Goldner, 1982), cross-cultural couples represent a new, more complex form of marriage than the traditional endogamous relationships of preindustrial societies. These intercultural systems may come closer to what Keeney (1983)—borrowing from biology—calls an "ecological climax," a "vital balance" of diverse forms of experience and behavior in an ecosystem. As Margaret Mead indicates in this chapter's opening quotation, a complex and challenging marriage may also be an antidote to boredom.

These theories offer a broad perspective for the clinician, but they are of limited application in the treatment of cross-cultural marriages in distress. Unlike the theories just described, less significance is given in this chapter to the actual magnitude of the cultural differences than to the perceptions and meanings intermarried spouses have developed about their cultural similarities and differences. This view is consistent with my working definition of culture (Falicov, 1988), which is applied here to cross-cultural couples.

DEFINITION OF CULTURE

In this chapter, a comprehensive, multidimensional definition of culture is utilized. *Culture is seen as those sets of shared worldviews and adaptive behaviors derived from simultaneous membership in a variety of contexts, such as ecological setting (rural, urban, suburban), religious background, nationality and ethnicity, social class, minority status, occupation, political leanings, migratory patterns and stage of acculturation, and values derived from belonging to the same generation, historical period, or particu-*

lar ideology (Falicov, 1988). Thus, cultural similarities and differences result from contextual inclusion, that is, participation and identification, in similar and in different types of groups. Because individuals select and combine features of the many groups to which they belong, in order to describe an individual's culture it is necessary to take into account all relevant contexts simultaneously.

Believing that ethnicity or social class has equal impact upon all individuals ignores the complex contexts that create variability. A husband and a wife may come from different ethnic groups and have very similar or very different cultural perspectives, as two couples living in Southern California illustrate. In one couple, the wife comes from a Swedish family and the husband has a Spanish background, yet they both went to college and graduate school in the same historical period. Now they are both marine biologists working on different aspects of the same research project and team, and they are both agnostic and liberal, and share many tastes in music, art, and cooking. They also agree on an egalitarian division of labor. Compare them to another couple, in which the American wife is from a rural, lower socioeconomic, German Protestant background, and the husband is the son of upper-class Latin American Catholics. After a rather carefree existence, the husband has recently returned to school to get a degree in business. Meanwhile, his hardworking wife continues her career in nursing. This couple is more likely to have conflicts of values, tastes, rituals, lifestyle, and goals.

Similarities and differences in contexts produce opportunities and constraints, resources and limitations, for the cross-cultural couple. Furthermore, individuals and couples vary in the extent to which they are able to define their cultural contexts and incorporate those definitions into their history and personal biography. A value implicit in this chapter is the concept of "sociological imagination" (Mills, 1959)—the view that awareness about how one's socialization affects one's identity and constructions about the world can be of help to cross-cultural spouses.

DEALING WITH DIFFERENCES

Although similarities and differences may be objectively and subjectively traced to experiences of inclusion or exclusion in various social settings, the totality of a couple's relationship involves many other areas of similarity and difference. One could argue that the way in which a couple deals with its cultural differences is similar or isomorphic to how the couple deals with other sources of similarity or difference, such as the spouses' characterological attributes, age, or gender differences. But this view ignores the complexity of the marital system, namely, that it may function differently depending on the area or type of problem. Furthermore, and perhaps most crucially, any difference or similarity can be maximized or minimized by the spouses at different times and in different areas for various psychological reasons or purposes. The position taken in this chapter is that the construction the intermarried spouses make of their cultural differences, whether these are large or small, is of great importance to the therapeutic process. The perspective that spouses develop of their similarities or differences can render a balanced, complex, and appropriately focused picture. Or, their view may appear imbalanced, impoverished, and inappropriately focused, either through maximizing or through minimizing their cultural differences in the context of their many similarities and differences.

A Balanced View

Many intermarried couples can offer a complex and balanced perspective about their relationship. This view encompasses experiences derived from their embeddedness in the spheres of social class, religion, occupation, historical moment, rural or urban setting, ethnic roots, or political ideology. Thus, a husband and wife may attribute their similarities to the fact that they both were raised in a small, middle-class nuclear family in an urban setting. They could point to differences in religious beliefs and practices, in the ethnic backgrounds of their grandparents, or in the political allegiances of their parents. And, again, they could find similarities in their own contemporary historical and ideological moments. Often the aspect of culture one selects to compare reveals one's personal biases and ideals. As one British-American Protestant man concluded about his and his Mexican Catholic wife's backgrounds after the couple underwent a complex analysis: "Our families' cultures were very similar in their traditions. On both sides, our parents slept in the same bed for 50 years." He underscored one definition of culture that mattered to him.

Within a balanced framework, cultural preferences are more easily integrated, negotiated, or allowed to remain parallel or autonomous from other areas. A balanced view is usually accompanied by harmony and helpful symmetry and complementarity.

An Unbalanced View

Intermarried couples in distress are more likely to have only a limited number of frames through which to screen their similarities and differences. Their views about the complexity of similarities and differences appear to be impoverished, unbalanced, or distorted. These couples may be unaware of the impact of cultural differences on their interactions. Or they may selectively submerge or highlight their cultural differences and similarities. Regardless of whether the cultural differences are objectively large or small, either or both spouses may maximize differences by overfocusing on them, or minimize differences by underfocusing on them.

An unbalanced view is usually accompanied by polarization and disharmony. Thus, cultural differences can be rather elastic and subjectively evaluated as foreground or background, depending on other personal and social processes. In so doing, couples may unwittingly use their differences and similarities as a constraint or a resource. The therapist needs to be sensitive to the ways in which marital partners introduce or omit culturally related experiences in presenting themselves. Particularly important seems to be whether intercultural couples make a balanced or unbalanced evaluation of their cultural differences in the context of other similarities and differences. This is not to imply that an unbalanced use of cultural differences is necessarily the cause of marital problems, but rather that this observation offers clues to the problematic involvement of culture in marital conflicts. Attention to the styles of adaptation that maximize or minimize cultural differences also offers therapeutic guidelines, as will be demonstrated later.

The therapist, like the family, uses cultural differences as reality, metaphor, or camouflage, maximizing or minimizing them in the service of therapeutic goals.

THE CONCEPT OF CULTURAL TRANSITION

The term "transition" derives from two Latin words meaning "to go across." Various uses of the word in the developmental literature converge on the notion of a passage or change from one place, state, or set of circumstances to another,

usually accompanied by a sense of instability or uncertainty in the individual and the family system.

Getting married can be defined as a crucial life transition. For the cross-cultural marriage, another transition is superimposed on the many changes involved in going from being single to being married. This is because, metaphorically speaking, a couple that intermarries enters, of necessity, a form of cultural transition. During the initial stages of the marriage, each member of the couple may experience confusion and conflict with the other's norms, values, meanings, and rituals in a manner akin to the dissonance that accompanies migration and cultural change. As time goes on, efforts at mutual adaptations and accommodations eventually lead to increased understanding and tolerance, and even to personal transformations that could be compared to a process of mutual acculturation.

The perspective proposed here is that the spouses' main developmental task during the cultural transition period of the marriage is to arrive at a balanced and flexible view of their cultural similarities and differences. This would make it possible to maintain some individuated values, to negotiate confusing and conflictual areas, and even to develop a new cultural code and a joint cross-cultural identity that integrates parts of both cultural heritages.

Framing couples' difficulties as the trials and growth potential offered by cultural transition has proven to be extremely helpful in offering an evolutionary and resource perspective for cross-cultural marriages in conflict.

UNBALANCED SOLUTIONS TO CULTURAL DISSONANCE

Difficulties in accepting and gradually resolving the state of cultural transition are manifested in a number of situations. Based on my clinical experience, I have selected three patterns wherein the cultural differences appear to be unbalanced in the context of other marital processes. These patterns are labeled as: (1) conflicts in cultural code, (2) cultural differences and permission to marry, and (3) cultural stereotyping and severe stress. In the first pattern, the marital conflicts are largely related to the lack of a shared cultural code. In the second pattern, the marital problems are tied to difficulties in the realignment of boundaries with the extended family, ostensibly because of the exogamous choice of marital partner. In the third pattern, the marital partners use their cultural differences stereotypically against each other to create a makeshift boundary that prevents painful emotional involvement in situations of severe stress.

These patterns can coexist simultaneously in the same couple; they can appear at different times during a couple's life span; or one pattern may remain more salient than the others throughout a couple's years together. It also seems possible, but remains to be studied, that some patterns may be more typical of one developmental stage than another. For example, in the initial stages of a marriage, there may be an overfocus or underfocus on developing a common cultural code, or on ignoring or defending against the families of origin. The third pattern could appear later, at the time of a threatened dissolution of the marriage (through divorce or death) or other crises that exacerbate an already problematic adaptation to the original tasks of cultural transition. Any difficult developmental transition can upset the balance of the marital situation to the point that any one pattern, or all three, can emerge. Clinical observations also indicate that individual or family life-cycle issues interact with the cross-cultural marriage in complex ways (McGoldrick & Preto, 1984; Crohn, 1986). The description of these three patterns and the corresponding therapeutic strategies that make use of the cultural issues are illustrated with clinical cases.

Conflicts in Cultural Code

Because it is very difficult to distinguish between conflicts linked to cultural differences and other types of marital conflicts, it is helpful for therapists to avail themselves of a conceptual framework to guide therapeutic conversations related to cultural matters. A framework of knowledge about the sociocultural beliefs, values, and meaning systems of different ethnic, racial, or religious groups helps the therapist to introduce relevant questions about possible cultural dissonances that otherwise may not be explored (McGoldrick, Pearce, & Giordano, 1982). The diversity of worldviews, interpersonal expectations, or childrearing values can be so broad that skills in conducting culturally sensitive inquiries are also essential. All inquiries about culture should be personal and nonstereotypic, because enculturation varies with the individual and may vary even more for those who intermarry (Murguia, 1982). Guidelines for these clinical tools are offered by Lappin (1983), Faulkner and Kich (1983), and Schwartzman (1983).

When working with interethnic and inter–social-class marriages, a conceptual framework that is particularly helpful focuses on differences in cultural values about marital and family organization. Some cultural expectations about marriage emphasize values that maintain contact and continuity with the extended family. Other conceptions of marriage favor more discontinuity and emotional autonomy from the parental families. Many ideal values and principles of organization that affect the functioning of the marital dyad stem from these two contexts. The differences in rules governing inclusion and exclusion of others in the marriage (proximity–distance) and in the rules about power and authority (hierarchies) are particularly important. These rules could be said to constitute a sort of cultural code that organizes expectations about marriage both internally and in relation to other subsystems. For a detailed discussion of this topic, see Falicov and Brudner-White (1983).

Intermarried partners often come from family backgrounds having different cultural codes that influence many aspects of relationships, from styles of communication to childrearing values. Some ethnic and religious groups have high expectations for family interdependence, whereas others favor greater autonomy and self-development. Using their circumplex model, Olson, Russell, and Sprenkle (1980) found that a frequent problem with many couples requesting treatment "is that each spouse is at the opposite extreme of the same dimension. On the cohesion dimension, one partner may want more cohesion in the relationship, while the other might want more autonomy and freedom" (p. 169). What often goes unrecognized by couples is that these expectations may stem from different cultural codes about relationships.

Spouses who experience conflicts in cultural code may be separated by many objective differences, such as ethnicity, race, religion, social class, nationality, and even language. At the same time, however, they may share similarities, such as profession, or political or social ideologies. They may also complement each other in cultural or personality aspects. Therefore, they may be able to achieve a balanced view of their differences.

In an attempt at mutual adaptation, some spouses minimize or ignore their cultural differences and end up with a superficial knowledge about each other's cultures. This premature closure of the cultural transition period prevents negotiation in important areas. There may be misunderstandings, problems in communication, and covert reciprocal anticipations of each other's behaviors. Errors based on either ethnocentric or stereotypic views of the other are also common. Cultural traits may be mistaken for negative personality traits. A case example of a couple that fits this pattern follows:

Case A

Jennifer, a young American wife, had been shocked recently by members of her husband's family when they announced their move to the United States from Iran. Her husband, Josef, acting in a culturally syntonic manner, felt willing and obliged to install his family in his and his wife's apartment, even though they were both graduate students and had limited means and time available. Jennifer had many reasons to want her in-laws to secure an apartment of their own. Some reasons were in her own self-interest, but others were considerate of the immigrant family's need to develop self-competence. Josef was extremely upset about what he thought was going to be perceived by his family as an unforgivable rejection. Jennifer finally compromised by agreeing to move to a building where the extended family could have a contiguous, separate apartment. But she remained covertly critical of her husband's "excessive attachment" to his family and, by implication, perceived herself as superior to him.

Shortly after this incident, she attended my lecture about families in cultural context. After the presentation, Jennifer requested a couple interview. During this session, it was clear that there were other tensions between husband and wife. Each complained of not feeling understood and supported by the other. Up to the time of attending the lecture, Jennifer minimized the differences between herself and her husband, although there appeared to be many. She believed that "a global culture" prevailed nowadays, particularly among graduate students, wherein the similarities overpowered the differences in ethnic background. They were both liberal, agnostic, and from middle-class backgrounds, which further reinforced the ideological commonalities. She could not see how their cultural backgrounds could affect their relationship. Speaking about her family, her grandfather had told her, "We are all Yankees, and that means we are the same as ninety percent of everybody else." Josef agreed with Jennifer in minimizing their cultural differences. Rather defensively, he described how, in spite of its traditional emphasis, Iran had continued to become westernized. Many women now studied, worked, and were generally "liberated." For Josef, minimizing the differences was a way of not devaluing his country in comparison to that of his wife.

The therapist continued to pursue a cultural theme by redefining the "global culture" as perhaps a goal for the future (a metaphor for their relationship). But at present, the therapist suggested, many couples all over the world are actually in "cultural transition." Continuing with the educational approach that had had an effect on Jennifer earlier, the therapist referred to cultural family forms that modify definitions about marital boundaries with the extended family. Thus, what Jennifer considered to be her husband's "excessive attachment" to his family would be seen as part of a cultural pattern.

Following this conversation, Josef said, "You are a product of your upbringing whether you like it or not, even if you don't agree with all the credos. The most important one that has stuck with me is that the man makes the decisions and the woman follows. I think, deep down, I don't really believe you can have two heads of household for everything." A lively discussion ensued regarding different cultural codes and the levels of power of men and women, whereupon the therapist facilitated a personal, rather than academic, interaction between the spouses. Through this personal interaction, it became clear that Josef had been fantasizing about having a baby, particularly since an Iranian friend's wife had just given birth. Josef felt quite inhibited about mentioning this to his wife, because she had been so adamant about pursuing her career. He also said that her contraceptive routines had become vaguely upsetting to him, and he had begun wondering whether she was rather cold and calculating. Jennifer felt hurt by this and claimed to be more affectionate than he was, a claim he could not deny.

The therapist looked at the meaning of Jennifer's behavior in cultural and gendered terms, wondering if what Josef saw as coldness could instead be viewed as "American practicality in pursuing goals." Furthermore, what he considered "calculating" could be seen as an example of the determination women need in order to change their subordinate position, since gender roles are in transition everywhere. The therapist also presented Josef's wish to have a baby as an important part of his cultural–familial orientation, an orientation that could be seen as complementary to Anglo-American individualism. The spouses' differences now stood in a complementary balance, opening up a more positive climate for negotiation. After this session, Josef and Jennifer reported that they were more communicative and had a greater sense of union and common purpose.

The spouses in this case example began by minimizing their cultural differences, which in turn prevented disclosure in many important areas. The therapist created balance, maximizing such differences in order to highlight, understand, and justify individual behaviors that the couple had been covertly interpreting as personality traits. The locus of the problem thus moved from the couple to the culture. A by-product of this externalization was to open up more productive communication and to help resolve conflictual issues.

When dealing with conflicts in cultural code, the therapist assumes the role of cultural mediator, interpreter, or "clarifier" of values. Although this role is often helpful, there are several pitfalls to be avoided when using this approach.

First, "cultural clarification" is insufficient and even problematic if the discussion remains at a content level only and does not attend to the process. At a content level, Jennifer and Josef professed to have an egalitarian relationship, but, in terms of process, she initiated many interactions and he deferred to her. While this could be partly due to her superior knowledge of the culture and language, other marital processes, incongruent with their egalitarian goals, seemed to be at work. The therapist then orchestrated the clarification of cultural differences in a therapeutic context that addressed necessary structural changes in the marital relationship: for example, facilitating the husband's expression of his desire for a baby and legitimizing it as a family orientation (rather than an individualistic one) made his contribution equal to his wife's. A move toward blending both orientations could be supported as part of a process of cultural and sex-role transition. A strict clarification of cultural content, without consideration for the complex hierarchical balance of this particular couple, could have led to the therapist's interpreting the husband's desire to see his wife pregnant as a vestige of his culture's traditionalism in sex roles and, thus, inadvertently diminish him further in his wife's eyes.

A second pitfall of cultural clarification may occur when the therapist, in raising consciousness about cultural differences, unwittingly implies a sense of hopelessness about the possibility of change. A cultural reframing could unfortunately suggest that a particular behavior, because it is rooted in the culture, is unchangeable: "Because of his Iranian upbringing, he thinks a wife is only for making babies"; "She can't stop flirting—it's in the Latin blood." Thus, the cultural reframing might inadvertently exonerate individuals from personal motivation or responsibility. It is better to view a cultural trait as a resource that can be used or not, depending on the circumstances, rather than as an inflexible feature. In the foregoing example, reframing the wife's efficiency in avoiding pregnancy as "American practicality" did not imply rigidity or an inability to be more romantic and less practical in other situations. In discussing hypotheses that marital partners formulate about each other's behaviors, Hurvitz (1975) coined the terms "terminal," which describes a behavior that is totally unchangeable, and "instrumental," a description that suggests something can be done about the behavior. Similarly, in cross-cultural situations, the marital partners and the therapist run the danger of using culture as a "terminal hypothesis."

The third pitfall is for the therapist to bring about further marital disengagement by emphasizing the gap in cultural differences too strongly. These differences may then become the "kiss of death" that supports justifications for incompatibility. To avoid it, conversations that underline cultural differences can be balanced by finding other connections, common ideologies, or cultural complementarities or bridges. Another way to prevent a static and disengaging use of culture is to label the couple as being in "cultural transition." This definition encourages them to promote the continuity of some of each spouses' traditions, while developing a "new culture," one that is more personal, unique, and encompassing.

Cultural Differences and Permission to Marry

Although, in Western cultures, parents no longer play an overt role in arranging marriages, parental approval of the marital partner one chooses is of great psychological import for most individuals. Often it is still difficult to secure tension-free, extended-family support for intermarriage. Parental disapproval complicates the expected realignment of generational boundaries to include the new spouse, and it either halts or precipitates too rapidly the stage of cultural transition. Each phase of the couple's life cycle is affected by the response of the extended family to the marriage (Faulkner & Kich, 1983). Interracial and interfaith couples may be forced by their families to skip parts of life cycle rituals, such as the wedding ceremony. Or they may decide on their own to skip the rituals in order to avoid further family tensions. An assessment of intermarried couples should always include the reactions that members of the extended family, and even friends, had to the marriage. It should also include the couples' subsequent relationships with their extended-family and friendship networks.

Racial, religious, or ethnic differences can certainly increase the probability of parental disapproval, particularly in families where generational continuity is expected and endogamy is the rule. In many cases, however, cultural prohibitions appear to be only part of the reason for family tensions around the marriage. The disapproval may also stem from other family processes that make it difficult for parents and their adult children to separate (Stanton, 1981; Friedman, 1982). Stanton (1981) describes some of the family processes behind the parental disapproval of a marriage:

> Such disapproval can loom like a malevolent specter over a marriage. It may occur because one of the partners is instrumental in keeping his or her parents' marriage together, because a parent is undergoing bereavement and is giving the message that "I need you more than your spouse," or for other reasons frequently tied into critical points in the family and parental life cycle. This disapproval is a way of not letting go of the son or daughter—they exert a pull on him/her—often because they feel their own needs are greater. (p. 22)

Cultural differences may not be the only, or even the main, cause of parental disapproval, but they certainly can provide a reinforcing concretization for the family's resistance to the marriage of the son or daughter. Based on his extensive experience with intermarried couples, Friedman (1982) attributes the difficulties of religious or ethnic families in accepting cross-cultural marriages not so much to a high degree of cultural commitment or religious devotion, but to other emotional processes. Marrying out may represent an attempt to create emotional distance, usually initiated by the child who has been most important to the balance of the parents' marriage. For the parents, the cultural differences act as a justification to reject the outsider and, in Friedman's words, become "cultural camouflage" to avoid dealing with the emotional reactions to the son's or daughter's departure.

Whether the content of the disapproval is ethnic or not, and the granting of the blessing religious or not, the more crucial problem is that a substantial number of intermarried couples suffer from a covert or overt lack of permission to marry, and this in turn may have an adverse impact on marital success. Stanton (1981) maintains that "80 percent of marriages that fail do so because one or both spouses have not had permission to succeed in the marriage." A similar point, stressing the importance of parental approval for marital success, is made by Boszormenyi-Nagy and Spark (1973).

In the case of intermarriage, it is as if the spouses do not have permission to enter the state of cultural transition, where they may begin to develop a new cultural code for their family unit. Instead, either a form of cohabitation takes place, or a new code develops, one that excludes relationships with the families of origin.

Marital difficulties can be compounded by divided loyalties or unresolved family ties, but an *unhappy* cross-cultural marriage can also be a "solution" to problems in the family of origin of one or both spouses. On the one hand, the ties with the family of origin are slackened because the cross-cultural configuration of the new couple draws a tighter boundary that excludes each spouse from certain interactions with his or her extended family. Both parties—the parents and the married son or daughter—can blame the necessary distance on the cultural outsider. On the other hand, the marital difficulties themselves could ensure continuity of family-of-origin patterns (cultural and idiosyncratic) if the son or daughter, by continuing to be the focus of parental attention, still detours parental problems, this time through his/her marital difficulties. A similar reasoning that interconnects the marital difficulties of the alcoholic or drug addict and his relationship with his parents (who refuse to accept his marriage) has been proposed by Stanton et al. (1978) and Stanton (1981).

I have observed two contrasting styles of adaptation in couples who do not obtain emotional permission to marry, ostensibly because of their cross-cultural union. The patterns may be distinguished by the boundary negotiations with the family of origin of one or both spouses, and the nature of the interpersonal boundaries within the marital subsystem. In the first pattern (Case B), the couple maximizes their cultural differences, and, in the second pattern (Case C), they minimize them.

Maximizing Differences

In the first pattern of adaptation, each member of the couple appears to emulate the reactions of his/her family of origin. The spouses polarize and maximize their differences, and do not blend, integrate, or negotiate their values and lifestyles.

They may lead parallel lives, each holding on to their culture and/or family of origin. Often the counterpoint of the marital distance is an excessive involvement of one or both parties with the family of origin. There also may be unresolved longings for the past ethnic or religious affiliations, even if these were of little importance previously. The following example illustrates a couple with these features:

Case B

John and his wife, Pat, married for 18 years, came to therapy complaining of chronic marital dissatisfaction and severe alienation from each other. They had minimal daily contact, leading parallel lives, each with his/her own group of friends and diverse interests. Their only common interest was the welfare of their 11-year-old daughter. Recently John had made an extramarital affair public. This altered the marital balance and called for some type of definition about their future together.

John and Pat had no explanation for their longstanding distance and lack of communication. They maximized their differences in personality, interests, lifestyle, and cultural values, while each vaguely blamed the other for not adjusting. The therapist focused the initial session on the beginning stages of the marriage, with the purpose of recreating connections through shared history. The following information was obtained.

John was born in New York City of Italian background, Pat, in upstate New York of French-Syrian parents. Both families were Catholic, but they varied greatly in their adherence to religion. John's family was very devout; Pat's was not. John had been raised in an Italian neighborhood surrounded by "hundreds of intrusive relatives." His nuclear family and extended family lived together in a three-story apartment building. Pat had had a lonely childhood, with almost yearly moves because of her father's position in the Army. When Pat's father was stationed in Europe, John was also in the Army. The couple met then and, after a brief courtship, married just prior to John's completing his tour of duty and returning to the United States. When asked about each family's reactions to their marriage, they responded with the following conversation.

PAT: His family never liked me; they never forgave me for depriving them of a big Italian wedding. They are New York Italians, a very ethnic cultural group.

JOHN (*interjects, laughing*): A culturally starved group.

PAT: Since my father was in the Army and we

lived in many different places around the world, my family is very open to differences. Plus, I was twenty-two and still living at home, so they were happy I found somebody to get married to. John's family's reaction was quite different. John is the prince of the family. His mother explained to me that most Italians are short, so they have this thing that the tallest one is the prince. [John is 6'2".] And I was overweight and my hair was too dark—Can you imagine an Italian saying my hair was too dark? [John is very fair and blue-eyed.]

JOHN: Pat and my family did not get off to a good start, for a lot of reasons. My family tried to be nice, to do their best . . .

PAT (*interrupting*): Well, we did not get married in New York. And, when we were going to return together from Europe, we were involved in an accident, and he had to stay in Europe for one-and-a-half months, while I had to come ahead and meet his parents. It was a true culture shock. I didn't know Italians or anything about Italians, and to be thrown into that environment . . . and his parents did not like me.

JOHN: I came back and there was tension, real or imagined, but there was tension. My mother is not tactful in certain areas. My dad tried, but I guess . . . I don't know . . . heated words were exchanged with Pat . . .

The parental disapproval was clear in some ways, but so was John's ambivalence about his family of origin, which is manifested in several of his answers.

PAT (*interrupting*): One reason you wanted to leave New York was to leave that environment, that Italian voodoo.

JOHN: That is not even fair . . . what is true is that when you are faced with decisions, you have twenty-five relatives trying to help, everyone with their own opinion. It's terrible. You take a job, and they say do this, do that. They have your own good at heart, really. But the reason I wanted to leave New York was because of the environment—too many people—it was stifling.

The husband attempts to deny that he wanted to leave New York to create some distance from his family, but then he says:

JOHN: I guess I did not want to get married in New York and have one-hundred or two-hundred wedding gifts and get caught in the same trade-off my brother got caught in. My parents were very annoyed because family weddings were their insurance policy. They'd been giving gifts for the past twenty-five years, and they keep a book on it. Then, when our family has a wedding, they invite the people they gave to, and in that way they get their gifts back. Not literally the same gifts, but other gifts. It's like a trade-off. I love my family, but they can drive you crazy—so much closeness and so many people. I guess I did not want to stay there.

John's wish to create distance from his family of origin stemmed from two sources: an overly responsible, parentified role in his family; and a perception of ethnic confinement. Because his mother was often ill and his father frequently absent, almost all of the household responsibilities, child care, and the mother's emotional support fell to John. Pat also played a crucial role in her family as her mother's confidant and detourer of marital conflicts. Her mother was chronically depressed and self-preoccupied. She sometimes blamed Pat for her problems, including marital ones.

Unlike Pat, who did not have a clear ethnic identity, and her parents, who minimized their own cultural differences, John lived in an intensely ethnic climate. Every person with whom he came in contact was Italian. All the stores, friends, and people in the neighborhood were Italian. His father played and composed only Italian music. As a second-generation immigrant, John felt embarrassed by so much ethnic emphasis. He looked up to the Anglo world, particularly to bohemians and hippies. With her dark good looks and unconventional clothes, Pat looked like the young women in Greenwich Village that John admired at a distance.

Almost 20 years later, John phones his parents from California weekly, visits them alone, and tells them about his marital problems. His parents put him in a no-win situation by disagreeing about how he should resolve his marital situation. About their position, John says, "My mother is in favor of us splitting up. I don't say, 'Me and Pat are miserable,' but my mother looks at me and she says, 'I know you are not happy,' and I know what she means, and she'll say one or two things about it, and that's all. She does not insist, but I know where she stands. My dad can beat you to death with, 'Don't break up the family.' " Although there had not been any cultural objections to her marriage, Pat had also continued to be overinvolved with her mother and her mother's troubles. Several items are noteworthy in John's relationship to his family. He did not have permission to marry or to have a wedding outside the extended-family setting. This may be because Pat was not Italian, but it is also clear that John played a crucial role as a parental child and as his mother's main companion. John purposefully avoided an Italian wedding (further rejecting his ethnic identification), but there are implications

that he allowed his parents to blame his wife for depriving them of the wedding and possibly for the subsequent marital problems. The cross-cultural marriage could be seen as a partial solution to John's difficulties with his family of origin. Marriage to an Italian woman would have restricted him to interact only with his ethnic group and would have made it more difficult to disengage from his triangulated position with his parents. Marrying outside the ethnic group distanced him from his family, although he still maintained ties and was able to regulate the emotional distance. The unhappiness in his marriage perpetuated his closeness to his parents and provided them with a focus for their disagreements.

Although there were many cultural differences in this case, focusing on them was not considered to be therapeutic at the time, because the spouses were very disengaged and already maximized their cultural differences. In labeling and elaborating on the differences, the therapist could have unwittingly provided yet another ready-made perch to hang their unhappiness on. The husband was ambivalent and defensive about his ethnic background and felt put down by his wife on this issue. Since his ethnic roots were most intense, an emphasis on culture could have implied a criticism of what he brought into the marriage. The couple had made a negative use of cultural metaphors, comparing the marriage to a union of two different countries, France and Germany. Here the therapist would expand the metaphor only if she could find a point of connection, such as the fact that France and Germany share a border, however small.

Circumscribing the cultural differences to the extended family was more appropriate. The therapist justified John's parents' behavior toward Pat as typical of Italian families' reactions to outsiders (Rotunno & McGoldrick, 1982), rather than as a rejection of Pat as a person. John was able to verbalize his conflict of loyalties between his wife and his parents. Pat suddenly realized that her own French mother had never been accepted by her Syrian father's extended family: "She was never good enough for them."

To avoid using culture to split or disengage, the therapist focused on the considerable similarity of positions that each spouse had in his/her own family. Cultural differences were regarded positively as the attraction of opposites: The diversity of Little Italy and Greenwich Village was used as a cultural metaphor for the interdependence and freedom they were both seeking. The cultural similarities and differences in values between generations (parents and adult children) and within generations (spouses) were used to create more appropriate boundaries, that is, more consonance between partners, and greater differentiation between parents and adult children.

The therapist made the loyalty aspects of the distant, unhappy marriage explicit. With a paradoxical intention, she called the unhappy marriage a necessary and valuable sacrifice to the families of origin (Stanton, 1981; Boszormenyi-Nagy & Spark, 1973). This positive connotation encompassed the past and the present, and began to shift the spouses' perceptions of their marriage, motivating them to work on modifying the boundary with their families.

Minimizing Differences

A second pattern of adaptation observed in couples who do not obtain emotional permission to marry consists of minimizing and even denying the cultural differences. They may join a third alternative "culture" and sever their cultural and/or family ties. These couples appear to have an attitude of "you and me against the world" or "we only have each other." The interface boundary with other family members is usually too rigid, and the individual boundaries of the spouses appear too permeable and diffuse.

The couple in the following example illustrates this style of adaptation. The example also shows that the disapproval of the marriage is not always parental. In this case, the lack of permission to marry was eventually found to arise from the children of a first marriage. It had a nearly devastating impact on the second marriage, and the symptoms abated only when this issue was confronted and resolved.

Case C

Sharon, an American, was the daughter of intermarried parents—a German Catholic mother and an English Protestant father. Her husband Michael, also American, was the son of a Chinese mother and an Indonesian father. The spouses had met through their association with an Eastern-type religion. They shared many similar values and a holistic lifestyle. They also had related occupations. Their original differences were balanced by these ideological similarities, but they denied that any cultural differences existed between them at all.

The couple had been married for 3 years and had a 1-year-old baby. They sought therapy because the wife was obsessed with the thought of the husband being unfaithful to her. Since they had recently had a baby, the first probes the therapist made were based on a developmental hypothesis. The birth of the baby placed many constraints on the couples' spontaneity and fun with each other. The wife was feeling unattractive, and the husband was so preoccupied with his new responsibilities as a father that he was less attentive to her. In this context, the therapist reframed the jealousy positively as a form of more intense and romantic involvement with each other, and wondered if the husband needed to be more expressive of his love for, and attraction to, his wife. The husband objected, arguing that, because of his Asian background, he could not be very open with his feelings. By maximizing the differences, the husband seemed to be making a selective and possibly homeostatic use of culture. Not only was he highly acculturated, he was also quite expressive verbally. It soon became clear, however, that the spouses did not need to be more cohesive.

The second hypothesis the therapist tested was one that tied the symptom to a hierarchical imbalance (Madanes, 1981). The wife was older, had more education and work experience, had been married before, and had raised children. She was the sole economic support of this new family, while the husband stayed home to take care of their baby. The husband had a history of drug involvement, procrastination in his studies, and difficulty in obtaining jobs. He was attractive and articulate, however, and women were often interested in him. In this context, the wife's jealousy could serve a balancing function: She was the one with the problem now. Although they joked about the label, they both called her behavior "paranoid." The jealousy was a constant reminder of the husband's superiority in the area of sexual attractiveness. It was, in fact, a form of flattery toward him. The jealousy also allowed the wife more intensive supervision over the husband than would have been possible otherwise. Because the supervision was ostensibly due to the wife's symptom, the husband could be spared from any criticism about his problems and thus save face.

When the therapist asked how the decision was reached about the husband staying home while the wife worked, they both related numerous instances of racial discrimination endured by the husband when he searched for jobs, since many people thought he was black. Both spouses appeared quite helpless and demoralized in the face of institutional racism. This explanation seemed to be realistic but nonetheless acted to prevent a search for strategies to ameliorate the situation. While acknowledging the reality of his social predicament, the therapist attempted to motivate the husband by using another cultural stereotype: "the bored housewife." The therapist said that she understood how his unemployment could fuel his wife's fears, since women know only too well that any person who stays home all day caring for a baby and watching soap operas on television would dream of a titillating affair that would save her/him from household drudgery. If it had not happened yet, it still could happen; the husband could, at some point, go off with another bored or overburdened housewife whom he had met at the supermarket. The husband did not like having yet another stereotype imposed on him, even if it was now being done humorously. This reframing, however, normalized the wife's jealousy and made outside employment of the husband a precondition for its disappearance.

As the husband mobilized himself, the wife's jealousy decreased, and the playfulness between the two of them returned. Within 2 weeks, the husband had found a part-time job that he liked. When he started working regularly, however, the wife's jealousy flared up again, this time with an additional problem. The wife was very reluctant to leave the baby with a sitter and was convinced that the child was now rejecting and turning away from her.

A third hypothesis was needed to account for the recurrence of symptoms. Exploration of the beginning of this marriage provided some leads. The wife had left an unhappy marriage to marry her present husband. After this decision, she became a total outcast, not only from her first husband, but also from her adolescent children and the two extended families. They scorned her for marrying into a different race and excluded her from family contacts. The newlyweds responded by encapsulating themselves behind an attitude of "you and me against the world." However, the wife felt terribly guilty toward her children and upset about their rejection. She said that although she had stopped being a "Roman Catholic" at age 12, she expected "punishment for her sins"—for "bringing unhappiness to so many people." What catastrophes would befall her? Because she was totally dependent emotionally on her new husband, in her view the most terrible thing that could happen would be his leaving her for another woman. When her husband went to work, and the baby was left with a sitter, she became fearful that this child, too, would end up disliking her, as her first children had.

The "lack of permission" from her children was thought by the therapist to be interfering with the trust and consolidation of the new couple. The jealousy was considered a constraint that was maintained by marital processes, but it was also linked with the rejection by the wife's children. The wife seemed to be expressing her loyalty to her children by not trusting her husband completely, because her jealousy and mistrust of her new husband were similar to her children's.

Continuation of contact with her children was thought to be developmentally and therapeutically necessary. Because the wife did not have direct access to her children, the therapist suggested that perhaps a symbolic continuity could be attempted. Both husband and wife were encouraged to use their imagination to devise cultural rituals of continuity (van der Hart, 1983). The customs of ancestor worship common to the Chinese culture provided one type of model, and the husband (himself of Chinese ancestry) could help the wife with the rituals. For example, they could arrange photographs and documents belonging to the maternal grandparents chronologically in albums and send them to the wife's children at the time of their high school graduation. They could also save her mementos from when the children were young, to be presented as gifts when the children grew up and had babies themselves. Working on these projects would keep the connection with the children alive and decrease the wife's sense of powerlessness and impending doom.

In the following session, both spouses reported finding the task extremely difficult. The husband said he could not, in all honesty, help the wife atone for "sins she had not committed." He was extremely supportive of her, saying that she had to leave her family for her own survival and sanity. Despite finding the task difficult, he said he would do what his wife requested of him. Christmas was near, and the wife felt that the best way to maintain continuity was to make gifts for her children, which she would deliver to her own parents' home on Christmas Eve. Thus, they would begin to "face the world." Husband and wife now became engrossed in the resolution of issues with her previous family and in planning the husband's continuation of his studies.

Cultural issues had been mentioned by each spouse (Asian lack of expressiveness by the husband, feelings of Catholic guilt by the wife) to justify or understand interpersonal behaviors and to indicate barriers to change. The therapist accepted, maximized, or minimized the cultural issues, depending on the therapeutic goals. For instance, the therapist did not focus on the husband's claim that his lack of expressiveness was due to his Asian background, primarily because supporting his cultural explanation would have justified his aloofness at an inappropriate time and place: early parenthood in a socially isolated couple. On the other hand, the therapist used a time-honored tradition belonging to the husband's culture as an example of recreating cultural rituals. The wife, in turn, ended up choosing to recreate gift-giving at Christmas, a ritual in her own culture.

The need to explore the relationships with the extended family became evident in this case. A problem that, on the surface, appeared to be exclusively marital could not be treated within the marital dyad. Only when the focus of treatment shifted to the relationship with other family members did the symptom take on a new meaning and become amenable to resolution.

Cultural Stereotyping and Severe Stress

Family members are quite capable of using cultural cliches against one another. This can be done in a friendly, humorous manner or in a manner that is distancing and disengaging. In certain clinical situations, the presenting problem is accompanied by cultural explanations, usually of a negative tone, given by one spouse for the behavior of the other. There is a strong negative emotional component to the cultural hypotheses: an overfocus on, and maximization of differences; or a polarization of views and values. As they begin therapy, however, spouses in such situations typically appear impoverished, offering simplistic explanations that maximize their differences. It seems possible that, in dealing with the stage of cultural transition, they have adapted through attempted solutions that have broken down under stress. Cultural disagreements, long suppressed for the sake of avoiding conflict, can emerge as "time bombs" full of intense feelings when spouses undergo family transitions or other trying times (P. Cowan & R. Cowan, 1987).

When the person being blamed is a member of a foreign or minority subgroup, a first impression suggests that the marital interactions replicate larger sociocultural tensions, such as ethnic or racial prejudice. A closer (and necessary) examination, however, reveals that other family processes are also at work. The distorted splitting content of the cultural explanation, and the degree of emotional intensity surrounding it, give the impression of a "cultural defense" or a massive denial that covers up other crucial processes. The question, "Why is culture an issue now?" is essential for understanding these cases. The answer reveals severe underlying stress, such as impending loss of a spouse through divorce or death. In this light, the communications about culture can be heard as metaphors for other relationship issues.

Case D

A couple who had recently separated and was contemplating divorce consulted a therapist as a last resort—albeit with little hope, since previous marital therapy had not resulted in any changes. Susan, an American with ancestors that went back 300 years in this country, spoke in a very derisive manner about her Cuban husband of 18 years: Luis, a successful engineer. She blamed many of his objectionable features on his ethnic origin and minority status. She said that he had an "inferiority complex" and was "very insecure," "insensitive and undemonstrative," "incapable of love," "selfish," "uncaring," "passive," and "crazy." She also said he was a poor Roman Catholic, even though she herself was of Protestant background and religion had never been an issue in their marriage.

There were several surprising aspects to these statements. First, in spite of the cultural frame used, the traits did not really have any identifiable ethnic roots. Second, during their nearly 20 years of marriage, the two had endured definite tensions due to cultural and language differences, but these had not been previously addressed by either one of them as insurmountable. If anything, the style of adaptation to their differences had been one in which the wife had joined the husband's culture—she had learned a little Spanish and gained considerable knowledge of Cuban history. There had been many attempts at integrating the cultures: for example, they had given each of their children two names—one Spanish, the other English. Third, although Luis was visibly disturbed by his wife's references to his ethnic background, he behaved like a gentleman and never returned in kind the cultural insults. In fact, he tacitly helped his wife to remain at this level of explanation for their problems.

The therapist did not question the content validity of the ethnic stereotypes or mention the spouses' previous attempts to adapt to their cultural differences, because she sensed that something else was happening. To explore matters further, she interviewed the spouses separately. When alone, Luis said his marital dissatisfaction had been longstanding, but he had never expressed it. Recently, he had abruptly taken the initiative to move out of the house. He was living in an apartment with a younger Mexican woman, with whom he had fallen in love. His wife knew this but had refused to take it seriously and had taken every opportunity to invite him to move back with her.

In the context of this marital crisis, the use of

ethnic stereotyping could be understood from various perspectives. By electing to blame her husband's background for his behavior, Susan protected herself from recognizing the possibility that he no longer loved her. A cultural explanation, of course, also excused him from responsibility for his behavior: "All Latin men have affairs." In attacking the Latin culture, Susan was indirectly criticizing her husband's choice of new partner, who was Mexican. The adjectives Susan used to describe Luis's character could be heard as metaphors for the feelings his behavior evoked in her: He was "insensitive" (toward her), "uncaring" (toward her), and "inconsiderate" (of her feelings toward him). Luis had been emotionally estranged from her for some time. Perhaps by voicing powerful ethnic stereotypes about him, she hoped to provoke an emotional reaction from him.

To confront Susan with the distortions of her husband's culture (by having an objective discussion about which of his traits were truly Hispanic and how these traits clashed or fit with her own cultural preferences) would have been therapeutically incorrect. It would have deprived her of a temporary means of protecting herself against the impending loss of her husband. Later on, consideration for the children (two adolescent boys) and the type of balanced picture about the father that would benefit them in the future became a therapeutic avenue to help this woman search for her strengths and a measure of equanimity. In this case, culture, in the form of an alliance with negative public stereotypes, was being used in the family's domain to attempt to correct excessive deviations, and thus gain a measure of psychological self-protection.

The following example, involving an interracial family, illustrates a similar use of cultural stereotyping under conditions of severe stress due to impending loss.

Case E

The presenting problem was arguments between the mother and the 15-year-old daughter, with the father acting as the peacemaker. The father, who was African American, and the children, blamed the mother's culture—she was born and raised in Spain—for the problem. They felt she was "too clean," "too particular" about the house, and also that she "nagged people." The unspoken truth was that the mother had recently had a mastectomy and was receiving frequent chemotherapy treatments that left her very tired. When she increased her demands for help with the house, the family group colluded to deny the reasons for the requests and

instead attributed them to the mother's cultural traits, traits that had been acceptable for over 20 years. Temporarily, it was more protective for everybody to blame the mother's changes on her culture rather than to recognize the serious nature of her illness.

The protective quality of using cultural stereotypes to explain the unexplainable should be given clinical consideration. The notion that differences are maximized and "prejudice" increases in the face of stress was the subject of many early social psychology experiments (Kretch & Crutchfield, 1948; Simpson & Yinger, 1958). There are several psychological and social hypotheses to account for these phenomena. One theory is that the cultural stereotyping of the other may be an attempt to maintain one's self-esteem when confronted with personal failure. The cultural explanation is a search for a reason, even an alibi, that provides a way out for oneself. Case D seems to fit this hypothesis well. Another theory fits the facts of Case E better. In the face of a situation that is hard to understand or accept, prejudices can be adopted to "explain" the crisis. These "situational prejudices" may be an attempt to bring meaning into a confusing and ambiguous crisis.

These cultural presentations need to be dealt with as an adaptation to a family crisis, rather than taking them at face value and focusing on the cultural stereotyping. The cultural stereotyping appears as a desperate boundary-making maneuver to prevent the passage of information and affect between people. Thus, it creates distance where there is too much proximity. From a therapeutic viewpoint, it appears advisable to respect this protective shield and work around it, until it becomes possible to deal directly or indirectly with the thwarted information or the painful affect. The strengths and resources inherent in the family system, both cultural and personal, need to be searched out and maximized to cope with the impending loss while halting the escalation of a distorted use of culture as a response to stress.

SUMMARY

This chapter presented a framework for exploring the conditions under which cultural differences between spouses interact with other processes in problematic ways. It advanced the hypothesis that cross-cultural couples undergo a form of cultural transition. The main task of this developmental phase of the relationship is to arrive at an adaptive and flexible view of the spouses' cultural similarities and differences. The accomplishment of this task would make it possible to maintain some individuated values, to negotiate conflictual areas, and even to develop a new cultural code that integrates parts of both cultural heritages.

Couples in distress usually have an impoverished, unbalanced, or distorted view of their cultural similarities and differences. In these couples, cultural differences are inappropriately focused on, either through maximizing and selectively highlighting them, or through minimizing and selectively submerging them. These signs are reliable indicators of problematic adaptations to the cultural transition.

Conversely, couples who achieve a balanced, complex, and appropriately focused style of dealing with their cultural differences are more likely to allow their differences to remain relatively autonomous of other processes or to integrate them in an enriching manner.

Three clinical patterns were described wherein the cultural differences are unbalanced. These were labeled as (1) conflicts in cultural code, (2) cultural differences and permission to marry, and (3) cultural stereotyping and severe stress. Each pattern involves a different presentation of the role of cultural differences in the marital problems. In each presentation, the therapist pays special attention to how the couple deals with its cultural differences, by maximizing or minimizing them, and/or by using them as reality, mask, or metaphor for the relationship issues. Each pattern requires a therapeutic approach that varies the intensity of the focus on the cultural issues. Common pitfalls were also described to help therapists avoid a use of culture that becomes more of a therapeutic liability than an asset.

Case examples illustrated a tactical use of cultural issues to further marital changes, particularly in terms of interpersonal and intergenerational boundaries. Culture becomes foreground or background, depending on these goals, but it is always used positively as a valuable resource for change.

REFERENCES

Barron, M. (Ed.). (1972). *The blending American: Patterns of intermarriage.* Chicago: Quadrangle Books.

Berman, L. (1968). *Jews and intermarriage.* New York: Thomas Yoseloff.

Boszormenyi-Nagy, I., & Spark, G. (1973). *Invisible loyalties.* New York: Harper & Row.

Cowan, P., & Cowan, R. (1987). *Mixed blessings: Overcoming the stumbling block in an interfaith marriage.* New York: Viking/Penguin.

Cretser, G., & Leon, J. (Eds.). (1982). *Intermarriage in the United States.* New York: Haworth Press, 1982.

Crohn, J. (1986). *Ethnic identity and marital conflict: Jews, Italians and WASPs.* New York: American Jewish Committee, Institute for Human Relations.

Falicov, C. J. (1982). Mexican-Americans. In M. McGoldrick, J. K. Pearce, & J. Giordano (Eds.), *Ethnicity and family therapy.* New York: Guilford Press.

Falicov, C. J. (1988). Learning to think culturally. In H. A., Liddle & D. C. Breunlin, & R. C. Schwartz (Eds.), *Handbook of family therapy training and supervision.* New York: Guilford Press.

Falicov, C. J., & Brudner-White, L. (1983). The shifting family triangle: The issue of cultural and contextual relativity. In C. J. Falicov (Ed.), *Cultural perspectives in family therapy.* Rockville, MD: Aspen Systems.

Falicov, C. J., & Karrer, B. (1984). Therapeutic strategies for Mexican-American families. *International Journal of Family Therapy, 6,* 1–18.

Faulkner, F., & Kich, G. K. (1983). Assessment and engagement stages in therapy with the interracial family. In C. J. Falicov (Ed.), *Cultural perspectives in family therapy.* Rockville, MD: Aspen Systems.

Friedman, E. (1982). The myth of the shiksa. In M. McGoldrick, J. K. Pearce, & J. Giordano (Eds.), *Ethnicity and family therapy.* New York: Guilford Press.

Goldner, V. (1982). Remarriage family: Structure, system, future. In L. Messinger (Ed.), *Therapy with remarriage families.* Rockville, MD: Aspen Systems.

Gordon, A. (1964). *Intermarriage: Interfaith, interracial, interethnic.* Boston: Beacon Press.

Ho, M. H. (1984). *Building a successful intermarriage.* St. Meinrad, IN: Abbey Press.

Hurvitz, N. (1975). Interaction hypothesis in marriage counseling. In A. Gurman & D. Rice (Eds.), *Couples in conflict.* New York: Jason Aronson.

Jeter, K. (1982). Analytic essay: Intercultural and interracial marriage. In G. Cretser & J. Leon (Eds.), *Intermarriage in the United States.* New York: Haworth Press.

Keeney, B. P. (1983). *Aesthetics of change.* New York: Guilford Press.

Kretch, D., & Crutchfield, R. (1948). *Theory and problems of social psychology.* New York: McGraw-Hill.

Lappin, J. (1983). On becoming a culturally conscious family therapist. In C. J. Falicov (Ed.), *Cultural perspectives in family therapy.* Rockville, MD: Aspen Systems.

Leslie, G. (1982). *The family in social context.* New York: Oxford University Press.

Madanes, C. (1981). *Strategic family therapy.* San Francisco: Jossey-Bass.

McGoldrick, M., Pearce, J. K., & Giordano, J. (Eds.). (1982). *Ethnicity and family therapy.* New York: Guilford Press.

McGoldrick, M., & Preto, N. G. (1984). Ethnic intermarriage: Implications for therapy. *Family Process, 23,* 347–364.

Mead, M. (1968). We must learn to see what's really new! *Life, 79,* p. 68.

Mills, C. W. (1959). *The sociological imagination.* London: Oxford University Press.

Murguia, E. (1982). *Chicano intermarriage: A theoretical and empirical study.* San Antonio, TX: Trinity University Press.

Olson, D. H., Russell, C. S., & Sprenkle, D. H. (1980). Circumplex model of marital and family systems, II: Empirical studies and clinical intervention. *Advances in Family Intervention, Assessment, and Theory, 1,* 129–179.

Reiss, I. (1976). *Family systems in America.* Hinsdale, IL: Dryden Press.

Rotunno, M., & McGoldrick, M. (1982). Italian families. In M. McGoldrick, J. K. Pearce, & J. Giordano (Eds.), *Ethnicity and family therapy.* New York: Guilford Press.

Schulz, D. (1976). *The changing family: Its function and future.* Englewood Cliffs, NJ: Prentice-Hall.

Schwartzman, J. (1983). Family ethnography: A tool for clinicians. In C. J. Falicov (Ed.), *Cultural perspectives in family therapy.* Rockville, MD: Aspen Systems.

Simpson, G., & Yinger, J. M. (1958). *Racial and cultural minorities.* New York: Harper & Bros.

Stanton, M. D. (1981). Marital therapy from a structural/strategic viewpoint. In G. P. Sholevar (Ed.), *The handbook of marriage and marital therapy.* Jamaica, NY: S. P. Medical and Scientific Books.

Stanton, M. D., Todd, T. C., Heard, D. B., Kirschner, S., Kleiman, J. I., Mowatt, D. T., Riley, P., Scott, S. M., & Van Deusen, J. M. (1978). Heroin addiction as a family phenomenon: A new conceptual model. *American Journal of Drug and Alcohol Abuse, 5,* 125–150.

van der Hart, O. (1983). *Rituals in psychotherapy: Transition and continuity.* New York: Irvington.

Winch, R. (1955). The theory of complementary needs in mate selection: Final results on the test of the general hypothesis. *American Sociological Review, 20,* 553–555.

12

Redefining the Past, Present, and Future: Therapy with Long-Term Marriages at Midlife

CAROL M. ANDERSON
SONA A. DIMIDJIAN
APRYL MILLER

AT MIDLIFE, FORGOTTEN dreams and age-old passions return to haunt us all. These visits from the past, along with an increased awareness of the passage of time and a host of current life-cycle events and changes, such as career plateaus, empty nests, loss of family and friends through death and illness, and decreased physical well-being, have led many to believe that midlife is inevitably a time of crisis for individuals, with a resulting disruptive impact on marital and family relationships.

Fortunately for those at midlife, there is a growing awareness among clinicians and researchers that such negative images are based more on myth than reality (Chiriboga, 1989a). Although midlife presents certain unique challenges, there is little to suggest it is universally a period of turmoil and crisis that culminates in the tragedy of aging and death. Midlife, it seems, is most fundamentally a period of change, affording individuals and couples opportunities to take stock of their past and chart new directions for their future. Many negotiate the transition smoothly and successfully without help, and move on to

the second half of life with a sense of enthusiasm and renewal. However, as with other developmental transitions, the challenges of negotiating midlife can also bring many couples to therapy. In fact, despite the fact that the divorce rate is significantly higher during the initial years of marriage (Turner, 1980; Collins, 1985), many marital therapists report that they see a disproportionate number of couples who are in their midlife years.

At midlife, distress within a couple can be generated by the interaction of four primary factors: (1) the impact of social change, (2) individual developmental changes, (3) outdated and inflexible early marital contracts, and (4) family life cycle changes. Negotiating these issues can often cause significant reverberations within a long-term marriage. At times, some couples even wonder whether their relationships can survive. And yet, although there is always the threat that one or both partners will conclude that the work necessary to preserve the marriage is not worth the effort, most partners are likely to be motivated to work out their difficulties, given the many years they have already invested in the relationship. Despite the challenges they face, they do have these years of commitment to one another on their side. Moreover, by midlife, most marriages are supported by a complex interdependency of shared history, a community of friends and extended family, and shared finances. Many also have enough life experience to know that substituting a new partner for an old one is no guarantee that the quality of their lives will improve.

AN APPROACH TO THERAPY

Many marital therapists today maintain an ahistorical–interactional orientation, believing that all that is relevant can be observed in the current interactional pattern of couples and can be modified by interrupting dysfunctional patterns and building behavioral skills in the here and now. Other marital therapists attend to the importance of past events, focusing predominantly on the influence of family of origin issues on marital functioning. While evidence exists for the effectiveness of these approaches in working with a wide range of problems, both have limitations with midlife couples, because they tend to look at marital problems as if they were the same, regardless of age or length of marriage.

In contrast, this approach emphasizes the influence of the changes of midlife in understanding and intervening in the marital distress experienced by midlife couples, focusing in particular on long-term marriages, defined as those approximately 10 years or longer, in which husbands and wives are in the middle decades of their lives. Although not discounting the importance of current interactional processes of family of origin issues, marital therapy with these couples requires attention to the ways in which developmental factors and existential challenges influence marital functioning and satisfaction. This attention does not require that therapists discard their focus on microrelationship issues, such as communication, positive exchanges, problem-solving skills, or their focus on the relevance of family of origin issues, but emphasizes that these issues are more relevant in the context of the wide range of life-cycle issues confronting midlife couples.

This approach builds on changes that have taken place within the field of marital and family therapy in recent years. In particular, there has been an increased recognition that no one theory or method of intervention works better

in all cases, and thus we have become convinced of the value of combining approaches, depending on the problems and needs of the people we see. In other words, the field has become more tolerant of integration. Limitations posed by any one method of intervention or understanding have caused us to look for ways of bringing the best of many approaches to bear on the complex problems facing couples and families. In addition, there have been an increased focus on the importance of family life cycle issues (Carter & McGoldrick, 1989; Falicov, 1988). Although the marital life cycle has not received primary attention, this work has highlighted the relevance of a developmental perspective.

ASSESSMENT

Considering the complex nature of midlife issues, a simple assessment of dysfunctional interactional patterns or attention to presenting problems alone is unlikely to address the major issues in a satisfying way. To determine the course of treatment, therapy must help partners to identify their dreams, needs, and the priorities they hope will guide the rest of their lives. This inevitably also leads to an assessment of whether their needs and goals can be met in the marriage and they ways in which their original contract and long-term patterns of relating must be modified. Thus, effective treatment is based on a comprehensive assessment of the following issues. Therapists must evaluate the ways in which the original marital contract has either evolved or become rigidified over time. Therapists must assess the ways in which these early contracts, particularly regarding gender based role behaviors and expectations, facilitate or compromise a couple's ability to negotiate normal midlife transitions. Finally, therapists must assess the impact of the current existential and family life cycle challenges with which a particular midlife couple might be contending.

Given these goals, it is obvious that a comprehensive assessment process is required. However, midlife couples often present for treatment at points of critical distress, and in need of immediate change. Thus, it is essential that therapists use the process of assessment not only to gather information but also to intervene quickly to alleviate a couple's distress. This can be achieved if therapists instill a sense of hope by providing a new framework or lens with which the couple can begin to understand their current difficulties.

Distress Generated by the Impact of Social and Cultural Change: The Loss of a Single Expected Path

The social and cultural changes that have occurred during the lifetimes of today's midlife couples are significant and pervasive and can crate increased pressure for many people. The models of marriage to which these couples were exposed as they were raised led them to anticipate few significant changes in the midlife phase. This expectation did not prepare them for the world in which they now live. There is no longer one way to live a life or have the support of a community. Today all couples of the same age do not experience similar stages and tasks at the same time. Some midlife couples today may find themselves in well seasoned marriages with children leaving for college, whereas others may be facing the arrival of their first child. Still others may be starting their first, or even their third or fourth marriage.

This diversity of marital patterns differs significantly from the enormous homogeneity that distinguished the marriages of many of the parents of today' midlife couples. During earlier generations, marriage was expected to follow a well-worn and stable path, based on widely accepted assumptions. Marriage was, first and foremost, based on an expectation of security and permanency. Although men and women may have married for love and romance, they also expected that marriage meant "until death do us part." Certainly there were couples who did divorce in earlier generations, but they were the exception, not the rule. Marriage was also based on highly structured complementary gender roles. As husbands, men were expected to put opportunities for interpersonal growth, freedom, and personal discovery after their responsibility for the economic survival of a family. In exchange, they gained the support of their wives in managing relationships and in maintaining the basic fabric of their daily lives. As women focused on the needs and goals of their husbands and children, they traded their chances to have a career and to develop identities outside of their roles as wives and mothers. They, gained however, security and financial support in a world that offered them few alternative options. Although there was little room for flexibility, experimentation, or personal choice in these arrangements, most men and women believed that this particular quid pro quo was their key to happiness, fulfillment, and social respectability. And for many couples, for many years, it was.

The 1960s and 1970s, however, shook this basic and widely accepted foundation of marriage and family life. Divorce, earlier viewed as anathema, became both more common and more acceptable, and the previously assumed lifetime commitment of marriage became less and less certain. The women's movement also gained force during this period, working to expand the opportunities for women in a wide range of areas. Women began to gain greater control over their bodies through more effective birth control and access to the right to abortion, and they began to increase their participation in the labor force in record numbers.

These social changes challenged many of the basic assumptions about marriage and the roles of husband and wife. They opened a world of opportunities that few midlife men and women were prepared to face. Today, midlife couples experience fewer absolutes, fewer constraints, more choices, and more alternative paths. With so many available and acceptable options, couples lack singular, clear models for "making it at midlife," and must cope with the burden of choice. In this context of rapid social change, midlife couples experience greater room for growth and change, as well as greater vulnerability to dissonance and stress (Nadelson, Polonsky, & Mathews, 1979; Siegel, 1982). These social changes, combined with the individual and family developmental changes of midlife, can place extraordinary pressure on long term marriages.

Distress Generated by Individual Developmental Issues

A profound shift occurs at midlife for individuals who gain an increased awareness of their own mortality and of the swift passage of time. For some, this awareness comes slowly, through the many physical changes that accompany midlife. Menopause, reduced physical stamina, the sudden need for glasses, wrinkles, hair loss, and other body changes are often gradual but unavoidable reminders of the aging process. For others, the shift at midlife occurs abruptly as they confront an increased number of personal losses, and experience the aging, illness, or death of parents and other family members or friends, coming face-to-face with their own mortality. In these ways, many begin to realize, often for the first time in their lives, what Olympia Dukakis's character expressed to her philandering husband in the movie *Moonstruck*, "No matter where you go or what you do, you're going to die." This awareness of death can stimulate many people to review their past choices, often with an emphasis on the paths not taken, creating an increased sense of urgency to experience all that life has to offer. Individuals focus their attention on the need to find deeper meaning and examine their decisions and behaviors accordingly. Often, they discover that postponing dreams no longer makes sense and their priorities begin to change. Previously accepted assumptions go up for grabs, as relationships, careers, lifestyles, and earlier commitments are reevaluated.

These midlife experiences can have a profound effect on long-term marriages. Guttman (1991), in fact, suggests that parental death is an often unidentified precipitant to sudden marital conflict and distress in midlife. The midlife review process can place pressure on some long-term marriages, particularly if one or both partners have a tendency to blame their spouse for what they feel they have missed—the career they could have had, the trips they could have taken, the man or woman they could have become, and the other relationships or affairs they could have experienced. These past regrets can become idealized when they are compared to the many mundane aspects of everyday marital life. Blinded to what they have gained from past choices and compromises, spouses blame one another for what they feel they have lost.

The following case demonstrates the ways in which compromises made during the early years of marriage can reemerge during midlife with increased intensity, causing disruption in relationships as spouses blame one another for regrets about the past:

Martha and Alan presented for therapy in extreme marital distress that began when Martha found out about Alan's 7-month extramarital affair with a 25-year-old woman he met in his workplace. At the time, Martha was also reporting a variety of symptoms of anxiety and depression. The couple, who had three adult children (aged 28, 26, 21), had been married for 30 years and reported a relatively stable history with little overt conflict.

During assessment, two common midlife experiences that had occurred in Alan's life were identified. His father had recently become very ill and his younger brother had abruptly decided to divorce his wife of 25 years. Discussion of these events revealed the ways in which Alan's father's illness had increased his awareness of his own mortality and the ways in which his brother's divorce had allowed him to see that he had choices about his future. Responding to these experiences, Alan began to review his past choices, questioning in particular

the many years he had devoted to his successful career and to his roles as husband and father. He believed that he had sacrificed adventure and excitement, explaining that as a young child and adolescent, he had wanted to become a major league football player. He was, in fact, quite talented and had been identified by several scouts. However, instead of pursuing this dream, he had decided to attend college and later decided to pursue a graduate degree. At midlife, Alan began to blame Martha for these past decisions. He often told the story of his and Martha's wedding day. As Martha and he were driving from the ceremony to the reception, Alan requested that they take a detour past the ball field where he had often played. Martha recalled feeling concerned that Alan would regret his choice to give up the chance of an athletic career. Although at the time, Alan expressed little regret about his choice to marry Martha, he now found himself plagued by thoughts of "what if." He did not perceive himself as responsible for his early choice or take into account the many factors and circumstances that encouraged him to choose college, graduate school, and his present career over a chance at being a professional athlete. He also did not acknowledge the many ways he had grown and benefitted from his choices. Instead, he focused only on a sense of regret and held Martha and their marriage responsible, explaining that she and their marriage had held him back from the life he could have had. His narrow understanding of his unhappiness led him to believe that there was only one solution: divorce.

This case illustrates how the changes of midlife can stimulate an increasing awareness of one's own mortality, ushering in a midlife review process in which past choices and compromises are examined. Because many past choices have invariably involved some compromise between individual and relationship needs in most long-term marriages, this individual review process is vulnerable to becoming "painted" a couple's "color," which can diminish rather than enhance a sense of personal responsibility. This, in turn, can create bitterness and place overwhelming pressure on their marriage to make up for past losses and regrets. It can also deprive individuals of the heightened sense of personal meaning that can arise from directly confronting the existential challenges of midlife.

Distress Generated by Outdated Marital Contracts

During the early years of a long-term relationship, implicit and explicit agreements and specific patterns of relating are established. During these years, which are often focused on parenting and career building, it is difficult for spouses to have the time and energy necessary to engage in an ongoing review and revision of these agreements. Although allowing their marital relationship to coast on "automatic pilot" during this life phase is often adaptive, these couples are vulnerable to being left at midlife with rigid patterns of relating and outdated contracts. For many couples, midlife is the first time in decades that they have actively attended to what is going on in their relationship. What often brings them to therapy is being confronted with the difficulty of changing these contracts to meet their needs during the midlife phase.

Couples whose marriages have been based on traditional gender values can be particularly vulnerable to distress at midlife if one partner begins to adopt nontraditional expectations or roles. Such a shift in gender-role behavior is not uncommon during midlife. Jung (1960), in fact, postulated that, at midlife, men and women begin to balance personal characteristics that were previously skewed to accommodate to traditional societal expectations. Support for these notions has been provided by Gutmann's research (1975, 1985), which suggests that men and women in many cultures balance stereotypical gender role behavior at midlife. These internal shifts experienced by today's midlife men and women have been amplified by the enormous changes in social expectations brought about by the impact of the women's movement and changing economic circumstances. Thus, many midlife men who previously concentrated on mastery, achievement, and their careers, begin to develop the more emotional, nurturing aspects of their personalities. Women, on the other hand, often having spent the first half of their lives nurturing others and taking care of relationships, begin to focus more on achievement. These individual changes impact the marital relationship as the husband, whose wife has long been asking for more time and intimacy, finds that he is prepared to give them just at the time she is likely to be wanting less of them, just at the time when she is interested in devoting more time to activities outside the home. Moreover, the wife, whose husband has long suggested that she find something to do with herself, something that would place less pressure on the relationship, suddenly finds that as she finally has one foot out the door, her husband wants more time to "smell the roses" with her by his side.

Although these shifts are both normal and can promote positive change for both individuals and couples, they can also create tension and serious distress. Couples are particularly vulnerable if either spouse clings rigidly to the early contract in an effort to preserve the status quo, or if either one pushes for changes that are particularly sudden or extreme. Couples may become "out of sync" with one another in ways so pervasive that the basic fabric of their relationship is questioned. They can become easily overwhelmed as they find they must renegotiate almost every aspect of their lives, including financial issues, division of labor, maintenance of relationships, and patterns of intimacy. The need to revise the original contract in such extensive ways can leave couples wondering whether anything still remains to unite them. Spouses can feel betrayed by the sudden changes in the other, just when they thought they knew their partner and the rules.

The following case demonstrates the impact of one partner's dramatic departure from traditional gender roles and the original martial contract of midlife:

Justin, a 40-year-old vice president of a major international company called to request marital therapy on an emergency basis, explaining that his wife, Sally, was threatening to leave him and that he had no idea why. Agreeing to a 4-session assessment, Sally and Justin told the story of their marriage.

They married straight out of college. Sally was a bright and popular young woman with the usual dreams of the time: to marry, have children, and live happily ever after. Tall, blond, and handsome, Justin had recently been offered a job at a successful company and his prospects appeared promising. He was crazy about her, and if she wasn't exactly head over heels in love, she liked and respected him and thought he seemed to be a good candidate to fulfill her dreams. Their first few years together went smoothly. They lived in the town in which they both were raised and soon had a child. Sally committed herself to being the "perfect" wife and mother and joined the PTA, civic groups, and entertained Justin's business associates. Soon, Justin was offered what was to be the first of many promotions that required the family to relocate. Sally was unhappy with the prospect of moving, because she was attached to family, friends, and her community, but she never questioned her assumption that Justin's job came first. She swallowed her negative feelings and made the best of it. Two years and two children later, just as she had begun to adjust to their new community, Justin was again promoted, this time to a position in Europe. It was a plum that could not be passed up, so Sally packed up the kids and went along.

In Europe, Sally continued to entertain and made friends easily, but she never allowed herself to get too involved. She knew that another move was likely and that putting down roots only made it harder to leave. Justin worked long hours and often wasn't very available to her and the children, but he was a faithful husband, a good provider, and extremely successful. At times, Sally felt unsatisfied, but reminded herself that he didn't drink, gamble, abuse her, or run around. They continued to move every 3 or 4 years for 18 years, and Sally always went along without complaint.

As Sally approached her 40th birthday, she began to look back over the years of their marriage and feel enormous resentment. For the first time, she felt angry about all the sacrifices she had made for Justin and his career, all the ways in which she had neglected her own needs and feelings in order to accommodate to his. She looked at him one morning over breakfast and said she wanted a divorce. Justin was devastated. From his perspective, nothing in their lives had changed that could explain such a drastic declaration. He had done nothing that he hadn't done for all the years of their marriage: He was no less or more available, no less considerate, no less successful. He could not understand why she wanted out.

During therapy, Justin expressed his confusion, explaining that he never knew that Sally had negative feelings about any of these issues. He did not want to divorce and saw her current complaints as completely unreasonable. Sally, however, expressed a feeling of hopelessness about their future together. She did not believe she could begin to figure out her own needs and goals within the context of their marriage. Their roles had become too rigid, and her impulse to accommodate to Justin, too deeply ingrained. Their traditional contract could not, in Sally's view, accommodate the changes she was seeking in midlife.

Several issues contributed to a poor prognosis for this marriage. Sally spent 18 years not expressing her anger, so that when she saw the various paths and adventures taken by women in a society that was allowing more autonomy for women, she was unprepared to handle her own rage over what she felt she had sacrificed. Moreover, Sally and Justin had lived so long with the automatic assumption that his needs and career came first, that they had no structure for conflict resolution or negotiation.

Distress Generated by Family Life-Cycle Issues

The midlife phase of a long-term marriage typically coincides with the family life-cycle phases of parenting and launching adolescents that have the potential to place additional emphasis, and sometimes stress, on the marital relationship. There is a large and growing number of both cross-sectional and longitudinal studies suggesting a curvilinear pattern in which marital satisfaction declines during the childrearing years, reaches a lowest point during the children's adolescence, and then increases in the postparental period (Rollins & Cannon, 1974; Schram, 1979; Spanier & Lewis, 1980; Glenn & McLanahan, 1982; Olson et al., 1983; Lee, 1988; Rollins, 1989). There are numerous theories regarding this decrease in marital satisfaction. Rollins (1989) suggests that the pattern relates generally to the responsibilities of parenting, as couples neglect needs for marital communication and companionship to meet parenting demands. White, Booth, and Edwards, (1986) suggest that marital satisfaction declines because parenting reduces time for marital interaction, financial achievement, and satisfaction with the division of labor in the home. Olson et al. (1983) theorize that much of the marital stress associated with midlife derives from a "pileup" phenomenon, whereby stressor events increase during earlier phases of childrearing, reaching an all-time high when children become teenagers.

The specific challenges of parenting adolescents can also place unique pressures on couples who are in midlife (Kidwell, Fischer, Dunham, & Baranowski, 1983). As these couples become increasingly aware of their own mortality and the sense of limited options, adolescents can bring their parents' forgotten dreams and past compromises into sharp focus. Adolescence is a time when the opportunities of life seem endless and one's personal power invincible; it is also a period of emerging sexuality. The passion that adolescents bring to both relationships and life can intensify midlife's existential issues regarding physical aging and sexuality. These issues may influence the standards by which couples judge their own satisfaction, causing them to wonder about the passion that is likely to have faded over the years in their own relationship. This phenomenon was well captured in Ethel Person's comments on the novel *Endless Love* in her book *Dreams of Love and Fateful Encounters* (1988):

... although Rose was not in love with him Arthur had adjusted to his marriage and accepted his lot in life, up until the time his own son fell in love and reminded him of what he was missing.

Adolescents, however, can also challenge their parents in far more direct and overt ways. Adolescents are, in fact, prone to challenge the meaning and relevance of nearly everything for which their parents stand. These judgements are often severe and penetrating. Ann Tyler's *Breathing Lessons* (1988) contains the following account of a mother talking about her adolescent daughter:

> You know what she told me the other day? I was testing out this tuna casserole. I served it up for supper and I said, "Isn't it delicious? Tell me honestly what you think." And Daisy said—Daisy just sat there and studies me for the longest time, with this kind of . . . fascinated expression on her face, and then she said, "Mom? Was there a certain conscious point in your life when you decided to settle for being ordinary?" (p. 43)

A few careless words from a 14-year-old, and suddenly midlife couples may unwittingly find themselves face-to-face with the compromises they made and the dreams they lost along the way ("When did we settle for being ordinary?" "Have we lived a second-rate life?" "Is it too late to fix it?").

Fortunately, and not surprisingly, marital satisfaction does appear to improve following launching of these adolescent children. Although this period, "the empty nest," has been commonly portrayed as one of the most depressing hallmarks of midlife, particularly for women, research seems to indicate otherwise (see Glenn, 1975; Lowenthal & Chiriboga, 1972; White & Edwards, 1990). In fact, women commonly encounter their empty nests with a sense of relief. The postparental stage seems to offer both men and women the opportunity to refocus the energy, which they had previously devoted to raising their children, on themselves and on their relationship. Many find that they are also less burdened by the financial pressures that dominated their childrearing years.

It should also be noted, however, that despite the relief most couples eventually experience in the postparental stage, the anticipation of, and immediate transition to, this stage can be particularly stressful for midlife couples. It is, in fact, often immediately during or preceding this transition that couples present for therapy. Adjusting to the impending postparental stage requires couples to make enormous shifts in their relationship. Many couples, whose roles as parents dominated their interactions for years, find that both the "glue" that held them together and the "buffer" that kept them apart are removed as their children are launched. They must refocus on one another to meet interpersonal needs, and may even have to become reacquainted with who their partner is as a person. If there are long-term conflicts that were not resolved during earlier years due to parenting demands, this stage can be particularly difficult, a struggle captured well in the following lines by Tillie Olson (1976):

> How deep back the stubborn, gnarled roots of the quarrel reached, no one could say—but only now, when tending to the needs of others no longer shackles them together, the roots swelled up visible, split the earth between them . . . (p. 86)

The following case illustrates the ways in which a couple was thrown into crisis as they anticipated the launching of their adolescent daughter:

Beth, a 39-year-old social worker, and Martin, a 41-year-old professor, had been married for 18 years when they were referred for marital therapy by the family therapist, whom they had consulted for help with their oldest daughter's (age 16) relatively mild symptoms of anxiety and depression. Because their daughter's main complaint during this consultation session was that her father wouldn't communicate and that she felt that she had to be her parents' marriage counselor, marital therapy was recommended.

During initial marital sessions, it became clear that Beth and Martin had a long history of chronic marital unhappiness. They had rarely overtly addressed or resolved conflicts over the years of their marriage, and tensions still existed from unresolved arguments that had occurred decades earlier. In therapy, Beth stated that she had always wanted Martin to be more physically affectionate and emotionally expressive while Martin explained that he wanted Beth to be less "controlling." Recently, their feelings of frustration with one another had significantly increased. Beth felt particularly discouraged and angry with Martin, overtly expressing for the first time feelings of hopelessness about the future of their marriage.

The assessment process revealed that the pressure on the relationship was increased, in large part, by the fact that their oldest daughter was preparing to apply to college and leave home. Although their younger daughter was only 11, they perceived their oldest daughter's departure as the indicator that their parenting years were coming to a close. They acknowledged anxiety about the loss of their roles as parents and about how their marriage would survive in their daughter's absence. Beth had also recently experienced the death of a close friend through cancer, a loss that compounded the intensity of her feelings about anticipating the loss of her daughter.

These changes triggered a disruption in the unsatisfying but stable patterns of relating that Beth and Martin had adopted over their years of parenting. Beth, in particular, felt motivated to try to fulfill her emotional needs through her relationship with Martin. This was the first time in years that she had sought out Martin in these ways. When he did not respond to her advances, Beth felt increasingly frustrated with him. He, in turn, felt that she had become hypercritical and was "nagging" him more than ever. Anticipating their daughter's departure had reinitiated their early and unresolved conflicts regarding patterns of intimacy that had been submerged during their years of active parenting, as Beth focused primarily on caring for their children.

Couples who have not had children do not face the struggles illustrated in cases like that of Beth and Martin; however, they must also negotiate midlife issues raised by the family life cycle. Midlife forces couples without children to confront the permanency of childlessness in their lives. With time running out on their "biological clocks" and the policies of adoption agencies, who give preference to younger couples, early midlife is likely to be the last chance they have to create a family. At this point, they must question how important parenting is to each of them individually and to their relationship. If couples have delayed confronting an underlying disagreement about whether to have children, the coming of midlife adds a time pressure that makes such conflicts harder to avoid. Couples who decide to have children at midlife can benefit from their years of experience and maturity, but they also face the unique challenge of adjusting to parenting at a time of life when they may have less energy, and when they may feel "out of sync" with many of their friends who are launching children. As both partners are likely to have well-developed careers or at least long-term work histories by midlife, they must also confront the difficult issues involved in negotiating professional and parenting responsibilities (Gilbert & Davidson, 1989).

Some couples who decide to have children at midlife face the possibility that conceiving will not be easy, and may even be impossible. The treatment of infertility is emotionally draining and stressful to the relationship, particularly if one partner is more committed to the process than the other. Couples who are unable to have children must often mourn lost dreams; and women, in particular, must come to terms with the response from a society that strongly links a woman's femininity and maturity to her status as a mother. The following case illustrates the ways in which dealing with these issues of childbearing at midlife can place stress on a marriage:

Jane and Henry presented for marital therapy with questions about divorce. They reported that most of their years together had been happy, but that once they reached midlife, they had begun to experience high levels of both conflict and distance. The assessment process revealed that this distress stemmed primarily from their feelings about childbearing and their experience of infertility. When Jane and Henry married, it was his second marriage, but her first. He had children from a previous marriage and wasn't particularly interested in having more. But he loved her and said if she really wanted a baby, he would go along. Soon after the wedding, however, he began to postpone such plans. He loved to travel and wanted Jane to be with him. Their lifestyle really couldn't incorporate children without major revisions. At first she didn't push the issue much, but as she approached midlife, she began to worry that her biological clock was running out. When she turned 38, Henry agreed, somewhat reluctantly, to have a child, and they began trying to conceive. After a year without results, they both went for tests and began a series of complicated and painful processes. Jane was placed on fertility drugs, and they began to try to have sex on schedule, when she was most likely to be fertile. The strain on their sex life was considerable and Henry claimed that the romance had been taken out of it. Jane became withdrawn from Henry because, as she explained in therapy, she felt that he wasn't really trying and never wanted a baby to begin with. She also revealed that she felt like a failure as a woman because she couldn't have a baby, and because she now felt that she couldn't keep her husband happy either. Henry thought she was depressed and moody all the time, and couldn't understand why she couldn't just let the whole thing be. Although Jane and Henry had been able to avoid dealing with their different feelings about childbearing during the early years of their marriage, the coming midlife and their experience of infertility pushed the issue to the center of their lives, causing great distress and disruption.

The other family life-cycle issue that gains prominence during the midlife years concerns relationships, not between midlife couples and their children, but between midlife couples and their parents. At midlife, couples today are facing an increasing need to provide care for aging parents, leading to a growing recognition of midlife couples as belonging to the "sandwich generation," caught between needs of the younger and older generations. A national survey of family caregivers of the elderly demonstrated that caregivers are, by and large, mostly female, middle-aged, white and married, fully one third of them being the adult children of the elderly (Stone, Cafferata, & Sangl, 1987). The impact of increased life expectancy, increased medical technology—leading to a shift from acute to chronic illness—and a public policy emphasis on family caregiving versus institutional care has contributed to this growing pressure placed on midlife adult children; this pressure is also increased by declining family size that reduce the number of individuals who can share caretaking responsibilities (Beigel, Sales, & Schultz, 1991). These changes have led some researchers to conclude that the caretaking needs of elderly parents are, in fact, surpassing the demands of caring for children (Beigel et al., 1991). Although caregiving for parents can provide positive opportunities for strengthening intergenerations bonds (Chiriboga, 1986b), the financial, physical, and emotional demands of caring for elderly parents, who increasingly require significant medical care, can also be enormously difficult for midlife couples to negotiate. These demands are further complicated by the fact that many couples have, during the years spent raising their children, looked forward to reaping the benefits of the "empty nest," and by the fact that an increasing number of women, who have traditionally done the real work of caretaking, are now in, or are joining, the labor force at midlife.

SPECIFIC INTERVENTIONS

This approach aims to help couples navigate the many challenges of midlife described previously by using therapeutic interventions to help them redefine their past, present, and future. Interventions to redefine the past attempt to decrease patterns of blaming and enhance individual responsibility for past choices. Interventions focused on redefining the present attempt to enable couples to broaden their understanding of their current distress to include the impact of midlife issues, thereby decreasing the responsibility placed on marriage to solve all of their problems. Interventions to redefine the future help couples to modify goals and dreams and make the necessary changes in their marital contract in order to achieve them.

The use of reframing is a critical intervention with midlife couples to achieve the goals of redefinition. Reframes based on individual and family developmental understanding can help couples shift their perspective, thus increasing their openness to the possibilities of change. For this reason, reframing provides the basic foundation of this approach. However, within this context, other interventions are also utilized. These interventions draw from models of marital therapy, ranging from behavioral and cognitive approaches to those that emphasize family-of-origin issues. Because these interventions have been well defined elsewhere, they will not be described in detail here. Instead, attention will be given primarily to the use of reframing to build the developmental framework in which midlife issues can be addressed in a variety of ways.

Redefining the Past

A focus on reframing the past is important in helping spouses redefine their choices in ways that help them let go of painful experiences, "bad" choices, lost dreams, and hopes. Individuals often find that they have more energy and less resistance to working on the present and the future if they can look back on their past with a focus on the ways in which they have grown and learned, rather than on the ways in which they have suffered and lost. Although past events obviously cannot be changed, an individual's perception of these events and their implications for the present and future can be redefined. This can be achieved primarily through the use of reframes that help individuals appreciate the contexts in which they made past choices, and help them understand the ways in which these choices made sense at the time. If individuals feel less guilt and regret about the past, they are more likely to see themselves as responsible for their choices and are less likely to blame their spouses.

The following case demonstrates how reframing was used to redefine the past in a way that decreased blaming patterns in the marriage and resistance to engaging in marital therapy:

Morgan and Joe had been married for 30 years when they presented for marital therapy. They reported that they had had a relationship without significant conflict but also without much joy. Morgan resented her decision to marry Joe, whom she perceived as a serious compromise made necessary by the fact that she saw herself as "damaged goods" because she had been sexually abused as a child. She also felt bitter about the fact that they had moved into his parents' home right after the wedding, and had lived there most of their married life. They were, she saids, treated like brother and sister, with his intrusive mother monitoring everything about their lives, including any sexual relationship that could have blossomed, but clearly didn't. Morgan saw Joe as limited and sometimes crude, but also knew that he asked little of her and expected little in their relationship, and was dependable and loyal. They got by without crises until their only son married and Joe's parents died. At that time, Morgan began to have what came to be a series of medical problems and serious depression requiring hospitalization. She began to think seriously about the paths not taken, and increasingly began to resent Joe and the years she had spent in their marriage.

At the time they came to therapy, Morgan was ready to leave Joe, claiming that her decision to marry him 30 years earlier had been a mistake that now must be corrected. She reported that he had brought her 30 years of unhappiness. Joe was devastated and wanted to do anything he could to save the marriage.

Morgan's level of anger and resentment about the past created a sense of bitterness toward Joe, hopelessness about their future, and resistance even to becoming involved in marital therapy. To begin work with Morgan, much less their marriage, it was necessary to help her develop a more useful view of herself and her past. Morgan was out of touch with her own strengths, as well as anything good about Joe or their marriage. The therapist chose to reframe her past decisions as good ones for her survival at the time, emphasizing the ways in which they made sense in the context of her background and her needs as a young woman. The goal was to help her forgive herself and Joe, and to test whether there was a strong enough foundation between them to work on their marriage if the blame and bitterness could be dissipated.

After listening to their accounts of the history of the marriage, the therapist offered the following reframe of Morgan's experience of not being protected from sexual abuse as a child and her later decision to marry Joe.

THERAPIST: Nobody was there for you at a time when every little girl deserves to have someone there for her. Nobody was there to protect you, no one was there to help you, no one was there for you to talk to, so you learned to keep it all in and to do it yourself. I think that you learned that so well that is was hard to give up when it was time to give it up. And I think that, in part, you chose Joe because he was the perfect man for you. I don't think you thought it at the time, but it isn't at all surprising that there was no big romance between you. You chose Joe because he wasn't going to push you too hard to share those kinds of things that you weren't willing to share with anybody. On some level, you weren't ready to trust being sexual and you knew Joe wasn't either. I think the other reason you might have chose Joe is for his family. (*Laughs, as Morgan looks very skeptical.*) I'm just guessing now, but I don't think it's any accident you moved in with his folks right after the wedding. I think they were the family you never had, a family that could be there for you.

MORGAN: But I didn't choose that. Joe chose that.

THERAPIST: Yes, you didn't choose that. But you chose Joe and you knew what Joe was about. And, in a way, I think as negative as living with a bossy mother-in-law may have been, it was a kind of belonging that you never had growing up. It made a place in your life for something you never got. I think at that point you were willing to give up the romance for that, because you needed that more. You didn't get it as a little girl, and if you don't get it, it's till there as an aching need. You didn't get romance with the choice you made, but you got parenting and security, which you instinctively knew you needed.

This reframe gave Morgan a new perspective, enabling her to see herself, not as a passive victim of life, but as a person in a position of power, capable of making choices that were good for her survival. In this way, reframing laid the foundation for further interventions by decreasing patterns of blame and creating a greater sense of hope about the marriage.

Redefining the Present

In order to redefine the present, therapists must help couples to shift their understanding of current problems to include the impact of developmental issues. Many couples enter therapy with a narrow definition of their distress. They often focus exclusively on the marriage as the source and therefore the solution to all of their current unhappiness and dissatisfaction. They lack an appreciation for the ways in which social change, existential challenges, gender-role shifts, and family life-cycle changes are influencing their marital functioning. In therapy, these basic, underlying issues can become obscured by the details of a couple's presenting problems, making it necessary for the therapist to introduce and emphasize the importance of the developmental perspective. Again, this is achieved primarily by the use of reframing. Developmental reframes can instill a sense of hope by helping couples see their current struggles as only a part of their long-term history, reminding them that they have weathered difficult times in the past. Also, these reframes can normalize distress and, most importantly, relieve the marriage of the burden of being exclusively responsible for the impact of all of midlife's changes.

The following case, introduced earlier, illustrates the use of reframing to help to shift a couple's focus from the presenting problem to the underlying midlife issues.

A major focus of treatment with Martha and Alan was reframing Alan's affair and the distress they were experiencing as reactions to midlife issues. In particular, the therapist emphasized the way in which they were each experiencing midlife's challenges in ways that were "out of sync" with one another. Martha was mourning the passing of her active mothering years and struggling with the transition to the empty nest. She was grieving the loss of the security of her role as homemaker, which she felt was slipping away. In contrast, the therapist explained, Alan's father's illness and his brother's divorce had heralded an intense need for him to recapture the sense of adventure and excitement he felt he had sacrificed for his work and family responsibilities. Far from mourning the coming of midlife, Alan was relishing it.

Redefining their present difficulties in this way allowed Martha to feel less hurt and personally rejected by Alan's affair, as she developed a greater understanding of the issues with which Alan was struggling. Alan also began to see his desire to have an affair with a younger woman in a new light. A crucial turning point in therapy occurred when Alan called the therapist between sessions, asking whether he would really be happier if he left Martha. He was able to recognize that pursuing an affair or ending his relationship with Martha would not "fix" his growing sense of mortality or his awareness of the swift passage of time.

In addition, Alan was able to begin to appreciate that Martha needed more time to adjust to their new postparental lifestyle. she was not unwilling to share in his future dreams, but she did require more time to grieve the loss of their past and prepare for upcoming years. Understanding Martha's feelings allowed Alan to recognize the positive aspects of their marriage and family life, which in turn reduced his sense of regret for his early choices and his tendency to blame Martha.

As this case demonstrates, highlighting developmental issues can open a couple to new avenues of change that would have remained blocked had the therapist allowed the couple to maintain their narrow definition of the presenting problem.

Redefining the Future

Once couples have a more useful view of the past and a broader understanding of the present, the task of therapy is to help them envision realistic dreams for the future and develop the skills necessary to achieve them. Often this involves evaluating and revising the marital contract and assessing which of their needs and goals they can meet within the marriage and which are best met by each partner learning to pursue other activities and relationships. As couples are helped to let go of dreams that are no longer realistic, they become more open to the option of creating new ones for their future. Towards this end, behavioral and problem-solving interventions may be indicated. For example, after midlife dilemmas have been explored and highlighted, therapists may ask couples to write out an updated list of their current needs and goals. These goals can be used by therapists to design behavioral tasks to help couples to implement the specific changes they seek.

In the following case, introduced earlier, the therapist worked to help the couple clarify their current needs, to assess the degree to which they could be met in the marriage, and then assigned tasks to allow them to achieve these goals:

When Beth and Martin began treatment, they explained that they had been in marital therapy 5 years earlier. With this therapist, they had focused on trying to learn new communication skills, but reported that these efforts are largely unsuccessful in changing their level of bitterness or dissatisfaction with one another. As a result, the current therapist chose to place an emphasis on helping Beth and Martin to be more realistic about what needs they would be able to have met within their marriage. Instead of working to teach new skills in relating to one another, the therapist focused on highlighting the ways in which their marriage had been successful, particularly in terms of their success in creating a family together. Simultaneously, however, interventions focused on generating alternative ways in which they could fulfill some of their old dreams. In particular, Beth was encouraged to develop other relationships to meet some of her needs for intimacy, reinvesting in friendships with other women that she had not had time to develop during her active parenting years. This reduced the intensity of the emotional needs that she had been asking Martin to fulfill which, in turn, gave Martin the opportunity to identify and act on his own needs for intimacy. Specific tasks were designed for him to initiate intimate, emotional contact with Beth between sessions (i.e., planning a birthday celebration for Beth, planning a weekend outing, etc.). These interventions created the basis for new patterns of relating and intimacy that Beth and Martin were able to build on over time.

THERAPISTS' ISSUES

The personal and professional characteristics of a therapist impact the process of therapy with couples at all life-cycle stages. In working with midlife couples in particular, however, one of the most significant issues concerns the therapist's own age and life experience. Both inexperienced, young therapists and those with many years of life and professional experience possess certain strengths and are vulnerable to certain pitfalls. It is important for therapists to develop an awareness of the ways in which these issues influence therapy, because treatment with midlife couples is not likely to follow a highly structured format. Because midlife issues do not lend themselves to a series of clear treatment stages of predictable groups of interventions, more latitude exists for therapists to impose their own issues and agendas.

Young therapists have the advantage of enthusiasm, energy, and optimism—qualities that can be contagious. They often have not had enough experience to cause them to believe that what they are trying to do cannot be done. They thus approach even the most challenging of cases with an unparalleled eagerness and excitement. A young therapist, however, also carries the burden of having to establish credibility with couples who often see him/her as not much older, and thus not automatically wiser, than their children. For this reason, it is important for these less experienced therapists to try to sensitize themselves to dealing with common midlife themes: loss, the failing health of parents, emancipated children, and the existential pressures born of a sense of time running out. Listening closely to these concerns and providing evidence that they have heard the issues and have understood their meaning for each partner goes a long ways toward establishing their credibility with the couple for a positive therapeutic relationship.

Young therapists must also be careful that, in their enthusiasm, they do not fall into the trap of trying to do too much, fixing things midlife couples do not want to fix, or do not even define as a problem (Anderson & Stewart 1983). A carefully negotiated contract that respects the couple's own priorities is vital, because it provides some protection against the therapist's own issues becoming primary. Therapists must leave the responsibility for change with each individual, and carefully avoid giving answers, even when they think they know them. The role of the marital therapist is that of a guide who helps to contain the anxiety generated by discussing painful and threatening issues, while providing a safe place for the couple to take the risk to hash them out.

Midlife therapists bring their own set of skills and advantages. They possess life experiences and wisdom, and they often benefit from a greater sense of mastery and competence in their work. These factors often allow midlife therapists to gain automatic credibility with midlife couples, thereby minimizing potential early resistance to therapy. However, midlife therapists may also be vulnerable to undermining these strengths by exposing bitterness, hopelessness, or jaded views of life that have grown from their own battles in insurmountable problems over time. They must guard against setting too limited goals, giving up too easily, and inappropriately imposing the solutions that have worked for them on the couples they treat.

Finally, both younger and older therapists, at least in part, must have come to grips with their own mortality, because this issue is central to many of the struggles of midlife couples. Effective therapy at this life-cycle stage requires an ability to deal directly with the pain of loss through death, abandonment, broken dreams, and lost chances. Unless therapists have faced these issues in their own lives, they will be uncomfortable with the pain inherent in discussing them, moving too quickly to reassurance or resolution. It also helps the course of therapy if therapists have been able to obtain or maintain a respect for the mystery and impermanence of life, the unknown and the unknowable. This diminishes the likelihood that therapists will offer easy answers or try to cure life—approaches that are bound to meet with resistance for most midlife couples

CONCLUSION

For many long-term marriages, midlife is a time of tremendous challenge. The impact of unexpected social change, outdated early contracts, and individual and family life-cycle issues can create marital distress and disruption. Yet, midlife can also be a period of great opportunity. By redefining the past, present, and future, therapy can help couples to gain strength from their early years together and create new visions for the second half of life. Therapists can help couples to let go of lost dreams and patterns of blame and bitterness to gain increased satisfaction in their own lives and in their relationship.

REFERENCES

Anderson, C. M. & Stewart, S. (1983). *Mastering resistance: A practical guide to family therapy.* New York: Guilford Press.

Beigel, D. E., Sales, E., & Schulz, R. (1991). *Family caregiving in chronic illness.* Newbury Park, CA: Sage.

Carter, E., & McGoldrick, M. (1989). *The changing family life cycle.* Boston: Alllyn & Bacon.

Chiriboga, D. A. (1989a). Mental health and the midpoint: Crisis, challenge, or relief? In S. Hunter and M. Sundel (Eds.) *Midlife myths: Issues, findings and practice implications* (pp. 116–144). Newbury Park, CA: Sage.

Chiriboga, D. A. (1989b). Stress and loss in middle age. In R. Kalish (Ed.), *Midlife loss: Coping strategies* (pp. 42–88). Newbury Park, CA: Sage.

Collins, R. (1985). *Sociology of marriage and the family.* Chicago, IL: Nelson-Hall.

Falicov, C. J. (1988). *Family transitions: Continuity and change over the life cycle.* New York: Guilford Press.

Gilbert, L. A., & Davidson, S. (1989). Dual career families at midlife. In S. Hunter & M. Sundel (Eds.), *Midlife myths: Issues, findings and practice implications* (pp. 195–209). Newbury Park, CA: Sage.

Glenn, N. D. (1975). Psychological well-being in the post parental stage: Some evidence from national surveys. *Journal of Marriage and the Family, 37,* 105–110.

Glenn, N. D., & McLanahan, S. (1982). Children and marital happiness: A further specification of the relationship. *Journal of Marriage and the Family, 44,* 63–72.

Gutmann, D. (1975). Parenthood: A key to the comparative study of the life cycle. In N. Datan & L. H. Ginsberg (Eds.), *Lifespan developmental psychology: Normative life crises* (pp. 167–184). New York: Academic Press.

Gutmann, D. (1985). The parental imperative revisited: Towards a developmental psychology of adulthood and later life. *Contributions to Human Development, 14,* 31–60.

Guttman, H. A. (1991). Parental death as a precipitant of marital conflict in middle age. *Journal of Marriage and Family Therapy, 17,* 81–87.

Jung, C. G. (1960). The stages of life. In *Collected works: Vol. 8. The structure and dynamics of the psyche.* New York: Pantheon.

Kidwell, J., Fischer, J. L., Dunham, R. M., & Baranowski, M. (1983). Parents and adolescents: Push and pull of change. In H. I. McCubbin & C. R. Figley (Eds.), *Stress and the family: Vol. 1. Coping with normative transitions* (pp. 74–89). New York: Brunner/Mazel.

Lee, G. R. (1988). Marital satisfaction in later life: The effects of non-marital roles. *Journal of Marriage and the Family, 50,* 775–783.

Lowenthal, M. F. & Chiriboga, D. (1972). Transition to the empty mest: Crisis, challenge, or relief? *Archives of General Psychiatry, 26,* 8–14.

Nadelson, C. C., Polonsky, D. C. & Mathews, M. A. (1979). Marriage and midlife: The impact of social change. *Journal of Clinical Psychiatry, 40,* 292–298.

Olsen, T. (1976). *Tell me a riddle.* New York: Dell.

Olson D. E., McCubbin, H. I., Barnes, H., Larsen, A., Muxen, M., & Wilson, M. (1983). *Families: What makes them work.* Newbury Park, CA: Sage.

Person, E. S. (1988). *Dreams of love and fateful encounters: The power of romantic passion.* New York: Norton.

Rollins, B. C. (1989). Marital quality at midlife. In S. Hunter & M. Sundel (Eds.), *Midlife myths: Issues, findings and practice implications* (pp. 184–194). Newbury Park, CA: Sage.

Rollins, B. C., & Cannon, K. L. (1974). Marital satisfaction over the family life cycle: A reevaluation. *Journal of Marriage and the Family, 36,* 271–282.

Schram, R. W. (1979). Marital satisfaction over the life cycle: A critique and proposal. *Journal of Marriage and the Family, 41,* 7–12.

Seigel, R. J. (1982). The long-term marriage: Implications for therapy. *Women and Therapy*, 1(1), 3–11.

Spanier, G. B., & Lewis, R. A. (1980). Marital quality: A review of the seventies. *Journal of Marriage and the Family*, 42, 825–839.

Stone, R., Cafferata, G. L., & Sangl, J. (1987). Caregivers of the frail elderly: A national profile. *Gerontologist*, 27, 616–626.

Turner, N. W. (1980). Divorce in midlife: Clinical implications and applications. In H. Norman & T. J. Scaramella (Eds.), *Midlife: Developmental and clinical issues* (pp. 149–177). New York: Brunner/Mazel.

Tyler, A. (1988). *Breathing Lessons*. New York: Knopf.

White, L. K., Booth, A., & Edwards, J. N. (1986). Children and marital happiness. Why negative correlation? *Journal of Family Issues*, 7, 131–147.

White, L., & Edwards J. N. (1990). Emptying the nest and parental well-being: An analysis of national panel data. *American Sociological Review*, 55, 235–242.

13

Gendered Aspects of Marital Therapy

CHERYL RAMPAGE

There is by now a very considerable body of
well-authenticated research to show that there really are
two marriages in every marital union, and that they do
not always coincide.
—BERNARD (1982, p. 5)

A FEMINIST CRITIQUE OF MARRIAGE

The core of a feminist critique of marriage is that,
as an institution, marriage has privileged men at
women's expense. Furthermore, the critique
holds, this discrepancy of advantage has been obfuscated by the promulgation of a myth that
women are the main beneficiaries of marriage.
This paradox has made it difficult for any particular woman to call into question the perceived
inequities of her marital relationship. The ideology underpinning this discrepancy in power and
privilege according to sex is called "patriarchy,"
a sociopolitical philosophy that considers men,
by virtue of their anatomy, more fit than wom-
en to rule and control in all domains of public
and private life (de Beauvoir, 1953; Lerner,
1986).

The effect of patriarchy on marriage has been
to reify the categories of "male" and "female" by
prescribing rigidly differentiated roles to each.
Thus breadwinning, car repair, and carving the
Thanksgiving turkey became associated with the
husband's role in the family, whereas homemaking, raising children, and creating a facilitating
environment for all family members became a
wife's job. Of the many differences prescribed under patriarchy, two are most salient: first, the
tasks women do are more private, and therefore
receive less recognition in the public world. Conversely, men's roles position them so as to be noticed in the world, to have their contribution
publicly acknowledged and appreciated. Second,
to the extent that wives' roles facilitate other
peoples' development and well-being rather than
their own, women as wives have seldom been
able to pursue their own personal agendas or to
demonstrate their own nonfamilial talents. The
pain and frustration associated with this condition has long been the theme of a branch of literature written by women (see, e.g., Gilman's *The
Yellow Wallpaper* [1973], Chopin's *The Awakening* [1977], or de Beauvoir's *The Second Sex*
[1953]), but it was not until *The Feminine Mystique* (Friedan, 1963) was published that a feminist dialogue about marriage began in earnest in
the United States.

As Friedan and others have noted (cf. Bernard,
1982; Dobash & Dobash, 1979; Hochschild,
1989; Rubin, 1976; Russell, 1982), marriage frequently has not been good for women. Whereas
married men live longer, are more healthy, and
suffer less depression than unmarried men, almost
the exact opposite is true for women. Far from

the stereotype of spinsters (never-married women) being miserable and unhappy, women who are not married actually have a lower incidence of emotional as well as physical illness.

In spite of ideology to the contrary, marriage has not assured women of physical safety (Dutton, 1988). Women are in greater danger of being physically and sexually abused by their husbands than by other, nonrelated men. Between 18% and 36% of all women in the United States are physically abused by a male partner at some time in their lives (Straus & Gelles, 1986), 14% are raped by their husbands (Russell, 1982), and thousands are murdered by their male partners or ex-partners every year.

Given the many serious disadvantages that marriage holds for women, how does it retain its appeal? The answer to this question requires a hard look at the alternatives available to women. Historically, those alternatives have been very limited, particularly given the lack of economic parity women experienced in the workplace, and the limited control they had over their reproductive capacity until well into this century. But it is more than economic and reproductive constraints that have kept women in the thrall of marriage. Rather, marriage has retained its popularity among women largely because of a widespread and powerful myth that it is the prerequisite and guarantee to a "happy ever after" sort of life, and because of a lack of a positive alternative vision of what adult female life could be.

It is not marriage per se that has been so appealing, but rather marriage as a myth or narrative, an outline within which women have constructed their particular marriages and lives. A primary difference between men and women is the availability of diverse life narratives. Whereas men can construct their lives according to many cultural narratives, such as poet, adventurer, hero, priest, or wise man, women's narratives largely have been confined to two types, both defined by marital status (Heilbrun, 1988).

The marriage narrative promotes a vision of woman as wife, supporting and nurturing husband and children and finding both identity and satisfaction in doing so. The alternative narrative casts woman as spinster, witch, old maid, or any of a number of other equally unattractive characters, all defined primarily by the lack of a husband and the social ostracism that accompanies such a degraded status.

Women (and men) are exposed to the marriage narrative in an endless variety of ways, beginning early in childhood. Fairy tales that end with beautiful young women being shepherded by handsome young princes into that "happy ever after" life are just one of the numerous and ubiquitous ways that the narrative is revealed to children. Religious doctrine, popular culture, public policy, and moral philosophy have all been used to promote marriage as the feminine ideal.

Feminists argue that the sad, stark truth about marriage is that it is *the* primary vehicle of female subordination. As Miller (1986) argues, marriage creates a union of two people of clearly unequal power. The demographics alone are revealing: On average, men marry women who are smaller, younger, less educated and less materially wealthy than themselves. These differences contribute to the truly significant distinction between husbands and wives: a difference in power. The loss of her name, the right to say no to sex, and the right to possess independent wealth, are but a few of the ways that women have historically been disempowered by marriage. Although some of the most blatantly unfair consequences of marriage for women have been modified in the past two decades, the asymmetry of the burden marriage creates for men and women continues (Hochschild, 1989). Women feel responsible for both the practical aspects of marital life (i.e., managing the household, children, social life, and relations with both extended families) and the emotional and intimate health of the relationship.

A feminist vision of marriage is founded on the notion of the relationship as a partnership of equals (Eisler, 1987; Pogrebin, 1983; Miller, 1986; Napier, 1988), each of whom feels accountable to the relationship and responsible for maintaining it. In such a relationship each partner has equal access to opportunities and rewards, while sacrifices and responsibilities are also equally distributed.

A FEMINIST CRITIQUE OF MARITAL THERAPY

Critiques of marital and family therapy can be found in much of the feminist scholarship that has been published in the field during the past decade (e.g., see Goldner, 1985; Goodrich, Rampage, Ellman, & Halstead, 1988; James & McIntyre, 1983; Luepnitz, 1988; Margolin, Fernandez, Talovic, & Onorato, 1983; McGoldrick, Anderson, & Walsh, 1989; Walters, Carter, Papp, & Silverstein, 1988). These authors challenge the notion that marital therapists are any less contaminated by sexist bias than the rest of the population raised in this patriarchal culture. As sexism has informed the making of individual marital relationships, it has also informed the making of theories, both about marriage and about marital therapy. The central tenet of the feminist critique of marital therapy is that it has not addressed, and at times has even obfuscated, differences in power between marital partners. Such power differences, whether at the level of financial resources or sheer physical strength, will inevitably affect all other aspects of the marital relationship.

Several of the concepts that have been crucial in the adaptation of systems theory to marital relationships have simultaneously served to render the role of power invisible in marriage. "Complementarity," for example, has commonly been used to describe the interdependency of distinct and seemingly independent patterns of marital partners. Complementary roles in marriage are held to be a normal, even desirable, system of managing the many varied tasks and responsibilities of married life. But, embedded in the notion of complementarity is the premise that all tasks and roles are divided fairly, that both partners are equally free to choose their tasks and roles, and that any apparent differences in status, power, or privilege of partners are offset at a deeper structural level by actual parity. Furthermore, complementarity predicts that dramatic shifts in role and function may occur between marital partners. Thus, the theory would predict, if one spouse typically withdraws from intense emotional encounters, while the other spouse loses no opportunity to pursue such moments, all that is necessary to change the pattern is for one partner to take on the other partner's position. If the pursuer stops pursuing, the distancer will stop distancing. Broadly applying complementarity to marital struggle will lead the therapist down a number of wrong paths, such as: "If she would stop overfunctioning regarding the children, he would step in and be a more consistent parent" or "If he would stop pressing her sexually, she would spontaneously become more amorous." It is not that such hypotheses are universally incorrect, but rather that what holds women and men in place in their marital roles is much stronger and more complex than can be understood by so simple a notion as complementarity.

"Circular causality" is another systemic concept that feminists have called into question (Goldner, 1988; Goodrich, 1991; Taggart, 1985). That systems are recursive is a powerful idea, one that

has allowed marital therapists to better understand the interactional patterns of married life, and to avoid the trap of blaming one person for the existence of the problem, but circular causality has also impaired marital therapists' ability to hold people accountable for their misdeeds. Nowhere has this inability been more damaging than in the situation of wife battering, in which marital therapists have been impotent in holding violent men accountable for their behavior (Avis, 1992). Circular causality leads the therapist to focus on the battered woman's responsibility for the violence done to her, a stance that inevitably results in blaming the victim. Again, what is lost is that men and women are not (in most cases) equally able to inflict physical pain on each other. By obscuring power differences between men and women, circular causality leads the therapist to an inadequate analysis of the situation any time that those power differences are relevant.

The preeminence of independent, autonomous functioning as the goal of healthy human adulthood, an idea at the core of most theories of human development, has been uncritically incorporated into the canon of marital therapy. Thus, separateness achieved through the processes of individuation and differentiation has been positively valued, whereas togetherness, defined in its extremes as "enmeshment" or "fusion," has been more suspect. The field of marital therapy has given little attention to the consideration of what constitutes a healthy amount of interdependency between married people.

Defining separateness as preferable to togetherness is not a gender-neutral act, according to a number of contemporary thinkers on female development. According to these authors (Gilligan, 1982; Jordan, Kaplan, Miller, Stiver, & Surrey, 1991) girls' development is directed from early childhood to be relational in its form and its goal. The path to mature adulthood for women does not lie in autonomy, but rather in the formation of increasingly complex relationships with others. It is through these relationships that women learn to define a self. These same authors, as well as others (Bly, 1990; Keen, 1991; Meth, Pasick, & Gordon, 1990), have noted that, in contrast to girls, boys are encouraged to see the goal of development as independence, and distrust the relational expectations of others. Because marital therapy has been largely untouched by the influence of this new thinking in human development, it continues to define the woman's call for greater involvement from her husband as a sign of her excessive dependency, rather than her legitimate need or his relational constrict-edness.

A final critique that feminists level toward marital therapists has to do with the conduct of therapy itself (Rampage & Avis, in press). Seeking help for relational problems is a solution more likely to be invoked by wives than husbands (witness the enormous volume of self-help books aimed toward women consumers, the vast majority of which offer assistance in improving relationships). Women are also likely to be more comfortable in the therapy room, because they see the process of reflecting on and discussing their relationships as familiar and helpful. Given their early training on the virtue of autonomy, self-reliance, and not showing vulnerability, most men find the marital therapy situation uncomfortable. Furthermore, to the extent that they have absorbed the cultural mandate that making relationships work is their wives' responsibility, most men do not come to therapy well prepared to respond to the therapist's questions about the more subtle aspects of the interactional patterns of the marriage. Thus, too often, the therapist relies on the wife in marital therapy, both to define the problem and to implement the solution. If this is done without comment by the therapist, it leaves the impression with the couple that the wife *is* the problem, because she is the focus of both the conversation and the intervention. This impression reinforces the belief system the couple came in with, and ignores an opportunity to help them discuss the underlying assumptions of their relationship.

REQUISITES OF
FEMINIST-INFORMED THERAPY

Because the idea that marriage is a power relationship between two people is a central tenet of the feminist analysis of marriage, it follows that a feminist-informed approach to marital therapy exerts a considerable focus on how power is distributed and managed in the relationship. Although there is no monolithic, feminist method of marital therapy, all feminist-informed approaches carefully attend to the ways in which power differences are manifested in the marital relationship. This task is not easily accomplished, because the overarching myth about marriage in this culture is that it is primarily a relationship of equal partners, in which distinctions of role and function reflect differing but complementary competencies of men and women, rather than differences in status.

The consequences of looking at marriage as a power relationship are profound. It draws the therapist's attention to how agreements are established in the relationship, to distinctions between collaboration and consent versus coercion and control. Some tasks in marriage can be accomplished under the condition of unequal power, whereas others are rendered impossible. Many instrumental tasks of married life, such as paying bills, providing meals, and even raising children, can be handled under a model in which one spouse is the decision-making executive while the other implements those policies. Indeed, this has been a standard model of marital functioning. Feminists are pointing out, however, that other marital functions are simply precluded by the condition of unequal power between spouses. Intimacy, for example, requires that each partner be empowered to co-create the meaning of the intimate moment (Weingarten, 1991). One person in the dyad cannot define a moment as intimate without the agreement of the other.

Relative to power, a useful distinction that has been proposed by feminists (Goodrich, 1991) is the difference between *power over* and *power to*. The former refers to coercive power, the ability to get someone else to bend to your will because you can make them do so. In its more benign forms, this is the power exercised by good parents on behalf of their children. In its darker form, it is exemplified by the oppression of a dictator who forces people into action against their judgment or will. It is power exercised by someone of higher status over someone of lower status. In contrast, *power to* is more akin to personal authority, the ability to perform and produce, and the freedom to do so. Feminists assert that marriage has been characterized as a relationship in which men have exercised *power over* women, often while simultaneously denying that they were doing so.

The question of male power in marriage has also been made more confusing by the fact that men often do not feel powerful, even as they assert power over their spouses. Men who batter their wives, for example, often describe themselves as feeling powerless and frustrated, even as they are being violent and abusive. Furthermore, the fact that men may express *power over* in their marriages is not to deny that men are also victims of *power over* in other domains of their lives, where other, more powerful men control and dictate to them.

Women, it should be noted, have also gone to great lengths not to notice the role of submission in their marriages or not to face up to their own ambivalence about exercising power. Fear of success, equating helplessness with femininity, and making submission erotic (Benjamin, 1988) are just a few of the ways that women deny and avoid directly expressing their desire for power. Women are often as reluctant to claim power for themselves as men are to give it up. Whatever else is on the agenda in marital therapy, a feminist approach looks carefully at the distribution of power and works toward balancing it.

The assessment process in a feminist-informed marital therapy gathers information about the gender roles of each partner. There are an endless number of variations in how couples arrange their lives, and yet these variations tend to arrange themselves in patterns. One useful schema for identifying the pattern of gender roles in a marriage has been proposed by Breunlin and his colleagues (Breunlin, Schwartz, & Kune-Karrer, 1992). In this schema, couples are placed along a continuum from traditional gender positions to balanced, egalitarian relationships. Each position is defined by the level of role complementarity, flexibility, and collaboration between partners. The therapist uses the gender assessment to plan therapeutic tasks and conversations that will move the system toward gender balance.

CLINICAL SKILLS

Empowerment

Given that power disparities between men and women undergird many of the problems couples bring to therapy, the process of empowerment figures prominently in feminist clinical work with couples. The goal of empowerment in marital therapy is to promote relational equality and personal agency. This is not to say that marital partners can or should share every responsibility equally or be evenly matched on every skill relevant to successful married life. Rather, the purpose of empowerment is to allow both partners to have the widest possible access to the opportunities, rewards, and benefits of married life, and to encourage partners to pursue their own goals independently, so long as that pursuit is not disproportionately at the expense of the other person.

Because marriage has historically been more beneficial to men than to women, it follows that empowerment in the context of feminist marital therapy will redistribute rewards and opportunities in a manner that primarily favors women. For example, feminism has encouraged women not to see themselves as the sole caregivers to their children. As they have felt empowered to give up this solitary responsibility, women have turned to their husbands, urging, requesting or demanding that they participate more fully in parenting. To the extent that fathers have taken up this burden, it has constrained their time, freedom, and flexibility (notwithstanding that it may have had salutary effects, such as deepening the attachment between father and child).

Although power is the preeminent clinical issue feminists have considered regarding marital therapy, it is by no means the only issue. The following sections address several other clinical skills that have significant gendered aspects.

Creating Empathy

Given the often considerable difference in marital partners' experiences and expectations within a relationship, increasing the empathic understanding between them can play a critical role in improving their relationship. A number of gendered issues may block the expression of empathy within the relationship, including ignorance of the other's experience, premature problem solving, negative expectations, and differences in timing between partners. Each of these obstacles requires therapeutic management.

Many wives (and some therapists) believe that men are not as capable of an empathic response as women. Research has shown, however, that men are as capable of demonstrating empathy as women *when they are motivated to do so* (Hare-Mustin & Marecek, 1990). Men and women often differ with respect to their belief in what constitutes an adequate response to a conversational partner (Tannen, 1990). When women listen to their partners' problems, they assume that what is called for is a response that demonstrates their concern, caring, and understanding of the other person (Jordan et al., 1991). Men, on the other hand, tend to listen to problems with an expectation that *they* should provide solutions. These differences in expectation lead to conversational impasses in which the wife feels angry because she wants to solve her own problems and experiences her husband's suggested solutions as patronizing and unhelpful, while he feels frustrated that his caring and helpfulness are being misconstrued and rejected unreasonably.

Helping a couple define what they want from each other is often a valuable process in increasing their experience of conversational success. Because they have learned from early childhood that they are valued as problem solvers, men frequently believe that "simply" listening, understanding, and facilitating their partner's efforts to solve a problem is an inadequate response. When reassured that this is exactly what she wants, most husbands are able and willing to provide this sort of mirroring for their wives.

Often a wife enters marital therapy hoping for greater emotional responsivity from her husband but is discouraged that she has been hitherto unable to evoke the desired response. In conversation she attempts to stimulate him by sharing an experience of her own, or by asking him questions. If his response is not immediately forthcoming, she may interpret his silence as a lack of interest and give up, either withdrawing from the relationship or becoming angry, whereupon a fight may ensue. Encouraging her to be patient with the silence, to trust and expect that he will be responsive if given enough time, can be helpful in interrupting this sort of cycle and allowing an empathic bond to be deepened (Bergman, 1991).

Another facet of increasing marital empathy involves breaking down the barrier of ignorance and mistrust that each partner has about the other's experience. None of us raised under patriarchy is free of sexist bias, and this bias inevitably creeps into the beliefs we have about our spouses, as well as ourselves. This bias sometimes gets expressed directly in the form of statements that characterize one's spouse as a typical member of his/her gender class ("You're just like all men!" or "You women are all alike!"). More frequently, such bias is experienced and expressed more subtly as attributions are made to the other spouse, based on assumptions about his/her gender. To the extent that their point of view has been more widely represented in culture and public life, men's experience is probably more accessible to women than the reverse. Also, under patriarchy, women, as the subordinate gender class, needed to have a better understanding of men as the dominant class.

Information is an antidote to bias. Encouraging spouses to challenge their own gender biases, and to be curious about their partner's feelings, thoughts, beliefs, and attitudes can be critical elements in creating empathy. This can be done in a variety of ways, from letter-writing to conversation, from communicating their reactions to shared experiences to hearing each other's life story.

Social Analysis

Marital therapy is directed toward personal change rather than social transformation. However, contemporary marital therapy takes place in the context of enormous social change in the institution of marriage and the roles marital partners expect themselves (and each other) to play. Feminist-informed approaches to marital therapy address the social context of marriage, including cultural expectations about the roles each spouse assumes in the relationship.

Bringing social analysis into the therapy setting accomplishes three goals: First, it depathologizes the clients' particular relationship and struggles by emphasizing the external factors that are contributing to the pressure to change (or not change). Second, social analysis can be a useful tool in creating empathy between partners and reducing blame. For example, husbands are more likely to be understanding of their wives' frustrations about work–family conflicts if they bear in mind that this is the first generation of women to pursue the demands of full-time jobs and careers while also raising families.

Similarly, wives are more likely to be patient with their husbands' sometimes awkward or reluctant participation in child care if they remain cognizant of what a leap into the unknown such tasks are for men, whose own fathers may very well never have diapered a baby or gotten up in the night with a sick child. Third, social analysis allows the couple to realistically examine the cultural constraints which that whatever role transformation they might wish to make in their personal relationship. For example, because work institutions have lagged behind families in adjusting to the cultural shift in gender roles, men are still more severely penalized than women for making accommodations in their work schedules to meet the needs of their families. Recognizing this constraint in therapy allows couples to focus on what changes they can make without incurring sanctions from the outside (e.g., in the form of lost promotions) and on whether they are willing to incur those sanctions for the sake of feeling more empowered to shape their relationship to their own desires.

Working with Men

One of the earliest responses to the feminist critique of family therapy was the claim that promoting feminist values in the therapy setting was unethical, and would inevitably alienate men, driving them out of therapy. Implicit in this claim is the assumption that feminist values are inherently antimale, a belief that distorts fundamentally the core tenet of feminism: that women and men are equally qualified and entitled to participate fully in the human experience. Nonetheless, to the extent that feminism has been misrepresented and misunderstood in popular culture, bringing feminism into the marital therapy setting requires special attention to the alliance issues, particularly with male clients.

Building a working alliance with a man in feminist marital therapy requires that the therapist develop an empathic appreciation for the way that gender beliefs have constrained him in his marriage. These constraints are particularly salient around issues such as the expression of his own vulnerability, dependency needs, and inadequacies.

One of the imbalances in many marriages is that wives have multiple relationships in which their needs for close connections to others can be met, whereas most men rely exclusively on their wives for the gratification of their intimacy and dependency needs. This imbalance leads to other problems in the marriage, including an overfocus on his concerns, because he has no other outlet for expressing them. Many contemporary writers on men's issues (Bly, 1990; Keen, 1991; Meth et al., 1990) espouse the belief that men need to increase their emotional and spiritual contact with other men in order to free themselves from the gridlock of ambivalent overdependence on women. Recommending men's groups as an adjunct to marital therapy can facilitate this process.

Effective Conflict

Managing marital conflict is an issue that all marital therapists address on a daily basis. The feminist contribution to this therapeutic issue has been twofold: (1) to recognize and unravel the subtle ways that power differences between partners can shape the expression of their arguments and conflicts, and (2) to redefine conflict as the recognition of differences that, if fully understood by both partners, can lead to an increase of mutual empathy (Miller, 1986, 1988). The goal of conflict, from a feminist perspective, should be to enhance the connection of marital partners by allowing them to feel that they are heard, understood, and accepted.

Addressing Violence

Both in theory and practice, marital and family therapy have thus far failed to adequately address the issue of husbands' violence toward their wives. This failure is demonstrated by both the dearth of clinical articles addressing the issue (Avis, 1992), and the unwillingness of the field to use language that attributes agency to the perpetrator of the violence. Lamb (1991) found that family therapy used more vague language to describe wife abuse than any of the other disciplines she studied. Using euphemisms such as "marital aggression" or "spousal violence" diffuses the responsibility for the violence, and implies that it is just another example of complementarity or circularity in married life.

An adequate systemic response to the problem of wife battering must include not only an understanding of the recursive and interdependent relationship between the violent man and the battered woman, but also a clear ethic that the violent man is absolutely responsible for his behavior, and that such behavior is incompatible with a healthy marriage. Although taking such a stance makes the development of an alliance with the violent husband more challenging, Goldner and her colleagues in the Ackerman Institute's project on couples treatment with batterers (Goldner, Penn, Sheinberg, & Walker, 1990) demonstrated that it is not impossible.

KEY ISSUES

There are many reasons why couples come for marital therapy, and some of these reasons are highly charged with gender issues. A discussion of several common themes presented in marital therapy, follows with an analysis of the gender dimensions of each.

Intimacy and Sex

In no other domain of male–female relationships are the differences between men and women so inarguable, or the consequences of those differences so profound, as in the area of sexuality. Even in the late 20th century, males and females are socialized to have radically different attitudes and belief systems about sex. Males are socialized to enjoy sex as recreation, to equate sexual experience with masculine success, and to expect that women will say no when they mean yes (Henneberger, 1993). From early girlhood, females are taught to romanticize sex, to eroticize submission, and to bear in mind that the consequences of sex can be life-changing as well as life-creating.

These vastly different understandings and experiences regarding the meaning of sexuality follow women and men into marriage, and eventually, for some, into marital therapy. The prototypic sexual conundrum expressed in the marital therapist's office is a direct extension of gender socialization. She says: "I can't make love until I feel close to you." He replies: "How can we get close if we don't make love?" This dilemma is rooted in the early learning that each has received about the connection between sex and intimacy. Girls are taught that sex is the ultimate physical expression of intimacy, that it seals the connection between two people, rather than creates it. Men, trained from early childhood to suppress their vulnerable feelings and deny their dependency needs, often lack, or feel awkward with, the kind of affectively loaded conversation that women seem to want. Expressing those feelings physically, through sexual contact, allows men to enact their dependency needs without having to acknowledge that they are doing so, thus sparing them the conflict of violating the internal prohibitions they feel about expressing such feelings verbally.

Many women expect that intimacy, which they regard as the necessary precondition for sex, is established by a certain kind of "conversation" in which each partner feels deeply understood and accepted. Men often participate in this conversation because they see it as a demand characteristic of the situation, rather than as inherently pleasurable or meaningful activity. As Susan Sarandon's character put it in the film *Bull Durham*: "Men will listen to anything if they think it's foreplay." Because men often feel that they are on shaky ground in emotional conversations, they may be more comfortable expressing themselves and creating closeness through physical contact, including sex.

In a classic example of the solution becoming the problem, women have responded to their partners' awkwardness with intimate conversation by perpetually hostessing them, listening for the unspoken need, facilitating expression of the half-formed thought, and intuiting the barely conscious meaning. Men come not only to rely on such hostessing, but also to consider it their due, neither appreciating its value nor feeling obligated to reciprocate. Addressing this disparity in marital therapy requires that the therapist help the clients to appreciate the differences in their needs and styles, without pathologizing either person.

The most treacherous time in Ed and Sue's marriage was when one of them returned from a business trip. Ed would immediately want to have sex as a way of reestablishing contact with Sue. Sue invariably felt reluctant, but, because she could not articulate what she regarded as an adequate explanation for her reluctance, often acceded to Ed's desire. During sex she would dissociate or feel badly, and become angry with and alienated from Ed. The sequence they described to me in therapy was: say hello, have sex, fight. I validated for both their desires to have reunions between them go well, and suggested a change in the sequence, so that their reunions took place at their favorite restaurant after work, rather than at home. This change allowed Sue to immerse herself more gradually into the relationship, and significantly increased her enthusiasm for having sex when they got home. Ed's willingness to participate in this plan was directly related to my explicit validation of his legitimate need for sexual contact with Sue. We defined the intervention as a change in the sequence of their reunions, rather than the substance of them. I also suggested to them that they should interrupt the sexual experience whenever Sue found herself uncomfortable or psychologically absent, and talk about what she was feeling, in order to use the moment as an opportunity to become more intimate with Ed.

There are, of course, other factors that mediate each partner's interest in sex, and they often are not the same factors (tiredness, distraction with work or children, fear of pregnancy). The therapist must be sensitive to the possibility that coercion may be used as a means of persuading a reluctant partner. Women are vulnerable to being sexually coerced precisely because female submission has been eroticized. Cultural vehicles as diverse as pornography, popular music, and romance novels (to name but a few) portray the shared ethos that women find male dominance normal and sexy, even when it includes the infliction of pain and humiliation on women. Such attitudes find their way into the marital relationship, expressed as a wife's doubt about her right to say no to sex (a right only recently protected by law in most states), or a husband's complementary assertion that his sexual demands are no more than his due.

Housework

Housework is the spinach of married life. No sooner do two starry eyed lovers cross the threshold of their first shared domicile than the battle begins over who sets the standards for domestic cleanliness and who implements them. The dismal fact about housework is that hardly anyone enjoys labor, the effects of which endure so briefly, it only has to be done again. It is the repetitiveness and lack of creativity associated with housework that gives it its bad name. That, and the fact that it has been classified as "women's work" for ages untold.

Because housework is generally classified as no better than a necessary evil, doing it is consigned to the person of lowest status in the household who is capable of doing it. Historically, that person has been the wife. As more and more wives have entered the paid workforce, they have exerted increasing pressure on their husbands to participate in housework. So far, sociologists tell us, husbands, as a group, have been somewhat less than totally enthusiastic about signing up for such a transformation. In fact, according to Hochschild (1989) men whose wives work outside the home do only slightly more housework than men whose wives are full-time homemakers, although husbands *do* significantly increase their contribution to child care when their wives are working for pay. This shows that even child care is perceived by husbands as a higher status activity than housework.

Interestingly, there is research to suggest that housework is actually good for men. Gottman's (1991) longitudinal study of marital satisfaction made the fascinating discovery that men who do housework are physically healthier, less avoidant of marital conflict, and less overwhelmed by their wives' emotions than their peers who do not.

In marital therapy the key word indicating to the therapist that the issue of housework needs exploration is "help," as in the statement by an earnest husband: "I help with the housework." Such a statement makes clear that the speaker's contribution is entirely voluntary and not based on obligation. The actual responsibility for the job belongs clearly to whoever is the object of the verb "help." In the vast majority of families, that is the wife. As uninteresting as housework is to us all, there is a temptation on the part of the therapist to skim through it, so as to get down to the "real" issues of marital therapy, such as sex, anger, and conflict. But to give short shrift to housework is to give short shrift to women, because they are almost inevitably held (by themselves as well as others) to be responsible for it.

As Braverman (1991) has pointed out, the equitable redistribution of housework between spouses is not as simple as dividing the list of chores in half and letting them manage their chores in their own way. Are tasks to be divided up along lines of expertise? Such a method will almost certainly leave the wife feeling overburdened, since she has, over long and arduous years, painstakingly discovered such secrets of the universe as how to get Kool-Aid stains out of T-shirts, and exactly how long chicken can be broiled before it turns into leather. On the other hand, should an experienced husband who is also a novice homemaker be encouraged to develop a personalized approach to doing laundry, even if it means that clothes become faded or stains are allowed to set?

The real dilemma of redistributing housework is that it inverts the "natural" order of marital roles, placing the wife in an expert position compared to the relative inexperience of her husband. It is the challenge to things as they are represented in this reorganizing that must be addressed in marital therapy. For a husband to take on serious and regular household responsibilities, and allow himself to be directed and instructed by his wife in doing so, inevitably shifts the power in the relationship.

Ron and Carrie came to marital therapy for assistance in reducing the amount of conflict between them. Married 8 years, they had two young children, primarily cared for by Carrie, who also worked part-time. Early in therapy, Carrie voiced her anger at Ron's unwillingness to share in household responsibilities, particularly those having to do with cleaning and picking up. As an example, Carrie described her feeling of irritation and gloom upon entering the kitchen at 7:30 A.M. with the task of preparing breakfast for two ravenous children and packing lunches for them amid the detritus of the previous evening's dinner. Ron protested that he *often* cleaned the kitchen after dinner, and in any case, he could not imagine a more boring use of a therapy session than to sit around discussing who did the dishes.

Ron's protestations revealed two important beliefs that made it difficult to resolve the problem of housework in the marriage. First, he was unable to validate or be empathic to Carrie's experience, because he felt that he *did* participate, but that his contributions were unappreciated. Second, he believed the whole issue of housework was unworthy of the level of attention that Carrie wanted to draw to it.

In order to detoxify the issue sufficiently so that it could be resolved, each of these beliefs had to be challenged. First, Ron's participation in housework was unpredictable as well as unaccountable. His exercise of choice regarding whether he did the dishes on any particular evening reflected his lack of ownership of the chore. He did it *if* he felt sufficiently energetic. In other words, he saw himself as a volunteer, a helper. If he felt so inclined, he would do it; if not, he would not. He did not request Carrie's consent to his choice, because it was her job anyway. She was (as she, herself, put it) the "default option." Because she could not count on Ron, she always felt the full burden of responsibility for housework on her shoulders alone, and it created smoldering anger in her.

Ron's second assertion about the appropriateness of housework as a topic for conversation in therapy reveals an even more subtle dynamic. By trying to block a discussion about housework, Ron was trying to control the agenda of the therapy. Controlling the agenda of a conversation is an efficient way to control its outcome. If the topic cannot be legitimately brought up, the status quo is protected. In other words, Ron's reluctance to engage in a conversation about housework protected his privileged position as a volunteer participant rather than the responsible party. And yet, Ron did not see himself as a volunteer: in fact, he took pride in being more involved with his kids and domestic life in general than his own father had ever been. What he actively resisted was Carrie's attempt (as he experienced it) to micromanage him, and to unilaterally set the domestic agenda. Bolstered by the possibility of ending the stalemate that had developed around this issue, Ron and Carrie entered into an extended conversation about what needed to be done at home, and how well. Feeling themselves on equal footing for the first time, Carrie was able to let go of some of the control of how things should be done at home, and Ron was able to acknowledge and occasionally defer to Carrie's expertise in this arena. They developed a more collaborative approach to the issue, and it eventually ceased to be a matter of concern in their treatment.

Money

The relationship that married women have to money has certainly changed in the two decades since they began flooding into the paid workforce. More women than ever before have their own checking accounts and credit histories, and many of them do not think it unfeminine to be able to distinguish stocks from bonds. Many married women pay their families' monthly bills and organize whatever family budget exists. Yet, there remains a gendered aspect to the way that money figures into married life.

As money is one of the most concrete expressions of power in a capitalist and consumer-oriented society, it is not surprising that personal power in marriage is highly correlated to economic power (Blumstein & Schwartz, 1983). The more income spouses generate, the more entitled they feel to have their say in the marriage. Since

the average woman in 1994 still earns considerably less than her husband, she also comes to marital therapy in a disempowered position. A marital therapist who is blind to this fact, or who minimizes it in order to appear evenhanded or to maintain balance with the couple, implicitly, if unintentionally, strengthens the alliance with the husband, possibly at the cost of mystifying the wife. Some therapists (e.g., McGoldrick, 1991) believe that it is nigh unto impossible to do marital therapy until both partners are economically viable and independent of each other.

David and Liesel were in their mid-40s and raising two children, a son, aged 9, and a daughter, aged 5. They came to therapy for help in dealing with a pattern of chronic fights that revolved around Liesel's anger that David was not more participative in the children's lives. Both spouses were teachers, but Liesel had ceased working professionally when her first child was born. Although the couple shared the philosophy that children should be raised by both their parents, David frequently opted out of parenting responsibilities because of work commitments or tiredness.

David's behavior was a constant source of disappointment for Liesel, but she was reluctant to push harder for David's greater involvement as a parent for a number of reasons. The easiest reason for her to articulate was that she was empathic to David's exhaustion at the end of a long school day. Certainly she seemed more empathic to David's tiredness than to her own. Furthermore, it was clear to them both that she was more effective and better organized with the children than was David. Finally, on a deeper level that she could only communicate after some months of therapy, Liesel was afraid to push David too hard, lest he leave her. She was openly terrified of being left financially vulnerable, and so censored herself in her marriage, and never let her anger push the situation too far.

David was surprised to learn the extent of Liesel's concern about his leaving her impoverished, and tried to reassure her that he was not the sort of man who would do such a thing. His reassurances seemed to have little effect on Liesel's sense of security. She continued to pick up the slack in David's parenting, and to resent him at the same time.

When her daughter started kindergarten the following fall, Liesel also went back to work as a teacher, a change that was in keeping with the couple's long-term plan. Within weeks of Liesel's return to the paid workforce, several changes occurred in the system. First, Liesel stopped doing so much of the parenting. She and David instituted a system whereby they alternated the tasks of cleaning the kitchen in the evening and putting the children to bed. Second, David's efficiency at these tasks, and his willingness to do them, ceased to be issues. Third, Liesel became more willing to press David about some of the issues that made her dissatisfied with the marriage.

In this case, it was a change in the context that led to the most significant change in the marital arrangement. Returning to work led to a significant increase in Liesel's feeling of entitlement to David's participation in domestic life, and a substantial decrease in her availability to "cover the bases" for everyone in the family. For David, the necessity of managing the household without Liesel's direct supervision freed him of the resentment and inadequacy that had contributed to his previous underfunctioning in this arena. Also, his esteem for Liesel as a fellow professional seemed to lead to an increase in his regard for her in general.

Unlike David and Liesel, for whom money was an implicit and unprocessed issue, many couples in marital therapy report that they fight frequently about family finances. Such fights may take many forms, from disagreements about how much discretionary spending each spouse is allowed, to conflicts about access to information about family finances. Two gendered patterns are worth noting. First, men who earn more than their wives (meaning, of course, *most* men) also tend to feel entitled to make unilateral decisions on spending large amounts of money. Second, even well-educated, highly competent women often do not understand their family's financial condition, a problem that seems directly correlated to the amount of resources the family has. That is, in families where a savings account, a pension plan, and a home comprise the total assets, women clients seem to know and understand the financial picture. When assets also include stock portfolios, real estate investments, and other sorts of wealth, women are more likely to be ignorant or only partially informed of their financial condition. This ignorance puts women on poor footing in attempts to participate as equals in matters pertaining to family finances, and has repercussions for other aspects of the marriage as well. Furthermore, given that the average woman will outlive her husband by several years, not understanding her financial situation puts her at risk of being overwhelmed and easily taken advantage of at the point when she must assume control of managing the family assets by herself.

Stuart and Audrey were an affluent couple in their late 40s. They began therapy at Audrey's instigation. She expressed a great deal of anger at Stuart for being overbearing and dominant in the marriage. These accusations bewildered Stuart, who believed himself to be devoted to Audrey and their children, and was highly identified with his evenhandedness and generosity. Stuart's affability and confusion left me also feeling befuddled about the origins of Audrey's feelings until I asked them to tell me about how they handled financial matters.

Audrey described feeling deceived and condescended to about finances. She recounted the story of purchasing their first home. After spending many weekends looking for houses in an agreed on price range, Stuart had seen a house priced more than 25% higher than they had agreed upon as their upper limit. Within a matter of hours they had seen the house and made an offer. Stuart was thrilled with the house and thought Audrey should bem too. He could not understand her annoyance and bewilderment that they had exceeded their original budget, because he was confident that he could make enough money to afford it.

Other similar examples followed. It seemed that whenever they set a budget for some major purchase, Audrey would take it as a real constraint, whereas Stuart would usually end up spending considerably more than they had initially planned. He also occasionally made major expenditures without checking first with Audrey. When this subject was brought up in therapy, Stuart was defensive, saying that he never demanded that Audrey account to him for her expenditures, and pointing out that, in fact, she probably spent more money than he did. As it happened, Audrey was by nature fiscally conservative, and so would never dream of spending significant sums without Stuart's input and agreement.

I asked Audrey how well she understood the family's financial standing. She confessed that she did not understand it at all, and that every time Stuart tried to explain it to her, they ended up fighting. With Stuart's support, I asked Audrey to make an appointment with their accountant to become more familiar with this information. A week later, Audrey called to report that the appointment with the accountant had been helpful, although there were still a few things she had not understood. I encouraged her to call the accountant again, and not get off the phone until she was satisfied that she understood everything. After several more calls and another appointment with the accountant, Audrey at last felt that she understood her family's finances.

This understanding led to an immediate shift in

the tone and content of marital discussions about money. Audrey stopped blaming Stuart for being controlling, and instead began making observations about their different attitudes and values about money. This shift allowed Stuart to become less defensive and more curious about Audrey's opinions regarding money. Furthermore, their being on equal footing with regard to financial information resulted in better collaboration around decision making. For the first time, Audrey and Stuart were able to work together on a long-term financial plan for their family.

CONCLUSION

All of us are living through a historical moment in which the most fundamental assumptions we have had about gender are being challenged. Scenarios that a generation ago would have qualified as science fiction or burlesque (e.g., *two* women on the Supreme Court, the men's movement, women in military combat positions) are rapidly becoming commonplace. As a society we are in the process of what Kuhn (1970) called a "paradigm shift," in which our definitions of "male" and "female," of "husband" and "wife," no longer fit, and we struggle as a group, as couples, and as individuals to construct new patterns and definitions.

As marital therapists we are both part of this process, and called upon to mediate it on behalf of our clients. As women and men, we, too, struggle with complex feelings and seemingly contradictory beliefs about our genders. Those struggles follow us into the therapy room, where our choice is not *whether* to deal with gender, but only *how* to do so. Will we, by our silence, implicitly endorse the status quo? Will we maintain a naive neutrality, supporting whatever gender beliefs our clients present us, regardless of the self-loathing or the misogyny those beliefs connote? In the interest of promoting change, will we resort to preaching, to admonishing, to shaming?

Or can we, as marital therapists, take a different position, one that acknowledges the impossibility of our being objective on the issue of gender, but declares our willingness to participate with our clients in a dialogue about the meaning and experience of maleness and femaleness? This is the conversation that feminists would urge for marital therapy, a conversation in which the ideals of equality, mutual respect, and curiosity about the other's experience would be embodied in both the goals and the process of the work.

REFERENCES

Avis, J. M. (1992). Where are all the family therapists: Abuse and violence within families and family therapy's response. *Journal of Marital and Family Therapy, 18*(3), 225–232.

de Beauvoir, S. (1953). *The second sex.* New York: Knopf.

Benjamin, J. (1988). *The bonds of love: Psychoanalysis, feminism, and the problem of domination* . New York: Pantheon.

Bergman, S. (1991). *Men's psychological development: A relational perspective* (Works in Progress No. 48). Wellesley, MA: Stone Center Working Paper Series.

Bernard, J. (1982). *The future of marriage* (2nd ed.). New Haven, CT: Yale University Press.

Blumstein, P., & Schwartz, P. (1983). *American couples: Money, work, sex.* New York: Morrow.

Bly, R. (1990). *Iron John: A book about men.* New York: Addison-Wesley.

Braverman, L. (1991). The dilemma of housework: A feminist reply to Gottman, Napier and Pittman. *Journal of Marital and Family Therapy, 17*(1), 25–28.

Breunlin, D., Schwartz, R., & Kune-Karrer, B. (1992). *Metaframeworks: Transcending the models of family therapy.* San Francisco: Jossey-Bass.

Chopin, K. (1992). *The awakening: A solitary soul.* New York: Knopf.

Dobash, R., & Dobash, R. (1979). *Violence against wives.* New York: Free Press.

Dutton, D. G. (1988). *The domestic assault of women: Psychological and criminal justice perspectives.* Toronto: Allyn & Bacon.

Eisler, R. (1987). *The chalice and the blade.* New York: HarperCollins.

Friedan, B. (1963). *The feminine mystique.* New York: Norton.

Gilligan, C. (1982). *In a different voice: Psychological theory and women's development.* Cambridge, MA: Harvard University Press.

Gilman, C. P. (1973). *The yellow wallpaper.* Old Westbury, NY: The Feminist Press.

Goldner, V. (1985). Feminism and family therapy. *Family Process, 24*(1), 31–48.

Goldner, V. (1988). Gender and generation: Normative and covert hierarchies. *Family Process, 27*(1), 17–33.

Goldner, V., Penn, P, Sheinberg, M., & Walker, G. (1990). Love and violence: Gender paradoxes in volatile attachments. *Family Process, 29,* 343–364.

Goodrich, T. J. (Ed.). (1991). *Women and power: Perspectives for family therapy.* New York: Norton.

Goodrich, T. J., Rampage, C., Ellman, B., & Halstead, K. (1988). *Feminist family therapy: A casebook.* New York: Norton.

Gottman, J. (1991). Predicting the longitudinal course of marriages. *Journal of Marital and Family Therapy, 17*(1), 3–7.

Hare-Mustin, R. T., & Marecek, J. (Eds.). (1990). *Making a difference: Psychology and the construction of gender.* New Haven, CT: Yale University Press.

Heilbrun, C. (1988). *Writing a woman's life.* New York: Norton.

Henneberger, B. (1993, July 11). Youthful courting has become a game of abuse. *The New York Times,* p. 1.

Hochschild, A. (1989). *The second shift: Working parents and the revolution at home.* New York: Viking Penguin.

James, K., & McIntyre, D. (1983). The reproduction of families: The social role of family therapy? *Journal of Marital and Family Therapy, 9*(2), 119–129.

Jordan, J. U., Kaplan, A. G., Miller, J. B., Stiver, I. P., & Surrey, J. L. (1991). *Women's growth in connection: Writing from the Stone Center.* New York: Guilford Press.

Keen, S. (1991). *Fire in the belly: On being a man.* New York: Bantam.

Kuhn, T. (1970). *The structure of scientific revolutions* (2nd ed.). Chicago: University of Chicago Press.

Lamb, S. (1991). Acts without agents: An analysis of linguistic avoidance in journal articles on men who batter women. *American Journal of Orthopsychiatry, 61*(2), 250–257.

Lerner, G. (1986). *The creation of patriarchy.* New York: Oxford University Press.

Luepnitz, D. (1988). *The family interpreted: Feminist theory in clinical practice.* New York: Basic Books.

Margolin, G., Fernandez, R., Talovic, S., & Onorato, R. (1983). Sex role consideration and behavioral marital therapy: Equal does not mean identical. *Journal of Marital and Family Therapy, 9*(2), 131–145.

McGoldrick, M. (1991). For love or money. In T. J. Goodrich (Ed.), *Women and power: Perspectives for family therapy* (pp. 239–245). New York: Norton.

McGoldrick, M., Anderson, C., & Walsh, F. (Eds.). (1989). *Women in families: A framework for family therapy.* New York: Norton.

Meth, R. L., Pasick R. S., Gordon, B., Allen, J. A., Feldman, L. B., & Gordon, S. (1990). *Men in therapy: The challenge of change.* New York: Guilford Press.

Miller, J. B. (1986). *Toward a new psychology of women* (2nd ed.). New York: Beacon Press.

Miller, J. B. (1988). *Connections, disconnections and violations.* (Works in Progress No. 33). Wellesley, MA: Stone Center Working Paper Series.

Napier, A. (1988). *The fragile bond: In search of an equal, intimate and enduring marriage.* New York: Harper.

Pogrebin, L. C. (1983). *Family politics.* New York: McGraw-Hill.

Rampage, C. & Avis, J. M. (in press). Gender, feminism, and family therapy. In M. Elkaim (Ed.), *Principles of family therapy.* Brussels: Seuil.

Rubin, L. (1976). *Worlds of pain: Life in the working class family.* New York: Basic.

Russell, D. (1982). *Rape in marriage.* New York: Macmillan.

Straus, M. A., & Gelles, R. J. (1986). Societal change and family violence from 1975 to 1985 as revealed by two national surveys. *Journal of Marriage and the Family, 48,* 465–480.

Taggart, M. (1985). The feminist critique in epistemological perspective: Questions of context in family therapy. *Journal of Marital and Family Therapy, 11*(2), 113–126.

Tannen, D. (1990). *You just don't understand: Women and men in conversation.* New York: Morrow.

Walters, M., Carter, B., Papp, P., & Silverstein, O. (1988). *The invisible web: Gender patterns in family relationships.* New York: Guilford Press.

Weingarten, K. (1991). The discourses of intimacy: Adding a social constructionist and feminist view. *Family Process, 30,* 285–305.

14

Therapy with Same-Sex Couples: An Introduction

LAURA S. BROWN

COUPLES VARY FROM one another; no two are quite alike. Although any experienced relationship therapist would probably agree with such an assertion, its meaning becomes more important when the couple in question is composed of two women or two men. Although in the past two decades lesbian and gay male couples have become increasingly visible and in many cases appear to be integrated into the general culture, they continue to be affected by hostile social forces that no heterosexual couples, however embattled, will ever have to encounter simply by virtue of existing, and as a rule are still more hidden from view than the average heterosexual therapist can imagine.

Many of the concrete issues faced by same-sex couples are, at first glance, strikingly similar to those dealt with by any intimate adult pair: sharing of power, raising children, balancing relationship and career commitments, establishing boundaries, and dealing with the in-laws. Yet, beneath this surface, it is often the case that lesbian and gay male couples have very different sets of dynamics and issues than do heterosexual couples entering therapy for relationship distress. Knowledge of those differences and their sources forms the necessary background information for competent delivery of services to same-sex couples.

Two factors are of primary importance in understanding these differences. The first is the impact of gender-role socialization. In a same-sex couple, both partners possess variations on the theme of the same benefits and deficits of essentially similar patterns of gender-role development. Whatever complementarity of roles such socialization may yield in a heterosexual couple is absent in most same-sex relationships, even if there is the appearance of greater overt "masculinity" or "femininity" on the part of one or the other partner. Usually, both members of a same-sex couple are relatively well-socialized members of their own gender with a positive gender identification. To work well and competently with same-sex couples, a therapist must possess a clear comprehension of the strengths and deficits of each gender role as they affect relationship functioning.

A second factor differentiating same-sex couples is the phenomenon of cultural oppression, which takes the forms of homophobia and heterosexism. "Homophobia" can be defined operationally as the fear and hatred of same-sex intimacy, love, and sexuality, and of those individuals and institutions that are, or are perceived to, support, affirm, or participate in such couplings. "Heterosexism" is the privileging by the culture and its institutions of heterosexual forms of relating, while simultaneously devaluing nonheterosexual forms of relating. Both of these forms of oppression function in a variety of ways. Externally and culturally, homophobia may be seen in the rising tide of bias-motivated violence against lesbians and gay men (Berrill,

1990; Garnets, Herek, & Levy, 1990) or in the passage of laws forbidding gay men and lesbians to adopt or foster children. Heterosexism manifests itself as the absence of legal structures such as marriage for same-sex couples; in the fact that a same-sex partner is usually not eligible to share in such employment-related benefits as health insurance and may not be treated as her/his partner's next of kin at times of illness or death; in the absence of a legal relationship between lesbians and the children they raise who are biologically related only to the parent who gave birth to them.

Internalized as a form of self-hatred, homophobia and heterosexism may also manifest themselves in subtle and frequently nonconscious ways in lesbian and gay people themselves. Because many lesbian and gay people entering couple's therapy are consciously affirmative of their sexual orientation, a therapist who ignores the possibility of internalized homophobia and heterosexism may miss issues germane to the problems in relationship functioning. All lesbian and gay male couples, however privileged and insulated from the most overt manifestations of oppression by favorable local laws or access to financial or personal resources, function in the context of these two interlocking forms of oppression. The existence of stable, happy, well-functioning same-sex relationships defies the "truths" of homophobia and heterosexism. As a consequence, many of the difficulties faced by such couples have as their primary etiology the oppressive social and interpersonal environments in which lesbians and gay men are required to operate.

Because homophobia and heterosexism are never a factor in the healthy functioning of heterosexual relationships, and because the manifestations of both external and internalized oppression may be quite subtle, a therapist working with same-sex couples must take this variable into account. Data from research on therapy with lesbians and gay men (Committee on Lesbian and Gay Concerns, 1991) suggest, however, that this is the factor most commonly *ignored* by well-meaning heterosexual therapists whose own knowledge of the manifestations of homophobia and heterosexism alike is likely to be somewhat limited to only the most overt examples.

This chapter is designed as an introductory effort with a goal of raising consciousness about the common concerns unique to same-sex relationships. It is important to underscore the introductory nature of this material. Reading it will not qualify the reader for competency in working with same-sex couples. Instead, my hope is that this chapter will lead readers to become aware of gaps in their knowledge and seek further training, supervision, and consultation. My goal is introduce readers to a set of cultures with which they may not be familiar, cultures that are quite diverse, yet share in common the fact that their members are people attracted to, and in intimate relationships with, members of their own gender.

As with other cross-cultural excursions, it is impossible to become a native speaker of the lesbian and gay mother tongues upon initial attempts (Brown, 1990). However, I encourage readers to take this excursion and others similar to it. Until the advent of AIDS on the American scene, which has had the effort of making many gay men and their lesbian allies visible to the culture at large, the normal daily lives and cultural experiences of sexual minority persons were largely unknown to the average heterosexual mental health professional. Information available in formal professional training remains both biased and incomplete (Buhrke & Douce, 1991). Since the first version of this chapter was written (Brown & Zimmer, 1986), many more readers have become aware of their lesbian and gay friends, colleagues, and family members; still most of us are likely to remain invisible to most of the heterosexual majority, or so marginal to the dominant culture as to be glimpsed only in part, and not seen as a whole.

This selective visibility of lesbians and gay men to mental health professionals has left many well-meaning individuals with a picture of lesbian and gay lives that is informed more by myth and the popular media than by daily reality. Bias can also be generated when the majority of lesbians or gay men known to a mental health professional are clients. We easily forget that everyone we see, regardless of sexual orientation, is in some kind of pain or distress, and we ignore how much larger, more complete, and complex is our database regarding the lives of nonclient heterosexual people. Because problems of bias and lack of information constitute the most important issues in working with same-sex couples, this chapter does not attend to questions of therapeutic technique, but rather offers information that can be integrated into the work of most approaches to relationship therapy.

It continues to be axiomatic that scholarly work on lesbians and gay men is incomplete because our data do not reflect the overall population. This state of affairs has changed somewhat in the 11 years between first writing and revision of this chapter, and our sources of information regarding the range of experiences of Caucasian lesbians and gay men has become quite rich and varied. Data regarding lesbians and gay men of color remain sparse for reasons having to do with the complex interactions of racism with homophobia and heterosexism. Much of the material in this chapter refers primarily to white lesbians and gay men; whereas many of the issues for sexual minority couples of color are similar, there are also important differences that have to do with the various meanings of same-sex relationships within a particular racial or cultural group. Interracial, same-sex relationships are also not well described by the extant literature.

What is now known is that sexual minority persons, and the lesbian population in particular, use therapy as a resource at a significantly higher rate than the U.S. population in general, with findings ranging in the 80th percentile for national and regional samples of mostly Caucasian lesbians (Bradford & Ryan, 1987; Morgan, 1992). Although there are no similar empirical data regarding gay men's use of psychotherapy, anecdotal evidence suggests that it is similarly high. What is also known is that the average psychologist sees at least one lesbian or gay man (and by inference, same-sex couple) during her/his professional career (Committee on Lesbian and Gay Concerns, 1991), implying the importance of acquisition of this knowledge by therapists.

There has been an increase particularly in the written work on lesbian and gay couples and families in the decade of the 1980s. Most of this has been aimed at a popular audience that is hungry for the kind of bibliotherapeutic self-help traditionally available to heterosexual couples (Clunis & Green, 1988; McWhirter & Mattison, 1984, Berzon, 1988). Some work, particularly that looking at questions of parenting and family formation, has been more scholarly in nature (Bozett, 1987). This chapter reflects that literature, as well as my clinical experiences with same-sex couples both inside and out of the therapy office, and the clinical experiences of the many lesbian and gay, and lesbian and gay-affirmative therapists with whom I work and consult.

This chapter comes with a bias that I wish to make clear from the start. I am a lesbian, and one half of a happy, stable, 15-year lesbian relationship. My partner and I, and our gay and lesbian-couple friends and colleagues, many of whom live, as we do, in one of the most hospitable environments for sexual minority persons in North America, have had our own frequent, and at times, traumatic, encounters with cultur-

al homophobia and heterosexism. On the one hand, I know from experience that same-sex relationships can and do last long and work well, serving as a source of joy, satisfaction, and passion for all involved. I also know firsthand the challenges that an oppressive reality can throw in the faces of the most happy and well-functioning same-sex couples, even when both partners are skillful communicators with a strong commitment to the functioning and health of the relationship.

A second and related bias in this chapter is that because many of the problems faced by lesbian and gay male couples can be gender specific, it is essential to deal with these issues separately, rather than attempt a premature fusion of concerns. Only when problems are clearly held in common will they be addressed as such. The terms "lesbian," "gay man," and "same-sex relationship" are used here as the preferred nomenclature of most people in such relationships; the term "homosexuality" is seen by most North American sexual-minority persons as a clinicalizing and pathologizing one. (Although the term "queer" is coming back into vogue with younger and/or more politically radical gay men and lesbians, therapists who are not themselves members of sexual minorities should approach it with caution, as it is also used pejoratively by heterosexuals.) I encourage readers to inquire of clients as to their preferred usage, since nomenclature has important political and social meanings in regard to where and how a particular relationship and its members situate-themselves within the lesbian and gay communities.

A final and important bias here is that to be gay or lesbian is to have a minority rather than a deviant or pathological sexual orientation. This setting is too brief for a complete review of the literature in support of this perspective, which represents current scholarly findings on the subject (Herek, 1990; Gonsiorek & Weinrich, 1991). However, any therapist who cannot approach the members of a same-sex couple with this perspective should ethically refrain from working as a therapist with lesbian and gay male relationships. Essential to therapy with this population is the therapists's belief that such relationships are worth the time, energy, effort, and pain that it may take to make them successful. A therapist who is ambivalent, who sees a same-sex relationship as second best, a substitute, or a poor imitation of the "real thing," will harm her/his clients in ways that would be ethically unacceptable to any mental health professional, no matter what her/his attitudes are toward homosexuality. This caveat applies equally to therapists of all sexual orientations, because therapists' own sexual minority status is not an absolute protection against oppressive attitudes toward members of their own group.

THE IMPACT OF HOMOPHOBIA AND HETEROSEXISM ON RELATIONAL FUNCTION

Problems confronting all same-sex couples, no matter how well they function, are homophobia and heterosexism. This section of the chapter addresses the effects of both external and internalized oppression and attempts to identify some of the more common problems faced by same-sex couples as a result of these persistent phenomena.

External/cultural homophobia is the overtly punitive aspect of sexual minority oppression. As of this writing, more than half of the states of the United States continue to carry laws which criminalize the forms of sexual expression most common to lesbians and gay men. In 1989, the U.S. Supreme Court held, in the case of *Bowers v. Hardwick,* that although such activities were protected under the right to privacy for heterosexual people, no such right extended to the same acts performed in a same-sex context. Lesbians and gay men continue to be fired from their jobs when their sexual orientation becomes known, or to encounter a "glass ceiling" which, despite outstanding performance, blocks further professional advancement. Despite the advice of their own expert studies, all branches of the U.S. military bar service by acknowledged gay men and lesbians, and continue to punish sexual minority military personnel with long criminal sentences, dishonorable discharge, and loss of pay and benefits (Shilts, 1993). Lesbians and gay men continue to routinely be stripped of rights to custody or even visitation of children conceived in prior heterosexual relationships; more recently, several courts have upheld the notion that such rights can also be denied to lesbian nonbiological coparents who have raised a child from birth. We can be expelled from our homes, and cast out of our religious and spiritual groups. Data from a national lesbian and gay rights organization tell us that more than half of all sexual minority people surveyed have experienced bias-related violence, ranging from verbal abuse to fatal assault, based solely on our sexual orientation (Berrill, 1990).

Heterosexism operates culturally so as to render lesbians and gay men, and our relationships, invisible. We cannot legally marry our partners anywhere outside of Denmark, although a few cities in the United States allow the registration of "domestic partnerships." With few excecptions, lesbians and gay men cannot designate their partners for normal, work-related benefits such as health insurance or pension survivorship rights. We are not legally considered to be one another's family and thus can be excluded from visiting an intensive care unit or making medical decisions in an emergency, even when we have the appropriate legal documents to ensure such rights; the wishes of sometimes long-estranged families of origin can and often do take precedence over those of the partner who has lived with the patient for many years (Thompson & Andrzejewski, 1988). When we cannot take the risk to be "out" and have our sexual orientation known, we are considered "single" by families and employers, are easily transferred in our jobs without attention to the relocation concerns of our partners, or are the target of endless matchmaking attempts by well-meaning co-workers (Morgan & Brown, 1991). Although lesbians and gay men increasingly are creating commitment ceremonies of our own (Butler, 1990), most of our relationships exist without the banal yet meaningful events that surround marriage: wedding showers, announcements in the newspaper, and the like.

The net effect of these combined oppressions on the same-sex couple can be twofold. Because of the ongoing risks, there are few visible, happy, normal "Ozzie and Harriet"-style models of same-sex couples available to adolescent lesbians and gay men who are developing their images of relationships to come. One study (Blumstein & Schwartz, 1983) noted that long-term, successful, same-sex couples tend not to be visible and active in the official lesbian and gay communities. Unlike members of ethnic, racial, and cultural minorities who normally grow up within their own reference group, in which culture and traditions can be transmitted in an affirmative-manner, lesbians and gay men are raised by and raised to be, heterosexuals, with the expectations of heterosexual relationships as our sole relational paradigm, and with exposure to hostile attitudes regarding lesbian/gay culture. Our families do not usually respond with joy when we introduce them to the women or men we love; more frequently, lesbians and gay men are shunned, ignored, or distanced, or inspire parental prayers for the end of our relationships.

The metamessage of all of this risk and invisibility is that the well-functioning same-sex couple does not exist (recent exceptions to the rule of invisibility tend to occur when someone in the public eye, such as Martina Navratilova, is *breaking up* her relationship, which never received so much publicity when she and her partner were getting along well together) Recent articles in *People* magazine portraying happy lesbian celebrities suggest some change in this pattern. Blumstein and Schwartz (1983) have commented that the institution of marriage has as its symbolic function the official sanctioning and privileging of heterosexual relationships. The absence of that official blessing, and the deprivileging of same-sex relationships, can often be interpreted by lesbians and gay men as a message of prohibition. Cultural myths regarding lesbians and gay men complicate the matter; although the picture is gradually changing as more respected leaders of politics, business, and the professions come out, many lesbians and gay men see only a negative and distorted picture of same-sex relationships reflected in the mirror of popular culture. This can lead some lesbians and gay men to hold a nonconscious set of negative expectations about their own potential for having adult relationships that can ever transcend the merely sexual or superficial realm. Such negative metamessages are likely, to some degree, to be internalized by all sexual minority people growing up in dominant Western cultures, no matter what our race, class, or age cohort. These factors can vary with the intensity and negativity of homophobia and heterosexism in the environment, but they are rarely completely removed from the emotional atmosphere.

As a consequence, therapists working with same-sex couples should not make the error of believing that lesbians and gay men with a conscious lack of bias against themselves will also lack nonconscious negative attitudes. Nor is a positive self-image a perfect shield against everyday reality and its pressures against the success of a same-sex pair. Rather, in working with same-sex couples, it is important to probe for the subtle manifestations of such deeply held attitudes that may constitute a significant portion of the difficulties a couple is experiencing, and to be attentive to external events that may have served to trigger or underscore such material. Some illustrative clinical examples include the following:

1. A same-sex couple entering therapy states that the focus of conflict is the merging or keeping separate of financial resources and household goods. In therapy, one partner begins to talk about her/his fears of combining resources, because "we'll just break up someday and have to unentangle it all." Expecting that a relationship *will* break up, as distinguished from holding the healthy awareness that any relationship can meet its end, can become a self-fulling prophecy in many same-sex relationships. Cultural expectations regarding instability of lesbian and gay couples can result in problems of trust and intimacy from the outset, particularly when both partners agree that there are no external, verifiable reasons for their caution or distance. A related manifestation of this aspect of internalized oppression can be seen in an overemphasis on the longevity, as opposed to the quality, of a same-sex relationship, with the relationship becoming a sacrifice to the struggle to "prove" to self or society that same-sex couples can last. Some data do suggest a relationship, however, between willingness to have some important resources or property in common, and relationship satisfaction, for same-sex couples (Berzon, 1989).

2. A same-sex couple enters treatment to deal with the extreme jealousy or possessiveness of one partner as the presenting complaint. One partner is angry that the other forbids her/him to have close friendships with others who are gay or lesbian. Discussions in the session reveal that both partners hold the belief that all other lesbians or gay men are a threat to their relationships because of perceived lack of respect for the commitment boundaries of relationships in the couple's reference group. These fears of infidelity reflect a sense that no same-sex partner could make a genuine commitment or respect it in the face of temptation, because this relationship is not a "real" (i.e., heterosexually married) relationship, and thus is based on only the most flimsy and fleeting of attractions. Same-sex couples may even attempt to convince the therapist of the truth of this myth by listing the number of couple-friends of theirs who have split up recently, drawing the therapist and themselves into ignoring the statistics on the similarly fragile state of heterosexual marriage in late 20th-century North America.

3. A couple seeks therapy because of jealousy over one partner's close friendship with a heterosexual person of the same sex. Here, the implied threat is that a heterosexual person would be more valued a companion than the partner, a member of the stigmatized group of lesbians or gay men.

4. A same-sex couple seeks therapy because, although all other aspects of relational functioning are working well, there has been a serious

diminishing of sexual frequency. Both partners express concern; both describe themselves as still attracted to and in love with their partner. The therapist has screened out such variables as child sexual-abuse histories or substance abuse in either partner, but finds that standard techniques to enhance the couple's sexual functioning have little impact, although motivation for change seems high. Both members of the couple wonder if their relationship can survive a surfeit of sex, or if, lacking an active sexual life, they are really still lovers/partners, or if should now see themselves as "just friends" (Rothblum & Brehony, 1993).

This "worm in the bud" phenomenon, in which a well-functioning same-sex couple seems to contain one apparently fatal and insurmountable flaw, is an example of one of the most challenging and subtle aspects of internalized oppression, yet one of the most common. Whereas in the past this particular difficulty was found more frequently among lesbians, since the advent of AIDS and changes in the monogamy patterns of gay male couples, it is also appearing in that population. The function of such sexual problems appears to be communication to the partners that a same-sex relationship that function well in all variables is an impossibility. Additionally, it serves to bring to the surface the fear that the sole defining characteristic of the couple is their sexual relationship. Although no one would declare a heterosexually married-couple to be "just friends" if they ceased for a period of time to be genitally sexual with one another, the fragility of definition for same-sex couples can be observed in this type of problem.

These examples underscore the importance, for the therapist, of seeking to uncover how apparently mysterious problems in the functioning of a same-sex couple may be signifiers of internalized homophobia or heterosexism. If, on careful analysis, it appears that the function of this particular problem is to communicate to the partners that their relationship is illegitimate, inconsequential, ephemeral, or otherwise less than equal to a heterosexual marriage, then the chances are excellent that internalized oppression will be a primary, if not the only, source of difficulties in the couple's functioning. When the couple is dealing with large amounts of external oppression as well, the likelihood that this has triggered lingering self-hatred is particularly common.

It is important to stress here that the best same-sex relationships will encounter glimmerings of internalized oppression, as well as the slings and arrows of external oppression from time to time; this has certainly been the case for my relationship and the quality relationships of my lesbian and gay male friends. The fight over whether to finally come out to a set of parents, or accept, yet again, the exclusion of one's partner from "family" status at holiday or ritual occasions; or the grief at again having to go "single" to a company function for the unpteenth time can intrude into the most functional and committed of same-sex relationships. How much more likely, therefore, that a couple with other problems will have to confront their mutual and often nonconscious self-oppressive beliefs and values. If there are other problems in the relationship, they will be exacerbated by external and internalized oppression.

These difficulties for the same-sex couple can be further complicated by the therapist's homophobia. Recent data from a large study of psychologists indicate that many experienced practitioners hold attitudes toward sexual minority persons that range from ignorant, but well-meaning, to viciously attacking (Committee on Lesbian and Gay Concerns, 1991). When the therapist is well-meaning, she/he is usually unaware of her/his own homophobia and heterosexism. Some common manifestations of these biases in therapists include the following:

1. Failing to value the couple's commitment to one another; encouraging a same-sex couple to see their problem as insurmountable and to end a relationship more quickly than would be the case for a heterosexual couple with similar problems.

2. Refusing to recognize and name violence in a same-sex relationship, or accepting the falsehood that because both partners are of the same gender, that these are "mutual fights" between equals (Lobel, 1986; Ireland & Letellier, 1991).

3. Joining a couple in being overattached to the issue of longevity versus quality of relationship in a situation in which the therapist would support a similarly malfunctioning heterosexual couple to find a sane way to bring an end to the relationship. Therapists should not require their same-sex couple clients to refute myths on the therapist's behalf.

4. Failing to attend to the high risk of substance abuse as a complicating factor in problematic same-sex relationships. Research indicates that as many as one third of all lesbian and gay men may have serious problems with drugs and/or alcohol (Swallow, 1983; Ziebold & Mongeon, 1985). Although one positive conse-

quence of the advent of AIDS has been the sobering up and recovery of many lesbian and gay practicing alcoholics and addicts, the problem still occurs at a higher base rate than in white heterosexual communities. Even though bars continue to be one major, public social nexus available to sexual minority persons, a therapist must not minimize the meaning of the couple's social life revolving around settings where alcohol consumption is a norm.

5. Overglamorizing the same-sex relationship. Some well-meaning individuals feel that in order to combat oppressive stereotypes they must romanticize same-sex relationships as universally wonderful and full of high-quality communication and empathy. A therapist's telling clients how "brave" they are communicates to them the metamessage that they had better not reveal the full extent of their problems lest they burst her/his bubble. Denying a same-sex couple the equal opportunity to have serious difficulties is a more complex, but also potentially damaging manifestation of a biased attitude on the part of a well-intentioned therapist.

A useful check against therapist bias is to ask the question: "What messages am I communicating to these clients about the meaning, worth, and value of same-sex relationships." Denigration and idealization have equal potential for harm. It is essential that a therapist working with a same-sex couple tender to them the same respect, dignity, and opportunity to be banal and yet unique, as they do in to every heterosexual couple. The goal is for both the therapist and the client pair to take for granted the possibility of a happy, healthy well-functioning same-sex couple, and to do so in a way that does not require the couple to mirror the norms of heterosexuality. Lesbian and gay paradigms for relationships (Brown, 1989, 1991) may be at variance with those for heterosexual couple satisfaction; however, the outcome in terms of quality of relational life and functioning is likely to be the same. Therapists who are novices working with same-sex couples and/or sexual minority individuals are strongly urged to seek regular consultation from a therapist who does have this experience and can point out the subtle expressions of bias that are bound to appear. My experience as a lesbian therapist is that my own internalized heterosexist and homophobic biases are best detected by the observing eyes and listening ears of my trusted colleagues; how much more so is this the case for the therapist who, culturally, is only barely literate in lesbian or gay male lives.

SPECIAL ISSUES AND CONCERNS OF LESBIAN COUPLES

One of the most salient facts regarding a lesbian couple is that it is composed of two women. This self-evident phenomenon is the richest source of both strengths and difficulties that such a couple brings to their relationship. A therapist working with a lesbian couple confronts a female gender-role development multiplied by two. Although each woman will vary in her degree of assimilation to this socialization, it is usually the case that even the most "masculine"-appearing lesbian will be a quite average woman when it comes to such issues as sharing power, expression of anger and hostility, initiation of sexual activity, boundary maintenance, and tolerance of distance and difference. In order to work well with lesbian couples, a therapist should first have a thorough grounding in the scholarship on women's adult development. Readers are referred to Miller (1976) or Jordan, Kaplan, Miller, Stiver, and Surrey (1991) for a more complete discussion of these issues. Without clearly comprehending the process of adult female development within a sexist cultural context in which women are devalued, it may be difficult for a therapist, no matter how skillful, to comprehend some common lesbian couple problems.

A lesbian couple, because it contains two women, is also twice as likely to include a survivor of childhood or adult sexual abuse, or assault. Base rates for both of these experiences in women's lives are quite high, with studies of nonpatient populations yielding figures revealing that approximately one-third of all women are violence survivors. It is not unusual for both partners to be incest survivors, with one woman's derepression of memory triggered by her partner's recall. Thus, the impact on adult relationship functioning of childhood abuse is more likely to be a factor in working with lesbian couples, simply because double the number of women doubles the likelihood of such a survivor being present.

As is the case with other forms of internalized bias, the phenomenon of cultural devaluation of women merits careful analysis in helping lesbian couples to confront their problems. Lesbians, like other women, have learned in most instances to place little value on such stereotypically "feminine" ways of behaving as being nurturant, empathic, and relationally oriented, although some groups of lesbians, familiar with the academic literature on the self-in-relation model, have embraced it enthusiastically as a corrective against such devaluation (Boston Lesbian Psychologies Collective, 1987). Blumstein and Schwartz (1983) have commented that, because the lesbian couples that they studied were in the process of rejecting and reevaluating both male and female gender roles as commonly socially constructed, they are more likely to experience relational conflict as they draw the maps to their relational territories from scratch. Clunis and Green (1988) point out that lesbian partners must struggle with learning how to treat a woman in a relationship with fairness and respect, and to expect, as a woman, to be valued equally by a partner—a dynamic they often did not observe in their heterosexual families of origin. To value the other woman in one's lesbian relationship, *because* she is a woman, challenges the deep devaluation and denigration of women in Western cultures.

In some problematic lesbian relationships, this devaluation of women manifests itself in terms of unreasonably high and perfectionistic expectations held by one woman about the other (and often held mutually). It is as if, in order to make up for her deficiency of not being a man, a lesbian partner is unconsciously expected to be a perfect mirror, a perfect nurturer, endlessly available and interested, and yet simultaneously independent and capable of meeting her own needs at all times. This double-bind of expectation, in which ego-boundariless empathy and relationality are to be combines with perfect skills at separation and individuation, can become a rock on which many lesbian couples may founder, particularly as they move from the initial romance stage to more normative conflict (Clunis & Green, 1988). A complicating factor in this picture is that while women have been well trained to cope with such expectations coming from men, and tend to expect that they will do the emotional work in heterosexual relationships, they may find them unrealistic or even insulting when delivered by a (mere) woman, who is supposed to be doing the emotional work of the relationship! A case example may illustrate this phenomenon in operation.

A lesbian couple sought therapy with a presenting complaints of increased arguing and conflict. On intake, they shared with the therapist the fact that they had only been genitally sexual four times in the 5 years that they had been together. Their joint understanding of this fact was that one of the women, an incest survivor, was working through her childhood abuse issues. The nonsurvivor partner often attempted to or wished to initiate sexual con-

tact over the years, but tried to restrain herself because both she and her survivor lover expected her to be extremely understanding and supportive. However, in the past year the nonsurvivor found herself growing more angry and resentful of this covert agreement, and less willing to live in an atmosphere where overt sexuality was absent. She began to push for sexual contact, and to make angry and sarcastic remarks about the length of time her partner was taking to deal with her incest issues.

The other partner was equally angry; her annoyance was focused on her partner's inability to be sufficiently "womanly" and uninterested in sex. "I would have expected this from a man," she told the therapist, "but women aren't so sexually motivated, are they? She's always been so supportive before now and this pressure to be sexual reminds me of what happened when I was a kid, and shuts me down even more." Her partner's rejoinder was that she was *trying* to be supportive, but that she has feelings too, and what is she supposed to do with them? The couple had discussed the possibility of nonmonogamy for the more sexually interested partner, but were fearful that this would constitute the beginning of the end of their relationship. The nonsurvivor partner expressed her feelings of guilt at pushing for sex, interwoven with a strong resentment that she was in the part of the "bad guy." Both were fearful of the fact that, after 5 years of apparent good functioning, they were arguing frequently.

This couple had made a covert agreement with each other that one partner could and would be a perfect, quasi-therapeutic nurturer to the other with all behavioral problems instantly understood and encompassed, and without differences between them as to need or timing of desire, and no expression of anger or resentment. Both partners perceived the failure of perfect seamless empathy on the part of the first woman as a failure of her commitment to the relationship. Neither woman's nonconscious expectations about the sort of womanly nurturing had been met by her partner, yet neither was aware, at this point, of the reasonableness (or lack thereof) of their expectations in an adult intimate relationship. Simultaneously, each woman expected the other to be able to cope, independently, with the distress engendered by their relational configuration. The metamessage that a woman is expected to be perfect in her giving and empathy had created a tangle that this couple could not see their way out of.

Therapy with this lesbian couple, as is often the case with two-women pairs, had as a major focus the analysis and comprehension of how such gender-role related expectations infused not only the sexual aspect of the relationship, also other facets of the interaction. Each woman's gender-role development experiences were a contributing factor to her difficulties. Each had learned that women were not supposed to be interested in sex, and that sex might, in fact, be dangerous. Neither had learned that it was acceptable to express anger, and thus did so in nonstraightforward guilt- and shame-ridden ways; neither was tolerant of the expression of anger by another woman, consigning anger also to the male realm. Each expected the other to be completely, empathically available, and to have needs and feelings that were a mirror of her own. In short, each woman expected her partner to be a good "wife" and neither was expected to have the stereotyped shortcomings of a "husband."

Another problem common to lesbian (and gay male) couples is the question of "age in gay life," or the "who's the real lesbian" phenomenon. Women "come out," assume a lesbian identity to describe their sexual orientation and attraction to women, at various points during adolescence and adulthood, and commonly at a later point than gay men, who tend to self-identify as gay during adolescence. Consequently, a couple with similar chronological ages may have very different experiences as "out" lesbians. One woman may have identified herself as lesbian since early adolescence and may have had little or no heterosexual experience, but many relationships with other women. Her partner, on the other hand, may have been heterosexually identified, married, and may have borne children, not becoming lesbian-identified until later adulthood. One author (Adelman, 1986) describes coming out to herself at age 60. Members of a couple may also have come out into a different social milieu. One woman may have named herself lesbian under conditions of great cultural oppression and secrecy in the time before lesbian gay liberation; the other may have come out in a context in which there were supportive laws and many openly lesbian role models available. In a relationship in which there is significant divergence on this variable, conflicts can attach themselves to its manifestations. An example can be found in the following case.

A lesbian couple who had been in a committed monogamous relationship for the past 2 years sought counseling due to numerous conflicts. There were two principal, identified problem areas: one woman was pushing the other to be more "out" in her work environment, and was suggesting that the couple explore nonmonogamy. The two women, in the middle 30s, had much in common that would

seem to support healthy relationship functioning. They came from similar ethnic and class backgrounds, and had many interests and values in common. They both worked in branches of the same profession, and met and began their relationship via their contacts at a professional association meeting. However, there was a major difference, in that the woman identified as the "troublemaker," who was pushing for greater openness of several kinds, was a previously married woman experiencing her first lesbian relationship. Her partner came out as an adolescent in the context of a fundamental religious family who responded in a very punitive manner to her lesbianism; she spent years carefully nurturing her professional persona, in which she had concealed her lesbianism to a large degree, and saw this relationship as her mature adult attempt at "settling down" after spending her twenties in a series of shorter, less satisfactory pairings.

Her partner's needs and perspective were quite different. She could not understand the first woman's need for caution, pointing out that theirs was very nonhomophobic profession and that "everyone knows" that the two of them were together; she was angry that her lover would not bring her to company social events. She said that she felt as if she missed the opportunity to experiment more in relationships with other women, and was concerned that it might be inappropriate for her to label herself a lesbian if this partner was the only woman she had ever had sex with. She suggested the possibility that "bisexual" might be a more accurate description of her; this was a catalyst for expressions of anger and terror on the part of her partner, who heard this as a statement of lack of commitment. The women had polarized around these issues, and believed that their relationship would probably end as a result. They were especially afraid that making the relationship a sexual one had ruined the close friendship they once had.

In the course of therapy, the woman who was newer to lesbian life expressed that her desire to have a committed relationship with her partner was at variance with what she had perceived as the needs of her "lesbian adolescence." This term is one used commonly in lesbian communities to refer to the behavior patterns of "newly-out" women, a period of adolescent-like sexual and relational experimentation in which sexual identity development is shaped and crystallized. Lesbian adolescence rarely corresponds in time with chronological adolescence, although as the stigma attached to lesbianism recedes, we are see more lesbians who engage in this developmental process at more age-appropriate times than was possible in the past. Such adolescence does not simply extend to sexual activities, however; it also is a time in which one's values about how to live as a lesbian are developed. The question of how open to be in dominant culture settings is an important aspect of this identity development, and the decisions that a woman makes how to position her identity, both with lesbian and dominant cultures, will reflect her perceptions of the risks and benefits of openness.

In this couple, the first woman had had ample opportunity to engage in her own adolescence as a lesbian, and had moved past that point in her desires regarding relational choices. She was unsettled by having her earlier decisions about openness challenged, and by what she perceived as her lover's failure to comprehend what were, to her, the very real risks of their being out as a couple. She felt less powerful in the relationship to her partner because, as the "real lesbian" in the relationship, she felt herself to be a less valued person in the culture at large. Conversely, her partner felt less valuable in their joint lesbian community in which she was the suspect newcomer, and wondered whether she might not be more credible and feel more equal if she, like her partner, were more clearly interested in *women* rather than just this particular woman.

Therapy with this couple focused on the age-cohort phenomenon, giving each woman a clearer view of the other's own unique experiences as parts of two very different age cohorts of lesbians. The therapist pointed out that these differences had very real meaning and import, as well as having become symbolic of a number of unexpressed fears regarding what might happen in a committed relationship with another woman, and asked them to explore whether it was reasonable, or even possible, for them to function as a couple, given their very different life experiences within a lesbian identity. She encouraged the pair to attend a support group for lesbian couples in which they could explore, in a peer-oriented setting, the ways that other lesbian couples had dealt with these and similar problems.

This couple did not stay together; after 6 months in couple therapy, they came to a mutual agreement to continue as close friends, but realized that the age-cohort differences led to too many meaningful distinctions between the legitimate needs and concerns of each woman. They reported that the transformation of their relationship, although sad for them both, was eased by their ability to understand the importance of contextual factors in shaping what had happened in their relationship, and that this allowed them to continue to have the deep degree of friendship and emotional intimacy that had drawn them together in the first place. Several years later, the more recently out woman was the facilitator at her now good friend's commitment ceremony to a woman who both of the original pair agreed was a better match on these important developmental variables than the first woman could ever have been. The three women described themselves as "family," a very common configuration in lesbian and gay communities (Becker, 1988) and the more recently out woman felt that she had "older sisters" to whom she could bring her various romantic dilemmas.

Because lesbian identity development in an oppressive context does not parallel many other adult developmental tasks, many lesbian couples encounter problems when they enter relational territories for which they are unprepared, and where there are few models of how lesbians might voyage through safely. A paucity of role models for lesbian couple functioning, as well as a dearth of mythologies about how a happy lesbian couple operates, have required the creation of support structures by lesbian communities that give lesbian couples access to one another's experiences of good functioning and positive outcome. Clunis and Green (1988) point out that lesbian couples rarely wish to model themselves after the heterosexual pairs by which they find themselves surrounded, but are uncertain of what constitutes normal *lesbian* couple functioning. The past decade has seen an outpouring of self-help books, leaderless support groups and even a sort of marriage manual (Butler, 1990) for lesbians. All of these are manifestations of the desire to develop norms against which couple functioning can be measured, and suggest that a referral to a group for couples, or to lesbian social settings that are supportive of couple relationships, can be an important intervention for a troubled lesbian pair.

Another issue that frequently complicates the lives of even well-functioning lesbian couples is a problem with boundaries, often manifested as an intolerance for distance and difference within the couple. Over the past decade this problem has become something of a humorous cliché in political and academic lesbian communities, with lesbian stand-up comics telling jokes about the dreaded signs of fusion in a relationship, and lesbian cartoons poking gentle fun at the occasional tendency to appear merged, which can happen when both partners have the same blouse size and color preference.

This apparent difficulty in the establishment of boundaries in a lesbian relationship has been described by the feminist psychodynamic theorists (Chodorow, 1979; Jordan et al., 1991; Burch, 1987) as reflecting the early mother–daughter bond that is characterized by more permeable ego boundaries and a heightened capacity for intimacy, leading to the development of a more relational, less distanced sense of self. This paradigm may lead to nonconscious expectations by women that their relationships with other women will be similar to that early bond, with perceived mutuality of needs and perfection of empathy. In the context of a heterosexual relationship, such a relational self can be highly functional when paired with a man's tighter ego boundaries and less well-developed capacities for empathy (Luepnitz, 1988). But in a lesbian relationship, subjected to the pressure cooker of external oppression that may artificially enhance perceived needs for similarity and closeness, this pairing of two female selves may be a source of some problems if not named and recognized.

It is extremely common for lesbian couples to describe their initial attraction in terms of a falling away of boundaries, and to find this image mirrored in the large volume of lesbian romantic fiction published in the past decade. Partners make statements such as "We were so alike"; "She understood me without my ever having to say anything" or "I felt joined with her." It is also common for lesbian couples in conflict to describe the etiology of their problem in the gradual emergence of differences between them. Clunis and Green (1988) describe this "conflict" stage of the relationship as being particularly difficult for lesbian couples who may be intolerant of differences of opinion, needs, or politics, and lack skills at communicating about those differences without feeling devalued.

Problems may also develop when one partner wishes to spend leisure time apart from the other, or to have friends as an individual rather than in the context of the couple's relationship. In a problematic lesbian couple, such a bid for autonomy is often defined as indicative of a desire to end a relationship, rather than a step toward making it more balanced and strong. Enmeshment, or its outward appearance, may be perceived to be a desirable goal, whereas more boundaried interdependence appears as a threat to the couple's stability. Problems frequently develop when a move toward autonomy by one woman is greeted with increased dependency needs by the other, leading to a cycle in which the autonomy-seeking partner finds herself feeling trapped by her partner's heightened demands for apparent emotional and behavioral fusion.

This very common and delicate problem of lesbian couples is best approached by the therapist's willingness to name it, and describe its normative status in a lesbian couple. Giving the women a clear theoretical explanation of what may be happening is often the most essential component of the intervention. This, as with other "normalizing" strategies suggested in this chapter, allows the two women to gain some distance on their dilemmas by seeing them as part and parcel of an attempt to construct a lesbian relationship from the materials of a sexist, heterosexist society. Such an approach frequently reduces the degree of fear associated with difference–distance issues in a lesbian couple, so that they can be approached therapeutically in a constructive manner. When each woman can be clear that this struggle to create a personal paradigm of a lesbian relationship, with a healthy mixture of boundaries and relatedness, is a sign of the strength and good quality of her relationship rather than a portent of disaster, she is more likely to ally herself with this task. It is important in this context that the couple's therapist come prepared with tools for teaching the women strategies for assertive and open resolution of conflict, as well as tools for identifying and uncovering hidden and symbolic communications that might otherwise be subjected to an attempt at empathic "mind reading" by one or both women.

An invaluable tool for therapists working with lesbian couples is knowledge of the dynamics and normative struggles of healthy and functioning lesbian couples. Watching or reading about how a well-functioning lesbian couple deals with such questions as the decision to bear and raise children, job relocations, coming out to families of origin or co-workers, gives the therapist a wealth of information that can be shared with the couple experiencing difficulties. Such data-gathering can be accomplished in a number of ways, which can include social and professional contacts with a range of lesbian couples from a diversity of backgrounds, familiarity with the literature on lesbian couple functioning, and an awareness of the norms of the various communities in which lesbians currently work and live. Having a clinical feel as well as a behavioral model for the varieties of well-functioning lesbian couples reduces the possibility that the therapist will be as confused about how a lesbian couple can work well as her/his lesbian clients are when they begin therapy.

THERAPY ISSUES
WITH GAY MALE COUPLES

As with lesbian couples, the juxtaposition of two male gender-role socialization experiences acts as a source of both strength and problems. In many ways, men in white, Western cultures are less well prepared by their gender-role development to take part in an intimate relationship or to do the work of relationship maintenance (David & Brannon, 1976; Orbach & Eichenbaum, 1983; Pleck & Sawyer, 1974; Stoltenberg, 1989) than are women. Just as lesbians grow up socialized to expect the dynamics and norms of a heterosexual relationship, so do gay men. However, gay men learn to be "husbands"; to be in control, to express anger, to be territorial, to move for power, and to be sexually initiating, but not to be empathic, nurturing, expressive of tender emotions, or to cook the meals and pick up the towels off the bathroom floor. Many of the problems discussed in the section on lesbian couples are reflected in the reverse here. Because gay men are men, the problems of gay male couples reflect the deficits inherent in the male gender role, and the difficulties experienced in striving toward intimacy when both partners' strengths lie in the areas of competition and differentiation.

In the past decade, gay men have had another, more frightening cloud hanging over their relationships. AIDS and the HIV epidemic have disproportionately affected the gay white-male community; even with changing demographics in the early 1990s, this group accounts for more than 70% of new HIV infections and AIDS deaths in North America. The 1980s was a decade of rapid change in the lives of gay men. Many gay male couples are faced with the chronic illness or imminent death of one or both partners who are HIV-positive. New relationships between gay men may be pairings of recent widowers, each with their own baggage of grief. Social support systems for gay men, whereas on the one hand strengthened by the network of organizations that have arisen to fight AIDS, are also decimated by death. One of my colleagues, a gay man active in the politics of his community, estimated that he had lost over 100 friends and colleagues in less than 10 years. The need to practice safer sex, although embraced enthusiastically by many gay men, has also been a source of new difficulties for gay male couples who once encompassed a variety of forms of sexual nonmonogamy within the context of emotional commitment.

Both of these factors— male gender-role socialization and survival in the age of AIDS— contribute to a common problem in gay male relationships of learning to do the emotional work of relationship maintenance. Men are socialized in white, Western cultures to respond sexually as a primary strategy for relationship development, and many gay male couples in the past have had their beginnings within a purely sexual context. Dating without immediate overt sexual expression is a new, artificially created artifact of the AIDS era for many gay men. Once the novelty of a new sexual partner fades, and the realities of relationship building are introduced, however, many gay male couples find themselves at a loss how to proceed. The expression of tender feelings has been stigmatized for men (David & Brannon, 1976; Stoltenberg, 1989); for many gay men, already stereotyped as "sissies" or "fairies," an exaggeratedly masculine, "macho" persona may be adopted as a defense against such stigma. Additionally, many gay men describe themselves as having difficulty maintaining sexual interest and arousal in the context of a long-term and sexually monogamous relationship, and may have a history of avoiding or sabotaging such pairings. The result of these various factors is that the members of the gay male couple may have little experience and comfort with the emotional skills necessary for long-term intimacy, and find themselves at a loss as to how to make the relationship progress. Because the pressure to remain partnered has heightened tremendously since the advent of AIDS, these problems are more likely than ever to bring a gay male couple into therapy. The following example suggests some of the parameters of the problem.

A gay male couple entered therapy with a presenting complaint of poor communication. The two men were first sexual with one another 2 years prior to entering therapy, and have lived together for 6 months, the time from which they dated their difficulties. One of the men was HIV-negative; the other had been recently diagnosed as HIV-positive, although he was currently in good health. Neither of the men had lived with a partner before, although both had extensive histories of relationships with other men; both of them expressed a desire to make a commitment and, in particular, to be able to see one another through the possibility of the seropositive man's illness to come.

During therapy, it became apparent that neither of the men had skills at expressing his dependency needs and tender feelings. Each man became aware of, and voiced, some previously nonconscious expectations that a partner would be more like a "wife," that is, good at reading his feelings. Neither partner wished to be a "wife," or to be the first one to express feelings of need and vulnerability. One man commented, "I'm attracted to masculine men, not screaming queens," uncovering the degree to which a sexist culture has created the association between masculinity and affective expression. Both men agreed that this was getting to be especially problematic for them because of their feelings about the second man's HIV-positive status; both described a need to cry and be held, as well as an aversion to the exposure of that need to their partner. Each felt somewhat embarrassed in the role of comforter.

In this case, although each man had had adequate skills for initiating sexual contact and maintaining a superficial dating relationship in which contact was structured, infrequent, and centered on exciting and interesting activities, neither had a repertoire for coping with the requirements of increased physical proximity and emotional intimacy. The added distress engendered by the newly discovered HIV-positive status of one of the partners crystallized these difficulties very quickly; the partners had many strong feelings to process with one another, and few tools with which to accomplish their task.

For these men, as with many other gay men struggling to reconcile their needs with homophobic, heterosexist, and sexist stereotyping, therapy focused initially on a confrontation of their rules about appropriate masculine behavior. Both men were encouraged to see how their rigid thinking about masculinity was an attempt to avoid fitting into homophobic stereotypes about gay men, and how it colluded with heterosexist norms by creating an image of manhood that impeded healthy gay make couples functioning. In this case, as was true for the lesbian couples described earlier in this chapter, a normalizing intervention was an essential component of the therapy process. The therapist was able to point out the impossibility of any feeling human being maintaining his macho "cool" in the face of the life-and-death realities confronted by these men, and the importance of allowing themselves room to experiment with various forms of tender emotional expression. Such a learning model gave each man greater permission to attempt, by trial and error, to find a means of communication that fit within his overall self-image, and to find out how the despised "nelly queen" image might be a source of strength and skills when viewed from a gay-affirmative, nonheterosexist perspective in which the expression of tender emotions

in a man was reframed as a desirable and attractive trait rather than a sign of despised "sissiehood."

With gay men, as with lesbians, it is important to encourage couples to form connections with other well-functioning gay male pairs who are addressing similar issues and concerns in their relationships, and who are striving to transcend and disempower stereotypes in the search for a new image of masculinity that includes tenderness, empathy, nonsexual connection. This may be even more important for gay male couples than for lesbian couples, because of the degree to which male adult development precludes the learning of good relationship-building skills; consequently, many gay male couples have fewer models to chose from within their own social circles than might a lesbian couple, particularly if neither man has significant prior experience in a long-term partnership. Unlike the lesbian community, where couples are the more valued norm, many gay male social activities have a "singles" flavor to them; it is thus more challenging for a gay male couple to immediately identify the benefits of a committed relationship when the social supports are less easily available. Simultaneously, the pressure for gay men to find "Mr. Right" and settle down have grown logarithmically in the face of AIDS; thus, the pressure on the relationship to succeed has grown as well, increasing the performance anxiety that can affect two people with achievement-oriented self-images, which is likely to be the case for two men.

It can be particularly important at this juncture for the therapist to examine how or if she/he is communicating distorted messages about the possibilities for success of a gay male couple. Since homophobic myths about relationship instability are even more prevalent with regard to gay men than they are regarding lesbians, such an exploration may be particularly essential to good, quality work with a gay male couple. The therapist's own AIDS phobia, as well as that of the two men, needs to be explored, as well the assumptions about the feasibility of a relationship when one man is HIV-positive and the other is not.

A common issue confronting gay male couples, both prior to and since the advent of AIDS and knowledge regarding its means of transmission, is the question of how commitment and monogamy are to be defined. In the past, many gay male couples have had an agreement that allowed for nonmongamous sexual behavior (often referred to as "tricking out") as long as the emotional ties of the relationship were not violated. Since the appearance of AIDS, the institution of safer sex guidelines and their adoption by many gay men has appeared to detach sexual safety from sexual monogamy. Consequently, a number of gay male couples find themselves continuing to struggle with these issues. Whereas in the past the rules for tricking out might have primarily entailed the setting in which such sex occurred, the identity of any other man and his relationship to the couple (e.g., not at home in the shared bed, not with close friends), current questions arise about whether one man can trust the other to practice safe sex outside of the relationship. Because such tricking-out arrangements were often essential to a couple's ability to function long term in an emotional commitment, the withdrawal of this option, because of fears of infection or mistrust of a partner's ability to stay sexually safe, has led to an upsurge in the difficulties faced by many gay male couples, who are now having to negotiate new shoals of relational configuration.

In the past, it was important for therapists working with gay male couples to understand the existence of this norm and not to confuse an absence of sexual monogamy with a failure of genuine emotional commitment. Currently, as norms for gay male relationships are undergoing tremendous change in the crucible of AIDS, it is important for therapists not to overvalue the meaning of sexual monogamy or perceive it as a sign of heightened quality of relational functioning, because it may simply represent a fearful fleeing from the realm of sexuality that carries so much real and apparent risk. Rather, it is essential for therapists working with the gay male couples to place the issue in its social and cultural context, to explore the function that past tricking-out agreements might have held in the ecology of the relationship, to help the couples consider how and if they need to reconstruct these agreements, and to normalize the difficulties that gay male couples may face when they move from one degree of sexual openness to another. The therapist must be conversant with safer sex guidelines as well, so as not to inadvertently reinforce potentially life-threatening misconceptions about what behaviors are least likely to transmit HIV.

In the past, tricking-out agreements may have been the source of an imbalance of power between the more and less monogamous members of a gay male pair; if a new agreement is made to institute sexual as well as emotional fidelity, the balance of power may shift into the hands

of the man most at ease with a sexually exclusive commitment, leading to confusion about how the relationship will now function. When a couple decides to continue a past pattern of sexual openness, issues of trust are likely to emerge regarding practice of safer sex both within and outside of the couple. A case example illustrates some of these points.

A gay male couple who had been together for 6 years called for therapy after one partner had seduced/pushed the other to engage in unprotected anal intercourse. The issue for these two men was not that the sex had been coercive (neither was willing to describe it as such) but rather that it was a violation, in which both men had colluded, of their agreement to be sexually safe. Both men had tested HIV-negative, but were aware that they continued to be at some risk because past sexual partners of each were seropositive; both had, by agreement, occasional sexual encounters with other men, which they had agreed to limit to mutual manual stimulation, a form of safer sex. Each was aware of the possibility that he could seroconvert at some time in the future, and was well informed about safer sex guidelines.

However, this episode led the man who had not initiated the unsafe sex to begin to question whether and how he could ever trust his partner. He broached the question of whether this unsafe exchange was a harbinger of things to come, or perhaps, more frightening to him, an indicator that his partner had not been trustworthy all along and had perhaps been sexually unsafe with one of his other casual sexual partners. The man who had initiated the unsafe sex was adamant that he had not been sexually unsafe in any other circumstance, but insisted that it felt to him like a genuine expression of their love and intimacy to make love in this highly intimate and unprotected way. He protested that, as the person being penetrated, he was actually the one at greater risk, and stated that this, if nothing else, should have clarified to his partner what the real dynamics of this sexual encounter were about. Implied, but not stated, by this man was, "If you really love me, you'll have unprotected sex with me."

Therapy with this couple required a careful analysis of the symbolic meaning of sex in the lives of these two particular gay men, as well as the central position of sexual expression in gay male culture and male gender-role socialization. The couple was encouraged to explore their sense of loss of sexual freedom since the advent of AIDS, and the fantasy that love would somehow prove as potent a protector against HIV as latex. They were referred by the therapist to a safer sex party presented by a local AIDS service organization. Such gatherings focus on teaching gay men ways to eroticize safer sex techniques, so as to increase commitment to and compliance with safer sex guidelines, as well as to help create contact with other gay men committed to safer sex. This series of interventions allowed the couple to feel supported in their agreements with one another so as to explore questions of trust in an emotionally less-charged atmosphere, and helped to maintain an atmosphere that was positive about sexual expression while simultaneously open to discussion about the meaning of sex in the couple's lives.

Another issue common to gay male couples is that of competition for power and status. Men in white, Western cultures are often socialized to equate their value as a person with the power, prestige, and income of their work, and to see other men, at best, as worthy competitors and, at worst, as the enemy in this game of status and power. In a gay male relationship, it is likely that one man may be in an occupation that carries greater power, income, or status than the other. The potential for feelings of competitiveness to emerge and become a destructive thread in the fabric of the relationship can be quite great, and can be expressed in a variety of nonobvious ways. For instance, the couple may present with a problem of unequal sharing of home maintenance or social activity planning. On examination, what may emerge is that both men nonconsciously expect the one with the lower status or lower income occupation to do more of the homemaking tasks' that, in a heterosexual relationship, tend to dissolve to the woman irrespective of her occupational status (Hochschild, 1989). Or, the man with less income may feel that he has less rights to participate in plans for spending money as a couple because it is not "his" money, while being resented by the higher income partner for not taking an equal part in the task of decision making.

In such situations, as with many other problems common to gay male couples, the therapist's thorough grasp of gender-role issues is essential to problem resolution. It can be highly effective for the therapist to probe regarding the impact of differences in occupational status on the couple's functioning. It is common for neither man to be aware of how he is communicating either excess value or devaluation to his partner and himself based upon income and status criteria; it is not unusual for both men to accept an unequal division of tasks because, using the heter-

osexist model in which they were raised, this appears "fair." It is useful for the therapist in such a situation to challenge the healthiness of the heterosexual relationship norm, either for gay men, or for heterosexual men and women regarding sharing of emotional caretaking tasks, and to suggest ways in which the couple can explore the symbolic meanings and cultural messages that they carry regarding money, status, and power. The two men might have very good skills at negotiating who takes out the garbage, but a much less thorough comprehension of why the task feels demeaning or problematic to the one doing it, or why this feels like "losing" the competition, when there is no overt desire to compete.

As with therapists working with lesbian couples, the therapist dealing with gay male relationships needs to develop a rich and diverse experience base of data from the lives of nonclient gay couples to serve as the source of an internal norm and clinical sense regarding good functioning in gay male relationships. If the only gay or lesbian couples that a therapist knows are clients, this can serve to bias the therapist's perceptions about how such couples work.

PARENTING ISSUES

It has become increasingly common in the past decade for lesbian and gay male couples also to be parents. This topic cannot be subsumed under the material in this chapter, due to its complexity and the quickly changing nature of the legal and social context in which lesbians and gay men give birth to, adopt, and raise their children. However, it is important to keep some basic facts in mind when dealing with a same-sex couple who are already, or who consider becoming, parents.

Lesbian and gay families have a variety of configurations: "blended" families, in which one or both partners bring children from a prior, usually heterosexual relationship; "adoptive" families, in which one or both partners adopt children in the context of the already existing same-sex couple, but where only one parent has legal rights to the child; and "birth" families, in which one of the parents gives birth to a biological child in the same-sex relational context. Whereas the issues inherent in lesbian and gay parenting are too complex for consideration in this context (readers are referred to Bozett, 1987, as an initial resource), the therapist working with a same-sex couple should not make the naive assumption that, because this couple is not interfertile, decisions about whether and how to become parents together will not be problematic. Perhaps *because* same-sex couples cannot for the most part accidentally become parents, but must plan carefully for almost any possible childraising experiences, these decisions will be the subject of much discussion and debate, and may catalyze or exacerbate other problems in the relationship. Additionally, because lesbian and gay parenting is not protected by any legal institutions, and is threatened by them in most cases, the decision to become parents will restimulate feelings that each partner has regarding their deprivileged status as lesbians or gay men.

Couples may enter therapy in order to have a safe arena in which to discuss parenting issues or the desire to become parents. Again, as with other concerns faced by same-sex couples, the therapist must be extremely careful not to allow bias to enter the therapy process. It is particularly important to explore the effects on both partners, the children, and the family unit, of the absence of legal support, or even clearly fined terms for relationships of two mothers or two fathers. Readers interested in this topic in greater detail are referred to Bozett (1987) or Pollack and Vaughn (1987) as resources.

CONCLUSION

Any two people entering therapy together to heal breaches in their relationships run a risk. That risk is that their couple system is not amenable to change in such a way that the system still operates. This holds as true for same-sex as for heterosexual couples, and the measure of good outcome in couple treatment is not always that the relationship persists. Good therapy with same-sex couples does not mean keeping them all together; it means giving such couples an equal opportunity of success at remaining together, or success at ending the relationship in a fashion that opens doors for each partner, and preserves friendship and connection when this is the desire of both people.

One thing that supports success, no matter how it looks, for the same-sex couple is for the therapist to be aware of the legal ramifications and needs of nonmarried domestic partnerships. A couple should be encouraged to consult an attorney knowledgeable about same-sex relationships in order to create living-together agreements, with clear clauses regarding separation and division of property, and custody and visi-

tation of any children. Additionally, a couple should have wills and durable springing powers of attorney in each other's favor that will establish their rights to act as next of kin in medical emergencies and protect shared property rights in case of the death of one party.

Although recent court decisions in large metropolitan areas have tended to honor implied rights of same-sex partners, such rights are only protected with this set of documents in hand. Without them, lesbians and gay men can, and have been, turned out of shared homes that were not in their names, deprived of shared property and money, kept away from sickbeds and funerals, forbidden visitation of children they had raised from birth, and denied care and custody of a disabled partner, even when that person clearly expressed wished for contact. In the most infamous U.S. case, that of Sharon Kowalski and Karen Thompson, Kowalski, a lesbian disabled with severe head injuries 5 years into the relationship, was denied the companionship of her partner, Thompson, by the former's parents, who insisted that their daughter could not possibly be a lesbian, even in the face of Sharon's repeated insistence that she wished to live with her lover, with whom she had exchanged rings and bought a home.

It took 8 years and numerous court battles before Karen was allowed, first to even visit with Sharon, and finally in December of 1991, to become Sharon's guardian and finally bring her home. A therapist can greatly reduce the stresses on a same-sex couple by making the procurement of these documents a condition of therapy. Working out a living-together and separation agreement can also provide a useful focus for addressing a number of the common problems in the same-sex relationship.

Same-sex couples are functional and viable systems, enriching the lives of lesbians and gay men, their friends, and families. In their lineaments, we can see possibilities for intimate couple relationships that so beyond the paradigms generated by heterosexuality, and expand our notions, as helping professionals, of what constitutes healthy couple functioning. I have suggested (Brown, 1989, 1991) that such a lesbian/gay paradigm for relational development may offer important new ways for therapists and researchers working with couples to understand problems and their solutions for heterosexual as well as same-sex couples. Troubled same-sex relationships deserve the same chances at healing and competent therapeutic interventions as do heterosexual ones. When a therapist is aware of the obstacles put in the way, both for the couple and herself/himself, by homophobia and heterosexism, and devises strategies to address these problems, such a chance for successful outcome is inevitably enhanced.

REFERENCES

Adelman, J. (1986). Falling and rising in love. In M. Adelman (Ed.), *Long time passing: Lives of older lesbians* (pp. 35–50.). Boston: Alyson.

Becker, C. S. (1988). *Unbroken ties: Lesbian ex-lovers.* Boston: Alyson.

Berrill, K. T. (1990). Anti-gay violence and victimization in the United States: An overview. *Journal of Interpersonal Violence, 5,* 274–294.

Berzon, B. (1988). *Permanent partners.* New York: Dutton.

Blumstein, P., & Schwartz, P. (1983). *American couples.* New York: Morrow.

Bozett, F. W. (Ed.). (1987). *Gay and lesbian parents.* New York: Praeger.

Bradford, J., & Ryan, C. (1987). *National lesbian health care survey. Mental health implications.* Richmond: Virginia Commonwealth University Research Laboratory.

Brown, L. S. (1989). New voices, new visions: Towards a lesbian/gay paradigm for psychology. *Psychology of Women Quarterly, 13,* 445–458.

Brown, L. S. (1990, October). *Therapy in another mother tongue: Working with the sexual minority client.* Keynote address, Counseling with Gay, Lesbian, and Bisexual People Conference, Ithaca, NY.

Brown, L. S (1991, March). *Lesbian paradigms for a psychology of women.* Invited address, Division of Women, Georgia Psychological Association, Atlanta, GA.

Brown L. S., & Zimmer, D. (1986). An introduction to therapy issues of lesbian and gay male couples. In N. S. Jacobson & A. S. Gurman (Eds.), *Clinical handbook of marital therapy* (pp. 451–468). New York: Guilford Press.

Burch, B. (1987). Barriers to intimacy; Conflicts over power, dependency, and nurturing in lesbian relationships. In Boston Lesbian Psychologies Collective (Ed.), *Lesbian psychologies: Explorations and challenges* (pp. 126–141). Chicago: University of Illinois Press.

Buhrke, R. A., & Douce, L. A. (1991). Training issues for counseling psychologists in working with lesbian women and gay men. *The Counseling Psychologist, 19,* 216–234.

Butler, B. (1990). *Ceremonies of the heart.* Seattle: Seal Press.

Chodorow, N. (1979). *The reproduction of mothering.* Berkeley: University of California Press.

Clunis, D. M., & Green, G. D. (1988). *Lesbian couples.* Seattle: Seal Press.

Committee on Lesbian and Gay Concerns. (1991). *Final report of the Task Force on bias in psychotherapy with lesbians and gay men.* Washington, DC: American Psychological Association.

David, D., & Brannon, R. (1976). *The forty-nine percent majority: The male sex role.* Reading, MA: Addison-Wesley.

Garnets, L. D., Herek, G. M., & Levy, B. (1990). Violence and victimization of lesbians and gay men: Mental health consequences. *Journal of Interpersonal Violence, 5,* 366–383.

Gonsiorek, J., & Weinrich, J. (1991). *Homosexuality: Social, psychological, and biological issues* (2nd ed.). Newbury Park, CA: Sage.

Herek, G. M. (1990). Gay people and government security clearances. *American Psychologist, 45,* 1035–1042.

Hochschild, A. (1989). *The second shift.* New York, Viking.

Ireland, D., & Letellier, P. (1991). *Men who beat the men who love them.* New York: Harrington Park Press.

Jordan, J. V., Kaplan, A. G., Miller, J. B., Stiver, I. P., & Surrey, J. L. (1991). *Women's growth in connection: Writings from the Stone Center.* New York: Guilford Press.

Lobel, K. (Ed.). (1986). *Naming the violence: Speaking out about lesbian battering.* Seattle: Seal Press.

Luepnitz, D. (1988). *The family interpreted.* New York: Basic Books.

McWhirter, D., & Mattison, A. (1984). *The male couple.* Englewood Cliffs, NJ: Prentice-Hall.

Miller, J. B. (1976). *Toward a new psychology of women.* Boston: Beacon Press.

Morgan, K. S. (1992). Caucasian lesbians' use of psychotherapy: A matter of attitude? *Psychology of Women Quarterly, 16,* 127–130.

Morgan, K. S., & Brown, L. S. (1991). Lesbian career development, work behavior, and vocational counseling. *The Counseling Psychologist, 19,* 273–291.

Orbach, S., & Eichenbaum, L. (1983). *What do woman want?* New York: Basic Books.

Pleck, J., & Sawyer, J. (1974). *Men and masculinity.* Englewood Cliffs, NJ: Prentice-Hall.

Pollack, S., & Vaughn, J. (1987). *Politics of the heart: A lesbian parenting anthology.* Ithaca, NY: Firebrand Books.

Rothblum, E. D., & Brehony, K. (Eds.). (1993). *Boston marriages.* Amherst, MA: University of Massachusetts Press.

Shilts, R. D. (1993). *Conduct unbecoming: Gays and lesbians in the US military.* New York: St. Martins Press.

Stoltenberg, J. (1989) *Refusing to be a man.* Portland, OR: Breitenbush Books.

Swallow, J. (Ed.). (1983). *Out from under: Sober dykes and our friends.* San Francisco: Spinsters Ink.

Thompson, K., & Andrezejewski, J. (1988). *Why can't Sharon Kowalski come home?* San Francisco: Spinsters/Aunt Lute.

Ziebold, T. O., & Mongeon, J. E. (19985). *Gay and sober: Directions for counseling and therapy.* New York: Harrington Park Press.

B

Ruptures of
the Relational Bond

15

Crises of Infidelity

FRANK S. PITTMAN III
TINA PITTMAN WAGERS

THE DEFINITION OF "infidelity" varies widely among professionals, nonprofessionals, and marriage partners. To us, "infidelity" is a breach of trust, the breaking of the couple's agreement about their sexual exclusivity. In monogamous marriages, most couples agree to strict sexual exclusivity, but some couples make up their own rules. For example, one or both partners may prostitute themselves when sex is purely for business. Some marriages have permitted homosexual, but not heterosexual, behavior outside of the marriage. Others have allowed outside sex when partners are separated by time or distance. Marriages in some cultures used to permit males, but not females, to screw around. In these marriages, as in more strictly exclusive ones, the infidelity may not be in the sexual act itself, but in the breaking of whatever agreement has been accepted by both partners in the marriage. Obviously, this definition of "infidelity" differs from that of "adultery," in which the sexual act itself is the issue, as defined legally or religiously.

Secrecy, which is primary to this definition of "infidelity," causes confusion for couples. For example, when a husband has engaged in flirtation, clandestine meetings, or furtive sex play with someone else, and insists that because no intercourse occurred, he did nothing wrong, he may be confused when his wife is uncomfortable with the flirtation. One man flew into a jealous rage when he found his wife in a bar with her hand on another man's knee. She thought his reaction was silly and overreactive since, after all,

she was just holding the guy's leg, not any other part of his anatomy. Another man, by chance, had lunch with a former affair partner. Although only a sandwich and mild pleasantries were shared, his wife considered his failure to tell her about it a betrayal of the relationship.

Infidelity, then, depends a great deal on the couple's understanding of the contract they have with one another. Because they may be the only ones privy to the terms of the contract, when they wonder whether something constitutes an infidelity, they should ask their marriage partner.

Research has shown that men and women define and participate in extramarital involvement differently, with women more likely to engage in emotional relationships and men more likely to engage in sexual ones (see Brown, 1991; Glass & Wright, 1985). Thus, it is important that couples clarify their understanding of the marital agreement.

When marriage partners are not honest with one another, the situation gets confusing and disorienting, and can destroy the relationship. The sex itself seems to be less damaging than the deliberate effort to disorient one's partner to avoid the inevitable conflict over some breach of the marital agreement. Indeed, in our clinical experience, divorces rarely occur unless there has been such a betrayal or infidelity. People tell us that they divorced because "they married too young" or "grew apart" or "couldn't communicate." Yet, in our clinical experience, more than 90% of divorces in established first marriages have involved infidelity, often kept secret throughout the entire divorce process, or considered too insignificant to mention. Strangely, this observation of the correlation between infidelity and divorce is rarely acknowledged in the clinical literature. Are we seeing a skewed sample in our practices? Are we exerting such a promarriage influence that couples get back together unless there is a strong counterpull out of the marriage? Or are the researchers of the literature failing to make the connection because they don't ask the questions? It may be that clinical observers who oversee marital dissolution more dispassionately might find a correlation of only 80% or even a bit lower.

What shall we call the players in these painful domestic dramas? To describe the betrayer, the person committing the affair, we prefer the term "infidel," the term's dual meaning also implying a nonbeliever, one who does not keep the faith. The affair partner is referred to as the "affairee." Unlike the term "lover," which is frequently inappropriate since love is such a minor, irrelevant ingredient in these often hateful situations, the term we use purposely implies unreality, enchantment, illusion, and impermanence. Last, the victim of the affair, the marriage partner who is being betrayed, is called the "cuckold," which used to be a derisive term referring to a man whose wife was pregnant by someone else. The origin of this term is from "cuckoo," the bird with the peculiar habit of laying its eggs in the nests of other birds. The other bird is surprised when an egg, thought to be her own, hatches a cuckoo bird. The word "cuckoo" has entered our slang not only as "someone who is in the wrong nest," but as "a silly and addle-brained person." Someone who is unfaithful is certainly cuckoo, and the unfortunate spouse of someone who has gone cuckoo is, sadly, the cuckold.

Also, although we refer to "marriage partners" and "spouses," the same forces operate among partners of either gender who live in a committed relationship with some contract or understanding about sexual exclusivity.

A clinical discussion of infidelity necessitates an exploration of values. The idea that psychotherapists can and should avoid making value judgements is, we believe, naive. Responsible therapists have to examine their own, as well as the patient's and society's values, with some understanding of how all of these fit together. The very writing of this chapter implies that we believe that infidelity is a matter deserving of attention and treatment in couples therapy, rather than, as has been previously believed in mental health circles, a moral issue and not a mental health one, or, as believed in psychoanalytic circles, less important than sexual fantasies and best handled with secrecy. Some therapists have seen affairs as normal, healthy expressions of normal impulses, and marriage as an unhealthy, unnatural restriction on sexual freedom. Therapists holding this attitude, blaming marriage for interfering with affairs, will have a far different impact on the marriage partners that come into their practice. A recent patient had been told by his five-times-married therapist that, after the man's recent affair, he might as well give up on his marriage, because "marriages don't survive affairs because women don't understand men's need to screw around." The therapist went on, "Marriages should change partners every few years anyway, since your partner gets to know you too well after a while."

The emotion of guilt, which usually occurs in conjunction with affairs, is variably valued in this culture. We believe that it really is mentally healthy to experience guilt over harmful actions such as an infidelity. Bob Beavers (1985), in his book *Successful Marriage*, said, "Guilt is good for you if it lasts no longer than 5 minutes and brings a change in behavior." On the other hand, feeling guilty about one's fantasies seems sick and pointless. Engaging in sexual fantasies, without engaging in the forbidden activities with the fantasied partner(s) is one of life's safest and healthiest pleasures.

People's sexual choices impact other people. When extramarital sex occurs in a marriage in which partners have agreed to monogamy, it should be considered symptomatic, problematic behavior. Extramarital sex that does not violate a particular marital contract may be less of a problem for the participants than for outside observers. However, some of these contracts may be less benign than they seem. Whether people practice monogamy cannot be a unilateral decision. Certainly, we can no longer afford to keep sex secret in the era of AIDS.

MYTHS ABOUT INFIDELITY

Despite the severe consequences of infidelity and the significant amount of public attention it receives, several myths about infidelity persist in popular, and even professional, mythology. These myths may appear naive or even old-fashioned, but we encounter each of them daily:

1. Everybody is unfaithful; it is normal, expected behavior.
2. Affairs are good for you, and may even revive a dull marriage.
3. The infidel must not "love" the cuckold; the affair proves it.
4. The affairee must be "sexier" than the spouse.
5. The affair is the fault of the cuckold, proof that the cuckold has failed in some way that made the affair necessary.
6. The best approach to the discovery of a spouse's affair is to pretend not to know and thereby avoid a crisis.
7. If an affair occurs, the marriage must end in a divorce.

Although some of these myths are true some of the time, they are misleading as generalities.

Myth #1: Everybody has affairs. People who screw around assume that everyone else does, too, whereas those who don't assume that monogamy is normal. People whose families of origin had extramarital affairs are more likely to view infidelity as normal and expected, and to behave accordingly.

Recent surveys show that about 50% of husbands have been unfaithful, whereas 30% to 40%% of wives have been so. In older generations, infidelity was a predominantly male activity, whereas today younger women are being unfaithful at rates similar to their husbands.

These figures are somewhat misleading, though. Many adulterers have had only one affair; most, only a few. Much of the infidelity takes place (as cause or effect) in the last year of a dying marriage. Intact, continuing marriages are far less adulterous than the statistics would reflect. Furthermore, surveys also show that the vast majority of people believe strongly in marital fidelity, usually for themselves, and certainly for their spouses.

Truth #1: Infidelity is not normal behavior, but a symptom of some problem.

Myth #2: Affairs are good for a marriage. Although *Playboy* and *Cosmopolitan* readers, as well as some family therapists, want to believe this, all evidence points to the contrary. Perhaps this myth is perpetuated by folks who believe that marriage itself is dull, and that if people felt free to be unfaithful, they wouldn't be resentful of their marriage's monotonous monogamy. Although some people are indeed too angry and too passive–aggressive for fidelity, this does not

mean that all people are passive–aggressive, or that faithful marriages are unnatural or fragile. Generally, affairs are dangerous and damaging. Partners in marriages in which an affair has occurred require a lot of work and pain in order to recover. Although affairs may result in a crisis in which some long-standing problem is solved, infidelity is a dangerous way of getting someone else's attention. Having an affair in order to produce such a crisis is a convoluted approach to problem solving, to say the least.

Truth #2: Affairs are dangerous and can easily, and inadvertently, end marriages.

Myth #3: Affairs prove that love has gone from a marriage. Reasons for affairs observed in clinical practice vary from hate, to "hobby," to "politeness," to confusion. Affairs may just result from the sexualization of friendships by people who are overly conscious of gender differences. Glass and Wright (1992) reviewed predictors of extramarital affairs that have been established in the research, including liberal sexual attitudes, and premarital sexual attitudes and behaviors. Women are more likely to believe that an affair has to do with an unhappy marriage. Women involved in affairs seem to be more unhappy in marriages than their male counterparts. However, we wonder *when* this attribution is made by unfaithful women, as no data is available comparing marital satisfaction before affairs versus satisfaction after the affair has begun.

In our experience, people are less likely to fall out of love and decide to have affairs, than they are to fall into affairs, and then justify their actions by deciding that they must have fallen out of love before the affair began. While they are in the throes of the affair, they may be disoriented about which event happened first. The infidel makes the unilateral choice to abandon the marital commitment amidst a smoldering stew of emotions. The presence or absence of love is too simplistic a factor. Marriages abound in a complexity of emotions: love, hate, anger, joy, dependency, admiration, fear, guilt, disgust, pity, and all other emotions, known and unknown. A commitment must survive independently of the emotions of the moment. It must be tied to each partner's choices about his/her identity and system of values. Fidelity has to do with what one intends to do, and does do, rather than what one is inclined to do.

Some therapists who write about infidelity have applied systems thinking to formulate the theory that "an affair indicates that an important emotional element is missing, such as the ability to sustain intimacy or to resolve conflicts without losing self-esteem" (Brown, 1991, p. 16). Because marriages are naturally imperfect, if you look for the flaws in any marriage you'll find some element missing. The problems don't necessarily cause the affair; it is just as systemic to believe that the affair causes the problems. An affair, once embarked upon, has powerful systemic impact on everyone in the system, and the system in which an affair is taking place may seem to be a swamp of pathology. Therapy is very different with therapists who wonder why this marriage caused a partner to be unfaithful, and those therapists who wonder how this infidel came to include betrayal in his/her repertoire of interpersonal coping techniques. We tend not to ask infidels why they weren't satisfied in the marriage; we're more likely to ask how they made the decision to be unfaithful, and where that particular approach to marital problem solving was learned. Investigators who believe infidelity is a reasonable approach to marital imperfection and who then ask about marital imperfection can find a marital cause for the infidelity.

Truth #3: Affairs can occur in marriages that, prior to the affair, were quite good.

Myth #4: The affairee was sexier than the spouse. Just because affairs involve sex doesn't mean they are about sex, or about the sexiness of the affairee. A lot of affairs involve a little bad sex and a lot of time on the telephone. Affairees may be different in some way from the cuckold, but not necessarily better. For example, one man whose wife was a bright, successful corporate manager started an affair with a 22-year-old drugstore clerk whose IQ and salary were both significantly lower than his wife's. It seems that he was threatened by increasing evidence of his wife's success, so he chose someone with whom he could feel more like the hero he thought a man should be.

Many people just want a friend, and the friendship slips into something quite different from what they had in mind. They don't seem to realize they can have friendships with members of the other gender without sexualizing the relationship.

Truth #4: Affairs involve sex, but sex is usually not the purpose of the affair.

Myth #5: The affair is the fault of the cuckold. Although a spouse may ignore evidence of an affair, or even encourage a spouse to pursue an affair, one person cannot make another have an affair. Indeed, an affair actually requires the physical absence of the cuckold. Despite this, infidels

standing there with their pants down often cry out, "You made me do it." Some marital therapists try to pacify everybody by declaring affairs to be a collusive effort, thus blaming the victim. We did see one woman who tried everything she knew to get her husband to have an affair. He wouldn't. She got him drunk and put a strange woman in his bed. He merely passed out. She finally held a gun to his head and demanded at gunpoint that he screw the neighbor, but he couldn't get it up. It seems ludicrous to believe that one person can force another to be unfaithful.

As difficult as it is to work with marriages in which there is an affair, it is harder to stop an ongoing affair when the betrayer is not forced to take full responsibility for his/her actions. Similarly, as the betrayed partner cannot make an affair happen or stop, it is futile to hand him/her the reins of responsibility.

Truth #5: No one can drive someone else to have an affair.

Myth #6: There is safety in ignorance of a spouse's affair. When affairs are revealed, stopped, and explored by the couple, marriages get closer. This can be scary. Ignorance of affairs—pretending not to notice—avoids conflict, but also avoids defining solvable problems. Affairs thrive in secrecy and derive their power from the conspiracy formed by a secret alliance. The weakness of the marriage may be in its avoidance of the issues.

Some people, though, choose to remain ignorant and uninvolved because they prefer not to be happily married, and prefer to retain some limits on the intimacy in their marriages. Although the spouse's affair can create an undesirable state of distance for these people, the end-of-affair reunion and postaffair problem solving might produce an even less desired state of excessive closeness.

Truth #6: Affairs are fueled by secrecy and threatened by exposure.

Myth #7: After an affair, divorce is inevitable. As is the case with any marital crisis, a marriage in the aftermath of an affair may get better and it may get worse. Postaffair marriages may become more intimate and honest, with the realization of the damage incurred through dishonesty and distance. Or they may become more distant and less intimate, for example, if the affair remains a disorienting, strongly suspected, but vigorously denied secret; if the infidel feels too guilty to fully return to the marriage; if the cuckold gets more security from anger and retribution than he/she gets from the shaky trust of a damaged marriage. The outcome seems to depend a great deal on people's expectations of their relationships, and their ability or willingness to live in an imperfect, tarnished world.

Although therapy, while the affair is still continuing, can seem ineffectual, albeit necessary to keep everyone alive and sane, therapy after the affair ends can determine the outcome of the postaffair marriage. Although many marriages end when the cuckold is confronted with an affair, many more end with the infidel's effort to maintain the secrecy of the affair.

Truth #7: Marriages can, with effort, survive affairs if the affairs are exposed.

In addition to an examination of myths surrounding marital infidelity, it is also important for therapists to look at their own thinking and feeling about honesty, gender, jealousy, and the nature of marriage.

HONESTY

People have some strange ideas about dishonesty. Some think that dishonesty is necessary between men and women, that dishonesty can protect people from getting hurt, and that the real danger of infidelity is in getting caught, because nobody will get upset if affairs are kept secret. These ideas imply a belief that your mate is too different, too delicate, or too frightening to understand you. Lying to someone further undermines any chance of having closeness, intimacy, or understanding in a relationship. But traditional wisdom has held that what husbands or wives don't know won't hurt them: "Women wouldn't understand—they'd just get stirred up." "You can't talk to men, they just get violent." We have found that intimacy in marriages is developed through confessions, explanations, and soul-searchings. Equality is also crucial to intimacy, and lying gives the liar a disorienting power over his/her partner that disrupts the balance of a relationship.

Marital satisfaction involves some sort of balance between closeness and distance. Healthy marriages are likely to negotiate this openly. Whereas most dysfunctional marriages suffer from insufficient intimacy, there are some people who find intimacy frightening and struggle to maintain distance, perhaps by actual physical distance, perhaps by emotional distance, perhaps by avoiding necessary conflict, or perhaps by throwing in just enough dishonesty

and misunderstanding to keep the partner disoriented. Such dishonesty may backfire and create in the partner alarm and frantic efforts to move closer. Dishonesty is not an efficient and reliable technique for creating comfortable distance. It is only helpful as a cover for someone who is trying to make a quick getaway.

JEALOUSY

Jealousy can be a normal, appropriate, and even necessary emotion when it occurs in a bonded relationship and elicits behavior that brings the couple closer together. For example, normal couples may notice the distance between themselves and their partners during the day, or at a party when they are talking with other people. Most partners will respond to that distance by "touching base" with their partner: seeking her out at a party, going to the room where he is working, or calling her at work to check on plans for the evening. Married couples do this several times a day, but such a response to jealousy in a nonbonded relationship would be inappropriate.

Jealousy can also be a subliminal signal of a lie. People who are truly intimate know when they are being lied to, even when they're not sure they know what the lie is. Jealousy is the emotional manifestation of their perception. The normal elements of fear of abandonment and dependency, which are contained in low doses in everyday jealousy, can cause problems when they occur in excessive amounts. For example, when people who have had affairs become frightened about the consequences of their own infidelity, they are most likely to fly into a jealous rage. Marriages in which jealousy is most intense may be those with the highest level of possessiveness and the lowest levels of intimacy. In marriages like these, one partner reveals so little of what is going on that the other must be constantly snooping around and testing, just trying to stay oriented in a confusing relationship.

Jealousy is sometimes related to low self-esteem, as when a person who feels unworthy bonds desperately and dependently, sometimes forcing the partner to sacrifice his/her own self-confidence to equalize the marriage.

Jealousy can be in error, or it can be mistaken without actually being wrong. Accusations of affairs are sometimes made without a real physical basis, although the accusations may contain some emotional truth. Sometimes one spouse appropriately senses another's attempts to distance, but mistakenly attributes the cause of the distance to a presumed rival. Honesty can reduce jealousy.

Inappropriate jealousy occurs in relationships in which one partner feels coupled and the other does not, such as in a new relationship or a former marriage. Other people may want to control the partner's thoughts, fantasies, or even memories of past relationships. (Such concerns may drive insecure men to seek virgins for marriage.) Inappropriate jealousy also occurs when people's dependency and fear reach desperate levels, or when they imagine that they are in competition for their partners with someone whose talents and characteristics they themselves envy.

Angry jealousy or jealous rages just produce distance. Jealousy must be gentle and loving to be either healthy or effective. In any case, reaffirming the bonds of the relationship and achieving a state of trust in the relationship will help jealousy dissipate to a normal level.

GENDER ISSUES

One problem with marriage is that it ordinarily takes place between one male and one female—two equal but slightly different halves of the complete partnership. (A lesbian friend once commented on lamentable "mixed marriages.") Katherine Hepburn says she never lived with Spencer Tracy because she considered men and women different species, too different to actually cohabit.

Although we could perseverate on the few physiological differences that exist between men and women, the differences are relatively small, and nowhere near as significant or functional as they appeared during the patriarchal times past. Gender differences are almost completely cultural. The success of the human animal is attributed to our species' ability to adapt to whatever conditions we face. The stability of our life, our society, and our marriage requires that we keep our pants zipped in public. Whether we are male or female, we should be able to do that.

We'll do whatever we're taught to do. The problem is what we learn, the socially reinforced models of male and female behavior that cause difficulties for people who belong to one gender and marry someone who belongs to the other. Although less is known about female development than is known about male development (mostly because male psychologists decided that males were the standard, and women's deviations from the standard were abnormal), Chodorow

(1978) and Gilligan (1982), as well as other writers, have come up with some credible hypotheses. One involves gender differences related to morality. Both boys and girls in this culture are usually raised primarily by women. For girls to learn to be adults, they model and learn from their caretakers, whereas boys must learn to be different from their primary caretakers in order to be "men." Girls thus see themselves as less differentiated than boys, as more continuous and related to their external world. Their morality is one of connectedness, context, and care. Women decide what is "right" based on what their responsibilities are to others, and in what context their decisions are made. Men are more likely to arrive at a morality based on fair and just resolution of dilemmas, in which the guiding principles are freestanding rules, principles, and ethics. These differences can make it difficult for one man and one woman to understand the reasoning of the other.

More obvious differences are evident in the way we raise boys and girls, particularly in how we raise them to behave during courtship. Boys are supposed to be assertive, unemotional, anti-intellectual, active, risk-taking, and are also supposed to conquer women. Girls are supposed to be passive, helpful, constricted, emotional, self-sacrificing, and submissive to men. We are each raised to become half of a human being. After gender training, anyone who manages to become a whole human being, capable of understanding and appreciating things from both a male and a female perspective, does so by accident.

One possible consequence of these gender differences can be found in Glass and Wright's (1992) findings regarding how men and women justify affairs differently. Their study found that women are more likely to justify extramarital involvement on the basis of emotional intimacy, whereas men justify affairs on the basis of sexual excitement. Not surprisingly, men's actual affairs are more sexual and women's are more emotional (Glass & Wright, 1985).

Of course, when the reality of marriage sets in, each individual partner (we hope) realizes that the functions required of him/her to stay married are very different from, and much more inclusive than, the ones required to court successfully. The most important point is this: Marriage certainly cannot become personal enough to work or to bear the pain of affairs until the gender boundaries are breached, and each marital partner recognizes and celebrates his/her marriage to a whole human being, rather than to a gender characterization.

PATTERNS OF INFIDELITY

In *Private Lies: Infidelity and the Betrayal of Intimacy* (Pittman, 1989), one of us (FSP) wrote a follow-up on 100 of the thousands of cases of infidelity he'd seen in practice. Four groups were identified, based largely on the direction of the emotional energy of the infidel. The four groups are (1) accidental infidelity; (2) philandering (3) romantic affairs, and (4) marital arrangements.

Accidental Infidelity

These affairs were not expected, familiar, and predictable, and they were not sought out by their participants. They happened unexpectedly, by chance, even carelessly, with no real consideration of the consequences. Unplanned, they usually took one or both of their participants by surprise. Accidental infidels, prior to the unexpected affair, did not usually think of themselves as being in love with the affair partner. In their efforts at justification, postcoitally infidels might fancy themselves in love, and the nature of the affair thus changes radically. Usually however, they don't fall in love with the affairee, and don't expect to continue the affair. They feel awkward, uncomfortable, and embarrassed about the affair. They know they have done something wrong. They were, at the time of the affair, too curious, too polite, too accommodating, or too friendly. When they explain the circumstances, they realize that "it just happened." For a short but crucial period of time, they let their guard down too far.

Sometimes their guard was down because they lacked sexual experience and were curious about whether they were missing something at home. In the past, virginity was valued in women, creating sexually incompatible marriages between men who were casual and even promiscuous about sex, and women who valued the nonphysical aspects of sex and romance. This double standard led to marriages that might not be very physical, and might even include the expectation that husbands would supplement their marriages with infidelity. Similarly, in some couples who are sexually inexperienced and are enduring some sort of sexual dysfunction, their frustration can tempt them to try sex with another partner.

Fortunately, more recent cultural standards permit men and women to be sexually skilled before marriage. These expectations change the emphasis on sex, so that the relationship, rather than the genitality, becomes the part that is special.

Despite vast amounts of experience and sexual skill, some people remain curious about something they believe they have missed. They are convinced that there must be something better than what they know already. In the past, middle age seemed to be the point at which people's curiosity was most likely to overflow and lead to accidental infidelity, fueled by awareness of having reached the summit. These days, with people's sexual curiosity sated earlier in life, the highs being sought are not sexual, but emotional or romantic.

A little boy used to be taught to be sexually aggressive, as if he were socially required to offer his sexual services to a lady, in much the same way that he would offer her his arm as they walked together. Some women accept the compliment but decline the services, realizing it is merely a gallantry. Some women don't decline the polite offer. These women are either normal women who like sex, or women who have been socialized to believe they are objects for the pleasure of men. In either case, if the offer has been accepted, the man's choices are either to admit he was paying a pleasant but empty compliment, or to follow through.

Some men and women whom the world has considered largely sexually undesirable may nonetheless manage to get married. Unfortunately, they may also be suckers for sexual flattery, and may become disoriented to time, place and person when they are flattered. Men who have affairs in these circumstances don't usually feel guilty since, after all, they didn't go looking for the affair. In addition, a man may buy into the classic convention that the decision about sex should be made by the female, and if he should be chosen, he's lucky. Women may so deeply appreciate the sexual flattery embedded in the offer that they may accept an offer that wasn't truly an offer.

Another common pattern involving politeness occurs when a man and a woman have known one another for some time through work or social situations. Although they would not ordinarily consider having an affair, circumstances of a crisis, perhaps, lead these friends away from their usual socially correct conversation and toward a more intimate interaction. Unsure of how to handle or understand this intimacy, the couple may misinterpret it as sexual and find themselves in an affair.

Accidental affairs may also happen to a man who is "just one of the boys," who foregoes intimacy with his wife in favor of gender loyalty to his buddies. This man's "good buddies" are philanderers who amuse themselves by flirting with and bedding women. When women come in pairs, this man obliges his "good buddy" by taking care of the extra "babe." Although this immature man doesn't seek out affairs, he's trapped in a custody battle between his friend and his wife, who is viewed as the enemy.

People who are, quite literally, crazy may have accidental affairs. People who are otherwise unlikely to have affairs may do so when they are having a psychotic episode or are going through a manic phase. A depressed person may collapse on an amateur rescuer, who is protective of the vulnerable, needy individual and sexualizes his/her newfound caretaker responsibility.

Even if a person is not truly crazy, he/she can have a bad day. We human beings are needier at some times than others. If our spouse has a surplus of nurturance on those days, all goes well. But if we are needy at a time when we are alone, out of favor at home, or when our partner is unavailable, we are at risk of being our least wise and least discriminating selves. Accidental affairs can happen on those days—or so we hear.

Philandering

Although philanderers come in many shapes and sizes, they all have a few things in common. First of all, they require a steady change of partner, which prevents them from committing to just one person. They are obsessed with gender, and take gender and its stereotypes quite literally. Male philanderers are more concerned with being men than with being human beings: Being a man requires a philanderer to be different from women and to obtain victories over them.

Philanderers are in love with their masculinity. At the root of philandering may be the man's relationship with his father. If the father was a philanderer, he may become one too, because that becomes the mark of a man. If the father failed to make the boy feel like a man—perhaps because he was too busy practicing his model of masculinity to be there for his son—then the boy may look to women to define him as a man. He is stuck in his development, perpetually going through puberty and confusing his penis with his self.

Women, through sex, bestow upon men their masculinity—by responding sexually, they make men men. But women also have the power to take the masculinity away. By their anger, their dissatisfaction, their betrayal, their failure to respond, they make the man feel less of a man.

In cultures that worship masculinity, most philanderers are men. These societies' double standards state that whatever is masculine is better than whatever is feminine. Monogamy is not expected in these societies, because monogamy requires gender equality. Philanderers buy the notion that masculinity can be achieved by competing with other men and/or by exerting sexual dominance over women. A Philanderer's greatest fear is to come under the control of a woman. He may bolster his beliefs about the dominance of men and the dangerous sexuality of women with religious or cultural traditions. Philanderers may practice hostility and cruelty to women, or amiable depersonalization of women, or may just perceive women as a different species.

However we view them—as bad little boys; as tragic, naturally polygamous men mistakenly placed in a monogamous culture; or as dangerous evolutionary throwbacks—they consider their behavior normal and even enviable.

Philanderers come in many guises. Charming philanderers have polished social skills, and are usually attractive and confident. They have been loved well and often, and are frequently frantically pursued by women who have heard of their expertise or who want to compete with the other women the man has used and thrown away.

Friendly philanderers are helpful guys who don't appear to be hostile toward, or exploitative of women. Rather, they are in awe of women and will sacrifice their own sexual pleasure to pacify and tame them. They use sex to overcome their fear of women, and so, like all other philanderers, are not quite comfortable with friendly sex among equals.

Heroic philanderers, like James Bond, who got off by bedding down women sent to kill him, are too tough for mere sex. They find danger sexually exciting, and seek relationships that are hostile and overtly threatening. These relationships prevent them from relaxing and becoming too comfortable with women, and so reduce the risk of their being controlled or destroyed by women.

The hostile philanderer is overgendered and focuses on his own genitals, and on the genitals and breasts of women. He is angry with marriage, sees it as a weapon his wife uses to restrict his freedom, and reassures himself of his masculinity by controlling things. The less successful he is in his own life, the more dependent on women, the more likely he is to put women down. He blames his philandering on his wife. He takes on the difficult job of seducing and degrading women at the same time.

Psychopaths are often philanderers, but some

men are "mascupaths." They retain their honor and morality in their dealings with men, and affirm their masculinity by fucking over women in horrifying, even lethal ways. Their objectification of all women as the enemies of men may lead them to become rapists and serial killers. At the center of such gruesome acts are men who are intensely aware of the danger of letting a female have control of them.

Some philanderers are sexual hobbyists. Although it would be easier for them to marry women who would share their sexual hobbies, these philanderers maintain a myth that men's sexual needs are greater than women's. They have affairs that they keep secret from their wives, and reassure themselves that this is only fair, given the mythic proportions of their sexual needs. Women can be philanderers too, but only after they have given up all romantic and idealistic expectations of men and marriage. Few do it.

Borderline philanderers have the attitudes of philanderers, but for one reason or another—guilt, comfort, wisdom, laziness, or lack of time—don't engage in philandering. Some of these men, though, wind up in a midlife crisis. After perhaps failing to achieve financial success, they start competitive seductions of women. With their honor lost in one arena, they feel they can relax their standards in another arena.

The impersonal philanderer has no time or energy for personal attachments to his affairees, or to his wife, for that matter. He barely notices which woman is with him in bed, because he is just using women for exercise and relaxation. Some of these men discover that it is more efficient to stick to masturbation and leave women out altogether.

Despite the fact that homosexual infidelity is just as damaging to monogamous relationships as heterosexual infidelity, gay philandering was rampant, at least in the pre-AIDS era. If the criteria for philandering involve (1) an obsession with masculinity, (2) determination not to come under the control of the "opposite" sex, and (3) sexual competitiveness with other men, the ultimate philanderer would by gay. Also, those who pay the enormous price for being gay in our society are making quite a sacrifice for their sexual freedom, so they have tended to demand their rights to the promiscuity they have purchased.

In the past, people have made a big issue of the difference between gay and straight affairs—as if heterosexual impulses were voluntary, whereas homosexual impulses were irresistible

Obviously, this is nonsense, since no one, straight or gay, is required to act on sexual impulses. We all choose which impulses we will act on, whether the impulse is straight or gay. The era of AIDS has, of course, had an enormous impact on the acceptability of philandering, as infidelity is seen as tantamount to an act of suicide/homicide. Because, by chance, AIDS hit the gay community first, gay monogamy has been more highly valued.

Most women who screw around a lot are not female philanderers. They lack the hostility toward their partners, and do not aim to degrade them when they conduct their sexual rounds. Most of them are romantics on a quest for "Mr. Wonderful." The few women who are capable of philandering may engage in hostile seductions, using sex to exercise power over male philanderers and beat these men at their own game. Many of these women's attitudes toward sex and men have been shaped by sexual abuse, which has led them to see themselves as objects, and sex as an act of exploitation, degradation, and aggression. Their fury with sex and men is evident in their exploitations. Most female philanderers also have had fathers who were philanderers. They are determined not to come under the control of males or marriage. The women who have the dynamics and background that would make them philanderers are more likely to be single and not put that much energy into marriage—which they distrust. Instead, they take out their anger on men, women, and marriage by raiding other people's marriages.

Although male and female philanderers may stop their activities when their marriages need attention, they don't keep that up for long. For philanderers, marriage, particularly a comfortable one, is too threatening for them to remain monogamous.

Male philanderers are likely to be married to women who are as concerned with their femininity as their philandering husbands are with their own masculinity. Philanderers encourage their wives' preoccupation, because it makes them look more masculine to be married to a thin, dainty, domestic woman. Although they encourage their wives' attractiveness, they discourage their sexuality. Either sexuality or competence on their wives' part would be threatening to their ever-important masculinity. A woman stays married to such a man because he may be attractive and successful, and she, his wife, is the envy of all her friends. If he is unsuccessful enough, the wife hopes, usually futilely, then eventually her husband will need and appreciate her. A woman married to a philanderer sometimes works very hard not to notice her husband's infidelities. If she does discover and confront her husband with the affair, he may have to punish her with them even more. It's hard spending a lifetime being married to a man who sees you as the enemy because you married him, who loathes and fears your gender, and yet demands that you constantly exaggerate and display it.

Romantic Affairs

Love has to do with bringing pleasure, comfort, peace, and security to one another. By contrast, falling *in* love involves romance, a form of exotic and narcissistic suffering in which the specialness of a loving relationship gets distorted into an obsession with suffering and sacrifices to keep things intense enough to make the world and reality fade away. The true romantic experience would come from defying all the forces of civilization in order to pursue a love experience that seems most "natural" (i.e., most socially inappropriate, disorderly, and unreasonable). This phenomenon tends to occur at points of transition in people's lives, and it can serve the purpose of distracting them from having to change and adapt to new circumstances or a new stage of development. Despite the fact that romantics are clearly experiencing a form of temporary insanity, and are disregarding all manner of other people and obligations in the meantime, they expect us to excuse their behavior and irresponsibility. Somehow, falling *in* love has become a sacred form of insanity. Certainly it is exalted in the literature, on TV, and in *People* magazine.

For instance, a woman entered into an affair after several years of marriage to a kind, generous, devoted husband. Her kids, with whom she'd been home since their birth, were now in school. She was bored with a life that was too predictable, too comfortable, and certainly not on par with the excitement she'd had in years past as an extraordinary student, then as a corporate fast tracker, and later as the full-time mother of bright and active children. She didn't know how to handle the next phase, and it was a toss-up between a new job or an affair. She chose the latter, and excused herself out of her marriage by saying she'd fallen "*in* love." Her husband was too nice for her to leave for any other reason. The affair ended soon after the marriage did, and she was once again free to lead an exciting life.

Romantics don't fall in love when they meet someone wonderful—they fall in love when they can't keep living their real life and they're not quite ready for suicide. It's a *liebestod* in which there is an irrational hope for a happy ending. Romance is an escape from too much reality; it is running away into fantasyland. It resembles a manic episode.

Romances occur at predictable points in life, when reality is coming on too strong: when your marital romance settles into honest love, when your children come and adulthood is expected, when you reach the summit of your career and feel the need for trophies or solace, when your parents die and you see what's in store for you, when your children hit adolescence and make life hell at home, when they leave home for good, when you or your partner begin to age. A marriage can be quite compatible for years and decades, and hit a turning point at which the two people seem headed in different directions. Naive therapists or affair partners may assume it is a bad marriage rather than a crisis in the life cycle.

Even though couples can carry on a romance for only a short period of time before they will lose their jobs and tie up traffic, starting a marriage with a romance may be a good beginning (as long as it doesn't involve destroying another marriage or two to get there). When the romance is recalled years later, the true love is strengthened somehow. These marriages can become dangerously imbalanced, however, when one person is ready to move from the "romance" to the love, and the other partner is determined to go to any lengths to forego honest love in order to keep a fantasy alive. It can fall apart when one or both partners discover that despite their intense preoccupation with each other during their hot romance, they really have nothing in common: no friendship, no partnership, and no real love.

When a romantic falls into bed with someone having an accident, as in the movie *Fatal Attraction*, the romantic subsequently does what feels right (i.e., most romantic), passionately clamps to the unsuspecting partner like a snapping turtle, and won't let go.

The romantic and the philanderer make an interesting couple. Romantics are easy prey for philanderers, but the combination can be dangerous. Romantics want philanderers to fulfill all of their expectations about romance, and the philanderer will escape anything that looks controlling. Pairing between either gender combination—romantic woman and philandering man, or philandering woman and romantic man—can be explosive.

The "romantic marital aide" is recruited in

some situations by the wife whose marriage is suffering some temporary distress. A romantic man may gallantly and passionately give up everything, including his marriage and his money, to help the woman with her marriage. She, however, is only using him as a marital aide, and will disengage from the romance as soon as she gets things worked out at home. Meanwhile, he's out of luck.

Romantic pairs can also prove to be an explosive combination. These lovers mesh so perfectly that they go wild, and the landscape is typically strewn with bodies before they are through with each other. These people are, of course, crazy, but the two peas sit in their pod and reassure themselves of the intense sanity of their love.

A few generalizations about such romance: It has little to do with love; it rarely works out for long; the more illogical it is, the more intense it is likely to be, and the sooner it becomes a disappointment. Finally, whatever happens, everybody gets hurt.

Marital Arrangements

Clearly, marital problems don't have to precede affairs. Philanderers sometimes create marital problems, but only after they have decided that they are in need of justification to have affairs. In "marital arrangements," however, a couple has problems they don't want to solve, and so they decide to stay married while both partners have affairs on the side. These affairs are not necessarily secret and are part of the marital arrangement. These couples have decided that although their marriage is by no means blissful, it is easier for all concerned that they stay together. Some people value distance more than intimacy, and may take some pride in differentiating themselves from the happily married. However, if each marital partner wants something different from the other, when one partner wants distance and the other wants closeness, a marital arrangement may stabilize a less than ideal situation. A marital aide is someone who is willing to sacrifice or at least enormously complicate his/her own life so that a couple won't have to divorce. Triangles like this can be amazingly stable.

Types of arrangements can include the "permanent separation," in which both reconciliations and remarriages are prevented by a separation that lasts many years. The permanent separation can serve the purposes of a betrayed spouse, too angry to free the betrayer, or, more likely, of a philanderer who can seduce potential affairees with that age-old promise, "The divorce is in the works," without actually having to make a whole new commitment.

People, obviously, can make whatever arrangement they choose workable, be it marriage, divorce, or permanent separation. The crucial ingredient here is the affair partner who keeps hoping for a divorce. This partner is, of course, as interchangeable as a set of clothes.

The "permanent triangle" is an arrangement entered into by a man who doesn't really want to be divorced, separated or truly married, either. He wants to maintain control and ensure that he isn't dependent on one woman. He wants an efficient, comfortable arrangement with just the right amount of distance, so he takes a mistress. Or, when the tables are turned, a woman may take a mister. Typically, these arrangements begin when a philanderer makes an effort at being a romantic and falls partially *in* love, but can't quite let the self-destructiveness of romance overcome the self-protectiveness of gender war, so he settles into a permanent friendly relationship with his affair partner. The relationship can last as long as the affair partner agrees to stability, and may well end if he/she makes a serious bid for spousal status.

People who are "just shopping" will remain married to a spouse considered highly imperfect while they look for a mate who is just right. None of the merchandise is quite up to par, though, and these people return merchandise frequently. They may keep getaway drivers around, who can help them escape from their imperfect marriage in case of emergency. Shoppers who are in the midst of divorce will similarly complain about the imperfection of the divorce agreement, lawyers, and custody arrangements.

"Psychiatric nurses" marry their spouse/patients because of the patient's emotional neediness. Their marriages to alcoholics, schizophrenics, and manic–depressives require them to overfunction so that their spouses can remain incompetent. If the nurses need emotional support, they may enter into a friendly affair, sometimes with someone from whom they are trying to get help for their spouse. These marriages are usually stable unless the patient is manic–depressive and gets involved in romantic affairs during high periods.

In some emotionally flat but efficient marriages, marital arrangements may involve "importing love." The marriages in which these arrangements occur work well—financially, socially, and even sexually—with role assignments based on gender. The couple may find it easier not to discuss each other's lives too much in order to retain the desired amount of ennui. If such a wife gets lonely and depressed, she may find intimacy elsewhere after her spouse has told her he doesn't want to be bothered with anything as inefficient as emotional closeness. The resultant affairs are typically romantic, but not very sexual, and serve to stabilize the otherwise stagnant marriage.

Some marriages are so stormy, so prone to craziness and instability, that arrangements involve "importing sanity" so that each partner can have a sane buddy or rescuer in the wings to turn to in times of burnout. These intense, exciting marriages are typically second marriages that started as ill-matched romantic affairs. The stabilizing forces may be the first-marriage partners, who were boring to be married to, but come in handy when sanctuary is needed.

Other arrangements involve "importing sex." For a variety of reasons, one marital partner may enjoy or want sex more than the other. Some people never liked sex much to begin with, and others have gotten out of the habit. Still others place such demands on their own sexual performance that they are rarely ready to perform. One husband may decide that his wife no longer meets his fantasied specifications. (Of course, no human being could transform him/herself as often as the spouse's fantasies are changed, but that isn't important to the philanderer who is seeking justification for affairs.) At any rate, sex is imported into these marriages, with the arrangement balancing the sexual inequality between the spouses.

"Revenge affairs" are nasty arrangements that occur after the discovery that one's spouse has had an affair. The enraged wife may be remarkably cruel in her revelation of the gory details of her affair to her husband. Sometimes, the faithless partner will encourage a revenge affair, and even recruit a willing participant for the betrayed spouse. Revenge affairs hardly ever work, and usually leave both spouses feeling angry and betrayed in a way that no reciprocal affair can resolve. They are especially hard on the unsuspecting affairee, who is being screwed with no love, only anger.

"Guerilla theater" is an arrangement entered into by couples who need to go through elaborate rituals and competitions to keep their love alive. They may even put on shows in public, using a volunteer, nonprofessional supporting cast. The volunteers are not aware that this is a theatrical production, and the couple may not be, either. The action sequence usually goes something like this: One monogamous romantic has a wife, but enjoys competition with a rival more than he enjoys being married. So he encourages his wife to have romantic affairs with which he can compete. His partner is a willing participant in all of these courtships, separations, and reconciliations. But her affairee is disoriented when his role in the final act switches from hero to villain to comic relief, dashing his hopes that this romance was working toward marriage.

"Jealous lovers" go through the same contortions as the "guerilla actors," but need only one act, usually performed in one evening. The roles are that of fighter and flirter. The couple goes someplace where the flirter can flirt, and the fighter can step in and fight with the flirtee. The couple then goes home to make love, leaving the flirtee humiliated and sometimes bruised. If the fighter loses the fight, the flirter can rescue him and the couple can still go home together.

A simple version of the jealousy game is called "flirtation." The partner needing the most reassurance of his/her attractiveness finds someone to flirt with. Once the flirtation has been sufficiently reassuring to the partner in need, any additional contact is optional. (If any clothing is removed, the flirtation becomes guilt-producing and complicated, and changes to a new game.) Armed with reassurance and a powerful sense of self-control, the reassured spouse can relay the story of the flirtation to the partner for an additional response.

Couples who aren't very proficient at sex may initiate arrangements involving "sex therapists." Sexual do-it-yourselfers don't go to professional sex therapists, but instead find makeshift arrangements for sexual instruction. They recruit friends, neighbors or co-workers to help them learn the necessary skills, and then return home to rescue their marriage. A decade or two ago, these arrangements were more common in marriages of women who'd never learned how to achieve orgasm. These difficulties and some others have been helped by the public availability of sexual information.

Although "swingers" are nearly an extinct breed, as people's sexual curiosities are now sated earlier, and certainly as the AIDS epidemic looms over fantasies of sexual freedom, there are still a few people out there whose major hobby is exploring the joys of sex. They'll try anything, and take a lot of risks in doing so. They seem to get pleasure from defiance of the risks in obtaining different sexual experiences, and are equally defiant in other areas of their lives. Their numbers are waning, though, and swinging and "free sex" seem dated and dangerous now. Maybe they always were.

INTERVENTION WITH INFIDELITY

Infidelity can be treated within a crisis framework, such as that described in *Turning Points: Treating Families in Transition and Crisis* (Pittman, 1987). Infidelity often presents in the midst of crisis, with all hell breaking loose and all the participants running wildly in all directions with their emotions hanging out and flapping in the breeze. It may seem overwhelming, but it really is not. A therapeutic partner is helpful but not necessary in these cases. While we have done cotherapy together, we each, in our separate practices, ordinarily work alone.

The steps in family crisis therapy are as follows:

Step 1: Emergency response, that is, quickly intercept the participants who are trying to escalate the chaos, either by homicide, suicide, precipitous divorce, or just creating confusion and sabotaging efforts at understanding what is going on. The therapist conveys confidence that the crisis can be survived.

Step 2: Bringing everybody together, that is, provide a calm, safe setting in which the infidel and the cuckold, and maybe even the affairee, can sit down facing one another and examine what has happened. The therapist conveys confidence that the parties to this crisis can face one another and talk about it.

Step 3: Defining the problem, that is, come to an understanding about why this person chose to betray that person on this occasion and under these circumstances. The therapist conveys confidence that infidelity can be understood.

Step 4: Calm everybody down, that is, help everyone see that drastic maneuvers are not necessary. It is possible to consider courses of action before acting. The therapist conveys confidence that people can live through infidelity, can live with infidelity, can even live after infidelity.

Step 5: Find a solution, that is, help the participants choose a course of action: what will be done about the affair, what will be done about the marriage, and what will be done about the relationship. The therapist conveys confidence that even infidels, even cuckolds, even affairees get to make choices about their lives.

Step 6: Negotiate the resistance, that is, compare what the marital partners want (the affairee does not get a voice in decisions about the marriage) and help them negotiate compromises. The therapist conveys confidence that problems can be overcome and things can change for the better.

Step 7: Terminate, that is, find out what the couple's fears are about the future, and help them decide what courses of action they would take in the face of future crises in the relationship and future crises of infidelity. Figure out what further changes need to be made and what further therapy needs to be arranged. The therapist conveys confidence that postaffair marriages can survive and prosper.

The first step in family crisis therapy is providing the "emergency response." In cases in which cuckolds enter therapy first, knowing that something is wrong but not having confirmation of the suspicions, they are frequently depressed, anxious, disoriented to the marriage, and doubting their own sanity. When cuckolds know about the affair, they are angry, hurt, and terror-stricken about the consequences and the possible disruptions to the family structure. There is awareness of the possibility of AIDS, divorce, abandonment, humiliation. Cuckolds who know about the affair need emergency attention before they can realize that this is a common problem and one that does not require precipitous action. ("Killing the son of a bitch is not going to get him back; killing yourself is not going to be easier on the kids than a divorce. Such crises are as awful as you imagine, but they are solved gradually.") Medication, particularly antidepressants, may be in order. Infidels should be contacted immediately, probably by the therapist, with awareness that they are probably in even worse shape.

If infidels present for treatment first, they may be anxious, depressed, overwhelmed by the secret of the affair, and dreaming up drastic solutions. They may have already suggested divorce to a confused cuckold. An infidel may attempt to elicit a promise of confidentiality about the affair. More than one man has asked us, in effect, to put his wife through a conspiratorial mock therapy in which we were to join forces in convincing her that her suspicions are crazy, that she is crazy, and that his peculiar recent behavior is a reaction to her deficiencies. We were then asked to keep her busy perfecting herself while he decided what to do about his affair. This is a popular but sadistic approach to crises of infidelity. It should be considered malpractice.

One of the most dangerous errors a therapist can make in cases of infidelity is to agree to keep it secret and then proceed with the disorienting mock therapy anyway. As an alternative to avoid these messy ethical dilemmas, you could refer the couple to a therapist who screws around and likes to conspire with some people and keep other people confused, or you could refer the couple to a therapist who is too stupid to ever suspect what is going on. Or, of course, you can offer to proceed but refuse to agree to keep the secret confidential.

Obviously, if infidels reveal an affair and want you to keep it secret, you can urge them to reveal it, pointing out the advantages of confession over discovery. You can see infidels individually and deal with their fear of honesty and exposure. If they still balk, you don't have to directly reveal it yourself. You can proceed with the couple anyway, not quite revealing the secret directly, but refusing to leave the issue alone until the secret is out. You can raise it as a possible explanation for the crisis ("This would be just what I would expect if you were having an affair. Are you?"). You can explore it as a hypothesis ("Most cases like this, where someone suddenly wants to leave a marriage that seemed reasonably okay before the sudden divorce talk, involved affairs. Do you think he might be having an affair and lying to you about it? If so, what do you think you would do?") You can even raise it as a challenge ("You try so hard to keep your wife calm, I think you might have trouble telling her something that would really upset her, such as an affair you might be having. What do you think she would do?"). With any other possible, secret crisis, you would bring it up without hesitation. The failure to do so with suspected infidelity, the usual cause of marriage rejection, amounts to therapeutic collusion with the infidel to effect a cover-up.

Until the infidelity is revealed, the marriage and the therapy are merely subterfuge. Whether you've heard about it or not, you could easily smell it, so just ask about it as if it were a routine piece of information, like whether spouses have been married before. It should be a routine inquiry("Is this the first marriage for each of you? Do you have any children? Is either of you having an affair? Have you had affairs in the past? You say not, but what is the agreement between you about affairs—do you reveal them or do you keep them secret?"). The infidel may lie, but will likely signal confirmation or call later to check whether it really is safe to reveal the secret.

Spouses don't have to be frightened by the revelation. The most severe reactions from cuckolds are likely to come from the continuation of affairs that were sworn to be over, but weren't. In our combined experience of over 30 years of practice, the confession of an affair that is now over has not resulted in a single suicide or homicide.

There is an ethical issue here. If the affair is not revealed, a potentially messy, time-consuming crisis can be avoided, and a marriage can be saved from becoming too intimate. But it is arrogant for you to treat your clients as if they aren't up to understanding the circumstances under which they are choosing to live. A secret in this context belongs not to any one individual, and certainly not to the therapist, but to the marriage. The couple can and must decide what level of intimacy and what level of fidelity they can live with, and what they should do when they don't get what they want.

In their fear of revelation, infidels can present for therapy in strange ways. One woman came under an assumed name; one man came incognito and in disguise. One man, who had decided to run off with his girlfriend, set up an appointment for himself and his barely compensated schizophrenic wife, brought her to the office for the appointment, and then slipped out of the waiting room, leaving her with us.

Getting into an affair is so simple that even a fool can do it, but each step after that seems harder and harder.

Step 2 in the handling of this crisis involves "bringing everyone together." Essentially, this means getting both marriage partners to the office with the same information. If the infidel originally sought therapy, and the cuckold knows about the affair, he/she should be included immediately. If the cuckold is unaware of the affair, the infidel should reveal it.

The concept of privileged information should not apply in marital therapy, and both partners should understand this from the outset. It should be standard to have the infidel reveal the affair. Reasons not to do so would have to be compelling. There aren't many exceptions to this. We did see one woman who told us that her husband was a mafia chieftain and her affair partner was his top hit man. Her husband had murdered his first few wives, and would surely murder her if he knew. She had every intention of leaving as soon as the school year was over, but her son had an especially good teacher this year so she'd take the chance, even if it made her nervous. We didn't know if the woman's story was true, but the better part of valor was not to push the matter of informing the husband.

If an infidel seeks individual therapy with the intention of obtaining a financially advantageous divorce without revealing the true motivation behind the divorce action, individual therapy is possible. The cuckold can be seen a time or two for information and evaluation, but couple therapy would be a collusive effort at disorientation. Infidels who fancy themselves to be "in love" with a current affairee are in need of reality-based therapy, and if the affair remains secret, the therapy might have to start on an individual basis. The unsuspecting cuckold can be informed that a few visits with the spouse will be needed before he/she is ready for couple work.

Sometimes, an infidel seeks therapy with anxiety over a brief affair, now past and unsuspected by the cuckold. The infidel's goals regarding the degree of intimacy desired in the marriage will determine the appropriateness of a revelation. If some degree of emotional distance is valued by the infidel, and revelation of the affair would disrupt that polite, trusting distance, the infidel might prefer not to reveal the affair. If intimacy is desired, disclosure of the affair may "hurt" the cuckold in the short run, but long-range prospects for an intimate marriage may be improved. If distance is desired, that can be achieved more efficiently by negotiating it honestly.

With "in love" affairs, the ongoing affairee might be included in the therapy, although the process can be cumbersome and explosive. A mistress or mister is part of the family system. Even if the affairee won't agree to take part in family sessions, the therapist's persistent requests dramatize the affairee's centrality to the crisis at hand. Even if the affairee refuses participation, the cuckold should feel free to contact the affairee, despite the infidel's rules and the affairee's insistence of immunity.

We once saw a man who could not decide between his wife of many years and the new woman with whom he had been working and sleeping. The cuckolded wife threatened divorce if he could not make up his mind. He assured her that he was not seeing the other woman anymore, and although sex resumed in the marriage, the intimacy was not renewed, as would be expected if he really were away from his affairee. The wife kept finding clues, such as lipstick-stained cigarettes in his ashtray and a woman's underpants in his glove compartment. He told her it was her imagination. She found his car in the woman's driveway, and rammed it through the woman's laundry room, playing havoc with the plumbing. She demanded that the affairee come to a therapy session with the couple. In the session, she informed the affairee that she was still sleeping with her husband, and that he

was lying to them both. The affairee felt betrayed and stalked out, saying something to the effect that all men in her experience betray their wives, but only a real asshole would betray his girlfriend.

A therapist's office is usually the safest possible place for the inevitable, eventual meeting of the adulterous triangle. The only meeting with an adulterous triad that ever got out of control in our practice did not actually take place in our office. The triangular meeting had been planned, but the ever-patient betrayed wife and the long-standing affairee both failed to show up. As we discussed the matter with the infidel in the office, we heard a scuffling in the hall. The two women were fighting. The wife had been running late and the affairee had been hiding in the stairwell, waiting for her. The affairee was trying to hit the wife with a pocketbook when the husband came out and broke it up. He pushed his bruised wife away as he comforted his sobbing affairee, and thus finally made the decision that broke the impasse.

There is a good chance that children in the family may know about the affair before their cuckolded parent, which is a terrible burden. If the affair drags on interminably, the children must be informed of the reason for their parents' indecisive conflict. People have to realize that they cannot betray their marriage without betraying their children as well, and they don't relieve their burden by lying to the children. If there is any possibility that a child might know, or suspect, or learn from someone else about the affair, and not realize that the other parent knows about it, too, it is safer to explain and reassure the child that the other parent knows the secret, too, and the child does not have to carry that burden and can talk about it with either parent. Children do not need to believe their parents are saints, but they do have to understand the nature of marriage and the circumstances of their lives.

Step 3 in treatment involves "defining the problem." Therapy doesn't really begin until the revelation of the affair has been made. All that precedes that step is merely foreplay.

A middle-aged doctor got caught in a therapeutic cross fire. He had gotten into his first affair, felt horribly confused by it, and in a state of crisis, made two appointments, one with a psychoanalyst and one with a marriage therapist. He saw the psychoanalyst first, and she assured him that he should keep the affair secret, because she believed that a marriage that has been betrayed can never be reconstituted. The psychoanaylst urged him to disorient his wife as much as possible, and once she was confused enough, to make a quick getaway. So the doctor went ahead to the marriage therapy appointment and spent several months in couple therapy confusing both his wife and his therapist. He kept bringing up unsolvable problems that were easily solved. He complained about behavior that the wife quickly changed. She lost weight, changed her hairstyle, became sexually aggressive, went to work, stopped spending money, learned to cook Cajun food, sat through car-crash movies with him, and went months without fussing about anything. He could not define a problem in the marriage that couldn't be readily solved. We began to suspect that he was having an affair with his psychoanalyst. No matter how often we smelled an affair and sympathetically said so, he always insisted he was completely faithful—right up to the day he abruptly moved out of his marriage and thereby confirmed the suspicion.

A year later, the doctor was out of his affair, out of his psychoanalysis, and back in his marriage. Only then did we get the full story. It turned out that the psychoanalyst had been a student of his in medical school, and had had a crush on him. She somehow felt heroic when she saw herself as rescuing him from his marriage to a woman she had never met but always resented. In a way, the doctor really was in an affair with his psychoanalyst. If it walks like a duck and it quacks like a duck and it looks like a duck, any therapist who isn't an idiot assumes it is a duck.

Once the affair is revealed, the reasons for the affair must be explored. We know the reasons for such an action have more to do with the repertoire, character, experience, and vulnerability of the infidel, but the infidel is likely to make a connection with some problem in the marriage, much as alcoholics attribute each episode of drunkenness to something outside themselves. It is therapeutically polite to listen to such defensive thinking. So we ask for an assessment of marital satisfaction and then, more relevantly, we ask the reasons for deciding that infidelity would be an appropriate and helpful reaction to whatever problems are being defined. The reasons people give for having affairs aren't real reasons, but they are clues to the way infidels think about sex and marriage, honesty and intimacy. Nevertheless, an evaluation of whether the affair was real or imagined, overt or covert, intrinsic or extrinsic, unique or habitual, and permanent or temporary, is in order. Although the cuckold should not jump to take responsibility for the affair, other marital issues should be explored, which may be only peripherally

related to the affair. Both cuckold and infidel need to identify areas in which they can make changes.

Infidels, in their determination to avoid taking responsibility for their actions, can come up with amazing justifications. They explain how they had an affair because "You didn't bathe often enough"; "You weren't friendly to my mother"; "You gained weight"; "You fussed too much about little things"; "You didn't housebreak the dog well enough"; "You didn't put enough air in my tires." It is hard to see how an affair would solve any of those problems.

Some people insist they had their mate's permission to have an affair. One man ran his wife's family's business, and it seemed to be sinking deeper into debt. When his brother-in-law investigated the situation, he discovered that the man was in an affair with his loan officer at the bank. The infidel was outraged that anyone would challenge his behavior because he insisted that his wife had once left him a note saying "I don't care what you do." She insisted that she meant only that she didn't care whether he went to church with her that day. He persisted that her words meant that she was releasing him from any vow of fidelity, and she had no right to complain.

Another man insisted that his wife talked in her sleep and told him she wouldn't mind if he had an affair. A woman insisted that her husband's participation in a threesome she arranged for his birthday constituted a de facto repeal of their agreement about fidelity. And another woman argued that her husband's failure to learn to dance gave her the right to sleep with any man who would dance with her.

Well-mannered therapists are polite enough to listen to such things, but they try to get the focus onto the real issues of how infidelity came to be seen by a partner as the appropriate reaction to life's failure to be a constant state of ecstatic wonder.

Step 4 involves "calming everybody down." This is best done by ending the affair and affirming commitment to the marriage. In our experience, 75% of affairs end at or before the point of disclosure. However, some romances continue, leaving the future of the marriage in doubt. Frequently, the cuckolds who have thought themselves paranoid in their imaginings of the affair may calm down quickly. Their worst fears are confirmed, but at least they know they weren't out of their minds.

The therapist at this point in the therapy relaxes, smiles, and announces optimism that the problems at hand are solvable, not necessarily that they will be solved, but they certainly can be solved. There should be a sudden shift in the therapist's posture at this point, giving the cue that infidelity is survivable, forgivable, and controllable. It is not a psychosis: It is just a defect in toilet training and it can, with practice, be voluntarily controlled.

Optimism about infidelity requires the therapist to get everyone to focus on the behavior, which is controllable, rather than the emotions, which seem overwhelming and out of control. Infidels, however rigidly they impose logic on their justifications for their actions, feel themselves at the mercy of their feelings. Therapy must not concern itself too much with how people feel: That might convey support for the popular but disastrous notion that mental health and happiness are achieved by acting on one's impulses. Therapists can sympathize with emotions, but realize that emotions are there to be talked about, not to be acted upon. It is an error to ask infidels to compare their feelings about the competing partners in their life; the relationships aren't comparable. That would be tantamount to asking a man in a manic episode whether he thought his latest cockamamie scheme was likely to work out. If you treat people who are "*in love*" as if they were manic, you'll be on the right track. If you ask yourself the question, "But what if this is *real* love?" go back to Reality 101.

In Step 5, the aim of therapy is "finding a solution." There are few problems in which the simple solution is more obvious. First the infidel stops the behavior, both the outside sex and the lying. Then, after a decent interval, the cuckold stops carrying on about it. In "accidental infidelity," the simple solution is to reveal the secret and accept human fallibility. In "romantic infidelity," the infidel must give up the affairee; the cuckold is given the unfair job of holding the marriage together for a while, and the therapy focuses on the stage of development that is scaring the infidel into this escape from reality. "Marital arrangements" merely have to be renegotiated. The only complexity is with "philanderers," who must rethink everything they've learned about gender and sex. The therapy is about the philanderer and his father and his masculinity.

The solution to the problem of infidelity always involves stopping the behavior and then learning new and more direct ways to deal with interpersonal problem solving. Infidels can come up with amazing alternatives to giving up the affair. One woman kept begging her husband for just another 2 weeks with her affairee before she gave him up completely. Another man explained to his wife that she was lucky to be married to him because she was such an ugly woman. She should feel proud to be married to a man who was able to get such a beautiful affairee, and she should appreciate the increased status that would come from accepting the new woman into a *ménage à trois*. The wife didn't have much self-confidence, but she still had more than he gave her credit for. She was not convinced.

Step 6 involves "negotiating the resistance." For couples in which accidental affairs have occurred, the affairs are already over when revealed. The resistance may lie in the cuckold's anger and rejection, so reasons for this need to be explored.

For "marital arrangements," the couple is asked to fight out the issues without resorting to affairs. The denial of marital problems can be a resistance. The existence of marital problems is universal but not necessarily related to an affair. Although the infidel is the only one who can control the adulterous behavior, both partners must be willing to change for the marriage. The premature termination of therapy is a problematic resistance, and is frequently initiated by the cuckold who avoids intimacy by declaring the problems solved. An infidel's resistance through termination of therapy can be a setup for more affairs.

A philanderer's resistance may stem from a belief that philandering is universal or culturally required. He may resist openness with his partner by agreeing to fidelity without believing in equality. It is difficult to change a cultural pattern for the sake of a long-devalued relationship with someone who is the enemy in fantasy and now, in fact. Cuckolds may be weary and may not expect or even desire a change. The Rose Kennedys of this world may be content to live with the philanderer for a lifetime and beyond. However, other cuckolds may attempt to control the philanderer, which is inflammatory to the philanderer's attempt to escape, overpower, and degrade women. The cuckold's anger and attempt to produce guilt from the infidel just drive him/her further away. Sympathy is more useful, but hard to maintain in the face of further lies. It isn't that sympathy makes it better, it is that anger makes it worse. Many of these cuckolds finally leave, and the philanderers are free to start over with less angry women to whom they owe less emotionally.

The most obvious resistance is the "romantic affair." If the infidel is unable to leave the affair immediately, a therapeutic separation may be reasonable. Very resilient and resourceful cuckolds may be able to tolerate staying with their spouse even while affairs continue, and also may be able to correct any behavior attributed to marital problems during this time. If the cuckold is so dependent that suicide or psychosis seems a real danger, a separation may be too stressful. Divorce in these instances is less suspenseful, and may elicit more support from relatives. Separation isn't always as humane as it looks, and may be comparable to the man who loved his dog so much that he cut off its tail an inch at a time.

Of course, stopping the affair is only the first and simplest step in a delicate process. The couple must renegotiate the process by which the errant partner achieves forgiveness. Usually, all it takes is complete cessation of the adulterous relationship, total revelation of all secrets, some symbolic acts of contrition, dedicated efforts toward intimacy, and begging of forgiveness—nothing more difficult than the original courtship—only this time it has to done while swimming upstream. Most infidels manage to do it without skipping a beat.

But the cuckold may not want a renewal of the intimacy and may prefer to continue the punishment and rejection indefinitely. Failure to forgive is, of course, a trick to achieve maximum control with minimal intimacy. We saw a couple in their 80s who had been married for 50 years. The man had had an affair 30 years before and his wife punished him daily and reminded him of his betrayal of her. We asked her when she had first known that he would make her life miserable. She explained that at their wedding, he had parked the car at an awkward angle for showing off her train to the photographers. For 50 years, she had complained daily that he was insufficiently dedicated to her happiness. The affair had occurred at a time when things were fairly good. If she had relaxed for a moment and let herself be actually happy, there's no telling what he would have done.

Those people who are determined to be miserable will find some justification for it. Their partners' infidelity must seem to be a godsend. There really should be a statute of limitations to punishment for an infidelity. A year seems long enough. After that, all emotional rights should be restored to the infidel and the cuckold's continuing efforts at punishment might be considered a pathological barrier to intimacy. In those occasional cases where the infidel's guilt and contrition does not bring reconciliation, the therapist may have to teach the infidel to be adoringly attentive otherwise, but to brag proudly

about the affair whenever the cuckold brings it up, and thus detoxify the effort to induce guilt.

Step 7 is "termination." Crises of infidelity—and their aftermaths of guilt, doubt, rehashing of the crisis, and punishment—may go on for years. Even if the marriage is headed for divorce, the infidel will frequently attempt a reconciliation just before the divorce is final. By this time, many cuckolds have lost interest.

Cuckolds seem to discover before infidels that affairs are too frivolous and confusing to serve as the basis for ending a marriage. Divorce can save lives, but is too risky to apply during something as disorienting as an affair.

Recently, a couple came in to remind us that we had seen them a few years ago, when he left his wife and children for an affair with a woman who tried to burn down the wife's house to speed up the divorce. The relationship with this fiery lady had gone up in smoke and he had now come home to his wife and children. It had taken 3 years for him to appreciate what we had been telling him. But, he explained, it had taken him even longer to learn his multiplication tables.

Sometimes, all the king's horses and all the king's therapists cannot put reality back together again. But time will break any fantasy spell.

CASE EXAMPLES

An Accidental Infidelity

Evelyn thought her life was rocking along smoothly until the phone call came from a strange man who told her that her husband was having an affair with his wife. She went into full alert, called Adam, demanded that he come home from his business trip, and then dragged him in to see us. She wanted to know what was going on. Who was this woman? How long had this affair been going on? What did it mean? Had it happened before?

Adam insisted he had been faithful all these years. He never really considered not being so. Men in his family didn't do things like that. Adam mostly traveled and worked. More than anything in life, he wanted to be rich, and Evelyn shared his goal. She could raise the kids just fine without him, as her mother had raised her. Conflict was low and weekends together were pleasant. The crisis really began when Adam had taken on a new sales line, and began traveling with Cleo, a new woman at work who was indispensable in this latest scheme to get rich. They made a big sale, celebrated with champagne, and somehow ended up in bed together. It happened a few more times after that, but Adam was uncomfortable with it, and had told her he wanted to stop. Cleo didn't. She wanted them both to get divorced and then get married. Adam was horrified; Cleo was angry and determined. She told her husband, knowing he'd tell Evelyn, and hoping Evelyn would then give up and disappear.

Adam had no doubt that he wanted his marriage. He'd worried about Evelyn's response when she found out—he abhorred scenes—and he was grateful that she could be as calm as she was. But Evelyn was not as relieved as she might have been. Adam continued to travel with Cleo. An important decision had to be made: Should he stop the business relationship with Cleo?

We were clear that in our experience it is dangerous to try to continue friendship with people who want to destroy your marriage and your life and use you to rescue them from the mess they've made of their own lives. There was danger, but Cleo seemed Adam's best hope for finally getting rich.

The therapy consisted mostly of negotiating their goals. Were the anticipated financial rewards worth the danger of the continued working partnership? Adam continued to work with Cleo. Cleo's husband continued to give reports to Evelyn, and Adam continued to give reassurances. We couldn't get Evelyn to discuss it all with Cleo, but she got more comfortable with the situation as she planned to quit her job as a teacher and take over Adam's office and finances. He felt sad that he was causing her to give up her own career so that she could keep an eye on him. As they drifted from therapy, Adam hadn't quite gotten rich yet, but both he and Evelyn kept sacrificing all else in life for that goal.

A Philanderer in Crisis

Burns had been good at sports and good at making money, but he'd never been good at marriage, despite his many tries. His father had been no better, and both his brothers had been divorced a few times. Burns had been married three times and had screwed around on all three women. After 10 years of chomping at the bit, he left his ultrastable first wife while in a torrid affair with his second wife, a pretty young clerk from the country. Within a few months, Burns realized he had made an awful mistake, and began a series of angry, frantic seductions and rages at the baffled woman for whom he'd given up his marriage, his small son, and half his kingdom. She just cried pathetically as he finally beat her up and left, blaming her for the divorce, but refusing to go back home to his wife and child.

Burns's third wife, Ashley, was more sophisticated. She was an occasional TV actress who had spent most of her life in affairs with married men. Burns thought she would understand "the way men are," although he told her very little about himself and his life. Their relationship consisted of intermittent sex, a busy social life, and a lot of traveling, mostly separate—the way Burns wanted it. Occasionally Ashley would complain that she wanted a closer relationship, but he would ridicule her crazy insecurity. If she showed any anger about his distance or his insults, he would dismiss it as premenstrual syndrome. Ashley was actually fairly comfortable with the distance. She had never expected anything much different and was pleased that Burns didn't hit her the way her father had hit her mother when she complained about his affairs.

Burns had the life of his dreams—a beautiful wife who gave him status and did not challenge his doing whatever he liked. Into this idyllic life came a crisis. Burns barely knew his son, Cole, from his first marriage. The boy had been raised by his born-again mother. Burns was horrified that the boy, fresh out of high school, was planning to marry. Burns decided finally to become a hands-on father. Burns arranged a bachelor party for Cole. He got Cole drunk, and threw the virginal boy into bed with a female friend who not only deflowered him, but compared him favorably to his father. Cole was horrified and told his fiancée, who went wild and then confronted his father. Burns explained what he thought was a normal sex life for men. He bragged of hundreds of sexual conquests. Cole was not impressed; instead, he was so outraged that he informed everyone in the family, including his stepmother. Ashley had to face it, whether she wanted to or not, but she could not discuss it with Burns.

Ashley talked to friends, read *Private Lies*, and called us. She set up an appointment for herself, Burns, and Cole. In the office, Ashley was depressed and withdrawn, and very anxious about discussing these things. Cole was furious about the episode, about his own weakness, and about his father's lifelong neglect—especially since he felt he had been neglected so his father could spend his life on such a self-indulgent and dehumanizing hobby. Burns was defensive and baffled. He insisted that there was nothing wrong with what he had done, and complained that none of us understood "the way men are." We sent him out to discuss it with the others.

Burns returned feeling foolish. He got no respect from anyone except some kid at the filling station. His ex-wife and her husband were disgusted. He expected the other guys to understand, but his friends laughed at his naïveté. They used to carry on the way he did, but they had wised up, had seen that it was messing with their minds, messing up their marriages, and taking too much time. Some of them confessed that they would get a piece of "strange" every year or so, but for the most part they'd stopped the macho bullshit. Even Burns's father, the one man he thought would understand, told him, "I thought you'd outgrown that. I gave it up 20 years ago. I thought it might hurt you kids and I knew it could hurt your stepmother." Burns actually apologized to both Ashley and Cole. He'd never apologized to anyone before, certainly not to a woman.

Ashley had had the marriage she wanted—reliably distant—and she felt that being threatened. The focus of therapy was on Burns, and Burns's strange concept of masculinity. When he recognized that he was playing by a different set of rules than other men, he began to open himself up to Ashley, to clear away all his secrets, to break off all relationships that made her uncomfortable, and to prove his commitment to her. She hadn't really required much intimacy, and now found herself closer to her husband than she'd ever thought possible with a man. The changes in both were extensive, and they both liked it. Ashley had to become more involved with Burns, and they even began to go on some trips together.

We saw Burns and Cole together a few more times, too. Cole maintained his engagement, but postponed the marriage for another year of college. Cole wanted to be sure he wouldn't be like his father had been. He has now decided that men can change.

Will Burns screw around in the future? Perhaps, but the pattern will be different. The male-centered gynephobic innocence is gone forever.

A Romantic Affair

Camille had been bored with Arnie for 25 years, and was sorry that she had married for stability rather than for romance. Her life had been spent raising their three children, helping Arnie get his anesthesiology practice going, playing tennis, and running her little boutique. She told friends that Arnie was the perfect anesthesiologist: As soon as he touched her she went right to sleep. She said that he was good at his work, that when he was working on her, she didn't feel a thing. Although she ridiculed Arnie, she wouldn't leave him. She had no identity, no profession of her own—she was tied to Arnie forever and so she tended her marriage carefully. And he really didn't care whether she liked him or not. He wasn't into relationships.

But the time came for their lives to change. The last of their three children, their glorious son Junior, left for college. Camille felt suddenly lonely, called

an old boyfriend from college, and fell instantly and crazily in love. Uncharacteristically throwing caution to the wind, she announced to Arnie she was getting a divorce and was going to marry the still-married but unemployed Gus—who had no intention of marrying Camille and had merely told her, when she threw herself at him, that he wouldn't have sex with her while they were both married.

We had worked with this family a few years earlier when one of the older kids had gone through a bad time in school. We knew the marriage wasn't very exciting but it seemed to meet their needs. Camille's sudden decision that it was intolerable seemed discontinuous.

I saw the couple together, and also called Gus, who did not want out of his current marriage and thought an affair with Camille would be nice, but had no intention of going back to work and supporting Camille's lifestyle. He didn't really believe in marriage, because his parents had divorced when he was quite young. He didn't believe in therapy, either, but he had a relaxed view of life that really appealed to Camille.

Camille told Arnie everything and he responded blandly. Arnie wanted to stay married, but didn't want to put much energy into it. He really didn't like sex very much, never had, and didn't like being under Camille's control. He preferred just to throw money at her and turn over and go to sleep. Junior, though, dropped out of college, bounced back home, and raised hell about his mother's plans to threaten everyone's security. Junior was determined to keep them together.

We were able to talk Camille into slowing down enough to think this out, but over the next few months of examining her life and her marriage, she realized she had done her job of raising her kids—the emotional energy was between herself and Junior rather than Arnie, or even Gus. Camille wanted a life and she decided that the issue was not Gus and it wasn't even Arnie, but was what she was going to do for the rest of her life.

Camille could not do without Gus, and all the ways in which he was so different from Arnie. She left Arnie so she could be with Gus, but she had to have something to do, so she returned to law school, and planned to become self supporting so she could choose to live with a poor man if she liked. She also decided she'd spent a lifetime on her children, and she was through. Arnie would finally have to act like a parent. She sent Junior to Arnie's apartment, and in time he went back to school.

A few years later, Camille finished law school, and dumped Gus. Right at the time that the divorce was final, Arnie remarried. Everyone lived happily and sensibly ever after.

A Marital Arrangement

Dick and Jane were busy people, and they were a great team. They were raising five active children, two sets of twins and a single, and they divided that awesome responsibility. They were also taking care of Jane's invalid parents, and running a very complicated business of remodeling old houses. Jane was an architect with great aesthetic sense and imagination, and Dick could get anybody to do anything. It took enormous energy for them to lead the life they led, and for years they did it with gusto.

A few years ago, Jane began having health problems. It didn't really make sense, but it had to do with her hormones. She ran out of energy and lost interest in sex. Dick was a man who needed a lot of attention, and he gave a lot, too. But Jane was backing away, even from the business. She was taking naps, saving her energy for the kids, and especially for helping Alice with her math. She insisted she wasn't depressed, just tired. Dick and Jane were sinking into a traditional gender arrangement that neither of them wanted.

They came to therapy when they realized that this great marriage had become a hostile interdependency that wasn't satisfying anybody. Each pushed for more, and each resisted. The kids began to show symptoms. Alice, the older daughter, began begging them to separate so they'd stop fighting. She, at 14, offered to drop out of school to take care of the little ones.

Dick pushed Jane for sexual involvement, and for sexual response, not just for tired mechanical sex. In one session, Jane told him that if he wanted to go outside the marriage, just say so. We assured him that she didn't mean that. But a few weeks later, when Jane couldn't work up much enthusiasm for Dick, he started fussing and before long had challenged her: "I don't want to leave you, but I'm ready to go find a real woman. I'm ready to have an affair."

We don't know who said what to whom, but one of the middle daughters heard the conversation and went into hysterics, outraged at her father. Dick and Jane pulled together and agreed to stop all discussion of the matter until they could get to my office. Once one of the kids knew the secret, it could not be kept from the other four without isolating that child. It had to be discussed. We asked that they bring all five kids—twin boys, age 10; twin girls, age 12; and Alice, age 14.

At the session, 12-year-old Sally couldn't talk about it, whispered to us separately what she'd

heard, and we repeated it to her family. Whereas Alice demanded that their parents get a divorce, the other four kids hovered protectively around their mother, and confronted their father with his selfishness. The kids decided that their parents were letting them down by failing to work out their relationship, and they presented their parents with guidelines for their behavior. In turn, they decided they would just do things in a way that would take the pressure off their parents. They told their mother that she was refusing to acknowledge how bad it was, how hard her illness was on everybody else, and how important it was for her to set her priorities more carefully. They reminded her that her choices affected everyone in her family, that she couldn't neglect her marriage without hurting them all. They told their father that his selfishness was way out of hand—he could not betray his marriage without betraying his children as well.

The kids wanted both of them to shape up, and they wanted their older sister to stop using a family crisis to escape a math test she feared. The kids decided 4 to 1 that the family's biggest problem was that their older sister needed a math tutor.

Dick was contrite and tearful, but relieved when he realized that he was not alone in trying to deal with Jane's disability. All he'd wanted was a little love, and he got it from his kids. Jane was furious with him and unwilling to give him what he wanted quite yet, but she, too, was relieved to have some help with her overextended life.

Dick and Jane, like most couples with a crisis of infidelity, actually benefited from the crisis a lot more than they would have from an infidelity.

CONCLUSION

The most important things we have to say on the subject of infidelity are that it need not be a disaster, it need not destroy the marriage, but it must be dealt with openly and honestly. Dealing with infidelity in marriage therapy may be uncomfortable, because it has the effect, ready or not, of bringing about a more intense level of intimacy in the marriage. Infidelity seems like a risky way to bring about marital closeness, but if the marriage and all the parties to it survive, closeness might well be the ultimate outcome.

REFERENCES

Beavers, W. R. (1985). *Successful marriage.* New York: Norton.

Brown, E. M. (1991). *Patterns of infidelity and their treatment.* New York: Brunner/Mazel.

Chodorow, N. (1978). *The reproduction of mothering.* Berkeley: University of California Press.

Gilligan, Carol, (1982). *In a different voice.* Cambridge, MA: Harvard University Press.

Glass, S. P., & Wright, T. L. (1985). Sex differences in type of extramarital involvement and marital dissatisfaction. *Sex Roles, 12,* 9–10.

Glass, S. P., & Wright, T. L. (1992). Justifications for extramarital relationships: The association between attitudes, behaviors and gender. *Journal of Sex Research, 29*(3), 361–387.

Pittman, F. S. (1989). *Private lies: Infidelity and the betrayal of intimacy.* New York: Norton.

Pittman, F. S. (1987). *Turning points: Treating families in transition and crisis.* New York: Norton.

16

The Assessment and Treatment of Marital Violence: An Introduction for the Marital Therapist

AMY HOLTZWORTH-MUNROE
STACIA BEAK BEATTY
KIMBERLY ANGLIN

MARITAL VIOLENCE is a serious problem in this country. Data from a recent national survey indicate that one out of eight husbands engaged in at least one violent act toward his wife during the year of the study and that 1.8 million wives are beaten by their spouses each year (Straus & Gelles, 1990). In examining spousal (both husband and wife) violence, Straus and Gelles found that one out of six American couples (i.e., 16%) experienced violence during the year of the study, leading to estimates that 8.7 million couples experience marital violence each year and 3.4 million couples experience severe violence carrying a high risk of injury (Straus & Gelles, 1990).

Such violence often begins early in a relationship. In a study of approximately 400 couples planning to marry, O'Leary et al. (1989) found that 31% of the men and 44% of the women reported that they had been physically aggressive toward their partner in the year prior to marriage. Similarly, in a study of over 1,000 couples applying for a license for a first marriage, over 30% of the husbands had engaged in relation-

ship violence (K. E. Leonard, personal communication, July 1992).

Available data also suggest that relationship violence often continues to occur without intervention. In the O'Leary et al. (1989) study, rates of violence did decline, significantly for women and nonsignificantly for men, by 30 months postmarriage; however, at that time, 25% of women and 32% of men still had engaged in violence during the previous year. In addition, if a partner had been violent at one point in time, there was a 46–72% probability that he/she would also report having used violence at the next follow-up assessment. Similarly, in another longitudinal study, Feld and Straus (1989) found that 42% of the couples who had experienced one to two severe husband assaults at Time 1 reported continuing husband violence at Time 2; this figure rose to 67% among couples who had originally reported three or more severe husband assaults.

The O'Leary et al. (1989) and Feld and Straus (1989) data suggest that, once begun, violence continues to occur. In addition, clinicians working with violent couples believe that violence escalates over time. Although longitudinal data addressing this issue are unavailable, retrospective reports from violent couples (e.g., Pagelow, 1981; Walker, 1979) indicate that many couples experience an escalation in the frequency, intensity, and severity of marital violence over time. These anecdotal data suggest that at least some proportion of violent newlyweds not only continue, but also escalate their marital violence.

The costs of marital violence are staggering. The most obvious consequence of marital violence is the increased likelihood of physical injury to one or both individuals; the most extreme consequence is death, with "15%–25% of all homicides committed in the U.S." being conjugal murders (Edelson, Miller, Stone, & Chapman, 1985, p. 230). In addition, marital violence has been associated with marital dissatisfaction (O'Leary et al., 1989, Rosenbaum & O'Leary, 1981) and physical and psychological health problems, including depression, alcohol abuse, and post-traumatic stress disorder (e.g., Hotaling & Sugarman, 1986; Houskamp & Foy, 1991; Sonkin, Martin, & Walker, 1985; Walker, 1979). Physical aggression in marriage has also been linked to child abuse and a variety of negative effects on the children of violent marriages (e.g., Grych & Fincham, 1990; McDonald & Jouriles, 1991).

Although both husbands and wives engage in physical aggression, researchers have consistently demonstrated that husband-to-wife violence results in more negative outcomes than wife-to-husband violence, in part due to husbands' greater physical size and strength. Husband-to-wife aggression results in more physical injury; wives are more likely than husbands to require medical care, to take time off from work, and to spend more time in bed due to illness as a consequence of a physical attack from a partner (Stets & Straus, 1990). Husband-to-wife violence also results in more health problems, stress, depression, and psychosomatic symptoms than does wife-to-husband aggression (Cascardi, Langhinrichsen, & Vivian, 1992; Stets & Straus, 1990). Thus, husband-to-wife violence is a particularly important problem and is the primary focus of this chapter.

Given the prevalence of marital violence, the likelihood that it will continue or escalate once begun, and the resulting negative consequences, the problem of marital violence should be of particular interest to marital therapists. Indeed, data indicate that violence is common among couples seeking marital therapy. For example, Holtzworth-Munroe et al. (1992) found that over half of the couples seeking marital therapy at several clinics had experienced husband-to-wife violence. Similarly, among 132 couples seeking marital therapy at a university clinic, O'Leary, Vivian, and Malone (1992a) found that 53% of the wives were the victims of husbands' physical aggression.

Despite the prevalence of marital violence among couples seeking treatment, marital therapists often fail to detect it. This is, in part, due to the fact that couples often do not spontaneously report this problem; rather, therapists must systematically seek information on violence. For example, O'Leary, Vivian, and Malone (1992) found that on written intake reports, only 6% of wives reported that physical aggression was a major problem in their marriage. However, when directly questioned about violence in individual interviews, 44% of these wives indicated that marital violence problems existed, and when asked to complete the Conflict Tactics Scale (CTS; Straus, 1979), a questionnaire measuring marital aggression, 53% of the wives reported the occurrence of husband-to-wife violence.

Even when couples do report problems with violence, many marital therapists do not incorporate this information into their conceptualization of marital therapy cases. Hansen, Harway, and Cervantes (1991) mailed marital/family therapists case descriptions of couples seeking therapy; the cases explicitly mentioned incidents of severe husband-to-wife violence. In their case conceptualizations, fully 40% of the therapists did not even allude to "conflict" as a problem; among those who did, only 22% explicitly identified the problem as violence or battering. Not one therapist indicated that lethality was of concern, despite the fact that one of the cases actually ended in the husband's murder of the wife. Only 55% of the therapists planned to intervene as if the violence required immediate action, and only 11% mentioned obtaining protection for the wife as a concern.

In summary, although it has been demonstrated that marital violence is prevalent among couples seeking marital therapy, such information often will only be obtained through a careful and direct assessment. Such an assessment is likely to be made only when marital therapists are sensitized to the problem of husband-to-wife violence and consider it important in case conceptualization and treatment planning.

ASSESSMENT OF MARITAL VIOLENCE

Is Marital Violence Occurring?

Given the prevalence of marital violence among couples seeking therapy, marital therapists must consider the possibility of violence in every case. In addition, since many couples do not spontaneously discuss this problem, therapists must directly assess the occurrence of marital violence. To do so, we recommend that spouses be separated and independently asked about the occurrence of violence, because battered wives may be afraid to speak truthfully in front of their abusers.

Perhaps the quickest way to screen for the occurrence of marital violence is to administer the CTS. Despite its limitations, this questionnaire is the most widely used measure of marital violence. It lists 19 behaviors couples may engage in during conflicts, ranging from nonviolent (e.g., discussing the issue calmly) to violent (e.g., using a knife or gun) behaviors. Respondents first report whether they or their partners have ever engaged in any of the listed behaviors. If so, they are then asked how often each behavior has occurred in the past year (i.e., responses range from *"never"* to *"more than 20 times"*).

Researchers have found low interspousal reliability in reports of marital violence on the CTS; in particular, partners rarely agree on the occurrence of specific violent behaviors (e.g., Arias & Beach, 1987; Browning & Dutton, 1986; Jouriles & O'Leary, 1985; Szinovacz, 1983). Relative to wives' reports, husbands tend to underreport their own use of violence. Thus, therapists should accept either spouse's report of the occurrence of violence and, given the tendency of husbands to minimize and deny their use of violence, should not ignore a wife's report of a husband's violence, even if these are not confirmed by the husband.

Assessing the Violence in More Detail

Although the CTS is a popular measure for identifying violent couples, it suffers from several shortcomings. First, some versions of the CTS only assess the occurrence of marital violence during conflicts. However, many battered women report that physical aggression can occur at other times also (e.g., husband who comes home upset and is violent without an immediately preceding disagreement). Second, the number of violent behaviors assessed by the CTS is limited; CTS responses will not provide therapists with a full picture of the extent of violence occurring between couples. Third, the CTS does not assess the context of the violence (i.e., the sequence of events leading to the violence, the sequence of events during a violent incident, the intentions behind each violent action, or the consequences of the violence); however, such factors are important for understanding the role violence plays in a relationship. For example, researchers have found that although while wives most frequently cite self-defense as the reason for their violence (Saunders, 1986), husbands report that they engage in violence for instrumental reasons, for example, to punish the wife or stop her from leaving (Cascardi, Vivian, & Meyer, 1991). In addition, as noted, husband-to-wife violence results in more injuries and negative consequences than does wife-to-husband violence (Cascardi et al., 1992; Stets & Straus, 1990).

Given these limitations of the CTS, a therapist who detects the occurrence of marital violence will need to conduct clinical interviews to gain additional information about the context, extent, intent, and consequences of the violence. More detailed information should be sought about the severity and frequency of the violence and about any resulting injuries (e.g., severity of injuries, what medical attention was sought, etc.). In addition, the therapist should assess any involvement of third parties in the violence (e.g., Have the police ever been called?) and the possibility of danger to other individuals (e.g., Is child abuse occurring or has the husband threatened other individuals?).

Is There a Risk of Lethality? Is the Wife Safe?

If the therapist establishes that severe and/or frequent marital violence is occurring, he/she should immediately assess the dangerousness and potential lethality of the situation. Although it is difficult to predict whether, and when, a client will engage in lethal behavior, it is important to be aware that this risk exists between violent couples.

Of obvious relevance is information about the severity and consequences of the violence. In addition, the therapist should investigate whether guns or other weapons are present in the household; if so, the therapist may require that all weapons be removed from the home during therapy (Saunders, 1992a). The therapist should investigate whether alcohol or other substance use is associated with the violence; such substances may reduce individuals' inhibitions, making lethal behavior more likely.

Assessing the female victim's potential for committing homicide is also important, given the fact that a battered woman may choose to kill her abuser rather than continue to live with constant fear and abuse (e.g., Browne, 1987, Hart, 1991). Saunders (1992a) suggests that therapists assess the type and extent of the wife's violent fantasies and should discuss with the female victim the types of resources she has employed in the past and, more important, which resources have previously failed her. These questions may identify the extent to which the female victim considers herself trapped in the violent relationship and believes that no alternatives exist besides homicide.

In many cases, the therapist should also discuss safety planning with the couple, particularly the wife. If the probability of continuing or escalating violence is high, this discussion should take place immediately. The wife should be made aware of local resources (e.g., shelters or safe houses, social service agencies) and legal options (e.g., restraining orders). The therapist should discuss practical issues, such as whether the wife can get herself and her children out of the house if she fears for her safety and where she can go (e.g., a relative, friend, shelter). She should be helped to develop a plan for such situations (e.g., Where are the keys and money in case a quick exit is needed? Does she have access to important papers and documents?).

Similarly, the husband should be warned of the dangerous nature of his violence and of the possibility of an escalation in violence. He should be asked to consider methods of stopping himself from using violence (see anger management techniques reviewed in this chapter). In some cases, the couple should be asked to temporarily separate to lower the risk of dangerous violence.

Assessing Other Relevant Variables

In addition to a careful assessment of the physical violence, therapists should assess other variables that may be relevant to treatment planning. A brief discussion of some of these is presented here.

Physical violence is often accompanied by *psychological and emotional abuse* of the wife. Such abuse includes actions that denigrate and humiliate the victim (e.g., calling the victim names, controlling her behavior, and putting her down), as well as threatening behaviors and actions that damage her property (e.g., driving recklessly with

her in the car, threatening her with bodily harm, and destroying a prized possession). Women often report that these behaviors are equally, or more, harmful psychologically than the physical abuse they suffer. Psychological abuse can be assessed through interviews and/or with several new questionnaire measures (e.g., Marshall's [1992] Severity of Violence Against Women Scales; Shepard & Campbell's [1992] Abusive Behavior Inventory; Tolman's [1989] Psychological Maltreatment of Women Inventory; Hudson & McIntosh's [1981] Index of Spouse Abuse). Since some forms of psychological abuse (e.g., the monitoring of the wife's activities) may take the guise of *jealousy* (e.g., Tolman & Bennett, 1990; Saunders, 1992a), therapists should also assess the extent and pervasiveness of the husband's jealousy.

Violent husbands describe themselves as experiencing significantly more *anger and hostility* than nonviolent men (e.g., Maiuro, Cahn, Vitaliano, Wagner, & Zegree, 1988). Although anger is not always a precursor for violent behavior, the level of anger experienced by violent husbands is relevant to treatment planning and the assessment of therapy outcome, since many marital violence treatment programs include anger management components. A variety of questionnaire measures of anger and hostility are available, including Novaco's Anger Index (1977), the Buss–Durkee Hostility Inventory (Buss & Durkee, 1957), and the State–Trait Anger Scale (Spielberger, Gorsuch, & Lushene, 1970). These questionnaires often must be modified to directly assess anger and hostility within marital interactions. In addition, researchers have recently developed anger measures specific to violent men (e.g., Maiuro, Vitaliano, & Cahn, 1987).

Alcohol is involved in many battering incidents (e.g., Hotaling & Sugarman, 1986; Kantor & Straus, 1987, 1989; Leonard & Blane, 1992; Leonard, Bromet, Parkinson, Day, & Ryan, 1985). Thus, practitioners should obtain a detailed history of the couple's *alcohol and drug use* and of the role alcohol and drugs play in the violent episodes. Some violent husbands may require alcohol or substance-abuse counseling prior to addressing their problems with marital violence.

Given the psychological consequences of violence, therapists may also wish to assess the presence of other *psychological problems*, including post-traumatic stress disorder among battered wives (Houskamp & Foy, 1991), and depression and risk of suicide among both spouses. Although standard measures of these problems may be employed (e.g., the Beck Depression Inventory; Beck, Ward, Mendelson, Mock, & Erbaugh, 1961), therapists should keep in mind that these problems may exist solely as a consequence of the marital violence. Cessation of the violence may lead to improvements in these problems without the need for further interventions. In addition, a substantial proportion of male batterers have been found to have personality disorders (e.g., Hamberger & Hastings, 1986); obtaining such information may aid in treatment planning.

Research has indicated that violent husbands have difficulty with *spouse-specific assertion* (e.g., Rosenbaum & O'Leary, 1981; O'Leary & Curley, 1986) and lack the skills to generate *competent solutions* in certain types of marital conflicts (Dutton & Browning, 1988; Holtzworth-Munroe & Anglin, 1991). In addition, observational studies have revealed that violent couples have poorer problem-solving, more negative, and less positive *marital interactions* than nonviolent couples (e.g., Boeke & Markman, 1992; Margolin, Burman, & John, 1989; Margolin, John, & Gleberman, 1988a; Vivian & O'Leary, 1987). Thus, therapists may wish to assess the communication and problem-solving skills of violent couples, using either paper and pencil measures (e.g., the Spouse-Specific Assertion/Aggression Scale, Rosenbaum & O'Leary, 1981) or direct observation of marital interactions.

Given feminist theories that men may use violence as a means of asserting their dominance over women, therapists may choose to assess husbands' and wives' *beliefs about sex roles* and the relationship between men and women, using such measures as the Attitudes Toward Women's Scale (Spence & Helmreich, 1972) and the Adversarial Sexual Beliefs Questionnaire (Burt, 1980). In addition, practitioners may wish to gather information regarding violent husbands' *beliefs about violence*, using new measures (Saunders, Lynch, Grayson, & Linz, 1987) to identify batterers who believe that there are situations in which violence is productive and necessary.

Many violent husbands grew up in violent homes, witnessing parental violence and having, themselves, been the victim of parental aggression (Hotaling & Sugarman, 1986). Both husbands' and wives' past experiences with violence may have influenced their perceptions of their own, current marital violence. Thus, it is often useful to assess each partner's experiences with violence in their family of origin and in past relationships.

Assessment Summary

In summary, therapists must recognize that marital violence will have occurred in over 50% of the couples seeking marital therapy. They should screen for the occurrence of marital violence, using the CTS and direct questions about violence, among all couples seeking therapy. For those couples who report violence, clinical interviews will be needed to determine the severity, frequency, and context of the violence; the consequences of the violence; and the risk of lethality. If imminent danger is detected, then more careful assessment of the risks must be undertaken and safety plans must be developed. Finally, related problems (e.g., psychological abuse, alcohol–drug abuse) should be assessed to aid in treatment planning.

TREATMENT OF MARITAL VIOLENCE

Treatment Goals and Format

Elimination of Violence as the Primary Treatment Goal

Regardless of theoretical orientation or therapeutic modality, the primary goal of therapy when working with violent couples is the elimination of physical aggression. Interestingly, this is not always the couple's primary goal, particularly among couples who have not experienced severe violence. In fact, when marital violence is identified as a problem by the therapist, many couples will disagree, stating their beliefs that the violence is not serious, will not occur again, and so on. Spouses sometimes believe that their use of physical aggression was justified or had positive benefits (e.g., "She was hysterical and we couldn't talk about the issue calmly; I had to calm her down") and sometimes deny responsibility for their aggression. Thus, it is the therapist's responsibility to stress the dangerousness of the violence and the importance of targeting violent behavior for therapeutic intervention.

To do so, it is useful to firmly adopt the stance that it is the therapist's "expert opinion" that the violence is a serious problem, even if the couple does not necessarily agree, and that no violent acts are acceptable within the relationship. It should be pointed out that, even if serious consequences have not yet occurred and the spouses' intentions do not involve harm, violence always carries the potential for serious injury and destructive outcomes. Examples help to make this point (e.g., a case where the husband pushed his wife, not hard and with no intent to hurt her; however, she slipped and hit her head on the kitchen counter, losing consciousness). In addition, it is useful to point out that research and clinical experience suggest that unless it is stopped, marital violence will continue and may even escalate. Finally, the therapist should explain that therapy may actually increase the risk of violence, because the couple will be asked to examine and discuss many of their most difficult and affect-laden issues. As a result of these factors, the therapist should explain that he/she has no option but to be concerned about the occurrence of violence and that therapy must focus on this problem.

It is also necessary to help spouses accept responsibility for their violent actions. The fact that spouses are able to "choose" where, when, and against whom to aggress can be used as proof of their responsibility. For example, many spouses' descriptions of their violence are inconsistent with their claims that they are "out of control" when angry and violent (e.g., a man who beat his wife severely but when asked why he did not kill her said, "Oh, I couldn't do that"; or a man who, in a "fit of rage," carefully and with precise aim shot each and every one of his wife's knickknacks with his gun). In addition, violence is framed as a learned behavior; this is often easily understood by spouses who grew up in violent homes. Framing violence as a learned behavior and as a choice opens the possibility that spouses can learn to choose nonviolent, constructive methods of handling marital conflict.

Conjoint or Individual/Group Treatment?

Based upon information gathered during the assessment of marital violence, the therapist must decide whether to proceed with conjoint marital therapy or to refer the individual spouses for relevant marital violence therapy. No firm guidelines have been established for making this decision, and no data currently exist regarding the relative efficacy of conjoint versus individual/group therapy for treating marital violence, although two empirical investigations of this issue are underway (e.g., O'Leary, Neidig, & Arias, 1992b; Dunford, 1992a). Thus, at this point in time, common sense and theoretical orientation often dictate the therapist's decision.

Conjoint treatment is generally recommended if the occurrence of past violence is relatively "mild" and infrequent and if the wife is not in immediate or serious danger. In addition, the perpetrator must be willing to acknowledge that the violence has occurred and is problematic, and be willing to address this issue in therapy. In our opinion, conjoint therapy is a viable option if the violence that has occurred is not severe, if there is a genuine commitment to the avoidance of physical aggression, and if both partners wish to remain in the relationship.

Other researchers and clinicians have outlined the potential advantages of conjoint therapy (e.g., Mantooth, Geffner, Franks, & Patrick, 1987; Margolin & Burman, 1993; Margolin, Sibner, & Gleberman, 1988b), including (1) giving the therapist a more accurate picture of the violence that is occurring (i.e., the husband and wife's reports may differ significantly); (2) introducing both spouses to the same information and techniques, thus helping to ensure that both understand the therapist's conceptualization of the violence (i.e., the wife is not responsible) and how to implement various procedures (e.g., when and how to take a time-out); (3) changing interactional patterns that precede the violence, helping the husband to monitor his anger and communicate with his wife; (4) helping the wife to recognize danger cues and take steps to protect herself; and (5) allowing the couple to postpone discussion of emotionally laden issues until therapy sessions.

However, there are potential disadvantages and dangers involved in conjoint treatment (e.g., Margolin & Burman, 1993). These include the fact that (1) the wife's safety may be jeopardized (e.g., if she accurately reports her husband's behavior, he may retaliate with further aggression after the session); (2) it may be difficult, with both spouses present, to accurately assess their desire to continue their marriage; and (3) conjoint interventions and the involvement of the wife in treatment may send the message that the wife is responsible for the violence (e.g., Bograd, 1984).

Given these potential disadvantages, conjoint treatment is contraindicated if the wife is in grave danger, if the husband refuses to take steps to reduce the danger (e.g., remove weapons from the house, seek help for alcohol problems, agree to a temporary separation), or if the wife is too afraid of the husband to be a full and equal participant in conjoint treatment. In such cases, the violent husband should be referred to a batterer's treatment program. These programs usually involve group treatment in which the husband will get extensive interventions targeted specifically at eliminating his violence and abusive behaviors. The wife should be referred to a local battered women's support group (e.g., groups run by the local shelter), where she will receive access to resources for battered women and support to make her own decisions about her life and the future of her relationship.

After the spouses have sought such help, many marital therapists will treat the couple conjointly (e.g., Rosenbaum & Maiuro, 1989), although no data regarding the efficacy of doing so are currently available. To be seen in conjoint therapy, the therapist should require that the husband has completed a batterer's program, accepted responsibility for his violence, and taken steps to reduce it; the therapist should also verify that the wife has made a decision, free of fear, to work on her relationship.

Janet and Bill

Janet and Bill, who presented at our clinic asking for marital therapy, did not volunteer any information about violence and did not mention fighting as a problem during their intake interview. However, as part of the routine clinic assessment, the couple completed the CTS. Both indicated that Bill had pushed/grabbed/shoved Janet and that she had slapped Bill; these actions reportedly had not occurred in the past year. At the next interview, the therapist specifically asked about these incidents. The couple reported that in their first year of marriage, which was over 3 years ago, they had "two or three" fights that ended with Janet hitting Bill and his shoving Janet "out of the way" so that he could leave the room. They reported that these incidents never resulted in injuries and that neither spouse was currently fearful of the other. Bill and Janet both reported that there had been no physical aggression in at least 3 years. They both agreed with the therapist's concern about violence; Bill volunteered his own concerns and the fact that he did not want their child to witness violence. The couple agreed to report any problems with escalating conflict and any incidents of violence that occurred during the course of treatment; they also agreed to work with the therapist to learn nonviolent methods of settling their conflicts. The therapist decided to work with the couple conjointly.

Mary and Jack

Mary and Jack also did not discuss physical aggression as a problem during their intake interview. However, Mary mentioned concerns about Jack's "anger" and both mentioned problems with "heated arguments." Based upon these hints, the therapist specifically asked the couple to describe their worst arguments and whether "physical contact" had ever occurred. The couple volunteered that, over the course of their 5-year relationship, they had regularly engaged in physical aggression, with fights escalating to the point of slapping and pushing several times per year. They did not say more; however, the therapist asked them to independently complete the CTS. Based upon their responses to this measure, the therapist chose to interview Mary and Jack separately during the next session.

Mary was interviewed first and volunteered that she was increasingly fearful of Jack and his violence. She reported that, in the past 6 months, Jack had twice pulled a knife and threatened her with it during fights. In another recent argument, Jack had begun beating the walls and throwing objects, breaking several possessions and hitting Mary in the head by throwing a vase before he ran out of the house; several hours later he had returned home drunk, and punched her several times before leaving the house again for 2 days. Mary reported that she had considered calling the police during this argument. Mary told the therapist that she wasn't sure that marital therapy was the "best idea" for her marriage; Mary and the therapist agreed to discuss these issues with Jack in a conjoint interview. Mary was helped to develop a safety plan, was given referrals to a local battered women's support group and the local shelter, and was informed of some of her legal options; she was explicitly warned about the danger of Jack's violence, was warned that Jack might not seek help and that, even if he did, it was not clear that therapy would be successful. In his interview, Jack expressed concerns about the couple's violence but depicted them both as violent; he described himself as "out of control" in arguments, but attributed his worsening violence to the stress of having recently lost his job.

In the conjoint session, the therapist explained her concerns regarding the seriousness of the violence and the potential danger of their escalating situation; she concluded that their level of violence was too high to permit conjoint therapy. She told Jack about the referrals she had given Mary and explained to him the possible consequences of his actions, including the legal consequences. She gave him referrals to a batterer's program in town and encouraged him to seek help there, offering to see the couple in the future, if Jack completed the program and the couple was no longer experiencing violence. She then met individually with Mary to assess whether Mary felt comfortable leaving the session with Jack, to further validate Mary's fears and concerns, and to encourage Mary to protect herself.

Conjoint Behavioral-Cognitive Therapy with Violent Couples

Once a therapist and couple have decided to engage in conjoint marital therapy, the therapist should again note his/her concern about the issue of marital violence; in addition, the couple should again be cautioned regarding the affective arousal that occurs concurrently with marital therapy and the resulting risk of violence reoccurring. The couple should be informed that treatment may be terminated if the violence continues and should be asked to make a "no violence" contract with the therapist.

Couples experiencing more serious or frequent violence should be told that the violence must be brought under control before work on other issues can begin; therapy should then focus on reducing the violence. Couples experiencing lower levels of violence can be offered a "two-pronged" therapy approach.

These couples are told that, given the potential dangers of the violence, they must learn methods for reducing and managing their destructive conflicts; these are reviewed in this chapter. However, focusing only on eliminating negative, aggressive interactions may be frustrating, because it does not provide couples with other, more constructive methods of resolving disputes. To deal with this issue, work on relationship improvement may be done concurrently with the anger management treatment: for example, part of each therapy session may be spent on violence/anger management and the rest of the session may be used to develop other relationship skills (e.g., communication training). Training in communication and problem-solving skills itself helps to lower levels of anger and subsequent violence. This dual-treatment approach can be explained to the couple by stating that anger control techniques help to prevent the escalation of conflicts, and problem-solving and communication training give the couple skills to use after the time-out to solve problems and to avoid future conflicts.

Given our behavioral-cognitive orientation, we utilize skill-based interventions when teaching couples new ways to handle conflict; these are discussed elsewhere and will not be reviewed here (see Chapter 4 by Baucom, Epstein, & Rankin, and Chapter 3 by Christensen, Jacobson, & Babcock, both in this volume; Holtzworth-Munroe & Jacobson, 1991; Jacobson & Margolin, 1979). Anger and violence management techniques are introduced below.

Group Therapy with Violent Husbands

As noted previously, if severe violence is occurring, the husband should be referred to a batterer's treatment group. Although no controlled studies regarding this issue have been conducted, it is widely assumed that group therapy provides the best setting for treating violent men, and most available programs utilize this format. The group provides an opportunity for exchanging social support and reducing the isolation and stigma that violent men might feel. Yet, a group is also an excellent vehicle for confrontation, and group members are typically encouraged to interact with each other in a direct manner, pointing out instances of denial and minimization of violence among themselves and other group members.

In our experience with various programs, the usual format for group therapy involves weekly sessions of approximately 1.5 to 2 hours for periods ranging from 8 to 36 weeks. Having a male and a female as cotherapists is generally recommended, since the therapists can model a positive, egalitarian relationship; group members can benefit from the opportunity to relate to an authority figure of each sex who, in turn, treats the members with respect and caring (Arias & O'Leary, 1988).

Groups for male batterers usually are primarily psychoeducational, although psychotherapeutic interventions are often included. They may be run as self-help groups involving peer counseling, or as therapist-led groups run by women's shelters or established mental health agencies (Margolin & Burman, 1993). Although there is much variability across group treatments for male batterers, the primary goal of most available programs is to end the violence. Men are asked to accept responsibility for their abuse and for ending their violence. Many of the programs use behavioral-cognitive interventions for teaching anger management and violence cessation, as outlined in more detail later (e.g., time-outs, self-talk, relaxation). They also often involve interventions from a feminist perspective, including sex-role education, resocialization, and discussions of patriarchal, male power issues. Finally, these programs often include skills training designed to improve the marital relationship and derived from both a behavioral-cognitive and family systems orientation (e.g., social skills training, assertion skills training).

Group Therapy with Battered Women

Groups for women who have been victims of marital violence are also prevalent (e.g., Cox & Stoltenberg, 1991; Douglas & Strom, 1988; Hartman, 1983; Gottlieb, Burden, McCormick, & Nicarthy, 1983; Miller, 1980); they are often offered through battered women's shelters. Such groups typically function as support systems and advocates for women who are working to achieve independence from the men who have battered them. Treatment typically involves the provision of instrumental help, including assistance in dealing with social and legal services (e.g., aid in obtaining welfare or employment; help getting housing; survival skills, such as budgeting; and information on possible legal interventions, including restraining orders and court procedures). In addition, with their nonjudgmental and supportive atmosphere, these groups offer battered women emotional support and the opportunity to build their self-esteem; they are designed to empower women to make their own decisions regarding their relationships (Margolin & Burman, 1993; O'Leary & Vivian, 1990).

Behavioral-Cognitive Therapeutic Interventions Designed to Eliminate Violence

Whether couples are seen conjointly or in individual/group therapy, the major and initial goal of therapy is to eliminate marital violence. Many of the available treatment programs are derived from behavioral-cognitive theories of husband-to-wife violence (e.g., Hamberger & Lohr, 1989; Saunders, 1989; Sonkin & Durphy, 1989).

Behavioral-cognitive models of marital violence are derived from social learning theory (e.g., Bandura, 1977; Dutton, 1988). These models view battering as a learned behavior. Violence is learned through direct observation of role models (e.g., observation of parental violence in one's family of origin) and indirect observation (e.g., TV, film, peers). Once learned, violence continues to be used because it is functional for the user (e.g., it may release tension or achieve victim compliance).

Behavioral-cognitive treatments are based on the combined assumptions that violent husbands have difficulty controlling their anger, and have deficits in relationship and communication skills. It is assumed that as an unskilled husband encounters marital conflicts and is unable to effectively handle the conflict and his anger, he is at increased risk to engage in violence. His inability to handle negative affect is associated with hostile withdrawal and physical abuse (e.g., Boeke & Markman, 1992). His use of violence may inadvertently be reinforced (e.g., it ends the conflict and/or decreases his anger), increasing the probability that he will choose violence again in future marital situations and decreasing the probability that he will learn more constructive methods for handling anger and conflict (e.g., Holtzworth-Munroe, 1991, 1992; O'Leary, 1988).

Available data support many of these theoretical assumptions (reviewed in Holtzworth-Munroe, 1992). For example, research indicates that violent husbands are more likely than nonviolent husbands to have witnessed parental violence as a child or adolescent (Hotaling & Sugarman, 1986). In addition, past researchers have demonstrated that violent husbands experience more anger than other men (e.g., Maiuro et al., 1988), especially in marital situations (e.g., Dutton & Browning, 1988; Margolin et al., 1988a). In observations of marital interactions, violent couples have been found to lack communication skills, engaging in more negative and fewer positive behaviors than other couples (e.g., Boeke & Markman, 1992; Margolin et al., 1988a; Vivian & O'Leary, 1987). Violent husbands have also been found to provide less competent responses to standardized problematic marital situations than nonviolent men (Holtzworth-Munroe & Anglin, 1991).

Given these data, therapists trained in the behavioral-cognitive orientation teach anger management skills to violent husbands. They also teach violent men and couples other communication and conflict-resolution skills (e.g., listening, expressing feeling, problem solving, assertiveness).

Anger Control Strategies

A variety of behavioral-cognitive interventions are available to help violent spouses recognize and reduce their anger and choose nonviolent actions, even when angry (e.g., Novaco, 1975; Goldstein & Rosenbaum, 1982; Sonkin & Durphy, 1989). These interventions often begin by teaching clients to recognize the cues that they are experiencing anger and then to implement responses that are incompatible with violence when angry.

Anger recognition strategies allow the client to identify the physiological, behavioral, and cognitive cues of anger that precede acts of violence.

Physiological cues include a racing heart, feeling flushed or hot, feeling tense, and clenched jaw or fists. Behavioral cues may involve such activities as standing up, pacing, and exaggerated gestures. Cognitive cues include thoughts or statements to oneself that result in increasing anger levels (e.g., ruminating about how one was wronged).

Cue recognition can be facilitated by having clients self-monitor their feelings, thoughts, and behaviors during experiences in which they felt angry. This is often done with anger logs in which clients record a description of incidents in which they felt angry, including the time, place, people involved, and their thoughts, behaviors, emotions, and physical reactions in these situations. Situational analyses of clients' anger experiences are then reviewed with the therapist; common elements are identified as specific anger cues (e.g., for one client, a clenched jaw and flushed face was a consistent sign that he was close to using violence) and high-risk situations are identified (e.g., one couple realized that their most destructive arguments occurred when they were running late for important appointments).

Once high-risk situations are identified, the clients and therapist can plan ways to avoid or prevent high-risk situations from occurring (e.g., better communication about expected departure times and better planning helped the couple to avoid running late). In addition, once anger cues are identified, clients can be taught to implement responses that are incompatible with violence when anger cues occur. These responses may be behavioral, such as taking a time-out or using relaxation techniques, and/or cognitive, such as changing one's self-talk.

Time-out procedures are almost universally used in marital violence programs. These procedures are designed to help a violent spouse leave an escalating argument before violence occurs; they involve recognizing and acknowledging one's anger, removing oneself from the situation before violence occurs, and returning after one has calmed down.

Interestingly, many couples object to the use of time-outs. These procedures initially seem paradoxical and undesirable to couples, given our culture's emphasis on the cathartic benefits of "getting it all out" and never leaving issues unresolved (e.g., "Never go to bed angry with one another"). Thus, the therapist must remind the couple that, given their past use of violence, such immediate emotional expression is ill-advised and that it is better to end the day with issues

unresolved than to engage in further physical violence. Time-out can be framed for the clients as a way to stop themselves from engaging in destructive behavior that they will later regret; most couples can understand this when reminded of the sadness and guilt they felt after past violent incidents.

The basic time-out procedure is as follows: When individuals first recognize that they are angry, they make a statement such as, "I feel angry and am going to take a time-out." They then state a specific and reasonable amount of time for the time-out and say that they will be back after that time period; this can range from 15 minutes to 2 hours, depending on the couple, the level of anger experienced, and the danger of violence. The person who called the time-out then leaves the interaction and, preferably, the setting (e.g., house, apartment) altogether. During the time-out, individuals should engage in techniques designed to decrease their anger. These may include nonaggressive physical exercise (e.g., running) and other calming techniques, such as deep breathing, positive self-talk, and relaxation. Activities that may escalate anger or endanger the person, such as alcohol or drug use, aggressive exercise, ruminating about the anger-provoking interaction, or driving, should be avoided. At the conclusion of the time-out period, the individual should return to the partner. If the couple can *calmly* resume their discussion, they may do so; if not, such a discussion should be postponed until it can be conducted safely, perhaps in the presence of the therapist.

Each step in the time-out is important and must be reviewed carefully with the couple. First, stating that one is angry and needs a time-out necessitates taking responsibility for one's feelings (i.e., as opposed to "You make me angry") and for one's behaviors when angry. It should be emphasized that each individual is responsible for his/her own time-outs. Telling the other person to take a time-out is *not* allowed, although many spouses will attempt to do so. Similarly, each partner must respect the other's right to take a time-out. We have encountered problems in which one partner tried to stop the other from leaving, wishing to finish the discussion. To avoid this, the couple must be prompted to remember the function and importance of the time-out: to stop destructive arguments.

Second, setting a limited length of time for the time-out is important, as is the couple's agreement to resume communication once the woman is again safe. The qualitative difference between this and the "unilateral cessation of an argument" (Margolin, 1979, p. 17) should be stressed. Without attention to this issue, many husbands will simply use time-out as one more abusive technique (e.g., a man who said he needed a time-out and then left home, not contacting his wife for over 3 days). Similarly, the couple must be reassured that therapy will teach them the skills necessary to constructively resolve their unfinished discussions.

Finally, one's actions during the time-out must be directed at reducing, rather than escalating, the anger. The first impulse of many men is to jump in the car, go get a drink, or punch a punching bag. The potential dangerousness of these actions should be discussed (e.g., Is it safe to drive when so angry? Can one calm down when punching a bag and envisioning revenge?).

In our experience, it is often useful to employ a sports analogy when discussing time-outs with men. In Indiana, where basketball engenders religious fervor, we ask the couple to consider when, and why, Bobby Knight (the infamous Indiana University basketball coach) calls a time-out during a game. The point is that coaches call time-outs to allow their team to regroup, to implement new plays or strategies, and to help their team regain control of a ball game before they "blow" the game with destructive, out-of-control, actions. Violent couples should use time-outs for the same reasons.

Time-out procedures are often initially difficult for couples to incorporate into their interactions; with practice, however, couples become increasingly proficient. After practicing the procedures during a therapy session, couples should be asked to take several practice time-outs per week, even if they do not really need them or feel only mildly irritated. Practicing these skills, in this manner, greatly increases the likelihood that the couple will learn the time-out procedures and use them when they are truly needed. It also allows the therapist to troubleshoot problems that the couple encounters when using the procedure. If a couple has had difficulty using time-outs, we often ask them to enact a time-out in the therapy session. This provides an excellent opportunity to examine what is interfering with the couple's execution of this procedure (e.g., one spouse is telling the other to leave, rather than taking responsibility for his/her own anger; one spouse is concerned that the issue will never be resolved if the partner leaves the discussion, etc.).

Self-talk strategies are grounded in the belief that self-statements and thoughts play a critical role in the initiation and intensification of anger. Several researchers have discussed cognitions that are related to anger (e.g., Beck, 1988; Ellis, 1977; Meichenbaum, 1977; Novaco, 1975). For example, Deffenbacher (1988) suggests that different types of thought lead to an increase in anger. These include catastrophizing thoughts, demanding/coercing thoughts (i.e., those that change wants and desires into demands and necessities), and the tendency to consistently personalize the reasons for a particular situation occurring. Following identification of the types of thoughts that clients have, they can be trained to engage in more productive thoughts that, in turn, enable them to deal more appropriately with frustrating situations.

Relaxation training can also be implemented to help violent spouses calm down during an angry incident or during a time-out. Detailed descriptions of relaxation procedures can be found elsewhere (e.g., Sonkin & Durphy, 1989).

Other Treatment/Theoretical Approaches Designed to Eliminate Marital Violence

Descriptions of behavioral-cognitive treatments for marital violence, such as those introduced previously, are prevalent in the marital violence literature. However, other approaches exist as well.

Another major approach includes programs based upon feminist theories of marital violence (e.g., Ganley, 1989). For example, Pence (Pence & Paymar, 1985; Pence, 1989) has developed treatment programs for violent men derived from feminist theories (also see Adams, 1989). These programs view marital violence as a sociopolitical issue; they assume that male violence toward women is based in, and supported by, our patriarchal society, which allows men to dominate and control women through a variety of economic and institutional mechanisms. Men are assumed to be more powerful than women: physically, politically, and economically. Thus, a husband's use of physical violence is simply one of the many methods he uses to control his wife's actions; others include psychological abuse, control of economic resources, and sexual abuse. Such tactics are supported by society, both directly (e.g., peer support of violence; the stated doctrine of some religious groups that the husband is the head of the household), and indirectly (e.g., lack of police response to domestic violence calls, lack of prosecution of marital violence as a crime, lack of training of physicians and psychologists to recognize the needs of battered women).

Previous research has provided data consistent that are with this model, for example, physically aggressive husbands are also likely to engage in psychologically abusive, controlling behaviors and to sexually abuse (e.g., Pagelow, 1988) their wives. Smith (1990) reviewed a variety of studies supporting a connection between a patriarchal ideology and wife beating. These studies demonstrated (1) a relationship between rates of violence against women and the status of women across states in the United States. (Yllo, 1983a, 1983b); (2) high rates of wife beating among husband-dominant couples (Yllo, 1984); (3) a positive relationship between patriarchal norms and wife beating (Yllo & Straus, 1984); (4) a positive relationship between marital conflict and husband violence, with husband-dominant couples having the most conflict about family responsibilities and the lowest consensus about the legitimacy of patriarchal norms (Coleman & Straus, 1986); and (5) high rates of wife beating in states with greater structural inequality for women (Straus, 1987). In addition, Smith's own survey of Toronto women revealed that, based upon wives' reports, men who beat their wives are more likely than men who do not to hold patriarchal beliefs and approve of violence against wives (Smith, 1990) and to have male friends who approve of violence against wives (Smith, 1991). Other researchers have similarly found that male batterers believe that wife beating is justified under certain conditions (Saunders et al., 1987) and that at least a subgroup of male batterers holds sexist attitudes toward women (e.g., Saunders, 1992b; although note, as reviewed in Smith, 1990, that data regarding general group differences between maritally violent and nonviolent men's sex-role expectations have been mixed and inconclusive).

Feminist intervention programs target men's views of women and their belief that they should be able to control their wives. Therapy focuses on helping men to examine their sexist assumptions and beliefs about relationships between men and women. Men are also asked to examine the various methods they use to control their wives and how society sanctions those actions. The critical dimensions in feminist treatment are power and control; a didactic approach is often used to help violent men explore the sociopolitical meaning of abuse.

In addition, feminist programs emphasize the need for community support of marital violence intervention programs. These programs are ideally only one part of active, coordinated efforts by all relevant community agencies (e.g., police, prosecutors, probation officers, judges, thera-

pists, battered women's advocates). Such coordination is designed to provide a consistent message that abuse will not be tolerated and that the violent husband is responsible for his actions. Through such efforts, it is hoped that changes can be made in societal norms and attitudes toward male domination and marital violence.

Treatment programs derived from family systems theories of marital violence also exist (e.g., Lane & Russell, 1989; Madanes, 1990; Neidig, Friedman, & Collins, 1985). According to systems theory, relationship violence is seen

> as a symptom of dysfunctional interactions in a couple's relationship. Violent episodes are seen as part of an interactional sequence in which both batterer and victim contribute to an escalation of tension that ends in a violent outburst. (Harris et al., 1988, p. 148)

This approach views marital violence as a relationship issue, as the function of the couple's interactional patterns; the causation of violence is believed to be circular, not linear, with both partners contributing to the escalation of conflicts.

This treatment approach usually includes the wife in therapy. It is designed to help spouses identify their role in relationship processes and to break the couple's rigid patterns of interaction, allowing constructive change to take place. Specific therapy techniques that are systemic in nature include behavioral prescriptions, paradoxical interventions, use of a treatment team, and triangulation interpretations. These techniques may be helpful in countering the resistance and avoidance of violent men (Madanes, 1990; Rosenbaum & O'Leary, 1986).

Systems therapy has been extensively criticized (e.g., Adams, 1989; Bograd, 1984; Margolin & Burman, 1993). Critics charge that this approach implies that the abused wife is, in some way, responsible for the solution to the problem and, perhaps, for the violence itself (i.e., blaming the victim). There is also concern that the wife's safety may be jeopardized by requiring her to actively participate in therapy (e.g., the husband may retaliate with violence if the wife discusses issues that he believes should not have been discussed with the therapist). In general, systems theory is criticized for ignoring gender issues and the inherent power of the men in our society, thus confusing the issue of who is responsible for male violence.

Clinical Issues for Marital Violence Therapists to Consider

Therapists' Emotional Reactions to Marital Violence

Marital violence is a complex, emotionally charged, and potentially dangerous problem. The intensity of spouses' emotions during violent conflicts and the despicable nature of some batterers' abusive behaviors may elicit intense emotional responses in therapists. In addition, given the prevalence of marital violence in our society, many therapists will have experienced physical aggression themselves, either in their own adult relationships or in their families of origin. Such experiences may color and shape therapists' reactions to reports of violence among their clients. Sometimes therapists become particularly concerned about their own safety when working with violent couples or batterers.

Therapists beginning work in this area should be aware of the potential for a variety of strong reactions to couples' reports of marital violence and should seek consultation and supervision as needed. Therapists' fears regarding their own safety should be dealt with by receiving training in the treatment of marital violence. Such training should help therapists to conduct better assessments of the level of danger in each case and to develop contingency safety plans for the protection of all involved parties.

Therapists' Beliefs about Marital Violence and Related Issues

In addition to emotional reactions, therapists who work with violent clients need to examine their personal beliefs about family violence. As noted by other researchers and clinicians, it is impossible to offer "value-free" therapy for marital violence (Margolin & Burman, 1993); every choice made by therapists will reflect and convey their own beliefs about domestic violence.

It is essential that therapists are clear in their own minds as to which behaviors are violent and which are not (e.g., Is an occasional push or shove "violence"? If not, what is? When, if ever, should conjoint treatment be terminated because the violence has become too severe?). In addition, marital therapists need to consider whether they believe that violence is simply an extreme version of marital conflict in general, or whether violence qualitatively differs from other marital conflict (e.g., by inducing fear in the wife, by involving possible injury, by altering the power structure of the relationship). Confusion on such

matters leads to an inconsistent therapy approach with violent cases.

Similarly, a therapist should confront his/her personal beliefs regarding male power and control. Does the therapist view violence in the context of our patriarchal society and our culture's assumptions of male domination? Is the therapist sensitive to the terror felt by the female victim of violence? Is he/she aware of gender differences in our culture and how these are translated into various power structures within marital relationships?

Finally, it is important that therapists carefully consider their goals when working with violent couples. Is the primary goal to end the violence, as we have suggested? If so, marital therapists who are accustomed to working with nonviolent couples may find it difficult to shift to, and maintain their attention on, the violence; they may find themselves ignoring the violence, believing that relationship improvement is the major treatment goal. Again, seeking additional training in the treatment of marital violence should help clinicians to consider such issues.

Therapeutic Alliances

Therapeutic alliances are always an issue when conducting conjoint therapy, but perhaps are a more prominent issue when working with violent couples. The therapist must ensure the safety of the wife, as outlined previously. However, it is also critical that therapists working with violent men be able to accept them as human beings fully deserving of respect. Batterers may enter therapy anticipating rejection or punishment from therapists and thus adopt a resistant posture. Therapists can circumvent this dynamic by emphasizing their acceptance of the batterer *and* their concurrent rejection of his violent behavior. This nonjudgmental status regarding the batterer's worth as a person must be balanced against a condemnation of his violence. We have encountered therapists who simply state that they cannot work with violent men, given their anger at such men's behavior; such personal awareness is necessary.

In addition, a marital therapist often serves as an advocate for the marital relationship, rather than for either spouse. In fact, marital therapy, by definition, is designed to preserve and improve the marriage. However, in the case of violent couples, a marital therapist must reconsider this assumption. For example, at what point is it better for a violent relationship to be dissolved? Can one be an advocate for the relationship, for the wife, and for the husband?

Legal Issues

Therapists must bear in mind the legal, ethical, and moral responsibilities involved in working with violent couples. Mandatory reporting laws for child abuse exist in all states; thus, any knowledge or reasonable suspicion of child abuse must be reported to a child protective agency. Although there are no such regulations concerning wife abuse, legal rulings regarding the duty to warn and protect potential victims are relevant (e.g., *Tarasoff v. Regents of University of California*, 1976). The relevance of such rulings to the treatment of marital violence are reviewed more completely elsewhere (Hart, 1988; Sonkin, 1986; Sonkin & Ellison, 1986) and are only briefly discussed here.

The major ruling relevant to marital violence, with which most therapists are familiar, was the *Tarasoff* decision (*Tarasoff v. Regents of the University of California*, 1976). In this case, the client, Mr. Poddar, was interested in dating a woman who was not interested in a romantic relationship with him. During treatment, Poddar specifically threatened to kill this woman. The therapist decided that Poddar should be hospitalized and asked the campus police to take him into custody. They did so, but released him after he agreed to stay away from the intended victim. He then murdered the woman. Her family brought a civil suit against the therapist, and the court found the therapist liable for not warning the victim about Poddar's intentions and for not hospitalizing him. The court ruled that the therapist had a duty to use "reasonable care" to protect an intended victim; this might include warning the victim, hospitalizing the patient, or warning the police. In a 1985 California Assembly Bill, the therapist's duty to "protect potential victims" was defined to include cases "where the patient has communicated a serious threat of violence against a reasonably identifiable victim"; such protective actions must include both "reasonable efforts to communicate the threat to the victim and a law enforcement agency" (California State Psychological Association, 1985).

Sonkin (1986; Sonkin & Ellison, 1986) argues that these legal rulings and guidelines are applicable to virtually all cases of marital violence. He reasons that, given data demonstrating the continuation and escalation of marital violence, continued violence in such cases is predictable without a specific verbal threat. Thus, he recommends that therapists dealing with a violent couple should warn both the husband and wife of the "high probability of continued violence." Given the overlap between marital violence and child abuse, he also recommends that therapists consider warning the couple of the potential danger to their children. In summary, Sonkin and Ellison (1986) conclude that

> those who routinely treat individuals with an established history of violent behaviors—such as men who are physically, sexually, or psychologically assaultive toward their mates—will be confronted with situations quite frequently in which the client has not made a verbal threat but nevertheless may pose a serious danger to family members or friends. In responding to this type of situation, it is advisable to use the "danger to self or others" clause as reason for violating confidentiality. "Others" may include intended (spouse) and unintended (children, friends, in-laws, etc.) victims of violence. The most appropriate course of action may include notifying the potential victim(s) and the law enforcement authorities. Although this intervention may be viewed as an extreme response and may actually be unnecessary, it seems the most ethical course of action. (pp. 210–211)

Many marital therapists are unaccustomed to working with the legal system. However, such cooperation is often required in marital violence cases (e.g., the husband has been court-ordered to seek therapy). Therapists lacking such experience may wish to seek consultation regarding such issues as confidentiality, reports to probation officers, and court appearances (see Sonkin et al., 1985, for discussion of these issues).

RESEARCH ON INTERVENTIONS FOR MARITAL VIOLENCE

Empirical Evidence of the Effects of Arrest

Many battered women's advocates have argued that marital violence should be treated in the same manner as any assault, resulting in arrest. Arrest and prosecution of batterers would empower women, sending the message that society will not tolerate spouse abuse and letting victims know that protection is available to them.

Empirical data from an early study conducted in Minneapolis (Sherman & Berk, 1984) support this position. In this study, over 300 cases of misdemeanor domestic assault were randomly assigned to one of three conditions: (1) arrest of the suspect, (2) mediation and advice, or (3) separation of the couple. Over a 6-month follow-up period, the rate of additional arrests among suspects in the arrest condition was approximately half of the rate of arrest among suspects who had not been arrested (i.e., 10% vs. 20%), indicating that arrest was an effective deterrent against domestic violence.

The Minneapolis study has been criticized on a variety of grounds, including the limited sample size, inadequate controls over whether the treatments delivered actually matched the treatments assigned, and the low proportion of victims who were available for follow-up interviews. Despite these possible limitations, shortly after the study results were released, the Attorney General of the United States recommended that arrest be made the standard treatment in cases of misdemeanor domestic assault (U.S. Attorney General's Task Force on Domestic Violence, 1984).

As a result of the Minneapolis findings, along with efforts made by battered women's advocates and fear of litigation (i.e., a variety of law suits were filed by battered women against the police for lack of protection, as listed in Frisch, 1992), many police departments decided to either allow or mandate arrest as the standard procedure for dealing with cases of misdemeanor domestic assault. By 1989, a survey demonstrated that 84% of big city police agencies had adopted a preferred arrest policy for such cases (Hirschel & Hutchison, 1991). Given interest in the effects of arrest, the National Institute of Justice funded replications of the Minneapolis study in six cities (Atlanta, Charlotte, Colorado Springs, Miami Metro-Dade, Milwaukee, and Omaha). At this point, initial results from five of the studies (all but Atlanta) have been published. Many of these findings are published in a special issue of *Journal of Criminal Law and Criminology* (Vol. 83, No. 1, 1992). This series also includes reviews of the history of police policies regarding domestic violence (Sherman, 1992) and a series of commentaries on the results of the replication studies, written by women's advocates, police, and legal scholars. The replication studies are reviewed in some detail here. Given their recent publication, we assume that therapists may not yet be familiar with these findings.

In all of the replication studies, cases of misdemeanor spouse assault were examined. Felony cases were excluded, as were cases in which the victim demanded arrest, and cases in which an outstanding arrest warrant had been issued for the suspect. All of the studies improved upon the initial Minneapolis study by separating deter-

mination of the eligibility of a case from random assignment to treatment. Police arrived at the scene and determined eligibility; officers then called a central number and were given a treatment assignment. Rates of compliance with assigned treatment (i.e., delivered treatment matches assigned treatment) were high. In addition, the replications all involved a minimum of 6 months of follow-up; outcome was determined, using both official records (e.g., further arrests of the suspect) and interviews with the victims.

In Omaha, Dunford and his colleagues (Dunford, Huizinga, & Elliott, 1990; Dunford, 1992b) randomly assigned over 300 cases of misdemeanor spouse assault, coming to the attention of the police during the evening hours, to one of three treatments: (1) mediation, (2) separation, or (3) arrest. In contrast with the Minneapolis findings, at the 6-month follow-up, arrest was no more effective in reducing recidivism than were mediation or separation. In addition, at the 12-month follow-up, cases assigned to the informal treatments, particularly mediation, tended to have a lower rates of arrest recidivism than did those assigned to the arrest condition.

In the Milwaukee replication study conducted by Sherman and his colleagues (Sherman et al., 1991, 1992), similar findings emerged. In this study, all eligible cases (n = 1,200) of misdemeanor domestic battery encountered by special teams of police officers, working from 7 P.M. to 3 A.M. in the city districts with high rates of domestic violence, were randomly assigned to one of three treatments: (1) long-custody arrest (i.e., mean of 11 hours of custody), (2) short-custody arrest (i.e., mean of 2.8 hours of custody), or (3) warning (i.e., no arrest, but warning of future arrest). In the first month following intervention, calls generated by the police and recorded by a domestic violence hotline indicated that arrest, either short or long, had a deterrent effect on violence, reducing violence by almost 50%. However, by the 1-year follow-up, there was no longer a deterrent effect of arrest. In the second year of follow-up, the short-arrest condition actually resulted in more reports of continued violence than did the other conditions; in fact, the total frequency of hotline reports increased twice as much in the short-arrest group as in the warning group, although the same criminogenic effects were not observed in the long-arrest group.

The Charlotte replication (Hirschel & Hutchison, 1992) involved the entire police force and operated 24 hours per day. Over 600 cases of spouse abuse were randomly assigned to one of three conditions: (1) advice and possible separation, (2) issuance of a citation (i.e., an order requiring the suspect to appear in court to answer charges), or (3) arrest. Examining arrest recidivism at a 6-month follow-up, the data indicate that there were no significant group differences in prevalence of recidivism and that arrest did not differ from the other conditions in incidence of recidivism. Thus, the authors concluded that arrest is neither more nor less effective in deterring subsequent violence than the other two interventions.

In an interesting exploration of interaction effects, Sherman (1992) proposed that arrest will have differing effects on different groups of men. Specifically, Sherman hypothesized that socially marginal men, characterized by such factors as unemployment, cohabitation, and previous arrest records, will be less deterred by arrest than "socially bonded" men who have a high stake in social conformity. An examination of data from the Milwaukee replication supported his thesis (Sherman et al., 1992), demonstrating that arrest deterred violence among men who were employed or married, but it actually escalated violence among men who had a prior record of arrest, were unemployed, had less than a high school education, were not married, or were black. The highest levels of escalation occurred among unemployed men who received the short-arrest treatment. Sherman concluded that the data "consistently show arrest to make those with less stake in conformity more violent, and those with more stake in conformity less violent" (p. 160).

Berk and his colleagues (Berk, Campbell, Klap, & Western, 1992) further examined this hypothesis, using their own data from the Colorado Springs replication and data from the Milwaukee and Omaha studies. Their analyses indicate that arrest has a deterrent effect among "good risk" (i.e., employed) offenders. Results for "bad risk" (i.e., unemployed) offenders differed, depending upon the source of the outcome data and the data analyses employed; however, in general, arrest either had no effect or, worse, an escalating effect on violence among this group.

In summary, unlike the original Minneapolis study, none of the replication studies published to date supports an overall deterrent effect of arrest relative to other police interventions. In contrast, arrest, particularly short arrest, may actually escalate violence over time. However, the data suggest that arrest will deter future violence among employed men; such men presumably have more to lose from arrest and involvement

with the criminal justice system. In contrast, arrest seems to have no effect, or perhaps even an escalating effect, among men who are unemployed and otherwise "socially marginal."

These findings have already generated controversy and debate. In general, critics argue that the data should not translate into the abandonment of mandatory arrest policies. They suggest that it is naive and unrealistic to assume that arrest alone will deter violence; rather, arrests are a necessary, but not a sufficient, condition for the deterrence of violence (Lerman, 1992). This approach suggests that even greater intervention, involving coordination and response from the entire community, will be necessary to deter violence among "socially marginal" men. For example, perhaps prosecution and conviction, with resulting legal sanctions, will be necessary to deter violence; indeed, data from the replication studies indicate that only a small proportion of the men who are arrested for spouse abuse are actually prosecuted. Similarly, perhaps community monitoring or treatment interventions would be effective with such a group. In addition, resources must be provided to the victims of violence. Arrest may be insufficient to deter violence unless the community also provides adequate support services to abused women and their children, allowing them to leave the abuser if they so desire (Bowman, 1992). Finally, even if arrest is not an effective deterrent, there are other rationales for the continued use of arrest, including the notion of equal treatment under the law (Frisch, 1992), the affirmation that abuse will not be tolerated in our society, and the opportunity that arrest may provide a battered woman to seek safety (Bowman, 1992). In these ways, arrest may empower battered women, even if it does not directly deter violence.

The Treatment Outcome Literature: Methodological Problems

Assuming that a violent husband seeks treatment, either through a court referral or voluntarily, one must examine whether the available treatments serve as effective means of eliminating marital violence. Unfortunately, at this time, few methodologically sound studies have been conducted to examine the efficacy of treatment programs for marital violence. As mentioned, at the present time, no studies comparing conjoint therapy to group/individual therapy have been completed. The majority of studies conducted to date examined group treatment for male batterers, although a few researchers have studied conjoint treatment (e.g., Harris et al., 1988; Lindquist, Telch, & Taylor, 1983). However, interpretation of the results of these studies is difficult, because a variety of methodological problems plague the marital violence treatment outcome literature. These problems have been discussed in detail elsewhere (Hamberger & Hastings, 1993; Rosenbaum, 1988; Rosenfeld, 1992; Saunders, 1988; Weis, 1989) and are only briefly reviewed here.

First, many treatment outcome studies lack control groups or are quasi-experimental in nature (e.g., no comparison group is included, or men completing treatment are compared to men who drop out, or who were untreated for other reasons). Rarely is random assignment, to a control group or alternative treatment, used (see Edleson & Syers, 1990, and Harris et al., 1988, for two exceptions).

Second, most batterer treatment programs suffer from low recruitment rates and high rates of client dropout. Judges may refer only those men who are most motivated to treatment programs (Rosenfeld, 1992) and many researchers exclude men with other problems, such as alcohol abuse or lack of motivation, from treatment (e.g., Dutton, 1986; Saunders & Hanusa, 1986). Estimates of treatment success under such conditions may not generalize to programs that accept more problematic clients. In addition, many studies are based on very small sample sizes, with some involving as few as 9 (Edleson et al., 1985) or 12 clients (Deschner, 1984). Given high rates of dropout and differences between men who drop out and those who complete marital violence treatment programs (e.g., dropouts are generally younger, less educated, and more likely to be unemployed; Edleson & Grusznski, 1988; Grusznski & Carrillo, 1988; Hamberger & Hastings, 1988; Saunders & Hanusa, 1986; Saunders & Parker, 1989), it is difficult to determine the efficacy of treatment programs.

It also is often difficult to compare findings across treatment outcome studies because researchers often define critical terms, such as "violence," "recidivism," and "dropout," differently. In addition, researchers use different methods of obtaining information on outcome variables; for example, the continuation of marital violence can be measured by husband self-report, partner/victim report (e.g., Edleson & Grusznski, 1988; Edleson & Syers, 1990) or police records (e.g., Dutton, 1988). Given discrepancies in husbands' and wives' reports of physical aggression (discussed previously) and the limited probability that acts of physical aggres-

sion will attract the attention of the criminal justice system, these various methods of evaluating treatment programs may create widely varying estimates of treatment success.

Despite the fact that a follow-up assessment period of at least 6 months has been recommended, because violence occurs only intermittently and recidivism is more likely as time following treatment increases (Rosenbaum, 1988), most therapy outcome studies have involved unacceptably short follow-up periods. Thus, it is still unknown whether the effects of treatment are maintained over time. In addition, very low response rates at follow-up assessments are common in these studies, and subjects who do not participate in follow-up assessments have been found to differ from those who do (e.g., DeMaris & Jackson, 1987; Edleson & Syers, 1990), suggesting that conclusions drawn from follow-up data must be interpreted carefully and may not be generalizable to men who do not participate in follow-up assessments.

Treatment Outcome Findings

Despite these methodological limitations, two recent reviews of the available data regarding treatment outcome have been conducted. Hamberger and Hastings (1993) reviewed 28 outcome studies; they present a brief discussion of each study reviewed, as well as a critique of this literature and suggestions for future research. Rosenfeld (1992) reviewed 25 studies of treatment programs for marital violence, making general conclusions across the studies. We draw on both papers in presenting this brief overview of the data.

Hamberger and Hastings (1993) essentially conclude:

> After reviewing much of the research literature, what do we "know" about the short- and long-term effects of treatment on spouse abuse? The answer, unfortunately, is "not much." . . . We cannot confidently say whether "treatment works." . . . While there are some moderately good studies, many have one or more significant methodological or conceptual flaws which render them unhelpful at best, and at worst, misleading. Taken together, these studies are so varied in their make-up, process, and reporting as to make cross-study generalization impossible. (pp. 64–65)

Rosenfeld (1992) acknowledges the same limitations in the currently available data as Hamberger and Hastings (1993); however, he chooses to make conclusions based upon these data rather than waiting until better studies have been conducted. Across the studies, Rosenfeld found an average recidivism rate, weighted by study sample size, of 27%; in other words, by the time of the follow-up assessment in each study, 27% of the men had been violent at least once since treatment. Based on this figure, Rosenfeld (1992) concludes that men who complete treatment have only slightly, and often nonsignificantly, lower recidivism rates than men who refuse treatment, drop out of treatment, or remain untreated. He also notes that studies examining the efficacy of treatment in reducing psychological abuse have demonstrated "only modest gains" (e.g., Edelson & Grusznski, 1988; Edelson & Syers, 1990; Saunders & Azar, 1989).

Focusing on the efficacy of court-ordered treatment for marital violence, he concludes:

> Although men and couples completing a treatment program (whether court-ordered or voluntary) report renewed violence at rates lower than those found when no form of intervention has occurred, men arrested but not referred to treatment appear to resume their violent behavior no more frequently than men arrested *and* treated. In addition, court-ordered men withdraw from treatment as often as do voluntary subjects, indicating that legal-system involvement may not be sufficient to motivate men who would otherwise be unmotivated to change their behavior. (Rosenfeld, 1992, p. 221)

Others have suggested that some treatment programs for violent husbands may not only be ineffectual but actually may also be detrimental (e.g., programs that focus exclusively on anger control, rather than recognizing that violence is used to control women; Gondolf & Russell, 1986). In addition, Gondolf (1988) has demonstrated that whether a batterer has sought counseling is the most influential predictor of whether his wife will return to him after leaving a shelter. However, given the current lack of evidence demonstrating the efficacy of marital violence treatment programs, these data suggest that the very existence of such programs may actually increase the wife's risk, by leading to a false sense of security among battered women whose husbands have sought treatment.

Questions have also been raised regarding whether it is reasonable to assume that the currently available short-term interventions for marital violence can effectively treat what is often a chronic and severe problem; suggestions for incorporating relapse prevention interventions into treatment programs have been made (Jennings, 1990). In addition, at the present time, virtual-

ly no information is available regarding which batterers or violent couples are most likely to benefit from treatment or how to match clients to the appropriate treatment approaches; in fact, research aimed at identifying subtypes of maritally violent men has only recently been undertaken (see review in Holtzworth-Munroe & Stuart, 1994).

Overall, one must conclude that treatments for marital violence have not been well researched, because past studies have been plagued by methodological problems. Thus, it is difficult to interpret the currently available data; however, these data do not indicate great success of available programs in reducing either physical or psychological abuse. In addition, questions regarding the possible detrimental effects of marital violence treatment programs have recently been raised. In summary, we concur with Hamberger and Hasting's (1993) and Rosenfeld's (1992) conclusion that questions regarding the efficacy of these programs remain unanswered until more, and better, research is conducted to clarify these issues.

REFERENCES

Adams, D. (1989). Feminist-based interventions for battering men. In P. L. Caesar & L. K. Hamberger (Eds.), *Treating men who batter: Theory, practice, and programs* (pp. 3–23). New York: Springer.

Arias, I., & Beach, R. H. (1987). Validity of self-reports of marital violence. *Journal of Family Violence, 2,* 139–142.

Arias, I., & O'Leary, K. D. (1988). Cognitive-behavioral treatment of physical aggression in marriage. In N. Epstein, S. E. Schlesinger, & W. Dryden (Eds.), *Cognitive-behavioral therapy with families* (pp. 118–150). New York: Brunner/Mazel.

Bandura, A. (1977). *Social learning theory.* Englewood Cliffs, NJ: Prentice-Hall.

Beck, A. T. (1988). *Love is never enough: How couples can overcome misunderstandings, resolve conflicts, and solve relationship problems through cognitive therapy.* New York: Harper & Row.

Beck, A. T., Ward, C. H., Mendelson, M., Mock, J., & Erbaugh, J. (1961). An inventory for measuring depression. *Archives of General Psychiatry, 4,* 53–63.

Berk, R. A., Campbell, A., Klap, R., & Western, B. (1992). A Bayesian analysis of the Colorado Springs spouse abuse experiment. *Journal of Criminal Law and Criminology, 83,* 170–200.

Boeke, K., & Markman, H. J. (1992). *The interaction patterns of violent couples: A home observation study.*

Unpublished manuscript, University of Denver, Denver, CO.

Bograd, M. (1984). Family systems approaches to wife battering: A feminist critique. *American Journal of Orthopsychiatry, 54,* 558–568.

Bowman, C. G. (1992). The arrest experiments: A feminist critique. *Journal of Criminal Law and Criminology, 83,* 201–208.

Browne, A. (1987). *When battered women kill.* New York: Free Press.

Browning, J., & Dutton, D. (1986). Assessment of wife assault with the Conflict Tactics Scale: Using couple data to quantify the differential reporting effect. *Journal of Marriage and the Family, 48,* 375–379.

Burt, M. R. (1980). Cultural myths and supports for rape. *Journal of Personality and Social Psychology, 38,* 217–230.

Buss, A. H., & Durkee, A. (1957). An inventory for assessing different kinds of hostility. *Journal of Clinical and Consulting Psychology, 21,* 343–349.

California State Psychological Association. (1985). New laws of interest to psychologists enacted during the 1985 session. *California State Psychologist, 20*(7), 1.

Cascardi, M, Langhinrichsen, J., & Vivian, D. (1992). Marital aggression: Impact, injury, and health correlates of husbands and wives. *Archives of Internal Medicine, 152,* 1178–1184.

Cascardi, M., Vivian, D., & Meyer, S. (1991, November). *Context and attributions for marital violence in discordant couples.* Poster presented at the 25th Annual Meeting of the Association for Advancement of Behavior Therapy, New York.

Coleman, D. H., & Straus, M. A. (1986). Marital power, conflict, and violence in a nationally representative sample of American couples. *Violence and Victims, 1,* 141–157.

Cox, J. W., & Stoltenberg, C. D. (1991). Evaluation of a treatment program for battered wives. *Journal of Family Violence, 6,* 395–414.

Deffenbacher, J. L. (1988). *A cognitive-relaxation approach to anger reduction: A treatment manual.* Fort Collins, CO: Colorado State University.

DeMaris, A., & Jackson, J. K. (1987). Batterers' reports of recidivism after counseling. *Social Casework, 68,* 458–465.

Deschner, J. (1984). *The hitting habit: Anger control for battering couples.* New York: Free Press.

Douglas, M. A., & Strom, J. (1988). Cognitive therapy with battered women. *Journal of Rational-Emotive and Cognitive-Behavior Therapy, 6,* 33–49.

Dunford, F. (1992a). *The San Diego Navy Spouse Assault/Treatment Experiment.* Ongoing project, National Institute of Mental Health grant/funded by the U.S. Navy.

Dunford, F. W. (1992b). The measurement of recidivism in cases of spouse assault. *Journal of Criminal Law and Criminology, 83,* 120–136.

Dunford, F. W., Huizinga, D., & Elliott, D. S. (1990). The role of arrest in domestic assault: The Omaha Police Experiment. *Criminology, 28,* 183–206.

Dutton, D. G. (1986). The outcome of court-mandated treatment for wife assault: A quasi-experimental evaluation. *Violence and Victims, 1,* 163–175.

Dutton, D. G. (1988). *The domestic assault of women: Psychological and criminal justice perspectives.* Boston: Allyn & Bacon.

Dutton, D. G., & Browning, J. J. (1988). Concern for power, fear of intimacy, and aversive stimuli for wife assault. In Hotaling, G., Finkelhor, D., Kirkpatrick, J. T., & Straus, M. A. (Eds.), *Family abuse and its consequences: New directions in research* pp. 163–175). Newbury, Park, CA: Sage.

Edelson, J. L., & Grusznski, R. J. (1988). Treating men who batter: Four years of outcome data from the domestic abuse project. *Journal of Social Service Research, 12,* 3–22.

Edelson, J. L., Miller, D. M., Stone, G. W., & Chapman, D. G. (1985). Group treatment for men who batter. *Social Work Research and Abstract, 26,* 10–17.

Edelson, J. L., & Syers, M. (1990). Relative effectiveness of group treatments for men who batter. *Social Work Research and Abstracts, 26,* 10–17.

Ellis, A. (1977). *How to live with—and without—anger.* New York: Reader's Digest Press.

Feld, S. L., & Straus, M. A. (1989). Escalation and desistance of wife assault in marriage. *Criminology, 27,* 141–159.

Frisch, L. A. (1992). Research that succeeds, policies that fail. *Journal of Criminal Law and Criminology, 83,* 209–216.

Ganley, A. L. (1989). Integrating feminist and social learning analyses of aggression: Creating multiple models for intervention with men who batter. In P. L. Caesar & L. K. Hamberger (Eds.) *Treating men who batter: Theory, practice, and programs* (pp. 196–235). New York: Springer.

Goldstein, A. P., & Rosenbaum, A. (1982). *Aggress-less: How to turn anger and aggression into positive action.* Englewood Cliffs, NJ: Prentice-Hall.

Gondolf, E. W., & Russell, D. (1986). The case against anger control treatment programs for batterers. *Response to the Victimization of Women and Children, 9,* 2–5.

Gottlieb, N., Burden, D., McCormick, R., & Nicarthy, G. (1983). The distinctive attributes of feminist groups. *Social Work with Groups, 6,* 81–93.

Grusznski, R. J., & Carrillo, T. P. (1988). Who completes batterer's treatment groups? An empirical investigation. *Journal of Family Violence, 3,* 141–150.

Grych, J. H., & Fincham, F. D. (1990). Marital conflict and children's adjustment: A cognitive-contextual framework. *Psychological Bulletin, 108,* 267–290.

Hamberger, L. K., & Hastings, J. E. (1988). Skills training for treatment of spouse abusers: An outcome study. *Journal of Family Violence, 3,* 121–130.

Hamberger, L. K., & Hastings, J. E. (1993). Court-mandated treatment of men who batter their partners: Issues, controversies, and outcomes. In Z. Hilton (Ed.), *Legal responses to wife assault* (pp. 188–229). Newbury Park, CA: Sage.

Hamberger, L. K., & Lohr, J. M. (1989). Proximal causes of spouse abuse: A theoretical analysis for cognitive-behavioral interventions. In P. L. Caesar & L. K. Hamberger (Eds.), *Treating men who batter: Theory, practice, and programs* (pp. 53–76). New York: Springer.

Hansen, M., Harway, M., & Cervantes, N. (1991). Therapists' perceptions of severity in cases of family violence. *Violence and Victims, 6,* 225–234.

Harris, R., Savage, S., Jones, T., & Brooke, W. (1988). A comparison of treatments for abusive men and their partners within a family-service agency. *Canadian Journal of Community Mental Health, 7,* 147–155.

Hart, B. (1988). Beyond the "duty to warn": A therapist's "duty to protect" battered women and children. In M. Bogard & K. Yllo (Eds.), *Feminist perspectives on wife abuse* (pp. 234–248). Newbury Park, CA: Sage.

Hart, B. (1991, August). *Duties to warn and protect.* Paper presented at the annual meeting of the American Psychological Association, San Francisco.

Hartman, S. (1983). A self-help group for women in abusive relationships (pp. 133–145).

Hirschel, J. D., & Hutchinson, I. W. (1991). Police-preferred arrest policies. In M. Steinman (Ed.), *Woman battering: Police responses* (pp. 49–72). Cincinnati, OH: Anderson Publishing Co. and Academy of Criminal Justice Sciences.

Hirschel, J. D., & Hutchinson, I. W. (1992). Female spouse abuse and the police reponse: The Charlotte, North Carolina experiment. *Journal of Criminal Law and Criminology, 83,* 73–119.

Holtzworth-Munroe, A. (1991). Applying the social information processing model to maritally violent men. *The Behavior Therapist, 14,* 129–132.

Holtzworth-Munroe, A. (1992). Social skill deficits in maritally violent men: Interpreting the data using a social information processing model. *Clinical Psychology Review, 12,* 605–617.

Holtzworth-Munroe, A., & Anglin, K. (1991). The competency of responses given by maritally violent versus nonviolent men to problematic marital situations. *Violence and Victims, 6,* 257–269.

Holtzworth-Munroe, A., & Jacobson, N. S. (1991). Behavioral marital therapy. In A. S. Gurman & D. P. Kniskern (Eds.), *Handbook of family therapy* (Vol. 2, pp. 96–133). New York: Brunner/Mazel.

Holtzworth-Munroe, A., & Stuart, G. (1994). Typologies of male batterers: Three subtypes and the differences among them. *Psychological Bulletin, 116,* 476–497.

Holtzworth-Munroe, A., Waltz, J., Jacobson, N. S., Monaco, V., Fehrenbach, P. A., & Gottman, J. M. (1992). Recruiting nonviolent men as control subjects for research on marital violence: How easily can it be done? *Violence and Victims, 7,* 79–88.

Hotaling, G. T., & Sugarman, D. B. (1986). An analysis of risk markers in husband to wife violence: The current state of knowledge. *Violence and Victims, 1,* 101–124.

Houskamp, B. M., & Foy, D. W. (1991). The assessment of posttraumatic stress disorder in battered women. *Journal of Interpersonal Violence, 6,* 367–375.

Hudson, W. W., & McIntosh, S. R. (1981). The assessment of spouse abuse: Two quantifiable dimensions. *Journal of Marriage and the Family, 43,* 873–888.

Jacobson, N. S., & Margolin, G. (1979). *Marital therapy: Strategies based on social learning & behavior exchange principles.* New York: Brunner/Mazel.

Jennings, J. L. (1990). Preventing relapse versus "stopping" domestic violence: Do we expect too much too soon from battering men? *Journal of Family Violence, 5,* 43–60.

Jouriles, E. N., & O'Leary, K. D. (1985). Interspousal reliability of reports of marital violence. *Journal of Consulting and Clinical Psychology, 53,* 419–421.

Kantor, G. K., & Straus, M. A. (1987). The "drunken bum" theory of wife beating. *Social Problems, 34,* 213–230.

Kantor, G. K., & Straus M. A. (1989). Substance abuse as a precipitant of wife abuse victimizations. *American Journal of Drug and Alcohol Abuse, 15,* 173–189.

Lane, G., & Russell, T. (1989). Second-order systemic work with violent couples. In P. L. Caesar & L. K. Hamberger (Eds.), *Treating men who batter: Theory, practice, and programs* (pp. 134–162). New York: Springer.

Leonard, K. E., & Blane, H. T. (1992). Alcohol and marital aggression in a national sample of young men. *Journal of Interpersonal Violence, 7,* 19–30.

Leonard, K. E., Bromet, E. J., Parkinson, D. K., Day, N. L., & Ryan, C. M. (1985). Patterns of alcohol use and physically aggressive behavior in men. *Journal of Studies on Alcohol, 46,* 279–282.

Lerman, L. G. (1992). The decontextualization of domestic violence. *Journal of Criminal Law and Criminology, 83,* 217–240.

Lindquist, C. U., Telch, C. F., & Taylor, J. (1983). Evaluation of a conjugal violence treatment program: A pilot study. *Behavioral Counseling and Community Interventions, 3,* 76–89.

Madanes, C. (1990). *Sex, love, and violence: Strategies for transformation.* New York: Norton.

Maiuro, R. D., Cahn, T. S., Vitaliano, P. P., Wagner, B. C., & Zegree, J. B. (1988). Anger, hostility, and depression in domestically violent versus generally assaultive men and nonviolent control subjects. *Journal of Consulting and Clinical Psychology, 56,* 17–23.

Maiuro, R. D., Vitaliano, P. P., & Cahn, T. S. (1987). A brief measure for the assessment of anger and aggression. *Journal of Interpersonal Violence, 2,* 166–178.

Mantooth, C. M., Geffner, G., Franks, & Patrick, J. (1987). *Family preservation: A treatment manual for reducing couple violence.* Tyler, TX: University of Texas at Tyler Press.

Margolin, G. (1979). Conjoint marital therapy to enhance anger management and reduce spouse abuse. *American Journal of Family Therapy, 7,* 13–23.

Margolin, G., & Burman, B. (1993). Wife abuse versus marital violence: Different terminologies, explanations, and solutions. *Clinical Psychology Review, 13,* 59–73.

Margolin, G., Burman, B., & John, R. S. (1989). Home observations of married couples reenacting naturalistic conflicts. *Behavioral Assessment, 11,* 101–118.

Margolin, G., John, R. S., & Gleberman, L. (1988a). Affective responses to conflictual discussions in violent and nonviolent couples. *Journal of Consulting and Clinical Psychology, 56,* 24–33.

Margolin, G., Sibner, L. G., & Gleberman, L. (1988b). Wife battering. In V. B. Van Hasselt, R. L. Morrison, A. S. Bellack, & M. Hersen, (Eds.), *Handbook of family violence* (pp. 89–117). New York: Plenum.

Marshall, L. L. (1992). Development of the severity of violence against women scales. *Journal of Family Violence, 7,* 103–121.

McDonald, R., & Jouriles, E. N. (1991, September). Marital aggression and child behavior problems: Research findings, mechanisms, and intervention strategies. *The Behavior Therapist,* 189–192.

Meichenbaum, D. (1977). *Cognitive-behavior modification: An integrative approach.* New York: Plenum.

Miller, D. (1980). Innovative program development for battered women and their families. *Victimology, 5,* 335–346.

Neidig, P. H., Friedman, D. H., & Collins, B. S. (1985). Domestic conflict containment: A spouse abuse treatment program. *Social Casework: The Journal of Contemporary Social Work, 66,* 195–204.

Novaco, R. W. (1975). *Anger control: The development and evaluation of an experimental treatment.* Lexington, MA: Lexington Books.

Novaco, R. W. (1977). Stress inoculation: A cognitive therapy for anger and its application to a case of depression. *Journal of Consulting and Clinical Psychology, 41,* 600–608.

O'Leary, K. D. (1988). Physical aggression between spouses: A social learning perspective. In V. B. Van Hasselt, R. L. Morrison., A. S. Bellack, & M. Hersen (Eds.), *Handbook of family violence* (pp. 31–55). New York: Plenum.

O'Leary, K. D., Barling, J., Arias, I., Rosenbaum, A., Malone, J., & Tyree, A. (1989). Prevalence and stability of physical aggression between spouses: A longitudinal analysis. *Journal of Consulting and Clinical Psychology, 57,* 263–268.

O'Leary, K. D., & Curley, A. D. (1986). Assertion and family violence: Correlates of spouse abuse. *Journal of Marital and Family Therapy, 12,* 284–289.

O'Leary, K. D., Neidig, P. H., & Arias, I. (1992). [Ongoing study of conjoint versus individual/group therapy for marital violence]. Unpublished data.

O'Leary, K. D., & Vivian, D. (1990). Physical aggression in marriage. In F. D. Fincham & T. N. Bradbury (Eds.), *The psychology of marriage: Basic issues and applications* (pp. 323–348). New York: Guilford Press.

O'Leary, K. D., Vivian, D., & Malone, J. (1992). Assessment of physical aggression against women in marriage: The need for multimodal assessment. *Behavioral Assessment, 14,* 5–14.

Pagelow, M. D. (1981). *Woman-battering: Victims and their experiences.* Newbury Park, CA: Sage.

Pagelow, M. D. (1988). Marital rape. In V. B. Van Hasselt, R. L. Morrison, A. S. Bellack, & M. Hersen (Eds.), *Handbook of family violence* (pp. 207–231). New York: Plenum.

Pence, E. (1989). Batterer programs: Shifting from community collusion to community confrontation. In P. L. Caesar & L. K. Hamberger (Eds.), *Treating men who batter: Theory, practice, and programs* (pp. 24–50). New York: Springer.

Pence, E., & Paymar, M. (1985). *Power and control: Tactics of men who batter.* Duluth, MN: Domestic Abuse Intervention Project.

Rosenbaum, A. (1988). Methodological issues in marital violence research. *Journal of Family Violence, 3,* 91–104.

Rosenbaum, A., & Maiuro, R. D. (1989). Eclectic approaches in working with men who batter. In C. L. Caesar & L. K. Hamberger (Eds.), *Treating men who batter: Theory, practice, and programs.* New York: Springer.

Rosenbaum, A., & O'Leary, K. D. (1981). Marital violence: Characteristics of abusive couples. *Journal of Consulting and Clinical Psychology, 49,* 63–71.

Rosenbaum, A., & O'Leary, K. D. (1986). The treatment of marital violence. In N. S. Jacobson & A. S. Gurman (Eds.), *Clinical handbook of marital therapy* (pp. 385–405). New York: Guilford Press.

Rosenfeld, B. D. (1992). Court-ordered treatment of spouse abuse. *Clinical Psychology Review, 12,* 205–226.

Saunders, D. G. (1986). When battered women use violence: Husband-abuse or self defense? *Violence and Victims, 1,* 47–60.

Saunders, D. G. (1988). Issues in conducting treatment research with men who batter. In G. T. Hotaling, D. Finkelhor, J. T. Kirkpatrick, & M. A. Straus (Eds.), *Coping with family violence: Research and policy perspectives* (pp. 145–156). Newbury Park, CA: Sage.

Saunders, D. G. (1989). Cognitive and behavioral interventions with men who batter: Application and outcome. In P. L. Caesar & L. K. Hamberger (Eds.), *Treating men who batter: Theory, practice, and programs* (pp. 77–100). New York: Springer.

Saunders, D. G. (1992a). Domestic Abuse. In R. T. Ammerman & M. Hersen (Eds.), *Assessment of family violence: A clinical and legal sourcebook* (pp. 208–235). New York: John Wiley.

Saunders, D. G. (1992b). A typology of men who batter women: Three types derived from cluster analysis. *American Journal of Orthopsychiatry, 62,* 264–275.

Saunders, D. G., & Azar, S. T. (1989). Treatment programs for family violence. In L. Ohlin & M. Tonry (Eds.), *Family violence: Crime and justice: A review of research* (Vol. 2, pp. 481–545). Chicago: University of Chicago Press.

Saunders, D. G., & Hanusa, D. (1986). Cognitive-behavioral treatment of men who batter: The short-term effects of group therapy. *Journal of Family Violence, 1,* 357–372.

Saunders, D. G., Lynch, A. B., Grayson, M., & Linz, D. (1987). The inventory of beliefs about wife beating: The construction and initial validation of a measure of beliefs and attitudes. *Violence and Victims, 2,* 39–57.

Saunders, D. G., & Parker, J. C. (1989, September). Legal sanctions and treatment follow-through among men who batter: A multivariate analysis. *Social Work Research and Abstracts,* pp. 21–29.

Shepard, M. F., & Campbell, J. A. (1992). The abusive behavior inventory: A measure of psychological and physical abuse. *Journal of Interpersonal Violence, 7,* 291–305.

Sherman, L. W. (1992). The influence of criminology on criminal law: Evaluating arrests for misdemeanor domestic violence. *Journal of Criminal Law and Criminology, 83,* 1–45.

Sherman, L. W., & Berk, R. A. (1984). The specific deterrent effects of arrest for domestic assault. *American Sociological Review, 49,* 261.

Sherman, L. W., Schmidt, J. D., Rogan, D. P. Gartin, P. R., Cohn, E. G., Collins, D. J., & Bacich, A. R. (1991). From initial deterrence to long-term escalation: Short-custody arrest for poverty ghetto domestic violence. *Criminology, 29,* 821–850.

Sherman, L. W., Schmidt, J. D., Rogan, D. P., Smith, D. A., Gartin, P. R., Cohn, E. G., Collins, D. J., & Bacich, A. R. (1992). The variable effects of arrest on criminal careers: The Milwaukee domestic violence experiment. *Journal of Criminal Law and Criminology, 83,* 137–169.

Smith, M. D. (1990). Patriarchal ideology and wife beating: A test of a feminist hypothesis. *Violence and Victims, 5,* 257–273.

Smith, M. D. (1991). Male peer support of wife abuse: An exploratory study. *Journal of Interpersonal Violence, 6,* 512–519.

Sonkin, D. (1986). Clairvoyance vs. common sense: Therapist's duty to warn and protect. *Violence and Victims, 1,* 7–22.

Sonkin, D. J., & Durphy, M. (1989). *Learning to live without violence: A book for men.* Volcano, CA: Volcano Press.

Sonkin, D. J., & Ellison, J. E. (1986). The therapist's duty to protect victims of domestic violence: Where we have been and where we are going. *Violence and Victims, 1,* 205–214.

Sonkin, D. J., Martin, D., & Walker, L.E.A. (1985). *The male batterer: A treatment approach.* New York: Springer.

Spence, J. T., & Helmreich, R. L. (1972). The attitudes toward women scale: An objective instrument to measure attitudes toward the rights and roles of women in contemporary society. *JSAS Catalogue of Selected Documents in Psychology, 2,* 66.

Spielberger, C. D., Gorsuch, R. L., & Lushene, R. E. (1970). *Manual for the State–Trait Anxiety Inventory.* Palo Alto, CA: Consulting Psychologist Press.

Stets, J. E., & Straus, M. A. (1990). Gender differences in reporting marital violence and its medical and psychological consequences. In M. A. Straus & R. J. Gells (Eds.), *Physical violence in American families: Risk factors and adaptations to violence in 8,145 families* (pp. 151–166). New Brunswick, NJ: Transaction.

Straus, M. A. (1979). Measuring intrafamily conflict

and violence: The Conflict Tactics (CT) Scales. *Journal of Marriage and the Family, 41,* 75–88.

Straus, M. A. (1987). *Social stratification, social bonds, and wife beating in the United States.* Paper presented at the American Society of Criminology Meeting, Montreal.

Straus, M. A., & Gelles, R. J. (1990). How violent are American families? Estimates from the national family violence resurvey and other studies. In M. A. Straus & R. J. Gelles (Eds.), *Physical violence in American families: Risk factors and adaptations to violence in 8,145 families* (pp. 95–112). New Brunswick, NJ: Transaction.

Szinovacz, M. E. (1983, August). Using couple data as a methodological tool: The case of marital violence. *Journal of Marriage and the Family,* pp. 633–644.

Tarasoff v. the Regents of the University of California, 17 Cal. 3d. 425. 55 − 2d 334 (1976).

Tolman, R. M. (1989). The development of a measure of psychological maltreatment of women by their male partners. *Violence and Victims, 4,* 159–177.

Tolman, R. M., & Bennett, L. W. (1990). A review of quantitative research on men who batter. *Journal of Interpersonal Violence, 5,* 87–118.

U.S. Attorney General's Task Force on Domestic Violence Report. (1984). (Rep. 17).

Vivian, D., & O'Leary, K. D. (1987, July). *Communication patterns in physically aggressive engaged couples.* Paper presented at the Third National Family Violence Conference. University of New Hampshire, Durham.

Walker, L. E. (1979). *The battered woman.* New York: Harper & Row.

Weis, J. G. (1989). Family violence research methodology and design. In L. Ohlin & M. Tonry (Eds.), *Family violence: Crime and justice: A review of research* (Vol. 11, pp. 117–162). Chicago: University of Chicago Press.

Yllo, K. (1983a). Sexual equality and violence against wives in American states. *Journal of Comparative Family Studies, 14,* 67–86.

Yllo, K. (1983b). Using a feminist approach in quantitative research: A case study. In D. Finkelhor, R. J. Gelles, G. T. Hotaling, & M. A. Straus (Eds.), *The dark side of families: Current family violence research* (pp. 277–288). Newbury Park, CA: Sage.

Yllo, K. (1984). The status of women, marital equality, and violence against wives. *Journal of Family Issues, 5,* 307–320.

Yllo, K., & Straus, M. A. (1984). Patriarchy and violence against wives: The impact of structural and normative factors. *Journal of International and Comparative Social Welfare, 1,* 1–13.

17

Facilitating Healthy Divorce Processes: Therapy and Mediation Approaches

FROMA WALSH
LYNN JACOB
VIRGINIA SIMONS

DIVORCE IS NOT SIMPLY a discrete event. It involves transactional processes that unfold over time, from the first consideration of separation, through tangled emotions and legal proceedings, to transitional upheavals in the immediate aftermath, and, into varying postdivorce reconfigurations. This chapter addresses important couple issues through the divorce process, focusing on both immediate and long-term challenges and adaptational tasks. Clinical guidelines are offered to deal effectively with predictable complications and distress associated with the multiple transitions and to promote optimal functioning in the future life course of former partners and their children.

DIVORCE AND THE MYTH OF THE NORMAL FAMILY

A major task in divorce is to construct new models of postdivorce life in the context of a society that continues to define the intact nuclear family as the norm. Yet, with the social changes of recent decades, the intact nuclear family is no longer representative of the majority of American families (Walsh, 1993). Nearly half of all couples are expected to divorce during their lifetime (Bray & Hetherington, 1993; Glick & Lin,

1986). After divorce, spouses and their children reconfigure in increasingly varied structural arrangements.

The high divorce rates do not mean that individuals have given up on marriage. On the contrary, nearly two thirds of women and three fourths of men remarry after divorce (Glick, 1989). Yet, the tremendous stresses inherent in the transitional processes of divorce and remarriage, and the complexity of these relationship networks, contribute to a divorce rate of nearly 60% among remarried couples, highest among those with children from former unions.

Images of "the normal intact family" complicate adjustment to divorce and remarriage. In fact, the happy intact family of the distant past is largely a myth (Walsh, 1992). Because the average life expectancy was only in the mid-40s before 20th-century medical advances, death commonly disrupted family units, with widow(er)s and surviving children moving into a variety of single parent and stepfamily arrangements (Walsh & McGoldrick, 1991). The traditional marital vow "till death do us part" must be viewed in that context. In fact, more recent increases in divorce owe in part to the lengthening life expectancy of 20–30 years postlaunching, posing a challenge for marriage to last a lifetime.

Although the modern nuclear family image of the 1950s became the standard for all to emulate, in fact, all was not as ideal as nostalgic depictions (Walsh, 1993). In reality, wives were isolated and devalued as homemaker/mothers. Breadwinner husbands were peripheral to family life and emotionally constrained from intimate connections. The accelerated divorce rate in the late 1960s and '70s occurred largely in reaction to those unsatisfying marriages and stifling gender roles (Skolnick, 1991).

Nevertheless, the myth of the intact family has persisted as not only descriptive of "normal" or "typical" family life, but also is deemed essential for the healthy development of adults and their children. Any deviation from that model has been viewed as inherently pathological (Walsh, 1993), with divorce regarded as a failure caused by deficits in one or both partners and as necessarily damaging to children. Single-parent households have been presumed to be deficient, with therapy commonly aimed at replacing the missing spouse by promoting remarriage (Herz, 1989). Yet stepfamilies, too, have been disparaged as a poor substitute for the "natural" family unit (Visher & Visher, 1988, 1993). Our society's idealization of the intact biological nuclear family leads divorced and remarried families to try in vain to emulate an inappropriate standard and contributes to problems in adjustment.

Clinically biased impressionistic studies of poorly functioning divorced families (Wallerstein & Kelly, 1980; Wallerstein & Blakeslee, 1989) have been cited widely, reinforcing the belief that divorce is inevitably destructive to all children—if not immediately, then surely in later development. A growing body of empirical research does not substantiate such a dim view of divorce (Bray & Hetherington, 1993). Such claims fail to take into account the mediating effects of numerous variables, particularly the quality of pre- and postdivorce relationships and the economic situation. In fact, a wide range of postdivorce adjustment is found. While couple therapists value family stability, we should not assume that *any* marriage is always better than divorce. Studies comparing divorced and nondivorced families find that children also tend to fare poorly in high-conflict and abusive families that remain together (Hetherington, Law, & O'Connor, 1993).

In summary, accumulating evidence suggests that while transitional stresses do generate emotional turmoil and short-term distress with divorce, well-functioning—and dysfunctional—families can be found in a variety of structures.

How the couple handles the divorce process is as crucial to adjustment as the fact of the divorce itself. Clinicians need to understand the factors in family resilience that make a difference so that we can facilitate healthy divorce processes (Abelsohn, 1992; Ahrons, 1994; Walsh, in press) by helping couples to minimize destructive conflict, buffer stress, achieve workable parenting arrangements, and move on with their lives.

A FAMILY DEVELOPMENTAL PERSPECTIVE

There are many pathways to divorce. It is important for clinicians and divorcing couples to track the developmental passage of their relationship to understand when and how it broke down. From a life-cycle vantage, it is useful to gain perspective on the evolution of the marriage and family unit and stressful changes that occurred over time, as with the untimely birth of a child or a move for one spouse's career advancement. It is vital also to gain a sense of future directions that couples anticipated, in order to understand their hopes, dreams, and disappointments. It is also important to consider the problem situation in the context of the multigenerational relationship system. One husband, asked in couple therapy when he first had considered divorce, reported that at the wedding his father had congratulated him on finding a woman just like his mother—whom the father had constantly berated throughout their marriage. He remarked, "That was like the kiss of death for my marriage—before we even had our honeymoon."

Divorce sets in motion a series of transitions in family roles and relationships, residential arrangements, and economic circumstances, all with strong impact for adjustment (Bray & Hetherington, 1993). The inherent complexity and fragmentation common in divorced and remarried families make the genogram (McGoldrick & Gerson, 1985) an essential tool for assessment. In constructing the diagram, clinicians and family members can visualize the total family system—including past marriages and exrelatives—and the positions of various members and subsystems in relation to others. The genogram can assist therapists in sorting out the complicated network of relationships: noting conflicts, cutoffs, and replication of dysfunctional patterns; identifying potential resources; and determining who should be involved in any intervention plan.

PATHWAYS TO DIVORCE

Many couples do not seek marital therapy until they are on the brink of divorce and it may be too late to repair the relationship. For some, divorce hits like a bolt out of the blue. Others question the viability of the marriage for years. Some divorcing couples shock friends who viewed them as an ideal couple. In other cases, signs and symptoms that the marriage is heading toward dissolution are evident in attitudes and interactions long before the decision is reached.

Relationships at risk of early divorce can be identified even before marriage. PREPARE, a self-report inventory for premarital couples developed by Olson and colleagues (Fowlers & Olson, 1986, 1989; Larsen & Olson, 1989), has been found to predict with 80–85% accuracy which couples will be happily married and which will be unhappy, separate, or divorce within 3 years of marriage. Since 40% of separations and divorces occur within the first 3–4 years of marriage, identifying key variables can inform early intervention, or more careful consideration of marital plans. The best predictors were found to be poor communication and conflict resolution, unrealistic expectations, and faulty role relationships. Of note, the researchers could not discriminate those who would divorce from those who would stay unhappily married, supporting the clinical observation that the decision to divorce is complicated by many factors not yet well understood.

In early marriage, interactional precursors to divorce have been found in relationships in which repeated "disconnections" occurred as spouses became emotionally detached. Gottman (1991, 1993) describes the following patterns of interaction that frequently lead to lack of resolution and marital unhappiness: complaining and criticism, defensiveness, "stonewalling" by husbands, contemptuousness, and withdrawal by one or both partners. A pileup of these processes and perceptions in multiple dimensions of the relationship tend to produce a cascade effect leading to divorce. A triad of elements involving thoughts, behaviors, and physiological responses is activated. Flooding and negative attributions contribute to the distancing cascade and to a negative recasting of the history of the relationship.

If detachment continues, the person questioning the relationship often begins to try out new or uncharacteristic behaviors, increasing involvement in an area of life separate from the spouse,

such as work, travel, and education, or having an affair. These new, unshared experiences can become fatal to the relationship (Vaughan, 1990) as separateness and secrecy increase, uncomprehended by the partner. What is often said in couples therapy is "We have become strangers." The discovery of an affair, accompanied by a deep sense of betrayal and abandonment, is impossible for some partners to forgive.

Financial strains, job loss, and relocation can also shake the foundation of a relationship. Added stressors, such as dealing with a chronic illness (Rolland, 1994), can compound marital discontent, precipitating a decision to separate. Other traumatic losses, especially the death of a child, pose a high risk for marital distancing and divorce, unless a couple can be helped to console and support each other (Walsh & McGoldrick, 1991).

In clinical practice, it is our experience that it is difficult and unwise to predict divorce in any particular case. Some couples with many strengths may be unable to reconcile a fundamental difference or regain trust after an extramarital affair. Others in chronically troubled relationships may decide to stay together, especially those with long and deep attachments, or determination to keep the family unit intact for the sake of children.

Reaching the Decision to Divorce

Despite the high divorce rate, most couples do not quickly or easily decide to divorce. Many are strongly influenced by cultural, religious, and familial sanctions discouraging divorce. Powerful expectations from family heritage may be expressed as "Our family never gives up" or "Once you've made your bed, you lie in it." Individuals may stay on for years in emotionally deadened, highly conflictual, or even abusive relationships. One depressed woman sought individual therapy to "adjust" to her chronically unhappy marriage. Her husband had adamantly refused couples therapy. Having not allowed herself to consider divorce, she felt trapped, admitting ashamedly, "Every night I pray for early widowhood."

Some couples enter therapy with the stated aim of working on their marriage when the decision to divorce has all but been made by one partner. As the therapist attempts to help the couple make progress on their relationship, such couples remain stuck, not following through with tasks and directives, or disqualifying any gain with another complaint. In many of these cases, one partner has already concluded that the marriage is hopeless or that the partner cannot change sufficiently, and uses each failed intervention as confirmation of that belief in order to justify and reinforce the decision to divorce. Often the therapist is looked to as a witness who will validate an individual's grievances or as a judge to make the decision for the couple, in order for them to avoid responsibility and reduce guilt for ending the marriage. These issues need to be addressed by the therapist and normalized in the context of the stigma and shame associated with divorce. It is important to help an individual, and wherever possible, both partners, to take responsibility for the decision to divorce. Divorce adjustment is facilitated when each partner can own his/her part in the process.

When someone is serious about a divorce and has decided to proceed, indicators may range from contacting an attorney, seeking another residence, and going over finances, to more indirect signs such as establishing new and separate relationships with others (even a therapist) without knowledge of the partner. The individual may no longer put effort into the relationship or even provoke the partner to end it. Most often, the decision to leave the relationship is made by one partner rather than by mutual agreement. Regardless, once a decision is made and others become involved in knowing or spreading the news, reconciliation becomes less likely.

As they consider divorce, the onslaught of decisions and their ramifications can overload the couple's emotional and relational capacities. Core beliefs and assumptions about oneself and the relationship are all reexamined, for example, "Who am I if not in relation to you?"; "What is shared and will no longer be shared?"; "What are the parent–child bonds and how are they to be redefined?"; "What is the financial and emotional responsibility for our children and for each other?" As events unfold, both partners and their children may experience an unsettling loss of security and control over their lives. The ways in which both spouses deal with these concerns can contribute to healthy or problematic adjustment as much as the actual decision to divorce.

As options are considered, some orienting questions are useful for the therapist and the couple. For instance, have they ever had a similar loss experience? What did they learn, and can something constructive be applied to this situation? How can they get information about the procedures they will be going through? Do they know people who have been through this who can answer questions and offer perspective? The therapist may offer suggestions or strategies that

have worked for others, to be considered in light of their relevance and usefulness in a particular case. Discussing the purpose and meaning of the therapy, both from the beginning contact and as changes occur, helps to clarify realistic objectives as well as the potential limitations of therapy. Does one spouse expect the therapist to "save the marriage" despite the partner's firm decision to end it? Do clients expect help in finding an attorney? Working in collaboration with clients to openly consider different pathways through the divorce process actively engages and empowers them in the ongoing decision making and facilitates the development of a mutually respectful postdivorce relationship.

Mixed feelings and confusion are quite common in couples. Within marriages people may say, "I must be crazy to stay in this," while also enjoying other parts of the relationship. During separation and divorce, some couples may want to end the relationship and yet simultaneously have feelings of attachment and familiarity that they do not want to lose. The mixed emotions create turmoil, leading some couples to alternate back and forth between separation and reunion, whereas others can become frozen in limbo, unable to move in either direction. Some couples break the tension and run from painful feelings and indecision by acting precipitously, which usually only compounds the emotional fallout in the long run.

When couples are considering divorce, it is important for therapists to help individuals not to make abrupt or premature decisions, which tend to be promoted by our cultural bent toward simply putting problems behind us and moving on. In one case, a wife entered couple therapy unsure whether to continue or end the marriage, while the husband was consistent in wanting to keep the relationship. When asked if she knew what it would take for her to clarify her position, she said, "Probably more time." She and her husband agreed to several months in therapy to give their 15-year relationship a chance. Over that period, she became more sure that she could not stay in the relationship. Even with the changes her husband had made, she felt that she was the one tackling the emotional issues for both of them. The therapy process helped her to reach a firm decision, concluding, "He could go on this way, but I cannot."

Often, individuals who are considering divorce frame their dilemma in a "to be or not to be" manner: whether to stay in the marriage or leave. Such framing carries a "take it or leave it" connotation, with the implication that staying means accepting the status quo, which may be intolerable. Often individuals ruminate endlessly on whether to stay, without fully exploring possibilities for change in either direction. It is important to help them identify and communicate to the partner the changes they would need for the relationship to be good enough for them to reinvest in it. When partners are able to reframe complaints as requests for positive change, they can better assess whether they are both willing and able to make such changes. In some cases, they may make such attempts but be unsuccessful in reshaping their relationship. In other cases, clarification of changes needed by one may help both to realize that those aims are unshared or unrealistic. Either way, if a couple's decision to divorce evolves out of the therapy process, they usually reach it with the sense of having made an effort, of greater clarity and mutual understanding, and of shared ownership of the decision, all of which facilitate a less acrimonious divorce process.

It is useful to help couples explore the full range of complicated feelings they may be experiencing, including relief or elation at freedom from a problematic relationship in which they have felt trapped, feelings of loss, a sense of failure, fears of the unknown, and intense anger or hurt. People have an easier time when helped to realize that confused, mixed feelings are to be expected in ending most relationships, and are understandable in their particular situation. It is helpful to explore each partner's assumptions and fantasies about expected consequences of the divorce, from idealized scenarios of total freedom, to catastrophic fears of loneliness and isolation. People commonly hold quite unrealistic views of postdivorce finances and parenting arrangements that need to be reappraised.

Marriage and Divorce Stories

Unique to each couple are the evolving beliefs created from each person's perceptions of the partner and self, as well as their views of cultural and familial values about committed relationships. Such beliefs underlie the "marital quid pro quo," the covert relationship bargain or set of rules defining interactional patterns and the position of each partner in relation to the other (Walsh, 1989). These beliefs both shape and are shaped by marital events, creating meaning that is usually understood and described by the couple in some form of marital story (Combs & Freedman, 1990). Considering divorce as an at-

tempted solution to relationship problems may generate fundamental shifts in these beliefs.

As divorce decisions are contemplated and acted upon, the "divorce story" begins to take shape. Each person's developing narrative about the marriage and its breakdown influences present and subsequent relationships in the family for years and even generations (Ahrons & Rodgers, 1987; Isaacs, Montalvo, & Abelson, 1986). As they approach divorce, both partners actively revise their beliefs about their collective history, present interactions, and anticipated future. Hetherington found that following the divorce, the account of the marriage and breakup told by each spouse is so different that blind raters could not match ex-spouses (Hetherington & Tryon, 1989). In other words, from their divorce stories it was not evident which individuals had been in the same marriage.

The predominant stories that people construct can restrain choices and keep them stuck in a problematic situation. Alternately, their stories may offer potential for solutions to their dilemmas. Therapists can help couples shift a rigid problem definition to enable them to see their situation in new ways that may offer greater potential for positive change (White & Epston, 1990). When one partner cannot accept the other's decision to divorce, the impasse may be broken by exploring the meanings of the marriage and the divorce. In other cases, a spouse stuck in an abusive relationship may be held back from exploring options for an independent life by insecurity and dread. Such fears of the unknown become the problem to be dealt with.

The use of systemic questions in therapy (Tomm, 1987) can be helpful in reflecting different perspectives, clarifying aspects of the situation and possible options, and furthering collaborative decision making in the divorce process. When clients are caught up in a reactive position relative to unwanted actions and events over which they feel powerless, it is important for therapists to help them consider their own choices and take more control of their own lives.

Keeping Separation/Divorce in Its Place

As people approach divorce, their positions can be intensified. A devaluing of the relationship or the other person or both can occur, often functioning to loosen attachments and ease the pain of loss. Therapists might be helpful in posing questions that encourage people to balance their negative view to include valued aspects of the partner and the relationship. Such questions might including the following:

> What strengths do you see the two of you having that would lead you through this period of time?
>
> What might a friend to both of you tell us about you and your relationship that you might have lost sight of during these difficult times?
>
> Have you noticed ways in which you have worked together in spite of feeling that you want to separate?
>
> How might you continue to work together around coparenting after divorce?
>
> As you think about the various parts of yourselves and the relationship, what would be most important to take with you into the future?
>
> What can you learn from this experience and what would you want to do differently?

Pacing/Timing Interventions

The reflections and revelations that lead to a final decision to divorce are difficult to predict. Some couples take years to reach a final decision, whereas others move very quickly through a decision and into action. Some marriages end traumatically when a partner abruptly moves out, goes away for a trip and does not come back, or dramatically reveals an affair. Such couples come to therapy in crisis, with one partner experiencing intense feelings of sudden abandonment, rejection, betrayal, and rage. The clinical work initially may need to be intensive to sort out the couple's complex feelings and actions before they experience any relief.

One couple began therapy after the husband had exposed an affair of 18 months and announced that he wanted a divorce and planned to move to another state to live with his girlfriend. During their marriage the wife had believed they were acceptably happy. This belief and trust were shattered. She was struggling with raw emotions, and simultaneously needed to find a job to support herself for the first time in her life. The husband felt guilty but was impatient with her struggle, wanting only to distance himself and move on with his life.

The movement toward the separation or divorce may be pivotal, for it is here that tolerance, flexibility, and consideration for the other person are reshaped or lost. The following questions can help with issues of timing and pacing:

1. Questions for the more eager partner:
   a. Do you think there could be any advantages in being able to wait a little while for your partner to adjust to this change?
   b. Have you ever had an experience in which waiting was best in the end?
   c. What difference could this make to your future?
2. Questions for the reluctant partner:
   a. What do you experience that gives you hope about this relationship?
   b. Have you ever known a good relationship in which one person truly wanted out? What happened? What helped them through it?
   c. As you look into the future beyond a divorce, what might help you through this time (or might be holding you back)?
   d. What have you already done to take care of yourself? What steps might you take?
   e. Do you know someone who could be a support to you through a separation/divorce?

The spouse wishing to preserve the relationship may refuse to deal directly with the partner about the possibility of divorce or may mount a strong defense of the old relationship. This avoidance and failure to acknowledge the marital breakdown may only exacerbate the partner's sense of hopelessness. The split can persist through the divorce process, with the reluctant partner dragging out the settlement and legal procedures. A prolonged separation process with ambiguity about the outcome, particularly around custody matters, can be very anxiety-provoking for children, who may become symptomatic. A combination of individual and conjoint sessions may be needed to help the reluctant partner accept the fact that the marriage cannot succeed without the commitment of both parties.

Emotionality

Profound and sudden changes occur during the uncertain period of deciding to separate or work through the decision made by a partner. At one session there can be grief about the impending loss of the relationship, and at the next, accusations of theft or escalation of mistrust. At one time the couple may feel they can settle things themselves; at the next meeting, one partner has hired an attorney and is not speaking directly to the other. In sessions, each partner can be so sensitive to what the other is saying or doing that clinicians need to be careful not to get caught up in the emotional reactivity. Therapists must be prepared to handle the couple's intense emotional outbursts, conflict, blame or threats toward the other, or a partner's abrupt departure from a session. Clear yet flexible structure and active intervention are needed to interrupt destructive interactions; therapists may need to call "timeouts," or see each person separately for part of a session.

Gender, Power, and Abuse

The gendered differential in power and influence in our society tends to favor men and disadvantage women in divorce (McGoldrick, Anderson, & Walsh, 1989). Most men are genuine in their concern to be full, active parents. Yet, clinicians should be alert to abuses of power. In some cases, men are prompted by their friends, family, or attorneys to file for sole custody as a strategy to contest the mother's custody bid, to intimidate her to agree to joint custody, or to win other concessions. Threats of lengthy court battles often coerce women into compliance in order to avoid prolonged conflict for the sake of the children and to avoid ugly court scenes that question her parental fitness.

The Bully

One wife entered therapy and filed for divorce and sole custody of four children after having been abused by her husband over many years. He threatened that if she left him, he would go after—and win—sole custody on the grounds that she was mentally unstable, as evidenced by her "wild claims" and lack of proof of abuse, and by her need for therapy. Frightened by the prospect of losing her children, she withdrew from therapy and dropped her divorce suit. When she entered therapy again, 3 years later, for help in going through with divorce, he tried to bully her into a joint-custody agreement by threatening to publically expose her deceased father's marital infidelity, a source of pain and shame in her deeply religious family. When, with the help of therapy, she did not back down, he delayed the divorce process and refused to move out of the house, taunting her whenever no one was present to witness his threats. Over the next several months, the children's behavior became increasingly wild and out of control, until one son ran away from home.

In such cases, therapists should make every attempt to deescalate the destructive situation. If possible, they should attempt conjoint sessions, preferably with two therapists, providing safety, support, and balance. Consultation with the clients' attorneys (with written consent), alerting them to the potential volatility of the situation, may be imperative. Often one attorney can persuade the other to recommend therapy or mediation for the offending spouse in order to avert legal complications.

Statistics indicate a heightened risk of abuse and injury to spouses and children during the final months of a relationship and the first few months of separation (Lerman, Kuehl, & Brygger, 1989). It is imperative for therapists to screen for dangerous situations and threatening behavior. They should inquire about hitting, slapping, coercion, intimidation, sexual misconduct, and also ask about possession of guns, which heightens the risk of serious or fatal injury, especially at times of confrontational episodes. Threats and stalking of women by former partners should be taken seriously: There is an alarmingly high incidence of homicide of "estranged" wives, particularly when the woman has initiated the separation or is involved with another man.

Planning Child-Custody Arrangements

Much conflict in divorce occurs over child-custody arrangements. In bitter divorces, couples may fight over "possession" of children, as if they were property to be won, lost, or divided up. In such battles, couples may lose sight of the best interests of their children, who become pawns in a struggle for power or revenge, or in attempts by partners to hold onto something in the face of loss. It is important to help divorcing parents carefully consider their parenting responsibilities and options and to plan for custody and visitation arrangements that will be best for their children in their situation.

Clinicians need to be informed about custody laws and practices. Over the past 150 years, child-custody laws have changed from a "parental rights" premise regarding children as property of the father, to a "tender years" doctrine entrusting the care of young children to mothers. By current principles, custody decisions are to be guided by the criterion of the "best interests of the child." In practice, mothers continue to be awarded sole custody in nearly 90% of all cases. For most fathers, modest initial contact immediately after divorce tends to drop off sharply over time. Studies have found that within 2 years of divorce, only one child in six saw the father at least once a week, on average; nearly half had not seen him in the past year (Amato & Keith, 1991a; Furstenberg & Cherlin, 1991). Therapists working with couples at the time of divorce can lay important groundwork to prevent this serious drop-off.

Whereas relatively few fathers gain sole custody, increasing numbers have sought joint custody, based on an equal rights doctrine. It is important to distinguish joint "legal" custody, involving shared authority, rights, and responsibilities, from joint "physical" custody, whereby children live part-time with each parent. Most families with joint legal custody have experienced merely a change in labels from what was formerly termed "liberal visitation," allowing fathers to define themselves as joint parents. The impetus of the movement has centered on equalizing fathers' "rights." However, it has not rebalanced the disproportionate "responsibilities" shouldered by mothers for the day-to-day care of most children.

With either joint or sole *legal* custody, couples can work out any of a variety of coparenting and residential arrangements. Many children live in a primary residence with their mothers and spend alternate weekends and some vacation time at their father's residence, with other additional contact, such as midweek dinners. Less frequently, children split parts of the week or the year between two homes, or may alternate weeks or years with each parent. Infrequently, siblings are split up in separate households. Each arrangement holds costs as well as benefits for children and their parents.

Although joint custody has been heralded by advocates for assuring involvement of both parents and enlarging fathers' rights, recent research finds mixed results and raises some serious questions (Hetherington et al., 1993). On the positive side, it facilitates more regular father–child contact than traditional visitation decrees. Split residence, however, is problematic in the heavy burden of adjustment it places on children, who must shuttle back and forth and may not feel that they fully belong in any home (Walsh, 1991). When parents do not live in the same neighborhood, daily peer contacts are hard for a child to maintain and practical problems arise constantly, such as having needed schoolwork, clothing, or medicine. Younger children are more likely to need the security and stability of one primary home and to experience confusion and upset at frequent shifts between two residences, without a sense of settling in. Adjustment to the arrangement often does not improve with time. After

2 years, one 7-year-old said that going back and forth felt "like a roller coaster that broke and can't stop."

The mechanics of transporting a child back and forth between homes, in addition to covering school functions and medical emergencies, absorb considerable energy and require continual coordination. Arrangements demand a high level of mutual trust, cooperation, and communication between ex-spouses that only some can achieve. Researchers caution that which severe conflict persists between ex-spouses, joint custody is likely to be harmful to children who are caught in the middle of hostilities, power struggles, and the battleground of two residences (Furstenberg & Cherlin, 1991). Joint custody is also contraindicated when a parent cannot be relied upon to maintain a responsible role, as in cases of severe mental illness, addiction, or a history of physical or sexual abuse and neglect. A case-by-case evaluation is needed to determine the safe, appropriate nature and degree of parental contact.

In sum, long-term follow-up studies (Furstenberg & Cherlin, 1991; Hetherington et al., 1993; Isaacs et al., 1986; Maccoby & Mnookin, 1992) indicate that when divorce is amicable and both parents remain involved with children, there may be little, if any, difference between joint or sole custody for a child's development. Successful adaptation depends less on shared living arrangements and more on the ability of the parents to *collaborate* in coparenting without serious, chronic conflict. When this is not possible, emerging research suggests that children fare better in sole custody and a primary residence, with predictable, structured visits with the noncustodial parent. A reasonable arrangement of "parallel parenting" (Furstenberg & Cherlin, 1991) can more realistically be achieved in most cases when each parent assumes responsibility and authority for his/her own parenting, with minimal contact with the ex-spouse and an agreement not to interfere with each other's arrangements. Clinicians can help divorcing couples by emphasizing that the most important key to child adjustment is the effective functioning of the custodial parent, supported to every extent possible by the noncustodial parent. Minimization of hostilities and mutual respect between parents enables reliable, nonconflictual *access* to both parents.

The Legal System and Consultants

The powerful influences of the legal system can be overwhelming and even run counter to therapeutic work with separating couples. Knowledge of local and state laws and legal processes is crucial for the therapist to understand what clients are going through and to help them examine options and ramifications and use the system most constructively. Clinicians may find legal consultation extremely useful in complicated cases.

Some couples have found a trial separation to be very helpful in reaching a divorce decision. If they separate without filing for legal separation or divorce, they should be apprised of financial risks and implications regarding positioning for custody of children. Formal legal separation agreements do include financial arrangements, such as temporary support orders. Clarification is needed for clients to make an informed choice.

Confidentiality laws regarding therapy are important in working with all clients during separation and divorce. Proper releases of information are needed for consultation with an attorney or other professional. Clinicians should be cautious not to make assumptions or evaluative statements, or to give assessment reports about someone without direct knowledge of the family by seeing everyone involved.

Therapists may be concerned about being subpoenaed to testify in divorce cases. Actually, the vast majority of divorce cases never go to trial, but are settled by attorneys. Many therapists take the position that they prefer not to testify or release records, and that the work with divorcing couples be kept private. In any case, a therapist who works systemically with a couple must maintain a bipartial stance, remaining empathic with the position of each partner, siding with neither against the other, and being aware of the circularity of influences in relationship problems. Fortunately, this systemic orientation, when explained to the couple at the outset of therapy—or to an attorney calling in hopes of expert testimony for a client against the other spouse—is most often a sufficient deterrent to being drawn into a legal battle.

A good, working collaboration with attorneys is most important for optimal divorce processes. In some situations a broad range of services may be needed. Discussions with the attorney or others in the divorce system can be constructive, for instance, when someone has difficulty understanding the laws or is intimidated, or when there is concern that a child may need representation. Other consultants may be needed, such as accountants for financial planning, therapists or other professionals regarding special needs of children, evaluators for offering recommendations that may be needed for court proceedings, and child protection authorities for dealing with abuse issues or supervised visitation.

POSTDIVORCE CHALLENGES

Divorce sets in motion a number of difficult transitions. The first postdivorce phase, typically lasting 1 to 2 years, is a period of high stress and turmoil. Because many individuals are more distressed after 1 year than immediately following the divorce, they may feel hopeless and discouraged at that time. However, longitudinal research (Hetherington et al., 1993) has found in most cases a remarkable period of recovery by the end of the second year. By the 6-year follow-up, most individuals—both adults and children—have restabilized and are functioning well. It can be reassuring to offer this long-range perspective to families still in crisis.

Therefore, it is important for clinicians to normalize the initial postdivorce crisis period as transitional, framing problems in relation to the process and identifying common issues that are likely to arise. It is crucial not to overpathologize distress or to assume that long-term treatment is needed before offering information and support, building resources, and promoting restabilization. It is most useful to help clients gain a normative developmental perspective, distinguishing both immediate and long-term challenges and expectations. Divorce groups for individuals who are navigating various stages of the process can be especially helpful at this time (Weiss, 1975).

Over time, families typically experience multiple dislocations and reorganizations as residences and custody arrangements change. With remarriage, the complicated process of restructuring old relationships to accommodate the new can require as long as 4 to 5 years for restabilization, especially if there are children in early adolescence (Visher & Visher, 1993).

Emotional Turmoil in the Immediate Aftermath

Given all the pressures and changes, it is not surprising that the early phase of separation involves considerable emotional turmoil. The most intense emotions concern the varied and complicated losses, involving the loss of the partner, the couple/parental relationships, and the intact family unit. Unlike loss through widowhood, divorce carries inherent ambiguities (Boss, 1991). The marriage is dead, but the former partner lives on, moving into a separate life and other relationships. It is especially painful to accept that the ex-spouse can love and share his/her life and home with someone else. The individuals are no longer a marital couple, and yet both remain forever parents to their children. Interactions around parenting can be disconcerting, the familiar interchanges and memories of shared experiences juxtaposed with new and different roles and rules for interaction. Even if the marriage or the partner was deeply disappointing, divorce involves the loss of the intact family unit, as well as the hopes and dreams for the future of the marriage and family. In our view, it is the avoidance of painful encounters rekindling these complicated feelings of loss that leads to so much postdivorce conflict, distancing, and cutoff.

Divorce has a profound impact on an individual's sense of self (Amato & Keith, 1991b). It can be most devastating for women in traditional marriages who lose their identities, as well as their financial security, with the loss of a husband (McGoldrick, Anderson, & Walsh, 1989). For men, the loss of a helpmate and emotional caretaker contributes to loneliness and a high rate of illness, depression, and suicide following divorce (Bray & Hetherington, 1993). For both men and women, changes in self-concept can be pervasive and enduring. They are most marked in the first year, when individuals commonly report "not me" experiences and behavior that is different from the past and discordant with their self-image. Many peopl make striking, but often short-lived, changes in their images. They commonly take active steps to improve themselves.

The "emotional" divorce may lag behind the "legal" divorce, especially when continuing involvement around children requires collaboration and restimulates old attachments and conflicts. Therapy can help not only in working through the loss, but also in transforming attachments into new coparenting partnerships. Some couples maintain their attachment through intense and bitter conflict (Isaacs et al., 1986). In a study of highly conflicted, divorcing couples, Johnston and Campbell (1988) describe the conflict as "multilayered" and "multileveled," with elements of the impasse occurring at external, interactional, and intrapsychic levels. They found that externally, the dispute can be fueled by relatives and close friends, new partners, and even helping professionals. Interactionally, it can be either a continuation of a conflictual marital relationship or the product of a traumatic separation. At the intrapsychic level, the issue can

be a traumatic reaction to rejection or loss. In cases of serious mental illness, such issues can be further complicated by extreme emotional reactions.

Involvement between children and fathers often ceases, because ongoing contact between the former spouses is too painful for either or both of them. One man, divorced 6 months earlier by his wife, found it so upsetting to have to ring the doorbell of his former home and wait on the porch to take his children out, that he became enraged at his ex-spouse, smashed a window, and would not go back. Increasingly problematic drinking brought him to a therapist, who helped him work through the emotional divorce and held time-limited conjoint sessions with the ex-spouse and her therapist to work out a better visitation arrangement. Pickup at school, day care, or other neutral places, with minimal contact between ex-spouses, is found by many to be more workable in such situations.

Former spouses commonly experience extreme fluctuations in mood. Such lability may be expressed in waves of intense emotion, from crashing depressions, outbursts of rage, or even death wishes toward the ex-spouse, to relief at being free of the former marital tension and momentary surges of euphoria. The partner who initiated the divorce is prone to lingering guilt, while a spouse who did not want it is likely to carry feelings of abandonment or betrayal and may seek retaliation through custody battles or by later witholding child visitation rights or financial support. The polarization of positions into victim and villain too often is intensified by the legal process, impeding emotional resolution of the divorce. The greater the ambiguity and ambivalence in the divorce process, the more difficult it is to make sense of the situation and to grieve the loss.

Among the most disturbing feelings for many people are persistent attachment and nostalgic thoughts of the ex-spouse or the intact family. At 1-year postdivorce, many individuals wonder if the divorce was the right thing or whether they had worked hard enough to make it work, and may view the alternatives less optimistically. Such doubts do tend to fade with time. Predivorce couple therapy, by clarifying the divorce decision, can prevent or lessen such later doubts.

The tendency to vilify an ex-spouse is as strong as the overromanticization of a new lover. The stigma, shame, and guilt surrounding divorce, further inflamed by the adversarial legal system, often lead to brutal character assasinations that serve as a rationale for the divorce or a desired settlement. The pressure for an explanation for a divorce to children, extended family, and friends can be intense. As one newly divorced woman stated, "He didn't drink too much or beat me. What can I tell people about why I left him?" Ambiguity about the cause of breakup in a marriage that appeared good to outsiders can stir in others' anxiety that their own relationships might not last. In response to a slur on her ex-husband's character by a well-intentioned friend, an exceptionally mature woman replied, "Please don't say anything against my former husband. He was a wonderful man or I never would have married him."

Individuals who are stuck in destructive stereotypical villain–victim images can be helped in therapy to restory the marriage, the relationship, and themselves as persons into fuller and more meaningful accounts that allow for mixed feelings, memories, and images of the self and ex-partner. Clinicians can be most helpful by encouraging divorced clients to review their courtship, marriage, and divorce process. It is useful to coach them to gather clarifying information and perspectives from the ex-spouse, other important family members, and friends, and to examine the factors in the breakdown of the marriage. Helping clients to make sense of the process, to take ownership of their part, and to accept what was beyond their control, can greatly facilitate the emotional resolution of the divorce that is necessary to move on with life.

Kin and Social Support

Loss of family and friendship networks compounds the difficulty of adjustment to divorce. It is crucial for therapists to assess these losses and help clients find ways to reclaim or replenish them. Although in-laws may back off or choose sides in the midst of loyalty conflicts during the divorce process, it is possible to maintain or renew important connections. Clinicians can help each individual find ways to continue valued relationships to the ex-spouse's family, who are also the children's grandparents, aunts, uncles, and cousins. It may be necessary to coach them not to involve the extended family in disputes or triangle them into coalitions against the ex-spouse.

A strong factor for couples in overcoming separation distress is the positive attitude and encouragement of parents (Issacs et. al., 1986). Following divorce, former spouses tend to turn to their own families of origin for help and solace. They also need to develop new supports, drawing on friends and neighbors, or sharing a household with another parent. They may need to overcome presumptions that others will be unavailable to them, or that a request will be burdensome or imply their failure to be self-sufficient. Some spouses may avoid contact with family, friends, or their religious community out of shame or stigma of divorce. When a clinician encourages hesitant clients to tell family members and others about their situation, to ask directly for help, and to be clear and specific about what is needed, they are most often surprised and relieved to receive a caring and helpful response. In any case, clients can feel good about asserting their own needs and position.

Economic and cultural factors influence intergenerational patterns of postdivorce support. In white, middle-class families, custodial mothers tend to live nearby, but separately from, their parents. Low-income blacks and other ethnic families are more likely to share a residence and resources. Structural interventions can be useful to address common hierarchical conflicts over who is in charge of children or a shared household. Where finances permit, a housekeeper/babysitter arrangement allows a parent to remain in charge, delegate authority and responsibility, and turn to family members for backup support.

Social relationships change dramatically with divorce. Ex-spouses are likely to confront issues of social isolation (Hetherington et al., 1993; Isaacs et al., 1986). Former friends of the couple may distance, take sides, or extend invitations only for child-focused events. Women in traditional marriages lose a vital social network connected to their husband's work. Noncustodial fathers may find school gatherings with other parents uncomfortable. Ex-spouses may feel awkward when both are attending children's events. A custodial parent may feel too depleted to socialize alone or initiate contact, and child-care coverage is an ever-present dilemma. Phone calls are important lifelines, as are cards and letters to keep in contact with family and friends living elsewhere.

Whereas extramarital affairs are quite common at the time of divorce, only 15% of such transitional relationships continue on to marriage (Hetherington et al., 1993). Hetherington and associates found that at divorce, men commonly initiated a frenetic phase of socializing or casual sexual activity, but by 1 year, they tended to seek more serious relationships. Most divorced women found casual sexual encounters unsatisfying, and felt depressed, controlled, and bad about themselves afterward. Even more than men, they yearned for a mutually caring relationship. The formation of an intimate relationship was the best predictor of happiness for both men and women. However, being a custodial parent interfered with this aim for women. Also, the prospect of intimacy made many individuals fearful of unlovability or of attachment that could replicate past conflict and loss. Fears of coping and remaining alone, as well as concerns about financial survival, propel some individuals into premature remarriage.

Parenting Issues and Children's Adjustment

Divorce ends a marriage, but does not end parent–child relationships and parental obligations. As couples with children struggle to cope with the disruption of their marriage and financial and social resources, they must simultaneously work out custody and visitation arrangements that were agreed to, but may not seem workable (Maccoby, Buchanan, Mnookin, & Dornbusch, 1993). It can be helpful for therapists to offer information about normative challenges for children and suggest strategies for coping that enable realistic planning, buffering of transitional stresses, and crisis prevention.

After divorce, nearly 90% of children live with their mothers. Although paternal custody arrangements remain uncommon, some differences have been noted. Visitation by noncustodial mothers tends to be more regular and frequent, contributing to children's adjustment. As in the predivorce period, it is helpful for therapists to share with clients the fact that emerging data on various custody and visitation arrangements suggest that successful adaptation is facilitated by the active, reliable involvement and responsibility of both parents and on their ability to cooperate without serious conflict. Children need structure and predictability, as well as warmth and responsiveness, for optimal functioning.

Whereas a good coparenting relationship is most desirable after divorce, interactional conflict between former spouses is common (Kline, Johnston, & Tschann, 1991), particularly in the early postdivorce phase and around subsequent transitions, such as remarriage. Conflict is more likely to persist with continued attachment and to diminish as those bonds started to fade. Clinically, it is helpful to work through lingering attachments to help let go of the old relationship and to enable a respectful, if not collaborative, relationship in parenting.

Parents should anticipate that, with any custody arrangement, distress is common for children in the first year postdivorce. Most often, especially for boys, it is externalized in aggressive, noncompliant, antisocial behavior. A child's sense of rejection by a noncustodial parent's unreliable contact or support is most often expressed in misbehavior in school or at home. Custodial mothers and sons tend to get into coercive cycles: A mother, overwhelmed by multiple stresses, is unable to control misbehavior, which escalates, increasing her sense of failure and incompetence. Problems worsen if the noncustodial father fails to set limits or support the mother. In some cases, a parent may fear losing a new relationship unless the problem child is removed. A frustrated parent's threat of rejection or abandonment may reinforce a child's belief that his/her badness had caused the earlier marital breakup. An escalating interactional spiral may provoke a residential shift. Clinicians can interrupt this dysfunctional cycle by facilitating more balanced, supportive coparental collaboration.

A custodial mother must establish herself as the sole daily manager of the children and household, providing nurturing and discipline while challenged by other demands, especially a full-time job. To function effectively, she needs emotional reserves and confidence in her own abilities. Clinicians can most effectively help parents with practical problems through psychoeducational, structural, and behavioral approaches, with concrete directives and support to reduce behavior problems and improve parent–child relationships. As mothers are helped to feel more competent and able to manage their situations, their self-esteem is also enhanced (Hetherington et al., 1993). A range of extended family, social, and community resources can be mobilized to support and enable overburdened single-parent heads of households to function most effectively.

In postdivorce single-parent households, whereas mother–son relationships may remain problematic and conflictual over time, mother–daughter relationships are more likely to be close and companionate (Hetherington et al., 1993). Such a bond can become dysfunctional if generational boundaries become blurred, as when a parent relates as a peer, or if roles are reversed, as when a child monitors a parent's dating. Girls may also act out distress later than boys. Adjustment for both is most complicated when divorce occurs in early adolescence.

Herz (1989) offers a clinically useful framework for handling the complexities in the process of reorganization in single-parent households over time. Guidelines for successive phases of adjustment focus on three interrelated challenges in establishing a viable unit: (1) financial pressures, (2) parenting, and (3) social relationships. In the early phase of adjustment, clinicians can help clients consider many potentially viable options and yet take things a step at a time, so they will not be overwhelmed by the unclarity and complexities of the postdivorce situation. Given the paucity of models in our society, it is important to offer information and linkage to community resources for support and practical assistance in developing such competencies as basic financial and legal knowledge. Single-parent groups and community drop-in centers may do more to sustain long-term adjustment than traditional therapies.

We can also counter the tendency in clinical assessment to overpathologize divorced parents who are overwhelmed, undersupported, and depleted by the challenges inherent in their situation (Walsh, 1992). We need to avoid assumptions of underlying psychopathology or blaming the "failure" to stay married, or to remarry, on individual character deficits. Single-parent mothers are frequently stereotyped as "chaotic," "excessively needy," and "deficient" in exerting executive leadership and controls. Clinicians need to be careful not to further overload a custodial parent with expectations and tasks without appreciating the overburdened situation and constraints imposed by limited resources. Viewing single-parent families as understaffed reframes deficiencies as structural problems that can be addressed.

Similarly, clinicians need to counter the tendency to ignore or negatively prejudge a noncustodial father's potential contributions. Secondhand reports of a father's unwillingness to be involved should not be relied on. Clinicians need to check out presumptions that an absent parent is uncaring, destructive, crazy, incompetent, or hopeless and to attempt to change that situation if appropriate and possible. Often that parent is willing to come in and to become more involved. Many parents are able to develop better relationships with their children after divorce than they had in the midst of a troubled marriage. It is important to contact the noncustodial parent directly and meet to assess and work toward new possibilities for parent–child involvement and more adequate financial support of children. It is essential first to gain the custodial parent's (usually the mother) agreement for such contact, helping her to understand how to do so will be in her interests as well as those

of the children. The aims of intervention, through either conjoint or individual sessions, need to be made explicit: not to reunite the former couple or to rehash old marital grievances, but rather to promote better parenting and the well-being of all members. Clinicians should make every effort to facilitate contact and support by noncustodial fathers and work through barriers to cooperative parenting whenever appropriate. However, in cases of destructive conflict or physical or sexual abuse, only limited, supervised contact, if any, may be indicated. A careful systems assessment is imperative.

A major postdivorce problem concerns the large number of children who grow up without the continuing involvement of their biological fathers (Furstenberg, 1990). Even when fathers are involved initially, most often their contact and child support declines steadily over time, particularly with remarriage (Furstenberg & Cherlin, 1991; Hetherington et al., 1993). Reports of the negative effects of divorce on children must be viewed in the context of the fact that so many men fail to maintain regular contact and adequate financial support.

A number of factors contribute to this general decline. Most often, traditional gender-based patterns of parenting in the marriage continue after divorce, with mothers in the central role and fathers only peripherally involved (Furstenberg & Cherlin, 1991). Although most men are well intentioned, without their wives and marriages to knit them to their children, they feel uncomfortable and inept in a parenting role on their own and easily feel unappreciated and rejected when children are difficult or unresponsive. Too often, both contact and financial support become erratic or stop altogether.

Transitions around the visit are often awkward and difficult. Residential mothers may react when children return drained and unruly from visits and fathers fail to enforce rules, instead offering only "good times." Visits can can be painful and guilt-provoking when contact is brief, intense, and insufficient and may stir up old affections, angers, or disappointments between former spouses. A vicious cycle of witholding support and decreased contact can escalate over time. An ex-wife who is angry and jealous at having been left for another relationship may block access to the children or turn them against her ex-husband.

In most families, the need to reevaluate custody or parenting arrangements arises over the course of time to accommodate to changes in children's developmental needs or parents' living situations. Residential changes are not uncommon, especially for boys at adolescence. Most arrangements are altered or break down altogether when one parent remarries or moves from the community. Since most parents do remarry or change job situations, initial plans should be viewed as modifiable. Parents should be encouraged to envision possible future scenarios and contingency plans and to be flexible in altering agreements to fit changing needs and circumstances. It is important in all custody arrangements to help parents consider their children's developmental priorities and recognize needs for change over time.

Economic Distress

Financial strain is the most significant factor in postdivorce adjustment problems, especially for women with children, whose standard of living declines markedly, whereas men's tends to increase (Furstenberg & Cherlin, 1991). Custodial mothers and children often suffer serious financial hardship and may be forced to move from homes and neighborhoods, resulting in a chain of social transitions and dislocations.

Forty percent of all divorcing couples make no property settlement because there is nothing of value to decide. The burden is greatest for poor, minority women lacking in education, job opportunity, and child-care resources. African–American couples have separation and divorce rates that are even higher than those for white families, and are also less likely to remarry (Cherlin, 1992). Seventy-five percent of black children experience the separation or divorce of their parents by age 16, and most will live for long periods in a mother-headed single-parent family.

Clinical interventions may need to address several sources of economic distress. First, inadequate divorce settlements and poor enforcement of support by fathers have become a serious and widespread problem. The shift in divorce laws toward "no-fault" divorce and "equal division" of property was intended to facilitate the divorce process and to compensate women who assumed the primary homemaking and childrearing responsibilities. However, equal division of property proves neither equitable nor adequate for women who continue to bear most childrearing obligations and who experience job discrimination (McGoldrick, 1989). With divorce reform laws in many states, alimony, now termed "rehabilitative maintenance," is awarded in only a small percentage of cases and for only a short time. The average amount of child support decreed by the court is inadequate in most cases, and furthermore, most fathers fail to comply with the amount decreed. Without the support of fathers, custodial mothers confront an inherent conflict in managing financial, homemaking, and child-care responsibilities. Low-paying, inflexible jobs as well as inadequate and unaffordable child-care complicate their dilemma. Researchers underscore the importance of financial support by fathers for both the immediate and long-term adjustment of their children (Furstenberg & Cherlin, 1991).

Clinicians should not shy away from inquiry about postdivorce finances. Given the common hardships and inequities of divorce, it is crucial to learn how ex-spouses' standard of living has been affected, the level of financial support mandated and actually received, and their attempts to manage economic needs. Enabling the custodial parent to deal with a financial situation may involve coaching a mother to obtain needed support from a father or contacting him directly to achieve a more workable agreement and follow-through. Because financial support is usually related to degree of involvement, a therapist may need to interrupt a vicious cycle in which mothers withhold visitation as fathers withhold support, each reacting to the other, using the leverage in their power. Clinicians should be aware of and share with each parent the local laws and court attitudes regarding child support enforcement as well as consequences for withholding visitation. Moreover, because economic viability and child-care supports involve work systems and larger social policies, clinicians need to actively promote such changes as flexible work schedules and affordable, quality child care.

Physical and Structural Dislocation

In the initial adjustment to the loss of the intact family unit and to new patterns of living, individuals are likely to experience a sense of disorientation in a transitional living situation lacking in structure and definition. Residential shifts and moves to new communities generate a sense of dislocation. Also, shared rituals and pleasurable interactions typically start breaking down. Daily routines, such as dinnertime, are disrupted as attention is demanded for immediate tasks of reordering a household or setting up a new home. Some clients may need help setting schedules to promote a sense of some order and predictability. Others may rigidly hold onto old patterns of living in an attempt to preserve a sense of stability and continuity with the past, as if the family were still an intact unit. While restabilizing, continuity can be fostered in the face of loss and change by preserving valued rituals, such as bedtime stories, and inventing new ones, such as Sunday brunch at Dad's.

Added to the lack of behavioral guidelines and ambivalent feelings is the ambiguity of norms in flux regarding the degree of involvement between former spouses, between parents and children, and with new partners (Ahrons & Rodgers, 1987). Role definitions are unclear. Clinicians need to evaluate the changes that have occurred in transition from the former intact family to the present structure. Helping them to negotiate and clarify new relationship rules, expectations, and reallocation of responsibilities will greatly facilitate the transition.

With divorce, parental roles shift as the custodial parent attempts to cover all bases, combining nurturing, disciplinary, and breadwinning roles. Undersupported custodial parents are likely to become overloaded when expecting themselves to do what two parents usually do. The "visiting" parent loses a clear role, power, and functions. Many men discuss the frustration in having precious little time with their children; in wanting it to be enjoyable, without having to discipline them; and in feeling the they have lost authority by not living in the primary home. Couples who have conformed to traditional gender roles before divorce commonly find themselves at a loss in handling the functions formerly carried by the spouse:

Lady with a Wrench

One divorced woman who had depended on her handyman husband around the house described one night when she had to restrain herself from calling her ex-spouse to fix her leaking drainpipe. Instead, she searched for the wrench, called a friend for instructions by phone, and fixed the leak herself, with a great sense of accomplishment.

Given limited resources, children and extended family members may be called upon to assume a larger share of responsibilities. It is common and not necessarily pathological for a mother to turn to children for comfort and affection in the father's absence. However, it is important that generational boundaries not be breached in mate-like role assignment, as in the following case.

The Burning Bed

A recently divorced mother and her four children were referred for therapy for the "out of control" behavior of the 15-year-old son who had "accidentally" set fire to his mother's bed. After the father moved out, the oldest son, age 17, quit school to help support the family, and the mother, telling him, "You're now the man of the house," gave him her bedroom, while she moved to the living room sofa.

Such an arrangement and accompanying message poses conflict and anxiety for a child about what may be expected in a mate-like role when signals become dangerously sexualized. Here, the therapist helped the mother to clarify boundaries and her parental status by reclaiming the master bedroom, telling her that as a working single parent she deserved more than ever to have her own space and privacy.

Postdivorce Belief Systems

Divorce, like other major life transitions, disrupts a family's paradigm, the worldview and basic premises that underlie the family identity and guide its actions. Parents' sense of mastery and competence are shaken. When individuals share unrealistic expectations that the family should function like an intact two-parent family, there is a sense of disappointment and deficiency when those fantasies cannot be met. Similarly, although most divorced adults do eventually remarry, it is crucial that clinicians view single parent households not merely as way stations in transition to remarriage, but rather as viable family structures in their own right (Herz, 1989). Many men rush into remarriage to fill the gap. Over a third of custodial mothers never remarry. In any case, the therapeutic goal should not be to help clients to seek a replacement or endure a waiting period, implying that living alone or heading a single parent household is inherently deficient. Such a frame perpetuates the belief that a new spouse/parent is needed to rescue the single parent—and children—who cannot function or live a satisfying life without the leadership of a man—or the caretaking of a woman—in the home. Such premises intensify feelings of being overwhelmed and powerless in coping with the real overload that single parents experience. In place of an intact family model, divorced individuals need help in creating new ways to meet socioemotional and to economic needs and reorganize relationship patterns, responsibilities, and expectations (Lindblad-Goldberg, 1989).

Because marital disruption calls into question many core values and fantasies associated with the intact family, it is important to review the beliefs held by family members and to promote transformation to fit new family requisites. Helping families to reconstruct beliefs and practices to find new expression can preserve a vital sense of meaning in the face of so much loss and upheaval.

Separation Issues in Gay and Lesbian Relationships

The end of a relationship for gay and lesbian couples is additionally complicated by the lack of the legal status of marriage, which leaves them unprotected by divorce laws regarding financial settlement and property rights (Laird, 1993). Lesbian and gay couples are increasingly raising children together, either through adoption or when one is the biological parent from a previous marriage, or by insemination. When these relationships end, nonbiological parents lack the protection of custody laws, leaving their relationships with children ambiguous, at best, or cut off without recourse. Separation therapy and mediation can be most beneficial.

STEPS TO REMARRIAGE

Remarriage most often occurs within 3 to 5 years of a divorce, with men tending to remarry sooner than women. Over half of remarrying adults have children from previous marriages and are twice as likely to redivorce in early remarriage due to child-related problems, despite congenial marital relations. However, couples who can survive the transitional period are no more likely to divorce than those in first marriages. Therefore, it is useful for clinicians to be aware of predictable emotional and organizational challenges as remarriage is contemplated (McGoldrick & Carter, 1989; Visher & Visher, 1988, 1993; Walsh, 1991).

When divorced individuals remarry, clinicians can be most helpful in facilitating establishment of an open, flexible structure with permeable boundaries and clear roles and rules. McGoldrick and Carter identify three key "enabling attitudes" that ease transition through the steps involved in the formation and stabilization process of remarriage: (1) resolution of the emotional attachment to ex-spouses; (2) giving up the unrealistic and inappropriate ideal of first-family structure and forming a new conceptual model of family; and (3) accepting the time and space involved in stepfamily organization, as well as the ambivalences and difficulties. Clinicians

need to help families to examine their beliefs and to work out feelings and expectations.

The framework of McGoldrick and Carter identifies tendencies toward dysfunction and guides clinical intervention. First, clinicians need to promote permeable boundaries between households to permit children easy access, as agreed upon in custody and visitation arrangements. Second, new couples need to be helped to solidify the marital bond, because the presence of children precludes a "honeymoon period." Concomitantly, they need to understand the difficult position of the stepparent and to accept and support the biological parent's attachments and responsibilities for children. Third, couples need to revise traditional gender roles that are dysfunctional in remarriage, so that each parent takes primary responsibility for his/her own children and financial support is equitably shared.

Remarriage thrusts all participants into instant multiple roles and childrearing responsibilities, without the stepwise progression of a first marriage. Confusion abounds concerning kinship labels, different names, interactional rules, and guidelines for functioning. Members must navigate complex and ambiguous boundaries of the system involving such basic issues as membership (Who are the "real" family members?); space and time (Where do children really belong? How much time is spent where, when, with whom?); authority (Who is in charge and who should a child obey?). This cluster of issues must continually be renegotiated. Enormous flexibility is required to enable the new family to expand and contract boundaries, to include visiting children and then let them go while also establishing a stable family unit.

Many problems stem from an attempt to replicate the intact family or its ideal image, with inappropriate roles and rules (McGoldrick & Carter, 1989). Rigid boundaries may shut out members and serve as reminders of the former family unit. Because the strong parent–child bond predates the marital bond, competition for primacy with the spouse/parent may blur the distinction that the relationships are not on the same generational level. Traditional gender role expectations pressure women to take responsibility for the emotional well-being of the family and generate adversarial relations with stepdaughters and the ex-wife/mother.

Therapists need to help individuals to counteract the wish for instant unity and tendencies toward fusion and conflict avoidance stemming from their past pain, vulnerability, and fear of failing in the new marriage. It is useful to examine and alter fantasies that foster denial of normal adjustment problems or a sense of failure when unrealistic expectations are not quickly met. Families gain a more realistic perspective when clinicians normalize the process, offering information about common transitional dilemmas (Whiteside, 1982). It is important for them to take the process a step at a time and to realize that successful remarried family integration can require as much as 5 years (Visher & Visher, 1993).

Reworking Previous Divorce Issues

Every remarriage is grounded in loss. When the previous task of mourning the loss of a past marriage and family unit has not been dealt with, the step of remarriage can reactivate painful feelings. Unresolved issues from the past marriage, the process of divorce, and the period between marriages, are all carried into remarriage. To the extent that each spouse can resolve emotional issues with significant people from the past, the new relationship can proceed on its own merits.

Remarried family integration can be more difficult following divorce than widowhood, given the emotional and practical complications. The remarriage of a former spouse is often accompanied by feelings of depression, helplessness, anger, and anxiety. Financial and custody battles frequently ensue at this time. With remarriage, distant but cordial relationships with ex-spouses and their new marital partners are typically preferred.

Clinicians may need to assist resolution of the emotional divorce between former spouses as marital partners while facilitating a viable, open collaboration in parenting that will increasingly involve stepparents. If ex-spouses are not speaking directly to each other or are in continual conflict, destructive bonds maintained by anger and communicated through children need to be altered so that they will not undermine remarried family formation. Loyalty conflicts for children are a common source of difficulty, in their fears that becoming close to a stepparent will hurt or alienate the other parent. Divided loyalties, confusion, and mixed feelings about where a child "belongs" may be expressed in transitional behavior problems or triangulations, taking sides, or playing off one side against the other.

Difficulty in forming new attachments may arise from persistent conflict or cutoffs from one's ex-spouse, children, or other family members as a result of a bitter divorce. Men who have been disengaged from their own children may be unable to develop a relationship with stepchildren out of feelings of disloyalty or guilt. Others may seek to compensate for a sense of failure in the first family by attempting to be a "perfect wife" or "superparent" in remarriage. With the normal tensions of remarried family life and the unresponsiveness of children, the sense of failure may fuel anger and futility. Repairing earlier cutoffs and addressing issues of conflicting loyalty and guilt are therapeutic priorities in such cases.

Remarriage signifies the permanent loss of the previous intact family and shatters lingering reunion fantasies. Parents and stepparents may need help in encouraging and tolerating expression of the range of feelings children are likely to have and the the need for continual involvement with the other parent. Reassuring children that the new stepparent relationship does not replace the bond with the biological parent reduces conflict for the child.

In work with remarried families on child-focused problems, it is recommended that ex-spouses be routinely contacted and invited to meet separately or with the children to hear their views on the presenting problem and their role as parent (McGoldrick & Carter, 1989). Clinicians are frequently warned by a client that the ex-spouse is "crazy," "uncaring," and certain to be unresponsive. Nevertheless, a phone call frequently reaches a concerned parent who is willing to come in. A remarriage partner should be involved in order to structurally reinforce that marital unit and to facilitate that stepparent connection. Ex-spouses are included in joint sessions with the remarried family only to deal with specific, child-focused, coparental issues. Even then, the level of tension may be counterproductive. Such a meeting may have primarily diagnostic value or underscore the seriousness of a situation. Only the passage of time helps some ex-spouses to deal with each other. Discussion of unresolved marital issues is not advised at such sessions that aim to develop a collaborative parental team across households.

DIVORCE MEDIATION

The process of "mediation," in which a neutral third person helps parties resolve a dispute, dates back thousands of years to the ancient Chinese, where mediation was the principal means of dispute resolution (Brown, 1982). The role of the mediator is much akin to that of the African headman or lineage spokesman and the role of the rabbis in the Jewish rabbinic courts (Gulliver, 1973; Brown, 1982). In the last twenty years, mediation has been applied to a range of marital and family disputes, particularly divorce.

Despite its visibility in government, labor management, neighborhood, and community settings, the direct application of mediation to divorce is relatively new. Until the 1970s, divorce was possible only on certain grounds, essentially a marital offense. One party was required to file suit against the other, typically charging either abandonment, adultery, or mental cruelty. In most cases, this charge went unchallenged by the spouse, who regardless of the veracity of the claim, bore the onus of "guilt" for the marital failure, while the aggrieved party was designated the victim. Such a system, in which attorneys vied to have their client found innocent, forced divorcing couples to become adversaries. Mediation was difficult (if not impossible) as long as divorce was based on the legal requirement of admission of wrongdoing by one partner. The spread of no-fault divorce, beginning in the 1970s, made possible the development of a no-fault dispute resolution procedure.

There is growing consensus among both legal and mental health professionals that litigation and the adversarial legal system contribute to the acrimony and conflict typically associated with divorce. It is in this atmosphere of dissatisfaction that mediation has emerged. With mediation, the parties work together in consultation with attorneys to determine issues of custody, property, and support, that is, how they want to coparent their children, divide their joint assets, and handle issues of financial support.

The field of family mediation, which includes divorce, is growing rapidly, with membership in the national Academy of Family Mediators expanding at the rate of roughly 20% per year. Increasingly, the strategies and techniques are also being incorporated within the practices of marital and family therapists as well as those of attorneys. Although most private mediators work with clients at middle- and upper-income levels, mediation is becoming more available in both the private and public sectors on a sliding-scale fee basis through family service agencies and training programs for mediators.

Public-Sector Mediation

Public-sector services are typically court-ordered or court-referred and funded through the courts or available at a reduced fee, with court mediators typically coming from mental health backgrounds. Court programs vary. Some court systems refer divorcing couples to mediation primarily when custody or visitation rights are at issue. In some jurisdictions, mediation is required by the court prior to the granting of a trial; in others, it is available to the couple on a voluntary basis or at the discretion of the judge.

Several concerns have been raised about court-ordered mediation. Many court programs, because of budget constraints, limit to three the number of sessions offered to clients, severely restricting needed service to deal with complex and conflictual cases. The involuntary nature of mandated mediation is especially problematic in cases of spouse abuse, in which trust, safety, and fairness are serious concerns. Client confidentiality is an issue in jurisdictions in which the option of "open mediation" is made available to disputants. Prior to beginning mediation, the parties decide whether they want the mediation to be totally "closed," meaning totally confidential, or "open," which means that should the mediation fail, the mediator will make a report and recommendations to the court. This nonconfidential use of mediation, which judges find helpful but may operate against a client, has been controversial.

Private-Sector Mediation: Process and Procedures

The experience of mediation can be quite different for a couple from that of a litigated divorce. Lawyers frame the issues related to divorce from a legal-rights perspective as custody, property, and support. Mediators, in contrast, come from a needs or relational perspective and discuss with the couple how they wish to share their parenting obligations and responsibilities, and their joint assets. In mediation, at the very least, clients' feelings and needs are recognized.

Mediation can be an empowering experience for clients, unlike litigation, in which they experience little control over decisions that affect their future. In addition to resolving the issues related to their divorce, mediation facilitates shared control in the process and deescalates relational conflict. Unlike lawyers who typically insist that their legally unsophisticated clients not discuss issues together out of fear that they might "give away the store" or their strategies, mediators encourage clients to work together as long as this is useful. With mediation, clients virtually write their own divorce agreements. Additionally, when a problem or a new issue arises, they are able to return to mediation, typically with the same mediator, for additional work.

A typical case referred for private mediation might be a couple whose therapist suggested that they consult a mediator prior to seeking the services of a lawyer. They might see a mediator for an initial orientation session simply because it has been recommended by their therapist, whom they both trust and respect. In such cases, the mediator offers information about the mediation process and describes the divorce process. Issues likely to be discussed include the couple's thoughts or plans about separating, whether the children and extended families have been informed, and how they are thinking of handling child support. Couples typically sign a contract agreeing to the confidentiality of the process, stating that they will not ask the mediator to report to the court, should the mediation break down.

After the initial orientation, the couple and the mediator usually meet in sessions lasting longer than the typical therapeutic hour, often for 1½ or 2 hours. In cases in which all the issues related to the children, as well as finances, are to be mediated, the process typically involves five stages:

1. Orientation and introduction in which the mediator sets ground rules and begins to establish trust.
2. Gathering information when relevant data are discussed in an effort to clarify the goals and positions of the parties.
3. Framing the issues and developing options that will be resolved by negotiation, compromise, and mutual accommodation.
4. Reaching an initial settlement and drafting a tentative agreement for review and discussion with attorneys and, if appropriate, with the whole family.
5. Finalizing the agreement in court.

Over the first few sessions, couples are given guidance in listing and valuing all of their assets and debts. They each note their preferences, such as who wants or does not want to stay in their home. Often, after consulting an attorney or an accountant, couples determine together how they will divide their joint assets. Issues on which there is disagreement are negotiated throughout the process. It is not uncommon for a couple to "fight" over items that may be of little material worth but hold strong sentimental or symbolic value, such as a souvenir, a favorite lamp, or cookware. Custody of a pet may be at issue.

Often the disagreement is primarily a power struggle over control of resources, who wins and who loses, or who gets more or less than the other. One partner may feel "owed" for past grievances or for the partner's having initiated the divorce, or may withhold something valued by the other. One wife smashed her husband's guitar rather than let him keep it after learning of his extramarital affair. Sorting out these issues in mediation can deescalate destructive reactions. One couple fought bitterly over a cutting board until the end of negotiations, when the disagreement melted and one spouse delivered it to the other at the last mediation session.

Couples are also helped to plan postdivorce budgets, using current expenses as a guideline. Asked to determine how much money they will need to maintain a household at the same level as their current standard of living, they often discover that they have been unrealistic or that there is not enough money between them, and they will both need to cut back.

When fathers have been the sole provider, courts seldom award mothers and children more that 33–40% of the father's net income, disadvantaging custodial mothers. Recently, states have set child support guidelines either as a percentage of the noncustodial parent's net income or as a percentage of the family's joint income. Although these support guidelines were designed as a floor, they are often taken as a ceiling. In Illinois, for example, if a couple has two children, a noncustodial father would typically pay 25% of his net income as child support until the children reach age 18. Spousal maintenance, if awarded at all, is roughly an additional 10% and, seen as rehabilitative, is limited to 6 years. Consideration of college expenses is often neglected in decrees. Mediation is useful in redressing these issues.

Quite frequently, couples separate during the mediation process. It is emotionally very difficult for them to remain in the same residence once the decision to divorce has been made. Yet, either may be reluctant to move until the amount of support has been agreed upon. Attorneys sometimes advise their clients not to move out until the divorce is finalized, fearing that should the mediation fail, they will either jeopardize their case for joint custody or for being awarded the family home. However, when parents in the process of divorce are still living together, the intense emotional mix of grief, anger, or longing for reunion can become volatile and can be extremely confusing and upsetting for children. It can be helpful for mediators to suggest to attorneys that they draft a statement to the effect that neither client's case will be prejudiced by the move.

Partway through the mediation, the mediator might draw up the first draft of the couple's Memorandum of Understanding for discussion of questions and concerns in session. The mediator then recommends that the parties review the agreement with their respective attorneys. The following session can be bristly and difficult when attorneys tell their clients that they should be getting more than they are asking for. Clients can be forewarned that this is a predictable crisis, and it can usually be worked through successfully.

Once the mediation ends, couples are informed that they still need to have one of their attorneys draft the formal Dissolution of Marriage Agreement and have the other party's attorney review it. To empower both clients to maintain control of their divorce process, they are coached to tell their attorneys assertively that they prefer to return to mediation rather than have the attorneys discuss discrepancies in the agreement between themselves.

Mediation is a flexible process that can address any or all of the issues related to the dispute. Attorneys are most comfortable when mediation is used just for the nonfinancial issues related to the child custody and visitation. They frequently question a (non-attorney) mediator's ability to handle the finances. For some, this is a turf issue that may involve concerns about control, perceived competence, or loss of fees. Collaboration by a clinician/mediator requires sensitivity to these issues.

It is considered good practice in mediation to encourage all couples to consult separate attorneys while negotiating their agreement. Clients can negotiate more effectively with full knowledge of the law and court practices. Currently, attorneys in most states cannot represent both parties to a dispute. It is possible for one party to waive the right to legal representation in order to have one attorney handle the divorce for a couple, but the client should be apprised of the risk of his/her position not being adequately represented by foregoing separate legal counsel. Unless the parties choose to represent themselves, an attorney must translate the mediation agreement into legal terms and formalize it in court.

Postdecree Mediation

Mediation can be extremely useful, not only at the time of divorce, but as the need for review and change arises over time. After the legal divorce has been finalized, some issues can continue to be unresolved for ex-spouses and new issues are likely to arise over time. Many long-term complications over custody, visitation, and financial support stem from the adversarial legal system in divorce settlements or from rigid adherence to decisions that prove to be inequitable or no longer workable. There is likely to be difficulty when a child chooses to move from one household to the other, or when a parent wants to move out of state with the child. As families evolve and children grow older, their needs and interests change; their parenting arrangements may also need to change. When there is conflict, however, it can easily escalate to a legal dispute. Before mediation was introduced, the only arena in which to work out postdivorce conflicts was in the courts.

Postdecree mediation is more complex but is especially useful when former spouses are locked in old battles. When such couples are unable to resolve a dispute, it is not that they are incapable of thinking of a variety of ways of compromising, but rather that an underlying issue may not have been addressed. If these emotional blocks can be at least partially dealt with, ex-spouses are better able to resolve their dispute and move on with their lives. Both mediation and therapeutic skills are needed in such cases. Often, with a multilayered conflict, the mediator must work with both lawyers and therapists and should be aware of legal, emotional, and systemic dimensions of any case.

Dad's Girlfriend

One child's therapist and mother both reported that the girl was very anxious when at her father's home with his girlfriend in his absence. The father shrugged this off as insignificant and could only think how good it felt to have her run up and hug him when he walked in the door. His own intense needs to feel loved by her and to see himself as a good parent blocked awareness of her concerns. The mediator collaborated with the daughter's therapist, who helped the daughter express her concerns more directly to her father and helped him to see that he could better achieve his aims by more sensitive consideration of her needs. It was also important to address the mother's feelings about her ex-husband's new relationship and her fears of losing her daughter's affections to the other woman. A child tunes in to such feelings and may express loyalty through misbehavior with the "replacement." Such triangles need to be addressed for resolution of the dispute.

There are many sources of impasse in post-divorce disputes (Jacob, 1991), such as: (1) inflexibility, (2) inability to effectively problem solve, (3) competition with the ex-spouse over who is the better parent, (4) need for punishment or retribution of the ex-spouse for perceived grievances, (5) inability to separate a child's needs from one's own, and (6) a traumatic response to loss or separation.

Some ex-spouses remain fixed in the last pattern or way of communicating that they had known and have been fighting since divorce papers were filed. They have not developed an effective postdivorce style of problem solving. Typically, these individuals feel powerless, mistakenly assuming that the other has all the power when, in fact, without some cooperation, neither of them has much power. In most instances, when two people are fighting, they both have the option of refusing to engage in the conflict, although they are seldom aware of this, and instead, tend to blame each other and feel helpless. Except in cases of serious abuse, unprovoked violence, or threatened harm toward an ex-spouse, both individuals have the power to end the conflict, and can be helped in mediation to do so.

It is helpful in postdivorce disputes to see all adults involved in parenting, such as a stepparent or a grandparent in the home. The most useful sequence is to begin with the parents together for one session, for it is their dispute and they need to be treated equally. It should be clearly framed for the parents and children that the purpose of meeting jointly is to work out better postdivorce relations, and not to reunite the former family or rehash of old grievances. The parents are then each seen separately and subsequently, with their current partners or spouses. After this, when necessary, children or grandparents can be seen. It is in these various sessions that the issues needing to be negotiated emerge.

Postdecree cases tend to take from three to six meetings. A relatively uncomplicated situation might require an initial joint meeting, then a session with each party individually or with a current partner, and one joint meeting to work out differences. The following case, which initially appeared complicated, worked easily, quickly, and well in mediation.

Who's in Control

Francine requested mediation, seeking more time with her son who lived with his father and stepmother. She had been unable to negotiate an acceptable schedule despite repeated attempts. Jeff,

age 8, had lived with his father since the marital breakup when he was 5. A year later, his father remarried, to a woman with two children of her own.

When the mediator suggested that Francine and her ex-husband, Tom, come in for the first meeting, Francine said that she preferred including his wife, Tina, who seemed to make all the decisions in that household. At the joint meeting, Tina explained that she and Tom could not be flexible with scheduling for Jeff because Tina's two children spent alternate weekends with their father in a schedule that was almost never changed. Tina insisted that she needed to coordinate the two schedules; otherwise she and Tom would never have any time alone.

In the individual meeting with Francine, the mediator listened to her frustration with her ex-husband's passivity. Francine insisted that he, not Tina, should be in charge of their son. The mediator agreed that this would be preferable, but asked if she realistically thought it would happen. Francine shrugged, admitting she was most upset that he always deferred to his new wife, when he had never accommodated to her needs. The mediator acknowledged her frustration, noting that she seemed to be still trying to change her ex-husband. Francine laughed, agreed, and realized that she needed to give that up and focus on a schedule that would work for all of them. An acceptable compromise was worked out in the next three-way meeting.

In a more complex situation, for instance, if Tina's ex-husband's rigidity precluded compromise, there might be additional individual and joint sessions with involved persons, or even telephone conversations with attorneys. Although postdecree disputes can be difficult, it is possible to tease apart the issues and emotions in order to achieve a workable solution. In some cases it is useful to have follow-up sessions, either regularly scheduled or as needed. It is also helpful for parties to agree that in the future, if either of them feels that a mediation session would be helpful, they will both come in for at least one session.

Roles and Skills of the Mediator

The mediator plays several roles with couples: at times a problem solver, an educator, a therapist, and a child advocate (Jacob, 1991). In each of these roles, the mediator, while working on behalf of both partners ending the marriage, should always uphold the best interests of the child. The mediator can teach parents about normal postdivorce parenting and difficulties that children typically have, such as the importance of not having children carry messages between the parents, and coaching them on how to help children talk about the divorce and their fear of losing one or both parents. Helping parents and stepparents appreciate the universality of loyalty conflicts and replacement issues can facilitate better ways to recognize the divorce or remarriage while respecting the continuity of parent–child bonds. In addition to teaching parenting and stepparenting skills, the mediator can recommend books, classes, support groups, and, when needed, therapists.

Underlying assumptions in mediation include honesty, openness, fairness, and the ability to keep an agreement on the part of both clients. Good mediation depends on at least some degree of justice and good will between them. Mediators need to be aware that both parties may not enter negotiation on a level playing field if the relationship is skewed in power and entitlement. A mediator's neutral stance may unwittingly reinforce an unfair or inequitable contract when a more flexible or intimidated spouse accommodates the more rigid, controlling one. It is important to be mindful of socially constructed gender imbalances in any negotiation process, whereby women are raised to defer to men, who are socialized to be more assertive negotiators on their own behalf (Walsh, 1989).

Although mediators are often described as neutral, more accurately, they need to be balanced, fair, and bipartial. They must weave back and forth between potential adversaries to make sure that each is heard and both reach an equitable settlement. At times in the process, a mediator may take the part of the less powerful, or more emotionally reactive, person to negotiate a particular issue. There are subtle shifts within a session as the mediator shapes the process and moves a couple toward agreement (Rifkin, Millen, & Cobb, 1991).

There are limits to mediation. If a client is untrustworthy and lies, hides assets, or refuses to keep to an agreement, the mediation should be terminated. Mediation may not be workable if a client is sociopathic or seriously distorts a reality situation, or when power is so skewed that one partner bullies or blackmails the other, who may be too fragile or frightened and accommodates to end conflict. Some experts in domestic violence believe that mediation should never be attempted when abuse has ever occurred or is a significant risk (*Mediation in Cases of Domestic*

Abuse, 1992). There is consensus that in cases of serious, ongoing abuse, mediation is contraindicated. In recent years, efforts at dialogue and collaboration have increased among mediators and women's advocates to address the benefits and risks associated with mediation and the unique needs of abused women.

Although it is useful for a mediator to have therapeutic skills, it should be emphasized that mediation is not therapy. Blurring the boundaries can be very confusing for clients (Kelly, 1983). Nonetheless, an important part of the mediator's role is to create a safe place where the disputants can come together and be heard in a respectful way. To be effective, a mediator must be comfortable with conflict and able to manage it. There are a variety of techniques for controlling conflict, such as having both parties talk to the mediator rather than to each other and, when necessary, working individually (in caucus) with both individuals, a go-between process sometimes referred to as "shuttle diplomacy." It is important not to permit blaming or name calling. Clients are coached to assert their own positions rather than speak for each other or take a reactive stance. It is suggested that they can change only one person—themselves. Yet, in doing so, they will alter negative cycles of interaction that will free them up to move on with their lives. It is most important to focus on the future rather than the past.

DIVORCE INTERVENTIONS IN CONTEXT

As therapists, we need to be aware of how our own assumptions and biases about family health and normality—based on clinical theory, personal experience, and cultural norms—influence our work with people considering divorce and those reorienting their lives in its aftermath (Walsh, 1993). We also need to examine how the hierarchical systems encountered by people in this process may foster stigma, alienation, and polarization. Our interventions should be conducted in ways that reduce these destructive tendencies and offer nonjudgmental, collaborative means to carry out the divorce process. In this context, conjoint therapy and mediation offer a constructive coming together in order to separate amicably.

Language, Beliefs, and Practice

Our language, influenced by socially constructed beliefs, in turn influences our clinical vision and practice with couples undergoing divorce (Walsh, 1991). Traditionally, the stigmatizing label "divorcee" connoted personal failure and disgrace. The use of the term "single-parent family" for both never-married and divorced sole-parent households has confounded quite different family situations and led to nonsystemic clinical intervention. Since the label is generally applied to the custodial parent (usually the mother), the noncustodial parent (usually the father) is left without designation, rendering his involvement invisible. Moreover, the label "single parent" narrows focus to the primary residential parent and ignores the ongoing or potential coparental relationship.

For divorced families with coparenting arrangements, Ahrons (Ahrons & Rodgers, 1987) has coined the term "binuclear family," that better describes and promotes the continuity of parent–child and coparenting relationships when children live part-time in two separate households. Yet, even this term poses a dilemma when parents remarry to partners who also have children from previous marriages, creating family systems that are "trinuclear" or even "quadrinuclear." (Walsh, 1991).

Where ex-spouses are unable to collaborate in "coparenting," the term "primary parent" is preferable. In the skewed situation experienced in the majority of postdivorced families, mothers head the primary residence and carry the bulk of responsibilities, while paternal contact and support may diminish over time. The term "primary parent" clarifies this arrangement, implying a secondary or backup role of the noncustodial parent, unlike the misnomer "single parent."

The term "single-parent family" is more appropriate when one parent carries all parental obligations and ongoing involvement, or when support by the other parent is precluded, as in widowhood, abandonment, or cases of serious abuse. For many families, the term "single parent" reflects the reality of a father's cutoff position and his failure to provide ongoing financial and emotional support to his children. On the one hand, we need to be cautious not to accept the stereotype that single-parent households are inherently dysfunctional without the leadership role of the father. At the same time, we must be careful that use of the label "single parent" does not reinforce a dysfunctional cutoff that may be reparable. In order to ameliorate a mother's overburden and to support the well-being of children, it may be crucial to bring the father from the periphery of the frame into focus for clinical assessment and intervention. In most cases children adjust best when both parents can remain involved with their children and cooperate in childrearing.

Moreover, we need to be careful that the term "single-parent household" not blind us to current influences and potential resources in the household and relational network, especially grandparents, other extended family members, a new partner, or a housemate, who share expenses and mutual child-care responsibilities. A systems perspective is essential for assessment and intervention.

With divorce and remarriage, the inherent ambiguity and changing nature of family boundaries, membership, and roles over time defy easy definition. Our kinship labels for remarried families also are inadequate and carry negative connotations, such as the "wicked stepmother." Even the term "step" implies a more distant and less "natural" relationship than with the "real" parent. Because the term "blended" family suggests greater integration than is realistic, we prefer the term "remarried family" "to emphasize that it is the marital bond that forms the basis for the complex arrangement of several families in a new constellation" (McGoldrick & Carter, 1989, p. 400).

Individual, Conjoint, and Combined Modalities

Thinking and working systemically with couple issues through the divorce process requires flexibility in our intervention approaches to fit the changing needs of clients over the long-term course of adaptation. A systems perspective keeps us sensitive to multiple considerations in determining when individual or conjoint sessions are most appropriate and how they can be combined effectively. For instance, when individual therapy is being conducted in the context of a marital relationship at risk, it may inadvertently contribute to problems of secrecy and separateness and the development of a new self-definition not shared with the partner. The special private, empathic relationship with the therapist may, like an extramarital affair, provide gratification that can further cause alienation from the marital partner.

Although Kitson and Holmes (1992) found that couple therapy is very helpful before the divorce is obtained, couples often do not seek therapy at this point. Those who are in therapy may withdraw altogether at the point when divorce is seriously considered. They may take a period to just live through the numerous adjustments. At other times, they may request individual sessions or be referred to other alternatives, such as divorce adjustment groups.

Some couple therapists who have been working to save a marriage, may feel a sense of failure, along with the couple, and discontinue contact at their decision to separate. Some therapists will continue to work on the marriage during a period of separation. However, most separated couples remain permanently separated or go on to divorce. Couple therapists need to feel comfortable shifting gears, from investment in the marriage to helping the couple end their relationship or recommending mediation. It is not advisable in most cases to switch from couple therapy to individual therapy with one partner at that time, which may be perceived as a coalition against the other partner and complicate or preclude further couple work. It is preferable to refer clients to another therapist for the individual work. There are times when a therapist can work collaboratively with a divorce mediator who takes the couple through the negotiations to a settlement, while the therapist focuses on personal needs and emotional resolution of the divorce. In later postdivorce disputes or child-focused problems, time-limited focused conjoint sessions may be held, including any new partners.

FACILITATING LONG-TERM ADAPTATION

In summary, postdivorce processes involve a number of developmental steps and psychosocial tasks. The intensity of feelings associated with the dissolution of the former marriage is reactivated and must be dealt with at each successive step, including the separation and divorce, the remarriage of either spouse, shifts in custody, changes in residence of either spouse, illness or death of the ex-spouse, and life-cycle transitions of the children (graduations, marriage, illness).

A number of variables must be kept in mind in helping a family achieve a functional postdivorce arrangement. It is not divorce, per se, but a problem divorce, in which transitional tasks were not accomplished, that holds particular jeopardy for long-term adjustment. In fact, the tremendous diversity in postdivorce adjustment should be underscored. Emerging research reveals that most children and their families do fairly well after divorce and some demonstrate remarkable resilience. Our task as researchers and clinicians is to identify and support the crucial

processes that facilitate resilience and long-term adaptation (Vemer, Coleman, Ganong, & Cooper, 1989; Walsh, in press).

Rituals are powerful experiences in the acknowledgement and integration of divorce and remarriage events (Imber-Black, 1988; Whiteside, 1988). Our culture lacks established patterns and rituals to assist in these difficult transitions, making individual adjustment and reconstruction of complex relationship networks all the more difficult. Divorce and remarriage rituals are especially valuable in sharing the realities of loss, change, and reinvestment, in marking the structural shifts, and in facilitating movement forward in the life course. As life moves on, weaving together practices from previous family traditions and creating new patterns, from dinnertime rituals to major holidays, helps to establish a sense of cohesion and continuity.

The important issues for research and clinical practice are threefold. First, we need to specify the normative challenges and tasks associated with the establishment and viability of postdivorce structures. Second, we need to identify the mediating variables that differentiate successful adaptation and dysfunction through transitional processes, relative to varying socioeconomic, cultural, and life-cycle imperatives. Third, we need to develop strategies and methods that are most effective for dealing with these issues in clinical practice. Regardless of the dynamics operating in any particular family, divorce processes are major disruptions in the family system that generate a series of changes in structure and relationships. Each requires a fundamental shift in how the family functions and how members define "normal family life." Increasingly, we are advancing beyond the deficit view of divorce, single-parent households, and remarriage, to examine their strengths and resources and their potential for individual and relational growth. The predictability of transitional upheaval underscores the importance of early interventions aimed at facilitating *legal* and *emotional* divorce processes.

REFERENCES

Abelsohn, D. (1992). A "good enough" separation: Some characteristic operations and tasks. *Family Process, 31,* 61–83.

Ahrons, C. (1994). *The good divorce.* New York: HarperCollins.

Ahrons, C., & Rodgers, R. (1987). *Divorced families: Meeting the challenge of divorce and remarriage.* New York: Norton.

Amato, P. R., & Keith, B. (1991a). Parental divorce and the well-being of children: A meta-analysis. *Psychological Bulletin*, 110, 26–46.

Amato, P. R., & Keith, B. (1991b). Parental divorce and adult well-being: A meta-analysis. *Journal of Marriage and the Family*, 53, 43–58.

Boss, P. (1991). Ambiguous loss. In F. Walsh & M. McGoldrick (Eds.), *Living beyond loss: Death in the family*. New York: Norton.

Bray, J. (1992). Family relationships and children's adjustment in clinical and nonclinical stepfather families. *Journal of Family Psychology*, 6, 60–68.

Bray, J. & Hetherington, E.M. (1993). Families in transition: Introduction and overview. *Journal of Family Psychology*. 7, 3–8.

Brown, D. G. (1982). Divorce and family mediation: History, review, future directions. *Conciliation Courts Review*, 20, 1–44.

Camera, K. A., & Resnick, G. (1988). Interparental conflict and cooperation: Factors moderating children's post-divorce adjustment. In E. M. Hetherington & J. D. Arasteh (Eds.), *Impact of divorce, single-parenting and stepparenting on children*. Hillsdale, NJ: Erhbaum.

Castro Martin, T., & Bumpass, L. (1989). Recent trends and differentials in marital disruption. *Demography*, 26, 37–51.

Cherlin, A. (1992). *Marriage, divorce, remarriage* (rev. ed). Cambridge, MA: Harvard University Press.

Combs, G., & Freedman, J. (1990). *Symbol, story, and ceremony*. New York: Norton.

Depner, C., & Bray, J. (Eds.). (1993). *Nonresidential parenting: New vistas in family living*. Newbury Park, CA: Sage.

Fowlers, B., & Olson, D.H. (1986). Predicting marital success with PREPARE: A predictive validity study. *Journal of Marital and Family Therapy*, 12, 403–413.

Fowlers, B. J., & Olson, D. H. (1989). The ENRICH marital inventory: A discriminant validity and cross-validation assessment. *Journal of Marital and Family Therapy*, 15, 65–79.

Furstenberg, F. (1990). Divorce and the American family. *Annual Review of Sociology*, 16, 379–403.

Furstenberg, F., & Cherlin, A. (1991). *Divided families: What happens to children when parents part*. Cambridge, MA: Harvard University Press.

Glick, P. (1989). Remarried families, stepfamilies, and stepchildren: A brief demographic profile. *Family Relations*, 38, 24–27.

Glick, P., & Lin, S. (1986). Recent changes in divorce and remarriage. *Journal of Marriage and the Family*, 48, 433–441.

Gottman, J. (1991). Predicting the longitudinal course of marriages. *Journal of Marital and Family Therapy*, 17, 3–7.

Gottman, J. (1993). A theory of marital dissolution and stability. *Journal of Family Psychology*, 7, 57–75.

Gulliver, P. H. (1973). Negotiations as a mode of dispute settlement: Toward a general model. *Law and Society Review*, 7, 667–691.

Herz, F. (1989). The postdivorce family. In B. Carter & M. McGoldrick (Eds.), *The changing family life cycle*. Boston: Allyn & Bacon.

Hetherington, E. M., & Tryon, A. S. (1989). His and her divorces. *Family Therapy Networker*, 13, 58–61.

Hetherington, E. M., Law, T. C., & O'Connor, T. G. (1993). Divorce: Challenges, changes, and new chances. In F. Walsh (Ed.), *Normal family processes* (2nd. ed.). New York: Guilford Press.

Imber-Black, E. (1988). Normative and therapeutic rituals in couples therapy. In E. Imber-Black, J. Roberts, & R. Whiting (Eds.), *Rituals in families and family therapy*. New York: Norton.

Isaacs, M., Montalvo, B., & Abelsohn, D. (1986). *The difficult divorce*. New York: Basic Books.

Jacob, L. C. (1991). Mediating postdecree disputes. *Mediation Quarterly*, 8, 171–183.

Johnston, J. R., & Campbell, L.E.G. (1988). *Impasses of divorce: The dynamics and resolution of family conflict*. New York: Free Press.

Kelly, J. (1983). Mediation and psychotherapy: Distinguishing the differences. *Mediation Quarterly*, 1, 33–44.

Kitson, G. C., & Holmes, W. A. (1992). *Portrait of divorce: Adjustment to marital breakdown*. New York: Guilford Press.

Kline, M., Johnston, J. R., & Tschann, J. (1991). The long shadow of marital conflict: A model of postdivorce adjustment. *Journal of Marriage and the Family*, 53, 297–309.

Laird, J. (1993). Lesbian and gay families. In F. Walsh (Ed.), *Normal family processes* (2nd. ed.). New York: Guilford Press.

Larsen, A. S., & Olson, D. H. (1989). Predicting marital satisfaction using PREPARE: A repilcation study. *Journal of Marital and Family Therapy*, 15, 313–324.

Lerman, L., Kuehl, S., & Brygger, M. (1989). *Domestic abuse and mediation: Guidelines for mediators and policy makers*. Washington, DC: National Women Abuse Prevention Project.

Lindblad-Goldberg, M. (1989). Successful minority single-parent families. In L. Combrinck-Graham (Ed.), *Children in family contexts: Perspectives on treatment*. New York: Guilford Press.

Maccoby, E., Buchanan, C., Mnookin, R., & Dornbusch, S. (1993). Postdivorce roles of mothers and fathers in the lives of their children. *Journal of Family Psychology*, 7, 24–38.

Maccoby, E., & Mnookin, R. (1992). *Dividing the child:*

Social and legal dilemmas of custody. Cambridge, MA: Harvard University Press.

McGoldrick, M., Anderson, C., & Walsh, F. (Eds.). (1989). *Women in families: Framework for family therapy.* New York: Norton.

McGoldrick, M., & Carter, B. (1989). Forming a remarried family. In B. Carter & M. McGoldrick (Eds.), *The changing family life cycle: Framework for family therapy.* Boston: Allyn & Bacon.

McGoldrick, M., & Gerson, R. (1985). *Genograms in family assessment.* New York: Norton.

Mediation in cases of domestic abuse: Helpful options or unacceptable risk? (1992). Final Report of the State of Maine Domestic Abuse and Mediation Project. Golden Valley, MN: Academy of Family Mediators.

Rolland, J. S. (1994). *Families, illness, and disability: A biopsychosocial model.* New York: Basic Books.

Rifkin, J., Millen, J., & Cobb, S. (1991). Toward a new discourse for mediation: A critique of neutrality. *Mediation Quarterly, 9,* 151–164.

Seltzer, J. A. (1991). Relationships between fathers and children who live apart: The father's role after separation. *Journal of Marriage and the Family, 53,* 79–101.

Skolnick, A. (1991). *Embattled paradise: The American family in an age of uncertainty.* New York: Basic Books.

Tomm, K. (1987). Interventive interviewing. Part II: Reflexive questioning as a means to enable self-healing. *Family Process, 26,* 167–183.

Vaughan, D. (1990). *Uncoupling: Turning points in intimate relationships.* New York: Random House.

Vemer, E., Coleman, M., Ganong, L., & Cooper, H. (1989). Marital satisfaction in remarriage: A meta-analysis. *Journal of Marriage and the Family, 51,* 713–735.

Visher, E., & Visher, J. (1988). *Old loyalties, new ties: Therapeutic strategies with step-families.* New York: Brunner/Mazel.

Visher, E. B., & Visher, J. S. (1993). Remarriage families and stepparenting. In F. Walsh (Ed.), *Normal family processes* (2nd. ed.), New York: Guilford Press.

Wallerstein, J., & Blakeslee, S. (1989). *Second chances: Men, women, and children a decade after divorce.* New York: Ticknor & Fields.

Wallerstein, J., & Kelly, J. B. (1980). *Surviving the breakup: How children and parents cope with divorce.* New York: Basic Books.

Walsh, F. (1989). Re-examining gender in the "marital quid pro quo". In M. McGoldrick, C. Anderson, & F. Walsh (Eds.), *Women in families: Framework for family therapy.* New York: Norton.

Walsh, F. (1991). Promoting healthy functioning in divorced and remarried families. In A. Gurman & D. Kniskern (Eds.), *Handbook of family therapy* (Vol. 2). New York: Brunner/Mazel.

Walsh, F. (1992). Beyond the myth of "the normal family" (Plenary address, 50th Anniversary Meeting). *Monograph of the American Association for Marriage and Family Therapy.* Washington, DC: AAMFT Publications.

Walsh, F. (1993). Conceptualization of normal family processes. In F. Walsh (Ed.), *Normal family processes* (2nd ed.). New York: Guilford Press.

Walsh, F. (in press). *Strengthening family resilience.* New York: Guilford Press.

Walsh, F., & McGoldrick, M. (Eds.). (1991). *Living beyond loss.* New York: Norton.

Weiss, R. (1975). *Marital separation.* New York: Basic Books.

Weitzman, L. (1985). *The divorce revolution.* New York: Free Press.

White, M., & Epston, D. (1990). *Narrative means to therapeutic ends.* New York: Norton.

Whiteside, M. (1982). Remarriage: A family developmental process. *Journal of Marital and Family Therapy, 8,* 59–68.

III

COUPLE THERAPY AND COMMON PSYCHIATRIC DISORDERS

18

Marital Therapy in the Treatment of Alcohol Problems

BARBARA S. McCRADY
ELIZABETH E. EPSTEIN

T HE 1990s ALCOHOLISM literature is filled with books on codependency, adult children of alcoholics, adult grandchildren of alcoholics, enablers, recovering alcoholics, chemically dependent people, and addictive personalities. In 1990, at least 21 books on codependency alone covered bookstore shelves (Kaminer, 1990), and undoubtedly many more have been published since. Self-help groups for family members of addicts abound in every community, and popular language embraces the terminology of addiction and codependency. In this chapter, we provide a different way to think about alcohol problems and relationships that is grounded in a scientific psychology and that provides an alternative to the popular psychology of addictions dominating American culture in the late 20th century. In the chapter, we present a model for conceptualizing and treating alcoholics and their partners, and then address clinical techniques and issues in the implementation of our treatment model.

MARITAL DISTRESS AND ITS RELATIONSHIP TO ALCOHOL PROBLEMS

Definitions and Diagnosis of Alcohol Problems

Before considering the relationships between marital functioning and drinking problems, it is important to consider the nature of drinking problems themselves. Contemporary approaches to the diagnosis of alcohol problems focus on a hypothetical construct, the "alcohol dependence syndrome" (Edwards & Gross, 1976), which is a constellation of behavior patterns and problems resulting from drinking. The diagnosis of alcohol problems in the fourth edition of the *Diagnostic and Statistical Manual of Mental Disorders* (DSM-IV; American Psychiatric Association, 1987) is based on the alcohol dependence syndrome. Thus, in addition to organically based alcohol-related problems, two primary alcohol diagnoses are included: alcohol dependence and alcohol abuse. To be diagnosed as alcohol dependent, an individual must meet at least three of seven criteria that relate to loss of control, physical tolerance and withdrawal, unsuccessful attempts to cut down, excessive time spent in drinking or recovering from drinking, interference of alcohol with functioning, and use of alcohol despite knowledge of physical or psychological problems related to alcohol use. Alcohol dependence may be with or without physiological dependence. In contrast, alcohol abuse is diagnosed based on problem use, including drinking resulting in failure to fulfill major social roles, drinking repeatedly in a manner that creates the potential for harm (such as drinking and driving), recurrent alcohol-related legal problems, or continuing to drink despite known social or interpersonal problems caused by drinking.

In contrast to the formal psychiatric diagnosis of alcohol dependence, behavioral researchers and clinicians have suggested that alcohol problems are part of the continuum of drinking that ranges from abstinence, to nonproblem use, to different types of problem use. From this perspective, problems may be exhibited in a variety of forms, some of which are consistent with a formal diagnosis, and some of which are milder or more intermittent. Babor, Kranzler, and Lauerman (1989) have suggested that persons with drinking problems be classified as vulnerable drinkers, hazardous drinkers, or harmful drinkers. Vulnerable drinkers are those persons whose current drinking does not create any harm to self or others, but who, because of family history or other vulnerabilities, are at particularly high risk for developing alcohol problems. Hazardous drinkers are those whose current drinking creates current or potential hazards in their lives or the lives of others. Harmful drinkers have begun to experience serious negative consequences of their alcohol use, or their pattern of use has become stereotypic and repetitive.

The alcohol problems perspective exemplified by Babor and behavioral researchers stands in contrast to the psychiatric diagnostic approach of DSM-IV. The alcohol problems perspective makes no a priori assumption that certain symptoms constellate together, nor does it assume an underlying syndrome or disease state. The alcohol problems perspective does not exclude the possibility of a syndrome, it just does not assume its existence. The psychiatric diagnostic approach assumes some underlying pathology that drives the observed symptoms. Our treatment model uses an alcohol problems perspective, working with the behaviors presented by the couple, but can be used with clients who hold a disease perspective on their own drinking if they can accept that changing their behavior is necessary to controlling the disease.

The alcohol problems perspective does create semantic difficulties that have not been addressed satisfactorily. Willoughby (1979) has suggested "alcohol-troubled person" as a neutral descriptive term. "Problem drinker" has been suggested as well, but may be misconstrued as referring only to those with less serious alcohol problems. We prefer the phrase "alcohol problem" or "person with an alcohol problem," but both of these are cumbersome in written and spoken language. Over time, the terms "alcoholism" and "alcoholic" have been sustained because of their simplicity, but these terms imply a syndromal model of drinking problems. For linguistic simplicity, we use both "alcoholic" and "person with an alcohol problem" interchangeably in this chapter, but the reader should not assume that we are assuming any particular syndrome associated with the terminology—rather, we are referring to persons who experience drinking-related problems of varying degrees of severity.

Interrelationships between Marital Functioning and Alcohol Problems

Theoretical Perspectives on the Relationship between Drinking and Family Functioning

Drinking and the marital relationship are often so closely bound that clinicians have referred to the "alcoholic marriage" (e.g., Paolino & McCrady, 1977). Early theoretical models suggested that women married alcoholic men as a defense against neurotic conflicts with control or dependency. These models suggested that wives of alcoholics needed their partners to continue to drink in order to avoid more serious decompensation themselves (e.g., Lewis, 1937; Whalen, 1953). These early psychodynamic models firmly placed responsibility for the alcoholic's continued drinking in the hands of the disturbed spouse. Sociological perspectives, predominant in the 1950s and '60s, viewed the spouse as responding to the chronic stress introduced by living with an alcoholic partner (e.g., Jackson, 1954), placing responsibility for the problems of the family with the alcoholic rather than with the spouse. Family systems models, predominant in the 1970s and '80s, emphasized the homeostatic balance between drinking and family functioning, hypothesizing that drinking stabilized the family system and allowed for the expression of certain facets of family relationships that could not be expressed during sober periods (e.g., Steinglass, Wolin, Bennett, & Reiss, 1987).

Theoretical Model of Problem Drinking and the Family

Our theoretical model draws from sociological, family systems, and behavioral models. We conceptualize many behaviors of the spouse of an alcoholic as attempts to cope with a difficult situation, but we also emphasize the reciprocal interactions between spouse and alcoholic behavior in determining repetitive and dysfunctional interaction patterns. Most generally, we use a social learning framework to conceptualize drinking problems and family functioning. The model assumes that drinking can best be treated by examining current factors that maintain the drinking, rather than historical factors. Factors that maintain the drinking can be nondyadic and/or rooted in the interpersonal relationship. The model assumes external antecedents to drinking that have a lawful relationship to drinking, through repeated pairings with positive or negative reinforcement or through the anticipation of reinforcement. The model assumes that cognitions and affective states mediate the relationship between external antecedents and drinking behavior, and that expectancies about the reinforcing value of alcohol play an important role in determining subsequent drinking behavior. Finally, the model assumes that drinking is maintained by its consequences, and that these consequences may occur at a physiological, individual psychological, or interpersonal level.

To integrate these assumptions into a model for conceptualizing drinking, we use an S-O-R-C model that conceptualizes the drinking *response* (R) as elicited by environmental *stimuli* (S) which occur antecedent to drinking, mediated by cognitive, affective, and physiological *organismic* (O) factors, and maintained by positive *consequences* (C) of drinking.

A variety of individual, familial, and other interpersonal factors may be associated with drinking. At the individual level, environmental antecedents may be associated with specific drinking situations, times of the day, or the mere sight or smell of alcohol. Organismic variables may include craving for alcohol; withdrawal symptoms; negative affects such as anger, anxiety or depression; negative self-evaluations or irrational beliefs; or positive expectancies about the effects of alcohol in particular situations. Individual reinforcers may include decreased craving or withdrawal symptoms, decreases in negative affect or increases in positive affect, decreased negative self-evaluations, or being able to forget problems.

At the familial level, a variety of antecedents to drinking occur. Alcohol is integral to many families, and may be a usual part of family celebrations or daily rituals (such as a shared cocktail before dinner). Family members may engage in a variety of attempts to influence the drinker's behavior, such as nagging him/her to stop drinking, or attempting to control the drinking through control of the finances or the liquor supply. Families in which alcohol problems are present often have evolved poor patterns of

communication and problem solving, and develop a variety of marital, sexual, financial, and childrearing problems over time. All of these can serve as antecedents to further drinking. The drinker may have a range of reactions to these familial antecedents, experiencing negative affect, low self-efficacy for coping with problems, or retaliatory thoughts (such as "She's not going to control me!").

Positive consequences of drinking may also come from the family. For example, families often engage in caretaking of the drinker, cleaning up after him/her, covering at work, or being particularly gentle and nonconfrontational during drinking episodes. Although these behaviors can be understood as normal reactions when a family member is sick, such behavior in alcoholic families may serve to reinforce drinking. A number of investigators have observed positive changes in marital interactions associated with drinking, suggesting that drinking may be reinforced by its positive marital consequences (e.g., Billings, Kessler, Gomberg, & Weiner, 1979; Frankenstein, Hay, & Nathan, 1985).

Families also provide a number of negative consequences for drinking. These include withdrawal from and avoidance of the drinker, negative verbal comments about the drinking (either during or after a drinking episode), and, in some families, physical violence directed at the drinker. These negative consequences, instead of suppressing the drinking, usually have two undesired effects. First, the drinker begins to avoid interactions with the family when drinking, or tries to hide the drinking. In some couples, hiding the drinking leads to a pattern of interactions characterized by avoidance of negative interactions and lying by the drinker, and hypervigilance on the part of the spouse. Second, negative consequences from family members often serve as cues to further drinking, thus maintaining a complex circular interaction between the drinking and family interactions.

Drinking also has a number of negative effects on the functioning of the family. Spouses of alcoholics are more likely to experience psychological or physical problems (Moos, Finney, & Gamble, 1982). Children growing up with an alcoholic parent experience a variety of psychological, behavioral, and school problems (Moos & Moos, 1984) and are at increased risk for developing drinking problems themselves (Cloninger, Bohman, & Sigvardsson, 1981). The role of alcohol in familial violence is somewhat unclear, but some studies suggest an increased incidence of spousal violence but not an increased incidence of child abuse among alcoholic men (U.S. Department of Health and Human Services, 1983). More generally, the decreased functioning of the drinking partner may place increased role responsibilities on the other members of the family, often leading to role overload for the nonalcoholic partner. The behavior of the drinker may be less predictable, and the drinking itself may interfere with effective communication and problem-solving between the partners. (The couple may also have communication and problem solving deficits that predate the drinking problem, but no research to date has been able to discriminate between preexisting communication problems and alcohol-related marital problems.)

Other interpersonal antecedents to drinking also occur. These may revolve around social pressures to drink, work-related drinking situations, friendships in which alcohol consumption plays a major role, or interpersonal conflicts with work associates, friends, or acquaintances. The drinker may react to interpersonal antecedents to drinking with craving, positive expectancies for alcohol use, social discomfort, or negative self-evaluations for not drinking. Positive interpersonal consequences of drinking may include decreased craving or social anxiety, or increased social comfort or assertiveness.

In summary, our model assumes that the drinking behavior of the alcoholic or problem drinker is embedded in a complex network of factors relating to the individual physiology and psychology of the drinker, the family, and other social networks. In each component of the network, there is a reciprocal relationship between the drinking and the functioning of network—the drinker's behavior influences the social network and is influenced by it.

Nondyadic Factors Contributing to Etiology and Maintenance of Alcohol Problems

In addition to the general individual psychological factors noted previously, there are a number of important nondyadic factors that contribute to the etiology and maintenance of alcohol problems. First, there is fairly strong evidence for the familial transmission of more severe forms of drinking problems (Cloninger et al., 1981). Persons with an alcoholic parent are at increased risk for developing alcoholism, particularly males with a male alcoholic parent. Risk of familial transmission is increased even among offspring who are not raised by their biological parents. It should be emphasized, however, that the risk

of developing an alcohol problem, given an alcoholic parent, is not high (Fingarette, 1988), even though that risk is greater than that of a person without alcoholism in the family.

A second important individual factor in conceptualizing alcohol problems is the comorbidity of alcoholism with other psychiatric disorders. Research has shown that a high percentage of alcoholics suffer from other psychiatric problems, which are either concurrent with, antecedent to, or resulting from their alcohol problem (Hasin, Grant, & Endicott, 1988; Hesselbrock, Meyer, & Keener, 1985; Ross, Glaser, & Germanson, 1988; Schuckit, 1985). The most common comorbid Axis I disorders, aside from drug abuse, are depression and anxiety disorders. For men, Ross et al. (1988a, 1988b) found a 23% lifetime prevalence rate of primary depression, 17% for dysthymia, and 60% for anxiety disorders. Ross and her colleagues found lifetime prevalences of 35% for affective disorders and 67% for anxiety disorders in women. Hasin et al. (1988) and Schuckit (1985) have reported that up to 60% of male alcoholics can manifest a major depression that is secondary to alcohol abuse. A secondary depression is likely to lift shortly (within a few weeks, less often after 2–3 months) after abstinence is achieved. The most common comorbid Axis II disorder found with alcoholism in males is antisocial personality disorder. Rates ranging from 20% to 50% have been cited (Hesselbrock et al., 1985; Read et al., 1990; Ross et al., 1988b). Females more often present with depressive disorders than with Axis II disorders.

A third important set of nondyadic factors affecting the etiology and maintenance of drinking revolve around interactions with the families of origin of both the drinker and the marital partner. Bennett and Wolin (1990) have reported a strong association between continuing interactions between offspring of alcoholics and their parents, and the probability of developing alcoholism in the offspring: that is, if an adult male who grew up in an alcoholic family continues to have contact with that family, he is more likely to develop drinking problems himself. Additionally, if there was alcoholism in his wife's family, and they continue to have contact with her family, his risk of developing alcoholism is also significantly increased.

In summary, the etiology of alcoholism is embedded in a psychological as well as genetic web, and the continuing interactions between the generations contribute to the risk for developing alcohol problems.

THEORY OF
THERAPEUTIC CHANGE

How Treatment Follows
from the Model of Dysfunction

Our model for conceptualizing drinking problems necessitates our intervening at multiple levels — with the individual, the spouse, the relationship as a unit, the family, and the other social systems in which the drinker is involved. Implicit in the model is the need for detailed assessment to determine the primary factors contributing to the maintenance of the drinking, the skills and deficits of the individual and the couple, and the sources of motivation to change (i.e., what potential reinforcers could maintain changes in drinking behavior?). At the individual level, the treatment helps the client to assess potential and actual reinforcers for continued drinking and for decreased drinking or abstinence, as well as assessing negative consequences of drinking and abstinence. Assessment of the relative strength of incentives to maintain versus change drinking patterns provides an incentive framework for the rest of the therapy. A number of other strategies (to be described) are also used to enhance motivation to change. Teaching *individual coping skills* to deal with alcohol-related situations are a second important individual intervention. Skills include self-management planning, stimulus control, drink refusal, and self-monitoring of drinking and drinking impulses. Behavioral and cognitive coping skills, individually tailored to the types of situations that are the most common antecedents to drinking ("high-risk situations"), are a third type of individually focused intervention, and include assertiveness, cognitive restructuring, relaxation, lifestyle balance, recreational activities, and so on. Finally, we believe that providing clients with a model for conceptualizing drinking problems and how to change is an important part of the therapy for both partners.

A second set of interventions that flow logically from our model revolves around the *coping behaviors of the nonalcoholic partner*. The partner's own motivation for entering and continuing in treatment, and the partner's perceptions of the positive and negative consequences of changes in drinking patterns and the marital relationship are important factors contributing to the partner's willingness to engage in new behaviors and be an active participant in the therapy. The model also suggests that the nonalcoholic spouse learn a variety of coping skills to deal with drinking and abstinence. An individualized assessment of spousal behaviors that may either cue drinking or maintain it is essential. Spousal coping skills might include learning new ways to discuss drinking and drinking situations, learning new responses to the partner's drinking and alcohol-related behavior, or individual skills to enhance his/her own individual functioning.

The third treatment component is a focus on the *interactions between the two partners*, around both alcohol and other issues. Alcohol-focused couple interventions use alcohol-related topics as vehicles to introduce communication and problem-solving skills. Questions such as how the couple could manage a situation in which alcohol is present, whether they will keep alcohol in the house, how the partner could assist the drinker in dealing with impulses to drink, or what the couple will tell family and friends about the alcoholic's treatment, are all relevant topics that the couple must face in the process of dealing with the drinking. By using such topics as vehicles for discussion, the couple is taught basic communication skills. Additionally, the model suggests that many alcoholic couples need to learn general communication and problem-solving skills, to decrease marital conflicts that may cue drinking, and to increase the rate of positive exchanges. When appropriate, the treatment also incorporates general reciprocity-enhancement interventions to increase the overall reward value of the relationship.

The fourth set of interventions focuses on *other social systems* in which the drinker and partner are currently or potentially involved. Clients are helped to identify interpersonal situations and persons who are associated with heavy drinking, and are also helped to identify potential social situations and people who would be supportive of abstinence or decreased drinking. Social skills such as refusing drinks or general assertiveness may be taught. Additionally, some clients are encouraged to become involved with Alcoholics Anonymous (AA). AA provides a strong social support network for abstinence, opportunities to meet nondrinkers, and a set of time-structuring activities that are incompatible with drinking.

Finally, the model includes *techniques to increase generalization to the natural environment* and *maintenance of new behaviors*. Homework assignments, teaching clients how to anticipate high-risk situations, and planned followup treatment sessions all are designed to contribute to maintenance of change.

Overall Strategy for Bringing about Change

General Strategies

To implement the therapeutic model, we provide conjoint therapy throughout the treatment. Couples are seen together in order to educate both partners about the nature of drinking problems and the model of change; to decrease the avoidance, lying, and hypervigilance that may characterize the relationship; to improve communication and problem-solving skills; and to use the differing perspectives of each partner to increase the information available to the therapist. Under certain circumstances in clinical practice, individual sessions may be appropriate. Most often, an individual assessment is appropriate when there are concerns about domestic violence, nonmonogamy by one or both marital partners, or when the volatility of the couple's relationship dramatically interferes with the therapist's ability to work directly on the drinking. Therapy typically follows a sequence in which alcohol is the primary focus of the early treatment sessions, and the couple's relationship becomes an increasing target for attention as therapy progresses. By focusing on alcohol at the beginning of treatment, the therapist allies with both partners, who have presented with drinking as their major concern. If the client is successful in changing his/her drinking, the spouse may be more amenable to examining and changing his/her own behavior. Discussing alcohol-related topics that affect the couple as a unit, encouraging simple, shared activities, and teaching the spouse to provide reinforcement for the positive changes in drinking behavior, are the earliest interventions directed at the couple as a unit, and provide a medium for the introduction of communication and problem-solving skills. As treatment progresses, the therapist focuses more explicitly on the marital relationship as a whole.

Diagnostic/Assessment Procedures

The primary goals of assessment are to evaluate the immediate needs of the couple, to assess the extent and severity of the drinking problem in order to determine the appropriate level of care, to identify antecedents to drinking and consequences that maintain the drinking, to identify cognitive and affective aspects of the drinking, to identify positive and negative aspects of the spouse's behavior around drinking, and to assess the strengths and weaknesses in the couple's relationship.

A number of different assessment strategies are necessary to complete a comprehensive evaluation that can be used for treatment planning: Intensive interviews; self-report questionnaires; observation of videotaped samples of interactional behavior; use of physiological measures, such as blood alcohol levels and tests of liver functioning; and the use of self-recording cards all contribute to the assessment. Specific assessment techniques and instruments are discussed in the second half of this chapter.

Treatment Goals

Selection of treatment goals around drinking is an area of significant controversy (e.g., McCrady, 1992; Peele, 1992), with vigorous debate around the necessity of abstinence for all clients with drinking problems, or the appropriateness of moderate drinking as a goal for some clients. Our treatment emphasizes abstinence as the preferable drinking goal for treatment for several reasons. First, most of our clients have experienced serious medical, social, legal, or occupational consequences of their drinking. The potential for problems if they continue to drink in an uncontrolled manner is fairly substantial. Second, if we want clients who have limited social support systems to use AA as a resource, then abstinence is a necessary goal. (Recently, a new self-help program, Rational Recovery [RR], has begun to develop. Based on rational-emotive therapy, RR offers an alternative support group that is more accepting of moderation as a goal. As RR develops, we may be able to accommodate clients who may be appropriate for moderate drinking goals but also need to access social networks that support abstinence or reduced drinking.) Third, we believe that many clients overvalue alcohol, underestimate the seriousness of the consequences of their drinking, or overestimate the negative aspects of abstinence. With such clients, we believe that part of the responsibility of the therapist is to help them make a more realistic appraisal of the positive and negative consequences of drinking and abstinence. Fourth, many couples enter treatment at the specific request of the nonalcoholic spouse, who may not agree to a goal of moderation.

For all of the reasons cited previously, we ask clients to agree to an initial goal of abstinence. For clients with medical sequelae of drinking, or severe and chronic drinking problems, we stress the importance of continued abstinence. For other clients, we may define abstinence as a provisional goal that allows them to be the most "clearheaded" during treatment, and gives them the opportunity to evaluate the experience of abstinence. We also suggest that as they evaluate their experience with abstinence during the treatment, they may decide eventually to return some other pattern of drinking. Most clients agree to abstinence, given the provisional rather than absolute nature of the goal.

In addition to drinking goals, there are several other major goals for the treatment. These goals include the following:

Development of coping skills to deal with alcohol-related situations (for both partners)
Development of positive reinforcers for abstinence or changed drinking
Enhancement of relationship functioning
Development of general coping skills
Development of effective communication and problem-solving skills
Development of strategies to maintain therapeutic gains and to deal with relapses.

Other couple-specific goals may also be negotiated.

Structure of Therapy Sessions

Therapy is conducted as conjoint sessions, typically 90 minutes in length, with a single therapist working with the couple. Sessions begin with the use of a handheld Breathalyzer to assess whether the problem drinker has any alcohol in his/her system. If the blood alcohol level is above .05 mg% but does not represent a serious relapse and no emergency attention is needed, the therapist reschedules the therapy session and asks the client to return sober. The nondrinking partner is asked to drive home.

The therapy session typically proceeds with a review of self-recording cards (described later), and a discussion of other homework. The balance of the session revolves around specific topics introduced by the therapist, as well as work on therapeutic issues introduced by the couple. Even if the focus of a particular session is on individual behavior change (such as self-management skills to avoid drinking situations), both partners are actively engaged in the treatment, and the therapist encourages the couple to interact, providing guidance and coaching on specific communication skills during these interactions.

Hypothesized Active Ingredients in the Treatment

Four major factors are hypothesized to contribute to therapeutic change. First, the *intensive assessment* of drinking and its consequences, feedback from the nonalcoholic spouse, and the increased knowledge about drinking problems, should facilitate motivation to engage in new behaviors that support change. Second, the treatment is designed to *enhance self-efficacy* by introducing a series of small, successful changes in the behavior of each partner, thus increasing each partner's self-efficacy for engaging in more difficult behavior change. Third, the treatment is designed to *increase positive reinforcers* for abstinence in general, and to *increase the overall reinforcement value of the relationship* as a way to provide a strong incentive to maintain changed drinking behavior. Fourth, *learning new cognitive and behavioral coping skills* provides couples with an expanded behavioral repertoire for coping with high-risk situations.

THE ROLE OF THE THERAPIST

Establishing and Fostering a Working Alliance

As with any form of therapy, the therapist's relationship to the couple and his/her therapeutic stance are important. Empathizing, active listening, instilling hope, and establishing a sense that the therapist and couple are working toward mutually agreed upon goals are essential (Miller, 1985). However, in couple work with alcoholics and their partners, such a therapeutic stance is sometimes difficult to attain or sustain. By treating a client with a drinking problem along with a spouse who wants that client to stop or decrease drinking, the therapist is allied de facto with the nonalcoholic partner. Because of the inherent imbalance in the treatment relationship, the therapist must make particular efforts to ally with the drinker. Developing such an alliance may be difficult for the therapist, both because of the problem drinker's behavior during treatment, and because of the history of drinking-related behaviors that the therapist may find repugnant or upsetting. The client also may lie or minimize drinking during treatment. To further complicate the therapist's task, the spouse may attempt to enhance her/his alliance with the therapist by echoing the therapist's comments, expressing anger at the client's behavior, being confrontational, or alternatively, being submissive and allowing the alcoholic partner to be verbally aggressive or dominant.

To handle the difficulties of the inherently imbalanced nature of the therapeutic situation, the therapist uses several techniques. First, the therapist must be able to *separate the person from the person's actions around alcohol.* The therapist must find aspects of the client as a person that are likable and begin to form a connection around these characteristics. Second, the therapist needs to *validate the perceptions and information provided by each partner.* Empathizing with how difficult the drinker finds honesty after having tried to hide his drinking from everyone, and also empathizing with the spouse's frustration with deceit communicates the fact that the therapist is concerned with both of their experiences, and sees both partners' experiences as valid and worthy of discussion. Third, the therapist must always *ally* him/herself *with the goals of the therapy as agreed upon by the couple.* Before a formal treatment contract has been developed, the therapist assumes that the implicit therapeutic goal is change in drinking behavior and diminution of problems that have arisen from the drinking. Thus, if the alcoholic partner appears to be lying or minimizing, the therapist can emphasize that lying has probably been adaptive in the past, but that part of therapy will involve learning how to be honest as a way to support change. Or, if the spouse is confrontational and hostile, the therapist can reframe anger as a problem that the spouse must learn to deal with differently as the client changes.

In addition to managing the potentially imbalanced therapeutic relationship, the therapist uses a variety of other techniques to foster a working alliance with the couple. First, the therapist may *predict for the couple that new information will emerge during the course of therapy,* and can normalize these discoveries as a positive part of the change process. Such a prediction is intended to reduce hostile confrontations and accusations in the therapy sessions. Second, the therapist *defines him/herself as an expert consultant* who has particular knowledge about alcohol, alcohol problems, and how to change drinking and marital problems, and uses this knowledge to educate the couple. Taking the stance of teacher and consultant, a familiar stance for behavior therapists, the therapist becomes a teacher rather than a person who will judge the rightness or wrongness of either partner's position. To support the stance of therapist as teacher, the therapist explains that each partner will have to learn a variety of new skills in therapy. Taking a neutral, teaching approach decreases the couple's sense that they are being judged as flawed or pathological.

Finally, the *therapist forms an alliance with the couple by making the therapist's expectations for the couple's behavior clear:* coming to scheduled sessions on time, calling if unable to attend, paying the bill for therapy, coming in sober, and completing assigned homework. The *therapist also makes his/her own commitment to the therapy clear,* by being at sessions on time, being reasonably available by telephone, providing coverage when away, and providing treatments with the best empirical support for their effectiveness. Being clear about expectations for therapy behavior emphasizes the therapist's commitment to therapy as a serious process.

Use of the Therapist–Patient Relationship to Foster Change

Our model of therapy does not view the therapist–patient relationship as a central agent of change in any specific or technical sense. We do not foster or interpret a transference relationship, for example. However, the therapist's positive relationship with the couple can be used to reinforce positive behavior change. Also, if the therapist has established a good working alliance with the couple, he/she can use that relationship as a vehicle for confrontation if either partner is being noncompliant. The therapist may also use self-disclosure at times as a way to validate some of the difficult or embarrassing experiences of the clients, or as a way to model active coping with life problems.

Therapeutic Stance

As described, the therapist takes the role of teacher or expert consultant. Working with couples with drinking problems requires the ability to be flexible and able to respond to the unexpected. The therapist may be supportive, empathic, and encouraging in one session, and limit-setting and confrontational in the next. In general, the therapist is fairly active and directive, although he/she may follow the lead of the clients at times.

Changes in the Therapist's Role during Therapy

As therapy progresses, the therapist may become less directive, fostering the clients' ability to direct their own behavior in the session and to select issues that they see as most important to discuss. The therapist may also use more self-disclosure as therapy progresses. The focus of the therapist gradually shifts from teaching new skills in the therapy session to emphasizing generalization to the natural environment, with the therapist prompting the use of skills learned in the sessions, rather than teaching clients new skills.

Typical Technical Errors by the Therapist

There are several common errors that therapists make in working with problem drinkers and their partners. First, *therapists often overestimate client motivation to change, and underestimate ambivalent feelings about change.* We assume that every couple enters treatment with mixed feelings about change. Alcohol is familiar to the couple, has provided many positive experiences in the past, and not drinking requires a new set of unfamiliar skills and experiences. The therapist who ignores this fundamental ambivalence will have difficulty in the therapy. A second common error made by therapists is *overestimating the skills of these couples.* Many alcoholics have good verbal skills that cover significant cognitive deficits (resulting from long-term heavy alcohol intake) in abstraction and problem solving (Parsons, Butters, & Nathan, 1987). The therapist may not observe these deficits in the course of a therapy session, and may assume that the drinker can apply concepts to situations outside the therapy without detailed discussion, explanation, and planning. The more concrete, detailed, and specific the therapist is, the easier the therapy will be for the drinker.

A third common therapeutic error occurs when the therapist *underestimates the degree of anger or other "lethal" pathology in the couple.* Some couples with drinking problems appear superficially to be committed to each other, but at the same time have a wealth of anger, based on years of disappointment, hurt, and vicious interactions. Some couples begin therapy with a rather positive stance, but after several sessions, the degree of the negative feeling between them becomes much more apparent.

A fourth common error that therapists commit occurs when the therapist *allows the couple to avoid homework or avoid discussing or dealing with alcohol-related issues.* Some couples are highly compliant with homework assignments, whereas others do not complete assignments, forget the assignments completely, or attempt to avoid discussing them in the treatment session. Because, for some of these couples, such a pattern of avoidance and lack of follow-through on commitments has been characteristic of their relationship, allowing them to engage in the same behavior in therapy undermines the therapist's credibility and cheats the couple out of the op-

portunity to have a different learning experience in therapy.

Finally, as discussed at the beginning of this section on the role of the therapist, a common technical error occurs when the *therapist allies with the nonalcoholic spouse against the noncompliant, alcoholic client.* Although easy to do, such an alliance probably assures that the therapy will not come to a successful conclusion.

In the second half of the chapter, we turn to a discuss of specific therapeutic techniques and the therapeutic process, and illustrate the application of our therapeutic model to an actual couple seen in our clinical research program.

CASE STUDY: HANK AND SHARON

The following case study illustrates several techniques and strategies used in cognitive-behavioral conjoint therapy for alcoholism. In this illustrative case, specific techniques from a relapse prevention (RP) model (Marlatt & Gordon, 1985) and also from a 12-step (AA) approach. (McCrady & Irvine, 1989) are used, in addition to the basic cognitive-behavioral model for the treatment of alcoholism. Despite controversy in the field regarding the mutually exclusive nature of RP and AA treatment for alcoholism (e.g., Marlatt & Gordon, 1985), we believe that the cognitive-behavioral model may be enhanced by specific techniques of these other treatment modalities, with no resultant confusion or compromise of integrity either on the therapists' or clients' part. Presentation of this case study is designed to highlight therapeutic interventions; therefore a relatively "straightforward" case was chosen. This couple's marital distress was relatively minimal, only one spouse (the husband) was alcoholic, and both spouses were relatively free of comorbid psychopathology, including other substance abuse. Factors that complicate delivery of these therapeutic techniques will be covered separately under "Common Obstacles to Successful Treatment."

Presenting Problem

Hank, age 26, and Sharon, age 29, have been married 2 years and cohabited for 2 years before marriage. This is Sharon's second marriage; from her first marriage she has two children, Kevin and Julia, ages 9 and 11, who live with Hank and Sharon and spend every other weekend visiting their father. This is Hank's first marriage. Sharon works full-time as a medical secretary, and Hank works full-time as an administrator in an accounts receivable department. Hank is also on call as a volunteer fireman in their hometown during all nonworking hours.

Hank and Sharon were referred by friends who were participating in a research/treatment program in our addictions clinic. Hank and Sharon wanted to participate in the hopes that Hank would "find something that would make me want to stop drinking." Hank was finding it difficult to stop drinking, although he had been able to reduce his alcohol intake on his own. He reported that he had tried AA, but that it had not entirely worked for him. Sharon agreed with Hank's assessment of the situation, and with his evaluation of their marriage as "basically very good." She said that as far as his drinking was concerned, she "wants to ignore it" but she tends to get upset and nervous about it.

Assessment Procedures (Two Extended Sessions, or 4 Hours)

Hank and Sharon underwent a rather extensive evaluation, which is a routine part of our research/treatment program. The assessment focused on history and severity of the alcohol problem, current drinking status, and parameters of the marital relationship, in addition to basic information about the presenting problems and motivation to stop drinking. The information was obtained during two clinical interviews that the client and spouse attended together; both semistructured interview protocols and self-report questionnaires were used.

At the start of the first meeting, as would be the case before every meeting thereafter, the clinician administered a Breathalyzer test to Hank to ascertain that his blood-alcohol level was below 0.05 mg%. While preparing to administer the test, the therapist asked the patient if he was familiar with the test, and went on to explain the rationale behind its administration. Hank was told that clinicians here routinely administer the breath test to all patients to ensure that the client is sober, because intoxication make it difficult to think clearly and benefit fully from the evaluation and therapy sessions. The therapist informed Hank that she would need to reschedule any session to which he arrived with an elevated blood-alcohol level. The Breathalyzer test, when explained in this respectful and positive light, serves both to educate the clients and to model clear, reasonable limit setting. Rather than being insulted by the breath test procedure, most clients seem to appreciate it if it is explained fully and administered consistently.

During the initial screening interview the need for detoxification should be evaluated, and should continue to be monitored throughout the course of treatment. If, for example, a client arrives intoxicated to a session, the clinician reviews options available for detoxification, and may direct the patient and spouse to the nearest acceptable option. Often, by this point, the spouse is at a loss as to how to help the client, and the therapist's limit setting (i.e., refusal to conduct a therapy session, and the firm directive "Get thee to detox") is both a relief and a role model for the spouse who feels frustrated and helpless. Two other strong indicators of need for detoxification before therapy begins are (1) daily drinking of large quantities of alcohol, and/or (2) history of withdrawal symptoms during prior attempts at abstinence.

Hank's blood-alcohol level was 0 at his initial interview, so the therapist began to evaluate the presenting problem by asking first Hank and then Sharon what led them to seek treatment at this time, how they each perceived the drinking problem, how the problem affected them, and whether there were any other personal problems that concerned them. The therapist also inquired about Hank's family history for alcoholism (which was positive: Hank's father had a drinking problem), and then asked some general questions about frequency, quantity, and types of alcohol currently used by Hank. From this initial set of questions, the clinician learned that approximately 18 months ago, Hank had been treated voluntarily for alcohol dependence at an 8-day inpatient detoxification program. Prior to detoxification, he had been drinking daily and heavily, and he and Sharon were arguing a great deal about his drinking. Following detoxification, he had been able to stay sober for 8 months, during which time he and Sharon rarely argued and began to enjoy each other's company much more. While in the detox program and for several subsequent months, Hank attended AA meetings at the hospital where he had been detoxified. After approximately 8 months of sobriety, according to Hank's report, he began to be "turned off" at the AA meetings because of his perceived lack of commonality between himself and the other AA members. Around the time Hank stopped attending AA, Sharon also stopped attending Alanon, which she had been attending during the same period. Hank started to drink again "behind Sharon's back" and gradually increased his intake. By the time the couple came to therapy, Hank was drinking at least one fourth of a pint of vodka several days a week after work. Sharon and Hank both viewed their marriage as essentially strong and satisfying, but agreed that Sharon's dislike of Hank's "personality change when drunk," her inability to believe or trust him, and the gradual erosion of communication and enjoyment of each other over the past year, indicated a need for abstinence on his part and a "face-lift" for their relationship. Both partners were afraid that Hank's drinking would gradually increase if not treated, and would eventually lead them back to the extremely unpleasant situation they were in 1½ years ago.

From the patient's self-report on the Michigan Alcoholism Screening Test (Selzer, 1971), the therapist learned that Hank had a relatively severe alcohol problem, as determined by the number of negative consequences he had experienced as a result of alcohol use: blackouts, complaints about drinking by Sharon, inability to stop drinking, drinking before noon, feeling bad about drinking, and not feeling that he was a normal drinker. Over the past 12 months, his alcohol problem was moderately severe in that negative consequences were limited to problems in his marriage and feeling bad about drinking. His self-report on the Symptom Checklist—90 (SCL-90; Derogatis, Lipman, & Covi, 1973) revealed no evidence of psychotic processes and some problems with depression and irritability. Sharon's Michigan Alcoholism Screening Test indicated that she had never had an alcohol problem. From her SCL-90 the therapist learned that she also had no psychotic symptomatology, did suffer from mild depression and irritability, and was also bothered by several somatic symptoms.

During the initial session the clinician assessed Hank's need for detoxification before beginning outpatient therapy. While in detoxification previously, he had experienced some minor withdrawal symptoms, including shaking, nausea, and sweating, for 2 days following cessation of drinking. He had, however, been drinking daily and much more heavily immediately prior to that detoxification. He reported no history of major withdrawal symptoms such as hallucinations and seizures. Based on his current, sporadic drinking pattern and relatively minimal intake, the therapist suspected that no detoxification would be necessary after abstinence was achieved. To be sure, she asked about Hank's last drink prior to the session. He had drunk one-fourth pint of vodka 2 days ago on his way home from work. He had not experienced any withdrawal symptoms since then. Thus, the therapist explained to Hank and Sharon that there was no need to refer him now for detoxification, and that he could safely cut down and stop drinking without medical supervision.

Finally, the clinician administered the Mini-Mental Status Exam (Folstein, Folstein, & McHugh, 1975) to rule out cognitive dysfunction that might preclude Hank's participation in the treatment program. He scored perfectly on 10 questions and tasks assessing orientation, short-term memory, concentration, and ability to name common objects, follow a three-stage direction, and write a sentence spontaneously.

In the second evaluation session, a detailed lifetime drinking history was obtained using the Composite International Diagnostic Interview-Substance Abuse Module (CIDI-SAM; Robins et al., 1988), as was an even more detailed account of amount and frequency of daily drinking during the past 180 days using the Time-Line Follow-Back Interview (M. Sobell, Maisto, L. Sobell, Cooper, & Saunders, 1980). In Hank's case the information obtained was used in part for research purposes; for strictly clinical use, a 90-day time-line procedure would suffice to give the therapist a clear indication of the client's drinking pattern and high-risk situations. Also, a more informal lifetime drinking history might be obtained to give the therapist perspective on the patient's current drinking pattern, prior periods of abstinence and relapse, and prior periods of heavy drinking.

The CIDI-SAM revealed that Hank began drinking enough to get drunk at age 14, and began drinking at least once a month at age 15. Heavier, more regular drinking began when he was 18 and continued until age 24. Hank developed a noticeable tolerance to alcohol around the age of 22 and felt loss of control over drinking by age 23. Around the age of 24, drinking began to interfere with family and employment obligations. His parents, relatives, and later, his spouse complained about his drinking from age 18 until the present. Thus, information gleaned from the CIDI-SAM indicated that Hank's drinking problem began when he was approximately 18 and worsened over the years until it began to intrude on his daily obligations and disrupt his work routine and close relationships, until he felt little control over drinking, and until he had to drink more and more to get the same effect (i.e., tolerance).

We determined daily drinking quantities in the 6 months prior to treatment. After establishing that Hank had no extended period of abstinence during the 6-month period, it was fairly easy to estimate Hank's alcohol intake. He drank 2 to 4 days per week, typically on 3 days—Monday,

Wednesday, and Friday. Occasionally he had a few beers in the evenings or on weekends. On the three regular drinking days he always drank the same thing: one-fourth pint (4 ounces) of vodka. The information obtained in this interview would be crucial for later use to develop a functional analysis of Hank's drinking behavior. Hank was surprised to realize, during the course of the interview, how consistent and predictable his drinking pattern really was. Hank's reaction was typical of many of our clients. Providing such information about daily drinking often helps clients to be more objective about their alcohol intake and to begin to view their drinking behavior as part of a pattern of behavior that they can perhaps change and control. Thus, a great deal of therapeutic gain can be made during the assessment. Remembering and describing one's drinking history and pattern can often start the process of self-awareness and seems to be a powerful motivational technique for many clients, because they hear themselves describing just how much they drink, how much time and energy it had taken out of the rest of their life, and how much it bothers people they care about. The therapeutic impact of this self-revelation is reinforced by the therapist, who gently gives feedback to clients about the severity of their drinking in terms of their drinking pattern (i.e., quantity and frequency) and the negative consequences they and their family have suffered.

The presence of the alcoholic's wife at the evaluation session can enhance the therapeutic value of the assessment. Often the spouse comments that this is the first time she has heard her husband talk about his alcohol consumption at any length. Many alcoholics attempt to "protect" their drinking habits from those around them who might try to interfere, and thus rarely discuss their use of alcohol. The assessment procedure, during which the alcoholic is required to talk about alcohol in front of his spouse to a nonjudgmental, encouraging third party, is a first step in the client's being able to ally himself with his spouse "against" alcohol.

In addition to assessment of the alcohol problem, the therapist begins to evaluate the marital relationship. From the initial interview, the therapist develops a sense of how the alcoholic spouse's drinking affects the relationship, and may also have ideas about the nondrinker's contribution to the drinking problem. The therapist has also been able to observe the couple interact with each other during the interview and should begin to formulate hypotheses about the quality of the marital relationship. It is important to assess which marital problems seem direct-

ly related to the alcohol problem, and which are likely to persist long after abstinence is attained. Examples of problems that tend to persist and require a good deal of attention in therapy include severely disrupted communication patterns, and a sense of "mutual dislike."

As part of the research protocol in our clinic, Hank and Sharon completed self-report questionnaires designed to assess marital satisfaction and content areas in which they want behavior change from their spouse. From the Dyadic Adjustment Scale (Spanier, 1976), the therapist noticed that both Hank and Sharon indicated that they agree more often than not on major marital issues, that they were "extremely happy" (Hank) and "very happy" (Sharon) with their relationship, and that they wanted very much for their relationship to succeed. Likewise, their Areas of Change Questionnaires (Margolin, Talovic, & Weinstein, 1983) identified only a few areas in which either partner wanted a behavior change from the other. These areas had to do with engagement in the relationship (e.g., items like "start interesting conversations with me somewhat more,"; "express his/her emotions clearly much more") and pointed to a need in therapy to enhance interactive behavior in the relationship.

From these two extended evaluation sessions the therapist knew a great deal about Hank and Sharon even before "therapy" began. She had information about Hank's drinking history and parameters of his current problem, the initial information about alcohol's effects on his marriage, Sharon's perception of, and her contribution to, the drinking problem, and information regarding the status of Hank and Sharon's mutual liking and commitment to their relationship. The therapist could proceed to the first therapy session, using these data as the groundwork for further analyzing Hank's drinking behavior and for teaching both spouses how to change destructive habits contributing to his alcohol intake. In addition, the therapeutic process had already begun—with Hank's self-disclosure, Sharon's relief at their seeking help together and the opportunity to model the therapist's calm, reasonable limit setting, and the development of rapport between the couple and the therapist.

Therapy Sessions 1–4:
Motivational Techniques
and Analysis of the Drinking Pattern

The therapist used the first therapy session to learn more about Hank and Sharon as a couple and individually, to deepen the developing rapport between herself and the couple, and to explain the program of treatment ahead. Subsequent early sessions focus on enhancing motivation to stop drinking, and mapping out and analyzing the client's drinking pattern and the spouse's role in it. Also, assessment of potential AA and Al-Anon involvement is made early on in therapy so that the therapist can facilitate participation and understanding of the program during the subsequent sessions.

Both Hank and Sharon viewed the conjoint therapy model as a welcome alternative to individual therapy for Hank or separate 12-Step programs of recovery for each. They hoped that Hank would be able to become more open about his drinking and allow Sharon to help him stop. Sharon's major frustration, in addition to and compounded by Hank's alcohol problem, was his reticence to actively engage her in conversation and his reluctance to "open up." Hank's chief complaint about Sharon was that she was very moody. Hank saw Sharon as "jabbering" too much sometimes, whereas at other times she suddenly became quiet and irritable for days at a time. Sharon agreed with this description of herself, and attributed the moodiness to hormonal changes during her menstrual cycle. At these times the couple barely communicated. In general, both Hank and Sharon showed genuine warmth toward each other, and these "complaints" were discussed in an almost lighthearted way. The only problem that seemed really to upset both spouses was Hank's drinking and Sharon's belief that he often lied to her about it. Hank claimed that keeping the drinking a secret from Sharon actually helped him control his intake, because during his prior heavier drinking period, he simply drank around the house in front of her; now he was limited to the time between leaving work and arriving home. The therapist reframed the lies as a method Hank used to protect his drinking from Sharon. The therapist observed that Hank currently saw Sharon as "the enemy of the drink" and so kept his drinking a secret from her, because he wanted to satisfy his cravings for alcohol. On the other hand, Hank very much wanted to fight these cravings and become abstinent. The therapist said that one of the goals of the conjoint therapy was to help Sharon to be supportive of Hank's efforts to stop and to understand how hard it is to give up drinking, and thus help Hank to more explicitly ally himself with Sharon, to "use her as a resource" in his "fights with alcohol." In the RP model, imagery can be used extensively to help the client strengthen resolve to refuse alcohol.

Because Hank was already quite eager to become

abstinent, little work was needed to enhance motivation. On his Decisional Matrix (Marlatt & Gordon, 1985), Hank listed positive consequences of drinking (easing of irritability after work, feeling a passing high, finding it easier to feel and act sociable); negative consequences of drinking (letting himself down, arguing with Sharon, needing to lie to Sharon, fearing the of eventual loss of control over drinking, health consequences, i.e., liver damage, potential for DWIs and loss of license); positive consequences of quitting drinking (feeling proud of himself, feeling closer to Sharon, feeling no danger of reverting back to the "predetoxification" situation); and negative consequences of quitting drinking (difficulty relaxing after work, no more feeling high, feeling left out at firehouse, feeling shy at social gatherings).

It was important for Hank to identify positive aspects of his drinking, so that he could begin to think about alternative ways to attain the positive things alcohol did for him. For Hank, the negative consequences of drinking, although usually longer term than the positive consequences, were much more damaging and dangerous than the short-term positive consequences. The therapist also had Hank and Sharon write an "alcohol autobiography" (Marlatt & Gordon, 1985) for homework. This exercise helped Hank see just how extensively alcohol—first his father's drinking and then his own—had impacted on almost every aspect of his life since childhood. Understanding the role of alcohol in his life and being forced to write down his thoughts and feelings helped to ready Hank emotionally for the task of giving up drinking. Sharon was also able to put into perspective her "relationship" with alcohol, both in her family of origin and in its overwhelming effect on her second marriage.

Functional analysis began with an assignment for Hank and Sharon to separately fill out a "Drinking Patterns Questionnaire" (Zitter & McCrady, 1979). This was used in the second session to help identify all the triggers and "high-risk situations" (Marlatt & Gordon, 1985) to which Hank responded by drinking. The therapist explained a "drinking chain" (the S-O-R-C analysis of drinking) as a learned sequence of events.

Analysis of Hank's drinking pattern revealed two major high-risk situations:

1. *On the days he drank after work.* He would leave work at 5:00 P.M., park his car in a nearby empty lot, smoke a cigarette, and drink

vodka out of small bottles he kept in the car for these occasions. Then he would drive home, sometimes finishing the vodka while driving, smoke cigarettes, and chew on mint candies.

2. *At the volunteer firehouse either after a fire call, during meetings, or just "hanging out" with the other firemen.* The firehouse actually had a wet bar and was stocked with beer and hard liquor at all times.

Other triggers included 5:00 P.M., especially on Mondays and Fridays, the two most stressful days at work; feeling bored at home on Sundays; and having an argument at work with either a client or a co-worker. *Spouse-related triggers* were reviewed, and neither Hank nor Sharon believed that Sharon did anything to promote Hank's drinking. She did not condone his drinking, and she did not get openly angry, even though she usually knew when Hank had been drinking. In fact, in order to avoid tension and arguments, Sharon tended to ignore the times when Hank drank on the way home from work or at the firehouse. On those days, she said, he would be "a chatterbox, even obnoxious." But, she said, she had learned in Al-Anon to detach, and so she had adopted a coping strategy of pretending that Hank had not had a drink. Drinking was, in fact, rarely mentioned between the two of them. Sharon could not, however, ignore her rising resentment and worry about Hank's drinking, which she also did not discuss with Hank. To complicate matters, Hank knew that Sharon knew when he had been drinking, and he also knew that she would ignore it, and they could both pretend that nothing was wrong. The therapist suggested that Sharon's pattern of ignoring the drinking was a subtle form of a spouse-related trigger, because Hank knew that he could drink under certain circumstances and would "get away with it." In other words, Sharon was protecting him from some of the negative consequences of his drinking. The price they were paying for the "quiet," however, was an erosion of trust in Hank on Sharon's part, a growing worry on Hank's part that sooner or later Sharon would no longer put up with the drinking if no other negative consequence came first, and a gradual lessening of intimacy for them both.

The therapist brought up AA and Al-Anon attendance. Discussion of Hank's attitude toward AA revealed that he preferred to use the skills training approach offered at our clinic, because he had tried AA in the past and had found it helpful but not sufficient. As a rather shy person, Hank felt uncomfortable in the group, and

found it difficult to open up there. The therapist encouraged Hank to reconsider AA, and suggested that he and Sharon go to a meeting together, perhaps a couples meeting. The therapist thought that Hank might benefit from the availability of the meetings, from contact with a sponsor with whom he could discuss his urges, and especially from a "sober network" of friends to see instead of his drinking buddies at the firehouse. Hank and Sharon had both felt out of place at meetings and were hesitant to try again. The therapist did not insist, but did from time to time in subsequent sessions bring up the possible value of AA.

Early in treatment both Hank and Sharon learned to fill out daily self-recording cards. Each day Hank monitored the frequency and intensity of his urges to drink, the number of drinks consumed, and his daily marital satisfaction. Sharon kept records of her daily estimate of Hank's alcohol consumption and intensity of his urges, along with her daily marital satisfaction. Sharon proved to be remarkably accurate in her estimations of Hank's urges, which underscored the potential for her to be a supportive "coach" to help Hank fight urges.

By the end of the fourth session Hank reported that he was still having very strong urges to drink after work, but had stopped keeping vodka in his car (at the therapist's suggestion) and had stopped at a liquor store only three times since then. He was still drinking when he went to the firehouse once a week, but on another occasion, after a fire, had gone home directly afterward instead of staying to have a beer. Sharon reported that she and Hank were talking much more than usual and that he was beginning to talk to her about alcohol outside of the therapy session.

Therapy Sessions 5–8: Developing a Self-Management Plan and Enhancing the Marital Relationship

By now the clients and therapist felt that they understood Hank's drinking pattern, his high-risk situations, his triggers, and Sharon's role. Thus, Sessions 5 through 8 were devoted to developing and practicing stimulus-control procedures so that Hank would have a self-management plan to help him respond without alcohol to his trigger situations. Also, a rearrangement of consequences was begun by Hank, to increase the salience of negative consequences of drinking and the positive consequences of abstinence. One positive consequence was a better marital relationship, which was also given more attention during these sessions.

Hank decided to deal with his "highest risk" situation—drinking vodka in his car after work—by changing and avoiding aspects of this situation, and by identifying antecedent emotional triggers at work. First, he began keeping Tootsie Roll candy (his favorite) rather than vodka in his glove compartment. On days when he had an urge to drink at 5:00 P.M. after work, he made it a point to walk briskly to his car, jot down the urge information on his self-recording card, and then drive away immediately, going out of his way to avoid passing the parking lot, where he normally stopped to drink, and the liquor store, where he bought the vodka. As he drove, if urges got particularly intense, he would eat Tootsie Roll candy, turn up the volume of the radio, and sing along loudly. He found these substitute activities helpful in battling the cravings for alcohol.

To make negative consequences more salient, Hank carried a 3″ × 5″ card on which he had listed negative consequences of drinking, and sometimes spent a moment after work in his car smoking a cigarette to relax and study this card. At these times Hank sometimes practiced the relaxation and imagery techniques that he learned in therapy: After taking a minute to relax, he would close his eyes and imagine in as vivid detail as possible the course of events if he drank, got stopped by the police for speeding, lost his license, had an angry Sharon drive him to work everyday, or alternately, got into an accident and injured someone. Other "negative" scenarios were worked out in session for Hank to conjure up in situations in which the urge to drink was very strong.

At the end of particularly trying days at work, Hank often felt frustrated, tired, resentful of his coworkers, "and really looking forward to that drink to calm (him) down." Hank and Sharon decided that when Hank felt this way, he should do one of two things: (1) pay an informal visit to his boss, who was also a friend, to chat about the day's activities, or (2) call Sharon for an "urge discussion." These were role-played in session as alternatives to drinking. Hank began to develop a closer relationship with his boss, who was able to give him several suggestions to increase his effectiveness with his staff. He also began to call Sharon regularly from work to chat, and sometimes to tell her how strong his urges to drink were and how difficult it was to avoid drinking. Sharon learned to respond supportively in these conversations: not to confuse his wish to drink with the act of drinking. She might suggest an alternative: "It sounds like you've had

a hell of a day. If you leave now, you can be home in half an hour and then we can take the kids out for dinner at the diner."

Hank found that calling Sharon before leaving work and making plans for the evening was helpful in reducing the intensity of his urges. Before, he had avoided his reactions to problems at work by using vodka as a solution. He then would feel guilty, worry about his drinking, and spend the evening trying to avoid Sharon. Now he was talking about his feelings to Sharon and left work feeling more relaxed and looking forward to spending his evening with her. The therapist built on this initial deepening of supportiveness and intimacy by assigned "marital enhancement" homework: Sharon was to give Hank at least four compliments each week as "verbal rewards" for abstinence. Hank was to return the favor by saying at least four nice things to Sharon during the week. Over the weeks, other homework was introduced to stimulate interchange of positive feelings and goodwill toward one another. For instance, a weekly "date" was planned, when Hank and Sharon went out, without the children, to a movie and dinner. One of their "dates" in the eighth week of therapy was a weekend at a nearby motel! Clearly, by this time in treatment, the marriage had become much more rewarding for each partner.

The most difficult issue—trust—was addressed in the context of self-management planning. In the past, when Hank would come home mildly intoxicated, Sharon would pretend not to notice, but the two would avoid each other all evening. Sharon had learned not to "give Hank the fifth degree" when he was drinking heavily. To stop Sharon from protecting Hank from the negative consequences of drinking, and to begin to sharpen their communication skills, Sharon and Hank practiced the following in session and at home:

HANK (*upon coming in the door, kissing Sharon hello*): Hi, Honey. See? No drink today.
SHARON: That's great! Let's have dinner.

If Hank neglected to approach Sharon:

SHARON: Hi, Honey. Did you have a good day? How were your urges today? What did you do about them?
HANK: I really wanted a drink after work but I had some candy instead. What's for dinner?

Or, if he had had a drink:

SHARON: Hi, Honey. You don't look so happy. What's the matter?

HANK: I really wanted a drink after work. I stopped at the liquor store and bought a small bottle of vodka and drank some. I threw out the rest. I feel like an idiot. I was doing so well, and now I blew it.

SHARON: Well, I'm glad you told me, but I can't say I'm happy about this. We can talk about it more when you're sober. For now, I'm going to watch TV for awhile. Why don't you eat dinner and sleep it off.

In this way, the therapist hoped to strengthen the dwindled trust Sharon had for Hank. The goal was to teach Sharon to be appropriately supportive while relinquishing responsibility to Hank to inform her of his drinking. Thus, Hank gradually found it easier to confide in Sharon, rather than perceive her as the "enemy" of his drinking, and was able to enlist her support in preventing "slips" from becoming full-blown relapses.

By the end of the eighth session, Hank had not had a drink in 3 weeks, and was reporting 40% fewer urges at an average of 20% less intensity that at the start of treatment.

Therapy Sessions 9–12: Additional Self-Control Skills

During these sessions Hank practiced self-management plans already in place and continued to develop new plans for other high-risk situations, particularly at the firehouse. In addition, the therapist introduced several other skills. Self-control skills, such as drink refusal training (as part of assertiveness training), and Sharon's role in drink refusal related directly to Hank's drinking. Other skills, such as general assertiveness training, problem solving, and cognitive restructuring (challenging irrational thoughts) were more indirectly related to Hank's urges to drink.

An entire session was spent on Hank's second, major high-risk situation—the firehouse—where he felt strong peer pressure to drink. Hank claimed that it is extremely important to be perceived as "one of the guys" so that in a fire, a fellow fireman would go out of his way, no matter what, to save him in a dangerous situation. Hank translated "one of the guys" to mean "drinking buddy," and therefore was quite concerned about his ability to refuse drinks at the firehouse. Also, Hank enjoyed the drinking scene in the firehouse, and a beer or two relaxed him sufficiently to be more sociable than usual. It was decided in session that the goal was to avoid being pressured to have a drink while remaining

on a friendly, joking level with the other firemen, as this tact would decrease his chances of being rejected because of his abstinence. The therapist challenged Hank's belief that drinking beer was a prerequisite to being accepted by the group. She asked Hank to think of nondrinking firemen who were popular nonetheless. Hank was able to name three, and decided to seek them out when the other men were drinking together. The therapist also challenged Hank's belief that drinking was the crucial link in "bonding" enough to have another fireman save one's life. Hank gradually began to consider the possibility that other ways of perceiving the drinking situation at the firehouse were valid. When the therapist finally expressed concern that the town's volunteer firemen force was comprised of intoxicated people and questioned their uncompromised ability to perform well in an emergency, Hank had enough objectivity to agree that it was not necessarily a good thing that the volunteer firehouse also served as a local bar and that the "volunteer firemen social system" revolved around drinking. In order to help him refuse drinks, a straightforward response was modeled, but Hank said that he did not yet want the other firemen to know that he was trying to stop drinking. He decided, after role-playing several alternative responses, and at Sharon's suggestion, to tell the "pushers" that he has given up beer for Lent, and then when Lent was over, to tell them that he had stopped drinking and there was no reason to start again. This solution was acceptable to Hank and was one that he thought he could carry out. The therapist told Hank that after a while the other men would begin to perceive him as a nondrinker and would stop "heckling" him about not accepting beers. In reality, after a few weeks, Hank reported that he was surprised to find that no one had even asked him twice to have a beer and he found that he was still able to feel relaxed and sociable, even without drinking. He also found that he preferred to spend more of his free time at home or out with Sharon, rather than "hanging out" at the firehouse.

During drink refusal training, it became apparent that both Hank and Sharon needed to sharpen their assertiveness skills.

At work, Hank supervised five people in an accounts receivable department of a mail-order company. He spent most of his time on the phone with delinquent customers. He felt a pressure at work to "produce" (i.e., to receive payment for the delinquent bills for which he and his staff were accountable). The therapist initially thought this an interesting choice of profession for someone as shy and reserved as Hank, but soon realized that although generally unassertive, he could become quite hostile and stubborn with slight provocation. On the phone, Hank could discharge some of his hostility while not having to be assertive in personal encounters. Hank complained in therapy that he had become dissatisfied with his supervisees' performance and instead of giving them feedback about their work, began to assume more of their responsibilities until he felt overburdened and resentful. These feelings made him want to drink. Sharon commented that she, too, tended to "stuff her feelings" at work and then be "bitchy" at home with Hank. Both spouses benefited from a session devoted to problem solving. The problem solving provided additional assertiveness training, and homework was assigned for both to practice their new skills during the week. Other topics that the couple discussed in the context of the problem-solving model were Hank's desire to improve his relationship with Sharon's children, and Sharon's moodiness.

Therapy Sessions 13–16: Communication Skills Training

Hank and Sharon consistently rated their marriage a "7" on a 1 to 7 scale (Sharon even rated it a "20" after a weekend away!), so communication training for this couple was less intense than for many other couples we see. However, three topics were discussed in the context of communication skills training: (1) Sharon's moodiness and her need to respectfully inform Hank when she felt depressed or irritable and needed time alone; (2) Hank's increasing eagerness to talk with Sharon about his feelings and stressful situations that might arise, and (3) how to avoid relapse back to their former pattern of minimal verbal interchange. Gottman, Notarius, Gonso, and Markman's (1976) model of communication was used during these sessions. Both spouses found it useful to have a framework for good versus poor communication to facilitate their increasing intimacy.

Therapy Sessions 17–20: Consolidating Skills and Maintenance Planning

In the final sessions we reviewed and continued to practice skills learned thus far. Hank was becoming more comfortable with his sobriety and both he and Sharon were beginning to settle into a new, sober lifestyle. The last few sessions focused on establishing "marital meetings," on

identifying signs of possible relapse, handling relapses, developing a relapse contract, and finally, scheduling booster sessions.

Hank and Sharon agreed on a weekly "marital meeting" that would take place at a restaurant in lieu of their appointment at the clinic. In therapy, they role-played establishing an effective agenda and good communication skills (Jacobson & Margolin, 1979). They decided that they would use these meetings to clear the air of any conflict or negative feelings about one another that had come up during the week, to discuss any family topics that needed attention that week, to anticipate high-risk situations that might be coming up in the week ahead and to problem solve about how Hank could deal with them and how Sharon could help him, and to discuss the frequency and intensity of Hank's urges to drink that week.

In order to facilitate identification and handling of relapses, the couple decided on the following "relapse contract" (Marlatt & Gordon, 1985):

1. Hank needs to be as honest as possible and inform Sharon of any drinking or strong urges to drink.
2. Sharon and Hank will discuss the necessity of returning to treatment if: Hank has a drink once a week for 3 weeks in a row, stress or no stress, or if Hank stays at the firehouse late more frequently, or Hank is very quiet for more than a week.
3. Hank will start to consider return to treatment after even one drink.
4. If Hank or Sharon notices a steady pattern of drinking, even if once every 3 weeks, or every month for 3 months, or if urges get stronger, return to therapy will be discussed.
5. If any of items 2, 3, or 4 occur, Hank should contact the therapist and discuss the need to schedule an impromptu booster session.

At the last meeting "booster sessions" were scheduled with the therapist for the following year. One session was scheduled for every 3 months. Hank and Sharon were invited to call to schedule an additional booster session whenever one of them felt it necessary.

By the end of 20 sessions, Hank had been abstinent for 15 weeks. Both Hank and Sharon noticed improvements in several areas of their lives, including their relationship, their handling of stress at work, and Hank's relationship with the children. Hank no longer felt the burden of keeping "drinking secrets" from Sharon, and the couple spent more time together enjoying each other's company. Hank also felt free of guilt and self-doubt that he would be able to control his drinking. He was aware that he would most likely continue to have urges to drink, but felt that the more his lifestyle was alcohol-free and satisfying, the less he would think about drinking.

COMMON OBSTACLES TO SUCCESSFUL TREATMENT

Resistance and Noncompliance

In this type of treatment, resistance comes in many forms, some more blatant than others. Resistance can be characterized as a conscious or unconscious unwillingness on either the alcoholic or the spouse's part to comply with the components or goals of treatment. In general, the alcoholic's resistance stems from ambivalence about giving up drinking and all the positive consequences associated with it. The nonalcoholic spouse may be ambivalent about change in the family or marital system that will occur as the alcoholic stops drinking. Many nonalcoholic spouses assume more responsibility over time to "keep the family going" as the alcohol interferes more with the alcoholic's abilities to meet family obligations. When the alcoholic first stops drinking, the spouse often hesitates to relinquish control of family decisions and caretaking duties. Both spouses may be ambivalent about changing their marital relationship, because they are used to the current relationship, regardless of how unsatisfying it may be. In a conjoint model of alcoholism treatment, the therapist must be aware of potential resistance not only from the alcoholic about sobriety, but also from both spouses about relationship change.

Resistance in its more subtle form is minimization of the alcohol problem, often called "denial" by traditional alcoholism-treatment professionals. It is not atypical during the initial assessment session to hear some variation of the following: "I don't think I have drinking problem. My wife said she'd leave me if I didn't come here. So, I'm here. But I think it's her problem—she freaks out if the word "beer" is even mentioned." In response to quantity–frequency questions, this person might reply, "Well I don't drink every day. I never miss work because of drinking. I drink on weekends (Friday, Saturday, Sunday). Usually I drink between 10 and 30 (12-ounce) beers a night," or, "I only drink two six-packs a day." He may also minimize the negative consequences

he has suffered. It is not uncommon for the wife to respond to the husband's minimization with anger and an intense intolerance, even disgust, for any drinking by her husband. Often, the wife's intense reaction further polarizes the couple.

Reduction of minimization usually happens gradually, and the therapist must be aware that confronting the alcoholic too forcefully before rapport has been established or supporting the spouse's view too strongly can result in attrition from treatment. As noted, the act of reporting one's drinking history and negative consequences often facilitates awareness. The therapist can help by gently "lending perspective" of his/her expertise.

> "It sounds like compared to what your brothers and your friends at the bar drink, you don't drink much. But I must tell you that compared to a wide range of patients I have seen, and based on the severity of the negative consequences you have suffered, I see your drinking as a problem for you. Most people don't drink two six-packs every night after work. Most people come home after work and think about what's for dinner, or what's on TV that night, or what they need to repair around the house, or whether they will go out with their wife to the mall . . . not how many cold beers there are left in the refrigerator, and how many they can drink before an argument starts between them and their wives. The major reason I see your alcohol as a problem, though, is because you've have two DWIs in the past 2 years, because alcohol is really affecting the quality of your marriage . . . " and so on.

This information must be imparted in a respectful, didactic manner. The therapist must remain aware of the patient's ambivalence and convey understanding of the difficulty involved in giving up drinking. The therapist's empathy in the context of limit setting can serve as a role model for the nonalcoholic spouse, who also needs to be made aware that becoming sober is a very difficult task.

Resistance on the wife's part can manifest itself in various ways, perhaps in her coming in every session with a "marital crisis" that must be dealt with in lieu of focusing on the drinking, or with comments such as, "You can try all you want—he'll give you lip service but he won't follow through. He'll never stop drinking," or otherwise sabotaging her husband's efforts to change. An interesting example of the latter developed in our clinic. After 8 weeks of intense work by the therapist and several other events (including getting into a car accident when drunk), this client decided he needed to stop drinking. He was sober for 4 weeks when his wife, who had been livid at the assessment session while describing her husband's drinking, began going out to local bars with her friends and drinking until the early morning hours, leaving her husband home to babysit. The wife was, in fact, beginning to develop a drinking problem. At the very least, she was undermining the work her husband had done, and was on the verge of effectively sabotaging the treatment. The therapist began to focus on the wife's angry feelings toward her husband, residual from his years of drinking all night and leaving her home to baby-sit. Most of the rest of therapy dealt with marital issues, in particular, the deep hostility the wife felt toward her husband and her ambivalence about wanting to remain in the relationship, even if he were to be sober. When he was drinking, it was easy to blame alcohol for their marital difficulties. It was harder for her to accept that she "just didn't like him," sober or drunk. She began to realize that she was acting out her anger toward him rather than more constructively dealing with unsatisfying aspects of their relationship.

Resistance can take a more blatant form—noncompliance in treatment. The most obvious type of noncompliance is unwillingness to attend treatment. Typically at our clinic, it is the nonalcoholic spouse who calls to make a first appointment, and in many cases her next task is to convince her husband that he needs to attend. We have endured many canceled appointments that were explained similarly: "He won't come. He says he doesn't have a problem." In these cases, we encourage the spouse to have the alcoholic call us directly so that we can do a short assessment over the phone, give him some feedback, and describe the program in the hope that he will be less fearful of a treatment session. If the husband refuses, we offer the nonalcoholic spouse four or five individual sessions to work on strategies for getting the alcoholic into treatment. This approach is somewhat similar to "unilateral marital therapy" for alcoholism (Thomas & Santa, 1982) in which the spouse of a treatment-refusing alcoholic comes to therapy alone and learns skills such as reinforcing sober behavior, ignoring drinking behavior, and not protecting the alcoholic from negative consequences of drinking.

Other types of noncompliance include refusal to complete homework assignments, frequent cancellations or "no shows" for therapy sessions,

refusal to stop drinking, and dropping out of treatment. Usually, these behaviors can be seen as "acting out" resistance, and the source of resistance must be identified and explored.

Acute Marital Distress

It is difficult and sometimes irrelevant to proceed calmly through functional analysis and self-management skills when spouses are very angry with one another in-session. If the marital distress is at a lower level, it is usually best to explain that the first few sessions will be devoted to helping the alcoholic become sober, and then marital issues will be dealt with in more detail.

Of course, if the spouses are screaming, threatening, or not speaking to one another in session, marital issues must be deemed acute and need to be addressed. As long as the alcoholic is sober and not going through withdrawal (which can cause irritability, and in which case, the argument can be framed as a direct negative consequence of drinking), these behaviors in-session should be managed according to standard cognitive-behavioral marital techniques (e.g., Baucom & Epstein, 1990). Similarly, if spouses report physical violence at home, this must be the first topic addressed. The therapist should assess whether the violence occurs in the absence of alcohol, or only when one or both spouses is intoxicated. A cognitive-behavioral treatment model of domestic violence (see Rosenbaum & O'Leary, 1986) can be used, taking into account that in most cases, intoxication will be a primary "high-risk" situation for the violence. Often, domestic violence can be framed as an intense negative consequence for the alcoholic who abuses his spouse when intoxicated. He typically feels very guilty afterward, and finds his loss of control repugnant. Unfortunately, domestic violence is often the negative consequence that finally brings the couple in for treatment.

Finally, acute marital distress can be manifested in-session as excessive bickering, nasty comments, negative nonverbal behavior, and/or references to separation or divorce. In these cases, the marital problems are too pressing to take the back burner to treatment of alcohol problems. The therapist can choose to spend the first half of the session exploring marital issues and then make an explicit shift to the alcohol problem. This technique should be announced beforehand: "You two are so mad at each other today, you won't be able to hear what I have to say about alcohol. But I think it's important that we discuss the alcohol problem and I have some very important skills to introduce to you today. So let's spend the first half of the session—say, 45 minutes, on discussing what's bothering you both, and then we'll switch to talk about alcohol for the second half."

Polydrug Use

Figures on comorbid drug abuse in alcoholic populations hover around 50% for males (Ross et al., 1988b; Hesselbrock et al., 1985); a figure of up to 80% of all substance abusers using multiple substances has been cited (Carroll, 1986). Thus, clients who come for conjoint therapy of alcoholism must be carefully evaluated for other drug abuse. Polydrug use can complicate the therapy model in several ways:

1. Abstinence from alcohol may result in "symptom substitution" and patients may increase their use of other drugs. New problems relating to the other drugs may then be created, such as excessive money spent on cocaine.
2. It may be difficult to link negative consequences specifically to either alcohol or other drugs.
3. Different measures may need to be taken to wean the client off different drugs: for example, outpatient detoxification may suffice for the alcohol problem, but the client may also require methadone maintenance.
4. Using other drugs may create "high risk situations" for alcohol use.
5. A client does not experience and adjust to a "drug-free lifestyle" if abstinent from alcohol but using other drugs. There remains a "place" in his daily lifestyle for substance use, which could result more readily in a relapse to alcohol use.
6. Marital issues are complicated by polydrug use. A nonalcoholic spouse may object to alcohol but not to her husband's smoking two or three joints every day. In fact, she may join her husband in smoking pot or using cocaine occasionally. It becomes difficult for the therapist and the spouse to set limits when the limits of what is acceptable and what is not are unclear.

For the aforementioned reasons, it typically is better to treat every addiction, not just the ones the client or spouse dislikes. Strategies for dealing with polydrug use vary depending on the nature of each substance and its negative consequences. For instance, the client can keep a separate self-recording card for each substance and monitor urges separately. In some cases, it may be prudent to treat the more disruptive substance problem first, and then address other substances. For instance, one client reported that he had urges to use cocaine only after drinking a certain number of beers. After achieving abstinence from alcohol, he still used cocaine and, in fact, began to use it more often. Attention was turned to control of his cocaine problem, separate from his alcohol use. In general, the conjoint model can be modified to handle polydrug use. This requires, however, that the therapist be knowledgeable about effects, dosages, withdrawal symptoms, and treatment of a wide range of substances.

Other Comorbid Psychopathology

As noted, research has shown that a high percentage of alcoholics suffer from other psychiatric problems that are either concurrent with, antecedent to, or resulting from, their alcohol problems. Rates of psychopathology among alcoholics are much greater than in the general population, and thus have several implications for treatment of alcoholics. In the context of the conjoint model, this means that assessment should include screening for other Axis I and Axis II disorders. Diagnosing depression, anxiety and antisocial personality disorder (ASP) can be problematic in an alcoholic patient, because several of the symptoms and consequences of alcohol abuse mimic other disorders, and vice versa. For instance, withdrawal from heavy alcohol use can result in anxiety, irritability, sleeplessness, and/or depression—all of which are symptoms of other diagnostic entities. The therapist should be careful to assess the primary or secondary nature of the comorbid psychopathology before deciding if separate treatment is necessary. Just as marital issues emerge as the "smoke screen" of alcohol and its withdrawal symptoms lift, so does the true nature of depressive or anxious symptoms. Of course, if depression is extremely severe at any point during treatment, the client should be referred either for treatment for the depression—psychotherapy, medication, or inpatient treatment. In such cases, the depression would preclude further work on alcohol and marital issues, which can resume after the depression is treated. If the depression does not warrant such immediate action, it should nonetheless be monitored closely. If the alcoholic stays depressed for several weeks after abstinence, if the depression worsens, or if a client reports a history of depression that is antecedent to alcohol abuse or occurred during a long period of abstinence, depression should, at the very least, be assessed as a separate disorder. Likewise, anxiety symptoms that do not abate or that get worse with treatment of alcohol problems indicate that the patient may have a comorbid anxiety disorder; in fact, he/she may have been "self-medicating" the anxiety with alcohol. The following example illustrates a case complicated by comorbid psychopathology.

John, a 33-year-old divorced sales representative, came to conjoint treatment with Amy, age 27, his live-in girlfriend of 5 years. John had a 15-year history of heavy drinking. At intake he described feeling very depressed during the past year and had begun seeing a psychiatrist 8 months prior to treatment. He was put on imipramine, which he used for 3 months and before weaning himself off it. He typically consumed large quantities of beer several times a week. His alcohol intake had increased at age 19 when his mother died of cancer, while John was away at college. Since then, this elevated intake had been constant. Because Amy decided that unless John became sober she would leave the relationship, John was extremely motivated to stop drinking and was able to do so by the fifth week of treatment. At the seventh session, John reported that he was feeling very depressed and that it seemed to be getting worse, not better, with abstinence. John said that, aside from all the financial and relationship problems he had caused himself with the abuse of alcohol, he found himself thinking frequently of his mother's death and of the subsequent dispersal of his siblings and the end of his relationship with all of his six older siblings. Having lost his father at age 15, the death of his mother and "loss" of his siblings essentially left John an orphan at age 19. He said that he had never really mourned his mother—rather, he had a drink (which led to several more beers) whenever he began to feel bad about her or sorry for himself. The therapist commented that she was not surprised that John was feeling more and more depressed, since this was the first extended period since his mother's death in which he had not used alcohol as a way of coping with, or "drowning" his sad feelings about losing his mother and family. Another hypothesis that the therapist entertained nonverbally was that John suffered from a true depressive disorder that he had self-medicated for years with heavy drinking. At the ninth session, John and Amy arrived late, highly agitated. John had had a panic attack while driving to the session and had narrowly avoided an accident with a truck on the highway. John then informed the therapist that he had suffered many such panic attacks in the preceding year, until his psychiatrist prescribed Xanax for him. Aware of the addictive potential of Xanax, John had weaned himself off it and since then had not experienced any attacks. John continued to have worsening panic attacks on the way to subsequent conjoint sessions. Because these attacks were quite disabling, John was referred to an anxiety disorders clinic at a local teaching hospital. John was resistant to pursuing this type of treatment and preferred instead to visit his psychiatrist again. By this point in treatment, John had not had a drink in 7 weeks, and he and Amy were getting along much better. The therapist recommended that the couple remain in conjoint treatment, because there were several long-standing relationship issues left to address. John, however, decided to terminate treatment. Medication did not eliminate the panic symptoms he had on the way to our sessions, and he was no longer willing to tolerate the drive.

In John's case, his Axis I disorder gradually worsened with abstinence and began to affect John's motivation for continuing couple therapy. His primary goals had been reached, he felt, and both he and his psychiatrist were resistant to recommendations made by the therapist to seek treatment at an anxiety disorders clinic for behavioral treatment of his anxiety disorder (the safest method of treatment for an alcoholic who is at increased risk for abuse of addictive medications such as benzodiazepines).

Axis II disorders, in particular, ASP, have been shown to negatively affect the course of alcoholism and response to treatment (Rounsaville, Dolinsky, Babor, & Meyer, 1987; Yates, Petty, & Brown, 1988). Since a hallmark of ASP is a history of unstable relationships, it is unlikely that a large number of persons in their 20s with ASP will seek marital treatment for alcoholism: Most people with ASP in that age range are not married or are not invested enough in their relationships to attempt to solve problems. It is more common for "aging ASPs"—past age 35—to come to treatment with their wives (often the second or third wife) for treatment. It is, however, quite complicated and difficult to treat even these older clients with ASP. Often their relationships are still markedly unstable. They are more likely to have severe polydrug abuse and/or gambling problems, and marital issues around trust are intensified. Such clients are less likely to remain in treatment, to demonstrate tolerance for negative affect that is usually involved in therapy, and to have a positive outcome. Patient–treatment research is beginning to indicate that a skills training approach may be best suited for an ASP alcoholic population (Kadden, Cooney, Getter, & Litt, 1989). It may also be that external coercion or other "external" measures such as the use of disulfiram (Antabuse) are more effective for these patients. More research is necessary to determine if this is indeed so.

When Both Spouses Have an Alcohol Problem

The conjoint model can be modified to allow treatment of both spouses. Treatment of both spouses, however, might necessitate a longer therapy program than described previously, because cognitive-behavioral skills would have to be covered for both spouses' drinking patterns. The spouses would almost certainly benefit from sharing and watching each other go through the learning experience, from learning the additional marital skills of reinforcing sobriety, eliminating spouse-related triggers, and so on, and from the marital skills training aspects of the therapy. In a way, the therapist is in for "double trouble," but if she/he and the patients are prepared for a great deal of hard work, then there is no reason to avoid conjoint therapy when both partners are alcoholics.

Difficult Couples

In our experience, couples who are described as "difficult" by the therapist usually fall into one or more of the aforementioned categories under "Obstacles to Treatment." Minimization of the alcohol problem, noncompliance in treatment, acute marital distress or extreme marital discord, comorbid psychopathology in the alcoholic, or evidence of psychopathology in the spouse are all factors that alone or in combination (and they often interact with one another) result in complications in delivering the conjoint model of treatment for alcoholism. As a general rule, for difficult couples, the therapist must use clear limit-setting techniques and remain flexible in both theoretical approach and clinical interventions. The heterogeneity of the current alcoholic population and the complications that can arise require case-by-case decisions for extent of modification of the therapeutic model. In some cases, the individual (or marital) pathology or resistance of either spouse may be intense enough to disrupt conjoint therapy to the point that individual therapy for either or both partners is advisable. In these cases, the "difficult" partner(s) must first resolve, or at least control, some degree of pathology before conjoint treatment can be resumed. This can be accomplished either by referring the partner(s) to individual therapy with a different therapist (each partner should see a different therapist), or by trying a series of individual therapy sessions with the marital therapist within the context of conjoint treatment.

LIMITATIONS AND CONTRAINDICATIONS OF MARITAL TREATMENT OF ALCOHOLISM

Limitations

Sometimes the client (or the spouse) requires a higher level of care. For instance, if an alcoholic client simply is not having success in stopping or substantially decreasing drinking by perhaps the 10th session, it may be wise to consider more intensive treatment. If a client or spouse presents with a worsening depression or "substitute drug dependence," it may be advisable to refer him/her either to a psychiatric unit, a drug-rehabilitation unit, or, if need be, a dual-diagnosis treatment program.

A different kind of limitation of marital therapy for alcoholism involves the complicated nature of the cases seen and the need to focus on so many levels of treatment. The limitation here—not insurmountable, of course—is the need to set treatment priorities and try systematically to address each set of treatment issues. These couples often present with severe marital discord—enough to keep any therapist quite busy for many sessions—yet the conjoint model therapist must handle the additional, not insignificant, problem of alcoholism.

Several factors can render what seems an overwhelmingly complicated case manageable:

1. The therapist should use good diagnostic tools at the start so that he/she is more knowledgeable about and prepared for potential complications.

2. The therapist should have at his/her disposal an excellent referral network, including local detoxification centers; local rehabilitation programs; a physician who has expertise in the addictions and can supervise an outpatient detoxification or a course of Antabuse therapy; and therapists and psychiatrists with special expertise in the addictions, who are available to hand-

le referrals for individual therapy or medication consultations.

3. The therapist needs to know when to make use of the referral network, that is, he/she needs to be aware of the limitations of the conjoint model and to know when to supplement the treatment with other interventions.

Contraindications

There currently are no published data on patient–treatment matching for marital treatment of alcoholism with a heterogeneous sample. Some contraindications to beginning conjoint treatment have been implied previously: for instance, if a patient is suicidal at the first assessment session, a higher level of care is appropriate. Aside from such extreme examples, however, this model of therapy is multifaceted enough to lend itself to a good deal of modification based on the type and degree of marital and individual psychopathology presented.

A large-scale randomized outcome study of marital treatment for a heterogeneous population of alcoholic males and their partners is currently underway at our clinic. Results of this study should shed some light on which patients, based on several patient characteristics and treatment factors, are likely to benefit most, in terms of abstinence and increased marital satisfaction, from this treatment model.

Termination

Termination raises an interesting problem in the context of alcoholism treatment in light of the fact that a substantial portion of treatment professionals in this field view alcoholism as a relapsing disorder or habit that requires chronic treatment. Thus, defining therapy as either time-limited, or lengthy but eventually ending, may well be altered in the treatment of alcoholism as research begins to document the benefits of continued periodic contact between the alcoholic and therapist after a block of more intense treatment.

Currently, the conjoint model of treatment for alcoholism is a time-limited approach, with the option of "booster" or maintenance sessions continuing for as long as the involved parties see fit. The case study presented here spanned twenty, 90-minute sessions. Depending on the case, the number of sessions needed to cover assessment and the alcohol and marital skills can range from 15 to perhaps even 30 or more sessions. Two major criteria should be used to assess when it is time to terminate:

1. *Resolution of the alcohol use.* Has the alcoholic been abstinent long enough to feel comfortable with changes made in his/her life to support sobriety or decreased drinking? Have the cravings and urges for alcohol become manageable (i.e., less intense and intrusive)? Have other pleasurable activities been substituted for positive consequences that the alcoholic formerly derived from drinking (i.e., Is the alcoholic reasonably pleased with the new sober lifestyle he or she has created?).

2. *Improved marital relationship.* Do both the client and spouse report greater satisfaction with the relationship? In session is there evidence of increased goodwill toward one another? Is there evidence of better communication and more effective problem solving? Have they both adjusted to the changes in their relationship that resulted when the alcohol was eliminated?

If these criteria are met, and the therapist feels comfortable that he/she has introduced at least most of the skills that would be potentially helpful to the couple, the process of terminating the intensive weekly portion of the therapy can begin. One way to ease termination and to help the couple continue to discuss issues regularly is to introduce the concept of "marital meetings," and have the couple practice these meetings in sessions and as homework between sessions toward the end of therapy.

In the cognitive-behavioral conjoint model, termination need not be a particularly jarring event for the clients, because of several factors built into the model:

1. The therapist–patient relationship is not the core component of treatment, as it is in more psychoanalytic treatment models.
2. The entire focus of the therapy is on teaching the client and spouse skills that ideally, by the end of treatment, come naturally and will remain in the clients' behavior and marital repertoire. Thus, the couple should feel a decreasing need for continued weekly sessions.
3. The relapse prevention model recommends the use of maintenance sessions on a "chronic" basis, if necessary.
4. The spouses should have learned in the course of treatment to use each other as resources, and as a support system, so that dependence on the therapist to fulfill such a function should have waned as the treatment progressed.
5. At the last session, a relapse contract should

be drawn up and signed by both spouses, explicitly stating the conditions under which they should seek treatment again, or call the therapist for help.

SUMMARY AND CONCLUSIONS

Working with problem drinkers and their partners is challenging, difficult therapeutic work, with the potential for substantial rewards and substantial frustrations. The model presented in this chapter represents a blending of empirically supported approaches and our own clinical experiences with these couples. Research suggests that involving the spouse in treatment increases the probability of a positive outcome in terms of drinking, and that addressing the marital relationship increases the chances of the couple's remaining together and having a more satisfying relationship (McCrady, Stout, Noel, Abrams, & Nelson, 1991). We believe that the outcomes justify the difficulties inherent in this work.

ACKNOWLEDGMENT

Preparation of this chapter was supported in part by National Institute on Alcohol Abuse and Alcoholism Grant No. AA 07070.

REFERENCES

American Psychiatric Association. (1994). *Diagnostic and statistical manual of mental disorders* (4th ed.). Washington, DC: Author.

Babor, T. F., Kranzler, H. R., & Lauerman, R. J. (1989). Early detection of harmful alcohol consumption: Comparison of clinical, laboratory, and self-report screening procedures. *Addictive Behaviors, 14,* 139–157.

Baucom, D. H., & Epstein, N. (1990). *Cognitive-behavioral marital therapy.* New York: Brunner/Mazel.

Bennett, L. A., & Wolin, S. J. (1990). Family culture and alcoholism transmission. In R. L. Collins, K. E. Leonard, & J. S. Searles (Eds.), *Alcohol and the family: Research and clinical perspectives* (pp. 194–219). New York: Guilford Press.

Billings, A. S., Kessler, M., Gomberg, C. A., & Weiner, S. (1979). Marital conflict resolution of alcoholic and nonalcoholic couples during drinking and nondrinking sessions. *Journal of Studies on Alcohol, 40,* 183–195.

Carroll, J. F. X. (1986). Treating multiple substance abuse clients. *Recent Developments in Alcoholism, 4,* 85–103.

Cloninger, C. R., Bohman, M., & Sigvardsson, S. (1981). Inheritance of alcohol abuse. *Archives of General Psychiatry, 38,* 861–868.

Derogatis, L.R., Lipman, R. S., & Covi, L. (1973). The SCL-90. An outpatient psychiatric rating scale. *Psychopharmacology Bulletin, 9,* 13–28.

Edwards, G., & Gross, M. M. (1976). Alcohol dependence: Provisional description of a clinical syndrome. *British Medical Journal, 1,* 1058–1061.

Fingarette, H. (1988). *Heavy drinking: The myth of alcoholism as a disease.* Berkeley, CA: University of California Press.

Folstein, M. F., Folstein, S. E., & McHugh, P. R. (1975). "Mini-mental state": A practical method for grading the cognitive state of patients for the clinician. *Journal of Psychiatric Research, 12,* 189–198.

Frankenstein, W., Hay, W. M., & Nathan, P. E. (1985). Effects of intoxication on alcoholics' marital communication and problem solving. *Journal of Studies on Alcohol, 46,* 1–6.

Gottman, J., Notarius, C., Gonso, J., & Markman, H. (1976). *A couples guide to communication.* Champaign, IL: Research Press.

Hasin, D. S., Grant, B. F., & Endicott, J. (1988). Lifetime psychiatric comorbidity in hospitalized alcoholics: Subject and family correlates. *International Journal of the Addictions, 23,* 827–850.

Hesselbrock, M., Meyer, R., & Keener, J. J. (1985). Psychopathology in hospitalized alcoholics. *Archives of General Psychiatry, 42,* 1050–1055.

Jackson, J. K. (1954). The adjustment of the family to the crisis of alcoholism. *Quarterly Journal of Studies on Alcohol, 15,* 562–586.

Jacobson, N. S., & Margolin, G. (1979). *Marital therapy.* New York: Brunner/Mazel.

Kadden, R. M., Cooney, N. L., Getter, H., & Litt, M. D. (1989). Matching alcoholics to coping skills or interactional therapies: Posttreatment results. *Journal of Consulting and Clinical Psychology, 57,* 698–704.

Kaminer, W. (1990, February 11). Chances are you're codependent too. *New York Times Book Review,* pp. 3, 26–29.

Lewis, M. L. (1937). Alcoholism and family casework. *Social Casework, 35,* 8–14.

Margolin, G., Talovic, S., & Weinstein, C. D. (1983). Areas of Change Questionnaire: A practical approach to marital assessment. *Journal of Consulting and Clinical Psychology, 51,* 920–931.

Marlatt, G. A., & Gordon, J. R. (Eds.). (1985). *Relapse prevention.* New York: Guilford Press.

McCrady, B. S. (1992). A reply to Peele: Is this how

you treat your friends? *Addictive Behaviors, 17,* 67–72.

McCrady, B. S., & Irvine, S. (1989). Self-help groups in the treatment of alcoholism. In R. Hester & W. R. Miller (Eds.), *Comprehensive handbook of alcoholism treatment approaches: Effective alternatives.* New York: Pergamon Press.

McCrady, B. S., Stout, R., Noel, N., Abrams, D., & Nelson, H. F. (1991). Effectiveness of three types of spouse-involved behavioral alcoholism treatment. *British Journal of Addiction, 86,* 1415–1424.

Miller, W. R. (1985). Motivation for treatment: A review with special emphasis on alcoholism. *Psychological Bulletin, 98,* 84–107.

Moos, R. H., Finney, J. W., & Gamble, W. (1982). The process of recovery from alcoholism. II. Comparing spouses of alcoholic patients and matched community controls. *Journal of Studies on Alcohol, 43,* 888–909.

Moos, R. H., & Moos, B. S. (1984). The process of recovery from alcoholism: III. Comparing functioning of families of alcoholics and matched control families. *Journal of Studies on Alcohol, 45,* 111–118.

Paolino, T. J., Jr., & McCrady, B. S. (1977). *The alcoholic marriage: Alternative perspectives.* New York: Grune & Stratton.

Parsons, O. A., Butters, N., & Nathan, P. E. (Eds.). (1987). *Neuropsychology of alcoholism: Implications for diagnosis and treatment.* New York: Guilford Press.

Peele, S. (1992). Alcoholism, politics, and bureaucracy: The consensus against controlled-drinking therapy in America. *Addictive Behaviors, 17,* 49–62.

Read, M. R., Penick, E. C., Powell, B. J., Nickel, E. J., Bingham, S. F., & Campbell, J. (1990). Subtyping male alcoholics by family history of alcohol abuse and co-occurring psychiatric disorder: A bi-dimensional model. *British Journal of Addiction, 85,* 367–378.

Robins, L. N., Helzer, J. E., Croughan, J., & Ratcliffe, K. S. (1981). The NIMH Diagnostic Interview Schedule: Its history, characteristics and validity. *Archives of General Psychiatry, 38,* 381–389.

Robins, L. N., Wing, J., Wittchen, H. U., Helzer, J. E., Babor, T. F., Burke, J., Farmer, A., Jablenski, A., Pickens, R., Regier, D. A., Sartorius, N., & Towle, L. H. (1988). The prevalence of psychiatric disorders in patients with alcohol and other drug problems. *Archives of General Psychiatry, 45,* 1023–1031.

Rosenbaum, A., & O'Leary, K. D. (1986). The treatment of marital violence. In N. S. Jacobson & A. S. Gurman (Eds.), *Clinical handbook of marital therapy* (pp. 385–405). New York: Guilford Press.

Ross, H. E., Glaser, F. B., & Germanson, T. (1988a). The prevalence of psychiatric disorders in patients with alcohol and other drug problems. *Archives of General Psychiatry, 45,* 1023–1031.

Ross, H. E., Glaser, F. B., & Stiasny, S. (1988b). Sex differences in the prevalence of psychiatric disorders in patients with alcohol and drug problems. *British Journal of Addiction, 83,* 1179–1192.

Rounsaville, B. J., Dolinsky, Z. S., Babor, T. F., & Meyer, R. E. (1987). Psychopathology as a predictor of treatment outcome in alcoholics. *Archives of General Psychiatry, 44,* 505–513.

Schuckit, M. A. (1985). The clinical implications of primary diagnostic groups among alcoholics. *Archives of General Psychiatry, 42,* 1043–1049.

Selzer, M. L. (1971). The Michigan Alcoholism Screening test: The quest for a new diagnostic instrument. *American Journal of Psychiatry, 127,* 1653–1658.

Sobell, M. B., Maisto, S. A., Sobell, L. C., Cooper, T., & Saunders, B. (1980). Developing a prototype for evaluating alcohol treatment effectiveness. In L. C. Sobell, M. B. Sobell, & E. Ward (Eds.), *Evaluating alcohol and drug abuse treatment effectiveness: Recent advances* (pp. 129–150). New York: Pergamon.

Spanier, G. (1976). Measuring dyadic adjustment: New scales for assessing the quality of marriage and similar dyads. *Journal of Marriage and the Family, 38,* 15–28.

Steinglass, P., Bennett, L. A., Wolin, S. J., & Reiss, D. (1987). *The alcoholic family.* New York: Basic Books.

Thomas, E. J., & Santa, C. A. (1982). Unilateral family therapy for alcohol abuse: A working conception. *American Journal of Family Therapy, 10,* 49–60.

U.S. Department of Health and Human Services. (1983). *Fifth special report of the U.S. Congress on alcohol and health* (DHHS Pub. No. (ADM) 84-1291). Washington, DC: U.S. Government Printing Office.

Whalen, T. (1953). Wives of alcoholics: Four types observed in a family service agency. *Quarterly Journal of Studies on Alcohol, 14,* 632–641.

Willoughby, A. (1979). *The alcohol troubled person: Known and unknown.* Chicago: Nelson-Hall.

Yates, W. R., Petty, F., & Brown, K. (1988). Alcoholism in males with antisocial personality disorder. *International Journal of the Addictions, 23,* 999–1010.

Zitter, R. E., & McCrady, B. S. (1979). *The Drinking Patterns Questionnaire.* Unpublished manuscript, Brown University, Providence, RI.

19

Anxiety Disorders: The Role of Marital Therapy

MICHELLE G. CRASKE
LORI A. ZOELLNER

T HE PURPOSE of this chapter is to review the evidence concerning the use of marital couple therapy in the treatment of anxiety disorders. In addition, the methods for incorporating marital/couple therapy into an overall cognitive-behavioral treatment approach are described.

Several trends are important to note at the outset. First, theorizing about the role of family and marital relations in the etiology and maintenance of anxiety disorders has quite a long history. However, inclusion of marital therapy as a specific intervention component, and evaluation of its efficacy, is a relatively recent advance. Second, unlike depression, in which therapies that focus on the interpersonal context have been found to be useful in their own right for alleviating personal distress (e.g., Elkin et al., 1989; McLean & Hakstian, 1979), couple therapy is usually an adjunct intervention strategy for the treatment of anxiety. Third, by far the majority of the discussion and empirical research about couple therapy has been limited to agoraphobia and panic disorder with agoraphobia. The role of couple therapy for other anxiety disorders has received very little consideration.

It is conceivable that the role of couple therapy becomes more paramount as the effects of anxiety disorders become more pervasive. Pervasiveness of anxiety disorders occurs along two dimensions. The first dimension is the number of situations with which anxiety is associated and/or the constancy over time with which anxiety is experienced. For example, generalized anxiety disorder is characterized by anxious apprehension across a variety of situations, whereas specific phobias are more limited and circumscribed. Typically, obsessive–compulsive disorder, generalized anxiety disorder, agoraphobia/panic disorder with agoraphobia, and posttraumatic stress disorder are more constant than social phobia and specific phobias. It is likely that the more "constant" the individual's distress, the greater the impact upon interpersonal interactions. For example, topics of discussion between a couple may become oriented to anxiety-related issues instead of mutual interests. Furthermore, more "constant" states of anxiety tend to be associated with more depressed mood (e.g., Moras, 1989), which in turn may detrimentally affect interpersonal relations. Under these conditions, couple therapy would alleviate the detrimental effects of anxiety upon the interpersonal relationship. In turn, aversive or conflictual interactional styles that develop as a result of "constant" anxiety can contribute to anxiety problems. Under these conditions, couple therapy would alleviate a source of distress that contributes directly to the anxiety.

The second dimension, is the degree to which daily functioning is impaired by the behavioral-avoidance component of anxiety. For example, agoraphobia often leads to restructure of child-rearing and housekeeping roles (i.e., who does the shopping, drives the children around) and limitations on social/leisure activities (i.e., eating out, attending social gatherings, movies, etc.), due to avoidance of situations from which escape might be difficult or help unavailable. In contrast, generalized anxiety disorder tends to have a lesser impact on daily activities, although a cautiousness in style is likely to be present: that is, whereas the person with generalized anxiety does not necessarily avoid travel, extra precautions may be taken with regard to road safety or check-in points along the way. The anxiety disorders that place most restrictions on daily activities and interpersonal functioning include agoraphobia, obsessive–compulsive disorder and social phobia. It is likely that the more pervasive the behavioral-avoidance component, the greater the impact upon interpersonal relations. Furthermore, avoidance or restriction of activities may affect the interpersonal relations in ways that ultimately contribute to the maintenance of the anxiety problem. For example, a spouse's assumption of roles formerly carried out by the agoraphobic partner, such as shopping and driving, may reinforce the agoraphobic avoidance pattern. Similarly, a spouses's compliance with the obsesive–compulsive person's cleaning rituals is likely to contribute to their maintenance. Therefore, couple therapy seems appropriate for improving the quality of the relationship, as well as facilitating recovery from the anxiety problem.

Nevertheless, regardless of the specific anxiety-disorder diagnosis, effective treatment planning warrants a complete functional analysis that includes consideration of the ways in which (1) interpersonal relations might contribute to the maintenance of the anxiety problem, and (2) interpersonal relations are negatively impacted by the anxiety problem.

This chapter begins with a review of the significance of interpersonal relationships for the onset and/or maintenance of anxiety disorders, and the interaction between the quality of couple relations and treatment outcome. Then, the methods of marital/couple therapy are described, including evaluation of the efficacy of these strategies. Finally, potential mechanisms of therapeutic efficacy and areas in need of further research and evaluation are considered. Throughout this chapter, the term "marital" refers to significant couple relationships.

THEORETICAL CONCEPTUALIZATIONS

The marital system has been hypothesized to relate to anxiety disorders in two main ways. First, it has been posited that the marital system precedes and is responsible for the development of certain anxiety disorders. Related to this is the notion that a motivation exists on the part of the nonanxious partner to maintain the significant other's distressed, anxious state, and that improvement by the anxious partner is distressing for the nonanxious partner. Second, it is posited that marital conflict develops as a result of an anxiety disorder, and in turn interferes with recovery from the anxiety disorder. The conceptualizations and empirical evidence are reviewed, with particular reference to agoraphobia.

Marital Distress as a Precursor of Anxiety Disorders

In their major paper on the topic of agoraphobia, Goldstein and Chambless (1978) outlined specifically the role of marital relations in the onset of agoraphobic symptoms. They distinguished between two types of agoraphobia: (1) "simple agoraphobia" refers to individuals who develop panic attacks in relation to physical disorders, such as hypoglycemia or drug experiences; (2) "complex agoraphobia," on the other hand, describes an entire syndrome: fear of fear; low levels of self-sufficiency or lack of skills; a tendency to misinterpret causal factors for panic attacks; and the onset of the symptoms under conditions of serious conflict. According to their conceptualization, this conflict is virtually always associated with interpersonal relationships. Specifically, Goldstein and Chambless emphasized the marital relationship. They suggested that interpersonal conflict may arise from the desire to achieve autonomy versus the desire to stay in a protective environment. Usually, the outbreak of agoraphobia occurs when this conflict surfaces. Prior to the onset of agoraphobia, the conflict can be avoided by substituting dependency on a spouse for parental protection. The marital situation may be exacerbated by several years of a bad marriage or the birth of children. Unfortunately, with his/her fears of separation and lack of coping skills, the person is trapped in a situation that cannot be resolved. When conflicts between autonomy and a familiar environment persist long enough, the preagoraphobic person is likely to experience sharp outbreaks of anxiety, otherwise known as "panic attacks." Furthermore, misattribution about causal factors may occur. For example, anxiety associated with an interpersonal problem may be interpreted as fear of being alone in the street. In summary, this theoretical conceptualization views the preagoraphobic as trapped in a domineering relationship without the skills needed to activate change in the situation.

Issues of dependency in the development of agoraphobia are also central from a psychodynamic perspective. In accord with this theoretical orientation, the agoraphobic adult is believed to regress into an infantile style of emotional dependence on the spouse. In turn, the spouse is strengthened as a result of the dependence placed upon him/herself (Fry, 1962). The marital relationship, therefore, is perceived to meet mutual needs or deficiencies for both partners. The spouse of the agoraphobic lacks self-confidence and this deficiency is reduced by his/her role in the relationship. The agoraphobic, in contrast, needs to rely on or requires the aid of the partner for the sense of support. Therefore, the development of agoraphobia is understood as arising from this complementary relationship between the phobic and the spouse.

Support for these conceptualizations of agoraphobia is mostly in the form of clinical case reports. However, the personality features of the agoraphobic partner, which are conceptualized as contributing to the "pathology" of the marital relationship (i.e., overdependence, immaturity, social anxiety, nonassertiveness, and fear of responsibility), are partially supported by studies of comorbidity between personality disorders and panic/agoraphobia. Barlow (1988) concluded that the comorbidity between personality disorders and panic disorder with agoraphobia ranges from 25% to 50%. Most of the personality disorders are from the "anxious" cluster: dependent, avoidant, obsessive– compulsive, and passive-aggressive. However, the causal significance of dependent and avoidant features is questionable. For example, Arrindell and Emmelkamp (1987) found that agoraphobic individuals are not significantly more dependent than are persons with other psychiatric conditions. Furthermore, Mavissakalian and Hamann (1987) found that dependent features tend to decline with successful treatment of agoraphobia (on the other hand, avoidant and histrionic characteristics are more enduring). Also, Reich, Noyes, Hirschfeld, Coryell, and O'Gorman (1987) failed to find any personality measures that differentiate re-covered panic patients from recovered depressed patients.

One fairly consistent pattern that has emerged is that individuals who develop severe agoraphobia tend to be more interpersonally sensitive than individuals whose agoraphobic avoidance remains relatively mild (Noyes et al., 1986; Thyer, Himle, Curtis, Cameron, & Nesse, 1985). Similarly, the more agoraphobic the individual, the stronger the likelihood of a diagnosis of dependent personality disorder (Reich, Noyes, & Troughten, 1987).

In conclusion, it would seem that the concept of a distinct marital system that predisposes to agoraphobia is almost devoid of empirical support, whereas evidence for distinct personality characteristics that predispose to the development of panic disorder/agoraphobia is mixed. The most consistent finding is an interpersonal sensitivity characteristic of agoraphobia. However, the way that such interpersonal sensitivity affects marital relations is not known.

An alternative conceptualization of the etiological significance of marital relationships for the development of agoraphobia, and anxiety disorders in general, is a stress–diathesis model. That is, most anxiety disorders tend to develop within the context of stressful life circumstances (e.g., Barlow, 1988; Craske, Miller, Rotunda, & Barlow, 1990; Pollard, Pollard, & Corn, 1990). Moreover, there is some evidence to suggest that interpersonal stress is a particularly common form of life event that precedes the development of anxiety disorders. In one study conducted by Doctor (1982), over 400 agoraphobics were interviewed concerning negative life events. He found that separation from or loss of a spouse (31%), relationships problems (30%), and new responsibilities (20%) were the most common antecedents of panic and agoraphobia. A similar finding was reported by Last, Barlow, and O'Brien (1984). Although these data suggest a special link between marital stress and panic/agoraphobia, it is unclear whether marital stress is simply a more common form of stress, or whether it has particular significance in comparison to other types of stressors.

Marital Distress as a Function of Anxiety Disorders

Although Lazarus (1966) speaks of the spouse as contributing to the development of agoraphobia by complying with the inevitable demands of the sufferer, the marital relationship itself may change as a result of these demands. Those changes in the relationship may, in turn, contribute to the anxiety problem. For example, an agoraphobic woman who previously was able to grocery shop now relies on her husband to do the shopping. The husband has new demands placed upon him that, in turn, lead to marital discord. The marital distress adds to background stress, making progress and recovery even more difficult.

Buglass, Clarke, Henderson, and Presley (1977) suggest that marital difficulties are primarily a product rather than a cause of agoraphobia. These authors compared 30 married agoraphobic women with married, nonpsychiatric controls selected from a general outpatient population. All subjects and spouses were interviewed and asked to complete a series of questionnaires. The results highlighted the sexual-relations aspect of the interpersonal context. Agoraphobic women did not differ from controls in their sexual adjustment prior to the onset of agoraphobia. After the onset of agoraphobia, however, 16 of 24 agoraphobics (who were married prior to the onset of their agoraphobia) reported a marked loss of sexual drive: a significantly higher proportion than in the nonagoraphobic control group. Furthermore, the husbands of the agoraphobic women complained of experiencing adverse effects from their wives' disorders.

Marital Relations as Predictor of Phobia Treatment Outcome

Regardless of whether marital distress is a cause or a consequence of panic and agoraphobia, an association between marital distress and the success with which agoraphobia is treated would suggest the value of marital therapy. The influence of the quality of marital relations on outcome from exposure therapy for agoraphobia has been studied by numerous investigators. ("Exposure therapy" is the treatment of choice for phobias, and refers to repeated confrontations with feared and avoided objects or situations.) Milton and Hafner (1979) reported that couples with disturbed marriages show the least improvement with exposure treatment. They suggested that problematic marriages may adversely affect response to exposure therapy. Furthermore, they found a clear relationship between worsening of marital relations and partial relapse during follow-up intervals, which was attributed to removal of the therapist's support and encouragement. Bland and Hallam (1981) tested a similar hypothesis and found that agoraphobics who had good marriages prior to treatment responded well

to the graded therapist-aided exposure and maintained their improvement over the 3-month follow-up interval. Agoraphobics who had poor marriages prior to treatment initially responded well to treatment, but later lost most of their gains. Also, maritally satisfied clients exhibited better generalization of treatment effectiveness to nontargeted areas. Other studies have supported the conclusion that the quality of the marital relationship prior to treatment may be an important predictor of treatment outcome (Hudson, 1974; Monteiro, Marks, & Ramm, 1985) Reviews conducted by Kleiner and Marshall (1985) and Dewey and Hunsley (1989) reached similar conclusions. From their analysis of six, well-controlled studies, Dewey and Hunsley found that higher pretreatment marital functioning was associated with greater reductions in agoraphobic symptomatology at posttreatment and up to 1 year following treatment completion. They suggested that patient ratings of a positive marital adjustment reflected a supportive interpersonal environment in which attempts to alter dysfunctional behaviors are reinforced.

Peter and Hand (1988) examined couple interaction from the perspective of "expressed emotion" (EE). The concept of EE was measured in 25 agoraphobics who were either married or in a marriage-like relationship. Couples' interactional styles were classified as either "high EE" or "low EE." High-EE couples were characterized by more disagreement, more personal and specific criticism, more negative affect, and more negative mutual reinforcement than couples with low EE. Treatment consisted of therapist-aided *in vivo* group exposure. During the follow-up period, clients from high-EE dyads showed significantly better treatment outcome than clients in low-EE dyads. The authors hypothesized that high criticism by clients of their spouses at pretreatment reflected a dissatisfaction with their perceived dependence on the spouse, a high motivation for change, and one of the first steps toward more open communication. On the other hand, low-EE couples may have a low motivation for change due to role compatibility and satisfaction with current lifestyle: that is, clients may want a caring and supportive spouse, while their partners may be happy with their dependence and housebound lifestyle.

On the other hand, several studies point to no specific relationship between marital satisfaction and treatment outcome. Emmelkamp (1980) divided 17 agoraphobics into groups of high and low marital satisfaction and also high and low assertiveness. Very few differences emerged between these groups after exposure treatment, albeit only 4 sessions in length, either at post-treatment or at 1-month follow-up. Similarly, Arrindell and Emmelkamp (1987) and Hafner and Ross (1983) found that improvement in agoraphobic complaints was unrelated to pretreatment levels of marital or sexual adjustment. Also, Himadi, Cerny, Barlow, Cohen, and O'Brien (1986) failed to establish a relationship between marital status and treatment outcome. However, the treatment for the majority of the agoraphobic sample studied by Himadi et al. (1986) involved spouses. As discussed next, involvement of spouses may override the detrimental effects of poor marital satisfaction upon treatment outcome.

Effect of Phobia Treatment on Marital Relations

A related issue is the extent to which an exposure-based treatment affects marital functioning. The research in this area is contradictory. Some researchers have noted that treatment can have a deleterious effect on the marriages of agoraphobic patients (Hafner, 1979, 1984; Hand & Lamontagne, 1976). Others have reported that successful treatment either has no effect or a positive effect on the marital functioning of agoraphobics (Barlow, O'Brien, Last, & Holden, 1983; Himadi et al., 1986). For example, Hand and Lamontagne (1976) noted that 7 couples experienced acute marital crises following the removal of the client's phobic symptoms. In a similar vein, Hafner (1977) noted that a significant proportion of husbands exhibited increased neurotic symptomatology and self-dissatisfaction that coincided with improvement in their wives' phobic symptoms. In contrast, Barlow, Mavissakalian, and Hay (1981) did not find a general pattern of marital dissatisfaction with improvement in phobic difficulties. Barlow et al. (1983) suggested that studies revealing negative effects of exposure therapy upon marital relations typically entail intensive *in vivo* exposure conducted without the spouses' involvement. They suggested that this type of treatment may negatively affect the spouses because major role changes occur beyond the spouses' perceived control. Accordingly, they proposed that spacing the treatment over a longer time allows the spouses to adapt to changes in the marriage relationship and the phobia. Furthermore, involvement of the spouse may offset those types of marital distress situations that occur as a result of exposure treatment (as reviewed later).

In summary, there is evidence to suggest that poor marital relations can predict poorer phobia outcome, that certain types of phobia treatments may have detrimental effects upon marital relations, and that marital distress may contribute to the maintenance, if not the etiology, of panic and agoraphobia. Taken together, these findings form the basis of marital therapy in the treatment of panic and agoraphobia.

MARITAL TREATMENT METHODS

Spouse as Coach

By far the most common method of incorporating marital therapy is to use the spouse as a coach who assists the agoraphobic client in becoming less agoraphobic in much the same way as would a therapist. This type of coaching has been conducted in individual- as well as group-treatment formats.

The following treatment description is derived from standardized intervention research protocols developed at the Center of Stress Anxiety Disorders, the University at Albany, State University of New York. The results from these types of treatment (which are reviewed next) are presented by Barlow, O'Brien, and Last (1984), and Cerny, Barlow, Craske, and Himadi (1987). The purpose of involving the spouse in treatment is to (1) alleviate marital distress that may surround and even contribute to the agoraphobic's problem, and (2) facilitate recovery by the agoraphobic client through enhanced generalization to the home setting, and increased practice of skills and strategies taught in therapy.

The treatment involves 12 clinic sessions conducted weekly for the first 8 sessions, and biweekly for the last 4 sessions. Each session is attended by the client and his/her spouse. The basic treatment strategy for agoraphobic problems entails *in vivo* exposure therapy, with the aid of various coping skills, such as relaxation training; self-statement training; or more recently, panic-management strategies, including breathing retraining and interoceptive exposure (e.g., Barlow, Craske, Cerny, & Klosko, 1989). What follows is a step-by-step description of how the *spouse is incorporated into the treatment*.

Education Phase

The purpose of the education phase is to provide a conceptual framework by which the client and spouse can understand the anxiety problem, and to provide information that corrects misappraisals about the nature of panic and anxiety. From the very beginning, the spouse is encouraged to become an active participant by providing his/her perception of the client's behavior and fearfulness, and the impact on the home environment. Sometimes spouses provide information of which the client was not fully aware, particularly in relation to how the client's behavior affects the spouse's own daily functioning. Consequently, the spouse helps generate a complete response profile and hierarchy of situations for exposure practice.

By acquiring an understanding of the client's agoraphobic behavior, the spouse is less frustrated and makes fewer negative attributions about the client's emotional functioning, which in turn is likely to alleviate distress between the couple. The basic rationale is that since agoraphobia represents avoidance due to anticipation of experiencing panic, treatment involves learning that the symptoms of panic are not dangerous, and that the avoided situations can be confronted without aversive consequences. In addition, the rationale emphasizes the importance of involving both partners of the couple in treatment, given the importance of the interpersonal context. The way that the agoraphobic problem has disrupted daily routines and distribution of home responsibilities is explored and discussed. Examples might include social activities, leisure activities, and household chores. The therapist explains that family activities may be structured around the agoraphobic fear and avoidance in order to help the client function without intense anxiety. At the same time, the reassignment to the spouse of tasks that were previously conducted by the client may actually reinforce the agoraphobic pattern of behavior. At this point, the couple is asked to identify those behaviors or task assignments that might be reinforcing the agoraphobic pattern.

Coping Strategies

Coping strategies are taught for dealing with heightened anxiety and panic. These include cognitive and somatic strategies. The role of self-statements about inability to cope, and expectancies of danger associated with panic attacks (e.g., fainting, going crazy), is discussed and explored. Clients and spouses are instructed in ways of questioning what clients envision happening, or what they think could occur if they panicked in a specific situation.

Next, specific methods of cognitive restructur-

ing are taught. Challenging self-statements take the form of Meichenbaum's (1974) 4-stage coping model or are based on Beck and Emery's (1985) errors in thinking (e.g., overgeneralizing, absolute thinking). The spouse is encouraged to help the client question and challenge his/her own "anxious" thoughts. Role plays of this type of questioning and challenging between the client and spouse can be conducted in-session, where the therapist provides corrective feedback to each partner.

In addition, this phase of treatment includes discussion of how the spouse can reinforce the agoraphobic problem through style of verbal response. For example, spouses may positively reinforce agoraphobic behavior with increased attention and sympathy when the client expresses fearfulness. Spouses are discouraged from magnifying the experience of panic and encouraged to help the client apply coping statements when anxious. At the same time, spouses are encouraged to be supportive and patient, especially because progress for the client may be erratic.

Other coping strategies taught to clients include relaxation (Bernstein & Borkovec, 1973) or slowed breathing exercises (Barlow & Craske, 1988). Spouses learn about these strategies through observation of the training process. During the *in vivo* exposure phase, the spouses are asked to prompt clients to use these coping strategies.

Communication Surrounding Exposure Tasks

The next step involves preparation for *in vivo* exposure by instructing couples in the methods of communicating and dealing with heightened anxiety. The client and spouse are encouraged to use a 0-to 8-point rating to communicate with each other about the client's current level of anxiety or distress, as a way of diminishing the awkwardness associated with discussion of this topic, especially in public situations. Clients are forewarned about preferring not to discuss their feelings with their spouse, due to (1) embarrassment or (2) attempts to avoid their anxiety due to the concern that anxiety levels will intensify as a function of being the focus of discussion. Avoidance of feelings is discouraged, because distraction is viewed as less beneficial in the long term than direct exposure. Clients are reassured that the initial discomfort and embarrassment will most likely be reduced as they become more familiar with discussing anxiety levels and their management.

Furthermore, clients' concerns about their spouses being insensitive or too pushy are addressed. For example, spouses may presume to know the client's level of anxiety and anxious thoughts without confirmation from the client, or spouses may become angry toward the client for avoiding or escaping from situations or being fearful. All of these issues are described as relatively common and understandable patterns of communication, but they nevertheless are detrimental. In-session role playing of more adaptive communication styles during episodes of heightened anxiety is a useful learning technique, especially in combination with participant modeling from the therapist.

In Vivo Practice

The next step involves structured in vivo exposure practices, with the aid of the spouse as a coach to encourage practice and use of coping strategies. In the Albany treatment protocol, the in vivo exposure strategies begin around the fifth treatment session, and continue for the remainder of the 12 sessions. Together, the client and spouse generate a hierarchy of situational tasks that impact their lives. Using a graduated approach, the items are listed in order of difficulty, or fear level, and practices begin at the lower end of the hierarchy. Time is spent in-session discussing exactly how the task is to be approached and accomplished. Clients are instructed to practice a particular task at least three times before the next clinic session (over the next week). The spouse must accompany the client on at least one occasion, usually the first time, whereas the client must complete the task alone on at least one other occasion. The reason for the latter requirement is to prevent overdependence, so that the client learns that he/she can perform the task without relying on the safety-signal presence of the spouse.

The remaining clinic sessions involve discussion of in vivo exposure assignments, with corrective feedback and reinforcement for the client and the spouse, followed by planning of the tasks to be conducted over the following week.

Specific Communication Training

In addition to incorporating the spouse as a coach, the couple can be taught specific techniques to enhance the quality of their communication. It is believed that enhanced communication facilitates completion of in vivo exposure tasks and reduces levels of background frustration and anxiety. In the studies to date, communication training has focused on issues related directly to agoraphobia, rather than more general topics of conflict. The communications training has been conducted in parallel with in vivo exposure practices, or as a separate treatment component following in vivo exposure (e.g., Arnow, Taylor, Agras, & Telch, 1985).

The communication training methods to be described are derived from a detailed research-intervention protocol currently under investigation at the Center for Stress and Anxiety Disorders in New York. The Albany protocol is derived from Arnow et al. (1985), who in turn drew heavily from Stuart (1980). Specific communication training is not introduced until the second half of the 12-session treatment program. After the couple has acquired a cognitive-behavioral framework for understanding agoraphobia, has realized behaviors and reinforcement patterns that may be contributing to the maintenance of agoraphobia, is familiar with the coping strategies, and has begun in vivo exposure practices, a problem-solving approach to communications skills is introduced. It is emphasized that because collaboration between partners is an integral part of treatment, it is important to enhance communication while working on phobic symptoms.

Communication Education

The basic elements of communication are described as "intent" and "impact" of messages, which are introduced in the following way.

"Good communication means having the impact that is intended. In other words, impact equals intent. For that type of equation to occur, the communication must be clear and precise. The speaker must clarify the intent of his/her message by stating exactly what it is he/she is thinking, wanting, or feeling and does not assume that the listener knows what is going on inside his/her head. The good listener tries to make sure that the intent of the message is understood and does not assume to know what is going on inside the speaker's mind."

"Cognitive filters" are described as mechanisms that distort messages in the following way.

"For example, after returning home from a hard day at work, spouses may sound very angry toward their partners, even though they were actually very irritated at their boss or some other aspect of the work setting. In this case, the spouse returning home may not even be aware of the impact he/she is creating, and the listener may distort the message with his/her own filter and not hear it the way the message was intended. Feedback is required in order to equate intent and impact. Feedback involves telling the speaker what impact the message had."

After discussion along the lines just described, the couple is instructed to think about examples of misinterpretations due to potential distortion of intent. In addition, they are asked to list agoraphobic issues that cause problems for them, either because they never seem to get resolved, or because they tend to escalate into arguments. The issues are structured into a hierarchy according to difficulty level. Examples might include the nonphobic spouse wanting to go to a party or restaurant to which the phobic partner refuses to go, vacation time, household and childrearing duties, or issues relating to the client's being afraid to stay home alone. The hierarchy is used for applied practice of communication skills that are taught over the next few weeks of treatment.

Summarizing Self-Syndrome

Next, the concept of "summarizing self-syndrome" is introduced as a basic communication flaw. It is presented as a restating of one's own position without listening to the other person. Each person is so sure that he/she is right that they both feel it is a waste of time to hear the other person's point of view, and so neither person really listens. Instead, both persons restate their own position again and again, resulting in feelings of frustration about not being listened to or respected. Indicators of this type of miscommunication are described to the couple in the form of a checklist that includes the following:

1. Drifting off beam: the sense that the other person never sees one's own point of view. This is caused by drifting into other problem areas when trying to resolve a specific issue.
2. Mind reading: the feeling of knowing someone so well that one can read his/her mind. Couples are told that since it is almost impossible to know what another person is thinking or feeling without asking, mind reading can lead to misconceptions.

3. Kitchen sinking: bringing in other issues when discussing a specific area of conflict. This usually ends with one or both parties feeling overwhelmed because they cannot solve any of their problems.
4. Yes butting: consistently finding something wrong with the speaker's point of view, which can be very frustrating for the speaking partner, who may decide that it is useless to speak if he/she is always wrong.
5. Cross-complaining: each partner stating a complaint in response to a complaint, so that each thinks in terms of winning.
6. The final indicators of the summarizing self-syndrome are the standoff (both partners holding fast to their own position, believing themselves to be right, with a sense of dignity and pride preventing them from backing down), quarrels, and heavy silences.

An example of a summarizing self-syndrome interaction about an agoraphobic topic follows:

NONPHOBIC PARTNER: Did you find a babysitter for Saturday night when we go to Mark and Joan's 20th anniversary party?

PHOBIC PARTNER: No . . . I've decided that I'm not going.

NONPHOBIC PARTNER: But I really want to go and everyone will be expecting us.

PHOBIC PARTNER: I won't enjoy myself.

NONPHOBIC PARTNER: But you don't enjoy yourself anywhere anymore . . . you're not even happy when you stay here, and you certainly aren't doing anything to help yourself by staying at home.

PHOBIC PARTNER: You just don't understand. You don't even care how bad I feel. You don't care about me at all.

NONPHOBIC PARTNER: Now you're just being ridiculous. I've put up with as much as I can from you. You let me know when you're ready to help yourself.

The couple is instructed to record independently the presence of any of these indicators in their own communication with their spouse over the next week. This self-monitoring of each person's own communication style is designed to increase awareness of errors, in much the same way that errors in thinking about the dangers of anxiety must be identified before being corrected with counterstatements.

In the next session, the couple is taught ways of ending the summarizing self-syndrome. They are instructed to see the validity of the other person's perspective in whatever way possible, to communicate that validation to the other person, to ask what can be done to "make things better," to assume a task focus, and to state what they is willing to do to correct the situation clearly and specifically. This involves taking a problem-solving approach in reference to agoraphobic issues. For example, phobic partners are encouraged to recognize the validity of their spouse's desire to socialize with friends, and to state what they are willing to do in order to attempt to achieve their spouses' goal, such as a willingness to attend the social event for the first 5 or 10 minutes. Similarly, the nonphobic partner is encouraged to recognize the phobic partner's fear of social situations and suggest how the situation could be best approached. The interaction described earlier could proceed in the following, more adaptive way:

NONPHOBIC PARTNER: Did you find a babysitter for Saturday night when we go to Mark and Joan's 20th anniversary party?

PHOBIC PARTNER: No . . . I've been thinking about it and I don't think I'm ready for that kind of event yet.

NONPHOBIC PARTNER: Is it because you're worried that you will feel too anxious when you get there?

PHOBIC PARTNER: Yes—I'm afraid. But I know that you really want to go to their party.

NONPHOBIC PARTNER: Is there anything I can do that would make you feel more comfortable about going?

PHOBIC PARTNER: Maybe by letting me leave early if I feel like I really have to leave . . . then we could at least try it to see how it goes.

Other strategies for ending the summarizing self-syndrome include calling for a "stop action," which means calling for an end to the discussion at hand and "discussing the discussion," asking for clear and brief feedback, listening to the feedback, paying attention to the content, and summarizing and validating the content and feelings in what each partner has said.

The between-session homework assignment is to practice the suggested communication strategies in relation to a topic from the lower end of the hierarchy of agoraphobic-related topics.

Leveling Techniques

Next, "leveling techniques" are discussed as skills for dealing with issues that have potential for resolution, or when communication regarding an issue is at a minimum, although each partner has a lot to say about the issue, for fear of conflict and disagreement. Leveling involves stating one's thoughts and feelings without blame or insult. For example, if going to the movies is a very anxiety-provoking situation for the agoraphobic partner, he/she could say to the nonphobic partner: "You are really cruel to keep asking me to go to the movies when you know that I am scared." This statement blames the nonphobic person and mind reads as well. A more effective way of communicating would be to say: "I realize that you really want to go to the movies and I can understand that, but I get very nervous and I don't think I would enjoy myself." In this second statement, no one feels attacked and the couple can continue to feel like a team facing a problem together. In addition, the phobic person is paraphrasing and therefore validating the nonphobic person's desire to go to the movies.

Another example of ineffective communication occurs when the nonphobic spouse says to the phobic partner: "You are really being selfish. You never want to go anywhere." In this statement, the nonphobic partner avoids stating his/her own feelings and is insulting and attacking. A more effective strategy would be to say: "I understand that you are frightened, but I would enjoy myself more if we would go places together the way we used to. What can I do to help?" In this statement, the nonphobic partner is being supportive and understanding, while simultaneously being honest about his/her own feelings. With this information, the couple is instructed to choose the next item from their hierarchy of agoraphobic issues to discuss, and attempt to reach a resolution.

Editing

A new communication skill called "editing" is introduced in the next session. "Editing" refers to politeness and consideration. Couples are informed of the common irony that we are often ruder to those we are closest to than we would be to total strangers. It has been found that spouses tend more to interrupt, put each other down, hurt each other's feelings, and be less complimentary to each other than they are to strangers. The couple is told that being considerate and polite should be independent of what the partner is doing. Editing means choosing the more positive way of communicating, such as responding to a request by stating what can be done instead of what cannot be done. For example, if the phobic spouse asks his/her partner to practice an *in vivo* exposure task, and the nonphobic spouse is busy, it would be preferable for the latter to state "I'll practice with you this weekend, when I finish this project" rather than "I'll be working on this project, and if I get a chance we can practice."

Another editing skill is to express appreciation for each other's actions. For example, if the nonphobic spouse is having a busy week and helps the phobic spouse practice one time only, the phobic spouse is encouraged to show appreciation for time taken out of a busy week rather than to complain about a lack of help.

A final editing skill is "empathy," described to couples as thinking of how the other person is feeling. For example, the nonphobic spouse may feel upset because he/she agreed to leave work early in order to help his/her spouse with an exposure practice. Upon arriving home, he/she finds the phobic spouse unwilling to attempt the exposure practice. Under these circumstances, the nonphobic spouse could say, "You always do this. You never want to try, besides the house is filthy. If you can't get out, the least you can do is clean up this place." A more effective communication might be "I know how much you want to get better. You must be feeling pretty anxious today if you are hesitant to try to practice. Why don't you try part of it." Again, the couple is instructed to practice communicating about and resolving another item from their topics hierarchy, using all of the communication skills described so far.

Problem Solving

Problem solving is introduced as a final communication skill, with particular reference to the development of the phobic partner's independent behavior over the months after treatment completion. "Problem solving" is described as learning how to approach an issue as a team, brainstorming potential courses of action, evaluating and selecting the most appropriate courses of action, and instituting the chosen course.

An important topic to brainstorm is how the phobic partner can deal most effectively with an unexpected panic attack when away from home and alone. Possible solutions might include self-reliance on coping strategies, contacting the nonphobic spouse for support and encouragement, or planned *in vivo* practice with the nonphobic spouse soon after the panic attack, in the situation in which the panic occurred. Another important topic for posttreatment planning concerns the phobic partner's interest in returning to a job or career, and how that might effect the daily living arrangements, care of children, and so on. Similarly, other changes in lifestyle that have become realizable since gaining control over panic attacks and agoraphobia (e.g., taking night classes for further education, socializing, vacationing) may warrant problem solving.

MARITAL TREATMENT EFFICACY

Evaluation of the efficacy of marital therapy in the treatment of agoraphobia can be addressed in one of three ways. First, what is the relationship between marital status at pretreatment and the efficacy of marital therapy for agoraphobia? Second, what is the effect of marital therapy on agoraphobia? Third, what is the effect of marital therapy on the marriages of agoraphobics in treatment for agoraphobia?

Marital Satisfaction as a Predictor of Phobia Treatment Outcome

As noted earlier, the predictive value of the quality of pretreatment marital relations is mixed, although several studies would suggest that a poorer marriage at pretreatment predicts poorer outcome from behavioral treatments for agoraphobia. In 1983, Barlow and colleagues found an interaction between whether the spouse was involved in treatment, and the predictive value of pretreatment marital status. That is, in initially maladjusted marriages, marked phobic improvement occurred only when the spouse was included in the treatment. Including the spouse seemed to overcome the deleterious effects of poor marital relations noted in previous investigations. This finding was corroborated by Himadi et al. (1986), who examined a group of agoraphobics whose treatment in the majority of cases involved a spouse. Overall, they found an improvement in phobic symptomatology and in marital satisfaction, regardless of initial levels of marital satisfaction.

Craske, Burton, and Barlow (1989) examined the relationship between communication and phobia outcome in agoraphobics whose treatment involved spouses. Measures of marital satisfaction were unrelated to treatment outcome. On the other hand, posttreatment responders rated themselves and their partners as more communicative regarding their fears at pretreatment assessment than did nonresponders. Furthermore, measures of communication related inversely to levels of anxiety reported during exposures.

Therefore, within this group of agoraphobics whose spouses were involved in all aspects of treatment, it was those who rated their communication as best at the start of treatment that benefited most from treatment. Interestingly, frequency of communication tended to improve from pre- to midtreatment in the subgroup that initially reported a low level of communication with their partners. Furthermore, phobic improvement was most apparent after the midtreatment point in this subgroup of subjects. Consequently, the authors suggested that communication training may be particularly helpful for couples who self-report low levels of communication at pretreatment.

Efficacy of Marital Therapy: Phobia Treatment Outcome

In 1981, Barlow, Mavissakalian, and Hay examined 6 agoraphobic women who were treated for agoraphobia with the aid of their spouse in the manner described earlier: that is, the husbands acted as coaches or cotherapists. These authors recognized that programs had occasionally included the spouses as cotherapists (e.g., Mathews, Teasdale, Nunby, Johnston, & Shaw, 1977), but the effects of this clinical strategy had not been evaluated up until that time. Overall, they found that all clients improved after 10 to 13 treatment sessions of graduated in vivo exposure therapy with the aid of cognitive restructuring and covert rehearsal of coping. In 1984, Cobb, Mathews, Childs-Clarke, and Blowers compared two types of behavioral treatment that were similar in all respects except that the nonphobic spouse was actively involved in only one. The treatment was home based. In one group (n = 10), the spouse was seen at the initial assessment only. The treatment began with therapist-accompanied in vivo exposure, and continued with homework assignments for exposure practices, with the aid of a therapy manual. In the second group (n = 9), the spouses were given copies of the treatment manual also and were present at all treatment sessions. The spouse was instructed to help the client carry out homework assignments and to encourage efforts of self-help rather than dependence. The results suggested that including the spouse in the treatment program produced broadly similar results to treating the client alone, and changes were maintained in the follow-up period equally well in both groups. However, therapists noted that the spouses of the client-alone group showed considerable interest in the treatment, because it was conducted in their home environment. That is, as suggested by Barlow et al. (1984), the group comparison was potentially confounded, since spouses of the non-spouse group were more involved than intended. The authors noted that the majority of spouses were prepared to be involved and proved to be enthusiastic cotherapists.

In 1984, Barlow and associates reported the results of a similar comparison between spouse (n = 14) and non-spouse (n = 14) treatment for agoraphobia. In contrast to the Cobb et al. (1984) study, the treatment sessions were clinic-based, thus eliminating the potential confound of spouses becoming inadvertently involved in non-spouse treatment conditions. (All spouses were willing to be involved in treatment.) Treatment was conducted in group therapy formats of 3 to 6 couples, and consisted of 12 weekly group sessions, involving coping skills training, and self-directed in vivo exposure practice. In the spouse condition, spouses became coaches for in vivo exposure practice (as outlined earlier). Couples in the spouse condition were encouraged to communicate more effectively during periods of anxiety or panic, and they negotiated strategies for handling anxiety that were acceptable to both partners during treatment sessions. The strategies were structured to prevent the nonphobic spouse from either ignoring anxiety-related behavior or trying to force the agoraphobic partner to attempt tasks with threats or ridicule. Significantly more of the spouse condition participants were classified as responders at posttreatment in comparison to the non-spouse condition: 12 of 14 spouse condition members versus 6 of 14 non-spouse-condition members. Thus, the authors concluded that including spouses directly in the treatment of agoraphobic women provided a substantial clinical advantage by posttreatment.

The follow-up results from this treatment comparison were reported by Cerny et al. (1987). Thirteen additional subjects were added to the spouse condition, for a total sample size of 27 spouse-condition members and 14 non-spouse-condition members. However, due to missing data, the final follow-up analysis was based on 17 spouse-treated clients and 11 non-spouse-treated clients. Overall, the results showed that the posttreatment advantage of including the spouse in treatment was maintained. This was particularly apparent on measures of phobic behavior 1 year after treatment, in which the spouse group had continued to improve while the non-spouse group demonstrated no further improvement, and even a slight deterioration. Unfortunately, results 2 years later were clouded by the small number in the non-spouse group, but in general, the non-spouse group resumed its improving trend. The composite measure of change indicated an even greater advantage for the spouse group at the 2-year follow-up. At that time, 82% of the spouse group versus 46% of the non-spouse group were classified as responders. The proportions for high-end state functioning (i.e., "symptom free") were 47% and 27%, respectively. As found in other studies, measures of marital satisfaction showed improvement in correlation with improvement in phobic behavior.

Arnow et al. (1985) noted that although including spouses as cotherapists may in some cases facilitate more efficient and effective exposure practice, it does not necessarily address directly the problem of marital issues that may interfere with treatment gains, or spouse behaviors that may unwittingly maintain or exacerbate the patients' symptoms. Therefore, they investigated the efficacy of providing communication skills training for couples following exposure therapy. The focus of communication training was the behavioral sequences between partners that may be instrumental in maintaining agoraphobic symptoms. Twenty-five agoraphobic subjects were given 4 weeks of in vivo exposure therapy with their spouses. Half received communication skills training for Weeks 5 through 12, while the other half received relaxation training for the same period of time. The communication skills training focused on procedures outlined by Stuart (1980), as described earlier. The marital interaction coding system (Hopps, Wills, Patterson, & Weiss, 1972) was used as a pre- to posttreatment measure of change in communication skills. Subjects who were given communication skills training gained significantly greater reductions in measures of agoraphobia by posttreatment. The between-group differences were maintained to some extent over the 8-month follow-up interval.

In another study, Oatley and Hodgson (1987) were interested in comparing the value of a spouse versus a friend as cotherapist. They hypothesized that spouses may be detrimental as cotherapists if they were invested in "keeping agoraphobic wives at home." Thirty agoraphobics were randomly assigned to conditions involving spouses or friends as cotherapists. The treatment was conducted in a home-based manner. Clients met with a therapist at specific times: 1 week, 1 month 2 months, 6 months, and 12 months. Both groups improved over the

12-month interval in terms of behavioral items completed and anxiety ratings. Overall, husbands proved to be as competent as friends in assisting the agoraphobic women to go out alone: The behavioral gains were only slightly stronger for the friend as cotherapist condition. Therefore, the results did not support the initial hypothesis that spousal involvement may be detrimental to phobic improvement. Futhermore, their results suggest that the benefits derived from spousal involvement shown by Barlow et al. (1984) may reflect the benefit of a supportive interpersonal context in general versus a supportive marital context in particular.

Some studies have examined the efficacy of marital therapy alone for agoraphobia. Cobb, McDonald, Marks, and Stern (1980) used a crossover design to compare the effects of in vivo exposure and marital therapy for 11 couples with coexisting marital and mixed phobic problems. Results revealed that marital therapy had a positive impact on marital problems but did not affect phobic ratings. In vivo exposure therapy, however, led to positive changes on both marital and phobic target behaviors. Although this study has been criticized, the results suggest that exposure treatment can lead to positive changes in phobic problems with a concomitant increase in marital satisfaction. Furthermore, these results suggests that marital therapy alone is not a sufficient treatment for phobias.

To the extent that assertiveness training influences interpersonal relations with nonphobic partners, the investigation conducted by Emmelkamp, van den Hout, and de Vries (1983) is relevant to the efficacy of marital therapy as a sole therapeutic strategy for agoraphobia. They compared in vivo exposure to assertiveness training and the combination of both therapies for agoraphobic women who were unassertive. Specific treatment effects were observed, with assertiveness leading to greater improvements in assertive behavior, and in vivo exposure leading to greater improvements in agoraphobic behavior. Furthermore, the addition of assertiveness training to in vivo exposure did not enhance the outcome from in vivo exposure alone. Similar results were obtained by Thorpe, Freedman, and Lazar (1985).

Efficacy of Marital Therapy: Marital Outcome

The general finding is that the inclusion of spouses in treatment tends to improve marital satisfaction ratings, in parallel with improvements in agoraphobic behavior. In the initial study, Barlow et al. (1981) found that spousal involvement in treatment improved marital satisfaction in 4 couples, while decreasing satisfaction in only 2 couples. Similarly, Himadi et al. (1986) found that a majority of couples in spousal treatment groups shifted from the dissatisfied to the satisfied marital classification from pre- to post-treatment. On the other hand, there was no change in marital classification for couples whose spouses were not involved in treatment. Also, Barlow et al. (1984) found that overall marital adjustment tended to improve as agoraphobic symptoms were reduced, suggesting that successful treatment of phobias does not necessarily result in a worsening of a marital situation.

In addition, Himadi et al. (1986) examined the effect of phobic improvement upon the emotional functioning of the spouse and failed to find any evidence for consistent deterioration. Although there was deterioration on certain isolated variables for some partners, it rarely approached a clinically problematic level. Himadi and associates suggested that their results confirmed the earlier impressions that including the spouse in treatment and using an extensive behavioral treatment format may preclude the negative effects on a marriage or a spouse of a more intensive, client-only behavioral treatment.

Attrition

Finally, there is clear indication that attrition rates from spouse-involved treatments are consistently below what is usually found. The review conducted by Dewey and Hunsley (1989) showed a 5% attrition rate for spouse-treatments, which is well below the usual 12% dropout rate from exposure-based treatments or the 25–40% dropout rate in pharmacological treatments. Thus, as noted by Dewey and Hunsley (1989), even if controlled investigations demonstrate that spouse-involved treatment is not significantly more effective than non-spouse treatment in terms of phobia improvement, reducing treatment attrition is a significant advantage for spouse treatment approaches.

MECHANISMS OF MARITAL THERAPY

Several therapeutic mechanisms have been mentioned throughout this review of the methods and efficacy of marital therapy for agoraphobia.

These have included (1) reduction in background stress by the generation of a more supportive interpersonal context; (2) removal of sources of sabotage or obstacles to improvement, especially in situations in which the spouse benefits psychologically from the dependency of the client or unwittingly reinforces dependency; (3) enhanced communication skills; and (4) improvement in the quality and/or quantity of exposure practices.

The results from Oatley and Hodgson (1987), who found that friends were as effective as spouses in the cotherapist role, are consistent with the first hypothesis. By establishing a generally supportive interpersonal environment, it is assumed that background stress is reduced. For example, Barlow et al. (1984) proposed that a cooperative and supportive spouse may reduce levels of tension and anxiety arising from marital conflict, thereby facilitating reduction in agoraphobic behavior. In terms of the second hypothesis, there is no direct evidence concerning the significance of modifying unwitting reinforcement of agoraphobic behavior by the nonphobic partner. On the other hand, the data showing that neither marital relations nor spousal emotional status deteriorates as phobic status improves tend to discount the hypothesis that marital therapy modifies reinforcement patterns from spouses who benefit from the phobic's psychological dependency.

Barlow et al. (1984) hypothesized that any advantage to a spousal involvement would be due to substantially greater self-initiated exposure between sessions, supported and encouraged by a cooperative spouse. However, their spouse and non-spouse treatment conditions did not differ on measures of self-initiated exposure. Moreover, treatment responders did not differ from nonresponders on this variable. They proposed that their measures of practice and exposure were insufficiently sensitive. As an alternative, they additionally suggested that a supportive and cooperative partner may facilitate more efficient and effective practice, rather than more total time practicing. The study by Craske et al. (1989) partially supported this hypothesis, because agoraphobics who indicated the highest levels of communication with their spouses reported the lowest level of anxiety during exposure practice. In turn, anxiety level during exposure corrrelated with overall improvement in phobic status.

Himadi et al. (1986) proposed that any improvement in marital satisfaction following therapy for agoraphobia could be directly attributed to modified communication patterns. These changes in communication may, in turn, improve the quality of exposure practices. However, the results from Arnow et al. (1985) are not entirely consistent with this speculation, because changes in communication as a result of direct communication skills training were not accompanied by improvement in ratings of marital satisfaction. Similarly, Craske et al. (1989a) found that marital satisfaction did not relate to any measure of exposure therapy, whereas, as stated previously, communication ratings were highly predictive of level of anxiety during exposure, and posttreatment outcome status.

OTHER ANXIETY DISORDERS

As noted, the major focus for marital therapy in the anxiety disorders is agoraphobia. However, research incorporating the spouse in the treatment of obsessive–compulsive disorder, social phobia, generalized anxiety disorder, and posttraumatic stress disorder is beginning to emerge. This trend seems to be developing from a realization of the importance of targeting marital and family factors relevant to maintenance of therapeutic gains.

Steketee (1987) investigated factors predictive of short- and long-term outcome after behavioral treatment for obsessive–compulsive disorder. In her study, greater availability of social support was found to relate to superior outcome. Social and familial functioning, as well as negative household interactions, correlated significantly with posttreatment anxiety levels. Similarly, problems with home and familial functioning immediately after treatment were predictive of more return of obsessive–compulsive symptoms over the long term. In particular, criticism, anger, urging of confrontation with feared obsessional cues, negative interactions in the household, and the spouse's belief that patients could control their symptoms if they wished, were all predictors of poor outcome over the follow-up. Greater emphasis on empathy and positive household feelings were indicative of a better prognosis. Steketee (1987) concluded that, rather than the broader social network, it is the specific reactions of close family members to patients after treatment that influences maintenance or loss of treatment benefits.

In the treatment of obsessive–compulsive disorder, marital therapy by itself has proven ineffective. For example, Cobb et al. (1980) showed that marital therapy did not reduce obsessive–compulsive symptoms for 11 married clients. Similarly, Hafner (1982) reported 5 cases of obsessive–compulsive disorder in which conjoint marital therapy failed to reduce the anxiety symptoms.

As with agoraphobic problems, Hafner (1982) and Hand and Lamontagne (1976) advocated spouse-aided therapy for the treatment of obsessions and compulsions, particularly in patients with unsatisfying marriages. Cobb (1982) compared exposure treatment with behavioral marital therapy for a group of patients with obsessive–compulsive neuroses. Incorporating the spouse as a cotherapist for exposure- and response-prevention treatment was effective for the obsessive–compulsive behavior, as well as the marital relationship. In contrast, the behavioral marital therapy improved the marriage but not the obsessive–compulsive problems. In an uncontrolled study, Julien, Riviere, and Note (1980) studied 20 patients with obsessions and complusions. They concluded that the inclusion of sexual therapy and marriage counseling along with other behavioral techniques improved the long-term outcome for obsessive–compulsive symptoms.

FUTURE RESEARCH

A review of the field of anxiety disorders in general indicates that most investigations of the behavioral treatment of anxiety disorders have concerned the individual in isolation from his/her interpersonal context. Investigation of the efficacy of marital therapies and including the significant other directly in the treatment for anxiety disorders remains a relatively new area of research. Obviously, replication of the few controlled studies comparing spouse and non-spouse treatments, and incorporating specific communication training, is needed. Little has been done to examine the value of couples treatments for obsessive–compulsive disorder, social phobia, generalized anxiety disorder, and posttraumatic stress disorder. The need for empirical investigation with these types of anxiety disorders is clear. Exploration of the rich and complex relationship between the clients' symptoms and the behavior of spouses and family members is needed, along the lines begun by Steketee (1987) and others. Such research may provide innovative alternatives to, and further development of, currently existing modes of treatment.

Ultimately, a marital therapy approach in the

treatment of anxiety disorders may be most beneficial under two conditions. First, it may be particularly helpful for more pervasive anxiety problems. Second, it appears that individuals with unsatisfying marriages prior to treatment may obtain the strongest benefits from a couple approach. Therefore, individuals with pervasive anxiety and unsatisfying marriages may benefit the most from including the spouse in therapy. Because including the spouse as a cotherapist is not marital therapy explicity, the couple is unlikely to fear that the marriage will be the focus of therapy. Once a therapeutic alliance has developed, it is possible for the spouse's role in symptom maintenance to be examined, discussed, and modified within the framework of the marital interaction.

Finally, the specific mechanisms through which the couple approach adds to treatment efficacy warrant further investigation. The reduction in background stress, the role of effective communication, the removal of phobic reinforcement patterns, and the effect upon self-directed exposure practices, have been identified as potential mechanisms. To the extent that specific mechanisms can be identified, therapeutic strategies might be modified to maximize treatment outcome and reduce the likelihood of relapse.

REFERENCES

Arnow, B. A., Taylor, C. B., Agras, W. S., & Telch, M. J. (1985). Enhancing agoraphobia treatment by changing couple communication patterns. *Behavior Therapy, 16,* 452–456.

Arrindell, W. A., & Emmelkamp, P. M. (1987). Psychological states and traits in female agoraphobics: A controlled study. *Journal of Psychopathology and Behavioral Assessment, 9,* 237–253.

Arrindell, W. A., Emmelkamp, P. M., Sanderman, R. (1986). Marital quality and general life adjustment in relation to treatment outcome in agoraphobia. *Advances in Behaviour Research and Therapy, 8,* 139–185.

Barlow, D. H. (1988). *Anxiety and its disorders: The nature and treatment of anxiety and panic.* New York: Guilford Press.

Barlow, D. H., & Crasko, M. G. (1988). *Mastery of your anxiety and panic.* Albany, NY: Graywind Publications.

Barlow, D. H., Caske, M. G., Cerny, J. A., & Klasko, J. S. (1989). Behavioral treatment of panic disorder. *Behavior Therapy, 20,* 261–282.

Barlow, D. H., O'Brien, G. T., & Last, C. G. (1984). Couples treatment of agoraphobia. *Behavior Therapy, 15,* 41–58.

Barlow, D. H., O'Brien, G. T., Last, C. G., & Holden, A. E. (1983). Couples treatment of agoraphobia: Inital outcome. In K. D. Craig & R. J. McMahon (Eds.), *Advances in clinical behavior therapy.* New York: Brunner/Mazel.

Barlow, D. H., Mavissakalian, M., & Hay, L. R. (1981). Couples treatment of agoraphobia: Changes in marital satisfaction. *Behaviour Research and Therapy, 19,* 245–255.

Beck, A. T., & Emery, G. (1985). *Anxiety disorders and phobias: A cognitive perspective.* New York: Basic Books.

Bernstein, D. A., & Borkover, T. D. (1973). *Progressive relaxation training.* Champaign, IL: Research Press.

Bland, K., & Hallam, R. S. (1981). Relationship between response to graded exposure and marital satisfaction in agoraphobics. *Behaviour Research and Therapy, 19,* 335–338.

Buglass, P., Clarke, J., Henderson, A. S., & Presley, A. S. (1977). A study of agoraphobic housewives. *Psychological Medicine, 7,* 73–86.

Cerny, J. A., Barlow, D. H., Craske, M. G., & Himadi, W. G. (1987). Couples treatment of agoraphobia: A two-year follow-up. *Behavior Therapy, 18,* 401–415.

Cobb, J. P. (1982). The interaction between neurotic problems and marriage: Implications for the therapist. *Partnerberatung, 19*(3), 105–111.

Cobb, J. P. (1983). The interaction between neurotic problems and marriage: Implications for the therapist. *Irish Journal of Psychotherapy, 2*(2), 65–66.

Cobb, J. P., Mathews, A. M., Childs-Clark, A., & Blowers, C. M. (1984). The spouse as co-therapist in the treatment of agoraphobia. *British Journal of Psychiatry, 144,* 282–287.

Cobb, J. P., McDonald, R., Marks, I. M., & Stern, R. S. (1980). Marital versus exposure therapy: Psychological treatments of co-existing marital and phobic. obsessive problems. *European Journal of Behavioural Analysis and Modification, 4,* 3–17.

Craske, M. G., Burton, T., & Barlow, D. H. (1989). Relationships among measures of communication, marital satisfaction and exposure during couples treatment of agoraphobia. *Behaviour Research and Therapy, 27,* 1–9.

Craske, M. G., Miller, P., Rotunda, R., & Barlow, D. H. (1990). Features of initial panic attacks in minimal and extensive avoiders. *Behaviour Research and Therapy, 28,* 395–400.

Dewey, D., & Hunsley, J. (1989). The effects of marital adjustment and spouse involvement on the behavioral treatment of agoraphobia: A meta-analytic view. *Anxiety Research.* .

Doctor, R. M. (1982). Major results of a large-scale pretreatment survey of agoraphobics. In R. L.

DuPont (Ed.), *Phobia: A comprehensive summary of modern treatments*. New York: Brunner/Mazel.

Elkin, I., Shea, M. T., Watkins, J., Imber, S. D., Sotsky, S. M., Collins, J., Glass, D., Pilkonis, P., Leber, W., Docherty, J., Fiester, S., & Parloff, M. (1989). National Institute of Mental Health treatment of depression collaborative program: General effectiveness of treatments. *Archives of General Psychiatry, 46*(11), 971–982.

Emmelkamp, P. M. (1980). Agoraphobic's interpersonal problems. *Archives of General Psychiatry, 37,* 1303–1306.

Emmelkamp, P. M., van den Hout, A., & de Vries, K. (1983). Assertive training for agoraphobics. *Behaviour Research and Therapy, 21*(1), 63–68.

Fry, W. F. (1962). The marital context of an anxiety syndrome. *Family Process, 1,* 245–252.

Goldstein, A. J., & Chambless, D. L. (1978). A reanalysis of agoraphobia. *Behavior Therapy, 9,* 47–59.

Hafner, R. J. (1977). The husbands of agoraphobic women and their influence on treatment outcome. *British Journal of Psychiatry, 131,* 289–294.

Hafner, J. (1979). Agoraphobic women married to abnormally jealous men. *British Journal of Medical Psychology, 52*(2), 99–104.

Hafner, J. (1982). Marital interaction in persisting obsessive–compulsive disorders. *Australian and New Zealand Journal of Psychiatry, 16,* 171–178.

Hafner, J. (1984). Predicting the effects on husbands of behaviour therapy for wives' agoraphobia. *Behaviour Research and Therapy, 22*(3), 217–226.

Hafner, R. J., & Ross, M. W. (1983). Predicting the outcome of behaviour therapy for agoraphobia. *Behaviour Research and Therapy, 21*(4), 375–382.

Hand, I. & Lamontagne, Y. (1976). The exacerbation of interpersonal problems after rapid phobia-removal. *Psychotherapy: Theory, Research, and Practice, 13,* 405–411.

Himadi, W. A., Cerny, J. A., Barlow, D. H., Cohen, S., & O'Brien, G. T. (1986). The relationship of marital adjustment to agoraphobia treatment outcome. *Behaviour Research and Therapy, 24*(2), 107–115.

Hopps, H., Wills, T. A., Patterson, G. R., & Weiss, R. L. (1972). *Marital Interaction Coding System.* Eugene, OR: University of Oregon and Oregon Research Institute.

Hudson, C. J. (1974). The families of agoraphobics treated by behaviour therapy. *British Journal of Social Work, 4,* 51–59.

Julien, R. A., Riviere, B., & Note, I.D. (1980). Behavioral and cognitive treatment of obsessions and compulsions: Results and discussion. *Annales Médico Psychologiques, 138*(9), 1123–1133.

Kleiner, L., & Marshall, W. L. (1985). Relationship

difficulties and agoraphobia. *Clinical Psychology Review, 5,* 581–595.

Last, C. G., Barlow, D. H., & O'Brien, G. T. (1984). Precipitants of agoraphobia: Role of stressful life events. *Psychological Reports, 54,* 567–570.

Lazarus, A. (1966). Broad-spectrum behaviour therapy and the treatment of agoraphobia. *Behaviour Research and Therapy,* 95–97.

Mathews, A. M., Teasdale, J., Nunby, M., Johnston, D., & Shaw, P. M. (1977). A home-based treatment program for agoraphobics. *Behavior Therapy, 8,* 915–924.

Mavissakalian, M., & Hamann, M. S. (1987). DSM-III personality disorder in agoraphobia: II. Changes with treatment. *Comprehensive Psychiatry, 28*(4), 356–361.

McLean, P., & Hakstain, A. (1979). Clinical depression: Comparative efficacy of outpatient treatments. *Journal of Consulting and Clinical Psychology, 47*(5), 818–836.

Meicherbaum, D. H. (1974). *Therapist manual for cognitive behavior modification.* Unpublished manuscript, University of Waterloo, Ontario, Canada.

Milton, F., & Hafner, J. (1979). The outcome of behavior therapy for agoraphobia in relation to marital adjustment. *Archives of General Psychiatry, 36,* 807–811.

Monteiro, W., Marks, I. M., & Ramm, E. (1985). Marital adjustment and treatment outcome in agoraphobia. *British Journal of Psychiatry, 146,* 383–390.

Moras, K. (1989). *Diagnostic comorbidity in DSM-III and DSM-III-R anxiety and mood disroders: Implications for the DSM-IV.* Unpublished manuscript.

Noyes, R., Crowe, R. R., Harris, E. L., Hamra, B. J., McChesney, C. M., & Chavdhry, D. R. (1986). Relationship between panic disorder and agoraphobia: A family study. *Archives of General Psychiatry, 43,* 227–232.

Oatley, K., & Hodgson, D. (1987). Influence of husbands on the outcome of their agoraphobic wives' therapy. *British Journal of Psychiatry, 150,* 380–386.

Peter, H., & Hand, I. (1988). Patterns of patient–spouse interaction in agoraphobics: Assessment by Camberwell Family Interview (CFI) and impact on outcome of self-exposure. In I. Hand & U. Wittchen (Eds.), *Panic and phobias.* Berlin: Spinger Verlag.

Pollard, H., Pollard, H., & Corn, K. (1990). Panic onset and major events in lives of agoraphobics: A test of contiguity. *Journal of Abnormal Psychology, 98*(3), 318–321.

Reich, J., Noyes, R., & Troughten, E. (1987). Dependent personality disorder associated with phobic avoidance in patients with anxiety disorder. *American Journal of Psychiatry, 144*(3), 323–326.

Reich, J., Noyes, R., Hirschfel, R., Coryell, W., & O'Gorman, T. (1987). State and personality in depressed and panic patients. *American Journal of Psychiatry, 144*(2), 181–187.

Steketee, G. (1987). Behavioral social work with obsessive compulsive disorder special issue: Progress in behavioral social work. *Journal of Social Service Research, 10*(2–4), 53–72.

Stuart, R. B. (1980). *Helping couples change: A social learning approach to marital therapy.* New York: Guilford Press.

Thorpe, G. L., Freedman, E. G., & Lazar, J. D. (1985). Assertiveness training and exposure *in vivo* for agoraphobics. *Behavioral Psychotherapy, 13,* 132–141.

Thyer, B. P., Himle, J., Curtis, G. C., Cameron, O. G., & Nesse, R. M. (1985). A comparison of panic disorder and agoraphobia with panic attacks. *Comprehensive Psychiatry, 26,* 208–214.

20

A Marital/Family Discord Model of Depression: Implications for Therapeutic Intervention

IAN H. GOTLIB
STEVEN R. H. BEACH

O F ALL THE PSYCHIATRIC disorders, depression is by far the most common. Each year, more than 100 million people worldwide develop clinically recognizable depression, an incidence 10 times greater than that of schizophrenia. During the course of a lifetime, it is estimated that between 8% and 18% of the general population will experience at least one clinically significant episode of depression (Boyd & Weissman, 1981; Karno et al., 1987), and that approximately twice as many women as men will be affected by depression (Frank, Carpenter, & Kupfer, 1988; Robins et al., 1984). For a significant proportion of these individuals, the depressive episode will result in suicide. Hirschfeld and Goodwin (1988), for example, report that approximately 15% of clinically depressed individuals will commit suicide. Consistent with this estimate, Minkoff, Bergman, E. Beck, and R. Beck (1973) suggest that more than 80% of individuals who commit suicide experience a clinically significant depressive episode in the months prior to their deaths. Indeed, the mortality risk from all causes appears to be considerably elevated in depressed individuals. For example, in a 16-year prospective study, Murphy, Monson, Olivier, Sobol, and Leighton (1987) found that depressed persons have death rates that are 1.5 to 2 times those of their nondepressed counterparts. When one considers the various medical and diagnostic categories of which depression is an integral part, therefore, or with which it is frequently associated, it is clear that the problem of depression is considerable, and its consequences are potentially lethal.

The term "depression" has a number of meanings, covering a wide range of emotional states, that range in severity from normal, everyday moods of sadness, to psychotic episodes with increased risk of suicide. Although everyone has at some time felt "sad," or "blue," clinically significant depression is differentiated from these more common emotions by the increased severity, pervasiveness, and persistence of the alteration in day-to-day functioning. The current diagnostic system in North America, the *Diagnostic and Statistical Manual of Mental Disorders* (DSM-IV; American Psychiatric Association, 1994), divides mood disorders into depressive disorders and bipolar disorders. Whereas a diagnosis of bipolar disorder essentially requires the presence of one or more manic or hypomanic episodes, a diagnosis of depressive disorder requires one or more periods of clinically significant depression without a history of either manic or hypomanic episodes. Because of the absence of manic episodes, depressive disorders are often referred to as "unipolar depression."

DSM-IV further divides depressive disorder into major depressive disorder and dysthymic disorder. For a diagnosis of major depressive disorder, the occurrence of one (single episode) or more (recurrent) major depressive episodes must be established. In a major depressive episode, the individual exhibits, over at least a 2-week period, depressed mood or a loss of interest or pleasure in almost all daily activities, as well as a number of other symptoms of depression, such as weight loss or gain, loss of appetite, sleep disturbance, psychomotor agitation or retardation, fatigue, feelings of guilt or worthlessness, and difficulties in thinking and concentration. In contrast, a diagnosis of dysthymic disorder requires a more chronic but less intense disturbance of mood. For this diagnosis to be made, the individual must have exhibited at least two symptoms of depression for most of a 2-year period (1 year in children and adolescents), without having experienced a major depressive episode.[1]

Given these diverse aspects of depression, it is doubtful that a single set of factors can adequately explain the full range of phenomena associated with this disorder. Investigators examining psychological factors in depression have focused primarily on psychoanalytic (e.g., Abraham, 1911/1985; Freud, 1917/1961), cognitive (e.g., Abramson, Metalsky, & Alloy, 1989; Beck, 1976), or behavioral (e.g., Ferster, 1973; Lewinsohn, Hoberman, Teri, & Hautzinger, 1985) constructs. Recently, however, researchers have increasingly expressed an appreciation of the significance of interpersonal aspects of depression (e.g., Brown & Harris, 1978; Gotlib & Whiffen, 1991; Kessler, Price, & Wortman, 1985). In this context, investigators have begun to assess the role of intimate relationships, and particularly marital and family relationships, in the etiology and course of depression, as well as the negative impact of depression on these relationships. Equally important, investigators have also begun to develop and examine the efficacy of marital- and family-oriented approaches to the treatment of depression (e.g., Beach, Sandeen, & O'Leary, 1990).

There is little question of a consistent association between marital or family distress and depression. Sager, Gundlach, and Kremer (1968), for example, estimate that 50% of all patients who seek psychotherapy do so because of marital difficulties; from a different perspective, Beach, Jouriles, and O'Leary (1985) suggest that in 50% of couples experiencing marital problems, one spouse is clinically depressed. Vaughn and Leff (1976) found that depressives are more vulnerable than are schizophrenics to family tension and to hostile statements made by family members, and Schless, Schwartz, Goetz, and Mendels (1974) demonstrated that this vulnerability to marriage- and family-related stresses persists after depressed patients recover. Consistent with these results, Merikangas (1984) found the divorce rate in depressed patients 2 years after discharge to be nine times that of the general population (see Beach & Nelson, 1990, and Gotlib & Hammen, 1992, for more detailed reviews of this literature).

As Gotlib and Hooley (1988) point out, there are a number of explanations for the association between depression and marital discord. For example, marital distress may be implicated directly in the development of a depressive episode. Thus, one can imagine a marriage in which neither partner has a history of depression, but which nevertheless sours and leads to a depressive episode in one of the spouses. Stressful life events may be implicated in this model as well, and may function either as direct or as indirect causes of marital distress; moreover, they may also function either addictively or interactively with the domestic tension in leading to a depressive episode. For example, financial strains may cause a direct increase in marital discord, which may in turn trigger the onset of depressive symptoms in one of the spouses. Alternatively, poor marital relationships may interact with negative life events to produce depression, either by increasing the total level of stress experienced or by failing to provide an adequate buffer against the impact of the events (Hobfoll & Lieberman, 1987). Finally, depression in one spouse may lead to marital distress, even in those cases in which the premorbid marital relationship is sound (Barling, MacEwen, & Kelloway, 1991). Living with a depressed individual, for example, may strain the coping resources of the nondepressed partner to such an extent that marital tension results. Furthermore, a vicious cycle may develop, in which these marital difficulties then exacerbate or prolong the depressive symptomatology (Beach & Fincham, 1994).

The purpose of this chapter is to further examine the association between interpersonal dysfunction and depression through an exploration of a marital/family discord model of depression. We have two main objectives in writing this chapter. First, we briefly present the results of research that have formed the empirical foundation for the development of marital/family therapies for depression by documenting the strength of the association between depression and interpersonal dysfunction. Then, we discuss studies that have examined the social behaviors of depressed persons with strangers, with their spouses, and with their children, further establishing the robust link between depression and interpersonal problems. We also examine the impact of depression on others in the depressed person's social environment. Second, we outline in some detail a marital/family discord model of depression that not only builds on the foundation established by studies of the marriages of depressed persons, but also goes beyond the marital subsystem and explicates the potential of other subsystems in the family to contribute to the exacerbation or maintenance of ongoing depressive symptomatology. We discuss implications of this model for intervention with depressed persons, and we present the results of investigations that have tested different aspects of the model. To aid in focusing this chapter, we discuss only unipolar forms of depression. Moreover, because the body of research that we review in this chapter is diverse, we use the term "depression" as a descriptor of a general negative emotional state, rather than as a label for a specific diagnostic category. We turn now to a discussion of the interpersonal functioning of depressed individuals.

THE SOCIAL BEHAVIOR OF DEPRESSED PERSONS

In order to gain a more comprehensive understanding of the association between depression and marital dysfunction, it is instructive to consider both the behavior of depressed persons in interpersonal interactions and the responses of others to depressed individuals. In this section, therefore, we examine the social behaviors of depressed persons in interactions with strangers, with their spouses, and with their children and, where possible, the responses of these persons to the depressed individual.

Depressed Persons with Strangers

The vast majority of interactional studies have been conducted with depressives in one-time encounters with strangers. The results of these studies indicate that depressed individuals are less socially skillful in interpersonal interactions than are their nondepressed counterparts. Compared to nondepressed controls, depressed persons have been found to maintain less eye contact (Gotlib, 1982; Hinchliffe, Hooper, & Roberts, 1978); to be less verbally productive (Hinchliffe et al., 1978); to speak more softly, more slowly, and more monotonously (Gotlib, 1982; Gotlib & Robinson, 1982; Hinchliffe et al., 1978); and to take longer to respond to the verbalizations of others (Libet & Lewinsohn, 1973; Youngren & Lewinsohn, 1980). Depressives' conversational behavior is frequently self-focused and negatively toned (Jacobson & Anderson, 1982), and in interpersonal situations they tend to communicate self-devaluation, sadness, and helplessness (Blumberg & Hokanson, 1983). Not surprisingly, perhaps, with few exceptions (e.g., Gotlib & Meltzer, 1987; Youngren & Lewinsohn, 1980) the interpersonal behaviors of depressed persons are judged both by the depressed person and by others as less socially competent (e.g., Dykman, Horowitz, Abramson, & Usher, 1991; Gotlib, 1982; Lewinsohn, Mischel, Chaplin, & Barton, 1980).

Given these behavioral patterns, it is not surprising to find that many of these studies have further demonstrated that depressed individuals elicit a variety of negative reactions from those with whom they interact (e.g., Coyne, 1976a; Gotlib & Robinson, 1982; Howes & Hokanson, 1979), although this is not invariably the case (cf. King & Heller, 1984). Persons interacting with depressed individuals, compared to controls, have been found to emit a greater number of negative statements and fewer positive statements (Gotlib & Robinson, 1982; Howes & Hokanson, 1979), to report experiencing more negative affect (Coyne, 1976b; Marks & Hammen, 1982), to perceive themselves as less skillful (Gotlib & Meltzer, 1987), and to be less willing to interact again with the depressed individual (Coyne, 1976a; Howes & Hokanson, 1979). Interestingly, the rejection of depressed individuals by others does not seem to be mediated by their ability to induce negative affect in others (Gurtman, 1986). Rather, it may be the perceived dissimilarity of the depressed person from the self that mediates both the negative reaction and rejection (Rosenblatt & Greenberg, 1988).

In addition, it is well known that emotions can prompt attention, influence cognitive capacity, and recruit congruent cognitive material (Bower, 1981, 1991; Forgas, Bower, & Moylan, 1990; Mandler, 1984; Pietromonaco & Rook, 1987). These processes, in turn, can profoundly affect social judgments. Of particular relevance for marital discord, and for the emergence of depression in the context of marital discord, is the likelihood that depressed mood may facilitate recall of previous anger- (or anxiety-) provoking situations (cf. Blaney, 1986), leading depressed spouses to be more prone to experience dissatisfaction with their marriages. Similarly, it seems plausible that depressed spouses will find their attention more readily drawn to negative behaviors or mannerisms than will nondepressed spouses. Depressed spouses also may be particularly likely to recall and react strongly to partner behavior that they perceive as nonsupportive or critical, further fueling their negative affective response to conflictual marital interactions and their tendency to withdraw. Given these formulations, combined with the likelihood that meaningful social relationships are affected by depression to a greater extent than are more superficial interactions with strangers (cf. Feldman & Gotlib, 1993), we turn now to an examination of the marital functioning of depressed persons.

Depressed Persons with Spouses

Earlier in this chapter we noted the consistent empirical association between marital dysfunction and depression. From a more theoretical perspective, Coyne's (1976b) interpersonal description of depression clearly implicates spouses as playing a critical role in the development and maintenance of depression. Similarly, systems theorists have also highlighted the importance of examining the marriages of depressed persons (cf. Gotlib & Colby, 1987). Finally, behavioral theorists have suggested that marital functioning plays a central role in the maintenance of depressive symptomatology (e.g., Beach et al., 1990; Jacobson, Holtzworth-Munroe, & Schmaling, 1989).

Marital Functioning

In the area of marital functioning, the role of relationship difficulties in exacerbating or precipitating depressive episodes has received particular attention. Indeed, several investigations have found that negative marital events precede the onset of depressive symptoms. For example, Paykel et al. (1969) and Paykel and Tanner (1976) used semistructured interviews of hospitalized patients to examine event occurrence and event timing to determine the ordering of marital discord and depression. In both cases, marital arguments and other stressors

preceded depression, and they were especially prominent during the month preceding depression onset. Using a different methodology, Ilfeld (1977) had community couples make a judgment about the length of their depression, social stressors, and marital problems. On average, marital distress was of considerably longer duration than the depressive symptomatology. Likewise, using a retrospective-interview approach with working-class women in England, Brown and Harris (1978) found that lack of a confiding relationship with a boyfriend or spouse was a significant vulnerability factor in the development of depression. Thus, in the aggregate, the data suggest that marital problems are more likely to precede depression than vice versa (cf. Birchnell & Kennard, 1983). Moreover, it also appears that the marital relationship is the most common source both of salient social stresses and salient social support, highlighting the central role of the marital relationship in affect regulation (cf. Beach, Martin, Blum, & Roman, 1993).

There is now also some prospective work examining the impact of marital variables on the development and remission of depressive symptomatology. Monroe, Bromet, Connell, and Steiner (1986), for example, found that with nonsymptomatic women in nondiscordant marriages, social support within a marriage predicted lower risk for depressive symptoms 1 year later. Using an index of marital conflict, Lewinsohn, Hoberman, and Rosenbaum (1988) found that those married persons who subsequently became depressed were more likely to be experiencing marital discord than were those who remained nondepressed. Beach and Nelson (1990) also reported an effect of marital discord on later depressive symptomatology. These investigators found that with newly married couples, marital discord at 6 months predicted higher levels of depressive symptoms at 18 months, even after controlling for initial symptoms and intervening levels of life stress. In addition, the magnitude of the relationship between marital discord and level of depressive symptomatology increased over time. Whereas the concurrent correlation between symptoms of depression (Beck Depression Inventory) and symptoms of marital discord (Short Marital Adjustment Test) at the premarital assessment was − .35, 6 months after marriage it had increased significantly to − .45, and by the 18-month assessment the concurrent correlation had again increased significantly to − .56.

More recently, Jacobson, Fruzzetti, Dobson, Whisman, and Hops (1993) examined the impact of behaviors assessed during marital interactions on changes in wives' depression status immediately following treatment, and at 6- and 12-month follow-ups. These investigators found that wives' recovery from depression posttreatment was associated with high rates of husbands' facilitative behavior. Moreover, husbands' facilitative behavior was also predictive of low levels of wives' depression at a 1-year follow-up. In summary, therefore, the available longitudinal evidence suggests a causal flow from marital dissatisfaction to depression, and an increasingly strong association between marital discord and depression over time (see also Shaefer & Burnett, 1987; Markman, Duncan, Storaasli, & Howes, 1987). Jacobson and associates' (1993) data also indicate that marital behaviors have an impact on the subsequent expression of depressive symptoms. Further implicating the primary role of marital distress, Rutter and Quinton (1984) reported that, when women whose marital difficulties preceded their depression divorce their husbands, their symptomatic outcome is most similar to that of women in good marriages: that is, for some women, ending a discordant marriage may help terminate an episode of depression.

Finally, recent work by Beach and O'Leary (1993) suggests that marital quality may be particularly predictive for certain "types" of individuals. Specifically, Beach and O'Leary found that although marital-relationship variables predicted later depressive symptomatology for all spouses, a chronically dysphoric subsample was particularly reactive to changes in marital adjustment. These results support the hypothesis that those who are chronically dysphoric are more vulnerable to stresses within the marital relationship. This, in turn, supports the inclusion of personality variables in models of the relationship of marital discord and depressive symptomatology (cf. Gotlib & Hooley, 1988).

Interactions with Spouses

The results of a number of self-report studies, many of which we discussed earlier, indicate that the marital relationships of depressed individuals are problematic. One difficulty with these data, however, is that the investigators relied almost exclusively on the self-reports of depressed persons. A number of theorists have postulated that, congruent with their mood, depressed individuals demonstrate negatively distorted perceptions of their environments (cf. Beck, Rush, Shaw, & Emery, 1979; Johnson & Magaro, 1987). In fact, several studies have found that

negative mood states facilitate the recall of negatively toned information (e.g. Bower, 1981; Derry & Kuiper, 1981; Gotlib, 1981, 1983). Consequently, studies based on data derived from self-report are at risk of being influenced by response or recall biases, as well as by situational demand characteristics (cf. Blaney, 1986; Coyne & Gotlib, 1983). It is important, therefore, that we examine the overt behavior of depressed persons in the context of marital interactions.

In early observational studies, Hinchliffe et al. (1978) and Hautzinger, Linden, and Hoffman (1982) examined the behavior of depressed persons with their spouses. Hinchliffe et al. found that couples with a depressed spouse showed greater conflict, tension, and negative expressiveness in their interactions than did nondepressed control couples. Interestingly, the depressed patients in this study were more verbally productive and laughed more often with a stranger than they did with their spouses, highlighting the importance of the marital system in understanding depression. Consistent with these results, Hautzinger et al. found that communication patterns in couples with a depressed spouse were more disturbed than in couples without a depressed partner. Spouses of depressed partners seldom agreed with their spouses, offered help in an ambivalent manner, and evaluated their depressed partner negatively. Drawing on their own similar findings, Merikangas, Ranelli, and Kupfer (1979) suggested that the behavior of the patients' spouses may be as influential in predicting clinical outcome as the patients' own symptoms and behaviors. Indeed, Hooley (1986; Hooley, Orley, & Teasdale, 1986; Hooley & Teasdale, 1989) not only found a high rate of negative comments in the spouses of depressed patients, but perhaps more important, also demonstrated that this high rate of criticism predicted relapse in the patients (see Gotlib & Hooley, 1988, for a more detailed discussion of these investigations).

Interestingly, several studies have found that the interactions of depressed persons and their spouses are characterized by hostility. Arkowitz, Holliday, and Hutter (1982) found that following interactions with their wives, husbands of depressed women reported feeling more hostile than did husbands of psychiatric and nonpsychiatric control subjects. Comparable findings were reported by Kahn, Coyne, and Margolin (1985), who found that couples with a depressed spouse were more sad and angry following marital interactions, and experienced each other as more negative, hostile, mistrusting, and detached than did nondepressed couples. Kowalik and

Gotlib (1987) had depressed and nondepressed psychiatric outpatients and nondepressed non-psychiatric controls participate in an interactional task with their spouses while simultaneously coding both the intended impact of their own behavior and their perception of their spouses' behavior. These investigators found that the communications of the depressed patients were more intentionally negative and less intentionally positive than were the communications of the nondepressed controls.

Ruscher and Gotlib (1988) examined the marital interactions of mildly depressed persons from the community, and found that couples in which one partner was depressed emitted a greater proportion of negative verbal and nonverbal behaviors than did nondepressed control couples. Gotlib and Whiffen (1989) reported that the interactions of depressed male and female psychiatric inpatients and their spouses were characterized by negative affect and hostility. Finally, McCabe and Gotlib (1993) examined perceptions and actual problem-solving behaviors of couples in which the wife was either clinically depressed (depressed couples) or nondepressed (nondepressed couples). Depressed couples, and particularly depressed wives, perceived their family lives to be more negative than did nondepressed couples. Depressed wives also became increasingly negative in their verbal behavior over the course of the interaction. Depressed couples perceived their interactions to be more hostile, less friendly, and more dominated by their partners than did nondepressed couples. Interestingly, only the depressed couples appeared to be immediately reactive to their spouses' behaviors in the interactions, indicating that behaviors in marital interactions likely reflect long-standing and ingrained patterns of communication.

A recent series of interactional studies was spawned when investigators at the Oregon Research Institute identified a constellation of "depressive" behaviors, which included self-derogation, physical and psychological complaints, and displays of depressed affect. Although defining depressive behavior in slightly different ways, three studies have found "depressive" behavior to be elevated among depressed persons, but not among their nondepressed partners or in community controls (Biglan et al., 1985; Nelson & Beach, 1990; Schmaling & Jacobson, 1990). In their pioneering study, Biglan et al. (1985) found that in couples in which the wife was both depressed and maritally discordant, depressive behavior had the effect of suppressing subsequent aggressive responses

from the husbands. Because there was no discordant, nondepressed comparison group, however, it was not possible to determine whether the effect was due to depression, marital discord, or their interaction. In a subsequent study, Schmaling and Jacobson (1990) attempted to disentangle the effects of marital discord and depression by comparing four groups of couples: (1) nondepressed, nondiscordant; (2) nondepressed, discordant; (3) depressed, nondiscordant; and (4) depressed, discordant. Unfortunately, Schmaling and Jacobson were unable to replicate the basic suppression effect. They did, however, find that spouses responded differently to depressive than to aggressive behavior. Specifically, discordant spouses tended to reciprocate aggressive behavior with aggressive responses. Depressive behavior, however, produced no tendency toward increased aggressive behavior on the part of spouses. Accordingly, although failing to replicate the ability of depressive behavior to suppress aggressive responding, Schmaling and Jacobson did find depressive and aggressive behavior to be functionally distinct in the interactions of discordant couples.

In the third study, Nelson and Beach (1990) compared the marital interactions of three groups of couples: (1) nondepressed, nondiscordant; (2) nondepressed, discordant; and (3) depressed, discordant. Again, depressed and aggressive behavior were found to be functionally distinct. In this study, depressive behavior was found to suppress aggressive responding by the spouse and to do so most strongly in the nondepressed, discordant group. Taken together, the results of these three studies strongly suggest that depressive behavior is functionally distinct from aggressive behavior. In addition, because neither Schmaling and Jacobson (1990) nor Nelson and Beach (1990) found an effect of diagnostic status on the observed associations, it seems likely that the effect of depressive behavior on aggressive spousal responding is primarily a function of level of marital discord rather than of level of depression. Indeed, Nelson and Beach found a nonsignificantly stronger suppression effect in the nondepressed, discordant group and found the magnitude of the suppression effect to be correlated with duration of marital discord. For couples who reported longer standing marital discord, the suppression effect was reduced. Thus, Schmaling and Jacobson may have failed to find an effect of depressive behavior in reducing subsequent spousal behavior either because their sample was insufficiently maritally discordant (none of the couples was seeking marital therapy), or because those couples who were maritally discordant had been discordant for a long time (cf. McGonagle, Kessler, & Gotlib, 1993). Clearly, further research is necessary to resolve these issues.

An additional finding of the Schmaling and Jacobson (1990) study was that depressive behavior, as defined by the Oregon research group, was elevated for depressed wives during a problem-focused discussion, but not during a discussion of "how their day had gone." This suggests that depressive behavior is elicited by a conflictual task involving interaction with the spouse, but not by a neutral task involving interaction with the spouse. Again, this finding underscores the linkage of marital conflict and displays of depressive symptomatology among the depressed.

Finally, in a follow-up to the Schmaling and Jacobson (1990) study, Schmaling, Whisman, Fruzzetti, and Truax (1991) examined the behavior of 100 couples as they attempted to decide which problem areas to discuss during their upcoming videotaped problem-solving discussion. Schmaling et al. found that both husbands' attempts to involve the interviewer and wives' active summarizing of proposed topics for discussion predicted wives' level of depression. In both cases, more active behavior was associated with less depression in the wife. This result fits well with recent findings by Christian, O'Leary, and Vivian (1991), indicating that among discordant couples, depression is associated with poorer self-reported problem-solving skills in both husbands and wives.

Considered collectively, these data lead to the conclusion that marital problems play an important role in depressive symptomatology. Results of retrospective and cross-sectional research appear to link marital discord to clinically significant depression, and longitudinal research demonstrates that marital variables can predict future levels of depressive symptomatology. Finally, evidence also links the presence of marital discord and perceived criticism by the spouse with relapse following successful somatic treatment for depression (Hooley & Teasdale, 1989). Thus, marital discord appears to be a powerful factor in determining the course of depression. Indeed, it seems to be sufficiently powerful both to make someone who is already depressed more depressed, and to make someone who has recently recovered from a depression more likely to relapse. Although additional work is necessary to fully document the influence of marital discord on the course of depression, sufficient evidence is already available to suggest, at a minimum, that the marital relationship should be assessed when the presenting problem is depression. In addition, the evidence also indicates the likely value of attending to, and directly addressing, marital discord when it co-occurs with depression.

Depressed Persons and Their Children

The final area that we shall discuss briefly before turning to an examination of marital/family treatment for depression concerns the impact of depressed parents on the functioning of their children. Although the relationships of depressed persons with their children have received less attention than have their marital relationships, the results of the studies that have been reported to date paint a similarly negative picture. At the level of self-report, there is evidence to indicate that depressed women find it difficult to be warm and consistent mothers, derive less satisfaction in being mothers, and feel inadequate in this role (e.g., Bromet & Cornely, 1984; Weissman, Paykel, & Klerman, 1972). Furthermore, depressed mothers have been found to report various psychological and physical problems in their children, including depressed and anxious mood, suicidal ideation, unexplained headaches, fighting, loss of interest in usual activities, hypochondriacal concerns, crying, and difficulties in school (e.g., Billings & Moos, 1983; Lee & Gotlib, 1989; Webster-Stratton & Hammond, 1988; Weissman et al., 1984). Interestingly, recent research suggests that *paternal* depressive mood can also contribute unique variance to problem behaviors in children and adolescents beyond that contributed by the mother's mood state (e.g., Carro, Grant, Gotlib, & Compas, 1993; Thomas & Forehand, 1991). Moreover, Billing and Moos (1986) and Lee and Gotlib (1991) found that problems in the children persisted even after remission of the parent's symptoms.

Although the results of these studies indicate that children of depressed parents function more poorly than do children of nondepressed parents, it is important to bear in mind that these data are based on parental reports, rather than on direct observations of children. Again, as we noted earlier, depressed parents' reports may be biased by a tendency to see both their parenting and their children's behavior in a negative light (cf. Gotlib, 1983; Rickard, Forehand, Wells, Griest, & McMahon, 1981). Thus, it is critical that the functioning of children of depressed parents be assessed more directly.

In addressing this issue, several investigators

have directly interviewed children of depressed parents in order to examine the rates of diagnosable disorder in these offspring. The results of these studies are remarkably consistent, yielding rates of psychiatric disorder, and particularly major depression, among children of depressed parents ranging from 41% (Orvaschel, Walsh-Allis, & Ye, 1988) to 77% lifetime disorder (Hammen et al., 1987). Winters, Stone, Weintraub, and Neale (1981) reported that children of unipolar depressed parents demonstrate deficits in their cognitive and attentional processing. Finally, there is also evidence of an association between parental depressed parents and poor functioning in their adolescent children (Forehand, McCombs, & Brody, 1987).

These findings clearly indicate that children of depressed parents are at considerable risk for experiencing difficulties in their psychosocial functioning, and for developing disorders themselves. In an attempt to examine how this risk might be transmitted, a small number of investigators have examined the interactional behavior of depressed mothers with their children. In this context, compared with their nondepressed counterparts, depressed mothers have been found to gaze less often at their infants (Livingood, Daen, & Smith, 1983), and to be less active, less playful, and less contingently responsive in face-to-face interactions with their infants (Bettes, 1988; Field, Healy, Goldstein, & Guthertz, 1990; Fleming, Ruble, Flett, & Shaul, 1988). Indeed, depressed mothers have also been found to be explicitly negative in interactions with their children (e.g., Cohn, Campbell, Matias, & Hopkins, 1990; Lyons-Ruth, Zoll, Connell, & Grunebaum, 1986).

Similar findings have been obtained in observational studies of depressed mothers interacting with their older children. Radke-Yarrow, Cummings, Kuczynski, and Chapman (1985) and Kochanska, Kuczynski, Radke-Yarrow, and Welsh (1987) found that depressed mothers exhibited less positive and more negative affect toward their older children than did nondepressed mothers; the children also displayed more insecure attachment to their mothers. These depressed mothers also spoke less to their children and responded more slowly to their children's speech than did the nondepressed control mothers (Breznitz & Sherman, 1987). Finally, depressed mothers have been found to be less responsive and involved with their children, to use less structure and discipline with them, and to engage in more disapproval and shouting (e.g., Goodman & Brumley, 1990; Gordon et al.,

1989; Mills, Puckering, Pound, & Cox, 1985; Panaccione & Wahler, 1986; see Feldman & Gotlib, 1993, for a more detailed discussion of this literature).

Summary

In sum, compared with nondepressed individuals, many depressed persons exhibit behaviors that are characterized as socially dysfunctional when interacting with strangers and with intimates. More specifically, whereas depressed persons exhibit social skills deficits in their interactions with strangers, their interactions with their spouses and children are more likely to be characterized by hostility and anger. Furthermore, it is clear that depression in one family member has a significant influence on the emotions and behavior of other members and, indeed, on the functioning of the couple or family as a unit. Conversely, negative interactions with spouses or other family members are powerfully related to level of depressive symptomatology. Accordingly, depression can produce dysfunctional interactions with family members that, in turn, can maintain or exacerbate the depressive episode. For the depressed, maritally discordant individual, therefore, it is important to consider both the powerful role that may have been played by the marital relationship in the development and maintenance of depression, and the potential utility of marital intervention in promoting recovery and maintenance of gains (Beach et al., 1990). At a minimum, the marital situation holds considerable influence over feelings of well being (Diener, 1984) and, as we have demonstrated, may often play a central role in the etiology and maintenance of a depressive episode. Furthermore, in the absence of direct intervention, disturbances in marital and family functioning are likely to persist (Bothwell & Weissman, 1977).

Using the studies reviewed here as a foundation, in the next section of the we present a marital/family discord model of depression. This model is designed to help identify an integrated set of "points of intervention" to guide clinical activity aimed at harnessing the marital dyad, and the family, in the process of recovery from depression. To the extent that it achieves this goal, the model will help organize clinical activity in a natural and fluid manner, allowing the clinician to tailor interventions to the particular couple, while maintaining a focus on the mediating goals of therapy, that is, those targets of therapy that are held to produce positive outcome (Beach & Bauserman, 1990). We focus in particular on the marital dyad; indeed, this model is developed from our work with depressed persons and their spouses. Nevertheless, we should note that much of the following discussion can also be applied to the family unit. Following this presentation, we discuss implications of the model for interventions with couples in which one spouse is depressed, and we present the results of investigations that have tested different aspects of the model in the treatment of depressed couples. Finally, we raise a cautionary note concerning the choice of treatment in the case of an actively suicidal patient, and we discuss directions for further work in this area.

THE MARITAL/FAMILY DISCORD MODEL OF DEPRESSION: BASIC POINTS OF INTERVENTION

An overview of the basic marital/family discord model of depression is presented in Figure 20.1. The model highlights the support obtainable through spousal and family systems and the areas of overt hostility and stress produced within these systems. The model underscores the way in which marital and family processes can exacerbate or maintain depressive symptomatology, as well as the processes through which depressive symptomatology can reciprocally influence and maintain dysfunctional marital and family processes. In the following paragraphs, we discuss components of the model in greater detail, beginning with the six aspects of support provision.

Support Provision

Cohesion

"Cohesion" within marriage or the family can be defined most simply as the amount of positive time spent together engaging in joint, pleasant activities. Cohesive behaviors include taking part in common, everyday, interactional events such as simple displays of affection, shared positive time together, making time to be together for routine enjoyable activities such as mealtime, or routine discussions of the day. These behaviors constitute a great reservoir of stability, familiarity, and positive experience, whether they involve the entire family or only particular subsystems. In addition, cohesive activities provide reassurance that occasional arguments or strained interactions with the spouse or other family

members are not as serious as they might otherwise seem. In marital work we have found that interventions aimed at increasing couple cohesion, such as "caring gestures" (Stuart, 1980; Weiss & Birchler, 1978), are particularly helpful in alleviating depression; it is likely that interventions targeted at the broader family system would be similarly effective.

More specifically, one effective way to enhance couple cohesion involves the direct prescription of "please and companionship" activities (Jacobson & Margolin, 1979). These are behaviors that focus on mutual relationship pleasures on which the spouses agree. It is important that the behaviors prescribed by the therapist already be "doable" for the couple: that is, no new learning should be required. In addition, the activities suggested by the therapist should be small actions that could be repeated often. The goal of prescribing these small activities is to increase the frequency of positive, enjoyable experiences that the couple can share.

The main task of the therapist is to help both spouses identify, prompt, recognize, and reward these small positive activities. We have found that many spouses need considerable help in discovering what is really pleasing to their partners. In this context, it is often helpful to have each spouse compile a list of small gestures or behaviors he/she would like the partner to perform. The therapist must ensure that these lists are conceptualized as menus, rather than as demands. Moreover, spouses should be educated about the importance of performing these behaviors frequently, and of the partners' recognition and reinforcement of the behaviors. Although this aspect of therapy may sound simple, we should note that because many people come to therapy focused exclusively on the negative aspects of their spouses' behavior, helping discordant and depressed couples increase their positive activities typically requires considerable therapeutic acumen and input. The following transcript illustrates the identification of "caring" behaviors:

THERAPIST: Okay, let's look at the lists of things you can do to show caring to your partner.

JIM: I had a little trouble thinking of little things.

THERAPIST: Okay, Well let's just look at the lists and use these as a starting point. Okay? (*Couple nods. Therapist quickly scans lists for obvious "problem" items, items that are "just right," and items that need some work.*) You both came up with twelve things. That's a great start! And some of the things you came

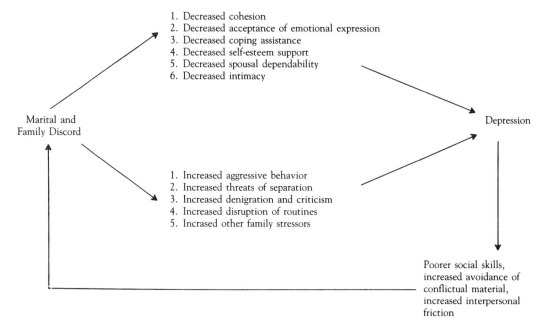

1. Decreased cohesion
2. Decreased acceptance of emotional expression
3. Decreased coping assistance
4. Decreased self-esteem support
5. Decreased spousal dependability
6. Decreased intimacy

Marital and
Family Discord

Depression

1. Increased aggressive behavior
2. Increased threats of separation
3. Increased denigration and criticism
4. Increased disruption of routines
5. Incrased other family stressors

Poorer social skills,
increased avoidance of
conflictual material,
increased interpersonal
friction

FIGURE 20.1. A marital/family discord model of depression.

up with are very similar. On both your lists I see asking how your partner's day went, telling partner "I love you," and giving partner a backrub. Are those things that both of you feel comfortable with right now?

KIRI: I am, but I think Jim has trouble telling me he loves me.

THERAPIST: Would it help you feel cared for and make it easier for you to see that Jim has loving feelings if he were to say "I love you" sometime?

KIRI: Yes, I think I would be surprised, but I would like it.

THERAPIST: Jim, I don't want to put anything on the final list that won't come naturally right now. If you want to say "I love you" more often but you find it a little awkward that's okay. It will be a good thing for us to work on a little later and there are a lot of important things we can learn about in the process. So, it's no problem to leave it off for now and come back to work on it later. Which do you think?

JIM: No, I do love Kiri and I often want to tell her. It's true that I don't say it very often, especially not recently, but it's how I feel.

THERAPIST: Kiri, how does it make you feel to hear Jim say he loves you?

KIRI: It makes me feel cared for . . . special . . . it is sort of a warm feeling, like being held.

THERAPIST: Jim, it seems like you can tell Kiri you love her and convey what you are feeling pretty well after all. Should we leave that one on the list?

JIM: Yes, definitely yes.

(*Therapist proceeds to rework items that are too large, phrased negatively, or touch on obvious problem areas. At the end of the session therapist gives an assignment to engage in caring items discussed, to keep track of things partner is doing, and note impact of each. Specific times for record keeping are discussed.*)

Acceptance of Emotional Expression

A second element of social support that has been discussed in the literature is the opportunity to express one's feelings and to feel understood and accepted by another. Indeed, B. Sarason, Shearin, Pierce, and I. Sarason (1987) suggest that being involved in a relationship that yields a sense of acceptance and of being loved may be the most central component of effective social support. Importantly, it is disclosure of *feelings* to one's partner, rather than facts, that appears to be related most strongly to marital satisfaction (Hendrick, 1981). It is also likely that it is the perception that one's spouse will be accepting of disclosure of one's feelings that is most protective against depression. Interventions aimed at enhancing listening skills in the dyad can often function to improve both reported marital satisfaction and mood. Communication skills training is particularly useful in this regard and is a standard component of marital therapy for depression (Beach et al., 1990).

Husbands of depressed wives often show a minimal response to their wives' complaints. Unfortunately, this lack of response only serves to further aggravate their marital problems (Gottman & Krokoff, 1989) and decrease feelings of acceptance. Thus, empathic listening can be introduced as one way for spouses to better understand each other. Empathic-listening skills training may begin with a brief didactic overview of the listening skills of summarizing, reflecting, validating, and question asking. The therapist first models the desired skills for the couple, and then the spouses practice the skills with feedback from the therapist. Primary-level empathy skills (Egan, 1986) are introduced first. This type of summarizing is very content-oriented; only as this skill is mastered are more inferential empathic responses encouraged. Validating the other's statements and asking questions in order to clarify potential misunderstandings are also introduced as important listening skills. Emphasis is placed on the appropriate expression of nonverbal behavior and on monitoring the couple's affective behaviors. In this context, "hot" topics are typically left until later in the training. Empathic listening could also be used to improve parent–child interactions and, potentially, to decrease unnecessary misunderstandings. Thus, as spousal listening and acceptance of disclosure are enhanced, it is likely that inappropriate self-disclosures to children will also decrease. Accordingly, building greater acceptance of self-disclosure by the nondepressed spouse may serve broader systemic goals, such as firming the boundaries between generations and decreasing dysfunctional alliances across generations. The following transcript illustrates the communication difficulties common in couples with a depressed spouse:

JIM: Wednesday night came first and I've had this happen before, to explain to you, somebody called up, one of our clients, and asked if I wanted to go out to dinner with him . . . and usually in that kind of situation, I come home and Kiri is asleep. That night you were sitting up. It was just puzzling for me. Why? You knew that Thursday was a workday.

KIRI: Is this the paraphrasing you're talking about? You're puzzled as to why I was waiting. When you had called, you said that you

would be home at ten or eleven . . . ten or eleven came and went and you weren't home, so I was getting worried. It was twenty after one when you came home. The later it got, the more awake I got. I was worried, that's all.

JIM: I wouldn't have expected you to be awake, because normally, by that time, you would have been tired and you would have gone to sleep.

KIRI: Yeah, but before that you said . . .

THERAPIST: Why don't you try paraphrasing that before you do anything else?

KIRI: You didn't expect me to be awake because usually I'm too tired to stay up that late. Normally, maybe I couldn't have stayed up that late but the later . . . it got so late and I thought something was wrong. I couldn't imagine a restaurant that would be open that late, where people were allowed to stay and talk over business. The other thing that was keeping me awake was that when you had called to say you were going out to dinner. You said that he called on your night number and I didn't even have a night number for you and this client has a night number? The more I thought about it the more upset I got.

JIM: Okay, so you didn't . . . you became upset because of not knowing about this night number . . . So, you were thinking about the night number and that's what kept you awake.

KIRI: Yes, I wanted to discuss that with you.

JIM: Why?

KIRI: Why? . . . there are a million things running around in my mind right now . . . umm . . .

THERAPIST: Why were you hurt?

KIRI: Because I thought that you didn't want me to be able to reach you . . . that if you left the building . . . I think it was a lack of trust and the more I thought about it, it was getting to be a lack of trust. What if you wanted to leave the building? I would have no way of knowing. If I called, I would not able to reach you. You could leave the building at 4:30 and not come home until 8:00 and say you were there, but I can't reach you, I don't know . . . I have no way of checking on you.

JIM: So, you were hurt really from not knowing about the number.

KIRI: Right . . . first of all. But also, you have had this new night number in for a week or two and you're telling me that the occasion hasn't come up for you to tell me about it. This is what I'm talking about.

THERAPIST (*interrupting*): Can you rephrase that more positively?

KIRI: More positively . . . it would have been nice if you had come home from work the day that they did that and said, "Guess what, you can reach me" . . . It would make me feel very good for you to offer me a way of communicating with you that I haven't been able to do.

THERAPIST: That was good.

KIRI: It would make me feel very . . . you know, like I'm part of your life. That you want me to be able to reach you when I need to.

JIM: So you're more comfortable with the situation when you can contact me.

KIRI: Yeah.

THERAPIST: Did he get all of what you wanted to say? If not, maybe you can say it again in a different way and give him another chance to paraphrase.

KIRI: Yeah. (*to husband*) There are little things that are going on in your life day to day, there has to be, and they don't seem very important to you or very earth shattering . . . you don't have to wait for major things in your life to let me know that is happening. If you could come home and share little things along the way then that let me into what's going on with you. I try to do that with you, talk about very insigificant things. and I don't even know whether you're listening to me or not. but I communicate to you.

JIM: So, what you're looking for is really the little communication, the little things that are going on in my life, just like your conversation to me as to what's going on in your class.

KIRI: The difference I can see is . . . I feel very . . . I feel like a very unimportant part of your life when you don't share with me. I feel . . . that I'm not worth your time. . . . It makes me get down on myself if you can't talk to me.

JIM: So, you feel basically down. You don't feel important if I don't talk to you about these little things. It affects your confidence . . . because I'm not telling you the little things that are going on.

THERAPIST: Kiri, that was pretty good as far as accepting responsibility for your feelings instead of attacking or criticizing Jim. And Jim, that was a pretty good job of paraphrasing and staying with Kiri instead of just nodding or giving a very short response.

Note: Clearly the therapist did not get at all aspects of the concerns felt by these clients. In particular, the wife's concern about her husband's possible infidelity and the husbands discomfort with being controlled were not fully explored. Because each partner felt listened to by the other, however, these "hot" topics could be more adequately explored later in therapy.

Coping Assistance

Actual and perceived coping assistance offered by a patient's spouse buffers stress and can protect against depression. Whether the stressor exists inside or outside of the marital relationship, joint problem solving and direct communication between spouses allow concrete assistance to be provided, provide the patient with an enhanced sense of environmental mastery, and so reduce symptoms (cf. Abramson et al., 1989). By reducing the perceived threat of stressors, coping assistance from the spouse may help the depressed patient to reappraise the level of threat more methodically. Indeed, Pearlin and Schooler (1978) found that the ability to address problems directly appeared to reduce stress effectively in the domain of marriage. Thus, helping couples address problems directly in a joint problem-solving format provides direct as well as indirect benefits for the reduction of depression. Joint problem-solving training is one usual component of our work with discordant, depressed couples. Often, work on enhancing joint parenting skills will dramatically increase the depressed patient's sense of coping assistance and will directly address a major stressor.

Enhancing a couple's joint problem-solving skills typically begins by sharing a basic "problem-solving attitude." It is important that the therapist convey the belief that problems are a normal part of married life, that family problems have solutions (or partial solutions) worth searching for, and that win-win solutions are always preferable to outcomes in which one spouse or other family member "loses." However, it is the parental subsystem of the family that is in greatest need of effective joint problem-solving skills, because spouses bear the greatest responsibility for regulating the decision-making process. Recently, considerable useful detail regarding problem solving as a therapeutic modality has been presented by D'Zurilla (1988) and A. Nezu, C. Nezu, and Perri (1989). It is useful to help couples distinguish among the six basic phases of problem solving: (1) problem definition, (2) brainstorming, (3) solution evaluation, (4) solution selection, (5) solution enactment, and (6) evaluation of the outcome.

The problem definition stage is especially important for depressed, discordant couples. Because of depressed persons' tendencies to perceive and talk about negative events in global, general terms, it is particularly important that couples be helped to make their concerns as concrete and specific as possible. In evaluating possible solutions to problems, it is often helpful to have couples give a percentage score to each solution in terms of how much it satisfies the desires of each partner. This procedure helps couples remain cognizant of the importance of mutual satisfaction. Finally, after couples learn to select and implement solutions, it is important that the therapist be involved in teaching them how to effectively evaluate outcomes of their solutions (cf. Beach et al., 1990). Couples may be led through a series of increasingly difficult applications at problem-solving skills, progressing from hypothetical problems to nonemotional, practical problems to increasingly "hot," ongoing problems.

Self-Esteem Support

This type of support is generally considered to include behaviors such as expressing appreciation, complimenting, and noticing positive traits in the partner or other family members. Interestingly, in a study conducted by Vanfossen (1986), it was the variable of affirmation that was most strongly and consistently related to feelings of well-being for wives. This type of support may be particularly important to wives, since they tend to be more self-critical than are husbands (Carver & Ganellen, 1983). Moreover, it is more common for wives to feel unappreciated by their husbands, and for discordant wives to actually receive less in the way of nonverbal positive behaviors from their husbands (Noller, 1987). Likewise, the perception that the spouse is critical or negative can promote relapse of depression (Hooley & Teasdale, 1989). In contrast, a woman who sees her husband or other family members as being appreciative, complimentary, and affirming will likely be better able to tolerate threats to her self-esteem arising from stresses external to the relationship, and to remain symptom-free despite challenging circumstances.

We have found it important to focus on each spouse's ability to notice positive attributes and behaviors, and to comment on them. Indeed, work aimed at enhancing this ability has been necessary for most discordant, depressed couples with whom we have worked. As the data reviewed earlier indicate, enhancing the ability to notice and comment on positive behaviors and attributes of offspring is also likely to be necessary and helpful for most depressed individuals. Enhancing depressed persons' ability to notice positive attributes is also likely to enhance their receipt of positive comments from other family members as well, although it must be emphasized that these positive communications should be independent of others' reciprocity.

This form of positive communication is typically presented as "expressing what you normally take for granted." The therapist's task is to help spouses verbalize positive feelings about their partners, in the form of thanks, acknowledgments, or compliments. Often the therapist will be required to prompt spouses in this behavior, and to explain the importance of positive verbalizations in enhancing the marital relationship. The therapist can explain to couples with a depressed spouse that being able to express positive feelings and appreciation is important both for helping to keep the marriage on the best course and for providing a more accurate view of themselves and their relationship. Positive communications that are begun during the session can be increased as homework over the course of therapy.

Spousal Dependability

A fifth aspect of social support can be labeled "spousal dependability," or the perceived presence of a "reliable alliance" (Weiss, 1974). It has been hypothesized that the most important aspect of social support may not be supportive behavior that actually occurs, but rather, the perception that supportive others *would be available* if they were needed. This perception may directly increase the individual's perceived control over the environment, reducing reactivity to stressful situations. Confirming the importance of perceived spousal dependability, Lieberman (1982) found that persons who perceived their world as containing significant others (particularly spouses) who could be counted on were less likely to be adversely affected by stress. At a minimum, the spouse who believes that his/her partner can be counted on will perceive him/herself as having greater resources with which to face difficulties as they arise. It is probably not the case that offspring can adequately provide a credible dependable other. Accordingly, efforts to increase the perception of a dependable other should focus on the spouse. Establishing an increased sense of spousal dependability sometimes occurs as an outgrowth of other positive changes in the relationship over the course of marital therapy for depression. When it does not improve spontaneously, however, we have found it important to address this issue directly.

Enhancing the depressed person's perception that his/her partner is dependable and committed to the relationship may require helping a committed spouse express commitment in clear, direct ways. However, it may also require a focus on dysfunctional attributions of blame for "old" behaviors that obstruct one spouse from giving the other credit for all the positive "new" behaviors that have been forthcoming in therapy. We have found that it is possible to decrease blame by examining the "old" problem behaviors to determine whether they can be seen as having been positively motivated, involuntary, or done in the absence of any negative intent (Fincham, Beach, & Nelson, 1987). Often, in the aftermath of positive and constructive marital change, spouses are willing to review and change their previous constructions about partner behavior and accept more benign interpretations. The therapist will often have to deal with the task of increasing both the level commitment of the less committed spouse to the marriage, and the perception of this spouse as actually committed to the relationship. Dealing with the spouses' attitudes or beliefs about the marriage is typically beneficial in this regard, as is training spouses to spontaneously express feelings of commitment in order to make commitment more observable (cf. Beach et al., 1990).

Intimacy and Confiding

The final aspect of social support that is relevant to mood is the concurrent sense of well-being that can result from intimate exchanges with a spouse or partner (Weiss, 1974). Although confiding can occur with offspring, it may be burdensome for them, and it is not recommended, particularly when the children are younger. Intimacy refers to a relationship state in which spouses' innermost feelings, thoughts, and dispositions can be revealed and explored (cf. Waring, 1988). Taking a risk by revealing something deeply personal to one's spouse, when coupled with spousal acceptance, can be a powerful mood elevator and can engender or rekindle strong feelings of attraction and love. Conversely, when sharing one's feelings is coupled with subsequent criticism or rejection, intense dysphoria and anger can result. In the context of marital dis-

cord, the loss of trust engendered by the ongoing discord likely serves to inhibit self-disclosure. Moreover, when a spouse does self-disclose, the probability of a rejecting response by the partner is likely to be higher in the context of marital discord than would be the case in a nondiscordant marriage. Given the depressed person's tendency to avoid negative outcomes and to use passive coping strategies (Feldman & Gotlib, 1993), one might anticipate a general pattern of withdrawal from marital conflict, which may in turn lead to further marital deterioration (Gottman & Krokoff, 1989; McGonagle et al., 1993). In the context of avoidance of significant marital issues, one might expect that intimacy would be particularly vulnerable to deterioration.

For many couples, intimate exchanges will begin to occur more frequently as a natural outgrowth of the marital interventions we outlined previously, aimed at improving listening and speaking skills, and at engendering a calmer and more cohesive marital atmosphere. However, on occasion we have found that, despite gains in other areas, couples lack the usual settings for relaxed, positive self-disclosure. In these cases the therapist may need to help the couple begin to develop new routines that create comfortable, natural, relaxed time together. More specifically, the therapist may focus on helping the couple structure their time to allow for shared mealtimes, a common bedtime, shared time over tea or coffee, or other regular time together. When such settings are lacking, the therapist might consider encouraging the couple's development of new daily routines that produce similar settings. Finally, the therapist must be sure to monitor the ratio of negative to positive self-disclosure. Because negative self-disclosures do not typically deepen feelings of intimacy (cf. Tolstedt & Stokes, 1984), it is important that the therapist work with the couple to help them express their positive feelings and observations to each other. This increased, positive self-disclosure should also promote positive tracking and increased mutual reinforcement of positive behavior in the marriage.

The Creation of Stress in the Marriage and Family

As research on stress has proliferated, various perspectives have emerged (cf. Avison & Gotlib, 1994). From the standpoint of guiding therapeutic intervention, however, it is the concrete, high-frequency negative marital stressors that often occur in the context of depression and marital discord, and are highly related to stress and depressive symptomatology that need to be highlighted. Thus, we focus on the *quality* of life events (i.e., their positive or negative nature) rather than simply on the amount of change entailed in adjusting to them (Monroe & Depue, 1991; Pearlin, 1982), on the *chronicity* or repetitiveness of stressors, and on stressors that carry the possibility of considerable threat or danger (Brown & Harris, 1978; Wheaton, 1994). We noted earlier in this chapter that depressed patients report feeling more vulnerable to marriage- and family-related stresses than to other types of stressors (Schless et al., 1974). Indeed, stresses related both to the marital and to the parenting relationships have been found to represent prominent concerns for depressed persons (Bothwell & Weissman, 1977). Although support most often comes from a spouse, it is important to realize that stress is often produced in other family relationships, and that it is stress that most powerfully predicts level of depressive symptomatology (Beach et al., 1993).

When high-intensity stressors can be identified, they often need to be given priority in treatment. When not addressed, they appear to block recovery for the patient. However, because the individual's perception or appraisal of the event is often critical in determining the magnitude of the stress response (Lazarus & Folkman, 1986), there is often considerable value in therapeutic intervention aimed at changing perceptions of behavior or attributions for spousal behavior, in addition to a focus on changing dysfunctional interaction patterns (Fincham, Bradbury, & Beach, 1990).

There are several patterns of marital behavior that are chronic, negative, and threatening, and that occur commonly in discordant and depressed couples. In particular, we have found it clinically useful to address marital patterns involving (1) verbal and physical aggression; (2) threats of separation and divorce; (3) explicitly denigrating references, severe criticism, and blame; and (4) unilateral disruption of major marital routines. Also important, these events may exacerbate feelings of depression, whether the depressed person initiated the negative exchange or was the recipient. Typically, negative exchanges of the sort just outlined are reciprocated. We should also note, of course, that there are often other idiosyncratic areas that function as major stressors for the couple. These patterns may be perceived as intensely stressful by a given couple or individual and cannot be ignored simply because they do not fit into one of previous categories. In addition, high-intensity arguments with their children and repetitive aversive behavior on the part of their children are often reported by depressed individuals and may contribute to their level of depressive symptomatology (Beach et al., 1993).

Overt Hostility: Verbal and Physical Aggression

Earlier in this chapter we discussed the results of studies demonstrating that discordant, depressed couples show considerable hostility and tension in their interactions. Clinically, we have seen couples in whom long periods of perceived isolation and relative silence were punctuated by outbursts of accusation and recrimination. This pattern may be played out in the domain of parenting interactions as well. Even more destructive is a pattern we have observed that involves rapidly escalating arguments, culminating in violence. Interactional patterns of this type leave even nondepressed spouses exhausted and drained. For depressed spouses, they provide a level of stress well beyond the level that permits symptomatic recovery. Indeed, for recovered individuals, this pattern may be expected to lead to relapse of depression. Yet, depressed persons are likely to find themselves locked in coercive patterns of stressful interaction with both their children and their spouses (Biglan et al., 1985; Hops et al., 1987). Thus, a pattern of high-intensity arguments associated with physical or verbal abuse, whether between the spouses or involving the children, should be a very early target of treatment.

Threats of Leaving

A less discussed stressor associated with marital discord is the fear of separation. Depressed, discordant couples often are plagued by a sense of uncertainty about the future of their relationships. In many cases this uncertainty will be echoed by their children. A frequent concern of couples entering therapy is that if the problems they are experiencing are not quickly resolved, marital separation may be imminent. Marital separation and divorce have been documented as major stressors in their own right (Bloom, Asher, & White, 1978); however, the role of fear of separation in the production of stress has not been so frequently investigated. With a 49% divorce rate projected for first marriages forming in the 1980s (Glick, 1984), however, concern about divorce could represent a significant element linking marital discord to stress, and may be one element leading to increased behavior problems in children. This uncertainty about the future of the relationship can often be conceptualized as a low level of perceived spousal dependability, to be dealt with in due course during marital therapy. However, when spouses use the threat of divorce as a potent way of underscoring a point during disagreements, particularly when this is done in front of their children, or tell their children that they are being driven away, the uncertainty is a stressor that deserves early attention in therapy.

For the depressed spouse, the idea of divorce can create ambivalence. On the one hand, the notion of divorce can represent escape and surcease of conflict; on the other hand, the idea of separation or divorce can be extremely threatening, given the elevated dependency needs that are characteristic of many depressed individuals (cf. Gotlib & Hammen, 1992). For the nondepressed spouse, the threat of divorce may be presented as a realistic representation of the level of frustration with the depressed partner. Divorce represents an opportunity to create needed distance from the spouse, and the use of the threat of divorce is often rewarded by some increased distance. Thus, explicit statements about divorce or actions that strongly imply thoughts of divorce can become established aspects of a couple's ongoing interaction in the context of discord and depression. In our clinical experience such events are not uncommon and can be disruptive to therapy if not addressed promptly. Accordingly, when this pattern is observed, it constitutes an early direct target of intervention.

Explicitly Denigrating Spousal References, Severe Criticism, and Blame

As we have discussed, it is clear that feedback from the spouse plays an important role in self-evaluation. Thus, the chronic use of statements that denigrate or devalue the partner can be expected to take a considerable toll on the spouse's self-esteem over time. Within the family, both children and spouses can be a source of such utterances. In the context of depression and marital discord, devaluation of the partner can progress from being nonverbal and implicit, to being stated directly, in harsh and uncompromising terms. A spouse may refer to the depressed patient in vulgar terms or may explicitly call him/her lazy, worthless, and bad. When done in front of offspring, this behavior may prompt modeling of the behavior and increase noncom-

pliance, further elevating the leve of marital and family stress. At low levels, this type of behavior represents a lack of self-esteem support or affirmation. As such, it may be dealt with as positive interactions are encouraged throughout therapy or as parenting skills are taught. However, when a shift occurs from "low-level stress" to the "high-level stress" of explicit denunciation, devaluation represents a major stressor, a threat to remission of depressive symptoms, and a likely source of relapse. As such, it must be managed explicitly and very early in marital or family therapy for depression.

Severe Disruption of Scripted Routines

A fourth common source of stress in discordant, depressed marriages arises from the breakdown of cohesion and the resulting disruption of routine, scripted spousal and family behavior (e.g., no goodbye kiss in the morning, disobedient children, a breakdown of responsibilities previously taken for granted in the dyad, nonresponsiveness to partner-initiated interaction). When a script is disrupted, the individual is forced to search for new ways to cope with the situation. This is likely to lead to increasingly erratic and random attempts at coping, which in turn increase the likelihood of sustained emotional arousal and exhaustion. In the presence of preexisting low self-esteem, this process appears likely to be intensified. As Lewinsohn et al. (1985) point out, disruption of scripts also produces increased self-awareness, the symptoms of which include self-criticism, negative expectancies, and an intensification of mood induction procedures.

Disruption of scripted behavior can occur from such low-level events as increased hesitancy in interaction and reluctance to communicate, both of which have been found to be characteristic of the interpersonal behavior of depressed persons. In such cases, the disruption is likely to be adequately resolved by interventions aimed at building new forms of marital support and cohesion. When the disruption introduced is severe, however, such as the disruption produced by spouses' threats to leave, routinely missing the family dinner hour, routinely staying late at work to minimize contact with the partner, or by refusing all physical contact with the partner, it may set into motion powerful depressogenic processes. In such cases, the disruption of major routines may need to be addressed before any progress is likely to be forthcoming. In particular, it may be necessary to help couples reengage in routines from an earlier stage in their relationship.

In summary, therefore, identifying major stressors in the marriage or family early in therapy, and either reducing them or decreasing their perceived impact, is critical if a positive focus is to emerge in the early phase of therapy. Accordingly, careful assessment of the more common major stressors outlined previously, as well as the more idiosyncratic major stressors, should have high priority in the initial sessions of therapy.

The Comorbidity of Depression and Marital Discord

The literature clearly suggests that explicitly discordant couples in which one member is depressed resemble other, nondepressed, explicitly discordant couples (Beach & Nelson, 1990). But, what of depressed couples who report themselves to be relatively nondiscordant. Do these couples really act like discordant couples? If so, then perhaps they need to receive some marital therapy as well. Interestingly, the work to date suggests that depressed couples who report satisfactory marriages do *not* have interactions that appear discordant, nor are they likely to benefit from marital therapy. Nondiscordant, depressed couples do not show prototypical discordant, negative interactional patterns (Biglan et al., 1985; Hooley, 1986), although there is some evidence to suggest that they are still characterized by elevated verbal aggression (Schmaling & Jacobson, 1990). Indeed, the available evidence, although limited, suggests that marital intervention with couples who deny marital problems is unlikely to be helpful to them (Jacobson, Dobson, Fruzzetti, Schmaling, & Salusky, 1991). Thus, at present there is no reason to routinely consider marital therapy for depressed persons in the absence of evidence of problems in the marriage. We suspect that the same is true regarding parenting difficulties: If the depressed person sees this as an area of relative strength, intervention may not be warranted. As discussed previously, when their children are not difficult, depressed individuals may have quite positive relationships with them.

Clinical reports persist, however, of cases in which a spouse (or an entire family) had adapted to one person's depression and experienced difficulty with symptomatic improvement. Similarly, clinical reports suggest the possibility that in some cases depression may "mask" severe marital discord until symptomatic improvement brings the problems into the open, typically as the formerly depressed spouse becomes more assertive (Jacobson, 1985). Our own findings do not suggest that this is always (or even typically) the case for mildly maritally discordant couples receiving individual therapy, or persons complaining of minor parenting concerns. Indeed, in our work, when individuals receive cognitive therapy for depression, their marital relationships have been as likely to im prove as to deteriorate (Beach & O'Leary, 1986; O'Leary & Beach, 1990). Similarly, in their nondiscordant subsample, Jacobson et al. (1991) found cognitive therapy to be associated with nonsignificantly greater improvement in the marital relationship and significantly greater improvement in depressive symptomatology than was marital therapy. Thus, given the current evidence, it is probably inappropriate to recommend marital therapy as a treatment for depression in the absence of overt marital discord.

A related issue involves the temporal relation between depression and marital discord when both are present in couples who are being assessed for treatment. As we noted earlier, Gotlib and Hooley (1988) presented a number of alternative temporal explanations for the association between depression and marital discord. In an important empirical examination of this issue, O'Leary, Risso, and Beach (1990) asked depressed wives whether they believed that their marital discord or depression came first, and to indicate the primary cause of their depression. Not suprisingly, perhaps, those wives who thought that their marital problems preceded their depression were also likely to rate marital problems as the primary cause of their depression. Moreover, depressed patients who reported that their marital problems preceded their depression had poorer marital outcomes if they were treated in cognitive therapy rather than marital therapy. In contrast, those patients who reported that their depression preceded their marital discord did equally well in cognitive and marital therapy.

Outcome of Marital Interventions for Depression

Although there is a growing literature attesting to the efficacy of marital- and family-oriented therapies for the treatment of depression (cf. Gotlib, Wallace, & Colby, 1990), three outcome studies in particular have examined reasonably well-specified examples of marital therapy for depression, and have compared their effectiveness to individual treatment approaches. We now examine these three studies in turn. No studies have investigated parent training or broader family treatment, although at least one such study is currently in progress.

O'Leary and Beach (1990)

O'Leary and Beach (1990) randomly assigned 36 couples to individual cognitive therapy (CT), conjoint behavioral marital therapy (BMT), or to a 15-week waiting-list condition. Both partners had to score in the discordant range of the Dyadic Adjustment Scale (Spanier, 1976), and to present themselves as being discordant. In each couple, the wife met diagnostic criteria for major affective disorder. At both posttherapy and 1-year follow-up assessments, CT and BMT were found to be effective in reducing depressive symptomatology. Indeed, at posttherapy, 67% of those who received individual cognitive therapy and 83% of those who received marital therapy no longer met the initial symptom-level criteria for inclusion into the study (i.e., Beck Depression Inventory scores above 14). There was no significant difference between CT and BMT with respect to their effects on depressive symptomatology. However, only BMT was found to be effective in improving the marital relationship. At posttherapy, only 25% of persons receiving CT, compared with 83% of those receiving BMT, had at least 15-point increases in their scores on the Dyadic Adjustment Scale from pretest to posttest. The same general pattern of results held at follow-up: Both the decreases in depression and the increases in marital satisfaction were maintained for at least 1 year following treatment.

What can be concluded from this study? If replicated, the results suggest that individual cognitive therapy is an acceptable intervention for depression, even in the face of continuing marital discord. Cognitive therapy appears to be quite effective in alleviation of guilt, shame, and depressive symptomatology. At a 1-year follow-up, the results obtained at posttherapy were maintained, both by the couples who had received marital therapy and by those who had received individual cognitive therapy. There was no significant difference between the two treated groups with respect to level of depression, but there continued to be a significant advantage for the marital therapy condition in level of marital satisfaction. Again, there was no evidence of compromised effectiveness or reduced maintenance of gains in depression for those persons who received only individual cognitive therapy. The primary advantage of marital therapy, documented in this study, was its ability to ef-

fectively reduce depressive symptomatology while simultaneously enhancing marital satisfaction.

Interestingly, as we described earlier, subsequent work by O'Leary et al. (1990) suggests that the unique advantage of marital therapy in producing better outcome on marital measures may be restricted to a subset of the overall population of maritally discordant and depressed couples: those depressed–discordant couples who reported that their marital problems preceded the onset of their depression. Conversely, depressed–discordant couples who reported that the depressed partner's symptoms preceded the onset of their marital problems responded quite well to cognitive therapy. This subgroup showed a pattern of change very similar to the marital therapy group, exhibiting improvements both in depressive symptomatology and in marital satisfaction. It appears, therefore, that some persons reporting both depression and marital discord may respond well to both individual and marital therapy. In a subsequent examination of the predictors of change, Beach and O'Leary (1992) found that persons in more negative pretherapy marital environments did more poorly in cognitive therapy, whereas persons with more negative pretherapy cognitive styles did more poorly in marital therapy. This provides strong support for the "matching hypothesis": that is, that depressed, discordant couples will do best when therapy targets the area of greatest relative disturbance and focuses on their primary concerns. Clearly, this is a critical direction for additional research.

Jacobson, Dobson, Fruzzetti, Schmaling, and Salusky (1991)

A recent study conducted by Jacobson et al. (1991) further suggests that individual cognitive therapy may be quite robust with regard to the presence of marital discord. Jacobson et al. randomly assigned 60 married women who had been diagnosed as depressed to either individual CT, BMT, or a treatment combining BMT and CT. Couples were not selected for the presence of marital discord. Accordingly, it was possible to examine directly the effect of marital therapy for nondiscordant–depressed couples. Contrary to the investigators' predictions, marital therapy was not found to be helpful for persons who were not maritally discordant: Only persons with significant marital complaints benefited from marital therapy.

Replicating O'Leary and Beach's (1990) results,

Jacobson et al. (1991) found that within the more discordant half of the sample, BMT was as effective as CT in reducing depression. Also replicating O'Leary and Beach, only BMT was found to be successful in enhancing marital satisfaction among discordant–depressed couples. Finally, and once again replicating O'Leary and Beach's results, CT was effective in reducing depressive symptomatology, even among the maritally discordant–depressed individuals. However, Jacobson et al. found no unique advantage of marital therapy over cognitive therapy among the discordant–depressed couples, with no significant differences between CT and BMT at posttherapy with respect to measures of depression or measures of marital discord. No data on long-term follow-up were presented in this study. Thus, the basic analyses suggest that individual cognitive therapy is better than marital therapy for some depressed persons (the nondiscordant–depressed), and is equivalent to marital therapy even for the discordant–depressed.

A major limitation of the Jacobson et al. (1991) study, however, is that there were very few couples in which both members of the dyad met the usual cutoff for marital discord on the Dyadic Adjustment Scale (< 97). Furthermore, couples were not seeking marital therapy and so many may not have viewed themselves as having marital problems. Although there were too few subjects to allow meaningful between-group comparisons, the authors report some comparisons within and between the small groups of "truly discordant" couples. They reported that the magnitude of change in marital satisfaction among the "truly" discordant who received marital therapy was greater than that observed in the larger "somewhat distressed" sample. In addition, only BMT showed a significant impact on the marital satisfaction of the "truly" discordant, whereas CT did not. Also of interest, all the "truly" discordant persons receiving BMT recovered from their depressive episodes, whereas this was not true of the larger "somewhat distressed" sample, nor was it true of all "truly" discordant persons receiving CT. Given this reanalysis, the Jacobson et al. study again suggests the possibility of unique advantages for marital therapy when administered to a depressed and clearly discordant population.

Foley, Rounsaville, Weissman, Sholomskas, and Chevron (1989)

In a final study of direct relevance to marital therapy for co-occurring marital discord and depression, Foley et al. (1989) randomly assigned 18 depressed outpatients to either individual interpersonal psychotherapy (IPT; Klerman, Weissman, Rounsaville, & Chevron, 1984) or to a newly developed couple-format version of IPT. Although patients in this study appear to have been only slightly more symptomatic than in the O'Leary and Beach (1990) or the Jacobson et al. (1991) studies, spouses appear to have been considerably more symptomatic, with 78% having a lifetime history of some form of psychiatric disorder. Unlike the other two studies discussed, in this investigation patients were either to be male or female, rather than being restricted to wives. Accordingly, the sample consisted of 5 male and 13 female patients. Because individual IPT is designed to treat marital disputes, among other interpersonal problems, the use of a conjoint format represented only a minor change in the format of the therapy.

Foley et al. (1989) found that the inclusion of the spouse in cases in which there were ongoing marital disputes was well received by patients and, even in their small sample, resulted in marginally greater improvement in the marital relationship than did the standard individual format of IPT. Both formats produced significant and comparable reductions in symptoms of depression. Of interest, given our previous discussion, is that depressed wives had mean intake Dyadic Adjustment Scale scores of 103 and 90.9 respectively, in the individual and conjoint formats. Given the Jacobson et al. (1991) suggestion that moderately discordant couples may show a greater advantage of marital therapy than do very mildly discordant couples, it seems possible that the sample may not have been sufficiently discordant to demonstrate the full potential of the conjoint format of IPT. Nevertheless, the obtained results suggest that the pattern reported by O'Leary and Beach (1990) and replicated by Jacobson et al. in their "truly discordant" subsample may be generalizable to other couple formats as well. Thus, direct attention to dyadic processes in structured, directive couple therapy may enhance marital functioning, while providing relief of depressive symptomatology comparable to standard individual treatments. Because follow-up data were not reported in this study, the issue of the relative merits of the two formats in terms of maintenance of gains was not addressed.

What can we conclude from this study? Again, an individual treatment, in this case IPT, appears to be a robust intervention for depression even in the context of ongoing (mild) marital discord. In addition, however, there is a tantalizing suggestion based on a small sample size and marginally significant results, that the conjoint format may offer greater potential for enhancing marital functioning than does the individual format.

Summary

Taken together, the three studies provide a strong basis for arguing that conjoint format interventions for the maritally discordant and depressed may have some unique benefits in the treatment of this population. The apparent consistency in the results, particularly for couples in which both partners are reporting significant levels of marital discord, should excite advocates of marital therapy for depression. In addition, the fact that change in the marital quality mediates the impact on depressive symptomatology of marital therapy, but not of cognitive therapy (Beach & O'Leary, 1992), serves to strengthen the belief that marital therapy offers a new approach to the treatment of depression that is distinct from more individually focused alternatives. Certainly, the results are sufficiently encouraging to support further investigation of the potential effectiveness of marital therapy for depression. At present, the advantage of using marital interventions for depression rather than individual approaches appears to lie primarily in the finding that marital intervention for depression is more efficient when used with persons with co-occurring marital discord and depression. For the truly discordant, marital therapy may simultaneously resolve both marital discord and depression. Given the prominence of parent–child disputes among the concerns of depressed parents, it seems likely that greater attention of parent training and nonmarital sources of stress in the family could further enhance the positive results obtained to date.

As a final cautionary note, we should point out that, although patients were not excluded from any of these studies if they simply reported suicidal ideation, actively suicidal patients were excluded. Accordingly, the positive results of marital therapy for depression that we described here cannot be generalized readily to actively suicidal depressed patients. Indeed, O'Leary, Sandeen, and Beach (1987) examined the efficacy of cognitive and marital therapies in a small sample of actively suicidal patients. They found that, whereas CT was quite effective in treating these patients, BMT was difficult to implement and, on average, did not produce positive results. In particular, it was difficult for both therapists and spouses to remain focused on enhancing the marriage while one member of the dyad was contemplating suicide. Although this was a relatively small sample of patients, the greater efficacy of CT over BMT in this study was clear. Accordingly, our experience suggests that actively suicidal patients may be better served, at least initially, by an individual approach to treatment, even when the focus of their concerns is marital disputes.

CONCLUDING COMMENTS

In the first section of this chapter, we reviewed data indicating that marital disturbance and discord are common and are of considerable consequence with regard to depressive symptomatology. It is clear, however, that disturbances also occur in other subsystems of the families of depressed patients. Just as effects of depression on spousal relationships may be bidirectional in nature, so too may the effects of depression on relationships with offspring or other family members be reciprocal. In particular, conflictual interactions with offspring may be a potent and frequent source of stress for the depressed patient. Thus, the marital discord model proposed by Beach et al. (1990) appears to be applicable to the broader family system.

In the second section of the chapter, we examined therapeutic procedures designed to enhance the marital functioning of depressed persons and to reduce the level of depressive symptomatology. We also expanded the therapeutic implications of the marital discord model to include likely family interventions as well. As our review of a selected outcome literature suggests, interventions focusing on the marital subsystem seem very promising as a means of simultaneously enhancing the marital functioning of depressed spouses and ameliorating their depressive symptomatology. Although outcome research examining the effectiveness of broader family interventions, or of interventions specifically aimed at enhancing the parent–child relationship, is less well developed at present, the currently available research supports attempting this type of intervention. Because at least one major outcome study examining family intervention in depression is currently in progress, more conclusive data are likely to be forthcoming in the future.

Clearly, the role of marriage and the family in the onset, maintenance, and treatment of depression is beginning to receive the attention it deserves. Although many questions remain concerning the nature of the association between depression and marital/family functioning, the results of current work are sufficient to indicate that these two broad domains are robustly related. Further efforts to examine the association of marital and family discord with depression, and to assess potential points of therapeutic intervention for depression that may reside in these intimate relationships, seem timely. It is our hope that this chapter will serve to stimulate such efforts.

ACKNOWLEDGMENTS

Preparation of this chapter was supported in part by Grant No. 6606-3465-51 from Health and Welfare Canada and an Ontario Mental Health Foundation Senior Research Fellowship awarded to the first author, and by NIMH Grant No. MH41487-05 awarded to the second author.

NOTE

1. In addition to these diagnostic categories, numerous subtypes of depression have also been described (e.g., psychotic, neurotic, endogenous, reactive, involutional, agitated, primary, and secondary; see Gotlib & Colby, 1987, and Gotlib, 1993, for detailed descriptions of these various subtypes).

REFERENCES

Abraham, K. (1985). Notes on the psychoanalytic investigation and treatment of manic–depressive insanity and allied conditions. In J. C. Coyne (Ed.), *Essential papers on depression* (pp. 31–47) New York: New York University Press. (Original work published 1911)

Abramson, L. Y., Metalsky, G. I., & Alloy, L. B. (1989). Hopelessness depression: A theory-based subtype of depression. *Psychological Review, 96,* 358–372.

American Psychiatric Association. (1994). *Diagnostic and statistical manual of mental disorders* (4th ed.). Washington, DC: Author.

Arkowitz, H., Holliday, S., & Hutter, M. (1982, November). *Depressed women and their husbands: A study of marital interaction and adjustment.* Paper presented at the Annual Convention of the Association for Advancement of Behavior Therapy, Los Angeles.

Avison, W. R., & Gotlib, I. H. (Eds.). (1994). *Stress and mental health: Contemporary issues and prospects for the future.* New York: Plenum.

Barling, J., MacEwen, K. E., & Kelloway, E. K. (1991, November). *Effects of short term role overload on marital interactions.* Paper presented to the 25th Annual Convention of the Association for Advancement of Behavior Therapy, New York.

Beach, S. R. H., & Bauserman, S. A. (1990). Enhancing outcome in marital therapy. In F. D. Fincham & T. N. Bradbury (Eds.), *The psychology of marriage: Basic issues and applications* (pp. 349–374). New York: Guilford Press.

Beach, S. R. H., & Fincham, F. D. (1994). Towards an integrated model of negative affectivity in marriage. In S. M. Johnson & L. S. Greenberg (Eds.), *The heart of the matter: Perspectives on marital therapy* (pp. 225–252). New York: Brunner/Mazel.

Beach, S. R. H., Jouriles, E., & O'Leary, K. D. (1985). Extramarital sex: Impact on depression and commitment in couples seeking marital therapy. *Journal of Sex and Marital Therapy, 11,* 99–108.

Beach, S. R. H., Martin, J. K., Blum, T. C., & Roman, P.M. (1993). Effects of marital and co-worker relationships on negative affect: Testing the central role of marriage. *American Journal of Family Therapy, 21,* 312–322.

Beach, S. R. H., & Nelson, G. M. (1990). Pursuing research on major psychopathology from a contextual perspective: The example of depression and marital discord. In G. Brody & I. E. Sigel (Eds.), *Family research* (Vol. 2, pp. 227–259). Hillsdale, NJ: Erlbaum.

Beach, S. R. H., & O'Leary, K. D. (1986). The treatment of depression occurring in the context of marital discord. *Behavior Therapy, 17,* 43–49.

Beach, S. R. H., & O'Leary, K. D. (1992). Treating depression in the context of marital discord: Outcome and predictors of response for marital therapy vs. cognitive therapy. *Behavior Therapy, 23,* 507–528.

Beach, S. R. H., & O'Leary, K. D. (1993). Marital discord and dysphoria: For whom does the marital relationship predict depressive symptomatology? *Journal of Social and Personal Relationships, 10,* 405–420.

Beach, S. R. H., Sandeen, E. E., & O'Leary, K. D. (1990). *Depression in marriage: A model for etiology and treatment.* New York: Guilford Press.

Beck, A. T. (1976). *Cognitive therapy and the emotional disorders.* New York: International Universities Press.

Beck, A. T., Rush, A. J., Shaw, B. F., & Emery, G. (1979). *Cognitive therapy of depression.* New York: Guilford Press.

Bettes, B. A. (1988). Maternal depression and motherese: Temporal and intonational features. *Child Development, 59,* 1089–1096.

Biglan, A., Hops, H., Sherman, L., Friedman, L. S.,

Arthur, J., & Osteen, V. (1985). Problem solving interactions of depressed women and their spouses. *Behavior Therapy, 16,* 431–451.

Billings, A. G., & Moos, R. H. (1983). Comparisons of children of depressed and nondepressed parents: A social–environmental perspective. *Journal of Abnormal Psychology, 11,* 463–486.

Billings, A. G., & Moos, R. H. (1986). Children of parents with unipolar depression: A controlled 1-year follow up. *Journal of Abnormal Child Psychology, 14,* 149–166.

Birchnell, J., & Kennard, J. (1983). Does marital maladjustment lead to mental illness? *Social Psychiatry, 18,* 79–88.

Blaney, P. H. (1986). Affect and memory: A review. *Psychological Bulletin, 99,* 229–246.

Bloom, B., Asher, S. J., & White, S. W. (1978). Marital disruption as a stressor: A review and analysis. *Psychological Bulletin, 85,* 867–894.

Blumberg, S. R., & Hokanson, J. E. (1983). The effects of another person's response style on interpersonal behavior in depression. *Journal of Abnormal Psychology, 92,* 196–209.

Bothwell, S., & Weissman, M. M. (1977). Social impairments four years after an acute depressive episode. *American Journal of Orthopsychiatry, 47,* 231–237.

Bower, G. H. (1981). Mood and memory. *American Psychologist, 36,* 129–148.

Bower, G. H. (1991). Mood congruity of social judgements. In J. P. Forgas (Ed.), *Emotion, and social judgments* (pp. 31–53). Oxford: Pergamon Press.

Boyd, J. H., & Weissman, M. M. (1981). Epidemiology of affective disorders. *Archives of General Psychiatry, 38,* 1039–1046.

Breznitz, A., & Sherman, T. (1987). Speech patterning of natural discourse of well and depressed mother and their young children. *Child Development, 58,* 395–400.

Bromet, E. J., & Cornely, P. J. (1984). Correlates of depression in mothers of young children. *Journal of the American Academy of Child Psychiatry, 23,* 335–342.

Brown, G. W., & Harris, T. (1978). *Social origins of depression: A study of psychiatric disorders in women.* New York: Free Press.

Carro, M. G., Grant, K. E., Gotlib, I. H., & Compas, B. E. (1993). Postpartum depression and child development: An investigation of mothers and fathers as sources of risk and resilience. *Development and Psychopathology, 5,* 567–579.

Carver, C. S., & Ganellen, R. J. (1983). Depression and components of self-punitiveness: High standards, self-criticism, and over-generalization. *Journal of Abnormal Psychology, 92,* 330–337.

Christian, J. L., O'Leary, K. D., & Vivian, D. (1991,

November). *Discriminating between depressed and nondepressed maritally discordant spouses.* Paper presented to the 25th Annual Convention of the Association for Advancement of Behavior Therapy, New York, NY.

Cohn, J. F., Campbell, S. B., Matias, R., & Hopkins, J. (1990). Face-to-face interactions of postpartum depressed and nondepressed mother–infant pairs at 2 months. *Developmental Psychology, 23,* 583–592.

Coyne, J. C. (1976a). Depression and the response of others. *Journal of Abnormal Psychology, 85,* 186–193.

Coyne, J. C. (1976b). Toward an interactional description of depression. *Psychiatry, 39,* 28–40.

Coyne, J. C., & Gotlib, I. H. (1983). The role of cognition in depression: A critical appraisal. *Psychological Bulletin, 94,* 472–505.

Derry, P. A., & Kuiper, N. A. (1981). Schematic processing and self-reference in clinical depression. *Journal of Abnormal Psychology, 90,* 286–297.

Diener, E. (1984). Subjective well-being. *Psychological Bulletin, 95,* 542–575.

Dykman, B. M., Horowitz, L. M., Abramson, L. Y., & Usher, M. (1991). Schematic and situational determinants of depressed and nondepressed students' interpretation of feedback. *Journal of Abnormal Psychology, 100,* 45–55.

D'Zurilla, T. J. (1988). *Problem-solving therapy: A social competence approach to clinical intervention.* New York: Springer.

Egan, G. (1986). *The skilled helper: A systematic approach to effective helping.* Monterey, CA: Brooks-Cole.

Feldman, L., & Gotlib, I. H. (1993). Social withdrawal. In C. G. Costello (Ed.), *Symptoms of depression* (pp. 85–112). New York: Wiley.

Ferster, C. B. (1973). A functional analysis of depression. *American Psychologist, 28,* 857–870.

Field, T., Healy, B., Goldstein, S., & Guthertz, M. (1990). Behavior-state matching and synchrony in mother–infant interactions of nondepressed versus depressed dyads. *Developmental Psychology, 26,* 7–14.

Fincham, F. D., Beach, S. R. H., & Nelson, G. M. (1987). Attribution processes in distressed and non-distressed couples: 4. Self-partner attribution differences. *Journal of Personality and Social Psychology, 52,* 739–748.

Fincham, F. D., Bradbury, T. N., & Beach, S. R. H. (1990). To arrive where we began: A reappraisal of cognition in marriage and in marital therapy. *Journal of Family Psychology, 4,* 167–184.

Fleming, A., Ruble, D., Flett, G., & Shaul, D. (1988). Postpartum adjustment in first-time mothers: Relations between mood, maternal attitudes, and mother–infant interactions. *Developmental Psychology, 24,* 71–81.

Foley, S. H., Rounsaville, B. J., Weissman, M. M., Sholomskas, D., & Chevron, E. (1989). Individual versus conjoint interpersonal psychotherapy for depressed patients with marital disputes. *International Journal of Family Psychiatry, 10,* 29–42.

Forehand, R., McCombs, A., & Brody, G. H. (1987). The relationship between parental depressive mood-states and child functioning. *Advances in Behavior Research and Therapy, 9,* 1–20.

Forgas, J., Bower, G., & Moylan, S. (1990). Praise or blame? Affective influences on attributions for achievement. *Journal of Personality and Social Psychology, 59,* 809–819.

Frank, E., Carpenter, L. L., & Kupfer, D. J. (1988). Sex differences in recurrent depression: Are there any that are significant? *American Journal of Psychiatry, 145,* 41–45.

Freud, S. (1961). Mourning and melancholia. In J. Strachey (Ed. & Trans.), *The standard edition of the complete psychological works of Sigmund Freud* (Vol. 14). London: Hogarth Press. (Original work published 1917)

Glick, P. G. (1984). How American families are changing. *American Demographics, 6,* 20–27.

Goodman, S. H., & Brumley, H. E. (1990). Schizophrenic and depressed mothers: Relational deficits in parenting. *Developmental Psychology, 26,* 31–39.

Gordon, D., Burge, D., Hammen, C., Adrian, C., Jaenicke, C., & Hiroto, D. (1989). Observations of interactions of depressed women with their children. *American Journal of Psychiatry, 146,* 50–55.

Gotlib, I. H. (1981). Self-reinforcement and recall: Differential deficits in depressed and nondepressed psychiatric inpatients. *Journal of Abnormal Psychology, 90,* 521–530.

Gotlib, I.H. (1982). Self-reinforcement and depression in interpersonal interaction: The role of performance level. *Journal of Abnormal Psychology, 91,* 3–13.

Gotlib, I. H. (1983). Perception and recall of interpersonal feedback: Negative bias in depression. *Cognitive Therapy and Research, 7,* 399–412.

Gotlib, I. H. (1993). Depressive disorders. In A.. Bellack & M. Hersen (Eds.), *Psychopathology in adulthood: An advanced text* (pp. 179–194). New York: Pergamon.

Gotlib, I. H., & Colby, C. A. (1987). *Treatment of depression: An interpersonal systems approach.* New York: Pergamon.

Gotlib, I. H., & Hammen, C. L. (1992). *Psychological aspects of depression: Toward a cognitive-interpersonal integration.* Chicester, England: Wiley.

Gotlib, I. H., & Hooley, J. M. (1988). Depression and marital functioning. In S. Duck (Ed.), *Handbook of personal relationships: Theory, research and interventions* (pp. 543–570). Chichester, England: Wiley.

Gotlib, I. H., & Meltzer, S. J. (1987). Depression and the perception of social skill. *Cognitive Therapy and Research, 11,* 41–54.

Gotlib, I. H., & Robinson, L. A. (1982). Responses to depressed individuals: Discrepancies between self-report and observer-rated behaviour. *Journal of Abnormal Psychology, 91,* 231–240.

Gotlib, I. H., Wallace, P. M., & Colby, C. A. (1990). Marital and family therapy for depression. In B. B. Wolman & G. Stricker (Eds.), *Depressive disorders: Facts, theories, and treatment methods* (pp. 396–424). New York: Wiley.

Gotlib, I. H., & Whiffen, V. E. (1989). Depression and marital functioning: An examination of specificity and gender differences. *Journal of Abnormal Psychology, 98,* 23–30.

Gotlib, I. H., & Whiffen, V. E. (1991). The interpersonal context of depression: Implications for theory and research. In W. H. Jones & D. Perlman (Eds.), *Advances in personal relationships* (Vol. 3, pp. 177–206). Greenwich, CT: JAI Press.

Gottman, J. M., & Krokoff, L. J. (1989). Marital interaction and satisfaction: A longitudinal view. *Journal of Consulting and Clinical Psychology, 57,* 47–52.

Gurtman, M. B. (1986). Depression and the response of others: Reevaluating the reevaluation. *Journal of Abnormal Psychology, 95,* 99–101.

Hammen, C., Adrian, C., Gordon, D., Burge, D., Jaenicke, C., & Hiroto, D. (1987). Children of depressed mothers: Maternal strain and symptom predictors of dysfunction. *Journal of Abnormal Psychology, 96,* 190–198.

Hautzinger, M., Linden, M., & Hoffman, N. (1982). Distressed couples with and without a depressed partner: An analysis of their verbal interaction. *Journal of Behavior Therapy and Experimental Psychology, 13,* 307–314.

Hendrick, S. S. (1981). Self-disclosure and marital satisfaction. *Journal of Personality and Social Psychology, 40,* 1130–1159.

Hinchliffe, M., Hooper, D., & Roberts, F. J. (1978). *The melancholy marriage.* New York: Wiley.

Hirschfeld, R.M.A., & Goodwin, F. K. (1988). Mood disorders. In J. A. Talbott, R. E. Hales, & S. C. Yudofsky (Eds.), *Textbook of psychiatry* (pp. 403–441). Washington, DC: American Psychiatric Press.

Hobfoll, S. E., & Lieberman, J. R. (1987). Personality and social resources in immediate and continued stress resistance among women. *Journal of Personality and Social Psychology, 52,* 18–26.

Hooley, J. M. (1986). Expressed emotion and depression: Interactions between patients and high-versus-low-expressed emotion spouses. *Journal of Abnormal Psychology, 95,* 237–246.

Hooley, J. M., Orley, J., & Teasdale, J. D. (1986). Levels of expressed emotion and relapse in depressed patients. *British Journal of Psychiatry, 148,* 642–647.

Hooley, J. M., & Teasdale, J. D. (1989). Predictors of relapse in unipolar depressives: Expressed emotion, marital distress, and perceived criticism. *Journal of Abnormal Psychology, 98,* 229–237.

Hops, H., Biglan, A., Sherman, L., Arthur, J., Friedman, L., & Osteen, V. (1987). Home observations of family interactions of depressed women. *Journal of Consulting and Clinical Psychology, 55,* 341–346.

Howes, M. J., & Hokanson, J. E. (1979). Conversational and social responses to depressive interpersonal behavior. *Journal of Abnormal Psychology, 88,* 625–634.

Ilfeld, F. W. (1977). Current social stressors and symptoms of depression. *American Journal of Psychiatry, 134,* 161–166.

Jacobson, N. S. (1985, August). *Combining marital therapy with individual therapy in the treatment of depression.* Paper presented at the 93rd Annual Convention of the American Psychological Association, Los Angeles.

Jacobson, N. S., & Anderson, E. (1982). Interpersonal skills deficits and depression in college students: A sequential analysis of the timing of self-disclosures. *Behavior Therapy, 13,* 271–282.

Jacobson, N. S., Dobson, K., Fruzzetti, A. E., Schmaling, K. B., & Salusky, S. (1991). Marital therapy as a treatment for depression. *Journal of Consulting and Clinical Psychology, 59,* 547–557.

Jacobson, N. S., Fruzzetti, A. E., Dobson, K., Whisman, M., & Hops, H. (1993). Couple therapy as a treatment for depression. II: The effects of relationship quality and therapy on depressive relapse. *Journal of Consulting and Clinical Psychology, 61,* 516–519.

Jacobson, N. S., Holtzworth-Munroe, A., & Schmaling, K. B. (1989). Marital therapy and spouse involvement in the treatment of depression, agoraphobia, and alcoholism. *Journal of Consulting and Clinical Psychology, 54,* 518–522.

Jacobson, N. S., & Margolin, G. (1979). *Marital therapy: Strategies based on social learning and behavior exchange principles.* New York: Brunner/Mazel.

Johnson, M. H., & Magaro, P. A. (1987). Effects of mood and severity on memory processes in depression and mania. *Psychological Bulletin, 101,* 28–40.

Kahn, J., Coyne, J. C., & Margolin, G. (1985). Depression and marital disagreement: The social construction of despair. *Journal of Social and Personal Relationships, 2,* 447–461.

Karno, M., Hough, R. L., Burnam, A., Escobar, J. I., Timbers, D. M., Santana, F., & Boyd, J. H. (1987). Lifetime prevalence of specific psychiatric disorders among Mexican Americans and non-Hispanic whites in Los Angeles. *Archives of General Psychiatry, 44,* 695–701.

Kessler, R. C., Price, R. H., & Wortman, C. B. (1985). Social factors in psychopathology: Stress, social support, and coping processes. *Annual Review of Psychology, 36,* 531–572.

King, D. A., & Heller, K. (1984). Depression and the response of others: A re-evaluation. *Journal of Abnormal Psychology, 94,* 477–480.

Klerman, G. L., Weissman, M. M., Rounsaville, B. J., & Chevron, E. (1984). *Interpersonal psychotherapy of depression.* New York: Basic Books.

Kochanska, G., Kuczynski, L., Radke-Yarrow, M., & Welsh, J. D. (1987). Resolutions of control episodes between well and affectively ill mothers and their young children. *Journal of Abnormal Child Psychology, 15,* 441–456.

Kowalik, D. L., & Gotlib, I. H. (1987). Depression and marital interaction: Concordance between intent and perception of communication. *Journal of Abnormal Psychology, 96,* 127–134.

Lazarus, R. S., & Folkman, S. (1986). Cognitive theories of stress and the issue of circularity. In M. H. Appley & R. Turnbull (Eds.), *Dynamics of stress: Physiological, psychological, and social perspectives.* New York: Plenum.

Lee, C. M., & Gotlib, I. H. (1989). Maternal depression and child adjustment: A longitudinal analysis. *Journal of Abnormal Psychology, 98,* 78–85.

Lee, C. M., & Gotlib, I. H. (1991). Adjustment of children of depressed mothers: A ten-month follow-up. *Journal of Abnormal Psychology, 100,* 473–477.

Lewinsohn, P. M., Hoberman, H., & Rosenbaum, M. (1988). A prospective study of risk factors for unipolar depression. *Journal of Abnormal Psychology, 97,* 251–264.

Lewinsohn, P. M., Hoberman, H., Teri, L., & Hautzinger, A. (1985). An integrative theory of depression. In S. Reiss, & R. Bootzin (Eds.), *Theoretical issues in behavior therapy* (pp. 331–359). New York: Academic Press.

Lewinsohn, P. M., Mischel, W., Chaplin, C., & Barton, R. (1980). Social competence and depression: The role of illusory self-perceptions. *Journal of Abnormal Psychology, 89,* 203–217.

Libet, J., & Lewinsohn, P. M. (1973). The concept of social skill with special reference to the behavior of depressed persons. *Journal of Consulting and Clinical Psychology, 40,* 304–312.

Lieberman, M. A. (1982). The effects of social supports on responses to stress. In L. Goldberger & S. Breznitz (Eds.), *Handbook of stress* (pp. 764–781). New York: Free Press.

Livingood, A., Daen, P., & Smith, B. (1983). The depressed mother as a source of stimulation for her infant. *Journal of Clinical Psychology, 39,* 369–375.

Lyons-Ruth, K., Zoll, D., Connell, D., & Grunebaum, H. U. (1986). The depressed mother and her one-year-old infant: Environmental context, mother–infant interaction and attachment, and infant development. In E. Tronick & T. Field (Eds.), *Maternal depression and infant disturbance: New directions in child development* (pp. 61–82). San Francisco: Jossey-Bass.

Mandler, G. (1984). *Mind and body: Psychology of emotion and stress.* New York: Norton.

Markman, H. J., Duncan, S. W., Storaasli, R. D., & Howes, P. W. (1987). The prediction of marital distress: A longitudinal investigation. In K. Hahlweg & M. Goldstein (Eds.), *Understanding major mental disorder: The contribution of family interaction research* (pp. 266–289). New York: Family Process Press.

Marks, T., & Hammen, C. L. (1982). Interpersonal mood induction: Situational and individual determinants. *Motivation and Emotion, 6,* 387–399.

McCabe, S. B., & Gotlib, I. H. (1993). Interactions of couples with and without a depressed spouse: Self-report and observations of problem-solving situations. *Journal of Social and Personal Relationships, 10,* 589–599.

McGonagle, K. A., Kessler, R. C., & Gotlib, I. H. (1993). The effects of marital disagreement style, frequency, and outcome on marital disruption. *Journal of Social and Personal Relationships, 10,* 385–404.

Merikangas, K. R. (1984). Divorce and assortative mating among depressed. *American Journal of Psychiatry, 141,* 74–76.

Merikangas, K. R., Ranelli, C., & Kupfer, D. (1979). Marital interaction in hospitalized depressed patients. *Journal of Nervous and Mental Disease, 167,* 689–695.

Mills, M., Puckering, C., Pound, A., & Cox, A. (1985). What is it about depressed mothers that influences their children's functioning? In J. E. Stevenson (Ed.), *Recent research in developmental psychopathology* (pp. 11–17). Oxford: Pergamon.

Minkoff, K., Bergman, E., Beck, A. T., & Beck, R. (1973). Hopelessness, depression, and attempted suicide. *American Journal of Psychiatry, 130,* 455–459.

Monroe, S. M., Bromet, E. J., Connell, M. M., & Steiner, S. C. (1986). Social support, life events, and depressive symptoms: A 1-year prospective study. *Journal of Consulting and Clinical Psychology, 54,* 424–431.

Monroe, S. M., & Depue, R. A. (1991). Life stress and depression. In J. Becker & A. Kleinman (Eds.), *Psychosocial aspects of depression* (pp. 101–130). Hillsdale, NJ: Erlbaum.

Murphy, J. M., Monson, R. R., Olivier, D. C., Sobol, A. M., & Leighton, A. H. (1987). Affective disorders and mortality. *Archives of General Psychiatry, 44,* 473–480.

Nelson, G. M., & Beach, S. R. H. (1990). Sequential interaction in depression: Effects of depressive behavior on spousal aggression. *Behavior Therapy, 21,* 167–182.

Nezu, A. M., Nezu, C. M., & Perri, M. G. (1989). *Problem-solving therapy for depression: Theory, research, and clinical guidelines.* New York: Wiley.

Noller, P. (1987). Nonverbal communication in marriage. In D. Perlman & S. Duck (Eds.), *Intimate relationships: Development, dynamics, and deterioration* (pp. 149–175). Beverly Hills, CA: Sage.

O'Leary, K. D., & Beach, S. R. H. (1990). Martial therapy: A viable treatment for depression and marital discord. *American Journal of Psychiatry, 147,* 183–186.

O'Leary, K. D., Risso, L. P., & Beach, S. R. H. (1990). Attributions about the marital discord/depression link and therapy outcome. *Behavior Therapy, 21,* 413–422.

O'Leary, K. D., Sandeen, E., & Beach, S. R. H. (1987, November). *Treatment of suicidal, maritally discordant clients by marital therapy or cognitive therapy.* Paper presented at the 21st Annual Meeting of the Association for Advancement of Behavior Therapy, Boston.

Orvaschel. H., Walsh-Allis, G., & Ye, W. (1988). Psychopathology in children of parents with recurrent depression. *Journal of Abnormal Child Psychology, 16,* 17–28.

Panaccione, V. F., & Wahler, R. G. (1986). Child behavior, maternal depression, and social coercion as factors in the quality of child care. *Journal of Abnormal Child Psychology, 14,* 263–278.

Paykel, E. S., Myers, J. K., Dienelt, M. N., Kierman, G. L., Lindenthal, J. J., & Peper, M. P. (1969). Life events and depression: A controlled study. *Archives of General Psychiatry, 21,* 753–760.

Paykel, E. S., & Tanner, J. (1976). Life events, depressive relapse, and maintenance treatment. *Psychological Medicine, 6,* 481–485.

Pearlin, L. I. (1982). The social contexts of stress. In L. Goldberger & S. Breznitz (Eds.), *Handbook of stress* (pp. 367–379). New York: Free Press.

Pearlin, L. I., & Schooler, C. (1978). The structure of coping. *Journal of Health and Social Behavior, 19,* 2–21.

Pietromonaco, P. R., & Rook, K. S. (1987). Decision style in depression: The contribution of perceived risks and benefits. *Journal of Personality and Social Psychology, 52,* 399–408.

Radke-Yarrow, M., Cummings, E. M., Kuczynski, L., & Chapman, M. (1985). Patterns of attachment in two and three year olds in normal families and families with parental depression. *Child Development, 56,* 884–893.

Rickard, K. M., Forehand, R., Wells, K. C., Griest, D. L., & McMahon, R. J. (1981). Factors in the referral of children for behavioural treatment: A comparison of mothers of clinic-referred deviant, clinic-referred non-deviant, and non-clinic children. *Behaviour Research and Therapy, 19,* 201–205.

Robins, L. N., Helzer, J. E., Weissman, M. M., Orvaschel, H., Gruenberg, E., Burke, J. D., & Regier, D. A. (1984). Lifetime prevalence of specific psychiatric disorders in three sites. *Archives of General Psychiatry, 41,* 949–958.

Rosenblatt, A., & Greenberg, J. (1988). Depression and interpersonal attraction: The role of perceived similarity. *Journal of Personality and Social Psychology, 55,* 112–119.

Ruscher, S. M., & Gotlib, I. H. (1988). Marital interaction patterns of couples with and without a depressed partner. *Behavior Therapy, 19,* 455–470.

Rutter, M., & Quinton, P. (1984). Parental psychiatric disorder: Effects on children. *Psychological Medicine, 14,* 853–880.

Sager, C. J., Gundlach, R., & Kremer, M. (1968). The married in treatment. *Archives of General Psychiatry, 19,* 205–217.

Sarason, B. R., Shearin, E. N., Pierce, G. R., & Sarason, I. G. (1987). Interrelationship of social support measures: Theoretical and practical implications. *Journal of Personality and Social Psychology, 52,* 813–832.

Schless, A. P., Schwartz, L., Goetz, C., & Mendels, J. (1974). How depressives view the significance of life events. *British Journal of Psychiatry, 125,* 406–410.

Schmaling, K. B., & Jacobson, N. S. (1990). Marital interaction and depression. *Journal of Abnormal Psychology, 99,* 229–236.

Schmaling, K. B., Whisman, M. A., Fruzzetti, A. E., & Truax, P. (1991). Identifying areas of marital conflict: Interactional behaviors associated with depression. *Journal of Family Psychology, 5,* 145–157.

Shaefer, E. S., & Burnett, C. K. (1987). Stability and predictability of quality of women's marital relationships and demoralization. *Journal of Personality and Social Psychology, 53,* 1129–1136.

Spanier, G. B. (1976). Measuring dyadic adjustment: New scales for assessing the quality of marriage and similar dyads. *Journal of Marriage and the Family, 38,* 15–28.

Stuart, R. B. (1980). *Helping couples change: A social learning approach to marital therapy.* New York: Guilford Press.

Thomas, A. M., & Forehand, R. (1991). The relationship between paternal depressive mood and early adolescent functioning. *Journal of Family Psychology, 4,* 260–271.

Tolstedt, B. E., & Stokes, J. P. (1984). Self-disclosure, intimacy, and the depenetration process. *Journal of Personality and Social Psychology, 46,* 84–90.

Vanfossen, B. E. (1986). Sex differences in depression: The role of spouse support. In S. E. Hobfoll (Ed.) *Stress, social support, and women* (pp. 69–84). New York: Hemisphere.

Vaughn, C. E., & Leff, J. P. (1976). The influence of family and social factors on the course of psychiatric illness: A comparison of schizophrenic and depressed neurotic patients. *British Journal of Psychiatry, 129,* 125–137.

Waring, E. M. (1988). *Enhancing marital intimacy through facilitating cognitive self-disclosure.* New York: Brunner/Mazel.

Webster-Stratton, C., & Hammond, M. (1988). Maternal depression and its relationship to life stress, perceptions of child behavior problems, parenting behaviors, and child conduct problems. *Journal of Abnormal Child Psychology, 16*(3), 299–315.

Weiss, R. L., & Birchler, G. R. (1978). Adults with marital dysfunction. In M. Hersen & A. S. Bellack (Eds.), *Behavior therapy in the psychiatric setting* (pp. 331–364). Baltimore: Williams & Wilkins.

Weiss, R. S. (1974). The provision of social relationships. In Z. Rubin (Ed.), *Doing unto others* (pp. 17–26). Englewood Cliffs, NJ: Prentice-Hall.

Weissman, M. M., Paykel, E. S., & Klerman, G. L. (1972). The depressed woman as a mother. *Social Psychiatry, 7,* 98–108.

Weissman, M. M., Prusoff, B., Gammon, G. D., Merikangas, K. R., Leckman, J., & Kidd, K. K. (1984). Psychopathology in the children (ages 6–18) of depressed and normal parents. *Journal of the American Academy of Child Psychiatry, 23,* 78–84.

Wheaton, B. (1994). Sampling the stress universe. In W. R. Avison & I. H. Gotlib (Eds.), *Stress and mental health: Contemporary issues and prospects for the future* (pp. 77–114). New York: Plenum.

Winters, K. C., Stone, A. A., Weintraub, S., & Neale, J. M. (1981). Cognitive and attentional deficits in children vulnerable to psychopathology. *Journal of Abnormal Child Psychology, 9,* 435–453.

Youngren, M. A., & Lewinsohn, P. M. (1980). The functional relationship between depression and problematic behavior. *Journal of Abnormal Psychology, 89,* 333–341.

21

Conceptualization and Treatment of Eating Disorders in Couples

MARIA P. P. ROOT

Dear Ann Landers,

My wife has been on a diet since New Year's of 1989. The method she chose was advertised by a nationally known diet franchise. After "Debbie" reached her goal she decided she wasn't thin enough and refused to quit dieting.

I went in and spoke with the person in charge of the diet plan. I was told, "There is nothing we can do. We've tried. She is totally out of control. The woman needs psychological counseling." Just so you'll know, Ann, Debbie has gone from 235 pounds to 115. I'm not sure exactly, because that was the last figure she quoted. She is 5 feet 8 inches tall and looks like a skeleton.

Debbie refuses to acknowledge that she has a problem. She dismissed the advice from the five health professionals we have consulted. Her battle cry is, "They don't understand. I worked like a dog to take off all that weight and now they're telling me to put it back on."

. . . Her health is deteriorating rapidly, yet she insists the diet isn't the problem. She says it's our marriage.

Can you give me a hand, Ann? I can't just stand by while my wife breaks up our marriage and starves herself to death.—*Crying on the Inside*

—LANDERS (1990, p. C7)

FAMILY AND GROUP therapies have been the recommended treatment for anorexia and bulimia nervosa, eating disorders that typically emerge during adolescence. Whereas recovery from these disorders can be achieved (Root, 1990), the hallmark symptoms, that is, significant weight loss, refusal to gain weight, starvation, compulsive and excessive exercise, exaggerated and/or distorted perceptions of body size, binge eating, and purging (American Psychiatric Association, 1994), can be resistant to change and may become chronic. Thus, an eating disorder that started in adolescence may be carried over to adulthood and life partnerships. In fact, Theander (1970) has observed that the older the individual, the more likely she/he will be married.

The couple is often an overlooked system and couple therapy has received little attention. This chapter focuses on understanding the interplay between the dynamics of the couple and eating-disordered symptoms. Treatment interventions are offered. The use of "she" to refer to the person with the eating disorder and the use of "he" to refer to the partner replicates the gender discrepancies in the distribution of these disorders; the person with the eating disorder is likely to be female, and the partner, male, although same sex couples may also seek help.

The fact that eating disorders have been conceptualized as adolescent disorders contributes to our oversight of adults with eating disorders in committed relationships. Several factors shed light on this omission in the research and treatment literature. In adolescence, treatment is usually initiated by parents. Because of the secrecy involved, particularly with bulimia nervosa, and the tendency of male partners to be more oriented to physical appearance than women (Siever, 1989), male partners are often unaware of the eating disorder; the end result is often viewed as attractive, except in severe cases of anorexia nervosa. If and when male partners become aware of it, they do not have the control that parents had to mandate treatment. A hallmark symptom of anorexia, amenorrhea, is often disguised by the use of birth control pills, thereby making detection that much more difficult within a couple. Additionally, the cost of treatment can be expensive. Young couples outside of university and college settings may encounter obstacles to obtaining affordable help at a time when they have fewest resources. Research samples often are drawn from university students and clinics that will serve proportionally fewer married bulimics and anorexics than would be found in community samples. Last, as often observed in couples in which one partner is abusing alcohol or drugs, denial or avoidance of existing relational problems may prevent the eating disorder from being acknowledged.

REVIEW OF THE LITERATURE

Family approaches to treatment presume that the family in which an individual develops an eating disorder has structural problems in communication and or in interpersonal boundaries (Minuchin, Rosman, & Baker, 1978; Root, Fallon, & Friedrich, 1986) that compromise the emotional climate of the family and its ability to meet the needs of the individual (Bruch, 1978). Root et al. (1986) further observed that these families are very heterogeneous in their strengths and weaknesses.

As with adolescents and single, young women, studies of married women suggest that family-of-origin dynamics are integral to the development of eating disorders (Minuchin et al., 1978; Root et al., 1986). It is often observed that developmental difficulties with individuation and independence in one's family-of-origin are present within a marriage or even drive the choice of partner (Dally, 1984; Foster, 1986; Heavey, Parker, Vhat, Crisp, & Gowers, 1989; Root et al., 1986; Van den Broucke & Vandereycken, 1989a). Root et al. (1986) emphasize that the family be placed in its social context. As such, many gender-role proscriptions increase women's vulnerability for developing eating disorders as strategies for resolving personal crises.

Arrest at one stage of development may also increase the likelihood that an individual will not have the resources to face increasingly challenging and demanding developmental tasks, such as the ongoing intimacy, conflicts, and compromises associated with long-term romantic relationships. For example, Heavey et al. (1989) observed a triangular relationship between family-of-origin relationships, the anorexic, and the anorexic's marriage.

> When relationships are even more disengaged and impoverished, in the midst of poorly resolved conflict, the young person may also drift into an early marriage without yet developing anorexia nervosa. However, within her own marriage she may experience a reenactment of these earlier unresolved conflicts . . . in the face of a resulting mounting marital crisis, the marriage itself is threatened, anorexia nervosa may now supervene, at a much older age, to protect the integrity of her own marriage. (p. 283)

Although clinical folklore suggests that married bulimics, their marriages, and their partners are dysfunctional, the emerging research suggests that, at least on the surface, they and their partners may not be that different from other persons in distressed partnerships (Levine, 1988). In a controlled study, Van Buren and Williamson (1988) found that both bulimic women and nonbulimic women in distressed marriages were similar. They tended to withdraw from conflict, used fewer problem-solving skills than nondistressed women, and believed their partners could not change. Partners of bulimic women, although more dissatisfied with their marriages than control spouses, were not as dissatisfed as male partners in the distressed group. None of the three groups of men (partners of bulimics, distressed, nondistressed) differed on conflict resolution styles. The implications of these findings are that the basic interventions in couple therapy will be useful in working with these couples.

Incidence of Marriage

In general, it is observed that fewer anorexics than bulimics marry (Garfinkel & Garner, 1982), and more women than men with eating disorders are married (Mitchell & Goff, 1984; Schneider & Agras, 1987). In female samples, it is estimated that 10% to 21% of anorexics are married (Crisp, Hsu, Harding, & Hartshor, 1980; Garfinkel & Garner, 1982; Sykes, Leuser, Melia, & Gross, 1988; Van den Broucke & Vandereycken, 1989b; Heavey et al., 1989) and 7% to 33% of bulimics are married (Russell, 1979; Garfinkel & Garner, 1982; Huon, 1985; Sykes et al., 1988).

Few studies have included enough men with eating disorders to produce reliable estimates of the incidence of marriage. In two studies of small samples of male subjects with bulimia nervosa, approximately 8% of the men were married (Mitchell & Goff, 1984; Schneider & Agras, 1987). The difference in incidence of marriage between men and women may be confounded with sexual orientation. Schneider and Agras (1987) found that 8 of their 15 male subjects with bulimia nervosa identified as gay or bisexual. They did not inquire if any of these men were in committed relationships. Additionally, the emotional lability associated with eating-disordered symptomatology conflicts more with stereotyped male than female role and behavior expectations.

Marital Status and Prognosis

In the early literature, marital status was associated with poor prognosis (Crisp et al., 1980; Hsu, Crisp, & Harding, 1979), particularly if the symptoms included vomiting (Russell, 1979). However, duration of the disorder, marital status, and age of onset are confounded in most studies. Two recent studies attempted to untangle this confound. The Heavey et al. (1989) study of 250 anorexics found that the average age of married anorexics was higher than that of single anorexics, a finding similar to that of Van den Broucke and Vandereycken (1989c). Heavey and associates found that vomiting or severe symptoms among anorexics were associated with chronicity; thus, women who were anorexic prior to marriage had a more severe illness. When the symptom profile was controlled for chronicity, there were no differences between married and unmarried anorexics. Similarly, in the Van den Broucke and Vandereycken comparative study (1989c), symptoms, weight history, and weight status were similar between married and unmarried groups, a finding consistent with case studies reviewed by Van den Broucke and Vandereycken (1988). Using cluster analysis in another study comparing married to unmarried anorexics, Van den Broucke and Vandereycken (1989c) found that 75% of their sample of 34 married anorexics fell into one cluster; the relationship was not only coincidental with the onset of the eating disorder, but it was also associated with a different course. In this cluster, being married was associated with greater weight loss and a different personality constellation, although the researchers did not control for duration of the eating disorder to determine if these differences were a result of chronicity.

Onset

Increasingly, researchers are finding that "late onset" eating disorders that emerge in the context of marriage are not unusual (Dally, 1984; Heavey et al., 1989; Lafeber, 1981, cited Vandereycken, Kog, & Vanderlinder, 1989; Van den Broucke & Vandereycken, 1989b). Heavey et al. (1989) found that 29.6% of their London sample of married anorexics had a postmarital onset. In a Dutch study of 10 couples with anorexic, bulimic, or mixed eating disorders, Van den Broucke and Vandereycken (1989c) found that all of the subjects in their study had a postrelational onset. These same researchers (1989c), although conducting a comparison study of married and unmarried anorexics, did not specifically determine onset in relation to marital status. They noted, however, that the age of onset in the early 20s for married subjects suggests that the onset of the eating disorder for many subjects may be related to the marital relationship. In fact, Dally and Gomez (1979) observed that age of onset may be a significant factor in the marital status of persons with eating disorders. They found that 40% of their sample of women whose onset was age 19 or older were married. Dally (1984) found that his sample of 50 anorexic "late-onset" women could be divided into different groups. Late onset does not preclude a previous occurrence of it. Dally found that 44% of his sample of late-onset anorexics had had an occurrence of anorexia prior to marriage. Women with a prior history of anorexia had a reoccurrence during the engagement or after marriage, but before pregnancy. Nevertheless, a significant number of late-onset eating disorders are a first occurence. In his sample, first occurrence, late-onset anorexia was developed within 3 years of childbirth or at postmenopause.

Choice of Partner

Hypotheses generated from both systematic and case studies of married anorexics' relationships not only suggest that marital conflict or avoidance of conflict may be at the heart of the disorder (Andersen, 1985; Barrett & Schwartz, 1987; Bruch, 1978; Foster, 1986; Heavey et al., 1989; Lafeber, 1981, cited in Vandereycken et al., 1989; Madanes, 1981), but also that they integrally link the hypothesized relationship dysfunction to psychopathology and maturity deficits in the partners (Dally, 1984; Lafeber, 1981, cited in Vandereychen et al., 1989). In fact, Barrett and Schwartz (1987) state that "the bulimic marries . . . a person who makes it possible for her to continue her relationship with food and, therefore, with bulimia" (p. 25).

The bulimic or anorexic's choice of partner may reflect a romantic idealization of the partner's ability to provide in ways parents could not. For example, the individual with the eating disorder may look to the partner for the acceptance, approval, limit setting, protection, and attachment that were lacking in the family of origin. The choice of partner may also reflect an attempt to create an environment and life extremely different from the parental home. Subsequently, the bulimic or anorexic chooses or sees in the partner only those qualities that are opposite from her/his family or parents. The choice of a partner may increase the bulimic or anorexic's status in the family; thus, she/he attempts to gain family approval through the choice of partner. Last, the bulimic or anorexic may be drawn to a partner who will provide a semblance of "normality," but who will not make demands for intimacy or responsibility that are beyond the capacities of the partner with the eating disorder.

In essence, the partner may be developmentally similar to the anorexic and bulimic.

For example, a young couple, Dave and Jan, struggled with similar issues about being alone, which created an obstacle for both persons to act in a way they felt would be best for them. For Dave, setting reasonable limits on what he could tolerate about his partner's eating disorder in their relationship was hindered by his fear that she would leave. This fear originated in his unresolved issues of losing his mother. Jan felt anguished by the distress her symp-

toms caused her partner. She felt that she should end the relationship to spare his grief. However, Jan anticipated that ending the relationship would leave her feeling utterly lost and incomplete, a reenactment of feelings she had experienced in her family prior to the onset of her anorexia. Both Dave and Jan had traumatic losses that now manifested in intense anxiety about being without each other.

Characteristics of the Partner

Hypotheses about the psychological maturity and developmental needs of the eating-disordered individual's partner are related to whether there is a pre- or postrelationship onset. In the case of a preexisting and/or continuing eating disorder, it is difficult to suggest that the partner has had a significant role in the etiology of the disorder. In these cases, regardless of whether the partner knows about the eating disorder, hypotheses are likely to focus on the male partner's neurotic needs, maturity deficits, avoidance of intimacy, and need to be a protector or rescuer—a caricature of the male gender role (i.e., his role in maintaining the symptomatology). Some authors suggest that there is collusion between partners (Andersen, 1985; Dally, 1984) in which the symptoms provide some homeostatic function. Knowingly entering into a long-term relationship with someone with an eating disorder may represent fulfillment of the "prince" role. It may also reflect the partner's search for self-regard that is otherwise lacking and/or the need to define self in relationship to his partner's weakness or "need for him."

Several hypotheses suggest that the unresolved issues for many male partners are less visible with partners who are seemingly more distressed than they are. In a combined sample of pre- and postmarital-onset eating disorders, male partners were compared to nonclinical controls and psychiatric controls (Van den Broucke & Vandereycken, 1989b). Partners scored similarly to persons with depression or anxiety disorders in the control groups, although they were symptomatically less severe than their partners with eating-disorders; thus, the eating disordered partners were the identified patients.

In cases of postrelationship onset, it is hypothesized that the partner plays an active role in the etiology and maintenance of the eating disorder. In these cases, it is hypothesized that these relationships reflect developmental compatability. For example, Dally (1984) suggests that the development of anorexia nervosa in the marital relationship is a response to growing marital conflict for which the woman had not completely developed the skills in adolescence to cope. This "stuckness" is attributed to deficits in the maturity of both partners and is supported by numerous authors (e.g., Andersen, 1985; Crisp, 1980; Foster, 1986; Lafeber, 1981, cited in Vandereycken et al.. 1989; Van den Broucke & Vandereycken, 1989c).

However, not all relationships reflect uniform dynamics (Levine, 1988; Root et al., 1986). For example, Dally's research (1984) led him to describe three types of partners married to late onset anorexics. Across types of relationships there is a lack of balance between separateness and togetherness or individuation and integration, and there appear to be difficulties in communication about more intimate and conflictual matters (Van den Broucke & Vandereycken, 1989a) despite initial reports of marital satisfaction (Levine, 1988; Van den Broucke & Vandereycken, 1989a).

It is also possible that romantic idealizations of marriage and partners subsequently contribute to conflicts in these marriages in which neither partner is equipped to cope constructively. Dally (1984) noted that, although husbands of the anorexics in his sample initially described their wives in idealized terms, as the relationship progressed and the husbands obtained a more realistic perception of their wives, there was a mutual emotional withdrawal that preceded the onset of anorexia. This observation is consistent with that of many researchers (Lafeber, 1981; Heavey et al., 1989), suggesting that with anorexics, one pattern of dealing with disappointment or conflict in the marriage is to submerge conflicts through emotional withdrawal, as their parents had done in the family of origin. As Heavey et al. (1989) and Foster (1986) observed, this type of reenactment of family-of-origin issues might precipitate the anorexia, as observed by Dally (1984).

In the first study of marital partners with an eating-disordered spouse, Dally (1984) observed three different patterns of husbands' behaviors in his 4 groups of maritally-related-onset anorexia. The pattern into which 50% of the husbands belonged was characterized by passivity, avoidance of conflict, and an intense need for affirmation. The latter is obtained through the wife's increasing dependence on him as she becomes anorexic. An example of this pattern is illustrated by Gerri, a 43-year-old white womanm as she struggled to decide whether to remain with her partner or breakup. After several trial separations, she noted that she was much less symp-

tomatic, often going 1 to 2 months without symptoms when she was not living with her partner. She concluded that in order to be in the relationship, she had to be symptomatic so that she could be the "weaker" one. As she become more symptomatic, she felt more critical of herself and more indebted and grateful to her partner for staying and putting up with her. A second pattern described one third of the sample. The husband copes with the emotional distance that accompanies anorexia nervosa by emotionally withdrawing either into an affair or by working long hours. The third category captured one sixth of the sample, in which they husband is often characterized as being older. His kindness and regard for his wife rest on the degree to which she reflects positively on him. With this type of partner, the woman is regarded much more as a possession. The partner tends not to be aware, or does not want to concern himself with the welfare of his partner if it is not overtly affecting him; thus, the female partner is a possession who learns to hide her eating disorder well.

Relationship Dynamics

As Levine (1988) summarized, the case study literature of couples with eating disorders suggests several relationship functions of eating disorders, specifically bulimia, in marriage: an indirect rebellion against a dominant or overprotective spouse; a struggle for control and independence in the marriage; stress management in the marriage; avoidance of intimacy; an excuse for being less than perfect; a distraction from marital distress; a way to obtain nurturance and sympathy from a partner; and a desperate weight-control measure. Levine was not able to find confirmation for these functions in the five couples she interviewed. However, it is my experience that the therapist needs to be very specific about how an issue manifests. Many couples will not be able to identify issues that shape their interactions at the beginning of treatment. This is often the case when the dynamics resemble family-of-origin dynamics and are thus normative for them. Additionally, many of these couples are invested in believing that their relationships are functioning well; many of the women fear being blamed for the relationship problems.

Therapists who work with couples with eating disorders are well aware of the length of time it may take for certain issues to be raised in the therapy environment. Such offerings require individuals in the couple to become aware of their own feelings and needs, and to believe they have the right to air them. Thus, conjoint therapy may necessarily require simultaneous individual therapy. Power must be shared between partners for some of the issues to emerge. Without personal power, it is difficult for some persons to make requests. For example, with one couple, the bulimic wife's past history had been used against her by both her parents and her husband in a way that rendered her powerless to consider the fact that her unhappiness might reside in some marital issues. Her past history of shoplifting, of being identified as a problem in her family of origin, of being divorced by her first husband, and her current husband's status as a physician, provided major obstacles to her being able to feel that she had credibility in therapy or in the marriage. She readily accepted her husband's brutal criticisms. It took over a year of individual therapy—working on family-of-origin issues and increasing her awareness of her feelings—for her to assert that her unhappiness had something to do with her marriage.

The issue of intimacy has received the most attention in the research and clinical literature and is summarized here, particulary as it is related to emotional engagement, sexuality, and communication. There are multiple ways in which difficulties with intimacy originate, are manifested, or developed. Again, several researchers suggest that the basis of these difficulties is founded in the eating-disordered person's relationship with her/his parents (Bruch, 1978; Foster, 1986; Heavey et al., 1989; Minuchin et al., 1978; Root et al., 1986). More specifically, intimacy might be compromised by the parents' overprotectiveness (Heavey et al., 1989), their modeling of emotional disengagement for conflict resolution (Bruch, 1978; Heavey et al., 1989; Minuchin et al., 1978; Root et al., 1986), or by "loyalty wars." In the latter dynamic, persons feel that they must choose between their partner and their parents (Root et al., 1986).

The observations about sexual intimacy are varied. Dally (1984) noted that, except for women who had started anorexia postmenopausally, the late onset anorexics he studied were "sexually timid," anxious, and avoidant or disgusted by sex. Similarly, Heavey et al. (1989) found that few women, married or single, among her anorexic sample were interested in sex (10.3% and 13.6%, respectively), and in fact, women in both groups actively avoided sexual activity (71.8% and 80.3%). In contrast, Abraham's (1985) Australian sample of bulimics described their sexual libido as above average. However, negative feelings about higher body weights than

desired were associated with social and sexual withdrawal.

Avoidance, lack of interest, or fear of relating sexually may have different and multiple origins. A recent case study report by Simpson and Ramberg (1992) observed that for all five married women included in their report, aversion to sex coincided with the onset of their eating disorder. Several researchers have suggested that prior sexual traumas make sexual intimacy difficult (Root & Fallon, 1988; Simpson & Ramberg, 1992; Zerbe, 1992). Such histories are consistent with difficulties in sexual function. Additionally, the hormonal changes consequent to anorexia substantially influence the perception of and desire for sexual activity.

Despite the ability of many women with eating disorders to express significant dissatisfication and unhappiness in relationships, they are not able to leave. The reasons for staying in their relationships are varied and may include the following:

1. Feeling "undeserving" of a relationship and thus grateful that someone would stay or "put up" with them.
2. Fearing that they will forever be alone.
3. Having developmental limitations that preclude feeling whole when alone.
4. Fearing financial responsibilities.
5. Fearing family-of-origin repercussions.
6. Fearing that they will be blamed for "failing" their female responsibility to make a relationship work.
7. Lacking the clarity to determining what their own contributions or responsibilities are to the relationship problems.
8. Fearing violence against self, children, extended family, or friends, if they leave.

In the cases where violence is present, emotional brainwashing may be at the heart of ravaged self-esteem and severely decreased optimism that make it difficult to leave. The eating disorder numbs the awareness of danger or despair.

Summary

Those who research and study eating disorders have largely overlooked the population of anorexics and bulimics in committed relationships. Approximately 20% of persons with eating disorders are married, the likelihood of which increases with age (Theander, 1970). A significant number of women with eating disorders develop the problem in the context of the relationship. With increasing chronicity, symptoms may become more severe.

The origin and function of an eating disorder may vary from person to person. At the present time, conceptualizations of the function of the eating disorder are varied and outstrip the empirical study of symptomatology. Results of empirically designed research are still exploratory. They do suggest that a wide range of functions may be served by the eating-disorder symptomatology. The research that does exist overlaps with conceptual formulations that suggest that developmental crises and deficits in the family of origin continue into couple's relationships and contribute to the vulnerability of late onset. Hypotheses about the partners of persons with eating disorders suggest a complementarity that seems to allow an eating disorder that existed prior to the relationship to be maintained within it, or one that develops within the relationship as a result of a crisis, to become more chronic.

ASSESSMENT

> I didn't want my husband to know. I kept the check register and paid the bills in our relationship. I could hide the cost of my habit—$100.00 to $250.00 in a bad week. Initially, I was working and was able to cover up my expenses by using all of my salary at times to pay for food and laxatives. But then I lost my job, because I was caught stealing money. I was utterly humiliated. Even then I didn't tell my husband.

In this section, strategies for assessment and intervention are considered. Functioning in the couple is hypothesized to be influenced heavily by family-of-origin dynamics and developmental difficulties. Thus, the heuristic typology of families proposed by Root et al. (1986) is offered to highlight the heterogeneity that exists among couples with eating disorders.

Family Types

The family types, "perfect," "overprotective," and "chaotic," differ from the model of psychosomatic families described by Minuchin et al. (1978). The distinctions among family types explains why some observational research reports focus on the absence of overt conflict (e.g., Levine, 1988; Minuchin et al., 1978), and why others report overt hostility and negative interactions (Humphrey, 1986; Humphrey, Apple, & Kirschenbaum, 1986; Kog, Vandereycken, & Vertom-

men, 1985). Across types of families and couples there are differences in regard to the content and seriousness of boundary problems, alliances, dependency and interdependency, communication of feelings, facilitation and support of individual growth and identity formation, intimacy, power, and conflict resolution. The family types differentiate the strengths and liabilities, developmental challenges, and treatment focus. Each family type suggests implications for the development of identity, self-confidence, interpersonal attachment, expression of feelings, and resolution of conflict.

Perfect Type

The person from the "perfect" family has benefited from many strengths in the family of origin, including consistency and age-appropriate rules. The consistency and warmth of this family type provides a foundation for positive self-esteem and for developing and sustaining close relationships.

This family type also has liabilities that can impact future relationships: (1) expression of negative feelings is discouraged, and thus, there is a lack of practice in resolving overt conflict; (2) pressure to succeed at that which is valued by the family (which can prohibit divorce); and (3) the identity of the family or couple is a priority over the individual's identity. Emotional distancing—through avoidance, denial, repression of negative affect, and of course, the eating disorder—might occur in the couple in which one person feels particularly dissatisfied, resentful, or angry at the other, in order to maintain the picture of harmony and intimacy.

Persons from "perfect" families must implicitly choose someone who enhances the family credentials, or at the very least, is "up to standard." These couples often appear to have a "fairy-tale" romance. Their investment in this "tale" makes it hard to come to terms with major deficits and disappointments in the relationship or partner, which makes it hard to seek help; thus, in this relationship, the solutions to the problems are an enforcement of the "perfect" strategies that result in a vicious cycle, leading to severe unhappiness (e.g., denial, suppression of anger, and suppression of individual needs).

Overprotective Type

This family of origin provides a foundation for trust and attachment, and a very protective, safe environment. It is often a caricature of stereotyped gender roles that contribute to male partners being in adult roles, often parental in nature, and women being in child roles; power is not shared and partners are not considered equals.

This family type has several liabilities:

1. It instills dependence in the less powerful members, rather than fostering a functional interdependence among members.
2. It provides little opportunity for learning on one's own, thereby diminishing self-confidence.
3. It inhibits age-appropriate independence.

One might characterize the individual from this family as suffering from stunted or obstructed growth, particularly as it affects self-knowledge and identity.

A person from an "overprotective" family often gets involved with someone who appears stable, mature, and in control of him/herself. Becoming more assertive and developing one's sense of self ultimately may result in exposing a partner's unhealthy dependence upon him/her. With one's increasing sense of self and desire to assert needs in the relationship, the failure of a partner to be willing to negotiate leadership or share decision making precipitates relationship crises. Some crises are precipitated by relationship triangles. Subsequently, a retreat into anorexia or bulimia forestalls a ludicrous choice between partner and parents. In the family of origin, parents can join together to worry about their sick child or play good parent versus bad parent. Once married, parents and partner can join together with worry or take sides about their sick loved one.

Chaotic Type

There are few strengths this family type directly provides. Those who survive the experience of this family, however, have some resilience that is otherwise hard to come by. These families are inconsistent, overtly hostile, and vacillate unpredictably between warmth and rejection.

The liabilities are profound: (1) a survival-related precociousness is encouraged in children, without supplying basic tools for independent or healthy interdependent functioning; (2) there is no consistent regulation of emotions and impulses; (3) rules and structure are inconsistently applied, which contribute to children's difficulties in self-regulation; and (4) identity is brittle and likely to be attached to something (accomplishments or possessions), or to one's partner. Numerous and/or inflexible rules may be generated by people from such families to provide a constant structure that was missing in the family of origin.

Emotional abuse and traumas in the family of origin make attachments difficult for offspring. On the other hand, they may choose someone who appears stable and consistent—even "perfect." In these cases, the perfection is often brittle and originates as a reaction to a "chaotic" family of origin or rigidity in the partner's family of origin. However, such individuals may pair up with someone who comes from a similarly "chaotic" family, who is currently abusing alcohol, drugs, and/or food. With this latter choice, they may end up in the familiar role of assuming responsibility for their partner's problem at the expense of being responsible for themselves. Difficulties in self-regulation are often at the origin of the intensity, passion, and volatility common in these relationships.

Intake

CLIENT: No, I don't think he knows, though he might suspect something. I'd like to work on this without having to involve him.

THERAPIST: Why?

CLIENT: Well, I feel it is such a weakness; it's so opposite of how I am otherwise. I'd just like to get this part of my life in order without him having to know.

THERAPIST: You are protecting an image?

CLIENT: Hmmm . . . I guess so. I just don't see why he needs to be involved. He has nothing to do with it. I'm not even sure he knows about it. I just need to learn how to be more disciplined.

THERAPIST: How would you explain your being in therapy?

CLIENT (*laughing nervously*): Well, I did think of that. We respect each other's privacy. So unless I tell him, he won't necessarily know.

THERAPIST: You are telling me some important things about how you and your partner operate in this relationship. These patterns are likely to get in the way of your accomplishing what you want in therapy. I usually want to meet a person's partner and involve him to some extent. You are embarking on a significant growth process; if you do not include him in it, your growth may be at a rate or in a direction that creates a relationship crisis. Let us look at the risks you see in involving your partner in this process.

The drama of the symptomatology, particularly when it existed prior to the relationship, leads most couples and many therapists to view the disorder primarily as an individual issue as, with the woman in the excerpt above and with the husband who wrote to Ann Landers. And indeed, most anorexics and bulimics prefer to keep their eating disorder an individual issue, partly out of shame and fear of judgment. Insistence on this position probably signals that privacy and/or control are not only issues for the individual, but may also be significant issues in the relationship. Nevertheless, a combination of individual intakes with each member of the couple and conjoint assessment interviews is highly recommended. Even if the eating disorder was present before the couple came together, recovery will undoubtedly affect the couple's interactions.

Information gathering is an opportunity to intervene by providing feedback and education. Asking direct questions about the state of the relationship and how the eating disorder works within the relationship is also an intervention. The conjoint intake may repeat material gathered in the individual intakes, providing the therapist with an opportunity to compare the partners' presentations singularly and together (Foster, 1986). Before discussing the information that should be gathered in the intakes, a way of thinking and deciding about whether treatment should include couple therapy is offered.

Indications and Contraindications for Conjoint Therapy

Different rationales abound for suggesting couple therapy as an effective approach for working through an eating disorder. Foster (1986) indicates four reasons to consider the marital therapy context: (1) the onset of symptomatology is temporally correlated with the relationship; (2) individual therapy has not worked; (3) the individual sees marital conflict as part of the problem; and (4) the partner seems amenable to interpersonal change. I suggest that when someone is in an ongoing, long-term, committed relationship, the therapist might assume that she/he will benefit from couple work unless it is contraindicated. At the very least, the therapist is afforded the opportunity for a firsthand experience of the couple's interaction. Furthermore, successful recovery from an eating disorder results in anorexics or bulimics making some very significant changes in how they take care of themselves and others. Usually, the changes mean that anorexics or bulimics will be less responsible and responsive to partners' needs at times and be

more responsible for themselves, which may cause conflict. The offering and suggestion of couple therapy allows for the possibility of helping both partners toward individual and relationship growth. Root et al. (1986) emphasize that

> delaying marital treatment must be made with an appreciation of the systemic implications. . . . Clinical lore is clear that individual treatment of one spouse may distress a marriage or at least make the distress more overt. Individual treatment may also be the quickest route to maintaining the status quo in the system or preventing second-order change. . . . Delaying conjoint treament may be a means towards clarifying a marital relationship or establishing a necessary boundary between the members of the marital dyad. The increased emotional distance that may result could be the precipitant to the couple's doing some changing in those areas that seem to perpetuate the symptoms, e.g., conflict. (pp. 192–193)

At times there are contraindications for couple therapy. Foster (1986) observes that a history of unstable relationships, often associated with a history of personality disorder, may suggest individual therapy as the primary therapy modality. I further suggest that sometimes the partners' needs are so great, as is frequently the case in "chaotic" couples, that the anorexic or bulimic cannot get many needs met in couple therapy. Therapy can, in fact, recapitulate the relationship. In this case, I may use conjoint sessions as an occasional adjunct to individual or group therapy. The couple may be directed to develop skills in communication and awareness of individual strengths before proceeding with intense couple work. Teaching them to role play interactions highlights processes at home and provides an opportunity to practice new responses to one another.

The intake is an opportunity to intervene by being direct and respectful in information gathering, feedback, and the acknowledgment of differences; this style of communication within the intake may be a first step toward direct communication about the eating disorder and other issues. Thus, rather than providing the reader information on the many of ways in which one can ask questions, this section focuses on informing the reader of what information is unique and necessary to gather in intakes of eating-disordered couples and individuals.

Intake of the Anorexic or Bulimic

The therapist explores individuals' conceptualizations of the origin and maintenance of their eating disorder and ideas about what they need to do to become asymptomatic. For all family types, the eating disorder may be a "secret." Information can be gathered as to the reasons for keeping the secret or the feared consequences of revealing the secret. Some partners may be insistent about being involved from the beginning. In some cases, individual assessment can be a first step toward disengaging anxious partners from responsibility for "fixing" their partner's eating disorder, a dynamic salient in "overprotective" couples.

It is important to view a chronic eating disorder as representative of developmental "stuckness." Age of onset is important for anchoring the beginning of the eating disorder to specific developmental steps and challenges, and/or relationship beginnings or endings, (e.g., premarital vs. postmarital, breakups with partners, deaths, births, divorces). Additionally, age of onset determines chronicity of the disorder, which is related to prognosis (Garfinkel & Garner, 1982) and severity of symptoms. The therapist determines the clients' awareness of the extent to which life revolves around the eating disorder and is regulated by it. Information on attempts at symptom control and the partners' involvement in these solutions are essential, as this provides some information on the recovery phase and systemic aspects of the couple's functioning.

Assessment of the range of symptoms and their frequency and severity must be conducted. *The therapist must be knowledgeable and "nondisgusted" by symptoms the client may reveal; seeking treatment is usually an act of courage and desperation, in which the client is very sensitive to ignorance about the disorder and disgust.* The severity of the disorder may dictate initial or concurrent medical and nutritional interventions. For example, fainting, edema, muscle weakness, dizziness, bloating, or concentration difficulties require further medical evaluation. Misinformation about how the body utilizes food, the fuel value of food, and how much to eat, necessitate nutritional consultation.

The therapist gathers information about the following:

1. Weight history (losses and gains, discrepancies between desired vs. healthy weight).
2. Body-image perception and satisfaction/dissatisfaction.
3. Eating patterns (when, where, what, how much, and how frequently).
4. Rules about eating and exercise.
5. Food restrictions, deprivation, and dieting (including participation in organized weight-loss programs, over-the-counter diet pills).
6. Use of appetite controls. such as amphetamines, cigarettes, caffeine, and cocaine.
7. Purging behaviors, such as vomiting, laxative-induced diarrhea, dehydration (through diuretics), weight loss through abuse of insulin, if diabetic.
8. Bingeing and compulsive eating.
9. Frequency, intensity, and kind of exercise.

The therapist should inquire about the role of weight and appearance among peers, family of origin, and with one's partner. The presence of companion and competitive dieting between members of the couple, family-of-origin members, or friends, should be assessed. The therapist should explore how the marital relationship changes with weight gains or losses, or other symptoms.

Feelings toward one's body, and comfort with one's physical self are important to assess. The therapist might ask individuals to bring in both a picture of themselves prior to the eating disorder and a current one. Satisfaction with one's physical body has bearing on one's comfort level in being physically and sexually intimate with a partner (Raciti & Hendrick, 1992). Therapists must be aware that, like the persons they work with, they are susceptible to distorted images of what physical appearances are healthy and should be cautious about offering opinions about what is "overweight." The emphasis should be on what is healthy, a fact which cannot always be determined by the pictures.

Simultaneously, therapists assess the presence of other disorders frequently present in persons with eating disorders (e.g., depression, anxiety, post-traumatic stress disorder, personality disorders, alcohol and drug abuse, and stealing). Histories of these difficulties should also be obtained. If there is significant alcohol and or drug abuse, these behaviors should be addressed initially in treatment, as they significantly compromise the effectiveness of treatment. If there are questions as to the seriousness of the dependency on substances, the therapist can ask that both partners use no alcohol or recreational drugs for the 24-hour period preceding intake and subsequent therapy. Inability to comply for whatever reason, suggests a problem of the magnitude requiring that it to be addressed first.

The physical instability induced by bulimia, which contributes to lability, the irritability induced by starvation in both anorexia and bulimia nervosa, and the desperation to support a bulimic habit (which may include stealing food, money, or cosmetics) may overlap considerably with features of borderline personality. It is recommended that unless one can obtain a reliable history of the individual prior to the onset of the eating disorder (inclusive of sexual abuse and assault), personality disorder diagnoses should be withheld until treatment has been under way for some time, and preferably until symptom remission has been established, or symptoms have been significantly decreased, and the individual is receiving adequate nutrition.

The therapist is well advised to carefully inquire about individuals' histories of sexual abuse, rape, physical abuse, and battering as children and adults, and in the current relationship. The dynamics responsible for insisting on secrecy about the eating disorder may also make it difficult to disclose about physical or sexual abuse in the relationship (Root et al., 1986). The therapist might misattribute some symptoms, that is, lack of treatment compliance or styles of communicating, if this information is not gathered. Post-traumatic stress syndromes may not be apparent until some symptom remission has been achieved. With symptom remission, some persons begin to recall memories of sexual abuse and assault (Root, 1991). For some persons, particularly those with bulimia, the eating disorder may divert them from memories and feelings surrounding abuse. In such cases, the therapist is advised to carefully consider the implications and reality of requiring "abstinence" from binging, purging, deprivation, or compulsive exercise. Sometimes the consequences are extreme decompensation. Furthermore, the milieu in which various stages of therapy are conducted must be carefully considered.

Additionally, the therapist should gather information about the family of origin. Family strengths and weaknesses can be examined in order to understand how individuals were taught to cope, to participate in interpersonal relationships, and to start their own families. A family psychiatric history is important, particularly regarding depression, anxiety disorders, personality styles, disordered eating, and disorders of self-regulation, including alcohol problems. The role of food and the importance of weight and appearance in the family of origin, expectations of achievement and appearance, permission to marry or have a partner, patterns of communication, and the role of the eating disorder are also relevant information. The degree to which the family of origin and in-laws are involved in the relationship is also important. Much involve

ment is likely to indicate that one or both partners have not been "released" from their families.

Often, in seeking this information, the therapist can also obtain information about whether the client chose his/her partner, was chosen as a partner, or whether the choice was mutual. The therapist is encouraged to inquire into marital satisfaction, changes in the relationship, responsibilities, the partner's perceptions of the client, and the client's perceptions of the partner. Exploration as to the client's perception of how the marital relationship affects his/her eating disorder, and vice versa, is a logical segue into inviting the partner in for a separate, individual intake.

If the individual is unwilling to consider including his/her partner, the therapist ascertains whether this will be an obstacle to treatment. The therapist should consider whether individual treatment will be appropriate and/or the limits of what can realistically be achieved in individual therapy.

Partner Assessment

Therapists take a similar detailed psychological and family history of the clients' partners, asking the partners for their explanations for etiology and maintenance of the disorder, as well as what they think needs to take place for their partner to become asymptomatic. The therapist is encouraged to ask partners why they think they have been asked in, what they would like to see changed in the relationship, and the degree to which they are aware that they affect their partner's eating disorder and are affected by that eating disorder. Partners should be specifically asked about how they view their partner's physical attractiveness, their feelings about their own physical attractiveness, and comments they make about their partners, themselves, or others regarding weight and fitness.

Leichner, Harper, and Johnston (1985) described a support group for male partners of women with eating disorders that, if available, may be helpful even if the partner without the eating disorder is not directly involved in treatment. Intake may be delayed if the therapist thinks an ongoing course of marital therapy is inappropriate. Instead, sporadic couple sessions could occur during the course of individual treatment. In this case, some of the intake on the partner could occur during a conjoint session.

In the event that a partner does not know about the eating disorder, when and how this revelation occurs is a significant intervention.

The individual intake of the partner with the eating disorder might set the foundation for a conjoint session in which the eating disorder is revealed.

Assessment of the Couple

In assessing the couple, the therapist attends to the range and quality of affect, the appropriateness of responsibility assumed by each partner, how power is shared, and gender-role expectations. The interventions typically used during the assessment phase are varied and typically include but are not limited to (1) the use of "circular questioning" to determine the awareness and accuracy with which partners perceive each other; (2) educating the couple as to the role of dieting for weight loss versus true health; (3) coaching partners in reflective listening; and (4) clarification of needs and feelings. Almost always, the therapist will need to attend to boundaries between the individuals and help define them more clearly. For example, the therapist may point out and prevent partners' interrupting, answering, or speaking for each other, particularly with regard to the eating disorder. Essentially, anorexic or bulimic partners are responsible for describing their symptomatology and how it affects them; partners without the eating disorder are responsible for describing how the eating disorder affects them.

The differences in the expression of affect between partners of different sex couples often are an exaggeration of gender role prescriptions around affect. For the male partner, concern, hurt, and anger are often mixed-up, however, anger is usually the most visible and verbalized feeling. For the person with the eating disorder, shame, fear, anger, and low self-esteem are mixed-up, they often appearing with depression.

Responsibility is often misaligned. Partners may assume responsibility for each other, but neglect their own self-care. This can be one conceptualization offered to the couple. For example, one couple expressed their love for each by the degree to which they were essentially willing to make sacrifices to "hopefully" save the other person. Although both partners felt they could not live without the other, both were considering ending the relationship to "save" the other, despite how miserable they thought they would feel. The therapist directed the couple to take appropriate responsibility for their own choices in their own mental health, not for what they thought would be best for the other person. This intervention redirects the couple to iden-

tify their needs in the relationship. In fact, eating-disordered symptomatology can often be framed as a lack of responsibility on the eating disordered person's part. Often this is the result of being responsible for everyone else and not being responsible to oneself. Women may be willing to make more sacrifices and take more responsibility for problems in relationships, because of the responsibility society accords them for relationship success, and blame for relationship failure.

Exploring gender roles provides a way of talking about differences in communication and expression of feelings; permission to have certain feelings, values and expectations around physical appearance, work, and division of responsibilities; expressions of and needs for intimacy and companionship; and expectations of families of origin, and so on. The therapist should directly assess the degree to which one partner's physical appearance enhances the other's self-esteem and value by peers. Exporing gender roles and expectations also provides a window for assessing the power imbalances in the relationship.

Foster (1986) points out the importance of determining during the first session with a couple (1) the degree to which they can move away from a symptom focus on the eating disorder, and (2) how they process "trial hypotheses" about the relationship. If the eating disorder plays an integral part in the functioning of the couple, it is unlikely that they will be able to genuinely focus on other aspects of the relationship for long. A therapist unfamiliar with treatment of eating-disordered couples might be sidetracked by being impressed with the couple's willingness to talk about the eating disorder. The therapist must try to sort out the degree to which this is therapeutic or possibly whether it reflects a retreat to safe ground by talking about the agreed-on problem.

TREATMENT

The point at which couples seek treatment for an eating disorder, if not after the "honeymoon" phase of the relationship, surely ends the honeymoon. As an intervention, conjoint treatment facilitates awareness of the reciprocal influence of the couple's functioning and eating-disorder symptoms. Whereas couples are often aware that the eating disorder is affecting their relationship, they are less likely to be aware of how the relationship affects the eating disorder (Van den Broucke & Vandereycken, 1988). Whether the onset of the eating disorder is pre- or postrelationship, the eating disorder and relationship will eventually have a reciprocal influence.

Treatment of eating disorders is complex; there are no formula approaches to symptom remission. Aside from different theoretical perspectives on eating disorders, perspectives on intervention vary greatly regarding the degree to which symptoms and remission of symptoms should be an overt focus. "Abstinence"-focused models, dominant in hospital and residential facilities, are oriented to help stop disordered-eating behaviors immediately. It is often the assumption that treatment cannot start until overt symptom cessation of binge eating, purging, starving, and compulsive exercising. Such models utilize controlled environments toward this end. Couple therapy is an adjunct to intensive individual treatment.

In contrast, outpatient therapy is less intensive, with sessions typically scheduled once or twice a week. This chapter focuses on strategies for intervention based on models of outpatient therapy. The predominant expectation is that symptoms will gradually be relinquished during the course of treatment as *symptom functions are addressed, skills are acquired for coping with feelings, and issues are resolved in the relationship.* Each of these areas is given attention later. Generally, the therapist needs to take an active stance in facilitating skills development and awareness of how the relationship changes with changes in symptoms of the eating disorder. Mere resolution of issues, except in some dramatic cases, does not necessarily result in symptom cessation. In contrast to most inpatient programs, outpatient-treatment approaches assume that relapses will be a normal part of the recovery process; indeed, recent research supports this assumption (Root, 1990). I recommend that educational interventions precede more intensive interventions. The concreteness of most of the information makes sense to clients. It also allows for additional assessment and establishing a rapport with the couple.

Education

Several sources of information are helpful in the beginning of treatment even if the couple is not able to use the education immediately. Four areas should be covered: (1) nutritional issues; (2) management of eating-disorder symptoms; (3) lifestyle habits and routines, particularly as related to stress and relaxation; and (4) communication styles. Providing basic information in these areas constitutes intervention. Helping individuals to distinguish among the symptom sources described subsequently becomes an intervention in and of itself.

The therapist provides information on how *restrictive eating* precipitates and maintains symptoms, such as food preoccupation and binge eating. Use of a nutritionist may be essential in some cases. Restricting quantity or types of food can precipitate binge eating as a reaction to physical and psychological deprivation. Additionally, rigid, unrealistic rules about eating set the foundation for significant guilt around food consumption. Starvation also increases preoccupation with food. Imbalances in the types of food eaten (e.g., trying to eliminate virtually all fats) is not healthy and has negative health consequences. Intervening with this information allows some couples to alter meal plans in such a way that food consumption becomes more nutritionally sound, and the preoccupation with food decreases as deprivation is addressed. The therapist might help a couple strategize to reduce the amount of responsibility the partner with the eating disorder has related to food preparation, (e.g., grocery shopping, meal planning, and cooking), thus helping that partner to be less food-focused and to reduce the number of high-risk situations related to his/her eating disorder.

Having a third party provide education and guidance around *management of the eating-disorder symptoms* is often a relief, although it is a tense subject with the couple. This management specifically raises the issues of boundaries and responsibility. Therapists need to be very directive in their interventions around symptoms. Specific *"do's and don'ts"* can be helpful. For example, a man should not tell his anorexic or bulimic partner when to stop eating; he should not attempt to force her to eat; he should not follow her to the bathroom to prevent her from throwing up; he should not lock the refrigerator. The goal of this education is to emphasize that the non-eating-disordered partner cannot control his partner's eating disorder. To continue to do so will be a losing battle; such a struggle for control likely exists in other areas of the couple's life and provides a point of concrete entry for the therapist. Additionally, fights and food are not to be paired together; discussing topics that are stressful should not be done at meal time. He can be helpful by expressing what he feels, thinks, and needs. The therapist must realize that the behaviors and chaos associated with an eating disorder and its consequences can catalyze very desperate and bizarre behavior, even in some of the most reasonable individuals. The woman with the eating disorder is made wholly responsible for her behavior. This includes cleaning up after binges, making sure a sink or bathroom she used to purge is kept clean for others, replacing family food used for a binge within a specific period of time, and sitting at meals with a partner and/or family, even if she does not choose to eat. It is her choice on an outpatient basis to eat or not to eat *and* to determine how much and what to eat. In extreme cases, the therapist may consider having partners eat separately when they cannot follow the preceding guidelines as set forth by the therapist. Gradually, joint mealtime is reintroduced.

Education around *lifestyle* considerations includes focusing both on choices of recreation and coping with stress. The therapist must encourage the pursuit of recreation that does not have a food focus. This is often very difficult for couples and families to implement when eating has been the activity around which socializing has taken place. The therapist can facilitate a discussion that might expose voids in the couple's or individuals' recreational lives. Some couples live exhausting lifestyles that look very fun; often, food is used to try to keep energy levels up, and at times eating provides a ritual for a quick transition between parts of a day, much as another person might change their clothes or meditate to mark a transition.

A couple, married for over 10 years, sought therapy to help "cure" an eating disorder that surfaced after the birth of their first child. This was an insightful couple with many strengths and much education. They described "jet-setting" on at least two significant trips a month. The brunt of packing for all three family members and arranging details for when they were gone fell to Grace. Formerly a schoolteacher, she was very organized, but with the addition of a child and major responsibility, she often felt that life consisted of packing, unpacking, and washing clothes after a trip in preparation for the next trip. She felt that she was constantly failing to establish routines in her life and consequently felt very out of control. Jon, a physician whose practice often left little time for them to share aside from these trips, attributed her difficulties to her being higher strung and less organized than he. The therapist suggested they try reducing the number of trips away from home for 3 months. Such a plan required Jon to consider scheduling his practice responsibilities differently, so that he would have some time at home when they might otherwise be traveling; Grace was to deliberately choose the business trips on which to join him. Within that 3-month period of time, Grace was able to establish daily and weekly routines, reported feeling much less tired, and felt more in control of her life. With this change she did not feel as intensely preoccupied with her weight, and she decreased the frequency of her binge-eating, starving, compulsive exercising, and throwing up. With less distraction and lower levels of stimulation by new places and changes in people, Grace and Jon realized that, although they knew how to vacation well together and have fun on trips, they did not know how to comfortably relate to each other at home anymore. Developing a lifestyle and communication at home became a focus of therapy, which led to rebalancing the power in the relationship as Grace voiced more dissatisfaction with the role she had assumed in the relationship, and with Jon's absence in the relationship.

Last, psychoeducation about *communication* provides a common language for making subsequent observations and interventions within the therapy. I often have clients read excerpts from a book by Root et al. (1986) that describes the three family types, and ask each member of the couple to identify their family of origin, as well as how they would identify themselves as a couple. The therapist can do this by identifying slogans that are associated with the types and prohibit communication of feelings. In the "perfect" couple, slogans might include "Don't dwell on the negative"; "Focus on the positive"; or "Look at the bright side of things." The "overprotective" couple's dynamics render slogans such as "Think of others first" and "Don't hurt anyone's feelings." The ideas expressed in these slogans make the communication of resentments, disappointments, and anger difficult. Without the communication of these feelings, it may be impossible to define conflicts, much less resolve them. Sometimes one partner has a willingness and ability to communicate openly. However, the past family dynamics of the person who becomes symptomatic may define this "functional" communication as extremely stressful. Rather than engaging in discussion, she/he might interpret the communication as blame (as in "chaotic" dynamics), or assume responsibility for making things right (such as in the "perfect" dynamics). In contrast to the "perfect" and "overprotective" couples, the "chaotic" couple's communication is punctuated by inconsistencies, disrespect, blame, and overt hostility. The most common slogans in attempts at communication are "Its your problem"; "It's your fault"; and "Don't bother me with your problems."

Assessing the couple's family type will help the therapist to anticipate the communication problems more readily and discuss these possibilities at the beginning of therapy. For example, the "perfect" couple tends to avoid criticizing each other or expressing direct anger. Their respect for one another may have created too much emotional distance for them to offer or receive more intimacy and assistance when it is needed. The "overprotective" couple avoids conflict and any communications that might hurt each other's feelings. They may make excuses for each other's failures to comply with therapy interventions; interpersonal boundaries are blurred. The "chaotic" couple manifests overt hostility, intensity, and avoids responsibility for personal behavior. The therapist can facilitate boundaries by requiring people not to speak for each other and by intervening when necessary to prevent partners from interrupting or finishing each other's sentences. Furthermore, the therapist can ask couples to create privacy from each other for a set amount of time each day. This intervention toward setting boundaries can be very unsettling for some couples.

A simple example is offered to demonstrate how the areas of education discussed previously can be used as a simple intervention. Subsequently, the therapist and couple can deal with the issues that do not respond to education. Jeff hears that Lisa wants to lose 10 pounds for their high school reunion. In an attempt to be supportive, he offers to buy her any outfit she wants for one of the special events of the reunion. Lisa initially loves this idea and thinks that Jeff's offer will be an incentive to keep her on her weight-loss program. She asks him for assistance in reminding her to keep on her diet. This scenario illustrates several innocently derived problems. At a societal level, dieting has unfortunately become a normative, although still unhealthy, female behavior (Polivy & Herman, 1987). Dieting before a major event, especially reunions, symbolizes the American formula to which women are socialized and brainwashed: "If you are thin or able to diet successfully, you will be popular, beautiful, and successful." Her husband's support enlists him as society's agent, especially as he is asked to remind her to stay on her diet. Lisa has asked Jeff to take responsibility for something he should not be supporting and cannot realistically control. She has given him authority over her appetite and choices. With some partners, this can be an invitation for criticism and competition (as some partners will join their wife in the weight loss, and men lose weight initially more quickly than women). If her family of origin was or is controlling around food (i.e., her parents insisting or forcing her to eat), the couple may be setting up a similar dynamic. And because diets are the precursor to eating disorders, Lisa has just enlisted Jeff in enforcing a risk factor.

The therapist can intervene by educating the couple about the relationship between dieting and eating-disordered attitudes and behaviors at the beginning of treatment. She/he can then remind them of this information and relationship when the desire to diet resurfaces as a dysfunctional strategy. The therapist can help a couple anticipate the consequences of such an incentive plan and explore how unresolved issues between them might be acted out in this prescribed plan—issues such as struggles for control, imbalance of power, and inappropriate responsibility for one another. If the woman's weight does not pose a health risk (versus defying a societal standard or the therapist's own visual preferences) a reduction of 10 pounds may result in her becoming very preoccupied with food and irritable. She may begin, or increase her frequency or intensity of, binge eating as a reaction to semi-starvation. Furthermore, such an innocent "exchange" might reflect the roles and responsibilities the couple has assumed relative to one another. Their response to the therapist's education, observations, and hypotheses will further help direct the therapy.

Relationship Crises

Several authors suggest that marital crisis may be at the heart of either the etiology or maintenance of anorexia nervosa in marital relationships. Lefeber (1981, cited in Vandereyck-en et al., 1989) suggests that marital crises become exposed during the course of recovery. When a crisis is covert, the eating disorder may play a critical role in suppressing overt conflict.

Intervention requires attention to several developmental issues and crises that overlap or subsume the functions of eating disorders. I will use the example of one couple, Helen and Bill, to illustrate four areas for potential crisis in relationships: (1) identity, (2) communication, (3) power/status balance, and (4) intimacy.

Bill and Helen met working for an advertising firm in New Mexico. They have been a couple for 6 years, married for 4 years. Both are in their early 30s. Helen is a Chicana raised in the Southwest. Bill identifies as a "mongrel" white American with no particular ethnic alliances. Neither had sought psychotherapy before.

Bill had sought the consultation in early November due to a crisis in the relationship. Helen was adamant that she did not want to spend Thanksgiving with his family. She said they must spend it with her family or at home. Bill cannot understand Helen's sudden anger and ultimatum; they have always spent Thanksgiving with his family.

They have had little overt conflict in their relationship until recently. The conflict had increased after Helen had revealed her 6½-year eating disorder to him 3 months previously. She had become more openly resentful of his attempts to help her gain control over her eating disorder and subsequently more secretive. Bill prides himself on being a rational, even-tempered person with excellent problem-solving skills. Helen describes herself as a people-oriented person with a positive outlook on life; she, too, prides herself on being even-tempered and a resourceful person.

Although they see themselves as having some overlapping strengths and sharing much in common, their styles of communicating and perceptions of the relationship and each other are very different. Bill perceived the problem as having its basis in Helen is having low self-esteem and being over-reactive. He also worried that Helen was persisting in her eating disorder to irritate him. Helen described Bill as thinking he knows everything and as not listening to her needs when they were different than what he thought she needed.

Bill and Helen appeared to care about each other and to be invested in the relationship. They seemed to be engaged in a significant power struggle in which neither was winning. During this stressful time, Bill came across as frustrated, deliberate, and judgmental; Helen appeared depressed and angry.

Power/Status Balance

Root et al. (1986) identified power as one of the two most significant issues in relationships in which an eating disorder exists. Some clinicians have suggested that the symptomatology offers a strategy for balancing power in inequitable situations (e.g., Madanes, 1981), whereas others suggest that it is not a main feature of the relationships (Levine, 1988). This conflict in opinion likely reflects both the diversity of ways in which someone can develop an eating disorder

and the diversity of dynamics that can maintain it. Even within couples in which there are power struggles, the eating disorder may serve different purposes. In one couple, the eating-disorder may give the eating disordered partner a sense of control that she/he does not ordinarily possess in the relationship. In contrast, some clients suggest that it makes them appear less competent than their partner, which thereby equalizes their otherwise enviable position as perceived by their partner. Root et al. (1986) note:

> In systemic terms, the one-down position of the bulimic spouse serves a system-stabilizing function. What would otherwise be a tenuous relationship can maintain homeostasis and continue indefinitely as long a both parties agree that all problems in the relationship are a direct extension of the wife's bulimia. (p. 181)

If the bulimia or anorexia was known, divulged or discovered by the partner prior to a wedding or commitment to live together, the individual's shame (i.e., that she is not good enough) will be manifested in statements such as "I'm so lucky that he was willing to marry me." Simultaneously, many a bulimic or anorexic partner who feels this way also often simultaneously harbors the thought, "What is wrong with him that he chose such a difficult relationship?"

Power and status imbalances are not necessarily obvious, as they tend often to be normative in different-sex couples. Some male partners' investment in their partners' physical appearance may recapture the dynamics of the Pygmalion story in which the person with less social status is considered to be inferior and becomes a "project" to be "fixed." Accomplishment of this goal enhances the "fixer's" status. The failure of this agenda is often the crisis that brings couples into therapy. An example of how the eating disorder may figure into the power dynamic in a relationship is illustrated, again, in the case of Bill and Helen.

Helen had observed during the intake: "Bill is good at anything. He is also a great problem solver and I know he takes pride in this. I was attracted to his confidence in being able to master any situation. The only power I have had at times with Bill, since he found out about my eating disorder, is not to let him be successful in fixing me, too." Indeed, part of the crisis that brought Bill and Helen into therapy in November was that Bill could not fix Helen's "problem." Besides genuinely wanting

Helen to be relieved of her eating disorder, Bill sought therapy to enlist help to fix Helen—not to work on the relationship.

Being able to hold the eating disorder or other aspects of one's life secret (e.g., an affair) provides a feeling of power when power does not feel shared in the relationship. Many a woman has made a remark that Helen made in a session by herself after 10 conjoint sessions. "There was a time when I would make Bill into a less successful, less all-knowing person by telling myself, 'He isn't that smart; he hasn't figured out that I stay this thin by starving myself for days before a company dinner and throwing up every chance I get.'" Conversely, Bill felt "duped" and hurt that Helen had not trusted him with her "secret." He told her, "How was I supposed to know? You always had excuses for not joining me for a meal, and nothing seemed wrong. I basically trusted you."

The therapist can address power issues in a variety of ways. The simplest intervention is to repeatedly name the dynamic and point it out each time it happens. This task is eventually the couple's responsibility. A more intense intervention is to suggest the couple exaggerate the power differences. This exaggeration often makes the dynamic and, issues clearer, or creates the intensity of the dynamic in the home situation. This is one of the few times that I might suggest that the non-eating-disordered partner attempt to exercise inappropriate control over their partner's eating-disordered behaviors; it is very concrete. In between are several strategies, including a prediction of worsening or improving of eating-disordered symptoms based on the power dynamics operative in the relationship. This observing and predicting function is eventually turned over to the couple.

Identity

At the root of most eating disorders is a struggle for identity. This struggle may be intensified in partnerships in which the eating disorder was chronic before the relationships developed. The chronic eating disorder may become synonymous with the individual. Therefore, a partner's attempts to "take away" the eating disorder may be experienced as an crisis.

Identity is a key issue for new couples. It requires the successful negotiation of maintaining a separate self and developing a sense of "we-ness" with one's significant other. This is often more difficult for women in heterosexual relationships, as historically, American women have assumed

the identity of their husbands by taking their last name; additionally, they have been expected to accommodate to their husbands' lifestyles and needs. If one does not have a clear sense of self, one is vulnerable to being "consumed" by a partner, or to "consuming" one's partner in order to establish a sense of wholeness (much as one might consume food to temporarily feel full). When the couple's relationship does not accommodate individual needs for separateness and privacy, eating disorders can intensify or begin as a way to have a secret—something that is "all one's own." Such is often the case in "overprotective" families and couples. This function of the eating disorder can literally be defended to the death as "Crying for Help" describes in the letter to Ann Landers at the beginning of this chapter. The lack of completeness in identity or its superficial existence, leaves many persons relying on societal formulas for identity (e.g., occupation, appearance, or possessions).

Many identity crises became apparent in Helen and Bill's relationship. The we-ness was not a merging of traditions or individuals, but reflected Helen's trying to fit into Bill's family with little reciprocal expectation that Bill would do this with Helen's family. This situation subtly reinforced the superior–inferior dynamic operating within this relationship. Helen was distressed by this arrangement. She felt it was a sacrifice not to see her family during significant holidays. However, she did this feeling that her acceptance by his family was precarious because of her Mexican-American background, something about herself that she felt they judged as inferior. She starved herself before these reunions to gain acceptance; they were complimentary about her figure. Through the discussions of how to spend holiday time and with whose family, many issues arose. Helen identified the impact of letting go of her family name, which was part of her ethnic identification. The loss of ethnic celebrations without the contact with her family, and living in a community without a visible and organized Chicano community, also created a void in Helen's life—something that Bill and his family could not fill. As she clarified this, she was able to relate this resentment and grief to an increase in her symptoms around holiday time, particularly starvation. The reason for the crisis in the relationship in November became clearer to them; they realized that they must negotiate a different arrangement.

Therapists can explore identity issues by suggesting that clients think of what their identities were before entering the relationship and contrast this with what their identities are now. They can observe to what degree compromises and changes in identity have been conscious, voluntary, and/or positive. Therapists can also explore the meaning and implications of differences in partners' perceptions of their identity as a couple. Such explorations often lead to forays into family-of-origin work and the implicit models of being a couple as exemplified by their parents.

Communication

In virtually all couples with eating disorders, communication becomes difficult, because openness regarding the disorder conflicts with the secrecy that surrounds the disorder. The crises related to communication are precipitated by (1) letting go of the secret world of the eating disorder and risking shame and humiliation; (2) revealing or confirming secrets (e.g., sexual abuse, domestic violence, and child abuse); and (3) fearing the loss of control over voicing rage or depression (and the consequences of their expression). For couples who have not accomplished a balance between separateness and togetherness, the expression of unhappiness, hurt, anger, distress, or discontent threatens the sense of being a couple. This was essentially part of the crisis that brought Helen and Bill to seek therapy. Secrecy also maintains the disorder's specialness to the individual or protects her/him from shame and/or humiliation.

For example, after many months of couple therapy, Helen voiced intense anger at Bill for his "putting her and her family down." This anger was not only for Bill and his patronizing attitude toward her, but it also was aimed at the general oppressive attitude that Bill portrayed, and that Helen had experienced many times in her life from whites and had felt powerless to address. She had been very reluctant to express her anger for fear that she would open a bottomless pit of rage that would threaten their ability to be a couple. She was able to express this anger once she identified the issue in her marriage and the connection to the oppression she experienced on a larger scale. Additionally, she trusted Bill's commitment to the relationship, and she trusted herself to be able to handle Bill's arguments or defenses of himself. Bill was initially defensive, but gradually was able to understand how his assumed superiority was oppressive. Bill had some insight that unspoken anger between them hindered their communication. However, since he had found out about Helen's eat-

ing disorder, he had worried that his letting her know he was angry would set her back in her progress. Thus, he had tried to be encouraging and positive. The therapist eventually pointed out that this strategy had led him to build up resentment and then take out his anger on Helen in "put-down" statements.

Therapists' interventions may simply serve to make the communication more direct in order to minimize miscommunication. Additionally, therapists' roles allow differences in perception to be valid and help the couple to negotiate differences. Negotiation was a critical intervention throughout the therapy with Bill and Helen, as it rebalanced the superior/inferior position that was operating in the relationship. As this rebalancing occurred, the intensity and frequency of eating-disordered symptoms diminished.

Intimacy

Anorexia and bulimia are intimate affairs. Most anorexics and bulimics establish a tremendous number of rituals that are imbued with special significance and meaning. This secret world limits the degree to which they allow themselves to be emotionally dependent on their partners, and thus vulnerable. If their partners cannot provide social and emotional support, consistency of emotional availability, and acceptance, they may not be able to fulfill the intimacy needs served by the eating disorder. Turning to food for emotional gratification has minimal risks. Paradoxically, relying on food, creates obstacles against taking risks to build intimacy with a partner. Helen's eating-disordered behavior had become increasingly frequent in the relationship over the last 2 years, because she had not been able to express her anger at Bill; this became an obstacle to her wanting to rely on him or to letting herself be very vulnerable to him.

Root et al. (1986) observed that the eating disorder, whether known or unknown, can serve to regulate the intimacy boundaries in a relationship. They observed three general patterns of intimacy in bulimic couples: "(1) rigidly overinvolved or a pseudo-intimacy; (2) rigidly distant or pseudo-distance; and (3) a more variable fluctuating between closeness and intimacy" (p. 183). In the first pattern, partners may feel satisfied, except in times of greater emotional need, such as when a parent dies or in times of need and comfort. In the second pattern, individuals may initially appear very independent, but a significant dependence rather than a healthy interdependence between partners becomes apparent as treatment progresses. This dependence may reflect a power arrangement reminiscent of traditionally heterosexual, proscribed roles around who is sick (inferior) and who is well (superior), and the privileges assumed with each position. Last, partners may fluctuate in the degree to which they feel or need to be close and intimate. As long as their timing does not complement one another, this mismatch serves as a distance regulator for intimacy.

For a variety of reasons, sexual intimacy may be unwanted by the bulimic or anorexic. Severe anorexia curbs hormonal levels and, in clinical cases, reduces sexual drive. Bingeing and throwing up before being with one's partner can result in many different feeling states including (1) dissociating from the sexual experience (a indication of possible prior sexual abuse or assault history); (2) relaxing enough to be physically intimate (the way some people, and many of them women, with alcohol problems use alcohol); (3) distracting oneself from the relationship by being preoccupied with food and self; and (4) self-loathing and feeling unattractive. The need for several of these functions is consistent with the a history of sexual abuse (Root, 1991). Additionally, in some relationships in which the partner has a consistent parental role, this relationship may be incongruent with sexual relating, as it symbolically violates an incest taboo.

Whereas the eating disorder usually creates emotional lability, an effect of starvation (which cannot be judged solely on apparent weight status), it can also temper or dampen the awareness and expression of other feelings, such as anger and unhappiness with the partner. Subsequently, the relationship may superficially operate without any relationship crises, but rather focus on the eating-disordered individual's crisis.

As one starts recovery, it is likely that a marital crisis might arise out of any of the issues discussed here. Furthermore, in examining these crises, several different functions of the eating disorder have been observed: privacy, control, superiority, anger management, feelings management, equalization of status, invisible indulgence, self-punishment, punishment for defects/weaknesses, regulation of intimacy, engenderment of concern and protection, minimization of expectations, mutual dependency, disempowerment, and partnership/friendship.

Interventions around this issue rest on making many observations about the issues around power, communication, and feelings. With increasing mutual trust, intimacy increases.

REFLECTING ON THERAPY

Most therapists agree that disordered-eating symptomatology is difficult to treat and that some people may require long-term treatment. Many pitfalls exist for the therapist, including uncritical acceptance of systemic hypotheses. Although many researchers and clinicians have suggested that the symptoms of an eating disorder are sustained by unacceptable systemic solutions to prior or current developmental impasses (e.g., Barrett & Schwartz, 1987; Dally, 1984; Foster, 1986; Lafeber, 1981, cited in Vandereychen et al., 1989; Root et al., 1986; Schwartz, Barrett, & Saba, 1984), there is a fine line between invoking a valid systemic conceptualization, such as power imbalances (Madanes, 1981) that are inherently sustained and socialized by the cultural system, and assuming a "50–50" responsibility between partners for the maintenance or etiology of anorexic or bulimic symptoms (Luepnitz, 1988). I discourage therapists from using uncritical application of the language of "co-dependence" (e.g., Beattie, 1987) to either spouse. This language assumes equal power in relationships between women and men, which does not usually reflect reality, particularly in dysfunctional relationships. Furthermore, this language tends to invoke the implicit, societal-level contract that women are responsible for the dysfunction or failure of relationships.

In mismanaged cases, the person with the eating disorder can become victimized by both the therapist and partner's frustration. As in families, a partner's feelings of helplessness, powerlessness, frustration, and desperation can result in uncharacteristically bizarre behaviors, including psychological and physical abuse. Therapists rendered helpless and powerless to effect change may invoke destructive and inaccurate conceptualizations and interventions.

SUMMARY

Ultimately, an eating disorder is a strategy for addressing crisis around communication, intimacy, power, and/or identity. Therapists are responsible for observing how couples' interactions and strategies maintain the eating disorder and may steer them toward crises. They observe how couples' relationships and strategies mirror problematic social proscriptions for roles and unhealthy, simplistic solutions to alleviate unhappiness and distress.

The goal of intervention is to facilitate a language that both partners understand, with a respect for individual styles. In effect, the therapists might consider themselves culture brokers between partners and between the couples and their respective families. Interventions are provided by therapists, in the form of education, observations, and suggestions. Therapists do not assume responsibility for the eating-disorder symptoms, but provide education and linkages to help couples understand the reciprocal influence of relationships and eating-disorder symptomatology. Choices are clearly left to the individuals and to the couples to develop ways of integrating the therapy directives into workable relationships.

In summary, despite our ability as therapists to attempt to explain complex interactions, it is important to remember that, at times, it is hard to distinguish an etiological factor from a reaction. Whether the eating disorder starts before or after the relationship, the two mutually affect each other over time; thus, the justification for conjoint treatment.

ACKNOWLEDGMENTS

Special thanks are offered to my colleagues, Gary Wieder, Ph.D., and Laura Kastner, Ph.D., for the time they spent critiquing an earlier draft. Their suggestions and comments were helpful and are reflected in this chapter.

REFERENCES

Abraham, S. F. (1985). The psychosexual histories of young women with bulimia. *Australian and New Zealand Journal of Psychiatry, 19,* 72–76.

Andersen, A. E. (1985). Family therapy and marital therapy of anorexia nervosa and bulimia. In A. E. Andersen (Ed.), *Practical comprehensive treatment of anorexia nervosa and bulimia* (pp. 135–148, 160–164). Baltimore, MD: Johns Hopkins University Press.

American Psychiatric Association. (1989). *Diagnostic and statistical manual of mental disorders* (4th ed.). Washington, DC: Author.

Barrett, M. J., & Schwartz, R. (1987). Couples therapy for bulimia. In J. E. Harkaway (Ed.), *The family therapy collections: Eating disorders* (Vol. 20, pp. 25–39). Rockville, MD: Aspen.

Beattie, M. (1987). *Codependent no more.* San Francisco: Harper & Row.

Bruch, H. (1978). *The golden cage: The enigma of anorexia nervosa.* New York: Basic Books.

Crisp, A. H. (1980). *Anorexia nervosa: Let me be.* London: Grune & Stratton.

Crisp, A. H., Hsu, L. K. G., Harding, B., & Hartshor, J. (1980). Clinical features of anorexia nervosa: A study of a consecutive series of 102 female patients. *Journal of Psychosomatic Research, 24,* 179–191.

Dally, P. (1984). Anorexia tardive: Late onset marital anorexia nervosa. *Journal of Psychosomatic Research, 18,* 423–428.

Dally, P., & Gomez, J. (1979). *Anorexia nervosa.* London: W. Heinemann Medical Books.

Foster, S. W. (1986). Marital treatment for eating disorders. In N. S. Jacobson & A. S. Gurman (Eds.), *Clinical handbook of marital therapy* (pp. 575–593). New York: Guilford Press.

Garfinkel, P. E., & Garner, D. M. (1982). *Anorexia nervosa: A multidimensional perspective.* New York: Brunner/Mazel.

Heavey, A., Parker, Y., Vhat, A. V., Crisp, A. H., & Gowers, S. G. (1989). Anorexia nervosa and marriage. *International Journal of Eating Disorders, 8,* 275–284.

Humphrey, L. L. (1986). Family relations in bulimic–anorexic and nondistressed families. *International Journal of Eating Disorders, 2,* 377–383.

Humphrey, L. L., Apple, R. F., & Kirschenbaum, D. S. (1986). Differentiating bulimic–anorexic from normal families using interpersonal and behavioral observational systems. *Journal of Consulting and Clinical Psychology, 54,* 190–195.

Huon, G. F. (1985). Bulimia: Therapy at a distance. In S. W. Touyz & P. J. V. Beumont (Eds.), *Eating disorders: Prevalence and treatment* (pp. 62–73). Sydney, Australia: Williams & Wilkins.

Hsu, L. K. G., Crisp, A. H., & Harding, B. (1979). Outcome of anorexia nervosa. *Lancet, 1,* 62–65.

Kassett, J. A., Gwirtsman, H. E., Kaye, W. H., et al. (1988). Patterns of onset of bulimic symptoms in anorexia nervosa. *American Journal of Psychiatry, 145,* 1287–1288.

Kog, E., Vandereycken, W., & Vertommen, H. (1985). Towards a verification of the psychosomatic family model: A pilot study of ten families with an anorexia/bulimia nervosa patient. *International Journal of Eating Disorders, 4,* 525–538.

Landers, A. (1990, December 28). Dear Ann Landers. *Honolulu Advertiser,* p. C7.

Leichner, P., Harper, D., & Johnston, D. (1985). Adjunctive group support for spouses of women with anorexia nervosa and/or bulimia. *International Journal of Eating Disorders, 4,* 227–335.

Levine, P. (1988). "Bulimic" couples: Dynamics and treatment. In F. Kaslow (Ed.), *Couples therapy in a family context: Perspective and retrospective* (pp. 89–103). Rockville, MD: Aspen.

Luepnitz, D. A. (1988). *The family interpreted: Feminist theory in clinical practice.* New York: Basic Books.

Madanes, C. (1981). *Strategic family therapy.* San Francisco: Jossey-Bass.

Minuchin, S., Rosman, B. L., & Baker, L. (1978). *Psychosomatic families: Anorexia nervosa in context.* Cambridge, MA: Harvard University Press.

Mitchell, J. E., & Goff, G. (1984). Bulimia in males. *Psychosomatics, 25,* 909–913.

Polivy, J., & Herman, C. P. (1987). Diagnosis and treatment of normal eating. *Journal of Consulting and Clinical Psychology, 55,* 635–644.

Raciti, M., & Hedrick, S. S. (1992). Relationships between eating disorder characteristics and love and sex attitudes. *Sex Roles, 27,* 553–564.

Root, M. P. P. (1990). Recovery and relapse in former bulimics. *Psychotherapy, 27,* 397–403.

Root, M. P. P. (1991). Persistent, disordered eating as a gender-specific, post-traumatic stress response to sexual assault. *Psychotherapy, 28,* 96–102.

Root, M. P. P., & Fallon, P. (1988). The incidence of victimization experiences in a bulimic sample. *Journal of Interpersonal Violence, 3,* 161–173.

Root, M. P. P., Fallon, P., & Friedrich, W. N. (1986). *Bulimia: A systems approach to treament.* New York: Norton.

Russell, G. F. M. (1979). Bulimia nervosa—An ominous variant of anorexia nervosa. *Psychological Medicine, 5,* 355–371.

Schneider, J. A., & Agras, W. S. (1987). Bulimia in males: A matched comparison with females. *International Journal of Eating Disorders, 6,* 235–242.

Schwartz, R. C., Barrett, M. J., & Saba, G. (1984). Family therapy for bulimia. In D. M. Garner & P. E. Garfinkel (Eds.), *Handbook of psychotherapy for anorexia nervosa and bulimia* (pp. 280–307). New York: Guilford Press.

Siever, M. D. (1989). *Socio-culturally acquired vulnerability to eating disorders.* Unpublished doctoral dissertion, University of Washington, Seattle.

Simpson, W. S., & Ramberg, J. A. (1992). Sexual dysfunction in married female patients with anorexia and bulimia nervosa. *Journal of Sex and Marital Therapy, 18,* 44–54.

Sykes, D. K., Leuser, B., Melia, M., & Gross, M. (1988). A demograhic analysis of 252 patients with anorexia nervosa and bulimia. *International Journal of Psychosomatics, 35,* 5–9.

Theander, S. (1970). Anorexia nervosa: A psychiatric investigation of 94 female patients. *Acta Psychiatrica Scandinavica,* (Suppl. 214), 1–194.

Thelen, M. H., Farmer, J., Mann, L. M., & Pruitt, J. (1990). Bulimia and interpersonal relationships: A longitudinal study. *Journal of Counseling Psychology, 37,* 85–90.

Van Buren, D. J., & Williamson, D. A. (1988). Marital relationships and conflict resolution skills of bulimics. *International Journal of Eating Disorders, 7,* 735–741.

Van den Broucke, S., & Vandereycken, W. (1988). Anorexia and bulimia nervosa in married patients: A review. *Comprehensive Psychiatry.*

Van den Broucke, S., & Vandereycken, W. (1989a). Eating disorders in married patients: Theory and therapy. In W. Vandereycken, E. Kog, & J. Vanderlinden (Eds.), *The family approach to eating disorders: Assessment and treatment of anorexia nervosa and bulimia* (pp. 333–346). New York: PMA Publishing.

Van den Broucke, S., & Vandereycken, W. (1989b). The marital relationship of patients with an eating disorder: A questionnaire study. *International Journal of Eating Disorders, 8,* 541–556.

Van den Broucke, S., & Vandereycken, W. (1989c). Eating disorders in married patients: A comparison with unmarried anorexics and an exploration of the marital relationship. In W. Vandereycken, E. Kog, & J. Vanderlinden (Eds.), *The family approach to eating disorders: Assessment and treatment of anorexia nervosa and bulimia* (pp. 173–188). New York: PMA Publishing.

Vandereycken, W., Kog, E., & Vanderlinden, J. (Eds.). (1989). *The family approach to eating disorders: Assessment and treatment of anorexia nervosa and bulimia.* New York: PMA Publishing.

Zerbe, K. J. (1992). Why eating-disordered patients resist sex therapy: A response to Simpson and Ramberg. *Journal of Sex and Marital Therapy, 18,* 55–64.

22

Object Relations Marital Therapy of Personality Disorders

SAMUEL SLIPP

THIS CHAPTER first provides a brief overview of borderline and narcissistic personality disorders, because they represent the most frequently encountered personality disorders in the clinical practice of marital therapy. This background is essential for the clinician in diagnosing these disorders and in understanding how individual psychodynamics influence the marital relationship. Many of the problems that develop in the marriages of these individuals can also be found to varying degrees in other types of personality disorders. Therefore, what is discussed here about the marital therapy of individuals with borderline and narcissistic conditions is also generally applicable when treating marital partners with these other personality disorders.

Individuals with borderline and narcissistic conditions usually enter marriage with the following problems that they hope the relationship will remedy: They fear intimacy, are self-preoccupied, have considerable anger, and are acutely sensitive to feeling rejected. After the initial passion and idealization of each other in the courtship and honeymoon periods of the relationship, conflict usually begins to simmer and gradually increases in intensity. The spouses have come into the marriage with preexisting, profound distrust that others will be responsive to their emotional needs. Therefore, their need to control and manipulate each other to sustain their self-esteem or even personality integration. Problems tend to be acted out instead of being discussed reasonably and resolved equitably. Because they view issues in black-and-white terms, they experience themselves as innocent victims and their spouses as dangerous persecutors. By understanding the individual and interpersonal dynamics, the marital therapist can avoid the inevitable pitfalls that arise, and work more effectively with these couples.

BORDERLINE PERSONALITY DISORDER

In the past 50 years, clinicians have become aware of a group of patients whose problems are more severe than neurotic disorders, yet less severe than those in the psychotic range. These patients have previously been called "as if personalities" (Deutsch, 1942), "psychotic characters" (Frosch, 1964), "bad hysterics" (Zetzel, 1968), or persons having "borderline syndromes" (Grinker, Werble, & Drye, 1968). Now, they are diagnosed as suffering from borderline and narcissistic personality disorders.

The most original work to unify thinking about borderline personality organization was done by Kernberg (1967). Subsequently, a phenomenological diagnosis was developed by Gunderson and other (Gunderson & Singer, 1975; Gunderson, Kolb, & Austin, 1981), which was included in the *Diagnostic and Statistical Manual of Mental Disorders* (DSM-IV). The diagnostic criteria for borderline personality disorder are indicated by five or more of the following:

1. Intolerance of being alone: frantic efforts to avoid real or imagined abandonment or depression.
2. Unstable and intense relationships: shifts of attitudes—idealization, devaluation, manipulation.
3. Identity disturbance: uncertain self-image, gender, long-term goals or career, values, and loyalties.
4. Impulsivity in two areas that are self-damaging: spending, sex, gambling, substance use, shoplifting, overeating, reckless driving.
5. Self-damaging physical acts: suicidal gestures, self-mutilation, recurrent accidents or fights.
6. Instability of affect: shifts from normal mood to depression, irritability, and anxiety.
7. Chronic feelings of boredom or emptiness.
8. Lack of control of anger.
9. Transient stress-related paranoid or severe dissociative symptoms.

Kernberg (1984) considers this symptomatic categorization of borderline personality disorder to be more suited for research than clinical purposes. He states that it does not involve assessment of the patient's level of severity; it overlaps other personality disorders; and it has little application to etiology, treatment, or prognosis. Kernberg's structural criteria, based on object relations and ego psychology psychoanalytic theory, are as follows for "borderline personality organization":

1. *Identity diffusion:* lack of integration of a concept of self or significant other, with contradictory behavior and perceptions of self and other;
2. *Primitive defensive operations* to protect the ego:
   a. *Splitting* of the self and the other: each is seen as all-good or all-bad, with sudden reversals of feelings;
   b. *Primitive idealization:* intolerance of imperfections in the idealized other, who is then seen as persecutory or dangerous;
   c. *Projective identification:* need to control and unconsciously induce behavior in another, resulting from the projection of a good or bad aspect of an internal self or object representation. The induced

response in the other is then identified with, so that this split-off aspect of oneself can be vicariously expressed through the other person. While the more mature defense of projection is based on repression and firm ego boundaries, projective identification is founded on splitting or primitive dissociation and weak ego boundaries;
   d. *Denial:* aware that the perceptions and feelings toward the self and others previously had been totally opposite, but they do not affect the present perceptions and feelings; and
   e. *Omnipotence and devaluation:* a grandiose self relates to a depreciated and devaluated other, which is a projection of a negative self representation.

Kernberg notes that borderline patients have the capacity for reality testing, and can differentiate the self from others. However, they have structural personality weaknesses. They lack impulse control, tolerate anxiety poorly, and have insufficient channels for sublimation. They cannot contain tension and are overly dependent on others for self-esteem and ego integration. Their superego pathology is manifested in immature value systems, lying, or antisocial behavior. Because of identity diffusion and primitive defenses, they suffer chronically chaotic relations with others and are subject to brief psychotic episodes if they feel abandoned.

Most psychoanalytic investigators place the fixation of borderline pathology at the rapprochement subphase of the separation–individuation phase of child development (Mahler, Pine, & Bergman, 1975). Around 2 years of age, a rapprochement crisis occurs in which the child becomes aware of its separateness as well as of gender differences. The child becomes especially vulnerable and fearful of the loss of the mother and her love. Loss of the mother's emotional availability during this stage is devastating, and results in annihilation anxiety. This occurs because the child has not yet internalized the mother to develop a sense of constancy of the self and of the other.

The narcissistic individual retains a grandiose self for security, as a defense against annihilation anxiety and the loss of self-esteem. The borderline individual experiences the loss of the mother as not only devastating to self-esteem, but also to the very integrity of the self. The developmental fixation that occurs results in narcissistic individuals' being constantly needy of other's admiring responses to sustain their self-esteem, whereas borderline persons become clinging and dependent to prevent abandonment by the other.

Kernberg (1975), although recognizing deficits in early mothering in the etiology of these patients' conditions, also emphasizes a hereditary deficit or vulnerability. Masterson and Rinsley (1975) believe that the mother's withdrawal of her emotional availability, as the child attempts to separate, results in the child's equating separation with abandonment.

Most recently, there is increasing evidence to indicate that borderline conditions can result from a post-traumatic stress disorder in childhood. Studies by Herman (1988), Nielsen (1983), Stone (1981), van der Kolk (1986), and Wilson (1988) found about 33% of borderline patients suffered sexual abuse during childhood. However, Bryner, Nelson, Miller, and Krol (1987) and Stone (1981) noted that about 75% of borderline patients who required hospitalization suffered physical or sexual abuse during childhood. Recent studies are exploring possible neurological and hormonal changes, as well as psychological consequences, as a result of this early child abuse.

My study of female borderlines and their families (Slipp, 1977, 1984) indicated that seductive sexual abuse need not be actually physical but could be emotional. The fathers were found to be narcissistic and controlling, feeling entitled to demand that others in the family cater to them as a "good mother" to maintain their self-esteem. They employed splitting and projective identification in family relations. When their wives rebelled against simply being used as a need-satisfying good mother, they were demeaned as being "all-bad" by their husbands. The husbands then idealized their daughters and emotionally induced them into the role of "surrogate wife/go-between." The child functioned as an "all-good" wife–mother, and as a cohesive agent to hold the marriage together.

Despite this oedipal triumph for the daughter, her seductive binding by the father was always exploitative and conditional. Her involvement and idealization depended on gratification of the father's narcissistic needs. Most of all, the father was intrusive, did not respect individual boundaries, did not respond to the daughter's developmental needs, and interfered with normal separation and individuation. Subsequently, the fathers rejected and no longer idealized their daughters, often turning to another woman. The daughters then fell from grace, felt discarded,

worthlessness, and enraged. What was especially pathogenic was that the family itself used splitting and projective identification, thereby reinforcing these primitive defenses in the patient. The self and others continued to be polarized, and seen as "all-good" or "all-bad."

How can the psychoanalytic finding of early maternal interference with separation and the threat of rejection be reconciled with the described seductive experience occurring during later childhood? With male borderline patients, there seems to be a direct continuation of the close-binding, seductive relationship with the mother and abandonment later during, childhood or adolescence. However, most borderline patients are women, and our own and the previously mentioned studies implicate the fathers. This can be explained as follows. The daughters could separate in early childhood, despite experiencing withdrawal by their mothers, by turning to their fathers, who functioned as mother surrogates. Kernberg (1986) noted that this sequence of events creates premature oedipal strivings that make daughters more vulnerable to their father's loss. The fathers' actually facilitating an oedipal triumph over the mothers is damaging because of the following:

1. The daughters are exploited for their fathers' narcissistic or sexual needs, which reinforces their distrust that others will be sensitive to and affirm them as individuals.
2. Internalization of a good maternal object, self and object constancy, and the ability to sustain self-esteem (narcissistic equilibrium) is disturbed.
3. The identification with the mother in girls and consolidation of feminine gender identity is disrupted.
4. Oedipal fantasies are not simply worked out and resolved as a form of safe play but are actually acted out in reality. Thus, interpersonal relationships become sexualized and integration and control of sexual and aggressive impulses do not occur.

Fathers of borderline patients were found to later reject their daughters for other women, often because of the daughters' need to separate and individuate. Thus, the same relationship of being exploited for narcissistic needs and abandoned by their mothers in early childhood is repeated by their fathers in adolescence. The patients internalize this relationship and unconsciously repeat this victimized role of being seduced, exploited, betrayed, and abandoned by others. Stone (1990) considers that being thrown on the trash heap by the father is repeated later in adult life, which he termed the Marilyn Monroe syndrome. Borderline individuals then discard themselves as worthless through suicide attempts. Alternatively, these borderline patients may identify with the aggressor, and do to others what was done to them.

NARCISSISTIC PERSONALITY DISORDER

The DSM-IV diagnostic criteria for narcissistic personality disorder are indicated by at least five of the following:

1. Grandiose self-importance: exaggerate achievements and talents, even problems are special.
2. Fantasies of great success, power, intelligence, beauty, or love.
3. Feels special, arrogant, and haughty.
4. Craves constant attention and admiration.
5. Feelings of rage, inferiority, shame, or emptiness in responding to criticism, indifference, or defeat.
6. Entitlement: expect special favors without reciprocal responsibility.
7. Exploitativeness: use others for own desires or self-aggrandizement.
8. Alternatively overidealize or devalue relationships.
9. Lack empathy: unable to recognize and respond to other's feelings.
10. Envious of others or feels others are envious.

There is disagreement concerning the relationship of narcissistic personality to borderline personality. Kernberg (1975) views the narcissist as also having a borderline personality organization, and considers the grandiose self as resulting from fusion of aspects of the ideal self and ideal object with the real self. The grandiose self can also be projected onto the therapist who becomes idealized, which serves as a defense against feelings of envy and rage and a denial of the separateness of and dependency on others.

The treatment approach of Kernberg et al. (1989) is to systematically interpret these split-off negative feelings, as manifested in the here-and-now transference to the therapist. Patients can then reown and integrate their ambivalence to strengthen and differentiate their ego. Kernberg considers that once the patient has worked

through the primitive level of internalized object relations, genetic links to the past can be made.

Kohut (1971,1977; Kohut & Wolf, 1982), using a self-psychology psychoanalytic framework, considers the etiology of narcissistic personality disorder to be due to deprivation of adequate parenting during early childhood. The child needs to idealize and internalize its parents as "selfobjects" (the other is experienced as part of oneself) for a sense of security and safety, and to obtain appropriate "mirroring" (admiring responses) from them to validate achievements to form a positive self-image, develop confidence, and to regulate self-esteem. In narcissistic personalities, Kohut considers that these needed responses do not occur because of the parents' "empathic failure," and the grandiose self of the child is not changed by "transmuting internalizations." Idealization of the therapist in treatment is viewed as an attempt to relive the need to fuse with idealized parents during childhood. In Kohut's approach, the therapist serves as a "selfobject" to provide the patient with an empathic relationship and "mirroring" for a reconstructive experience that was lacking in childhood.

Kohut (1977) considers the narcissistic personality as more mature, having stable, cohesive self and selfobjects, while borderline personalities have fragmented, unstable self and selfobjects. Adler and Buie (1979) note that borderline patients lack object permanency, being unable to evoke the image of the mother and thus are more vulnerable to feeling abandoned and regressing to psychosis. They consider that narcissistic patients are more advanced and lack object constancy, although still dependent on others for their self-esteem. Rinsley (1985) notes that

> in both personalities, major overt or underlying themes of rejection and abandonment, loss of inner controls, split good–bad perceptions, and related thinking, impairment of self and sexual identity, pre-eruptive and eruptive rage, and depression and symptomatic behavior relfective of unrequited symbiotic needs are evident. (pp. 318–319)

The narcissistic personality has negotiated individuation but has not separated and remains dependent on others for self-esteem. The borderline personality is arrested in both these processes, and needs others to preserve self-esteem and personality integrity. Persons with narcissistic personality deny their dependency and helplessness and erect a psychological "plastic bubble" (Volkan, 1973) or "cocoon" (Modell, 1976) to distance themselves from empathic experiences with others and a world experienced as unpredictable and dangerous. Narcissistic patients tend to idealize those experienced as potential persecutors and to demean others who are seen as dependent.

In clinical work with narcissistic patients and their families (Slipp, 1988), a family pattern was found that employed and reinforced the existing primitive defenses of splitting and projective identification. As a child, the narcissistic patient was idealized and induced into a "savior" or "surrogate spouse/go-between" role, which alternated with being demeaned as a "scapegoat." As the "savior" the child was expected to perform socially to enhance the family prestige and self-esteem of the parent(s). As the "surrogate spouse/go-between," the child was seductively bound and achieved an oedipal victory over the parent of the same sex. In both these instances, the child's grandiose self was reinforced, and a sense of entitlement established. When the child was alternately scapegoated, his/her self-esteem was wounded. Thus, persons with narcissistic disorder learn to distrust others, since they expect to be controlled and exploited to sustain the other's emotional equilibrium. As an adult, narcissistic individuals reinforce this expectation by repeating the internalized family pattern of relationships they experienced in childhood. They try to rescue or perform for others and then feel controlled, used, and angry. They also do to others what was done to them: Using projective identification and splitting, they alternately idealize or demean others.

One form of this interaction is the "Solomon child syndrome" (Slipp, 1988), which was found when parents were hostile to each other and competed for the child's loyalty. This pattern occurred in marriages where clear sides were drawn, frequently occurring before or following divorce. If the child performed as a "savior" or "surrogate spouse/go-between" for one parent, rejection by the other parent occurred. The child was thus caught between conflicting loyalties and helplessly torn between the parents. The patient felt controlled and used by the parents in their conflict with one another, which resulted in profound distrust and the erection of narcissistic, self-protective defenses against intimacy with others. These patient as adults maintained the illusion of being self-sufficient and needing to depend on no one. Narcissistic individuals also seemed compelled to save, rescue, or heal others, just as occurred with their parents. They did not openly acknowledge or express needs of their own. Thus, unconsciously they felt exploited and angry that their own needs were ignored, which justified their distrust, anger, and distancing.

In individual therapy with persons with narcissistic personality disorders, Modell (1976) found that a combination of Winnicott's (1965), Kohut's (1977), and Kernberg's (1975) approaches was most effective. Initially, the establishment of a safe holding environment, by the therapist's being empathic, was essential. Here, Modell recommends acceptance of the patient's verbalizations without interpretation, in order to facilitate consolidation of the patient's ego. The patient eventually becomes able to lower defensiveness, to establish trust that the therapist is responsive, and to separate sufficiently from the therapist to express anger. In the second stage, the therapist can make interpretations, and there is less likelihood that the patient will feel personally attacked or rejected. Finally, the patient develops a more typical transference neurosis, which can be interpreted along with defenses.

THE NARCISSISTIC–BORDERLINE COUPLE

There seems to be an attraction between persons suffering from narcissistic and borderline personality disorders. The narcissistic person, who tends to be obsessional and emotionally dead, experiences the borderline person's expressiveness as stimulating. In addition, the narcissist's need for self-sufficiency and admiration is fulfilled by the borderline's dependency. From the borderline person's perspective, the narcissist appears to be a tower of strength and reason, who can calm and contain their emotionality. During their romantic infatuation, they each idealize the other. However, once this honeymoon period is over, conflicts usually arise and the marriage becomes dysfunctional and chaotic. Both partners experience themselves as a victim and the other as a persecutor, resulting in considerable anger and inability to resolve conflict.

Both find themselves in a marriage that is similar to the relationship they experienced in their childhood. The narcissist had been used as a "savior" or "surrogate spouse/go-between" to rescue and preserve the parents' egos and marriage. This role had alternated with the child's being "scapegoated" by one or both of the parents.

Thus, narcissists unconsciously feel that others will either feed their grandiosity or else abandon them, so that they alternately feel special or rejected. By choosing a borderline person who is seductive and needs to be saved, the narcissist recreates the same roles in the marriage as in the family of origin. However, the spouse's needs ultimately cannot be gratified and the borderline person becomes demanding, critical, rejecting, or threatens suicide. Just as they erected distancing defenses to avoid being invaded and to protect their identity from their parents, narcissistic individuals repeat this behavior with the spouse. Borderline spouses experience this withdrawal as an abandonment and either increase demands or superficially comply for a while. Ultimately, a to and fro dance ensues, with each partner attempting to manipulate, control, and punish the other into being the way he/she requires.

Complementary Projective Identifications

The underlying dynamic for the narcissistic–borderline couple is a shared, unconscious collusion involving dependency and anger. The narcissistic spouse withdraws behind a defense of self-sufficiency and represses rage, while the borderline spouse openly expresses anger; thus, the borderline spouse may be provoked to enact the narcissistic person's anger. This same process of putting an unacceptable aspect of onself into another through projective identification and inducing the other to act it out also holds true for the narcissistic individual's feelings of dependency. The narcissistic person has erected defenses against dependency, and thus he/she can live vicariously through the borderline spouse, who is openly clinging and dependent.

Narcissist persons are experienced by borderline spouse as being able to contain their deficit of impulse control. The hope is that the narcissistic spouse will function as a calming, protective, and limit-setting good parent, which was missing in their family of origin. Borderline spouses may also test limits, seeing how far they can be tolerated before they are rejected. Since they expect rejection, they also often unconsciously press to provoke it. When borderline patients are rejected, it fulfills their expectation that they will be exploited and abandoned, which occurred with their parent(s) during childhood. Similarly, narcissistic spouses also unconsciously select mates who will be self-centered and exploitative, reinforcing the distrustful expectations derived from their childhood relationship with their parent(s).

Even though real intimacy may not be achieved, sometimes these marriages operate a long time in a complementary fashion. The bor-

derline spouse can express the dependency and anger for the narcissistic spouse, and the narcissist controls the borderline's impulsivity. However, more often there is an ongoing battle for control with sadomasochistic interaction in these marriages. Although both narcissistic and borderline spouses may profoundly wish for intimacy, they also do not trust that others will be genuinely concerned and responsive. It is safer to hold onto this undifferentiated relationship, because separation and autonomy are equated with rejection. For real change to occur, both have to work through their past parental relationships that programmed their current negative expectations. They need to become less dependent on continued external affirmation for their self-esteem and survival, become more autonomous, and more willing to be more trustful and empathic in a genuinely intimate relationship.

OBJECT RELATIONS MARITAL THERAPY

The sequence described earlier by Modell, Kernberg, and Kohut for individual therapy was also found to be most suitable for working with couples having personality disorders. Initially, the therapist tries to empathically understand and connect to both spouses to develop a "working alliance" and a "safe holding environment." To achieve these objectives, the therapist needs to take an evenhanded approach, be nonjudgmental, and not side with one spouse against the other. This is often difficult, because the couple usually tries to induce the therapist to function as a judge to determine who is right and wrong. Each partner tries to draw in the therapist as an ally to his/her side. For the therapist to do so would only reinforce splitting and the view of one spouse as a persecutor and the other as a victim.

It is also important for the therapist not to take a controlling or manipulative stance, and to avoid being experienced transferentially as a dominating and exploitative parental figure. The object relations therapist does not attempt to do problem solving for the couple as a behavioral therapist might or to be directive in the manner of a systemic therapist. First of all, the therapist's changing the couple's overt behavior or symptoms without their understanding the underlying dynamics is not considered therapeutic. Second, a therapist's using power and authority to impose change is usually experienced by the couple as another attempt by a parental figure to be controlling, to deny autonomy, and to demand submission. The couple may respond to directives with superficial compliance, but they can feel demeaned, invaded, angry, and may terminate treatment. Third, if the therapist's directive is done by deceptive techniques out of the couple's conscious awareness, their distrust and defensiveness are only further reinforced. In summary, even if superifical symptoms are altered, the couple's basic inability to trust or have an intimate relationship is not changed.

The initial goal is for the therapist to establish a genuine "working alliance" with the couple. This alliance is egalitarian and will facilitate less defensiveness and more openness. A "safe holding environment" is also established by the therapist's ability to contain emotions. Only after their distrust and distance are lessened and the couple is engaged in treatment can an interpretive approach, using the techniques of object relations therapy, be employed. Here in the middle phase, the therapist's goals are to help them differentiate the boundaries between the self from the other by interpreting projective identification and to integrate ambivalence instead of the use of splitting. Intrapsychic conflict that had been acted out in the interpersonal sphere is now reowned. Both spouses are then better able to discriminate between their inner self and object representations, to observe themselves, empathize with others, and be more aware of their effect on others. In the marriage, self-defeating and self-destructive behavior is thereby diminished. In the last phase of treatment, both spouses can then work through their own inner conflicts to achieve a better sense of self with less vulnerability. A detailed discussion of the three phases of object relations couple therapy follows.

Engagement Phase of Treatment

Initially, the therapist establishes a *working alliance* by maintaining a neutral, evenhanded, and empathic position with respect to both parties in the relationship. The therapist serves as a model of an authority figure who can empathically listen and be responsive to each of the spouses' emotional needs. The therapist does not control, impose, or manipulate the couple for his/her own agenda, as was generally the case with the couple's parents during childhood. In this way the therapist does not stimulate or reinforce a negative transference reaction, but creates the condition for a corrective emotional experience.

This is especially helpful for narcissistic individuals who are out of touch with their own emotions and needs, which were not recognized or acknowledged in their families of origin. Trust and openness toward another human being who listens and is responsive becomes a possibility, so that narcissistic spouses can risk verbally expressing their own emotions and needs.

The therapist also needs to contain hostility that is expressed, and to set firm limits against its being acted out by the couple in ways destructive to the marital relationship. This needs to be done firmly without anger or assuming excessive control, which inhibits openness and spontaneity. A *safe holding environment* is thereby established, allowing for the expression of anger without fear of retaliation, or its going out of control and becoming self-destructive or damaging to the relationship.

An agreement can be made with the couple concerning the form of communication occuring between them, so as not to escalate conflict. For example, this includes both spouses using "I" to describe their reactions instead of "you," which tends to project blame and only leads to counter-defensive behavior. In fighting, they agree not to "hit below the belt," by not attacking each other personally or becoming witholding or rejecting. They need to try to stick to specific behavior or issues and not to generalize, so that their continued dialogue has a better chance at conflict resolution. Each partner is encouraged to make an effort to listen to the other and try to experience what the other is feeling before responding defensively.

It is important to let the couple know that even though they each want the therapist to side with them and judge the other spouse, this would interfere with being helpful to them. The role of the therapist is not to be a judge determining who is right or wrong, but to help them both improve their relationship with one another. The therapist is thus not induced to take sides, thereby reinforcing splitting. The therapist needs to function as an idealized selfobject or good parent who listens to, is supportive of, and tries to understand both spouses' perspectives. This therapeutic framework serves as a model to encourage empathic understanding by each spouse of the other's views and focuses on their resolution of problems and not simply on blaming each other.

Systemic Beginning Phase of Treatment

In the beginning phase of treatment, the here-and-now interaction between the couples is clarified by the therapist. This is similar to Kernberg's object relations approach in individual therapy of interpretation of the transference to the therapist in the here and now. However, in couple therapy the transference to the therapist is diluted, but there are existing transferences already in operation between the spouses. It is also similar to systemic forms of family therapy, which look for reverberating positive and negative feedback cycles in the present relationship that maintain or escalate conflict. Unlike systemic approaches, the object relations marital therapist maintains a neutral, nonintrusive position, and does not use the power vested in the position to manipulate or control the couple to produce change. The object relations therapist does not take sides to structure the interaction, nor provide obscure paradoxical prescriptions. Overcoming resistance to change because of family homeostasis need not be forced by the therapist, especially when it is outside the couple's awareness. Even being a benevolent despot, by the therapist's being directive for the couple's benefit, is infantilizing and not helpful toward their achieving independence and autonomy. The object relations marital therapist sides with the healthy aspects of the couple and engages in a collaborative effort with them to bring about change. In this way a negative transference to the therapist, as a controlling or manipulating parental figure, is not reinforced and a trusting relationship is maintained.

The therapist's employing an object relations approach points out and clarifies the cycles of systemic interaction that are clearly observable, so that the couple themselves can take responsibility for bringing about change. The therapist offers the following suggestions as a tentative hypothesis:

1. What the problem appears to be.
2. How spouse A dealt with it.
3. Its effects on spouse B, and B's response.
4. Which, in turn, influenced A, and A's response, to creat a vicious cycle that escalates conflict.

This serves to openly clarify dysfunctional cycles of interaction in the here and now that only increase conflict. The aim is to demonstrate how a blaming or fault-finding approach only generates cycles of defensiveness and hostility, which results in a stalemate and is ultimately self-defeating for both spouses. Blaming perpetuates the use of splitting, of seeing the other as the "all-bad" persecutor and the self as the "all-good"

victim. It sets up a condition in which both spouses feel self-righteous and entrenched in their position unaware of the others needs and motives, and thus entitled to demand that the other change.

Blaming also perpetuates an egocentric position and projective identification. Individuals are unaware of the linkage of their behavior to the effect on another person, thereby interfering with taking some responsibility for the interaction that follows. A healthier problem-solving method is encouraged, in which each partner assumes some share of the responsibility as a more productive way of dealing with and resolving conflict. Depending on the severity of pathology, seeing the couple during this initial phase on a once-a-week basis may last from several weeks to months.

Interpersonal Middle Phase of Treatment

After the couple is engaged, the middle phase of treatment focuses on interpretation of splitting and projective identification. The therapist notes how split off and repressed unacceptable aspects of one spouse are placed into the other. The goal is for both members to reown this aspect of themselves, to integrate their ambivalence, and to establish clearer boundaries between the self and other. In this way, the interpersonal acting out of intrapsychic conflict is halted and can be worked through on a verbal level. My method of interpreting splitting and projective identification is as follows:

1. *Reframing* its purpose into a positive aim.
2. *Linking* it to a genetic reconstruction.
3. *Clarifying* why an aspect of the self was felt unacceptable and needed to be projected.

In working with couples, the interpretation of how they relate to one another in the present is linked to past parental relations. This intervention occurs earlier than Kernberg suggests in individual therapy with personality disorders, because he feels it interferes with the differentiation of the present from the past. However, in couple work, it is more urgent that the relationship with the spouse in the present be differentiated from that with a parent from the past. The couple's current relationship is being threatened with dissolution by the unconscious repetition of past relationships. By providing a genetic interpretation, an empathic understanding, and not blame, is emphasized. The therapist tries to explain to the couple the reason why spouse A needed to disown an aspect of the self and use projective identification. This approach also offers a basis for reframing the interpretation of projective identification into a positive vein for both spouses. Now, spouse A is not simply a villain, but a victim also of past relationships from childhood. Now, spouse B, who contained and expressed the projection, is not viewed as being "all-bad" (the scapegoat), but as serving a helpful function (the savior).

Thus, the behavior of both spouses is reinterpreted and reframed from a negative into a positive light, so as to bring them closer together. The following case example of a man with a narcissistic character disorder who married a relatively normal woman, demonstrates how the therapist might interpret splitting and projective identification.

Bill and Mary came in for marital therapy because of mounting conflict and distance between them. Bill felt that Mary had a bad temper and was not nice to his mother. This always put him in the middle between Mary and his mother, which was uncomfortable. Mary felt that Bill did not value or respect her and resented this. Each week, Bill's mother would visit and tell Mary how to treat her son and grandchild. The mother would rearrange the dishes and silverware, tell them how to decorate the house, and dominate the conversation with her stories. It was as if the mother were Bill's wife and not Mary. Bill was detached and amused by his mother's behavior, but Mary resented this and felt his mother was intrusive and controlling. Mary would then confront Bill's mother and an argument would ensue. Bill complained that he was always caught between these fighting women and blamed Mary for being so argumentative.

In obtaining a family history, it was revealed that Bill's father had died in the war and his mother had never remarried. She had difficulty in coping with her two boys without her husband and became a strict taskmaster. Bill was the older sibling, was parentified, and functioned as a substitute spouse for his mother. However, he was severely punished and rejected for disobedience even if he answered back. One of the qualities that attracted Bill to Mary was her lively independence and her ability to speak up for herself. This had contributed to his choice of a mate, because it was what he himself wished he could do.

In therapy, it became clear that Bill's not setting firm limits with his mother unconsciously served to provoke Mary into anger. Then Bill would blame Mary for getting angry at his mother. Mary felt devalued, unprotected, and conflicted about how to deal with Bill's mother. She could not allow his mother to run rampant over her, yet if she stood up for herself, she was criticized by her husband.

The therapist hypothesized silently to himself that Bill was using projective identification in order to induce Mary to express his split-off anger at his mother. Then, by condemning Mary, Bill would appear to be an innocent victim and Mary would be the villain attacking his mother. In this way Bill did not risk rejection from his mother and could vicariously express his anger at his mother through Mary. During the middle phase of treatment, the therapist reframed and openly interpreted this splitting and projective identification as follows:

"You are very fortunate, Bill, that Mary was so helpful to you by expressing those parts of yourself that probably were unacceptable and had to be repressed from your conscious awareness. You told me how strict your mother was, and how she would not allow you to even speak up for yourself. Because you, Bill, feared rejection by your mother if you spoke up for yourself, you needed to repress that assertive part of yourself. With Mary's help in expressing that part of yourself, you were able to be what you wanted to be—a whole and complete person."

By linking the present to the past, Bill is reframed from being an exploitative, "bad" husband into being a victim of his past relationship with his mother. Mary is now redefined as his savior instead of being demeaned as the scapegoat. This reframing tends to diminish their entrenched positions arising from each partner's need to defend themself against being considered as bad by the other. With Bill's reowning of the projective identification and intergrating his ambivalence, firmer boundaries can be established between the couple. The therapist can then state the following:

"Now that you, Bill, are more in touch with that assertive aspect of yourself, you can function as a more complete person alone. You don't need Mary's help anymore in setting limits with your mother. You are no longer that helpless and dependent little boy, and your mother no longer has power over you as an adult man. You are now freer to express those parts of yourself that formerly were unacceptable and had to be expressed for you by Mary."

The interpretation of projective identification would be unsuccessful if the therapist stated that Bill was dumping his anger into Mary, then using her to express it, and disowning it by blaming her in order to avoid being rejected by his mother. This would only be experienced by Bill as his being called a bad, angry person, who is to blame for the couple's problems. It would only perpetuate splitting, insult Bill's self-esteem, and probably disrupt treatment. Through reframing the interpretation to include understanding from the past and a projection into the future, a positive direction and hope are instilled. No one is to blame, and each spouse can be more understanding of the other. In addition, Bill's sense of masculinity is enhanced, which provides an incentive for ego integration of his ambivalence, as well as for differentiation of the self from the other.

Working with a couple in which only one member is suffering from a personality disorder, especially when it is narcissistic, tends to be less difficult. Usually people marry others who have similar levels of personality development. Hence, the spouse with a narcissistic personality disorder who is able to marry a relatively normal individual tends to be higher functioning. Similarly, there are higher levels of borderline personality functioning. Because female borderline individuals seem sexy and exciting, they may be appealing to males who are generally repressed emotionally, but otherwise normal and without severe conflicts. Here again, these borderlines tend not to be grossly impulsive, self-destructive, or to have minipsychotic episodes. Thus, engagement in therapy is easier, and firm limit setting is not as necessary in the early phases of treatment. During the middle phase of treatment, projective identification and splitting are similarly reframed into a positive light and interpreted. The couple's acceptance of the interpretation tends to be resisted less, since their ability at forming a therapeutic alliance and self-observation is greater.

Countertransference

During this middle phase, the therapist can also examine and try to become aware of any countertransference reactions experienced toward the couple. The following indications of the likelihood of a countertransference reaction occur when the therapist:

1. Breaks the frame of treatment (e.g., not collecting fees, finding it difficult to listen, coming late to or forgetting appointments).
2. Does not remain neutral, but takes sides.
3. Acts, feels, or says things that are not customary or appropriate, or that feel uncomfortable.
4. Dreams or fantasizes about the couple.

The first step for the therapist in this situation is to try to capture the feeling or action and identify it. For example, does the therapist feel incompetent or bored? The next step is self-examination, which requires an honest investigation into whether these reactions arise from unresolved issues in the therapist's own background or current life. For example, does the husband remind the therapist of his/her father or husband? If this is the case, it would be called a "subjective" countertransference (Winnicott, 1949). The danger is that the therapist's countertransference will influence the reaction of one or both members of the couple to the therapist. It can result in the narcissistic spouse trying to cure the therapist, so that progress is halted or treatment is terminated. The therapist needs to work through and resolve this countertransference through self-analysis, so that it does not interfere with therapy.

If the reaction does not seem reminiscent of past or present relationships, the therapist's responses may be due to projective identification coming from the couple, which systemic family therapists sometimes call being "sucked into the system." This is the same process that occurs between the spouses in order to shape the other's responses. Unacceptable aspects of their own internalized object world are dumped into the other to form an unconscious collusive pattern of interaction. It is important that the therapist also not be induced into acting out interpersonally, but try to metabolize and comprehend this "objective" countertransference. On careful consideration of this countertransference reaction, it may reveal which split-off aspect, good or bad, self- or object representation is being projected into the therapist by the couple. This information can then be helpful in understanding the internal world of object relations existing in the couple.

For example, an experienced therapist may unaccountably feel incompetent and helpless. After identifying these feelings, it is necessary to explore whether they come from one's own background. Does either spouse remind one of relationships with his/her parents, spouse, or someone else? If not, these feelings may result from projective identification from one or both of the spouses in treatment. If it is the husband, did he feel incompetent and helpless as a child? Was this what he was projecting into his wife as well, who also was complaining of experiencing these feelings? If so, the therapist can search to see where and why the husband might have felt this way. Then, the therapist can openly acknowledge that he/she was experiencing feelings of incompetence and helplessness and interpret their possible source. From what we know of the family history, this was the way that the husband felt as a child, because his older brother and father were so critical of him. The therapist can then reframe and state that he/she wonders if the husband needed to evoke these feelings in the therapist, in order for the therapist to really understand and empathize with what the husband went through as a child. In this way, these split-off and projected feelings can be reowned by the husband without his feeling criticized and ego boundaries differentiated. Instead, a greater empathic bond is established between the husband and the therapist. The husband can then work these feelings through verbally in treatment instead of inducing others to act them out interpersonally. The interpersonal middle phase of treatment, on a once-a-week basis, usually lasts 3 to 6 months or longer, depending on the level of pathology.

Intrapsychic Ending Phase

In the last phase of treatment, both spouses own their individual conflicts and developmental arrests that now can be worked through intrapsychically. There is less of a tendency to employ the primitive defenses of splitting and projective identification and more of a tendency to use mature defenses. As the couple seems to be functioning better and no longer act out their intrapsychic conflicts in the interpersonal sphere, termination of marital treatment is brought up for discussion. When this is mutually agreed on, the termination phase begins. There may be a brief regression and return of symptoms, as the couple resists ending treatment. During the termination of treatment there is a mourning and acceptance of the limitations of their own background and awareness of how past issues have influenced their current spousal relationship. The ending phase of object relations marital therapy usually lasts 1 to 2 months. Marital therapy alone can diminish acting out and interpersonal conflict, but it is insufficient to bring about deep and long-lasting change in personality disorders. Because of the severe nature of character pathology, treatment often needs to continue into individual therapy for one or both of the spouses after the couple therapy has ended.

OTHER CLINICAL ISSUES

If there is severe pathology and low level of personality functioning in a couple, object relations marital therapy may not be effective. In fact, any form of intervention by the therapist may be experienced as criticism and an insult to self-esteem. Even sincere efforts by the therapist to try to work with this issue may not be successful. Thus, the couple may limit the therapist to being solely supportive, and treatment may not proceed beyond the first stage of marital therapy. What may be possible is for the couple to learn to minimize the use of splitting and to argue more constructively. However, they may resist the interpretation of projective identification, even when it is reframed into a positive light. The development of firmer ego boundaries and a better functioning personality may not develop if the pathology is very severe in both the spouses. If suicidal acting out is a possibility, the need for hospitalization may be necessary. Firm limit setting for other forms of destructive acting out may also be necessary at times to prevent couples from harming each other or interfering with the therapy.

Some couples repeatedly sabotage their therapy through self-defeating or provocative actions. Indeed, many of these couples have already made the rounds of other therapists, whom they have left because of dissatisfaction. If this is the case, it is important to recognize and discuss the probability that they will feel tempted to repeat this pattern again. The therapist needs to instruct the couple that when they feel unhappy about the treatment or have the urge to quit therapy, they need to bring this up as soon as possible. Openly discussing their dissatisfactions with the therapist and each other can serve as a helpful model in containing impulsivity and working out their relationship. This forewarning encourages verbalization of anger instead of the acting out of conflict in the transference. It communicates that the therapist will contain the anger that they express, and not be destroyed or abandon them. This may have been the experience with their parents, who were seen as emotionally fragile, concerned over their own issues, and unreliable. Therapy needs to become a corrective emotional experience, with internalization of the reactions of the therapist that allows for greater freedom of expression of a genuine self.

At times, the couples will disagree with or misinterpret what the therapist says, and they need to be instructed to bring this up also for discussion. If the therapist senses that this has occurred, it is important to bring this up for open discussion to clarify any distortions and misconceptions. The therapist's interpretations are merely attempts to try to understand and are only working hypotheses. In response, the couple can disagree or elaborate upon them as they see fit. It is their responsibility, as well as that of the therapist, to work together cooperatively to facilitate the movement in treatment.

When marital therapy is successful in persons with personalty disorders, it can enable the spouses to recognize their own problems and to share responsibility for the cause and resolution of marital problems. They establish firmer ego boundaries, integrate their ambivalence, diminish the use of primitive defenses such as splitting and projective identification, and employ more mature defenses. After successful marital therapy, long-term individual psychodynamic therapy is considered the treatment of choice for these personality disorders.

REFERENCES

Adler, G., & Buie, D. H. (1979). ALoneness and borderline psychopathology:: The possible relevance of child development issues. *International Journal of Psycho-Analysis, 60,* 83–96.

American Psychiatric Association. (1994). *Diagnostic and statistical manual of mental disorders* (4th ed.). Washington, DC: Author.

Bryner, J. B., Nelson, B. A., Miller, J. B., & Krol, P. A. (1987). Childhood sexual and physical abuse as a factor in adult psychiatric illness. *American Journal of Psychiatry, 144,* 1426–1430.

Deutsch, H. (1942). Some forms of emotional disturbance and their relationship to schizophrenia. *Psychanalytic Quarterly, 11,* 301–321.

Frosch, J. (1964). The psychotic character: Clinical psychiatric considerations. *Psychiatric Quarterly, 38,* 81–96.

Grinker, R. R., Werble, B., & Drye, R. C. (1968). *The borderline syndrome: A behavioral study of ego functions.* New York: Basic Books.

Gunderson, J. G., Kolb, J. E., & Austin, V. (1981). The diagnostic interview for borderline patients. *American Journal of Psychiatry, 138,* 896–903.

Gunderson, J. G., & Singer, M. (1975). Defining borderline patients: An overview. *American Journal of Psychiatry, 132,* 1–10.

Herman, J. (1988). Father–daughter incest. In F. Ochberg (Ed.), *Post-traumatic therapy and victims of violence* (pp. 175–195). New York: Brunner/Mazel.

Kernberg, O. F. (1967). Borderline personality organization. *Journal of the American Psychoanalytic Association, 15,* 641–685.

Kernberg, O. F. (1975). *Borderline conditions and pathological narcissim.* New York: Aronson.

Kernberg, O. F. (1984). *Severe personality disorders: Psychotherapeutic strategies.* New Haven, CT: Yale University Press.

Kernberg, O. F. (1986). Identification and its vicissitudes as observed in psychosis. *International Journal of Psycho-Analysis, 67,* 147–159.

Kernberg, O. F., Selzer, M. A., Koenigsberg, H. W., Carr, A. C., & Appelbaum, A. H. (1989). *Psychodynamic psychotherapy of borderline patients.* New York: Basic Books.

Kohut, H. S. (1971). *The analysis of the self.* New York: International Universities Press.

Kohut, H. S. (1977). *The restoration of the self.* New York: International Universities Press.

Kohut, H. S., & Wolf, E. S. (1982). The disorders of the self and their treatment. In S. Slipp (Ed.), *Curative factors in dynamic psychotherapy* (pp. 44–59). New York: McGraw-Hill.

Mahler, M. S., Pine, F., & Bergman, A. (1975). *The psychological birth of the human infant: Symbiosis and individuation.* New York: Basic Books.

Masterson, J. F., & Rinsley, D. B. (1975). The borderline syndrome: The role of the mother in the genesis and psychic structure of the borderline personality. *International Journal of Psycho-Analysis, 56,* 163–177.

Modell, A. H. (1976). The holding environment and the therapeutic action of psychoanalysis. *Journal of the American Psychoanalytic Association, 24,* 285–307.

Nielsen, G. (1983). *Borderline and acting-out adolescents: A developmental approach.* New York: Human Science Press.

Rinsley, D. B. (1985). Notes on the pathogenesis and nosology of borderline and narcissistic personality disorders. *Journal of the American Academy of Psychoanalysis, 13,* 317–328.

Slipp, S. (1977). Interpersonal factors in hysteria: Freud's seduction theory and the case of Dora. *Journal of the American Academy of Psychoanalysis, 5,* 359–376.

Slipp, S. (1984). *Object relations: A dynamic bridge between individual and family treatment.* New York: Jason Aronson.

Slipp, S. (1988). *The technique and practice of object relations family therapy.* New York: Jason Aronson.

Stone, M. H. (1981). Borderline syndomes: A consideration of subtypes and an overview: Directions for research. *Psychiatric Clinics of North America, 4,* 3–24.

Stone, M. H. (1990). *The fate of borderline patients: Successful outcome and psychiatric practice.* New York: Guilford Press.

van der Kolk, B. (1986). *Psychological trauma.* Washington, DC: American Psychiatric Press.

Volkam, V. (1973). Transitional fantasies in the analysis of a narcissistic personality. *Journal of the American Psychoanalytic Association, 21,* 351–376.

Wilson, J. (1988). Understanding the Vietnam veteran. In F. Ochberg (Ed.), *Post-traumatic therapy and* victims of violence (pp. 227–253). New York: Brunner/Mazel.

Winnicott, D. W. (1949). Hate in the countertransference. *International Journal of Psycho-Analysis, 30,* 36–74.

Winnicott, D. W. (1965). *The maturational process and the facilitating environment.* New York: International Universities Press.

Zetzel, E. (1968). The so-called good hysteric. *International Journal of Psycho-Analysis, 49,* 256–260.

23

Treating Sexual Desire Disorders in Couples

JULIA R. HEIMAN
PAMELA HILL EPPS
BEATRICE ELLIS

$\mathbf{A}$ THERAPIST FACED with an individual or couple reporting a problem with sexual desire is in an interesting but uneasy position. First, there are essentially no population-sampled data on the statistical frequencies and ranges of sexual desire in women and men. All assumptions about desire are based on behavioral (frequency of sexual activities) studies (e.g., Blumstein & Schwartz, 1983; Kinsey, Pomeroy, & Martin, 1948; Kinsey, Pomeroy, Martin, & Gebhard, 1953). However, such studies cannot take into account those instances in which sexual behavior occurs in the absence of desire, or when sexual activity is impossible or unavailable, despite high desire. How desire levels may vary depending on other factors such as relationship type (committed, noncommitted), sexual orientation (heterosexual, homosexual, bisexual), and age (of the individual, of the relationship) is also unknown. Second, there are no agreed-on definitions of sexual desire disorder among the variety of clinical reports published. Even in the *Diagnostic and Statistical Manual of Mental Disorders* published by the American Psychiatric Association (APA) the concept of sexual desire disorder is clearly an evolving one. It was not present prior to DSM-III (APA, 1980) and has changed in label and description in DSM-III-R (APA, 1987) and DSM-IV (APA, 1994). A third issue confronting the therapist is the plethora of treatment models and strategies recommended with little or no indication of their relative effectiveness (Leiblum & Rosen, 1988).

In spite of the lack of data and conceptual disarray, therapists who use the DSM-IV are expected to make a diagnosis of sexual desire disorder. This currently includes hypoactive sexual desire (HSD) and sexual aversion disorder. HSD is a "deficiency or absence of sexual fantasies and desire for sexual activity" taking into account factors that affect sexual functioning, such as "the individual's characteristics, the interpersonal determinants, the life context, and the cultural setting" (p. 496). This extensive reliance on therapists' opinions is troublesome when they themselves have almost nothing but subjective impression upon which to make even a diagnosis of HSD. To diagnose sexual aversion disorder, "the aversion to and active avoidance of genital sexual contact with a sexual partner" (p. 499), is less dependent on therapists' wisdom. It is of sociocultural note that the DSM does not identify hyperactive sexual desire as a disorder. A hyperactive sexual desire diagnosis would raise the same knowledge and judgment quandaries as hypoactive desire. Individuals with hyperactive desire either rarely come into treatment, or they are otherwise labeled as obsessive–compulsive, anxious, or in certain cases, paraphilic.

The perspective needed by a therapist dealing

with sexual desire disorders is therefore a broad and exploratory one, which recognizes that little is certain about the understanding and treatment of this disorder. The present chapter focuses on the most common, current clinical presentation of desire disorders—HSD—in couples who have ongoing committed relationships. Sexual aversion is only discussed as it relates to low sexual desire.

THEORETICAL MODELS

Although Masters and Johnson's (1970) work ushered in a new era of effective treatment for many sexual dysfunctions, disorders of desire were not part of the clinical (or cultural) landscape. Thus, no mention is made of treating sexual desire problems in *Human Sexual Inadequacy* (Masters & Johnson, 1970), or in Kaplan's (1974) *The New Sex Therapy*. As increasing complaints of low desire began to surface, therapists found that Masters and Johnson's approach was not very effective. Kaplan's (1977, 1979) later work was the first to formally articulate this problem. She proposed that desire problems signified deeper levels of sexual conflict than did other sexual dysfunctions, and required a more intensive psychodynamic approach. Other therapists similarly drew from broader theoretical strategies (e.g., Lazarus, 1988; J. LoPiccolo & Friedman, 1988), or more specifically conceptualized existing frameworks (e.g., Apfelbaum, 1988; D. Scharff, 1988) to increase their treatment effectiveness.

Currently there is not a predominating model in the treatment of low sexual desire. The field has been irrevocably changed by Masters and Johnson, who have never clearly articulated their adherence to a particular theoretical orientation. Most scholars would agree, however, that the therapy done by this team drew primarily from a cognitive-behavioral approach that focused on information, education, skills learning, *in vivo* desensitization to deal with performance anxiety, and directive intervention. Of tremendous importance was the focus on the couple, and on making their sexual response cycles more satisfying and coordinated through at-home exercises. A variety of other cognitive-behavioral therapists expanded and added new elements to this approach to the treatment of low sexual desire (e.g., Lazarus, 1988; J. LoPiccolo & Friedman, 1988; L. LoPiccolo, 1980; Rosen & Leiblum, 1988; Zilbergeld & Ellison, 1980).

Psychodynamic components with particular attention to varying types of anxiety, remote and immediate, which might unconsciously impair desire, were deemed important by Kaplan (1979). Apfelbaum (1988) took a further step by coining the term "response anxiety" to describe performance anxiety about desire or, more specifically, anxiety about not feeling aroused. He differentiates this from his view of Masters and Johnson's performance anxiety, which is the fear of not being able to perform, as a difference between a concern for subjective sexual response versus physical sexual response. Other analytic therapists have focused on an object relations approach, both in the individual and the couple (D. Scharff, 1988; D. Scharff & J. Scharff, 1987). Early experiences (relationships) with primary caregivers (objects), particularly with respect to the internalization of imprints of good as well as painful or rejecting others, are thought to be important in understanding patients prior to embarking on treatment. Projective identification in the transference–countertransference relationship is the basis of the actual object relations approach to sexual therapy with couples.

Another therapeutic model proposed to improve the capacity to treat low sexual desire is a systemic approach (Schnarch, 1991; Verhulst & Heiman, 1988). Conceptualization and treatment from a systemic perspective allows for interacting subsystems (physical, affective, symbolic) within an individual, as well as between individuals. It may be particularly useful in cases in which a relationship problem is an embedded part of the desire complaint and the pathway from the cause to the problem to the solution is not linear. Past and current interactional patterns, stuck or changing, are the usual focus of the therapeutic process.

The research on couple treatment of inhibited sexual desire consists primarily of studies using variations of Masters and Johnson's framework (see Table 23.1). Criticism that has been leveled at sex therapy outcome research in general (Hogan, 1978; J. LoPiccolo & Stock, 1986; Sotile & Kilmann, 1977; Zilbergeld & Kilmann, 1984) applies to these studies as well: None includes a control group; measures of sexual function and outcomes are often subjective or vague; and follow-ups often cover only limited periods of time. Furthermore, some studies incorporated heterogeneous samples. Presenting problems included desire problems, as well as sexual aversion (Schover & J. LoPiccolo, 1982), arousal difficulties (Carney, Bancroft, & Mathews, 1978; Mathews et al., 1976; Mathews, Whitehead, & Kellett, 1983; Whitehead & Mathews, 1977, 1986), or other sexual dysfunctions (DeAmicis,

TABLE 23.1. Summary of Clinical Studies Including Low Sexual Desire in Couples

Authors (year)	Subjects	HSD definition	Therapy	Outcome
Mathews et al. (1976)	36 couples, 18 male, 18 female identified patients. 13/18 wives of male patients, and 17/18 female patients had interest and/or arousal problems. Male complaints involved erectile and/or ejaculatory problems.	"Generally low interest in, and arousal by, sexual relations."	1. Systematic desensitization and counseling. 2. Directed practice[a] and counseling. 3. Directed practice[a] and minimal contact. All: 10 weeks (meeting with, or letter from, therapist). Individual therapist or male–female teams.	• Somewhat better outcome with (2), according to raters. • Male patients and their wives had more improvement in sexual function. • Therapist rated female enjoyment improved with (2). • Warned about possible adverse effects from (3).
Whitehead & Mathews (1977)	Same as above.	Same as above.	Same as above.	• Semantic differential, by subject, showed some improvement with (2) for self-ratings about sexuality.
Carney, Bancroft, & Mathews (1978)	32 couples, female identified patient. Half each high and low anxiety.	Seems to incorporate "lack of interest in sex as well as a lack of sexual arousability."	1. "Modified" M&J[a] and counseling sessions—16 weekly and 5 monthly. 2. Females given testosterone or Valium. All couples kept weekly diary. Discussed problems with therapist, therapist provided "encouragement."	• Blind ratings by second author. • Somewhat more improvement with testosterone. • Females' ratings showed improvement in sexual feelings, satisfaction, and thoughts. • Gains maintained after testosterone stopped. • Males better with monthly sessions—self-rated as calmer, females rated males more loving.
Mathews, Whitehead, & Kellett (1983)	48 couples, female identified patient. Excluded re: psychopathology or marital problems, if needed "urgent clinical attention outside of sex therapy."	"Lack of sexual responsiveness . . . in the absence of severe vaginismus or impotence."	1. M&J[a] and Heiman et al.[b] exercises, counseling re: sex; book as needed (*Book of Love*). 2. Females given testosterone 10 mg/day, decreased over time, versus placebo. 3. Male–female cotherapists versus female therapist. 4. Weekly versus monthly sessions.	• Blind raters: females increased enjoyment, interest/arousal, orgasm, decreased aversion; improved male ejaculatory control; improved general relationship and sexual relationship. • Increased intercouse frequency with weekly sessions/placebo. • Males negative re: reactions to weekly sessions and cotherapist teams. • No benefit from testosterone. • Some evidence that females preferred weekly sessions.

(cont.)

TABLE 23.1. (cont.)

Authors (year)	Subjects	HSD definition	Therapy	Outcome
Whitehead & Mathews (1986)	Same as above.	Same as above.	Same as above.	• Blind raters—quality of sexual relationship 1–5. • 25 couples improved, 22 not improved. • Somewhat better effects for weekly and placebo or monthly and testosterone—but did not hold at 6-month follow-up. • Quality of general relationship according to couple and therapist, was related to improvement. • Females' pretreatment ratings of more pleasant and less unpleasant feelings about sex associated with improvement.
Schover & J. LoPiccolo (1982)	152 couples, from 747 intakes 1974–1981. 1 member low sexual desire or aversion to sex. Male HSD 58 (38%). Female HSD 67 (44%). Female aversion 27 (18%). Exclusion criteria included: HSD in both parties, and severe marital conflict or psychopathology.	Multiaxial[c]: 1. Low frequency of sexual activity. 2. Subjective lack of desire for sexual activity. Aversion: "a more severe point on a continuum of sexual avoidance behavior."	1. Behavioral sex therapy—including "behavioral, cognitive-behavioral, Gestalt, and psychodynamic interventions to supplement the usual sex therapy format." 2. Homework—sexual awareness, communication, increasing caring behavior, decreasing performance anxiety. 3. Usually 15 sessions, occasionally 20. 4. 1 or 2 therapists.	• LW[d] nonsignifcantly increased after therapy. • Sexual satisfaction increased after therapy. • Sexual frequency increased after therapy follow-up. • Increased equitable initiation of sex. • HSD-identified patient—increased responsiveness to partner initiations after therapy. • Aversion: "backslide" at 3-month follow-up, okay for sexual satisfaction at 1 year. • Describe overall outcomes as nondistressed but not optimal.
McCarthy (1984)	20 couples. 12 female HSD: 7 primary, 5 secondary. 3: both HSD.	Not specified, but refers to Kaplan (1979); Kolodny, Masters, & Johnson (1979); Zilbergeld & Ellison (1980).	Assessment focuses on marital respect, trust, intimacy, inhibitors of sexual desire—anxiety (response, performance); anger, guilt, reaction to sexual trauma. Overall: labeled cognitive-behavioral.	• Follow-up 1 year after treatment—1–7 scale of change in sexual problems. • 15 couples improved. • 1 worse, 2 "minimal change," 2 separated.

(cont.)

TABLE 23.1. (*cont.*)

Authors (year)	Subjects	HSD definition	Therapy	Outcome
McCarthy (*cont.*)	Over 2/3 had at least one other sexual dysfunction. Ascertained marital bond not "broken."		Exercises: 1. Increase comfort. 2. Attraction and increasing it. 3. Identify trust, vulnerability, "safe" positions during sex. 4. "Design and initiate a positive sexual scenerio." 5. Beliefs about function of sex. Cognitive restructuring; increasing comfort, receptivity, increase orgasm, frequency; sexual involvement (fantasy, scripts).	
DeAmicis et al. (1985)	38 couples treated 3 years prior for sexual dysfuntion— out of 104 couples treated 1975– 1978. "Lack of interest" reported by 14 males and 25 females. Diagnosis of HSD made for 6 males, 3 females; of aversion for 2 females. Aversion: 2 females. Other sexual dysfunctions —could have more than one diagnosis. Excluded re: "psychosis or severe depressive symptoms; impending separation or divorce."	Multiaxial[c] 1. Low frequency of sexual activity. 2. Subjective lack of desire for sexual activity.	1. Couple treatment. 2. 1/week × 15 weeks, up to 20 when necessary. 3. 74% ($n = 28$) male–female team. 4. 10% ($n = 4$) male therapist. 13% ($n = 5$) female therapist. 5. (1 couple–format unavailable.) 6. Homework assignments, "focus on sexual interactions, and time-limited therapy." 7. Overall sounds behavioral and partly cognitive. 8. Increased communication, "awareness of affective states and consequences of behaviors."	For HSD: • Increase at posttreatment, decrease below pretreatment at follow-up, for sexual frequency and frequency of desire for sexual contact. • Improvement at posttreatment and at follow-up in sexual satisfaction for males and females and in orgasm frequency for females. • *Note.* only 47% of original sample in follow-up.

(*cont.*)

TABLE 23.1. (*cont.*)

Authors (year)	Subjects	HSD definition	Therapy	Outcome
Hawton, Catalan, & Fagg (1991)	60 couples, female HSD; 14 (23%) primary, 46 (77%) secondary. In 22 (37%), male also had a sexual problem. Excluded re: "Severe marital problems, major psychiatric disorder (including alcoholism), current infidelity or pregnancy."	"Persistent and marked impairment of interest in sex and, usually, a relatively low frequency of sexual activity."	• M&J,[a] individual therapists, weekly sessions. • Allowed for sessions with just one partner, if needed. • Homework assignments. • Mean of 11.6 ($\pm$ 4.9) session, range 2–25. • Mean of 13.9 ($\pm$ 3.6) sessions, range 7–25 for completers. • 14 (23%) dropped out, 6 (10%) terminated by therapist, 2 (3%) others did not complete treatment.	• Rating by therapist of change in presenting problem, 1–5 scale. • At 3 months, 28/42 (47%) improved. • Of 38 completers, 32 (84%) improved. • *Patient reports:* Increased pleasant, decreased unpleasant feelings about specific sexual situations. Significant for females, nonsignificant for males. • General relationship improved—significant for males, nonsignificant for females.

[a]Based on Masters & Johnson (1970).
[b]Based on Heiman, LoPiccolo, & LoPiccolo (1976).
[c]Schover, Friedman, Weiler, Heiman, & LoPiccolo (1982).
[d]Locke–Wallace Marital Adjustment Inventory.

Goldberg, J. LoPiccolo, Friedman, & Davies, 1985; Hawton, Catalan, & Fagg, 1991; McCarthy, 1984). Additionally, subjects were often excluded from these studies on the basis of individual psychopathology or marital conflict that was judged by the researchers as problematic enough to potentially interfere with a sex therapy treatment approach. Thus, the effectiveness of any treatment approach to cases with a wider range of psychopathology or marital problems remains unknown.

Overall, it appears that the studies summarized in Table 23.1 incorporated aspects of all or most of the following intervention techniques: education/information about sexual functioning, cognitive techniques (e.g., investigating and changing beliefs), and behavioral interventions (communication exercises, sexual homework assignments). Some studies also allowed for processing of affective reactions to the assignments (DeAmicis et al., 1985; Schover & J. LoPiccolo, 1982) and discussion of nonsexual marital issues (McCarthy, 1984). Interestingly, it was often observed by the researchers that sustained increases in sexual satisfaction were reported by clients, even when little or no change was made in specific sexual complaints.

Given the lack of specifics on therapy components, diversity of subjects and outcome criteria, and high rates of attrition during treatment and follow-up, one cannot readily attribute greater effectiveness to one therapeutic approach over another. Rather, until the definitional and conceptual problems in the area are more settled, the therapeutically most conscientious position is one that can accommodate multiple theoretical frameworks and permit the therapist flexibility of interpretation and action. We have selected a systemic approach for these reasons as well as the following advantages: (1) it is interactional while taking the individual into account, (2) it allows for the integration of the physical with the psychosocial, and (3) it does not require deficiency and pathology constructs in order to understand and treat sexual disorders.

A detailed systemic perspective on low sexual desire is presented elsewhere (Verhulst & Heiman, 1988). Here the model will be briefly summarized so that more attention can be devoted to therapeutic interventions derived from it. The model describes three levels of interactions— (1) symbolic, (2) affect-regulated and (3) sensate exchanges—each of which can enhance or diminish sexual desire between two people.

Symbolic interactions refer to the formal exchange of language and symbolic gestures. Individuals need some type of common language to communicate and need to be of sufficiently close cultural background to follow each other's reasoning and presentation. A poor symbolic interactional fit often leads to mistrust, as exemplified by religious disputes among nations and within couples. A good interactional fit on a symbolic level is marked by finding common ground and tuning into each other's worldviews. As should be clear, not everyone is attracted to people with whom they have a "good fit" on a symbolic level and that can be a source of fascinating complementarity or increasing distance in certain couples.

Affect-regulated interaction refers to those aspects of communication governed and coordinated by the affective states of the participants. When partners tune into their own sexual feelings and the others' sexual expressions, a sexual context of meaning is created. However, what can happen and often predominates in couples in sex therapy is that the sexual context breaks down and nonsexual interactions take over. Common nonsexual interactions include (1) attachment interactions that focus on the establishment, preservation, and intensity regulation of the affective bond; (2) exploratory interactions that focus on the establishment and maintenance of familiarity through sensory contact; (3) territorial interactions that focus on the acquisition, management, and defense of ownership rights over space, one's body and other possessions; and (4) ranking-order interactions that focus on the acquisition and defense of social position or status, conferring decision-making powers on the possessor. Nonsexual interactions are not antisexual interactions. Any of these affective interactions can augment or detract from sexual desire and response. It is only when they dominate the entire interaction that the sexual feelings and responses are impaired (see Verhulst & Heiman, 1979, for more details on this level).

It is quite common in low-desire cases to see some disturbance in territorial and ranking-order interactions.

In one couple, for example, the wife felt that it was her husband's responsibility to share his body with her sexually and she made it very difficult for him if he said no (i.e., she felt she had some ownership over his sexual feelings). Because he said "no" to sex anyway, he felt guilty and tended to never say "no" to his wife in the other areas of their marriage. This left him resentful and feeling dominated, which in turn maintained the struggle in the sexual area. This interactional pattern contributed to his chronic, low sexual desire.

In another instance a 42-year-old former bachelor, married for less than 1 year and recently the father of twins and an 11-year-old stepson, was experiencing no desire for his wife. The patient revealed a strong need to be a responsible and "superachieving" father and husband. He felt he needed to cook gourmet meals for his wife (he was a chef by trade), play sports with his stepson on demand, and allow his wife adequate rest from the twins when he arrived home from work. When the therapist examined the source of his drive to achieve, the patient described himself as the "shining light" in his family of origin, which was weighed down by his severely retarded sister. As a child, he felt unable to ask for anything and received positive feedback only by being helpful, "a good boy," always accessible. In the current relationship the patient's sexual desire was the only area that he kept for himself (he engaged in frequent masturbation). His wife had benefited from all of his effort around the home, but at the cost of a sexual relationship, which she felt was too high. When she understood a bit more about his history, and the necessity of needing his own territory, she was able to let go of her belief that he had just been withholding from her. As a result, her anger decreased and with the therapist's encouragement, she was able to express appreciation (both in-session and at home) for what he was, as opposed to what he did for her, and he began to allow himself more time and space. His sexual desire for his wife soon resurfaced.

Affect-regulated interactions are normal and continuous in relationships. They can enhance the sexual quality of the interaction with some couples under certain conditions (e.g., some ranking-order interactions, with dominance and submission roles, can augment sexual desire and arousal), or they can predominate and neutralize sexual feelings (e.g., a person being raped experiences a territorial invasion, robbed of any sexual feelings).

Sensate exchange of sexual interactions focuses on the sensory patterns, the direct neurophysiological responses, and the motor reflexes that each partner elicits in the other. An interactional fit at the sensory-exchange level means that each individual reacts to and produces sensory stimulation at a pace that does not interfere with, or even enhances, sexual response in the other. Some sexual desire problems originate out of a very different pace of sexual arousal and orgasm in each individual, such as premature ejaculation. Some partners of men with long-term premature ejaculation are at risk for losing their desire in part because the poor interactional fit at the sensory level interferes with a satisfying sexual experience. Attending to the sensory exchange pattern by dealing with any physical symptoms can help prevent later desire problems.

The three levels of interaction discussed here are intimately connected with each other. In part, one needs to imagine them interacting all the time within two larger systems: the individual and the couple. Feedback loops among each of these subsystems, as well as homeostatic and recursive properties help to determine which interactional patterns will predominate with different couples. It also helps to point to which interactional patterns may be useful in treatment recommendations.

The utility of this model for low sexual desire is that it allows the therapist to look for interactional patterns and interactional solutions, which are often less threatening and blaming for couples. Both the person complaining of low sexual desire and the partner often feel very uncomfortable about not having what they are supposed to have and not being desirable enough. This is a disorder that is more easily personalized than many of the disorders with a physical-symptom basis. It is easier to say "My body doesn't work" than it is to say "I've lost my desire." The latter implies a broader, more pervasive impairment to the person and between the partners. This factor may be related to the difficulty in treating these couples because on some level each feels to blame and defensive.

THE PROCESS OF CHANGE

Change of sexual desire comes from thinking, feeling and/or behaving differently, or more precisely in a systemic model, changes occur at symbolic, affective, and/or sensory levels. A change at one level does not predict anything specific at another. However, if change is of adequate intensity, one would expect some degree of ripple effect and coordination across other levels. Although couples expect a change in desire to manifest in their behavior of having more frequent sex, this is not necessarily the case. And the therapist who believes that decreasing conflict and hostility will automatically lead to an enhanced sexual relationship will be disappointed.

Therapists can be useful in the change process by arranging circumstances both during and outside of therapy in which different ways of thinking, feeling, and behaving can occur. As important, the therapist can also offer to the clients new ways of understanding and conceptualizing the problem on any one of the levels. To do this with some success, however, the therapist must find an explanation that fits several levels of the couple's reality. Reframing with an eye toward interactional fit is one approach. For an obvious example, a man with low sexual desire was married to a woman who as a 13-year-old had experienced repeated sexual fondling from her adoptive father. One of the starting points for the therapy was to reframe the woman's view of her husband as sexually rejecting to one of her husband as sexually protective. This intervention seemed to fit with the underlying feelings of the couple, and facilitated a more collaborative, less blameful working alliance in the early stages of treatment.

The primary ingredients for change, however, are the couple. How the partner reacts to change becomes part of the process that augments or inhibits further movement. Most people want conscious and unconscious assurances that change will be better than nonchange. This issue is at the heart of resistance/conflict about change. As suggested earlier, it is critical for the therapist to appreciate and understand the nonchange position. An example early in treatment is to avoid aligning with the non-HSD partner's overt quest to increase the HSD partner's sexual desire level. This addresses two basic messages: (1) that the therapist will not pressure for more sex in the relationship and will not collude with either partner against the other, and (2) the option of no change can be as soberly and nonjudgmentally entertained as the option to change. While this therapeutic position of aligning with the resistance is well known in couple and family work, it is particularly important in treating sexual problems. Lack of change in the sexual arena may be protecting a more threatening change elsewhere in the relationship. In addition, some couples feel internalized cultural pressure to be more sexual, although with some therapeutic permission, they would be quite satisfied with the status quo of infrequent sex.

Diagnosis and Assessment

In DSM-IV (APA, 1994), HSD disorder can be either primary or secondary to another sexual dysfunction; all other Axis I disorders (clinical psychiatric syndromes and V codes) and Axis III disorders (physical disorders and conditions) need to be ruled out as the primary diagnosis. In addition, the disorder should not be substance induced (drugs, medications) or due to a secondary sexual dysfunction. Similarly, other primary Axis I disorders, except for a sexual dysfunction, need to be ruled out in the diagnosis of sexual aversion disorder. A discussion of the problem of the DSM-IV nosology is beyond the scope of the present paper. However, it is important to note that absence and deficiency are decided on by the clinical assessor, based on variables such as age, sex, and life context about which there are essentially no data for sexual desire, and that one of the V codes is relationship problems, about which it is usually difficult to discern primary or secondary status.

What the DSM-IV definition does underscore is that HSD is not merely a difference in desire between two people (cf. Zilbergeld & Ellison, 1980). That clinical situation exists and sometimes requires intervention if it is distressing to a couple. However, the more troublesome problem is when one person is noticeably lacking in desire and that person or the partner is voicing a complaint. One of the helpful additions to the DSM-IV is the inclusion of the criterion that "the disturbance must cause marked distress or interpersonal difficulty" (APA, 1994, p. 496). A number of couples adjust to infrequent or no sex and thus no longer complain of it. They come to therapy, if at all, to be informed that the choice is theirs if it does not interfere with their sense of personal identity or their relationship satisfaction.

A careful *description* of the problem(s) is the first issue. Both partners are included in the assessment that centers around a careful description of the problem in formal assessment and interview. The categories of importance are as follows:

Individual patterns: Current and historical, physical health including illness, surgeries and medications; psychological functioning; solo sexual activity such as masturbation and fantasy; gender identity; sexual orientation.
Interpersonal patterns: Current and historical relationships; family patterns; sexual relationships.
Sociocultural patterns: Current and historical beliefs about sex; gender, sexual orientation; importance of religion.

Several comments on the above factors are in order. First, as in other sexual disorders, a variety of physical conditions may impair sexual desire. Illness or physical traumas that interfere with general vitality may interfere with sexual desire. In global loss of desire, a neuroendocrine imbalance is possible. For these reasons, men with hypoactive desire are often encouraged to have their levels of testosterone, luteinizing hormone, and prolactin tested. There is insufficient and inconsistent research on the female endocrine system and sexual desire to recommend endocrine testing. Changes throughout the menstrual cycle appear to be idiosyncratic rather than standard. Similarly, the evidence concerning desire changes with natural or surgical menopause does not convincingly show that endocrinological factors are etiologically involved. Interesting experimental work with androgen–estrogen replacement for surgically menopausal women has shown increases in desire, arousal, and fantasy (Sherwin, Gelfand, & Brender, 1985), but the clinical efficacy of this regimen has yet to be confirmed. Hyperprolactinemia can be associated with decreased sexual desire in women as well as men. However, there is minimal evidence pointing to the prevalence of serious pituitary disorders in women with an isolated complaint of low sexual desire. For this reason, routine serum prolactin evaluation is not currently advised for women. Segraves (1988a) has advised all female patients be referred for evaluation if there is evidence of menstrual irregularity. In either sex, a report of genital pain during or after coitus is an indication for referral to a physician with an interest in sexual medicine.

Depression is another condition that may present as the cause of low desire. In actual practice, it is rare for individuals to present with low desire as the primary symptom of depression. More likely is that a level of depression has been overlooked (more often by males) or adapted to (more common in females) for months or even years, and thus it has escaped diagnosis and treatment. Although in some cases the sexual disorder and depression can be treated nearly concurrently, depressive symptoms usually need to be treated first in order to clarify the role and possibly the source of the sexual problem. A middle-aged couple entered treatment after having been part of an experimental drug study for HSD over the previous 2 years. They had been married for 20 years and for the past 5 years described chronic low sexual desire in the husband. During the initial sessions he was quite tearful and described feelings of hopelessness, worthlessness, and that "life had passed [him] by." At this point the patient's symptoms of depression needed attention before the couple's sexual difficulties could be fully addressed.

Alcohol and recreational drug use have important effects on sexual response as they affect vascular and neural functioning. Narcotics consistently dampen desire as does longer term or heavy cocaine use, in spite of brief aphrodisiac-like effects. Alcohol can be used to mask discomfort at being sexual, lack of sexual desire, and various expressions of lack of intimacy with a partner. Conversely, an alcoholic partner can be one of the factors that contributes to embedded anger and low desire in the spouse. Even after removal of the active alcohol problem, bitter resentment may continue for years. A woman currently in treatment has lost all sexual desire for her husband. She described 8 of their 13 years of marriage, in which he drank heavily, as feeling treated sexually as "a thing, rather than a person." Her situation is complicated by the fact that this feeling replicated what she felt with her stepfather, who was a drug abuser and who had sexual contact with her when she was a preadolescent.

Prescription medications often have effects on sexual desire directly, or indirectly, by affecting sexual arousal or orgasmic ease. Drugs likely to affect libido are hypotensive agents (adrenergic-inhibiting agents as well as diuretics), psychiatric drugs, anticonvulsant drugs, chemotherapy agents for cancer, as well as drugs used to treat cardiac failure, glaucoma, and excessive appetite. Although many of these findings are based on case studies, the message to therapists is to check which medications a patient is taking, be aware of their side effects, and consider a consultation with the individual's physician to determine whether a dosage adjustment or medication change would be medically appropriate (see Segraves, 1988b, for further information).

The psychological effects of physical illness are unpredictable but need to be considered in evaluating patients' desire problems. A confrontation with mortality and loss, the loss of sensory acuity, and the effects of medical treatments (surgery, radiation, chemotherapy) on body image and well-being may contribute to persons' feeling undesirable themselves and undesiring of their partner. Partners also, unpredictably, may have their own reactions and be unable to confront a partner's illness and all its meanings.

In addition, a careful evaluation of the sexual problem needs to include a multiaxial diagnosis (Schover, Friedman, Weiler, Heiman, & J. LoPiccolo, 1982). Such an approach clarifies whether there are problems not just in sexual desire, but in *arousal, orgasm, pain,* and *satisfaction* dimensions, and any *qualifying information,* such as sexual orientation impacting partner choice, hurtful affairs, or paraphilias. A brief review of these domains should combine them with qualifiers as to whether they are generalized or situational, and lifelong or acquired. Assessing for other sexual dysfunctions is important because the presence of other sexual disorders may be impairing desire (e.g., sex becomes frustrating rather than enjoyable). Also, it is not uncommon for an arousal or orgasm problem to mask a sexual desire problem, either because the therapist was not observant or because the couple was afraid to raise it (e.g., Kaplan, 1979). Undiagnosed and untreated problems of low sexual desire have been blamed for the relapse rate noted in several longer term studies (3 months to 1 year) following sex therapy for arousal, orgasm, and pain disorders (J. LoPiccolo & Friedman, 1988).

Key aspects of the preceding material can be gathered in one to two sessions. Written and formal assessment tools that we often use to assist this process include a Medical History Form, the Dyadic Adjustment Scale (Spanier, 1976), the Brief Symptom Inventory (Derogatis & Spencer, 1982), and a Life Stress Scale (Sarason, Johnson, & Siegel, 1978), all completed by couples prior to the first session. A Sex Behavior Form (e.g., Nowinski & LoPiccolo, 1979), asking about sexual functioning, desire and satisfaction, is often completed at the end of Session 1. Cooperativeness in filling out these forms is usually excellent, partly because the time saved covering repetitive basic material is substantial. They also provide a mechanism of formal feedback for patients that is reassuring to some couples.

Assessment can extend well into the treatment as more difficult themes are explored.

For example, a couple who had been in treatment for 9 months for the husband's HSD was making no headway and the therapist decided to meet individually with each partner. During each individual session, very important new sexual information was obtained. For the husband, sex was not satisfying. He felt his partner was unresponsive and disconnected ("not there") during sex. However, he was too protective of himself and his partner to bring up these complaints when he was in session with her. Likewise she reported a 10-year sexual history of bondage and anal sex with her husband that had ended a few years earlier but still negatively affected her. She had been unable to discuss these issues for fear of betraying her husband. With the permission of each spouse, each person's reactions were explored in a joint session. The structure of the joint session preceded by a sense of safety and rehearsal alone with the therapist was useful. The husband was able to respond to the information by reflecting upon ways in which he felt powerless both within his relationship with his partner and children and also in his professional life. Sex had been the only area in which he had felt powerful. He was aware that his wife had been unhappy about his sexual interests and that he had consequently "shut down" his sexual desire. At this point, the couple could honestly engage in a discussion of their sexual preferences and the ways in which they both felt that their sexual needs were not getting met. She stated that sex for her was a more spiritual activity and that she was unhappy with her husband's inability to connect with these feelings. He stated that his sexual self was more aggressive than spiritual and that he wished his wife could join him on this level. Given their mismatched needs during sex, they discussed the value of a "no sex" relationship. Whereas this is not a good resolution for all couples, it can be a useful real or paradoxical position. They agreed to embark on this road while remaining committed to the relationship with reasonable success and satisfaction.

Thus the collaborative use of "reassessment" during therapy allows treatment to proceed to a more authentic level of understanding.

Treatment Goals

The goals of treatment center around two questions: (1) Can sexual desire become integrated into an individual's experience/identity of him/herself? (2) Can sexual desire become integrated into *each* spouse's experience of the relationship? If the answer, after some exploration in therapy, to either of these questions is "no," then the treatment goals typically shift to issues about individual and relationship identity. Commitment to the relationship is essential to explore.

Often, the answers to these questions are "maybe" or more precisely, "yes and no." In this case, the therapist's goals are to clarify the conflicted issues around this topic for both partners, confronting the cost of change, and searching for a fertile interactional environment in which sexual desire may be able to emerge.

It is important not to agree to a goal of directly pursuing increased sexual desire. Therapists who promise desire may find that they, through their promise to increase desire without knowl-

edge of its effects on the players, become embedded in the problem rather than a liaison to a solution. Sometimes the conflicts around the search for desire are obvious. One man involved with a woman for 2 years complained of a loss of desire and stated that until he was assured of a satisfying sexual relationship, he would not commit to marriage. When examined more fully, the man revealed significant fear attached to intimacy and primary relationships due to a history of humiliation and shame from parental relationships, peers, and romantic attachments. The sexual difficulties were conveniently distracting and protecting him from confronting deeper issues that themselves were very ingrained in his affective interactional experience.

Structure of Sessions

The original sex therapy model of daily sessions secluded from one's usual routine is still recommended by the Masters and Johnson Institute (Schwartz & Masters, 1988), but is rarely practiced because of its impracticality for most couples. Although there have been no outcome studies on sexual desire and treatment modality, at least one study has found no difference on sexual and marital variables in the effectiveness of daily versus weekly treatment sessions for other sexual dysfunctions (Heiman & J. LoPiccolo, 1983). However, the seclusion factor was not included in this study because all couples continued their daily work and home routines while engaged in therapy.

Most studies in Table 23.1 utilized weekly sessions. In Whitehead and Mathews (1986), an interactional effect was found for frequency (weekly vs. monthly) and medication condition (testosterone/placebo). This finding was not predicted or readily explainable, and effects did not last at 6-month follow-up, leaving the authors unable to make recommendations regarding frequency. Carney et al. (1978) reported some evidence that males had more negative reactions to weekly as opposed to monthly counseling, and Mathews et al. (1983) reported negative reactions of males to weekly sessions with male–female cotherapy teams.

Therapists are divided on how exclusively they prefer to work with the couple and are more likely to include some individual sessions in HSD cases than in other sexual dysfunctions. Once a therapeutic relationship is established with the couple, it can be helpful to meet individually with each partner, especially when the treatment appears to be stuck. New information may be obtained during these sessions. Because of mutual protectiveness in which the couple engages in joint therapy sessions, hurtful or potentially embarrassing information may be censored and thus the therapy process becomes stalemated. It is extremely useful to individually confront and explore this protective shield and help the couple to find a way to utilize this new information. Occasionally there are secrets revealed, such as current affairs that patients are unwilling to discuss or alter, that interfere with movement in the current relationship, or that stalemate the therapist's ability to function well. However, this is in fact rarer than one might imagine and should not by itself force the avoidance of any individual sessions.

An alternative approach is to force the issue in couple work by continuing to meet with the couple, acknowledge the stalemate, and suggest that either therapy may need to terminate or yet undiscussed issues may need to be addressed. Providing choices of action and enlisting the patients as coactors are important in this strategy.

Sessions are focused on encouraging both persons to express their view or experience of an issue at hand and watching to see that they are heard. A no-therapy framework may need to be set up for the first few sessions to decrease defensiveness and pressure on the low-desire partner and to allow a deeper level of discussion to surface. Assignments are a typical part of most sessions, so that feedback on the assignments, completed or not, takes some of the hour.

THE THERAPEUTIC PROCESS: INTERVENTIONS AND STRATEGIES

Early in therapy, the task of the therapist and clients is to explore the content, context, and function of the sexual desire complaint in order to propose interventions. As therapy progresses, the level of integration or isolation of sexual factors from other patterns becomes clearer. The evolution of the process of therapy for low sexual desire usually needs to attend to the following areas:

1. Careful description of the complaints from each person.
2. An understanding and formulation of key interactional themes for each person, especially as they relate to sexuality.
3. Flexible interventions based on interactional themes.

Describing the Complaint

A recent couple came in with her complaint consisting of lack of desire and his complaint being her lack of "pleasure," by which he meant orgasm. Upon discussion, a picture emerged in which she was never easily orgasmic and had begun a masturbation program that helped to achieve masturbatory orgasms but seemed to increase the pressure on her. Her partner inadvertently contributed to this pressure because her orgasm reassured him that he was a good sexual partner. The woman, sensitive to any sign of failure and judgment, gradually lost her desire.

In this case, the initial complaints of *both* partners give a lot of information about what may be the basis of the low desire, and certainly a first step is to describe this pattern leading from infrequent orgasm (with high desire) to pressure to be orgasmic, to greater difficulty with sexual response, to low desire. Interactionally, there was a descriptive fit between his need to be reassured and her need to please. This kind of beginning, when reflected back to the couple, can start the process of change.

Content is therefore important, and listening to how complaints are made, and the order and emphasis each person gives to them, is an important part of this process. It is important to ask and listen for what sexual desire (and its absence) means to each person and begin to understand how sex may summarize what the particular couple wants to say about themselves or their relationship. Often sex is a nonverbal expression for what is avoided or inaccessible verbally, such as marital unhappiness, a power struggle, emotional emptiness, or existential anxieties or losses.

A middle-aged man with a long-standing history of low sexual desire described a recent dream. Most powerful was the image of a man who was being beaten to death by a group of other men. The patient related this to his feeling that he had not only "beaten down" or "been beaten down" sexually but also felt this applied to his professional achievements and role in the family. He related this to early messages from his mother that men were "no good," and from his father that he was not "man enough." He felt that he had held himself back in an attempt to not be like "those kinds" of men and therefore never fully participated in any endeavor or relationship. Thus, the sexual symptom was one of a series of lost or unrealized experiences of his identity, while at the same time being a symbolic solution to the double bind his parents presented to him.

Context, both affective and symbolic, is also important. The verbal and nonverbal reactions of each person, the range of emotions expressed, apparent differences in emotional investment, and the responses evoked in the therapist are all important to incorporate in an understanding of the problem and its effect on the participants.

Finally, how the sexual symptom might serve the individuals and the relationship needs some exploration. Although sexual problems are not necessarily invented by a couple to solve other interactional problems, they are often maintained in part because they have some utility or become incorporated into broader relationship patterns. Removing them would make other aspects of the relationship change unpredictably or intolerably. One can ask couples what would happen, both positively and negatively, if the low desire problem were immediately removed. Often people respond with surprisingly helpful (to the therapist) comments. The expectation of increased demands to be sexual as well as giving up time, control, and autonomy are often voiced and give the therapist clues for what the issues of therapy will be. Individuals who claim that life and marriage will be wonderful when desire problems are better eventually need to probe or confront this conclusion in order to reduce the pressure on the symptom. It is also important to clarify whether each person is changing for him/herself or the other. If people acknowledge absolutely no reason that they are in treatment, except to please the other partner, the therapist is in for resentment and ranking-order interaction problems. Women with HSD are more likely than men to state that they are only there for their partner or the relationship, perhaps because it is more culturally acceptable for women to accept sexual disinterest in themselves. The therapist has several choices if this is the case. One direction would be to clarify each partner's interest in treatment and to develop some common ground from which to work. Alternatively, the therapist could "prescribe their symptom"—encourage change for the sake of the other until the partners realize the absurdity of that direction.

The relationship also helps to maintain and take the blame for each individual's intrapsychic issues. For example, the middle-aged man who felt he had "beaten down" or "been beaten down" sexually, initially blamed his wife's rejecting and disinterested sexual position. Although she contributed to his ambivalence about his masculinity, she did not create it. This is an important distinction for the therapist to examine in order

to create in the couple a sense of personal responsibility in the eventual solution. Sometimes this can be done very provocatively, if there is adequate rapport, by saying something like, "How was she powerful enough to crush your masculinity?" or more evocatively, by wondering with the patient, "How is it that you have never been able to develop enough of a sense of your masculinity to withstand her sexual disinterest?" In both cases the therapist would still examine the wife's investment in either image, given her experience with sexuality, men, and power.

The therapeutic atmosphere should be one that optimizes the development of a very custom-made sexual life. In some cases, this may be a greater sexual frequency and higher level of passion. A new level of intimacy and sexual experimentation may be required, which may be frightening to the participants and thus accompanied by therapeutic fits and starts. At the other end of the spectrum is the possibility of infrequent sex, or of eliminating sex. In these cases, the exploration needs to include discussion (and home trials) of physical but nonsexual affection, a loving and attentive but nonsexual atmosphere, and the role of sex outside of the relationship. Most therapists lean toward increasing sexuality in a relationship, perhaps because they evolve out of the same "be sexual" culture as their patients. Yet we have no idea whether it is reasonable to desire and have sexual contact with the same partner for more than a few years. Blumstein and Schwartz (1983) have made the point that there is considerable variability in sexual frequency. Comparing couples after 10 or more years of involvement in ongoing, committed relationships, those having sex $\leq$ 1/month included 15% of heterosexual couples, 33% of gay male couples, and 47% of lesbian couples (those having sex $\geq$ 3/week included 18% of heterosexual couples, 11% of gay male couples and 1% of lesbian couples).

In fact, no one has to have sex to be a loving and good person or partner. The therapist needs to believe that a nonsexual relationship is as adequate an option in some cases as increased sexual desire and activity. The effect on the therapy is greater freedom of choice and thus less pressure—which can also translate into a paradoxical effect that enhances desire.

Understanding Key Interactional Themes and Using Them Flexibly in Interventions

Interactional themes will become increasingly clear when asking each person about how the couple gets along outside of sex (e.g., around work, play, and family care) and in approaching sex. Details about how sex was when it was better are important, along with what happened around the time that changes began. Usually this is a gradual process, but occasionally it is sudden, subsequent to a discovered affair, childbirth, or an illness. Sometimes this information is sufficient, but more distant relationship themes, those from one's family of origin, can also be valuable in constructing an understanding of key themes in intimate relationships, with special but not exclusive attention to sexuality. What follows is a discussion of the most prominent common themes to appear in working with low-desire couples. The affect-regulative interactional levels discussed earlier are used as a framework for organizing issues and interactions.

Ranking-Order Themes

One of the most prominent themes across low-desire couples can be summarized by ranking-order interactions, in which there are frequent references to who is felt to be in control over communication in the relationship, or over the relationship itself. It is sometimes felt as a struggle for power in determining who makes the decisions. Often the person who appears to be in charge is merely under the authority of another, as any driver who has ridden with a "backseat driver" can readily attest. In sexual desire problems, this pattern often takes the form of one person expressing, even pushing for sex (the apparent driver) and the other person refusing (the one in control of the couple's sexuality).

Ranking-order or dominance themes thus have to do with the power of saying "yes" or "I want" and "no" or "I don't want" *and* having those messages decide the course of action. The person who says "no" to sex controls that interaction by stopping the initiation of the partner. The person who is disinterested in sex, who has far less interest than the partner, is always saying "no" in some sense and thus is in the more powerful position with respect to the sexual relationship. The frustration of the partner who unsuccessfully initiates is only partly the immediate rejection sting; the longer term resentment is born out of the sense of powerlessness.

It is important in these cases to further examine ranking-order interaction in other areas. Do many areas turn into ranking-order disputes? All couples are affected by dominance and power issues, and most work out ways to balance the areas of control. One balance is for one person to be

dominant and the other submissive most of the time. If those roles are agreeable and valued, they can work well. However, a substantial number of couples desire a more equivalent role structure, which requires a great deal of flexibility, clear understandings of who decides about what, and/or the willingness to periodically do battle over areas of mutual investment.

Decision making occurs around major and minor issues, for example, how money is saved and spent, household caretaking tasks, the raising of children, or the use of free time. In a number of heterosexual couples, particularly in which the male reports HSD, his partner either makes or tries to make the majority of decisions about the relationship, trying to steer things in her direction. The man is often so busy reacting to her controlling that he does not think about what he wants. There is a push from the woman for more, and a push back—either directly or passively—from the man. The area that remains protected from his partner is his sexual desire. Often both people feel powerless to influence the other. Insight into the problem rarely produces change by itself.

Issues to address depend on the couple. *Working on assertiveness* to help initiation and refusal, as well as positive and negative reactions to them, can be seen as affirmative by both people. Trying this in a nonsexual area can be an easier start, as it may create a better balance. In-session opportunities for assertiveness between partners or with the therapist and partners can be illuminating and should be sought out. However it may not, and usually does not, generalize to the sexual area, so specific attention is likely to be needed there. *Clarify why control is important* to each person and why each person wants neither to give in nor, in fact, to be in control of the other. Usually overcontrolling is a "default" position resulting from fears, self-preservation, and historical experiences with dominance–submission themes. Assignments to reverse control roles for several days can be helpful if the couple is not too withdrawn or hostile toward each other. *Pursue the pursuer* is a reliable guideline. The one who is trying to get sex will fail to do so if the pursuit of the partner continues—that is why they have come to treatment. The therapist needs to attend to the pursuer (as well as the pursued) in terms of why she/he wants sex, why it is so important and why it would be good, while looking for ranking-order and territoriality themes, such as "I need it to feel close"; "I need it to feel good about myself"; "It was part of 'our' agreement when we got together"; "That's what loving couples do." Confronting these assumptions about rights, ownership, and decision-making responsibility over the sexuality of the other is important in and of itself and to shift some of the pressure off of the HSD partner. *Reflecting and analyzing each person's contribution to the desire problem* should be an obvious intervention. This is not blame-oriented but solution-oriented, because it involves taking responsibility for one's own ideals, sensitivities, powers, and weaknesses in the relationship (and, thus, can help balance ranking-order interactions). Most couples have too many requirements for a sexual experience to be right (fatigue, energy levels, distress, anger, feeling distant), which need to be challenged in treatment. One couple in treatment, both of whom had desire problems following a history of bitter fighting and critique about each other's performance, gave themselves the exercise of just having sex four nights in a row, "no matter what." This was after several months of therapy. They managed two nights of sexual contact and felt that a spell was broken to allow them to move further.

A more extensive clinical example illustrates several of the above issues.

Susan and Daniel were a young couple who entered therapy on the verge of separating over what the wife called "infrequent and unsatisfying sex." She complained that her husband almost never initiated sex and that when he did so, he was tentative and "weak." After further exploration it became clear that she was constantly checking his performance not only sexually, but also in other areas—thus creating a series of ranking-order interactions. For example, when he took over the task of paying the bills, she would continually check to see that he had properly stapled the bill to the check, addressed the envelope correctly. He, in turn, would not challenge her interference but would respond with passive avoidance. He "forget" to do the bills and experienced little desire for his wife. During the course of treatment, he was encouraged to be more assertive (e.g., not complying with the submissive role, as he had been doing) in their relationship. A particularly important session occurred when the therapist made the couple aware of Susan's tendency to "speak for" her husband, telling him what he thought and felt. When the therapist repeatedly commented on this process, Daniel recognized that he felt infantilized by this behavior, as well as irritated by her assumption of knowing him better than he knew himself. The therapist, using ranking-order and territorial language, encouraged the husband to speak up when this was

happening and assisted Susan in hearing his position. For example, the therapist made comments about the necessity for Daniel to "take ownership over who you are and the tasks you commit to," and to resist Susan's attempts to exert quality control over him, giving her the message to stop "invading and directing" on these issues. As is often the case, Susan was hesitant to give up on her dominating interactions because they were her source of security and control, but at the same time was relieved to let go of the role of being a domineering nag. The therapist pushed this image a bit in order to allow Susan to let got more easily.

Outside of therapy, ranking-order themes began to change as well. For example, when the couple needed to have their car fixed, Daniel took total charge of investigating and repairing the problem because he knew more about this than did Susan. When she attempted to take over, he was able to tell her to "back off" and that he would take care of it. This was an extremely healing intervention, because she had wanted to be taken care of but was too anxious to allow him to do so. He wanted to feel "manly" and take care of her but had not been able to assert himself well enough to do so. This kind of interaction helped the husband feel more powerful and caretaking and helped her to feel less anxious and more nurtured. A similar ranking-order interaction occurred around sex. Daniel complained of entirely focusing on his wife's level of satisfaction during sex. It was suggested that he focus more on his desires and needs than on his wife's. For example, he had always wanted to watch an X-rated movie with his wife but had resisted suggesting this due to her previous statement that she was not excited by the idea. The therapist suggested he rent a movie that week and incorporate that into a sexual interaction. Susan did not like the video but also was not offended by it. Daniel reported enhanced sexual responsiveness as he was less concerned with her approval (or disapproval) during this interaction. He also found that he less wanted this specific activity, erotic videos, than he wanted to contribute to the definition of their sexual life. As these dominance–submission struggles decreased in several domains, and it was clear that both persons could meet some of their partner's needs without sacrificing their own identity, sex became more frequent and satisfying.

If we select out the role and activity of the therapist in this case, which is structurally like strategies used with other interactional themes, we have the following:

1. Looking for interactional patterns rather than individual personality pathology. Couples

come in with the blame-the-other perspective and it is obviously unhelpful for the therapist to contribute to this except perhaps during paradoxical interventions.

2. In this case the therapist made a deliberate intervention with the more submissive partner to be assertive, and at first in a nonsexual area that for initial change may be easier to tolerate (if there are indeed problems nonsexually). However, the assertive intervention took into account the wife's own role in the ranking-order interaction—her anxiety about not being taken care of. A pure, assertive response, without attention to the interactional context, could have resulted in increased hostility and dissatisfaction.

3. The therapist cocreated and used *in-session* interactions to illustrate the pattern and its emotional impact, getting the couple to remark on the experience rather than providing a lot of interpretation. The therapist also assigned, watched for, and discussed *out-of-session* examples of the target interactional pattern.

4. Territorial and ranking-order interactions were both involved in this example, as they often are with couples. The therapist may choose to bring out both interactional components or focus on the most prominent one.

5. A different but equally useful component would have been for the therapist to label the interaction as a ranking-order problem, explain what ranking-order interactions are and why they cause trouble. This allows the couple to participate in the same language and offers a conceptual reframing of the problem from "You're controlling—you're lazy" to "There are ranking order problems we need to solve." Notice that ranking order, as well as the other interactional patterns described are neither healthy or sick, but are in need of continuous balancing and adjusting depending on the individuals and the context involved.

Other therapists have taken different tacks in approaching low sexual desire and the subjective sense of control issues dominating the sexual interaction. Apfelbaum (1988), for example, proposes the concept of "response anxiety" (p. 81) to describe performance anxiety about desire. Low sexual desire, which he calls it "sexual apathy," is seen as a withdrawal response consequential to the pressure everyone is under to respond positively in relationships, especially to sex, since it is expected to be an automatic response. Sexual oppression does not easily disappear and is even embedded in different therapeutic approaches to its solution.

Psychodynamic sex therapists either see nonresponders as having an investment in their apathy or simply that this means the problem is deep-seated and therefore requires more extensive exploration or relationship therapy. Missing is the Masters and Johnson insight that the "sex-positive" reaction against what we call the "sexual drive phobia" represents a new tyranny. (Apfelbaum, 1988, p. 91)

His approach, an ego-analytic one, focuses on what is being resisted in the person who is not responding sexually. In a number of cases, resistance revolves around an avoidance of the awareness and the expression of dissatisfaction during sex. This expression is encouraged in conjoint sessions and with scheduled breaks during sensate focus exercises. Whatever reactions this engenders in the non-HSD partner allows the therapist to shift to that person's sexual issues, particularly as they relate to pressures around seeking and wanting sex, and thus decreases the pressure on the HSD partner to be solely responsible for change. Apfelbaum reports excellent success with this approach, although with numerous dropouts and greater difficulty if the male is the HSD partner.

Territorial Themes

Territorial interactions have to do with acquiring, managing and defending the ownership rights of physical or psychological space. For example, it is useful to have a sense of territorial ownership over one's own body. Some individuals have no sense of actively giving their body in sex—rather, their partner simply claims ownership. Women have more problems with this, perhaps because there are cultural messages, including legal and religious proscriptions, that their (male) marital partners own them. For sexual abuse survivors, physical territorial ownership is especially salient because they often feel that they experienced a territorial invasion during the abuse. However, there are also psychological territories. A number of years ago *The New Yorker* published a cartoon—a line drawing of a house in the form of an encompassing woman; the "woman" and "house" were the same form. Many heterosexual couples feel that the woman owns the home space, while the husband owns and manages the outside space. Because ownership implies decision making, ranking-order interactions often overlap with territorial ones. Thus, often subtly, the "woman" or "house person" in the case of gay and lesbian couples will set the standards about order, cleanliness, and decor that both people expect the non-home person to meet. But because this contract is covert, disagreements arise over style and perceived inconsideration, and perhaps even feeling neglected.

Territorial issues from other aspects of the relationship may invade the sexual arena. Sex is by definition a territorial interaction. Needs for territorial ownership vary. Some people need a lot of territory to feel comfortable, others do not. There are important differences in the extent to which one person will claim new territory and defend old territory. Since territoriality implies ownership, those aspects of the relationship seen as jointly owned (money, children) are more subject to ranking-order interactions (some people prefer to own more territory unilaterally, precisely because they can then call the shots and avoid getting into joint-decision squabbles). In therapy, one often sees couples in which the husband feels that the wife "owns" a lot of the social and family space in the relationship. Whereas this can be a good arrangement if agreed on (one does not have to be a territorial tyrant), it also leaves the husband on the outside of these spheres. Territorial issues arise even more for lesbian and gay couples, in which there are fewer guidelines for what is a committed relationship with separate and shared lives and goals.

A person's body is usually the basis from which a sense of territoriality develops. Except as young children or during serious illness, people develop a strong sense that their body belongs to them. Experiences such as abuse can alter that feeling, leaving questions about ownership over one's body. Similarly, disliking one's body is a form of territorial rejection that can lead to selecting partners for overt reassurance or covert confirmation of the negative feelings. Disliking one's body can also impair sexual desire, with great suspicions about any partner who might enjoy it.

For example, Paulette, who had been molested by her father at an early age, initially entered therapy complaining that her husband had lost all sexual desire. On further exploration, the therapist found that 10 years previously, when the couple stopped having regular sex, the husband, David, had reported a regular and angry rejecting response from his wife whenever he attempted to initiate sex. She called him "an animal" and was repulsed by his "pawing and constant need for sex." It was at this time that he decided he would no longer initiate sex with her and subsequently lost all desire for her. Thus, although his wife was unhappy about her husband's current low desire, on some level she was able to have rights to her body without having to reject or displease him. The therapist pointed this

out to the couple, emphasizing the fact that their current sexual difficulty was at the same time a problem and a solution. Stating this can have several related effects: It can reframe the nature of the problem; it can call into question the type of intervention needed; and it can refocus the pressure from the one everyone thought was to blame to a more complex and constructive picture.

Indeed, the couple corroborated and expanded the idea. They tentatively and then more convincingly agreed that because it was quite difficult for Paulette to directly make claims over her own body, and because it had been difficult for David to hear her (he would accuse her of not loving him when she refused to have sex), this no-sex arrangement was a less stressful solution for both partners than many others would have been. Subsequently in treatment, this couple was able to make use of therapeutic interventions that addressed the historical and current issues around the power of territorial themes for them. By conceptualizing the struggle as primarily a territorial one rather than just a difference in sexual desire, the couple was able to see themselves as mutually responsible for the current state of affairs. Previously the husband had blamed his wife for his HSD ("She got what she asked for"). Paulette entered treatment, stating that she had done everything she could think of to spark his desire, to no avail. During treatment David recognized that punishing his wife for her rejecting response was self-protective and avoidant. Paulette realized that in some ways her husband had listened to her messages of "Leave me alone" and was respecting her more unconscious wishes and fears. With this couple, a few sensate-focus exercises were used to gradually introduce sexual touching. The sensory exchange, combined with a different view of the problem, helped. David's sexual drive improved slowly and modestly and Paulette's enjoyment of sexual contact improved slightly. At the end of therapy their sexual satisfaction, while not what they had hoped for, and their relationship, were improved.

Another common pattern in low-desire couples is for there to have been a history of territorial battles, including sex as an issue in the marriage and about sex in particular.

One woman, Anna, married to a small-town physician, Frank, for 15 years, had spent the first 14 years being resentful of his work (which included required, frequent night call and Saturdays) and his lack of joint ownership of the home and family responsibilities. Her strategy was to doggedly pursue him. It was only when she stopped this strategy that he began to really commit in-person time and effort to the family, including writing thoughtful weekly letters to her that she honestly treasured. Sex had limped along in a rather boring fashion, until the last year when, consequent to her cessation of nagging, her desire dropped away. Although grateful her husband was now more of a family participant, she was still resentful in two areas—that her original strategy had been ineffective, and that she now had to share some of her territory (management of the children), whereas before she could unilaterally make decisions. In her case, the language of resentment was to withdraw sexually and at least not to allow him access to that territory.

To Anna the question was posed, "Are you willing to share your territory rather than make Frank own and manage it all while you criticize?" This was after six sessions of relationship development between the therapist and the couple. However, it introduced the issue of the wife's "reverse-the-tables" desire to punish her husband for his absence, the extent to which the old problematic territorial assignment had come to serve her own needs for autonomy and control, and a different level of therapeutic discourse. It was after this interaction that Anna revealed how upset she had been about his initial (15 years earlier) lack of commitment and desire for her. The therapist asked her to devise a punishment for him and she rejected the punishment idea, but wanted corrective historical revisions: She asked her husband to role play the same scene of 15 years earlier, but to say what he really would have wanted to have said. To the therapist's amazement, this he did immediately after leaving the therapy office. To Anna's credit, she was able to hear and thoroughly appreciate his response. Eventually this couple had infrequent but far more enjoyable sex and were less bitter and fixed in their own fossilized history.

Several comments deserve mention. First, the couple entered therapy with change already clearly in motion. Anna had stopped a long-term pattern and in response, Frank had reorganized his priorities in very visible ways. Second, the territorial issues were far from the major focus of the actual therapy. Territory and its management were concepts used to describe a problem in different terms than an individual impairment perspective. In our opinion, it aided the couple in more actively directing their own treatment, including the woman's revision of the therapist's suggested intervention. This is not to say that other interventions might not have been equally effective, but some interventions might well have interfered with the momentum the couple came with into treatment.

Women with child sexual-abuse histories can suffer a number of sexual dysfunctions—pain and low arousal being the most common. Some also have loss of desire, especially as a sense of intimacy, trust, and commitment increases. In addition, they may have great difficulty claiming their bodies and sexual responsiveness as their territory.

One woman currently in treatment, Helen, on examining this issue kept repeating, "My body betrayed me," meaning that not only had her body been sexually responsive to her father over 6 years of sexual abuse as a child, but also that she felt it was *her body* that encouraged him to be sexual in the first place. The clinical issue here was to help the client shift the sense of betrayal from herself onto her parent, so that she could reclaim her body, its responsiveness (she was orgasmic but with HSD), and her sexual desire. Although Helen, who was 46 when she entered treatment, was rapidly able to hold her father responsible for his part in the abuse (and evenually her mother, for her role), she remained very fixed on her body as the guilty culprit. In several attempts, using light hypnotic suggestions, to forgive and comfort herselfl as a young child, she was unable to do so. When the therapist invited her to bring in family photos from the time period of the abuse, she was able to find one that happened to show her mother not touching her and her father holding her firmly with both hands. This photo, along with several others, began to allow the patient, with the therapist probing for reactions, to see how she was terribly young, too young to force her father to do anything, and that she had been claimed by him.

This case is an example of common technique not particular to any specifc theoretical position (trance induction, assignments), but focused on the intense addressing of one key aspect of the incest experience—the impairment of a sense of territoriality over one's body. The resolution of territoriality issues for this patient remains a treatment goal rather than simply a theme and set of interventions. In the resolutions of this issue, much of the healing is expected to take place because territory requires recognition of boundaries, self- and other-respect, the necessity of assertiveness for defense, and the recognition of limits of the body as one's territory.

In cases in which there are territorial issues during sex, the partner's response is important. Greater attention to territorial reactions and showing respect for the territory of the partner's body can be useful bridges to sexual interaction.

For example, Helen's first husband had been very sexually demanding and not concerned with whether she was interested or responsive in sex. He also criticized her body and appearance as being unattractive and claimed she had poor skill as a lover. These critical remarks about her body and sexual behavior were accepted by Helen as valid, and for years she tried hard to improve, until she finally realized that the marriage was hopeless. Her second marriage, to Sam, was quite different. He liked and respected Helen's body, felt sexual toward her, but was able to understand the impact of her prior abusive relationships. In addition, he was willing to attend conjoint sessions and change "harmless" but problematic behaviors, such as affectionately touching her breasts while she was involved in various activities at home. Helen experienced this as a territorial invasion, as the therapist relabeled the experience for Sam. Sam's former wife had used sex to manipulate him, denying him sex when she did not get what she wanted. Thus, he was sensitive and anxious when he felt rejected. The therapist worked to separate refusal of sex from rejection of a sexual partner and use of sex as a manipulation. In Helen's case, giving in and agreeing to have sex had been a manipulation, and Sam appreciated this point. The major, usually nonverbal, corrective territorial messages that Sam consistently provided were: "I respect your preferences about sexual touching, both in and out of the bedroom," and, "Your body belongs to you; I will request access to it from time to time and will listen to your response." The therapist and Helen were very supportive of his effort and attempted to look for other ways Sam could feel sexually accepted. Eventually, he said, because he more fully understood Helen's predicament as being more about her own unresolved issues than his, sexual rejection receded as an issue for Sam. It was also possible that his sexual interest was decreasing somewhat and other life issues were becoming more important (he was 63, retired, and increasingly focused on their joint recreational activities).

A different slant on the systemic approach to understanding and treating HSD comes from Schnarch (1991) and is presented at this point because of its congruence with territorial and ranking-order interactions. Schnarch's opinion is that HSD couples are poorly "differentiated," a term from family therapist Bowen's original concept in family therapy (e.g., Kerr & Bowen, 1988). "Differentiation" is the process by which a person learns how to maintain a sense of individuality *and* togetherness in a relationship. Lack of differentiation creates an anxiety-driven pressure for togetherness, at the loss of autonomy, which in turn places the responsibility—and power—for a meaningful life and adequate functioning in the hands of the other person in the relationship. Schnarch's general approach is to (1) differentiate himself by declaring he is unwilling and unable to force sexual desire—he instead states that lack of desire is a reasonable response to one's actual experiences; (2) ask why each person thinks that she/he should want sex and that it should always be great; (3) encourage the asymptomatic partner to differentiate, develop a more internalized sense of self, and avoid the tendency to personalize the partner's HSD as a reflection on him/herself; (4) encourage sexual approaches that stem from desire versus need, and continue to stress that lack of contact is not equivalent to lack of validation; (5) increase differentiation of the asymptomatic partner to reduce pressure on the identified patient, which may also make the relationship potentially less "secure" (if being needed was the relationship's cement); (6) make the identified patient feel more pressure to deal with his/her own lack of desire, which the therapist does not dissipate; and (7) encourage the identified patient *not* to give into the pressure, and support (as previously done with the partner) the identified patient's sense of self, thus increasingly confronting the identified patient with the necessity to struggle with him/herself.

Several aspects of what Schnarch stresses in his approach have been mentioned by other clinicians. Examples include the relatively greater power of the HSD partner in the sexual arena, the necessity for the therapist to explore the nonsymptomatic partner, and a systems perspective that allows an integration of sexual and marital therapy (e.g., Apfelbaum, 1988; Heiman & Grafton-Becker, 1989; Verhulst & Heiman, 1988). What Schnarch offers in addition is the extensive and thoughtful use of the concept of differentiation, embedded in a systemic framework, to organize much of his work in sexual and marital problems. The discussion of differentiation, from its existential roots to its necessity for intimacy, has considerable utility potential for therapists working with HSD couples, although it begs to be researched. Whether higher desire individuals are in fact more highly differentiated has not been studied. In fact, one can imagine that very "in love" or limerent couples would not appear highly differentiated. Differentiation may be more useful as a change label, better applied to a process than a stage. The limitations of the differentiation concept remain to be elaborated, and future work will need to contend as much with such issues as to its cultural relativity and the problem of less undifferentiated being seen as "bad" and more differentiated being seen as "good," in spite of Schnarch's claim for his perspective to be nonpathologizing.

It is not unlikely that one or both members of the couple will need to confront the loss of the relationship in the process of clarifying the degree of change they are willing or not willing to accommodate. This may come about in discussing territorial and ranking-order disputes, or in attending to differentiation themes. S. Kirschner and D. Kirschner (1990), for example, have discussed the *fear of loss* dynamic as a means of challenging partners to progress by means of a carefully considered proposal by one partner to leave the relationship. The individual who threatens separation must believe that survival without the partner is possible.

For example, Larry and Anita unsuccessfully struggled in treatment for 1½ years with Larry's long-term loss of sexual desire. Larry stated that his loss of desire was a result of anger he "can't let go of," stemming from past experiences of rejections (mainly sexual) by his wife. For the last 3 years, Anita had tried everything to "get back in his good graces" but at this point felt "there is nothing I can do to make him happy." The therapist, in an individual session with the wife (although an individual session is not a necessity), encouraged her to take her feelings of frustration seriously and act assertively. At this point in treatment the therapist had worked with Anita on her feelings of competency and desirability. This was accomplished by both direct feedback (i.e., "You are an attractive woman") and by encouraging her to seek out activities that would prove her competencies. This laid the groundwork for her increased feelings of independence and strength. At this point, Anita was not tied to the relationship out of her fear of being alone. She had gained enough security within herself to enable her to *choose* whether she wanted this relationship in its present form. She decided to tell her husband that she was ready to separate because she did not want to live the rest of her life in a "sexually dead" relationship. In response, Larry became quite upset and began to reconnect with his deep longing and love for his wife. At some level Larry was aware of his wife's strength and courage in making this choice and was able to see her in a new light. She had stepped out of their patterned set of responses and he was grateful that the cycle had been broken. This change also forced him to face his own fears of losing his relationship and being alone. He

stopped taking her and his marriage for granted and gave up the assumption that regardless of what he did or did not do, she would always be there. At this juncture a temporary honeymoon period ensued, with frequent and satisfying sex. Once the couple experienced this shift they were able to work on their relationship and use therapeutic input in more productive and motivated ways.

This is not an intervention to be used in all difficult cases. The Kirschners advise as a prerequisite a strong therapeutic relationship with both partners in order to deal with the inevitable anger and fear that arises in both partners. It is the therapist's job to create a safe and supportive environment for the couple so that these frightening feelings can be explored in a therapeutically useful direction.

Attachment Themes

Whereas territoriality themes focus on managing separation in the face of togetherness, attachment themes focus more on managing togetherness in the face of aloneness. Attachment interactions deal with intimacy and affection, as well as their fluctuating intensity, between partners. Attachment themes have significance to individuals who are coupled because of early experiences with intimate family figures who provided (or failed to provide) care, protection, bonding, and closeness. If there was an attachment problem such as rejection, separation, withdrawal, or distancing (and most people do have imperfect attachment histories), a person will bring these sensitivities and strengths to the current relationship. One client, whose mother had committed suicide when he was 10, was very dependent on his wife's approval, although irritated by her requests. His sex drive decreased as the relationship became more committed and when she had their first child. His faith in close relationships and his belief that he might do something wrong (again) to destroy this one kept him in a defensive (trying to fix all problems) position, but the cost was his resentment and his loss of sexual desire.

Behaviorally, attachment requires that couples pay attention to each other, take time out to take the other into account, and do activities of mutual enjoyment. Affectively, the feelings created by attachment interactions have a soothing rather than a stimulating effect, tenderness being a prime example. Thus they are useful to counteract fear, guilt, or anxiety, which may allow sexual feelings to resurface or may just dissipate into sleepy relaxation. Therefore, attachment interactions may be important for a very hostile or resentful low-desire couple to focus on for awhile. They can also be useful in cases in which childhood sexual or physical abuse occurred, such as Helen and Sam mentioned earlier, in order to create a safe environment. For typical low-desire patients, this may not be directly helpful except as an antidote to other feelings that may compete with sexual desire and arousal. In some cases, attachment behaviors appear to interfere with desire. For example, a couple married for 2 years reported an excellent history of warmth, affection and nurturing, but were confused by the husband's complaints of low sexual desire. However, upon examination it became clear that he experienced his wife more as "a mother" than "a lover." Because he was uncomfortable having sexual feelings for *mothers*, he was frequently affectionate but not sexual. It was important to explore this patient's relationship with his mother in an attempt to differentiate it from his relationship with his wife. For this man, who had been taught always to please and take care of his mother, his concept of attachment behaviors served to extinguish his sexual responsiveness.

Specific Additional Interventions

In addition to addressing the previous themes, there are other interventions that several different therapists have found useful.

First, assigning sensate focus exercises can be useful, but they benefit from a different emphasis than that given by Masters and Johnson (1970). Specifically, couples are asked to attend to what, if any, stimulation feels sensual enough that it holds their attention. The first several times, each person takes turns touching in a way that they may find even mildly sensual and interesting. The time limit is suggested as 20–25 minutes and the couple is asked to individually write down as many reactions as possible to the exercise. They are not instructed to feel arousal or even pleasure. It is made quite clear that there are no "correct" feelings, and all feelings are legitimate and valuable to discuss in session. Initially, couples are often told *not* to discuss their reactions with each other outside the session. The reason for this suggestion is that it is useful for the therapist to witness the discussions without clients having preprocessed their reactions, and it is useful for the couples to build some tension around the affective aspects of sexual experience.

This exercise gives and supports an experience focused on nonperformance sensual feelings, permission to feel contradictory feelings as legitimate, and permission not to be aroused or pressured to feel pleasure. It focuses on what each person feels and wants for him/herself, not from the other. This is not "give to get" (Masters & Johnson, 1970). It can also provide information about specific behaviors during physical interactions that may be associated with *changes* in desire. For example, does increasing arousal actually lead one partner to "turn off?"

Variations on this exercise can be explored, given the couple's territorial and ranking-order issues (e.g., to teach how to correct a territorial battle during sexual initiation), teaching assertiveness, or stopping when one person begins to feel pressured and talking about these feelings before resuming the physical interaction as illustrated by Apfelbaum (1988). Sometimes these assignments can move rapidly from the less to the more sexual, depending upon the couple. If a couple finds the pace too rapid and excessively anxiety-provoking, separate assignments to have a sexual encounter with instructions to incorporate those principles from the sensate focus exercises can be useful.

Second, individuals are asked to pay attention to any sexual or sensual feelings during daily activities. Brief wisps of sexual feeling deserve note whether or not they include the partner. Recording the circumstances (affective and behavioral) when it happens can also be useful. Feeling a little sexual when the partner is unavailable can actually be a sign that sexual feelings might emerge. Feeling repulsed by the partner is usually very difficult to impact. This exercise is a step toward the awareness and responsibility that each partner needs to assume for his/her own erotic responses, and also can increase the awareness that the HSD person is not "sexually dead," a common expression for patients entering treatment.

Some therapists recommend taking this exercise a step further and experimenting with alternative ways of being sexual. Taking fantasy "breaks" during the day, attending films, or buying books with sexual content can be done individually. J. LoPiccolo and Friedman (1988), for example, prescribe this as part of a drive induction, "priming the pump" strategy and report it to be very helpful. In addition, some couples can benefit from sharing sexual fantasies or buying a sensual surprise together or as a gift for each other. This type of intervention may be more useful with HSD couples in which there are some inhibition issues surrounding their desire disorders, rather than to couples in which the HSD has become the scapegoat of multiple angry disputes.

THE THERAPIST'S ROLE

The therapist's primary role is to work with a couple to find a satisfactory solution to the sexual desire complaint presented. Incorporated in that task, the therapist has special responsibilities with regard to knowledge, awareness, and conduct.

Knowledge that is important relates to understanding when general factors influence sexual desire (e.g., individual, biological, psychological, interpersonal, and sociocultural). Vague notions or personal experience are usually inadequate in the sexuality area since the therapist is as subject to cultural bias as any patient, and it is the therapist's responsibility to monitor how and where assumptions are being made about satisfaction and adequacy. Knowledge is also important regarding the variable relationship between sexual and relationship satisfaction. One example is the consistent finding that many couples report being happily married in spite of the presence of low desire or another sexual dysfunction (e.g., Frank, Anderson, & Rubinstein, 1978). In addition, the importance of desire for a relationship appears to vary greatly depending upon the sexual orientation of the participants and the duration of the relationship (e.g., Blumstein & Schwartz, 1983).

Another type of knowledge that is important for therapists has to do with treatment. Therapists treating sexual desire disorders need to be familiar with change strategies within at least one of the theoretical frameworks. The major skill that therapists should know is how to adapt their framework to encompass couple and relationship issues in order to deal with "being stuck," "resistance" or "vicious cycles." It is the therapist's job to be flexible and to be convinced that the lack of change in the couple has potentially as much to do with the lack of ingenuity in the therapist as it does with the couple's issues.

It is important for therapists to keep in mind that both scientific and clinical knowledge about sexuality is very culturally determined. An obvious example is that 100 years ago in Victorian England, hypoactive sexual desire was a virtue, not a dysfunction. "Thus women who denied their husbands' sexual contact, except when procreation was desired were seen as actually

helping men to control their 'baser desires'" (Caplan, 1987, p. 204). Therapists today are embedded in a social web that allows them to collaborate in defining, with their patients, adequate and inadequate sexual functioning. The awareness that concepts such as healthy sexuality are not fixed and essential but can change over time is one of the factors that has gradually encouraged a social constructionist view of sexuality. "Social constructionism" is based on several intellectual traditions, including phenomenology, existentialism, and symbolic interactionism and emphasizes "an individual's active role, guided by his or her culture, in structuring reality" (Tiefer, 1987, p. 71). Knowledge is viewed as subjective and constructed (rather than objective) and therefore is based on existing available concepts, categories, and methods. Biological sexuality, from a constructionist perspective, is a necessary precondition of human sexuality, but it is always mediated by human culture. A dramatic scripting metaphor, most carefully articulated by Gagnon and Simon (1973), puts the power of sexuality in the script created by sociocultural forces rather than in a predetermined, universal biological drive. Scripting draws from concepts of learning, revising, and rehearsing to create identities and meanings.

The constructionist approach is raised here because it is so relevant to what therapists actually do with their clients: constructing and deconstructing reality. Rosen and Leiblum (1988) have paid direct attention to the use of sexual scripting in treating low sexual desire (although they do not discuss this as constructionism). However, all therapists participate in some degree of constructionism because they need to listen to their clients' stories of the origins and maintenance of the sexual desire problem and help the clients, through their own theoretical framework (also constructed), to develop, or to construct, a new reality. This new story, which may be developed from different symbolic, affective and/or sensory experiences, needs to be one that will allow a couple to move beyond their current inertia. "Reframing" is an example of what is usually a partial reconstruction of the problem in order to facilitate change.

In forming a therapeutic alliance with a couple and empathizing with each of their stories, the therapist connects on symbolic, affective and sensory levels with the clients and with their relationship. Elkaïm (1990) has written about how specific elements or "singularities" of the therapist–couple system "resonate" because of current and historical features of all parties involved. System singularities grow out of what Elkaïm calls a "cocktail" of elements tied to both the past and the present. In the therapist's case, this cocktail is drawn from professional as well as personal beliefs and experiences. It is these unique resonances that the therapist must develop with a couple in order to facilitate change, requiring a therapist to be aware of resonances that can and cannot facilitate change. The therapist may resonate with a couple in a way that inhibits change and supports homeostasis. Inexperienced therapists are especially prone to avoiding in a couple what is uncomfortable for them, not just as individuals but in relationships. For example, a therapist who has low tolerance of anxiety and uncertainty in his/her own relationship may have trouble with a couple whose sexual desire is diminished because of a covert agreement to pretend that nothing could ever really threaten their relationship, including lack of sex, hostility, frequent conflicts, or emptiness. Trial and error, or more accurately, testing hypotheses with the possibility of nonconfirmation, sometimes is necessary until the most useful singularity develops. This also means that different therapists are likely to have different resonances with the same couple, different sensitivities on which they connect in a therapeutically meaningful way.

CONCLUSION

One of the most common current sexual complaints is hypoactive sexual desire. In spite of DSM-IV, its definition is extremely inexact with operational criteria unevenly and inconsistently applied by clinicians and researchers. It is therefore a heterogeneous category that restricts treatment guidelines to general or broad spectrum approaches, until some subcategorizations are made. Given these issues, the present chapter has recommended a systemic approach to treatment, which can loosely integrate other types of therapeutic approaches in a change-oriented rather than pathologizing language. The systemic perspective presented here is unique in its focus on interactional patterns rather than on purely individual characteristics that impact the interactions. It offers, first of all, a conceptualization, and second, a therapeutic stance for organizing problems and solutions. There is no specific set of interventions or techniques, but rather a process of examining the problem and coming up with possible solutions. Therapists need to be aware of the socially constructed nature of sexual diagnoses, quite clearly illustrated

by the evolving definition of sexual desire as a disorder, in order to be alert and creative in response to couples coming in with desire disorder complaints.

ACKNOWLEDEMENT

The authors would like to thank Janet Woodford for her helpful assistance in manuscript preparation.

REFERENCES

American Psychiatric Association. (1980). *Diagnostic and statistical manual of mental disorders* (3rd ed.). Washington, DC: Author.

American Psychiatric Association. (1987). *Diagnostic and statistical manual of mental disorders* (3rd ed., rev.). Washington, DC: Author.

American Psychiatric Association. (1994). *Diagnostic and statistical manual of mental disorders* (4th ed.). Washington, DC: Author.

Apfelbaum, B. (1988). An ego analytic perspective on desire disorders. In S. R. Leiblum & R. C. Rosen (Eds.), *Sexual desire disorders* (pp. 75–106). New York: Guilford Press.

Blumstein, P., & Schwartz, P. (1983). *American couples: Money, work and sex.* New York: Morrow.

Caplan, P. (1987). Introduction. In P. Caplan (Ed.), *The cultural construction of sexuality* (pp. 1–30). New York: Tavistock.

Carney, A., Bancroft, J., & Mathews, A. (1978). Combination of hormonal and psychological treatment for female sexual unresponsiveness: A comparative study. *British Journal of Psychiatry, 132,* 339–346.

DeAmicis, L. A., Goldberg, D. C., LoPiccolo, J., Friedman, J., & Davies, L. (1985). Clinical follow-up of couples treated for sexual dysfunction. *Archives of Sexual Behavior, 14,* 467–488.

Derogatis, L. R., & Spencer, P. M. (1982). *The Brief Symptom Inventory: Administration, scoring and procedures manual—I.* Baltimore, MD: Clinical Psychometric Research.

Elkaïm, M. (1990). *If you love me, don't love me: Constructions of reality and change in family therapy.* New York: Basic Books.

Frank, E., Anderson, A., & Rubinstein, D. (1978). Frequency of sexual dysfunction in "normal" couples. *New England Journal of Medicine, 299,* 111–115.

Gagnon, J. R., & Simon, W. (1973). *Sexual conduct: The social sources of human sexuality.* Chicago: Aldine.

Hawton, K., Catalan, J., & Fagg, J. (1991). Low sexual desire: Sex therapy results and prognostic factors. *Behaviour Research and Therapy, 29,* 217–224.

Heiman, J., & Grafton-Becker, V. (1989). Orgasmic disorders in women. In S. R. Leiblum & R. C. Rosen (Eds.), *Principles and practice of sex therapy* (2nd ed., pp. 51–88). New York: Guilford Press.

Heiman, J. R., & LoPiccolo, J. (1983). Clinical outcome of sex therapy: Effects of daily vs. weekly treatment. *Archives of General Psychiatry, 40,* 443–449.

Hogan, D. R. (1978). The effectiveness of sex therapy: A review of the literature. In J. LoPiccolo & L. LoPiccolo (Eds.), *Handbook of sex therapy* (pp. 57–84). New York: Plenum.

Kaplan, H. S. (1974). *The new sex therapy.* New York: Brunner/Mazel.

Kaplan, H. S. (1977). Hypoactive sexual desire. *Journal of Sex and Marital Therapy, 3,* 3–9.

Kaplan, H. S. (1979). *Disorders of sexual desire.* New York: Brunner/Mazel.

Kerr, M. E., & Bowen, M. (1988). *Family evaluation.* New York: Norton.

Kinsey, A. C., Pomeroy, W. B., & Martin, C. E. (1948). *Sexual behavior in the human male.* Philadelphia: Saunders.

Kinsey, A. C., Pomeroy, W. B., Martin, C. E., & Gebhard, P. H. (1953). *Sexual behavior in the human female.* Philadelphia: Saunders.

Kirschner, S., & Kirschner, D. A. (1990). Comprehensive family therapy: Integrating indvidual, marital and family therapy. In F. Kaslow (Ed.), *Voices in family therapy* (Vol. 2, pp. 231–243). Newbury Park, CA: Sage.

Kolodny, R., Masters, W., & Johnson, V. (1979). *Textbook of sexual medicine.* Boston: Little, Brown.

Lazarus, A. A. (1988). Multimodal perspective on problems of sexual desire. In S. R. Leiblum & R. C. Rosen (Eds.), *Sexual desire disorders* (pp. 145–167). New York: Guilford Press.

Leiblum, S. R., & Rosen, R. C. (Eds.). (1988). *Sexual desire disorders.* New York: Guilford Press.

LoPiccolo, J., & Friedman, J. M. (1988). Broadspectrum treatment of low sexual desire: Integration of cognitive, behavioral and systemic therapy. In S. R. Leiblum & R. C. Rosen (Eds.), *Sexual desire disorders* (pp. 107–144). New York: Guilford Press.

LoPiccolo, J., & Stock, W. E. (1986). Treatment of sexual dysfunction. *Journal of Consulting and Clinical Psychology, 54,* 158–167.

LoPiccolo, L. (1980). Low sexual desire. In S. R. Leiblum & L. A. Pervin (Eds.), *Principles and practice of sex therapy* (1st ed., pp. 29–64). New York: Guilford Press.

Masters, W., & Johnson, V. (1970). *Human sexual inadequacy.* Boston: Little, Brown.

Mathews, A., Bancroft, J., Whitehead, A., Hackmann, A., Julier, D., Bancroft, J., Gath, D., & Shaw, P. (1976). The behavioural treatment of sexual inadequacy: A comparative study. *Behaviour Research and Therapy, 14,* 427–436.

Mathews, A., Whitehead, A., & Kellett, J. (1983). Psychological and hormonal factors in the treatment of female sexual dysfunction. *Psychological Medicine, 13,* 83–92.

McCarthy, B. W. (1984). Strategies and techniques for the treatment of inhibited sexual desire. *Journal of Sex and Marital Therapy, 10,* 97–104.

Nowinski, J., & LoPiccolo, J. (1979). Assessing sexual behavior in couples. *Journal of Sex and Marital Therapy, 5,* 225–243.

Rosen, R. C., & Leiblum, S. R. (1988). Sexual scripting approach to problems of desire. In S. R. Leiblum & R. C. Rosen (Eds.), *Sexual desire disorders* (pp. 168–191). New York: Guilford Press.

Sarason, I. G., Johnson, J. H., & Siegel, J. M. (1978). Assessing the impact of life changes: Development of the Life Experiences Survey. *Journal of Consulting and Clinical Psychology, 46,* 932–946.

Scarff, D. E. (1988). An object relations approach to inhibited sexual desire. In S. R. Leiblum & R. C. Rosen (Eds.), *Sexual desire disorders* (pp. 45–74). New York: Guilford Press.

Scarff, D. E., & Scarff, J. S. (1987). *Object relations family therapy.* Northvale, NJ: Jason Aronson.

Schnarch, D. M. (1991). *The sexual crucible: An integration of sexual and marital therapy.* New York: Norton.

Schover, L. R., Friedman, J. M., Weiler, S. J., Heiman, J. R., & LoPiccolo, J. (1982). Multiaxial problem-oriented system for sexual dysfunction: An alternative to DSM III. *Archives of General Psychiatry, 39,* 614–619.

Schover, L. R., & LoPiccolo, J. (1982). Treatment effectiveness for dysfunctions of sexual desire. *Journal of Sex and Marital Therapy, 8,* 179–197.

Schwartz, M. F., & Masters, W. H. (1988). Inhibited sexual desire: The Masters and Johnson Institute treatment model. In S. R. Leiblum & R. C. Rosen (Eds.), *Sexual desire disorders* (pp. 229–241). New York: Guilford Press.

Segraves, R. T. (1988a). Hormones and libido. In S. R. Leiblum & R. C. Rosen (Eds.), *Sexual desire disorders* (pp. 271–312). New York: Guilford Press.

Segraves, R. T. (1988b). Drugs and desire. In S. R. Leiblum & R. C. Rosen (Eds.), *Sexual desire disorders* (pp. 313–347). New York: Guilford Press.

Sherwin, B. B., Gelfand, M. M., & Brender, W. (1985). Androgen enhances sexual motivation in females: A prospective, crossover study of sex steroid administration in the surgical menopause. *Psychosomatic Medicine, 47,* 339–351.

Sotile, W. M., & Kilmann, P. R. (1977). Treatments of psychogenic female sexual dysfunctions. *Psychological Bulletin, 84*, 619–633.

Spanier, G. B. (1976). Measuring dyadic adjustment: New scales for assessing quality of marriage and similar dyads. *Journal of Marriage and Family Therapy, 38*(7), 15–28.

Tiefer, L. (1987). Social constructionism and the study of human sexuality. In P. Shaver & C. Hendrick (Eds.), *Sex and gender* (pp. 70–94). Newbury Park, CA: Sage.

Verhulst, J., & Heiman, J. (1979). An interactional approach to sexual dysfunction. *American Journal of Family Therapy, 7*, 19–36.

Verhulst, J., & Heiman, J. (1988). A systems perspective on sexual desire. In S. R. Leiblum & R. C. Rosen (Eds.), *Sexual desire disorders* (pp. 168–191). New York: Guilford Press.

Whitehead, A., & Mathews, A. (1977). Attitude change during behavioural treatment of sexual inadequacy. *British Journal of Social and Clinical Psychology, 16*, 275–281.

Whitehead, A., & Mathews, A. (1986). Factors related to successful outcome in the treatment of sexually unresponsive women. *Psychological Medicine, 16*, 373–378.

Zilbergeld, B., & Ellison, C. R. (1980). Desire discrepancies and arousal problems. In S. R. Leiblum & L. Pervin (Eds.), *Principles and practice of sex therapy* (1st ed., pp. 65–101). New York: Guilford Press.

Zilbergeld, B., & Kilmann, P. R. (1984). The scope and effectiveness of sex therapy. *Psychotherapy, 21*, 319–326.

Index

Acceptance
 credibility gap problem, 46
 detachment interventions to promote, 58–59, 63
 of differences, 42
 in integrative behavioral couple therapy, 31, 32,
  39–40
 minefield problem, 46
 mutual trap problem, 46
 promoting, strategies for, 43–44, 54–63
 strategies for, integrated with change strategies,
  48–51
 through tolerance building, 59–60
Accreditation, 2
Agoraphobia, 395
 communication training, 399–403
 comorbid personality disorders, 396
 coping strategies, 399
 dependency and, 396
 expressed emotion in couple functioning, 397
 marital distress and, 395–398, 403–407
 marital treatment methods, 398–403
 outcome predictors, 397–398, 403–406
 summarizing self-syndrome, 401–403
 in vivo practice intervention, 400
AIDS, 285–286, 287–288
Alcohol problem
 among gay and lesbian clients, 279–280
 assessment, 369–370, 373, 374, 378–382
 both spouses with, 390
 case study, 377–386
 clinical constructs, 369–370
 comorbid drug use, 388
 comorbidity, 372, 388–390
 conjoint therapy, 374
 contraindications, 391
 coping behaviors of nonalcoholic partner, 373
 coping skills training for, 373
 difficult couples, 390
 family functioning and, 370–372
 genetic risk, 372
 limitations of treatment, 390–391
 marital violence and, 320

 motivation for abstinence, 381
 nondyadic factors contributing to, 372
 obstacles to treatment, 386–390
 patterns of drinking, 379–380, 381–382
 rational emotive therapy for, 374
 relapse prevention model, 377, 381
 resistance issues, 386–387
 sexual desire disorder assessment and, 480
 termination work, 391–392
 theory of therapeutic change, 373, 375, 376
 therapy goals, 374–375
 therapy structure, 374, 375
 treatment compliance, 387
Alcoholics Anonymous, 373, 374, 377
Anger, 55–56
 assessment value, 36–37
 control strategies for marital violence, 325–327
 in narcissistic-borderline couple, 463
 as primary emotion, 126
 as secondary emotional response, 126
 in violent husbands, 320
Antisocial personality disorder, alcohol problem
  comorbid with, 388, 389–390
Anxiety/anxiety disorders
 about intimacy, 180–182
 chronic, 12
 differentiation of self and, 14
 emergence of triangle processes in, 15, 16
 future of marital therapy in treatment for,
  407–408
 marital distress and, 395–396, 407–408
 models of sexual desire disorder, 472
 pervasiveness, 394–395
 process reactions within couple, 21
 in psychoanalytic marital therapy, 173
 role of couple therapy for, 394
 as social process, 18
 state shifts vs. change, 19
 in symptom process in couples, 17–18
 therapist's, 20
 as threat response, 12
Areas of Change Questionnaire, 31, 35, 41, 69

Arguments communication training vs., 52
  problem-maintaining behavior in, 149–150
Assessment
  of alcohol problem, 369–370, 373, 374, 377–382
  of anxiety disorder, 394–395
  of attributional style, 69–70, 72
  in behavioral therapy, 35
  Bowen family system approach, 19–20, 20–21
  of capacity for change, 42–43
  of capacity for collaboration, 47–48
  categories of emotion, 126
  for change strategies, 42–43
  of cognitive variables, 68–75
  of communication skills/style, 73
  cross-cultural marriage, 234–245
  definition and specification, 37
  of depression, 411–412
  development of relationship theme in, 37–38,
      68–69, 71
  diaries and logs, 81–82
  of differentiation of self, 13
  for discussions to promote acceptance, 43–44
  of divisive issues for couple, 41
  divorce, life cycle perspective in, 341
  of divorce risk, 342
  of eating disorder, 441–442, 443–444, 455
  of emotional processes between spouses, 21–22
  in emotionally focused therapy, 128
  of family emotional systems, 20–21
  feedback session after, 44–48
  in feminist-informed practice, 265
  focused problem resolution, 145–146
  functional analysis of behavior, 35–38
  functional analysis of relationships, 32–33
  in group therapy with couples, 203–204
  history taking, 36, 71–72, 80–81
  individual interviews for, 41, 128, 147
  in integrative behavioral couple therapy, 35–38,
      40–44
  of level of commitment, 40–41
  of level of marital distress, 40
  of long-term marriage at midlife, 248–255
  of marital violence, 318, 319–321
  in psychoanalytic marital therapy, 166–167,
      172–173
  of relationship expectancies, 70, 72
  of relationship standards, 70–71, 72–73
  selection of strategies for, 73–75
  of sexual desire disorders, 471–472, 478–481
  in solution-focused therapy, 152
  strengths, 42
  value of affect, 36–37
Association for Couples in Marital Enrichment,
    221
Assumptions about marriage, 66, 70, 72, 82–83
  cognitive restructuring interventions, 85–87
Attachment processes in emotionally focused ap-
    proach, 121, 123–125
  in relationship patterns, 123
  themes in sexual desire disorder, 490–491
Attachment theory
  clinical trends, 139

  conceptual basis, 123–124
  of emotion experience, 125
  marital dysfunction in, 124–125
  separation distress in, 140
Attribution Questionnaire, 69
Attributions
  assessment instruments, 69–70
  assessment interview, 72, 73
  cognitive factors in couple functioning, 65
  cognitive restructuring interventions, 84
  expectancies and, 67
  implications for therapy, 67–68
  increasing spouse's awareness of, 82
  level of marital adjustment and, 66–67
  theory development, 65
Attunement, 124
Automatic thoughts, 80
Aversive stimulation, 34

B

Behavior exchange strategies, 38–39, 51, 52
Behavioral therapy, 2. See also Integrative be-
    havioral couple therapy
  change goals, 38
  with depression, outcome research, 428–429
  effectiveness, 32
  functional analysis in, 32
  misconceptions about, 32
  outcome research, 87, 88
  psychoanalytic marital therapy and, 185
  shifts to cognitive focus in, 76–77
  therapeutic goals, 75–76
  traditional assessment, 35
Biofeedback, 4, 22
Biological processes
  in Bowen family system theory, 11–12
  mating behaviors, 16
  midlife stress, 249–250
  physical response in emotional arousal, 122
Borderline personality disorder
  clinical features, 458–459
  developmental issues, 459–461
  narcissistic-borderline couple, 462–463
  narcissistic personality disorder and, 461
  object relations therapy with narcissistic-
      borderline couple, 463–469
  relationship problems, 458
  vs. borderline personality organization, 459
Bowen family system theory/therapy applications
    and development, 27, 29
  avoiding transference in, 28
  behavioral techniques, 4
  concept of change, 19
  conceptual basis, 11
  conflict processes in, 17
  controlling emotional reactiveness, 26
  couple's emotional system, 12
  defining emotional processes between spouses,
      21–22, 24–25
  demonstrating differentiation of self, 23–24
  determinants of individual capability in, 16

detriangling, 26–27
differentiation of self in, 12–14
eclectic practice and, 29–30
emotional cutoff concept, 18
emotional distance in, 17
emotional fields, family, 20–21
emotional process in society, 18
emotional system in, 11–12
emotional systems, instructing clients in function of, 23
family assessment, 19–20, 20–21
family projection processes, 16
feeling system in, 12
individual sessions in, 25
intellectual system in, 12
multigenerational transmission in, 16–17
nuclear family emotional process in, 17
process orientation, 24
projection of problem to a child, 17–18
resistance issues, 27–28
role of clinician in, 19–20
sibling position in, 18
symptom presentation in two-person system, 17–18
termination issues, 28, 29
therapeutic goals, 29
therapeutic involvement of extended family, 25–27
therapeutic relationship in, 28
therapist stance, 20, 28
triangle concept in, 14–16
triangling of therapist, 22–23
Brief therapy
advantages of, 142
clinical trends, 2

C

Causes and maintenance of relationship distress
anxiety disorders and, 396–397
attachment theory, 124
depression, 412
ego-analytic theory, 91, 97–101
in emotionally focused approach, 121–123
feminist-informed practice, 264–265, 267–272
in focused problem resolution, 145
functional symptoms, 5–6
in IBCT, 32–35
infidelity in, 295–296
in long-term marriage at midlife, 248
in marital/family discord model of depression, 424–427
marital violence, 325, 328
models of cultural differences in, 232, 233–234
object relations model, 168–171
psychoanalytic model, 165–168
relationship enhancement intervention, 213
for same-sex couple, social oppression as source of, 277–280
unique features of gay male relationships, 285–288
unique features of lesbian relationships, 280–284

Child abuse
borderline personality organization and, 460
late-onset eating disorders, 447
mandatory reporting, 330
Child custody issues, 346–347, 351, 352–353
Circular causality
cognitive restructuring intervention, 80–81
feminist critique of concept of, 263, 328
in marital violence, 263, 328
Coercion theory, 34, 264
Cognitive-behavioral marital therapy
assessment, 68–75
cognitive restructuring interventions, 83–87
conceptual development, 65
content focus vs. process focus, 78–80
duration of therapy, 87–88
focus on standards, 78–79
interaction of domains in, 65–66
outcome research, 87–88
self-monitoring interventions, 80–83
skills training in, 68
structure of therapy sessions, 75–77
therapeutic focus, 76, 78
therapist role in, 78–80
with violent couples, 324, 325–327
Cognitive processes
anger control strategies, 325–327
assessment of, 68–75
in behavioral models, 33
in Bowen family system theory, 12
clinical trends, 65
in couple functioning, 33, 213
decision to divorce, 342–344
in ego-analytic theory of relationship dysfunction, 97–101
in focused solution development concepts, 151
information processing model of emotion, 125
in marital behavior, 66–68
negative and distorted, 67
postdivorce belief systems, 354–355
schemata, 85–86
self-monitoring interventions, 79, 80–83
Commitment
couple assessment, 40–41
feedback discussion with couple after assessment of, 45
midlife marital distress and, 247–248
premarital intervention and, 218
in prevention and relationship enhancement program, 217
recognition of spousal dependability, 423–424
Communication
challenges for gay male couples, 285–286
depression effects, 413
divorce predictors, 342
ego-analytic approach to difficulty in, 95–96
ego-analytic concepts, 101–112
expectations about, 216
in family development model of couple functioning, 213, 214–215
gender issues, 265–266
interactions in sexual functioning, 476–477

Communication (*cont.*)
  interventions with adult with eating disorder, 450–451, 454
  language of emotional acceptance, 55–56
  in model of relationship distress, 33
  obstacles to assessment, 36
  paradoxical form, 149
  recovery conversations, 96
  role playing interventions for enhancing, 61
  self-reproach as obstacle to, 111
  skills assessment, 73
Communication skills training
  alcohol relapse prevention, 385
  anxiety reduction, couple therapy in, 399–403
  in communication/problem-solving training approach, 38–39
  ego-analytic approach, 115–116
  goals, 38, 51–52
  in group therapy with couples, 199–200
  in IBCT, 52, 53, 54
  in prevention and relationship enhancement program, 216, 217, 220
  to promote acceptance of emotional expression, 420–422
  promoting intimate exchanges, 424
  self-esteem support, 423
Compliance issues
  in alcohol problem intervention, 387
  in emotionally focused therapy, 132
  in psychoanalytic marital therapy, 187
Confidentiality
  divorce intervention, 348
  divorce mediation, 357
Conflict Tactics Scale, 40, 318, 319
Contingency-shaped behavior, 38–39, 49
Countertransference
  concordant and complementary identifications, 180
  ego-analytic interpretation, 105
  in object relations therapy with borderline-narcissistic couple, 467–468
  in psychoanalytic marital therapy, 173, 178–180
Couple functioning. *See also* Family functioning; Sexual desire disorders
  alcohol problems and, 370, 371
  anxiety disorders and, 395–398, 407–408
  assessment of cognitive variables, 68–75
  attachment theory, 124–125
  circular patterns, 80–81
  coercive processes, 34
  cognitive processes, 33
  cognitive processes in, 66–68
  collaborative set assessment, 43
  cultural consonance in, 232
  depression and, 414–417
  differentiation of self and, 14
  eating disorder and, 438–439, 441–443, 451–455
  ego-analytic theory of dysfunction, 97–101
  emotion as organizing principle in, 125–126
  empathy in, 265–266
  existential psychotherapy model, 198–199
  fun in, 216

  functional analysis of, 32–33
  gender differences in negative interactional patterns, 122
  honesty in, 299
  mating behavior, 16
  narcissistic-borderline couple, 462–463
  power distribution in, in feminist thought, 264–265
  problem definition, 52–53
  problem-solving attempts, assessment of, 41–42
  psychoanalytic marital therapy model, 166–168
  same-sex couples, unique features of, 274–275, 280–284
  sexism in clinical models of, 263
  skills, 33
  triangles in, 14–16
  unique concerns of gay male couples, 285–288
  unique concerns of lesbian couples, 280–284
Couple therapy
  clinical population, 1, 31
  conceptual development, 1–4, 6
  evaluation of models of intervention, 3
  family therapy and, 2
  individual psychiatric disorders and, 4, 5–6
  social context, 4–5
Couples Assessment Inventory, 203
Cross-cultural marriage
  conflicts of cultural code in, 234, 235–237
  cultural transition in, 234
  definition of culture, 232–233
  patterns of dissonance, 234–235, 245
  permission-to-marry issues, 237–243
  range of, 231
  stereotyping, 243–244
  theoretical models, 232, 233–234

D

Daily Record of Dysfunctional Thoughts, 81–82, 83
Death
  depression and mortality rates, 411
  emotional response in families, 21
  marital violence and, 318
  midlife issues, 249–250
  therapist conceptualization of, 258–259
Defenses, in psychoanalytic marital therapy, 173, 180
Demand–withdraw patterns of behavior, 145, 148–149
Dependency
  in couple conflict, 17
  in development of agoraphobia, 396
  differentiation of self and, 14
  in narcissistic-borderline couple, 462–463
  in narcissistic personality disorder, 461–462
  self-care strategies, 62–63
  sociocultural reinforcement of gender roles, 263–264
Depression. *See also* Marital/family discord model of depression clinical
  features, 411–412

comorbid marital discord and, 427
conversational behavior and, 413
incidence, 411
interpersonal factors in, 412–413
marital functioning and, 414–417, 418, 430–431
marital therapy outcome research, 427–430
parenting and, 417–418
prevalence in marital distress, 412
problem definition in, 422
recall of negative information and, 413–414, 415
separation distress and, 140
social behavior with strangers, 413–414
suicide risk, 411
Detachment strategy, 58–59, 63
Development. *See also* Midlife couple
behavioral theory, 32
borderline personality organization, 459–461
cognitive structures, 85
considerations in preventive interventions, 214–215
cultural transition in marriage, 234
depressed parent effects, 417–418
ego-analytic concepts, 117–119
family developmental perspective of divorce, 341
gender roles, sociocultural reinforcement of, 263–264
issues in psychoanalytic marital therapy, 166–167
in narcissistic personality disorder, 462
object relations theory of, 168
projective identification in, 169
psychoanalytic theory of, 165–166
socialization of sexual behavior, 267–268
of therapy groups, 204–205
unresolved emotional attachment, 13–14, 16, 18
Diaries, 81–82
Difficult client(s)
alcohol problem intervention, 390
psychoanalytic approach, 187
Divorce, 3
after remarriage, 340
ambiguous feelings after, 350
challenges after, 348
child-custody arrangements, 346–347, 351, 352–353
clinical terminology, 361–362
decision-making dynamics, 342–345
economic issues, 353, 358
emotional turmoil after, 348–350
emotionality in decision-making, 345–346
family developmental perspective, 341
family outcomes, 341
gay and lesbian couples, 355
gender issues, 346
infidelity and, 295–296, 298–299
legal issues, 346–348, 353
long-term adaptation, goals for, 363
mediation, 3, 356–361
narrative construction, 344
parent–child adjustment, 351–353
postdivorce belief systems, 354–355

risk assessment, 342
risk of violence in, 346
rituals for, 363
sexual behavior after, 350–351
social support networks, 350–351
sociocultural attitudes, 249, 340–341
steps to remarriage, 355–356
structural dislocation in, 353–354
therapist issues, 361–363
therapy structure, 362–363
as threat, 425–426
as transactional process, 340
trial separation, 348
Duration of treatment
cognitive-behavioral marital therapy, 87–88
group therapy with couples, 197
prevention and relationship enhancement program, 215
psychoanalytic marital therapy, 173–174
Dyadic Adjustment Scale, 40, 132
Dyadic Attributional Inventory, 69

E

Eating disorders in adults
assessment, 455
client education, 449–451
clinical challenges, 437–438
communication interventions, 450–451, 454
comorbid disorders, 446–447
conjoint therapy considerations, 445
couple assessment, 448
couple functioning and, 438–439, 441–443
current conceptualizations, 438–439, 443
family-of-origin issues, 438, 441, 443–444, 447
identity issues, 453–454
incidence of marriage and, 439, 442
intake assessment, 444–447
marital status and prognosis, 439
marriage partner characteristics, 440–441
onset, 439–440, 446
partner assessment, 447–448
prior sexual abuse and, 447
relationship assessment, 441–442, 443–444
relationship crises, 451–455
sexual behavior, 442, 454–455
therapeutic goals, 455–456
therapist considerations, 455
treatment, 448–449
Eclectic practice
Bowen family systems therapy and, 29–30
problem-focused and solution-focused integration, 156
psychoanalytic marital therapy techniques in, 184–187
Ego analysis
avoiding reproachful interpretation in, 92–93, 94
cognitive restructuring, 116
communication skills training and, 115–116
conceptual basis, 91
conceptual development, 97

Ego analysis (*cont.*)
  countertransference concept, 105
  developmental issues in, 117–119
  entitlement-to-feelings concept, 97, 98–99, 101,
      110, 112
  functional symptoms in, 96
  handling interruptions by spouse, 93
  hidden-validity principle, 94–95, 107, 110
  joint platform concept for problem-solving, 96,
      101–102, 103, 108, 109, 110, 113–115, 119
  leading-edge feelings, 101, 102–103, 105, 109,
      110
  need-to-get-something-across principle, 95–96,
      110
  paradoxical interventions, 116–117, 119
  resistance concept, 105
  self-reproach in, 91, 94
  symptom generation in, 101
  theory of relationship dysfunction, 97–101
  therapeutic course, 101–112
  therapeutic goals, 92, 109, 119
  therapeutic principles, 94–97
  therapist qualities, 112–113
  victims principle, 96, 110, 111–112
Ego psychology, 97
Emotion
  acceptance of emotional expression, 420–422
  assessment, 20–22, 36–37, 173
  in attachment model of relationships, 125–126
  in Bowen family system theory, 11–12
  categorization, 126
  in cognitive-behavioral marital therapy, 65
  constructivist information processing model, 125
  controlling emotional reactivity, 26–27
  couple interaction, clinical assessment of, 21–22
  in divorce decisionmaking, 345–346
  emotional cutoff, 18
  emotional distance, 17
  expressiveness training, 75
  family assessment, 20–21
  family system issues, 19–20
  language of emotional disclosure, 55–56
  as organizing principle, 125
  in psychoanalytic marital therapy, assessment of,
      173
  social context, 18
  therapeutic significance, 125–126
  unresolved emotional attachment, 13–14, 16, 18
Emotional abuse, 320
Emotionally focused therapy, 2
  assessment in, 121–122, 128
  attachment processes in, 123–125
  case example, 132–135
  compliance issues, 132
  concept of emotion in marriage and, 125–126
  conceptual basis, 121
  diagnostic picture intervention, 137
  difficulties in, 136–137
  future directions, 139–140
  model of relationship dysfunction, 121–123
  outcome predictors, 127, 130, 135–136
  outcome research, 121

  problematic interactions, 137–139
  stages of change, 129
  strategies, 128
  theory of change, 126–128
  therapeutic goals, 127, 130
  therapist role in, 130–132
  trends in couple therapy, 4
  violence in relationship and, 128
Empathy, 4, 265–266
Empty nest period, 253
Engagement encounter, 218
Enrichment methods, 3
Etiology
  in Bowen family system theory, 11
  ego-analytic approach, 91
Evolutionary biology, 15, 16
Existential psychotherapy
  in group therapy with couples, 198–199
  therapeutic goals, 198
Expectancies
  assessment of, 70, 72, 73
  cognitive processes in couple functioning, 66, 67
  cognitive restructuring interventions, 85
  communication, 216
  cultural, about marriage, 235
  increasing spouse's awareness of, 82

F

Family functioning. *See also* Couple functioning;
      Marital/family discord model of depression
  after divorce, 341
  alcohol problems and, 370–372
  assessment of emotional systems in, 19–20,
      20–21
  depression and, 417–418
  divorce effects, 353–354
  goals of Bowen family system therapy, 29
  nuclear family emotional process in, 17
  parenting issues for same sex couples, 288–289
  preventive interventions for couples and, 222
  projection of problem to a child, 17–18
  sibling position in, 18
Family-of-origin issues
  after divorce, 350
  in alcohol problem maintenance, 372
  in cross-cultural marriages, 231, 237–243
  in development of narcissistic disorders, 462
  in eating disorders in adults, 438, 441, 443–444,
      447
  in ego-analytic theory of relationship dysfunc-
      tion, 97, 100–101
  in emotionally focused therapy, 135, 137
  in family systems theory, 25–27
  in marital violence, 321, 325
  in midlife marriage, 255
  multigenerational transmission processes, 16–17
  parental death, 250
  parental level of differentiation of self, 16
  therapist's, 25
  unresolved emotional attachment, 13–14, 16,
      18

Feedback
    recorded, for communication/problem-solving
        training, 54
    recorded, for increasing awareness of selective
        attention, 81
    therapy session for, after assessment, 44–48
Feeling system, 12
Feminist thought
    clinical assessment in, 265
    marital therapy in, 262–264
    in marital violence interventions, 327–328
    marriage in, 261–262
    model of couple functioning, 264–265
    social analysis in, 266
    social and clinical trends, 272
    socialization of sexual behavior, 267–268
    themes in relationship dysfunction, 267–272
    therapeutic techniques informed by, 265–267
    on therapy with men, 266–267
Financial issues, 176, 209
    challenges for same-sex couples, 277, 278
    divorce effects, 353
    divorce mediation, 353, 359
    gender-related conflict, 270–272
Focused problem resolution, 142, 143
    assessment, 145–146
    conceptual development, 144
    control issues in therapy, 146–147
    couple therapy, 144, 148–150
    criticism of, 157–158
    demand-withdraw patterns, 145, 148–149
    effectiveness, 158–160
    future directions, 160–161
    interactional view, 144
    jamming technique, 149
    model of marital dysfunction, 145
    problem-maintaining solutions in, 146
    problem-solution loops in, 150
    strategic themes in, 156–157
    symmetrical patterns of problem-maintaining be-
        havior, 149–150
    therapeutic change in, 147–148
    therapeutic process/techniques, 145–147
    therapy structure, 144
Fun in relationships, 216
Functional analysis of behavior, 32, 35–38
Functional symptoms, 5–6, 18, 19
    in cross-cultural marriage, 238
    ego-analytic concepts, 96
    sexual desire disorders, 483

G

Gay and lesbian couples
    "age in gay life" issues, 282–283
    AIDS, 285–286
    boundary issues, 283–284
    clinical issues for lesbian couples, 280–284
    clinical research, 275–276
    gender-role socialization issues, 274
    implications for heterosexual relationship
        research, 289

    infidelity issues, 278, 302
    internalized homophobia, 275
    legal issues, 277, 289
    parenting issues, 288–289
    portrayals of long-term relationships, 277–278
    power issues, 287–288
    role models for, 277–278, 283
    separation issues, 355
    sexual functioning as presenting complaint,
        278–279
    social oppression, 274–275, 277–280
    social trends, 274, 275
    therapist bias, 276–277, 279–280
    unique clinical issues, 274–275
    utilization of psychotherapy, 276
Gender differences
    communication techniques, 265–266
    in divorce decisions, abuse of power and, 346
    emotional response to divorce, 349, 350–351
    in extramarital involvement, 295, 297, 300
    gender-role socialization, same-sex relationships
        and, 280–282, 285
    midlife couple developmental issues, 250–251
    in negative interactional patterns, 122
    patriarchical view, 261
    in patterns of marital violence, 318
    in philandering, 302–303
    in prevention and relationship enhancement
        program, 215–216
    role socialization, 263–264, 274
    socialization of sexual behavior, 267–268
    themes in relationship dysfunction, 267–272
    therapeutic process and, 264, 266–267
Genetics
    alcohol risk, 372
    behavioral theory and, 32
    in interpretation of projective identification,
        465–466
    in mating behaviors, 33
Genograms, 341
Getting the Love You Want: A Guide for Couples,
    221
Group therapy
    with battered women, 325
    marital violence, 322
    support for partners of adult with eating disord-
        er, 447
    with violent husbands, 324
Group therapy with couples
    assessment, 203–204
    benefits of, 207–209
    coleadership, 206–207
    communication skills interventions, 199–200
    conceptual development, 197–198
    existential psychotherapy in, 198–199
    future directions, 209–210
    group developmental stages, 204–205
    group policies, 202
    levels of intervention, 200–201
    membership issues, 202–203
    out-of-group work, 207
    outcome research, 208

Group therapy with couples (*cont.*)
   preparatory meetings, 202
   principle of isomorphism in, 198–199
   resistance in, 206
   self-disclosure in, 205
   termination issues, 205
   theoretical basis, 198–199
   therapist training for, 198, 209
   therapy structure, 197, 201, 208–209
   unstructured sessions, 201
Guided imagery, 205–206
Guilt, in infidelity, 296

H

Housework, 268–270

I

IBCT. *See* Integrative behavioral couples therapy
Incompatibility, sources of, 33–34
Individual dysfunction
   comorbidity of alcohol problem, 372, 388–390
   in couple therapy concepts, 4, 5–6
   functional role in relationships, 5–6
   in midlife marriage, 249–250
   in problem-focused therapy with couple, 150
   symptom presentation in two-person system, 17
Infertility, 254
Infidelity, 5
   accidental-type, 301–302, 311, 312–313
   as beneficial for marriage, 297
   blame in, 298, 310
   case examples of intervention with, 312–315
   categories of, 301
   children and, 309
   crisis intervention, 307
   definition, 295
   divorce and, 295–296, 298–299
   fear of, as presenting complaint for same-sex couple, 278
   forgiveness issues, 312
   gender issues, 295, 297, 300
   guilt issues, 296
   honesty and, 299
   implications for psychoanalytic marital therapy, 187
   intervention model, 307–312
   jealousy and, 299–300
   in lesbian and gay relationships, 278, 303
   myths about, 296–297
   as normal behavior, 297
   as part of marriage agreement, 305–307, 311, 316
   philandering-type, 302–304, 311, 313–315
   prevalence, 297
   quality of marriage and, 297–298
   reasons for, 297
   resistance issues, 307, 311
   revenge affairs, 306
   romantic affairs, 304–305, 311–312, 315–316
   secrecy and, 295, 298, 307–309

   sexual aspects in, 298
   termination work, 307, 312
   terminology, 296
   threat to relationship, 295–296
   values issues, 296
Integrative behavioral couples therapy
   acceptance in, 31
   assessment phase, 40–44
   clinical application, 31
   communication/problem-solving training, 38–39, 51–54
   concept of relationship distress, 32–33
   conceptual development, 31–32
   determinants of behavior in, 33
   development of relationship distress, model of, 33–35
   emotional acceptance in, 39–40
   feedback session, 44–48
   functional analysis of behavior in, 35–36
   implementation of treatment phases, 48–54
   promoting emotional acceptance in, 54–63
   role of affect, 36–37
   significance of, 31, 35
   theme development in, 37–38
   theory of therapeutic change, 35, 38–40
   therapeutic goals, 43
Intent-Impact Model, 216
Interactional view, 144
Interpersonal psychotherapy, 429–430
Inventory of General Relationship Standards, 70, 71
Inventory of Specific Relationship Beliefs, 82, 86
Inventory of Specific Relationship Standards, 68, 71
Isomorphism, 199

J

Jealousy
   infidelity and, 299–300
   same-sex couples, 278

L

Learned helplessness, 65
Legal issues
   arrest and prosecution of spouse batterers, 330–332
   child custody disputes, 346–347
   in divorce, 346–348, 353
   divorce mediation, 357–360
   duty to warn, 330
   for lesbian and gay couples, 277, 289
   mandatory reporting of child abuse, 330
   in marital violence intervention, 330
Logical analysis, 84–85, 87

M

Managed health care, 2
Marital Agendas Protocol, 70

Marital/family discord model of depression
  acceptance of emotional expression in, 420–422
  attacks on self-esteem in, 426
  cohesive behavior in, 419–420
  coping assistance in, 422–423
  disruption of scripted routines in, 426–427
  general features, 419, 430
  promoting intimate exchanges in, 424
  self-esteem support in, 423
  sources of stress in, 424–427
  spousal dependability in, 423–424
  therapeutic goals, 418–419
Marital Satisfaction Inventory, 40
Marital Status Inventory, 40–41
Marital violence
  alcohol abuse and, 320, 371–372
  alcohol problem intervention and, 387
  arrest and prosecution of batterers, 330–332
  assessment, 318, 319–321
  behavioral-cognitive therapy, 324, 325–327
  case examples, 323
  circular causality concept, 263, 328
  conjoint therapy, 322–324
  in depressed couples, 425
  in divorce process, 346
  emotional/psychological abuse, 320
  feminist-informed intervention, 327–328
  in feminist thought, 263, 264, 328
  group therapy, 322, 324–325
  incidence, 317
  interventions, 321–328
  legal issues, 330
  mortality rate, 318
  onset, 317
  outcomes, 318, 332–334
  patterns, 317–318
  prevalence, 262
  relapse prevention, 334
  safety consideration, 319–320
  social learning theory, 325
  systems therapy, 328
  therapeutic approaches, 318
  therapist issues, 329–330
  therapy goals, 321
  therapy structure, 322–323
Marriage, clinical meaning of, 1, 11, 31
Marriage Encounter, 221
Mental Research Institute, Palo Alto *See* Focused
    problem resolution
Midlife couple
  approach to therapy, 248
  assessment of, 248–255
  conceptions of marital distress in, 247–248
  individual developmental stress in, 249–250
  life-cycle stressors, 252–255
  misconceptions about midlife, 247
  outdated marital contracts, 250–251
  reframing strategies, 255–258
  reproductive dysfunction, 254–255
  sociocultural context, 249
  therapist issues, 258–259
  without children, 254

Miracle question, 152
Myers-Briggs Questionnaire, 203

N

Narcissistic personality disorder
  borderline personality disorder and, 461
  clinical features, 461–462
  etiology, 461
  family patterns, 462
  object relations therapy with narcissistic-
    borderline couple, 462–469
  relationship problems, 458
  therapeutic goals, 461
Narrative
  construction marriage and divorce stories,
    344
  social context, 5
  sociocultural, gender roles in, 262

O

Object relations
  marital therapy application, 463
  beginning phase, 464–465
  complicating factors, 468–469
  countertransference, 467–468
  ending phase, 468
  engagement phase, 464
  interpersonal middle phase, 465–467
  interpretation in, 465–467
  therapeutic relationship in, 464
  therapist stance, 463–464
Object relations theory
  attachment theory and, 123
  conceptual basis, 168
  individual development in, 168–169
  marriage in, 169
  projective and introjective identification,
    169–171
  therapeutic use of fantasy and inner object rela-
    tions, 182–183
Obsessive-compulsive disorder, 395, 407
Outcome predictors
  anxiety disorders, 407
  collaborative set, 43
  for cross-cultural marriage, 232
  for eating disorders, marital status as, 439
  in emotionally focused approach, 127, 130,
    135–136
  marital relations as, in phobia treatment,
    397–398, 403–406
  relationship, 67, 122, 213
Outcome research
  behavioral couple therapy, 32
  cognitive interventions, 75–76
  cognitive restructuring, 87–88
  emotionally focused therapy, 121
  focused problem resolution, 158–160
  group therapy with couples, 208
  marital therapy for depression, 427–430
  marital violence interventions, 332–334

Outcome research (*cont.*)
  prevention and relationship enhancement program, 218–219
  solution-focused therapy, 158–160
  treatment of sexual desire disorders, 476

P

Paradoxical interventions, 116–117, 119
Personality disorders, 396, 458. *See also* specific disorder
Philanderers, 302–304, 311, 313–315
Poststructuralism, 151, 156–157
Posttraumatic stress disorder, 407
  borderline personality organization and, 460
Practical Application of Intimate Relationship Skills, 220–221
Premarital counseling, 218
PREPARE inventory, 342
Prescribing the system, 62
Prevention and relationship enhancement program
  booster sessions, 222
  case example, 222–224
  gender issues in, 215–216
  as instilling hope and confidence, 220
  interpersonal communication concepts in, 216, 217, 220
  life cycle factors, 214–215
  model of marital distress, 213
  outcome evaluation, 218–219
  physical relationship issues in, 217
  problem-solving strategies, 217
  process and techniques, 215–218
  rationale, 212
  research needs, 212, 221
  social and cultural sensitivity, 222
  spiritual values in, 217
  therapist factors, 219–220
  therapy structure, 215
Preventive interventions, 3. *See also* Prevention and relationship enhancement program
  alcohol problem relapse prevention model, 377
  booster sessions, 222
  challenges to implementation, 212–213
  family outcomes, 222
  marital violence relapse, 334
  Marriage Encounter, 221
  Practical Application of Intimate Relationship Skills, 220–221
  rationale, 212
  relationship enhancement, 220
  research needs, 212, 221
  social and cultural sensitivity in, 221–222
Problem-focused therapy
  conceptual development, 2–3, 142, 143
  individual sessions in couple therapy, 147
  solution-focused therapy and, 143, 152, 155–158
  therapeutic change in, 143, 155
  therapeutic goals, 143
  See also Focused problem resolution
Problem-solving training, 38–39, 51–54, 75
  for anxiety reduction, 403

  model of, 422–423
  in prevention and relationship enhancement program, 217
  process focus in, 78
  for promoting coping assistance, 422–423
Projective identification
  in marriage, 169–170
  theory of, 169–170
Psychoanalytic marital therapy
  acute distress, 188
  assessment, 172–173
  classical psychoanalysis and, 164
  clinical features, 164–165
  conceptual development, 167–168
  confronting anxiety in, 173
  contract, 176
  difficult couple, 187
  infidelity issues, 187
  integration with other interventions, 184–187
  interpretation of defense, 173
  model of two-person system, 166–168
  noncompliance in, 187
  obstacles to treatment, 184
  resistance in, 187
  techniques, 175–184
  termination issues, 189
  therapeutic change, 172
  therapeutic goals, 172, 173
  therapist errors, 175
  therapist role, 174–175, 177
  therapist use of self in, 178–180
  therapy structure, 173–174
  transference and countertransference in, 173, 178–180
  trauma issues in, 187–188
sychoanalytic theory
  couple formulations, 166–167
  duality of instincts in, 165
  influence of, 165
  object relations theory in, 168–171
  oedipal development, 166
  preoedipal development, 165–166
  therapist-patient relationship in, 3

R

Race/ethnicity
  economic effects of divorce, 353
  gay and lesbian couples and, 276
Rational emotive therapy, 86
  for alcohol problem, 374
Rational Recovery, 374
Reframing
  interventions with long-term marriage at midlife, 255–258
  in object relations therapy with borderline-narcissistic couple, 466
  paradoxical interventions, 116–117
  positive features of negative behavior, 60–61
  in sexual desire disorder intervention, 478
Reinforced behavior, 33, 34
Relationship Attribution Questionnaire, 69

Relationship Belief Inventory, 67, 70, 82, 85, 86
Relationship enhancement, 220
Relaxation training, 4, 22, 327
Remarriage, 3
  risk of divorce, 340
  social and cultural attitudes, 340–341
  social trends, 355
  therapist role, 355–356
Resistance
  in alcohol problem intervention, 386–387
  in Bowen family system theory, 27–28
  ego-analytic interpretation, 105
  in group therapy with couples, 206
  in intervention with infidelity, 307, 311
  in psychoanalytic marital therapy, 187
Rituals, divorce and remarriage, 363
Role playing interventions
  behavior reversal of negative behavior, 61
  faked incidents of negative behavior, 61–62
Rule-shaped behavior, 38–39, 49

S

S-O-R-C model of alcohol abuse, 371
Safety, 135
Selective attention
  assessment, 72, 73
  cognitive restructuring interventions, 83–84
  in couple functioning, 66
  increasing spouse's awareness of, 80–82
elf-care strategies, 62–63
elf-differentiation
  in Bowen family systems theory, 12–14
  levels in couples, 17
  multigenerational transmission processes, 16–17
  sexual desire disorders and, 489–490
  therapeutic demonstration, 23–24
  therapist stance, 20, 28
  triangling processes and, 16
Self-monitoring interventions, 80–83
Self psychology, 167
Self-reproach
  in couple interaction, 100
  in ego-analytic concepts, 91, 94
  internalized homophobia in lesbians and gays, 275
  mistrustful blamer in emotionally focused therapy, 138–139
  as obstacle to communication, 111
  self-responsibility ethic in, 96
Self-talk strategies, 327
Separation, 3
  client fear of, 425–426
  during divorce mediation, 358–359
  gay and lesbian couples, 355
  trial, in divorce decisionmaking, 348
Sexism in marital therapy, 262–264
Sexual desire disorders
  affect-regulated interactions in, 477
  assessment, 480–481
  attachment themes, 490–491
  change process, 478

  clinical features, 471, 493
  differential diagnosis, 478–480
  functional symptomology, 483
  interactional themes in treatment, 483–484
  prevalence, 471, 493
  problem definition, 482–483
  ranking-order themes in, 484–486
  reframing, 478
  self-differentiation issues, 489–490
  sensate exchange in, 477–478
  sensate focus interventions, 491–492
  symbolic interactions in, 476–477
  territorial themes in, 486–490
  theoretical models, 472–478
  therapist role, 492–493
  therapy process, 482, 493
  treatment goals, 481
  treatment structure, 481–482
Sexuality/sexual behavior
  abuse history and, 188
  anxiety about intimacy, 180–182
  challenges for gay male couples, 285, 286–288
  culturally-influenced assessment, 492, 493
  eating disorders in adults, 442, 454–455
  as element of extramarital affair, 298
  feminist-informed therapy, 267–268
  post-divorce patterns, 350–351
  as presenting complaint for same-sex couple, 278–279
  in prevention and relationship enhancement program, 217
  problem-focused therapy for dysfunction, 150
  psychoanalytic marital therapy for, 185–187
  psychoanalytic model of development, 165–166
  social trends, 301
Sibling position, 18
Social constructionism, 492
Social learning theory, 325
  model of alcohol problem, 370–371
  model of marital distress, 213
Sociocultural context. *See also* Cross-cultural marriage
  assessment of sexual functioning, 492, 493
  attitudes toward divorce, 249, 340–341
  conceptual trends in couples therapy, 2
  definition of culture, 232–233
  emotional process in society, 18
  feminist critique of marriage, 261–262
  gender role socialization, 300
  gender-role socialization, gay male relationships and, 285
  gender-role socialization, lesbian relationships and, 280–282
  oppression of same-sex couples as source of relationship dysfunction, 277–280
  perception of infidelity, 296–299
  portrayals of long-term same-sex relationships, 277–278
  of same-sex couple therapy, 274–275
  sensitivity in design of preventive interventions, 221–222
  social analysis in therapeutic process, 266

Sociocultural context (*cont.*)
  as source of distress in midlife marriage, 249
  trends in couple therapy, 4–5
Solution-focused therapy
  assessment, 152
  categorization of clients in, 153
  conceptual development, 2–3, 142–143,
    150–151, 151–152
  coping questions, 153
  couple work, 154–155
  criticism of, 157–158
  effectiveness, 158–160
  future directions, 160–161
  future-oriented questions in, 153
  individual sessions in couple therapy, 154–155
  miracle question, 152
  poststructural themes in, 151, 156–157
  principles of practice, 152–154
  problem-focused therapy and, 143, 152, 155–158
  questions about presession change in, 153
  scaling questions, 153
  strategies, 151
  therapeutic change in, 143, 152, 155
  therapeutic goals, 143
  therapeutic relationship in, 152–153
  therapeutic tasks in, 153–154
  therapy structure, 151
Spiritual values, 217
  differences in marriage, 231
Spouse abuse. *See* Marital violence
Spouse Observation Checklist, 31, 35, 69, 81
Strategic therapy, 143, 156–157
Stress-diathesis model, 396
Substance abuse among gays and lesbians,
    279–280
  comorbid alcohol problem, 388
  sexual desire disorder assessment and, 480
Symptom Checklist, 203
Systems theory
  marital violence interventions, 328
  principle of isomorphism in, 198–199
  self-reinforcing relationship patterns in, 122–123
  therapist-patient relationship and, 4
  treatment of sexual desire disorders, 472

T

Tarasoff v. Regents of the University of California,
    330
Termination work
  alcohol problem intervention, 391–392
  Bowen family system therapy, 28, 29
  group therapy with couples, 205
  intervention with infidelity, 307, 312
  object relations therapy with borderline-
    narcissistic couple, 468
  psychoanalytic marital therapy, 189
Theoretical basis
  attachment theory, 123–124
  Bowen family system theory, 11–12
  cultural consonance in marriage, 232, 233–234
  ego analysis, 91

  emotionally focused therapy, 121
  existential psychotherapy with couples, 198–199
  group therapy with couples, 198–199
  integrative behavioral couples therapy, 32–38
  marital distress in course of anxiety disorders,
    395–397, 406–407
  marital violence, 325
  object relations theory, 168
  psychoanalytic marital therapy, 166–167
  psychoanalytic theory, 165–166
  relationship enhancement intervention,
    213–215
  sexist concepts in, 263
  therapist-patient relationship in change process,
    3–4
  treatment of sexual desire disorders, 472–478,
    493
  trends in couple therapy, 2, 3–4, 6
Therapeutic change
  alcohol problem intervention, 373, 375, 376
  assessment of capacity for, 43
  assessment of strategies for, 42–43
  behavioral therapy, 38
  Bowen family system therapy, 29
  communication training for, 52
  contingency-shaped behaviors in, 38–39
  in ego-analytic approach, 92, 109–110
  emotion in, 125–126
  emotionally focused approach, 122, 126–128,
    129
  extra-clinical preparation, 29
  focused problem resolution, 147–148
  goal setting, 46–47
  group therapy with couples, 207–208
  integrative behavioral couples therapy, 35,
    38–40
  problem-focused therapy, 143
  psychoanalytic marital therapy, 172
  rule-shaped behaviors in, 38–39
  sexual desire disorder, 478
  solution-focused therapy, 143, 152
  spontaneous, 49
  theoretical basis, 3
  therapist-patient relationship in, 3
  vs. emotional acceptance, 39–40
  vs. shifts of symptom state, 19
Therapeutic process/techniques, 3. *See also* specific
    therapeutic approach
  for alcohol problems, 373–375
  anger control strategies, 325–327
  attributional style and, 67–68
  for avoiding transference, 28
  behavior exchange strategies, 38–39, 51, 52
  boundary issues in lesbian couples, 284
  changing perceptions of stress, 425
  client participation in designing, 48
  cognitive restructuring interventions, 83–87
  collaborative probe, 47–48
  communication/problem-solving training, 38–39,
    51–54
  controlling emotional reactiveness, 26
  couple considering divorce, 343–345

couples group therapy techniques, 199–200, 204–207
delineation of couple's strengths, 47
demonstrating differentiation of self, 23–24
detriangling from emotional situations, 26–27
discussion of negative experiences, 58
eating disorders in adults, 445, 448–455
ego-analytic approach, 101–112
emotionally focused therapy, 128–130, 132–135, 137–139
family-of-origin research, 25–26
feedback session after assessment, 44–48
feminist critique, 262–264
feminist-informed, 265–267, 272
focused problem resolution, 145–150
in focused solution development, 151, 152–155
with gay men, unique issues in, 285–288
gender-related themes, 267–272
gender-role development issues for lesbian couple, 281–282
handling interruptions by spouse, 93
identification and discussion of positive interactions, 57–58, 81–82
identifying emotional reactivity, 21–22, 24–25
increasing awareness of assumptions, 82–83
increasing awareness of attributions, 82
increasing awareness of expectancies, 82
increasing awareness of relationship standards, 82–83
increasing awareness of selective attention, 80–81
individual sessions in couple therapy, 25, 147, 154–155
with infidelity, 307–315
integration of change and acceptance strategies, 48–51
integrative ego-analytic interventions, 115–119
joint platform concept in ego-analytic approach, 96, 101–102, 108, 109, 110, 113–115, 119
lesbian adolescence, 282–283
levels of intervention in group therapy, 199–200
logical analysis, 84–85, 87
with long-term marriage at midlife, 255–258
marital/family discord model of depression, 418–419
marital therapy with agoraphobic client, 398
marital violence, 321–328
object relations marital therapy with borderline-narcissistic couple, 463–469
paradoxical interventions, 116–117, 119
prevention and relationship enhancement program, 215–218
principles of ego-analytic approach, 94–97
problem definition, 52–53
promoting acceptance, 43–44
promoting acceptance of emotional expression, 421–422
promoting cohesive behaviors, 419–420
promoting emotional acceptance, 54–63
promoting spousal dependability, 423–424
psychoanalytic marital therapy, 173–174, 175–184

relaxation training, 4, 22, 327
reproachful interpretations in, 92, 93–94
role playing interventions, 61–62
selection of problems, 48
self-esteem support in, 423
self-monitoring of cognitions, 79, 80–83
self-protection strategies, 62–63
self-talk strategies, 327
sexual desire disorders, 482–492
social analysis in, 266
structure of couples therapy group, 198, 201
teaching about emotional systems, 23
therapist use of self in psychoanalytic marital therapy, 178–180
time-out procedures, 326–327
tolerance building strategies, 59–63
trends in couple therapy, 4, 6
Therapist–patient relationship
alcohol problem intervention, 375–377, 386
avoiding problems of, 28–29
coleadership of therapy group, 206–207
conceptual trends in couple therapy, 3–4
control issues, 146–147
in divorce interventions, 361
emotional contact with family system, 19–20, 24
in emotionally focused therapy, 130, 131
empathy in, 4
gender issues, 264, 266–267
in marital violence interventions, 329–330
in object relations marital therapy, 464
in prevention and relationship enhancement program, 219–220
resistance and, 27–28
safety in, 4
sexual desire disorder interventions, 492–493
in solution-focused therapy, 152–153
teaching, 23
therapist homophobia, 276–277, 279–280, 286
triangling of therapist, 22–23
as working alliance, 3
Therapist role
in alcohol problem intervention, 375–377
in Bowen family systems, 19–20
in cognitive-behavioral marital therapy, 78–80
in divorce mediation, 356–361
in ego-analytic approach, 112–113
in emotionally focused therapy, 127, 130–132
in group therapy with couples, 200–201
postdivorce effects, 348–355
in prevention and relationship enhancement program, 219–220
in psychoanalytic marital therapy, 174–175
remarriage interventions, 355–356
in revealing infidelity, 307–309
safety considerations in marital violence interventions, 319–320
sexual desire disorder interventions, 492–493
social values issues and, 5
theoretical basis, 3
treating eating disorder in adult, 455
working with midlife couple, 258–259
in working with same sex couples, 280, 286

Therapist stance
  in alcohol problem intervention, 375, 376
  differentiation of self in, 20, 28
  emotional neutrality, 20, 22, 24, 176–177
  object relations marital therapy, 463–464
  in problem-focused therapy, 143
  in psychoanalytic marital therapy, 174–175, 177
  research attitude, 22
  in solution-focused therapy, 143
Time-out procedures, 326–327
olerance building, 59–63
raining of therapists
  for group therapy with couples, 198, 209
  for same-sex couples work, 275
  sociocultural sensitivity, 235
  trends, 2
Transference
  avoiding, 28
  in psychoanalytic marital therapy, 173, 178–180

Triangulation
  Bowen family system theory concept, 14–16
  detriangling from emotional situations, 26–27
  of therapist, 22–23

V

Value differences, 231
  in lesbian couple, regarding public display of
      sexual orientation, 282–283
  perceptions of infidelity, 296
Values differences, 5
  gender role socialization and, 300
Violence
  as contraindication to emotionally focused thera-
      py, 128
  against gays and lesbians, 277
  joint-victim model of spouse abuse, 112
  problem-maintaining behavior in, 149